XSLT 2.0 Programmer's Reference
Third Edition

Michael Kay

WILEY

Wiley Publishing, Inc.

XSLT 2.0 Programmer's Reference, Third Edition

Published by
Wiley Publishing, Inc.
10475 Crosspoint Boulevard
Indianapolis, IN 46256
www.wiley.com

For general information on our other products and services please contact our Customer Care Department within the United States at (800) 762-2974, outside the United States at (317) 572-3993 or fax (317) 572-4002.

Library of Congress Cataloging-in-Publication Data:

ISBN: 0-764-56909-0

Printed in the United States of America

10 9 8 7 6 5 4 3 2 1

Credits

Vice President and Executive Group Publisher
Richard Swadley

Vice President and Executive Publisher
Robert Ipsen

Vice President and Publisher
Joseph B. Wikert

Executive Editorial Director
Mary Bednarek

Senior Acquisitions Editor
Jim Minatel

Editorial Manager
Kathryn A. Malm

Senior Production Editor
Fred Bernardi

Senior Development Editor
Emilie Herman

Production Editor
Pamela Hanley

Text Design & Composition
TechBooks

Technical Editor
Wiley-Dreamtech India Pvt Ltd

To the Peacemakers

Contents

Acknowledgments	**xxiii**
Introduction	**xxvii**
List of Examples	**xxxv**

Chapter 1: XSLT in Context   1

What is XSLT?	**1**
Why Version 2.0?	3
A Scenario: Transforming Music	3
How Does XSLT Transform XML?	**5**
XSLT and SQL: An Analogy	7
XSLT Processors	8
An XSLT 1.0 Stylesheet	9
An XSLT 2.0 Stylesheet	15
Where to Use XSLT	**17**
Data Conversion Applications	17
Publishing	19
When to Do the Conversion?	20
The Place of XSLT in the XML Family	**21**
XSLT and XSL	21
XSLT and XML	22
XSL and CSS	24
XSLT and XML Schemas	25
The History of XSL	**26**
Prehistory	26
The First XSL Proposal	28
The Microsoft WD-xsl Dialect	30
Saxon	31
Beyond XSLT 1.0	31
XQuery	32
XSLT 2.0 and XPath 2.0	33
XSLT 2.0 as a Language	**34**
Use of XML Syntax	34
No Side Effects	36
Rule-Based	37
Types Based on XML Schema	41
Summary	**41**

Contents

Chapter 2: The XSLT Processing Model   43

XSLT: A System Overview   **43**
  A Simplified Overview   43
  Trees, not Documents   44
  Different Output Formats   45
  Multiple Inputs and Outputs   47
The Tree Model   **48**
  XML as a Tree   48
  Nodes in the Tree Model   51
  What Does the Tree Leave Out?   56
The Transformation Process   **59**
  Invoking a Transformation   59
  Template Rules   60
  Sequence Constructors   61
  Push Processing   65
  Controlling Which Nodes to Process   68
  Modes   70
  Built-In Template Rules   70
  Conflict Resolution Policy   71
Error Handling   **71**
Variables and Expressions   **72**
  Variables   73
  Parameters   74
  Data Types   74
  Expressions   76
  Context   78
  Temporary Trees   79
Summary   **82**

Chapter 3: Stylesheet Structure   83

Changes in XSLT 2.0   **84**
The Modular Structure of a Stylesheet   **84**
The <xsl:stylesheet> Element   **91**
The <?xml-stylesheet?> Processing Instruction   **93**
Embedded Stylesheets   **95**
Declarations   **98**
  XSLT-Defined Declarations   99
  Implementor-Defined Declarations   100
  User-Defined Top-Level Elements   101

Contents

Instructions **103**
    XSLT Instructions 103
    Extension Instructions 105
    Literal Result Elements 106
    Attribute Value Templates 116
Simplified Stylesheets **119**
Writing Portable Stylesheets **121**
    Conditional Compilation 122
    Version Compatibility 123
    Extensibility 128
Whitespace **136**
    Whitespace Nodes in the Stylesheet 141
    The Effect of Stripping Whitespace Nodes 141
    Solving Whitespace Problems 142
Summary **144**

Chapter 4: Stylesheets and Schemas **145**

XML Schema: An Overview **145**
    Simple Type Definitions 146
    Elements with Attributes and Simple Content 148
    Elements with Mixed Content 149
    Elements with Element-Only Content 150
    Substitution Groups 151
Declaring Types **154**
Validating the Source Document **159**
Validating the Result Document **160**
Validating a Temporary Tree **163**
Validating Individual Elements **164**
Validating Individual Attributes **167**
The default-validation Attribute **168**
Importing Schemas **168**
Using xsi:type **170**
Nillability **171**
Summary **171**

Chapter 5: XSLT Elements **173**

xsl:analyze-string **176**
    Changes in 2.0 176
    Format 177

Contents

Effect 178
Usage and Examples 181
See Also 184
xsl:apply-imports **184**
Changes in 2.0 184
Format 184
Effect 185
Usage and Examples 185
See Also 187
xsl:apply-templates **187**
Changes in 2.0 187
Format 187
Effect 188
Usage and Examples 193
See Also 201
xsl:attribute **201**
Changes in 2.0 201
Format 201
Effect 202
Usage 208
Examples 211
See Also 214
xsl:attribute-set **214**
Changes in 2.0 214
Format 214
Effect 215
Usage 217
Examples 217
See Also 220
xsl:call-template **220**
Changes in 2.0 220
Format 220
Effect 221
Usage and Examples 222
See Also 229
xsl:character-map **229**
Changes in 2.0 229
Format 229
Effect 230
Usage and Examples 232
See Also 236

Contents

xsl:choose   **236**
Changes in 2.0   236
Format   236
Effect   236
Usage   237
Examples   237
See Also   238
xsl:comment   **238**
Changes in 2.0   238
Format   238
Effect   239
Usage   239
Examples   240
xsl:copy   **240**
Changes in 2.0   241
Format   241
Effect   242
Usage   243
Examples   244
See Also   244
xsl:copy-of   **245**
Changes in 2.0   245
Format   245
Effect   246
Usage and Examples   247
See Also   251
xsl:decimal-format   **251**
Changes in 2.0   252
Format   252
Effect   253
Usage   255
Examples   255
See Also   257
xsl:document   **257**
Changes in 2.0   257
Format   257
Effect   258
Usage and Examples   260
See Also   260
xsl:element   **260**
Changes in 2.0   260

Contents

Format	261
Effect	261
Usage and Examples	269
See Also	271
xsl:fallback	**271**
Changes in 2.0	271
Format	271
Effect	272
Usage	273
Examples	274
See Also	276
xsl:for-each	**276**
Changes in 2.0	276
Format	277
Effect	277
Usage and Examples	279
See Also	281
xsl:for-each-group	**281**
Changes in 2.0	281
Format	281
Effect	282
Usage and Examples	286
See Also	300
xsl:function	**300**
Changes in 2.0	300
Format	300
Effect	301
Usage and Examples	303
See Also	309
xsl:if	**309**
Changes in 2.0	309
Format	309
Effect	309
Usage	310
Examples	311
See Also	312
xsl:import	**312**
Changes in 2.0	312
Format	312
Effect	313
Usage	319

Contents

Examples	320
See Also	324
xsl:import-schema	**324**
Changes in 2.0	324
Format	325
Effect	325
Usage	326
Examples	328
xsl:include	**328**
Changes in 2.0	328
Format	328
Effect	329
Usage and Examples	330
See Also	332
xsl:key	**332**
Changes in 2.0	332
Format	332
Effect	333
Usage and Examples	335
See Also	342
xsl:matching-substring	**342**
Changes in 2.0	342
Format	342
Effect	343
Usage and Examples	343
See Also	343
xsl:message	**343**
Changes in 2.0	343
Format	343
Effect	344
Usage	344
Examples	345
See Also	346
xsl:namespace	**346**
Changes in 2.0	347
Format	347
Effect	347
Usage and Examples	348
See Also	350
xsl:namespace-alias	**350**
Changes in 2.0	350

Contents

Format   350
Effect   351
Usage and Examples   352
See Also   355
xsl:next-match   **355**
Changes in 2.0   355
Format   355
Effect   356
Usage and Examples   357
See Also   358
xsl:non-matching-substring   **358**
Changes in 2.0   359
Format   359
Effect   359
Usage and Examples   359
See Also   359
xsl:number   **359**
Changes in 2.0   360
Format   360
Effect   361
Usage and Examples   367
See Also   374
xsl:otherwise   **374**
Changes in 2.0   374
Format   374
Effect   374
Usage and Examples   375
See Also   375
xsl:output   **375**
Changes in 2.0   375
Format   375
Effect   377
Usage   390
Examples   391
See Also   391
xsl:output-character   **391**
Changes in 2.0   391
Format   392
Effect   392
See Also   392
xsl:param   **392**
Changes in 2.0   393

Contents

Format	393
Effect	394
Usage	397
Examples	399
See Also	404
xsl:perform-sort	**405**
Changes in 2.0	405
Format	405
Effect	405
Usage and Examples	406
See Also	406
xsl:preserve-space	**406**
Changes in 2.0	406
Format	406
Effect	407
Usage	409
Examples	410
See Also	411
xsl:processing-instruction	**411**
Changes in 2.0	411
Format	411
Effect	411
Usage	412
Examples	413
xsl:result-document	**414**
Changes in 2.0	414
Format	414
Effect	415
Usage	417
Examples	417
See Also	419
xsl:sequence	**420**
Changes in 2.0	420
Format	420
Effect	420
Usage and Examples	421
See Also	422
xsl:sort	**423**
Changes in 2.0	423
Format	423
Effect	424
Usage	429

Contents

Examples	431
See Also	432
xsl:strip-space	**432**
Changes in 2.0	433
Format	433
Effect, Usage, and Examples	433
See Also	433
xsl:stylesheet	**433**
Changes in 2.0	434
Format	434
Effect	437
Usage and Examples	445
See Also	450
xsl:template	**450**
Changes in 2.0	451
Format	451
Effect	452
Usage and Examples	455
See Also	459
xsl:text	**459**
Changes in 2.0	460
Format	460
Effect	460
Usage	460
See Also	465
xsl:transform	**465**
Format	465
See Also	465
xsl:value-of	**465**
Changes in 2.0	465
Format	465
Effect	466
Usage	467
Examples	470
See Also	471
xsl:variable	**471**
Changes in 2.0	471
Format	471
Effect	472
Usage	477
Examples	477
See Also	487

Contents

xsl:when   **487**

     Changes in 2.0   487

     Format   487

     Effect   487

     Usage and Examples   488

     See Also   488

xsl:with-param   **488**

     Changes in 2.0   489

     Format   489

     Effect   489

     Usage and Examples   490

     See Also   491

Summary   **491**

Chapter 6: Patterns   **493**

Changes in XSLT 2.0   **494**

The Formal Definition   **495**

     Patterns Containing Predicates   497

An Informal Definition   **497**

Conflict Resolution   **498**

Matching Parentless Nodes   **500**

The Syntax of Patterns   **501**

     Pattern   502

     PathPattern   503

     RelativePathPattern   505

     PatternStep   507

     IdKeyPattern   518

Summary   **522**

Chapter 7: XSLT Functions   **523**

current   **526**

     Changes in 2.0   526

     Signature   526

     Effect   526

     Usage   527

     Example   527

current-group   **529**

     Changes in 2.0   529

     Signature   530

     Effect   530

Contents

Usage and Examples   530
See Also   530
current-grouping-key   **530**
Changes in 2.0   531
Signature   531
Effect   531
Usage and Examples   531
See Also   532
document   **532**
Changes in 2.0   532
Signature   532
Effect   533
See Also   542
element-available   **542**
Changes in 2.0   543
Signature   543
Effect   543
Usage and Examples   544
See Also   548
format-date   **548**
Changes in 2.0   548
Signature   549
Effect   549
Usage and Examples   549
See Also   550
format-dateTime   **550**
Changes in 2.0   550
Signature   550
Effect   551
Usage and Examples   557
See Also   558
format-number   **558**
Changes in 2.0   558
Signature   558
Effect   559
Usage   561
Examples   561
See Also   562
format-time   **562**
Changes in 2.0   562
Signature   562
Effect   563

Contents

Usage and Examples 563

See Also 564

function-available **564**

Changes in 2.0 564

Signature 564

Effect 564

Usage 565

Example 1: Testing for xx:node-set() Extensions 566

Example 2: Testing Availability of a Java Method 568

See Also 568

generate-id **568**

Changes in 2.0 569

Signature 569

Effect 569

Usage and Examples 569

See Also 572

key **572**

Changes in 2.0 573

Signature 573

Effect 573

Usage and Examples 574

See Also 579

regex-group **580**

Changes in 2.0 580

Signature 580

Effect 580

Usage and Examples 580

See Also 581

system-property **581**

Changes in 2.0 581

Signature 582

Effect 582

Usage 583

Examples 584

See Also 584

unparsed-entity-public-id **584**

Changes in 2.0 584

Signature 584

Effect 584

Usage 585

Examples 585

See Also 585

Contents

unparsed-entity-uri **585**

 Changes in 2.0 585

 Signature 586

 Effect 586

 Usage 586

 Examples 587

 See Also 587

unparsed-text **587**

 Changes in 2.0 587

 Signature 588

 Effect 588

 Usage and Examples 589

 See Also 593

Summary **593**

Chapter 8: Extensibility 595

What Vendor Extensions Are Allowed? **595**

Extension Functions **597**

 When Are Extension Functions Needed? 597

 When Are Extension Functions not Needed? 598

 Calling Extension Functions 598

 What Language Is Best? 599

 Client-Side Script 599

 Binding Extension Functions 599

 Calling External Functions within a Loop 606

 Functions with Uncontrolled Side Effects 609

Keeping Extensions Portable **611**

Summary **612**

Chapter 9: Stylesheet Design Patterns 613

Fill-in-the-Blanks Stylesheets **613**

Navigational Stylesheets **616**

Rule-Based Stylesheets **620**

Computational Stylesheets **625**

 Programming without Assignment Statements 625

 So Why Are They Called Variables? 629

 Cheating 629

 Avoiding Assignment Statements 630

 Grouping 641

Summary **643**

Chapter 10: Case Study: XMLSpec — 645

Formatting the XML Specification — **646**
Preface — **647**
Creating the HTML Outline — **651**
Formatting the Document Header — **655**
Creating the Table of Contents — **661**
Creating Section Headers — **666**
Formatting the Text — **667**
Producing Lists — **670**
Making Cross-References — **672**
Setting Out the Production Rules — **676**
Variant Stylesheets — **684**
  diffspec.xsl — 685
  xslt.xsl — 687
  funcproto.xsl — 688
  xsl-query.xsl — 688
Summary — **689**

Chapter 11: Case Study: A Family Tree — 691

Modeling A Family Tree — **692**
  The GEDCOM Data Model — 692
  Creating a Schema for GEDCOM 6.0 — 695
  The GEDCOM 6.0 Schema — 696
Creating a Data File — **702**
  Converting GEDCOM Files to XML — 703
  Converting from GEDCOM 5.5 to 6.0 — 704
Displaying the Family Tree Data — **714**
  The Stylesheet — 715
  Putting it Together — 728
Summary — **738**

Chapter 12: Case Study: Knight's Tour — 739

The Problem — **739**
The Algorithm — **740**
Placing the Knight — **744**
Displaying the Final Board — **745**
Finding the Route — **746**
  Finding the Possible Moves — 747
  Trying the Possible Moves — 749
  Selecting the Best Move — 750

Contents

Running the Stylesheet   752
Observations   752
Summary   753

Appendix A: XPath 2.0 Syntax Summary   755
Appendix B: XPath Function Library   765
Appendix C: Microsoft XSLT Processors   799
Appendix D: JAXP: The Java API for Transformation   815
Appendix E: Saxon   851
Appendix F: Backwards Compatibility   865
Glossary   869
Index   893

Acknowledgments

Firstly, I'd like to acknowledge the work of the W3C XSL Working Group, who created the XSLT language, as well as many other experts inside and outside W3C who provided ideas and feedback. As the editor of the XSLT 2.0 specification I have to take responsibility not only for the imperfections in this book but also for some of the defects in the design of the language it describes; but the credit goes to the team as a whole, and particularly to James Clark, who created the solid technical foundation on which version 2.0 has been built.

I would like to thank the many readers of previous editions of this book who have provided feedback, criticism, and encouragement. Without the knowledge that the book has been so widely appreciated, I would not have embarked on the daunting task of producing a new edition. Please keep the feedback coming, whether positive or negative.

The bulk of this book was written while I was an employee of Software AG. I'd like to thank the company for allowing me to take this project on.

I must thank Wiley, who rescued this project when the old Wrox Press collapsed, and whose editor has applied a delicate touch both to reminding me of imminent deadlines and to correcting my prose.

And once again, I have to thank Penny and Pippa, who have sustained me through another winter in which I rarely left my desk.

About the Author

Michael Kay has been working in the XML field since 1997; he became a member of the XSL Working Group soon after the publication of XSLT 1.0, and took over as editor of the XSLT 2.0 specification in early 2001. He is also a member of the XQuery Working Group. He is well known not only through previous editions of this book, but also as the developer of the open-source Saxon product, a pioneering implementation of XSLT 2.0, XPath 2.0, and XQuery 1.0.

The author has recently formed his own company, Saxonica Limited, to provide commercial software and services building on the success of the Saxon technology. Previously he spent three years with Software AG, working with the developers of the Tamino XML server, a leading XQuery implementation. His background is in database technology: after leaving the University of Cambridge with a Ph.D., he worked for many years with the (then) computer manufacturer ICL, developing network, relational, and object-oriented database software products as well as a text search engine, and held the position of ICL Fellow.

Michael lives in Reading, England, with his wife and daughter. His hobbies, as you might guess from this book, include genealogy and choral singing (and once included chess). He has a croquet handicap of 9.

Introduction

XML today needs no introduction: as soon as it hit the streets in 1998 it immediately gained universal acceptance both as a practical tool for use by programmers, and as a strategic technology advocated by captains of industry. XSLT and XPath followed soon afterwards in 1999, and quickly became established as the preferred high-level languages for manipulating XML content, despite a reputation among some users for being difficult to learn (probably a fair comment) and sluggish in performance (less fair, certainly today).

The first edition of this book was published in the Spring of 2000, at the same time as the first complete XSLT implementations were appearing from companies such as Oracle, Microsoft, and IBM. The book quickly became recognized as the definitive reference on the XSLT and XPath languages, only second to the formal specifications from the World Wide Web Consortium (W3C). On the strength of the book, as well as my open-source XSLT implementation Saxon, I was invited to join the W3C Working Group developing the next version of the language, and I later became the editor of the XSLT 2.0 specification. So it's natural that I should now be rewriting the book to cover the new version.

XSLT 2.0 and XPath 2.0 have been a long time in the making. As so often happens with version two of anything, the requirements turned out to be very ambitious. Also, standards work tends to slow down as more people get involved, and with any technology as successful as XML, more people are going to get involved as things move forward. Chapter 1 explains how XPath 2.0 and many of the core ideas influencing the design of XSLT 2.0 were developed collaboratively between two separate Working Groups, whose members came from very different traditions in the IT community. One result is that the specifications are much more bulky than the original 1.0 version (the two languages, XSLT and XPath, are perhaps double the size of the originals, but the specifications are ten times the length). All the more need, therefore, for a book that collects the information together and presents it comprehensively and comprehensibly to the prospective users of the two languages.

The fact that the languages are bigger means that there are more features to learn about: new XSLT instructions for doing grouping and regular expression handling, new data types, a large number of new XPath functions. Paradoxically, however, I think it will now be easier for new users to become proficient in the language, because there is less need to discover the esoteric workarounds for straightforward problems that were the stuff of XSLT 1.0 programming.

In previous editions, XSLT and XPath were covered in a single volume. This time, they have been divided into two separate books: this one covers XSLT 2.0, while the companion book *XPath 2.0 Programmer's Reference* describes XPath. One reason for the split was that there is simply too much material to cover in detail in a single volume; the other reason is that XPath (as was always intended) has acquired a life of its own separate from XSLT, and there may well be readers who are interested in XPath, without wanting to use XSLT. For XSLT users, however, I would strongly recommend acquiring both volumes.

At the time of writing, the ink is not yet dry on the XSLT 2.0 and XPath 2.0 specifications. Both specifications went into their formal public consultation period on November 12, 2003, along with XQuery 1.0 ,which is a superset of XPath 2.0. This 3-month consultation generated over a thousand comments, which the working groups are still trawling through as I write in May. These range from simple typos that are easily corrected, to offbeat ideas that have no chance of acceptance. In between these extremes are some tricky bugs and usability problems that need to be fixed. Many of these, however, are corner cases where the final decision is unlikely to affect many everyday applications (an example is the detail of how arithmetic overflow should be handled). There will certainly be a few changes to the three languages as a result of the public consultation, and as a result of implementation experience gathered during the Candidate Recommendation phase that still lies ahead, but my prediction is that these will be minor. Some late changes already agreed have made it into this book. Where possible, we will draw attention to any further changes in the errata published at http://www.wrox.com/.

The big software companies have not rushed to upgrade their XSLT 1.0 implementations to the 2.0 standard; the signs are that they are waiting until they have confidence that the language is stable. At the time of writing, my own Saxon product is the only reasonably complete XSLT 2.0 implementation (there is also an early beta from Oracle). However, several other products are known to be in development. XPath 2.0 implementations have started to appear in products such as XMLSpy and Stylus Studio. Users, of course, have to make their own decisions about when to start moving forward. For many, the new functionality in XSLT 2.0 has proved compelling, and there are already production applications using the language even before the specifications are finalized.

Who This Book Is For

This book, as the title implies, is primarily a practical reference book for professional XSLT developers. It assumes no previous knowledge of the language, and many developers have used it as their first introduction to XSLT; however, it is not structured as a tutorial, and there are other books on XSLT that provide a gentler approach for beginners.

The book does assume a basic knowledge of XML, HTML, and the architecture of the Web, and it is written for experienced programmers. There's no assumption that you know any particular language such as Java or Visual Basic, just that you recognize the concepts that all programming languages have in common.

I have tried to make the book suitable both for XSLT 1.0 users upgrading to XSLT 2.0, and for newcomers to XSLT. This is easier to do in a reference book, of course, than in a tutorial. I have also tried to make the book equally suitable whether you work in the Java or .NET world.

As befits a reference book, a key aim is that the coverage should be comprehensive and authoritative. It is designed to give you all the detail, not just an overview of the 20 percent of the language that most people use 80 percent of the time. It's designed so that you will keep coming back to the book whenever you encounter new and challenging programming tasks, not as a book that you skim quickly and then leave on the shelf. If you like detail, you will enjoy this book; if not, you probably won't.

But as well as giving the detail, this book aims to explain the concepts, in some depth. It's therefore a book for people who not only want to use the language, but who also want to understand it at a deep level. Many readers have written to me saying that they particularly appreciate these insights into the language, and it's my sincere hope that after reading it you will not only be a more productive XSLT programmer, but also a more knowledgeable software engineer.

What This Book Covers

This book aims to tell you everything you need to know about the XSLT 2.0 language. It gives equal weight to the things that are new in XSLT 2.0, and the things that were already present in version 1.0.

The book is about the language, not about specific products. However, there are appendices about Saxon (my own implementation of XSLT 2.0), and about the Java and Microsoft APIs for controlling XSLT transformations, which will no doubt be upgraded to handle XSLT 2.0 as well as 1.0. The experience of XSLT 1.0 is that there has been a very high level of interoperability between different XSLT processors, and if you can use one of them, then you can use them all.

The book is intended to be used alongside the companion volume *XPath 2.0 Programmer's Reference*. Since XSLT 2.0 has such a strong dependence on XPath 2.0, you really need both books. Although there are a couple of appendices in this book summarizing details of XPath syntax and the function library, the information is not comprehensive and is provided purely for convenience on those occasions when you lent the other book to a colleague.

The book does not cover XSL Formatting Objects, a big subject in its own right. Nor does it cover XML Schemas in any detail. If you want to use these important technologies in conjunction with XSLT, there are other books that do them justice.

How This Book Is Structured

The material in this book falls broadly into three parts.

The first part, in Chapters 1 to 4, is concerned with explaining concepts. Chapter 1 is about the background to the language, about how it was created and about its role and purpose. In Chapter 2 we study the processing model: the inputs and outputs of a transformation, the data model and the type system. Chapter 3 looks at the structure of a stylesheet—it describes the way a stylesheet can be divided into modules, and surveys the different kinds of declaration and instruction that a stylesheet module may contain. Chapter 4 then examines the relationship of XSLT stylesheets to XML Schemas: this linkage is at the same time one of the more powerful new capabilities in XSLT 2.0, and also one of the most controversial.

The second part of the book, in Chapters 5 to 8, contains reference information. Chapter 5 is the central core of the book, providing an alphabetical listing of every XSLT element that can appear in a stylesheet, explaining its syntax and its effect, and giving usage advice and examples. Chapter 6 describes the syntax of match patterns, which are used to define which rules in a stylesheet affect which parts of an XML document. Chapter 7 describes the XSLT function library, that is, the functions provided by XSLT for use in XPath expressions within a stylesheet, over and above the core library of XPath functions described in *XPath 2.0 Programmer's Reference*. Then Chapter 8 discusses features in the language designed to provide extensibility, in particular the ability to link to extension functions written in other languages such as Java or JavaScript.

The third part of the book, comprising Chapters 9 to 12, is designed to show how the parts of the language come together when writing real XSLT applications. Chapter 9 discusses a number of design patterns that can be used when applying XSLT to different kinds of problem, taking time to explain the way that XSLT can be used as a functional programming language to tackle complex computational problems. The remaining three chapters are presented as case studies that exemplify these design patterns: Chapter 10 studies a stylesheet written to render technical specifications into HTML, Chapter 11 looks at a suite of stylesheets designed for transformation and presentation of structured genealogical data, and Chapter 12 looks at a purely computational problem, the calculation of a knight's tour around the chessboard. (I was pleased recently to be told that one of my readers had found this inspirational when working out how to calculate the placement of table cells on an HTML page in a far less exotic application.)

Finally, the appendices give ancillary information that will typically be of interest to some readers and not to others. The first two appendices summarize the XPath syntax and function library; the next two give information about the APIs used to control XSLT transformations in the Java and Microsoft environments. Appendix E is about the Saxon product, and Appendix F summarizes the main backwards-compatibility issues that arise when converting from XSLT 1.0 to XSLT 2.0. The book ends with a glossary and an index.

What You Need to Use This Book

Many of the examples in this book, as you would expect, require an XSLT 2.0 processor, and at the time of writing the only XSLT 2.0 processor that will run these examples is the Saxon product. You will need Saxon version 7.9 or later, which can be obtained from http://saxon.sf.net/.

The XSLT 2.0 specification describes two kinds of XSLT processor: a *basic* processor and a *schema-aware* processor. Saxon 7.9 is a basic XSLT processor. As I write this, I am currently testing Saxon 8.0, which will be a schema-aware processor. There are only two sections of the book that require the additional features of a schema-aware processor, namely Chapter 4, which discusses the relationships between XSLT and XML Schema, and Chapter 11, the case study where XSLT is applied to genealogical data. To run these examples you will need to acquire a schema-aware processor such as Saxon 8.0 (unlike the basic processor, this will not be free). The schema-aware version of Saxon will be available from http://www.saxonica.com/.

There is information on installing Saxon in Chapter 1 (see page 12). Before you can use Saxon you will need to install JDK 1.4, and if you're on Windows then it's a good idea to install a text editor such as jEdit (www.jedit.org) that provides a console for running operating system commands.

Of course, it is likely that during the months after this book is published, other XSLT 2.0 processors will become available from other vendors. Most of the examples should run with any processor that conforms to the standards.

Other XSLT Resources

Some of the sites that you might find useful for additional XSLT information are:

❑   http://www.w3.org/TR/xslt20: The latest version of the XSLT 2.0 specification from the W3C, including references to the other specifications (such as the data model) on which it depends.

❑   http://www.w3.org/Style/XSL/: Home page of the XSL Working Group.

❑   http://xml.coverpages.org/xsl.html: The Cover Pages, run by Robin Cover, provide a comprehensive set of links and summaries of everything in the world of XML and XSLT.

❑   http://msdn.microsoft.com/xml: A good jumping-off point to Microsoft's view on the XML and XSL world.

❑   http://www.mulberrytech.com/xsl/xsl-list: The home page of the xsl-list, a remarkably effective forum for all XSLT matters, from beginners' questions to advanced theoretical debates.

Conventions

To help you get the most from the text and keep track of what's happening, we've used a number of conventions throughout the book.

Worked examples—which you can download and try out for yourself—generally appear in a box like this:

A Specimen Example

Source

This section gives the XML source data, the input to the transformation. If the file name is given as `example.xml`, you will find that file in the archive that you can download from the Wrox Web site at `http://www.wrox.com/`, generally in a subdirectory holding all the examples for one chapter.

```
<source data="xml"/>
```

Stylesheet

This section describes the XSLT stylesheet used to achieve the transformation. Again, there will usually be a filename such as `style.xsl` so you can find the stylesheet in the Wrox download archive.

```
<xsl:stylesheet...
```

Output

This section shows the output when you apply this stylesheet to this source data, either as an XML or HTML listing, or as a screenshot.

```
<html...</html>
```

There are some further typographical conventions:

> **Boxes like this one hold important, not-to-be forgotten information that is directly relevant to the surrounding text.**

Tips, hints, tricks, and asides to the current discussion are offset and placed in italic like this.

As for styles in the text:

❑   We *highlight* important words when we introduce them.

❑   We show keyboard strokes like this: Ctrl+A.

❑   We show code within the text as follows. Element names are written as `<html>` or `<xsl:stylesheet>`. Function names are written as `concat()` or `current-date()`. Other names (for example of attributes or types) are written simply as `version` or `xs:string`. Fragments of code other than simple names are offset from the surrounding text by chevrons, for example «`substring($a,1,1) = 'X'`». Chevrons are also used around individual characters or string values: as a general rule, if a string is enclosed in quotation marks, then the quotes are part of the code example, whereas if it is enclosed in chevrons, the chevrons are there only to separate the code from the surrounding text.

❏ Blocks of code are shown as follows:

```
In examples we highlight code with a gray background.
```

Source Code

There are two kinds of code examples in this book: *code fragments* and *worked examples*.

Code fragments are incomplete, and are not intended to be executed on their own. You can build them into your own stylesheets if you find them useful, but you will have to retype the code.

Worked examples are provided in the form of complete stylesheets, accompanied by sample source XML documents to which they can be applied, and an illustration of the output that they are expected to produce. Worked examples are presented as shown in the specimen in the previous section. These stylesheets and source documents can be downloaded. In most cases both the source document and the stylesheet are listed in full in the book, though they are sometimes abbreviated to save space. In all cases, there is a reference to a filename where the full code can be found in the downloaded source code library.

All of this source code is available for download at http://www.wrox.com. Once at the site, simply locate the book's title (either by using the Search box or by using one of the title lists) and click the Download Code link on the book's detail page to obtain all the source code for the book.

Because many books have similar titles, you may find it easiest to search by ISBN; for this book the ISBN is 0-764-56909-0.

Once you download the code, just unzip it with your favorite compression tool. The files are organized according to the chapter that each example appears in, with one or two of the source files that are used repeatedly held in the top-level directory. Alternately, you can go to the main Wrox code download page at http://www.wrox.com/dynamic/books/download.aspx to see the code available for this book and all other Wrox books.

Errata

We make every effort to ensure that there are no errors in the text or in the code. However, no one is perfect, and mistakes do occur. If you find an error in one of our books, like a spelling mistake or faulty piece of code, we would be very grateful for your feedback. By sending in errata you may save another reader hours of frustration and at the same time you will be helping us provide even higher quality information.

To find the errata page for this book, go to http://www.wrox.com and locate the title using the Search box or one of the title lists. Then, on the book details page, click the Book Errata link. On this page you can view all errata that have been submitted for this book and posted by Wrox editors. A complete book list including links to each's book's errata is also available at www.wrox.com/misc-pages/booklist.shtml.

On the errata page for this book you may also find information about any significant changes that have been made to the XSLT 2.0 language after we went to press.

If you don't spot your error on the Book Errata page, go to www.wrox.com/contact/techsupport.shtml and complete the form there to send us the error you have found. We'll check the information and, if appropriate, post a message to the book's errata page and fix the problem in subsequent editions of the book.

p2p.wrox.com

For author and peer discussion, join the P2P forums at p2p.wrox.com. The forums are a Web-based system for you to post messages relating to Wrox books and related technologies and interact with other readers and technology users. The forums offer a subscription feature to e-mail you topics of interest of your choosing when new posts are made to the forums. Wrox authors, editors, other industry experts, and your fellow readers are present on these forums.

At http://p2p.wrox.com you will find a number of different forums that will help you not only as you read this book, but also as you develop your own applications. To join the forums, just follow these steps:

1. Go to p2p.wrox.com and click the Register link.

2. Read the terms of use and click Agree.

3. Complete the required information to join as well as any optional information you wish to provide and click Submit.

4. You will receive an e-mail with information describing how to verify your account and complete the joining process.

   You can read messages in the forums without joining P2P but in order to post your own messages, you must join.

Once you join, you can post new messages and respond to messages that other users post. You can read messages at any time on the Web. If you would like to have new messages from a particular forum e-mailed to you, click the Subscribe to this Forum icon by the forum name in the forum listing.

For more information about how to use the Wrox P2P, be sure to read the P2P FAQs for answers to questions about how the forum software works as well as many common questions specific to P2P and Wrox books. To read the FAQs, click the FAQ link on any P2P page.

And Finally. . .

This book has involved many long hours of work, and the feedback from readers of the previous editions has been a great encouragement to keep going. But as I look out on an English garden where the daffodils and cherry blossom of spring are competing with the last hail showers of winter, I find a particular poignancy in Rupert Brooke's poem, used so often throughout the book as an example text:

My heart all Winter lay so numb,
The earth so dead and frore,
That I never thought the Spring would come again
Or my heart wake any more.

But Winter's broken and earth has woken,
And the small birds cry again;
And the hawthorn hedge puts forth its buds,
And my heart puts forth its pain.

I hope you will find my efforts worthwhile.

List of Examples

This list includes all the worked examples in the book: that is, the examples consisting of entire stylesheets, for which working code can be downloaded from `http://www.wrox.com/`. It does not include the many examples that are provided as incomplete snippets.

The purpose of this list is to help you out when you know that you've seen an example somewhere that is relevant to your current problem, but you can't remember where you saw it.

Chapter 1

Description	Page
A Hello World Stylesheet	10
This stylesheet creates an HTML containing a greeting (such as "Hello, World!") read from the source XML document	
Tabulating Word Frequencies	15
Given any XML document, this stylesheet produces a list of the words that appear in its text, giving the number of times each word appears, together with its frequency. This illustrates features in XSLT 2.0 for analyzing text using regular expressions, and for grouping based on common values	
Displaying a Poem	37
This stylesheet shows how to use template rules to render the text of a poem in HTML	

Chapter 2

Description	Page
An XML Tree	48
This example shows how an XML document is represented as a tree in the data model	
Push Processing	65
This stylesheet shows the use of template rules to display a list of books in HTML	
Controlling the Sequence of Processing	68
This example shows a refinement of the previous stylesheet in which the `select` attribute of `<xsl:apply-templates>` is used to control the sequence of different parts of the output	

Continues

List of Examples

Description	Page
Selecting Nodes Explicitly	69
This shows a further refinement of the book list stylesheet in which some aspects of the output are generated using `<xsl:value-of>` instructions	

Chapter 3

Description	Page
Using <xsl:include>	85
This example shows the use of `<xsl:include>` to split a stylesheet into three modules performing distinct tasks: one to format the current date, one to construct a copyright statement, and one to control the rest of the processing	
Using <xsl:import>	89
This stylesheet extends the previous example, showing how `<xsl:import>` allows some of the declarations in one module to be overridden in the importing module	
Embedded Stylesheets	96
This example shows the use of a stylesheet embedded within the source document that it is designed to display	
A Simplified Stylesheet	120
This is an example of a simplified stylesheet module, that is, a stylesheet whose outermost element is a literal result element rather than an `<xsl:stylesheet>` element.	
Using An Extension Instruction	134
This stylesheet uses Saxon's `<saxon:while>` element to illustrate how a stylesheet can call extension instructions provided by a vendor or third party	

Chapter 5

Description	Page
Using Modes	194
The example uses a mode to display a list of characters appearing in a play	
Checking for Cycles in a Graph	199
This example provides a generic procedure to look for cycles in a graph, and then applies this procedure to data file to see if the ID/IDREF links are cyclic. It illustrates the use of `<xsl:apply-templates>` to simulate a higher-order function	

Description	Page
Generating an Attribute Conditionally	211
This example shows the use of `<xsl:attribute>` to generate an attribute only when certain conditions are true	
Deciding the Attribute Name at Runtime	213
This example shows the use of `<xsl:attribute>` to generate an attribute whose name is not known until execution time	
Using an Attribute Set for Numbering	218
This stylesheet shows an unusual way of using attribute sets, to illustrate that the attributes generated by an attribute set do not need to have fixed values	
Using Recursion to Process a Sequence of Nodes	224
This example illustrates how to use a recursive named template to process a sequence of nodes. It uses this technique to find the longest speech in a play	
Using Recursion to Process a Sequence of Strings	227
This example uses a recursive named template to process a sequence of strings, obtained by splitting a line of text into its constituent words. It uses this technique to find phrases of the form "A and B", where A and B are both the names of characters in a play	
Using Character Maps to Comment-Out Elements	234
This example shows the use of `<xsl:character-map>` to generate XML start and end comment delimiters around a section of an XML document that contains element markup.	
Using `<xsl:copy-of>` to Produce Repeated Output	247
This stylesheet uses `<xsl:copy-of>` to generate a standard table heading that appears repeatedly in the HTML output document (a listing of soccer matches)	
Converting Attributes to Child Elements	270
This example illustrates how `<xsl:element>` can be used to create element nodes whose names and content are taken from the names and values of attributes in the source document	
Showing the Ancestors of a Node	279
This example stylesheet can be applied to any XML document. For each element it processes all its ancestor elements, in reverse document order (that is, starting with the parent node and ending with the document element), and outputs their names to a comment that shows the position of the current node	
Single-Level Grouping by Value	286
This example uses `<xsl:for-each-group>` to group a set of employees according to the department in which they work	

Continues

List of Examples

Description	Page
Multilevel Grouping by Value	288
This example groups employees by department, and groups the departments by location	
Grouping Consecutive Elements by Name	291
This example shows how the `group-adjacent` attribute of `<xsl:for-each-group>` can be used to group adjacent elements having the same element name. It applies this technique to the adjacent `<speaker>` and `<line>` elements in a Shakespeare play	
Handling Repeating Groups of Adjacent Elements	294
This takes the previous example and makes the problem more difficult, by removing another layer of markup from the source document, so that it is necessary to infer multiple levels of hierarchic structure from the pattern of leaf elements in the tree	
Handling Flat XHTML Documents	296
This example shows how to use the `group-starting-with` attribute of `<xsl:for-each-group>` to process the implicit structure of an XHTML source document, in which an `<Hn>` element is followed by a number of `<P>` elements that are logically subordinate to the `<Hn>` element, but actually appear as its siblings	
Looking for Cycles Among Attribute Sets	307
This example illustrates the use of recursive stylesheet functions to analyze a graph structure. Specifically, it analyzes an XSLT stylesheet as its source document, to determine whether there are any cyclic dependencies among the attribute set definitions in the stylesheet	
Formatting a List of Names	311
This example shows the use of `<xsl:if>` to produce punctuation between the items in a list, where the punctuation depends on the position of the item within the list	
Precedence of Variables	320
This example shows how an importing stylesheet module can declare global variables with the same names as variables within the imported module, and how the variables in the importing module take precedence	
Precedence of Template Rules	321
This example shows how an importing stylesheet module can declare template rules that override template rules within the imported module. It also shows the use of `<xsl:apply-imports>` in an overriding template rule, to invoke the functionality of the template rule that was overridden	
Using `<xsl:include>` with Named Attribute Sets	331
This example illustrates the use of `<xsl:include>` to incorporate declarations (in this case, attribute set declarations) from one stylesheet module into another	

Description	Page
Multivalued non-Unique Keys	338
This example shows the use of an `<xsl:key>` definition in which several elements can have the same key value, and a single element can have multiple key values. Specifically, this situation arises when books are indexed by the names of their authors	
Generating a Stylesheet using `<xsl:namespace-alias>`	354
This example shows the way in which `<xsl:namespace-alias>` can be used when writing a stylesheet whose task is to generate (or modify) another XSLT stylesheet	
Numbering the Lines of a Poem	371
This stylesheet uses `<xsl:number>` to selectively number the lines of a poem	
Using `<xsl:param>` with a Default Value	399
This is an example of a named template that defines a default value for an optional template parameter. The stylesheet can be run against any source document, and displays the depth of nesting of the nodes in that document	
Tunnel Parameters	400
This example shows how tunnel parameters can be useful when customizing an existing stylesheet, for reducing the number of rules in the existing stylesheet that need to me modified. The specific example shows how to produce a modified rendition of a Shakespeare play in which the lines for each actor are highlighted	
Creating Multiple Output Files	418
This stylesheet uses the `<xsl:result-document>` instruction to split a source document into multiple result documents	
Sorting on the Results of a Calculation	431
This example uses `<xsl:sort>` to sort items on a value that does not appear explicitly in either the source or result documents, but is computed. (It produces a sales report for different flavors of jam)	
Template Rules	456
This is an illustration of the classic use of template rules to control the rendition of narrative text, in this case, short biographies of concert soloists	
Using Modes	458
This stylesheet modifies the previous example showing how modes can be used to process the same source data in more than one way, using different template rules. It illustrates this by including at the end of each biography a summary of the performances in which the artist has appeared	

Continues

List of Examples

Description	Page
Using a Variable for Content-Sensitive Values	478
This example shows how a variable can be used to hold on to information that depends on the context, for use when the context has changed	
Capturing the Result of a Template in a Variable	482
This stylesheet processes the source document using a template, and captures the result of this processing in a variable, so that the result can be further processed before producing the final result tree	
A Multiphase Transformation	484
Another example of a stylesheet that uses variables to capture the result of one phase of processing, so that further processing can be carried out before delivering the final result. In this case the first phase calculates the results of a soccer tournament, and the second phase displays these results as HTML	

Chapter 6

Description	Page
Using the key() Pattern to Format a Specific Node	520
This stylesheet shows how a match pattern for a template rule can use the `key()` function to apply distinctive formatting to one selected node in the source document	

Chapter 7

Description	Page
Using the current() Function	527
This stylesheet shows the use of the `current()` function within an XPath predicate, effectively to do a join: Given a book, it selects other books in the same category	
Using the document() Function to Analyze a Stylesheet	537
A stylesheet is an XML document, so it can be used as the input to another stylesheet. This makes it very easy to write little tools that manipulate stylesheets. This example shows such a tool, designed to report on the hierarchic structure of the modules that make up a stylesheet	
A Look-Up Table in the Stylesheet	540
This example uses data in a look-up table to expand abbreviations of book categories. Two techniques are shown: In the first example the look-up table is held in the stylesheet, and in the second example it is held in a separate XML document	

Description	Page
Creating Multiple Output Files	545
The main purpose of this example is to show how the `element-available()` function can be used to write stylesheets that are portable across different XSLT processors, even though they use facilities that are provided in different ways by different processors	
Testing for xx:node-set() Extensions	566
This example shows how the `function-available()` function can be used to write stylesheets that are portable across different XSLT processors, even though they use facilities that are provided in different ways by different processors	
Testing the Availability of a Java Method	568
This example shows the use of the «use-when» attribute to compile two different versions of a global variable declaration, depending on which version of the Java JDK is in use	
Using generate-id() to Create Links	570
This stylesheet produces information about holiday resorts as an HTML document; the hyperlinks within the document are generated by calling the `generate-id()` function to produce unique anchors	
Using Keys as Cross-References	575
This example uses two source files: The principal source document is a file containing a list of books, and the secondary one (accessed using the `document()` function) contains biographies of authors. The author name held in the first file acts as a cross-reference to the author's biography in the second file, rather like a join in SQL	
Using Keys for Grouping	578
This example shows the use of the XSLT 1.0 Muenchian grouping method to create a list of cities, grouped by country	
Processing a Comma-Separated-Values File	589
This example is a stylesheet that uses the `unparsed-text()` function to read a comma-separated-values file, given the URL of the file as a stylesheet parameter. It outputs an XML representation of this file, placing the rows in a `<row>` element and each value in a `<cell>` element	

Chapter 8

Description	Page
Using VBScript in an MSXML3 Stylesheet	600
This example shows a stylesheet that uses a VBScript extension function to convert dimensions in inches to the equivalent in millimeters	

Continues

List of Examples

Description	Page
A Java Extension Function to Calculate a Square Root	602
This example invokes a standard method in the Java class library to compute the square root of a number in the source document	
Calling External Functions within a Loop	606
This stylesheet calls external Java methods to read a source file, one line at a time, by means of recursive calls	
A Function with Uncontrolled Side Effects	609
This example shows what can go wrong with extension functions: Although it is apparently only a minor change to the previous example, it produces completely wrong results because it depends on the order in which instructions are executed	

Chapter 9

Description	Page
A "Fill-in-the-Blanks" Stylesheet	614
This stylesheet illustrates the fill-in-the-blanks design pattern. It is a simplified stylesheet that consists essentially of the target HTML page, with `<xsl:value-of>` instructions inserted at the points where variable data is to be fetched from the XML source document	
A Navigational Stylesheet	617
This example shows the use of a navigational stylesheet to produce a very simple sales report	
A Rule-Based Stylesheet	621
Rule-based stylesheets are often used to process narrative documents, where most of the processing consists in replacing XML tags by HTML tags. This example illustrates this by showing how a Shakespeare play can be rendered in HTML	
Aggregating a List of Numbers	634
This is an example of the computational design pattern: The stylesheet uses a recursive template to process a whitespace-separated list of numbers. Recursive processing is needed to produce cumulative totals efficiently, since none of the standard aggregation functions supports this directly	
Using Interleaved Structures	637
Lines of verse aren't neatly nested inside speeches, and speeches aren't nested inside lines of verse: The two structures are interleaved. The usual solution to this problem is to use the hierarchic XML tagging to represent one of the structures (say the speeches) and to use empty element tags to mark the boundaries in the other structure. This example shows a stylesheet that can convert from one of these representations to the other	

Chapter 10

Description	Page
Formatting the XML Specification	645
This entire chapter is devoted to the study of a single "real-life" application, the family of stylesheets used to process the XML specification and other related W3C documents	

Chapter 11

Description	Page
Converting from GEDCOM 5.5 to GEDCOM 6.0	703
This stylesheet converts genealogical data from one version of the GEDCOM standard to a subsequent version. The older version is a non-XML format, so part of the task is to convert this to XML, which is done by writing a GEDCOM parser that implements the SAX parser interfaces, so it can be called directly by an XSLT processor. This stylesheet is schema-aware, using the schema for GEDCOM 6.0 to validate the output as it is written	
Displaying the Family Tree Data	714
This stylesheet produces an XHTML representation of the information concerning one individual in a GEDCOM 6.0 data file. The stylesheet is schema-aware, using a schema both to validate the input document and to ensure that the output is valid XHTML	
Publishing Static HTML	728
This stylesheet incorporates the previous stylesheet, and uses it to create a set of linked XHTML pages displaying all the individuals in the input GEDCOM 6.0 data file	
Generating HTML Pages from a Servlet	730
This stylesheet shows an alternative way of displaying the family tree data: This time, HTML pages are generated on demand, by a transformation invoked from a Java servlet	
Generating HTML in the Browser	735
This stylesheet (which is restricted to use XSLT 1.0 facilities because of browser limitations) shows a third way of displaying the same data, this time by means of a transformation performed client side, and controlled by script on the HTML page	

Chapter 12

Description	Page
Knight's Tour of the Chessboard	739

Knight's Tour of the Chessboard

This entire chapter is devoted to the study of a single program, a computational stylesheet that calculates a route for a knight on a chessboard, in which from any starting square, each square on the board is visited exactly once. The stylesheet demonstrates how even quite complex algorithms can be implemented in XSLT by use of recursive functions

XSLT in Context

This chapter is designed to put XSLT in context. It's about the purpose of XSLT and the task it was designed to perform. It's about what kind of language it is, how it came to be that way, and how it has changed in version 2.0; and it's about how XSLT fits in with all the other technologies that you are likely to use in a typical Web-based application. I won't be saying very much in this chapter about what an XSLT stylesheet actually looks like or how it works: that will come later, in Chapters 2 and 3.

The chapter starts by describing the task that XSLT is designed to perform—**transformation**—and why there is the need to transform XML documents. I'll then present a trivial example of a transformation in order to explain what this means in practice.

Next, I cover the different ways of using XSLT within the overall architecture of an application, in which there will inevitably be many other technologies and components, each playing their own part. We then discuss the relationship of XSLT to other standards in the growing XML family, to put its function into context and explain how it complements the other standards.

I'll describe what kind of language XSLT is, and delve a little into the history of how it came to be like that. If you're impatient you may want to skip the history and get on with using the language, but sooner or later you will ask "why on earth did they design it like that?" and at that stage I hope you will go back and read about the process by which XSLT came into being.

What is XSLT?

XSLT (which stands for eXtensible Stylesheet Language: Transformations) is a language that, according to the very first sentence in the specification (found at `http://www.w3.org/TR/xslt20/`), is primarily designed for transforming one XML document into another. However, XSLT is also capable of transforming XML to HTML and many other text-based formats, so a more general definition might be as follows:

XSLT is a language for transforming the structure and content of an XML document.

Why should you want to do that? In order to answer this question properly, we first need to remind ourselves why XML has proved such a success and generated so much excitement.

XML is a simple, standard way to interchange structured textual data between computer programs. Part of its success comes because it is also readable and writable by humans, using nothing more complicated than a text editor, but this doesn't alter the fact that it is primarily intended for communication between software systems. As such, XML satisfies two compelling requirements:

❑ *Separating data from presentation*: the need to separate information (such as a weather forecast) from details of the way it is to be presented on a particular device. The early motivation for this arose from the need to deliver information not only to the traditional PC-based Web browser (which itself comes in many flavors), but also to TV sets and WAP phones, not to mention the continuing need to produce print-on-paper. Today, for many information providers an even more important driver is the opportunity to syndicate content to other organizations that can republish it with their own look-and-feel.

❑ *Transmitting data between applications*: the need to transmit information (such as orders and invoices) from one organization to another without investing in bespoke software integration projects. As electronic commerce gathers pace, the amount of data exchanged between enterprises increases daily, and this need becomes ever more urgent.

Of course, these two ways of using XML are not mutually exclusive. An invoice can be presented on the screen as well as being input to a financial application package, and weather forecasts can be summarized, indexed, and aggregated by the recipient instead of being displayed directly. Another of the key benefits of XML is that it unifies the worlds of documents and data, providing a single way of representing structure regardless of whether the information is intended for human or machine consumption. The main point is that, whether the XML data is ultimately used by people or by a software application, it will very rarely be used directly in the form it arrives: it first has to be transformed into something else.

In order to communicate with a human reader, this something else might be a document that can be displayed or printed: for example, an HTML file, a PDF file, or even audible sound. Converting XML to HTML for display is the most common application of XSLT today, and it is the one I will use in most of the examples in this book. Once you have the data in HTML format, it can be displayed on any browser.

In order to transfer data between different applications we need to be able to transform information from the data model used by one application to the model used by another. To load the data into an application, the required format might be a comma-separated-values file, a SQL script, an HTTP message, or a sequence of calls on a particular programming interface. Alternatively, it might be another XML file using a different vocabulary from the original. As XML-based electronic commerce becomes widespread, the role of XSLT in data conversion between applications also becomes ever more important. Just because everyone is using XML does not mean the need for data conversion will disappear.

There will always be multiple standards in use. For example, the NewsML format for exchanging news stories (`http://www.newsml.org/pages/index.php`) has wide support among Western newspaper publishers and press agencies, but attracts little support from broadcasters. Meanwhile, broadcasters in Japan are concentrating their efforts on the Broadcast Markup Language (`http://xml.coverpages.org/bml.html`). This has a very different scope and purpose; but ultimately, it can handle the same content in a different form, and there is therefore a need for transformation when information is passed from one industry sector to the other.

Even within the domain of a single standard, there is a need to extract information from one kind of document and insert it into another. For example, a PC manufacturer who devises a solution to a customer problem will need to extract data from the problem reports and insert it into the documents issued to field engineers so they can recognize and fix the problem when other customers hit it. The field engineers, of course, are probably working for a different company, not for the original manufacturer. So, linking up enterprises to do e-commerce will increasingly become a case of defining how to extract and combine data from one set of XML documents to generate another set of XML documents: and XSLT is the ideal tool for the job.

At the end of this chapter we will come back to specific examples of when XSLT should be used to transform XML. For now, I just wanted to establish a feel for the importance and usefulness of transforming XML. If you are already using XSLT, of course, this may be stale news. So let's take a look now at what XSLT version 2.0 brings to the party.

Why Version 2.0?

XSLT 1.0 came out in November 1999 and has been highly successful. It was therefore almost inevitable that work would start on a version 2.0. As we will see later, the process of creating version 2.0 has been far from smooth and has taken rather longer than some people hoped.

It's easy to look at version 2.0 and see it as a collection of features bolted on to the language, patches to make up for the weaknesses of version 1.0. As with a new release of any other language or software package, most users will find some features here that they have been crying out for, and other additions that appear surplus to requirements.

But I think there is more to version 2.0 than just a bag of goodies; there are some underlying themes that have guided the design and the selection of features. I can identify three main themes:

- ❑ *Integration across the XML standards family*: W3C working groups do not work in isolation from each other; they spend a lot of time trying to ensure that their efforts are coordinated. A great deal of what is in XSLT 2.0 is influenced by a wider agenda of doing what is right for the whole raft of XML standards, not just for XSLT considered in isolation.

- ❑ *Extending the scope of applicability*: XSLT 1.0 is pretty good at rendering XML documents for display as HTML on screen, and for converting them to XSL Formatting Objects for print publishing. But there are many other transformation tasks for which it has proved less suitable. Compared with report writers (even those from the 1980s, let alone modern data visualization tools) its data handling capabilities are very weak. The language is quite good at doing conversions of XML documents if the original markup is well designed, but it's much weaker at recognizing patterns in the text or markup that represent hidden structure. An important aim of XSLT 2.0 is to increase the range of applications that you can tackle using XSLT.

- ❑ *Tactical usability improvements*: Here we *are* into the realm of added goodies. The aim here is to achieve productivity benefits, making it easier to do things that are difficult or error-prone in version 1.0. These are probably the features that existing users will immediately recognize as the most beneficial, but in the long term the other two themes probably have more strategic significance for the future of the language.

Before we discuss XSLT in more detail and have a first look at how it works, let's study a scenario that clearly demonstrates the variety of formats to which we can transform XML, using XSLT.

A Scenario: Transforming Music

As an indication of how far XML has now penetrated, Robin Cover's index of XML-based application standards at http://xml.coverpages.org/xmlApplications.html today runs to over

580 entries. (The last one is entitled *Mind Reading Markup Language*, but as far as I can tell, all the other entries are serious.)

I'll follow just one of these 580 links, *XML and Music*, which takes us to http://xml.coverpages .org/xmlMusic.html. On this page we find a list of no less than 17 standards, proposals, or initiatives that use XML for marking up music.

Some of this diversity is unnecessary, and many of these initiatives will bear little fruit. Even the names of the standards are chaotic: there is a Music Markup Language, a MusicML, a MusicXML, and a MusiXML, all of which appear to be quite unrelated. There are at least two really serious contenders: the Music Encoding Initiative (MEI) and the Standard Music Description Language (SMDL). The MEI derives its inspiration from the Text Encoding Initiative, which is widely used by the library community for creating digital text archives, while SMDL is related to the HyTime hypermedia standards and takes into account requirements such as the need to synchronize music with video or with a lighting script.

The diversity of standards is inevitable before the industry can come up with a standard that works for everyone. Without variety, there can be no innovation or experimentation. In fact, the likely outcome is not a single standard, but a collection of three or four different standards that are optimized for different needs. The different notations were invented with different purposes in mind: a markup language used by a publisher for printing sheet music has different requirements from the one designed to let you listen to the music from a browser.

For most of us, music may be fun, a diversion from the world of work. But for others, it is a very serious billion-dollar business. Standards that make information interchange in this business easier have an enormous economic impact. Whether you're interested in the music or the money, we're not dealing here with something that's trivial. So it shouldn't be surprising that so much effort is going into the process of creating standards in this area.

In earlier editions of this book I introduced the idea of using XSLT to transform music as a theoretical possibility, something to make my readers think about the range of possibilities open for the language. Today, it is no longer a theoretical possibility—people are actually doing it.

With 17 different schemas for music in existence, all with different strengths and weaknesses (and fan clubs), there is a big need to convert information from one of these formats to any of the others. There is also a need to convert information from any of these formats to a printable score or an audible performance of the music, as well as a need to create XML representations of music from non-XML sources such as MIDI files (Figure 1-1). XSLT has a role to play in all of these conversions.

So you could use XSLT to:

❑ Convert music from one of these representations to another, for example from MEI to SMDL.

❑ Convert music from any of these representations into visual music notation, by generating the XML-based vector graphics format SVG.

❑ Play the music on a synthesizer, by generating a MIDI (Musical Instrument Digital Interface) file.

❑ Perform a musical transformation, such as transposing the music into a different key or extracting parts for different instruments or voices.

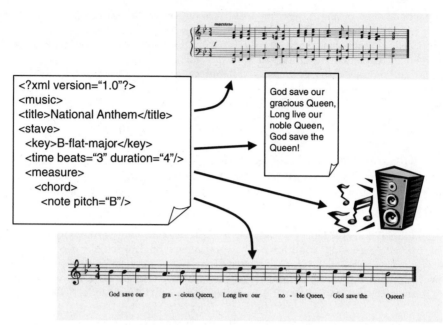

Figure 1-1

❑ Extract the lyrics, into HTML or into a text-only XML document.

❑ Capture music from non-XML formats and translate it to XML (XSLT 2.0 is especially useful here).

As you can see, XSLT is not just for converting XML documents to HTML.

For some real examples of XSLT stylesheets used to transform music, take a look at a thesis written by Baron Schwartz at the University of Virginia (http://www.cs.virginia.edu/~bps7j/thesis/).

How Does XSLT Transform XML?

By now you are probably wondering exactly how XSLT goes about processing an XML document in order to convert it into the required output. There are usually two aspects to this process:

1. The first stage is a structural transformation, in which the data is converted from the structure of the incoming XML document to a structure that reflects the desired output.

2. The second stage is formatting, in which the new structure is output in the required format such as HTML or PDF.

The second stage covers the ground we discussed in the previous section; the data structure that results from the first stage can be output as HTML, a text file, or as XML. HTML output allows the information to be viewed directly in a browser by a human user or be input into any modern word processor. Plain text output allows data to be formatted in the way an existing application can accept, for example comma-separated values or one of the many text-based data interchange formats that were developed before XML arrived on the scene. Finally, XML output allows the data to be supplied to one of the new breed of applications that accepts XML directly. Typically, this will use a different vocabulary of XML tags from the original document: for example, an XSLT transformation might take the monthly sales figures as its XML input and produce a histogram as its XML output, using the XML-based SVG standard for vector graphics. Or, you could use an XSLT transformation to generate Voice XML output, for aural rendition of your data.

Information about VoiceXML can be found at `http://www.voicexml.org/`.

Let's now delve into the first stage, transformation—the stage with which XSLT is primarily concerned and which makes it possible to provide output in all of these formats. This stage might involve selecting data, aggregating and grouping it, sorting it, or performing arithmetic conversions such as changing centimeters to inches.

So how does this come about? Before the advent of XSLT, you could only process incoming XML documents by writing a custom application. The application wouldn't actually need to parse the raw XML, but it would need to invoke an XML parser, via a defined Application Programming Interface (API), to get information from the document and do something with it. There are two principal APIs for achieving this: the Simple API for XML (SAX) and the Document Object Model (DOM).

The SAX API is an event-based interface in which the parser notifies the application of each piece of information in the document as it is read. If you use the DOM API, then the parser interrogates the document and builds a tree-like object structure in memory. You would then write a custom application (in a procedural language such as C#, Visual Basic, or Java, for example), which could interrogate this tree structure. It would do so by defining a specific *sequence of steps* to be followed in order to produce the required output. Thus, whatever parser you use, this process has the same principal drawback: every time you want to handle a new kind of XML document, you have to write a new custom program, describing a different sequence of steps, to process the XML.

So, how is using XSLT to perform transformations on XML better than writing custom applications? Well, the design of XSLT is based on a recognition that these programs are all very similar, and it should therefore be possible to describe what they do using a high-level *declarative* language rather than writing each program from scratch in C#, Visual Basic, or Java. The required transformation can be expressed as a set of rules. These rules are based on defining what output should be generated when particular patterns occur in the input. The language is declarative in the sense that you describe the transformation you require, rather than providing a sequence of procedural instructions to achieve it. XSLT describes the required transformation and then relies on the XSLT processor to decide the most efficient way to go about it.

XSLT still relies on an XML parser—it might be a DOM parser or a SAX-compliant one, or one of the new breed of "pull parsers"—to convert the XML document into a tree structure. It is the structure of this tree representation of the document that XSLT manipulates, not the document itself. If you are familiar with the DOM, then you will be happy with the idea of treating every item in an XML document (elements, attributes, processing instructions, and so on) as a node in a tree. With XSLT we have a high-level language that can navigate around a node tree, select specific nodes, and perform complex manipulations on these nodes.

The XSLT tree model is similar in concept to the DOM but it is not the same. The full XSLT processing model is discussed in Chapter 2.

The description of XSLT given thus far (a declarative language that can navigate to and select specific data and then manipulate that data) may strike you as being similar to that of the standard database query language, SQL. Let's take a closer look at this comparison.

XSLT and SQL: An Analogy

In a relational database, the data consists of a set of tables. By themselves, the tables are not of much use, the data might as well be stored in flat files in comma-separated values format. The power of a relational database doesn't come from its data structure: it comes from the language that processes the data, SQL. In the same way, XML on its own just defines a data structure. It's a bit richer than the tables of the relational model, but by itself it doesn't actually do anything very useful. It's when we get a high-level language expressly designed to manipulate the data structure that we start to find we've got something interesting on our hands, and for XML data the main language that does that is XSLT.

Superficially, SQL and XSLT are very different languages. But if you look below the surface, they actually have a lot in common. For starters, in order to process specific data, be it in a relational database or an XML document, the processing language must incorporate a declarative query syntax for selecting the data that needs to be processed. In SQL, that's the SELECT statement. In XSLT, the equivalent is the *XPath expression*.

The XPath expression language forms an essential part of XSLT, though it is actually defined in a separate W3C Recommendation (http://www.w3.org/TR/xpath) because it can also be used independently of XSLT (the relationship between XPath and XSLT is discussed further on page 21). For the same reason, I cover the details of XPath in a companion book, *XPath 2.0 Programmer's Reference*.

The XPath syntax is designed to retrieve nodes from an XML document, based on a path through the XML document or the context in which the node appears. It allows access to specific nodes, while preserving the hierarchy and structure of the document. XSLT is then used to manipulate the results of these queries, for example by rearranging selected nodes and constructing new nodes.

There are further similarities between XSLT and SQL:

❑   Both languages augment the basic query facilities with useful additions for performing arithmetic, string manipulation, and comparison operations.

❑   Both languages supplement the declarative query syntax with semiprocedural facilities for describing the processing to be carried out, and they also provide hooks to escape into conventional programming languages where the algorithms start to get too complex.

❑   Both languages have an important property called *closure*, which means that the output has the same data structure as the input. For SQL, this structure is tables, for XSLT it is trees—the tree representation of XML documents. The closure property is extremely valuable because it means operations performed using the language can be combined end-to-end to define bigger, more complex operations: you just take the output of one operation and make it the input of the next operation. In SQL you can do this by defining views or subqueries; in XSLT you can do it by passing your data through a series of stylesheets, or by capturing the output of one transformation phase as a temporary tree, and using that temporary tree as the input of another transformation phase. This last feature is new in XSLT 2.0, though most XSLT 1.0 processors offered a similar capability as a language extension.

In the real world, of course, XSLT and SQL have to coexist. There are many possible relationships but typically, data is stored in relational databases and transmitted between systems in XML. The two languages don't fit together as comfortably as one would like, because the data models are so different. But XSLT transformations can play an important role in bridging the divide. A number of database vendors have delivered (or at least promised) products that integrate XML and SQL, and some standards are starting to emerge in this area. Check the vendor's Web sites for the latest releases of Microsoft SQL Server, IBM DB2, and Oracle 10*g*.

Before we look at a simple working example of an XSLT transformation, we should briefly discuss a few of the XSLT processors that are available to effect these transformations.

XSLT Processors

The job of an XSLT processor is to apply an XSLT stylesheet to an XML source document and produce a result document.

With XSLT 1.0, there are quite a few good XSLT processors to choose from, and many of them can be downloaded free of charge (but do read the licensing conditions).

If you're working in the Microsoft environment, there is a choice of two products. The most widely used option is MSXML3/4 (Google for "Download MSXML4" to find it). Usually, I'm not Microsoft's greatest fan, but with this processor it's generally agreed that they have done an excellent job. This product comes as standard with Internet Explorer and is therefore the preferred choice for running transformations in the browser. The XSLT processor differs little between MSXML3 and MSXML4: the differences are in what else comes in the package. MSXML3 also includes support for an obsolete but still-encountered dialect of XSLT called WD-xsl (which isn't covered in this book), while MSXML4 includes more extensive support for XML Schema processing. For the .NET environment, however, Microsoft has developed a new processor. This doesn't have a product name of its own, other than its package name within the .NET framework, which is `System.Xml.Xsl`. This processor is often said to be slower than the MSXML3 product, but if you're writing your application using .NET technologies such as C# and ASP.NET, it's probably the one that you'll find more convenient.

In the Java world, there's a choice of open-source products. There's my own Saxon product (version 6.5.3 is the version that supports XSLT 1.0) available from `http://saxon.sf.net/`, there's the Xalan-J product available from Apache at `http://xml.apache.org/`, there is a processor from Oracle, and there is the less well known but highly regarded `jd.xslt` product from Johannes Döbler at `http://www.aztecrider.com/`, which is sadly no longer available for free download. The standard for all these products was set by James Clark's original xt processor, which has been updated by Bill Lindsay and is now available at `http://www.blnz.com/xt/index.html`. A version of Xalan-J is bundled with Sun's Java JDK software from JDK 1.4 onwards.

Other popular XSLT processors include the `libxslt` engine (`http://xmlsoft.org/XSLT/`), Sablotron (`http://www.gingerall.com/charlie/ga/xml/p_sab.xml`), and 4XSLT (part of 4suite, see `http://4suite.org/index.xhtml`).

Most of these products are XSLT interpreters, but there are two well-known XSLT compilers: XSLTC, which is distributed as part of the Xalan-J package mentioned earlier, and Gregor, from Jacek Ambroziak (`http://www.ambrosoft.com/gregor.html`).

The XSLT processor bundled with the Netscape/Mozilla browser is Transformiix (`http://www.mozilla.org/projects/xslt/`).

There are a number of development environments that include XSLT processors with custom editing and debugging capabilities. Notable examples are XML Spy (http://www.altova.com) and Stylus Studio (http://www.stylusstudio.com/).

However, these are all XSLT 1.0 processors, and this book is about XSLT 2.0. With XSLT 2.0, at the time of writing, you really have one choice only, and that is my own Saxon product. By the time you read this, you will be able to get the Saxon XSLT 2.0 processor in two variants, corresponding to the two conformance levels defined in the W3C specification: Standard Saxon 8.x (http://saxon.sf.net/) is an open-source implementation of a basic XSLT 2.0 processor, and Saxon-SA 8.x (http://www.saxonica.com/) is a commercial implementation of a schema-aware XSLT processor. You can run most of the examples in this book, using a basic XSLT processor, but Chapter 4 and Chapter 11 focus on the additional capability of XSLT when used with XML Schemas, with examples that will only run with a schema-aware product.

There are several other XSLT 2.0 processors under development, though it's not my job to pass on unofficial rumors. Oracle has released a beta implementation (http://otn.oracle.com/tech/xml/xdk/xdkbeta.html). Apache has said that they are developing an XSLT 2.0 version of Xalan, and although things have been very quiet in public since they announced this, if you poke around the archives of their internal developers' mailing list (which are all openly available) you can see that work is proceeding, slowly but steadily.

The biggest uncertainty at the moment is what Microsoft will do. The MSXML3/4 products have been highly successful technically, though whether Microsoft considers them a commercial success is anyone's guess. The .NET processor also appears to be a competent piece of engineering. However, the unofficial rumor from Reston is that there is no XSLT 2.0 version of this technology under development. Instead, most of Microsoft's efforts seem to be going into the development of their XQuery engine, designed as part of the SQL Server release code-named Yukon. I have heard speculation that if and when Microsoft implements XSLT 2.0, it is likely to be done using this engine. XSLT 2.0 and XQuery 1.0 are so close in their semantics that it's entirely possible to implement both languages, using the same processing engine, as Saxon has already demonstrated.

It shouldn't really be a surprise that commercial vendors are keeping fairly quiet about their plans while the specifications are still working drafts. When a specification first comes out at version 1.0, there is a great deal of commercial advantage to be gained by releasing beta implementations as early as possible. With a 2.0 draft, it's more prudent to wait until you know exactly what's in the final specification. W3C specifications these days spend a long time in their "Candidate Recommendation" phase, and this is the time to look for evidence of implementation activity. Although XSLT 2.0 is close to reaching that phase, it isn't there yet at the time of writing.

I think it's a little unlikely that there will be quite as many XSLT 2.0 processors as there are for XSLT 1.0 (there is bound to be some shakeout in a maturing market), but I'm confident there will be four or five, which should be enough.

Meanwhile, there is Saxon, and that's what I will be using for all the examples in this book.

An XSLT 1.0 Stylesheet

We're now ready to take a look at an example of using XSLT to transform a very simple XML document.

Example: A "Hello, world!" XSLT Stylesheet

Kernighan and Ritchie in their classic *The C Programming Language* (Prentice-Hall, 1988) originated the idea of presenting a trivial but complete program right at the beginning of the book, and ever since then the `Hello world` program has been an honored tradition. Of course, a complete description of how this example works is not possible until all the concepts have been defined, and so if you feel I'm not explaining it fully, don't worry—the explanations will come later.

Input

What kind of transformation would we like to do? Let's try transforming the following XML document.

```
<?xml version="1.0" encoding="iso-8859-1"?>
<?xml-stylesheet type="text/xsl" href="hello.xsl"?>
<greeting>Hello, world!</greeting>
```

This document is available as file `hello.xml` in the download directory for this chapter.

A simple node-tree representation of this document is shown in Figure 1-2.

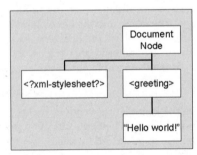

Figure 1-2

There are four nodes in this tree: a document node that represents the document as a whole; an `<?xml-stylesheet?>` processing instruction that identifies the stylesheet to be used; the `<greeting>` element; and the text within the `<greeting>` element.

The document node in the XSLT model performs the same function as the document node in the DOM model (it was called the root node in XSLT 1.0, but the nomenclature has been brought into line with the DOM). The XML declaration is not visible to the XSLT processor and, therefore, is not included in the tree.

I've deliberately made it easy by including an `<?xml-stylesheet?>` processing instruction in the source XML file. Many XSLT processors will use this to identify the stylesheet if you don't specify a different stylesheet to use. The `href` attribute gives the relative URI of the default stylesheet for this document.

Output

Our required output is the following HTML, which will simply change the browser title to "Today's Greeting" and display whatever greeting is in the source XML file:

```
<html>
<head>
   <title>Today's greeting</title>
</head>
<body>
   <p>Hello, world!</p>
</body>
</html>
```

XSLT Stylesheet

Without any more ado, here's the XSLT stylesheet hello.xsl to effect the transformation.

```
<?xml version="1.0" encoding="iso-8859-1"?>
<xsl:stylesheet
   version="1.0"
   xmlns:xsl="http://www.w3.org/1999/XSL/Transform">

<xsl:template match="/">
   <html>
   <head>
      <title>Today's greeting</title>
   </head>
   <body>
      <p><xsl:value-of select="greeting"/></p>
   </body>
   </html>
</xsl:template>

</xsl:stylesheet>
```

Running the Stylesheet

You can run this stylesheet in a number of different ways. The easiest is simply to load the XML file hello.xml into any recent version of Internet Explorer or Netscape. The browser will recognize the <?xml-stylesheet?> processing instruction and will use this to fetch the stylesheet and execute it. The result is a display like the one in Figure 1-3.

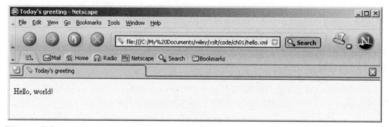

Figure 1-3

Note that this example is an XSLT 1.0 stylesheet. Current versions of Internet Explorer and Netscape don't yet support XSLT 2.0.

Saxon

Running the stylesheet with Saxon is a bit more complicated, because you first need to install the software. It's worth going through these steps, because you will need Saxon to run later examples in this book. The steps are as follows:

1. Ensure you have the Java SDK version 1.4 or later installed on your machine. You can get this from `http://java.sun.com/`. Saxon is pure Java code, and so it will run on any platform that supports Java, but I will usually assume that you are using a Windows machine.

2. Download the Saxon processor from `http://saxon.sf.net/`. Any version of Saxon will run this example, but we'll soon be introducing XSLT 2.0 examples, so install a recent version, say Saxon 7.9.

3. Unzip the download file into a suitable directory, for example `c:\saxon.`.

4. Within this directory, create a subdirectory called `data`.

5. Using Notepad, type the two files mentioned earlier into `hello.xml` and `hello.xsl` respectively, within this directory (or get them from the Wrox Web site at `http://www.wrox.com`).

6. Bring up an MSDOS-style console window (using Start | Programs | MSDOS Prompt on Windows 98 or NT, or look in the Accessories menu under Windows 2000 or Windows XT).

7. Type the following at the command prompt.

```
java -jar c:\saxon\saxon8.jar -a hello.xml
```

8. Admire the HTML displayed on the standard output.

If you want to view the output using your browser, simply save the command line output as an HTML file, in the following manner.

```
java -jar c:\saxon\saxon8.jar -a hello.xml >hello.html
```

(Using the command prompt in Windows isn't much fun. I would recommend acquiring a good text editor: most editors have the ability invoke a command line processor that is usually much more usable than the one provided by the operating system. I have recently started using `jEdit`, which is free and can be downloaded from `http://www.jedit.org/`. Be sure to install the optional Console plug-in.)

How It Works

If you've succeeded in running this example, or even if you just want to get on with reading the book, you'll want to know how it works. Let's dissect it.

```
<?xml version="1.0" encoding="iso-8859-1"?>
```

This is just the standard XML heading. The interesting point is that an XSLT stylesheet is itself an XML document. I'll have more to say about this, later in the chapter. I've used iso-8859-1 character encoding (which is the official name for the character set that Microsoft sometimes calls "ANSI") because in Western Europe and North America it's the character set that most text editors support. If you've got a text editor that supports UTF-8 or some other character encoding, feel free to use that instead.

```
<xsl:stylesheet
    version="1.0"
    xmlns:xsl="http://www.w3.org/1999/XSL/Transform">
```

This is the standard XSLT heading. In XML terms it's an element start tag, and it identifies the document as a stylesheet. The xmlns:xsl attribute is an XML Namespace declaration, which indicates that the prefix xsl is going to be used for elements defined in the W3C XSLT specification. XSLT makes extensive use of XML namespaces, and all the element names defined in the standard are prefixed with this namespace to avoid any clash with names used in your source document. The version attribute indicates that the stylesheet is only using features from version 1.0 of the XSLT standard.

Let's move on.

```
<xsl:template match="/">
```

An <xsl:template> element defines a template rule to be triggered when a particular part of the source document is being processed. The attribute «match="/"» indicates that this particular rule is triggered right at the start of processing the source document. Here «/» is an XPath expression that identifies the *document node* of the document: an XML document has a hierarchic structure, and in the same way as UNIX uses the special filename «/» to indicate the root of a hierarchic file store, XPath uses «/» to represent the root of the XML content hierarchy.

```
<html>
<head>
    <title>Today's greeting</title>
</head>
<body>
    <p><xsl:value-of select="greeting"/></p>
</body>
</html>
```

Once this rule is triggered, the body of the template says what output to generate. Most of the template body here is a sequence of HTML elements and text to be copied into the output file. There's one exception: an <xsl:value-of> element, which we recognize as an XSLT instruction, because it uses the namespace prefix xsl. This particular instruction copies the textual content of a node in the source document to the output document. The select attribute of the element specifies the node for which the value should be evaluated. The XPath expression «greeting» means "find the set of all <greeting> elements that are children of the node that this template rule is currently processing." In this case, this means the <greeting> element that's the outermost element of the source document. The <xsl:value-of> instruction then extracts the text of this element and copies it to the output at the relevant place—in other words, within the generated <p> element.

All that remains is to finish what we started.

```
    </xsl:template>

    </xsl:stylesheet>
```

In fact, for a simple stylesheet like the one shown earlier, you can cut out some of the red tape. Since there is only one template rule, the `<xsl:template>` element can actually be omitted. The following is a complete, valid stylesheet equivalent to the preceding one.

```
<html xsl:version="1.0"
      xmlns:xsl="http://www.w3.org/1999/XSL/Transform">
<head>
    <title>Today's greeting</title>
</head>
<body>
    <p><xsl:value-of select="greeting"/></p>
</body>
</html>
```

This simplified syntax is designed to make XSLT look familiar to people who have learned to use proprietary template languages that allow you to write a skeleton HTML page with special tags (analogous to `<xsl:value-of>`) to insert variable data at the appropriate place. But as we'll see, XSLT is much more powerful than that.

Why would you want to place today's greeting in a separate XML file and display it using a stylesheet? One reason is that you might want to show the greeting in different ways, depending on the context; for example, it might be shown differently on a different device, or the greeting might depend on the time of day. In this case, you could write a different stylesheet to transform the same source document in a different way. This raises the question of how a stylesheet gets selected at run-time. There is no single answer to this question: it depends on the product you are using.

With Saxon, we used the `-a` option to process the XML document using the stylesheet specified in its `<?xml-stylesheet?>` processing instruction. Instead, we could simply have specified the stylesheet on the command line:

```
java -jar c:\saxon\saxon8.jar hello.xml hello.xsl >hello.html
```

The same thing can also be achieved with the Microsoft XSLT product. Like Saxon, this has a command line interface; though, if you want to control it programmatically in the browser you will need to write an HTML page containing some script code to control the transformation. The `<?xml-stylesheet?>` processing instruction which I used in the example described earlier works only if you want to use the same stylesheet every time.

Having looked at a very simple XSLT 1.0 stylesheet, let's now look at a stylesheet that uses features that are new in XSLT 2.0.

An XSLT 2.0 Stylesheet

This stylesheet is very short, but it manages to use four or five new XSLT 2.0 and XPath 2.0 features within the space of a few lines. I wrote it in response to a user enquiry raised on the xsl-list at http://www.mulberrytech.com/ (an excellent place for meeting other XSLT developers with widely varying levels of experience); so it's a real problem, not an invention. The XSLT 1.0 solution to this problem is about 60 lines of code.

Example: Tabulating Word Frequencies

The problem is simply stated: given any XML document, produce a list of the words that appear in its text, giving the number of times each word appears, together with its frequency.

Input

The input can be any XML document. I will use the text of Shakespeare's *Othello* as an example; this is provided as othello.xml in the download files for this book.

Output

The required output is an XML file that lists words in decreasing order of frequency. For *Othello*, the output file starts like this.

```
<?xml version="1.0" encoding="UTF-8"?>
<wordcount>
   <word word="i" frequency="899"/>
   <word word="and" frequency="796"/>
   <word word="the" frequency="764"/>
   <word word="to" frequency="632"/>
   <word word="you" frequency="494"/>
   <word word="of" frequency="476"/>
   <word word="a" frequency="453"/>
   <word word="my" frequency="427"/>
   <word word="that" frequency="396"/>
   <word word="iago" frequency="361"/>
   <word word="in" frequency="343"/>
   <word word="othello" frequency="336"/>
   <word word="it" frequency="319"/>
   <word word="not" frequency="319"/>
   <word word="is" frequency="309"/>
   <word word="me" frequency="281"/>
   <word word="cassio" frequency="254"/>
```

Stylesheet

Here is the stylesheet that produces this output. You can find it in wordcount.xsl.

```
<?xml version="1.0" encoding="iso-8859-1"?>
<xsl:stylesheet
    version="2.0"
    xmlns:xsl="http://www.w3.org/1999/XSL/Transform">
```

```
<xsl:output method="xml" indent="yes"/>

<xsl:template match="/">
  <wordcount>
    <xsl:for-each-group group-by="." select="
          for $w in tokenize(string(.), '\W+') return lower-case($w)">
      <xsl:sort select="count(current-group())" order="descending"/>
      <word word="{current-grouping-key()}"
            frequency="{count(current-group())}"/>
    </xsl:for-each-group>
  </wordcount>
</xsl:template>

</xsl:stylesheet>
```

Let's see how this works.

The <xsl:stylesheet> element introduces the XSLT namespace, as before, and tells us that this stylesheet is designed to be used with an XSLT 2.0 processor.

The <xsl:output> element asks for the XML output of the stylesheet to be indented, which makes it much easier for humans to read.

There is one <xsl:template> element, as before, which defines the code to be executed when the document node of the source document is encountered. This generates a <wordcount> element in the result, and within this it puts the word frequencies.

To understand the <xsl:for-each-group> instruction, which is new in XSLT 2.0, we first need to look at its select attribute. This contains the XPath 2.0 expression

```
for $w in tokenize(string(.), '\W+') return lower-case($w)
```

This first calculates string(.), the string-value of the node currently being processed, which in this case contains the whole text of the input document, ignoring all markup. It then tokenizes this big string: that is, it splits it into a sequence of substrings. The tokenizing is done by applying the regular expression «\W+». Regular expressions are new in XPath 2.0 and XSLT 2.0, though they will be very familiar to users of other languages such as Perl. They provide the language with greatly enhanced text handling capability. This particular expression, «\W+», matches any sequence of one-or-more "non-word" characters, a convenient category that includes spaces, punctuation marks, and other separators. So the result of calling the tokenize() function is a sequence of strings containing the words that appear in the text.

The XPath «for» expression now applies the function lower-case() to each of the strings in this sequence, producing the lower-case equivalent of the word. (Almost everything in this XPath expression is new in XPath 2.0: the lower-case() function, the tokenize() function, the «for» expression, and indeed the ability to manipulate a sequence of strings.)

The XSLT stylesheet now takes this sequence of strings and applies the <xsl:for-each-group> instruction to it. This processes the body of the <xsl:for-each-group>

instruction once for each group of selected items, where a group is identified as those items that have a common value for a grouping key. In this case the grouping key is written as «group-by=" . "», which means that the values (the words) are grouped on their own value. (In another application, we might have chosen to group them by their length, or by their initial letter.) So, the body of the instruction is executed once for each distinct word, and the <xsl:sort> instruction tells us to sort the groups in descending order of the size of the groups (that is, the number of times each word appears). For each of the groups, we output a <word> element with two attributes: one attribute is the value we used as the grouping key, the other is the number of items in the group.

Don't worry if this example seemed a bit bewildering: it uses many concepts that haven't been explained yet. The purpose was to give you a feeling for some of the new features in XSLT 2.0 and XPath 2.0, which will all be explained in much greater detail elsewhere in this book (in the case of XSLT features) or in the companion book *XPath 2.0 Programmer's Reference*.

Having dipped our toes briefly into some XSLT code, I'd now like to step back to take a higher-level view, to discuss where XSLT as a technology fits into the big picture of designing applications for the Web.

Where to Use XSLT

This section identifies what tasks XSLT is good at, and by implication, tasks for which a different tool would be more suitable. I also look at alternative ways of using XSLT within the overall architecture of your application.

As I discussed at the beginning of the chapter, there are two main scenarios for using XSLT transformations: data conversion and publishing. We'll consider each of them separately.

Data Conversion Applications

Data conversion is not something that will go away just because XML has been invented. Even though an increasing number of data transfers between organizations or between applications within an organization are likely to be encoded in XML, there will still be different data models, different ways of representing the same thing, and different subsets of information that are of interest to different people (recall the example at the beginning of the chapter, where we were converting music between different XML representations and different presentation formats). So, however enthusiastic we are about XML, the reality is that there are going to be a lot of comma-separated-values files, EDI messages, and any number of other formats in use for a long time to come.

When you have the task of converting one XML data set into another, then XSLT is an obvious choice (Figure 1-4).

It can be used for extracting the data selectively, reordering it, turning attributes into elements or vice versa, or any number of similar tasks. It can also be used simply for validating the data. As a language, XSLT 1.0 was best at manipulating the structure of the information as distinct from its content: it was a good language for turning rows into columns, but for string handling (for example, removing any text that appears between square brackets) it was rather laborious compared with a language like JavaScript

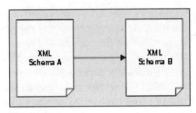

Figure 1-4

or Perl that offered support for regular expressions. This has changed considerably in version 2.0, and now there are few XML transformation tasks that I wouldn't tackle using XSLT.

XSLT is also useful for converting XML data into any text-based format, such as comma-separated values, or various EDI message formats (Figure 1-5). Text output is really just like XML output without the tags, so this creates no particular problems for the language.

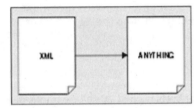

Figure 1-5

Perhaps more surprising is that XSLT can often be useful to convert from non-XML formats into XML or something else (Figure 1-6). In this case you'll need to write some kind of parser that understands the input format; but you would have had to do that anyway. The benefit is that once you've written the parser, the rest of the data conversion can be expressed in a high-level language. This separation also increases the chances that you'll be able to reuse your parser next time you need to handle that particular input format. I'll show you an example in Chapter 11, page 703, where the input is a rather old-fashioned and distinctly non-XML format widely used for exchanging data between genealogy software packages. It turns out that it isn't even necessary to write the data out as XML before using the XSLT stylesheet to process it: all you need to do is to make your parser look like an XML parser, by making it implement one of the standard parser interfaces: SAX or DOM. Most XSLT processors will accept input from a program that implements the SAX or DOM interfaces, even if the data never saw the light of day as XML.

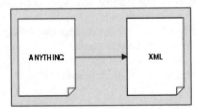

Figure 1-6

One caveat about data conversion applications: today's XSLT processors all rely on holding all the data in memory while the transformation is taking place. The tree structure in memory can be anything up to ten times the original data size, and so if you have 512MB of memory, I wouldn't advise tackling a transformation larger than 50MB, unless you do some performance tests first. Even at this size, a complex conversion can be quite time-consuming; it depends very much on the processing that you actually want to do.

One way around this is to split the data into chunks and convert each chunk separately—assuming, of course, that there is some kind of correspondence between chunks of input and chunks of output. But when this starts to get complicated, there comes a point where XSLT is no longer the best tool for the job. You would probably be better off-loading the data into an XML database such as Tamino or Xindice, and using the database query language to extract it again in a different sequence.

If you need to process large amounts of data serially, for example extracting selected records from a log of retail transactions, then an application written using the SAX interface might take a little longer to write than the equivalent XSLT stylesheet, but it is likely to run many times faster. Very often the combination of a SAX filter application to do simple data extraction, followed by an XSLT stylesheet to do more complex manipulation, can be the best solution in such cases.

Publishing

The difference between data conversion and publishing is that in the former case, the data is destined for input to another piece of software, while in the latter case it is destined to be read (you hope) by human beings. Publishing in this context doesn't just mean lavish text and multimedia, it also means data: everything from the traditional activity of producing and distributing reports so that managers know what's going on in the business, to producing online phone bills and bank statements for customers, and rail timetables for the general public. XML is ideal for such data publishing applications, as well as the more traditional text publishing, which was the original home territory of SGML.

XML was designed to enable information to be held independently of the way it is presented, which sometimes leads people into the fallacy of thinking that using XML for presentation details is somehow bad. Far from it, if you were designing a new format for downloading fonts to a printer today, you would probably make it XML-based. Presentation details have just as much right to be encoded in XML as any other kind of information. So, we can see the role of XSLT in the publishing process as being converting data-without-presentation to data-with-presentation, where both are, at least in principle, XML formats.

The two important vehicles for publishing information today are print-on-paper and the Web. The print-on-paper scene is the more difficult one, because of the high expectations of users for visual quality. XSL Formatting Objects attempts to define an XML-based model of a print file for high-quality display on paper or on screen. Because of the sheer number of parameters needed to achieve this, the standard has taken a while to come to maturity. But the Web is a less demanding environment, where all we need to do is convert the data to HTML and leave the browser to do the best it can on the display available. HTML, of course, is not XML, but it is close enough so that a simple mapping is possible. Converting XML to HTML is the most common application for XSLT today. It's actually a two-stage process: first convert to an XML-based model that is structurally equivalent to the target HTML, and then serialize this in HTML notation rather than strict XML.

The emergence of XHTML 1.0, of course, tidies up this process even further, because it is a pure XML format. But the emergence of XSLT has arguably reduced the need for XHTML, because once HTML becomes merely a transient protocol used to get information from the XSLT engine to the Web browser, its idiosyncrasies cease to matter so much.

When to Do the Conversion?

The process of publishing information to a user is illustrated in Figure 1-7.

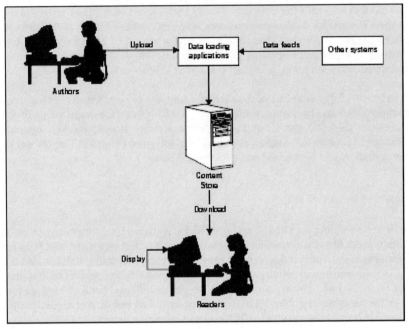

Figure 1-7

There are several points in such a system where XSLT transformations might be appropriate:

❑   Information entered by authors using their preferred tools, or customized form-filling interfaces, can be converted to XML and stored in that form in the content store.

❑   XML information arriving from other systems might be transformed into a different flavor of XML for storage in the content store. For example, it might be broken up into page-size chunks.

❑   XML can be translated into HTML on the server, when the users request a page. This can be controlled using technology such as Java servlets or Java Server Pages. On a Microsoft server you can invoke the transformation from script on ASP.NET pages.

❑   XML can be sent down to the client system and translated into HTML within the browser. This can give a highly interactive presentation of the information and remove a lot of the processing load from the server, but it relies on all the users having a browser that can do the job.

❑   XML data can also be converted into its final display form at publishing time and stored as HTML within the content store. This minimizes the work that needs to be done at display time and is ideal when the same displayed page is presented to very many users.

There isn't one right answer, and often a combination of techniques may be appropriate. Conversion in the browser is an attractive option when XSLT is widely available within browsers, but we still don't have universal availability of XSLT 1.0 in all browsers, let alone 2.0. Even when client-side conversion is done, there may still be a need for some server-side processing to deliver the XML in manageable chunks and to protect secure information. Conversion at delivery time on the server is a popular choice, because it allows personalization, but it can be a heavy overhead for sites with high traffic. Some busy sites have found that it is more effective to generate a different set of HTML pages for each section of the target audience in advance, and at page request time to do nothing more than select the right preconstructed HTML page.

It's time now to take a closer look at the relationship between XSLT and XPath and other XML-related technologies.

The Place of XSLT in the XML Family

XSLT is published by the World Wide Web Consortium (W3C) and fits into the XML family of standards, most of which are also developed by W3C. In this section I will try to explain the sometimes-confusing relationship of XSLT to other related standards and specifications.

XSLT and XSL

XSLT started life as part of a bigger language called *XSL (Extensible Stylesheet Language)*. As the name implies, XSL was (and is) intended to define the formatting and presentation of XML documents for display on screen, on paper, or in the spoken word. As the development of XSL proceeded, it became clear that this was usually a two-stage process: first a structural transformation, in which elements are selected, grouped and reordered; and then a formatting process in which the resulting elements are rendered as ink on paper, or pixels on the screen. It was recognized that these two stages were quite independent, so XSL was split into two parts: XSLT for defining transformations; and "the rest"—which is still officially called XSL, though most people prefer to call it *XSL-FO (XSL Formatting Objects)*—for the formatting stage.

XSL-FO is nothing more than another XML vocabulary, in which the objects described are areas of the printed page and their properties. Since this is just another XML vocabulary, XSLT needs no special capabilities to generate this as its output. XSL-FO is outside the scope of this book. It's a big subject (the specification is longer than XSLT). What's more, you're probably less likely to need it than to need XSLT. XSL-FO provides wonderful facilities to achieve high-quality typographical output of your documents. However, for many people translating documents into HTML for presentation by a standard browser is quite good enough, and that can be achieved using XSLT alone, or if necessary, by using XSLT in conjunction with Cascading Stylesheets (CSS or CSS2), which I shall return to shortly.

> *The XSL-FO specification became a Recommendation on 15 October 2001. It can be found at* `http://www.w3.org/TR/xsl`.

XSLT and XPath

Halfway through the development of XSLT 1.0, it was recognized that there was a significant overlap between the expression syntax in XSLT for selecting parts of a document and the XPointer language being developed for linking from one document to another. To avoid having two separate but overlapping expression languages, the two committees decided to join forces and define a single language, *XPath*, which would serve both purposes. XPath 1.0 was published on the same day as XSLT 1.0, 16 November 1999.

XPath acts as a sublanguage within an XSLT stylesheet. An XPath expression may be used for numerical calculations or string manipulations, or for testing Boolean conditions, but its most characteristic use (and the one that gives it its name) is to identify parts of the input document to be processed. For example, the following instruction outputs the average price of all the books in the input document:

```
<xsl:value-of select="avg(//book/@price)"/>
```

Here, the `<xsl:value-of>` element is an instruction defined in the XSLT standard, which causes a value to be written to the output document. The `select` attribute contains an XPath expression, which calculates the value to be written: specifically, the average value of the `price` attributes on all the `<book>` elements. (The `avg()` function too is new in XPath 2.0.)

Following its publication, the XPath specification increasingly took on a life of its own, separate from XSLT. Several DOM implementations (including Microsoft's) allowed you to select nodes within a DOM tree structure, using a method such as `selectNodes(XPath)`, and this feature is now included in the current version of the standard, DOM3. A subset of XPath is used within the XML Schema language, and bindings of XPath to other languages such as Perl are multiplying. The language has also proved interesting to academics, and a number of papers have been published analyzing its semantics, which provides the basis for optimized implementations.

The separation of XPath from XSLT works reasonably well, but as the earlier example shows, you need to understand the interaction between the two languages to see how a stylesheet works. In previous editions of this book I covered both languages together, but this time I have given each language its own volume, mainly because the amount of material had become too large for one book, and also because there are an increasing number of people who use XPath without also using XSLT. For the XSLT user, though, I'm afraid that at times you may have to keep both books open on your desk at once.

XSLT and XML

XSLT is essentially a tool for transforming XML documents. At the start of this chapter we discussed the reasons why this is important, but now we need to look a little more precisely at the relationship between the two. There are two particular aspects of XML that XSLT interacts with very closely: one is XML Namespaces; the other is the XML Information Set. These are discussed in the following sections.

XML Namespaces

XSLT is designed on the basis that *XML namespaces* are an essential part of the XML standard. So when the XSLT standard refers to an XML document, it really means an XML document that also conforms to the XML Namespaces specification, which can be found at `http://www.w3.org/TR/REC-xml-names`.

For a full explanation of XML Namespaces, see Chapter 11 of XML 1.1 Bible, Third Edition (Wiley, 2004).

Namespaces play an important role in XSLT. Their purpose is to allow you to mix tags from two different vocabularies in the same XML document. For example, in one vocabulary `<table>` might mean a two-dimensional array of data values, while in another vocabulary `<table>` refers to a piece of furniture. Here's a quick reminder of how they work:

❑ Namespaces are identified by a Uniform Resource Identifier (URI). This can take a number of forms. One form is the familiar URL, for example `http://www.wrox.com/namespace`. Another form, not fully standardized but being used in some XML vocabularies, is a URN, for example `urn:biztalk-org:biztalk:biztalk_1"`. The detailed form of the URI doesn't matter, but it is a good idea to choose one that will be unique. One good way of achieving this is to use the URL of your own Web site. But don't let this confuse you into thinking that there must be something on the Web site for the URL to point to. The namespace URI is simply a string that you have chosen to be different from other people's namespace URIs; it doesn't need to point to anything.

❏ The latest version, XML Namespaces 1.1, allows you to use an International Resource Identifier (IRI) rather than a URI. The main difference is that this permits characters from any alphabet; it is no longer confined to ASCII. In practice, most XML parsers have always allowed you to use any characters you like in a namespace URI.

❏ Since namespace URIs are often rather long and use special characters such as «/», they are not used in full as part of the element and attribute names. Instead, each namespace used in a document can be given a short nickname, and this nickname is used as a prefix of the element and attribute names. It doesn't matter what prefix you choose, because the real name of the element or attribute is determined only by its namespace URI and its local name (the part of the name after the prefix). For example, all my examples use the prefix `xsl` to refer to the namespace URI `http://www.w3.org/1999/XSL/Transform`, but you could equally well use the prefix `xslt`, so long as you use it consistently.

❏ For element names, you can also declare a default namespace URI, which is to be associated with unprefixed element names. The default namespace URI, however, does not apply to unprefixed attribute names.

A namespace prefix is declared using a special pseudo-attribute within any element start tag, with the form:

```
xmlns:prefix = "namespace-URI"
```

This declares a namespace prefix, which can be used for the name of that element, for its attributes, and for any element or attribute name contained in that element. The default namespace, which is used for elements having no prefix (but not for attributes), is similarly declared using a pseudo-attribute:

```
xmlns = "namespace-URI"
```

XSLT can't be used to process an XML document unless it conforms to the XML Namespaces Recommendation. In practice this isn't a problem, because most people are treating XML Namespaces as an intrinsic part of the XML standard, rather than a bolt-on optional extra. It does have certain implications, though. In particular, serious use of Namespaces is difficult to combine with serious use of Document Type Definitions (DTDs), because DTDs don't recognize the special significance of prefixes in element names; so, a consequence of backing Namespaces is that XSLT provides very little support for DTDs, having chosen instead to wait for the replacement facility, XML Schemas.

XML Namespaces 1.1 became a Recommendation on 4 February 2004, and the XSLT 2.0 specification makes provision for XSLT processors to work with this version, though it isn't required. Apart from the largely cosmetic change from URIs to IRIs mentioned earlier, the main innovation is the ability to undeclare a namespace, using a namespace undeclaration of the form «xmlns:prefix=""». This is particularly intended for applications like SOAP messaging, where an XML payload document is wrapped in an XML envelope for transmission. Without namespace undeclarations, there is a tendency for namespaces used in the SOAP envelope to stick to the payload XML when this is removed from the envelope, which can cause validation failures and other problems. For example, it can invalidate a digital signature attached to the document.

The XML Information Set

XSLT is designed to work on the information carried by an XML document, not on the raw document itself. This means that, as an XSLT programmer, you are given a tree view of the source document. This tree view is an abstraction of the original lexical XML, in which information that's deemed significant is retained, and other information is discarded. For example, you can see the attribute names and values, but you can't see whether the attribute was written in single or double quotes, you can't see what order the attributes were in, and you can't tell whether or not they were written on the same line.

One messy detail is that there have been many attempts to define exactly what constitutes the *essential* information content of a well-formed XML document, as distinct from its accidental punctuation. All attempts so far have come up with slightly different answers. The most definitive attempt to provide a common vocabulary for the content of XML documents is the *XML Information Set* definition (usually called the InfoSet), which may be found at http://www.w3.org/TR/xml-infoset.

Unfortunately, the InfoSet came too late to make all the standards consistent. For example, some treat comments as significant, others not; some treat the choice of namespace prefixes as significant, others take them as irrelevant. In Chapter 2, I shall describe exactly how XSLT (or more accurately, XPath) defines the tree model of XML, and how it differs in finer points of detail from some of the other definitions such as the Document Object Model or DOM.

One new piece of jargon is the concept of the *post schema validation infoset* or PSVI. This contains the significant information from the source document, augmented with information taken from its XML schema. It therefore allows you to find out not only that the value of an attribute was «17.3», but also that the attribute was described in the schema as a non-negative decimal number. A major change in XSLT 2.0 is that if you choose to use a schema processor to validate your documents, your XSLT stylesheets now make use of this additional information in the PSVI.

XSL and CSS

Why are there two stylesheet languages, XSL (that is, XSLT plus XSL Formatting Objects) as well as Cascading Style Sheets (CSS and CSS2)?

It's only fair to say that in an ideal world there would be a single language in this role, and that the reason there are two is that no one was able to invent something that achieved the simplicity and economy of CSS for doing simple things, combined with the power of XSL for doing more complex things.

CSS (by which I include CSS2, which greatly extends the degree to which you can control the final appearance of the page) is mainly used for rendering HTML, but it can also be used for rendering XML directly, by defining the display characteristics of each XML element. However, it has serious limitations. It cannot reorder the elements in the source document, it cannot add text or images, it cannot decide which elements should be displayed and which omitted, neither can it calculate totals or averages or sequence numbers. In other words, it can only be used when the structure of the source document is already very close to the final display form.

Having said this, CSS is simple to write, and it is very economical in machine resources. It doesn't reorder the document, and so it doesn't need to build a tree representation of the document in memory, and it can start displaying the document as soon as the first text is received over the network. Perhaps, most important of all, CSS is very simple for HTML authors to write, without any programming skills. In comparison, XSLT is far more powerful, but it also consumes a lot more memory and processor power, as well as training budget.

It's often appropriate to use both tools together. Use XSLT to create a representation of the document that is close to its final form, in that it contains the right text in the right order, and then use CSS to add the finishing touches, by selecting font sizes, colors, and so on. Typically, you would do the XSLT processing on the server and the CSS processing on the client (in the browser); so, another advantage of this approach is that you reduce the amount of data sent down the line, which should improve response time for your users and postpone the next expensive bandwidth increase.

XSLT and XML Schemas

One of the biggest changes in XSLT 2.0, and one of the most controversial, is the integration of XSLT with the XML Schema language. XML Schema provides a replacement for DTDs as a way of specifying the structural constraints that apply to a class of documents; unlike DTDs, an XML Schema can regulate the content of the text as well as the nesting of the elements and attributes. Many of the industry vocabularies being used to define XML interchange standards are specified using XML Schema definitions. For example, several of the XML vocabularies for describing music, which I alluded to earlier in the chapter, have an XML Schema to define their rules, and this schema can be used to check the conformance of individual documents to the standard in question.

When you write a stylesheet, you need to make assumptions about the structure of the input documents it is designed to process and the structure of the result documents it is designed to produce. With XSLT 1.0, these assumptions were implicit; there was no formal way of stating the assumptions in the stylesheet itself. As a result, if you try applying a stylesheet to the wrong kind of input document, the result will generally be garbage.

The idea of linking XSLT and XML Schema was driven by two main considerations:

❏ There should, in principle, be software engineering benefits if a program (and a stylesheet is indeed a program) makes explicit assertions about its expected inputs and outputs. These assertions can lead to better and faster detection of errors, often enabling errors to be reported at compile time that otherwise would only be reported the first time the stylesheet was applied to some test data that happened to exercise a particular part of the code.

❏ The more information that's available to an XSLT processor at compile time, the more potential it has to generate optimal code, giving faster execution and better use of memory.

So why the controversy? It's mainly because XML Schema itself is less than universally popular. It's an extremely complex specification that's very hard to read, and when you discover what it says, it appears to be full of rules that seem artificial and inconsistent. It manages at the same time to be specified in very formal language, and yet to have a worryingly high number of bugs that have been fixed through published errata. Although there are good books that present XML Schema in a more readable way, they achieve this by glossing over the complications, which means that the error messages you get when you do something wrong can be extremely obscure. As a result, there has been a significant amount of support for an alternative schema language, Relax NG, which as it happens was co-developed by the designer of XSLT and XPath, James Clark, and is widely regarded as a much more elegant approach.

The XSL and XQuery working groups responded to these concerns by ensuring that support for XML Schema was optional, both for implementors and for users. However, this has not entirely quelled the voices of dissent. Some have asked for XSLT to offer a choice of schema languages. However, this is technically very difficult to achieve, since the structure of data and the semantics of the operations that can be performed on the data are so closely coupled with each other.

The signs are that XML Schema is here to stay, whether people like it or not. It has the backing of all the major software vendors such as IBM, Oracle, and Microsoft, and it is being adopted by many of the larger user organizations and industries. And like so many things that the IT world has adopted as standards, it may be imperfect but it does actually work. Meanwhile, to simplify the situation rather cruelly, Relax NG is taking the role of the Apple Macintosh: the choice of the cognoscenti who judge a design by its intrinsic quality rather than by its list of heavyweight backers.

As I've already mentioned, W3C is not an organization that likes to let a thousand flowers bloom. It is not a loose umbrella organization in which each working group is free to do its own thing. There are strong processes that ensure the working groups cooperate and strive to reconcile their differences. There is therefore a determination to make all the specifications work properly together, and the message is that if XML Schema has its problems, then you work together to get them fixed. XSLT and XML Schema come from the same stable, so they are expected to work together. And I hope to show in this book that they can work together beneficially.

Chapter 4 provides an overview of how stylesheets and schemas are integrated in XSLT 2.0, and Chapter 11 provides a worked example of an application that uses this capability. In developing this application for the book (which I did at the same time as I developed the underlying support in Saxon) I was pleasantly surprised to see that I really was getting benefits from the integration. At the simplest level, I really liked the immediate feedback you get when a stylesheet generates output that does not conform to the schema for the result document, with error messages that point straight to the offending line in the stylesheet. This makes for a much faster debugging cycle than does the old approach of putting the finished output file through a schema validator as a completely separate operation.

The History of XSL

Like most of the XML family of standards, XSLT was developed by the World Wide Web Consortium (W3C), a coalition of companies orchestrated by Tim Berners-Lee, the inventor of the Web. There is an interesting page on the history of XSL, and styling proposals generally, at http://www.w3.org/Style/History/.

> *Writing history is a tricky business. Sharon Adler, the chair of the XSL Working Group, tells me that her recollections of what happened are very different from the way I describe them. This just goes to show that the documentary record is a very crude snapshot of what people were actually thinking and talking about. Unfortunately, though, it's all that we've got.*

Prehistory

HTML was originally conceived by Berners-Lee as a set of tags to mark the logical structure of a document; headings, paragraphs, links, quotes, code sections, and the like. Soon, people wanted more control over how the document looked; they wanted to achieve the same control over the appearance of the delivered publication as they had with printing and paper. So, HTML acquired more and more tags and attributes to control presentation; fonts, margins, tables, colors, and all the rest that followed. As it evolved, the documents being published became more and more browser-dependent, and it was seen that the original goals of simplicity and universality were starting to slip away.

The remedy was widely seen as separation of content from presentation. This was not a new concept; it had been well developed through the 1980s in the development of *Standard Generalized Markup Language (SGML)*.

Just as XML was derived as a greatly simplified subset of SGML, so XSLT has its origins in an SGML-based standard called *DSSSL (Document Style Semantics and Specification Language)*. DSSSL (pronounced *Dissel*) was developed primarily to fill the need for a standard device-independent language to define the output rendition of SGML documents, particularly for high-quality typographical presentation. SGML was around for a long time before DSSSL appeared in the early 1990s, but until then the output side had been handled using proprietary and often extremely expensive tools, geared toward driving equally expensive phototypesetters, so that the technology was really taken up only by the big publishing houses.

Michael Sperberg-McQueen and Robert F. Goldstein presented an influential paper at the WWW '94 conference in Chicago under the title *A Manifesto for Adding SGML Intelligence to the World-Wide Web*. You can find it at `http://www.ncsa.uiuc.edu/SDG/IT94/Proceedings/Autools/sperberg-mcqueen/sperberg.html`.

The authors presented a set of requirements for a stylesheet language, which is as good a statement as any of the aims that the XSL designers were trying to meet. As with other proposals from around that time, the concept of a separate transformation language had not yet appeared, and a great deal of the paper is devoted to the rendition capabilities of the language. There are many formative ideas, however, including the concept of fallback processing to cope with situations where particular features are not available in the current environment.

It is worth quoting some extracts from the paper here:

> *Ideally, the stylesheet language should be declarative, not procedural, and should allow stylesheets to exploit the structure of SGML documents to the fullest. Styles must be able to vary with the structural location of the element: paragraphs within notes may be formatted differently from paragraphs in the main text. Styles must be able to vary with the attribute values of the element in question: a quotation of type "display" may need to be formatted differently from a quotation of type "inline"*

> *At the same time, the language has to be reasonably easy to interpret in a procedural way: implementing the stylesheet language should not become the major challenge in implementing a Web client.*

> *The semantics should be additive: It should be possible for users to create new stylesheets by adding new specifications to some existing (possibly standard) stylesheet. This should not require copying the entire base stylesheet; instead, the user should be able to store locally just the user's own changes to the standard stylesheet, and they should be added in at browse time. This is particularly important to support local modifications of standard DTDs.*

> *Syntactically, the stylesheet language must be very simple, preferably trivial to parse. One obvious possibility: formulate the stylesheet language as an SGML DTD, so that each stylesheet will be an SGML document. Since the browser already knows how to parse SGML, no extra effort will be needed.*

> *We recommend strongly that a subset of DSSSL be used to formulate stylesheets for use on the World Wide Web; with the completion of the standards work on DSSSL, there is no reason for any community to invent*

their own style-sheet language from scratch. The full DSSSL standard may well be too demanding to implement in its entirety, but even if that proves true, it provides only an argument for defining a subset of DSSSL that must be supported, not an argument for rolling our own. Unlike home-brew specifications, a subset of a standard comes with an automatically predefined growth path. We expect to work on the formulation of a usable, implementable subset of DSSSL for use in WWW stylesheets, and invite all interested parties to join in the effort

In late 1995, a W3C-sponsored workshop on stylesheet languages was held in Paris. In view of the subsequent role of James Clark as editor of the XSLT Recommendation, it is interesting to read the notes of his contribution on the goals of DSSSL, which can be found at `http://www.w3.org/Style/ 951106_Workshop/report1.html#clark`.

Here are a few selected paragraphs from these notes.

DSSSL contains both a transformation language and a formatting language. Originally the transformation was needed to make certain kinds of styles possible (such as tables of contents). The query language now takes care of that, but the transformation language survives because it is useful in its own right.

The language is strictly declarative, which is achieved by adopting a functional subset of Scheme. Interactive stylesheet editors must be possible.

A DSSSL stylesheet very precisely describes a function from SGML to a flow object tree. It allows partial stylesheets to be combined ("cascaded" as in CSS): some rule may override some other rule, based on implicit and explicit priorities, but there is no blending between conflicting styles.

James Clark closed his talk with the remark:

Creating a good, extensible style language is hard!

One suspects that the effort of editing the XSLT 1.0 Recommendation didn't cause him to change his mind.

The First XSL Proposal

Following these early discussions, the W3C set up a formal activity to create a stylesheet language proposal. The remit for this group specified that it should be based on DSSSL.

As an output of this activity came the first formal proposal for XSL, dated 27 August 1997. Entitled *A Proposal for XSL*, it lists 11 authors: James Clark (who works for himself), five from Microsoft, three from Imso Corporation, one from ArborText, and one (Henry Thompson) from the University of Edinburgh. The document can be found at `http://www.w3.org/TR/NOTE-XSL.html`.

The section describing the purpose of the language is worth reading.

XSL is a stylesheet language designed for the Web community. It provides functionality beyond CSS (e.g. element reordering). We expect that CSS will be used to display simply structured XML documents and XSL will be used where more powerful formatting capabilities are required or for formatting highly structured information such as XML structured data or XML documents that contain structured data.

Web authors create content at three different levels of sophistication given as follows:

- *markup: relies solely on a declarative syntax*
- *script: additionally uses code "snippets" for more complex behaviors*
- *program: uses a full programming language*

XSL is intended to be accessible to the "markup" level user by providing a declarative solution to most data description and rendering requirements. Less common tasks are accommodated through a graceful escape to a familiar scripting environment. This approach is familiar to the Web publishing community as it is modeled after the HTML/JavaScript environment.

The powerful capabilities provided by XSL allow:

- *formatting of source elements based on ancestry/descendency, position, and uniqueness*
- *the creation of formatting constructs including generated text and graphics*
- *the definition of reusable formatting macros*
- *writing-direction independent stylesheets*
- *extensible set of formatting objects*

The authors then explained carefully why they had felt it necessary to diverge from DSSSL and described why a separate language from CSS (Cascading Style Sheets) was thought necessary.

They then stated some design principles:

- XSL should be straightforwardly usable over the Internet.
- XSL should be expressed in XML syntax.
- XSL should provide a declarative language to do all common formatting tasks.
- XSL should provide an "escape" into a scripting language to accommodate more sophisticated formatting tasks and to allow for extensibility and completeness.
- XSL will be a subset of DSSSL with the proposed amendment. *(As XSL was no longer a subset of DSSSL, they cannily proposed amending DSSSL so it would become a superset of XSL.)*
- A mechanical mapping of a CSS stylesheet into an XSL stylesheet should be possible.
- XSL should be informed by user experience with the FOSI stylesheet language.
- The number of optional features in XSL should be kept to a minimum.
- XSL stylesheets should be human-legible and reasonably clear.
- The XSL design should be prepared quickly.
- XSL stylesheets shall be easy to create.
- Terseness in XSL markup is of minimal importance.

As a requirements statement, this doesn't rank among the best. It doesn't read like the kind of list you get when you talk to users and find out what they need. It's much more the kind of list that designers write when they know what they want to produce, including a few political concessions to the people who might raise objections. But if you want to understand why XSLT became the language it did, this list is certainly evidence of the thinking.

The language described in this first proposal contains many of the key concepts of XSLT as it finally emerged, but the syntax is virtually unrecognizable. It was already clear that the language should be based on templates that handled nodes in the source document matching a defined pattern, and that the language should be free of side effects, to allow "progressive rendering and handling of large documents." I'll explore the significance of this requirement in more detail on page 36, and discuss its implications on the way stylesheets are designed in Chapter 9. The basic idea is that if a stylesheet is expressed as a collection of completely independent operations, each of which has no external effect other than generating part of the output from its input (for example, it cannot update global variables), then it becomes possible to generate any part of the output independently if that particular part of the input changes. Whether the XSLT language actually achieves this objective is still an open question.

Microsoft shipped its first technology preview 5 months after this proposal appeared, in January 1998.

To enable W3C to make an assessment of the proposal, Norman Walsh produced a requirements summary, which was published in May 1998. It is available at `http://www.w3.org/TR/WD-XSLReq`. It largely confirms the thinking already outlined.

The bulk of his paper is given over to a long list of the typographical features that the language should support, following the tradition that the formatting side of the language originally got a lot more column inches than did the transformation side.

Following this activity, the first Working Draft of XSL (not to be confused with the Proposal) was published on 18 August 1998, and the language started to take shape, gradually converging on the final form it took in the 16 November 1999 Recommendation through a series of Working Drafts, each of which made radical changes, but kept the original design principles intact.

> **A Recommendation is the most definitive of documents produced by the W3C. It's not technically a standard, because standards can only be published by government-approved standards organizations. But I will often refer to it loosely as "the standard" in this book.**

The Microsoft WD-xsl Dialect

Before the Recommendation came out, however, Microsoft took a fateful decision to ship an early implementation of their XSLT processor as an add-on to Internet Explorer 4, and later as a built-in feature of IE5. Unfortunately, Microsoft was too early, and the XSLT standard changed and grew. When the XSLT Recommendation version 1.0 was finally published on 16 November 1999, it had diverged significantly from the initial Microsoft product.

Many of the differences, such as changes of keywords, are very superficial but some run much deeper; for example, changes in the way the equals operator is defined.

Fortunately, the Microsoft IE5 dialect of XSL (which I refer to as WD-xsl) is now almost completely obsolete. Microsoft no longer actively promotes it, and their more recent products are very closely aligned with the W3C specifications. It's still possible, however, that you will come across stylesheets written in this language, or developers who aren't aware of the differences. You can recognize stylesheets written in this dialect by the namespace URI on the `<xsl:stylesheet>` element, which is «`http://www.w3.org/TR/WD-xsl`».

Saxon

At this point it might be a good idea to clarify how I got involved in the story. In 1998 I was working for the British computer manufacturer ICL, a part of Fujitsu. Fujitsu, in Japan, had developed an object database system, later marketed by Computer Associates as Jasmine, and I was trying to find applications for this technology in content management applications for large publishers. We developed a few successful large systems with this technology, but found that it didn't scale downwards to the kind of project that wanted something working in 6 weeks rather than 6 months. So I was asked to look at what we could do with XML, which was just appearing on the horizon.

I came to the conclusion that XML looked like a good thing, but that there wasn't any software. So I developed the very first early versions of Saxon to provide a proof-of-concept demonstration. At that stage Saxon was just a Java library, not an XSLT processor, but as the XSL standards developed I found that my own ideas were converging more and more with what the W3C working group was doing, and I started implementing the language as it was being specified. ICL had decided that its marketing resources were spread thinly over too many products, and so the management took the imaginative decision to make the technology available as open source. Seventeen days after the XSLT 1.0 specification was published in November 1999, I announced the first conformant implementation. And on the day it was published, I started work on the first edition of this book.

When the book was published, the XSL Working Group invited me to join and participate in the development of XSLT 1.1. Initially, being based in the United Kingdom and with limited time available for the work, my involvement was fairly sporadic. But early in 2001 I changed jobs and joined Software AG, which wanted me to take a full role in the W3C work. The following year James Clark pulled out of the Working Group, and I stepped into his shoes as editor.

The reason I'm explaining this sequence of events is that I hope it will help you to understand the viewpoint from which this book is written. When I wrote the first edition I was an outsider, and I felt completely free to criticize the specification when I felt it necessary. I have tried to retain an objective approach in the present edition, but as editor of the language spec it is much more difficult to be impartial. I've tried to keep a balance: it wouldn't be fair to use the book as a platform to push my views over those of my colleagues of the working group, but at the same time, I've made no effort to be defensive about decisions that I would have made differently if they had been left to me.

Software AG continued to support my involvement in the W3C work (on the XQuery group as well as the XSL group), as well as the development of Saxon and the writing of this book, through till February 2004, at which point I left to set up my own company, Saxonica.

Beyond XSLT 1.0

After XSLT 1.0 was published, the XSL Working Group responsible for the language decided to split the requirements for enhancements into two categories: XSLT 1.1 would standardize a small number of urgent features that vendors had already found necessary to add to their products as extensions, while XSLT 2.0 would handle the more strategic requirements that needed further research.

A working draft of XSLT 1.1 was published on December 12, 2000. It described three main enhancements to the XSLT 1.0 specification:

❑ *Multiple output documents*: an `<xsl:document>` instruction, modeled on extensions provided initially in Saxon and subsequently in other products including xt, Xalan and Oracle, allowing a source document to be split into multiple output documents. This instruction has become `<xsl:result-document>` in XSLT 2.0.

❑ *Temporary trees*: the ability to treat a tree created by one phase of processing as input to a subsequent phase of processing. This enhancement was modeled on the `node-set()` extension function introduced first in xt and subsequently copied in other products. It is retained largely unchanged in XSLT 2.0.

❑ *Standard bindings to extension functions*: written in Java and ECMAScript. XSLT 1.0 allowed a stylesheet to call external functions, but did not say how such functions should be written, with the result that extension functions written for Xalan would not work with xt or Saxon, or vice versa. XSLT 1.1 defined a general framework for binding extension functions written in any language, with specific mappings for Java and ECMAScript (the official name for JavaScript). This feature of the XSLT 1.1 draft has been dropped completely from XSLT 2.0. It proved highly controversial, particularly as it coincided with Microsoft's U-turn in its Java strategy.

For a number of reasons XSLT 1.1 never got past the working draft stage. This was partly because of the controversy surrounding the Java language bindings, but more particularly because it was becoming clearer that XSLT 2.0 would be a fairly radical revision of the language, and the working group didn't want to do anything in 1.1 that would get in the way of achieving the 2.0 goals. There were feelings, for example, that the facility for temporary trees might prejudice the ability to support sequences in 2.0, a fear which as it happens proved largely unfounded.

XQuery

By the time work on XSLT 2.0 was starting, the separate XQuery working group in W3C had created a draft of its own language.

While the XSL working group had identified the need for a transformation language to support a self-contained part of the formatting process, XQuery originated from the need to search large quantities of XML documents stored in a database.

Different people had different motivations for wanting an XML Query Language, and many of these motivations were aired at a workshop held in December 1998. You can find all 66 position papers presented at this workshop at `http://www.w3.org/TandS/QL/QL98/pp.html`. Quite how a consensus emerged from this enormous variety of views is difficult to determine in retrospect. But it's interesting to see how the participants saw the relationship with XSL, as it was then known. The Microsoft position paper states the belief that a query language could be developed as an extension of XSLT, but in this it is almost alone. Many of the participants came from a database background, with ideas firmly rooted in the tradition of SQL and object database languages such as OQL, and to these people, XSL didn't look remotely like a query language. But in the light of subsequent events, it's interesting to read the position paper from the XSL Working Group, which states in its summary:

1. The query language should use XSL patterns as the basis for information retrieval.

2. The query language should use XSL templates as the basis for materializing query results.

3. The query language should be at least as expressive as XSL is, currently.

4. Development of the pattern and transformation languages should remain in the XSL working group.

5. A coordination group should ensure either that a single query language satisfies all working group requirements or that all W3C query languages share an underlying query model.

(Remember that XPath had not yet been identified as a separate language, and that the expressions that later became XPath were then known as patterns.)

This offer to coordinate, and the strong desire to ensure consistency among the different W3C specifications, can be seen as directly leading to the subsequent collaboration between the two working groups to define XPath 2.0.

The XQuery group started meeting in September 1999. The first published requirements document was published the following January (`http://www.w3.org/TR/2000/WD-xmlquery-req-20000131`). It included a commitment to compatibility with XML Schema, and a rather cautiously worded promise to "take into consideration the expressibility and search facilities of XPath when formulating its algebra and query syntax." July 2000 saw a revised requirements document that included a selection of queries that the language must be able to express. The first externally visible draft of the XQuery language was published in February 2001 (see `http://www.w3.org/TR/2001/WD-xquery-20010215/`) and it was at this stage that the collaboration between the two working groups began in earnest.

The close cooperation between the teams developing the two languages contrasts strangely with the somewhat adversarial position adopted by parts of the user community. XSLT users were quick to point out that XSLT 1.0 satisfied every single requirement in the first XQuery requirements document, and could solve all the use cases published in the second version in August 2000. At the same time, users on the XQuery side of the fence have often been dismissive about XSLT, complaining about its verbose syntax and sometimes arcane semantics. Even today, when the similarities of the two languages at a deep level are clearly apparent, there is very little overlap between their user communities: I find that most users of the XQuery engine in Saxon have no XSLT experience. The difference between XSLT and XQuery is in many ways a difference of style rather than substance, but users often feel strongly about style.

XSLT 2.0 and XPath 2.0

The requirements for XSLT 2.0 and XPath 2.0 were published on 14 February 2001. In the case of the XPath 2.0 requirements, the document was written jointly by the two working groups. You can find the documents at the following URLs:

```
http://www.w3.org/TR/2001/WD-xslt20req-20010214

http://www.w3.org/TR/2001/WD-xpath20req-20010214
```

Broadly, the requirements fall into three categories:

❑ Features that are obviously missing from the current standards and that would make users' lives much easier, for example, facilities for grouping related nodes, extra string-handling and numeric functions, and the ability to read text files as well as XML documents.

❑ Changes desired by the XML Query working group. The difficulty at this stage was that the Query group did not just want additions to the XPath language; they wanted fundamental changes to its semantics. Many members of the XQuery group felt they could not live with some of the arbitrariness of the way XPath handled data types generally, and node-sets in particular, for example the fact that «a = 1» tests whether there is some «a» that equals one, whereas «a – 1 = 0» tests whether the first «a» equals one.

❑ Features designed to exploit and integrate with XML Schema. The W3C XML Schema specification had reached an advanced stage (it became a Candidate Recommendation on 20 October 2000), and implementations were starting to appear in products. The thinking was that if the schema specified that a particular element contains a number or a date (for example), then it ought to be possible to use this knowledge when comparing or sorting dates within a stylesheet.

It has sometimes been suggested that the adoption of XML Schema was forced on XSLT by the XQuery group. I don't think there is any truth in this. The big three database companies (IBM, Oracle, and Microsoft) were very active in both working groups, along with middle-tier players such as BEA and Software AG. Most of these companies saw XML Schema as a strategic way forward, and they carried both groups along with them. What is almost certainly true, however, is that when the XSL Working Group made the decision to work with XML Schema, this was based on a rather vague idea of the potential benefits; none of the members at that stage had a clear idea as to the detailed implications of this decision on the design of the language.

The development of XSLT 2.0 has been a long drawn out process. The timescale was dictated largely by the pace at which agreement could be reached with the XQuery group on the details of XPath 2.0. This took a long time firstly, because of the number of people involved; secondly, because of the very different places where people were coming from (the database community and the document community have historically been completely isolated from each other, and it took a lot of talking before people started to understand each others' positions); and finally, because of the sheer technical difficulty of finding a workable design that offered the right balance between backwards compatibility and rigorous, consistent semantics. A great deal of the credit for finding a way through these obstacles goes to Mary Fernandez, who chaired the joint XPath task force with remarkable patience and persistence.

So much for the history. Let's look now at the essential characteristics of XSLT 2.0 as a language.

XSLT 2.0 as a Language

What are the most significant characteristics of XSLT as a language, which distinguish it from other languages? In this section I shall pick four of the most striking features: the fact that it is written in XML syntax, the fact that it is a language free of side effects, the fact that processing is described as a set of independent pattern-matching rules, and the fact that it has a type system based on XML Schema.

Use of XML Syntax

As we've seen, the use of SGML syntax for stylesheets was proposed as long ago as 1994, and it seems that this idea gradually became the accepted wisdom. It's difficult to trace exactly what the overriding arguments were, and when you find yourself writing something like:

```
<xsl:variable name="y">
   <xsl:call-template name="f">
      <xsl:with-param name="x"/>
   </xsl:call-template>
</xsl:variable>
```

to express what in other languages would be written as «y=f(x);», then you may find yourself wondering how such a decision came to be made.

In fact, it could have been worse; in the very early drafts, the syntax for writing what are now XPath expressions was also expressed in XML, so instead of writing «select="book/author/first-name"» you had to write something along the lines of:

```
<select>
   <path>
      <element type="book">
      <element type="author">
      <element type="first-name">
   </path>
</select>
```

The most obvious arguments for expressing XSLT stylesheets in XML are perhaps as follows:

❑ There is already an XML parser in the browser; so it keeps the footprint small if this can be reused.

❑ Everyone had got fed up with the syntactic inconsistencies between HTML/XML and CSS and didn't want the same thing to happen again.

❑ The Lisp-like syntax of DSSSL was widely seen as a barrier to its adoption; so it would be better to have a syntax that was already familiar in the target community.

❑ Many existing popular template languages (including simple ASP and JSP pages) are expressed as an outline of the output document with embedded instructions; so this is a familiar concept.

❑ The lexical apparatus is reusable, for example Unicode support, character and entity references, whitespace handling, namespaces.

❑ It's occasionally useful to have a stylesheet as the input or output of a transformation (witness the Microsoft XSL converter as an example); so it's a benefit if a stylesheet can read and write other stylesheets.

❑ Providing visual development tools easily solves the inconvenience of having to type lots of angle brackets.

Like it or not, the XML-based syntax is now an intrinsic feature of the language that has both benefits and drawbacks. It does make the language verbose, but in the end, the number of keystrokes has very little bearing on the ease or difficulty of solving particular transformation problems.

In XSLT 2.0, the long-windedness of the language has been reduced considerably by increasing the expressiveness of the non-XML part of the syntax, namely XPath expressions. Many computations that required five lines of XSLT code in 1.0 can be expressed in a single XPath expression in 2.0. Two constructs in particular led to this simplification: the conditional expression (if..then..else) in XPath 2.0; and the ability to define a function in XSLT (using <xsl:function>) that can be called directly from an

XPath expression. To take the example discussed earlier, if you replace the template «f» by a user-written function «f», you can replace the five lines in the example with:

```
<xsl:variable name="y" select="f($x)"/>
```

The decision to base the XSLT syntax on XML has proved its worth in several ways that I would not have predicted in advance:

❑ It has proved very easy to extend the syntax. Adding new elements and attributes is trivial; there is no risk of introducing parsing difficulties when doing so, and it is easy to manage backwards compatibility. (In contrast, extending XQuery's non-XML syntax without introducing parsing ambiguities is a highly delicate operation.)

❑ The separation of XML parsing from XSLT processing leads to good error reporting and recovery in the compiler. It makes it much easier to report the location of an error with precision and to report many errors in one run of the compiler. This leads to a faster development cycle.

❑ It makes it easier to maintain stylistic consistency between different constructs in the language. The discipline of defining the language through elements and attributes creates a constrained vocabulary with which the language designers must work, and these constraints impose a certain consistency of design.

No Side Effects

The idea that XSL should be a declarative language free of side effects appears repeatedly in the early statements about the goals and design principles of the language, but no one ever seems to explain *why*: what would be the user benefit?

A function or procedure in a programming language is said to have side effects if it makes changes to its environment; for example, if it can update a global variable that another function or procedure can read, or if it can write messages to a log file, or prompt the user. If functions have side effects, it becomes important to call them the right number of times and in the correct order. Functions that have no side effects (sometimes called pure functions) can be called any number of times and in any order. It doesn't matter how many times you evaluate the area of a triangle, you will always get the same answer; but if the function to calculate the area has a side effect such as changing the size of the triangle, or if you don't know whether it has side effects or not, then it becomes important to call it once only.

I expand further on this concept in the section on Computational Stylesheets in Chapter 9, page 625.

It is possible to find hints at the reason why this was considered desirable in the statements that the language should be equally suitable for batch or interactive use, and that it should be capable of *progressive rendering*. There is a concern that when you download a large XML document, you won't be able to see anything on your screen until the last byte has been received from the server. Equally, if a small change were made to the XML document, it would be nice to be able to determine the change needed to the screen display, without recalculating the whole thing from scratch. If a language has side effects then the order of execution of the statements in the language has to be defined, or the final result becomes unpredictable. Without side effects, the statements can be executed in any order, which means it is possible, in principle, to process the parts of a stylesheet selectively and independently.

Whether XSLT has actually achieved these goals is somewhat debatable. Certainly, determining which parts of the output document are affected by a small change to one part of the input document is not easy, given the flexibility of the expressions and patterns that are now permitted in the language. Equally, most existing XSLT processors require the whole document to be loaded into memory (there is a version of jd.xslt that is disk-based, but this is the exception to the rule). However, there has been research work that suggests the goals are achievable (search for papers on "Incremental XSLT Transformation" or "Lazy XSLT Transformation"). When E. F. Codd published the relational calculus in 1970, he made the claim that a declarative language was desirable because it was possible to optimize it, which was not possible with the navigational data access languages in use at the time. In fact, it took another 15 years before relational optimization techniques (and, to be fair, the price of hardware) reached the point where large relational databases were commercially viable. But in the end he was proved right, and the hope is that the same principle will also eventually deliver similar benefits in the area of transformation and styling languages.

Of course, there will always be some transformations where the whole document needs to be available before you can produce any output; examples are where the stylesheet sorts the data, or where it starts with a table of contents. But there are many other transformations where the order of the output directly reflects the order of the input, and progressive rendering should be possible in such cases. Xalan-J made a start on this by running a transformation thread in parallel with the parsing thread, so the transformer can produce output before the parser has finished, and MSXML3 (from the evidence of its API) seems to be designed on a similar principle. The Stylus Studio debugging tool tracks the dependencies between parts of the output document and the template rules that were used to generate them, and so one can start to see the potential to regenerate the output selectively when small changes are made.

What it means in practice to be free of side effects is that you cannot update the value of a variable. This restriction is something many users find very frustrating at first, and a big price to pay for these rather remote benefits. But as you get the feel of the language and learn to think about using it the way it was designed to be used, rather than the way you are familiar with from other languages, you will find you stop thinking about this as a restriction. In fact, one of the benefits is that it eliminates a whole class of bugs from your code. I shall come back to this subject in Chapter 9, where I outline some of the common design patterns for XSLT stylesheets and, in particular, describe how to use recursive code to handle situations where in the past you would probably have used updateable variables to keep track of the current state.

Rule-Based

The dominant feature of a typical XSLT stylesheet is that it consists of a sequence of template rules, each of which describes how a particular element type or other construct should be processed. The rules are not arranged in any particular order; they don't have to match the order of the input or the order of the output, and in fact there are very few clues as to what ordering or nesting of elements the stylesheet author expects to encounter in the source document. It is this that makes XSLT a declarative language, because you specify what output should be produced when particular patterns occur in the input, as distinct from a procedural program where you have to say what tasks to perform in what order.

This rule-based structure is very like CSS, but with the major difference that both the patterns (the description of which nodes a rule applies to) and the actions (the description of what happens when the rule is matched) are much richer in functionality.

Example: Displaying a Poem

Let's see how we can use the rule-based approach to format a poem. Again, we haven't introduced all the concepts yet, and so I won't try to explain every detail of how this works, but it's useful to see what the template rules actually look like in practice.

Input

Let's take this poem as our XML source. The source file is called `poem.xml`, and the stylesheet is `poem.xsl`.

```xml
<poem>
    <author>Rupert Brooke</author>
    <date>1912</date>
    <title>Song</title>
    <stanza>
        <line>And suddenly the wind comes soft,</line>
        <line>And Spring is here again;</line>
        <line>And the hawthorn quickens with buds of green</line>
        <line>And my heart with buds of pain.</line>
    </stanza>
    <stanza>
        <line>My heart all Winter lay so numb,</line>
        <line>The earth so dead and frore,</line>
        <line>That I never thought the Spring would come again</line>
        <line>Or my heart wake any more.</line>
    </stanza>
    <stanza>
        <line>But Winter's broken and earth has woken,</line>
        <line>And the small birds cry again;</line>
        <line>And the hawthorn hedge puts forth its buds,</line>
        <line>And my heart puts forth its pain.</line>
    </stanza>
</poem>
```

Output

Let's write a stylesheet such that this document appears in the browser, as shown in Figure 1-8.

Stylesheet

It starts with the standard header.

```xml
<xsl:stylesheet
    xmlns:xsl="http://www.w3.org/1999/XSL/Transform"
    version="1.0">
```

Now we write one template rule for each element type in the source document. The rule for the `<poem>` element creates the skeleton of the HTML output, defining the ordering of the elements in the output (which doesn't have to be the same as the input order). The `<xsl:value-of>` instruction inserts the value of the selected element at this point in the output. The `<xsl:apply-templates>` instructions cause the selected child elements to be processed, each using its own template rule.

```xml
<xsl:template match="poem">
    <html>
    <head>
```

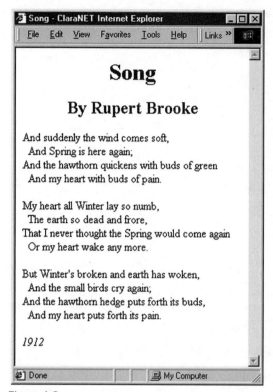

Figure 1-8

```
      <title><xsl:value-of select="title"/></title>
   </head>
   <body>
      <xsl:apply-templates select="title"/>
      <xsl:apply-templates select="author"/>
      <xsl:apply-templates select="stanza"/>
      <xsl:apply-templates select="date"/>
   </body>
   </html>
</xsl:template>
```

In XSLT 2.0 we could replace the four `<xsl:apply-templates>` instructions with one, written as follows:

```
<xsl:apply-templates select="title, author, stanza, date"/>
```

This takes advantage of the fact that the type system for the language now supports ordered sequences. The «,» operator performs list concatenation and is used here to form a list containing the `<title>`, `<author>`, `<stanza>`, and `<date>` elements in that order. Note that this includes all the `<stanza>` elements, so in general this will be a sequence containing more than four items.

The template rules for the `<title>`, `<author>`, and `<date>` elements are very simple; they take the content of the element (denoted by «`select="."`»), and surround it within appropriate HTML tags to define its display style.

```
<xsl:template match="title">
   <div align="center">
      <h1><xsl:value-of select="."/></h1>
   </div>
</xsl:template>

<xsl:template match="author">
   <div align="center">
      <h2>By <xsl:value-of select="."/></h2>
   </div>
</xsl:template>

<xsl:template match="date">
   <p><i><xsl:value-of select="."/></i></p>
</xsl:template>
```

The template rule for the `<stanza>` element puts each stanza into an HTML paragraph, and then invokes processing of the lines within the stanza, as defined by the template rule for lines:

```
<xsl:template match="stanza">
<p><xsl:apply-templates select="line"/></p>
</xsl:template>
```

The rule for `<line>` elements is a little more complex: if the position of the line within the stanza is an even number, it precedes the line with two non-breaking-space characters (` `). The `<xsl:if>` instruction tests a boolean condition, which in this case calls the `position()` function to determine the relative position of the current line. It then outputs the contents of the line, followed by an empty HTML `<br>` element to end the line.

```
<xsl:template match="line">
   <xsl:if test="position() mod 2 = 0">  </xsl:if>
   <xsl:value-of select="."/><br/>
</xsl:template>
```

And to finish off, we close the `<xsl:stylesheet>` element.

```
</xsl:stylesheet>
```

Although template rules are a characteristic feature of the XSLT language, we'll see that this is not the only way of writing a stylesheet. In Chapter 9, I will describe four different design patterns for XSLT stylesheets, only one of which makes extensive use of template rules. In fact, the Hello World stylesheet I presented earlier in this chapter doesn't make any real use of template rules; it fits into the design pattern I call *fill-in-the-blanks*, because the stylesheet essentially contains the fixed part of the output with embedded instructions saying where to get the data to put in the variable parts.

Types Based on XML Schema

I have described three characteristics of the XSLT language (the use of XML syntax, the principle of no side-effects, and the rule-based processing model) that were essential features of XSLT 1.0 and that have been retained essentially unchanged in XSLT 2.0. The fourth characteristic is new in XSLT 2.0, and creates a fundamental change in the nature of XSLT as a language. This is the adoption of a type system based on XML Schema.

There are two aspects to the type system of any programming language. The first is the set of types that are supported (for example, integers, strings, lists, tuples), together with the mechanisms for creating user-defined types. The second aspect is the rules that the language enforces to ensure type-correctness.

XSLT 1.0 had a very small set of types (integers, booleans, strings, node-sets, and result tree fragments), and the rules it applied were what is often called "weak typing": this means that the processor would always attempt to convert the value supplied in an expression or function call to the type that was required in that context. This makes for a very happy-go-lucky environment: if you supply an integer where a string is expected, or vice versa, nothing will break.

XSLT 2.0 has changed both aspects of the type system. There is now a much richer set of types available (and this set is user-extensible), and the rules for type-checking are stricter.

We will look at the implications of this in greater detail in Chapter 4.

Summary

This introductory chapter answered the following questions about XSLT:

- ❑   What kind of language is it?
- ❑   Where does it fit into the XML family?
- ❑   Where does it come from and why was it designed the way it is?
- ❑   Where should it be used?

You now know that XSLT is a declarative high-level language designed for transforming the structure of XML documents; that it has two major applications: data conversion and presentation; and that it can be used at a number of different points in the overall application architecture, including at data capture time, at delivery time on the server, and at display time on the browser. You also have some idea why XSLT has developed in the way it has.

Now it's time to start taking an in-depth look inside the language to see how it does this job. In the next chapter, we look at the way transformation is carried out by treating the input and output as tree structures, and using patterns to match particular nodes in the input tree and define what nodes should be added to the result tree when the pattern is matched.

2

The XSLT Processing Model

This chapter takes a bird's eye view of what an XSLT processor does. We start by looking at a system overview: what are the inputs and outputs of the processor.

Then we look in some detail at the data model, in particular the structure of the tree representation of XML documents. An important message here is that XSLT transformations do not operate on XML documents as text; they operate on the abstract tree-like information structure represented by the text.

Having established the data model, I describe the processing sequence that occurs when a source document and a stylesheet are brought together. XSLT is not a conventional procedural language; it consists of a collection of template rules defining output that is produced when particular patterns are matched in the input. As seen in Chapter 1, this rule-based processing structure is one of the distinguishing features of the XSLT language.

Finally, we look at the way in which variables and expressions can be used in an XSLT stylesheet, and also look at the various data types available.

XSLT: A System Overview

This section looks at the nature of the transformation process performed by XSLT, concentrating on the inputs and outputs of a transformation.

A Simplified Overview

The core task of an XSLT processor is to apply a stylesheet to a source document and produce a result document. This is shown in Figure 2-1.

As a first approximation we can think of the source document, the stylesheet, and the result document as each being an XML document. XSLT performs a *transformation* process because the *output* (the result document) is the same kind of object as the *input* (the source document). This has

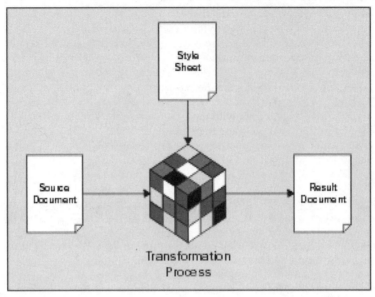

Figure 2-1

immediate benefits: for example, it is possible to do a complex transformation as a series of simple transformations, and it is possible to do transformations in either direction using the same technology.

> *The choice of Rubik's cube to illustrate the transformation process is not entirely whimsical. The mathematics of Rubik's cube relies on group theory, which is where the notion of closure comes from: every operation transforms one instance of a type into another instance of the same type. We're transforming XML documents rather than cubes, but the principle is the same.*

The name *stylesheet* has stuck for the document that defines the transformation, even though purists prefer to call it a *transformation sheet*. The name reflects the reality that a very common kind of transformation performed using XSLT is to define a display style for the information in the source document, so that the result document contains information from the source document augmented with information controlling the way it is displayed on some output device.

Trees, not Documents

In practice, we don't always want the input or output to be XML in its textual form. If we want to produce HTML output (a very common requirement) we want to produce it directly, rather than having an XML document as an intermediate form. When the Netscape browser displays the result of an XSLT transformation, it doesn't serialize the result to HTML and then parse the serial HTML; rather, it works directly from the result tree as a data structure in memory. Similarly, we might want to take input from a database or (say) an LDAP directory, or an EDI message, or a data file using comma-separated-values syntax. We don't want to spend a lot of time converting these into serial XML documents if we can avoid it, nor do we want another raft of converters to install.

Instead, XSLT defines its operations in terms of a representation of an XML document called the *tree*. The tree is an abstract data type. There is no defined application programming interface (API) and no defined data representation, only a conceptual model that defines the objects in the tree, their properties, and their relationships. The tree is similar in concept to the W3C DOM, except that the Document Object Model (DOM) does have a defined API. Some implementors do indeed use the DOM as their internal tree structure. Others use a data structure that corresponds more closely to the XPath tree model, while some use optimized internal data structures that are only distantly related to this model. It's a conceptual model we are describing, not something that necessarily exists in an implementation.

The data model for XSLT trees is shared with the XPath and XQuery specifications, which ensures that data can be freely exchanged between these three languages. With XSLT and XPath, this is of course essential, because XSLT always retrieves data from a source document by executing XPath expressions. The companion book *XPath 2.0 Programmer's Reference* contains a detailed description of this data model, and later in this section I will give a quick summary of the model for ease of reference.

Taking the inputs and output of the XSLT processors as trees produces a new diagram (Figure 2-2). The formal conformance rules say that an XSLT processor must be able to read a stylesheet and use it to transform a source tree into a result tree. This is the part of the system shown in the oval box. There's no official requirement to handle the parts of the process shown outside the box, namely the creation of a source tree from a source XML document (known as *parsing*), or the creation of a result XML document from the result tree (called *serialization*). In practice, though, most real products are likely to handle these parts as well.

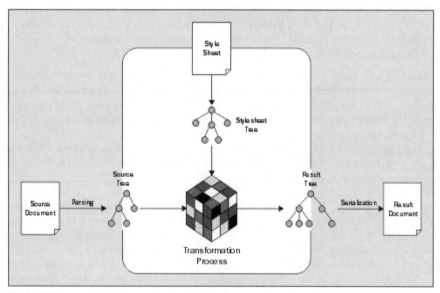

Figure 2-2

Different Output Formats

Although the final process of converting the result tree to an output document is outside the conformance rules of the XSLT standard, this doesn't mean that XSLT has nothing to say on the subject. In fact, there is a substantial section of the specification devoted to serialization, and although everything it says is nonbinding, most implementations have followed it very closely. The main control over this process is the `<xsl:output>` element, which is described in detail in Chapter 5, page 375.

The `<xsl:output>` element defines four output formats or methods, namely `xml`, `html`, `xhtml`, and `text`. In each case a result tree is written to a single output file.

❑ With the `xml` output method, the output file is an XML document. We'll see later that it need not be a complete XML document; it can also be an XML fragment. The `<xsl:output>` element allows the stylesheet writer some control over the way in which the XML is written, for example, the character encoding used and the use of `CDATA` sections.

❑ With the `html` output method, the output file is an HTML document, typically HTML 4.0, though products may support other versions if they wish. With HTML output, the XSLT processor recognizes many of the conventions of HTML and structures the output accordingly. For example, it recognizes elements such as `<hr>` that have a start tag and no end tag, as well as the special rules for escape characters within a `<script>` element. It may also (if it chooses) generate references to built-in entities such as «é».

Selecting `html` as the output method doesn't in any way automate the process of creating valid HTML, nor does it cause errors if the result tree produced by the transformation is invalid HTML. All it does is to tell the serializer to use HTML conventions when turning the nodes in the tree back into markup.

❑ The `xhtml` output method, as one might expect, is a compromise between the `xml` and `html` output methods. Generally speaking, it follows the rules of the `xml` output method, but sticks to the conventions described in the XHTML specification that are designed to make the output display properly in browsers that are designed to handle HTML. Such conventions include, for example, outputting an empty `<br>` element as `<br/>` (with a space before the «/»), and outputting an empty `<p>` element as `<p></p>`.

❑ The `text` output method is designed to allow output in any other text-based format. For example, the output might be a comma-separated-values file, a document in Microsoft's Rich Text Format (RTF), or in Adobe's Portable Document Format (PDF); or, it might be an electronic data interchange message, or a script in SQL or JavaScript. It's entirely up to you.

If the `<xsl:output>` element is omitted, the processor makes an intelligent guess, choosing HTML if the output starts with an `<html>` element in the null namespace, XHTML if it starts with an `<html>` element in the XHTML namespace, and XML otherwise.

Implementations may include output methods other than these four, but this is outside the scope of the standard. One mechanism provided by several products is to feed the result tree to a user-supplied document handler. In the case of Java products this will generally be written to conform to the `ContentHandler` interface defined as part of the SAX2 API specification (which since JDK 1.4 is part of the core class library in Java). Most implementations also provide mechanisms to capture the result as a DOM tree. Remember that if you use the result tree directly in this way, the XSLT processor will not serialize the tree, and therefore nothing you say in the `<xsl:output>` declaration will have any effect.

So, while the bulk of the XSLT Recommendation describes the transformation process from a source tree to a result tree, there is one section that describes another process, serialization. Because the serialization of a document tree as a file is a process that is relevant not only to XSLT but also to XQuery and potentially other applications in the future, the detail is no longer in the XSLT 2.0 Recommendation, but forms a W3C specification in its own right (see `http://www.w3.org/TR/xslt-xquery-serialization/`). The name *serialization* is used because it turns a tree structure into a stream of characters or bytes (but it mustn't be confused with serialization in distributed object systems such as Component Object Model

(COM) or Java, which produces a serial file representation of a COM or Java object). XSLT processors can implement this at their discretion, and it fits into our diagram as shown in Figure 2-3.

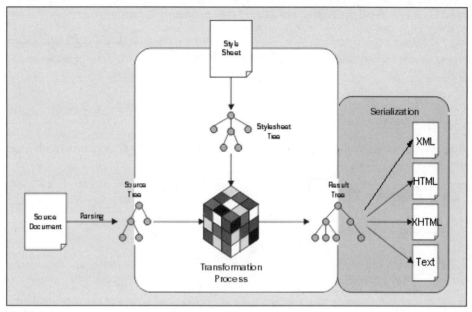

Figure 2-3

Multiple Inputs and Outputs

In real life, the processing model is further complicated because there can be multiple inputs and outputs. Specifically:

❑   There can be multiple input documents. The stylesheet can use the document() function (described in Chapter 7, page 532) to load secondary input documents, based on URI references held in the source document or the stylesheet. Each input document is processed as a tree in its own right, in exactly the same way as the principal input document. It is also possible to supply additional input documents as parameters to the stylesheet.

❑   The stylesheet may also consist of multiple documents. There are two declarations that can be used in the stylesheet, <xsl:include> and <xsl:import>, to load additional stylesheet modules and use them as extensions of the principal module. Splitting a stylesheet in this way allows modularity: in a complex environment different aspects of processing can be described in component stylesheets that can be incorporated into several different parent stylesheets. There is a detailed discussion of how to split a stylesheet into modules in Chapter 3.

❑   A single run of the XSLT processor can produce multiple output documents. This allows a single source document to be split into several output files: for example, the input might contain the text of an entire book, while the output contains one HTML file for each chapter, all connected using suitable hyperlinks. This capability, which is provided by the <xsl:result-document> element described in Chapter 5, is new in XSLT 2.0, though many vendors provided similar facilities as extensions to their XSLT 1.0 processors.

The Tree Model

Let's now look at the tree model used in XSLT, in a little more detail. This is a summary of the model; it is described in greater detail in Chapter 2 of *XPath 2.0 Programmer's Reference*.

The XSLT tree model is similar in many ways to the XML DOM. However, there are a number of differences of terminology and some subtle differences of detail. I'll point some of these out as we go along.

XML as a Tree

At a simple level, the equivalence of the textual representation of an XML document with a tree representation is very straightforward.

Example: An XML Tree

Consider the following document.

```
<definition>
    <word>export</word>
    <part-of-speech>vt</part-of-speech>
    <meaning>Send out (goods) to another country.</meaning>
    <etymology>
        <language>Latin</language>
        <parts>
            <part>
                <prefix>ex</prefix>
                <meaning>out(of)</meaning>
            </part>
            <part>
                <word>portare</word>
                <meaning>to carry</meaning>
            </part>
        </parts>
    </etymology>
</definition>
```

We can consider each piece of text as a leaf node, and each element as a containing node, and build an equivalent tree structure, which looks like Figure 2-4. It shows the tree after the stripping of all whitespace nodes: for discussion of this process, see Chapter 3, page 138. In this diagram each node is shown with potentially three pieces of information: in the top cell, the *type* of node; in the middle cell, the *name* of the node; and in the bottom one, its *string value*. For the root node and for elements, I show the string value simply as an asterisk: in fact, the string value of these nodes is defined to be the concatenation of the string values of all the element and text nodes at the next level of the tree.

It is easy to see how other aspects of the XML document, for example attributes and processing instructions, can be similarly represented in this tree view by means of additional kinds of node.

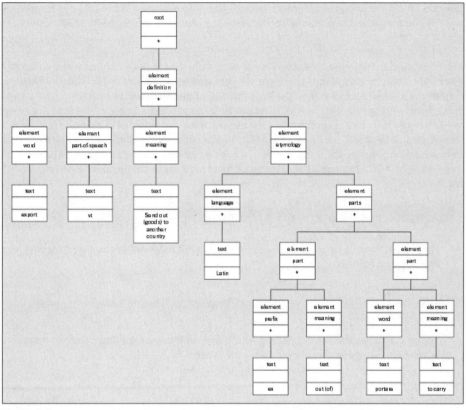

Figure 2-4

At the top of a tree that represents a well-formed XML document, there is a *document* node. This performs the same function as the document node in the DOM model in that it doesn't correspond to any particular part of the source document, but you can regard it as representing the document as a whole. The children of the document node are the top-level elements, comments, processing instructions, and so on.

The root node is not an element. In some specifications, the outermost element is described as the root of the document, but not in XPath or XSLT. In the XPath model, the root is the parent of the outermost element; it represents the document as a whole.

In XSLT 1.0, the document node was referred to as the root node. The terminology has changed, because trees that exist temporarily in the course of stylesheet execution can now have a different kind of node (for example, an element or an attribute node) as their root node.

The XSLT tree model can represent every well-formed XML document, but it can also represent structures that are not well formed according to the XML definition. Specifically, in well-formed XML, there must be a single outermost element containing all the other elements and text nodes; this element (the XML specification calls it the document element, though XSLT does not use this term) can be preceded and followed by comments and processing instructions, but cannot be preceded by other elements or text nodes.

The XSLT tree model does not enforce this constraint; a document node can have any children that an element might have, including multiple elements and text nodes in any order. The root might also have no children at all. This corresponds to the XML rules for the content of an *external general parsed entity*, which is a freestanding fragment of XML that can be incorporated into a well-formed document by means of an entity reference. I shall sometimes use the term *well balanced* to refer to such an entity. This term is not used in the XSLT specification; rather, I have borrowed it from the rarely mentioned XML fragment interchange proposal (`http://www.w3.org/TR/WD-xml-fragment`). The essential feature of a well-balanced XML fragment is that every element start tag is balanced by a corresponding element end tag.

Example: Well-Balanced XML Fragment

Here is an example of an XML fragment that is well balanced but not well formed, as there is no enclosing element.

```
The <noun>cat</noun> <verb>sat</verb> on the <noun>mat</noun>.
```

Figure 2-5 shows the corresponding XPath tree. In this case it is important to retain whitespace, so spaces are shown using the symbol ♦.

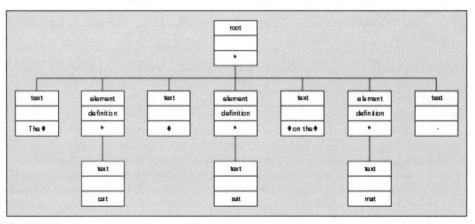

Figure 2-5

The string value of the root node in this example is simply «The cat sat on the mat.».

In practice, the input and output of the transformation will usually be well-formed documents, but it is very common for temporary trees constructed in the course of processing to have more than one element as a child of the root.

Nodes in the Tree Model

An XPath tree is made up of nodes. There are seven kinds of nodes, corresponding fairly directly to the components of the source XML document.

Node Type	Description
Document node	The document node is a singular node; there is one for each document. Do not confuse the document node with the document element, which in a well-formed document is the outermost element that contains all others.
Element node	An element is a part of a document bounded by start and end tags, or represented by a single empty-element tag such as `<TAG/>`.
Text node	A text node is a sequence of consecutive characters in a PCDATA part of an element. Text nodes are always made as big as possible: there will never be two adjacent text nodes in the tree, because they will have been merged together. In DOM terminology, the text nodes are *normalized*.
Attribute node	An attribute node includes the name and value of an attribute written within an element start tag (or empty-element tag). An attribute that was not present in the tag, but which has a default value defined in the Document Type Definition (DTD), is also represented as an attribute node on each separate element instance. A namespace declaration (an attribute whose name is `xmlns` or whose name begins with `xmlns:`) is, however, *not* represented by an attribute node in the tree.
Comment node	A comment node represents a comment written in the XML source document between the delimiters «`<!--`» and «`-->`».
Processing instruction node	A processing instruction node represents a processing instruction written in the XML source document between the delimiters «`<?`» and «`?>`». The *PITarget* from the XML source is taken as the node's name and the rest of the content as its value. Note that the XML declaration `<?xml version="1.0"?>` is not a processing instruction, even though it looks like one, and it is not represented by a node in the tree.
Namespace node	A namespace node represents a namespace declaration, except that it is copied to each element that it applies to. So each element node has one namespace node for every namespace declaration that is in scope for the element. The namespace nodes belonging to one element are distinct from those belonging to another element, even when they are derived from the same namespace declaration in the source document.

Each node can have a number of properties. Some of these are applicable to some kinds of nodes and not others (for example, elements and attributes have names, but text nodes do not), but for simplicity, the model is defined so that all properties are defined for all nodes, using a default value where nothing else makes sense.

The following table summarizes the properties of a node. There is more information on all these properties in Chapter 2 of *XPath 2.0 Programmer's Reference*.

Property	Description
Name	Elements and attributes have namespace-qualified names. The name is in two parts: a namespace URI (which may be null) and a local name. These can be obtained separately, using the functions `namespace-uri()` and `local-name()`, or together, in the form of an `xs:QName` value, using the function `node-name()`. The `name()` function attempts to reconstruct the node's name in the form of a lexical QName, by finding a prefix that is associated with the node's namespace URI.
	Processing instruction and namespace nodes also have names; in these cases this consists of a local name only. The name of a namespace node represents the namespace prefix.
	Document nodes, comment nodes, and text nodes are unnamed.
String value	Every node has a string value.
	❑ For elements and document nodes, this is the concatenation of all the text nodes within the element or document, at any depth
	❑ For attributes, it is the value of the attribute
	❑ For text nodes, it is the content of the text
	❑ For comments, it is the text of the comment
	❑ For processing instructions, it is the data part of the processing instruction (the part that follows the name)
	❑ For namespace nodes, it is the namespace URI
	The string value of a node can be obtained using the `string()` function in XPath.
Typed value	The typed value of a node represents the value after schema validation. For example, if the value of an element or attribute is described in the schema as a list of integers, then the typed value will be a sequence whose items are integers.
	For nodes other than elements and attributes, the typed value is the same as the string value.
	The typed value of a node can be obtained using the `data()` function in XPath, but this is rarely used explicitly because most operations that need access to the typed value extract it from the node automatically, through a process called *atomization*.
Type annotation	Element and attribute nodes have a type annotation, which is set by a schema processor when the node is validated, and indicates the schema type definition that the value conforms to. This may be a simple type or a complex type. For nodes that have not been validated, the type is set to `xdt:untyped` in the case of elements and `xdt:untypedAtomic` in the case of attributes. The type annotation of a node is not available directly to applications, but many operations on nodes depend on it.

Property	Description
Base URI	Document nodes, element nodes, and processing instructions have their own base URI, derived from the URI of the XML entity in which they were originally contained. Other nodes inherit their base URI from that of their parent node. The base URI may be overridden using the `xml:base` attribute. The base URI of a node is used when resolving a relative URI contained in that node (such as an «href» attribute in XHTML).
Parent	Every node except a document node can have a parent. In the XPath 2.0 model, however, other node kinds are not required to have a parent; any kind of node can also exist without a parent.
Children	Document nodes and element nodes can have children. In both cases, the children may be any sequence of elements, text nodes, comments, and processing instructions. The attributes of an element are not considered to be children of the element, even though the element is considered to be the parent of the attributes. For other nodes, this property is always an empty sequence.
Attributes	Element nodes can have attributes. For elements, this property is a sequence of zero or more attribute nodes; for other kinds of node, the property is always empty. The namespace declarations on an element are not considered to be attributes, and are not accessible via this property. The order in which attributes appear is not predictable.
Namespaces	Element nodes always have one or more namespace nodes. This property defines all the namespaces that are in scope for an element, whether they were declared on this element or on an outer element. There is always at least one namespace node, because the XML namespace is in scope for every element. For nodes other than elements, the set of namespace nodes is always empty.

Let's look in more detail at one particular feature of this model, the handling of names and, in particular, the use of namespaces.

Names and Namespaces

XSLT and XPath are designed very much with the use of XML Namespaces in mind, and although many source documents may make little or no use of namespaces, an understanding of the XML Namespaces Recommendation (found in `http://www.w3.org/TR/REC-xml-names`) is essential.

Expanding on the description in Chapter 1 (page 22), here's a summary of how namespaces work:

❑ A namespace declaration defines a namespace prefix and a namespace URI. The namespace prefix needs to be unique only within a local scope, but the namespace URI is supposed to be unique globally. Globally, here, really does mean globally: not just unique in the document, but unique across all documents around the planet. To achieve that, the advice is to use a URI based on a domain name that you control, for example `http://www.my-domain.com/namespace/billing`. XSLT doesn't impose any particular rules on the URI syntax, though it's a good idea to stick to a standard URI scheme in case this ever changes; in most of our examples we'll use URIs beginning with «http://».

❑ To avoid any ambiguity, it's also best to avoid relative URIs such as «billing.dtd». After a fierce debate on the issue, W3C issued a belated edict deprecating the use of relative namespace URIs in XML documents, and stating that the effect of using them is implementation defined. What this actually means is that they couldn't get everyone to agree. However, as far as most XSLT processors are concerned, the namespace URI does not have to conform to any particular syntax. For example, «abc», «42», and «?!*» are all likely to be acceptable as namespace URIs. It is just a character string, and two namespace URIs are considered equal if they contain the same sequence of Unicode characters.

❑ The namespace URI does not have to identify any particular resource, and although it is recommended to use a URL based on a domain name that you own, there is no implication that there is anything of interest to be found at that address. The two strings «c:\this.dtd» and «C:\THIS.DTD» are both acceptable as namespace URIs, whether or not there is actually a file of this name; and they represent different namespaces even though when read as filenames they might identify the same file.

> The fact that every stylesheet uses the namespace URI **http://www.w3.org/1999/ XSL/Transform** doesn't mean that you can't run a transformation if your machine has no Internet connection. The name is just an elaborate constant: it's not the address of something that the processor has to go and fetch.

❑ A namespace declaration for a non-null prefix is written as follows. This associates the namespace prefix my-prefix with the namespace URI http://my.com/namespace.

```
<a xmlns:my-prefix="http://my.com/namespace">
```

❑ A namespace declaration may also be present for the null prefix. This is known as the default namespace. The following declaration makes http://your.com/namespace the default namespace URI.

```
<a xmlns="http://your.com/namespace">
```

❑ The scope of a namespace declaration is the element on which it appears and all its children and descendants, excluding any subtree where the same prefix is associated with a different URI. This scope defines where the prefix is available for use. Within this scope, any name with the given prefix is automatically associated with the given namespace URI.

❑ A name has three properties: the prefix, the local part, and the namespace URI. If the prefix is not null, the name is written in the source document in the form prefix:local part: for example in the name xsl:template, the prefix is xsl and the local part is template. This format is referred to as a *lexical QName*. The namespace URI of the name is found from the innermost element that carries a namespace declaration of the relevant prefix. (In theory this allows you to use the same prefix with different meanings in different parts of the document, but the only time you'll ever need to do this is if you assemble a document from pieces that were separately authored.)

❑ The XML Namespaces Recommendation defines two kinds of names that may be qualified by means of a prefix: element names and attribute names. The XSLT Recommendation extends this to many other kinds of name that appear in the values of XML attributes, for example variable names, function names, template names, names of keys, and so on. All these names can be qualified by a namespace prefix.

❑ If a name has no prefix, then its namespace URI is considered to be the default namespace URI in the case of an element name, or a null URI in the case of an attribute name or any other kind of name (such as XSLT variable names and template names). Within an XPath expression, the default namespace URI is not used to qualify unprefixed names, even if the name is an element name. However, there is an attribute xpath-default-namespace that you can set on the <xsl:stylesheet> element, or on other elements, to qualify such names. This is described in Chapter 5 on page 442.

❑ Two names are considered equal if they have the same local part and the same namespace URI. The combination of the local part and the namespace URI is called the *expanded QName*. The expanded QName is never actually written down, and there is no defined syntax for it; it is a conceptual value made up of these two components.

> *The JAXP Application Programming Interface, described in Appendix D, allows expanded QNames to be written in the form* «{namespace.uri}local-name». *This is sometimes referred to as Clark notation.*

❑ The prefix of a name is arbitrary in that it does not affect comparison of names; however, it is available to applications, so it can be used as the default choice of prefix in the result tree, or in diagnostic output messages.

In the XPath tree model, there are two ways namespace declarations are made visible:

❑ For any node such as an element or attribute, the three components of the name (the prefix, the local part, and the namespace URI) are each available via the functions name(), local-name(), and namespace-uri(). The application doesn't need to know, and cannot find out, where the relevant namespace was declared. Technically, the prefix is not actually stored as part of the element or attribute name in the tree, but is reconstructed when the name() function is called. In some situations (for example, if your document uses more than one prefix to refer to the same namespace URI) the system might not use the original prefix, but another prefix that identifies the same namespace URI. In a few cases, typically where the source document uses the same prefix to refer to more than one namespace, it may be necessary for the processor to invent an arbitrary prefix.

❑ For any element, it is possible to determine all the namespace declarations that were in force for that element, by retrieving the associated namespace nodes. These are all made available as if the namespace declarations were repeated on that specific element. Again, the application cannot determine where the namespace declaration actually occurred in the source document. The name of a namespace node is the namespace prefix that was originally written in the source document; unlike the prefix returned by the name() function, the system is not free to change this.

Although the namespace declarations are originally written in the source document in the form of XML attributes, they are not retained as attribute nodes on the tree, and cannot be processed by looking for all the attribute nodes. Similarly, it is not possible to generate namespace nodes on the result tree by writing attributes with the names «xmlns:*» reserved for namespace declarations.

What Does the Tree Leave Out?

Many newcomers to XSLT ask questions like "How can I get the processor to use single quotes around attribute values rather than double quotes?" or "How can I get it to output « » instead of « »?"—and the answer is that you can't, because these distinctions are considered to be things that the recipient of the document shouldn't care about, and they were therefore left out of the XPath tree model. The principal output of an XSLT stylesheet is a tree, not a serialization.

Generally, the features of an XML document fall into one of three categories: definitely significant, definitely insignificant, and debatable. For example, the order of elements is definitely significant; the order of attributes within a start element tag is definitely insignificant; but the significance of comments is debatable.

Figure 2-6 illustrates this classification: the central core is information that is definitely significant; the "peripheral" ring is information that is debatable; while the outer ring represents features of an XML document that are definitely insignificant.

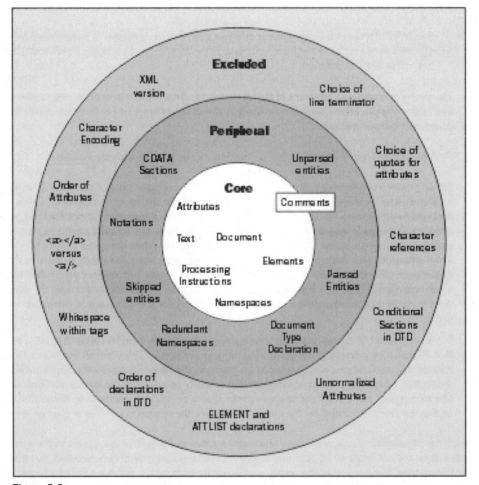

Figure 2-6

The choice of information items that are present in the XSLT/XPath tree model, and that therefore are accessible to an XSLT stylesheet follows the "core" as shown in the previous diagram fairly closely, but there are some very small differences of detail:

❑ The XSLT model includes comments. However, XML parsers aren't required to retain comments, so they can sometimes be lost before the stylesheet gets to see them.

❑ XSLT retains all the information derived from namespace declarations, unless the namespace declaration is redundant. It doesn't retain the actual namespace prefix used as part of an element or attribute name, but it will usually be possible to reconstitute the original prefix unless there are several prefixes declared for the same namespace.

❑ The XSLT model retains the base URI as a property of a node, unless you use the `xml:base` attribute; this property is not actually present in the original XML document, but is derived from the URI of the file or other resource containing the original document. As a result, this property will often not survive when documents are copied or moved, which can give problems when the document contains relative URIs.

Controlling Serialization

The transformation processor, which generates the result tree, generally gives the user control only over the core information items and properties (plus comments) in the output. The output processor or serializer gives a little bit of extra control over how the result tree is converted into a serial XML document. Specifically, it allows control over the following:

❑ Use of `CDATA` sections

❑ XML version

❑ Character encoding

❑ The `standalone` property in the XML declaration

❑ `DOCTYPE` declaration

Some of these things are considered peripheral in our classification given earlier and some are in the excluded category. The features that can be controlled during serialization do not include all the peripheral information items (for example, it is not possible to generate entity references), and they certainly do not include all the excluded features. For example, there is no way of controlling the order in which attributes are written, or the choice of `<a/>` versus `<a></a>` to represent empty elements, the disposition of whitespace within a start tag, or the presence of a newline character at the end of the document.

Although you get some control over these features during serialization, one thing you can't do is copy them from the source document unchanged through to the result. The fact that text was in a `CDATA` section in the input document has no bearing on whether it will be represented in as a `CDATA` section in the output document. The tree model does not provide any way for this extra information to be retained.

To underline all this, let's list some of the things you can't see in the input tree and some of the things you can't control in an XML output file.

Invisible Distinctions

In the following table, the constructs in the two columns are considered equivalent, and in each case you can't tell as a stylesheet writer which one was used in the source document. If one of them doesn't seem to have the required effect, don't bother trying the other because it won't make any difference.

Construct	Equivalent
`<item/>`	`<item></item>`
`&gt;`	`&#62;`
`<e>&quot;</e>`	`<e>"</e>`
`<![CDATA[ a < b ]]>`	`a &lt; b`

`<a xmlns="one.uri">`
`<b/>`
`</a>`
	`<a xmlns="one.uri">`
	`  <b xmlns="one.uri"/>`
	`</a>`

`<rectangle x="2" y="4"/>`	`<rectangle y='4'`
	`      x='2'`
	`/>`

In all these cases, except CDATA, it's equally true that you have no control over the format of the output. Because the alternatives are equivalent, you aren't supposed to care which is used.

Why make a distinction for CDATA on output? Perhaps because where a passage of text contains a large number of special characters, for example in a book where you want to show examples of XML, the use of character references can become very unreadable. It is after all one of the strengths of XML, and one of the reasons for its success, that XML documents are easy to read and edit by hand. Also, perhaps, because there is actually some controversy about the meaning of CDATA: there have been disputes, for example, about whether «`<![CDATA[ ]]>`» is allowed in circumstances where XML permits whitespace only.

DTD and Schema Information

The XPath designers decided not to include all the DTD information in the tree. Perhaps they were already anticipating the introduction of XML Schemas, which are widely expected to replace DTDs.

The XSLT processor (but not the application) needs to know which attributes are of type ID, so that the relevant elements can be retrieved when the id() function is used. It is part of the tree model that a particular element has a particular ID value, and this information will generally be available whether it comes from a DTD or from a schema. For other attribute types defined in a DTD, the specification is a little fuzzy. It does say that unless you use a schema-aware processor, the type annotations on all attributes will be xdt:untypedAtomic. But with a schema-aware processor, the system may take notice of DTD types as if they were defined in a schema rather than a DTD.

The information contained in the schema (for example, the type hierarchy) is not officially part of the data model, but there are implications that it is available to the XSLT processor in some form. In the formal data model, all you get is the type annotation property of element and attribute nodes, which is a reference to a type (a simple or complex type) defined in a schema. The specification doesn't say exactly how the information about this type is modeled, and there is no way for an application to access the type information directly (unlike languages such as SQL or Java, which offer this capability through a feature known as *reflection* or *introspection*). However, the implication is that internally the XSLT processor has access to any schema information needed to interpret a type annotation on a node in the tree.

We will be looking at the relationship between XSLT processing and XML schemas much more closely in Chapter 4.

The Transformation Process

I've described the essential process performed by XSLT, transformed a source tree to a result tree under the control of a stylesheet, and looked at the structure of these trees. Now it's time to look at how the transformation process actually works, which means taking a look inside the stylesheet.

Invoking a Transformation

The actual interface for firing off a transformation is outside the scope of the XSLT specification, and it's done differently by different products. There are also different styles of interface: possibilities include an API that can be invoked by applications, a GUI interface within a development environment, a command line interface, and the use of an `<?xml-stylesheet?>` processing instruction within a source document, which is described in Chapter 3 (see page 93). There's a common API for Java processors that was initially called TrAX, then became part of JAXP, and in JDK 1.4 has become part of the standard Java class library. For browsers, Microsoft and Netscape each has its own API, but there is at least one project (Sarissa, see `http://sarissa.sourceforge.net/`) that provides a common API that can be used on either browser.

What the XSLT 2.0 specification does do is to describe in abstract terms what information can be passed across this interface when the transformation is started. This includes the following:

❑ *The stylesheet itself:* Many products provide separate API calls to compile a stylesheet and then to run it, which saves time if the same stylesheet is being used to transform many source documents.

❑ *A source document:* This can be identified by any node in the document, which acts as the initial context node for the transformation. This will usually be the document node at the root of the tree, but it doesn't have to be. In fact, you don't have to supply an initial context node at all; you can instead supply the name of a template that will be the first template to be executed. The stylesheet can then fetch any data it needs from stylesheet parameters or from calls on the `document()` function.

❑ *An initial named template:* This acts as the entry point to the stylesheet and can be specified instead of supplying an initial context node, but it is also possible to supply both. If an initial named template is identified, the transformation starts with that template; otherwise, it starts by searching for a template rule that matches the initial context node, as described in the next section.

❑ *An initial mode:* Modes are described later in this chapter, on page 70. Normally, the transformation starts in the default (unnamed) mode, but you can choose to start in a different mode if you prefer. When the template rules in a stylesheet use a named mode, it becomes easier to combine two stylesheets into a single multiphase transformation, as described on page 82, and this feature ensures that you can still use the rules for each processing phase independently.

❑ *Parameters:* A stylesheet can define global parameters using `<xsl:param>` elements, as discussed on page 392. Interfaces for invoking a transformation will generally provide some kind of mechanism for setting values for these parameters. (A notable exception is that when you invoke a transformation using the `<?xml-stylesheet?>` processing instruction in a source document, there is no way of setting parameters.)

❑ *A base URI for output documents:* Many stylesheets will produce a single result document, and this URI effectively defines where this result document will be written. If the stylesheet produces multiple result documents, then each one is created using an `<xsl:result-document>` instruction with an `href` attribute, and the `href` attribute, if it is a relative URI, is interpreted as a location relative to this base URI.

Template Rules

As we saw in Chapter 1, most stylesheets will contain a number of template rules. Each template rule is expressed in the stylesheet as an <xsl:template> element with a match attribute. The value of the match attribute is a pattern. The pattern determines which nodes in the source tree the template rule matches.

For example, the pattern «/» matches the root node, the pattern «title» matches a <title> element, and the pattern «chapter/title» matches a <title> element whose parent is a <chapter> element.

When you invoke an XSLT processor to apply a particular stylesheet to a particular source document, the first thing it does is to read and parse these documents and create internal tree representations of them in memory. Once this preparation is complete, the transformation process can start.

The first step in the transformation process is usually to find a template rule that matches the document node of the source tree. If there are several possible candidates, there is a conflict resolution policy to choose the best fit (see page 71 for details). If there is no template rule that matches the document node, a built-in template is used. The XSLT processor then evaluates the contents of this template rule.

> XSLT 2.0 also allows you to start the transformation by supplying an initial node other than the document node. As discussed in the previous section, you can even start the transformation without supplying an initial node at all, by providing the name of the first template to be evaluated.

The content of an <xsl:template> element in the stylesheet is a sequence of elements and text nodes. Comments and processing instructions in the stylesheet are ignored, as are whitespace text nodes, unless they belong to an <xsl:text> element or to one with an appropriate xml:space attribute. This sequence of elements and text nodes is called a *sequence constructor*, because the result of evaluating it is itself a sequence.

Elements in the sequence constructor can be classified as either instructions or data, depending on their namespace. Text nodes are always classified as data. When the sequence constructor is evaluated, the instructions are evaluated, and the result of each instruction is added to the result sequence. The data nodes are copied to the result tree. Elements that are classified as data are officially termed *literal result elements*.

Contents of a Sequence Constructor

Consider the following template rule.

```
<xsl:template match="/">
   <xsl:message>Started!</xsl:message>
   <xsl:comment>Generated from XSLT</xsl:comment>
   <html>
      ...
   </html>
   The end
</xsl:template>
```

The body of this template rule consists of two instructions (<xsl:message> and <xsl:comment>), a literal result element (the <html> element), and some text («The end»). When this template is evaluated, the instructions are executed according to the rules for each individual instruction, and literal result elements and text nodes are copied (as element nodes and text nodes, respectively) to the result sequence.

It's simplest to think of this as a sequential process, where evaluating a sequence constructor causes evaluation of each of its components in the order they appear. Actually, because XSLT is largely side-effect-free, they could be executed in a different order, or in parallel. The important thing is that after evaluating this sequence constructor, the result sequence will contain a comment node (produced by the `<xsl:comment>` instruction), an `<html>` element node (produced by the `<html>` literal result element), and the text node «The end». The order of these items in the result sequence corresponds to the order of the instructions in the stylesheet, although in principle the XSLT processor is free to execute the instructions in any order it likes.

> `<xsl:message>` *is an exception to the rule that XSLT is side-effect-free. Evaluating an* `<xsl:message>` *instruction doesn't cause anything to be added to the result sequence; it merely causes the side effect of writing a message to some external device (perhaps standard output, or a log file). If there are several* `<xsl:message>` *instructions in a sequence constructor, then the order in which the messages appear is not guaranteed.*

If I hadn't included the «. . .» within the `<html>` element, this would be the end of the matter. But when a literal result element such as `<html>` is evaluated, its content is treated as a sequence constructor in its own right, and this is evaluated in the same way. It can again contain a mixture of instructions, literal result elements, and text. As we'll see in the next section, the result sequence produced by this sequence constructor is used to create the nodes that are attributes and children of the new `<html>` element.

Sequence Constructors

Sequence constructors play such an important role in the XSLT 2.0 processing model that it's worth studying them in some detail.

As we have seen, the content of an `<xsl:template>` element, after any parameter definitions contained in `<xsl:param>` elements, is a sequence constructor. (In XSLT 1.0, a sequence of instructions is officially called a *template*, though in practice everyone uses this term to mean "a template rule." In the previous edition of this book, I referred to the concept as a *template body*.) The new name *sequence constructor* reflects a change in the way the processing model is described, and a change in its capability: a sequence of instructions can now be used to produce any sequence of items, not only a sequence of sibling nodes in a tree.

Many other XSLT elements are also defined to have a sequence constructor as their content. For example, the contents of an `<xsl:variable>` or `<xsl:if>` element follow exactly the same rules as the content of an `<xsl:template>` (ignoring `<xsl:param>` elements), and these too are sequence constructors. It follows that one sequence constructor may be contained within another. For example, consider the following template rule.

```
<xsl:template match="para">
   <xsl:if test="position()=1">
      <hr/>- o - 0 - o -<hr/>
   </xsl:if>
   <xsl:apply-templates/>
   <xsl:if test="position()=last()">
      <hr/>- o - 0 - o -<hr/>
   </xsl:if>
</xsl:template>
```

Viewed as a tree, using the notation introduced in Chapter 2, this has the structure shown in Figure 2-7. There are three sequence constructors, indicated by the dotted lines. Within the sequence constructors on this tree, there are three kinds of nodes: text nodes, XSLT instructions (such as <xsl:if>), and literal result elements (such as <hr>), which are elements to be written to the result tree.

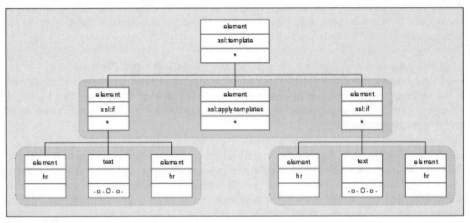

Figure 2-7

A sequence constructor is the nearest equivalent in XSLT to a block or compound statement in a block-structured programming language such as C or Java; and like blocks in C or Java, it defines the scope of any local variables declared within the block.

A sequence constructor is a sequence of sibling nodes in the stylesheet. Comment and processing instruction nodes are allowed, but the XSLT processor ignores them. The nodes of interest are text nodes and element nodes.

When a sequence constructor is evaluated, the result is, in general, a sequence of items. Many instructions such as <xsl:element>, <xsl:copy-of>, and <xsl:number> can create new nodes; a couple of the new instructions introduced in XSLT 2.0 such as <xsl:sequence> and <xsl:perform-sort> can also return references to existing nodes in a source document. It is also possible for the sequence to contain atomic values: these can be produced using the <xsl:sequence> and <xsl:copy-of> instructions.

Most likely, the sequence returned by a sequence constructor will be used to build the content of an element node in the result tree. In the example shown in Figure 2-7:

❑ The sequence constructors contained in the <xsl:if> elements always (if they are evaluated at all) produce a sequence of three nodes: two empty <hr> elements and a text node.

❑ The sequence constructor contained in the <xsl:template> instruction returns a sequence that is the concatenation of the nodes returned by the first <xsl:if> instruction, then the nodes returned by the <xsl:apply-templates> instruction, and finally the nodes returned by the second <xsl:if> instruction. The result of the template is this sequence of nodes.

Suppose that the template rule in our example is invoked using a construct such as the following.

```
<div>
   <xsl:apply-templates select="para"/>
</div>
```

The `<xsl:apply-templates>` instruction results in the sequence of nodes produced by evaluating the selected template rule. In fact, this instruction can select several `<para>` elements, and the template rule is invoked once for each one. The resulting nodes are all concatenated into a single sequence. Because the `<xsl:apply-templates>` instruction is the only instruction in the sequence constructor contained by the `<div>` element, the final sequence delivered to the `<div>` element contains the results of expanding the template rule for each of the selected `<para>` elements in the source document.

The `<div>` element is a literal result element, which when evaluated constructs a new element node. The name of this node will be `<div>`, and the content will be formed from the sequence produced by evaluating the sequence constructor contained within the literal result element in the stylesheet. In our example, this sequence contains elements and text nodes, and these are copied to form the content of the new `<div>` element.

This is by far the most common scenario: instructions are evaluated to produce a sequence of nodes, and the nodes are copied to form the contents of a result tree. However, in XSLT 2.0 it is also possible to process the sequence in other ways. In particular:

❏   A generated sequence can be captured in a variable. For example, the following variable will have a value that is a sequence of element nodes. These elements are not attached to a tree; they have no parent, and they are not siblings of each other:

```
<xsl:variable name="months" as="element()*">
   <month>January</month>
   <month>February</month>
   <month>March</month>
</xsl:variable>
```

You can then refer to the third element in this sequence as «$months[3]». But don't try doing «$months/month»; the $months variable holds a sequence of `<month>` elements, and the path expression «$months/month» (which is short for «$months/child::month») tries to find children of these elements that are named `<month>`. It won't find any.

This kind of variable is constructed when the «as» attribute is present to define the required type of the items in the sequence. If the «as» attribute were omitted, the `<month>` elements would be added to a temporary tree, and the variable $months would refer to the document node of this tree. For more information, see the section *Temporary Trees* on page 79.

❏   A generated sequence can also be returned by a function. Rather than defining the sequence of month elements in a variable, it could equally well be defined in a function.

```
<xsl:function name="m:months" as="element()*">
   <month>January</month>
   <month>February</month>
   <month>March</month>
</xsl:function>
```

You could then refer to the third month as «m:months() [3]». Note that user-defined functions must always be in a namespace, to avoid conflicts with system-defined functions.

❑ There is an important difference between using a variable and a function to capture the sequence: the variable will return the same elements every time, whereas the function will create new elements every time you call it. For example, this means that the expression «$months[3]is $months[3]» will be true, while «m:months()[3]is m:months()[3]» will be false. (The «is» operator in XPath 2.0 tests whether the values of the two operands are references to the same node.) In practice, you would want to use a function only if you were supplying parameters, because the data that came back depended on the parameters in some way.

Text nodes appearing within a template body are copied to the result sequence when the sequence constructor is evaluated. However, text nodes in a sequence constructor that consist entirely of whitespace will be ignored, unless the xml:space attribute is used on an enclosing element to define them as significant.

Text nodes containing whitespace only are also significant if they appear as the content of an <xsl:text> *element, but in that case they are not part of a sequence constructor.*

For more information on the treatment of whitespace see Chapter 3, page 136.

Nested Sequence Constructors

Suppose the template rule actually looks like this.

```
<xsl:template match="/">
    <xsl:message>Started!</xsl:message>
    <xsl:comment>Generated from XSLT</xsl:comment>
    <html>
        <head>
            <title>My first generated HTML page</title>
        </head>
        <body>
            <xsl:apply-templates/>
        </body>
    </html>
    The end
</xsl:template>
```

Here the <html> element contains two child elements, <head> and <body>. These are both literal result elements, so they are evaluated by copying them from the stylesheet to the result sequence.

Evaluating the <head> element in turn causes the sequence constructor within the <head> element to be evaluated. This sequence constructor contains a single literal result element, the <title> element, which in turn contains a sequence constructor containing a single text node, whose value is the string «My first generated HTML page».

What happens here (as far as the formal definition of the processing model is concerned) is a bottom-up process of tree construction. The sequence constructor containing the text node is evaluated to produce a result sequence containing a copy of the text node. The <head> element is then evaluated to produce a new <head> element node, which has this text node as its only child.

When the `<body>` element is evaluated, things get more interesting because it contains an XSLT instruction, namely `<xsl:apply-templates/>`. This particular instruction has critical importance: when written as here, without any attributes, it means "select all the children of the current node in the source tree, and for each one, find the matching template rule in the stylesheet, and evaluate it."

What actually happens at this point depends both on what is found in the source document, and on what other template rules are present in the stylesheet. Typically, because we are currently processing the root node of the source document tree, it will have just one child node, namely the document element (the outermost element of the source XML document). Suppose this is a `<doc>` element. Then the XSLT processor will search the stylesheet looking for a template rule that matches the `<doc>` element.

The simplest situation is where it finds just one rule that matches this element, for example one declared as:

```
<xsl:template match="doc">
```

If it finds more than one matching template rule, it has to use its conflict resolution policy to choose the best fit. The other possibility is that there is no matching template rule: in this case it invokes the built-in template rule for element nodes, which simply executes `<xsl:apply-templates/>`: in other words, it selects the children of this element, and tries to find template rules that match these children. There's also a built-in template rule for text nodes, which copies the text node to the output. If the element has no children, `<xsl:apply-templates/>` does nothing.

Whatever happens, however, the result of evaluating the `<xsl:apply-templates>` instruction is a sequence, usually a sequence of nodes. These nodes are added to the result of the sequence constructor contained by the `<body>` instruction, and are used to form the children (and potentially also the attributes) of the new `<body>` element. The new `<head>` and `<body>` elements now form a sequence that's used to make the children of the `<html>` element; and because this template rule was the first one to be activated, the transformation is now complete and the tree with this `<html>` element at the top becomes the final result tree of the transformation. (The `<html>` element is automatically wrapped in a document node, to complete the process.)

Hopefully, you never actually need to analyze what's going on to this level of detail. The name *template* was chosen because you can think of the whole process as producing a simple fill-in-the-blanks copy of the elements in the stylesheet as elements in the result tree. In the case of literal result elements and literal text, they are copied across unchanged; in the case of XSLT instructions, some processing is performed to fetch data from a source document for insertion at this point in the result tree.

Push Processing

The simplest way to process a source tree is thus to write a template rule for each kind of node that can be encountered, and for that template rule to produce any output required, as well as to call `<xsl:apply-templates>` to process the children of that node.

Example: Push Processing

This example demonstrates the push processing technique: a rule-based stylesheet in which there is one template rule to process each different kind of node.

Input

The source document, `books.xml`, is a simple book catalog.

```xml
<?xml version="1.0"?>
<books>
  <book category="reference">
      <author>Nigel Rees</author>
      <title>Sayings of the Century</title>
      <price>8.95</price>
  </book>
  <book category="fiction">
      <author>Evelyn Waugh</author>
      <title>Sword of Honour</title>
      <price>12.99</price>
  </book>
  <book category="fiction">
      <author>Herman Melville</author>
      <title>Moby Dick</title>
      <price>8.99</price>
  </book>
  <book category="fiction">
      <author>J. R. R. Tolkien</author>
      <title>The Lord of the Rings</title>
      <price>22.99</price>
  </book>
</books>
```

Stylesheet

Say you want display this data in the form of a sequentially numbered booklist. The following stylesheet, `books.xsl`, will do the trick.

```xml
<xsl:stylesheet
          xmlns:xsl="http://www.w3.org/1999/XSL/Transform"
          version="2.0"
>
<xsl:template match="books">
   <html><body>
   <h1>A list of books</h1>
   <table width="640">
   <xsl:apply-templates/>
   </table>
   </body></html>
</xsl:template>

<xsl:template match="book">
<tr>
   <td><xsl:number/></td>
   <xsl:apply-templates/>
   </tr>
</xsl:template>

<xsl:template match="author | title | price">
   <td><xsl:value-of select="."/></td>
```

```
    </xsl:template>

  </xsl:stylesheet>
```

What's happening here? There's no template rule for the document node, so the built-in template gets invoked. This processes all the children of the document node.

There's only one child of the document node, the <books> element. So the template rule for the <books> element is evaluated. This creates some standard HTML elements on the result tree, and eventually calls <xsl:apply-templates/> to cause its own children to be processed. These children are all <book> elements, so they are all processed by the template rule whose match pattern is «match="book"». This template rule outputs an HTML <tr> element, and within it a <td> element, which it fills by executing the <xsl:number/> instruction whose effect is to get the sequence number of the current node (the <book> element) within its parent element. It then calls <xsl:apply-templates/> once again to process the children of the <book> element in the source tree.

The children of the <book> element in the source document are all <author>, <title>, or <price> elements; so as it happens they all match the template rule whose match pattern is «match="author | title | price"» (you can read «|» as "or"). This template rule outputs an HTML <td> element that it fills by executing an instruction <xsl:value-of select="."/>. This instruction evaluates an XPath expression, and writes its result (a string) as text to the result tree. The expression is «.», which returns the string value of the current node, that is the textual content of the current <author>, <price>, or <title> element.

This template makes no further call on <xsl:apply-templates>, so its own children are not processed, and control returns all the way up.

Output

```
<html>
  <body>
    <h1>A list of books</h1>
    <table width="640">
      <tr>
        <td>1</td>
        <td>Nigel Rees</td>
        <td>Sayings of the Century</td>
        <td>8.95</td>
      </tr>
      <tr>
        <td>2</td>
        <td>Evelyn Waugh</td>
        <td>Sword of Honour</td>
        <td>12.99</td>
      </tr>
    etc..
      </table>
  </body>
</html>
```

This style of processing is called *push* processing. It is driven by the `<xsl:apply-templates>` instruction, as if the processor is pushing the nodes out of the door, saying "is anyone interested in dealing with this one?"

In this description I occasionally talk of instructions writing to the result tree. This is how the process was described in XSLT 1.0, and it accounts for the name push. It's a convenient way to think about what's going on. Technically, as we have seen, instructions don't write to the result tree; they are evaluated to produce a sequence (usually a sequence of nodes, but occasionally atomic values) and this sequence is then used by the calling instruction, often to construct the children of a new element. The importance of this model is that in XSLT 2.0, there are some situations in which the result of a sequence constructor is not used directly to build part of a result tree, but can be used in some other way, for example as the result of an XPath function call.

In such situations it is possible for an XPath expression to encounter nodes such as attributes and text nodes that have no parent, because they have not yet been attached to a result tree.

Controlling Which Nodes to Process

Simple push processing works very well when the data in the output is to have the same structure and sequence as the data in the input, and all we want to do is add or remove a few tags or perform other simple editing of values as we go along.

In the previous example, it wouldn't work so well if the properties of each book were less predictable, for example if some of the books had no price, or if the title and author could appear in either order. In this case the HTML table that we generated wouldn't be nicely arranged in columns any more, because generating a new cell for each property we encounter is not necessarily the right thing to do.

In such circumstances, there are two choices:

❑ Be more precise about which nodes to process, rather than just saying *process all children of the current node*.

❑ Be more precise about how to process them, rather than just saying *choose the best-fit template rule*.

Let's try the first option.

Example: Controlling the Sequence of Processing

We can gain greater control over *which* nodes are to be processed by changing the `<book>` template in `books.xsl`, as follows.

```
<xsl:template match="book">
   <tr>
     <td><xsl:number/></td>
     <xsl:apply-templates select="author, title, price"/>
   </tr>
</xsl:template>
```

Instead of selecting all child elements and finding the appropriate template rule for each one, this now explicitly selects first the `<author>` child element, then the `<title>` child element, and then the `<price>` child element.

This will still work, and it's more robust than our previous attempt, but it will still produce a ragged table if there are any `<book>` elements without an `<author>` (say), or with more than one.

> *The comma operator used in the expression «`select="author, title, price"`» is new in XPath 2.0. It simply concatenates several sequences (which might be single items, but could also be empty, or contain multiple items) into a single sequence, in the order specified.*

As we want a regular structure in the output and because we know a lot about the structure of the source document, we'd probably be better off in this situation defining all the processing in the `<book>` template rather than relying on template rules to match each of its child elements.

Example: Selecting Nodes Explicitly

We can gain greater control over *how* nodes are to be processed by writing the `<book>` template rule in the following manner.

```
<xsl:template match="book">
   <tr>
   <td><xsl:number/></td>
   <td><xsl:value-of select="author"/></td>
   <td><xsl:value-of select="title"/></td>
   <td><xsl:value-of select="price"/></td>
   </tr>
</xsl:template>
```

Some people call this *pull* processing, because instead of the template pushing nodes out of the door to be picked up by another template, it is pulling the nodes in and handling them itself.

The pattern-matching (or push) style of processing is the most characteristic feature of XSLT, and it works very well in applications where it makes sense to describe the handling of each type of node in the source document independently. However, there are many other techniques available, all of which are equally valuable. From within a template rule that is processing one particular node, the main alternatives if you want access to information in other nodes are as follows:

❑ Call `<xsl:apply-templates>` to process those nodes using their appropriate template rules.

❑ Call `<xsl:apply-templates>` in a particular *mode* (see later) to process those nodes using the template rules for the relevant mode.

❑ Call `<xsl:value-of>` to extract the required information from the nodes directly.

❑ Call `<xsl:for-each>` to perform explicit processing of each of the nodes in turn.

❑ Call `<xsl:call-template>` to invoke a specific template by name, rather than relying on pattern matching to decide which template to invoke.

Further discussion of the different approaches to writing a stylesheet is included in Chapter 9, "Stylesheet Design Patterns."

Modes

Sometimes you want to process the same node in the source tree more than once, in different ways. The classic example is to produce a table of contents. When generating the table of contents, you want to handle all the section headings in one way, and when producing the body of the document, you want to handle them in a different way.

One way around this problem is to use push processing on one of these passes through the data, and pull processing on all the other occasions. However, this could be very constraining. Instead, you can define different modes of processing, one for each pass through the data. You can name the mode of processing when you call `<xsl:apply-templates>`, and the only template rules that will be considered are those that specify the same mode. For example, if you specify:

```
<xsl:apply-templates select="heading-1" mode="table-of-contents"/>
```

Then the selected template rule might be one defined as:

```
<xsl:template match="heading-1" mode="table-of-contents">
...
</xsl:template>
```

Further details of how to use modes are in Chapter 5, page 194 and an example of how to use them to generate a table of contents is in Chapter 10, page 661.

Built-In Template Rules

What happens when `<xsl:apply-templates>` is invoked to process a node, and there is no template rule in the stylesheet that matches that node?

A *built-in template rule* is invoked.

There is a built-in template rule for each kind of node. The built-in rules work as follows.

Node Kind	Built-In Template Rule
Document	Call `<xsl:apply-templates>` to process the children of the document node, in the same mode as the calling mode
Element	Call `<xsl:apply-templates>` to process the children of this element, in the same mode as the calling mode
Attribute	Copy the attribute value to the result tree, as text—not as an attribute node
Text	Copy the text to the result tree
Comment	Do nothing

Node Kind	Built-In Template Rule
Processing instruction	Do nothing
Namespace	Do nothing

The built-in template rules will only be invoked if there is no rule that matches the node anywhere in the stylesheet.

There is no way to override the built-in template for namespace nodes, because there is no pattern that will match a namespace node. If you call `<xsl:apply-templates>` to process namespace nodes, nothing happens. If you want to process all the namespace nodes for an element, use:

```
<xsl:for-each select="namespace::*">
```

Conflict Resolution Policy

Conversely, what happens when there is more than one template rule whose pattern matches a particular node? As I mentioned earlier, the conflict resolution policy comes into play.

This works as follows:

❑ First the *import precedence* of each rule is considered. As Chapter 3 will show, one stylesheet may import another, using the `<xsl:import>` declaration, and this part of the policy basically says that when stylesheet A imports stylesheet B, the rules in A take precedence over the rules in B.

❑ Then the *priority* of each rule is examined. The priority is a numeric value, and the higher the number, the higher the priority. You can either specify the priority explicitly in the `priority` attribute of the `<xsl:template>` element, or leave the system to allocate a default priority. In this case, the system allocates a priority that is designed to reflect whether the pattern is very general or very specific: for example the pattern «subsection/title» (which matches any `<title>` element whose parent is a `<subsection>` element) gets higher priority than the pattern «*», which matches any element. System-allocated priorities are always in the range −0.5 to +0.5: user-allocated priorities will normally be 1 or more, but there are no restrictions. For more details see the description of the `<xsl:template>` element in Chapter 5, page 450.

❑ Finally, if there is more than one rule with the same import precedence and priority, the XSLT processor has a choice: it can either report an error, or choose whichever rule appears last in the stylesheet (some processors do both: they give you a warning, and then carry on processing). Different processors will behave differently in this situation, which gives you a slight portability problem to watch out for: it is best to ensure this ambiguity never happens, which you can achieve by setting explicit priorities on your template rules.

Error Handling

There are two kinds of error that can occur during an XSLT transformation: static errors and dynamic errors. Static errors occur while the stylesheet is being compiled, and dynamic errors occur while the transformation is actually running. If you invoke the transformation using a "single-shot" interface that doesn't distinguish compilation from execution then you may not notice the difference, but it is there all the same.

XSLT 1.0 was designed to minimize the number of things that could cause runtime errors. This was done largely by defining fallback behavior. For example, if you supplied the string "Africa" as input to an arithmetic operator, you would get the result NaN (not-a-number). This might not be a very useful result, but the thinking was that it was better than producing a pop-up on the browser saying "Error in stylesheet". For many runtime errors, implementors were in fact given a choice of reporting an error, or taking some defined fallback action.

The thinking in XSLT 2.0 has shifted significantly. There are now many more conditions that cause runtime errors, and many of these are not recoverable. There is also no try/catch mechanism to trap the errors when they occur: if a runtime error does occur in a stylesheet, it is fatal. In practice this means that you have to design your stylesheet to prevent them occurring. This means that you have to test whether the input data is valid before using it in an operation that could cause errors if it isn't valid. For example, before trying to convert a string to an integer using the `xs:integer()` constructor function, it is a good idea to test whether the conversion is possible using a construct such as «`if ($x castable as xs:integer) then ...`».

Although the language specification is very precise about what constitutes an error and what doesn't, there may well be variations between processors as to whether runtime errors are actually reported in particular circumstances. This is partly because the choice of reporting the error or taking fallback action is still there, as in XSLT 1.0; and it is also because the order of execution of instructions (or of subexpressions within an XPath expression) is not precisely defined. Suppose you write an expression such as «`exists(//employee[@retirement-date = current-date()])`» (which finds out whether any employees are retiring today). One XSLT processor might find such an employee, and return `true`. Another might find an employee whose `retirement-date` attribute is not a date (perhaps it is the string `"unknown"`) and report a runtime error. Processors are never required to do extra work just to look for runtime errors. In this example, the processor is allowed to stop searching the employees as soon as it finds one that satisfies the required conditions.

> *What if there are no employees retiring today, and there are some employees whose retirement dates are not valid dates? Does the processor have to raise a runtime error, or can it return `false`? A straightforward reading of the specification suggests that it has to report an error in this case. However, the rules that allow the processor to devise an optimal execution strategy are drawn up so broadly that I think an implementor could argue that returning `false` was conformant behavior.*

Variables and Expressions

The system of data types lies at the core of any language, and the way expressions are used to compute values and assign these to variables is closely tied up with the type system. The type system for XSLT is actually defined by the XPath language, and is fully explained in *XPath 2.0 Programmer's Reference* (in particular, Chapter 3). But here it's appropriate to look at how XSLT makes use of this type system. So this section will look in more detail at these aspects of the language.

The more sophisticated aspects of the XSLT type system interact closely with types as defined in XML Schema. We'll look in more detail in Chapter 4 at how stylesheets and schemas interact.

Variables

XSLT allows global variables to be defined, which are available throughout the whole stylesheet, as well as local variables, which are available only within a particular sequence constructor. The name and value of a variable are defined in an `<xsl:variable>` element. For example:

```
<xsl:variable name="width" select="50" as="xs:integer"/>
```

This defines a variable whose name is `width` and whose value is the number 50. The variable can subsequently be referenced in an XPath expression as `$width`. If the `<xsl:variable>` element appears at the top level of the stylesheet (as a child of the `<xsl:stylesheet>` element) then it declares a global variable; if it appears within the body of an `<xsl:template>` or `<xsl:function>` element then it defines a local variable.

The use of variables is superficially very similar to their use in conventional programming and scripting languages. They even have similar scoping rules. However, there is one key difference: *once a value has been given to a variable, it cannot be changed*. This difference has a profound impact on the way programs are written, so it is discussed in detail in the section *Programming without Assignment Statements* in Chapter 9, page 625.

The `as` attribute is optional, and defines the data type of the variable as being an integer. In this example, this doesn't add much: you can tell that it's an integer by looking at the value, and so can the XSLT processor. But there are cases where it's useful to specify the type. The `select` attribute doesn't have to be a constant, as it is in the previous example—it might, for example, be a call on a function. The `as` attribute acts both as an assertion about the type of the value (if the value is of the wrong type, you'll see an error message, either at compile time or at runtime) and also as a request to perform certain limited conversions from the supplied value to the specified type.

Broadly speaking, the type conversions that are possible in XSLT can be categorized as strong conversions and weak conversions. In a context like this, only weak conversions are applied. The weak conversions include the following:

❑ Treating a value of type T as a value of a supertype of T, for example an `xs:integer` as an `xs:decimal`, or an `xs:ID` as an `xs:string`.

❑ Extracting the typed value of a node, in cases where the supplied value is a reference to a node and the required type is atomic. This process is called *atomization*. The typed value of a node has the type determined by schema validation, for example if the node has been validated as an integer, you can use its value where an integer is expected, but not where (say) an `xs:anyURI` is expected. If there is no schema, then the typed value is the same as the string value.

❑ Numeric promotion of an `xs:integer` or `xs:decimal` to an `xs:float` or `xs:double`, and of an `xs:float` to an `xs:double`. In XML Schema, `xs:float` is not defined as a subtype of `xs:double`, but XPath and XSLT behave largely as if it were.

❑ Conversion of untyped atomic values (which usually arise as the values of nodes in documents, or parts of documents, that have not been schema-validated) to the required type. This conversion uses the rules defined in XML Schema: for example, if the required type is `xs:date`, then the supplied value must have the correct lexical form for an `xs:date`, as defined in the XML Schema specifications (that is, `YYYY-MM-DD` with an optional timezone).

These weak conversions are applied to the values of variables and parameters, and they are also used when converting the arguments supplied in a function call to the types declared in the function signature.

Strong conversions can be achieved by use of constructor functions, for example you can convert a string to an integer with the function «xs:integer($s)». Generally in XSLT 2.0, strong conversions are not applied automatically; you have to ask for them. Strong conversion is also referred to as *casting*, and the rules for casting are given in Chapter 9 of *XPath 2.0 Programmer's Reference*.

In the case of function calls, strong conversions are applied implicitly if you run the stylesheet in backwards-compatible mode. This is described in Chapter 3 on page 126. You can select backwards-compatible mode by specifying «version="1.0"» on the <xsl:stylesheet> element. However, even in backwards-compatible mode strong conversions are not applied to variables and parameters in the stylesheet. This is because in XSLT 1.0 it was not possible to declare the type of a variable or parameter, so there is no requirement here for backwards compatibility.

Parameters

Parameters in XSLT are very similar to variables. They are declared with an <xsl:param> element instead of <xsl:variable>, and they differ in that the value can be supplied externally. There are three places you can use parameters in a stylesheet:

❑ *Stylesheet parameters* (also known as global parameters) are supplied when the transformation is invoked, and they can be referenced from anywhere in the stylesheet. They are set from outside the stylesheet (for example, from the command line or from an API—the actual mechanism is implementation defined).

❑ *Template parameters* are defined within an <xsl:template> element, and are available only during the evaluation of that template. They are set by means of <xsl:with-param> elements within the instruction (for example <xsl:call-template> or <xsl:apply-templates>) that invokes the template. These parameters can take different values each time the template is invoked.

❑ *Function parameters* are defined within an <xsl:function> element, and are available only during the evaluation of that function. Functions are very similar to templates, except that they are invoked not by means of XSLT instructions, but by evaluating a function call within an XPath expression. The parameters to a function are supplied as part of this function call.

As with variables, the expected type of a parameter can be declared using an «as» attribute. Here it's much more useful to declare the expected type, because you can then fail cleanly if the caller supplies the wrong type of value, rather than crashing or producing wrong answers. It's also very valuable to the XSLT compiler to know in advance what type of value will be supplied, because it means that it can generate tighter code that doesn't have to deal with as many runtime possibilities. You don't have to declare the types of parameters, and if you don't, then any type of value will be accepted—but I would recommend it as good programming practice always to declare the types. I certainly find that it catches many of my sillier programming mistakes.

Data Types

The data type of a variable or parameter is described using the XPath 2.0 construct called SequenceType. The full syntax is explored in *XPath 2.0 Programmer's Reference*.

Every value in the XPath 2.0 data model is a sequence of items, and the `SequenceType` syntax is therefore in two parts: an `ItemType`, which describes the allowed content of each item, and an `OccurrenceIndicator`, which specifies how many items are allowed in the sequence. The possible occurrence indicators are «`*`» meaning any number of items (zero or more), «`?`» meaning zero or one item, and «`+`» meaning one or more items. If there is no occurrence indicator, then the sequence must contain exactly one item.

The values for `ItemType` that every XSLT processor is obliged to recognize (even if it doesn't support schema-aware stylesheets) are listed in the following table.

Item Type	Allowed Values
`item()`	Any item
`node()`	Any node
`document-node()`	Any document node
`element()`	Any element node. If a name is supplied within the parentheses, only elements with that name are allowed. A schema-aware processor allows further options to control which types of element node are allowed: see Chapter 4 for details.
`attribute()`	Any attribute node. If a name is supplied within the parentheses, only attributes with that name are allowed. A schema-aware processor allows further options to control which types of attribute node are allowed: see Chapter 4 for details.
`text()`	Any text node
`comment()`	Any comment node
`processing-instruction()`	Any processing instruction node. If a name is supplied within the parentheses, only processing instructions with that name are allowed.
`xdt:anyAtomicType`	Any atomic value
`xs:boolean`	A boolean value (true or false)
`xs:string`	A string of characters
`xs:decimal`	A decimal number
`xs:integer`	An integer (integers are considered to be a subtype of decimal numbers)
`xs:double`	A double-precision floating point number
`xs:dateTime`	A date and time
`xs:date`	A date
`xs:time`	A time

Continues

Item Type	Allowed Values
`xs:Qname`	A namespace-qualified name. Note that the value of an `xs:QName` contains the namespace URI and the local name, it does not contain a prefix.
`xs:anyURI`	A URI
`xdt:untypedAtomic`	An untyped atomic value, usually obtained by extracting the typed value of a node that has not been schema validated
`xdt:dayTimeDuration`	A duration expressed in days, hours, minutes, and seconds (and possibly fractions of a second)
`xdt:yearMonthDuration`	A duration expressed in years and months

The prefixes «xs» and «xdt» in this list are conventional. You can use any prefix that has been declared with the correct namespace URI (some people prefer to use «xsd» for the schema namespace). The «xs» prefix represents the namespace URI http://www.w3.org/2001/XMLSchema, while the «xdt» prefix represents a namespace that is given in the current draft specifications as http://www.w3.org/2003/11/xpath-datatypes, but this is likely to change in the final Recommendation.

Most of the time you can get by using only these data types. But if you are using a schema-aware XSLT processor, then you can also use the additional data types defined in the XML Schema Recommendation (for example, xs:positiveInteger or xs:hexBinary), as well as your own user-defined data types defined in a schema that has been imported into the stylesheet using an <xsl:import-schema> declaration. More on this in Chapter 4.

Expressions

The syntax of expressions is defined in the XPath Recommendation, and is described in detail in *XPath 2.0 Programmer's Reference*.

XPath expressions are used in a number of contexts in an XSLT stylesheet. They are used as attribute values for many XSLT elements, for example:

```
<xsl:value-of select="($x + $y) * 2"/>
```

In this example $x and $y are references to variables, and the operators «+» and «*» have their usual meanings of addition and multiplication.

Many XPath expressions, like this one, follow a syntax that is similar to other programming languages. The one that stands out, however, and the one that gave XPath its name, is the *path expression*.

A path expression defines a navigation path through the document tree. Starting at a defined origin, usually either the current node or the root, it follows a sequence of steps in defined directions. At each stage the path can branch, so for example you can find all the attributes of all the children of the origin node. The result is always a sequence of nodes in a fixed order (known as document order) with no duplicates. It might be empty or contain only one node, but it is still treated as a sequence.

The directions of navigation through the tree are called *axes*. The various axes are defined in detail in Chapter 7 of *XPath 2.0 Programmer's Reference*. They include the following:

- ❑ The child axis, which finds all the children of a node.

- ❑ The attribute axis, which finds all the attributes of a node.

- ❑ The ancestor axis, which finds all the ancestors of a node.

- ❑ The following-sibling axis, which finds the nodes that come after this one and share the same parent.

- ❑ The preceding-sibling axis, which finds the nodes that come before this one and share the same parent.

As well as specifying the direction of navigation through the tree, each step in a path expression can also qualify which nodes are to be selected. This can be done in several different ways:

- ❑ By specifying the name of the nodes (completely or partially).

- ❑ By specifying the kind of nodes (for example, elements or processing instructions).

- ❑ By specifying the schema-defined type of the nodes (for example, elements of type `person`, or attributes of type `xs:date`).

- ❑ By defining a predicate that the nodes must satisfy—an arbitrary boolean expression.

- ❑ By defining the relative position of the node along the axis: for example, it is possible to select only the immediately preceding sibling.

The syntax of a path expression uses «/» as an operator to separate the successive steps. A «/» at the start of a path expression indicates that the origin is the document node; otherwise it is generally the context node (we'll be looking at the notion of context in the next section). Within each step, the axis is written first, separated from the other conditions by the separator «::». However, the child axis is the default, so it may be omitted; and the attribute axis may be abbreviated to «@».

For example:

```
child::item/attribute::category
```

is a path expression of two steps, the first selects all the child `<item>` elements of the current node, and the second step selects their `category` attributes. This can be abbreviated to

```
item/@category
```

Predicates that the nodes must satisfy are written in square brackets, for example:

```
item[@code='T']/@category
```

This selects the `category` attributes of those child `<item>` elements that have a `code` attribute whose value is «T».

There are many ways of abbreviating path expressions to make them easier to write, but the basic structure remains the same. The full detail appears in Chapter 7 of *XPath 2.0 Programmer's Reference*.

Context

The way in which expressions are evaluated is to some extent context dependent. For example, the value of the expression $x depends on the current value of the variable x, and the value of the expression «.» depends on which node is currently being processed in the source document.

There are two aspects to the context: the static context, which depends only on where the expression appears in the stylesheet; and the dynamic context, which depends on the state of processing at the time the expression is evaluated.

The static context for an expression includes the following:

❑ The set of namespace declarations in force at the point where the expression is written. This determines the validity and meaning of any namespace prefixes used in the expression. As well as defining the namespace prefixes that are available, the context also defines the default namespace that will be used for unqualified element names appearing in path expressions.

❑ The set of variable declarations (that is, `<xsl:variable>` and `<xsl:param>` elements) in scope at the point where the expression is written. This determines the validity of any variable references used in the expression. As well as checking at compile time that the variable has been declared, the processor can also make checks on its type: for example it would be an error to use a variable of type `xs:date` as an argument to the `round()` function, and the processor can often detect such errors and report them at compile time.

❑ The functions that are available to be called. These always include the core library of functions defined in the XSLT and XPath specifications, and the constructor functions for built-in atomic types such as `xs:date`. They also include user-defined functions written using the `<xsl:function>` declaration, constructor functions for user-defined types in an imported schema (as described in Chapter 4), vendor-defined extension functions, and user-defined extension functions linked in to the stylesheet using vendor-defined mechanisms.

❑ The base URI of the stylesheet element containing the XPath expression. This only affects the result if the expression uses functions such as `document()` that make explicit use of the base URI.

All of these aspects of the static context for XPath expressions can be controlled from within the stylesheet, and may be different for different XPath expressions. There are other aspects of the XPath context that cannot be controlled using XSLT itself, but where implementors are likely to allow you some control via the API of their individual products. The most important example in this category is the set of URIs that are available for identifying collations (that is, rules for sorting and comparing strings according to the conventions of different languages).

The dynamic context is set only at stylesheet execution time. It consists of the following:

❑ The current values of all the variables that are in scope for the expression. These may be different each time the expression is evaluated.

❑ The focus, which reflects the current state of processing in the stylesheet. The focus comprises the following:

❑   The *context item*. This is the item (often a node in the source tree) that is currently being processed. An item becomes the context item when it is selected using the `<xsl:apply-templates>` or `<xsl:for-each>` instructions. The context item can also be set by the XPath processor when evaluating a subexpression. The context item can be referenced using the expression «.». In addition, the `current()` function (defined in Chapter 7) can always be used to reference the item that's the context item at the XSLT level, ignoring any changes made at the XPath level.

❑   The *context position*. This is an integer (≥1) that indicates the position of the context item in the sequence of items currently being processed. The context position can be referenced using the `position()` function. When `<xsl:apply-templates>` or `<xsl:for-each>` are used to process a sequence of items, the context position takes the values $1 \ldots n$ as each of the items in the list is processed. Similarly, when a predicate is used within a path expression, the context position is the position of the node being tested within the set of nodes being tested. For example, «child::a[position() != 1]» selects all the child elements named <a>, except the first.

❑   The *context size*. This is an integer (≥1) that indicates the number of items in the sequence of items currently being processed (that is, the highest value that `position()` will reach). The context size can be referenced using the `last()` function. For example, «child::a [position() != last()]» selects all the child elements named <a>, except the last.

❑   The set of documents that can be accessed using the `doc()` and `document()` functions is also regarded as being part of the dynamic context. This might include the whole of the Web, or it might be restricted by security policies to a local machine, or (if, say, the transformation is running on an embedded processor controlling the engine of your car) it might contain no documents at all. Modeling the set of addressable documents as part of the context is a formal device for describing the language semantics (it's a way of saying that the result of the `document()` function is defined by the environment in which the stylesheet runs, not by the language specification itself) and it turns out to be quite a neat device for distinguishing those aspects of these functions that are defined by the language spec from those that depend on the implementation.

Some system functions that can be used in XPath 2.0 expressions have other dependencies on the stylesheet context, for example the effect of the `key()` function depends on the set of `<xsl:key>` declarations in force; but the list given earlier covers all the context information that is directly accessible to user-written expressions.

Temporary Trees

As we described at the beginning of the chapter, a transformation takes a source tree as input (or perhaps more than one source tree) and produces a result tree (or several result trees) as output.

Very often, however, the easiest way to write a complex transformation is to split it into a number of phases, each of which performs one task. Like pipes in Unix, this creates a powerful way of reusing modules of code—on the basis that each module does only one job. For example, if your stylesheet involves selecting input records, sorting them, grouping them, numbering them, and then formatting the result as HTML, you could potentially carry out each of these five steps in a separate transformation phase. The result would be that if you wanted to change the output from HTML to PDF, the first four steps would be completely reusable.

One way of doing this is to write five separate stylesheets, and couple them together into a processing pipeline. The Java JAXP API, described in Appendix D, is well suited to this task. But often, you want rather closer coupling than this, and you don't necessarily want to write Java code to control the transformations. So the alternative is to write all the phases of the transformation in a single stylesheet, using *temporary trees* to represent the intermediate results between one phase of processing and the next.

A temporary tree is created by using an `<xsl:variable>` element with no «as» attribute, containing a sequence constructor to create the content of the tree. For example:

```
<xsl:variable name="author">
  <person>
    <first>Michael</first>
    <last>Kay</last>
    <nationality>British</nationality>
  </person>
</xsl:variable>
```

In this example, the value of the variable is a document node, which contains the `<person>` element as its only child node.

One popular way to use a temporary tree is as a lookup table. The following stylesheet fragment uses data held in a temporary tree to get the name of the month, given its number held in a variable $mm.

```
<xsl:variable name="months">
    <name>January</name><name>February</name><name>March</name>
    <name>April</name><name>May</name><name>June</name>
    <name>July</name><name>August</name><name>September</name>
    <name>October</name><name>November</name><name>December</name>
</xsl:variable>
    ...
    <xsl:value-of select="$months/name[position()=$mm])"/>
```

Of course, the sequence constructor does not have to contain constant values as in these two examples; it can also contain instructions such as `<xsl:value-of>` and `<xsl:apply-templates>` to build the content of the temporary tree dynamically. This is shown in the following example.

```
<xsl:variable name="tree">
  <xsl:text>AAA</xsl:text>
  <xsl:element name="x">
    <xsl:attribute name="att">att-value</xsl:attribute>
    <xsl:text>BBB</xsl:text>
  </xsl:element>
  <xsl:element name="y"/>
  <xsl:text>CCC</xsl:text>
</xsl:variable>
```

This creates the tree illustrated in Figure 2-8. Each box shows a node; the three layers are respectively the node kind, the node name, and the string value of the node. Once again, an asterisk indicates that the string value is the concatenation of the string values of the child nodes.

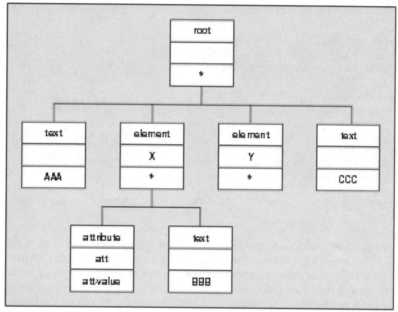

Figure 2-8

In XSLT 1.0, temporary trees went under the name of *result tree fragments*. I introduced the term *temporary tree* in an earlier edition of this book, because I felt that the phrase *result tree fragment* undervalued the range of purposes to which these structures can be applied. The term *temporary tree* is now the one used in the official language specification. In fact, result tree fragments in XSLT 1.0 were very limited in their capability because of a quite artificial restriction that prevented them being accessed using path expressions. Most vendors ended up circumventing this restriction using an extension function generally named xx:node-set(), where xx refers to the vendor's particular namespace. In XSLT 2.0, the restriction is gone for good, and temporary trees can now be used in exactly the same way as any source document: they can be used as the result tree for one phase of transformation, and the source tree for the next.

The restrictions in XSLT 1.0 were defined by making result tree fragments a separate data type, with a restricted range of operations available. In XSLT 2.0, a temporary tree is a tree just like any other, and is manipulated using variables or expressions that refer to its root node, which is always a document node. (In XSLT 2.0 you can have trees rooted at elements, or even at attributes or text nodes—though in that case there will only be one node in the tree. But the name temporary tree is reserved for trees with a document node at their root.)

A temporary tree does not necessarily correspond to a well-formed XML document, for example the document node can own text nodes directly, and it can have more than one element node among its children. However, it must conform to the same rules as an XML external parsed entity: for example, all the attributes belonging to an element node must have distinct names.

The ability to use temporary trees as intermediate results in a multiphase transformation greatly increases the options available to the stylesheet designer (which is why the xx:node-set() extension function was so popular in XSLT 1.0). The general structure of such a stylesheet follows the pattern:

```
<xsl:variable name="phase-1-output">
  <xsl:apply-templates mode="phase-1"/>
</xsl:variable>

<xsl:variable name="phase-2-output">
  <xsl:apply-templates select="$phase-1-output" mode="phase-2"/>
</xsl:variable>

<xsl:result-document>
  <xsl:apply-templates select="phase-2-output" mode="phase-3"/>
</xsl:result-document>
```

Some people prefer to use local variables for the intermediate results, some use global variables; it makes little difference.

One way that I often use multiphase transformations is to write a preprocessor for some specialized data source, to convert it into the format expected by an existing stylesheet module that renders it into HTML. For example, to create a glossary as an appendix in a document, you may want to write some code that searches the document for terms and their definitions. Rather than generating HTML directly from this code, you can generate the XML vocabulary used in the rest of the document, and then reuse the existing stylesheet code to render this as phase two of your transformation.

Since multiphase transformations are often used to keep stylesheets modular, some discipline is required to keep the template rules for each phase separate. I generally do this in two ways:

❑ Keep the rules for each phase of transformation in a separate stylesheet module. Stylesheet modules are discussed in Chapter 3.

❑ Use a different mode for each phase of the transformation. Modes were described earlier in this chapter, on page 70.

Summary

In this chapter we explored the important concepts needed to understand what an XSLT processor does, including the following:

❑ The overall system architecture, in which a stylesheet controls the transformation of a source tree into a result tree.

❑ The tree model used in XSLT, the way it relates to the XML standards, and some of the ways it differs from the DOM model.

❑ How template rules are used to define the action to be taken by the XSLT processor when it encounters particular kinds of node in the tree.

❑ The way in which expressions, data types, and variables are used in the XSLT language to calculate values.

The next chapter looks at the structure of an XSLT stylesheet in more detail.

Stylesheet Structure

This chapter describes the overall structure of a stylesheet. In the previous chapter we looked at the processing model for XSLT and the data model for its source and result trees. In this chapter we will look in more detail at the different kinds of construct found in a stylesheet such as declarations and instructions, literal result elements, and attribute value templates.

Some of the concepts explained in this chapter are tricky; they are areas that often cause confusion, which is why I have tried to explain them in some detail. However, it's not necessary to master everything in this chapter before you can write your first stylesheet—so use it as a reference, coming back to topics as and when you need to understand them more deeply.

The topics covered in this chapter are as follows:

- ❑ *Stylesheet modules*. We will discuss how a stylesheet program can be made up of one or more stylesheet modules, linked together with `<xsl:import>` and `<xsl:include>` elements.

- ❑ The `<xsl:stylesheet>` (or `<xsl:transform>` element). This is the outermost element of most stylesheet modules.

- ❑ The `<?xml-stylesheet?>` processing instruction. This links a source document to its associated stylesheet, and allows stylesheets to be embedded directly in the source document whose style they define.

- ❑ A brief description of the *declarations* found in the stylesheet, that is, the immediate children of the `<xsl:stylesheet>` or `<xsl:transform>` element. The full specifications are in Chapter 5.

- ❑ A brief description of each *instruction* that can be used in a stylesheet. In the previous chapter, I introduced the idea of a *sequence constructor* as a sequence of instructions that can be evaluated to produce a sequence of items, which will usually be nodes to be written to the result tree. This section provides a list of the instructions that can be used, with a quick summary of the function of each one. Full specifications of each instruction can be found in Chapter 5.

- ❑ *Simplified stylesheets*, in which the `<xsl:stylesheet>` and `<xsl:template match="/">` elements are omitted, to make an XSLT stylesheet look more like the simple template languages that some users may be familiar with.

❑ *Attribute value templates*. These define variable attributes not only of literal result elements, but of certain XSLT elements as well.

❑ Facilities allowing the specification to be extended, both by vendors and by W3C itself, without adversely affecting the portability of stylesheets.

❑ Handling of *whitespace* in the source document, in the stylesheet itself, and in the result tree.

Chapter 4 concludes the introductory section of this book with a discussion of how schemas are used with XSLT. The main reference section of the book then follows in Chapters 5 through 8.

Changes in XSLT 2.0

The important concepts in this chapter are largely unchanged from XSLT 1.0. The most significant changes are as follows:

❑ There are some terminology changes. Top-level elements are now called declarations. Templates (or *template bodies* as I called them in previous editions of this book) are now called sequence constructors—most people used the word template incorrectly to refer to an <xsl:template> element, and the new terminology bows to popular usage. Some of the terms previously used in this book but not in the official specification are now official (an example is the term *stylesheet module*).

❑ Some new declarations and instructions have been introduced.

❑ The concept of backwards-compatibility mode has been introduced. This is invoked when a stylesheet specifies «xsl:version="1.0"» and causes certain constructs to be handled in a way that is compatible with XSLT 1.0.

❑ The use-when attribute is introduced to allow parts of a stylesheet to be conditionally included or excluded at compile time.

❑ In other areas, there has been a general tightening up of the rules. For example, the effect of specifying «xml:space="preserve"» in a stylesheet is now described much more precisely.

The Modular Structure of a Stylesheet

In the previous chapter I described the XSLT processing model, in which a stylesheet defines the rules by which a source tree is transformed into a result tree.

Stylesheets, like programs in other languages, can become quite long and complex, and so there is a need to allow them to be divided into separate modules. This allows modules to be reused, and to be combined in different ways for different purposes: for example, we might want to use two different stylesheets to display press releases on screen and on paper, but there might be components that both of these stylesheets share in common. These shared components can go in a separate module that is used in both cases.

We touched on another way of using multiple stylesheet modules in the previous chapter, where each module corresponds to one phase of processing in a multiphase transformation.

One can regard the complete collection of modules as a *stylesheet program*, and refer to its components as *stylesheet modules*.

One of the stylesheet modules is the *principal stylesheet module*. This is in effect the main program, the module that is identified to the stylesheet processor by the use of an `<?xml-stylesheet?>` processing instruction in the source document, or whatever command-line parameters or application programming interface (API) the vendor chooses to provide. The principal stylesheet module may fetch other stylesheet modules, using `<xsl:include>` and `<xsl:import>` elements. These may in turn fetch others, and so on.

The following example illustrates a stylesheet written as three modules: a principal module to do the bulk of the work, with two supporting stylesheet modules: one to obtain the current date, and one to construct a copyright statement.

Example: Using <xsl:include>

Source

The input document, `sample.xml`, looks like this.

```
<?xml version="1.0" encoding="iso-8859-1"?>
<document>
    <author>Michael Kay</author>
    <title>XSLT 2.0 Programmer's Reference</title>
    <copyright/>
    <date/>
    <abstract>A comprehensive guide to the XSLT 2.0
       recommendation published by the World Wide Web Consortium
    </abstract>
</document>
```

Stylesheets

The stylesheet uses `<xsl:include>`. The effect of this stylesheet is to copy the source document unchanged to the result, except that any `<date>` elements are set to the current date, and any `<copyright>` elements are set to a string identifying the copyright owner.

There are three modules in this stylesheet program: `principal.xsl`, `date.xsl`, and `copyright.xsl`. The `date.xsl` module uses the XSLT 2.0 function `current-date()`; the other modules will work equally well with XSLT 1.0 or 2.0.

When you run the transformation, you only need to name the principal stylesheet module on the command line—the other modules will be fetched automatically. The way this stylesheet is written, all the modules must be in the same directory.

principal.xsl

The first module, `principal.xsl`, contains the main logic of the stylesheet.

```
<?xml version="1.0" encoding="iso-8859-1"?>
<xsl:stylesheet
      xmlns:xsl="http://www.w3.org/1999/XSL/Transform"
      version="1.0"
>
<xsl:include href="date.xsl"/>
<xsl:include href="copyright.xsl"/>
```

```
<xsl:output method="xml" encoding="iso-8859-1" indent="yes"/>
<xsl:strip-space elements="*"/>

<xsl:template match="date">
   <date><xsl:value-of select="$date"/></date>
</xsl:template>

<xsl:template match="copyright">
   <copyright>
      <xsl:call-template name="copyright"/>
   </copyright>
</xsl:template>

<xsl:template match="*">
   <xsl:copy>
      <xsl:copy-of select="@*"/>
      <xsl:apply-templates/>
   </xsl:copy>
</xsl:template>

</xsl:stylesheet>
```

It starts with two <xsl:include> elements to bring in the other modules. The <xsl:output> element indicates that the output should be in XML format, using the ISO 8859/1 character set (which makes it easy to view with a text editor), and with indentation to show the XML structure. The <xsl:strip-space> element indicates that whitespace nodes in the source document are to be ignored: I'll have a lot more to say about whitespace handling later in this chapter. Then there are three template rules, one for <date> elements, one for <copyright> elements, and one for everything else.

The template rule for <date> elements outputs the value of the variable named $date. This variable isn't defined in this stylesheet module, but it is present in the module date.xsl, so it can be accessed from here.

The template rule for <copyright> elements similarly calls the template named copyright. Again, there is no template of this name in this module, but there is one in the module copyright.xsl, so it can be called from here.

Finally, the template rule that matches all other elements («match="*"») has the effect of copying the element unchanged from the source document to the output. The <xsl:copy> (page 240) and <xsl:copy-of> (page 245) instructions are explained in Chapter 5.

date.xsl

The next module, date.xsl, declares a global variable containing today's date. This calls the current-date() function in the standard XPath 2.0 function library, and the XSLT 2.0 format-date() function, which is described in Chapter 7 of this book.

```
<xsl:stylesheet
      xmlns:xsl="http://www.w3.org/1999/XSL/Transform"
      version="2.0"
```

```
        xmlns:xs="http://www.w3.org/2001/XMLSchema"
   >
   <xsl:variable name="date" as="xs:string"
       select="format-date(current-date(), '[MNn] [D1o], [Y]')"/>

   </xsl:stylesheet>
```

Although this is a rather minimal module, there's a good reason why you might want to separate this code into its own module: it's dependent on XSLT 2.0, and you might want to write an alternative version of the function that doesn't have this dependency. Note that we've set «version="2.0"» on the <xsl:stylesheet> element to document this dependency; the other modules in this stylesheet have «version="1.0"».

copyright.xsl

Finally, the module copyright.xsl contains a named template that outputs a copyright statement. This template is called by the <xsl:call-template> instruction in the principal stylesheet. The template uses a variable $owner to construct the copyright statement: we'll see later how this is useful.

```
   <?xml version="1.0" encoding="iso-8859-1"?>
   <xsl:stylesheet
          xmlns:xsl="http://www.w3.org/1999/XSL/Transform"
          version="1.0">

   <xsl:variable name="owner">John Wiley and Sons</xsl:variable>

   <xsl:template name="copyright">
      <xsl:text>Copyright © </xsl:text>
      <xsl:value-of select="$owner"/>
      <xsl:text> 2004</xsl:text>
   </xsl:template>

   </xsl:stylesheet>
```

The reason for separating this stylesheet program into three modules is that the date.xsl and copyright.xsl modules are reusable in other stylesheets. Functionally, the stylesheet would have exactly the same effect if the variable $date and the template named copyright were defined directly in the principal stylesheet module.

Output

```
   <?xml version="1.0" encoding="iso-8859-1" ?>
   <document>
      <author>Michael Kay</author>
      <title>XSLT 2.0 Programmer's Reference</title>
      <copyright>Copyright © John Wiley and Sons 2004</copyright>
      <date>April 15th, 2004</date>
      <abstract>A comprehensive guide to the XSLT 2.0 recommendation
   published by the World Wide Web Consortium </abstract>
   </document>
```

There is no syntactic difference between a principal stylesheet module and any other module; in fact any module can be used as a principal module.

This means that `<xsl:include>` and `<xsl:import>` can be used in any module, not only the principal module. So the stylesheet program is actually a tree of stylesheet modules, with the principal module at its root.

A stylesheet module is generally a complete XML document (the exception, an *embedded stylesheet*, will be described later on page 95). The document element (the outermost element of the XML document) is then either an `<xsl:stylesheet>` element or an `<xsl:transform>` element: the two names are synonymous. The elements immediately subordinate to the `<xsl:stylesheet>` or `<xsl:transform>` element are called *declarations*. The XSLT-defined declarations are listed on page 99.

The `<xsl:include>` and `<xsl:import>` declarations are always children of the `<xsl:stylesheet>` or `<xsl:transform>` element. Usually, declarations can appear in any order, but `<xsl:import>` is an exception: it must appear before any other declaration. Both elements take an `href` attribute whose value is a URI. Most commonly, it will be a relative URI, defining the location of the included or imported stylesheet module relative to the parent module. For example, `<xsl:include href="mod1.xsl"/>` fetches the module `mod1.xsl` located in the same directory as the parent module.

The difference between `<xsl:include>` and `<xsl:import>` is that conflicting definitions are resolved differently:

❑ `<xsl:include>` effectively does a textual inclusion of the referenced stylesheet module, minus its containing `<xsl:stylesheet>` element, at the point where the `<xsl:include>` element is written. The included module is treated exactly as if its top-level elements, with their contents, appeared in the parent module in place of the `<xsl:include>` element itself.

❑ `<xsl:import>` also incorporates the top-level elements from the referenced stylesheet module, but in this case the declarations in the imported module have lower *import precedence* than the declarations in the parent module. If there are conflicting declarations, the one with higher import precedence will generally win. The detailed rules actually depend on the type of definition, and are given in the specification of `<xsl:import>` on page 312 in Chapter 5. Importing a module is thus rather like defining a subclass, in that the parent module can use some declarations unchanged from the imported module, and override others with declarations of its own.

> *It may not come naturally to think of the importing module as a subclass of the imported module, because in a class hierarchy, the most general classes are near the root of the tree, whereas in the* `<xsl:import>` *tree, the most general classes are at the leaves of the tree. Nevertheless, this is how* `<xsl:import>` *should be used: general-purpose modules should always be imported into special-purpose modules, not the other way around.*

The most common kind of declaration is the definition of a template rule, using an `<xsl:template>` element with a `match` attribute. As we saw in the previous chapter, if there are several template rules that match a particular node in the source tree, the first step in deciding which to use is to look at their import precedence, and discard all those with import precedence less than the highest. So a template rule defined in a particular stylesheet module will automatically take precedence over another matching rule in a module that it imports.

Where one module A imports two others, B and C, as shown in Figure 3-1, then A takes precedence over both B and C, and C also takes precedence over B, assuming that the `<xsl:import>` element that loads B precedes the `<xsl:import>` element that loads C.

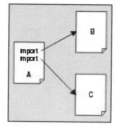

Figure 3-1

When a stylesheet incorporates another using `<xsl:include>`, the declarations in the included stylesheet have the same import precedence as those in the parent stylesheet.

Where two declarations have the same import precedence (because they were in the same stylesheet module, or because one was in a module incorporated in the other using `<xsl:include>`), the rules for resolving conflicts depend on the kind of declaration. In some cases, for example declarations of named templates or variables, duplicate declarations with the same name are always reported as an error. In other cases, for example declarations of template rules, the implementer has the choice of reporting an error or choosing the declaration that occurs later in the stylesheet. Some implementers may pass this choice on to the user. The detailed rules are given in Chapter 5 for each kind of declaration, and they are summarized in the section for `<xsl:import>`, page 312.

Example: Using <xsl:import>

This extends the previous `<xsl:include>` example, showing how to use `<xsl:import>` to incorporate the declarations in another stylesheet module while overriding some of them.

Source

The input document for this example is `sample.xml`.

Stylesheet

Recall that the `copyright.xsl` module used a variable, `$owner`, to hold the name of the copyright owner. Suppose that we want to use the `copyright` template, but with a different copyright owner. We can achieve this by writing a revised principal stylesheet as follows (this is called `principal2.xsl` in the downloadable sample files).

This stylesheet uses `<xsl:import>` instead of `<xsl:include>` to incorporate the `copyright.xsl` module, and it then contains a new declaration of the `$owner` variable, which will override the declaration in the imported module. Note that the `<xsl:import>` element must come first.

```
<?xml version="1.0" encoding="iso-8859-1"?>
<xsl:stylesheet
    xmlns:xsl="http://www.w3.org/1999/XSL/Transform"
    version="1.0"
>
```

```
<xsl:import href="copyright.xsl"/>
<xsl:variable name="owner">John Wiley Inc.</xsl:variable>
<xsl:include href="date.xsl"/>

<xsl:output method="xml" encoding="iso-8859-1" indent="yes"/>
<xsl:strip-space elements="*"/>

<xsl:template match="date">
    <date><xsl:value-of select="$date"/></date>
</xsl:template>
<xsl:template match="copyright">
    <copyright><xsl:call-template name="copyright"/></copyright>
</xsl:template>

<xsl:template match="*">
    <xsl:copy>
        <xsl:copy-of select="@*"/>
        <xsl:apply-templates/>
    </xsl:copy>
</xsl:template>

</xsl:stylesheet>
```

Output

```
<?xml version="1.0" encoding="iso-8859-1" ?>
<document>
    <author>Michael Kay</author>
    <title>XSLT Programmer's Reference</title>
    <copyright>Copyright © John Wiley Inc 2004</copyright>
    <date>April 15th, 2004</date>
    <abstract>A comprehensive guide to the XSLT 2.0 recommendation
published by the World Wide Web Consortium </abstract>
</document>
```

This example wouldn't work if you used `<xsl:include>` rather than `<xsl:import>`. It would complain that the variable `$owner` was declared twice. This is because with `<xsl:include>`, the two declarations have the same import precedence, so neither can override the other.

It is an error for a stylesheet module to import or include itself, directly or indirectly, because doing so would define an infinite loop.

It isn't an error, however, for a stylesheet module to be included or imported at more than one place in the stylesheet program. The following isn't an error.

```
<xsl:stylesheet xmlns:xsl="http://www.w3.org/1999/XSL/Transform"
version="1.0">
   <xsl:import href="date.xsl"/>
   <xsl:import href="date.xsl"/>
</xsl:stylesheet>
```

This may seem rather pointless, but in a highly modular structure it can sometimes happen by accident and be harmless. For example, several of your stylesheet modules might independently reference a commonly used module such as date.xsl. The effect is simply to load two copies of all the declarations in date.xsl, exactly as if two identical files with different names had been imported.

If the same module is fetched twice using <xsl:include>, the included declarations will have the same import precedence, which is likely to cause an error. If, for example, the included module defines a global variable or a named template, duplicate declarations will be reported. In other cases, for example where the file uses the <xsl:attribute-set> element to define named attribute sets, the duplicate declarations are harmless (the <xsl:attribute-set> element is described on page 214, in Chapter 5). However, if there is a risk of loading the same module twice, it makes sense to use <xsl:import> rather than <xsl:include>.

Note that with both <xsl:include> and <xsl:import>, the href attribute is fixed: it is possible for a stylesheet compiler to assemble all the modules in a stylesheet well before a source document is supplied to actually run the transformation. People often ask for some kind of facility to load stylesheet modules dynamically, based on a decision made while the transformation is running. The simple answer is that you can't do this: you have to construct the whole stylesheet before you can start running it.

Sometimes, this requirement arises when people try to use <xsl:import> "the wrong way round." It's fairly natural to think in terms of writing a general-purpose stylesheet G that imports A in some circumstances (say if the user is French) and imports B in other circumstances (if the user is Spanish). But that's the wrong way to do it: you should select A or B as the principal stylesheet module, and have both of these import the general-purpose module G. The special-purpose stylesheet module should always import the general-purpose module.

The XSL Working Group has recently added a facility for compile-time conditionals to the language. This allows you to write something like:

```
<xsl:include href="mod1.xsl" use-when="system-property('xsl:vendor')=
'Xalan'"/>.
```

This allows conditional inclusion of a module based on information that is known at compile time. There is more information on the use-when *attribute later in the chapter: see the section* Writing Portable Stylesheets.

The <xsl:stylesheet> Element

The <xsl:stylesheet> element (or <xsl:transform>, which is a synonym) is the outermost element of every stylesheet module.

The name <xsl:stylesheet> is a conventional name. The first part, xsl, is a prefix that identifies the namespace to which the element name belongs. Any prefix can be used so long as it is mapped, using a namespace declaration, to the URI http://www.w3.org/1999/XSL/Transform. There is also a mandatory version attribute. So the start tag of the <xsl:stylesheet> element will usually look like this.

```
<xsl:stylesheet
    xmlns:xsl="http://www.w3.org/1999/XSL/Transform"
    version="2.0"
>
```

The `<xsl:stylesheet>` element can also be written as `<xsl:transform>` if you prefer to think of XSLT as doing transformations rather than styling. The two names are completely interchangeable, but I usually use `<xsl:stylesheet>` for familiarity. Everything I say about the `<xsl:stylesheet>` element applies equally to `<xsl:transform>`.

As a general principle, it's advisable to specify «version="2.0"» if the stylesheet module uses any facilities from XSLT 2.0 or XPath 2.0, and «version="1.0"» if it relies only on XSLT 1.0 and XPath 1.0 features. This isn't purely documentary; as we'll see later (see page 123), XSLT processors have some subtle differences in behavior, depending on the setting of this attribute.

> *If you encounter a stylesheet that uses the namespace URI http://www.w3.org/TR/WD-xsl, then the stylesheet is written in a Microsoft dialect, based on an early working draft of the XSLT standard. This version was released with Internet Explorer 5, and although it has been obsolete for some years, you still come across it occasionally. There are many differences between the IE5 dialect (which I refer to as WD-xsl, but which Microsoft documentation often refers to simply as "XSL") and XSLT 1.0, and even more differences between WD-xsl and XSLT 2.0.*

The other attributes that may appear on this element are described under `<xsl:stylesheet>` in Chapter 5, page 433. Specifically, they are as follows:

❑ id, to identify the stylesheet if it appears as an embedded stylesheet within another document. Embedded stylesheets are described in the next section.

❑ extension-element-prefixes, a list of namespace prefixes that denote elements used for vendor-defined or user-defined extensions to the XSLT language.

❑ exclude-result-prefixes, a list of namespaces used in the stylesheet that should not be copied to the result tree unless they are actually needed. I'll explain how this works in the section *Literal Result Elements* on page 106.

❑ xpath-default-namespace, a namespace URI, which is used as the default namespace for unprefixed element names used in path expressions within the stylesheet, and also for unprefixed type names. This attribute is handy when all the elements in your source document are in a particular namespace, because it saves you having to use a namespace prefix every time you refer to an element in this namespace. Without this attribute, element names with no prefix are assumed to refer to names in the null namespace (neither the default namespace declared using «xmlns="uri"» in the stylesheet, nor the default namespace declared in the source document, has any effect on names used in path expressions).

❑ default-validation, which takes one of the values «strict», «lax», «preserve», or «strip». This attribute is used by a schema-aware processor to define the schema-based validation that is applied to elements created in a result tree. The value can be overridden on the instruction that creates a particular element. If the attribute is omitted, the value «strip» is assumed: this causes no schema-based validation to occur, and it also ensures that type annotations are not copied from the source tree to the result tree. You will find more details of how result trees are validated against a schema in Chapter 4.

These attributes affect only the stylesheet module in which this `<xsl:stylesheet>` element appears; they do not affect what happens in included or imported stylesheet modules.

The `<xsl:stylesheet>` element will often contain further namespace declarations. Many stylesheets are likely to reference the names of types defined in XML Schema, in which case the XML Schema namespace needs to be declared. Also, if the `extension-element-prefixes` or `exclude-result-prefixes` attributes are used, then any namespace prefixes they mention must be declared by means of a namespace declaration on the `<xsl:stylesheet>` element. For example, if you want to declare «saxon» as an extension element prefix, the start tag of the `<xsl:stylesheet>` element might look like this.

```
<xsl:stylesheet
    xmlns:xsl="http://www.w3.org/1999/XSL/Transform"
    xmlns:xs="http://www.w3.org/2001/XMLSchema"
    xmlns:saxon="http://saxon.sf.net/"
    version="1.0"
    extension-element-prefixes="saxon"
>
```

Namespace declarations on the `<xsl:stylesheet>` element, and indeed anywhere else in the stylesheet, apply only to the stylesheet module in which they appear. They are not inherited by included or imported modules.

The <?xml-stylesheet?> Processing Instruction

This processing instruction is not a part of the XSLT or XPath standard; rather it has a short W3C Recommendation all to itself, which you can find at `http://www.w3.org/TR/xml-stylesheet`. XSLT mentions it, but only in an example, so there is no implication that an XSLT processor is required to support it. However, most processors do.

The `<?xml-stylesheet?>` processing instruction is used within a source XML document to identify the stylesheet that should be used to process it. There can be several `<?xml-stylesheet?>` processing instructions present, defining different stylesheets to be used under different circumstances.

This way of controlling a transformation is particularly useful if you want to run the transformation on the client side (that is, in the browser). This is supported by both Internet Explorer and Netscape. It means you can simply send an XML file to the browser, with a processing instruction to identify the stylesheet to be used, and the browser will automatically invoke a transformation to HTML, which is then displayed. No special script is needed to control the process, which means the solution is very portable. Unfortunately, at the time of writing, none of the major browsers includes support for client-side transformation using XSLT 2.0. In fact it is likely to be a long time before support for XSLT 2.0 is sufficiently widespread in browsers for this to be a realistic option.

On the server side, which is where you are more likely to be using XSLT 2.0, it's less likely that you will want to control the transformation, using this processing instruction. It's much more likely that you will either want to drive the process from the operating system command line, or to use an API such as the Microsoft or Java APIs (described in Appendices C and D, respectively). These APIs give you much more control: they allow you to apply different stylesheets to the same documents on different occasions, to set parameters, and to compile a stylesheet once and then use it repeatedly.

So it's quite likely you can skip this section for now; but for completeness, I think it's still important to describe this mechanism.

The `<?xml-stylesheet?>` processing instruction has an `href` attribute whose value is the URI of the stylesheet (that is, the principal stylesheet module), and a `type` attribute that indicates the language in which the stylesheet is written. This doesn't have to be an XSLT stylesheet; it could be a Cascading Style Sheet (CSS).

There's considerable confusion about what the correct value of this attribute should be in the case of XSLT.

Until recently there was no registered media type (often called MIME type) for XSLT stylesheets, so Microsoft invented one: `text/xsl`. This has never been made official, and the XSLT 2.0 working draft proposes the registration of the name `application/xslt+xml`. However, the use of `text/xsl` is now so widespread that it is unlikely to go away.

> *Technically, XML processing instructions do not contain attributes; they contain a name (here* `xml-stylesheet`*) followed by character data. However, many people like to structure the character data as a sequence of* `name="value"` *pairs, like the attributes in an element start tag, and the xml-stylesheet recommendation follows this practice. It refers to the* `name="value"` *pairs as pseudo-attributes.*

Following is the full list of pseudo-attributes in the `<?xml-stylesheet?>` processing instruction.

Attribute Name	Value	Meaning
href (mandatory)	URI	The URI of the stylesheet. This may be an absolute or relative URL of the XML document, containing the stylesheet, or it may contain a fragment identifier (for example #styleB) used to locate the stylesheet within a larger file. See the section *Embedded Stylesheets* on page 95.
type (mandatory)	MIME type	Identifies the language in which the stylesheet is written; typically «application/xslt+xml» or «text/xsl» (see discussionearlier).
title (optional)	String	If there are several <?xml-stylesheet?> processing instructions, each should be given a title to distinguish them. The user can then be allowed to choose which stylesheet is wanted. For example, there may be special stylesheets that produce large print or aural rendition.
media (optional)	String	Description of the output medium, for example «print», «projection», or «aural». The list of possible values is defined in the HTML 4.0 specification. This value can be used to select from the available stylesheets.
charset optional	Character encoding name, for example iso-8859-1	This attribute is not useful with XSLT stylesheets, since as XML documents they define their character encoding themselves.
alternate (optional)	"yes" or "no"	If «no» is specified, this is the preferred stylesheet. If «yes» is specified, it is an alternative stylesheet.

As far as I have been able to discover, however, the only two attributes that influence Netscape or Internet Explorer are the `media` and `href` attributes.

An `<?xml-stylesheet?>` processing instruction must appear, if it appears at all, as part of the document prolog, that is, before the start tag of the document element. The `href` attribute identifies the location of the stylesheet by an absolute or relative URL. For example:

```
<?xml-stylesheet type="text/xsl" href="../style.xsl"?>
```

According to the W3C spec, it is possible to have several `<?xml-stylesheet?>` processing instructions that match the required criteria. The idea is that, as with CSS, the different stylesheets should be merged. Again, however, the practical reality seems to be different: it appears that Internet Explorer uses the first stylesheet specified, and Netscape uses the last. (Since this might be a bug that could be fixed at any time, I would advise against relying on this observation in the design of your application.)

It isn't mandatory to use the `<?xml-stylesheet?>` processing instruction, and most products will offer some other way of saying which stylesheet you want to apply to a particular document. It's mainly useful when you want to apply a stylesheet to an XML document within the browser; specifying this processing instruction means that the browser can apply a default stylesheet to the document, without any extra scripting being needed.

Clearly, one of the reasons for separating the stylesheet from the source XML document is so that the same information can be transformed or presented in different ways depending on the user, their equipment, or the particular mode of access. The various attributes of the `<?xml-stylesheet?>` processing instruction are designed to define the rules controlling the selection of an appropriate stylesheet. The mechanism is geared toward stylesheets that are used to display information to users: it has less relevance to the more general use of XSLT for performing data transformations.

Embedded Stylesheets

There is one exception to the rule that the stylesheet module must be an XML document. The principal stylesheet module can be *embedded* within another XML document, typically the document whose style it is defining.

The ability to embed stylesheets within the source document is best regarded as a carryover from CSS. It can be useful if you have a freestanding document that you want to distribute as a self-contained unit, but in most situations it is better to use an external stylesheet that can be used for many different source documents. I sometimes use an embedded stylesheet when I have a "one-of-a-kind" document such as a diary of events to be displayed on a Web site, as it simplifies things to keep the stylesheet and the data together. Some people like to embed stylesheets to reduce download time, but this can be counterproductive, because it means the browser cannot spot that the stylesheet is already present in its cache.

> **Not all products support embedded stylesheets. Check the documentation for your particular product before using them.**

The outermost element of the stylesheet is still an `<xsl:stylesheet>` or `<xsl:transform>` element, but it will no longer be the outermost element of the XML document (that is, the document element). The `<xsl:stylesheet>` element will generally have an `id` attribute to identify it, and will be referenced within its containing document using the `<?xml-stylesheet?>` processing instruction, as shown in the following example.

Example: Embedded Stylesheets

This example shows a stylesheet embedded within an XML source document containing a list of books.

Source

The data file, `embedded.xml`, containing both source document and stylesheet, is as follows.

```xml
<?xml version="1.0"?>
<!DOCTYPE books [
  <!ATTLIST xsl:stylesheet id ID #REQUIRED>
]>
<?xml-stylesheet type="text/xml" href="#style1"?>
<books>
    <book category="reference">
        <author>Nigel Rees</author>
        <title>Sayings of the Century</title>
        <price>8.95</price>
    </book>
    <book category="fiction">
        <author>Evelyn Waugh</author>
        <title>Sword of Honour</title>
        <price>12.99</price>
    </book>
    <book category="fiction">
        <author>Herman Melville</author>
        <title>Moby Dick</title>
        <price>8.99</price>
    </book>
    <book category="fiction">
        <author>J. R. R. Tolkien</author>
        <title>The Lord of the Rings</title>
        <price>22.99</price>
    </book>

    <xsl:stylesheet id="style1" version="1.0"
        xmlns:xsl="http://www.w3.org/1999/XSL/Transform">

    <xsl:template match="xsl:stylesheet"/>

    <xsl:template match="books">
        <html><body>
            <h1>A list of books</h1>
            <table>
                <xsl:apply-templates/>
            </table>
```

```
      </body></html>
  </xsl:template>

  <xsl:template match="book">
     <tr><xsl:apply-templates/></tr>
  </xsl:template>

  <xsl:template match="author | title | price">
     <td><xsl:value-of select="."/></td>
  </xsl:template>

  </xsl:stylesheet>
</books>
```

You can run this stylesheet using Saxon with a command of the form:

```
java -jar c:\saxon\saxon7.jar -a embedded.xml
```

The –a option tells Saxon to look for an `<?xml-stylesheet?>` processing instruction in the supplied source document, and to process the source document using that stylesheet. Saxon doesn't allow you (when using the command line interface) to specify the criteria for selecting a specific stylesheet, so if there are several, it uses a composite stylesheet that imports all of them.

Saxon will recognize the relative URI «#style1» only if it refers to the value of an attribute of type ID. The «id» attribute of the `<xsl:stylesheet>` element therefore needs to be declared as having this type: this is the purpose of the short `<!DOCTYPE>` entry. This isn't sufficient to invoke validation of the document (if you do try to invoke validation, by specifying the –v option on the command line, you will get a string of error messages referring to undeclared elements), but it is sufficient to register the attribute type of the «id» attribute.

Output

The output of this embedded stylesheet, when viewed in a Web browser, is shown in Figure 3-2.

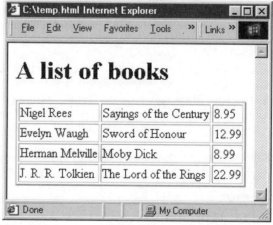

Figure 3-2

Note the empty template rule that matches the `<xsl:stylesheet>` element. This is needed because without it the stylesheet will try to process itself along with the rest of the document. The empty template rule ensures that when the `<xsl:stylesheet>` element is matched, no output is generated and its child elements are not processed. You may need to take care to avoid matching other elements in the stylesheet as well. For example, if the stylesheet looks for book titles using an expression such as «//title», this could accidentally match a `<title>` literal result element within the embedded stylesheet.

An embedded stylesheet module will generally be used as the principal stylesheet module. The standard doesn't explicitly say whether or not an embedded stylesheet can be included or imported into another. In practice, the details of what is supported are likely to vary from one product to another; few of the current products have much to say about embedded stylesheets in their documentation.

If namespace declarations occur outside the embedded stylesheet, they will still be in scope within the embedded stylesheet, which may result in extra namespace nodes being copied into the result tree. You can suppress such namespaces, using the `exclude-result-prefixes` attribute on the `<xsl:stylesheet>` element. If you are using an XML 1.1 parser, another solution would be to undeclare these namespaces (that is, to remove them from the set of namespaces that are in scope) by using a namespace undeclaration of the form «xmlns:prefix=""». (With XML 1.0, the only namespace that can be undeclared is the default namespace.)

Declarations

All elements that are immediate children of the `<xsl:stylesheet>` or `<xsl:transform>` element are called *top-level elements*. The top-level elements that are defined in the XSLT specification, and whose names are in the XSLT namespace, are called *declarations*. Those that are not defined in the XSLT specification are called user-defined data elements, and I will consider these in two categories: elements defined by the vendor of the XSLT processor, and elements defined by the stylesheet author.

It is not permitted to have text nodes as immediate children of the `<xsl:stylesheet>` or `<xsl:transform>` element, unless they consist entirely of whitespace characters. Processing instructions and comments may appear, and the XSLT processor will ignore them.

Top-level elements can appear in any order in the stylesheet, except that if there are any `<xsl:import>` declarations, these must come first. In most cases the order in which the elements appear is of no significance; however, if there are conflicting definitions, the XSLT processor sometimes has the option of either reporting an error or taking whichever definition comes last. If you want your stylesheet to be portable, you cannot rely on this behavior, and should ensure that conflicting declarations don't arise.

Let's now examine the three categories of elements that may appear as children of `<xsl:stylesheet>`.

❑   XSLT-defined declarations

❑   Implementer-defined declarations

❑   User-defined data elements

XSLT-Defined Declarations

An XSLT-defined declaration must be one of the following.

```
<xsl:attribute-set>
<xsl:character-map>
<xsl:decimal-format>
<xsl:function>
<xsl:import>
<xsl:import-schema>
<xsl:include>
<xsl:key>
<xsl:namespace-alias>
<xsl:output>
<xsl:param>
<xsl:preserve-space>
<xsl:strip-space>
<xsl:template>
<xsl:variable>
```

No other XSLT element (that is, no other element with the namespace URI `http://www.w3.org/1999/XSL/Transform`) may be used as a child of an `<xsl:stylesheet>` element.

The `<xsl:param>` and `<xsl:variable>` elements are exceptional in that they can be used both as declarations (of global variables and parameters) and as instructions within a sequence constructor.

The following table gives a quick introduction to the purpose of each of these declarations.

Declaration	Effect
`<xsl:attribute-set>`	Defines a named set of attribute nodes that can be added to any element in the result tree
`<xsl:character-map>`	Defines how individual characters in the result tree are to be output by the serializer
`<xsl:decimal-format>`	Defines a display format for numbers, used by the `format-number()` function described in Chapter 7
`<xsl:function>`	Defines a stylesheet function that can be invoked from any XPath expression
`<xsl:import>`	Incorporates declarations from another stylesheet module, with lower precedence than the declarations in the importing module
`<xsl:import-schema>`	Incorporates definitions from an XML Schema

Continues

Declaration	Effect
`<xsl:include>`	Incorporates declarations from another stylesheet module, with the same precedence as the declarations in the including module
`<xsl:key>`	Defines a key that may be referenced using the `key()` function (described in Chapter 7) to give fast access to elements if their key values are known
`<xsl:namespace-alias>`	Defines a translation from namespaces used in the stylesheet to namespaces used in the result tree
`<xsl:output>`	Defines how a result tree should be serialized
`<xsl:param>`	Defines a stylesheet parameter, a value that can be set from outside the stylesheet and accessed from anywhere within it
`<xsl:preserve-space>`	Defines a list of elements that contain whitespace text nodes that need to be retained
`<xsl:strip-space>`	Defines a list of elements that contain whitespace text nodes that must be removed
`<xsl:template>`	Defines a template that can be invoked either when specific nodes are matched, or explicitly by name
`<xsl:variable>`	Defines a global variable whose value can be accessed from anywhere in the stylesheet

The meaning of each of these elements is explained in full detail in Chapter 5.

Implementor-Defined Declarations

An implementor-defined declaration must belong to a namespace with a non-null URI, different from the XSLT namespace. This will generally be a namespace defined by the vendor: for example with the Saxon product, the relevant namespace URI is `http://saxon.sf.net/`. The meaning of elements in this category is entirely at the discretion of the vendor, though the specification states a rule that such elements must not be used to change the meaning of any standard XSLT constructs, *except to the extent that the behavior is implementation defined*. This is a very important caveat, because there are a great many things in XSLT that are implementation defined, and this clause allows vendors to use top-level elements to give the user control over the choices that are exercised. For example, they might be used to control the following:

❏   Binding of extension functions and extension instructions

❏   Collations used for sorting

❏   Details of result-tree serialization

❏   Localization of messages

❑   Options applied when building source trees, for example whether or not schema validation is performed

❑   Performance trade-offs, for example switches to control optimization or generation of diagnostics

❑   Error recovery policy

Note that these top-level elements are not technically extension instructions, and their namespace does not have to be declared in the `extension-element-prefixes` attribute for them to be effective.

Several vendors supply top-level elements that allow you to define extension functions that can be invoked from XPath expressions in the stylesheet (for example, Microsoft has an element called `<msxsl:script>` that can be used to define JavaScript functions to be called during the transformation). Others might use such elements to define debugging or tracing options. Saxon also uses top-level elements to describe details of collations used for sorting. Such extensions are described in the vendor's documentation for the particular product.

If the processor doesn't recognize the namespace used for an implementor-defined declaration, it simply ignores it. This means you can safely mix different vendors' extensions in the same stylesheet.

User-Defined Top-Level Elements

A *user-defined top-level element* must also belong to a namespace with a non-null URI, different from the XSLT namespace, and preferably different from the namespace URI used by any vendor. These elements are ignored by the XSLT processor.

With XSLT 1.0, user-defined top-level elements were useful as a place to put lookup data, error messages, and the like. It is possible to reference these elements from within the stylesheet, by treating the stylesheet as an additional source document, and loading it using the `document()` function, which is described in Chapter 7, page 532. If the first argument to this function is an empty string, it is interpreted as a reference to the stylesheet module in which the `document()` function appears.

So, for example, if the stylesheet contains a user-defined top-level element as follows:

```
<user:data xmlns:user="http://acme.com/">
   <message nr="1">Source document is empty</message>
   <message nr="2">Invalid date</message>
   <message nr="3">Sales value is not numeric</message>
</user:data>
```

then the same stylesheet can contain a named template to display a numbered message as follows.

```
<xsl:template name="display-message">
   <xsl:param name="message-nr"/>
   <xsl:message xmlns:user="http://acme.com/">
      <xsl:value-of
        select="document('')/*/user:data/message[@nr=$message-nr]"/>
   </xsl:message>
</xsl:template>
```

The `<xsl:value-of>` element evaluates the XPath expression in its `select` attribute as a string, and writes the value to the result tree. In this case the XPath expression is a path expression starting with «document('')», which selects the root node of the stylesheet module, followed by «*», which selects its first child (the `<xsl:stylesheet>` element), followed by «user:data», which selects the `<user:data>` element, followed by «message[@nr=$message-nr]», which selects the `<message>` element whose `nr` attribute is equal to the value of the $message-nr parameter in the stylesheet.

This named template might be invoked from elsewhere in the stylesheet using a sequence such as:

```
<xsl:if test="string(number(@sales))='NaN'">
    <xsl:call-template name="display-message">
        <xsl:with-param name="message-nr" select="3"/>
    </xsl:call-template>
</xsl:if>
```

The `<xsl:if>` element tests whether the `sales` attribute of the current source element is numeric: if not, the result of converting it to a number and then to a string will be the value NaN, meaning *Not-A-Number*. In this case, the code will call the template we defined earlier to display the message "Sales value is not numeric." (The destination of messages output using `<xsl:message>` is not defined in the standard. It might produce an alert box, or simply a message in the Web server log file.)

The advantage of this technique is that it gathers all the messages together in one place, for ease of maintenance. The technique can also be readily extended to use different sets of messages, depending on the user's preferred language.

With XSLT 2.0 this technique is no longer necessary, since it becomes more convenient to define fixed data as part of a global variable definition. Instead of writing:

```
<user:data xmlns:user="http://acme.com/">
    <message nr="1">Source document is empty</message>
    <message nr="2">Invalid date</message>
    <message nr="3">Sales value is not numeric</message>
</user:data>
```

you can write:

```
<xsl:variable name="data">
    <message nr="1">Source document is empty</message>
    <message nr="2">Invalid date</message>
    <message nr="3">Sales value is not numeric</message>
</xsl:variable>
```

and instead of:

```
<xsl:value-of select="document('')/*/user:data/message[@nr=$message-nr]"/>
```

you can write:

```
<xsl:value-of select="$data/message[@nr=$message-nr]"/>
```

The XSLT 1.0 technique still works, and you may want to continue using it when you write stylesheets that are to be portable between 1.0 and 2.0 processors.

Instructions

We saw in the previous chapter that a stylesheet is evaluated by a process that involves identifying template rules, evaluating the instructions contained in a template rule to produce nodes, and then adding the nodes to a result tree. This section explores in more detail the instructions that can be evaluated to produce nodes in the result tree.

The content of an `<xsl:template>` declaration, and of various other XSLT elements, is known as a *sequence constructor*. Element nodes within a sequence constructor are one of three kinds: XSLT instructions, extension elements, and literal result elements. I'll describe these in the next three sections.

XSLT Instructions

An XSLT instruction is one of the following elements.

```
<xsl:analyze-string>
<xsl:apply-imports>
<xsl:apply-templates>
<xsl:attribute>
<xsl:call-template>
<xsl:choose>
<xsl:comment>
<xsl:copy>
<xsl:copy-of>
<xsl:element>
<xsl:fallback>
<xsl:for-each>
<xsl:for-each-group>
<xsl:if>
<xsl:message>
<xsl:namespace>
<xsl:next-match>
<xsl:number>
<xsl:perform-sort>
<xsl:processing-instruction>
<xsl:result-document>
<xsl:sequence>
<xsl:text>
<xsl:value-of>
<xsl:variable>
```

No other element in the XSLT namespace may appear directly in a sequence constructor. Other XSLT elements, for example `<xsl:with-param>`, `<xsl:sort>`, and `<xsl:otherwise>`, are not regarded as instructions, because they cannot appear directly in a sequence constructor—they may appear only in very specific contexts. The `<xsl:param>` element is anomalous as it can appear as a child of an `<xsl:template>` element, but it is constrained to appear before other elements, and is therefore not considered to be part of the sequence constructor. So, it is not classified as an instruction. The same is true of an `<xsl:sort>` element appearing within `<xsl:for-each>` or `<xsl:for-each-group>`.

The following table gives a brief introduction to the effect of each XSLT instruction.

Instruction	Effect
`<xsl:analyze-string>`	Applies a regular expression to a string, causing subsidiary instructions to be evaluated for each matching and nonmatching substring
`<xsl:apply-imports>`	Searches imported stylesheets for another template rule to apply to the context node
`<xsl:apply-templates>`	Selects a sequence of nodes, and for each of these nodes identifies the template rule to be used to process that node, invokes the template rule, and returns the results
`<xsl:attribute>`	Constructs an attribute node
`<xsl:call-template>`	Invokes a named template and returns its result
`<xsl:choose>`	Chooses one of a number of instructions to evaluate, based on boolean conditions
`<xsl:comment>`	Constructs a comment node
`<xsl:copy>`	Copies the context node. This is a shallow copy; the content of the new node is determined by the contained instructions
`<xsl:copy-of>`	Returns a deep copy of selected nodes or atomic values
`<xsl:element>`	Constructs an element node
`<xsl:fallback>`	Defines fallback behavior to use if a particular instruction is not available
`<xsl:for-each>`	Invokes the contained instructions once for each item in a sequence of items
`<xsl:for-each-group>`	Selects a sequence of items and divides these into groups according to specified criteria; invokes the contained instructions once for each group of items
`<xsl:if>`	Evaluates the contained instructions if and only if a specified condition is true
`<xsl:message>`	Outputs a message to a system-defined destination
`<xsl:namespace>`	Constructs a namespace node
`<xsl:next-match>`	Selects another template rule that applies to the context node, and invokes it
`<xsl:number>`	Generates a sequence number for the context node and formats it for output
`<xsl:processing-instruction>`	Constructs a processing instruction node

Instruction	Effect
`<xsl:perform-sort>`	Selects a sequence of items and sorts them according to specified criteria
`<xsl:result-document>`	Constructs a document node to act as the root of a result tree, and optionally serializes it to a specified output destination
`<xsl:sequence>`	Produces a sequence of nodes and/or atomic values
`<xsl:text>`	Constructs a text node from literal text in the stylesheet, preserving whitespace
`<xsl:value-of>`	Constructs a text node
`<xsl:variable>`	Defines a local variable whose value can be accessed from other instructions within its scope

All of these XSLT instructions are explained in full detail in Chapter 5.

If an unknown element in the XSLT namespace is encountered in a sequence constructor, the action taken depends on whether *forwards-compatible mode* is enabled. This is discussed later on page 124.

Extension Instructions

An *extension instruction* is an instruction defined by the vendor or the user, as distinct from one defined in the XSLT standard. In both cases, they are recognized as extension elements because they belong to a namespace that is listed in the `extension-element-prefixes` attribute of the containing `<xsl:stylesheet>` element, or in the `xsl:extension-element-prefixes` attribute of the element itself, or of a containing literal result element or extension instruction.

In practice, extension instructions are more likely to be defined by vendors than by users. With XSLT 1.0, several vendors provided extension instructions to direct the stylesheet output to multiple output files (with XSLT 2.0, this is superseded by a standard facility, the `<xsl:result-document>` instruction). The Saxon product also provided the `<saxon:group>` extension element, which has been superseded by the `<xsl:for-each-group>` instruction in XSLT 2.0. An example of an extension that has not been superseded by any XSLT 2.0 feature is Saxon's `<sql:query>` element, which returns the result of performing a query on a relational database.

Not all products allow users to implement their own extension instructions, and with those that do, it may well involve some rather complex system-level programming. In practice, it is usually simpler to escape to user-written code by using extension functions, which are much easier to write. Extension functions are discussed later in this chapter, on page 129.

The following example shows an `<acme:instruction>` element that would be treated as a literal result element were it not for the `xsl:extension-element-prefixes` attribute, which turns it into an extension instruction.

```
<acme:instruction
   xmlns:acme="http://acme.co.jp/xslt"
   xsl:extension-element-prefixes="acme"/>
```

The way in which new extension instructions are implemented is not defined in the XSLT specification, and is likely to vary for each vendor. In fact, XSLT processors are not required to provide a mechanism for defining new extension elements. The only requirement is that they should recognize an extension instruction when they see one, and distinguish it from a literal result element.

What happens if a stylesheet that uses an extension instruction defined in the Xalan product (say) is processed using a different product (say Microsoft's)? If the processor encounters an extension instruction that it cannot evaluate (typically because it was invented by a different vendor), the action it must take is clearly defined in the XSLT standard: if the stylesheet author has defined an `<xsl:fallback>` action, it must evaluate that, otherwise it must report an error. The one thing it must not do is to treat the extension instruction as a literal result element and copy it to the result tree.

> The `<xsl:fallback>` instruction allows you to define how an XSLT processor should deal with extension instructions it does not recognize. It is described in more detail on page 136, and full specifications are on page 271 in Chapter 5.

Any element found in a sequence constructor that is not an XSLT instruction or an extension instruction is interpreted as a *literal result element* (for example, the `<hr/>` elements in the example discussed earlier). When the sequence constructor is evaluated, the literal result element will be copied to the result sequence.

So in effect there are two kinds of nodes in a sequence constructor: instructions and data. Instructions are obeyed according to the rules of the particular instruction, and data nodes (text nodes and literal result elements) are copied to the result sequence.

Literal result elements play an important role in the structure of a stylesheet, so the next section examines them in more detail.

Literal Result Elements

A literal result element is an element within a sequence constructor in the stylesheet that cannot be interpreted as an instruction, and which is therefore treated as data to be copied to the current output destination.

The notation I'm using here to describe literal result elements will be used extensively in Chapter 5, so it's worth explaining it.

❑   The *Format* section explains where the element can appear in the stylesheet; it lists the permitted attributes and their meanings and defines what child elements can appear in this element, if any. For each attribute it gives the name of the attribute, states whether the attribute is mandatory or optional, gives the permitted values for the attribute, and explains how the attribute is used. It also indicates whether the attribute may be an attribute value template.

❑   The *Usage* section explains what the element does and how it is used.

❑   The *Examples* section gives examples of how the element is used. In some cases, especially where an element has several distinct usages, the examples are merged into the *Usage* section.

Format

A literal result element can have any name, provided it is not in the XSLT namespace and is not in a namespace declared to contain extension instructions.

Position

A literal result element always appears directly within a sequence constructor.

Attributes

Name	Value	Meaning
xsl:exclude-result-prefixes (optional)	Whitespace-separated list of namespace prefixes (see the following note)	Each prefix in the list must identify a namespace that is in scope at this point in the stylesheet module. The namespace identified is not to be copied to the result tree.
xsl:extension-element-prefixes (optional)	Whitespace-separated list of namespace prefixes (see the following note)	Each prefix in the list must identify a namespace that is in scope at this point in the stylesheet module. Elements that are a descendant of this literal result element, and whose names are in one of these identified namespaces, are treated as extension instructions rather than literal result elements.
xsl:version (optional)	Number	The value «1.0» invokes backwards-compatible processing for this element and its descendants (see page 124). A value greater than 2.0 enables forwards-compatible processing (see page 126).
xsl:use-attribute-sets (optional)	Whitespace-separated list of QNames identifying named **<xsl:attribute-set>** elements (see the following note)	The attributes defined in the named attribute sets are instantiated and copied as attributes of this literal result element in the constructed sequence.
xsl:type (optional)	The name of a global type (simple type or complex type), which is either a built-in type such as xs:date, or a type defined in an imported schema	The constructed element in the result tree will be validated against this type definition. If it is valid, the element will be annotated with this type; if not, the transformation will fail.

Continues

Name	Value	Meaning
xsl:validation (optional)	One of the values «strict», «lax», «strip», or «preserve»	Describes the validation action to be performed. This attribute cannot be combined with the xsl:type attribute. The value «strict» or «lax» causes the processor to look in the available schemas for an element declaration that matches the name of the literal result element, and to validate the constructed element against this declaration. *Validation* is described in more detail in Chapter 4.
Other attributes (optional)	Attribute value template	Any XPath expressions occurring between curly braces in the value are evaluated, and the resulting string forms the value of an attribute copied to the result sequence. *Attribute Value Templates* are described on page 116.

Note: Several of the attributes take the form of whitespace-separated lists. This is simply a list of names (or prefixes) in which the various names are separated by any of the XML-defined whitespace characters: tab, carriage return, newline, or space. For example, you could write:

```
<TD xsl:use-attribute-sets="blue italic centered"/>
```

Here the names blue, italic, and centered must match the names of <xsl:attribute-set> elements elsewhere in the stylesheet.

Content

The content of a literal result element is a sequence constructor. It may thus contain XSLT instructions, extension elements, literal result elements, and/or text nodes.

Usage

The sequence constructor contained in the literal result element is evaluated, and this sequence is used to form the content of the new result element. This result element is then returned as the result of the instruction, to be combined with other items produced by sibling instructions in the stylesheet.

Consider a template body containing a single literal result element.

```
<TD>Product code</TD>
```

In this case a <TD> element will be written to the result tree with a child text node whose content is «Product code». When the result tree is output to an XML or HTML file, it will regenerate the text as it appeared in the stylesheet—or something equivalent. There is no guarantee that it will be character-for-character identical, for example the processor may add or remove whitespace within the tags, or it may represent characters using character or entity references.

If the literal result element has content, then the content must be another sequence constructor, and this sequence constructor is itself evaluated; any nodes generated in the result sequence in the course of this process will become children of the element created from the literal result element.

For example, if the template body is:

```
<TD><xsl:value-of select="."/></TD>
```

then when the <TD> element is evaluated, its content will also be evaluated. The content in this case is a sequence constructor consisting of a single XSLT instruction, and the effect is that this instruction is evaluated to create a text node that will be a child of the <TD> element in the result tree. The instruction <xsl:value-of select="."> outputs the typed value of the current node in the source tree, converted to a string. So if this value is «$83.99», the result would be as follows.

```
<TD>$83.99</TD>
```

It is tempting to think of this as a sequence of three steps:

❑ The <TD> start tag causes a <TD> start tag to be written to the output

❑ The <xsl:value-of> element is evaluated and the result («$83.99») is written to the output

❑ The </TD> end tag causes a </TD> end tag to be written to the output

However, this is not a true picture of what is going on, and it is best not to think about it this way, otherwise you will start wondering, for example, how to delay writing the end tag until some condition is encountered in the input.

> **The transformation process writes nodes to the result tree; it does not write tags to a sequential file. The <TD> element in the stylesheet causes a <TD> element to be written to the result tree. You cannot write half a node to the tree—the start and end tags are not written as separate operations. The <TD> and </TD> tags are generated only when the result tree is serialized as XML or HTML.**

Figure 3-3 helps illustrate this.

If you do find yourself thinking about where you want tags to appear in the output, it is a good idea to draw a sketch showing the required shape of the result tree, and then think about how to write the stylesheet to produce the required nodes on the tree. Since the element in the result tree will always be produced by evaluating one sequence constructor in the stylesheet, this amounts to asking "what condition in the input tree should cause this result element to be generated?"

For example, suppose you want to generate an HTML table with five columns, arranging the <item> elements from the source XML five to a row. Then the condition in the source XML that causes an output row to be generated is an <item> element whose position is 1, 6, 11, and so on. The logic can be written:

```
<xsl:template match="item[position() mod 5 = 1]">
<tr>
  <xsl:for-each select=".,  following-sibling::item[position() lt 5]">
    <td><xsl:value-of select="."/></td>
  </xsl:for-each>
</tr>
</xsl:template>

<xsl:template match="item"/>
```

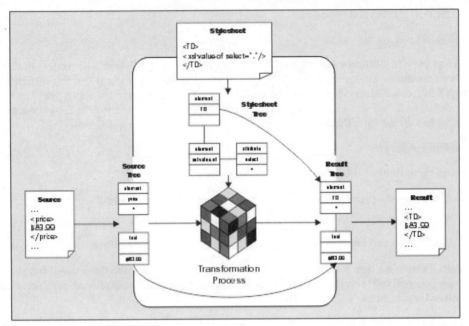

Figure 3-3

The first template rule matches `<item>` elements that should appear at the start of a new row; it outputs the `<tr>` element, and five `<td>` elements corresponding to this `<item>` and its four following siblings. The second rule matches `<item>` elements that should *not* appear at the start of a new row, and does nothing, because these will already have been processed by the first template rule.

> *In XSLT 2.0 problems like this one can also be solved conveniently using the `<xsl:for-each-group>` instruction, which is described with examples in Chapter 5 on page 281. However, for simple cases like this, the approach shown above works just as well.*

Attributes of a Literal Result Element

If the literal result element has attributes, other than the special `xsl`-prefixed ones in the list above, then these attributes too will be copied to the current output destination. So if the sequence constructor contains:

```
<TD><IMG src="picture1.gif"/></TD>
```

then the output will contain a copy of this whole structure. The outer `<TD>` element is copied to the result tree as before, and this time its content consists of another literal result element, the `<IMG>` element, which is copied to the result tree as a child of the `<TD>` element, along with its `src` attribute. This time both the stylesheet tree and the result tree take the form shown in Figure 3-4.

If the value of an attribute of a literal result element contains curly braces («{» and «}»), then it is treated as an *attribute value template* (discussed further in the next section). The text between the curly braces is treated as an XPath expression, and is evaluated as a string; the attribute written to the result tree contains this string in place of the expression. For example, suppose we apply the following template to the `books.xml` file used earlier.

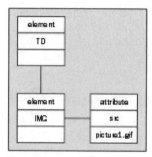

Figure 3-4

```
<xsl:template match="/">
  <xsl:for-each select="//book">
    <div id="div{position()}">
      <xsl:value-of select="title"/>
    </div>
  </xsl:for-each>
</xsl:template>
```

Because the `position()` function takes the values 1, 2, 3, and 4, as we move through the set of books, the output will take the following form.

```
<div id="div1">Sayings of the Century</div>
<div id="div2">Sword of Honour</div>
<div id="div3">Moby Dick</div>
<div id="div4">The Lord of the Rings</div>
```

It is also possible to generate attributes for a literal result element by two other mechanisms:

❑   The attribute can be generated by an `<xsl:attribute>` instruction. This instruction does not need to be textually within the content of the literal result element in the stylesheet, but attributes generated in the result sequence must appear before any child nodes (elements or children).

The reason for this rule is to allow the XSLT processor to avoid building the result tree in memory. Many processors will serialize XML syntax directly to an output file as the nodes are generated, and the rule that attributes must be generated before child elements or text nodes ensures that this is possible. Technically, it's not the order in which the instructions are evaluated that matters (that's up to the implementation); rather, the rule is that attribute nodes in the result of evaluating a sequence constructor must appear earlier in the sequence than nodes to be used as children.

❑   A collection of attributes can be generated by use of a named attribute set. The literal result element must contain an `xsl:use-attribute-sets` attribute that names the attribute sets to be incorporated: these names must correspond to `<xsl:attribute-set>` declarations at the top level of the stylesheet. The named attribute sets each contain a sequence of `<xsl:attribute>` instructions, and these cause attributes to be added to the generated element as if they were present directly in the content of the literal result element. Named attribute sets are useful to maintain a collection of related attributes such as font name, color, and size, which together define a style that will be used repeatedly in the output document; they are a direct parallel to the styles found in simpler languages such as CSS.

Attributes are added to the generated element node in a defined order: firstly, attributes incorporated using `xsl:use-attribute-sets`, then attributes present on the literal result element itself, and finally attributes added using `<xsl:attribute>` instructions. The significance of this sequence is that if two or more attributes with the same name are added, it is the last one that counts. It doesn't mean that they will necessarily appear in this order when the result tree is serialized.

Namespaces for a Literal Result Element

The namespace nodes of a literal result element are also copied to the result sequence of the sequence constructor. This is often the source of some confusion. The literal result element in the stylesheet will have a namespace node for every namespace declaration that is in scope: that is, every «xmlns» or «xmlns:*» attribute on the literal result element itself, or on any of its ancestor elements in the stylesheet. The only exception is that the attribute «xmlns=""» does not act as a namespace declaration, rather it cancels any earlier declaration for the default namespace.

> With XML Namespaces 1.1, it is also possible to cancel declarations of non-default namespaces, using an attribute of the form «xmlns:prefix=""». This undeclaration, if supported by the XSLT processor, ensures that the literal result element will not have a namespace node for that namespace prefix.

In the result tree, the element created from the literal result element is guaranteed to have a namespace node for every namespace node that was present on the literal result element in the stylesheet, except the following:

❑ A namespace node for the XSLT namespace URI `http://www.w3.org/1999/XSL/Transform` will not be copied.

❑ A namespace node for a namespace declared as an extension instruction namespace will not be copied. A namespace is declared as an extension instruction namespace by including its prefix in the value of the `[xsl:]extension-element-prefixes` attribute of the literal result element, or of any enclosing element in the stylesheet. (The attribute must be prefixed with the XSLT namespace if it appears on a literal result element, but must be unprefixed if it appears on an XSLT element.)

❑ A namespace node for an excluded namespace will not be copied. A namespace is declared as an excluded namespace by including its prefix in the value of the `[xsl:]exclude-result-prefixes` attribute of this literal result element or of any ancestor element in the stylesheet. (Again, the attribute must be in the XSLT namespace when it appears on an element that is *not* in the XSLT namespace.)

These exceptions don't apply if the name of the element, or the name of one of its attributes, actually uses one of these namespaces. The system will always ensure that the namespaces used for the element and attributes in the result tree are declared, however hard you try to prevent it. If this isn't what you want, then the chances are you should be generating the element in a different namespace to start with. To achieve this, you might need to use the `<xsl:element>` instruction instead of using literal result elements.

Consider the following stylesheet.

```
<xsl:stylesheet
    xmlns:xsl="http://www.w3.org/1999/XSL/Transform"
    version="2.0"
```

```
    xmlns:Date="java:java.util.Date"
>

<xsl:template match="/" xmlns="urn:acme-com:gregorian">
    <date><xsl:value-of select="$today"/></date>
</xsl:template>

<xsl:param name="today" select="Date:toString(Date:new())"/>

</xsl:stylesheet>
```

There are three namespaces in scope for the <date> element, namely the XSLT namespace, the namespace «java:java.util.Date», and the default namespace «urn:acme-com:gregorian». The XSLT namespace is not copied to the result tree, but the other two are. So, the <date> element added to the result tree is guaranteed to have these two namespaces in scope: «java:java.util.Date», and «urn:acme-com:gregorian».

> *This stylesheet uses two extension functions «Date:new()» and «Date:toString()». This means that it will not be portable between different XSLT processors.*

If the $today parameter is supplied as the value «2000-13-18», the output would be as follows (regardless of the source document).

```
<date xmlns="urn:acme-com:gregorian"
        xmlns:Date="java:java.util.Date">2000-13-18</date>
```

The first namespace declaration is necessary, because it defines the namespace for the element name <date>. However, you probably don't really want the xmlns:Date declaration here. It's not doing any harm, but it's not doing any good either. It's there because the XSLT processor can't tell that it's unwanted. If you want this declaration to be omitted, use the xsl:exclude-result-prefixes attribute as follows.

```
<xsl:stylesheet
    xmlns:xsl="http://www.w3.org/1999/XSL/Transform"
    version="2.0"
    xmlns:Date="java:java.util.Date"
>

<xsl:template match="/" xmlns="urn:acme-com:gregorian">
    <date xsl:exclude-result-prefixes="Date">
        <xsl:value-of select="$today"/>
    </date>
</xsl:template>

<xsl:param name="today" select="Date:toString(Date:new())"/>

</xsl:stylesheet>
```

The fact that an element in the result tree has a namespace node does not necessarily mean that when the result tree is written out as an XML document, the corresponding element will have a namespace declaration for that namespace. The XSLT processor is likely to omit the namespace declaration if it is redundant, in other words, if it duplicates a namespace declaration on a containing element. It can't be omitted, however, simply on the basis that it is not used. This is because namespace declarations might affect the meaning of the data in the output document in a way that the XSLT processor is unaware of. Applications are perfectly entitled to use namespace declarations to scope identifiers and names appearing in attribute values or text.

The `xsl:exclude-result-prefixes` *attribute is used to remove namespace declarations that are unused and unwanted. It can't be used to remove the declaration of namespace prefixes that are actually used in the result tree. And it isn't used to remove duplicate namespace declarations, as most processors will do that automatically.*

When an element is generated in the result tree, it doesn't automatically acquire copies of the namespace nodes attached to its parent in the result tree. Suppose your stylesheet has the following form.

```
<xsl:template match="product" xmlns:p="product.uri">
  <p:product>
    <xsl:call-template name="generate-description"/>
  </p:product>
</xsl:template>

<xsl:template name="generate-description">
  <text>This product is brilliant!</text>
</xsl:template>
```

There is nothing in the rules that causes the `<text>` element in the result tree to acquire a namespace node for the «`product.uri`» namespace. Despite this, the result of applying these two rules to a `<product>` element in the source document will probably look like this:

```
<p:product xmlns:p="product.uri">
    <text>This product is brilliant!</text>
</p:product>
```

Note that in this serialized output, the namespace «`product.uri`» is in scope for the `<text>` element. However, in the result tree itself, the `<text>` element does not have a namespace node for this namespace URI. In XML 1.0, there is no way to serialize the document in a way that faithfully reflects this fact. But with XML Namespaces 1.1, the result tree can be serialized more accurately as follows.

```
<p:product xmlns:p="product.uri">
    <text xmlns:p ="">This product is brilliant!</text>
</p:product>
```

To get this serialization, your stylesheet needs to contain the following declaration.

```
<xsl:output method="xml" version="1.1" undeclare-namespaces="yes"/>
```

In this example, the difference is unimportant. But if the `<p:product>` element were the envelope of a SOAP message, and the `<text>` element were the payload of the SOAP message, then the namespace undeclarations could be useful: the effect is that if the recipient of the SOAP message extracts the payload using another XSLT transformation, it will be in precisely its original form, not polluted with any declarations of SOAP namespaces.

For information about SOAP, see `http://www.w3.org/TR/soap12-part0/`

Namespace Prefixes

When a literal result element is copied to the result tree, the element name and attribute names of the new nodes in the result tree will have the same expanded name (that is, local name and namespace URI) as the corresponding nodes in the stylesheet. Usually, the names that are eventually output will also use the same namespace prefix.

There are unusual circumstances when the XSLT processor may need to change the prefix for a namespace. For example, it is possible to create two attributes that use the same namespace prefix to refer to different namespace URIs, as in the following example.

```
<output>
    <xsl:attribute name="out:file"
        xmlns:out="http://domain-a.com/">a</xsl:attribute>
    <xsl:attribute name="out:dir"
        xmlns:out="http://domain-b.com/">b</xsl:attribute>
</output>
```

The generated output in this case will look something like this.

```
<output
    out:file="a"
    ns1:dir="b"
    xmlns:out="http://domain-a.com/"
    xmlns:ns1="http://domain-b.com/"/>
```

The XSLT processor has no choice but to invent a prefix for one of the namespaces, because the supplied prefix is already in use with a different meaning. But because namespace prefixes are essentially arbitrary (it's only the URI that has any real significance) the meaning of the output file is not affected.

When namespace nodes are copied from the source or stylesheet tree to the result tree, the namespace prefix and namespace URI are both copied unchanged. When element or attribute nodes are copied, the expanded name of the element or attribute (that is, its local name and namespace URI) is always preserved, but the namespace prefix may occasionally need to be changed. If this happens, however, an extra namespace node will be added to the result tree to associate the new namespace prefix with the correct namespace URI.

Namespace Aliasing

In some circumstances, instead of changing the namespace prefix when a literal result element is copied to the result tree, it is necessary to change the namespace URI.

The most obvious situation where this arises is when the output document is itself a stylesheet. This isn't as esoteric a requirement as it may appear; generating a stylesheet can be a very useful technique. For example, if your company changes its house style to use different fonts and colors, you could write an XSLT transformation to convert all your existing stylesheets to the new standard.

When you generate a stylesheet, you will want to generate XSLT elements such as `<xsl:template>` in the result tree; but you can't include such elements as literal result elements in the stylesheet, because they would be mistaken for instructions. One approach is to generate these elements using the `<xsl:element>` instruction instead of literal result elements. But there is another way of doing it: you can include them in the stylesheet with a different namespace, and then declare in an

<xsl:namespace-alias> element that the URI should be changed when the literal result element is copied to the result tree.

For more details of this mechanism, see <xsl:namespace-alias> in Chapter 5, on page 350.

Attribute Value Templates

As we've seen, an attribute value template is a special form of parameterized attribute value. There are two ways they can be used:

❑ On a literal result element, an attribute value template provides a way of generating an attribute whose value is computed at runtime rather than always taking the same value, for example `<td width="{$width}">`. You could achieve the same effect with the `<xsl:attribute>` instruction, but attribute value templates are easier to write and understand.

❑ On some XSLT elements, certain attributes can be computed at runtime. For example, when sorting, instead of writing «order="ascending"» or «order="descending"», you could write «order="{$order}"» so that the order varies, depending on a runtime parameter. Note that there are very few attributes where this facility is available. They are listed later in this section.

The term *template* here has nothing to do with XSLT template rules or `<xsl:template>` elements. Attribute value templates simply provide a notation for embedding variable components into an otherwise fixed attribute value.

An attribute value template is a string in which XPath expressions may be embedded within curly braces («{» and «}»). The XPath expression is evaluated, and in general the result will be a sequence. Each item in this sequence is converted to a string, using the rules for the XPath `string()` function (see Chapter 10 of *XPath 2.0 Programmer's Reference*). These strings are then concatenated, with a single space character inserted as a separator between each string. The resulting concatenated string is substituted into the attribute value in place of the original XPath expression and curly braces.

> *If backwards-compatibility mode is in use (that is, if «version="1.0"» is specified), then all strings after the first in the sequence are discarded; only the first string is included in the output. See the section* Version Compatibility *on page 123 for details.*

For example, suppose you have a set of images representing an alphabet such as the following, and you want to use these to represent the first character of a paragraph of text.

| fancyA.gif | FancyB.gif | fancyC.gif | fancyD.gif | FancyF.gif |

You could write a template rule to achieve this as follows (ignoring practical details such as how to deal with paragraphs that don't start with a capital letter). It uses the `substring()` function, which is described in Chapter 10 of *XPath 2.0 Programmer's Reference*.

```
<xsl:template match="para">
   <p><img src="fancy{substring(.,1,1)}.gif"/>
   <xsl:value-of select="substring(.,2)" /></p>
</xsl:template>
```

A paragraph that starts with the letter A (like this one) will cause the `src` attribute of the `<img>` element to be evaluated as «img src="fancyA.gif"», so it will be displayed in the browser as shown in Figure 3-5.

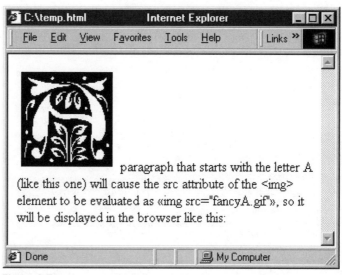

Figure 3-5

If you want to include the characters «{» or «}» in an attribute value with their ordinary meaning, they should be doubled as «{{» or «}}». This is sometimes necessary when generating dynamic HTML, and it also happens often with the `regex` attribute of the `<xsl:analyze-string>` instruction, whose value is a regular expression. However, you should do this only in an attribute that is being interpreted as an attribute value template. In other attributes, curly braces have no special meaning.

Curly brackets can never be nested. You can use them only to include an XPath expression in the text of a stylesheet attribute; they cannot be used within an XPath expression itself. You can always achieve the required effect some other way; for example, instead of:

```
<a href="#{id( 'A{@nr}' )}"> <!-- WRONG -->
```

write:

```
<a href="#{id( concat('A', @nr) )}">
```

The `concat()` function, described in Chapter 10 of *XPath 2.0 Programmer's Reference*, performs concatenation of strings.

Attribute value templates cannot be used anywhere you like in the stylesheet. They can be used only for those attributes that are specifically identified as attribute value templates in the XSLT Recommendation. The following table gives a complete list of all the places you can use attribute value templates.

Element	Attributes Interpreted as Attribute Value Templates
Literal result elements	All attributes except those in the XSLT namespace
Extension elements	As defined by the specification of each extension element
`<xsl:analyze-string>`	`regex, flags`
`<xsl:attribute>`	`name, namespace, separator`
`<xsl:element>`	`name, namespace`
`<xsl:for-each-group>`	`collation`
`<xsl:message>`	`terminate`
`<xsl:namespace>`	`name`
`<xsl:number>`	`format, lang, letter-value, ordinal, grouping-separator, grouping-size`
`<xsl:processing-instruction>`	`name`
`<xsl:result-document>`	`href`
`<xsl:sort>`	`lang, order, collation, data-type, case-order`
`<xsl:value-of>`	`separator`

In all other contexts, don't even think of trying to use them because the curly braces will either be ignored, or cause an error to be reported. It can be very tempting, if you want to use `<xsl:call-template>`, for example, and the name of the template you want to call is in a variable, to want to write:

```
<!- WRONG -->
<xsl:param name="tname"/>
<xsl:call-template name="{$tname}"/>
<!- WRONG -->
```

However, you can't, because the `name` attribute (or any other attribute of `<xsl:call-template>` for that matter) of `<xsl:call-template>` is not in the above list of places where attribute value templates can be used.

Why are attribute value templates rationed so severely? The restrictions are there deliberately to make life easier for the XSLT processor:

❑ Attribute value templates are never allowed for attributes of declarations. This ensures that the values are known before the source document is read, and are constant for each run of the stylesheet.

❑ Attribute value templates are never allowed for attributes whose value is an XPath expression or a pattern. This ensures that expressions and patterns can be compiled when the stylesheet is read, and do not need to be re-parsed each time they are evaluated.

❑ Attribute value templates are generally not allowed for attributes whose value is the name of another object in the stylesheet, for example a named template or a named attribute set. This ensures that references from one stylesheet object to another can be resolved once and for all when the stylesheet is first read. They are allowed, however, for names of nodes being written to the result tree.

❑ Attribute value templates are not allowed for attributes interpreted by the XML parser, specifically `xml:space`, `xml:lang`, and namespace declarations (`xmlns` and `xmlns:prefix`). This is because the XML parser reads the value before the XSLT processor gets a chance to expand it. The `xml:base` attribute, when used on a literal result element, is anomalous: the value of the attribute as seen by the XML parser will be the value before any attribute-value-template expansion, while the value copied to the result tree will be the value after attribute-value-template expansion. It's therefore best to avoid using curly braces within the value of the `xml:base` attribute. (The `xml:base` attribute is defined in a separate W3C Recommendation called XML Base: see `http://www.w3.org/TR/xmlbase/`.)

When an XPath expression within an attribute value template is evaluated, the context is the same as for any other expression in the stylesheet. The idea of an expression having a context was introduced in Chapter 2, on page 78: it determines the meaning of constructs such as «`.`», which refers to the context node, and «`position()`», which refers to the context position. Variables and namespace prefixes may be used within the expression only if they are in scope at that point in the stylesheet. The context item, context position, and context size are determined from the sequence being processed in the most recent call of `<xsl:apply-templates>`, `<xsl:for-each>`, or `<xsl:for-each-group>`. Outside such a call (for example, while a global variable is being evaluated), the context item is set to a value supplied by the caller of the stylesheet (generally the document node of the source document), and the context position and size are set to 1 (one).

On entry to a stylesheet function defined using `<xsl:function>`, the context item, position, and size are undefined—trying to use their values will raise an error. The idea is that the result of a function should depend only on its explicit arguments. This principle makes it possible for the XPath processor to perform optimizations on function calls that would otherwise be very difficult.

Simplified Stylesheets

A simplified stylesheet uses an abbreviated syntax in which the `<xsl:stylesheet>` element and all the top-level declarations are omitted.

The original purpose of this facility was to allow people with HTML-authoring skills but no programming experience to write simple stylesheets with a minimum of training. A simplified stylesheet has a skeleton that looks like the target document (which is usually HTML, though it doesn't have to be), and uses XSLT instructions to fill in the variable parts.

A stylesheet module is interpreted as a simplified stylesheet if the outermost element is not `<xsl:stylesheet>` or `<xsl:transform>`. The outermost element can have any name, provided it is not in the XSLT namespace. It must still contain a declaration of the XSLT namespace, and it must have an `xsl:version` attribute. For XSLT 2.0 the value should be «`1.0`» or «`2.0`» (use «`2.0`» if your stylesheet depends on features defined in XSLT 2.0, or «`1.0`» if you also want it to work with XSLT 1.0 processors). When the `xsl:version` attribute is greater than «`2.0`», forwards-compatible processing mode is enabled. This is discussed later in this chapter on page 124.

Example: A Simplified Stylesheet

This example shows a stylesheet that takes the form of an HTML skeleton page, with XSLT instructions embedded within it to pull data from the source document. The stylesheet is in the download file available from `http://www.wrox.com/`. It has the filename `simplified.xsl`, and can be used together with the data file `books.xml`.

The complete stylesheet is as follows.

```
<html xmlns:xsl="http://www.w3.org/1999/XSL/Transform"
      xsl:version="1.0">
<head><title>A list of books</title></head>
<body>
<h1>A list of books</h1>
    <table border="2">
    <xsl:for-each select="//book">
        <xsl:sort select="author"/>
        <tr>
          <td><xsl:value-of select="author"/></td>
          <td><xsl:value-of select="title"/></td>
          <td><xsl:value-of select="@category"/></td>
          <td><xsl:value-of select="price"/></td>
        </tr>
    </xsl:for-each>
    </table>
</body>
</html>
```

When you run this against the file `books.xml` (which is listed on page 66 in Chapter 2), the output is a sorted table showing the books (Figure 3-6).

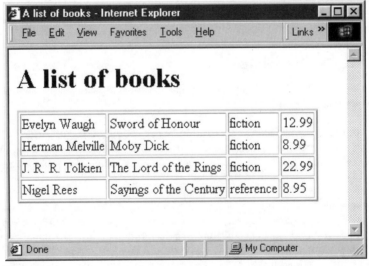

Figure 3-6

A simplified stylesheet is equivalent to a stylesheet in which the outermost element (typically the `<html>` element) is wrapped first in an `<xsl:template>` element with «`match="/"`», and then in an `<xsl:stylesheet>` element. The `xsl:version` attribute of the outermost element becomes the `version` attribute of the `<xsl:stylesheet>`. So the expanded form of the above example would be as follows.

```
<xsl:stylesheet xmlns:xsl="http://www.w3.org/1999/XSL/Transform"
                version="1.0">
<xsl:template match="/">
<html>
<head><title>A list of books</title></head>
<body>
<h1>A list of books</h1>
    <table border="2">
    <xsl:for-each select="//book">
       <xsl:sort select="author"/>
       <tr>
          <td><xsl:value-of select="author"/></td>
          <td><xsl:value-of select="title"/></td>
          <td><xsl:value-of select="@category"/></td>
          <td><xsl:value-of select="price"/></td>
       </tr>
    </xsl:for-each>
    </table>
</body>
</html>
</xsl:template>
</xsl:stylesheet>
```

The significance of «`match="/"`» is that this identifies the template rule as the first one to be processed when the stylesheet is activated. As we saw in Chapter 2, processing generally starts at the root node of the source document tree, and whichever template rule matches this root node is the first one to be invoked. The match pattern «`/`» matches a document node. In a simplified stylesheet, this will be the only template rule invoked.

There are many things a simplified stylesheet cannot do, because it cannot contain any declarations. For example, a simplified stylesheet can't include or import another stylesheet, it can't have global variables or parameters, and it can't define keys. But when you need these extra capabilities, you can always "unsimplify" the stylesheet by adding the surrounding `<xsl:stylesheet>` and `<xsl:template>` elements.

It is possible in theory for a stylesheet to include or import a simplified stylesheet, which would be expanded exactly as described above—but it would be a rather unusual thing to do.

Writing Portable Stylesheets

In this section we will examine a range of facilities that are included in XSLT to help you write portable stylesheets: that is, stylesheets that can run across different XSLT processors, possibly supporting different versions of the XSLT language.

We will look at the question of version compatibility: that is, how to write stylesheets that work with both XSLT 1.0 and XSLT 2.0. Then we will look at how to use vendor extensions, without sacrificing portability.

But before we do either of these things, I will describe a new feature that has been added to XSLT 2.0 to aid portability, namely the use-when attribute, which allows you to include or exclude stylesheet code conditionally at compile time.

Conditional Compilation

The use-when attribute serves a similar purpose to ifdef in the C language: it allows you to define conditions under which a section of the stylesheet can be conditionally included or excluded at compile time.

At the time of writing, this feature has been agreed by the XSL Working Group, but it is not present in any published language draft. Because it is a recent addition, the details could change, so check the latest specifications.

The use-when attribute can be used on any XSLT element. This includes declarations and instructions, and other elements such as <xsl:sort> and <xsl:with-param>. Written as «xsl:use-when», it is also allowed on literal result elements. The value of the attribute is a condition to be evaluated at compile time. If the condition is false, then the element and the subtree rooted at that element are effectively eliminated from the stylesheet, before any further processing takes place: it is as if the element were not there. One consequence is that no XSLT errors will be reported in respect of this element or its descendants.

Here is an example, which defines two alternative entry points, one for an XSLT 1.0 processor and one for an XSLT 2.0 processor. This assumes that the <xsl:stylesheet> element specifies «version=2.0». This means that an XSLT 1.0 processor will be running in forwards-compatible mode (explained in the next section) and will therefore ignore attributes such as use-when that it does not understand. An XSLT 1.0 processor will use the first template rule as the entry point, because it has higher priority. An XSLT 2.0 processor, however, will behave as if the first template rule is not present, and will use the second one, which differs in that it invokes schema validation of the result document.

```
<xsl:template match="/" priority="2"
              use-when="system-property('xsl:version')='1.0'">
  <xsl:apply-templates/>
</xsl:template>

<xsl:template match="/" priority="1">
  <xsl:result-document validation="strict">
    <xsl:apply-templates/>
  </xsl:result-document>
</xsl:template>
```

The expression contained in the use-when attribute is in principle any XPath expression; however, it is constrained to have a very restricted evaluation context. This means there is no context item, there are no variables available, and no access to external documents. In practice, this means that the only things the expression can usefully do is to examine the results of functions such as system-property(), element-available(), and function-available(), to see what environment the stylesheet is running in. These three functions are fully described in Chapter 7.

One important reason for the introduction of the use-when attribute was to allow stylesheets that work both on schema-aware and non-schema-aware XSLT processors to be written. For example, you can use the `system-property()` function in a use-when attribute on the `<xsl:import-schema>` declaration so that a schema is imported only when using a schema-aware processor. For details of how schemas are imported into a stylesheet, see Chapter 4.

Version Compatibility

Version compatibility is about how to achieve resilience to differences between versions of the XSLT standard.

There are currently two versions of the XSLT Recommendation, version 1.0, and a draft of version 2.0 (the many intermediate working drafts don't count). So compatibility between versions has now become an issue. However, the language designers had the foresight to anticipate that it would become an issue, and made provision even in version 1.0 to allow stylesheets to be written in a portable way.

The stylesheet is required to carry a version number (typically «version=1.0» or «version=2.0») as an attribute of the `<xsl:stylesheet>` element. Specifying «version=1.0» declares that the stylesheet is designed primarily for use with XSLT 1.0 processors, while specifying «version=2.0» indicates that it is designed for XSLT 2.0.

The term *backwards compatibility* refers to the ability of version N of a language to accept programs or data that worked under version $N-1$, while *forwards compatibility* refers to the ability of programs that worked under version N to move forward to version $N+1$. The two concepts are therefore opposite sides of the same coin. However, the XSLT language specification distinguishes carefully between them. As far as an XSLT 2.0 processor is concerned, a stylesheet that specifies «version="1.0"» is operating in backwards-compatible mode, while a stylesheet that specifies «version="3.0"» is operating in forwards-compatible mode.

If you specify «version="1.0"» in the stylesheet, then you are signaling the fact that the stylesheet was designed to be run under XSLT 1.0, and that in some specific cases where XSLT 2.0 defines different behavior from 1.0, the 1.0 behavior should be used. For example, if you supply a sequence of nodes as the value of the `select` attribute of `<xsl:value-of>`, the XSLT 1.0 behavior is to output the first value in the sequence and ignore the others; the XSLT 2.0 behavior is to output all the values, space separated.

Specifying «version="1.0"» does *not* mean that it is an error to use facilities that were newly introduced in XSLT 2.0. It only means that an XSLT 2.0 processor should use the 1.0 behavior in certain specific cases where there are incompatibilities.

If you specify «version="2.0"» in a stylesheet, and then run it under an XSLT 1.0 processor, you are indicating that the stylesheet makes use of facilities that were newly introduced in XSLT 2.0, and that the 1.0 processor should not treat these constructs as an error unless they are actually evaluated. The stylesheet can use various mechanisms to avoid evaluating the constructs that depend on XSLT 2.0 when these features are not available. This only works, of course, because the need for it was anticipated in the XSLT 1.0 specification, and even though no details were known of what new features would be introduced in a later version of the language, XSLT 1.0 processors were required to behave in a particular way (called forwards-compatibility mode) when the version attribute was set to a value other than «1.0». XSLT 2.0 similarly carries forward these provisions so that when the time comes, stylesheets that take advantage of new features in XSLT 3.0 or beyond will still be able to run under an XSLT 2.0 processor.

If you use facilities defined in XSLT version 1.0 only, but want your stylesheet to run under both XSLT 1.0 and 2.0 processors, then you should specify «version=1.0», and every conformant XSLT processor will then handle the stylesheet correctly, unless you rely on one of the few areas that are incompatible even in backwards-compatible mode. There is a list of these in Appendix F, and for the most part they are things that few reasonable users would do.

If you use facilities that are new in XSLT version 2.0, and you don't need the stylesheet to run under an XSLT 1.0 processor, then it's best to specify «version=2.0». If there are parts of the stylesheet that you haven't converted from XSLT 1.0, where you want backward-compatible behavior to be invoked, then you can leave those parts in a separate stylesheet module that specifies «version="1.0"». It's quite OK to mix versions like this. In fact XSLT 2.0 allows you to specify the version attribute at any level of granularity, for example on an <xsl:template> element, or even on an element that encloses one small part of a template. If you use it on a literal result element, the attribute should be named xsl:version to distinguish it from user-defined attributes. Bear in mind, however, that XSLT 1.0 processors allow the version attribute to appear only on the <xsl:stylesheet> element, or, as xsl:version, on a literal result element: it's not permitted, for example, on <xsl:template>.

If you use facilities that are new in XSLT version 2.0, but you also want the stylesheet to run under an XSLT 1.0 processor, then you may need to write it in such a way that it defines fallback behavior to be invoked when running under 1.0. There are various techniques you can use to achieve this. You can use the element-available() function to test whether a particular XSLT instruction is implemented; you can use <xsl:fallback> to define what the processor should do if a construct is not available; or you can use the system-property() function (described in Chapter 7) to test which version of XSLT is supported, and execute different code, depending on the result. Whichever technique you use, you need to ensure that those parts of the stylesheet that use XSLT 2.0 facilities are within the scope of an element that specifies «version="2.0"», otherwise an XSLT 1.0 processor will reject them at compile time.

The following sections look in more detail at the rules for backwards-compatible and forwards-compatible behavior.

Forwards Compatibility in XSLT 1.0

At present, you are probably more concerned with migration of XSLT 1.0 stylesheets to XSLT 2.0 than with migration from 2.0 to 3.0, so it makes sense to look at the forwards-compatibility rules as they were defined in the XSLT 1.0 specification. In fact these rules are not greatly changed in XSLT 2.0, so if you are reading this perhaps in 2008 and planning the transition to a new version 3.0, the advice should still be relevant.

Forwards-compatibility mode is invoked, as far as an XSLT 1.0 processor is concerned, by setting the version attribute on the <xsl:stylesheet> element to any value other than «1.0» (even, surprisingly, a value lower than «1.0»). For an XSLT 2.0 processor, forwards-compatibility mode is invoked by a version attribute greater than «2.0».

This mode has static scope rather than dynamic scope: it affects the instructions in the stylesheet that are textually within the element that carries the relevant version attribute. It only affects the behavior of the compiler, it does not alter the way that any instruction or expression is evaluated at runtime.

In forwards-compatible mode, the XSLT processor must assume that the stylesheet is using XSLT facilities defined in a version of the standard that has been published since the software was released. The processor, of course, won't know what to do with these facilities, but it must assume that the stylesheetauthor is using them deliberately. It treats them in much the same way as vendor extensions that it doesn't understand:

- ❑ It must report an error for XSLT elements it doesn't understand only if they are actually evaluated, and if there is no child `<xsl:fallback>` instruction.

- ❑ It must ignore attributes it doesn't recognize, and unrecognized values for recognized attributes. One particular consequence of this is that if the stylesheet specifies «version="2.0"», then an XSLT 1.0 processor will ignore any «use-when» attributes that it finds on XSLT elements.

- ❑ It must report an error for functions it doesn't recognize, or that have the wrong number of arguments, only if the function is actually called. You can avoid this error condition by using `function-available()` to test whether the function exists before calling it.

- ❑ It must report syntax errors in XPath expressions that use syntax that isn't allowed in the relevant version of XPath if the expression is actually evaluated. (XSLT 1.0 works only with XPath 1.0, while XSLT 2.0 works only with XPath 2.0.)

This behavior occurs only if the `<xsl:stylesheet>` element specifies a version other than «1.0» (or for XSLT 2.0, a value greater than «2.0»). Forwards-compatible mode can also be specified for a portion of a stylesheet by specifying the `xsl:version` attribute on any literal result element, and in the case of XSLT 2.0, by specifying the `version` attribute on any XSLT element. If forwards-compatible mode is not enabled, then any use of an XSLT element, attribute, or function that isn't in the version of XSLT that the processor supports, or any use of XPath syntax that isn't in the corresponding XPath specification, is an error and must be reported, whether it is actually executed or not.

If you specify «version=1.0» and then use XSLT 2.0 facilities such as `<xsl:result-document>`, then an XSLT 1.0 processor will reject this as an error. An XSLT 2.0 processor, however, will process your stylesheet successfully. An XSLT 2.0 processor when given a stylesheet that specifies «version="1.0"» is not expected to check that the stylesheet actually conforms to XSLT 1.0.

Forwards-compatible processing was specified to allow you to write a stylesheet that exploits facilities in version 2.0 while still behaving sensibly when run with an XSLT processor that supports version 1.0 only, or, at some point in the future, to use facilities in version 3.0 and still behave sensibly with an XSLT 2.0 processor. To achieve this, you can use the `system-property()` function (described on page 581, in Chapter 7) to discover which version of XSLT the processor implements, or which processor is being used. For example, you could write code such as follows.

```
<xsl:if test="system-property('xsl:version')=2.0 or
        starts-with(system-property('xsl:vendor'), 'xalan')">
    <xsl:new-facility/>
</xsl:if>
```

Relying on the version number this returns is a rather crude mechanism: there are likely to be processors around that implement some of the new features in XSLT 2.0 but not yet all of them. Testing which vendor's processor is in use is therefore handy for portability, especially when vendors have not kept strictly to the conformance rules. Another possibility is to use the `element-available()` and `function-available()` functions described later in the chapter: although these are primarily intended to allow you to test whether particular vendor or user-defined extensions are available, they can also be used to test for the availability of specific XSLT instructions and functions in the core language.

Technically, a processor that implements some of the new XSLT 2.0 features but not all of them doesn't conform either with XSLT 1.0 or with XSLT 2.0. But since many XSLT processors are developed incrementally with new releases every few weeks, you might well find products that occupy this no man's land. A product will presumably return «2.0» as the value of «system-property ('xsl-version')» when the vendor is confident that the product is "almost" conformant: past experience suggests that different vendors will interpret this in different ways.

> *There was a suggestion that one should ban processors from returning «2.0» unless they are fully conformant with the spec. But there is little point in such a prohibition, because a product that isn't fully conformant with the spec is by definition doing things that the spec doesn't allow.*

Backwards Compatibility in XSLT 2.0

For an XSLT 2.0 processor, you can invoke backwards-compatibility mode by setting the `version` attribute on the `<xsl:stylesheet>` element (or in fact on any XSLT element) to the value «1.0». In fact, any value less than «2.0» will do. You can also set the `xsl:version` attribute on a literal result element in the same way.

Like the switch for forwards-compatibility mode, this has static scope: it applies to all instructions and XPath expressions contained within the element where the `version` attribute is set. Unlike forwards-compatibility mode, however, this mode affects the results of evaluating instructions and expressions, rather than being purely a compile-time switch.

XSLT 2.0 processors aren't obliged to support backwards-compatible processing. If they don't, they must reject any attempt to specify «version="1.0"» as an error. In the early life of XSLT 2.0, I imagine that most vendors will want to support backwards-compatibility mode because their customers are likely to require it. The reason it is optional is that this need may gradually decline as XSLT 1.0 recedes into history. If XSLT 2.0 turns out to have a long life, and is not superseded by a subsequent version for 5 years or so, it's quite likely that a vendor developing a new XSLT 2.0 processor might decide that there is no longer a market need for 1.0 backwards compatibility.

How does backwards compatibility actually affect the results of the stylesheet? One thing that it does *not* do is to say "process this according to the rules in the XSLT 1.0 specification." This wouldn't work, because the parts of the stylesheet that use 2.0 facilities and the parts that use backwards-compatibility mode need to work with the same data model, and the data model used by an XSLT 2.0 processor is the 2.0 data model, not the 1.0 data model. Instead, backwards-compatibility mode changes the behavior of a small number of specific XSLT and XPath constructs, in quite specific ways.

Here is a checklist of the things that are done differently. The left-hand column indicates the normal XSLT 2.0 (or XPath 2.0) behavior, the right-hand column the behavior in backwards-compatibility mode.

First, the differences covered by the XSLT 2.0 specification are given as follows.

2.0 Behavior	1.0 Behavior
When the value selected by the `<xsl:value-of>` instruction is a sequence, all the values are output, separated by spaces	When the value selected by the `<xsl:value-of>` instruction is a sequence, the first value is output, and the rest are ignored
When the value produced by an expression in an attribute value template is a sequence, all the values are output, separated by spaces	When the value produced by an expression in an attribute value template is a sequence, the first value is output, and the rest are ignored
When the value returned by the expression in the `value` attribute of `<xsl:number>` is a sequence, all the numbers in the sequence are output, according to the format described in the format attribute	When the value returned by the expression in the `value` attribute of `<xsl:number>` is a sequence, the first number in the sequence is output, and the rest are discarded
When the value of a sort key is a sequence containing more than one item, a type error is reported	When the value of a sort key is a sequence containing more than one item, the first item is used as the sort key, and remaining items are ignored
When `<xsl:call-template>` supplies a parameter that's not defined in the template being called, a static error is reported	When `<xsl:call-template>` supplies a parameter that's not defined in the template being called, the extra parameter is ignored

Backwards-compatibility mode also affects the way that XPath expressions in the stylesheet are evaluated. Here are the differences.

2.0 Behavior	1.0 Behavior
When a function expects a single node or a single item as an argument, and the supplied value of the argument is a sequence containing more than one item, a type error is reported	When a function expects a single node or a single item as an argument, and the supplied value of the argument is a sequence containing more than one item, all items except the first are ignored
When a function expects a string or a number as an argument, and the supplied value is of the wrong type, a type error is reported	When a function expects a string or a number as an argument, and the supplied value is of the wrong type, the system convert the supplied value to a number using the `string()` or `number()` function as appropriate
When one of the operands to an operator such as «=» or «<» is a number, and the other is not, a type error is reported	When one of the operands to an operator such as «=» or «<» is a number, and the other is not, the non-numeric operand is converted to a number using the `number()` function (see the following note)

Continues

2.0 Behavior	1.0 Behavior
When one of the operands of an arithmetic operator such as «+» or «*» is a sequence containing more than one item, a type error is reported	When one of the operands of an arithmetic operator such as «+» or «*» is a sequence containing more than one item, all items except the first are ignored
When the operands of an arithmetic operator such as «+» or «*» have types for which this operator is not defined, a type error is reported	When the operands of an arithmetic operator such as «+» or «*» have types for which this operator is not defined, the supplied operands are converted to numbers (if possible) using the number() function

Note: The November 2003 draft of XPath 2.0 states that in backwards-compatible mode, non-numeric operands of an arithmetic operator are converted to numbers by casting. However, I believe this is incorrect and the conversion should be done using the number() function. The difference is that casting treats non-numeric values as an error, while the number() function converts them to the special value NaN.

My personal preference when moving forward to a new software version or language version is to take the pain of the conversion all at once, and try to make the program or stylesheet look as if it had been written for the new version from the word go. Most of the changes listed above are to reflect the fact that XSLT 2.0 and XPath 2.0 no longer use the "first node" rule when a sequence is supplied in a context where a singleton is needed. You can always get the effect of selecting the first item in the sequence, by using the predicate «[1]». For example, if an XSLT 1.0 stylesheet contains the instruction:

```
<xsl:value-of select="following-sibling::*"/>
```

then it should be changed to:

```
<xsl:value-of select="following-sibling::*[1]"/>
```

But doing the conversion all at once is a luxury that you can't always afford. Backwards-compatibility mode is there to allow you to spread the cost of making the changes by doing it gradually.

Extensibility

Bitten by years of experience with proprietary vendor extensions to HTML, the W3C committee responsible for XSLT took great care to allow vendor extensions in a tightly controlled way.

The extensibility mechanisms in XSLT are governed by several unstated design principles:

❑   Namespaces are used to ensure that vendor extensions cannot clash with facilities in the standard (including facilities introduced in future versions), or with extensions defined by a different vendor.

❑   It is possible for an XSLT processor to recognize where extensions have been used, including extensions defined by a different vendor, and to fail cleanly if it cannot implement those extensions.

❑   It is possible for the writer of a stylesheet to test whether particular extensions are available, and to define fallback behavior if they are not. For example, the stylesheet might be able to achieve the same effect in a different way, or it might make do without some special effect in the output.

The principal extension mechanisms are extension functions and extension instructions. However, it is also possible for vendors to define other kinds of extensions, or to provide mechanisms for users or third parties to do so. These include the following:

❑ XSLT-defined elements can have additional vendor-defined attributes, provided they use a non-null namespace URI, and that they do not introduce nonconformant behavior for standard elements and attributes. For example, a vendor could add an attribute such as acme:debug to the <xsl:template> element, whose effect is to pause execution when the template is evaluated. But adding an attribute «acme:repeat="2"» whose effect is to execute the template twice would be against the conformance rules.

❑ Vendors can define additional top-level elements; again provided that they use a non-null namespace URI, and that they do not cause nonconformant behavior for standard elements and attributes. An example of such an element is Microsoft's <msxsl:script> element, for defining external functions in VBScript or JScript. Any processor that doesn't recognize the namespace URI will ignore such top-level elements.

❑ Certain XSLT-defined attributes have an open-ended set of values, where vendors have discretion on the range of values to be supported. Examples are the lang attribute of <xsl:number> and <xsl:sort>, which provides language-dependent numbering and sorting; the method attribute of <xsl:output>, which defines how the result tree is output to a file; and the format attribute of <xsl:number>, which allows the vendor to provide additional numbering sequences beyond those defined in the standard. The list of system properties supplied in the first argument of the system-property() function is similarly open ended.

Extension Functions

Extension functions provide a mechanism for extending the capabilities of XSLT by escaping into another language such as Java or JavaScript. The most usual reasons for doing this are as follows:

❑ To improve performance

❑ To exploit system capabilities and services

❑ To reuse code that already exists in another language

❑ For convenience, as complex algorithms and computations can be very verbose when written in XSLT

XSLT 2.0 allows functions to be written using the <xsl:function> declaration in a stylesheet (these are referred to as stylesheet functions, and they are not considered to be extension functions). This facility, together with the increase in the size of the core function library, greatly reduces the need to escape into other programming languages. However, it is still necessary if you need access to external resources or services from within the stylesheet.

The term *extension function* is used both for functions supplied by the vendor beyond the core functions defined in the XSLT and XPath standards (those described in Chapter 7 of this book, and Chapter 10 of *XPath 2.0 Programmer's Reference*), and also for functions written by users and third parties.

The XSLT Recommendation allows extension functions to be called, but does not define how they are written, or how they should be bound to the stylesheet, or which languages should be supported. This means that it is quite difficult to write extension functions that work with more than one vendor's XSLT processor, even though in the Java world there are some conventions that several vendors have adopted.

In December 2000 the XSL Working Group in W3C published a working draft for XSLT 1.1, which proposed detailed conventions for writing extension functions in Java and JavaScript. These proposals met a rather hostile reception, for a variety of reasons. The working draft was subsequently withdrawn and the work hasn't been taken forward. It is still available, if you are interested, at http://www.w3.org/TR/xslt11.

A function name in the XPath expression syntax is a QName, that is, a name with an optional namespace prefix. Under XSLT, the default namespace for functions (the namespace that is assumed when the function name has no prefix) is always the namespace for the core function library. This function library includes the XSLT-defined functions listed in Chapter 7 of this book, as well as the functions defined in the XPath 2.0 specifications, which are listed in Chapter 10 of *XPath 2.0 Programmer's Reference*. For example the core function not() can be invoked as follows.

```
<xsl:if test="not( @name = 'Mozart' )">
```

If the function name has a prefix, the function can come from a number of other sources, depending on its namespace:

❑ Functions in the XML Schema namespace http://www.w3.org/2001/XMLSchema (traditionally associated with the prefix «xs», though «xsd» is also used) are used to construct values of built-in types. For example, the function call «xs:date('2004-02-29')» is used to convert a string to an xs:date value.

❑ Supplementing the XML Schema built-in types, there are four additional types defined in XPath 2.0: xdt:untyped, xdt:untypedAtomic, xdt:yearMonthDuration, and xdt:dayMonthDuration. The last three of these have constructor functions in the same way as the XML Schema built-in types. The «xdt» prefix here is used to represent the namespace http://www.w3.org/2003/11/xpath-datatypes. (There is no constructor function for xdt:untyped because it is a complex type rather than an atomic type.)

❑ XSLT vendors will often provide additional functions in their own namespace. For example, Saxon provides a number of functions in the namespace http://saxon.sf.net/. An example is saxon:evaluate(), which allows an XPath expression to be constructed dynamically from a string, and then executed.

❑ Third parties may also define function libraries. Of particular note is the EXSLT library at http://www.exslt.org/. This provides, among other things, a useful library of mathematical functions. (It also provides capabilities such as date and time handling, and regular expression processing, that have largely been overtaken by standard facilities in XSLT 2.0 and XPath 2.0.) This is primarily a library of function specifications, but implementations of the functions are available for many popular XSLT processors, either from the XSLT vendor or from some other party. This ensures that you can use these functions in a stylesheet and still retain portability across XSLT processors. Note, however, that implementations of these functions are not generally portable: an implementation of math:sqrt() that's written for MSXML3 won't work with Xalan, for example.

❑ You can write your own functions in XSLT, using the <xsl:function> declaration. These will be completely portable across XSLT 2.0 implementations, but of course they are restricted to things that can be coded in XSLT and XPath. These functions can be in any namespace apart from a small number of reserved namespaces. The namespaces that are reserved are the obvious ones such as the XSLT, XML, and XML Schema namespaces.

❑ The `<xsl:function>` element has an attribute `override` that can be set to «yes» or «no» to indicate whether the stylesheet function should override any vendor-defined function of the same name. This is useful because there might be a portable cross-platform implementation of a function such as `math:sqrt()` specified in a third-party library such as EXSLT, as well as a native implementation provided by the XSLT vendor. This attribute allows you to choose which implementation is preferred.

❑ Finally, if the XSLT processor allows it, you may be able to write functions in an external programming language. Microsoft's XSLT processors, for example, allow you to invoke functions in scripting languages such as JavaScript, and all the Java-based processors such as Xalan-J, Saxon, and jd.xslt allow you to invoke methods written in Java. Saxon also allows you to call functions written in XQuery. Other processors will tend to support the native language of the processor: Xalan-C++ allows you to write extension functions in C++ (you need to be aware that installing these is lot more complex than in the case of Java), while the 4XSLT processor (`http://4suite.org`) focuses on Python.

The language specification says nothing about how extension functions are written, and how they are linked to the stylesheet. The notes that follow are provided to give an indication of the kind of techniques you are likely to encounter.

In the case of Java, several processors have provided a mechanism in which the name of the Java class is contained in the namespace URI of the function, while the name of the method is represented by the local name. This mechanism means that all the information needed to identify and call the function is contained within the function name itself. For example, if you want to call the Java method `random()` in class `java.lang.Math` to obtain a random number between 0.0 and 1.0, you can write:

```
<xsl:variable name="random-number" select="Math:random()"
    xmlns:Math="ext://java.lang.Math"/>
```

Unfortunately, each processor has slightly different rules for forming the namespace URI, as well as different rules for converting function arguments and results between Java classes and the XPath type system, so it won't always be possible to make such calls portable between XSLT processors. But the example above works with both Saxon and Xalan.

This example calls a static method in Java, but most products also allow you to call Java constructors to return object instances, and then to call instance methods on those objects. To make this possible, the processor needs to extend the XPath type system to allow expressions to return values that are essentially wrappers around external Java objects. The XSLT and XPath specifications are written to explicitly permit this, though the details are left to the implementation.

For example, suppose you want to monitor the amount of free memory that is available, perhaps to diagnose an "out of memory" error in a stylesheet. You could do this by writing:

```
<xsl:message>
    <xsl:text>Free memory: </xsl:text>
    <xsl:value-of select="rt:freeMemory(rt:getRuntime())"
                  xmlns:rt="ext://java.lang.Runtime"/>
</xsl:message>
```

Again, this example is written to work with both Saxon and Xalan.

There are two extension function calls here: the call on `getRuntime()` calls a static method in the class `java.lang.Runtime`, which returns an instance of this class. The call on `freeMemory()` is an instance method in this class. By convention, instance methods are called by supplying the target instance as an extra first parameter in the call.

Another technique that's used for linking an extension function is to use a declaration in the stylesheet. Microsoft's processors use this approach to bind JavaScript functions. Here is an example of a simple extension function implemented using this mechanism with Microsoft's MSXML3/4 processor, and an expression that calls it.

```
<xsl:stylesheet version="1.0"
    xmlns:xsl="http://www.w3.org/1999/XSL/Transform"
    xmlns:ms="javascript:my-extensions">

<msxsl:script
    xmlns:msxsl="urn:schemas-microsoft-com:xslt"
    language="VBScript"
    implements-prefix="ms"
>
Function ToMillimetres(inches)
    ToMillimetres = inches * 25.4
End Function
</msxsl:script>

<xsl:template match="/" >
    <xsl:variable name="test" select="12"/>
    <size><xsl:value-of select="ms:ToMillimetres($test)"/></size>
</xsl:template>
</xsl:stylesheet>
```

This is not a particularly well-chosen example, because it could easily be coded in XSLT, and it's generally a good idea to stick to XSLT code unless there is a very good reason not to; but it illustrates how it's done.

People sometimes get confused about the difference between script in the stylesheet, which is designed to be called as part of the transformation process, and script in the HTML output page, which is designed to be called during the display of the HTML in the browser. When the transformation is being done within the browser, and is perhaps invoked from script in another HTML page, it can be difficult to keep the distinctions clearly in mind. I find that it always helps in this environment to create a mock-up of the HTML page that you want to generate, test that it works as expected in the browser, and then start thinking about writing the XSLT code to generate it.

Sometimes you need to change configuration files or environment variables, or call special methods in the processor's API to make extension functions available; this is particularly true of products written in C or C++, which are less well suited to dynamic loading and linking.

In XSLT 2.0 (this is a change from XSLT 1.0), it is a static error if the stylesheet contains a call on a function that the compiler cannot locate. If you want to write code that is portable across processors offering different extension functions, you should therefore use the new `use-when` attribute to ensure that code containing such calls is not compiled unless the function is available. You can test whether a particular extension function is available by using the `function-available()` function. For example:

```
<xsl:sequence xmlns:acme="http://acme.co.jp/xslt">
   <xsl:value-of select="acme:moonshine($x)"
                 use-when="function-available('acme:moonshine')"/>
   <xsl:text use-when="not(function-available('acme:moonshine'))"
          >*** Sorry, moonshine is off today ***</xsl:text>
</xsl:sequence>
```

Extension functions, because they are written in general-purpose programming languages, can have side effects. For example, they can write to databases, they can ask the user for input, or they can maintain counters. At one time Xalan provided a sample application to implement a counter using extension functions, effectively circumventing the restriction that XSLT variables cannot be modified in situ. However, extension functions with side effects should be used with great care, because the XSLT specification doesn't say what order things are supposed to happen in. For example, it doesn't say whether a variable is evaluated when its declaration is first encountered, or when its value is first used. The more advanced XSLT processors adopt a lazy evaluation strategy in which (for example) variables are not evaluated until they are used. If extension functions with side effects are used to evaluate such variables, the results can be very surprising, because the order in which the extension functions are called becomes quite unpredictable. For example, if one function writes to a log file and another closes this file, you could find that the log file is closed before it is written to. In fact, if a variable is never used, the extension function contained in its definition might not be evaluated at all.

Before writing an extension function, there are a number of alternatives you should consider:

❑   Can the function be written in XSLT, using an `<xsl:function>` element?

❑   Is it possible to supply the required information as a stylesheet parameter? Generally this provides a cleaner and more portable solution.

❑   Is it possible to get the result by calling the `document()` function, with a suitable URI? The URI passed to the `document()` function does not have to identify a static file; it could also invoke code on an ASP page or a Java servlet. The Java JAXP API allows you to write a `URIResolver` class that intercepts the call on the `document()` function, so the `URIResolver` can return the results directly without needing to access any external resources. The `System.Xml.Xsl` interface in the Microsoft .NET framework has a similar capability, referred to as an `XmlResolver`.

Extension Instructions

An extension instruction is an element occurring within a sequence constructor, that belongs to a namespace designated as an extension namespace. A namespace is designated as an extension namespace by including its namespace prefix in the `extension-element-prefixes` attribute of the `<xsl:stylesheet>` element, or in the `xsl:extension-element-prefixes` attribute of the element itself, or of a containing extension element or literal result element.

For example, Saxon provides an extension instruction `<saxon:while>` to perform looping while a condition remains true. There is no standard XSLT construct for this because without side effects, a condition once true can never become false. But when used in conjunction with extension functions, `<saxon:while>` can be a useful addition.

Example: Using an Extension Instruction

The following stylesheet uses the `<saxon:while>` element to process all the Java system properties. It can be run with any source document.

Stylesheet

The stylesheet calls five methods in the Java class library:

- ❑ `System.getProperties()` to get a `Properties` object containing all the system properties

- ❑ `Properties.propertyNames()` to get an `Enumeration` of the names of the system properties

- ❑ `Enumeration.hasMoreElements()` to determine whether there are more system properties to come

- ❑ `Enumeration.nextElement()` to get the next system property

- ❑ `Properties.getProperty()` to get the value of the system property with a given name. For this method, the `Properties` object is supplied as the first argument, and the name of the required property in the second

```
<xsl:stylesheet version="2.0"
   xmlns:xsl="http://www.w3.org/1999/XSL/Transform"
>
<xsl:output indent="yes"/>
<xsl:template match="/">
   <system-properties
       xmlns:System="ext://java.lang.System"
       xmlns:Properties="ext://java.util.Properties"
       xmlns:Enumeration="ext://java.util.Enumeration"
       xsl:exclude-result-prefixes="System Properties Enumeration">
   <xsl:variable name="props"
                 select="System:getProperties()"/>
   <xsl:variable name="enum"
                 select="Properties:propertyNames($props)"/>
   <saxon:while test="Enumeration:hasMoreElements($enum)"
           xsl:extension-element-prefixes="saxon"
           xmlns:saxon="http://saxon.sf.net/">
       <xsl:variable name="property-name"
                     select="Enumeration:nextElement($enum)"/>
       <property name="{$property-name}"
           value="{Properties:getProperty($props, $property-name)}"/>
   </saxon:while>
   </system-properties>
</xsl:template>
</xsl:stylesheet>
```

Note that for this to work, «saxon» must be declared as an extension element prefix, otherwise `<saxon:while>` would be interpreted as a literal result element and would be copied to the output. The `xsl:exclude-result-prefixes` attribute is not strictly necessary, but it prevents the output being cluttered with unnecessary namespace declarations.

Technically, this code is unsafe. Although it appears that the extension functions are read-only, the `Enumeration` object actually contains information about the current position in a sequence, and the call to `nextElement()` modifies this information: it is therefore a function call with side effects. In practice you can usually get away with such calls. However, as optimizers become more sophisticated, stylesheets that rely on side effects can sometimes work with one version of an XSLT processor, and fail with the next version. So you should use such constructs only when you have no alternative.

A tip: if you have problems getting such stylesheets to work in Saxon, the `-TJ` option on the command line can be useful for debugging. It gives you diagnostic output showing which Java classes were searched to find methods matching the extension function calls.

As with extension functions, the term `extension instruction` covers both nonstandard instructions provided by the vendor, and nonstandard instructions implemented by a user or third party. There is no requirement that an XSLT implementation must allow users to define new extension instructions, only that it should behave in a particular way when it encounters extension instructions that it cannot process.

Where a product does allow users to implement extension instructions (two products that do so are Saxon and Xalan), the mechanisms and APIs involved are likely to be rather more complex than those for extension functions, and the task is not one to be undertaken lightly. However, extension instructions can offer capabilities that would be very hard to provide with extension functions alone.

If there is an extension instruction in a stylesheet, then all XSLT processors will recognize it as such, but in general some will be able to handle it and others won't (because it is defined by a different vendor). As with extension functions, the rule is that a processor mustn't fail merely because an extension instruction is present; it should fail only if an attempt is made to evaluate it.

There are two mechanisms to allow stylesheet authors to test whether a particular extension instruction is available: the `element-available()` function and the `<xsl:fallback>` instruction.

The `element-available()` function works in a very similar way to `function-available()`. You can use it in a `use-when` attribute to include stylesheet code conditionally. In this case, however, you can also do the test at evaluation time if you prefer, because calls to unknown extension instructions don't generate an error unless then are executed. For example:

```
<xsl:choose xmlns:acme="http://acme.co.jp/xslt">
   <xsl:when test="element-available('acme:moonshine')">
     <acme:moonshine select="$x" xsl:extension-element-prefixes="acme"/>
   </xsl:when>
   <xsl:otherwise>
      <xsl:text>*** Sorry, moonshine is off today ***</xsl:text>
   </xsl:otherwise>
</xsl:choose>
```

Note that at the time `element-available()` is called, the prefix for the extension element (here «acme») must have been declared in a namespace declaration, but it does not need to have been designated as an extension element.

The `<xsl:fallback>` instruction (which is fully described on page 271, in Chapter 5) provides an alternative way of specifying what should happen when an extension instruction is not available. The following example is equivalent to the previous one.

```
<acme:moonshine select="$x"
    xmlns:acme="http://acme.co.jp/xslt"
    xsl:extension-element-prefixes="acme">
    <xsl:fallback>
        <xsl:text>*** Sorry, moonshine is off today ***</xsl:text>
    </xsl:fallback>
</acme:moonshine>
```

When an extension instruction is evaluated, and the XSLT processor does not know what to do with it, it should evaluate any child `<xsl:fallback>` element. If there are several `<xsl:fallback>` children, it should evaluate them all. Only if there is no `<xsl:fallback>` element should it report an error. Conversely, if the XSLT processor can evaluate the instruction, it should ignore any child `<xsl:fallback>` element.

> *The specification doesn't actually say that an extension instruction must allow an `<xsl:fallback>` child to be present. There are plenty of XSLT instructions that do not allow `<xsl:fallback>` as a child, for example `<xsl:copy-of>` and `<xsl:value-of>`. However, an extension instruction that didn't allow `<xsl:fallback>` would certainly be against the spirit of the standard.*

Vendor-defined or user-defined elements at the top level of the stylesheet are not technically extension instructions, because they don't appear within a sequence constructor; therefore the namespace they appear in does not need to be designated as an extension namespace.

Whitespace

Whitespace handling can be a considerable source of confusion. When the output of a stylesheet is HTML, you can get away without worrying too much about it, because except in some very specific contexts HTML generally treats any sequence of spaces and newlines in the same way as a single space. But with other output formats, getting spaces and newlines where you want them, and avoiding them where you don't, can be crucial.

There are two issues:

❑ Controlling which whitespace in the source document is significant, and therefore visible to the stylesheet.

❑ Controlling which whitespace in the stylesheet is significant, because significant whitespace in the stylesheet is likely to get copied to the output.

Whitespace is defined as any sequence of the following four characters.

Character	Unicode Symbol
Tab	#x9
Newline	#xA
carriage return	#xD
Space	#x20

The definition in XSLT is exactly the same as in XML itself. Other characters such as non-breaking-space (#xA0), which is familiar to HTML authors as the entity reference « », may use just as little black ink as these four, but they are not included in the definition.

There are some additional complications about the definition. Writing a character reference « » is in many ways exactly the same as hitting the space bar on the keyboard, but in some circumstances it behaves differently. The character reference « » will be treated as whitespace by the XSLT processor, but not by the XML parser, so you need to understand which rules are applied at which stage of processing.

The XML standard makes some attempt to distinguish between significant and insignificant whitespace. Whitespace in elements with element-only content is considered insignificant, whereas whitespace in elements that allow #PCDATA content is significant. However, the distinction depends on whether a validating parser is used or not, and in any case, the standard requires both kinds of whitespace to be notified to the application. The writers of the XSLT specification decided that the handling of whitespace should not depend on anything in the DTD or schema, and should not depend on whether a validating or nonvalidating parser was used. Instead the handling of whitespace is controlled entirely from the source document (using the xml:space attribute) or from the stylesheet (using the <xsl:strip-space> and <xsl:preserve-space> declarations), which are fully described in Chapter 5.

The first stages in whitespace handling are the job of the XML parser, and are done long before the XSLT processor gets to see the data. Remember that these apply both to source documents and to stylesheets:

❑ End-of-line appearing in the textual content of an element is always normalized to a single newline «#xA» character. This eliminates the differences between line endings on Unix, Windows, and Macintosh systems. XML 1.1 introduces additional rules to normalize the line endings found on IBM mainframes.

❑ The XML parser will normalize attribute values. A tab or newline will always be replaced by a single space, unless it is written as a character reference such as «	» or «&#A;»; for some types of attribute (anything except type CDATA), a validating XML parser will also remove leading and trailing whitespace, and normalize other sequences of whitespace to a single space character.

This attribute normalization can be significant when the attribute in question is an XPath expression in the stylesheet. For example, suppose you want to test whether a string value contains a newline character. You can write this as follows.

```
<xsl:if test="contains(address, '&#xA;')">
```

It's important to use the character reference «
» here, rather than a real newline, because a newline character would be converted to a space by the XML parser, and the expression would then actually test whether the supplied string contains a space.

What this means in practice is that if you want to be specific about whitespace characters, write them as character references; if you just want to use them as separators and padding, use the whitespace characters directly.

> The XSLT specification assumes that the XML parser will hand over all whitespace text nodes to the XSLT processor. However, the input to the XSLT processor is technically a tree, and the XSLT specification claims no control over how this tree is built. If you use Microsoft's MSXML3, the tree is supplied in the form of a DOM, and the default option when building a DOM in MSXML3 is to remove whitespace text nodes. If you want the parser to behave the way that the XSLT specification expects, you must set the `preserveWhitespace` property on the `Document` object to true before you load the document.

Once the XML parser has done its work, further manipulation of whitespace may be done by the schema processor. This is more likely to affect source documents than stylesheets, since there is little point in putting a stylesheet through a schema processor. For each simple data type, XML Schema defines whitespace handling as one of three options:

❑ *Preserve*: All whitespace characters in the value are preserved. This option is used for the data type xs:string.

❑ *Replace*: Each newline, carriage return, and tab character is replaced by a single-space character. This option is used for the data type xs:normalizedString and types derived from it.

❑ *Collapse*: Leading and trailing whitespace is removed, and any internal sequence of whitespace characters is replaced by a single space. This option is used for all other data types (including those where internal whitespace is not actually allowed).

When source documents are processed using a schema, the rules for the XPath 2.0 data model say that for attributes, and for elements with simple content (that is, elements that can't have child elements), the typed value of the element or attribute is the value after whitespace normalization has been done according to the XML Schema rules for the particular data type. In the current draft (November 2003) it is not entirely clear whether the *string* value of an element or attribute is the value before or after the schema whitespace rules are applied: this will probably be clarified in later versions of the specification. However, the only thing that depends on the string value of a node is the string() function itself: everything else uses the typed value.

Finally, the XSLT processor then applies some processing of its own. By this time entity and character references have been expanded, so there is no difference between a space written as a space and one written as « »:

❑ Adjacent text nodes are merged into a single text node (*normalized* in the terminology of the DOM).

❑ Then, if a text node consists entirely of whitespace, it is removed (or *stripped*) from the tree if the containing element is listed in an <xsl:strip-space> definition in the stylesheet. The detailed rules are more complex than this, and also take into account the presence of the xml:space attribute in the source document: see the <xsl:text> element on page 459, in Chapter 5 for details.

This process never removes whitespace characters that are adjacent to non-whitespace characters. For example, consider the following.

```
<article>
   <title>Abelard and Heloise</title>
   <subtitle>Some notes towards a family tree</subtitle>
   <author>Brenda M Cook</author>
   <abstract>
      The story of Abelard and Heloise is best recalled nowadays from the
stage drama of 1970 and it is perhaps inevitable that Diana Rigg stripping
off for Keith Mitchell should be the most enduring image of this historic
couple in some people's minds.
   </abstract>
</article>
```

Our textual analysis will focus entirely on the whitespace—the actual content of the piece is best ignored.

There are five whitespace-only text nodes in this fragment, one before each of the child elements `<title>`, `<subtitle>`, `<author>`, and `<abstract>`, and another between the end of the `<abstract>` and the end of the `<article>`. The whitespace in these nodes is passed by the XML parser to the XSLT processor, and it is up to the stylesheet whether to take any notice of it or not. Typically, in this situation this whitespace is of no interest and it can be stripped from the tree by specifying `<xsl:strip-space elements="article"/>`.

The whitespace within the `<abstract>` cannot be removed by the same process. The newline characters at the start and end of the abstract, and at the end of each line, are part of the text passed by the parser to the application, and it is not possible in the stylesheet to declare them as being irrelevant. If the `<abstract>` element is defined in the schema as being of type `xs:token` (or a type derived from this) then the schema processor will remove the leading and trailing whitespace characters, and convert the newlines into single spaces. But if it is of type `xs:string`, or if no schema processing is done, then all the spaces and newlines will be present in the tree model of the source document. What you can do is to call the `normalize-space()` function when processing these nodes on the source tree, which will have the same effect as schema processing for a type that specifies the collapse option (that is, it will remove leading and trailing whitespace and replace all other sequences of one or more whitespace characters by a single space). The `normalize-space()` function is described in Chapter 10 of *XPath 2.0 Programmer's Reference*.

The processing done by a schema processor for data of type xs:normalizedString *is to replace each newline, tab, and carriage return by a single space character. This is not the same as the processing done by the* normalize-space() *function in XPath. The term* normalization, *unfortunately, does not have a standard meaning.*

So we can see that XSLT makes a very firm distinction between text nodes that comprise whitespace only, and those that hold something other than whitespace. A whitespace text node can exist only where there is nothing between two pieces of markup other than whitespace characters.

To take another example, consider the following document.

```
<person>
   <name>Prudence Flowers</name>
   <employer>Lloyds Bank</employer>
```

```
        <place-of-work>
            71 Lombard Street
            London, UK
            <zip>EC3P 3BS</zip>
        </place-of-work>
    </person>
```

Where are the whitespace nodes? Let's look at it again, this time making the whitespace characters visible.

```
<person>↵
→<name>Prudence Flowers</name>↵
→<employer>Lloyds Bank</employer>↵
→<place-of-work>↵
→♦♦♦71 Lombard Street↵
→♦♦♦London, UK↵
→♦♦♦<zip>EC3P 3BS</zip>♦↵
→<place-of-work>↵
</person>↵
```

The newline and tab between <person> and <name> are not adjacent to any non-whitespace characters, so they constitute a whitespace node. So do the characters between </name> and <employer>, and between </employer> and <place-of-work>. However, most of the whitespace characters within the <place-of-work> element are in the same text node as non-whitespace characters, so they do not constitute a whitespace node. To make it even clearer, let's highlight the whitespace characters in whitespace nodes, and show the others as ordinary spaces.

```
<person>↵
→<name>Prudence Flowers</name>↵
→<employer>Lloyds Bank</employer>↵
→<place-of-work>
            71 Lombard Street
            London, UK
            <zip>EC3P 3BS</zip>♦↵
→</place-of-work>↵
</person>
```

Why is all this relevant? As we've seen, the <xsl:strip-space> element allows you to control what happens to whitespace nodes (those shown in the immediately preceding example), but it doesn't let you do anything special with whitespace characters that appear in ordinary text nodes (those shown in as ordinary spaces).

All the whitespace nodes in this example are immediate children of the <person> element, so they could be stripped by writing:

```
<xsl:strip-space elements="person"/>
```

Whitespace nodes are retained on the source tree unless you ask for them to be stripped, either by using <xsl:strip-space>, or by using some option provided by the XML parser or schema processor during the building of the tree.

Whitespace Nodes in the Stylesheet

For the stylesheet itself, whitespace nodes are all stripped, with two exceptions, namely whitespace within an `<xsl:text>` element, and whitespace controlled by the attribute «`xml:space="preserve"`». If you explicitly want to copy a whitespace text node from the stylesheet to the result tree, write it within an `<xsl:text>` element, like this.

```
<xsl:value-of select="address-line[1]"/>
<xsl:text>&#xA;</xsl:text>
<xsl:value-of select="address-line[2]"/>
```

The only reason for using «`&#xA;`» here rather than an actual newline is that it's more clearly visible to the reader; it's also less likely to be accidentally turned into a newline followed by tabs or spaces. Writing the whitespace as a character reference doesn't stop it being treated as whitespace by XSLT, because the character references will have been expanded by the XML parser before the XSLT processor gets to see them.

Another way of coding the previous fragment in XSLT 2.0 is to write:

```
<xsl:value-of select="address-line[position() = 1 to 2]"
              separator="&#xA;"/>
```

You can also cause whitespace text nodes in the stylesheet to be retained by using the option «`xml:space="preserve"`». Although this is defined in the XML specification, its defined effect is to advise the application that whitespace is significant, and XSLT (which is the application in this case) will respect this. In XSLT 1.0 this sometimes caused problems because certain elements, such as `<xsl:choose>` and `<xsl:apply-templates>`, do not allow text nodes as children, even whitespace-only text nodes. Many processors, however, were forgiving on this. XSLT 2.0 has clarified that in situations where text nodes are not allowed, a whitespace-only text node is now stripped, despite the `xml:space` attribute. (However, an element that must always be empty, such as `<xsl:output>`, must be completely empty: whitespace-only text nodes are not allowed within these elements.)

Despite this clarification of the rules, I wouldn't normally recommend using the `xml:space` attribute in a stylesheet, but if there are large chunks of existing XML that you want to copy into the stylesheet verbatim, the technique can be useful.

The Effect of Stripping Whitespace Nodes

There are two main effects of stripping whitespace nodes, as done in the `<person>` element in the earlier example:

❑ When you use `<xsl:apply-templates/>` to process all the children of the `<person>` element, the whitespace nodes aren't there, so they don't get selected, which means they don't get copied to the result tree. If they had been left on the source tree, then by default they would be copied to the result tree.

❑ When you use `<xsl:number>` or the `position()` or `count()` functions to count nodes, the whitespace nodes aren't there, so they aren't counted. If you had left the whitespace nodes on the tree, then the `<name>`, `<employer>`, and `<place-of-work>` elements would be nodes 2, 4, and 6 instead of 1, 2, and 3.

There are cases where it's important to keep the whitespace nodes. Consider the following.

```
<para>
Edited by <name>James Clark</name>◆<email>jjc@jclark.com</email>
</para>
```

The diamond represents a space character that needs to be preserved, but because it is not adjacent to any other text, it would be eligible for stripping. In fact, whitespace is nearly always significant in elements that have mixed content (that is, elements that have both element and text nodes as children).

If you want to strip all the whitespace nodes from the source tree, you can write:

```
<xsl:strip-space elements="*"/>
```

If you want to strip all the whitespace nodes except those within certain named elements, you can write:

```
<xsl:strip-space elements="*"/>
<xsl:preserve-space elements="para h1 h2 h3 h4"/>
```

If any elements in the document (either the source document or the stylesheet) use the XML-defined attribute «xml:space="preserve"», this takes precedence over these rules: whitespace nodes in that element, and in all its descendants, will be kept on the tree unless the attribute is cancelled on a descendant element by specifying «xml:space="default"». This allows you to control on a per-instance basis whether whitespace is kept, whereas <xsl:strip-space> controls it at the element-type level.

Solving Whitespace Problems

There are two typical problems with whitespace in the output: too much of it, or too little.

If you are generating HTML, a bit of extra whitespace usually doesn't matter, though there are some places where it can slightly distort the layout of your page. With some text formats, however (a classic example is comma-separated values) you need to be very careful to output whitespace in exactly the right places.

Too Much Whitespace

If you are getting too much whitespace, there are three possible places it can be coming from:

❑ The source document

❑ The stylesheet

❑ Output indentation

First ensure that you set «indent="no"» on the <xsl:output> element, to eliminate the last of these possibilities.

If the output whitespace is adjacent to text, then it probably comes from the same place as that text.

❑   If this text comes from the stylesheet, use `<xsl:text>` to control more precisely what is output. For example, the following code outputs a comma between the items in a list, but it also outputs a newline after the comma, because the newline is part of the same text node as the comma:

```
<xsl:for-each select="item">
   <xsl:value-of select="."/>,
</xsl:for-each>
```

If you want the comma but not the newline, change this so that the newline is in a text node of its own, and is therefore stripped.

```
<xsl:for-each select="item">
   <xsl:value-of select="."/>,<xsl:text/>
</xsl:for-each>
```

❑   If the text comes from the source document, use `normalize-space()` to trim leading and trailing spaces from the text before outputting it.

If the offending whitespace is between tags in the output, then it probably comes from white-space nodes in the source tree that have not been stripped, and the remedy is to add an `<xsl:strip-space>` element to the stylesheet.

Too Little Whitespace

If you want whitespace in the output and aren't getting it, use `<xsl:text>` to generate it at the appropriate point. For example, the following code will output the lines of a poem in HTML, with each line of the poem being shown on a new line.

```
<xsl:for-each select="line">
   <xsl:value-of select="."/><br/>
</xsl:for-each>
```

This will display perfectly correctly in the browser, but if you want to view the HTML in a text editor, it will be difficult because everything goes on a single line. It would be useful to start a newline after each `<br>` element—you can do this as follows.

```
<xsl:for-each select="line">
   <xsl:value-of select="."/><br/><xsl:text>&#xa;</xsl:text>
</xsl:for-each>
```

Another trick I have used to achieve this is to exploit the fact that the non-breaking-space character (#xa0), although invisible, is not classified as whitespace. So you can achieve the required effect by writing:

```
<xsl:for-each select="line">
   <xsl:value-of select="."/><br/> 
</xsl:for-each>
```

This works because the newline after the «` `» is now part of a non-whitespace node.

Summary

The purpose of this chapter was to study the overall structure of a stylesheet, before going into the detailed specification of each element in the next chapter. We've now covered the following:

❑ How a stylesheet program can be made up of one or more stylesheet modules, linked together with `<xsl:import>` and `<xsl:include>` declarations. I described how the concept of import precedence allows one stylesheet to override definitions in those it imports.

❑ The `<xsl:stylesheet>` (or `<xsl:transform>`) element, which is the outermost element of most stylesheet modules.

❑ The `<?xml-stylesheet?>` processing instruction, which can be used to link from a source document to its associated stylesheets, and which allows a stylesheet to be embedded directly in the source document whose style it defines.

❑ The declarations found in the stylesheet, that is, the immediate children of the `<xsl:stylesheet>` or `<xsl:transform>` element, including the ability to have user-defined or vendor-defined elements here.

❑ How the `<xsl:stylesheet>` and `<xsl:template match="/">` elements can be omitted to make an XSLT stylesheet look more like the simple template languages that some users may be familiar with.

❑ The idea of a sequence constructor, a structure that occurs throughout a stylesheet, which is a sequence containing text nodes and literal result elements to be copied to the result tree, and instructions and extension elements to be executed. This led naturally to a discussion of literal result elements, and of attribute value templates, which are used to define variable attributes not only of literal result elements, but of certain XSLT elements as well.

❑ How the W3C standards committee has tried to ensure that the specification can be extended, both by vendors and by W3C itself, without adversely affecting the portability of stylesheets. You saw how to make a stylesheet work even if it uses proprietary extension functions and extension elements that may not be available in all implementations.

❑ How XSLT stylesheets handle whitespace in the source document, in the stylesheet itself, and in the result tree.

The next chapter describes how to use XSLT stylesheets together with an XML Schema for the source and/or result documents. If you are not interested in using schemas, you can probably skip that chapter and move straight to Chapter 5, which starts the main reference section of the book with an alphabetically organized set of specifications for each of the XSLT elements that can appear in a stylesheet.

Stylesheets and Schemas

One of the most important innovations in XSLT 2.0 is that stylesheets can take advantage of the schemas you have defined for your input and output documents. This chapter explores how this works.

This feature is an optional part of XSLT 2.0, in two significant ways:

- ❏ Firstly, an XSLT 2.0 processor isn't required to implement this part of the standard. A processor that offers schema support is called a *schema-aware processor*; one that does not is referred to as a *basic processor*.

- ❏ Secondly, even if the XSLT 2.0 processor you are using is a schema-aware processor, you can still process input documents, and produce output documents, for which there is no schema available.

There is no space in this book for a complete description of XML Schema. If you want to start writing schemas, I would recommend you read a book such as *XML Schema Essentials* by R. Allen Wyke and Andrew Watt (Wiley, 2002), or *XML Schema* by Eric van der Vlist (O'Reilly & Associates, 2002). XML Schema is a large and complicated specification, certainly as large as XSLT itself. However, it's possible that you are not writing your own schemas, but writing stylesheets designed to work with a schema that someone else has already written. If this is the case, I hope you will find the short overview of XML Schema in this chapter a useful introduction. This overview, with minor variations, is included both in this book and in *XPath 2.0 Programmer's Reference*, because understanding the basic concepts is essential to both languages; however, you don't need to read both.

XML Schema: An Overview

The primary purpose of XML Schema is to enable documents to be validated: they define a set of rules that XML documents must conform to, and enable documents to be checked against these rules. This means that organizations using XML to exchange invoices and purchase orders can agree on a schema defining the rules for these messages, and both parties can validate the messages against the schema to ensure that they are right. So the schema, in effect, defines a type of document, and this is why schemas are central to the type system of XSLT.

In fact, the designers of XML Schema were more ambitious than this. They realized that rather than simply giving a "yes" or "no" answer, processing a document against a schema could make the application's life easier by attaching labels to the validated document indicating, for each element and attribute in the document, which schema definitions it was validated against. In the language of XML Schema, this document with validation labels is called a Post Schema Validation Infoset or PSVI. The data model used by XSLT and XPath is based on the PSVI, but it only retains a subset of the information in the PSVI: specifically, the type annotations attached to element and attribute nodes.

We begin by looking at the kinds of types that can be defined in XML Schema, starting with simple types and moving on to progressively more complex types.

Simple Type Definitions

Let's suppose that many of our messages refer to part numbers, and that part numbers have a particular format such as ABC12345. We can start by defining this as a type in the schema:

```
<xs:simple-type name="part-number">
  <xs:restriction base="xs:token">
    <xs:pattern value="[A-Z]{3}[0-9]{5}"/>
  </xs:retriction>
</xs:simple-type>
```

Part number is a simple type because it doesn't have any internal node structure (that is, it doesn't contain any elements or attributes). I have defined it by restriction from xs:token, which is one of the built-in types that come for free with XML Schema. I could have chosen to base the type on xs:string, but xs:token is probably better because with xs:string, leading and trailing whitespace is considered significant, whereas with xs:token, it gets stripped automatically before the validation takes place. The particular restriction in this case is that the value must match the regular expression given in the <xs:pattern> element. This particular regular expression says that the value must consist of exactly three letters in the range A to Z, followed by exactly five digits.

Having defined this type, I can now refer to it in definitions of elements and attributes. For example, I can define the element:

```
<xs:element name="part" type="part-number"/>
```

This allows documents to contain <part> elements whose content conforms to the rules for the type called part-number. Of course, I can also define other elements that have the same type, for example:

```
<xs:element name="subpart" type="part-number"/>
```

Note the distinction between the name of an element and its type. Many element declarations in a schema (declarations that define elements with different names) can refer to the same type definition, if the rules for validating their content are the same. It's also permitted, though we won't go into the detail just yet, to use the same element name at different places within a document with different type definitions.

We can also use the same type definition in an attribute, for example:

```
<xs:attribute name="part-nr" type="part-number"/>
```

As we will see later in the chapter, we can declare variables and parameters in a stylesheet whose values must be elements or attributes of a particular type. Once a document has been validated using this schema, elements that have been validated against the declarations of part and subpart given above, and attributes that have been validated against the declaration named part-nr, will carry the type annotation part-number, and they can be assigned to a variable such as

```
<xsl:variable name="part" as="element(*, part-number)">
```

This variable is allowed to contain any element node that has the type annotation part-number. If further types have been defined as restricted subtypes of part-number (for example, Boeing-part-number), these can be assigned to the variable too. The «*» indicates that we are not concerned with the name of the element, but only with its type.

There are actually three kinds of simple types that you can define in XML Schema: atomic types, list types, and union types. Atomic types are treated specially in the XPath/XSLT type system, because values of an atomic type (called, naturally enough, atomic values) can be manipulated as free-standing items, independently of any node. Like integers, booleans, and strings, part numbers as defined above are atomic values, and you can hold a part number or a sequence of part numbers directly in a variable, without creating any node to contain it. For example, the following declaration defines a variable whose value is a sequence of three part numbers:

```
<xsl:variable name="part" as="part-number*"
              select="part-number('WZH94623'),
                      part-number('BYF67253'),
                      part-number('PRG83692')"/>
```

Simple types in XML Schema are not the same thing as atomic types in the XPath data model. This is because a simple type can also allow a sequence of values. For example, it is possible to define the following simple type:

```
<xs:simpleType name="colors">
  <xs:list>
    <xs:simpleType>
      <xs:restriction base="xs:NCName">
        <xs:enumeration value="red"/>
        <xs:enumeration value="orange"/>
        <xs:enumeration value="yellow"/>
        <xs:enumeration value="green"/>
        <xs:enumeration value="blue"/>
        <xs:enumeration value="indigo"/>
        <xs:enumeration value="violet"/>
      </xs:restriction>
    </xs:simpleType>
  </xs:list>
</xs:simpleType>
```

There are actually two type definitions here. The inner type is anonymous, because the <xs:simpleType> element has no name attribute. It defines an atomic value, which must be an xs:NCName, and more specifically, must be one of the values «red», «orange», «yellow», «green», «blue», «indigo», or «violet». The outer type is a named type (which means it can be referenced

147

from elsewhere in the schema), and it defines a list type whose individual items must conform to the inner type.

This type therefore allows values such as «red green blue», or «violet yellow» or even «red red red». The values are written in textual XML as a list of color names separated by spaces, but once the document has been through schema validation, the typed value of an element with this type will be a sequence of xs:NCName values.

The term *simple type* in XML Schema rules out types involving multiple attribute or element nodes, but it does allow composite values consisting of a sequence of atomic values.

Elements with Attributes and Simple Content

One thing that might occur quite frequently in an invoice or purchase order is an amount in money: there might be elements such as:

❑   <unit-price currency="USD">50.00</unit-price>

❑   <amount-due currency="EUR">1890.00</amount-due>

What these two elements have in common is that they have a currency attribute (with a particular range of allowed values) and content that is a decimal number. This is an example of a complex type. We defined part-number as a simple type because it didn't involve any nodes. The money-amount type is a complex type, because it involves a decimal number and an attribute value. We can define this by declaring two elements in the schema with the same type:

```
<xs:simpleType name="currency-type">
  <xs:restriction base="xs:token">
    <xs:enumeration value="USD"/>
    <xs:enumeration value="EUR"/>
    <xs:enumeration value="GBP"/>
    <xs:enumeration value="CAD"/>
  </xs:restriction>
</xs:simpleType>

<xs:complexType name="money-amount">
  <xs:simpleContent>
    <xs:extension base="xs:decimal">
      <xs:attribute name="currency" type="currency-type"/>
    </xs:extension>
  </xs:simpleContent>
</xs:complexType>
```

Here we have defined two new types in the schema, both of which are named. The first defines the type of the currency attribute. We could have used the same name for the attribute and its type, but many people prefer to keep the names of types distinct from those of elements and attributes, to avoid confusing the two. In this case I've chosen to define it (again) as a subtype of xs:token, but this time restricting the value to be one of four particular world currencies. In practice, of course, the list might be much longer. The currency-type is again a simple type, because it's just a value; it doesn't define any nodes.

The second definition is a complex type, because it defines two things. It's the type of an element that has a `currency` attribute conforming to the definition of `currency-type`, and has content (the text between the element start and end tags) that is a decimal number, indicated by the reference to the built-in type `xs:decimal`. This particular kind of complex type is called a *complex type with simple content*, which means that elements of this type can have attributes, but they cannot have child elements.

Again, the name of the type is quite distinct from the names of the elements that conform to this type. We can declare the two example elements above in the schema as follows:

```
<xs:element name="unit-price" type="money-amount"/>
<xs:element name="amount-due" type="money-amount"/>
```

But although the type definition doesn't constrain the element name, it does constrain the name of the attribute, which must be «currency». If the type definition defined child elements, it would also constrain these child elements to have particular names.

In an XSLT 2.0 stylesheet, we can write a template rule for processing elements of this type, which means that all the logic for formatting money amounts can go in one place. For example, we could write:

```
<xsl:template match="element(*, money-amount)">
  <xsl:value-of select="@currency, format-number(., '#,##0.00')"/>
</xsl:template>
```

This would output the example `<amount-due>` element as «EUR 1,890.00». (The `format-number()` function is described in Chapter 7, on page 558). The beauty of such a template rule is that it is highly reusable: however much the schema is extended to include new elements that hold amounts of money, this rule can be used to display them.

Elements with Mixed Content

The type of an element that can contain child elements is called a *complex type with complex content*. Such types essentially fall into three categories, called *empty content*, *mixed content*, and *element-only content*. Mixed content allows intermingled text and child elements, and is often found in narrative XML documents, allowing markup such as:

```
<para>The population of <city>London</city> reached
  <number>5,572,000</number> in <year>1891</year>, and had risen
  further to <number>7,160,000</number> by <year>1911</year>.</para>
```

The type of this element could be declared in a schema as:

```
<xs:complex-type name="para-type" mixed="true">
  <xs:choice minOccurs="0" maxOccurs="unbounded">
    <xs:element ref="city"/>
    <xs:element ref="number"/>
    <xs:element ref="year"/>
  </xs:choice>
</xs:complex-type>
```

In practice, the list of permitted child elements would probably be much longer than this, and a common technique is to define *substitution groups* which allow a list of such elements to be referred to by a single name.

Narrative documents tend to be less constrained than documents holding structured data such as purchase orders and invoices, and while schema validation is still very useful, the type annotations generated as a result of validation aren't generally so important when the time comes to process the data using XSLT: The names of the elements are usually more significant than their types. However, there is plenty of potential for using the types, especially if the schema is designed with this in mind.

When schemas are used primarily for validation, the tendency is to think of types in terms of the form that values assume. For example, it is natural to define the element <city> (as used in the example above) as a type derived from xs:token by restriction, because the names of cities are strings, perhaps consisting of multiple words, in which spaces are not significant. Once types start to be used for processing information (which is what you are doing when you use XSLT), it's also useful to think about what the value actually means. The content of the <city> element is not just a string of characters, it is the name of a geographical place, a place that has a location on the Earth's surface, that is in a particular country, and that may figure in postal addresses. If you have other similar elements such as <county>, <country>, and <state>, it might be a good idea to define a single type for all of them. Even if this type doesn't have any particular purpose for validation, because it doesn't define any extra constraints on the content, it can potentially be useful when writing XSLT templates because it groups a number of elements that belong together semantically.

Elements with Element-Only Content

This category covers most of the "wrapper" elements that are found in data-oriented XML. A typical example is the outer <person> element in a structure such as:

```
<person id="P517541">
   <name>
      <given>Michael</given>
      <given>Howard</given>
      <family>Kay</family>
   </name>
   <date-of-birth>1951-10-11</date-of-birth>
   <place-of-birth>Hannover</place-of-birth>
</person>
```

The schema for this might be:

```
<xs:element name="person" type="person-type"/>

<xs:complexType name="person-type">
   <xs:sequence>
      <xs:element name="name" type="personal-name-type"/>
      <xs:element name="date-of-birth" type="xs:date"/>
      <xs:element name="place-of-birth" type="xs:token"/>
   </xs:sequence>
   <xs:attribute name="id" type="id-number"/>
</xs:complexType>
```

```
<xs:complexType name="personal-name-type">
  <xs:sequence>
    <xs:element name="given" maxOccurs="unbounded" type="xs:token"/>
    <xs:element name="family" type="xs:token"/>
  </xs:sequence>
</xs:complexType>

<xs:simpleType name="id-number">
  <xs:restriction base="xs:ID">
    <xs:pattern value="[A-Z][0-9]{6}"/>
  </xs:restriction>
</xs:simpleType>
```

There are a number of ways these definitions could have been written. In the so-called *Russian Doll* style, the types would be defined inline within the element declarations, rather than being given separate names of their own. The schema could have been written using more top-level element declarations, for example the <name> element could have been described at a top level. When you use a schema for validation, these design decisions mainly affect your ability to reuse definitions later when the schema changes. When you use a schema to describe types that can be referenced in XSLT stylesheets, however, they also affect the ease of writing the stylesheet.

In choosing the representation of the schema shown above, I made a number of implicit assumptions:

❑ It's quite likely that there will be other elements with the same structure as <person>, or with an extension of this structure: perhaps not at the moment, but at some time in the future. Examples of such elements might be <employee> or <pensioner>. Therefore, it's worth describing the element and its type separately.

❑ Similarly, personal names are likely to appear in a number of different places. Elements with this type won't always be called <name>, so it's a good idea to create a type definition that can be referenced from any element.

❑ Not every element called <name> will be a personal name, the same tag might also be used (even in the same namespace) for other purposes. If I were confident that the tag would always be used for personal names, then I would probably have made it the subject of a top-level element declaration, rather than defining it inline within the <person> element.

❑ The elements at the leaves of the tree (those with simple types) such as <date-of-birth>, <place-of-birth>, <given>, and <family> are probably best defined using local element declarations rather than top-level declarations. Even if they are used in more than one container element, there is relatively little to be gained by pulling the element declarations out to the top level. The important thing is that if any of them have a user-defined type (which isn't the case in this example) then the user-defined types are defined using top-level <xs:simpleType> declarations. This is what I have done for the id attribute (which is defined as a subtype of xs:ID, forcing values to be unique within any XML document), but I chose not to do the same for the leaf elements.

Substitution Groups

The type of an element or attribute tells you what can appear inside the content of the element or attribute. Substitution groups, by contrast, classify elements according to where they can appear.

There is a schema for XSLT 2.0 stylesheets published as part of the XSLT Recommendation (see `http://www.w3.org/TR/xslt20`). Let's look at how this schema uses substitution groups.

Firstly, the schema defines a type that is applicable to any XSLT-defined element, and that simply declares the standard attributes that can appear on any element:

```
<xs:complexType name="generic-element-type">
  <xs:attribute name="extension-element-prefixes" type="xsl:prefixes"/>
  <xs:attribute name="exclude-result-prefixes" type="xsl:prefixes"/>
  <xs:attribute name="xpath-default-namespace" type="xs:anyURI"/>
  <xs:attribute ref="xml:space"/>
  <xs:attribute ref="xml:lang"/>
  <xs:anyAttribute namespace="##other" processContents="skip"/>
</xs:complexType>
```

There's a good mix of features used to define these attributes. Some attributes use built-in types (`xs:anyURI`), some use user-defined types defined elsewhere in the schema (`xsl:prefixes`), and two of them (`xml:space` and `xml:lang`)) are defined in a schema for a different namespace. The `<xs:anyAttribute>` at the end says that XSLT elements can contain attributes from a different namespace, which are not validated. (Perhaps it would be better to specify lax validation, which would validate the attribute if and only if a schema is available for it.)

Every XSLT element except the `<xsl:output>` element allows a standard `version` attribute (the `<xsl:output>` element is different because its `version` attribute is defined for a different purpose and has a different type). So the schema defines another type that adds this attribute:

```
<xs:complexType name="versioned-element-type">
  <xs:complexContent>
    <xs:extension base="xsl:generic-element-type">
      <xs:attribute name="version" type="xs:decimal" use="optional"/>
    </xs:extension>
  </xs:complexContent>
</xs:complexType>
```

The XSLT specification classifies many XSLT elements as *instructions*. This is not a structural distinction based on the attributes or content model of these elements (which varies widely), it is a distinction based on the way they are used. In particular, instruction elements are interchangeable in terms of where they may appear in a stylesheet: If you can use one instruction in a particular context, you can use any instruction. This calls for defining a substitution group:

```
<xs:element name="instruction"
            type="xsl:versioned-element-type"
            abstract="true"/>
```

Note that although the substitution group is defined using an element declaration, it does not define a real element, because it specifies «`abstract="true"`». This means that an actual XSLT stylesheet will never contain an element called `<xsl:instruction>`. It is a fictional element that exists only so that others can be substituted for it.

What this declaration does say is that every element in the substitution group for `<xsl:instruction>` must be defined with a type that is derived from `xsl:versioned-element-type`. That is, every XSLT instruction allows the attributes `extension-element-prefixes`, `exclude-result-prefixes`, `xpath-default-namespace`, `xml:space`, `xml:lang`, and `version`. This is in fact the only thing that XSLT instructions have in common with each other, as far as their permitted content is concerned.

Individual instructions are now defined as members of this substitution group. Here is a simple example, the declaration of the `<xsl:if>` element:

```
<xs:element name="if" substitutionGroup="xsl:instruction">
  <xs:complexType>
    <xs:complexContent mixed="true">
      <xs:extension base="xsl:sequence-constructor">
        <xs:attribute name="test" type="xsl:expression" use="required"/>
      </xs:extension>
    </xs:complexContent>
  </xs:complexType>
</xs:element>
```

This shows that the `<xsl:if>` element is a member of the substitution group whose head is the abstract `<xsl:instruction>` element. It also tells us that the content model of the element (that is, its type) is defined as an extension of the type `xsl:sequence-constructor`, the extension being to require a `test` attribute whose value is of type `xsl:expression`—this is a simple type defined later in the same schema, representing an XPath expression that may appear as the content of this attribute.

The type `xsl:sequence-constructor` is used for all XSLT elements whose permitted content is a *sequence constructor*. A sequence constructor is simply a sequence of zero or more XSLT instructions, defined like this:

```
<xs:complexType name="sequence-constructor">
  <xs:complexContent mixed="true">
    <xs:extension base="xsl:versioned-element-type">
      <xs:group ref="xsl:sequence-constructor-group" minOccurs="0"
                                                      maxOccurs="unbounded"/>
    </xs:extension>
  </xs:complexContent>
</xs:complexType>

<xs:group name="sequence-constructor-group">
  <xs:choice>
    <xs:element ref="xsl:variable"/>
    <xs:element ref="xsl:instruction"/>
    <xs:group ref="xsl:result-elements"/>
  </xs:choice>
</xs:group>
```

The first definition says that the `xsl:sequence-constructor` type extends `xsl:versioned-element-type`, whose definition we gave earlier. If it didn't extend this type, we wouldn't be allowed to put `<xsl:if>` in the substitution group of `<xsl:instruction>`. It also says that the content of a sequence constructor consists of zero or more elements, each of which must be chosen from those in the group `sequence-contructor-group`. The second definition says that every element in `sequence-contructor-group` is either an `<xsl:instruction>` (which implicitly allows any element in the substitution group for `<xsl:instruction>`, including of course `<xsl:if>`), or an `<xsl:variable>`.

The `<xsl:variable>` element is not defined as a member of the substitution group because it can be used in two different contexts: either as an instruction or as a top-level declaration in a stylesheet. This is one of the drawbacks of substitution groups: they can't overlap. The schema defines all the elements that can act as declarations in a very similar way, using a substitution group headed by an abstract `<xsl:declaration>` element. It's not possible for the same element, `<xsl:variable>`, to appear in both substitution groups, so it has been defined in neither, and needs to be treated as a special case.

If you need to use XSLT to access an XSLT stylesheet (which isn't as obscure a requirement as it may seem; there are many applications for this) then the classification of elements as instructions or declarations can be very useful. For example, you can match all the instructions that have an attribute in the Saxon namespace with the template rule:

```
<xsl:template match="schema-element(xsl:instruction)[@saxon:*]">
```

assuming that the namespace prefix «saxon» has been declared appropriately. Here the expression «schema-element(xsl:instruction)» selects elements that are either named `<xsl:instruction>`, or are in the substitution group with `<xsl:instruction>` as its head element, and the expression «[@saxon:*]» is a filter that selects only those elements that have an attribute in the «saxon» namespace.

The penalty of choosing a real schema for our example is that we have to live with its complications. As we saw earlier, the `<xsl:variable>` element isn't part of this substitution group. So we might have to extend the query to handle `<xsl:variable>` elements as well. We can do this by writing:

```
<xsl:template match="(schema-element(xsl:instruction)|xsl:variable)[@saxon:*]">
```

A detailed explanation of this match pattern can be found in Chapter 6.

So, to sum up this section, substitution groups are not only a very convenient mechanism for referring to a number of elements that can be substituted for each other in the schema, but can also provide a handy way of referring to a group of elements in XSLT match patterns. But they do have one limitation, which is that elements can only belong directly to one substitution group (or to put it another way, substitution groups must be properly nested, they cannot overlap).

At this point I will finish the lightning tour of XML Schema. The rest of the chapter builds on this understanding to show how the types defined in an XML Schema can be used in a stylesheet.

Declaring Types

As we saw in the overview section, XSLT 2.0 allows you to define the type of a variable. Similarly, when you write functions or templates, you can declare the type of each parameter, and also the type of the returned value.

Here is an example of a function that takes a string as its parameter, and returns an integer as its result:

```
<xsl:function name="my:length" as="xs:integer">
  <xsl:param name="in" as="xs:string"/>
  <xsl:sequence select="max((string-length(upper-case($in)),
                         string-length(lower-case($in))))"/>
</xsl:function>
```

And here's a named template that expects either an element node or nothing as its parameter, and returns either a text node or nothing as its result:

```
<xsl:template name="sequence-nr" as="text()?">
  <xsl:param name="in" as="element()?"/>
  <xsl:number level="any" select="$in" format="i"/>
</xsl:template>
```

You don't have to include type declarations in the stylesheet: If you leave out the «as» attribute, then as with XSLT 1.0, any type of value will be accepted. However, I think it's a good software engineering practice always to declare the types as precisely as you can. The type declarations serve two purposes:

❑ The XSLT processor has extra information about the permitted values of the variables or parameters, and it can use this information to generate more efficient code.

❑ The processor will check (at compile time, and if necessary at runtime) that the values supplied for a variable or parameter match the declared types, and will report an error if not. This can detect many errors in your code, errors that might otherwise have led to the stylesheet producing incorrect output. As a general rule, the sooner an error is detected, the easier it is to find the cause and correct it, so defining types in this way leads to faster debugging. I have heard stories of users upgrading their stylesheets from XSLT 1.0 to XSLT 2.0 and finding that the extra type checking revealed errors that had been causing the stylesheet to produce incorrect output which no one had ever noticed.

These type declarations are written using the «as» attribute of elements such as <xsl:variable>, <xsl:param>, <xsl:function>, and <xsl:template>. You don't need to use a schema-aware processor to use the «as» attribute, because many of the types you can declare (including those in the two examples above) are built-in types, rather than types that need to be defined in your schema. For example, if a function parameter is required to be an integer, you can declare it like this:

```
<xsl:param name="in" as="xs:integer"/>
```

which will work whether or not your XSLT processor is schema-aware, and whether or not your source documents are validated using an XML Schema.

The rules for what you can write in the «as» attribute are defined in XPath 2.0, not in XSLT itself. The construct that appears here is called a *sequence type descriptor*, and it is explained in detail in Chapter 9 of *XPath 2.0 Programmer's Reference*. Here are some examples of sequence type descriptors that you can use with any XSLT processor, whether or not it is schema-aware:

Construct	Meaning
xs:integer	An atomic value labeled as an integer
xs:integer *	A sequence of zero or more integers
xs:string ?	Either a string, or an empty sequence
xs:date	A date

Continues

Construct	Meaning
`xdt:anyAtomicType`	An atomic value of any type (for example integer, string, and so on)
`node()`	Any node in a tree
`node() *`	Any sequence of zero or more nodes, of any kind
`element()`	Any element node
`attribute() +`	Any sequence of one or more attribute nodes
`document-node()`	Any document node

The types that are available in a basic XSLT processor are shown in Figure 4-1, which also shows where they appear in the type hierarchy:

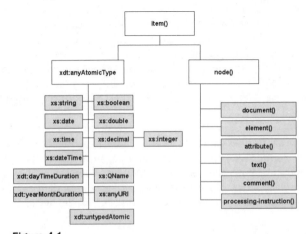

Figure 4-1

The shaded boxes show concrete types, and the empty boxes represent abstract types. The difference is that a value can never belong to an abstract type unless it also belongs to one of the concrete subtypes of that type.

The most general type here is «`item()`», which allows any kind of item. The two kinds of items are atomic values, shown on the left-hand branch of the type hierarchy, and nodes, shown on the right-hand branch.

In a sequence type descriptor, any of the item types listed in Figure 4-1 may be followed by one of the occurrence indicators «`*`», «`+`», or «`?`». The occurrence indicator defines how many items (of the given item type) may appear in the value. They have the following meanings:

Occurrence indicator	Meaning
`*`	Zero or more occurrences allowed
`+`	One or more occurrences allowed
`?`	Zero or one occurrence allowed

If there is no occurrence indicator, then the value must contain exactly one item of the specified type.

In a schema-aware processor, this type hierarchy is extended in the following two ways:

❑   Firstly, all the built-in atomic types defined in the XML Schema specification become available. These include additional primitive types such as xs:hexBinary and xs:gYearMonth, and types derived from xs:string and xs:integer, for example xs:normalizedString and xs:nonNegativeInteger. A full list of these types, with explanations of their meanings, is given in Chapter 3 of *XPath 2.0 Programmer's Reference*.

❑   Secondly, user-defined types can be imported from an XML Schema definition.

To make user-defined types available for use in type declarations in a stylesheet, the schema must first be imported into the stylesheet. This can be done with an <xsl:import-schema> declaration, which might take the form:

```
<xsl:import-schema namespace="http://acme.org/ns" schema-location="acme.xsd"/>
```

The <xsl:import-schema> declaration is described in more detail later in this chapter (see page 168). You can import any number of schemas into a stylesheet, provided that the namespaces do not clash. If you want to refer to types defined in a schema by name, then you must import that schema into the stylesheet using an <xsl:import-schema> declaration. However, you don't need to import a schema simply because you are using it to validate source or result documents.

The types defined in a schema are either complex types or simple types, and simple types in turn divide into union types, list types, and atomic types.

When atomic types are imported from a schema, they can be used in a stylesheet in just the same way as the built-in atomic types. For example, if the schema defines an atomic type mf:part-number as a subtype of xs:string constrained to conform to a particular pattern, then in the stylesheet you can declare a variable:

```
<xsl:variable name="part" as="mf:part-number" select="EXPRESSION"/>
```

which informs the system that the value of the $part variable will always be a part number. The expression in the select attribute must return a valid part number according to these rules, or the transformation will fail.

> Note that to conform to this type, it's not enough to supply a string that matches the schema-defined pattern. The value must actually be labeled as an mf:part-number. To achieve this, you typically have to convert the value to the required type using a constructor function. For example, you could write:
>
> ```
> <xsl:variable name="part" as="mf:part-number"
>                           select="mf:part-number('BFG94623')"/>
> ```

Atomic values can exist independently of any node in a document, which is why you can use an atomic type directly as the type of a value. In contrast, instances of complex types, union types, and list types can exist only as the content of a node in a document. This means that the names of these types can't be used directly in an «as» attribute defining the type of (say) a variable or parameter. You can use them, however, to qualify a type that describes a node. Examples of such sequence type descriptors are shown in the table below:

Construct	Meaning
element(*, mf:invoice)	An element node validated against the complex type mf:invoice defined in an imported schema
attribute(*, xs:NMTOKENS)	An attribute validated against the built-in schema list type xs:NMTOKENS
document-node(element (*, mf:invoice))	A document node representing a well-formed XML document whose outermost element has been validated against the complex type mf:invoice defined in an imported schema

Often the structure of an element is defined in the schema not by creating an explicitly named <xs:complexType> definition, but rather by means of an <xs:element> declaration that contains an unnamed <xs:complexType>. Here's a typical example, taken from the schema for XSLT 2.0 stylesheets:

```
<xs:element name="apply-imports" substitutionGroup="xsl:instruction">
  <xs:complexType>
    <xs:complexContent>
      <xs:extension base="xsl:versioned-element-type">
        <xs:sequence>
          <xs:element ref="xsl:with-param" minOccurs="0" maxOccurs="unbounded"/>
        </xs:sequence>
      </xs:extension>
    </xs:complexContent>
  </xs:complexType>
</xs:element>
```

To allow for the fact that many of the types defined in a typical schema are anonymous, there is another form of the element() test that is used to refer to elements conforming to this named element declaration. If you write:

```
<xsl:param name="ai" as="schema-element(xsl:apply-imports)"/>
```

then you are saying that the value of the parameter must be an element that has been validated against the element declaration xsl:apply-imports in this schema. The name of the element passed as the parameter must either be xsl:apply-imports, or must match an element defined in the schema to be a member of the substitution group of xsl:apply-imports.

You can similarly refer to top-level attribute declarations in the schema using the syntax «schema-attribute(nnn)», though this form is not seen very often because it is unusual to find top-level attribute declarations in a schema.

Sequence type descriptors can also be used within XPath expressions. The expressions that use them are described in Chapter 9 of *XPath 2.0 Programmer's Reference*, which also defines the syntax and semantics in much greater detail than defined here. The operators that use sequence type descriptors are as follows:

❑ «instance of», which tests whether a given value is an instance of a given type. For example, «@dob instance of attribute(*, xs:date)» returns true if the attribute @dob is labeled with the type annotation xs:date (or a type derived from xs:date), which will be true only if the attribute contains a valid date and has been validated using a schema that declares the type of the attribute as xs:date.

❑ «treat as», which asserts that a given value is an instance of a given type, causing a runtime failure if it is not. This operator is useful mainly with XPath processors that do strict static type-checking, which is unlikely to apply in an XSLT environment unless the processor has a diagnostic mode to do this extra level of checking.

Validating the Source Document

Validation is the process of taking a raw XML document and processing it using an XML Schema. The most obvious output of this process is a success or failure rating: the document is either valid or invalid against the schema. But this is not the only output. Validation also annotates the document, marking each element and attribute node with a label indicating its type. For example, if validation checks that a <shippingAddress> element is valid according to the «us-postal-address» type in the schema, then this element will be annotated as having the type «us-postal-address». There are various ways the stylesheet can then use this information:

❑ Many operations on nodes extract the typed value of the nodes. This process is called *atomization*, and it is sensitive to the type annotations on the nodes. For example, when you compare two attributes using an expression such as «@discount gt $customer/@max-discount», the values that are compared are the typed values of @discount and @max-discount respectively. If the schema defines these values to be numbers (for example, using the type xs:decimal), then they will be compared numerically, so the value «10.00» will be considered greater than the value «2.50». If the same values were compared as strings, «10.00» would be less than «2.50». Adding type annotations to nodes, through the process of schema validation, enables operations on the values of the nodes to be performed more intelligently.

❑ There are many operations that only make sense when applied to a particular kind of data. At the top level, the stylesheet as a whole might be designed to process purchase orders, and will produce garbage if you make the mistake of feeding it with input that's actually a delivery note. At a more fine-grained level, you might have a stylesheet function or template rule that's designed to process US postal addresses, and that won't work properly if you give it a phone number instead. XSLT 2.0 allows you to define the type of data that you expect your functions and template rules to process, and to define the type of result that they produce as their output. A schema-aware processor will then automatically check that when the function or template is actually called, the data is of the right type, and if it isn't, the error will be reported.

At times these errors can become frustrating. But remember, every time you get one of these error messages, it tells you about a programming mistake that might otherwise have been much harder to track down. With XSLT 1.0, most programming mistakes don't give you an error message, they simply give you wrong output, and it can be a tortuous process debugging the stylesheet to find out where you went wrong. With XSLT 2.0, if you choose to define data types for your stylesheet functions and templates, you can get error messages that make it much clearer where the mistake lies.

You don't request validation of the input document from within the stylesheet. It's assumed that you will request this as part of the way you invoke the transformation, and details of how you do this will vary from one XSLT processor to another. (With Saxon, for example, you can use the `-val` option on the command line.) What you can do is test in your stylesheet whether the input has actually been validated. For example, you can write the first template rule in the stylesheet as follows:

```
<xsl:template match="/">
  <xsl:if test="not(* instance of schema-element(purchase-order))">
    <xsl:message terminate="yes">
        Source document is not a validated purchase order
    </xsl:message>
  </xsl:if>
  <xsl:apply-templates/>
</xsl:template>
```

The effect of writing the template rule this way is that if the stylesheet is presented with a document that is not a validated purchase order, it will immediately fail and display an error message, rather than trying to process it and producing garbage output.

Note the carefully chosen phrase *a validated purchase order*. It's not enough to supply an XML document that would be deemed valid if you tried to validate it. To pass this test, the document must already have been through a schema processor, and must have passed validation.

If you prefer, you could code the stylesheet to invoke the validation explicitly, by writing the following:

```
<xsl:template match="/">
  <xsl:variable name="input">
    <xsl:copy-of select="*" type="purchase-order-type"/>
  </xsl:variable>
  <xsl:apply-templates select="$input"/>
</xsl:template>
```

This defines a variable to hold a copy of the input document. The «type» attribute on the `<xsl:copy-of>` instruction asks the XSLT processor to invoke schema validation on the document, and if this succeeds, the element and attribute nodes in the new copy will have type annotations reflecting the result of this process. There is no explicit logic here to test whether validation has succeeded. It isn't needed, because a validation failure will always cause the transformation to be aborted with an error message.

However, I wouldn't normally recommend this approach. Creating a copy of the input document is likely to be expensive. It's better to do the validation on the fly while the input document is being parsed in the first place.

The value of the «type» attribute in this example, like the type named in the «instance of» expression in the previous example, is a type that's defined in a schema. We'll see later how the XSLT processor locates a schema containing this type definition.

Validating the Result Document

You can also request validation of the output of the transformation. For example, if you have written the stylesheet to generate XHTML, you can ask for it to be validated by writing your first template rule as follows:

```
<xsl:template match="/">
  <xsl:result-document validate="strict">
    <xsl:apply-templates/>
  </xsl:result-document>
</xsl:template>
```

In this example, there is nothing that says what the expected type of the output is. What «validate="strict"» means is that the outermost element of the result document (for example, <xhtml:html>) must correspond to an element declaration that's present in some schema known to the system, and the system is then required to check that the contents of the element conform to the rules defined in that element declaration.

You could argue that validating the output from within the stylesheet is no different from running the transformation and then putting the output through a schema processor to check that it's valid. However, once you try developing a stylesheet this way, you will find that the experience is very different. If you put the output file through a free-standing schema processor once the transformation is complete, the schema processor will give you error messages in terms of a position within the result document. You will then have to open the result document in a text editor, find out what's wrong with it, find the instruction in the stylesheet that generated the incorrect output, and then correct the stylesheet. Working with a schema processor that's integrated into your XSLT processor is much more direct: In most cases the error message will tell you directly which instruction in the stylesheet needs to be changed. This makes for a much more rapid development cycle.

In principle there is another advantage—in many cases it should be possible for a schema-aware XSLT processor to tell you that the output will be invalid before you even try running the stylesheet against a source document. That is, it should be able to report some of your errors at compile time. This gives you an even quicker turnaround in fixing errors, and more importantly, it means that the ability to detect bugs in your code is less dependent on the completeness of your test suite. Stylesheet programming is often done without much regard to the traditional disciplines of software engineering—testing tends to be less than thorough. So anything that reduces the risk of failures once the stylesheet is in live use is to be welcomed.

At the time of writing this chapter, the only schema-aware XSLT processor available is Saxon 8.0. This doesn't do any compile-time checking of the stylesheet against the schema, other than checking that the type names used in the stylesheet are actually declared in the schema. This feature is bound to appear as the technology matures.

Validation of a result document can be controlled using either the `validation` attribute or the `type` attribute of the `<xsl:result-document>` element. You can use only one of these: they can't be mixed. The `validation` attribute allows four values, whose meanings are explained in the table below.

Attribute value	Meaning
strict	The result document is subjected to strict validation. This means that there must be an element declaration for the outermost element of the result document in some schema, and the structure of the result document must conform to that element declaration

Continues

Attribute value	Meaning
`lax`	The result document is subjected to lax validation. This means that the outermost element is validated against a schema if a declaration for that element name can be located; if not, the system assumes the existence of an element declaration that allows any content for that element. The children of the element are also subjected to lax validation, and so on recursively. So any elements in the tree that are declared in a schema must conform to their declaration, but for other elements, there are no constraints
`preserve`	This option means that no validation is applied at the document level, but if any elements or attributes within the result tree have been constructed using node-level validation (as described in the next section), then the type annotations resulting from that node-level validation will be preserved in the result tree. These node annotations are only relevant, of course, if the result tree is passed to another process that understands them. If the result tree is simply serialized, it makes no difference whether type annotations are preserved or not
`strip`	This option means that no validation is applied at the document level, and moreover, if any elements or attributes within the result tree have been constructed using node-level validation (as described in the next section), then the type annotations resulting from that node-level validation will be removed from the result tree. Instead, all elements will be given a type annotation of `xdt:untyped`, and attributes will have the type annotation `xdt:untypedAtomic`

The other way of requesting validation of the result tree is through the `type` attribute. If the `type` attribute is specified, its value must be a QName, which must match the name of a global type definition in an imported schema. In practice this will almost invariably be a complex type definition. The rules to pass validation are as follows:

1. The result tree must be a well-formed document: That is, it must contain exactly one element node, and no text nodes, among the children of the document node. (In the absence of validation, this rule can be relaxed. For example, it is possible to have a temporary tree in which the document node has three element nodes as its children.)

2. The document element (that is, the single element node child of the document node) must validate against the schema definition of the specified type, according to the rules defined in XML Schema.

3. The document must satisfy document-level integrity constraints defined in the schema. This means:

   ❑ Elements and attributes of type `xs:ID` must have unique values within the document.

   ❑ Elements and attributes of type `xs:IDREF` or `xs:IDREFS` must contain valid references to `xs:ID` values within the document.

   ❑ Any constraints defined by `<xs:unique>`, `<xs:key>`, and `<xs:keyref>` declarations in the schema must be satisfied.

Document-level validation rules must also be satisfied when validation is requested using the option «validate="strict"» or «validate="lax"».

The language of the XSLT specification that describes these rules is somewhat tortuous. This is because XSLT tries to define what validation means in terms of the rules in the XML Schema specification, which means that there is a need to establish a precise correspondence between the terminologies of the two specifications. This is made more difficult by the fact that XML Schema is not defined in terms of the XSLT/XPath data model, but rather in terms of the XML Infoset and the Post Schema Validation Infoset (PSVI), which is defined in the XML Schema specification itself. To make this work, the XSLT specification says that when a document is validated, it is first serialized, and then re-parsed to create an Infoset. The Infoset is then validated, as defined in XML Schema, to create a PSVI. Finally, this PSVI is converted to a document in the XPath data model using rules defined in the XPath data model specification. However, you should regard this description of the process as a purely formal device to ensure that no ambiguities are introduced between the different specifications. In practice, an XSLT processor is likely to have a fairly intimate interface with a schema processor, and both are likely to share the same internal data structures.

If you request validation by specifying «validation="strict"» or «validation="lax"», this raises the question of where the XSLT processor should look to find a schema that contains a suitable element declaration. The specification leaves this slightly open. The first place a processor will look is among the schemas that were imported into the stylesheet using <xsl:import-schema> declarations: see *Importing Schemas* on page 168. The processor is also allowed (but not required) to use any xsi:schemaLocation or xsi:noNamespaceSchemaLocation attributes that are present in the result document itself as hints indicating where to locate a suitable schema. My advice, however, would be to make sure that the required schemas are explicitly imported.

Validating a Temporary Tree

In the previous two sections, we have seen how you can validate a source document that is to be processed by the stylesheet, and how you can validate result documents produced as output by the stylesheet. It's also possible to apply validation to temporary documents created and used internally during the course of stylesheet processing (these documents are known as temporary trees).

The most common way to create a temporary tree is as follows:

```
<xsl:variable name="temp">
  <xsl:apply-templates select="." mode="phase-1"/>
</xsl:variable>
```

There is no «as» attribute here: the default type for a variable whose value is defined by a contained sequence constructor, rather than by means of a select attribute, is document-node(), which means that the value of the variable will be the document node at the root of a newly constructed temporary tree. The body of the tree in this case is produced by the <xsl:apply-templates> instruction.

The example above can be regarded as shorthand for the more detailed construction:

```
<xsl:variable name="temp" as="document-node()">
  <xsl:document>
    <xsl:apply-templates select="." mode="phase-1"/>
  </xsl:document>
</xsl:variable>
```

This shows more explicitly how the sequence constructor contained in the `<xsl:variable>` element creates a single document node, whose content is populated by the `<xsl:apply-templates>` instruction.

If you expand the variable definition in this way, you can also use the attributes `validation` and `type` on the `<xsl:document>` instruction to invoke validation of the temporary tree. These attributes work exactly the same way on `<xsl:document>` as they do on `<xsl:result-document>`, which produces a final result tree.

Another way of creating temporary trees is by copying an existing document node using either of the instructions `<xsl:copy>` (which makes a shallow copy) or `<xsl:copy-of>` (which makes a deep copy). These instructions both have `validation` and `type` attributes, and when the instructions are used to copy a document node, these attributes work the same way as the corresponding attributes on the `<xsl:document>` and `<xsl:result-document>` instructions.

Validating Individual Elements

Rather than applying validation at the document level, it is possible to invoke validation of specific elements as they are constructed. This can be useful in a number of circumstances:

❏ Sometimes you do not have a schema definition for the result document as a whole, but you do have schema definitions for individual elements within it. For example, you may be creating a data file in which the contents of some elements are expected to be valid XHTML.

❏ If you are running a transformation whose purpose is to extract parts of the source document, then you may actually know that the result document as a whole is deliberately invalid—the schema for source documents may require the presence of elements or attributes, which you want to exclude from the result document, perhaps for privacy or security reasons. The fact that the result document as a whole has no schema should not stop you from validating those parts that do have one.

❏ You may be creating elements in temporary working storage (that is, in variables) that are to be copied or processed before incorporating them into a final result document. It can be useful to validate these elements in their own right, to make sure that they have the type annotations that enable them to be used as input to functions and templates that will only work on elements of a particular type.

The usual way of creating a new element node in XSLT is either by using a literal result element, or by using the `<xsl:element>` instruction.

The `<xsl:element>` instruction has attributes `validation` and `type`, which work in a very similar way to the corresponding attributes of `<xsl:result-document>` and `<xsl:document>`; however, in this case it is only element-level validation that is invoked, not document-level validation.

The same facilities are available with literal result elements. In this case, however, the attributes are named `xsl:validation` and `xsl:type`. This is to avoid any possible conflict with attributes that you want copied to the result document as attributes of the element you are creating.

For example, suppose you want to validate an address. If there is a global element declaration with the name `address`, you might write:

```
<address xsl:validation="strict">
  <number>39</number>
  <street>Lombard Street</street>
  <city>London</city>
  <postcode>EC1 3CX</postcode>
</address>
```

If this matches the schema definition of the element declaration for address, this will succeed, and the resulting element will be annotated as an address—or more strictly, as an instance of the type associated with the address element, which might be either a named type in the schema, or an anonymous type. In addition, the child elements will also have type annotations based on the way they are defined in the schema, for example the <number> element might (perhaps) be annotated as type xs:integer. If validation fails, the whole transformation is aborted.

What if there is no global element declaration for the <address> element (typically because it is defined in the schema as a local element declaration within some larger element)? You can still request validation if the element is defined in the schema to have a named type. For example, if the element is declared as:

```
<xs:element name="address" type="address-type"/>
```

then you can cause it to be validated by writing:

```
<address xsl:type="address-type">
  <number>39</number>
  <street>Lombard Street</street>
  <city>London</city>
  <postcode>EC1 3CX</postcode>
</address>
```

If neither a top-level element declaration nor a top-level type definition is available, you can't invoke validation at this level. The only thing you can do is either (a) change the schema so that some of the elements and/or types are promoted to be globally defined, or (b) invoke validation at a higher level, where a global element declaration or type definition is available.

You don't need to invoke validation at more than one level, and it may be inefficient to do so. Asking for validation of <address> in the above example will automatically invoke validation of its child elements. If you also invoked validation of the child elements by writing, say:

```
<address xsl:type="address-type">
  <number xsl:type="xs:integer">39</number>
  ...
```

then it's possible that the system would do the validation twice over. If you're lucky the optimizer will spot that this is unnecessary, but you could be incurring extra costs for no good reason.

If you ask for validation of a child element, but don't validate its parent element, then the child element will be checked for correctness, but the type annotation will probably not survive the process of tree construction. For example, suppose you write the following:

```
<address>
  <number xsl:type="xs:integer">39</number>
```

```
      <street>Lombard Street</street>
      <city>London</city>
      <postcode>EC1 3CX</postcode>
   </address>
```

Specifying the xsl:type attribute on the <number> element causes the system to check that the value of the element is numeric, and to construct an element that is annotated as an integer. The result of evaluating the sequence constructor contained in the <address> element is thus a sequence of four elements, of which the first has a type annotation of xs:integer. Evaluating the literal result element <address> creates a new <address> element, and forms children of this element from the result of evaluating the contained sequence constructor: The formal model is that the elements in this sequence are copied to form these children. The xsl:validation attribute on the <address> element determines what happens to the type annotations on these child elements. If the value is strict or lax, the type annotations on the child elements are ignored, and the type annotation in the final tree depends only on the result of validation of <address> against the schema. If the value is preserve, the type annotation on the child element is preserved, and if the value is strip, then the type annotation on the child element is replaced by xdt:untyped.

The type of an element never depends on the types of the items used to form its children. For example, suppose that the variable $i holds an integer value. Then you might suppose that the construct:

```
<xsl:element name="x">
   <xsl:sequence select="$i"/>
</xsl:element>
```

would create an element whose type annotation is xs:integer. It doesn't—the type annotation will be xs:untyped. Atomic values in the sequence produced by evaluating the sequence constructor are always (at least conceptually) converted to strings, and any type annotation in the new element is obtained by validating the resulting string values against the desired type.

> *This might not seem a very satisfactory design—why discard the type information? The working groups agonized over this question for months. The problem is that there are some cases like this one where retaining the type annotation obviously makes sense; there are many other cases, such as a sequence involving mixed content, where it obviously doesn't make sense; and there are further cases such as a sequence containing a mixture of integers and dates where it could make sense, but the definition would be very difficult. Because the working group found it difficult to devise a clear rule that separated the simple cases from the difficult or impossible ones, they eventually decided on this rather blunt rule: everything is reduced to a string before constructing the new node and validating it.*

When there is no xsl:validation or xsl:type attribute on a literal result element, the default value is taken from the default-validation attribute on the containing <xsl:stylesheet> element; and if this attribute isn't specified either, the default is taken as strip. So in this example, assuming there is no default-validation attribute, all the elements in the resulting tree will be annotated as xdt:untyped.

Note that when you use the xsl:type attribute to validate an element, the actual element name can be anything you like. There is no requirement that it should be an element name declared in the schema. It can even be an element name that is declared in the schema, but with a different type (though I can't see any justification for doing something quite so confusing, unless the types are closely related).

All the same considerations apply when creating a new element using the `<xsl:element>` or `<xsl:copy>` instruction rather than a literal result element. The only difference is that the attributes are now called `validation` and `type` instead of `xsl:validation` and `xsl:type`.

The value of the `type` or `xsl:type` attribute is always a QName, and this must always be the name of a top-level complex type or simple type defined in an imported schema. This isn't the same as the «as» attribute used in declaring the type of variables or functions. Note the following differences:

❑ If the «as» attribute is a QName, the QName must identify an atomic type. The «type» attribute is always a QName, and this may be any type defined in an imported schema: complex types are allowed as well as all three kinds of simple type, list types, union types, and atomic types.

❑ The «as» attribute can include an occurrence indicator («?», «*», or «+»). The «type» attribute never includes an occurrence indicator.

❑ The «as» attribute may define node kinds, for example «node()», «element()», or «comment()». Such constructs are never used in the «type» attribute.

This means that to create an element holding a sequence of `IDREF` values, you write:

```
<xsl:element name="ref" type="xs:IDREFS"
    select="'id001 id002 id003'"/>
```

whereas to declare a variable holding the same sequence, you write:

```
<xsl:variable name="ref" as="xs:IDREF*"
    select="xs:IDREF('id001'), xs:IDREF('id002'), xs:IDREF('id003')"/>
```

In the case of `<xsl:copy>`, note that the option «validation="preserve"» applies to the children (and attributes) of the copied element, but not to the copied element itself. This instruction does a shallow copy, so in general the content of the new element will be completely different from the content of the old one. It doesn't make sense to keep the type annotation intact if the content is changing, because this could result in the type annotation becoming inconsistent with the actual content.

By contrast, the `<xsl:copy-of>` instruction does a deep copy. Since the content remains unchanged, it's safe to keep the type annotation unchanged, and the option «validation="preserve"» is useful in achieving this. When you request validation at the element level, the system does not perform any document-level integrity checks. That is, it does not check that `ID` values are unique, or that `IDREF` values don't point into thin air, and it does not check constraints defined by `<xs:unique>`, `<xs:key>`, and `<xs:keyref>` definitions in the schema. To invoke this level of validation, you have to do it at the document level.

Validating Individual Attributes

XSLT 2.0 also allows you to request validation at the level of individual attributes. The `<xsl:attribute>` instruction, like `<xsl:element>`, has attributes `validation` and `type`, which can be used to validate an attribute node independently of its containing element.

It's relatively unusual for a schema to contain global attribute declarations, so the options «validation="strict"» and «validation="lax"» are unlikely to be very useful at the attribute level. Also, because attributes don't have children, the options «validation="strip"» and «validation="preserve"» both mean the same thing: The new attribute node will be annotated as «xdt:untypedAtomic». The most useful option for attributes is to specify «type» to validate the attribute value against a specific type definition in the schema. This will always be the name of a simple type, and in many cases it will be the name of a built-in atomic type, for example «type="xs:date"» or «type="xs:ID"». But it can also be a list or union type, for example «type="xs:IDREFS"».

If «xsl:copy» or «xsl:copy-of» is used to create attribute nodes by copying nodes from a source document, attribute-level validation can be invoked using the validation and type attributes in the same way. Unlike the situation with elements, «preserve="yes"» on either of these instructions means what it says: The attribute is copied together with its type annotation.

At the time of writing this chapter, there are gaps in the language specification concerning the validation of attributes whose type is xs:QName or xs:NOTATION. Since these types require a namespace context to perform the validation, it doesn't really make sense to validate standalone attributes that have these types.

The default-validation Attribute

The default-validation attribute on the <xsl:stylesheet> element can take one of the four values «strict», «lax», «preserve», or «strip», and it defines the default that is used on any of the instructions <xsl:attribute>, <xsl:copy>, <xsl:copy-of>, <xsl:document>, <xsl:element>, and <xsl:result-document> when neither a type nor a validation attribute is specified explicitly.

The default value for the default-validation attribute is «strip». Personally, I would be cautious about changing it to any other value for the following reasons:

❑ Changing it to «strict» will give you problems unless every element and attribute that you create is declared globally in a schema, which is unlikely.

❑ Changing it to «lax» is more likely to give acceptable results, but could lead to performance problems through excessive validation. Validation is an expensive thing to do, and should probably be requested explicitly at the point where you want it.

❑ Changing it to «preserve» may lead to rather patchy results in terms of which elements and attributes carry a type annotation, and which are left as untyped. Preserving type annotations makes most sense when you are explicitly copying data from one document to another, and it's probably best to request it explicitly on the instructions that do the copying.

But there may well be use cases I haven't thought of, and if you find yourself using the same value of the validation attribute throughout the stylesheet, then defining a default at the stylesheet module level may turn out to be a useful thing to do.

Importing Schemas

The facilities that we've been discussing in this chapter work only if schema information is available to the XSLT processor. The primary way that the processor gets this information is through the <xsl:import-schema> declaration, which can be used at the top level of any stylesheet module.

The `<xsl:import-schema>` declaration is modeled on the `<xs:import>` element within the XML Schema specification, but with some concessions to the XSLT house style (for example, the `schemaLocation` attribute in `<xs:import>` becomes `schema-location` in XSLT). Importantly, it adopts the same deliberate vagueness about exactly where the schema comes from, giving implementations the freedom to implement local schema caches or catalogs.

The most important attribute is the `namespace` attribute. This gives the target namespace of the schema being imported. If the attribute is omitted, this represents a request for a schema with no target namespace. You can only import one schema for any given namespace, plus one for the null namespace. This can create a problem if both your source document and your result document are defined by schemas with no target namespace: You won't be able to import both schemas. You can use the `<xs:redefine>` mechanism in XML Schema to map one of them (say the result schema) into a namespace, but you will then have to generate the result elements in this namespace, and perhaps apply a second transformation subsequently to get rid of the unwanted namespace.

You should import each schema that contains a type definition, element declaration, or attribute declaration that your stylesheet refers to by name. Importing a schema that in turn imports another schema isn't good enough: The only names that become available for use in your stylesheet are those defined in the schemas for the namespaces that you import explicitly. The XSLT processor is given some leeway to implicitly import schemas that aren't requested explicitly in the stylesheet. This is intended particularly for use in highly controlled environments, such as running a transformation within an XML database engine where the available schemas are all known in advance. But it's unwise to rely on this if you want your stylesheet to be portable.

The `schema-location` attribute of `<xsl:import-schema>` defines a URI where the schema can be located. This is described in the specification as a hint, which means that if the XSLT processor knows a better place to look, it is free to do so. For example, it might already have a precompiled copy of the schema held in memory. If you don't supply a `schema-location` attribute, then the schema import will work only if the XSLT processor already knows where to look. It's possible, for example, that some XSLT processors might have built-in knowledge of common schemas such as the XHTML schema, so they never need to fetch the XML source. However, if you want your stylesheet to be portable, it's probably a good idea to specify the schema location.

You don't need to import schemas into every stylesheet module individually. Importing a schema into one stylesheet module makes its definitions available in all stylesheet modules. (This is a notable difference from the equivalent facility in XQuery.)

What happens if you have two `<xsl:import-schema>` declarations for the same namespace URI (or, more probably, for the null namespace)? This can easily happen when different stylesheet modules are combined into a single stylesheet. Firstly, the system chooses the one with the highest import precedence, as explained in Chapter 3. If this leaves more than one, then they are all used. The XSLT specification explains how conflicts are resolved by reference to the XML Schema specification: It's defined to be the same as if you have two `<xs:import>` declarations for the same namespace in a schema. This is rather passing the buck, as it happens, because XML Schema leaves a lot of latitude to implementations in deciding how far they will go in analyzing two different schemas for conflicts. It's best not to do it. Since the processor is perfectly entitled to ignore the `schema-location` hint, it is also entitled to assume that if it already has a schema for a given namespace loaded, then this is the one that the user wanted.

As with validation, the XSLT specification describes the semantics of schema import by means of a rather artificial device: It defines the effect by reference to a synthetic schema document that is assembled to contain `<xs:import>` declarations representing each of the `<xsl:import-schema>` declarations in the stylesheet. The reason for this artifice is that it provides a way of invoking the rules of XML Schema and saying that they apply equally to XSLT, without actually copying the rules and repeating them, which would inevitably lead to inconsistencies. No real implementation is likely to integrate the XSLT processor and the schema processor in the clumsy manner described in the spec.

You don't need to import a schema merely because it is used to validate source documents. However, I would recommend doing so. If you don't, this creates the possibility that a source document will contain type annotations that mean nothing to the XSLT processor. There are various ways an XSLT processor can deal with this problem (no less than four possible approaches are described in the specification, one of which is to raise an error) but the simplest approach is to avoid the problem by ensuring that all the schemas used in your transformation are explicitly imported.

Using xsi:type

I haven't yet mentioned the use of `xsi:type` in this chapter (I did mention `xsl:type`, but that's a completely different thing, despite the similar name). In fact, the XSLT 2.0 specification mentions `xsi:type` only in notes and examples, which means that it plays no formal role in the XSLT language.

You can use `xsi:type` as an attribute on an element within a document that's being assessed by a schema processor. Its effect is to ask the schema processor to apply a stricter check to the element than it would otherwise. An `xsi:type` can't override the constraints defined in the schema, but it can make assertions about the document content that go beyond what the schema requires. For example, if the schema allows a particular element (by means of a union type) to contain either an integer or a QName, then specifying «`xsi:type="xs:QName"`» will cause it to be validated as if only a QName were allowed. This can also result in the element node acquiring a more specific type annotation than would otherwise be the case.

The effect of `xsi:type` on schema validation applies just as much when the validation is happening under the control of XSLT as it does in free-standing schema processing. If you write an `xsi:type` attribute to the result tree (which you can do in exactly the same way as you write any other attribute), then the element will be validated against that type definition.

Although I started by saying that `xsi:type` and `xsl:type` were quite different things, this description shows that there are cases where their effects are very similar. For example, writing:

```
<cost xsi:type="xs:decimal">23.44</cost>
```

and

```
<cost xsl:type="xs:decimal">23.44</cost>
```

can both produce a `<cost>` element validated and annotated as being of type `xs:decimal`. However, there are some important differences:

- ❑ `xsl:type` (or `type`) invokes validation as well as specifying the expected type of the element. `xsi:type` specifies the expected type, but it is ignored unless validation is requested by some other mechanism.

- ❑ The `xsi:type` attribute is copied to the result document; the `xsl:type` and `type` attributes are not.

❑ The `xsi:type` attribute can only be used to specify the type of element nodes. A `type` attribute (when it is used on the `<xsl:attribute>` instruction) can also control the type of attribute nodes.

Nillability

The `xsi:nil` attribute was defined in XML Schema because there were some people from the relational database tradition who felt that omitting an element or attribute from an XML document was not an adequate way of representing the SQL concept of null values. I have to say I find the facility completely unnecessary: Null was invented in SQL so that a cell in a table could hold no data, but XML already has perfectly good ways of representing absence of data, namely an absent element or attribute. But `xsi:nil` exists, and it can't be uninvented, and you may need to use it if it has been built in to the semantics of the vocabulary for your source or result documents.

As with `xsi:type`, the `xsi:nil` attribute is mentioned in the XSLT specification only in notes and examples. However, it gets a rather more detailed treatment in the XPath formal semantics, because it has a significant effect in complicating the rules for type matching.

You can use `xsi:nil` on an element only if the schema defines the element as nillable. If you do set «`xsi:nil="true"`» on an element, then the element is valid only if it is empty; moreover, it is allowed to be empty in this case even if the content model for the element would otherwise not permit it to be empty.

The possibility of encountering an `xsi:nil` potentially plays havoc with the type safety of your stylesheet. If you write a function that is designed to process valid book elements, and every book must have an ISBN, then the function should be allowed to access the ISBN without adding conditional logic to check that it is there. For this reason, a function or variable that accepts nilled elements has to declare that it does so. If a function parameter is declared with the type «`as="element(*, book-type)"`», then passing the element `<book xsi:nil="true"/>` to this function will cause a type error. If you want to write a function that accepts this element, you must instead write «`as="element(*, book-type?)"`» to show that your function can handle this input.

Apart from this, `xsi:nil` behaves in XSLT just like any other attribute.

You do need to be a little careful if you want to put your stylesheets through a schema processor (which you might do, for example, if you store your stylesheets in an XML database). The schema processor attaches a special meaning to attributes such as `xsi:nil`, `xsi:type`, and `xsi:schemaLocation`, even though XSLT does not. It's therefore best to avoid using these attributes directly on literal result elements. Two possible ways round this problem are:

❑ Generating these attributes using the `<xsl:attribute>` instruction instead.

❑ Using a namespace alias for the `xsi` namespace: See the description of the `<xsl:namespace-alias>` declaration in Chapter 5 (page 350).

Summary

Firstly, a reminder of something we said at the beginning of the chapter, and haven't touched on since: schema processing in XSLT 2.0 is optional. Some XSLT 2.0 processors won't support schema processing at all, and even if you are using a processor that is schema-aware, you can still use it to transform source documents that have no schema into result documents that have no schema.

We started this chapter with a very quick tour of the essentials of XML Schema, describing the main concepts of element and attribute declarations and simple and complex types, and discussing the role that they play in XSLT processing.

There are two main roles for schemas in XSLT, which are strongly related. Firstly, XML Schema provides the type system for XSLT and XPath, and as such, you can define the types of variables, functions, and templates in terms of types that are either built into XML Schema, or defined as user-defined types in a specific schema.

Secondly, you can use an XML Schema to validate your source documents, your result documents, or intermediate working data. This not only checks that your data is as you expected it, which helps debugging, but also annotates the nodes in the data model, which can be used to steer the way the nodes are processed, for example by defining template rules that match particular types of node.

The mechanism that binds a stylesheet to one or more schemas is the `<xsl:import-schema>` declaration, and we looked in some detail at the way this works.

This concludes the introductory section of this book, where I have tried to explain all the key concepts that you need to understand in order to use the language effectively.

The next four chapters form the reference section of the book: Chapter 5, in particular, contains detailed specifications of every XSLT element, arranged alphabetically. Chapter 6 describes XSLT match patterns, Chapter 7 describes the functions available in the XSLT function library as additions to the core XPath function library, and Chapter 8 is concerned with extensibility.

The final chapters of the book then step back again from the detail, to look at how the facilities of the language can be used to construct real applications. Having reached the end of this chapter, you will probably be particularly interested in Chapter 11, which describes a sample application using schema-aware XSLT stylesheets to process genealogical data, which I chose as a good example of data that goes beyond the narrow confines of the relational rows-and-columns world view.

5

XSLT Elements

This chapter provides an alphabetical list of reference entries, one for each of the XSLT elements. Each entry gives:

❑ A short description of the purpose of the element

❑ *Changes in 2.0*: A quick summary of changes to this element since XSLT 1.0

❑ *Format*: A pro forma summary of the format, defining where the element may appear in the stylesheet, what its permitted attributes are, and what its content (child elements) may be

❑ *Effect*: A definition of the formal rules defining how this element behaves

❑ *Usage*: A section giving usage advice on how to exploit this XSLT element

❑ *Examples*: Coding examples of the element, showing the context in which it might be used. (where appropriate, the *Usage* and *Examples* sections are merged into one)

❑ *See also*: Cross-references to other related constructs

The *Format* section for each element includes a syntax skeleton designed to provide a quick reminder of the names and types of the attributes and any constraints on the context. The format of this is designed to be intuitive: It only gives a summary of the rules, because you will find these in full in the *Position, Attributes,* and *Content* sections that follow.

There are a number of specialized terms used in this chapter, and it is worth becoming familiar with them before you get in too deeply. There are fuller explanations in Chapters 2 and 3, and the following descriptions are really intended just as a quick memory-jogger.

For a more comprehensive definition of terms, refer to the glossary.

Term	Description
attribute value template	An attribute whose value may contain expressions nested with curly braces, for example «url="../{$href}"». The term *template* here has nothing to do with any other kind of template in XSLT.

Continues

Term	Description
	Embedded expressions may only be used in an attribute value (or are only recognized as such) if the attribute is one that is explicitly designated as an attribute value template. Attribute value templates are described in more detail in Chapter 3, page 116
document order	An ordering of the nodes in the source tree that corresponds to the order in which the corresponding items appeared in the source XML document: An element precedes its children, and the children are ordered as they appeared in the source
expression	Many XSLT elements have attributes whose value is an *expression*. This always means an XPath expression: a full definition of XPath Expressions is given in XPath 2.0 Programmer's Reference, and a summary is given in Appendix A. An expression returns a value, which may be any sequence of items (nodes, atomic values, or a mixture of the two). These data types are described fully in Chapter 2.
Extension instructions	Any element used in a sequence: specifically, an XSLT instruction, a literal result element, or an extension element. The `<xsl:if>` element is an instruction, but `<xsl:strip-space>` isn't, because `<xsl:if>` appears in a sequence constructor and `<xsl:strip-space>` doesn't. Extension instructions are described in Chapter 3, page 105
literal result element	An element in the stylesheet, used in a *sequence constructor*, which is copied to the output document: for example (if you are generating HTML) `<p>` or `<td>`. Literal result elements are described in Chapter 3, page 106
pattern	Some XSLT elements have attributes whose value must be a pattern. The syntax of patterns is defined in Chapter 6. A pattern is a test that can be applied to nodes to see if they match. For example, the pattern «title» matches all `<title>` elements, and the Pattern «text()» matches all text nodes
lexical QName	An XML name, optionally qualified by a namespace prefix. Examples of lexical QNames with no prefix are «color» and «date-due». Examples of prefixed QNames are «xsl:choose» and «html:table». The adjective *lexical* is used to distinguish a QName in this form from a value of type xs:QName, which contains a namespace URI and a local name. Where the lexical QName has a prefix, this must always match a namespace declaration that is in scope at the place in the stylesheet where the QName is used. For more information on namespaces see Chapter 2, page 53
stylesheet	In general, references to the *stylesheet* mean the principal stylesheet module plus all the stylesheet modules incorporated into it using `<xsl:include>` and `<xsl:import>` elements. When I want to refer to one of these components individually, I call it a *stylesheet module*

Term	Description
sequence constructor	A sequence of instructions and literal result elements contained within (that is, that are children of) another XSLT element. Many XSLT elements, such as `<xsl:template>`, `<xsl:if>`, and `<xsl:variable>`, have a sequence constructor as their content.
SequenceType	A number of XSLT elements take an «as» attribute whose value is a SequenceType. This is a sequence type descriptor such as «`xs:integer*`», or «`node()?`», or «`element(part,*)`». The syntax for sequence type descriptors is outlined in Chapter 4 of this book, and is given in full in Chapter 9 of *XPath 2.0 Programmer's Reference*
template rule	An `<xsl:template>` element that has a `match` attribute
temporary tree	The value of a variable established using an `<xsl:variable>` element that contains a sequence constructor, for example `<xsl:variable>A <b>very</b> nice language</xsl:variable>`. This construct was referred to in the XSLT 1.0 specification as a *result tree fragment*. In XSLT 2.0, however, the term result tree fragment is no longer used, reflecting the fact that the restrictions on use of temporary trees have been relaxed, making them much more versatile
XSLT element	Any of the standard elements in the XSLT namespace listed in this chapter, for example `<xsl:template>` or `<xsl:if>`

The elements in this chapter are listed alphabetically rather than on functional lines, for ease of reference. This is fine when you know what you are looking for, but if you are using this book as your introduction to XSLT, it does create the problem that related things won't be found together. And if you try to read sequentially, you'll start with `<xsl:analyze-string>`, which is not one of the instructions that you are likely to use every day of the week.

So here's an attempt at some kind of ordering and grouping, to suggest which entries you might look at first if you're new to the subject:

Grouping	Elements

Elements used to define template rules and functions and control the way they are invoked	`<xsl:template>`
	`<xsl:apply-imports>`
	`<xsl:apply-templates>`
	`<xsl:call-template>`
	`<xsl:function>`
	`<xsl:next-match>`

Elements defining the structure of the stylesheet	`<xsl:stylesheet>`
	`<xsl:include>`
	`<xsl:import>`
	`<xsl:import-schema>`

Continues

Grouping	Elements

Elements used to create nodes	`<xsl:element>`
	`<xsl:attribute>`
	`<xsl:comment>`
	`<xsl:document>`
	`<xsl:namespace>`
	`<xsl:processing-instruction>`
	`<xsl:text>`
	`<xsl:value-of>`

Elements used to define variables and parameters	`<xsl:variable>`
	`<xsl:param>`
	`<xsl:with-param>`

Elements used to copy information from the source document to the result	`<xsl:copy>` `<xsl:copy-of>`

Elements used for conditional processing and iteration	`<xsl:if>`
	`<xsl:choose>`
	`<xsl:when>`
	`<xsl:otherwise>`
	`<xsl:for-each>`
	`<xsl:for-each-group>`

Elements to control sorting, searching, and numbering	`<xsl:perform-sort>`
	`<xsl:sort>`
	`<xsl:number>`
	`<xsl:key>`
	`<xsl:decimal-format>`

Elements used to control the output of the stylesheet	`<xsl:output>`
	`<xsl:result-document>`
	`<xsl:character-map>`
	`<xsl:output-character>`

This covers all the most commonly used elements; the rest can only really be classified as 'miscellaneous'.

xsl:analyze-string

The `<xsl:analyze-string>` instruction is used to process an input string using a regular expression (often abbreviated to *regex*). It is useful where the source document contains text whose structure is not fully marked up using XML elements and attributes, but has its own internal syntax: For example, the value of an attribute might be a list of numbers separated by commas.

I use the term *regex* to refer to regular expressions in this section, because it helps to avoid any confusion with XPath expressions.

Changes in 2.0

This instruction is new in XSLT 2.0.

Format

```
<xsl:analyze-string
  select = expression
  regex = { string }
  flags? = { string }>
  <!-- Content: (xsl:matching-substring?,
                 xsl:non-matching-substring?,
                 xsl:fallback*) -->
</xsl:analyze-string>
```

Position

`<xsl:analyze-string>` is an instruction, and is always used within a sequence constructor.

Attributes

Name	Value	Meaning
select mandatory	Expression	The input string to be analyzed using the regex. A type error occurs if the value of the expression cannot be converted to a string using the standard conversion rules described on page 476
regex optional	Attribute value template, returning a regular expression, as defined below	The regular expression (regex) used to analyze the string
flags optional	Attribute value template, returning regex flags, as defined below	Flags controlling how the regex is interpreted. Omitting the attribute is equivalent to supplying a zero-length string (no special flags)

The construct *expression* (meaning an XPath expression) is defined at the beginning of this chapter and more formally in Chapter 5 of *XPath 2.0 Programmer's Reference*.

The syntax of regular expressions permitted in the `regex` attribute is the same as the syntax accepted by the functions `matches()`, `replace()`, and `tokenize()` in XPath 2.0. This is described fully in Chapter 11 of *XPath 2.0 Programmer's Reference*, and is summarized below. It is based on the syntax used for regular expressions in XML Schema, with some extensions.

The `regex` attribute is an attribute value template. This makes it possible to construct the regex at runtime, using an XPath expression. For example, the regex can be supplied as a stylesheet parameter. The downside of this is that curly braces within the attribute value must be doubled if they are to be treated as part of the regex, rather than having their special meaning for attribute value templates. For example, to match a sequence of three digits, write «regex=" [0-9]{{3}} "».

The `flags` attribute controls how the regex is to be interpreted. Four flags are defined, each denoted by a single letter, and they can be written in any order. Like the `regex` attribute, `flags` may be written as an attribute value template. The flags have the following meaning:

Flag	Meaning
i	Selects case-insensitive mode. In simple terms, this means that «X» and «x» will match each other. The detailed definition is much more complex, and is specified by reference to character properties in the Unicode character database. Without this flag, characters match only if the Unicode codepoints are identical
m	Selects multiline mode. In multiline mode, the metacharacters «^» and «$» match the beginning and end of a line, while in string mode, they match the beginning and end of the entire string. (People sometimes find the name confusing: think of multiline as meaning "treat each line separately," and string as meaning "treat all the lines as a single string")
s	Selects dot-all mode (this is called single-line mode in Perl—hence the abbreviation—but this term is confusing since it suggests the opposite of multiline mode). In dot-all mode the metacharacter «.» matches any character, whereas normally it matches any character except a newline (x0A)
x	Allows whitespace to be used as an insignificant separator within the regex. Without this setting, whitespace characters in a regex are ordinary characters that represent themselves

Content

Zero or one `<xsl:matching-substring>` element

Zero or one `<xsl:non-matching-substring>` element

Zero or more `<xsl:fallback>` elements

These must appear in the order specified, if they appear at all. An XSLT 2.0 processor will ignore any `<xsl:fallback>` instructions; they are allowed so that a stylesheet can specify fallback actions to be taken by an XSLT 1.0 processor when it encounters this element, if it is working in forward-compatible mode.

The elements `<xsl:matching-substring>` and `<xsl:non-matching-substring>` take no attributes, and their content is in each case a sequence constructor.

Effect

The XPath expression given in the `select` attribute is evaluated, and provides the input string to be matched by the regex. A type error occurs if the value of this expression can't be converted to a string using the standard conversion rules described on page 476.

The regex must not be one that matches a zero-length string. This rules out values such as «regex=" "» or «regex=" [0-9]*"». The reason for this rule is that languages such as Perl have different ways of handling this situation, none of which are completely satisfactory, and which are sensitive to additional parameters such as "limit," which XSLT chose not to provide.

The input string is formed by evaluating the select expression, and the processor then analyzes this string to find all substrings that match the regex. The substrings that match the regex are processed using the instructions within the <xsl:matching-substring> element, while the intervening substrings are processed using the instructions in the <xsl:non-matching-substring> element. For example, if the regex is «[0-9]+», then any consecutive sequence of digits in the input string is passed to the <xsl:matching-substring> element, while consecutive sequences of non-digits are passed to the <xsl:non-matching-substring> element.

Within the <xsl:matching-substring> or <xsl:non-matching-substring> element, the substring in question can be referenced as the context item, using the XPath expression «.». It is also possible within the <xsl:matching-substring> element to refer to the substrings that matched particular parts of the regex: see *Captured Groups* below.

Neither a matching substring nor a nonmatching substring will ever be zero-length. This means that if two matching substrings are adjacent to each other in the input string, there will be two consecutive calls on the <xsl:matching-substring> element, with no intervening call on the <xsl:non-matching-substring> element.

Omitting either the <xsl:matching-substring> element or the <xsl:non-matching-substring> element causes the relevant substring to be discarded (no output is produced in respect of this substring). It is legal, though pointless, to omit both these elements.

In working its way through the input string, the processor always looks for the first match that it can find: That is, it looks first for a match starting at the first character of the input string, then for a match starting at the second character, and so on. There are several situations that can result in several candidate matches occurring at the same position (that is, starting with the same character in the input). The rules that apply are:

❑ The quantifiers «*» and «+» are *greedy*: They match as many characters as they can, consistent with the regular expression as a whole succeeding. For example, given the input «Here [1] or there [2]», the regex «[.*]» will match the string «[1] or there [2]».

❑ The quantifiers «*?» and «+?» are *non-greedy*: They match as few characters as they can, consistent with the regular expression as a whole succeeding. For example, given the input «Here [1] or there [2]», the regex «[.*?]» will match the strings «[1]» and «[2]».

❑ When there are two alternatives that both match at the same position in the input string, the first alternative is preferred, regardless of its length. For example, given the input «size = 5.2», the regular expression «[0-9]+|[0-9]*\.[0-9]*» will match «5» rather than «5.2».

Regular Expression Syntax

The regular expression syntax accepted in the regex attribute is the same as that accepted by the match(), tokenize(), and replace() functions, and is fully described in Chapter 11 of *XPath 2.0 Programmer's Reference*. This section provides a quick summary only; it makes no attempt to define details such as precedence rules.

In this summary, capital letters A and B represent arbitrary regular expressions. n and m represent a number (a sequence of digits). a, b, c represent an arbitrary character, which is either a normal character, or one of the metacharacters «.», «\», «?», «*», «+», «{», «}», «(», «)», «[» or «]» escaped by preceding it with a backslash «\», or one of the symbols «\n», «\r», «\t» representing a newline, carriage return, or tab respectively.

Construct	Matches a string S if...
A|B	S matches either A or B
AB	The first part of S matches A and the rest matches B
A?	S either matches A or is empty
A*	S is a sequence of zero or more strings that each match A
A+	S is a sequence of one or more strings that each match A
A{n,m}	S is a sequence of between n and m strings that each match A
A{n,}	S is a sequence of n or more strings that each match A
A{n}	S is a sequence of exactly n strings that each match A
Q?	Where Q is one of the regular expressions described in the previous six rows: matches the same strings as Q, but using nongreedy matching
(A)	S matches A
c	S consists of the single character c
[abc]	S consists of one of the characters a, b, or c
[^abc]	S consists of a single character that is not one of a, b, or c
[a-b]	S is a character whose Unicode codepoint is in the range a to b
\p{prop}	S is a character that has property prop in the Unicode database
\P{prop}	S is a character that does not have property prop in the Unicode database
.	S is any single character (in dot-all mode) or any single character other than a newline (when not in dot-all mode)
\s	S is a single space, tab, newline, or carriage return
\S	S is a character that does not match \s
\i	S is a character that can appear at the start of an XML Name
\I	S is a character that does not match \i
\c	S is a character that can appear in an XML Name
\C	S is a character that does not match \c
\d	S is a character classified in Unicode as a digit
\D	S is a character that does not match \d
\w	S is a character that does not match \W
\W	S is a character that is classified in Unicode as a punctuation, separator, or "other" character
^	Matches the start of the input string, or the start of a line if in multiline mode
$	Matches the end of the input string, or the end of a line if in multiline mode

The most useful properties that may be specified in the «\p» and «\P» constructs are described below; for a full list see Chapter 11 of *XPath 2.0 Programmer's Reference*:

Property	Meaning
L	All letters
Lu	Uppercase letters, for example, A, B, Š, Σ
Ll	Lowercase letters, for example, a, b, ñ, λ
N	All numbers
P	Punctuation (full stop, comma, semicolon, and so on)
Z	Separators (for example, space, newline, no-breaking space, en space, em space)
S	Symbols (for example, currency symbols, mathematical symbols, dingbats, and musical symbols)

Captured Groups

Within the `<xsl:matching-substring>` element, it is possible to refer to the substring that matched the regular expression as «.», because it is provided as the context item. Sometimes, however, it is useful to be able to determine the strings that matched particular parts of the regular expression.

Any subexpression of the regular expression that is enclosed in parentheses causes the string that it matches to be available as a *captured group*. For example, if the regex «([0-9]+)([A-Z]+)([0-9]+)» is used to match the string «13DEC1987», then the three captured groups will be «13», «DEC», and «1987». If the regular expression were written instead as «([0-9]+)([A-Z]+([0-9]+))», then the three captured groups would be «13», «DEC1987», and «1987». The subexpression that starts with the *n*th left parenthesis in the regular expression delivers the *n*th captured group in the result.

Some parenthesized subexpression might not match any part of the string. For example if the regex «([0-9]+)|([A-Z]+)» is used to match the string «12», the first captured subgroup will be «12» and the second will be empty.

A parenthesized expression might also match more than one substring. For example, if the regex «([0-9]+)(,[0-9]+)*» is used to match the string «12,13,14», then the second part in parentheses matches both «,13» and «,14». In this case only the last one is captured. The first captured group in this example will be «12», and the second will be «,14».

While the `<xsl:matching-substring>` element is being evaluated, the captured groups found during the regular expression match are available using the `regex-group()` function. This takes an integer argument, which is the number of the captured group that is required. If there is no corresponding subexpression in the regular expression, or if that subexpression didn't match anything, the result is a zero-length string.

Usage and Examples

There are three functions in the core function library (see *XPath 2.0 Programmer's Reference*, Chapter 10) that use regular expressions: `matches()`, `replace()`, and `tokenize()`. These are used as follows:

Function	Purpose
matches()	Tests whether a string matches a given regular expression
replace()	Replaces the parts of a string that match a given regular expression with a different string
tokenize()	Splits a string into a sequence of substrings, by finding occurrences of a separator that matches a given regular expression

There are many ways to use the XPath regex functions in an XSLT stylesheet. For example, you might write a template rule that matches customers with a customer number in the form 999-AAAA-99 (this might be the only way, for example, that you can recognize customers acquired as a result of a corporate takeover). Write this as:

```
<xsl:template
    match="customer[matches(cust-nr, '^[0-9]{3}-[A-Z]{4}-[0-9]{2}$')]">
```

There is no need to double the curly braces in this example. The match *attribute of* <xsl:template> *is not an attribute value template, so curly braces have no special significance.*

The <xsl:analyze-string> instruction is more powerful (but also more complex) than any of these three functions. In particular, none of the three XPath functions can produce new elements or other nodes. The <xsl:analyze-string> instruction can do so, which makes it very useful when you want to find a non-XML structure in the source text (for example, the comma-separated list of numbers mentioned earlier) and convert it into an XML representation (a sequence of elements, say). This is sometimes called up-conversion.

There are two main ways of using <xsl:analyze-string>, which I will describe as single-match and multiple-match applications. I shall give an example of each.

A Single-Match Example

In the single-match use of <xsl:analyze-string>, a regex is supplied that is designed to match the entire input string. The purpose is to extract and process the various parts of the string using the captured groups. This is all done within the <xsl:matching-substring> child element, which is only invoked once. The <xsl:non-matching-substring> element is used only to define error handling, to deal with the case where the input doesn't match the expected format.

For example, suppose you want to display a date as 13th March 2005. To achieve this, you need to generate the output «13th March 2005» (or rather, text nodes and element nodes corresponding to this serial XML representation). You can achieve the basic date formatting using the format-date() function described in Chapter 7, but to add the markup you need to post-process the output of this function.

Here is the code:

```
<xsl:analyze-string
            select="format-date(current-date(), '[Do] [Mn] [Y]')"
            regex="^([0-9]+)([a-z]+)(.*)$">
```

```
    <xsl:matching-substring>
        <xsl:value-of select="regex-group(1)"/>
        <sup><i><xsl:value-of select="regex-group(2)"/></i></sup>
        <xsl:value-of select="regex-group(3)"/>
    </xsl:matching-substring>
    <xsl:non-matching-substring>
        <xsl:value-of select="."/>
    </xsl:non-matching-substring>
</xsl:analyze-string>
```

Note that the regex is anchored (it starts with «^» and ends with «$») to force it to match the whole input string. Unlike regex expressions used in the pattern facet in XML Schema, a regex used in the `<xsl:analyze-string>` instruction is not implicitly anchored.

In this example I chose in the `<xsl:non-matching-substring>` to output the whole date as returned by `format-date()`, without any markup. This error might occur, for example, because the stylesheet is being run in a locale that uses an unexpected representation of ordinal numbers. The alternative would be to call `<xsl:message>` to report an error and perhaps terminate.

A Multiple-Match Example

In a multiple-match application, you supply a regular expression that will match the input string repeatedly, breaking it into a sequence of substrings. There are two main ways you can design this:

1. Match the parts of the string that you are interested in. For example, the regex «[0-9]+» will match any sequence of consecutive digits, and pass it to the `<xsl:matching-substring>` element to be processed. The characters that separate groups of digits are passed to the `<xsl:non-matching-substring>` element, if there is one (you might choose to ignore them completely).

   There is a variant of this approach that is useful where there are no separators as such. For example you might be dealing with a format such as the one used for ISO 8601 durations, which look like this: «P12H30M10S», with the requirement to split out the components «12H», «30M», and «10S». The regex «[0-9]+[A-Z]» will achieve this, passing each component to the `<xsl:matching-substring>` element in turn.

2. Match the separators between the parts of the string that you are interested in. For example, if the string uses comma as a separator, the regex «,\s*» will match any comma followed optionally by spaces. The fields that appear between the commas will be passed, one at a time, to the `<xsl:non-matching-substring>` element, while the separators (if you want to look at them at all) are passed to the `<xsl:matching-substring>` element.

The following example blends these techniques. It analyzes an XPath expression and lists all the variable names that it references. The regex chosen is one that matches things you're interested in (the variable names) but it also uses parentheses to provide access to a captured group from which the leading «$» sign is left out. It's not an industrial-quality solution to this problem, for example it doesn't try to ignore the content of comments and string literals. But it does allow for the fact that a space between the «$» sign and the variable name is permitted. You can extend it to handle these extra challenges if you like. (And if you are really keen, you can extend it to extract the namespace prefix from the variable name, and look up the corresponding namespace URI using the `get-namespace-uri-for-prefix()` function.)

```
<xsl:analyze-string select="$param" regex="\$\s*(\i\c*)"
   <xsl:matching-substring>
       <ref><xsl:value-of select="regex-group(1)"/></ref>
   </xsl:matching-substring>
</xsl:analyze-string>
```

Note in this example that a «$» sign used to represent itself must be escaped using a backslash, and that we are taking advantage of the rather specialized regex constructs «\i» and «\c» to match an XML name. The output is a sequence of <ref> elements containing the names of the referenced variables.

See Also

<xsl:matching-substring> on page 342
<xsl:non-matching-substring> on page 358
matches() in *XPath 2.0 Programmer's Reference (Chapter 10)*
replace() in *XPath 2.0 Programmer's Reference (Chapter 10)*
tokenize() in *XPath 2.0 Programmer's Reference (Chapter 10)*
regex-group() on page 580 (Chapter 7)

xsl:apply-imports

The <xsl:apply-imports> instruction is used in conjunction with imported stylesheets. A template rule in one stylesheet module can override a template rule in an imported stylesheet module. Sometimes, you want to supplement the functionality of the rule in the imported module, not to replace it entirely. <xsl:apply-imports> is provided so that the overriding template rule can invoke the overridden template rule in the imported module.

There is a clear analogy here with object-oriented programming. Writing a stylesheet module that imports another is like writing a subclass, whose methods override the methods of the superclass. <xsl:apply-imports> behaves analogously to the super() function in object-oriented programming languages, allowing the functionality of the superclass to be incorporated in the functionality of the subclass.

Changes in 2.0

In XSLT 2.0, the instruction is extended to allow parameters to be passed using enclosed <xsl:with-param> elements.

XSLT 2.0 also introduces a new <xsl:next-match> instruction, which will often be a more suitable solution in situations where <xsl:apply-imports> might have previously been used.

Format

```
<xsl:apply-imports>
   <!-- Content: xsl:with-param* -->
</xsl:apply-imports>
```

Position

<xsl:apply-imports> is an instruction, and is always used within a sequence constructor.

Attributes

None.

Content

The element may be empty, or it may contain one or more `<xsl:with-param>` elements.

Effect

`<xsl:apply-imports>` relies on the concept of a *current template rule*. A template rule becomes the current template rule when it is invoked using `<xsl:apply-templates>`, `<xsl:apply-imports>`, or `<xsl:next-match>`. Using `<xsl:call-template>` does not change the current template rule. However, using `<xsl:for-each>` makes the current template rule null, until such time as the `<xsl:for-each>` terminates, when the previous value is reinstated. The current template rule is also null while global variables and attribute sets are being evaluated.

`<xsl:apply-imports>` searches for a template rule that matches the current node, using the same search rules as `<xsl:apply-templates>`, but considering only those template rules that (a) have the same mode as the current template rule and (b) are defined in a stylesheet module that was imported into the stylesheet module containing the current template rule. For details of import precedence, see `<xsl:import>` on page 312.

The specification defines what this means in terms of the import tree. If a stylesheet module A includes another module B using `<xsl:include>`, then A and B are part of the same stylesheet level. If any module in stylesheet level L imports a module in stylesheet level M, then M is a child of L in the import tree. The template rules that are considered are those that are defined in a stylesheet level that is a descendent of the stylesheet level containing the current template rule.

It is possible to specify parameters to be supplied to the called template, using `<xsl:with-param>` elements contained within the `<xsl:apply-imports>` element. These work in the same way as parameters for `<xsl:call-template>` and `<xsl:apply-templates>`; if the name of the supplied parameter matches the name of an `<xsl:param>` element within the called template, the parameter will take that value, otherwise it will take the default value supplied in the `<xsl:param>` element. It is not an error to supply parameters that don't match any `<xsl:param>` element in the called template rule, they will simply be ignored. However, if the called template specifies any parameters with «required="yes"», then a runtime error occurs if no value is supplied for that parameter.

Usage and Examples

The intended usage pattern behind `<xsl:apply-imports>` is illustrated by the following example.

One stylesheet, `a.xsl`, contains general-purpose rules for rendering elements. For example, it might contain a general-purpose template rule for displaying dates, given as follows:

```
<xsl:template match="date">
   <xsl:value-of select="day"/>
   <xsl:text>/</xsl:text>
   <xsl:value-of select="month"/>
```

```
    <xsl:text>/</xsl:text>
    <xsl:value-of select="year"/>
</xsl:template>
```

A second stylesheet, `b.xsl`, contains special-purpose rules for rendering elements. For example, you might want it to display dates that occur in a particular context in the same way, but in bold face. It could be written as:

```
<xsl:template match="timeline/date">
    <b>
    <xsl:value-of select="day"/>
    <xsl:text>/</xsl:text>
    <xsl:value-of select="month"/>
    <xsl:text>/</xsl:text>
    <xsl:value-of select="year"/>
    </b>
</xsl:template>
```

However, this involves duplicating most of the original template rule, which is a bad idea from a maintenance point of view. So, in `b.xsl` we could import `a.xsl`, and write instead:

```
<xsl:import href="a.xsl"/>
<xsl:template match="timeline/date">
    <b>
    <xsl:apply-imports/>
    </b>
</xsl:template>
```

Note that the facility only allows a template rule to invoke one of lower *import precedence*, not one of lower *priority*. The import precedence depends on how the stylesheet module was loaded, as explained under `<xsl:import>` on page 312. The priority can be specified individually for each template rule, as explained under `<xsl:template>` on page 450. The code above will work only if the «`timeline/date`» template rule is in a stylesheet that directly or indirectly imports the «`date`» template rule. It will not work, for example, if they are in the same stylesheet but defined with different priority. In this respect, `<xsl:apply-imports>` differs from `<xsl:next-match>`.

In many situations the same effect can be achieved equally well by giving the general-purpose template rule a name, and invoking it from the special-purpose template rule by using `<xsl:call-template>` (see page 220). But this approach doesn't work if you want one rule that overrides or supplements many others. One example I encountered was a developer who had a working stylesheet, but wanted to add the rule "output an HTML `<a>` tag for any source element that has an `anchor` attribute." Rather than modifying every rule in the existing stylesheet, this can be achieved by defining a new stylesheet module that imports the original one, and contains the single rule:

```
<xsl:template match="*[@anchor]">
    <a name="{@anchor}"/>
    <xsl:apply-imports/>
</xsl:template>
```

There is a more complete example of the use of `<xsl:apply-imports>` in the section for `<xsl:import>`.

See Also

<xsl:import> on page 312
<xsl:next-match> on page 355
<xsl:param> on page 392
<xsl:with-param> on page 488

xsl:apply-templates

The <xsl:apply-templates> instruction defines a set of nodes to be processed, and causes the system to process them by selecting an appropriate template rule for each one.

Changes in 2.0

The mode attribute may now take the value «#current» to continue processing in the current mode.

Built-in template rules now pass parameters through unchanged.

Format

```
<xsl:apply-templates
  select? = expression
  mode? = token>
  <!-- Content: (xsl:sort | xsl:with-param)* -->
</xsl:apply-templates>
```

Position

<xsl:apply-templates> is an instruction, and is always used within a sequence constructor.

Attributes

Name	Value	Meaning
select optional	*Expression*	The sequence of nodes to be processed. If omitted, all children of the current node are processed
mode optional	*QName* or «#current»	The processing mode. Template rules used to process the selected nodes must have a matching mode. If omitted, the default (unnamed) mode is used. The value «#current» indicates that the current mode should be used

The constructs *Expression* and *QName* are defined at the beginning of this chapter and more formally in Chapter 5 of *XPath 2.0 Programmer's Reference*.

187

Content

Zero or more `<xsl:sort>` elements.

Zero or more `<xsl:with-param>` elements.

Effect

The `<xsl:apply-templates>` element selects a sequence of nodes in the input tree, and processes each of them individually by finding a matching template rule for that node. The sequence of nodes is determined by the `select` attribute; the order in which they are processed is determined by the `<xsl:sort>` elements (if present), and the parameters passed to the template rules are determined by the `<xsl:with-param>` elements (if present). The behavior is explained in detail in the following sections.

The select Attribute

If the `select` attribute is present, the *expression* defines the nodes that will be processed. This must be an XPath expression that returns a sequence of (zero or more) nodes. For example `<xsl:apply-templates select="*"/>` selects the set of all element nodes that are children of the current node. Writing `<xsl:apply-templates select="@width+3"/>` would cause a type error, because the value of the expression is a number, not a sequence of nodes.

The expression may select nodes relative to the context node (the node currently being processed), as in the example above. Alternatively it may make an absolute selection from the root node (for example `<xsl:apply-templates select="//item"/>`), or it may simply select the nodes by reference to a variable initialized earlier (for example `<xsl:apply-templates select="$sales-figures"/>`).

If the `select` attribute is omitted, the nodes processed will be the children of the context node: that is, the elements, text nodes, comments, and processing instructions that occur directly within the context node. It's then an error if the context item isn't a node. Text nodes that consist only of whitespace will be processed along with the others, unless they have been stripped from the tree; for details, see `<xsl:strip-space>` on page 432. In the XPath tree model (described in Chapter 2) attribute nodes and namespace nodes are *not* regarded as children of the containing element, so they are not processed: If you want to process attribute nodes, you must include an explicit `select` attribute, for example `<xsl:apply-templates select="@*"/>`. However, it is more usual to get the attribute values directly using the `<xsl:value-of>` instruction, described on page 465.

Omitting the `select` attribute has exactly the same effect as specifying the expression «`child::node()`». This selects all the nodes (elements, text nodes, comments, and processing instructions) that are children of the context node. If the context node is anything other than a root node or an element node, then it has no children, so `<xsl:apply-templates/>` does nothing, because there are no nodes to process.

For each node in the selected sequence, in turn, one template rule is selected and the sequence constructor contained in its body is evaluated. In general there may be a different template rule for each selected node. Within this sequence constructor, this node becomes the new context node, so it can be referred to using the XPath expression «`.`».

The called template can also determine the relative position of this node within the list of nodes selected for processing: Specifically, it can use the `position()` function to give the position of that node in the list of nodes being processed (the first node processed has position()=1, and so on), and the last() function to give the number of nodes in the list being processed. These two functions are described in detail in Chapter 10 of *XPath 2.0 Programmer's Reference*. They enable the called template to output sequence numbers for the nodes as they are processed, or to take different action for the first and the last nodes, or perhaps to use different background colors for odd-numbered and even-numbered nodes.

Sorting

If there are no child <xsl:sort> instructions, the selected items are processed in the order of the sequence produced by evaluating the select expression. If the select expression is a path expression, the nodes will be in *document order*. In the normal case where the nodes all come from the same input document this means they will be processed in the order they are encountered in the original source document: for example, an element node is processed before its children. Attribute nodes belonging to the same element, however, may be processed in any order, because the order of attributes in XML is not considered significant. If there are nodes from several different documents in the sequence, which can happen when you use the document() function (described in Chapter 7, page 532), the relative order of nodes from different documents is not defined, though it is consistent if the same set of nodes is processed more than once.

> *The direction of the axis used to select the nodes is irrelevant. (The direction of different axes is described in Chapter 7 of* XPath 2.0 Programmer's Reference.*) For example,* «select="preceding-sibling::*"» *will process the preceding siblings of the current node in document order (starting with the first sibling) even though the preceding-sibling axis is in reverse document order. The axis direction affects only the meaning of any positional qualifiers used within the select expression. For example,* «select="preceding-sibling::*[1]"» *will select the first preceding sibling element in the direction of the axis, which is the element immediately before the current node, if there is one.*

Although most XPath expressions return nodes in document order, not all do so. For example, the expression «title, author, publisher» returns a sequence containing first the child title elements, then the child author elements, and then the child publisher elements of the context node, regardless of the order that these nodes appear in the source document. The nodes returned by the XPath expression will be processed in the order of the sequence that is returned, not necessarily in document order.

If there are one or more <xsl:sort> instructions as children of the <xsl:apply-templates> instruction, the nodes are sorted before processing. Each <xsl:sort> instruction defines one sort key. For details of how sorting is controlled, see <xsl:sort> on page 423. If there are several sort keys defined, they apply in major-to-minor order. For example if the first <xsl:sort> defines sorting by country and the second by state, then the nodes will be processed in order of state within country. If two nodes have equal sort keys (or if the same node is included more than once in the sequence), they will be processed in the order that they appeared in the original result of the select expression.

Choosing a Template Rule

For each node to be processed, a template rule is selected. The choice of a template rule is made independently for each selected node; they may all be processed by the same template rule, or a different template rule may be chosen for each one.

The template rule selected for processing a node will always be either an <xsl:template> element with a match attribute, or a built-in template rule provided by the XSLT processor.

An <xsl:template> element will be used to process a node only if it has a matching *mode*: That is, the mode attribute of the <xsl:apply-templates> element must match the mode attribute of the <xsl:template> element. An <xsl:template> element can define a list of modes that it matches, or it can specify «#all» to indicate that it matches all modes. If the <xsl:template> element has no mode attribute, or if its mode attribute includes the keyword «#default», then the template rule matches the default mode, which is the mode that is used when <xsl:apply-templates> has no mode attribute. If the <xsl:apply-templates> instruction does have a mode attribute, then the value of the attribute must be a name that matches one of the names listed in the mode attribute of the <xsl:template> element. If the mode name contains a namespace prefix, it is the namespace URI that must match, not necessarily the prefix itself. Alternatively, the <xsl:apply-templates> instruction can specify «mode="#current"» to continue processing in the current mode. This is useful when the instruction is contained in a template rule that can be invoked in a number of different modes. The concept of the *current mode* is explained more fully in the section for <xsl:apply-imports>.

Note that if the mode attribute is omitted, it makes no difference what mode was originally used to select the template rule containing the <xsl:apply-templates> instruction. The mode is not sticky; it reverts to the default mode as soon as <xsl:apply-templates> is used with no mode attribute. If you want to continue processing in the current mode, either specify the mode explicitly, or set «mode="#current"».

An <xsl:template> element will be used to process a node only if the node matches the pattern defined in the match attribute of the <xsl:template> element.

If there is more than one <xsl:template> element that matches a selected node, one of them is selected based on its *import precedence* and *priority*, as detailed under <xsl:template> on page 450.

If there is no <xsl:template> element that matches a selected node, a built-in template rule is used. The action of the built-in template rule depends on the kind of node, as follows:

Node Kind	Action of Built-In Template Rule
Document node Element node	Call apply-templates to process each child of the selected node, using the mode specified on the call to <xsl:apply-templates>. This is done as if the contents of the template were `<xsl:apply-templates mode="#current"/>`. The parameters passed in the call of <xsl:apply-templates> are passed transparently through the built-in template to the template rules for the child elements
Text node Attribute node	Copy the string value of the node to the result sequence, as a text node. This is done as if the contents of the template were `<xsl:value-of select="string(.)">`
Comment node Processing Instruction Namespace node	No action

For the document node and for element nodes, the built-in template rule processes the children of the selected node in document order, matching each one against the available template rules as if the template body contained an explicit `<xsl:apply-templates>` element with no `select` attribute. Unlike the situation with explicit template rules, the mode *is* sticky; it is carried through automatically to the template rules that are called. So if you execute `<xsl:apply-templates mode="m"/>` for an element that has no matching template rule, the built-in template rule will execute `<xsl:apply-templates mode="m"/>` for each of its children. This process can, of course, recurse to process the grandchildren, and so on.

In XSLT 2.0, the built-in template rules not only pass on the mode they were called with, they also pass on their parameters. This is a change from XSLT 1.0.

Parameters

If there are any `<xsl:with-param>` elements present as children of the `<xsl:apply-templates>` element, they define parameters that are made available to the called template rules. The same parameters are made available to each template rule that is evaluated, even though different template rules may be invoked to process different nodes in the list.

Each `<xsl:with-param>` element is evaluated in the same way as an `<xsl:variable>` element. Specifically:

- ❑ if it has a `select` attribute, it is evaluated as an XPath expression.

- ❑ if there is no `select` attribute and the `<xsl:with-param>` element is empty, the value is a zero-length string, unless there is an `as` attribute, in which case it is an empty sequence.

- ❑ otherwise, the value of the parameter is determined by evaluating the sequence constructor contained within the `<xsl:with-param>` element. If there is an `as` attribute, this sequence forms the value of the parameter; if not, a temporary tree is constructed from this sequence, and the document node at the root of the temporary tree is passed as the value of the parameter. Tree-valued variables are described under `<xsl:variable>` on page 471.

If the `<xsl:with-param>` element has an `as` attribute, then the value of the parameter must match the type specified in this attribute, and if necessary the value is converted to this type using the standard conversion rules described on page 476. In theory it is possible for a parameter value to be converted twice, first to the type defined on the `<xsl:with-param>` element, and then to the type defined on the corresponding `<xsl:param>` element.

It is not defined whether the parameter is evaluated once only, or whether it is evaluated repeatedly, once for each node in the sequence. If the value isn't needed (for example, because the `select` expression selected no nodes, or because none of the nodes match a template that uses this parameter) then it isn't defined whether the parameter is evaluated at all. Usually this doesn't matter, because evaluating the parameter repeatedly will have exactly the same effect each time. But it's something to watch out for if the parameter is evaluated by calling an external function that has a side effect, such as reading the next record from a database.

If the name of a child `<xsl:with-param>` element matches the name of an `<xsl:param>` element in the selected template rule, then the value of the `<xsl:with-param>` element is assigned to the relevant `<xsl:param>` variable name.

If there is a child `<xsl:with-param>` element that does not match the name of any `<xsl:param>` element in the selected template rule, then it is ignored. This is not treated as an error.

If there is an `<xsl:param>` element in the selected template rule with no matching `<xsl:with-param>` element in the `<xsl:apply-templates>` element, then the parameter is given a default value: see `<xsl:param>` on page 392 for details. This is an error only if the `<xsl:param>` element specifies «required="yes"».

If the selected template rule is a built-in rule, then any parameters that are supplied are passed on to any template rules called by the built-in rule, in the same way that the mode is passed on. This is a change from XSLT 1.0. For example, consider:

```
<xsl:template match="section">
<ol>
  <xsl:apply-templates>
    <xsl:with-param name="in-section" select="true()"/>
  </xsl:apply-templates>
</ol>
</xsl:template>

<xsl:template match="clause">
  <xsl:param name="in-section" select="false()"/>
  ...
</xsl:template>
```

When a `<clause>` is contained directly within a `<section>`, the parameter `$in-section` will of course take the value «true» as expected. If there is an intervening element, with no explicit template rule, so that the `<clause>` is the grandchild of the `<section>` element, the `<clause>` template rule will still be invoked, and the parameter `$in-section` will still have the value «true». The reason is that the built-in template rule for the intermediate element calls `<xsl:apply-templates>` to process its `<clause>` children, supplying all the parameters that were supplied when it itself was invoked.

Result

The result of evaluating the `<xsl:apply-templates>` instruction is an arbitrary sequence, which may include both nodes and atomic values. This sequence is formed by concatenating the sequences produced by each of the template rules that is invoked. These sequences are concatenated in the order of the selected nodes (after any sorting), so that if the selected nodes after sorting were (A, B, C), and the template rule for node A generates the sequence T(A), then the final result sequence is (T(A), T(B), T(C)).

This doesn't mean that the XSLT processor has to process the nodes sequentially. It can process them in any order it likes, or in parallel, so long as it assembles the results in the right order at the end.

Usually, `<xsl:apply-templates>` is used to produce a sequence of nodes that become siblings in the result tree. This is what happens when `<xsl:apply-templates>`, or any other instruction, is used in the sequence constructor within an element such as an `<xsl:element>` instruction or a literal result element. But `<xsl:apply-templates>` is not confined to such uses. For example, the following code (which is written to take an XSLT stylesheet as input) uses `<xsl:apply-templates>` to decide which version of XSLT the current element belongs to:

```
<xsl:template match="*">
  <xsl:variable name="version" as="xs:decimal">
    <xsl:apply-templates select="." mode="get-version"/>
  </xsl:variable>
```

```
    <xsl:if test="version='2.0'">
       ...
    </xsl:if>
  </xsl:template>

  <xsl:template mode="get-version" as="xs:decimal"
        match="xsl:analyze-string | xsl:for-each-group |
          xsl:character-map | xsl:next-match | ...">
    <xsl:sequence select="2.0"/>
  </xsl:template>

  <xsl:template mode="get-version" as="xs:decimal" match="*">
    <xsl:sequence select="1.0"/>
  </xsl:template>
```

In this example, the result returned by <xsl:apply-templates> is a single decimal number.

Note that it's quite legitimate to use <xsl:apply-templates> within the body of a global variable definition, for example:

```
<xsl:variable name="table-of-contents">
    <xsl:apply-templates mode="toc"/>
</xsl:variable>
```

In this situation the context node is taken as the root of the principal source document, so the <xsl:apply-templates> processes the children of the root node. If the transformation is invoked without supplying a principal source document, this causes a runtime error. There will also be an error reported if a template rule that is invoked attempts to access the value of the global variable: This kind of error is referred to in the specification as a *circularity*.

Usage and Examples

First, some simple examples are given below:

Construct	Effect
`<xsl:apply-templates/>`	Processes all the children of the context node
`<xsl:apply-templates select="para"/>`	Processes all the <para> elements that are children of the context node
`<xsl:apply-templates select="//*"` `                mode="toc"/>`	Processes every element in the document in mode «toc»

`<xsl:apply-templates select="para">`
`  <xsl:with-param name="indent"`
`                select="$n+4"/>`
`</xsl:apply-templates>`
	Process all the <para> elements that are children of the context node, setting the value of the indent parameter in each called template to the value of the variable $n plus 4

`<xsl:apply-templates select="//book">`
`  <xsl:sort select="@isbn"/>`
`</xsl:apply-templates>`
	Process all the <book> elements in the document, sorting them in ascending order of their isbn attribute

The following sections give some hints and tips about using `<xsl:apply-templates>`. First I'll discuss when to use `<xsl:apply-templates>` and when to use `<xsl:for-each>`. Then I'll explain how to use modes.

`<xsl:apply-templates>` versus `<xsl:for-each>`

`<xsl:apply-templates>` is most useful when processing an element that may contain children of a variety of different types in an unpredictable sequence. This is a *rule-based* design pattern: the body of each individual template rule declares which nodes it is interested in, rather than the template rule for the parent node defining in detail how each of its children should be processed. The rule-based approach works particularly well when the document design is likely to evolve over time. As new child elements are added, template rules to process them can also be added, without changing the logic for the parent elements in which they might appear.

This style of processing is sometimes called *push* processing. It will be familiar if you have used text processing languages such as awk or Perl, but it may be unfamiliar if you are more used to procedural programming in C++ or Visual Basic.

Where the structure is more regular and predictable, it may be simpler to navigate around the document using `<xsl:for-each>`, or by accessing the required data directly using `<xsl:value-of>`. This is sometimes called *pull* processing. The `<xsl-value-of>` instruction allows you to fetch data from the XML document using an arbitrarily complex XPath expression. In this sense it is similar to a SELECT statement in SQL.

A unique strength of XSLT is the ability to mix these two styles of programming. I'll discuss both approaches, and their relative merits, in more detail in Chapter 9.

Modes

Modes are useful where the same data is to be processed more than once.

A classic example is when building a table of contents. The main body of the output can be produced by processing the nodes in default mode, while the table of contents is produced by processing the same nodes with «mode="TOC"».

The following example does something very similar to this: it displays a scene from a play, adding at the start of the page a list of the characters who appear in this scene:

Example: Using Modes

This example uses a mode to create a list of characters appearing in a scene of a play.

Source

The source file, `scene.xml`, contains a scene from a play (specifically, Act I Scene 1 of Shakespeare's *Othello*—marked up in XML by Jon Bosak).

It starts like this:

```
<?xml version="1.0"?>
<SCENE><TITLE>SCENE I. Venice. A street.</TITLE>
<STAGEDIR>Enter RODERIGO and IAGO</STAGEDIR>
```

```
<SPEECH>
<SPEAKER>RODERIGO</SPEAKER>
<LINE>Tush! never tell me; I take it much unkindly</LINE>
<LINE>That thou, Iago, who hast had my purse</LINE>
<LINE>As if the strings were thine, shouldst know of this.</LINE>
</SPEECH>


<SPEECH>
<SPEAKER>IAGO</SPEAKER>
<LINE>'Sblood, but you will not hear me:</LINE>
<LINE>If ever I did dream of such a matter, Abhor me.</LINE>
</SPEECH>
etc.
</SCENE>
```

Stylesheet

The stylesheet `scene.xsl` is designed to display this scene in HTML. This is how it starts:

```
<xsl:transform
    xmlns:xsl="http://www.w3.org/1999/XSL/Transform"
    version="2.0">

<xsl:template match="SCENE">
<html><body>
   <xsl:apply-templates select="TITLE"/>

   <xsl:variable name="speakers" as="element()*">
     <xsl:for-each-group select="//SPEAKER" group-by=".">
       <xsl:sequence select="current-group()[1]"/>
     </xsl:for-each-group>
   </xsl:variable>

   <h2>Cast: <xsl:apply-templates select="$speakers"
                                  mode="cast-list"/></h2>
   <xsl:apply-templates select="* except TITLE"/>
</body></html>
</xsl:template>
```

The template rule shown above matches the <SCENE> element. It first displays the <TITLE> element (if there is one) using the appropriate template rule. Then it sets up a variable called «speakers» to be a sequence containing all the distinct <SPEAKER> elements that appear in the document. This is constructed by grouping all the <SPEAKER> elements using the <xsl:for-each-group> instruction, and then taking the first one in each group. The result is a list of the speakers in which each one appears once only.

The template rule then calls <xsl:apply-templates> to process this set of speakers in mode «cast-list» (a nice side effect is that they will be listed in order of appearance). Finally it calls <xsl:apply-templates> again, this time in the default mode, to process all elements («*») except <TITLE> elements (because the title has already been processed).

The stylesheet carries on as follows:

```
<xsl:template match="SPEAKER" mode="cast-list">
    <xsl:value-of select="."/>
    <xsl:if test="not(position()=last())">, </xsl:if>
</xsl:template>
```

This template rule defines how the <SPEAKER> element should be processed when it is being processed in «cast-list» mode. The sequence constructor has the effect of outputting the speaker's name, followed by a comma if it is not the last speaker in the list.

Finally the remaining template rules define how each element should be output, when processed in default mode:

```
<xsl:template match="TITLE">
<h1><xsl:apply-templates/></h1>
</xsl:template>

<xsl:template match="STAGEDIR">
<i><xsl:apply-templates/></i>
</xsl:template>

<xsl:template match="SPEECH">
<p><xsl:apply-templates/></p>
</xsl:template>

<xsl:template match="SPEAKER">
<b><xsl:apply-templates/></b><br/>
</xsl:template>

<xsl:template match="LINE">
<xsl:apply-templates/><br/>
</xsl:template>
</xsl:transform>
```

Output

The precise layout of the HTML depends on which XSLT processor you are using, but apart from layout details it should start like this:

```
<html>
    <body>
        <h1>SCENE I. Venice. A street.</h1>
        <h2>Cast: RODERIGO, IAGO, BRABANTIO</h2>
        <i>Enter RODERIGO and IAGO</i>
        <p>
            <b>RODERIGO</b><br>
            Tush! never tell me; I take it much unkindly<br>
            That thou, Iago, who hast had my purse<br>
            As if the strings were thine, shouldst know of this.<br>
        </p>
```

```
        <p>
            <b>IAGO</b><br>
            'Sblood, but you will not hear me:<br>
            If ever I did dream of such a matter, Abhor me.<br>
        </p>
        ...
    </body>
</html>
```

It is sometimes useful to use named modes, even where they are not strictly necessary, to document more clearly the relationship between calling templates and called templates, and to constrain the selection of template rules rather more visibly than can be achieved by relying on template rule priorities. This might even improve performance by reducing the number of rules to be considered, though the effect is likely to be marginal.

For example, suppose that a <poem> consists of a number of <stanza> elements, and that the first <stanza> is to be output using a different style from the rest. The orthodox way to achieve this would be as follows:

```
<xsl:template match="poem">
...
    <xsl:apply-templates select="stanza"/>
...
</xsl:template>
<xsl:template match="stanza[1]">
...
</xsl:template>
<xsl:template match="stanza">
...
</xsl:template>
```

This relies on the default priority rules to ensure that the correct template rule is applied to each stanza—as explained in Chapter 6, the default priority for the pattern «stanza[1]» is higher than the default priority for «stanza».

Another way of doing this, perhaps less orthodox but equally effective, is as follows:

```
<xsl:template match="poem">
...
    <xsl:apply-templates select="stanza[1]" mode="first"/>
    <xsl:apply-templates select="stanza[position()>1]" mode="rest"/>
...
</xsl:template>

<xsl:template match="stanza" mode="first">
...
</xsl:template>

<xsl:template match="stanza" mode="rest">
...
</xsl:template>
```

Another solution, giving even finer control, would be to use `<xsl:for-each>` and `<xsl:call-template>` to control precisely which template rules are applied to which nodes, avoiding the pattern-matching mechanisms of `<xsl:apply-templates>` altogether.

Which you choose is largely a matter of personal style, and it is very hard to argue that one is better than the other in all cases. However, if you find that the match patterns used in defining a template rule are becoming extremely complex and context dependent, then you probably have both a performance and a maintenance problem on your hands, and controlling the selection of template rules in the calling code, by using modes or by calling templates by name, may well be the answer.

Simulating Higher Order Functions

In functional programming languages, a very useful programming technique is to write a function that accepts another function as an argument. This is known as a higher order function. For example, you might write a function that does a depth-first traversal of a tree, and processes each node in the tree using a function that is supplied as an argument. This makes it possible to use one tree-walking routine to achieve many different effects.

In XSLT (and XPath), functions are not first-class objects, so they cannot be passed as arguments to other functions. The same is true of templates. However, the template-matching capability of `<xsl:apply-templates>` can be used to simulate higher order functions.

This use of `<xsl:apply-templates>` has been developed to a fine art by Dimitre Novatchev in his FXSL library (`http://fxsl.sourceforge.net/`), which provides many examples of the technique.

A simple example of a higher order function found in many functional programming languages is the `fold` function. Given as an argument a function that adds two numbers, `fold` will find the sum of all the numbers in a sequence. Given a function that multiplies two numbers, it will find the product of the numbers in the sequence. In fact `fold` takes three arguments: the sequence to be processed, the function to process two values, and the initial value. It turns out that the `fold` function can be used, with suitable arguments, to perform a wide variety of aggregation functions on sequences.

The key to the technique is that although you cannot pass a function or template as an argument to another function or template, you can pass a node, and can use `<xsl:apply-templates>` to trigger execution of a template associated with that node.

Rather than show you how `fold` works, which you can find out on the FXSL Web site, I will use another example that makes greater use of the new capabilities in XSLT 2.0. A common problem is to check whether there are cycles in your data. For example, your data might represent a part explosion, and you want to check that no part is a component of itself, directly or indirectly. Or you might be checking an XSLT stylesheet to check that no attribute set is defined in terms of itself. (There is an example that shows how to do this conventionally, without a higher order function, under `<xsl:function>` on page 307.) The problem is that there are many ways one can represent a relationship between two nodes in XML, and we don't want to have to write a new function to check for cycles each time we come across a new way of representing a relationship. So we write a general higher order function that looks for cycles, and pass it as a parameter, a function (actually represented by a node that will trigger a template rule) that knows how a particular relationship is represented.

Example: Checking for Cycles in a Graph

This example provides a generic procedure to look for cycles in a graph, and then applies this procedure to a data file to see if the ID/IDREF links are cyclic.

The algorithm to check for a cycle is this. Given a function `links(A)` that returns the set of nodes to which A is directly linked, the function `refers(A,B)` is true if `links(A)` includes B (that is, if there is a direct reference) or if there is a node C in the result of `links(A)` such that `refers(C,B)` is true (this is an indirect reference via C). This is a recursive definition, of course, and it is implemented by a recursive function. Finally, you know that A participates in a cycle if `refers(A,A)` is true.

Stylesheet

The stylesheet that searches for cycles in a graph is in `cycle.xsl`.

You can implement the `refers` function like this:

```
<xsl:function name="graph:refers" as="xs:boolean">
   <xsl:param name="links" as="node()"/>
   <!-- $links is a node that represents the template to be called -->
   <xsl:param name="A" as="node()"/>
   <xsl:param name="B" as="node()"/>

   <!-- find the directly-connected nodes -->
   <xsl:variable name="direct" as="node()*">
      <xsl:apply-templates select="$links">
         <xsl:with-param name="from" select="$A"/>
      </xsl:apply-templates>
   </xsl:variable>

   <!-- return true if B is directly or indirectly connected from A -->
   <xsl:sequence select="if (exists($direct intersect $B)) then true()
                    else if (some $C in $direct
                                 satisfies graph:refers($links, $C, $B))
                          then true()
                          else false()"/>
</xsl:function>
```

When you call this higher order function, you need to supply a node as the `$links` argument that will always cause a particular template rule to be invoked. Let's do this for the case where the link is established by virtue of the fact that the first node contains an `idref` attribute whose value matches the `id` attribute of the node that it references. This is in `idref-cycle.xsl`:

```
<xsl:variable name="graph:idref-links" as="element()">
     <graph:idref-link/>
</xsl:variable>
```

```
<xsl:template match="graph:idref-link" as="node()*">
  <xsl:param name="from" required="yes" as="node()"/>
  <xsl:sequence select="$from/id($from/@idref)"/>
</xsl:template>
```

And now you can test whether the context node participates in a cycle like this:

```
<xsl:template name="check-context-node">
  <xsl:if test="graph:refers($graph:idref-links, ., .)">
    <xsl:message terminate="yes">Cycle detected!</xsl:message>
  </xsl:if>
</xsl:template>
```

Let's look at the details of how this works:

The higher order function is implemented using <xsl:function>. It can't actually take a function or a template as a parameter, so what it takes instead is a node, which uniquely identifies the specific code to be executed to follow a link.

The code to follow a link is implemented as a template rule, and is invoked using <xsl:apply-templates>. An element is created (<graph:idref-link>) whose sole purpose is to trigger the execution of the associated template rule. Note that because of the «as="element()"» attribute on the <xsl:variable> element, the variable holds a single (parentless) element node, not a temporary tree.

Unlike conventional template rules that create new nodes, this particular rule returns a reference to a sequence of existing nodes: specifically, the nodes selected by the select attribute of the <xsl:sequence> instruction. The result of the <xsl:apply-templates> instruction is also captured in a variable with an as attribute, which means that the result of the variable is the sequence of nodes returned by the template. Without the as attribute, the nodes would be copied to make a temporary tree, which wouldn't work, because the XPath intersect operator relies on the nodes in the variable $direct having their original identity (used in the way it is used here, it tests whether $B is one of the nodes in $direct).

The important thing about this stylesheet is that the module cycle.xsl is completely general-purpose: it has no knowledge of how the links between nodes are represented, and can therefore be used to look for cycles in any graph, however it is implemented.

Source

Two source files are supplied: acyclic-data.xml and cyclic-data.xml. Here is the one containing a cycle:

```
<!DOCTYPE parts [
  <!ATTLIST part id ID #REQUIRED>
]>
<parts>
  <part id="p10" idref="p20"/>
  <part id="p20" idref="p30 p40"/>
  <part id="p30"/>
  <part id="p40" idref="p10"/>
</parts>
```

Output

> Running the stylesheet `idref-cycle.xsl` against the source file `cyclic-data.xml` simply produces an error message saying that the data contains a cycle.

Higher order functions such as this are a powerful programming technique, particularly when handling complex data structures.

See Also

`<xsl:for-each>` on page 276
`<xsl:function>` on page 300
`<xsl:sequence>` on page 420
`<xsl:sort>` on page 423
`<xsl:template>` on page 450
`<xsl:with-param>` on page 488

xsl:attribute

The `<xsl:attribute>` instruction constructs an attribute node and adds it to the result sequence.

Changes in 2.0

The content of the attribute can be specified using a `select` attribute, as an alternative to using a sequence constructor. The `separator` attribute can be used to format the attribute value when the content is supplied as a sequence.

With a schema-aware XSLT processor, the `type` and `validation` attributes can be used to control the type annotation given to the new attribute node.

Format

```
<xsl:attribute
  name = { qname }
  namespace? = { uri-reference }
  select? = expression
  separator? = { string }
  validation? = "strict" | "lax" | "preserve" | "strip"
  type? = qname>
  <!-- Content: sequence-constructor -->
</xsl:attribute>
```

Position

`<xsl:attribute>` may be used either as an instruction within a *sequence constructor*, or within an `<xsl:attribute-set>` element.

Attributes

Name	Value	Meaning
name mandatory	Attribute value template returning a lexical QName	The name of the attribute node to be generated
namespace optional	Attribute value template returning a URI	The namespace URI of the generated attribute node
select optional	Expression	Provides the value of the attribute
separator optional	Attribute value template returning a string	Separator string to be inserted between items when the value is a sequence
validation optional	«strict», «lax», «preserve», or «skip»	Indicates whether and how the attribute should be subjected to schema validation
type optional	lexical QName	Identifies a type declaration (either a built-in type, or a user-defined type imported from a schema) against which the new element is to be validated

The `type` and `validation` attributes are mutually exclusive: If one is present, the other must be absent.

Content

A sequence constructor.

Effect

The effect of this instruction is to create a new attribute node, and to return this node as the result of the instruction. In some error cases, the results may be different: These situations are described below.

In the usual case where the sequence constructor containing the `<xsl:attribute>` instruction is used to construct the content of an element, the attribute must not be preceded in the result sequence by any node other than a namespace node or another attribute node. The processor can either treat this as a fatal error, or discard the attribute node.

The name of the generated attribute node is determined using the `name` and `namespace` attributes. The way in which these attributes are used is described below in the section *The Name of the Attribute*.

The value of the new attribute node may be established either using the `select` attribute, or using the sequence constructor contained in the `<xsl:attribute>` instruction. These are mutually exclusive: If the `select` attribute is present, the `<xsl:attribute>` element must be empty. If neither is present, the value of the attribute will be a zero-length string. The way the value of the attribute is established is described in more detail in the section *The Value of the Attribute*.

When a schema-aware XSLT processor is used, the new attribute may be validated to ensure that it conforms to a type defined in a schema. This process results in the new attribute node having a type annotation. The type annotation affects the behavior of subsequent operations on this attribute node even though it is not visible when the result tree is serialized as raw XML. The validation and annotation of the new attribute node are controlled using the `type` and `validation` attributes. This is described in the section *Validating and Annotating the Attribute*.

The Name of the Attribute

The name of an attribute node has two parts: the local name and the namespace URI. These are controlled using the `name` and the `namespace` attributes.

Both the `name` and the `namespace` attributes may be given as attribute value templates; that is, they may contain expressions nested within curly braces. One of the main reasons for using the `<xsl:attribute>` instruction in preference to attributes on a literal result element (described in the section *Literal Result Elements* in Chapter 3, page 106) is that `<xsl:attribute>` allows the name of the attribute node to be decided at runtime, and this is achieved by using attribute value templates in these two attributes.

The result of expanding the `name` attribute value template must be a lexical QName; that is, a valid XML name with an optional namespace prefix, for example, «code» or «xsi:type». If there is a prefix, it must correspond to a namespace declaration that is in scope at this point in the stylesheet, unless there is also a `namespace` attribute, in which case it is taken as referring to that namespace.

If the name is not a valid QName, the XSLT processor can either report the error, or ignore it and continue processing. If the error is ignored, the `<xsl:attribute>` instruction returns an empty sequence.

The local part of the name of the created attribute node will always be the same as the local part of the QName supplied as the value of the `name` attribute.

If the `<xsl:attribute>` instruction has a `namespace` attribute, it is evaluated (expanding the attribute value template if necessary) to determine the namespace URI part of the name of the created attribute node:

❑ If the value is a zero-length string, the attribute will have a null namespace URI. It will therefore be serialized without a prefix. Any prefix in the value of the `name` attribute will be ignored.

❑ Otherwise, the value should be a URI identifying a namespace. This namespace will be used as the namespace URI of the new attribute node. The namespace URI associated with any prefix in the QName obtained from the name attribute will then be ignored (though it must still be valid). This namespace does not need to be in scope at this point in the stylesheet, in fact it usually won't be. The system does not check that the value conforms to any particular URI syntax, so in effect any string can be used.

If there is no `namespace` attribute:

❑ If the supplied QName includes a prefix, the prefix must be a namespace prefix that is in scope at this point in the stylesheet: In other words, there must be an `xmlns:prefix` declaration either on the `<xsl:attribute>` instruction itself or on some containing element. The namespace URI in the output will be that of the namespace associated with this prefix in the stylesheet.

❑ Otherwise, the attribute will have a null namespace URI. The default namespace is *not* used.

Attribute nodes, according to the formal data model, do not contain a namespace prefix, only a namespace URI and a local name. The only way to establish a prefix is to look at the namespace nodes for the element node that is the parent of this attribute, to find one that binds a prefix to the namespace URI of this attribute. These namespace nodes are created by virtue of the namespace fixup process that occurs whenever an element node is created: For a description of this process, see page 265.

Namespace fixup is not performed at the level of an individual attribute node. This is because attributes can only be associated with namespace nodes via their parent element. In consequence, if you call the `name()` function on an attribute node that has not yet been attached to an element, any prefix in the returned name will be meaningless. It's better to use the `node-name()` function instead: This returns an `xs:QName` value that can be properly compared with other `xs:QName` values, without relying on unpredictable namespace prefixes.

In principle, XSLT processors can choose any prefix they like when generating namespace nodes during the namespace fixup process. (Choosing a prefix in this discussion also includes the option of using the empty prefix, which is how the data model represents the default namespace.) In practice, processors will usually be able to make a sensible choice, resulting in prefixes that are recognizable to users, rather than random alphanumeric noise. For example, if the lexical QName used as the value of the name attribute of `<xsl:attribute>` includes a prefix, then most processors will choose this prefix during the namespace fixup process. Occasionally a processor might choose a different prefix:

❑ There might be another prefix available that is just as good. For example, if two attributes on the same element use the same namespace URI, then it makes sense to give both the same prefix.

❑ The preferred prefix might already be in use to refer to a different namespace URI. For example, two `<xsl:attribute>` instructions can create attributes for the same element that are in different namespaces, and in this case they must also have different prefixes. Conflicts are unlikely to happen, but when they do, the system has to invent an arbitrary prefix such as «ns0001».

❑ Some prefixes, notably «xml» and «xmlns» are reserved.

If the name attribute provides a name that has no prefix, but a `namespace` attribute is present so that the namespace URI is not null, then the system has no choice but to invent a namespace prefix for the attribute. For example, if you write:

```
<table>
<xsl:attribute name="width" namespace="http://acme.org/">
    <xsl:text>200</xsl:text>
</xsl:attribute>
</table>
```

then the output might be

```
<table ns0001:width="200" xmlns:ns0001="http://acme.org"/>
```

The XSLT specification explicitly states that you cannot use `<xsl:attribute>` to generate namespace declarations by giving an attribute name of «xmlns» or «xmlns:*». In the XPath data model, attributes and namespaces are quite different animals, and you cannot simulate a namespace declaration by creating an attribute node with a special name. Namespace declarations will be added to the output automatically whenever you generate elements or attributes that require them, and if you really need to, you can also force them to be generated using the `<xsl:namespace>` instruction.

The new attribute, when initially created, has no parent node. Usually, however, the result of the instruction will form part of a sequence that is used to construct the content of a new element node. This will always be the case when the parent of the `<xsl:attribute>` instruction is an `<xsl:element>` or `<xsl:copy>` instruction, or a literal result element, and it will also be the case when the `<xsl:attribute>` is contained in an `<xsl:attribute-set>`.

Very often the `<xsl:attribute>` instruction will be contained directly in the instruction that writes the element, for example:

```
<table>
    <xsl:attribute name="border">2</xsl:attribute>
</table>
```

but this is not essential, for example you could also do:

```
<table>
    <xsl:call-template name="set-border"/>
</table>
```

and then create the attribute from within the «set-border» template. Less commonly, parentless attribute nodes may be created and held in variables, for example:

```
<xsl:variable name="three-atts" as="attribute()*">
   <xsl:attribute name="color">red</xsl:attribute>
   <xsl:attribute name="color">green</xsl:attribute>
   <xsl:attribute name="color">blue</xsl:attribute>
</xsl:variable>
```

In this particular case, just to show what is possible, we have created a variable whose value is a sequence of three parentless attributes, each of which has the same attribute name. These attributes could later be added to elements using instructions such as:

```
<table>
    <xsl:copy-of select="$three-atts[2]"/>
</table>
```

Whether the attribute node is added immediately to an element, or whether it is perhaps stored in a variable and added to an element later, at the point where the attribute is attached to an element, it must appear in the sequence before any child nodes (text nodes, elements, comments, or processing instructions) that are being added to the same element node.

This rule is there for the convenience of implementors. It means that the XSLT processor can execute the stylesheet and build the result tree sequentially, if it wishes. If it does so, the attributes for an element will always be evaluated before the children of the element, which means that the processor doesn't actually need to build the result tree in memory. Instead, each node can be serialized to an XML file as soon as it is generated. If it weren't for this rule, the software wouldn't be able to write the first start tag until right at the end, because there would always be a chance of an attribute being added to it.

When a sequence of nodes containing several attribute nodes is used to form the content of an element, and several of the attributes have the same name, the one that is used is the one that appears last in the sequence. This is not an error: In fact, when named attribute sets are used to add attributes to an output element, it is an important mechanism. Named attribute sets are described under `<xsl:attribute-set>` on page 214.

XQuery does this differently. In XQuery 1.0, adding two attributes with the same name to the same element is an error.

The Value of the Attribute

The string value of the new attribute node is obtained by evaluating the `select` attribute or the sequence constructor. The value of the `separator` attribute, if present, also plays a role.

Whether the `select` attribute or the sequence constructor is used, it is evaluated to produce a sequence of items, and this sequence of items is processed as follows:

1. The sequence is atomized. Atomization is described in Chapter 2 (page 73). This process replaces any nodes in the sequence by their typed values.

2. Every value in the atomized sequence is converted to a string by applying the XPath casting rules. An error may occur if there are values that cannot be converted to strings (specifically, `xs:NOTATION` or `xs:QName` values).

3. The strings in the resulting sequence are concatenated, with an optional separator between adjacent strings. If the `separator` attribute is present, its value is used as the separator (this may be a zero-length string). If the `select` attribute is used, then the default separator is a single space; otherwise, it is a zero-length string—in other words, there is no separator.

4. The resulting string is used as the value of the new attribute node.

The following examples illustrate the effect:

Instruction	Result
`<xsl:attribute name="x"` `              select="1 to 5"/>`	`x="1 2 3 4 5"`

`<xsl:attribute name="x">`
`  <xsl:sequence select="1 to 5"/>`
`</xsl:attribute>`
	`x="12345"`

`<xsl:attribute name="x"`
`          select="1 to 5"`
`          separator=","/>`
	`x="1,2,3,4,5"`

`<xsl:attribute name="x"`
`              separator="-">`
`  <xsl:sequence select="1 to 5"/>`
`</xsl:attribute>`
	`x="1-2-3-4-5"`

In XSLT 1.0, it was an error if the evaluating the content of an attribute produced a node other than a text node. Processors were allowed to recover by ignoring such nodes. In XSLT 2.0, any kind of node is allowed, and is handled by the atomization process. If your stylesheet contains this error, and your XSLT 1.0 processor chose to ignore it, then it will produce different results under XSLT 2.0.

Validating and Annotating the Attribute

This section is relevant only if you are using a schema-aware XSLT processor. With a non–schema-aware processor, you cannot use the `type` and `validation` attributes, and the type annotation on the new attribute node will always be `xdt:untypedAtomic`, which you can effectively ignore because it imposes no constraints.

With a schema-aware processor, you can validate the new attribute to ensure that it conforms to relevant definitions in a schema. If validation fails, a fatal error is reported. If it succeeds, the new attribute node will have a type annotation that reflects the validation that was performed. This type annotation will not affect the way the attribute node is serialized, but if you want to do further processing on the attribute, the type annotation may affect the way this works. For example, if you sort a sequence of attributes annotated with type `xs:integer`, you will get different results than if they are annotated as `xs:string`.

If you use the `type` attribute, the value of the attribute must be a lexical QName that identifies a known type definition. Generally this means that it must either be a built-in type such as `xs:string` or `xs:dateTime`, or it must be the name of a global simple type defined in a schema that has been imported using an `<xsl:import-schema>` declaration in the stylesheet. (That is, the local part of the QName must match the `name` attribute of a top-level `<xs:simpleType>` element in the schema for the namespace that matches the namespace URI part of the QName.)

> *The XSLT specification allows the implementation to provide other ways of accessing type definitions, perhaps through an API or configuration file, and it also allows the type definition to originate from a source other than an XML Schema, but since it provides no details of how this might work, we won't explore the possibility further.*

The processor validates that the value of the new attribute node conforms to the named type definition. If it does, the attribute is annotated with the name of this type. If it doesn't, processing fails.

Validating an attribute using the `type` attribute places no constraints on the name of the attribute. It doesn't need to be an attribute name that is defined in any schema, and it does not matter whether or not the attribute name is in a namespace. The validation is concerned with the content of the attribute and not with its name.

In contrast, validation using the `validation` attribute is driven by the attribute's name.

For symmetry with other instructions, the `validation` attribute has four possible values: «preserve», «strip», «strict», and «lax». However, in the case of `<xsl:attribute>`, «preserve» and «strip» have exactly the same effect: No validation takes place, and the type annotation on the attribute node will be `xdt:untypedAtomic`. Let's focus on the other two options.

❑ «validation="strict"» causes the processor to look for an attribute declaration that matches the name of the attribute. That is, it looks for a top-level `<xs:attribute>` whose `name` attribute matches the local name of the attribute being validated, in a schema whose namespace matches the namespace URI of the attribute being validated. If it can't find such a definition, a fatal error is reported. Otherwise, the value of the attribute node is validated against the schema-defined rules implied by this attribute declaration. Note that global attribute declarations are used only for namespace-qualified attribute names, so this facility has rather limited use.

❑ If the attribute declaration in the schema refers to a named type definition, then on successful validation, the attribute is annotated with this type name. If the attribute declaration contains an inline (and therefore unnamed) type definition, the XSLT processor invents a name for this implicit type, and uses this invented name as the type annotation, just as in the case described earlier for the `type` attribute.

❑ «`validation="lax"`» behaves in the same way as «`validation="strict"`», except that no failure occurs if the processor cannot locate a top-level schema definition for the attribute. Instead of reporting an error, the attribute is annotated as `xdt:untypedAtomic`.

If neither the `type` nor `validation` attribute is present, then the system behaves as if the `validation` attribute were present, and had the value given by the `default-validation` attribute of the containing `<xsl:stylesheet>` element. If no default is specified, the effect is the same as «`validation="strip"`».

XSLT does not provide any way of requesting validation of an attribute against a local attribute or type definition in a schema. The way around this is to request validation only when you create an element for which there is a top-level definition in the schema. This will then implicitly validate the whole subtree contained by that element, including elements and attributes that have local definitions in the schema.

Usage

You will sometimes see stylesheets that use the `<xsl:attribute>` instruction whenever they need to output an attribute value. However, in XSLT there are several different ways of generating an attribute in the result tree. This section compares the different approaches. It then looks specifically at the problem of creating an attribute whose value is a QName, such as an «`xsi:type`» attribute.

Different Ways of Creating Attributes

Where an output element is generated using a literal result element, the simplest way to specify attributes is normally to include them as attributes on the literal result element itself. You can do this even when the value is derived from information in the source document, because the value can be generated using an attribute value template, for example:

```
<body bgcolor="#{@red}{@green}{@blue}">
```

This concatenates three attributes of the current node in the source tree to create a single attribute in the result tree. Attribute value templates are described in Chapter 3, page 116.

Using `<xsl:attribute>` gives you more control than writing the attribute directly using attribute value templates. It is useful where one of the following conditions applies:

❑ The parent element is output using `<xsl:element>` or `<xsl:copy>` (rather than a literal result element).

❑ There is conditional logic to decide whether to output the attribute or not.

❑ The name of the attribute is computed at runtime.

❑ There is complex logic to calculate the value of the attribute.

❑ The attribute is one of a set that can conveniently be grouped together using `<xsl:attribute-set>`.

❑ The output attribute belongs to a namespace that is not present in the source document or the stylesheet.

A third way to output attributes is to copy them from the source tree to the result tree by using `<xsl:copy>` or `<xsl:copy-of>`. This works only if the attribute you want to generate has the same name and same value as an attribute in the source.

`<xsl:copy>` can be used when the context node in the source document is an attribute node. It's not necessary that the owning element was output using `<xsl:copy>`, for example the following code ensures that the `width`, `height`, and `depth` attributes of the source `<parcel>` element are copied to the output `<package>` element, but its `value` and `owner` attributes are discarded:

```
<xsl:template match="parcel">
<package>
    <xsl:apply-templates select="@*"/>
</package>
</xsl:template>

<xsl:template match="parcel/@width | parcel/@height | parcel/@depth">
    <xsl:copy/>
</xsl:template>

<xsl:template match="parcel/@value | parcel/@owner"/>
```

This example uses `<xsl:apply-templates>` to process all the attributes of the `<parcel>` element. Some of these match one template rule, which copies the attribute to the output element, while others match an empty template rule that does nothing.

The same effect could be achieved more easily with `<xsl:copy-of>`, as follows:

```
<xsl:template match="parcel">
<package>
    <xsl:copy-of select="@width, @height, @depth"/>
</package>
</xsl:template>
```

The `select` expression here selects a sequence containing all the `width`, `height`, and `depth` attributes of the context node, and the `<xsl:copy-of>` instruction copies this sequence. The «, » operator, described in *XPath 2.0 Programmer's Reference*, concatenates two sequences (or in this case, two nodes) to form a single sequence.

If you want to copy all attributes of the current node to the result tree, the simplest way to achieve this is `<xsl:copy-of select="@*"/>`. If you want to copy all the attributes except certain particular ones, you can use the XPath 2.0 «except» operator:

```
<xsl:copy-of select=@* except (@value, @owner)"/>
```

Finally, if you want to add a bundle of commonly used attributes to an element, a convenient mechanism is available in the form of attribute sets. These can be defined using an `<xsl:attribute-set>` declaration, described on page 214.

Creating an Attribute whose Value is a QName

XML Schema allows an attribute to have a value whose type is xs:QName. A typical example of such an attribute is «xsi:type="xs:decimal"», which happens to be an attribute whose meaning is defined in the XML Schema specification itself. But they can also be defined in any other XML vocabulary. In fact, QName-valued elements can also be defined, though I haven't come across them in practice.

If you are generating an XSLT stylesheet as the output of the transformation you will often have to generate QNames in the content of attributes: not only attributes like the name attribute of <xsl:template> and <xsl:variable>, but any attribute that contains an XPath expression or a pattern. In fact, any attribute that is an attribute value template can potentially contain a QName.

The tricky thing about these attributes is that they contain a namespace prefix, and you need to ensure that the output document contains a namespace declaration that binds this prefix to the correct URI.

It turns out that the fact that the attribute is declared in the schema as an xs:QName doesn't help with this. Firstly, not all these attributes are declared as QNames. Attributes containing XPath expressions obviously can't be declared as QNames, but less obviously, the schema for XSLT doesn't define the name attribute of <xsl:template> or <xsl:variable> as an xs:QName either. The reason for this is subtle: Although XML Schema would apply the right validation rules if they were declared as QNames, it would not follow the correct rules when converting the lexical value into a value in the QName value space. This is because the XML Schema definition of xs:QName (you'll need to look in the errata or the second edition to find it) says that an unprefixed QName is assumed to be in the default namespace, whereas the QNames used in these XSLT contexts never use the default namespace.

But even where the type is known to be an xs:QName, you can't rely on this to ensure that the right namespaces are declared. This is because the process of creating an attribute node for an element in XSLT is typically:

1.   Evaluate the expression that delivers the attribute value; atomize the result of this expression and convert the resulting sequence to a single string. This process loses any type information associated with the values from which the string was constructed.

2.   Create an attribute node with this string value.

3.   When the attribute is attached to an element, perform namespace fixup on the element. Namespace fixup is described on page 265.

4.   Finally, if required, perform schema validation on the element.

In this process, there is no type annotation associated with the attribute at the time namespace fixup is performed. The namespace nodes need to be in place before validation of the attribute as a QName will succeed, so the only way of constructing them automatically would be to do it during validation, which would require a rewrite of the (already hideously complex) rules defined in XML Schema for validating elements.

The consequence of all this is that when you construct one of these attributes, it is your responsibility firstly, to choose a prefix and to output the attribute in its correct lexical form, and secondly to ensure that the containing element node has a namespace node that maps this prefix to the required namespace URI. The simplest way to be sure of this is by using the <xsl:namespace> instruction described on page 346.

So to generate the element `<e xsi:type="xs:decimal">93.7</e>`, write:

```
<e>
  <xsl:attribute name="xsi:type"
                 namespace="http://www.w3.org/2001/XMLSchema-instance"
                 select="'xs:decimal'">
  <xsl:namespace name="xs"
                 select="'http://www.w3.org/2001/XMLSchema'"/>
  <xsl:value-of select="93.7"/>
</e>
```

An alternative to using `<xsl:namespace>`, in a case like this where the containing element is generated using a literal result element, is simply to ensure that the literal result element has a namespace node that will be copied to the result tree. This can be achieved by writing:

```
<e xmlns:xs="http://www.w3.org/2001/XMLSchema">
  <xsl:attribute name="xsi:type"
                 namespace="http://www.w3.org/2001/XMLSchema-instance"
                 select="'xs:decimal'">
  <xsl:value-of select="93.7"/>
</e>
```

The cases where `<xsl:namespace>` is needed are (a) where the element is produced using `<xsl:element>` rather than a literal result element, and (b) where the namespace prefix or URI is not known at compile time.

Note that it's not a good idea to generate special attributes such as `xsi:type` by including them directly as attributes on the literal result element. This is because if the stylesheet is ever passed through a schema processor, the schema processor will try to check that the content of the `<e>` element in the stylesheet is `xs:decimal`, and of course it isn't. You could avoid such problems by using namespace aliasing (see `<xsl:namespace-alias>` on page 350), but in my view generating the attribute using `<xsl:attribute>` is easier.

Examples

The following example outputs an HTML `<OPTION>` element, with a `SELECTED` attribute included only if the boolean variable `$selected` is true. (The XML output would be `<OPTION SELECTED="SELECTED">`, but the HTML output method will convert this to `<OPTION SELECTED>`.)

Example: Generating an Attribute Conditionally

This example shows the use of `<xsl:attribute>` in a situation where the attribute is generated only if certain conditions are true in the source data.

Source

The source file is `countries.xml`.

```
<?xml version="1.0"?>
<countries>
<country name="France"/>
<country name="Germany"/>
```

```
<country name="Israel"/>
<country name="Japan"/>
<country name="Poland"/>
<country name="United States" selected="yes"/>
<country name="Venezuela"/>
</countries>
```

Stylesheet

The stylesheet file is `options.xsl`.

This is a complete stylesheet using the simplified stylesheet syntax described in Chapter 3, page 119. It outputs an HTML selection box in which the `selected` attribute is set for the option marked as «`selected="yes"`» in the XML source document.

```
<html xsl:version="1.0"
      xmlns:xsl="http://www.w3.org/1999/XSL/Transform">
<body>
<h1>Please select a country:</h1>
<select id="country">
<xsl:for-each select="//country">
  <option value="{@name}">
    <xsl:if test="@selected='yes'">
       <xsl:attribute name="selected">selected</xsl:attribute>
    </xsl:if>
    <xsl:value-of select="@name"/>
  </option>
</xsl:for-each>
</select>
<hr/>
</body>
</html>
```

Output

The output (shown with the selection box opened) is shown in Figure 5-1.

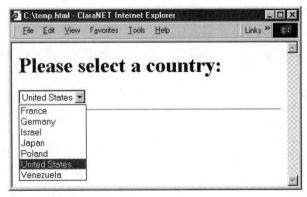

Figure 5-1

The following example outputs a `<promotion>` element with either a `code` or `reason-code` attribute depending on the variable `$schema-version`. This kind of logic can be useful in an application that has to handle different versions of the output document schema.

Example: Deciding the Attribute Name at Runtime

This example shows the use of `<xsl:attribute>` in a situation where the name of the generated attribute is decided at runtime.

Source

This example works with any source file.

Stylesheet

The stylesheet can be found in the file `conditional.xsl`.

The stylesheet declares a global parameter «schema-version», which controls the name of the attribute used in the output file.

```
<xsl:stylesheet version="2.0"
      xmlns:xsl="http://www.w3.org/1999/XSL/Transform">

<xsl:param name="schema-version" select="4.0"/>

<xsl:template match="/">
<promotion>
   <xsl:variable name="attname"
        select="if ($schema-version lt 3.0)
                then 'code'
                else 'reason-code'"/>
   <xsl:attribute name="{$attname}" select="17"/>
</promotion>

</xsl:template>
</xsl:stylesheet>
```

Output

With the default value of the parameter «schema-version», the output is:

```
<promotion reason-code="17"/>
```

When run with the parameter «schema-version» set to 2.0, the output is:

```
<promotion code="17"/>
```

In the above example it would be equally valid, of course, to use `<xsl:attribute>` with a fixed attribute name in both arms of the `<xsl:choose>` element; the advantage of doing this the way we have shown would start to become apparent if the sequence constructor of the `<xsl:attribute>` instruction were more complicated than the simple constant «17».

In XSLT 1.0, it was often necessary to use `<xsl:attribute>` because the value required a calculation. In the following example, the value of the `value` attribute is a whitespace-separated list of the `id` attributes of the child `<item>` elements of the context node:

```
<basket>
    <xsl:attribute name="value">
        <xsl:for-each select="item">
            <xsl:value-of select="@id"/>
            <xsl:if test="not(position()=last())">
                <xsl:text> </xsl:text>
            </xsl:if>
        </xsl:for-each>
    </xsl:attribute>
</basket>
```

In XSLT 2.0, the work can often be done at the XPath level. This example can now be written:

```
<basket value="{item/@id}"/>
```

because when the value of an expression in an attribute value template is given as a sequence, the processor will automatically convert the items in this sequence to strings and concatenate them using a single space as a separator.

See Also

`<xsl:element>` on page 260
`<xsl:copy>` on page 240
`<xsl:copy-of>` on page 245

xsl:attribute-set

The `<xsl:attribute-set>` element is a top-level XSLT declaration used to define a named set of attribute names and values. The resulting attribute set can be applied as a whole to any output element, providing a way of defining commonly used sets of attributes in a single place.

Changes in 2.0

None.

Format

```
<xsl:attribute-set
  name = qname
  use-attribute-sets? = qnames>
  <!-- Content: xsl:attribute* -->
</xsl:attribute-set>
```

Position

<xsl:attribute-set> is a declaration, so it must always occur as a child of the <xsl:stylesheet> element.

Attributes

Name	Value	Meaning
name mandatory	QName	The name of the attribute set
use-attribute-sets optional	Whitespace-separated list of QNames	The names of other attribute sets to be incorporated into this attribute set

Content

Zero or more <xsl:attribute> elements.

Effect

Named attribute sets provide a capability similar to named styles in CSS.

The name attribute is mandatory, and defines the name of the attribute set. It must be a lexical QName: a name with or without a namespace prefix. If the name uses a prefix, it must refer to a namespace declaration that is in scope at this point in the stylesheet, and as usual it is the namespace URI rather than the prefix that is used when matching names. The name does not need to be unique; if there are several attribute sets with the same name, they are effectively merged.

The use-attribute-sets attribute is optional. It is used to build up one attribute set from a number of others. If present, its value must be a whitespace-separated list of tokens each of which is a valid lexical QName that refers to another named attribute set in the stylesheet. For example:

```
<xsl:attribute-set name="table-cell"
   use-attribute-sets="small-font gray-background centered"/>

<xsl:attribute-set name="small-font">
   <xsl:attribute name="font-name">Verdana</xsl:attribute>
   <xsl:attribute name="font-size">6pt</xsl:attribute>
</xsl:attribute-set>

<xsl:attribute-set name="gray-background">
   <xsl:attribute name="bgcolor">#xBBBBBB</xsl:attribute>
</xsl:attribute-set>

<xsl:attribute-set name="centered">
   <xsl:attribute name="align">center</xsl:attribute>
</xsl:attribute-set>
```

The references must not be circular: If A refers to B, then B must not refer directly or indirectly to A. The order is significant: Specifying a list of named attribute sets is equivalent to copying the <xsl:attribute> elements that they contain, in order, to the *beginning* of the list of <xsl:attribute> elements contained in this <xsl:attribute-set> element.

If several attribute sets have the same name, they are merged. If this merging finds two attributes with the same name, then the one in the attribute set with higher import precedence will take precedence. Import precedence is discussed under <xsl:import> on page 312. If they both have the same precedence, the XSLT processor has the option of using the one that came later in the stylesheet, or reporting an error. (Note that it isn't generally possible to detect this error at compile time, because the attribute names can be calculated at runtime using an attribute value template.)

The order in which this merging process takes place can affect the outcome. When use-attribute-sets appears on an <xsl:attribute-set> or <xsl:copy> element, or xsl:use-attribute-sets on a literal result element, it is expanded to create a sequence of attribute nodes. This is essentially done by a recursive process:

❑ To expand an [xsl:]use-attribute-sets attribute, process all the attribute set names in the order they are listed.

❑ To process an attribute set name, expand each of the <xsl:attribute-set> declarations having that name, taking them in increasing order of import precedence, and within each import precedence, in declaration order. For definitions of *import precedence* and *declaration order*, see <xsl:import> on page 312.

❑ To expand an <xsl:attribute-set> declaration, first expand its use-attribute-sets attribute (if any) by a recursive application of these rules, then add the attribute nodes generated by evaluating the contained <xsl:attribute> instructions to the result sequence.

It's best to illustrate this by an example. Suppose you have the following attribute-set definition:

```
<xsl:attribute-set name="B" use-attribute-sets="A1 A2">
  <xsl:attribute name="p">percy</xsl:attribute>
  <xsl:attribute name="q">queenie</xsl:attribute>
  <xsl:attribute name="r">rory</xsl:attribute>
</xsl:attribute-set>
```

If there is more than one attribute set named A1 these must be merged first (taking import precedence into account), and then the merged contents must be substituted into B.

Then the same process is applied to A2. The referenced attribute sets are expanded in order. The attributes that result from expanding A1 are output before those that result from expanding A2. This means that attributes from A2 take priority over those from A1 if there is a clash.

In turn, the attribute set B must be fully expanded before it is merged with any other attribute set called B. That is, the processor must replace the references to attribute sets A1 and A2 with an equivalent list of <xsl:attribute> instructions before it merges this B with other attribute sets of the same name.

When B is expanded, the attributes derived from A1 and A2 will be output before the attributes p, q, and r, so if expanding A1 and A2 generates any attributes called p, q, and r, these will be overwritten by the values specified within B (percy, queenie, and rory).

Normally when describing the processing model for XSLT instructions, we distinguish between the process of generating a sequence of nodes, and attaching these nodes to a tree. Eliminating attribute nodes with duplicate names is technically part of the second process. However, attribute sets can only be expanded from instructions that create elements, so the resulting attributes will always be attached to an element. This means we can treat it as if generating the attribute nodes and attaching them to an element are done as a single process.

In general, duplicate attribute names or attribute set names do not cause an error. If several attributes have the same name, the one that comes last (in the order produced by the merging rules given above) will take precedence. There is one situation only that is defined as an error, namely if two different attribute-sets with the same name and the same import precedence both produce attributes with the same name. Another way of saying this is: It is an error if the final result depends on the relative positions of the attribute-set definitions in the stylesheet. However, the processor is allowed to recover from this error by taking the definitions in stylesheet order, and in this particular case it's so much easier to take the recovery action than to detect the error that I suspect this is what most processors are likely to do.

Usage

The most common use of attribute sets is to define packages of attributes that constitute a display style, for example a collection of attributes for a font or for a table.

A named attribute set is used by referring to it in the `use-attribute-sets` attribute of the `<xsl:element>` or `<xsl:copy>` element, or in the `xsl:use-attribute-sets` attribute of a literal result element, or, of course, in the `use-attribute-sets` attribute of another `<xsl:attribute-set>`. The first three cases all create an element node, and have the effect of adding the attributes in the named attribute set to that element node. Any attributes added implicitly from a named attribute set can be overridden by attribute nodes added explicitly by the invoking code.

An attribute set is not simply a textual macro. The attributes contained in the attribute set each have a `select` attribute or sequence constructor to define the value, and although this will often return a fixed value, it may also, for example, declare variables or invoke other XSLT instructions such as `<xsl:call-template>` and `<xsl:apply-templates>`.

The rules for the scope of variables, described under `<xsl:variable>` on page 471, are the same as anywhere else, and are defined by the position of the definitions in the source stylesheet document. This means that the only way to parameterize the values of attributes in a named attribute set is by reference to global variables and parameters: There is no other way of passing parameters to an attribute set. However, the value of the generated attributes may depend on the context in the source document. The context is not changed when the attribute set is used, so the current item («.») and current position and size are exactly the same as in the calling instruction.

Examples

The following example defines an attribute set designed for generated HTML `<table>` elements:

```
<xsl:attribute-set name="full-width-table">
  <xsl:attribute name="border">1</xsl:attribute>
```

```
      <xsl:attribute name="cellpadding">3</xsl:attribute>
      <xsl:attribute name="cellspacing">0</xsl:attribute>
      <xsl:attribute name="width">100%</xsl:attribute>
</xsl:attribute-set>
```

This attribute set can be used when generating an output element, as follows:

```
<table xsl:use-attribute-sets="full-width-table">
   <tr>...</tr>
</table>
```

This produces the following output:

```
<table border="1" cellpadding="3" cellspacing="0" width="100%">
   <tr>...</tr>
</table>
```

Alternatively it is possible to use the attribute set while overriding some of its definitions and adding others, for example:

```
<table border="2" rules="cols" xsl:use-attribute-sets="full-width-table">
   <tr>...</tr>
</table>
```

The output now becomes:

```
<table border="2" rules="cols" cellpadding="3" cellspacing="0" width="100%">
   <tr>...</tr>
</table>
```

If this combination of attributes is also used repeatedly, it could be defined as an attribute set in its own right, as:

```
<xsl:attribute-set name="ruled-table" use-attribute-set="full-width-table">
   <xsl:attribute name="border">2</xsl:attribute>
   <xsl:attribute name="rules">cols</xsl:attribute>
</xsl:attribute-set>
```

Then this new attribute set could also be invoked by name from a literal result element, an `<xsl:element>` instruction, or an `<xsl:copy>` instruction.

The next example shows that the values of the attributes in an attribute set need not be constants.

Example: Using an Attribute Set for Numbering

Suppose you want to copy an XML file containing a poem, but with the `<line>` elements in the poem output in the form `<line number="3" of="18">` within the stanza.

Source

The source file `poem.xml` has the following structure (I'm only showing the first stanza):

```
<?xml version="1.0"?>
<poem>
<author>Rupert Brooke</author>
<date>1912</date>
<title>Song</title>
<stanza>
<line>And suddenly the wind comes soft,</line>
<line>And Spring is here again;</line>
<line>And the hawthorn quickens with buds of green</line>
<line>And my heart with buds of pain.</line>
</stanza>
</poem>
```

Stylesheet

The stylesheet `number-lines.xsl` copies everything unchanged except the <line>
elements, which are copied with a named attribute set:

```
<xsl:transform
 xmlns:xsl="http://www.w3.org/1999/XSL/Transform"
 version="2.0"
>
<xsl:strip-space elements="*"/>
<xsl:output method="xml" indent="yes"/>

<xsl:template match="*">
   <xsl:copy>
     <xsl:apply-templates/>
   </xsl:copy>
</xsl:template>

<xsl:template match="line">
   <xsl:copy use-attribute-sets="sequence">
     <xsl:apply-templates/>
   </xsl:copy>
</xsl:template>

<xsl:attribute-set name="sequence">
   <xsl:attribute name="number" select="position()"/>
   <xsl:attribute name="of" select="last()"/>
</xsl:attribute-set>

</xsl:transform>
```

Output

The output (again showing only the first stanza) looks like this:

```
<poem>
   <author>Rupert Brooke</author>
   <date>1912</date>
   <title>Song</title>
   <stanza>
```

```
         <line number="1" of="4">And suddenly the wind comes soft,</line>
         <line number="2" of="4">And Spring is here again;</line>
         <line number="3" of="4">And the hawthorn quickens with
                     buds of green</line>
         <line number="4" of="4">And my heart with buds of pain.</line>
      </stanza>
   </poem>
```

See Also

<xsl:element> on page 260
<xsl:copy> on page 240
Literal Result Elements in Chapter 3, page 106

xsl:call-template

The <xsl:call-template> instruction is used to invoke a named template. Its effect is analogous to a procedure call or subroutine call in other programming languages.

Changes in 2.0

There are no syntactic changes to this instruction in XSLT 2.0. However, using the <xsl:sequence> instruction in the called template (see page 420) now allows the result of the <xsl:call-template> instruction to be any sequence, not only a sequence of nodes.

In many cases where it was appropriate to use <xsl:call-template> in XSLT 1.0, it may be more appropriate in 2.0 to use an XPath expression containing a call on a stylesheet function defined using <xsl:function>, which is described on page 300.

Many problems that required recursive use of <xsl:call-template> to process a string can be solved more conveniently in XSLT 2.0 using the <xsl:analyze-string> instruction (see page 176), and many problems that used recursion to process a sequence of nodes can now be tackled more easily using <xsl:for-each-group>, described on page 281.

It is now a compile-time error to supply a parameter that the called template does not declare: In XSLT 1.0, such a parameter was silently ignored. To preserve backwards compatibility, this rule is not enforced when the stylesheet specifies «version="1.0"».

Format

```
<xsl:call-template
   name = qname>
   <!-- Content: xsl:with-param* -->
</xsl:call-template>
```

Position

`<xsl:call-template>` is an instruction; it is always used within a sequence constructor.

Attributes

Name	Value	Meaning
name mandatory	QName	The name of the template to be called

Content

Zero or more `<xsl:with-param>` elements.

Effect

The sections below describe the rules for the template name, the rules for supplying parameters to the called template, and the way the context is affected.

The Template Name

The mandatory `name` attribute must be a lexical QName, and it must match the `name` attribute of an `<xsl:template>` element in the stylesheet. If the name has a namespace prefix, the names are compared using the corresponding namespace URI in the usual way. If there is no prefix, the namespace URI is null (the default namespace is not used). It is an error if there is no `<xsl:template>` element with a matching name.

If there is more than one `<xsl:template>` in the stylesheet with a matching name, they must have different `import precedence`, and the one with highest import precedence is used. For information about import precedence, see `<xsl:import>` on page 312.

The name of the template to be called must be written explicitly in the `name` attribute. There is no way of writing this name as a variable or an expression to be evaluated at runtime. If you want to make a runtime decision on which of several named templates to call, the only way to achieve this is to write an `<xsl:choose>` instruction. Alternatively, there is a technique for using templates as if they were higher order functions: This is described under *Simulating Higher Order Functions* on page 198.

Parameters

If the name of a child `<xsl:with-param>` element matches the name of an `<xsl:param>` element in the called `<xsl:template>`, then the `<xsl:with-param>` element is evaluated (in the same way as an `<xsl:variable>` element) and the value is assigned to the relevant `<xsl:param>` variable name within that named template.

In XSLT 2.0 a compile-time error is reported if there is a child `<xsl:with-param>` element that does not match the name of any `<xsl:param>` element in the selected `<xsl:template>`. However, if the `<xsl:call-template>` instruction is in a part of the stylesheet that specifies «[xsl:]version="1.0"», the extra parameter is ignored as it was in XSLT 1.0.

If there is an `<xsl:param>` element in the selected `<xsl:template>` with no matching `<xsl:with-param>` element in the `<xsl:call-template>` element, then the `<xsl:param>` variable is given a default value. But if the `<xsl:param>` element specifies «required="yes"», this is a compile-time error. See `<xsl:param>` on page 392 for details.

Context

The selected `<xsl:template>` is evaluated with no change to the context: It uses the same context item, context position, and context size as the calling template. There is also no change to the *current template rule* (a concept that is used only by `<xsl:apply-imports>`, described on page 184, and `<xsl:next-match>`, described on page 355).

Usage and Examples

The `<xsl:call-template>` element is similar to a subroutine call in conventional programming languages, and the parameters behave in the same way as conventional call-by-value parameters. It is useful wherever there is common logic to be called from different places in the stylesheet.

Using the Result

The result of an `<xsl:call-template>` instruction is the sequence returned by the sequence constructor inside the template that is called. Usually, this consists of nodes that are to be added to the result tree. However, you can also capture the result by calling `<xsl:call-template>` from a sequence constructor enclosed within an `<xsl:variable>` element, in which case the result of the called template becomes the value of the variable.

For example, the following template outputs the supplied string enclosed in parentheses:

```
<xsl:template name="parenthesize">
    <xsl:param name="string"/>
    <xsl:sequence select="concat('(',$string,')')"/>
</xsl:template>
```

This may be called as follows:

```
<xsl:variable name="credit-in-paren" as="xs:string">
    <xsl:call-template name="parenthesize">
        <xsl:with-param name="string" select="@credit"/>
    </xsl:call-template>
</xsl:variable>
```

If the value of the credit attribute is «120.00», the resulting value of the variable «$credit-in-paren» will be the string «(120.00)».

If you omitted the «as="xs:string"» from the `<xsl:variable>` element, the result would not be a string, but a temporary tree consisting of a root node that owns a single text node, and the contents of that text node would be «(120.00)»; but for all practical purposes the value could still be used as if it were a string. One difference is that you won't get such good type checking: For example, if you try to use the variable $credit-in-paren as defined above in a context where a number is required, this will be reported as an error, quite possibly at compile time. But if you leave off the as attribute, you will probably not get an error at all, just a wrong answer: The system will treat the value of the variable as NaN (not a number).

Changing the Context Item

If you want to use <xsl:call-template> to process an item that is not the context item, the easiest way to achieve this is to nest the <xsl:call-template> inside an <xsl:for-each> instruction. An alternative, however, is to give the target template a distinctive mode name, and call it using <xsl:apply-templates> with the specified mode.

For example, suppose you have written a template that returns the depth of the current node (the number of ancestors it has). The template has been given a unique name and an identical mode name:

```
<xsl:template name="depth" mode="depth" match="node()">
   <xsl:sequence select="count(ancestor::node())"/>
</xsl:template>
```

Now, suppose you want to obtain the depth of a node other than the current node—let's say the depth of the next node in document order, which need not be on the same level as the current node. You can call this template in either of two ways.

Using <xsl:call-template>:

```
<xsl:variable name="next-depth" as="xs:integer">
   <xsl:for-each select="following::node()[1]">
      <xsl:call-template name="depth"/>
   </xsl:for-each>
</xsl:variable>
```

or using <xsl:apply-templates> with a special mode:

```
<xsl:variable name="next-depth" as="xs:integer">
   <xsl:apply-templates select="following::node()[1]" mode="depth"/>
</xsl:variable>
```

In both cases the variable $next-depth will, on return, hold a value, which is the depth in the tree of the node following the context node. If the context item is not a node, a runtime error will occur. Because the <xsl:variable> element has an «as» attribute, the result is of type xs:integer. Without the «as» attribute, the result would be a temporary tree containing a single text node, whose value is the string representation of this integer. For details, see <xsl:variable> on page 471.

Recursion: Processing a List of Values

Named templates are sometimes used to process a list of values. As XSLT has no updateable variables like a conventional programming language, it also has no conventional *for* or *while* loop, because these constructs can only terminate if there is a control variable whose value is changing.

In XSLT 2.0 (and XPath 2.0) most processing of sequences can be done iteratively, using the XSLT `<xsl:for-each>` instruction or the XPath 2.0 «for» expression, for example:

```
sum(for $i in //item return $i/price * $i/quantity)
```

When things get difficult, it is possible to use functions such as `tokenize()` or `distinct-values()` to define the sequence that needs to be processed, and to use instructions such as `<xsl:analyze-string>` and `<xsl:for-each-group>` to do the processing. In XSLT 1.0 it was often necessary to write recursive templates to perform such calculations.

Recursion is still needed in XSLT 2.0 to handle more complex algorithms, particularly those that navigate a hierarchy or a graph, but it will often be done more conveniently using XPath function calls and stylesheet functions written using `<xsl:function>` rather than using `<xsl:call-template>`. Nevertheless, recursive use of `<xsl:call-template>` still has a role to play, so I will present a couple of examples.

The typical logic used to process a sequence using recursion is illustrated by the following pseudocode:

```
function process-sequence(sequence L) {
   if (not-empty(L)) {
      process(first(L));
      process-sequence(remainder(L));
   }
}
```

That is, the function does nothing if the sequence is empty; otherwise it processes the first item in the sequence, and then calls itself to process the sequence containing all items except the first. The net effect is that each item in the sequence will be processed and the function will then exit. This particular approach to writing recursive algorithms is often known as *head-tail recursion*.

There are two main kinds of sequence that this logic is applied to: sequences of nodes, and strings containing separator characters. I will show one example of each kind; more complex examples can be found in Chapters 9 and 12.

Example: Using Recursion to Process a Sequence of Nodes

Here's an example for processing a sequence of node. XPath 2.0 provides `min()` and `max()` functions for finding the minimum and maximum of a set of atomic values, but it doesn't provide a way of processing a set of nodes and returning the one whose value for some expression is least or greatest. This can be done by computing the value of the expression for each of the nodes, passing these values into the `min()` or `max()` function, and then searching the nodes to see which of them had this value; but this approach is rather inefficient because it involves visiting each node and calculating the expression twice. So we'll do it ourselves, using a recursive scan of the nodes, in a single pass. The specific task we will tackle is to look for the longest speech in a scene of a play.

Conceptually it's trivial: The maximum value of a set of numbers is either the first number or the maximum of the set of the numbers after the first, whichever is larger. We use XPath predicates for manipulating the node sequences: in particular, «[1]» to find the first node in the sequence, and «[position()!=1]» to find the remainder.

Source

The source file scene.xml is the scene of a play. It starts like this:

```
<?xml version="1.0"?>
<SCENE><TITLE>SCENE I. Venice. A street.</TITLE>
<STAGEDIR>Enter RODERIGO and IAGO</STAGEDIR>

<SPEECH>
<SPEAKER>RODERIGO</SPEAKER>
<LINE>Tush! never tell me; I take it much unkindly</LINE>
<LINE>That thou, Iago, who hast had my purse</LINE>
<LINE>As if the strings were thine, shouldst know of this.</LINE>
</SPEECH>

<SPEECH>
<SPEAKER>IAGO</SPEAKER>
<LINE>'Sblood, but you will not hear me:</LINE>
<LINE>If ever I did dream of such a matter, Abhor me.</LINE>
</SPEECH>
etc.
</SCENE>
```

Stylesheet

The stylesheet longest-speech.xsl is shown below. It starts by defining a named template «max». This template takes a node sequence called «list» as its parameter.

The first thing it does is to test whether this node sequence is nonempty (<xsl:when test="$list">). If it isn't, it gets the number of <LINE> element children of the first node in the list into a variable «$first». Then the template calls itself recursively, passing all nodes except the first as the parameter, to determine the maximum value for the rest of the list. It then returns either the first value, or the maximum for the rest of the list, whichever is greater. Finally, if the supplied list was empty, it returns zero.

The template rule for the root node of the source document simply calls the «longest-speech» template, passing the list of all <SPEECH> elements as a parameter.

```
<xsl:transform
 xmlns:xsl="http://www.w3.org/1999/XSL/Transform"
 xmlns:xs="http://www.w3.org/2001/XMLSchema"
 exclude-result-prefixes="xs"
 version="2.0"
>
<xsl:template name="longest-speech" as="element(SPEECH)?">
<xsl:param name="list" as="element(SPEECH)*"/>
<xsl:choose>
<xsl:when test="$list">
    <xsl:variable name="first" select="count($list[1]/LINE)"
                  as="xs:integer"/>
```

```
            <xsl:variable name="longest-of-rest" as="element(SPEECH)?">
                <xsl:call-template name="longest-speech">
                    <xsl:with-param name="list"
                                    select="$list[position()!=1]"/>
                </xsl:call-template>
            </xsl:variable>
            <xsl:choose>
            <xsl:when test="$first gt count($longest-of-rest/LINE)">
                <xsl:sequence select="$list[1]"/>
            </xsl:when>
            <xsl:otherwise>
                <xsl:sequence select="$longest-of-rest"/>
            </xsl:otherwise>
            </xsl:choose>
        </xsl:when>
        </xsl:choose>
        </xsl:template>

        <xsl:template match="/">
        <longest-speech>
            <xsl:call-template name="longest-speech">
                <xsl:with-param name="list" select="//SPEECH"/>
            </xsl:call-template>
        </longest-speech>
        </xsl:template>
        </xsl:transform>
```

Output

The output gives the text of the longest speech in this scene. It starts like this:

```
<?xml version="1.0" encoding="UTF-8"?>
<longest-speech>
<SPEECH><SPEAKER>IAGO</SPEAKER>
<LINE>O, sir, content you;</LINE>
<LINE>I follow him to serve my turn upon him:</LINE>
<LINE>We cannot all be masters, nor all masters</LINE>
<LINE>Cannot be truly follow'd. You shall mark</LINE>
<LINE>Many a duteous and knee-crooking knave,</LINE>
<LINE>That, doting on his own obsequious bondage,</LINE>
<LINE>Wears out his time, much like his master's ass,</LINE>
<LINE>For nought but provender, and when he's old, cashier'd:</LINE>
<LINE>Whip me such honest knaves...
```

Note that this is taking advantage of some of the new features of XSLT 2.0. The template uses `<xsl:sequence>` to return a reference to an existing node, rather than creating a copy of the node using `<xsl:copy-of>`. It also declares the type of the parameters expected by the template, and the type of the result, which is useful documentation, and provides information that the XSLT processor can use for generating optimized code. I also found that while I was developing the stylesheet, many of my errors were trapped by the type checking. Note that the form «as="element(SPEECH)"» can be used even when there is no schema. The example could have been rewritten to make much heavier use of XSLT 2.0 features, for example it could have been written using `<xsl:function>` rather than `<xsl:template>`, and the `<xsl:choose>` instruction could have been replaced by an XPath 2.0 «if» expression. The result would have occupied fewer lines of code, but it would not necessarily have been any more readable or more efficient.

There is another solution to this problem that may be more appropriate depending on the circumstances. This involves sorting the node-set, and taking the first or last element. It goes like this:

```
<xsl:variable name="longest-speech" as="element(SPEECH)?>
    <xsl:for-each select="SPEECH">
      <xsl:sort select="count(LINE)"/>
      <xsl:if test="position()=last()">
        <xsl:sequence select="."/>
      </xsl:if>
    </xsl:for-each>
</xsl:variable>
```

In principle, the recursive solution should be faster, because it only looks at each node once, whereas sorting all the values requires more work than is strictly necessary to find the largest. In practice, though, it rather depends on how efficiently recursion is implemented in the particular processor.

Another case where recursion has traditionally been useful is processing of a list presented in the form of a string containing a list of tokens. In XSLT 2.0, most such problems can be tackled much more conveniently using the XPath 2.0 `tokenize()` function, which breaks a string into a sequence by using regular expressions, or by using the `<xsl:analyze-string>` instruction described on page 176. But although these functions are excellent at breaking a string into a sequence of substrings, they don't by themselves provide any ability to process the resulting sequence in a nonlinear way. Sometimes recursion is still the best way of tackling such problems.

Example: Using Recursion to Process a Sequence of Strings

Suppose that you want to find all the lines within a play that contain the phrase «A and B» where A and B are both names of characters in the play.

Source

There is only one line in the whole of *Othello* that meets these criteria. So you will need to run the stylesheet against the full play, `othello.xml`.

Stylesheet

The stylesheet `naming-lines.xsl` starts by declaring a global variable whose value is the set of names of the characters in the play, with duplicates removed and case normalized for efficiency:

```
<xsl:transform
  xmlns:xsl="http://www.w3.org/1999/XSL/Transform"
  xmlns:xs="http://www.w3.org/2001/XMLSchema"
  xmlns:local="local-functions.uri"
  exclude-result-prefixes="xs local"
  version="2.0"
>
```

```
<xsl:variable name="speakers" as="xs:string*"
  select="for $w in distinct-values(//SPEAKER) return upper-case($w)"/>
```

We'll write a function that splits a line into its words. This was hard work in XSLT 1.0, but is now much easier.

```
<xsl:function name="local:split" as="xs:string*">
  <xsl:param name="line" as="xs:string"/>
  <xsl:sequence select="tokenize($line, '\W')"/>
</xsl:function>
```

The next step is a function that tests whether a given word is the name of a character in the play:

```
<xsl:function name="local:is-character" as="xs:boolean">
  <xsl:param name="word" as="xs:string"/>
  <xsl:sequence select="upper-case($word)=$speakers"/>
</xsl:function>
```

This way of doing case-independent matching isn't really recommended, it's better to use a collation designed for the purpose, but it works with this data. Note that we are relying on the "existential" properties of the «=» operator: that is, the fact that it compares the word on the left with every string in the $speakers sequence.

Now I'll write a named template that processes a sequence of words, and looks for the phrase «A and B» where A and B are both the names of characters.

```
<xsl:template name="scan-line">
   <xsl:param name="words" as="xs:string*"/>
   <xsl:if test="count($words) ge 3">
     <xsl:if test="local:is-character($words[1]) and
                   lower-case($words[2]) = 'and' and
                   local:is-character($words[3])">
       <hit>
         <xsl:value-of select="$words[position()=1 to 3]" separator=" "/>
       </hit>
     </xsl:if>
     <xsl:call-template name="scan-line">
       <xsl:with-param name="words"
                       select="$words[position() gt 1]"/>
     </xsl:call-template>
   </xsl:if>
</xsl:template>
```

Then comes the "main program," the template rule that matches the root node. This simply calls the named template for each <LINE> element in the document, which causes <hit> elements to be output for all matching sequences:

```
<xsl:template match="/">
  <naming-lines>
    <xsl:for-each select="//LINE">
```

```
        <xsl:call-template name="scan-line">
          <xsl:with-param name="words" select="local:split(.)"/>
        </xsl:call-template>
      </xsl:for-each>
    </naming-lines>
  </xsl:template>

  </xsl:transform>
```

Output

The output is simply:

```
<?xml version="1.0" encoding="UTF-8"?>
<naming-lines>
    <hit>Othello and Desdemona</hit>
</naming-lines>
```

See Also

<xsl:apply-templates> on page 187
<xsl:function> on page 300
<xsl:param> on page 392
<xsl:template> on page 450
<xsl:with-param> on page 488

xsl:character-map

The <xsl:character-map> element is a top-level XSLT declaration used to provide detailed control over the way individual characters are serialized. A character map is used only when the result of the transformation is serialized, and when the <xsl:output> declaration that controls the serialization references the character map.

Changes in 2.0

Character maps are a new feature in XSLT 2.0, designed as a replacement for disable-output-escaping, which is now deprecated.

Format

```
<xsl:character-map
  name = qname
  use-character-maps? = qnames>
  <!-- Content: (xsl:output-character*) -->
</xsl:character-map>
```

Position

`<xsl:character-map>` is a top-level declaration, so it must always occur as a child of the `<xsl:stylesheet>` element.

Attributes

Name	Value	Meaning
name mandatory	Lexical QName	The name of this character map
use-character-maps optional	Whitespace-separated list of lexical QNames	The names of other character maps to be incorporated into this character map

Content

Zero or more `<xsl:output-character>` elements.

Effect

The `name` attribute is mandatory, and defines the name of the character map. It must be a lexical QName: a name with or without a namespace prefix. If the name uses a prefix, it must refer to a namespace declaration that is in scope at this point in the stylesheet, and as usual it is the namespace URI rather than the prefix that is used when matching names. If several character maps in the stylesheet have the same name, then the one with highest import precedence is used; an error is reported if this rule does not identify a character map uniquely. Import precedence is explained on page 314.

The character map contains zero or more `<xsl:output-character>` elements. Each `<xsl:output-character>` element defines a mapping between a single Unicode character and a string that is used to represent that character in the serialized output. For example, the element:

```
<xsl:output-character char=" " string=" "/>
```

indicates that the nonbreaking space character (Unicode codepoint 160) is to be represented on output by the string « ». This illustrates one of the possible uses of character maps, which is to render specific characters using XML or HTML entity references.

The `use-character-maps` attribute is optional. It is used to build up one character map from a number of others. If present, its value must be a whitespace-separated list of tokens each of which is a valid QName that refers to another named character map in the stylesheet. For example:

```
<xsl:character-map name="NBSP">
    <xsl:output-character char=" " string=" "/>
</xsl:character-map>

<xsl:character-map name="latin-1-symbols">
    <xsl:output-character char="&#161;" string="&amp;iexcl;"/>
    <xsl:output-character char="&#162;" string="&amp;cent;"/>
    <xsl:output-character char="&#163;" string="&amp;pound;"/>
```

```
      <xsl:output-character char="&#164;" string="&amp;curren;"/>
      ...
  </xsl:character-map>

  <xsl:character-map name="latin-1-accented-letters">
      <xsl:output-character char="&#192;" string="&amp;Agrave;"/>
      <xsl:output-character char="&#193;" string="&amp;Aacute;"/>
      <xsl:output-character char="&#194;" string="&amp;Acirc;"/>
      <xsl:output-character char="&#195;" string="&amp;Atilde;"/>
      ...
  </xsl:character-map>

  <xsl:character-map name="latin-1-entities"
      use-character-maps="NBSP
                          latin-1-symbols
                          latin-1-accented-characters"/>
```

This example creates a composite character map called `latin-1-entities` that is effectively the union of three underlying character maps. The effect in this case is as if all the `<xsl:output-character>` elements in the three underlying character maps were actually present as children of the composite character map.

The rules for merging character maps are as follows. Firstly, there must be no circularities (a character map must not reference itself, directly or indirectly). The *expanded content* of a character map can then be defined (recursively) as the concatenation of the expanded content of each of the character maps referenced in its `use-character-maps` attribute, in the order in which they are named, followed by the `<xsl:output-character>` elements that are directly contained in the `<xsl:character-map>` element, in the order that they appear in the stylesheet. If the expanded content of a character map contains two mappings for the same Unicode character, then the one that comes last in this sequence is the one that is used.

A character map is used during serialization when it is named in the `use-character-maps` attribute of an `<xsl:output>` declaration. This is itself a list of named character maps; these character maps are combined using the same rule—they are concatenated in the order that they are listed, and conflicts are resolved by choosing the mapping for a character that is last in the list. It is also possible to merge the lists of character maps defined in several `<xsl:output>` declarations: the rules for this are given in the description of the `<xsl:output>` element on page 375.

During serialization, character mapping is applied to characters appearing in the content of text nodes and attribute nodes. It is not applied to other content (such as comments and processing instructions), nor to element and attribute names. It is not applied to characters for which `disable-output-escaping` has been specified, nor to characters in CDATA sections (that is, characters in the content of elements listed in the `cdata-section-elements` attribute of `<xsl:output>`). It is also not applied to characters in URI-valued attributes that are subjected to URI escaping under the rules of the HTML and XHTML output methods.

If a character is included in the character map, this bypasses the normal XML/HTML escaping. For example if the ampersand character «&» is mapped to the string «###», then an ampersand appearing in the content of a text or attribute node will be output as «###» (and not as «###amp;»). But the character map is not applied to the output of XML/HTML escaping: A «<» character will still be output as «<», not as «###lt;».

The string that is substituted for a character using character mapping is inserted into the stream of characters produced by the serializer, and is processed along with the other characters in this stream by the final two stages of serialization, namely Unicode normalization and character encoding. Unicode normalization (if requested using the `normalization-form` attribute of `<xsl:output>`) affects the way that combining characters are represented, for example it may cause a sequence consisting of a lowercase letter «c» followed by a cedilla «ˌ» to be replaced by the single character «ç». Finally, character encoding (which is determined by the encoding attribute of `<xsl:output>`) converts logical Unicode characters into actual bytes or octets; for example if the encoding is UTF-8 then the character «ç» will be represented by the two octets «x3C xA7». You cannot use character maps to alter the effect of the Unicode normalization and character encoding processes.

Usage and Examples

Character maps are useful in many situations where you need precise control over the serialization of the result tree.

In general, if you are producing XML output that is to be used by another application, or if you are producing HTML output that is destined to be displayed in a browser, then the standard serialized output should be perfectly adequate. The situations where you need a finer level of control are typically:

❑ If the output is designed to be edited by humans rather than processed by a machine. In this case you may want, for example, to control the use of entity references in the output.

❑ If the output format is not standard HTML or XML, but some proprietary extension with its own rules. Such dialects are commonly encountered with HTML, though fortunately they are very rare in the case of XML. A similar requirement arises where the required output format is SGML.

❑ If the application that processes the HTML or XML that you produce is buggy. You live in the real world and life isn't perfect. For example, it is rumored that some older browsers will not accept an «&» in a URL that has been escaped as «&», even though the HTML standard requires the escaped form. If you encounter such bugs, you may need to work around them.

❑ If the required output format uses what I call "double markup." By this I mean the use of XML tags in places where tags are not recognized by an XML parser, generally within CDATA sections or comments. I don't think that this is a particularly good design pattern for XML, because it is not possible to model the structure correctly as a tree using the XPath data model, but document structures such as this exist and you may be obliged to produce them. You can solve this problem using character maps by choosing two characters to map to the CDATA start and end delimiters («<![CDATA[» and «]]>») or the comment start and end delimiters («<!--» and «-->»). An example is shown below.

❑ Finally, there are some transformations where generating the correct result tree is really difficult, or really slow. An example might be where the document structure uses interleaved markup. This is used where there are two parallel hierarchies running through the same document, for example one for the chapter/section/paragraph structure and one for the paginated layout. An expert will know when it's time to give up and cheat—which in this case means producing markup in the result document by direct intervention at the serialization stage, rather than generating the correct result tree and having the markup produced automatically by the serializer. The problem, of course, is that beginners are inclined to give up and cheat far too soon, which leads to code that is very difficult to extend and maintain.

Character Maps versus disable-output-escaping

The mechanism provided in XSLT 1.0 to handle these requirements was the `disable-output-escaping` attribute of the `<xsl:text>` and `<xsl:value-of>` elements. This was always an optional feature. XSLT processors were not obliged to implement it, and of course it would have no effect unless serialization was invoked. In XSLT 2.0, `disable-output-escaping` has become deprecated, so it's rather more likely that processors will be encountered that don't support the feature.

Character maps are less powerful than `disable-output-escaping`, because you can't switch them on and off for different parts of the result tree. But this is also their strength. The problem with `disable-output-escaping` is that it requires some extra information to pass between the transformation engine and the serializer, in addition to the information that's defined in the data model. (As evidence for this, look at the clumsy way that `disable-output-escaping` requests are encoded in a `SAXResult` stream in the Java JAXP interface.) This information is generally lost if you want to pass the result tree to another application before serializing it. The problem gets worse in XSLT 2.0, which allows temporary trees and parentless text nodes to be created and processed within the course of a transformation. One of the difficulties in designing this feature was whether a request to disable output escaping should be meaningful when the data being written was not being passed straight to the serializer, but was being written to a temporary tree or a parentless text node.

Most of the things that can be done with `disable-output-escaping`, including the bad things, can also be done with character maps. The big advantage of character maps is that they don't distort the data model, which means that they don't impact your ability to use a stylesheet-based transformation as a component in an application with clean interfaces to other components.

Choosing Characters to Map

Applications for character maps probably fall into two categories: those where you want to choose a nonstandard string representation of a character that occurs naturally in the data, and those where you want to choose some special character to trigger some special effect in the output.

An example in the first category would be the example shown earlier:

```
<xsl:character-map name="NBSP">
   <xsl:output-character char=" " string=" "/>
</xsl:character-map>
```

This forces the nonbreaking space character to be output as an entity reference. If the document is to be edited, many people will find the entity reference easier to manipulate because it shows up as a visible character, whereas the nonbreaking space character itself appears on the screen just like an ordinary space.

An example in the second category would be choosing two characters to represent the start and end of a comment. Suppose that the requirement is to transform an input document by "commenting out" any element that has the attribute «delete="yes"». By commenting out, I mean outputting something like:

```
<!--
  <para delete="yes">
     This paragraph has been deleted
  </para>
-->
```

This is tricky, because the result cannot be modeled naturally as a result tree—comment nodes cannot have element nodes as children. So we'll choose instead to output the `<para>` element to the result tree unchanged, but preceded and followed by special characters, which we will map during serialization to comment start and end delimiters.

The best characters to choose for such purposes are the characters in the Unicode Private Use Area, for example the characters from xE000 to xF8FF. These characters have no defined meaning in Unicode, and are intended to be used for communications where there is a private agreement between the sender and the recipient as to what they mean. In this case, the sender is the stylesheet and the recipient is the serializer.

If you assign private use characters in information that is passed between applications, especially applications owned by different organizations, you should make sure that your use of the characters is well documented.

Here is a stylesheet that performs the required transformation:

Example: Using a character-map to comment-out Elements

This example copies the input unchanged to the output, except that any element in the input that has the attribute «`delete="yes"`» is output within a comment.

Stylesheet

The stylesheet is `comment-out.xsl`:

```
<?xml version="1.0"?>
<!DOCTYPE xsl:stylesheet [
  <!ENTITY start-comment "&#xE501;">
  <!ENTITY end-comment "&#xE502;">
]>

<xsl:stylesheet version="2.0"
    xmlns:xsl="http://www.w3.org/1999/XSL/Transform">

<xsl:output use-character-maps="comment-delimiters"/>

<xsl:character-map name="comment-delimiters">
  <xsl:output-character char="&start-comment;" string="&lt;!--"/>
  <xsl:output-character char="&end-comment;" string="--&gt;"/>
</xsl:character-map>

<xsl:template match="*">
  <xsl:copy>
    <xsl:copy-of select="@*"/>
    <xsl:apply-templates/>
  </xsl:copy>
</xsl:template>

<xsl:template match="*[@delete='yes']">
  <xsl:text>&start-comment;</xsl:text>
```

```
    <xsl:copy-of select="."/>
    <xsl:text>&end-comment;</xsl:text>
</xsl:template>

</xsl:stylesheet>
```

Source

One of the paragraphs in the source file `resume.xml` is:

```
<p delete="yes">Aidan is also in demand as a consort singer, performing
with groups including the Oxford Camerata and the Sarum Consort, with
whom he has made several acclaimed recordings on the ASV label of
motets by Bach and Peter Philips sung by solo voices.</p>
```

Output

When the stylesheet is applied to the source file `resume.xml`, the above paragraph appears as:

```
<!--<p delete="yes">Aidan is also in demand as a consort singer,
performing with groups including the Oxford Camerata and the Sarum
Consort, with whom he has made several acclaimed recordings on the ASV
label of motets by Bach and Peter Philips sung by solo voices.</p>-->
```

Limitations

A character map applies to a whole result document; you cannot switch character mapping on and off at will.

The character map must be fixed at compile time. You cannot compute the output string at runtime, and there is no way the process can be parameterized. (You can, however, substitute a different character map by having different definitions of the same character map in different stylesheet modules, and deciding which one to import using `<xsl:import>`.)

Character mapping may impose a performance penalty, especially if a large number of characters are mapped.

Character mapping has no effect unless the result of the transformation is actually serialized. If the result tree is passed straight to another application that doesn't understand the special characters, it is unlikely to have the desired effect.

Character mapping only affects the content of text and attribute nodes. It doesn't affect characters in element and attribute names, or markup characters such as the quotes around an attribute value.

The character to be mapped, and all the characters in the replacement string, must be valid XML characters. This is because there is no way of representing invalid characters in the `<xsl:output-character>` element in the stylesheet. This means that character maps cannot be used to generate text files containing characters not allowed in XML, such as the NUL character (x00).

See Also

`<xsl:output>` on page 375

`<xsl:output-character>` on page 391

`<xsl:text>` on page 459

xsl:choose

The `<xsl:choose>` instruction defines a choice between a number of alternatives.

If there are two alternatives it performs the equivalent of `if-then-else` in other languages; if there are more than two, it performs the equivalent of a `switch` or `select` statement.

Changes in 2.0

There are no changes to the syntax of `<xsl:choose>` in XSLT 2.0. However, by using `<xsl:sequence>` instructions within the `<xsl:when>` or `<xsl:otherwise>` branch, it is now possible to use `<xsl:choose>` in cases where the required result is an atomic value, or a reference to an existing node. In XSLT 1.0, the result always consisted of newly constructed nodes.

Format

```
<xsl:choose>
  <!-- Content: (xsl:when+, xsl:otherwise?) -->
</xsl:choose>
```

Position

`<xsl:choose>` is an instruction; it is always used within a sequence constructor.

Attributes

None.

Content

One or more `<xsl:when>` elements.

Optionally, an `<xsl:otherwise>` element, which must come last if it is present at all.

Effect

The `<xsl:choose>` element is evaluated as follows:

❑ The first `<xsl:when>` element whose `test` *expression* is true is selected. Subsequent `<xsl:when>` elements are ignored whether or not their `test` *expression* is true. The `test` expression is evaluated to obtain its *effective boolean value*: The rules for this are given under `<xsl:if>`, on page 310.

- ❑ If none of the <xsl:when> elements has a test *expression* that is true, the <xsl:otherwise> element is selected. If there is no <xsl:otherwise> element, no element is selected, and the <xsl:choose> element therefore has no effect (it returns an empty sequence).

- ❑ The selected child element (if any) is executed by evaluating its sequence constructor in the current context. So the effect is as if the relevant sequence constructor appeared in place of the <xsl:choose> instruction.

The test expression in <xsl:when> elements after the selected one is not evaluated.

Usage

The <xsl:choose> instruction is useful where there is a choice of two or more alternative courses of action. It thus performs the functions of both the if-then-else and switch or Select Case constructs found in other programming languages.

Using <xsl:choose> with a single <xsl:when> instruction and no <xsl:otherwise> is permitted, and means exactly the same as <xsl:if>. Some people suggest writing every <xsl:if> instruction this way, to save rewriting it later when you discover that you want an else branch after all.

When <xsl:choose> is used within the body of an <xsl:variable> (or <xsl:param> or <xsl:with-param>) element, the effect is a conditional assignment: the relevant variable is assigned a different value depending on the conditions.

Examples

The following example returns the name of a state in the USA based on a two-letter abbreviation for the state. If the abbreviation is not that of a recognized state, it outputs the abbreviation itself.

```
<xsl:choose>
    <xsl:when test="state='AZ'">Arizona</xsl:when>
    <xsl:when test="state='CA'">California</xsl:when>
    <xsl:when test="state='DC'">Washington DC</xsl:when>
    ......
    <xsl:otherwise><xsl:value-of select="state"/></xsl:otherwise>
</xsl:choose>
```

The following example declares a variable called width and initializes its value to the width attribute of the current node, if there is one, or to 100 otherwise.

```
<xsl:variable name="width" as="xs:integer">
    <xsl:choose>
        <xsl:when test="@width">
            <xsl:sequence select="@width"/>
        </xsl:when>
        <xsl:otherwise>
            <xsl:sequence select="100"/>
        </xsl:otherwise>
    </xsl:choose>
</xsl:variable>
```

You might be tempted to write this as follows:

```
<!--WRONG-->
<xsl:choose>
   <xsl:when test="@width">
       <xsl:variable name="width" select="@width"/>
   </xsl:when>
   <xsl:otherwise>
       <xsl:variable name="width" select="100"/>
   </xsl:otherwise>
</xsl:choose>
<!--WRONG-->
```

This is legal XSLT, but it does not achieve the required effect. This is because both the variables called «width» have a scope that is bounded by the containing element, so they are inaccessible outside the <xsl:choose> instruction.

Everyone has personal preferences when coding. I tend to prefer constructs that are more compact than <xsl:choose>. I would probably write the above example as:

```
<xsl:variable name="width" select="(@width, 100)[1]" as="xs:integer"/>
```

See Also

<xsl:when> on page 438
<xsl:otherwise> on page 374
<xsl:if> on page 309

xsl:comment

The <xsl:comment> instruction is used to write a comment node to the result sequence.

Changes in 2.0

A select attribute is added in XSLT 2.0, allowing the content of the comment to be defined by an XPath expression rather than by a sequence constructor.

Format

```
<xsl:comment
  select? = expression>
  <!-- Content: sequence-constructor -->
</xsl:comment>
```

Position

<xsl:comment> is an instruction; it is always used within a sequence constructor.

Attributes

Name	Value	Meaning
select optional	Expression	Defines the string value of this comment node

The select attribute and the sequence constructor are mutually exclusive; if one is present, the other must be absent.

Content

A sequence constructor.

Effect

The value of the comment is produced by evaluating either the `select` attribute or the sequence constructor. If neither is present, the comment will be empty.

The sequence produced by evaluating the `select` attribute or the contained sequence constructor is first atomized, and each item in the atomized sequence is then converted to a string. If the `select` attribute is present, these strings are concatenated with a single space between adjacent strings; if a sequence constructor is used, they are concatenated with no separator. The resulting string forms the string value of the new comment node. For more details of this process, including error conditions that can arise, see `<xsl:attribute>` on page 201, which works exactly the same way.

The comment should not include the sequence «--», and it should not end in «-», because these sequences are not allowed in XML comments. The XSLT processor may recover from these errors by adding extra spaces to the comment, or it may report an error. If you want your stylesheet to be portable, you must therefore avoid generating these sequences.

In XML or HTML output, the comment will appear as:

```
<!-- comment text -->
```

Usage

In theory, a comment has no meaning to the software that processes the output document—it is intended only for human readers. Comments are therefore useful to record when and how the document was generated, or perhaps to explain the meaning of the tags.

Comments can be particularly useful for debugging the stylesheet. If each `<xsl:template>` in the stylesheet starts with an `<xsl:comment>` instruction, you will find it much easier to trace back from the output to your stylesheet.

Comments in HTML output are used for some special markup conventions, for example surrounding Dynamic HTML scripts. The purpose of the comment here is to ensure that browsers that don't understand the script will skip over it rather than display it as text. An example is shown below.

Examples

The following example generates a comment showing the date and time at which the output file was generated, and identifying the XSLT processor that was used.

```
<xsl:comment>
    <xsl:text> Generated on: </xsl:text>
    <xsl:value-of select="format-dateTime(
                          current-dateTime(),
                          '[D] [MNn] [Y] at [H]:[m01]:[s01]')"/>
    <xsl:text> using </xsl:text>
    <xsl:value-of select="system-property('xsl:product-name')"/>
    <xsl:text> version </xsl:text>
    <xsl:value-of select="system-property('xsl:product-version')"/>
</xsl:comment>
```

Typical output might be:

```
<!-- Generated on: 23 March 2004 at 12:13:02 using SAXON version 7.9-->
```

The following example outputs a piece of client-side JavaScript to an HTML output file:

```
<script language="JavaScript">
    <xsl:comment>
        function bk(n) {
            parent.frames['content'].location="chap" + n + ".1.html";
        }
    //</xsl:comment>
</script>
```

The output will look like this:

```
<script language="JavaScript">
    <!--
        function bk(n) {
            parent.frames['content'].location="chap" + n + ".1.html";
        }
    //-->
</script>
```

The comment cannot be written as a comment in the stylesheet, of course, because then the XSLT processor would ignore it entirely. Comments in the stylesheet are not copied to the output destination.

xsl:copy

The `<xsl:copy>` instruction copies the context node in the source document to the result sequence. This is a shallow copy; it does not copy the children, descendants, or attributes of the context node, only the context node itself and (if it is an element) its namespaces. For a deep copy, you need to use `<xsl:copy-of>`, see page 245.

Changes in 2.0

A new attribute `copy-namespaces` has been added, which allows control over whether namespace nodes for an element should be copied or not.

New attributes `validation` and `type` have been added to control whether and how the copied element is validated against a schema.

Format

```
<xsl:copy
   copy-namespaces? = "yes" | "no"
   use-attribute-sets? = qnames
   validation? = "strict" | "lax" | "preserve" | "strip"
   type? = qname>
   <!-- Content: sequence-constructor -->
</xsl:copy>
```

Position

`<xsl:copy>` is an instruction. It is always used within a sequence constructor.

Attributes

Name	Value	Meaning
copy-namespaces optional	«yes» or «no»	Indicates whether the namespace nodes of an element should be copied; default is «yes»
use-attribute-sets optional	Whitespace-separated list of lexical QNames	The names of attribute sets to be applied to the generated node, if it is an element
validation optional	«strict», «lax», «preserve», or «skip»	Indicates whether and how the copied nodes should be subjected to schema validation, or whether existing type annotations should be retained or removed
type optional	Lexical QName	Identifies a type declaration (either a built-in type, or a user-defined type imported from a schema) against which copied nodes are to be validated

Content

An optional sequence constructor, which is used only if the item being copied is a document node or an element.

Effect

The action depends on what kind of node the context node is, as follows:

Node kind	Action
document	A new document node is added to the result sequence. The sequence constructor is evaluated to provide the content for the document node. This works in the same way as the content of an <xsl:document> instruction, as described on page 242. The attributes use-attribute-sets and copy-namespaces are ignored. The type and validation attributes have the same effect as <xsl:document>.
element	An element node is added to the result sequence, as if by a call on <xsl:element>. This will have the same name as the context node. Although the local name and namespace URI are guaranteed to be the same as the original, the prefix may change. The namespace nodes associated with the current element node are also copied, unless «copy-namespaces="no"» is specified.
	The use-attribute-sets attribute is expanded: It must be a whitespace-separated list of QNames that identify named attribute sets in the stylesheet. The attributes within these named attribute sets are evaluated in the order they appear, and added to the new element node. The sequence constructor is then evaluated.
	Namespace fixup is applied to the new element, to ensure that it has all the namespace nodes it needs, in the same way as for the <xsl:element> instruction.
	With a schema-aware processor, the new element may be validated and may acquire a type annotation: This depends on the values of the type and validation attributes, and works exactly as for <xsl:element> described on page 260. Note the surprising consequence that «validation="preserve"» does not cause the type annotation of the original element to be retained: This is not feasible, because the content of the element is not being copied.
text	A new text node is added to the result sequence, with the same string value as the context node. The attributes use-attribute-sets, copy-namespaces, type and validation, and the sequence constructor are ignored
attribute	A new attribute node is added to the result sequence, as if by a call on <xsl:attribute>. This will have the same name and value as the context node. The use-attribute-sets and copy-namespaces attributes and the sequence constructor are ignored. Although the local name, namespace URI, and string value of the output attribute are guaranteed to be the same as the original, the prefix may change (for example, if two attributes added to the same element use the same prefix to refer to different namespace URIs)
	With a schema-aware processor, the new attribute may be validated and may acquire a type annotation: This depends on the values of the type and validation attributes, and works exactly as for <xsl:attribute> described on page 201.

Node kind	Action
processing instruction	A processing instruction node is added to the result sequence, with the same name and value (target and data in XML terminology) as the context node. The attributes `use-attribute-sets`, `copy-namespaces`, `type`, and `validation`, and the sequence constructor are ignored
comment	A comment node is added to the result sequence, with the same content as the context node. The attributes `use-attribute-sets`, `copy-namespaces`, `type`, and `validation`, and the sequence constructor are ignored
namespace	The namespace node is copied to the result sequence. The new namespace node will have the same name and value (that is, the same namespace prefix and URI) as the original. The attributes `use-attribute-sets`, `copy-namespaces`, `type`, and `validation`, and the sequence constructor are ignored

Usage

The main use of `<xsl:copy>` is when doing an XML-to-XML transformation in which parts of the document are to remain unchanged. It is also useful when the source XML document contains XHTML fragments within it, for example if the simple HTML formatting elements such as `<i>` and `<b>` are used within textual data in the source, and are to be copied unchanged to an HTML output document.

Although `<xsl:copy>` does a shallow copy, it is easy to construct a deep copy by applying it recursively. The typical manner of use is to write a template rule that effectively calls itself:

```
<xsl:template match="@*|node()" mode="copy">
    <xsl:copy>
        <xsl:copy-of select="@*"/>
        <xsl:apply-templates mode="copy"/>
    </xsl:copy>
</xsl:template>
```

This is sometimes referred to as the *identity template*. This template rule matches any node except a namespace or document node. This is because «@*» matches any attribute node, and «node()», which is short for «child::node()», matches any node that is allowed to be the child of something (that is, an element node, text node, comment, or processing instruction). Once this template rule is applied to a node, it copies that node, and if it is an element node, it copies its attributes unchanged and then applies itself to its child nodes—on the assumption that there is no other template rule with `mode="copy"` that has a higher priority.

An easier way of doing a deep copy is to use `<xsl:copy-of>`. However, the recursive use of `<xsl:copy>` allows modifications to be made to the tree while it is being copied, by adding further template rules. For example, if you want to copy the whole document except for the subtree rooted at a `<note>` element, you can achieve this with a stylesheet that contains the identity template as above, together with the rule:

```
<xsl:template match="note" mode="copy"/>
```

which does nothing when a <note> element is found. Because it does nothing, nothing is written to the result tree, so the <note> element is effectively deleted.

Examples

The following template rule is useful if the source document contains HTML-like tables that are to be copied directly to the output, without change to the structure.

```
<xsl:template match=" table | tbody | tr | th | td ">
   <xsl:copy>
      <xsl:copy-of select="@*"/>
      <xsl:apply-templates/>
   </xsl:copy>
</xsl:template>
```

The effect is that all of these elements are copied to the output destination, along with their attributes, but their child elements are processed using whatever template rule is appropriate, which might be the same one in the case of a child element that is part of the table model, or it might be a different template for some other element.

The following template rule matches any elements in the source document that are in the SVG namespace, and copies them unchanged to the output, along with their attributes. The SVG namespace node itself will also be included automatically in the output tree. (SVG stands for Scalable Vector Graphics, which is an XML-based standard that became a W3C Recommendation on September 4, 2001, and was designed to fill the long-standing need for including vector graphics in Web pages.)

```
<xsl:template match="svg:*"
             xmlns:svg="http://www.w3.org/2000/svg">
   <xsl:copy copy-namespaces="no">
      <xsl:copy-of select="@*">
      <xsl:apply-templates/>
   </xsl:copy>
</xsl:template>
```

This example uses «copy-namespaces="no"» to avoid copying the namespace nodes attached to the SVG elements. It is safe to do this because SVG elements and attributes do not include data that depends on in-scope namespaces. The namespaces used in the element and attribute names will automatically acquire namespace nodes as a result of the namespace fixup process described on page 265. It may be useful to get rid of extraneous namespace nodes. For example, if the SVG document was embedded in an XHTML document, and the purpose of the copy operation is to make it into a free-standing SVG document, then the default value «copy-namespaces="yes"» would mean that the free-standing SVG document would contain an unwanted reference to the XHTML namespace.

See Also

<xsl:copy-of> on the opposite page.

xsl:copy-of

The main purpose of the `<xsl:copy-of>` instruction is to copy a sequence of nodes to the result sequence. This is a deep copy—when a node is copied, its descendants are also copied.

Changes in 2.0

A new `copy-namespaces` attribute is introduced: This gives you control over whether or not the unused namespaces of an element should be copied.

Two new attributes `validation` and `type` are available, to control whether and how the copied nodes are validated against a schema.

Format

```
<xsl:copy-of
  select = expression
  copy-namespaces? = "yes" | "no"
  validation? = "strict" | "lax" | "preserve" | "strip"
  type? = qname />
```

Position

`<xsl:copy-of>` is an instruction. It is always used within a sequence constructor.

Attributes

Name	Value	Meaning
select mandatory	Expression	The sequence of nodes or atomic values to be copied to the output destination
copy-namespaces optional	«yes» or «no»	Indicates whether the namespace nodes of an element should be copied; default is «yes»
validation optional	«strict», «lax», «preserve», or «skip»	Indicates whether and how the copied nodes should be subjected to schema validation, or whether existing type annotations should be retained or removed
type optional	Lexical QName	Identifies a type declaration (either a built-in type, or a user-defined type imported from a schema) against which copied nodes are to be validated

The `type` and `validation` attributes are mutually exclusive: if one is present, the other must be absent.

Content

None; the element is always empty.

Effect

The result of evaluating the `select` expression can be any sequence, containing nodes, atomic values, or a mixture of the two. Each of the items is copied to the result sequence, as follows:

❑ If the item is an atomic value, it is copied directly to the result sequence. So the instruction `<xsl:copy-of select="1 to 5"/>` has exactly the same effect as the instruction `<xsl:sequence select="1 to 5"/>`.

❑ If the item is a text node, comment, processing instruction, or namespace node, then it is copied in exactly the same way as the `<xsl:copy>` instruction. The new node has the same name and string value as the original, but it has a new identity. For example, `generate-id()` applied to the new node will give a different result from `generate-id()` applied to the original.

❑ If the item is an attribute node, then it is copied to create a new attribute node. The new attribute node has the same name and string value as the original, but has a new identity. The type annotation on the new attribute node depends on the values of the `type` and `validation` attributes, in the same way as for `<xsl:attribute>` as described on page 201.

❑ If the item is an element node, then it is copied to create a new element node. This is a deep copy: All the attributes and children of the element node are also copied. The namespace nodes of this element, and of any descendant elements, are copied unless the `copy-namespaces` attribute is present with the value «no». The base URIs of copied element nodes are unchanged (which means that any relative URIs in the content of these nodes retain their original meaning).

The type annotation of the new element node depends on the values of the `type` and `validation` attributes. If the `type` attribute is specified, or if validation is set to «strip», «strict», or «lax», then the effect is exactly as if new content were being constructed from scratch: Existing type annotations are discarded, and the copied content is revalidated to construct type annotations. In the case of «validation="preserve"», the existing type annotations are copied over unchanged type annotations.

❑ If the item is a document node, then it is copied to create a new document node. This is a deep copy: All the children of the document node are also copied. All copied nodes below this document node retain the name, string value, base URIs, and type annotations of their respective originals. If «validation="preserve"» is specified, then existing type annotations are copied unchanged; in other cases, document-level validation may occur to create new type annotations. This follows the rules for the `<xsl:document>` instruction, which means that it includes checks on uniqueness and referential constraints such as `<xs:unique>`, `<xs:key>`, and `<xs:keyref>`.

Usage and Examples

There are two principal uses for <xsl:copy-of>: It can be used when copying data to and from a temporary tree, and it can be used for copying a subtree unchanged from the input document to the output.

Copying Nodes to and from Temporary Trees

One use of <xsl:copy-of> in conjunction with temporary trees arises when you want to write the same collection of nodes to the output in more than one place. This might arise, for example, with page headers and footers. The construct allows you to assemble the required output fragment as the value of a variable, and then copy it to the final output destination as often as required.

Example: Using <xsl:copy-of> for Repeated Output

Source

The source file soccer.xml holds details of a number of soccer matches played during the World Cup finals in 1998.

```xml
<?xml version="1.0"?>
<results group="A">
<match>
<date>10-Jun-98</date>
<team score="2">Brazil</team>
<team score="1">Scotland</team>
</match>
<match>
<date>10-Jun-98</date>
<team score="2">Morocco</team>
<team score="2">Norway</team>
</match>
<match>
<date>16-Jun-98</date>
<team score="1">Scotland</team>
<team score="1">Norway</team>
</match>
<match>
<date>16-Jun-98</date>
<team score="3">Brazil</team>
<team score="0">Morocco</team>
</match>
<match>
<date>23-Jun-98</date>
<team score="1">Brazil</team>
<team score="2">Norway</team>
</match>
<match>
<date>23-Jun-98</date>
```

```
     <team score="0">Scotland</team>
     <team score="3">Morocco</team>
     </match>
     </results>
```

Stylesheet

The stylesheet is in the file soccer.xsl.

It constructs an HTML table heading as a global tree-valued variable, and then uses <xsl:copy-of> every time it wants to output this heading. In this particular case the heading is fixed, but it could contain data from the source document, so long as the heading is the same each time it is output. If it contained calculated values, there would be a possible performance benefit by coding it this way rather than regenerating the heading each time.

```
<xsl:stylesheet version="1.0"
     xmlns:xsl="http://www.w3.org/1999/XSL/Transform">

<xsl:variable name="table-heading">
    <tr>
        <td><b>Date</b></td>
        <td><b>Home Team</b></td>
        <td><b>Away Team</b></td>
        <td><b>Result</b></td>
    </tr>
</xsl:variable>

<xsl:template match="/">
<html><body>
    <h1>Matches in Group <xsl:value-of select="/*/@group"/></h1>
    <xsl:for-each select="//match">
    <h2><xsl:value-of select="concat(team[1], ' versus ', team[2])"/>
    </h2>
    <table bgcolor="#cccccc" border="1" cellpadding="5">
        <xsl:copy-of select="$table-heading"/>
        <tr>
        <td><xsl:value-of select="date"/> </td>
        <td><xsl:value-of select="team[1]"/> </td>
        <td><xsl:value-of select="team[2]"/> </td>
        <td><xsl:value-of select=
            "concat(team[1]/@score, '-', team[2]/@score)"/> </td>
        </tr>
    </table>
    </xsl:for-each>
</body></html>
</xsl:template>

</xsl:stylesheet>
```

Output

(Apologies to soccer fans who know fully well that all these matches were played in France, on neither team's home territory. It's only an example!) See Figure 5-2.

Figure 5-2

In XSLT 1.0, temporary trees (then known as result tree fragments; the term has been dropped in XSLT 2.0) were very limited in functionality. There were only two things you could do with them: You could copy them to another tree using `<xsl:copy-of>`, and you could convert them to a string. Most XSLT 1.0 implementations provide an extension function to convert a result tree fragment to a node set (containing the document node at the root of the tree), which greatly increases the usefulness of result tree fragments because it allows them to be used as working data structures. In XSLT 2.0, this capability has become part of the standard, so a temporary tree can be used in exactly the same way as a source document. In fact, in XSLT 2.0 a temporary tree *is* a node, so there is no need for a special conversion function.

Deep Copy

The other use for `<xsl:copy-of>` is that it provides a simple way of copying an entire subtree of the input document directly to the output. As `<xsl:copy-of>` does a deep copy, this is simpler than using `<xsl:copy>`, although it can only be used when the whole subtree is to be copied without change. For example, an XML document defining a product description might have an element called `<overview>` whose content is pure XHTML. You could copy this to the output HTML document with a template rule such as:

```
<xsl:template match="overview">
   <div>
      <xsl:copy-of select="node()"/>
   </div>
</xsl:template>
```

Unlike the examples using `<xsl:copy>`, there is no recursive application of template rules here: each child node of the `<overview>` element is copied to the output destination in a single operation, along with all its children.

The most common example of this technique is using `<xsl:copy-of select="@*"/>` to copy all the attributes of the current element. You can also use this selectively. To copy specific attributes use the following code:

```
<xsl:copy-of select="@name | @height | @width"/>
```

Copying all the attributes with specific exceptions is also straightforward using the new «except» operator in XPath 2.0:

```
<xsl:copy-of select="@* except @note"/>
```

Copying Namespace Nodes

The `copy-namespaces` attribute provides a choice as to whether the namespace nodes in a tree are copied or not. By default, all the namespaces are copied.

If namespaces are used only in the names of elements and attributes, then there is no need to copy namespace nodes. In the new tree, all the necessary namespace nodes will be created by virtue of the namespace fixup process, which is described under `<xsl:element>` on page 265 but applies equally to elements constructed using `<xsl:copy>` or `<xsl:copy-of>`. Copying unwanted namespace nodes generally does no harm, but they are unnecessary and can clutter the result document, and in some cases they can cause DTD-based validation to fail.

The real problem arises when namespace prefixes are used in the values of attributes or text nodes. This happens, for example, if the document is an XSLT stylesheet containing XPath expressions, if it is an XML Schema, if it uses «xsi:type» attributes that identify schema-defined types (the value of this attribute is a QName, and therefore contains a namespace prefix), or if it uses any other XML vocabulary that contains references to the names of elements or attributes within the document content. Since the XSLT processor cannot know that these references exist, and since the references depend on the existence of namespace nodes to resolve namespace prefixes to a URI, it is unsafe to shed the namespace nodes.

There are some cases where losing namespace nodes is very desirable. For example, if an XML document is wrapped in a SOAP envelope, and then subsequently removed from the envelope, the round trip can easily cause the SOAP namespaces defined for use in the envelope to stick to the content when it is extracted using `<xsl:copy-of>`. Under these circumstances, using «copy-namespaces="no"» can be useful to remove unwanted namespaces from the result. But it is only safe to use this option if you know that there are no namespace prefixes in the content of text nodes and attribute nodes.

Copying Type Annotations

The `validation` attribute of the `<xsl:copy-of>` instruction gives you four options on how to handle type annotations:

❑ The «strip» option removes all type annotations from the element and attribute nodes being copied, leaving them only with the generic type annotations `xdt:untyped` and `xdt:untypedAtomic` respectively. The main advantage of doing this is that you know exactly where you stand. This is the default, unless overridden using the default-validation attribute of the `<xsl:stylesheet>` element, and it means that the behavior will be the same whether or not the processor is schema-aware.

Sometimes the «strip» option is needed because the existing type annotations do not make sense in a new context. For example, you might be copying a price-range attribute from an element in which the name is constrained to be a sequence of two numbers, to an element in which any string is allowed. Retaining the type annotation would cause spurious effects, or errors, if the attribute in its new context is then used for comparisons or sorting.

❑ The «preserve» option leaves all the type annotations intact. One might expect that this would be the default, but the value «strip» was chosen for consistency with other instructions. Generally speaking, if the source nodes have been validated and annotated, this will often be the option that makes most sense on `<xsl:copy-of>`.

This option works because the validity of an element or attribute depends only on its content (that is, on its attributes, its descendant elements, and their attributes). Cross-validation constraints that might be defined in the schema, such as id/idref or key/keyref constraints, are not taken into account by the XPath type system. This means that if the source data has a particular type annotation, you can take it on trust that the data is valid against that type, and if you copy the whole subtree, then the new nodes will still be valid against these types.

❑ The «strict» and «lax» options discard all existing type annotations, and then invoke the schema processor to validate the copied nodes. The same happens when you use the type attribute instead of the validation attribute. The way that validation works is exactly as described for the `<xsl:element>` instruction in the case of element nodes (see page 267), or the `<xsl:attribute>` instruction in the case of attribute nodes (see page 207), or the `<xsl:document>` instruction in the case of document nodes (see page 259). For other nodes and atomic values the validation and type attributes are ignored.

There may be cases where the existing nodes had a specific type annotation, but where revalidating the copied subtree either fails, or produces a different type annotation from the original. This is because the validation context may be different. If the subtree was originally validated as part of some larger tree, then it is possible that local element and attribute declarations were used on that occasion, whereas top-level element and attribute declarations are used this time. The top-level declarations may be either more or less permissive than the local declarations.

See Also

`<xsl:copy>` on page 240
`<xsl:variable>` on page 471

xsl:decimal-format

The `<xsl:decimal-format>` element is used to define the characters and symbols used when converting numbers into strings using the format-number() function.

Note that `<xsl:decimal-format>` applies only to the format-number() function. It has no effect on the way `<xsl:number>` formats numbers for display, nor on the default number-to-string conversion used by the `string()` function, nor on the format used when `<xsl:value-of>` is used to output a number as a string.

Import precedence now applies to decimal formats in a similar way as to other declarations.

Changes in 2.0

The specification of the `format-number()` function, which uses the `<xsl:decimal-format>` declaration, is substantially rewritten in XSLT 2.0, though users should notice few changes except in a few corner cases. The `<xsl:decimal-format>` declaration itself is unchanged.

Format

```
<xsl:decimal-format
  name? = qname
  decimal-separator? = char
  grouping-separator? = char
  infinity? = string
  minus-sign? = char
  NaN? = string
  percent? = char
  per-mille? = char
  zero-digit? = char
  digit? = char
  pattern-separator? = char />
```

Position

`<xsl:decimal-format>` is a top-level declaration. It may appear any number of times in a stylesheet, but only as an immediate child of the `<xsl:stylesheet>` element.

Attributes

Name	Value	Meaning
name optional	QName	The name of this decimal format. If omitted, the attributes apply to the default decimal format
decimal-separator optional	character	Character to be used to separate the integer and the fraction part of a number. Default is «.» (x2E)
grouping-separator optional	character	Character used to separate groups of digits. Default is «,» (x2C)
infinity optional	string	String used to represent the numeric value infinity. Default value is «Infinity»
minus-sign optional	character	Character used as the default minus sign. Default is «-» (x2D)

Name	Value	Meaning
NaN optional	string	String used to represent the numeric value NaN (not a number). Default value is «NaN»
percent optional	character	Character used to represent a percentage sign. Default value is «%» (x25)
per-mille optional	character	Character used to represent a per-mille (per-thousand) sign. Default value is «‰» (x2030)
zero-digit optional	character	Character used in a format pattern to indicate a place where a leading or trailing zero digit is required, even if it is not significant. Default value is «0» (x30). This character must be one that is classified in the Unicode database as a digit character, with the numeric value zero
digit optional	character	Character used in a format pattern to indicate a place where a digit will appear, provided it is a significant digit. Default value is «#» (x23)
pattern-separator optional	character	Character used in a format pattern to separate the subpattern for positive numbers from the subpattern for negative numbers. Default value is «;» (x3B)

Content

None; the element is always empty.

Effect

If a name attribute is supplied, the `<xsl:decimal-format>` element defines a named decimal format; otherwise it defines attributes of the default decimal format. A named decimal format is used by the `format-number()` function when it is called with three arguments (the third argument is the name of a decimal format); the default decimal format is used when the `format-number()` function is called without a third argument.

It is an possible to have more than one `<xsl:decimal-format>` element for the default decimal format, or more than one for a decimal format with a given name. The effective value of a given attribute (such as `zero-digit`) is taken from the declaration with the highest import precedence that specifies a value for the required attribute. It is an error if this selects more than one declaration, unless the values specified are the same.

The `<xsl:decimal-format>` element does not directly define the display format of a number. Rather it defines the characters and strings used to represent different logical symbols. Some of these logical symbols occur in the *picture string* used as an argument to the `format-number()` function, some of them occur in the final output number itself, and some are used in both. The actual display format of a number depends both on the picture string and on the choice of decimal format symbols.

For example, if there is a `<xsl:decimal-format>` element as follows:

```
<xsl:decimal-format name="european"
                    decimal-separator=","
                    grouping-separator="." >
```

then the function call:

```
format-number(1234.5, '#.##0,00', 'european')
```

will produce the output:

```
1.234,50
```

The use of the «.» and «,» characters in both the picture string and the output display is determined by the named `<xsl:decimal-format>` element, but the number of digits displayed, and the use of leading and trailing zeros, is determined solely by the picture string.

The structure of a picture string is defined in the description of the `format-number()` function in Chapter 7, page 558. The syntax of the picture string uses a number of special symbols: the actual characters used for these symbols are defined in the relevant `<xsl:decimal-format>` element. These symbols are:

```
decimal-separator
grouping-separator
percent
per-mille
zero-digit
digit
pattern-separator
```

The `<xsl:decimal-format>` element also defines characters and strings that are used, when required, in the actual output value. Some of these are the same as characters used in the picture string, others are different. These characters and strings are:

```
decimal-separator
grouping-separator
infinity
minus-sign
NaN
percent
per-mille
zero-digit
```

For example, if the `<xsl:decimal-format>` element defines the infinity string as «***», then the output of «`format-number(1 div 0, $format)`» will be «***», regardless of the picture string.

Usage

The `<xsl:decimal-format>` element is used in conjunction with the `format-number()` function to output numeric information. It is designed primarily to provide localization of the format for display to human readers, but it can also be useful when you need to produce an output data file using, for example, a fixed number of leading zeroes. It is typically used for numbers in the source data or computed from the source data, whereas the `<xsl:number>` element, which has its own formatting capabilities, is generally used for sequence numbers.

Each `<xsl:decimal-format>` element defines a style of localized numbering, catering for the variations that occur in different countries and languages, and for other local preferences such as the convention in the accountancy profession whereby parentheses are used to indicate negative numbers.

Examples

The tables in the following examples illustrate some of the effects achievable using the `<xsl:decimal-format>` element in conjunction with different picture string.

Example 1

This decimal format is used in many Western European countries; it uses a comma as a decimal point and a period (full stop) as a thousand separator, the reverse of the custom in Britain and North America.

The left-hand column shows the number as it would be written in XSLT. The middle column shows the picture string supplied as the second argument to the `format-number()` function. The right-hand column shows the string value returned by the `format-number()` function.

The patterns used in this example use the following symbols:

- «.», which I have defined as my thousands separator
- «,», which I have defined as my decimal point
- «#», which is a position where a digit can occur, but where the digit is omitted if it is an insignificant zero
- «0», which is a position where a digit will always occur, even if it is an insignificant zero
- «%», which indicates that the number should be expressed as a percentage
- «;», which separates the subpicture used for positive numbers from the subpicture used for negative numbers

```
<xsl:decimal-format decimal-separator="," grouping-separator="."/>
```

Number	Picture String	Result
1234.5	#.##0,00	1.234,50
123.456	#.##0,00	123,46
1000000	#.##0,00	1.000.000,00

Continues

Number	Picture String	Result
-59	#.##0,00	-59,00
1 div 0	#.##0,00	Infinity
1234	###0,0###	1234,0
1234.5	###0,0###	1234,5
.00035	###0,0###	0,0004
0.25	#00%	25%
0.736	#00%	74%
1	#00%	100%
-42	#00%	-4200%
-3.12	#,00;(#,00)	(3,12)
-3.12	#,00;#,00CR	3,12CR

Example 2

This example shows how digits other than the Western digits 0–9 can be used. I will use the Indic Arabic digits (that is, the Arabic digits used in many Arabic countries, as distinct from the so-called Arabic digits used in the West):

```
<xsl:decimal-format zero-digit="&#x0660;"/>
```

Number	Format pattern	Result
12345	·(x0660)	١٢٣٤٥

The digits will be output in the output XML or HTML file in the usual order (most significant digit first). Displaying the number correctly when it appears as part of text that runs from right to left is the job of the browser or other display software, and you shouldn't worry about it at the XSLT level.

Example 3

This example shows how the exceptional numeric values NaN and Infinity can be shown, for example in a statistical table.

```
<xsl:decimal-format NaN="Not Applicable" infinity="Out of Range"/>
```

Number	Format pattern	Result
number('a')	any	Not Applicable
1e0 div 0	any	Out of Range
-1e0 div 0	any	-Out of Range

See Also

`format-number()` function in Chapter 7, page 558
`<xsl:number>` on page 359

xsl:document

The `<xsl:document>` instruction creates a document node and adds it to the result sequence. The most likely reason for using it is to perform document-level validation on a temporary tree.

Changes in 2.0

This instruction is new in XSLT 2.0. It should not be confused with the `<xsl:document>` instruction described in the abandoned XSLT 1.1 working draft, which was the precursor to the `<xsl:result-document>` instruction in XSLT 2.0. The document created by `<xsl:document>` is a temporary document that becomes available for further processing within the stylesheet; the document created by `<xsl:result-document>` is a final output from the transformation.

Format

```
<xsl:document
  validation? = "strict" | "lax" | "preserve" | "strip"
  type? = qname>
  <!-- Content: sequence-constructor -->
</xsl:document>
```

Position

`<xsl:document>` is used as an instruction within a sequence constructor.

Attributes

Name	Value	Meaning
validation optional	«strict», «lax», «preserve», or «skip»	Indicates whether and how the document should be subjected to schema validation
type optional	lexical QName	Identifies a type declaration (either a built-in type, or a user-defined type imported from a schema) against which the outermost element of the new document is to be validated

The `type` and `validation` attributes are mutually exclusive: If one is present, the other must be absent.

Content

A sequence constructor.

Effect

The following sections describe firstly, how the content of the document node is constructed, and secondly how document-level validation works.

The Content of the Document

The `<xsl:document>` instruction creates a new document node. The content of the document is constructed by evaluating the sequence constructor within the `<xsl:document>` element.

The child nodes of the new document node are constructed in a process that is very similar to that used for constructing the content of an element node, described under `<xsl:element>` on page 263. There are differences, however, because unlike an element node, a document node cannot have attribute or namespace nodes.

Although the XML specification requires a well-formed document to contain exactly one element node, optionally preceded or followed by comments and processing instructions, this restriction is not carried forward into the XPath data model. In this model, a document node can contain any sequence of elements, text nodes, comments, and processing instructions (including an empty sequence) as its children. In fact, a document node can have any content that is allowed for an element node, except for the namespaces and attributes.

The process of forming the content of the document node is described below.

The first stage is to evaluate the sequence constructor contained in the `<xsl:document>` instruction (or in any other instruction that is being used to create a new document node, for example, `<xsl:copy>`, `<xsl:message>`, `<xsl:result-document>`, or `<xsl:variable>`). The sequence constructor is a sequence of instructions, and as its name implies, the result of evaluating these instructions is a sequence of items. Usually these values will all be newly constructed nodes but the sequence might also contain atomic values and/or references to existing nodes.

The way that the instructions in the sequence constructor are evaluated is described in the rules for each instruction; the items produced by each instruction are concatenated together (in the order in which the instructions appear in the stylesheet) to produce the final result sequence.

The second stage of the process is to use the result sequence delivered by evaluating the sequence constructor to create the content of the new document node. This process works as follows:

1. If there are any atomic values in the sequence, they are converted to strings using the XPath casting rules. Errors may arise if the value has a data type that cannot always be cast to a string, specifically `xs:NOTATION` and `xs:QName`.

2. Any sequence of adjacent strings is converted to a single text node, using a single space as a separator between adjacent strings.

3. If there is a document node in the sequence, then it is replaced in the sequence by its children (this may produce an arbitrary sequence of elements, text nodes, comments, and processing instructions).

4. Adjacent text nodes within the sequence are combined into a single text node, *without* any space separator. Zero-length text nodes are removed completely.

It is an error if the resulting sequence contains an attribute or namespace node. The processor has the choice of reporting this error, or ignoring these nodes.

Finally, the nodes in the sequence are attached to the document node as its children. Officially, this involves making a deep copy of each node: This is because nodes in the data model are immutable, so you cannot change the parent of an existing node. In practice, making a copy at this stage is very rarely necessary, because in most cases the node being attached has only just been created and will never be used independently of its new parent. The only case where it is necessary is where the result sequence contains references to existing nodes, which can be produced using the `<xsl:sequence>` instruction:

```
<xsl:document>
    <xsl:sequence select="//email[@date=current-date()]"/>
</xsl:document>
```

Even in this case, copying the nodes can be avoided if the result tree is to be immediately serialized.

Validating and Annotating the Document

The `validation` and `type` attributes control whether and how the new document is validated. They are available only if you are using a schema-aware processor. As usual, validation has two effects: It triggers a failure if the result document is invalid according to the schema, and it creates type annotations on the nodes in the tree.

The `validation` attribute has the same four values as on other elements: «`strip`», «`preserve`», «`strict`», and «`lax`». If the `validation` attribute is not specified, then the default is provided by the `default-validation` attribute on the `<xsl:stylesheet>` element, which in turn defaults to «`strip`».

- ❑ «`strip`» removes all type annotations, replacing them with `xs:untyped` for elements and `xs:untypedAtomic` for attributes.

- ❑ «`preserve`» leaves the type annotations as they are, determined by the `validation` and `type` attributes on the instructions that created individual elements and attributes.

- ❑ «`strict`» and «`lax`» firstly check that the tree represents a well-formed XML document, that is, that the children of the document node comprise exactly one element node, no text nodes, and any number of comments and processing instructions. If not, a failure is reported. Then the top-level element node (the document element) is validated against the schema definitions, with the difference being that «`lax`» validates an element only if a schema definition for that element can be found, while «`strict`» fails if no declaration of this element can be found.

- ❑ Validation of a document node works in the same way as validation of individual elements but with one important exception: Identity constraints defined in the schema are checked when validation is done at the document level, but not when it is done at element level. Identity constraints are those defined by the `<xs:key>`, `<xs:keyref>`, and `<xs:unique>` elements in XML Schema, as well as checking that `xs:ID` values are unique and that `xs:IDREF` and `xs:IDREFS` values reference an ID value somewhere in the document.

The «`type`» attribute gives the required type of the document element (not the document node). For example, if «`type="mf:invoiceType"`» is specified, then the single element child of the document node is validated against the schema type «`mf:invoiceType`».

Usage and Examples

The most likely reason for using `<xsl:document>` is to invoke validation of a temporary tree.

It is possible to perform element-level validation of the document element in a tree without using `<xsl:document>`, for example by writing:

```
<xsl:variable name="temp">
  <invoice xsl:type="mf:invoiceType">
    <xsl:call-template name="build-invoice"/>
  </invoice>
</xsl:variable>
```

However, this does not perform document-level validation: It doesn't check the `<xs:key>` and `<xs:keyref>` constraints defined in the schema, for example. To perform these extra checks, it is necessary to write the `<xsl:document>` instruction explicitly:

```
<xsl:variable name="temp">
  <xsl:document type="mf:invoiceType">
    <invoice>
      <xsl:call-template name="build-invoice"/>
    </invoice>
  </xsl:document>
</xsl:variable>
```

There are certain other situations where `<xsl:document>` might be needed. For example, this is the only way of producing a sequence containing several new document nodes. It is also necessary if you want the value of a variable, or the default value of a parameter, to be a document node, and you also want to use the «as» attribute of `<xsl:variable>` or `<xsl:param>` to define the type of the variable, for example «as="document(element(*, mf:invoiceType))"».

See Also

`<xsl:result-document>` on page 414
`<xsl:message>` on page 343

xsl:element

The `<xsl:element>` instruction is used to create an element node and write it to the result sequence. It provides an alternative to using a literal result element, and is useful especially when the element name or namespace is to be calculated at runtime.

Changes in 2.0

Two new attributes `validation` and `type` are available, to control whether and how the copied nodes are validated against a schema.

Format

```
<xsl:element
  name = { qname }
  namespace? = { uri-reference }
  use-attribute-sets? = qnames
  validation? = "strict" | "lax" | "preserve" | "strip"
  type? = qname>
  <!-- Content: sequence-constructor -->
</xsl:element>
```

Position

`<xsl:element>` is used as an instruction within a sequence constructor.

Attributes

Name	Value	Meaning
name mandatory	Attribute value template returning a lexical QName	The name of the element to be generated
namespace optional	Attribute value template returning a URI	The namespace URI of the generated element
use-attribute-sets optional	Whitespace-separated list of lexical QNames	List of named attribute sets containing attributes to be added to this output element
validation optional	«strict», «lax», «preserve», or «skip»	Indicates whether and how the element should be subjected to schema validation, or whether existing type annotations on attributes and child elements should be retained or removed
type optional	lexical QName	Identifies a type declaration (either a built-in type, or a user-defined type imported from a schema) against which the new element is to be validated

The `type` and `validation` attributes are mutually exclusive: If one is present, the other must be absent.

Content

A sequence constructor.

Effect

The effect of this instruction is to create a new element node, and to return this node as the result of the instruction. In some error cases, the results may be different: These situations are described below.

The name of the generated element node is determined using the `name` and `namespace` attributes. The way in which these attributes are used is described below in the section *The Name of the Element*.

261

The sequence constructor contained in the `<xsl:element>` instruction, together with the `use-attribute-sets` attribute, is used to form the content of the new element: that is, its namespaces, attributes, and child nodes. The way this works is described in the section *The Content of the Element*.

When a schema-aware XSLT processor is used, the new element (and its contained elements and attributes) may be validated to ensure that they conform to a type defined in a schema. This process results in the new element node having a type annotation. The type annotation affects the behavior of subsequent operations on this element node even though it is not visible when the result tree is serialized as raw XML. The validation and annotation of the new element node are controlled using the `type` and `validation` attributes. This is described in the section *Validating and Annotating the Element*.

The XSLT specification is written in terms of writing nodes to a result sequence. Sometimes it is convenient to think in terms of the start tag of the `<xsl:element>` element producing a start tag in the output XML file and the end tag of the `<xsl:element>` element producing the corresponding end tag, with the intervening sequence constructor producing the contents of the output element. However, this is a dangerous simplification, because writing the start tag and end tag are not separate operations that can be individually controlled, they are simply two things that happen together as a consequence of the `<xsl:element>` instruction being evaluated. This is explained in more detail in the section *Literal Result Elements* in Chapter 3, page 106.

The Name of the Element

The name of an element node has two parts: the local name and the namespace URI. These are controlled using the `name` and the `namespace` attributes.

Both the `name` and the `namespace` attributes may be given as attribute value templates; that is, they may contain expressions nested within curly braces. One of the main reasons for using the `<xsl:element>` instruction in preference to a literal result element (described in the section *Literal Result Elements* in Chapter 3, page 106) is that `<xsl:element>` allows the name of the element to be decided at runtime, and this is achieved by using attribute value templates in these two attributes.

The result of expanding the `name` attribute value template must be a lexical QName; that is, a valid XML name with an optional namespace prefix, for example, «`table`» or «`fo:block`». If there is a prefix, it must correspond to a namespace declaration that is in scope at this point in the stylesheet, unless there is also a `namespace` attribute, in which case it is taken as referring to that namespace.

If the name is not a valid QName, the XSLT processor is required either to report the error, or to leave this element node out of the generated tree, while still including its children (but not its attributes). Different processors may thus handle this error differently.

The local part of the name of the created element node will always be the same as the local part of the QName supplied as the value of the `name` attribute.

If the `<xsl:element>` instruction has a `namespace` attribute, it is evaluated (expanding the attribute value template if necessary) to determine the namespace URI part of the name of the created element node:

❑ If the value is a zero-length string, the element will have a null namespace URI.

❑ Otherwise, the value should be a URI identifying a namespace. This namespace does not need to be in scope at this point in the stylesheet, in fact it usually won't be. The system does not check that the value conforms to any particular URI syntax, so in effect any string can be used.

If there is no `namespace` attribute:

❑ If the supplied QName includes a prefix, the prefix must be a namespace prefix that is in scope at this point in the stylesheet. In other words, there must be an «`xmlns:prefix="uri"`» attribute either on the `<xsl:element>` instruction itself or on some containing element. The namespace URI in the output will be that of the namespace associated with this prefix in the stylesheet.

❑ Otherwise, the default namespace is used. This is the namespace declared, in some containing element in the stylesheet, with an «`xmlns="uri"`» declaration. If there is no default namespace declaration in scope, then the element will have a null namespace URI. Note that this is one of the few places in XSLT where the default namespace is used to expand a QName having no prefix; in nearly all other cases, a null namespace URI is used. The reason is to ensure that the behavior is consistent with that of an element name used in the start tag of a literal result element.

Element nodes, according to the formal data model, do not contain a namespace prefix, only a namespace URI and a local name. There are two situations in which a prefix needs to be generated for the element node: Firstly, when the `name()` function is called, and secondly, when the tree is serialized into textual XML. The XSLT specification leaves the choice of a prefix to some degree up to the implementation; however, the choice is constrained by the process known as *namespace fixup*, described below on page 265.

The Content of the Element

The attributes, namespaces, and child nodes of the new element node are constructed in what is conceptually a three-stage process, though in practice most implementations are likely to collapse the three stages into one.

The first stage is to evaluate the sequence constructor contained in the `<xsl:element>` instruction. The sequence constructor is a sequence of instructions, and as its name implies, the result of evaluating these instructions is a sequence of items. Usually these values will all be newly constructed nodes but the sequence might also contain atomic values and/or references to existing nodes.

The way that the instructions in the sequence constructor are evaluated is described in the rules for each instruction; the items produced by each instruction are concatenated together (in the order in which the instructions appear in the stylesheet) to produce the final result sequence.

> *The instructions in a sequence constructor can be evaluated in any order, or in parallel, but their results must be assembled in the correct order on completion.*

If the `use-attribute-sets` attribute is present it must be a whitespace-separated list of lexical QNames that identify named `<xsl:attribute-set>` declarations in the stylesheet. The `<xsl:attribute>` instructions within these named attribute sets are evaluated, and the resulting sequence of attribute nodes is added to the start of the result sequence. For more details, see `<xsl:attribute-set>` on page 214.

The second stage of the process is to use the result sequence delivered by evaluating the sequence constructor (and the `use-attribute-sets` attribute if present) to create the content of the new element node. This process works as follows:

1. If there are any atomic values in the sequence, they are converted to strings using the XPath casting rules. Errors may arise if the value has a data type that cannot always be cast to a string, specifically `xs:NOTATION` and `xs:QName`.

2. Any sequence of adjacent strings is converted to a single text node, using a single space as a separator between adjacent strings. This allows list-valued content to be constructed, for example where the schema for the result document requires the content of an element to be a sequence of integers.

3. If there is a document node in the sequence, then it is replaced in the sequence by its children (document nodes in the data model are not constrained to represent well-formed XML documents, so this may produce an arbitrary sequence of elements, text nodes, comments, and processing instructions).

4. Adjacent text nodes within the sequence are combined into a single text node, *without* any space separator, and zero-length text nodes are removed.

5. Duplicate attribute nodes are removed. If several attributes in the sequence have the same name, all but the last are discarded.

6. Duplicate namespace nodes are removed. If several namespace nodes in the sequence have the same name *and string-value* (that is, they bind the same namespace prefix to the same namespace URI), then all but one of them are discarded. It makes no difference which one is kept.

It is an error if the resulting sequence contains an attribute or namespace that is preceded by a node that is not an attribute or namespace node. The processor has the choice of reporting this error, or ignoring the relevant attribute or namespace node.

The reason for this rule is to allow the implementation the flexibility to generate the output as an XML file, without having to build the result tree in memory first. If attributes could be added at any time, the whole result tree would need to be kept in memory.

Another error that can arise is that the sequence contains two conflicting namespace nodes, that is, two namespace nodes that bind the same prefix to different namespace URIs. Again, the processor can either report this error or ignore all but the last of the duplicates.

Finally, the attribute nodes in the sequence are attached to the new element as its attributes, the namespace nodes are attached as its namespaces, and the other nodes are attached as its children. Officially, this involves making a deep copy of each node: This is because nodes in the data model are immutable, so you cannot change the parent of an existing node. In practice, making a copy at this stage is very rarely necessary, because in most cases the node being attached has only just been created and will never be used independently of its new parent. The only case where it is necessary is where the result sequence contains references to existing nodes, which can be produced using the `<xsl:sequence>` instruction:

```
<xsl:element name="digest">
   <xsl:sequence select="//email[@date=current-date()]"/>
</xsl:element>
```

In this situation, the result is exactly the same as if `<xsl:copy-of>` had been used instead of `<xsl:sequence>`.

The third stage of the process is called *namespace fixup*. Conceptually this is done after all the nodes produced by the sequence constructor have been added to the new element. In practice all the information needed to do namespace fixup is available once all the attributes and namespaces have been added, and a processor that serializes the result tree "on the fly" is likely to perform this operation at that stage, so that the start tag of the serialized element can be output as early as possible. Namespace fixup is described in the next section.

Namespace Fixup

Namespace fixup is applied to any element node as soon as its content has been constructed, whether the node is created using the `<xsl:element>` instruction, or using another mechanism such as a literal result element, `<xsl:copy>`, or `<xsl:copy-of>`. The process ensures that the new element node will automatically contain all the namespace nodes it needs to bind unique namespace prefixes to the namespaces used in the element name itself and on the names of all its attributes.

Although namespace fixup is described in terms of creating namespace nodes for an element, another way of thinking about it is that it is the process that allocates namespace prefixes for the namespace URIs used in the element name and in the names of its attributes. It just happens that in the formal data model, namespace nodes are where these prefixes are held.

In principle, XSLT processors can choose any prefix they like when generating namespace nodes during the namespace fixup process. (Choosing a prefix in this discussion also includes the option of using the empty prefix, which is how the data model represents the default namespace.) In practice, processors will usually be able to make a sensible choice, resulting in prefixes that are recognizable to users, rather than random alphanumeric noise. For example, if the QName used as the value of the name attribute of `<xsl:element>` includes a prefix, then most processors will choose this prefix during the namespace fixup process. There are only really two reasons why a processor might choose a different prefix:

❑ There might be another prefix available that is just as good. For example, if the parent of the new element is in the same namespace, then the processor might decide to use the same prefix that was used for the parent element, which will reduce the number of namespace declarations required when the result tree is serialized.

❑ The prefix might already be in use to refer to a different namespace URI. This is more of a theoretical possibility than something that happens often in practice; it is most likely to occur in the case of the empty prefix (the prefix that identifies the default namespace). When this happens, the system may be forced to invent an arbitrary prefix such as «ns0001».

The main importance of namespace nodes is that they determine the namespace declarations that will be output when a result tree is serialized. Namespace nodes are not the same as namespace declarations, but they contain essentially the same information. Usually namespace nodes are handled automatically behind the scenes, and users don't need to worry about them. The only time they really become important is if your XML document uses QNames in the content of elements and attributes. In this situation, the XSLT processor doesn't necessarily know that your content is dependent on particular namespaces being in scope, and so it can't automate the process of generating the right namespace nodes in the same way as namespace fixup does for element and attribute names. You can use an `<xsl:namespace>` instruction to create a namespace node explicitly, in the rare cases where it isn't generated automatically through namespace fixup.

Namespace fixup also ensures that every element has a namespace node that maps the prefix «xml» to the namespace URI `http://www.w3.org/XML/1998/namespace`. At any rate, this is what the specification says. In practice, implementations probably won't store a real node for this namespace, instead they will simply behave as if it always existed.

It's worth observing one thing that namespace fixup *doesn't* do. When you create an element `<b>` as a child of `<a>`, namespace fixup does not try to give the `<b>` element a copy of every namespace node that is present for the <a> element. This reflects a new freedom that comes with the XML Namespaces 1.1 specification, which introduces the ability to undeclare namespaces. It was always possible under XML Namespaces 1.0 to write:

```
<a xmlns="one.uri">
    <b xmlns=""/>
</a>
```

which has the effect that the «one.uri» namespace is in scope for <a> but not for <b>. This is represented in the data model by the fact that the <a> element has a namespace node that maps the empty prefix to the namespace URI «one.uri», while the <b> element has no such namespace node. With XML Namespaces 1.1 it becomes possible to do the same thing with a nondefault namespace. You can now write:

```
<a xmlns:one="one.uri">
    <b xmlns:one=""/>
</a>
```

Again, this is represented in the data model by the fact that the <a> element has a namespace node that maps the prefix «one» to the namespace URI «one.uri», while the <b> element has no such namespace node. And if the above code appears in your stylesheet rather than your source document, it will have the same effect, as you would expect.

This also means that if you have a source document, which is simply:

```
<b/>
```

and you then write in your stylesheet

```
<a xmlns:one="one.uri">
    <xsl:copy-of select="/b"/>
</a>
```

then you will create the same data model. There is nothing in the rules that says the <b> element will acquire a namespace node for the «one.uri» namespace.

The only way to serialize this result tree into an XML document in such a way that you get exactly the same data model back when it is parsed (a property known as *round-tripping*) is as follows:

```
<?xml version="1.1"?>
<a xmlns:one="one.uri">
    <b xmlns:one=""/>
</a>
```

Unfortunately an XML 1.0 parser will throw this out, so it's not a very practical proposition as long as 99% of the XML users in the world are still using version 1.0. Therefore, to get this serialized output, you have to request both «version="1.1"» and «undeclare-namespaces="yes"» in your <xsl:output> declaration. Unless you do this, the serialized output will be:

```
<?xml version="1.1"?>
<a xmlns:one="one.uri">
    <b/>
</a>
```

This won't round-trip accurately, because the <b> element will acquire an extra namespace node in the process, but few people are likely to notice, and in any case, the behavior is consistent with what happened with XSLT 1.0.

For more details of serialization options, see <xsl:output> on page 375.

One final observation about namespace fixup: it doesn't create namespace nodes in respect of namespaces that are referenced in the content of the element, or the content of its attributes. For example, if you create the attribute «xsi:type="mf:part-number"», namespace fixup won't automatically create a namespace node for the «mf» namespace, even if you use a schema-aware processor that knows that the type of the «xsi:type» attribute is xs:QName. The problem is that namespace fixup has to be done before validation, because validation would reject an element on which the relevant namespaces haven't been declared; and until validation is done, there is no way of knowing that the attribute in question has type xs:QName. To find out how to generate an attribute whose value is an xs:QName, see page 210.

Validating and Annotating the Element

This section is relevant only if you are using a schema-aware XSLT processor. With a non–schema-aware processor, you cannot use the type and validation attributes, and the type annotation on the new element will always be xs:untyped, which you can effectively ignore because it imposes no constraints.

With a schema-aware processor, you can validate the new element to ensure that it conforms with relevant definitions in a schema. If validation fails, a fatal error is reported. If it succeeds, the new element will have a type annotation that reflects the validation that was performed. This type annotation will not affect the way the element node is serialized, but if you want to do further processing on the element, the type annotation may affect the way this works. For example, if you sort a sequence of elements annotated with type xs:integer, you will get different results than if they are annotated as xs:string.

If you use the type attribute, the value of the attribute must be a lexical QName that identifies a known type definition. Generally this means that it must either be a built-in type such as xs:string or xs:dateTime, or it must be the name of a global simple or complex type defined in a schema that has been imported using an <xsl:import-schema> declaration in the stylesheet. (That is, the local part of the QName must match the name attribute of a top-level <xs:simpleType> or <xs:complexType> element in the schema whose target namespace matches the namespace URI part of the QName.)

> *The XSLT specification allows the implementation to provide other ways of accessing type definitions, perhaps through an API or a configuration file, and it also allows the type definition to originate from a source other than an XML Schema, but since it provides no details of how this might work, we won't explore the possibility further here.*

The processor validates that the constructed element conforms to the named type definition. If it does, the element is annotated with the name of this type. If it doesn't, processing fails.

Validating an element is a recursive process, which also involves validating all its attributes and child elements. So these contained elements and attributes may also acquire a different type annotation.

In general, it's likely that some of the contained elements and attributes will be validated against anonymous type definitions in the schema, that is, types defined inline as part of another type definition (or element or attribute declaration), rather than named global types. In this case, the XSLT processor invents a name for each such type definition, and uses this invented name as the type annotation. The invented name is not visible to the application, though it might appear in diagnostics, but it is used during subsequent processing whenever there is a need to check that the element or attribute conforms to a particular type. (In practice, of course, the invented "name" might not really be a name at all, but a pointer to some data structure containing the type definition.)

There is potentially a lot of redundant processing if you validate every element that you add to the result tree, because elements at the bottom level of the tree will be validated repeatedly each time an ancestor element is validated. It's up to the XSLT processor to handle this sensibly; one approach that it might use is to mark the element as needing validation, but to defer the actual validation until it really needs to be done.

Validating the element may also have other effects, in particular, it may cause default values for elements and attributes within the element's content to be expanded. Default values can be defined in the schema using `<xs:element default="ABC">` or `<xs:attribute default="XYZ">`. So the element after validation may contain element and attribute values that were not put there explicitly by the stylesheet. The XSLT specification does not attempt to describe exactly how validation works, instead it simply points to the XML Schema specification, which describes the process in minute detail.

Validating an element using the `type` attribute places no constraints on the name of the element. It does not need to be an element name that is defined in any schema. The validation is concerned with the content of the element (including, of course, the names of its attributes and children) and not with its name.

In contrast, validation using the `validation` attribute is driven by the element's name.

There are two options for the `validation` attribute that cause schema validation to happen, and two options that cause it not to happen. Let's take the last two first:

❑ «validation="preserve"» means that the new element will have a type annotation of `xs:anyType`, and the attributes and elements in its content will have their original type annotation. During the (formal) process of copying nodes from the sequence produced by evaluating the sequence constructor, the nodes are copied with their type annotations intact.

❑ «validation="strip"» means that the new element will have a type annotation of `xs:untyped`, and in this case the attributes and elements in its content (at any depth) will have their type annotation changed to `xs:untypedAtomic` or `xs:untyped` respectively. (The type annotations are changed in the course of copying the nodes; the original nodes are, of course, unchanged).

The difference between `xs:anyType` and `xs:untyped` is rather subtle, and most applications won't notice the difference. However, the XSLT processor knows when it sees an `xs:untyped` element that all its descendants will also be `xs:untyped`, and this makes certain optimizations possible.

The other two options are «strict» and «lax»:

❑ «validation="strict"» causes the processor to look in the schema for an element declaration that matches the name of the element. That is, it looks for a top-level `<xs:element>` whose name attribute matches the local name of the element being validated, in a schema whose target namespace matches the namespace URI of the element being validated. If it can't find such a definition, a fatal error is reported. Otherwise, the content of the element is validated against the schema-defined rules implied by this element declaration.

If the element declaration in the schema refers to a named type definition, then on successful validation, the element is annotated with this type name. If the element declaration contains an inline (and therefore unnamed) type definition, the XSLT processor invents a name for this implicit type, and uses this invented name as the type annotation, just as in the case described earlier for the `type` attribute.

If the element declaration requires it, then strict validation of an element proceeds recursively through the content of the element. It is possible, however, that the element declaration is liberal. It may, for example, define the permitted contents of the element using `<xs:any>`, with `processContents` set to «lax» or «skip». In this case, validation follows the schema rules. If «skip» is specified, for example, the relevant subtree is not validated. All nodes in such a subtree will be annotated as if «validation="strip"» were specified.

❑ «validation="lax"» behaves in the same way as «validation="strict"», except that no failure occurs if the processor cannot locate a top-level schema definition for the element. Instead of reporting an error, the element is annotated as `xs:anyType`, and validation continues recursively (again, in lax mode) with its attributes and child elements. Once an element is found that does have a schema definition, however, it is validated strictly against that definition, and if validation fails, a fatal error is reported.

I said that the processor looks in the schema for an appropriate element declaration, but where does it find the schema? It knows the namespace of the element name at this stage, so if a schema for this target namespace has been imported using `<xsl:import-schema>` (see page 324) then there is no problem. Otherwise, the specification leaves things rather open. It recognizes that some processors are likely to have some kind of catalog or repository that enables the schema for a given namespace to be found without difficulty, and it allows this to happen where the implementation supports it. You can also create an `xsi:schemaLocation` attribute node on the element being validated, to provide guidance on where a schema document might be found. In other cases, the implementation is allowed to report an error.

If neither the `type` nor `validation` attribute is present, then the system behaves as if the `validation` attribute were present, and had the value given by the `default-validation` attribute of the containing `<xsl:stylesheet>` element. If no default is specified at that level, the effect is the same as «validation="strip"».

XSLT does not provide any way to request validation of an element against a local element or type definition in a schema. The way around this is to request validation only when you create an element for which there is a top-level definition in the schema. This will then implicitly validate the whole subtree contained by that element, including elements that have local definitions in the schema. Alternatively, many locally-declared elements make use of a globally-defined type, and you can then use the `type` attribute to validate against the type definition.

Usage and Examples

In most cases, elements in a result tree can be generated either using literal result elements in the stylesheet, or by copying a node from the source document using `<xsl:copy>`.

The only situations where `<xsl:element>` is absolutely needed are therefore where the element name in the result document is not fixed, and is not the same as an element in the source document.

Using `<xsl:element>` rather than a literal result element can also be useful where different namespaces are in use. It allows the namespace URI of the generated element to be specified explicitly, rather than being referenced via a prefix. This means the namespace does not have to be present in the stylesheet itself, thus giving greater control over exactly which elements the namespace declarations are attached to.

Example: Converting Attributes to Child Elements

This example illustrates how `<xsl:element>` can be used to create element nodes whose names and content are taken from the names and values of attributes in the source document.

Source

The source document `book.xml` contains a single `<book>` element with several attributes:

```
<?xml version="1.0"?>
<book title="Object-oriented Languages"
    author="Michel Beaudouin-Lafon"
    translator="Jack Howlett"
    publisher="Chapman &amp; Hall"
    isbn="0 412 55800 9"
    date="1994"/>
```

Stylesheet

The stylesheet `atts-to-elements.xsl` handles the book element by processing each of the attributes in turn (the expression «@*» selects all the attribute nodes). For each one, it outputs an element whose name is the same as the attribute name and whose content is the same as the attribute value.

The stylesheet is as follows:

```
<xsl:transform
  xmlns:xsl="http://www.w3.org/1999/XSL/Transform"
  version="1.0"
>
<xsl:output indent="yes"/>
<xsl:template match="book">
  <book>
    <xsl:for-each select="@*">
      <xsl:element name="{name()}">
        <xsl:value-of select="."/>
      </xsl:element>
    </xsl:for-each>
  </book>
</xsl:template>
</xsl:transform>
```

This selects all the attributes of the `<book>` element (using the expression «@*»), and for each one, it generates an element whose name is the same as the name of that attribute, and whose content is the value of that attribute.

Output

The XML output (on my system) is shown below. Actually, this stylesheet isn't guaranteed to produce exactly this output. This is because the order of attributes is undefined. This means that the `<xsl:for-each>` loop might process the attributes in any order, so the order of child elements in the output is also unpredictable. With Saxon, it actually depends on which XML parser you are using.

```
<book>
    <author>Michel Beaudouin-Lafon</author>
    <date>1994</date>
    <isbn>0 412 55800 9</isbn>
    <publisher>Chapman &amp; Hall</publisher>
    <title>Object-oriented Languages</title>
    <translator>Jack Howlett</translator>
</book>
```

See Also

`<xsl:attribute>` on page 201
`<xsl:copy>` on page 240
Literal Result Elements in Chapter 3, page 106

xsl:fallback

The `<xsl:fallback>` instruction is used to define processing that should occur if no implementation of its parent instruction is available.

Changes in 2.0

None.

Format

```
<xsl:fallback>
    <!-- Content: sequence-constructor -->
</xsl:fallback>
```

Position

`<xsl:fallback>` is an instruction. It is generally used within a sequence constructor. However, some new XSLT 2.0 instructions (`<xsl:analyze-string>`, `<xsl:next-match>`) allow an `<xsl:fallback>` element as a child even though they do not contain a sequence constructor. This is to allow fallback behavior to be defined for use when these instructions are encountered by an XSLT 1.0 processor.

Attributes

None.

Content

A sequence constructor.

Effect

There are two circumstances where `<xsl:fallback>` can be useful:

❑ In a stylesheet that uses XSLT features defined in version 2.0, to indicate what should happen if the stylesheet is used with an XSLT 1.0 processor. For example, the draft XSLT 2.0 specification introduces the new instruction `<xsl:result-document>`. If you want to use the `<xsl:result-document>` instruction in a stylesheet, and also want to specify what an XSLT 1.0 processor that doesn't understand this instruction should do, you can define the required behavior using `<xsl:fallback>`. XSLT 1.0 was carefully designed with extensibility in mind, so every XSLT 1.0 processor should implement this fallback behavior correctly even though the new XSLT 2.0 instructions were not defined at the time the processor was written.

❑ In a stylesheet that uses extension elements provided by a vendor, by the user, or by a third party, to indicate what should happen if the stylesheet is used with an XSLT processor that does not support these extensions.

If the `<xsl:fallback>` instruction is encountered in a sequence constructor that the processor can evaluate normally, it is ignored, along with its contents.

An instruction (as distinct from a literal result element) is an element that occurs in a sequence constructor and is:

❑ either in the XSLT namespace

❑ or in a namespace designated as an extension namespace by its inclusion in the `[xsl:]extension-element-prefixes` attribute of the element itself or a containing element. This attribute must be in the XSLT namespace if the element containing it is *not* in the XSLT namespace, and vice versa.

If an instruction is recognized by the XSLT processor, it is evaluated. The standard doesn't define exactly what "recognized by the XSLT processor" means. Typically it means that either the instruction is a vendor-specific extension implemented by that vendor, or it is a user-defined extension that has been installed or configured according to the instructions given by the vendor. It is also quite permissible for one vendor, say Oracle, to recognize extensions defined by another vendor, say Microsoft.

If an instruction is *not* recognized by the XSLT processor, the action taken by an XSLT 2.0 processor is as follows:

❑ For an element in the XSLT namespace, if the effective version is «2.0» or less, an error is reported. If the effective version is higher than «2.0», fallback processing is invoked.

❑ For an extension element, fallback processing is invoked.

Similarly, an XSLT 1.0 processor invokes fallback processing when it sees an instruction in the XSLT namespace if the effective version is «2.0» (or indeed, any value other than «1.0»).

The effective version is the value of the [xsl:]version attribute on the nearest enclosing element that has such an attribute (the attribute must be in the XSLT namespace if the element is *not* in the XSLT namespace, and vice versa). The value is a decimal number (for example «2.3», «10.852», or «17», and it is compared numerically. The idea is that a stylesheet, or a portion of a stylesheet, that uses facilities defined in some future XSLT version, 2.1 (say), should be given an effective version of «2.1».

Note that while XSLT 2.0 allows the version attribute to appear on any element in the XSLT namespace, XSLT 1.0 allowed it only on the <xsl:stylesheet> element. This means that if you want an XSLT 1.0 processor to invoke fallback behavior on a stylesheet that uses XSLT 2.0 features, you must either specify «version="2.0"» on the <xsl:stylesheet> element, or specify «xsl:version="2.0"» on a containing literal result element. In practice, it is a good idea to put the templates and other declarations that depend on XSLT 2.0 in a separate stylesheet module, and label that module with «version="2.0"» on the <xsl:stylesheet> element.

Fallback processing means that if the unknown instruction has an <xsl:fallback> child element, the <xsl:fallback> instruction is evaluated; otherwise, an error is reported. If there is more than one <xsl:fallback> instruction, they are all evaluated.

<xsl:fallback> is concerned only with fallback behavior for instructions within sequence constructors. Top-level declarations that the implementation doesn't recognize are simply ignored, as are unrecognized elements in another context (for example, an unrecognized child of an <xsl:choose> or <xsl:call-template> instruction).

Note that both the [xsl:]version attribute and the [xsl:]extension-element-prefixes attribute apply only within the stylesheet module in which they occur: They do not apply to stylesheet modules incorporated using <xsl:include> or <xsl:import>.

Usage

The <xsl:fallback> mechanism allows a stylesheet to be written that behaves sensibly with XSLT processors that handle different versions of XSLT. This is motivated by the experience of Web developers with HTML, and especially by the difficulty of writing Web pages that work correctly on different browsers. The design aimed to cater for a world in which some browsers would include an XSLT 2.0 processor and others would provide an XSLT 1.0 processor; in this situation, it would become necessary to write stylesheets that would work with either.

Similarly, it is very likely that each vendor of an XSLT processor (or each browser vendor) will add some bells and whistles of their own—indeed, this has already happened with XSLT 1.0. For server-side stylesheet processing you might be prepared to use such proprietary extensions and thus lock yourself into the products of one vendor; but more likely, you want to keep your stylesheets portable. The <xsl:fallback> mechanism allows you to do this by defining within any proprietary extension element what the XSLT processor should do if it doesn't understand it. This might be, for example:

❑   Do nothing, if the behavior is inessential, such as keeping statistics.

❑   Invoke an alternative implementation that achieves the same effect.

❑   Output fallback text to the user explaining that a particular facility cannot be offered and suggesting how they should upgrade.

An alternative way of defining fallback behavior when facilities are not available is to use the `element-available()` function, and to avoid executing the relevant parts of a stylesheet. This function is described in Chapter 7, page 542. The two mechanisms have overlapping functionality, so use whichever you find most convenient.

Examples

The two examples that follow illustrate the principal use cases for `<xsl:fallback>`: creating stylesheets that are forwards compatible across XSLT versions, and creating stylesheets that use vendor extensions while maintaining portability. The third example is not actually an example of `<xsl:fallback>` at all: It shows another method of achieving fallback behavior when `<xsl:fallback>` won't do the job.

Example 1: XSLT Forwards Compatibility

The following example shows a stylesheet written to exploit a hypothetical new XSLT feature in version 6.1 of the standard that inserts a document identified by URI straight into the result tree. The stylesheet is written so that if this feature is not available, the same effect is achieved using existing facilities.

```
<xsl:template match="boilerplate" version="6.1">
    <div id="boilerplate">
        <xsl:copy-to-output href="boilerplate.xhtml">
            <xsl:fallback>
                <xsl:copy-of select="document('boilerplate.xhtml')"/>
            </xsl:fallback>
        </xsl:copy-to-output>
    </div>
</xsl:template>
```

Example 2: Vendor Portability

Writing a stylesheet that uses vendor extensions but is still portable is not particularly easy, but the mechanisms are there to achieve it, especially in the case where several vendors provide similar extensions but in slightly different ways.

For example, several XSLT 1.0 processors (certainly xt, Saxon, and Xalan) provide a feature to generate multiple output files from a single stylesheet. With XSLT 2.0 this popular facility has made it into the XSLT standard, but before that happened, each product had to invent its own syntax. If you want to write a stylesheet that uses the XSLT 2.0 facility when it is available, but with fallback implementations for these three products, you could do it like this:

```
<xsl:template match="preface">
<a href="preface.html" xsl:version="2.0"
      xmlns:saxon="http://icl.com/saxon"
      xmlns:xt="http://www.jclark.com/xt"
      xmlns:xalan="com.lotus.xsl.extensions.Redirect"
      xsl:extension-element-prefixes="saxon xt xalan">
  <xsl:result-document href="preface.html">
    <xsl:call-template name="write-preface"/>
    <xsl:fallback>
      <saxon:output file="preface.html">
        <xsl:call-template name="write-preface"/>
```

```
            <xsl:fallback/>
        </saxon:output>
        <xt:document href="preface.html">
            <xsl:call-template name="write-preface"/>
            <xsl:fallback/>
        </xt:document>
        <xalan:write file="preface.html">
            <xsl:call-template name="write-preface"/>
            <xsl:fallback/>
        </xalan:write>
      </xsl:fallback>
    </xsl:result-document>
  Preface</a>
  </xsl:template>
```

Hopefully this little nightmare will disappear once XSLT 2.0 is finalized and becomes widely implemented. However, by then the vendors, no doubt, will have thought of other good ideas to include as nonstandard extensions.

Example 3: Temporary Trees

This example doesn't actually use `<xsl:fallback>`; it's an example of where the same effect needs to be achieved by different means.

One of the most important new features introduced in XSLT 2.0 is the ability to process a tree-valued variable as a document in its own right, using facilities such as XPath path expressions and `<xsl:for-each>`. The following code, which is perfectly legal in XSLT 2.0, will be flagged as an error by an XSLT 1.0 processor:

```
<xsl:variable name="us-states">
  <state abbr="AZ" name="Arizona"/>
  <state abbr="CA" name="California"/>
  <state abbr="NY" name="New York"/>
</xsl:variable>
...
<xsl:value-of select="$us-states/state[@abbr='CA']/@name"/>
```

The change to make this legal in XSLT 2.0 involves no new instructions, so it isn't possible to write an `<xsl:fallback>` template that defines what an XSLT 1.0 processor should do with this code: There's no suitable instruction to contain it. The only way of defining fallback behavior in this case is to test the XSLT version using the `system-property()` function. The following stylesheet will work with both XSLT 1.0 and XSLT 2.0. This accesses a lookup table defined as a global variable in the stylesheet. With a 2.0 processor, it accesses the variable containing the lookup table directly. With a 1.0 processor, it does it by using the «`document('')`» construct to read the stylesheet as a secondary input document.

```
<xsl:stylesheet version="2.0"
      xmlns:xsl="http://www.w3.org/1999/XSL/Transform">

<xsl:variable name="us-states">
  <state abbr="AZ" name="Arizona"/>
  <state abbr="CA" name="California"/>
  <state abbr="NY" name="New York"/>
</xsl:variable>
```

```
<xsl:param name="state" select="'AZ'"/>

<xsl:variable name="is-1.0"
   select="system-property('xsl:version')=1.0"/>

<xsl:variable name="lookup-table-1.0"
  select="document('')/*/xsl:variable[@name='us-states']"/>

<xsl:template match="/">
  <xsl:choose>
    <xsl:when test="$is-1.0">
      <xsl:value-of select="$lookup-table-1.0/state[@abbr=$state]/@name"/>
    </xsl:when>
    <xsl:otherwise>
      <xsl:value-of select="$us-states/state[@abbr=$state]/@name"/>
    </xsl:otherwise>
  </xsl:choose>
</xsl:template>

</xsl:stylesheet>
```

I used «version="2.0"» on the <xsl:stylesheet> element here, but in fact «version="1.0"» works just as well, because there is nothing in the forwards compatibility rules that relates to this situation, where the syntax is legal at both versions but the runtime behavior is an error for version 1.0. In theory, an XSLT 1.0 processor could legitimately reject the above stylesheet at compile time, regardless of whether it specifies «version="1.0"» or «version="2.0"», but fortunately the XSLT 1.0 processors that I've tried accept it without quibble.

In this example I used the standard document() function to provide fallback processing that works with all XSLT 1.0 processors. In more complex examples, the fallback processing might need to use vendor extensions such as Microsoft's msxml:node-set() extension function. In this situation different fallback mechanisms would be needed for different processors.

See Also

Extensibility in Chapter 3, page 128
Literal Result Elements in Chapter 3, page 106
element-available() function in Chapter 7, page 542
system-property() function in Chapter 7, page 581

xsl:for-each

The <xsl:for-each> instruction selects a sequence of items using an XPath expression, and performs the same processing for each item in the sequence.

Changes in 2.0

There are no changes to the syntax of this instruction in XSLT 2.0. However, the ability to process sequences of atomic values as well as sequences of nodes greatly increases its power.

Format

```
<xsl:for-each
  select = sequence-expression>
  <!-- Content: (xsl:sort*, sequence-constructor) -->
</xsl:for-each>
```

Position

`<xsl:for-each>` is an instruction, which is always used within a sequence constructor.

Attributes

Name	Value	Meaning
select mandatory	Expression returning a sequence of nodes and/or atomic values	The sequence of items to be processed

Content

Zero or more `<xsl:sort>` elements, followed by a sequence constructor.

Effect

The effect of the `<xsl:for-each>` instruction is to evaluate the sequence constructor that it contains once for each item in the selected sequence of items. The following sections describe how this is done.

The select Attribute

The `select` attribute is mandatory. The expression defines the items that will be processed. This may be any XPath expression, because every XPath expression returns a sequence. It is quite legitimate, and occasionally useful, to select a single item or an empty sequence.

The expression will often be a path expression, which may select nodes relative to the context node (the node currently being processed). Alternatively it may make an absolute selection from the root node, or it may simply select the nodes by reference to a variable initialized earlier. By referencing a tree-valued variable, or by using the `document()` function (described in Chapter 7, page 532) it may also select the root node of another XML document.

The `<xsl:for-each>` instruction can also be used to process a sequence of atomic values. The following example causes five empty `<br>` elements to be output:

```
<xsl:for-each select="1 to 5"><br/></xsl:for-each>
```

The sequence constructor contained within the `<xsl:for-each>` element is evaluated once for each item in the `select` sequence. Within this sequence constructor, the context item is the item being processed (one of the selected items); the `position()` function gives the position of that item in order of processing (the first item processed has `position()=1`, and so on), and the `last()` function gives the number of items being processed.

A common mistake is to forget that `<xsl:for-each>` changes the context item. For example, the following code will probably produce no output:

```
<xsl:for-each select="para">
  <p><xsl:value-of select="para"/></p>
</xsl:for-each>
```

Why? Because within the `<xsl:for-each>` element, the context node is a `<para>` element, so the `<xsl:value-of>` instruction is trying to display another `<para>` element that is a child of the first one. What the author probably intended was:

```
<xsl:for-each select="para">
  <p><xsl:value-of select="."/></p>
</xsl:for-each>
```

Sorting

If there are no child `<xsl:sort>` instructions, the selected items are processed in the order of the sequence produced by evaluating the `select` expression. If the `select` expression is a path expression, the nodes will be in *document order*. In the normal case where the nodes all come from the same input document, this means they will be processed in the order they are encountered in the original source document: For example, an element node is processed before its children. Attribute nodes belonging to the same element, however, may be processed in any order, because the order of attributes in XML is not considered significant. If there are nodes from several different documents in the sequence, which can happen when you use the `document()` function (described in Chapter 7, page 532), the relative order of nodes from different documents is not defined, though it is consistent if the same set of nodes is processed more than once.

> *The direction of the axis used to select the nodes is irrelevant. (The direction of different axes is described in Chapter 5.) For example, «`select="preceding-sibling::*"`» will process the preceding siblings of the context node in document order (starting with the first sibling) even though the preceding-sibling axis is in reverse document order. The axis direction affects only the meaning of any positional qualifiers used within the select expression. So «`select="preceding-sibling:: *[1]"`» will select the first preceding sibling element in the direction of the axis, which is the element immediately before the context node, if there is one.*

Although most XPath expressions return nodes in document order, not all do so. For example, the expression «`title, author, publisher`» returns a sequence containing first the child `title` elements, then the child `author` elements, and then the child `publisher` elements of the context node, regardless of the order that these nodes appear in the source document. The nodes returned by the XPath expression will be processed in the order of the sequence that is returned, not necessarily in document order.

If there are one or more `<xsl:sort>` instructions as children of the `<xsl:for-each>` instruction, the items are sorted before processing. Each `<xsl:sort>` instruction defines one component of the sort key. If the sort key contains several components, they apply in major-to-minor order. For example if the first `<xsl:sort>` defines sorting by country and the second by state, then the nodes will be processed in order of state within country. If two items have equal sort keys (or if the same item is included more than once in the sequence), they will be processed in the order that they appeared in the original result of the `select` expression. For a more complete specification of how sorting works, see `<xsl:sort>` on page 423.

If you want to process the items in the reverse of their original order, specify:

```
<xsl:sort select="position()" order="descending">
```

Alternatively, call the `reverse()` function. The following instruction will process the preceding siblings of the context node in reverse document order (that is, starting with the sibling closest to the context node and working backwards).

```
<xsl:for-each select="reverse(preceding-sibling::*)">
```

Usage and Examples

The main purpose of `<xsl:for-each>` is to iterate over a sequence of items. It can also be used, however, simply to change the context item. These two styles of use are illustrated in the following sections.

Iterating over a Sequence of Nodes

The most common use of `<xsl:for-each>` is to iterate over a sequence of nodes. As such it provides an alternative to `<xsl:apply-templates>`. Which you use is largely a matter of personal style, arguably `<xsl:apply-templates>` (*push* processing) ties the stylesheet less strongly to the detailed structure of the source document and makes it easier to write a stylesheet that can accommodate some flexibility in the structures that will be encountered, while `<xsl:for-each>` (*pull* processing) makes the logic clearer to the reader. It may even improve performance because it bypasses the need to identify template rules by pattern matching, though the effect is likely to be very small.

The following example processes all the attributes of the current element node, writing them out as elements to the result tree. This example is presented in greater detail under `<xsl:element>` on page 270.

```
<xsl:template match="book">
   <book>
      <xsl:for-each select="@*">
         <xsl:element name="{local-name()}"
                      namespace="{namespace-uri()}">
            <xsl:value-of select="."/>
         </xsl:element>
      </xsl:for-each>
   </book>
</xsl:template>
```

The next example is a general one that can be applied to any XML document.

Example: Showing the Ancestors of a Node

The following example stylesheet can be applied to any XML document. For each element it processes all its ancestor elements, in reverse document order (that is, starting with the parent node and ending with the document element), and outputs their names to a comment that shows the position of the current node.

Source

This stylesheet can be applied to any source document.

Stylesheet

This stylesheet is in the file `nesting.xsl`.

```
<xsl:transform
 xmlns:xsl="http://www.w3.org/1999/XSL/Transform"
 version="1.0"
>
<xsl:template match="*">
   <xsl:comment>
       <xsl:value-of select="name()"/>
       <xsl:for-each select="ancestor::*">
          <xsl:sort select="position()" order="descending"/>
          <xsl:text> within </xsl:text>
          <xsl:value-of select="name()"/>
       </xsl:for-each>
   </xsl:comment>
   <xsl:apply-templates/>
</xsl:template>

</xsl:transform>
```

Output

An example of the output this might produce is:

```
<!--BOOKS within BOOKLIST-->
   <!--ITEM within BOOKS within BOOKLIST-->
   <!--TITLE within ITEM within BOOKS within BOOKLIST-->Number, the
                                              Language of Science
   <!--AUTHOR within ITEM within BOOKS within BOOKLIST-->Danzig
   <!--PRICE within ITEM within BOOKS within BOOKLIST-->5.95
   <!--QUANTITY within ITEM within BOOKS within BOOKLIST-->3
```

Changing the Context Item

Another use of `<xsl:for-each>` is simply to change the context item. The need for this is reduced in XSLT 2.0, but it is still convenient on occasions. In XSLT 1.0, if you wanted to use the `key()` function (described in Chapter 7, page 572) to locate nodes in some ancillary document, it was necessary first to establish some node in that document (typically the root) as the context node, because the `key()` function will only find nodes in the same document as the context node.

For example, you might write:

```
<xsl:variable name="county">
   <xsl:for-each select="document('county-code.xml')">
      <xsl:value-of select="key('county-code', $code)/@name"/>
   </xsl:for-each>
</xsl:variable>
```

The effect is to assign to the variable the value of the name attribute of the first element whose county-code key matches the value of the $code variable.

In XSLT 2.0 this particular example becomes simpler, because the key() function now accepts a third argument identifying the document to be searched. You can now write:

```
<xsl:variable name="county"
        select="key('county-code', $code, document('county-code.xml'))/@name"/>
```

But there are other cases where the technique is still useful, for example if you need to call a named template that is designed to operate on the context node.

In a stylesheet that handles multiple input documents, it is always a good idea to declare a global variable:

```
<xsl:variable name="root" select="/"/>
```

Then you can always return to the original source document by writing:

```
<xsl:for-each select="$root">
    ...
</xsl:for-each>
```

See Also

<xsl:apply-templates> on page 187
<xsl:sort> on page 423
document() function in Chapter 7, page 532
key() function in Chapter 7, page 572

xsl:for-each-group

The <xsl:for-each-group> instruction selects a set of items, arranges the items into groups based on common values or other criteria, and then processes each group in turn.

Changes in 2.0

This instruction is new in XSLT 2.0.

Format

```
<xsl:for-each-group
   select = expression
   group-by? = expression
   group-adjacent? = expression
   group-starting-with? = pattern
   group-ending-with? = pattern
   collation? = { uri }>
   <!-- Content: (xsl:sort*, sequence-constructor) -->
</xsl:for-each-group>
```

Position

`<xsl:for-each-group>` is an instruction, which is always used within a sequence constructor.

Attributes

Name	Value	Meaning
select mandatory	Expression	The sequence of items to be grouped, known as the population
group-by optional	Expression	Grouping key. Items with common values for the grouping key are to be allocated to the same group
group-adjacent optional	Expression	Grouping key. Items with common values for the grouping key are to be allocated to the same group if they are adjacent in the population
group-starting-with optional	Pattern	A new group will be started for each item in the population that matches this pattern
group-ending-with optional	Pattern	A new group will be started following an item that matches this pattern
collation optional	Collation URI	Identifies a collation used to compare strings for equality when comparing group key values

The attributes `group-by`, `group-adjacent`, `group-starting-with`, and `group-ending-with` are mutually exclusive. Exactly one of these four attributes must be present.

Content

Zero or more `<xsl:sort>` elements, followed by a sequence constructor.

Effect

Grouping takes as input a collection of items (usually nodes) and allocates each of these items to one of a number of subcollections called groups. It then processes each of the groups in turn.

The effect of the `<xsl:for-each-group>` instruction is summarized as follows:

❑ The expression in the `select` attribute is evaluated. This can return any sequence (of nodes or atomic values). This sequence is known as the *population*, and the order of the items in the sequence is called *population order*.

❑ Each item in the population is allocated to one or more groups. The way this is done depends on which of the four attributes `group-by`, `group-adjacent`, `group-starting-with`, and `group-ending-with` is specified, and is described in detail below. When `group-by` is used, an item may have more than one grouping key and may therefore be allocated to any number of groups (zero or more). In all other cases, each item in the population is allocated to exactly one group. (For the benefit of mathematicians, the groups are then said to *partition* the population.)

❑ The initial item of each group is identified. This is the item in the group that is first in *population order*, as defined above. If one or more sort keys have been defined using `<xsl:sort>` elements within the `<xsl:for-each-group>` element, these sort keys are used to determine the processing order of the groups. Otherwise, the groups are processed in *order of first appearance*, that is, based on the position of their initial items in population order.

❑ There is a special rule covering what happens if an item is allocated to two groups and is the initial item in both of them. This can only happen if the item had several values for its grouping key, and the *order of first appearance* then relates to the order of these grouping keys in the result of the `group-by` expression. If the expression was «`group-by="author"`», and the value of this expression for the node in question was the sequence «`("Gilbert", "Sullivan")`», then the group for author Gilbert will be processed before the group for author Sullivan.

❑ The sequence constructor contained in the `<xsl:for-each-group>` element is evaluated once for each group. Within the sequence constructor, the function `current-group()` may be called to obtain the items that are members of this group (in population order); and if the groups were defined using `group-by` or `group-adjacent` then the function `current-grouping-key()` may be called to obtain the value of the grouping key that characterizes this group of items.

❑ The sequences that result from evaluating the sequence constructor once for each group are concatenated (in processing order) to form the final result of the `<xsl:for-each-group>` instruction.

If the population is empty, then the number of groups will be zero. No group is ever empty. Whether the population contains nodes or atomic values, no attempt is made to remove duplicates. This means that if the same node appears twice in the population, it will generally appear twice in each group that it is allocated to.

The following sections describe the effect of each of the four attributes `group-by`, `group-adjacent`, `group-starting-with`, and `group-ending-with` in turn.

group-by

The most common way of using `<xsl:for-each-group>` is to group items based on common values for a grouping key, which is achieved using the `group-by` attribute.

The `group-by` attribute is an XPath expression, which is evaluated once for each item in the population. It is evaluated with this item as the context item, with the position of this item in the population as the context position, and with the size of the population as the context size.

The value of the `group-by` expression is in general a sequence. This sequence is first atomized (as described in Chapter 2, page 73), and duplicate values are then removed from the atomic sequence that results. For each distinct value that remains in the sequence, the item is allocated to a group identified by this value. The total number of groups is equal to the number of distinct values present in the grouping keys for all items in the population.

Duplicate nodes are not removed from the population, but duplicate grouping keys calculated for a single node are removed. So if the authors of a book are J. Smith and P. Smith, and your grouping key is «`author/surname`», then when you process the group for Smith, this book will be processed once, not twice.

Grouping keys are compared based on their data type: For example numbers are compared as numbers, and dates are compared as dates. Two grouping keys are considered equal based on the rules of the XPath «eq» operator. Strings are compared using the collation specified in the `collation` attribute if present (for more details on collations, see under `<xsl:sort>` on page 427). Two NaN (not-a-number) values are considered equal to each other even though they are not equal when compared using «eq». If two values cannot be compared (because they are of noncomparable types, for example `xs:date` and `xs:integer`, or because they belong to a type such as `xs:duration` where no equality operator is defined) then they are considered not equal, which means the items end up in different groups.

If the `group-by` expression for any item in the population evaluates to an empty sequence, then the item will not be allocated to any groups, which means it will not be processed at all.

group-adjacent

When the `group-adjacent` attribute is used to define the grouping criteria, items are assigned to groups on the following basis:

❑   The first item in the population starts a new group.

❑   Subsequent items in the population are allocated to the same group as the previous item in the population if and only if they share the same value for the grouping key defined by the `group-adjacent` attribute; otherwise they are allocated to a new group.

The `group-adjacent` expression is evaluated once for each item in the population. During this evaluation, the context item is this item, the context position is the position of this item in population order, and the context size is the size of the population. The value that results from evaluating the `group-adjacent` expression is atomized (see page **000**). Unlike the `group-by` attribute, the result of evaluating the `group-adjacent` expression, after atomization, must be a single value. A type error is reported if the value is an empty sequence, or if it is a sequence containing more than one atomic value.

Values of the grouping key are compared in the same way as for the `group-by` attribute. This means, for example, that strings are compared using the collation defined in the `collation` attribute if specified, and that NaN values compare equal.

There are two main reasons for using `group-adjacent` in preference to `group-by`:

❑   Firstly, when there is a genuine requirement not to group items with the same grouping key unless they are adjacent. For example, a sequence of temperature readings might be presented so that the only readings actually shown are those that differ from the previous reading. This can be achieved by grouping adjacent readings, and only displaying the first reading in each group.

❑   Secondly, when it is known that the items with common grouping keys will always be adjacent in the population. In this case using `group-adjacent` might give the same result as `group-by`, but might be more efficient because the XSLT processor can perform the grouping in a single pass through the data.

group-starting-with

The `group-starting-with` attribute is a pattern (not an expression). Patterns are described in Chapter 6. Patterns apply only to nodes, so this attribute must be used only when the population consists entirely of nodes. The nodes in the population are assigned to groups on the following basis:

❑   The first node in the population starts a new group.

❑   Subsequent nodes in the population start a new group if they match the pattern, and are assigned to the same group as the previous node otherwise.

The result is that the initial node in each group (the one that comes first in population order) will always match the pattern, with the possible exception of the first group, which may contain no node that matches the pattern.

The group-starting-with attribute is useful where the population consists of a repeating group of nodes whose first member can be readily identified: for example, a <header> element followed by a sequence of <para> elements, then another <header>, and so on. In this case the grouping can easily be defined using «group-starting-with="header"».

group-ending-with

This attribute behaves in a very similar way to group-starting-with, except that the pattern identifies the last item in a group instead of the first. The nodes in the population are assigned to groups on the following basis:

❑   The first node in the population starts a new group

❑   Subsequent nodes in the population start a new group if the previous node in the population matches the pattern, and are assigned to the same group as the previous node otherwise.

The most common use case for this option is where input records contain a continuation marker of some kind. For example, the population might consist of elements that have the attribute «continued="yes"» or «continued="no"». A group can then be defined using the criterion «group-ending-with="*[@continued='no']"».

Sorting the Groups

If there are any <xsl:sort> elements as children of the <xsl:for-each-group>, these affect the order in which the groups are processed. They do not affect the order of the items within each group, nor which item in a group is considered to be the initial item.

The select expression in an <xsl:sort> element calculates a sort key that affects the group as a whole, but it is always evaluated with respect to the initial item in the group. The initial item in a group is the item within the group that was first in population order. The select expression is evaluated with this item as the context item, with the position of this item relative to the initial items of other groups as the context position, and with the number of groups as the context size.

If any of the attributes of the <xsl:sort> elements are attribute value templates, then the XPath expressions in these attribute value templates are evaluated with the same context item, position, and size as the select expression of the containing <xsl:for-each-group> element.

If there are no <xsl:sort> elements, or in cases where the initial items in two groups have the same values for their sort keys, the groups are processed in order of first appearance; that is, if the initial item of group G appeared in the population before the initial item of group H, then group G is processed before group H.

> *"Processed before" does not refer to the actual order of execution: the system can process the groups in any order, or in parallel. What it means is that the results of processing group G appear in the final result sequence ahead of the results of processing group H.*

In practice, if the groups are sorted at all then they are nearly always sorted by the value of the grouping key: *group the addresses in each city, sorting the groups by city*. This can be conveniently coded as:

```
<xsl:for-each-group select="//address" group-by="city">
    <xsl:sort select="current-grouping-key()"/>
    <city-group>
        <xsl:copy-of select="current-group()"/>
    </city-group>
</xsl:for-each-group>
```

The functions `current-group()` and `current-grouping-key()` are described on page 529 in Chapter 7.

An `<xsl:sort>` element within `<xsl:for-each-group>` is used to sort the groups. To sort the items within each group, use an `<xsl:sort>` element within the inner `<xsl:for-each>`, or write:

```
<xsl:perform-sort select="current-group()"/>
```

The `<xsl:perform-sort>` instruction is described on page 405.

You can also use the `<xsl:perform-sort>` instruction to sort the population before grouping starts.

Usage and Examples

The following sections give a number of examples of how `<xsl:for-each-group>` can be used to solve grouping problems. They are organized according to the four ways of defining the grouping criteria: `group-by`, `group-adjacent`, `group-starting-with`, and `group-ending-with`.

Using group-by

This is by far the most common kind of grouping. We'll start with a simple case.

Example: Single-Level Grouping by Value

This example groups a set of employees according to the department in which they work.

Source

We'll start with the following simple data file (`staff.xml`):

```
<staff>
    <employee name="John Jones" department="sales"/>
    <employee name="Barbara Jenkins" department="personnel"/>
    <employee name="Cormac O'Donovan" department="transport"/>
    <employee name="Wesley Thomas" department="personnel"/>
    <employee name="Maria Gomez" department="sales"/>
</staff>
```

Output

The requirement is to output an HTML document in which the staff are listed by department:

```
<h2>sales department</h2>
<p>John Jones</p>
<p>Maria Gomez</p>

<h2>personnel department</h2>
<p>Barbara Jenkins</p>
<p>Wesley Thomas</p>

<h2>transport department</h2>
<p>Cormac O'Donovan</p>
```

Stylesheet

This output is simple to achieve. The full stylesheet is in group-by-dept.xsl:

```
<xsl:template match="staff">
  <xsl:for-each-group select="employee" group-by="@department">
    <h2><xsl:value-of select="current-grouping-key()"/>
          <xsl:text> department</xsl:text></h2>
    <xsl:for-each select="current-group()">
      <p><xsl:value-of select="@name"/></p>
    </xsl:for-each>
  </xsl:for-each-group>
</xsl:template>
```

A number of variations are possible on this theme. To sort the deparments, use an <xsl:sort> element within the <xsl:for-each-group>. To sort the employees within each department, use an <xsl:sort> element within the <xsl:for-each>. The solution then becomes (sorted-depts.xsl):

```
<xsl:template match="staff">
  <xsl:for-each-group select="employee" group-by="@department">
  <xsl:sort select="current-grouping-key()"/>
    <h2><xsl:value-of select="current-grouping-key()"/>
          <xsl:text> department</xsl:text></h2>
    <xsl:for-each select="current-group()">
      <xsl:sort select="@name"/>
      <p><xsl:value-of select="@name"/></p>
    </xsl:for-each>
  </xsl:for-each-group>
</xsl:template>
```

This general design pattern, where <xsl:for-each-group> is used at the outer level to iterate over the groups, and an inner <xsl:for-each> is used to iterate over the items within a group, is typical. But there are a number of useful variations:

❑ The inner loop is sometimes better done using `<xsl:apply-templates select="current-group()"/>`, especially if the group includes elements of different types.

❑ Sometimes the entire inner loop can be written as `<xsl:copy-of select="current-group()"/>`, especially when generating XML output.

❑ Sometimes the requirement is not to display the items in each group, but to calculate some aggregate function for these items: for example to list for each department, the name of the department, the number of employees, and the maximum salary. In this case, the inner loop might not be explicit. The number of employees in the group is easily computed as «count(current-group())». Our sample data doesn't show salary, but if this was available as an extra attribute on the `<employee>` element then you could easily calculate the maximum salary as «max(current-group()/@salary)».

❑ If the requirement is to eliminate duplicates rather than to group all the items (in our example, to output a list of departments) then the inner loop can be omitted entirely. But in this case it may be simpler to use the `distinct-values()` function described in *XPath 2.0 Programmer's Reference*.

❑ If you need to number the groups, or test whether you are processing the last group, then within the `<xsl:for-each-group>` element you can use `position()` and `last()` in the usual way. At this level, the context item is the initial item of the group being processed, and `position()` and `last()` refer to the position of this item in a list that contains the initial item of each group, in processing order.

The example above was expressed as a grouping problem ("list the employees grouped by department"), so it is easy to see that `<xsl:for-each-group>` can be applied to the problem. Sometimes grouping problems are not so easy to recognize. This might be the case if the example above were expressed as "for each department, list the name of the department and the number of employees."

Example: Multilevel Grouping by Value

Sometimes there is a need to do multilevel grouping. For example, you might want to group the employees by department, and the departments by location. Assume that the `<employee>` element now has a location attribute as well as a department attribute. It doesn't really matter whether departments can span locations, the code will work either way.

Source

The data is now like this (`staff-locations.xml`):

```
<staff>
   <employee name="John Jones"
             department="sales"
             location="New York"/>
   <employee name="Barbara Jenkins"
             department="personnel"
             location="Los Angeles"/>
   <employee name="Cormac O'Donovan"
             department="transport"
             location="New York"/>
```

```
    <employee name="Wesley Thomas"
            department="personnel"
            location="Los Angeles"/>
    <employee name="Maria Gomez"
            department="sales"
            location="Seattle"/>
</staff>
```

Output

You might want the output presented like this:

```
Location: Los Angeles
    Department: Personnel
        Barbara Jenkins
        Wesley Thomas
Location: New York
    Department: Sales
        John Jones
    Department: Transport
        Cormac O'Donovan
Location: Seattle
    Department: Sales
        Maria Gomez
```

Stylesheet

Assume that the indentation is achieved using CSS styles, so you can concentrate on getting the structure of the information right. To do this multilevel grouping, just use two levels of `<xsl:for-each-group>` elements (multi-level.xsl):

```
<xsl:template match="staff">
  <xsl:for-each-group select="employee" group-by="@location">
    <xsl:sort select="current-grouping-key()"/>
    <p class="indent0">
      <xsl:text>Location </xsl:text>
      <xsl:value-of select="current-grouping-key()"/>
    </p>
    <xsl:for-each-group select="current-group()" group-by="@department">
      <xsl:sort select="current-grouping-key()"/>
      <p class="indent1">
        <xsl:text>Location </xsl:text>
        <xsl:value-of select="current-grouping-key()"/>
      </p>
      <xsl:for-each select="current-group()">
        <xsl:sort select="@name"/>
        <p class="indent2">
          <xsl:text>Location </xsl:text>
          <xsl:value-of select="@name"/>
        </p>
      </xsl:for-each>
    </xsl:for-each-group>
  </xsl:for-each-group>
</xsl:template>
```

A similar requirement is where there is a composite grouping key ("group employees that have the same department and the same location"). There are two ways of handling this. You can either treat it as a single level of grouping, using the concatenation of the two values as the grouping key, or you can treat it as two nested groupings in which the outer level does nothing (composite.xsl):

```
<xsl:for-each-group select="employee" group-by="@location">
  <xsl:for-each-group select="current-group()" group-by="@department">
    ...
  </xsl:for-each-group>
</xsl:for-each-group>
```

The two techniques are not completely identical. For example, with a single-level grouping using a concatenated key, the value of position() while processing a department will run continuously from 1 up to the total number of groups, but with a two-level grouping, position() will start again at 1 for each location.

The group-by option also allows an item to belong to more than one group. Suppose that an employee can work for several departments, and that the department attribute is extended to be a whitespace-separated list of department names. If you are using a schema-aware processor that annotates this attribute as belonging to a list-valued type, then all the examples we have written above will handle this situation without change. When you write «group-by="@department"», the value of the expression is atomized, and if the type is a list-valued type, this will return the sequence of atomic values contained in the attribute. The item with this grouping key is then allocated to one group for each department. I was careful to output the department name by referring to <xsl:value-of select="current-grouping-key()"/>; if I had written <xsl:value-of select="@department"/> the output would have been rather confusing, because instead of listing the name of the single department to which all the employees in this group belong, the code would list all the deparments to which the first employee in the group belongs.

Using group-adjacent

The group-adjacent option attaches significance not only to the value of the grouping key, but to the order of items in the population. So it shouldn't be a surprise to find that most of its applications come with document-oriented XML, where order is typically much more signicant than with data-oriented XML.

Here's a simple example: Given a sequence consisting of <para> elements and <bullet> elements, you want to convert the <para> elements into <p> elements, and the <bullet> elements into <li> elements, with a <ul> element wrapped around a sequence of consecutive bullets. You can do this as follows:

```
<xsl:template match="para">
  <p>
    <xsl:for-each-group
                group-adjacent="if (self::bullet) then 0 else position()">
      <xsl:apply-templates/>
    </xsl:for-each-group>
  </p>
</xsl:template>
```

The grouping condition ensures that adjacent <bullet> elements go in a group together, while each <para> element goes in a group by itself (calling position() ensures each <para> element gets a unique grouping key—you could also have used generate-id()). We are only interested in the rule that processes the first bullet:

```
<xsl:template match="bullet">
  <ul>
    <xsl:apply-templates select="current-group()" mode="each-bullet"/>
  </ul>
</xsl:template>
```

This template rule processes the group of adjacent bullets by outputting the necessary <ul> element to the result tree, and inside this it creates the elements that represent each individual bullet, by calling another template rule (in a different mode) to process each one.

Now look at a more complex example, involving the formatting of a Shakespeare play. You can download the text of all Shakespeare's plays, marked up in XML by Jon Bosak, at http://metalab.unc.edu/bosak/xml/eg/shaks200.zip.

Example: Grouping Consecutive Elements by Name

This example shows how to tackle a problem in which the content of an element (in this case, a <SPEECH>) consists of a number of <SPEAKER> elements followed by a number of <LINE> elements.

Source

You can run this example on any of the Shakespeare plays. For convenience, the download directory contains the file ado-scene1.xml, containing the first scene from *Much Ado About Nothing*.

In this markup, a <SCENE> element consists of a sequence of <SPEECH> elements interleaved with stage directions. A <SPEECH> contains one or more <SPEAKER> elements indicating who is speaking, and one or more <LINE> elements indicating what they are saying. So in *Hamlet* you have speeches like this:

```
<SPEECH>
<SPEAKER>HAMLET</SPEAKER>
<LINE>My fate cries out,</LINE>
<LINE>And makes each petty artery in this body</LINE>
<LINE>As hardy as the Nemean lion's nerve.</LINE>
<LINE>Still am I call'd. Unhand me, gentlemen.</LINE>
<LINE>By heaven, I'll make a ghost of him that lets me!</LINE>
<LINE>I say, away! Go on; I'll follow thee.</LINE>
</SPEECH>
```

and also speeches with multiple speakers:

```
<SPEECH>
<SPEAKER>ROSENCRANTZ</SPEAKER>
<SPEAKER>GUILDENSTERN</SPEAKER>
<LINE>We'll wait upon you.</LINE>
</SPEECH>
```

There are very few occasions where Shakespeare allows two characters to speak together for more than a single line (the witches' speech in *Macbeth* is tagged as `<SPEAKER>ALL</SPEAKER>`), but here is an example from *Timon of Athens*:

```
<SPEECH>
<SPEAKER>PHRYNIA</SPEAKER>
<SPEAKER>TIMANDRA</SPEAKER>
<LINE>Well, more gold: what then?</LINE>
<LINE>Believe't, that we'll do any thing for gold.</LINE>
</SPEECH>
```

Output

Suppose that you want to output each speech as a row in a table, with the speakers listed in one column, and the text in the other. It should look like this (you wouldn't normally make the table cells visible in this way, but it helps to be able to see the structure):

PHRYNIA TIMANDRA	More counsel with more money, bounteous Timon.
TIMON	More whore, more mischief first; I have given you earnest.
ALCIBIADES	Strike up the drum towards Athens! Farewell, Timon: If I thrive well, I'll visit thee again.
TIMON	If I hope well, I'll never see thee more.

Stylesheet

So what does the stylesheet look like?

The content of a `<SPEECH>` element consists of two groups: a group containing consecutive `<SPEAKER>` elements and a group containing consecutive `<LINE>` elements. So you can write it like this:

```
<xsl:template match="SPEECH">
  <tr>
  <xsl:for-each-group select="*" group-adjacent="name()">
    <td valign="top">
      <xsl:for-each select="current-group()">
        <xsl:apply-templates select="."/>
        <xsl:if test="position()!=last()"><br/></xsl:if>
      </xsl:for-each>
    </td>
  </xsl:for-each-group>
  </tr>
</xsl:template>
```

Here we are using the name of an element as its grouping key.

Actually, I omitted one complication. Within the sequence of <LINE> elements there can also be a <STAGEDIR> representing a stage direction, thus:

```
<SPEECH>
<SPEAKER>TIMON</SPEAKER>
<LINE>Long live so, and so die.</LINE>
<STAGEDIR>Exit APEMANTUS</STAGEDIR>
<LINE>I am quit.</LINE>
<LINE>Moe things like men! Eat, Timon, and abhor them.</LINE>
</SPEECH>
```

When this happens you would want to output it, in its proper place, in italics:

TIMON	Long live so, and so die.
	Exit APEMANTUS
	I am quit.
	Moe things like men! Eat, Timon, and abhor them.

What does this do to the stylesheet?

The second group, the one that comprises the right-hand column of the table, no longer shares a common element name. What you can do, however, is allocate <SPEAKER> elements to one group, and anything else to a different group.

```
<xsl:template match="SPEECH">
  <tr>
  <xsl:for-each-group select="*"
                      group-adjacent="if (self::SPEAKER) then 0 else 1">
    <td valign="top">
       <xsl:for-each select="current-group()">
          <xsl:apply-templates select="."/>
          <xsl:if test="position()!=last()"><br/></xsl:if>
       </xsl:for-each>
    </td>
  </xsl:for-each-group>
  </tr>
</xsl:template>
```

The fact that you output the content of the <SPEAKER> and <LINE> elements using <xsl:apply-templates> means that you don't have to change the body of this rule to handle <STAGEDIR> elements as well, all you need to do is add a template rule with «match="SPEECH/STAGEDIR"» to handle them.

To complete the stylesheet, you need to add template rules for the individual elements such as <STAGEDIR>. These are straightforward, so I will not list them here. You can find the complete stylesheet in speech.xsl.

You could actually have used a boolean grouping key, «group-adjacent="boolean (self::SPEAKER)"», but that would be a little obscure for my taste.

All these examples so far would work equally well using group-by rather than group-adjacent, because there are no nonadjacent items that would have been put in the same group if you had used group-by. But it's still worth using group-adjacent, if only because it's likely to be more efficient—the system knows that it doesn't need to do any sorting or hashing, it just has to compare adjacent items.

Example: Handling Repeating Groups of Adjacent Elements

This example is a slightly more difficult variant of the previous example, in which the <SPEECH> elements have been omitted from the input markup.

Source

If the Shakespeare markup had been done by someone less capable than Jon Bosak, the <SPEECH> elements might have been left out. You would then see a structure like this:

```
<SPEAKER>PHRYNIA</SPEAKER>
<SPEAKER>TIMANDRA</SPEAKER>
<LINE>More counsel with more money, bounteous Timon.</LINE>
<SPEAKER>TIMON</SPEAKER>
<LINE>More whore, more mischief first; I have given you earnest.</LINE>
<SPEAKER>ALCIBIADES</SPEAKER>
<LINE>Strike up the drum towards Athens! Farewell, Timon:</LINE>
<LINE>If I thrive well, I'll visit thee again.</LINE>
```

I have modified the markup of this (very long) scene from *Timon of Athens* and included it as timon-scene.xml.

Output

The required output is the same as in the previous example: that is, a table, in which each row represents one speech, with the names of the speakers in one column and the lines spoken in the other.

Stylesheet

There are various ways of handling such a structure, none of them particularly easy. One approach is to do the grouping bottom-up: First you put a group of consecutive speakers in a <SPEAKERS> element and a group of consecutive lines and stage directions in a <LINES> element; then you process the sequence of alternating <LINES> and <SPEAKERS> elements. Here's the logic, which is expanded into a full stylesheet in the download file alternate-groups.xsl:

```
<xsl:template match="SCENE">
<table>
  <xsl:variable name="sequence" as="element()*">
    <xsl:for-each-group select="*"
                        group-adjacent="if (self::SPEAKER)
                                        then 'SPEAKERS' else 'LINES'">
      <xsl:element name="{current-grouping-key()}">
        <xsl:copy-of select="current-group()"/>
      </xsl:element>
```

```
      </xsl:for-each-group>
    </xsl:variable>
    <xsl:for-each-group select="$sequence"
                        group-starting-with="SPEAKERS">
      <tr>
        <xsl:for-each select="current-group()">
          <td valign="top">
            <xsl:for-each select="*">
              <xsl:apply-templates/>
              <xsl:if test="position() != last()"><br/></xsl:if>
            </xsl:for-each>
          </td>
        </xsl:for-each>
      </tr>
    </xsl:for-each-group>
  <table>
  </xsl:template>
```

This does the grouping in two phases. The first phase creates a sequence of alternating elements named <SPEAKERS> and <LINES>, which you constructed by choosing these as your grouping keys. This sequence is held in a variable. The second phase uses group-starting-with to recognize a group consisting of a <SPEAKERS> element followed by a <LINES> element. All that remains is to process each group, which of course consists of a <SPEAKERS> element holding one or more <SPEAKER> elements, followed by a <LINES> element holding one or more <LINE> and <STAGEDIR> elements.

If I had presented an example query "find all the speeches in Shakespeare involving two or more speakers and containing two or more lines," and had presented the solution as «collection ('shakes.xml')//SPEECH[SPEAKER[2] and LINES[2]]», you would probably have found the example rather implausible. But if you want to know how I found the Timon of Athens quote, you have your answer.

Using group-starting-with

Like group-adjacent, the group-starting-with option selects groups of items that are adjacent in the population, and it therefore tends to be used with document-oriented XML. The difference is that with this option, there doesn't have to be any value that the adjacent nodes have in common: All that you need is a pattern that matches the first node in each group.

I used this technique for the Shakespeare example. In fact, given a scene consisting of alternating sequences of <SPEAKER> elements and <LINE> elements, with no <SPEECH> elements to mark the boundaries, I could have reconstructed the <SPEECH> elements by writing:

```
<xsl:template match="SCENE">
<xsl:copy>
  <xsl:for-each-group select="*" group-starting-with=
      "SPEAKER[not(preceding-sibling::*[1] [self::SPEAKER])]">
    <SPEECH>
      <xsl:copy-of select="current-group()"/>
    </SPEECH>
```

```
    </xsl:for-each-group>
   </xsl:copy>
  </xsl:template>
```

Here the pattern that marks out the first element in a new group is that it is a <SPEAKER> element whose immediately preceding sibling element (if it has one) is not another <SPEAKER> element.

A common use for group-starting-with is the implicit hierarchies one sees in XHTML. We will explore this in the next example.

Example: Handling Flat XHTML Documents

This example shows how to create a hierarchy to represent the underlying structure of an XHTML document in which headings and paragraphs are all represented as sibling elements.

Source

A typical XHTML document looks like this (flat.xml):

```
<html>
 <body>
  <h1>Title</h1>
  <p>We need to understand how hierarchies can be flat.</p>
  <h2>Subtitle</h2>
  <p>Let's get to the point.</p>
  <p>The second paragraph in a section often says very little.</p>
  <p>But the third gets to the heart of the matter.</p>
  <h2>Subtitle</h2>
  <p>To conclude, we are dealing with a flat hierarchy.</p>
 </body>
</html>
```

This fragment consists of a <body> element with eight child elements, all at the same level of the tree. Very often, if you want to process this text, you will need to understand the hierarchic structure even though it is not explicit in the markup. For example, you may want to number the last paragraph as «1.2.1».

Output

To manipulate this data, you need to transform into a structure like the one below that reflects the true hierarchy:

```
<body>
   <div><head>Title</head>
      <p>We need to understand how hierarchies can be flat.</p>
      <div><head>Subtitle</head>
        <p>Let's get to the point.</p>
        <p>The second paragraph in a section often says very little.</p>
        <p>But the third gets to the heart of the matter.</p>
      </div>
      <div><head>Subtitle</head>
```

```
    <p>To conclude, we are dealing with a flat hierarchy.</p>
  </div>
  </div>
</body>
```

Stylesheet

The `group-starting-with` option is ideal for this purpose, because the `<h1>` and `<h2>` elements are easy to match. Here is the code (`unflatten.xsl`):

```
<xsl:template match="body">
<xsl:copy>
  <xsl:for-each-group select="*" group-starting-with="h1">
    <xsl:apply-templates select="." mode="group"/>
  </xsl:for-each-group>
</xsl:copy>
</xsl:template>

<xsl:template match="h1" mode="group">
<div><head><xsl:value-of select="."/></head>
  <xsl:for-each-group select="current-group() except ."
                      group-starting-with="h2">
    <xsl:apply-templates select="." mode="group"/>
  </xsl:for-each-group>
</div>
</xsl:template>

<xsl:template match="h2" mode="group">
<div><head><xsl:value-of select="."/></head>
  <xsl:for-each-group select="current-group() except ."
                      group-starting-with="h3">
    <xsl:apply-templates select="." mode="group"/>
  </xsl:for-each-group>
</div>
</xsl:template>

<xsl:template match="h3" mode="group">
<div><head><xsl:value-of select="."/></head>
  <xsl:copy-of select="current-group() except ."/>
</div>
</xsl:template>

<xsl:template match="p" mode="group">
  <xsl:copy-of select="current-group()"/>
</xsl:template>
```

I've shown this down to three levels; it should be obvious how it can be extended.

When an `<h1>` element is matched, it is processed as part of a group that starts with an `<h1>` element and then contains a number of `<p>` and `<h2>` elements interleaved. The template rule first outputs the contents of the `<h1>` element as a heading, and then splits the contents of this group (excluding the first `<h1>` element, which is of no further interest) into subgroups. The first subgroup will typically start with an ordinary `<p>` element, and all subsequent subgroups will start with an `<h2>` element. Call `<xsl:apply-templates>` to process the first element in the subgroup, and this fires off either the «`match="p"`» template (for the first group) or the «`match="h2"`» template (for others). The «`match="p"`» template simply copies the group of `<p>` elements to the result tree, while the «`match="h2"`» template starts yet another level of grouping based on the `<h3>` elements, and so on.

If you wanted to be clever you could handle the `<h1>`, `<h2>`, `<h3>`, ..., `<h8>` elements with a single generic rule. This could be done by writing the pattern as:

```
group-starting-with=
        "*[name()=translate(name(current()), '12345678', '23456789')]"
```

Using group-ending-with

The `group-ending-with` option complements `group-starting-with` by matching the last item in a group instead of the first. This requirement is far less common, but it does arise. The classical example for it is where a large document has been broken up, for transmission reasons, into small arbitrary chunks, and the last chunk carries some distinguishing characteristic such as the absence of an attribute saying «`continued="yes"`». To reconstitute the documents from the sequence of chunks, `group-ending-with` is the answer:

```
<xsl:template match="sequence-of-chunks">
<xsl:for-each-group group-ending-with="*[not(@continued='yes')]">
    <doc>
        <xsl:copy-of select="current-group()/*"/>
    </doc>
</xsl:for-each-group>
</xsl:template>
```

Arranging Data in Tables

Arranging data in tables is a common requirement when generating HTML pages, and the `<xsl:for-each-group>` instruction can help with this in a number of ways. I will not present any detailed worked examples here, just a checklist of techniques. However, the examples are expanded in the download files: see `towns.xml`, `towns-by-rows.xsl` and `towns-by-columns.xsl`.

If you need to arrange data in rows, like this:

Andover	Basingstoke	Crawley	Dorking
Egham	Farnham	Guildford	Horsham
Ironbridge	Jarrow	Kingston	Leatherhead

the simplest approach is this, where «`$cols`» is the number of columns required:

```
<xsl:for-each-group select="town"
                    group-adjacent="(position()-1) idiv $cols">
<tr>
```

```
    <xsl:for-each select="current-group()">
    <td>
       <xsl:value-of select="."/>
    </td>
    </xsl:for-each>
</tr>
</xsl:for-each-group>
```

If the data needs to be sorted first, use the `<xsl:perform-sort>` instruction. For example:

```
<xsl:variable name="sorted-towns" as="element()*">
  <xsl:perform-sort select="town">
     <xsl:sort/>
  </xsl:perform-sort>
</xsl:variable>

<xsl:for-each-group select="$sorted-towns"
                    group-adjacent="(position()-1) idiv $cols">
  ...
</xsl:for-each-group>
```

The `<xsl:perform-sort>` instruction is described on page 405.

If you need to generate empty table cells to fill up the last row, one convenient way is to add them to the sequence before you start:

```
<xsl:variable name="gaps"
   select="(count(towns) idiv $cols)*$cols + $cols -- count(towns)"/>

<xsl:variable name="padding" select="
   if ($gaps = $cols) then ()
   else for $i in 1 to $gaps return ' '"/>

<xsl:variable name="cells" select="towns, $padding"/>

<xsl:for-each-group select="$cells">
  ...
</xsl:for-each-group>
```

If you want to arrange the data in columns, like this:

Andover	Dorking	Guildford	Jarrow
Basingstoke	Egham	Horsham	Kingston
Crawley	Farnham	Ironbridge	Leatherhead

then it is probably simplest to use `group-by`. The grouping key (the things that the towns in a particular row have in common) is the value of «`position() mod 3`» where 3 is the number of rows, which you can calculate as «count($cells) idiv $cols»):

```
<xsl:for-each-group select="$cells"
                    group-by="position() mod (last() idiv $cols)">
<tr>
   <xsl:for-each select="current-group()">
   <td>
      <xsl:value-of select="."/>
   </td>
   </xsl:for-each>
</tr>
</xsl:for-each-group>
```

See Also

<xsl:perform-sort> on page 405
<xsl:sort> on page 423
Collations on page 427
current-group() function on page 529
current-grouping-key() function on page 530
distinct-values() function in *XPath 2.0 Programmer's Reference*

xsl:function

The <xsl:function> declaration defines a stylesheet function that can be invoked using a function call from any XPath expression.

Changes in 2.0

This element is new in XSLT 2.0.

Format

```
<xsl:function
  name = qname
  as? = sequence-type
  override? = "yes" | "no">
  <!-- Content: (xsl:param*, sequence-constructor) -->
</xsl:function>
```

Position

<xsl:function> is a top-level declaration, which means that it always appears as a child of the <xsl:stylesheet> element.

Attributes

Name	Value	Meaning
name mandatory	Lexical QName	The name of the function
as optional	SequenceType	The type of the value returned when this function is evaluated. A type error is reported if the result does not match this type
override optional	«yes» or «no»	Indicates whether this function overrides any vendor-supplied function of the same name

The construct SequenceType is outlined in Chapter 4, and is described in full in Chapter 9 of *XPath 2.0 Programmer's Reference*.

Content

Zero or more <xsl:param> elements, followed by a sequence constructor.

Effect

Stylesheet functions can be called from XPath expressions in the same way as system-provided functions. The function defined by this <xsl:function> element is added to the static context for every XPath expression in the stylesheet, which means that the function will be invoked when evaluating a function call in an XPath expression that has a matching name and number of arguments (*arity*).

When a stylesheet function is called from an XPath expression, the parameters supplied in the function call are evaluated and bound to the variables defined in the <xsl:param> elements, the sequence constructor contained in the <xsl:function> element is evaluated, and the result of this evaluation is returned as the result of the XPath function call.

The name of the function is given as a lexical QName in the name attribute. This name must have a namespace prefix: This is to ensure that the name does not clash with the names of functions in the standard function library. The XSLT 2.0 specification defines several namespaces (all starting with «http://www.w3.org/») that are reserved—that is, they cannot be used for the names of user-defined functions, variables, or other stylesheet objects.

The stylesheet is allowed to contain two functions of the same name if they have different arity.

It is an error to have two functions in the stylesheet with the same name, arity, and import precedence, unless there is another with higher import precedence. When a function call in an XPath expression is evaluated, the function with highest import precedence is chosen.

The parameters to a function (which are defined using <xsl:param> elements as children to the <xsl:function> element) are mandatory parameters; it is not possible to use the required attribute to specify that a parameter is optional, or to specify a default value. The parameters are interpreted positionally: the first argument in the function call binds to the first `<xsl:param>` element, the second argument binds to the second `<xsl:param>`, and so on.

The values supplied as arguments to the function in the XPath function call are converted to the types defined by as attributes on the corresponding `<xsl:param>` elements if required, using the standard conversion rules described on page 476. If this conversion fails, a type error is reported. If an `<xsl:param>` element has no as attribute, then any value of any type is acceptable, and no checking or conversion takes place. This is equivalent to specifying «`as="item()*"`».

On entry to the function, the context item, position, and size are undefined. It is therefore an error to use the expression «`.`», or any relative path expression, or the functions `position()` and `last()`. Even a path expression beginning with «`/`» is not allowed, because such path expressions select from the root of the tree containing the context node. This means that all information needed by the function must either be passed explicitly as a parameter, or be available in a global variable. Path expressions such as «`$par/a/b/c`» can be used to navigate from nodes that are supplied as parameters to other nodes in the same tree.

Other values in the dynamic context, such as the current template, current mode, current group, and current grouping key, are also either undefined or empty on entry to a stylesheet function.

The result of the function is obtained by evaluating the sequence constructor. This result may be a sequence consisting of nodes (either newly constructed nodes or references to existing nodes) or atomic values or both. If there is an as attribute on the `<xsl:function>` element, then the result of evaluating the sequence constructor is converted, if necessary, to the specified type. Once again, the standard conversion rules defined on page 476 are used. A type error is reported if this conversion fails. If the `<xsl:function>` element has no «`as`» attribute, then a result of any type may be returned, and no checking or conversion takes place.

The override Attribute

The `override` attribute controls what happens if a user-written function and a vendor-supplied function have the same name.

❑ «`override="yes"`» means that the user-written function wins. This is the default. This value maximizes portability: The same implementation of the function will be used on all XSLT processors.

❑ «`override="no"`» means that the vendor-supplied function wins. This setting is useful when the stylesheet function has been written as a fallback implementation of the function, for use in environments where no vendor-supplied implementation exists. For example, at `http://www.exslt.org/` there is a definition of a mathematical function library including the function `math:sqrt()`, which evaluates the square root of its argument. This function is likely to be available with a number of XSLT processors, but not all. By supplying an XSLT implementation of this function, and specifying «`override="no"`», the stylesheet author can ensure that a call to `math:sqrt()` will execute on any XSLT processor, and will take advantage of the vendor's native implementation when available.

You can find a square root function implemented in XSLT on Dimitre Novatchev's FXSL site at `http://fxsl.sourceforge.net/`. It's not as inefficient as you might imagine. Nor is it a purely academic exercise. XSLT can be used to create graphical renditions of your data in SVG format, and this will often require such computations.

Usage and Examples

In this section I will first outline a few ways in which stylesheet functions can be used. I will then look more specifically at the differences between stylesheet functions and named templates. Then I will discuss the use of recursive functions, which provide an extremely powerful programming tool.

Using Stylesheet Functions

Stylesheet functions can be used in many different ways. Here is a simple function, which can be applied to an `<employee>` element to calculate the employee's annual leave entitlement in days:

```
<xsl:function name="pers:annual-leave" as="xs:integer"
              xpath-default-namespace="http://ns.megacorp.com/hr">
  <xsl:param name="emp" as="element(employee)"/>
  <xsl:variable name="service"
                as="xdt:yearMonthDuration"
                select="subtract-dateTimes-yielding-yearMonthDuration(
                           current-date(),
                           $emp/date-of-joining)"/>
  <xsl:choose>
    <xsl:when test="$service gt xdt:yearMonthDuration('P10Y')">
      <xsl:copy-of select="20"/>
    </xsl:when>
    <xsl:when test="$service gt xdt:yearMonthDuration('P3Y')">
      <xsl:copy-of select="17"/>
    </xsl:when>
    <xsl:otherwise>
      <xsl:copy-of select="15"/>
    </xsl:otherwise>
  </xsl:choose>
</xsl:function>
```

This function can now be called from any XPath expression. For example, you can process all the employees with more than 16 days' annual leave by writing:

```
<xsl:apply-templates select="//employee[pers:annual-leave(.) gt 16]"/>
```

Or you could process the employees sorted according to the number of days they are entitled to:

```
<xsl:apply-templates select="//employee">
  <xsl:sort select="pers:annual-leave(.)"/>
</xsl:apply-templates>
```

This function could be packaged in a library module with other similar functions, allowing reuse of the code, and allowing the algorithms to be changed in one place rather than having them scattered around many different stylesheets. For calculating properties of nodes, functions are much more flexible than named templates because of the way they can be called.

As well as encapsulating properties of elements, functions can be used to encapsulate relationships. For example, the following function determines the responsible line manager for an employee:

```
<xsl:function name="pers:line-manager" as="element(pers:employee)"
        xpath-default-namespace="http://ns.megacorp.com/hr">
  <xsl:param name="emp" as="element(employee)"/>
  <xsl:variable name="mgr_nr"
                select="doc('departments.xml')
                          /departments
                          /department[@dept-no = $emp/department]
                          /manager-nr"/>
  <xsl:sequence select="doc('employees.xml')
                          /key('emp', $mgr-nr)"/>
</xsl:function>
```

Users of this function do not need to know how the relationship between employees and their line manager is actually represented in the XML source documents, only that the information is obtainable. This function can then be used in a path expression, rather like a virtual axis:

```
<xsl:template match="pers:employee">
  <xsl:text>Manager: </xsl:text>
  <xsl:value-of select="pers:line-manager(.)/name"/>
</xsl:template>
```

In these examples I have declared the types of the parameters and the result by reference to types defined in a schema. This helps to document what the function is intended for, and it ensures that you will get an error message (rather than garbage output) if you call the function with incorrect parameters, for example a department rather than an employee element.

I have used the xpath-default-namespace attribute, which can be used on any XSLT element to define the namespace that is used for unprefixed element and type names occurring in XPath expressions. For details of this attribute, see the entry for <xsl:stylesheet> on page 433.

I also chose to put the functions in the same namespace as the elements that they operate on. This is not the only approach possible, but to my mind it establishes clearly that there is a close relationship between the types (such as pers:employee) and the functions designed to operate on those types—the functions act like methods on a class.

Functions versus Named Templates

XSLT offers two very similar constructs: named templates and stylesheet functions. This section discusses the differences between them, and suggests when they might be used.

The main difference between named templates and stylesheet functions is the way they are called: templates are called from the XSLT level using the <xsl:call-template> instruction, while stylesheet functions are called from XPath expressions using a function call.

In earlier working drafts of XSLT 2.0, the differences between named templates and stylesheet functions were considerably greater. Named templates were always implemented using XSLT instructions, while stylesheet functions were largely implemented using XPath expressions. Named templates always returned newly constructed nodes, while stylesheet functions returned references to existing nodes, or atomic values.

In the final version of the specification, these differences have largely disappeared. The content model for the <xsl:template> and <xsl:function> elements is identical, and there is no difference in the way they are evaluated to produce a result, or in the kinds of result they can return. The only difference is in the way they are called.

If you need to invoke the same functionality from both the XSLT and the XPath levels, it is very easy to define a named template as a wrapper for a stylesheet function:

```
<xsl:template name="my:func">
    <xsl:param name="p1" required="yes"/>
    <xsl:param name="p2" required="yes"/>
    <xsl:sequence select="my:func($p1, $p2)"/>
</xsl:template>
```

or to define a stylesheet function as a wrapper for a named template,

```
<xsl:function name="my:func">
    <xsl:param name="p1" required="yes"/>
    <xsl:param name="p2" required="yes"/>
    <xsl:call-template name="my:func">
        <xsl:with-param name="p1" select="$p1"/>
        <xsl:with-param name="p2" select="$p2"/>
    </xsl:call-template>
</xsl:function>
```

My own preference is to use stylesheet functions when I want to compute a value or to select existing nodes, and to use a named template when I want to construct new nodes. This reflects the fact that in general, the role of XSLT instructions is to construct nodes in the result tree, while the role of XPath expressions is to select nodes in the source tree and compute values derived from their content. Implementations are quite likely to reflect this distinction, with an XPath engine that is better at one kind of job and an XSLT engine that is better at another. In particular, XSLT engines are very likely to be able to bypass the formal process of constructing a sequence of nodes, then copying the nodes in this sequence to construct a tree, and serializing the tree. Many XSLT engines will be able to collapse this into a single operation, where the new nodes are serialized as soon as they are constructed. This optimization is much more difficult if the constructed nodes have to be passed to an XPath engine first, as the result of a function call.

The fact that stylesheet functions do not have access to the context item may seem at first to be an inconvenience. But I think that the fact that all parameters to the function are explicit greatly helps programming discipline, and produces code that is easier to maintain. It also makes life much easier for the optimizer, which brings another benefit in terms of faster execution.

Functions with side effects can cause some surprises at the XPath level, and creating a new node is a kind of a side effect. For example, one might expect that the result of the expression:

```
my:f($x) is my:f($x)
```

is always true. But if the function my:f() creates a new node, this is not the case. It is no longer a pure function, because it returns different results on different invocations. An optimizer has to recognize this possibility when rearranging such an expression: It must make sure that the function is actually called twice.

Another example of this effect is the (admittedly rather perverse) expression:

```
count(//a/../my:f(.))
```

Normally when evaluating a path expression, the processor can first find all the nodes that the path expression locates, then sort them into document order and eliminate duplicates. But with the expression above, if «my:f()» creates new nodes then the result of the final count() depends critically on how many times the function «my:f()» is called, and the correct answer is that it must be called exactly once for each distinct parent of an <a> element in the source document.

This is the kind of expression that is used to sort out the sheep from the goats when doing XPath conformance testing. At the time of writing, I have to confess that Saxon fails this test miserably: It only eliminates duplicates from the final result of a path expression, and not from intermediate results.

The bottom line is that functions that create and return new nodes are likely to play havoc with XPath optimization and are best avoided. Creating a temporary tree as local working data within the function is, of course, a different matter: the thing that causes problems is two invocations of the same function, with the same parameters, returning different results.

Recursion

Stylesheet functions can be recursive: They can call themselves either directly or indirectly. Because XSLT is a functional programming language without side effects (specifically, without updateable variables), recursion plays a key role in writing algorithms of any complexity.

In XSLT 1.0, such algorithms were written using recursive named templates. Apart from being rather long-winded, this had the drawback that it was difficult to return certain kinds of result: Templates in XSLT 1.0 could only return results by constructing new nodes. In XSLT 2.0 both templates and functions offer much more flexibility in the types of result they can return, and stylesheet functions offer additional flexibility in the way they can be called (for example, they can be called from within a predicate used in a match pattern).

As it happens, many of the simple problems where recursion was needed in XSLT 1.0 can now be solved in other ways, because XPath 2.0 offers a wider range of aggregation functions, and functions such as tokenize() to break up a string into its parts. But there are still cases where recursion is needed, and even when it isn't, many people find the recursive solution more elegant than an iterative solution using <xsl:for-each> or the XPath «for» expression.

Here is a function that extracts the part of a string after the last «/» character:

```
<xsl:function name="str:suffix" as="xs:string">
   <xsl:param name="in" as="xs:string"/>
   <xsl:sequence select="
           if (contains($in, '/')
           then str:suffix(substring-after($in, '/'))
           else $in"/>
</xsl:function>
```

Note how all the logic is contained in a single XPath expression. I could have used <xsl:choose> to express the same logic, but with this kind of function I personally find it clearer to write the whole algorithm at the XPath level.

The function result is returned using an `<xsl:sequence>` instruction. It sometimes feels a little strange to use `<xsl:sequence>` when the value being computed is a single integer or string, but in the XPath data model a single value is the same as a sequence of length 1, so it's worth getting used to the idea that everything is a sequence. When returning an atomic value, one could just as easily use `<xsl:copy-of>`, but I prefer `<xsl:sequence>` because it works in all cases: When you are returning nodes, you don't want to copy them unnecessarily. You might also be tempted to use `<xsl:value-of>`, and in this case it would work, but the semantics aren't quite what we want: `<xsl:value-of>` would convert the selected string into a text node, which would then be atomized back to a string by virtue of the function's declared return type. Even if the optimizer can sort this out, it's making unnecessary work.

Another observation about this function is that it is tail-recursive. This means that after calling itself, the function does nothing else before it returns to its caller. This property is important because tail-recursive functions can be optimized to save memory. Sometimes a problem with recursion is that if you recurse too deeply, say to 1000 levels or so, the system runs out of stack space and terminates with a fatal error. A good XSLT processor can optimize a tail-recursive function so that this doesn't happen. Basically the trick is that instead of making the recursive call and then unwinding the stack when it regains control, the function can unwind the stack first, and then make the recursive call. This is because the stack frame isn't needed once the recursive call returns.

I mentioned earlier that many functions can now be implemented easily without using recursion, and this one is no exception. It could also be written using regular expressions:

```
<xsl:function name="str:suffix" as="xs:string">
  <xsl:param name="in" as="xs:string"/>
  <xsl:sequence select="replace($in, '.*/([^/]*)', '$1')"/>
</xsl:function>
```

But this is a matter of personal style. It's a good idea to have more than one tool in your kitbag, and recursion is the most powerful one available.

One kind of problem where you will need recursion is when you need to analyze a graph (that is, a network of related objects). The next example shows the technique.

Example: Looking for Cycles among Attribute Sets

This example examines a stylesheet module (we'll stick to a single module for simplicity) and determines whether it contains any cycles among its attribute set definitions. Also to keep it simple, I'll assume that attribute sets have simple names and ignore the complications caused by namespace prefixes.

Source

The source document is any stylesheet module. But the example is only interesting if you run it on a stylesheet module that contains attribute sets that are (incorrectly) defined in terms of themselves. I've included such a sample as `cyclic-stylesheet.xsl`.

This example requires a schema-aware processor, and assumes that the source document is validated against the schema for XSLT 2.0 stylesheets, which is included in the download as `xslt20.xsd`.

Output

The stylesheet will report the name of any attribute set that is defined directly or indirectly in terms of itself.

Stylesheet

This stylesheet is available as `find-cycles.xsl`. We'll start with a function that returns the attribute sets that are directly referenced from a given attribute set:

```
<xsl:function name="cyc:direct" as="schema-element(xsl:attribute-set)*">
  <xsl:param name="in" as="schema-element(xsl:attribute-set)"/>
  <xsl:sequence select="$in/../xsl:attribute-set
                               [@name=$in/@use-attribute-sets]"/>
</xsl:function>
```

This returns any `attribute-set` in the containing document whose `name` attribute is equal to any of these strings. Notice what's going on: The schema for XSLT stylesheets tells us that the `use-attribute-sets` attribute is a sequence of strings. The «=» operator causes this attribute to be atomized, which returns the typed value of the attribute, namely this sequence of strings; it then returns true if any of the strings in this sequence is equal to the other operand. This will only work if the input document has been validated against its schema.

Now observe that an attribute set A references another attribute set B if either `cyc:direct(A)` includes B, or there is an attribute set in `cyc:direct(A)` that references B. This translates into the recursive function:

```
<xsl:function name="cyc:references" as="xs:boolean">
  <xsl:param name="A" as="schema-element(xsl:attribute-set)"/>
  <xsl:param name="B" as="schema-element(xsl:attribute-set)"/>
  <xsl:sequence select="
      if (cyc:direct($A) intersect $B)
      then true()
      else some $X in cyc:direct($A) satisfies cyc:references($X, $B)"/>
</xsl:function>
```

Now, finally, you can discover whether there are any cycles, that is, any attribute sets that reference themselves directly or indirectly:

```
<xsl:value-of select="some $X in /*/xsl:attribute-set
                    satisfies cyc:references($X, $X)"/>
```

Note that once again, the function is tail-recursive.

An interesting observation about this function is that it is written entirely using constructs that are new in XSLT 2.0 and XPath 2.0: stylesheet functions, type checking based on schema-defined types, atomization of a list-valued attribute, the `<xsl:sequence>` instruction that allows XSLT instructions to return values other than nodes, the XPath `intersect` operator, and the XPath `some..satisfies` expression.

For a more generalized function that looks for cycles in any source data file, regardless how the relationships are represented, see the section *Simulating Higher Order Functions* under <xsl:apply-templates> on page 198.

See Also

<xsl:template> on page 450

xsl:if

The <xsl:if> instruction encloses a sequence constructor that will be evaluated only if a specified condition is true. If the condition is true, it returns the result of this evaluation; otherwise, it returns the empty sequence.

<xsl:if> is analogous to the *if* statement found in many programming languages.

Changes in 2.0

None.

Format

```
<xsl:if
  test = expression>
  <!-- Content: sequence-constructor -->
</xsl:if>
```

Position

<xsl:if> is an instruction. It is always used within a sequence constructor.

Attributes

Name	Value	Meaning
test mandatory	Expression	The boolean condition to be tested

Content

A sequence constructor.

Effect

The test expression is evaluated. If the *effective boolean value* of the result is true, the contained sequence constructor is evaluated; otherwise, no action is taken (an empty sequence is returned).

Any XPath expression may be evaluated to obtain an effective boolean value. In brief, the rules are:

❑ If the value of the expression is an empty sequence, the effective boolean value is `false`.

❑ If the value of the expression is a single atomic value, the effective boolean value is `false` if the value is a zero-length string, the boolean value `false`, a number (integer, decimal, float, or double) equal to zero, or the special value NaN (not a number). Otherwise the effective boolean value is `true`.

❑ If the value of the expression is a single node, the effective boolean value is `true`.

❑ If the value of the expression is a sequence of two or more items, the effective boolean value is `true`.

These rules are the same as XPath itself uses in boolean contexts, for example in «if» expressions and for the operands of the «and» and «or» operators. They are also the same as the rules used by the `boolean()` function, and they are designed to be fully compatible with XPath 1.0. Note that the effective boolean value of a sequence can be evaluated without looking beyond the second item in the sequence, which makes the rules very efficient.

Usage

The `<xsl:if>` instruction is useful where an action is to be performed conditionally. It performs the functions of the `if-then` construct found in other programming languages. If there are two or more alternative actions (the equivalent of an `if-then-else`, `switch`, or `Select Case` in other languages), use `<xsl:choose>` instead.

One common use of `<xsl:if>` is to test for error conditions. In this case it is often used with `<xsl:message>`.

Try to avoid using `<xsl:if>` as the entire content of a template rule. It's better to use a predicate instead, because this gives the processor more scope for optimization. For example,

```
<xsl:template match="para">
  <xsl:if test="@display='yes'">
    <p><xsl:apply-templates/></p>
  </xsl:if>
</xsl:template>
```

can be rewritten as:

```
<xsl:template match="para[@display='yes']">
  <p><xsl:apply-templates/></p>
</xsl:for-each>

<xsl:template match="para"/>
```

(Of course, it's always possible that the processor will perform this optimization anyway, but you can't rely on it.)

Examples

The following example outputs an `<hr>` element after processing the last of a sequence of `<para>` elements:

```
<xsl:template match="para">
   <p><xsl:apply-templates/></p>
   <xsl:if test="position()=last()">
      <hr/>
   </xsl:if>
</xsl:template>
```

The following example reports an error if the `percent` attribute of the current element is not a number between 0 and 100. The expression returns true if:

- ❏ the `percent` attribute does not exist
- ❏ the value cannot be interpreted as a number (so that «`number(@percent)`» is NaN)
- ❏ the numeric value is less than zero, or
- ❏ the numeric value is greater than 100

```
<xsl:if test="not(@percent) or
                    (string(number(@percent))='NaN') or
                    (number(@percent) lt 0) or
                    (number(@percent) gt 100)">
   <xsl:message>
      percent attribute must be a number between 0 and 100
   </xsl:message>
</xsl:if>
```

The next example shows the use of `<xsl:if>` in the context of a complete stylesheet.

Example: Formatting a List of Names

This example formats a list of names, using `<xsl:if>` to produce punctuation that depends on the position of each name in the list.

Source

The source file `authors.xml` contains a single `<book>` element with a list of authors.

```
<?xml version="1.0"?>
<book>
     <title>Design Patterns</title>
     <author>Erich Gamma</author>
     <author>Richard Helm</author>
     <author>Ralph Johnson</author>
     <author>John Vlissides</author>
</book>
```

Stylesheet

The stylesheet `authors.xsl` processes the list of authors, adding punctuation depending on the position of each author in the list.

```
<xsl:transform
  xmlns:xsl="http://www.w3.org/1999/XSL/Transform"
  version="1.0">

<xsl:template match="book">
   <xsl:value-of select="title"/>
  by <xsl:for-each select="author">
      <xsl:value-of select="."/>
      <xsl:if test="position()!=last()">, </xsl:if>
      <xsl:if test="position()=last()-1">and </xsl:if>
</xsl:for-each>
</xsl:template>

</xsl:transform>
```

Output

```
Design Patterns
by Erich Gamma, Richard Helm, Ralph Johnson, and John Vlissides
```

See Also

`<xsl:choose>` on page 236

xsl:import

`<xsl:import>` is a top-level element used to import the contents of one stylesheet module into another. The declarations in the importing stylesheet module have a higher *import precedence* than those in the imported module, which usually means that they will be used in preference, but the detailed rules vary for each type of declaration.

Changes in 2.0

There are no changes to the syntax of this instruction in XSLT 2.0. The rules for the `href` attribute have been reformulated: In effect, the way in which the URI is dereferenced to obtain a stylesheet module is now largely implementation defined. This allows for options such as catalogs or user-specified URI resolvers, as well as implementations that cache or precompile stylesheet modules.

Format

```
<xsl:import
  href = uri-reference />
```

Position

<xsl:import> is a top-level element, which means that it must appear as a child of the <xsl:stylesheet> element. Within an <xsl:stylesheet> element, the <xsl:import> child elements must come before any other children.

Attributes

Name	Value	Meaning
href mandatory	URI	The URI of the stylesheet to be imported

Like all other XSLT elements, the <xsl:import> declaration may also have a «use-when» attribute. This is described in Chapter 3 (see page 122).

Content

None; the element is always empty.

Effect

The <xsl:import> declaration loads the stylesheet module identified in its href attribute. First we'll look at how this module is located, and then at the question of import precedence, which determines how the declarations in the imported module are used.

Locating the Stylesheet Module

The URI contained in the href attribute may be an absolute URI or a relative URI. If relative, it is interpreted relative to the base URI of the XML document or external entity containing the <xsl:import> element. For example, if a file main.xsl contains the element <xsl:import href="date.xsl"/> then the system will, by default, look for date.xsl in the same directory as main.xsl. You can change this behavior by using the xml:base attribute, as described in Chapter 2 on page 53. This allows you to specify a different base URI for resolving the relative URI.

The URI must identify an XML document that is a valid XSLT stylesheet module. The declarations in the imported stylesheet are logically inserted into the importing stylesheet at the point where the <xsl:import> element appears. However:

❏ Imported declarations have lower import precedence than the declarations that appear directly in the importing stylesheet, or are incorporated into it using <xsl:include>. This is explained in more detail below.

❏ Imported elements retain their base URI, so anything that involves referencing a relative URI is done relative to the original URI of the imported stylesheet. This includes, for example, expansion of further <xsl:import> elements, or use of URIs as arguments to the document() function.

❏ When a namespace prefix is used (typically within a QName, but it also applies to freestanding prefixes such as those in the xsl:exclude-result-prefixes attribute of a literal result element), it is interpreted using only the namespace declarations in the original stylesheet module in which the QName occurred. An imported stylesheet module does not inherit namespace declarations from the module that imports it. This includes QNames constructed at execution time as the result of evaluating an expression, for example an expression used within an attribute value template for the name or namespace attribute of <xsl:element>.

❑ The values of the version, extension-element-prefixes, exclude-result-prefixes, and xpath-default-namespace attributes that apply to an element in the imported stylesheet, as well as xml:lang and xml:space, are those that were defined in the <xsl:stylesheet> element of their own stylesheet module, not those on the <xsl:stylesheet> element of the importing module.

The imported stylesheet module may use the simplified stylesheet syntax described in Chapter 3. This allows an entire module to be defined as the content of an element such as <HTML>. It is then treated as if it were a stylesheet module containing a single template, whose match pattern is «/» and whose content is the literal result element.

The imported stylesheet module may contain <xsl:include> statements to include further stylesheet modules, or <xsl:import> statements to import them. A stylesheet module must not directly or indirectly import itself.

It is not an error to import the same stylesheet module more than once, either directly or indirectly, but it is not usually a useful thing to do. The effect is that the same definitions or templates will be present with several different import precedences. The situation is exactly the same as if two stylesheet modules with different names but identical contents had been imported.

The href attribute must be a fixed value—it isn't possible to compute its value at runtime. This is because the first thing an XSLT processor does, long before any source document is available, is assemble the stylesheet from all its constituent modules and compile it into some internal representation. As with every other modern programming language, a program cannot change its own source code while executing. However, there is a new facility in XSLT 2.0 that allows stylesheets to be tailored to different environments. The «use-when» attribute is allowed on <xsl:import> (and indeed on any other XSLT element) to define a compile-time condition defining whether this element should be included or ignored. For example, you can write:

```
<xsl:import href="xalan-rules.xsl"
            use-when="system-property('xsl:product-name') = 'Xalan'"/>
<xsl:import href="saxon-rules.xsl"
            use-when="system-property('xsl:product-name') = 'SAXON'"/>
```

to import different modules depending on whether you are running Saxon or Xalan.

Determining the Import Precedence

Each stylesheet module that is imported has an import precedence. The rules are:

❑ The precedence of a module that is imported is always lower than the precedence of the module importing it.

❑ If one module imports several others, then the one it imports first has lower precedence than the next, and so on.

This means that in the structure shown in Figure 5-3, the highest precedence module is A followed by C, F, B, E, and finally D.

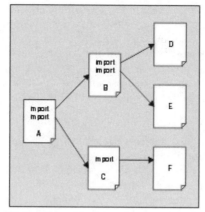

Figure 5-3

If one stylesheet module incorporates another using `<xsl:include>` rather than `<xsl:import>`, it has the same import precedence as the module that includes it (Figure 5-4).

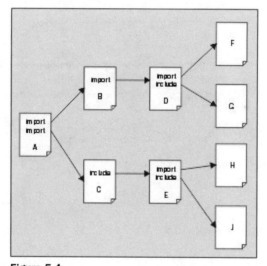

Figure 5-4

Here J is included in E, so it has the same import precedence as E, and similarly E has the same import precedence as C. If you attach numeric values to the import precedence to indicate the ordering (the absolute values don't matter, the only significance is that a higher number indicates higher precedence), you could do so as follows:

A	B	C	D	E	F	G	H	J
6	3	5	2	5	1	2	4	5

The import precedence of a stylesheet module applies to all the declarations in that module, so for example the <xsl:template> elements in module E have a higher import precedence than those in G.

As <xsl:import> statements must occur before any other declarations in a stylesheet module, the effect of these rules is that if each <xsl:import> statement were to be replaced by the content of the module it imports, the declarations in the resulting combined stylesheet would be in increasing order of import precedence. This makes life rather easier for implementors. However, it does not mean that <xsl:import> is a straightforward textual substitution process, because there is still a need to distinguish cases where two objects (for example template rules) have the same import precedence because they came originally from the same stylesheet or from stylesheets that were included rather than imported.

The XSLT 2.0 specification introduces the concept of a *stylesheet layer*, which is a group of stylesheet modules that have the same import precedence because they refer to each other using <xsl:include> rather than <xsl:import>. In the example above modules D and G are in the same layer; C, E, and J are in the same layer; and each of the other modules is in a layer of its own. Within a stylesheet layer the specification describes the concept of *declaration order*, which is the order that the declarations (top-level elements) would appear in if included stylesheets were expanded at the point of the <xsl:include> statement. The stylesheet layers (rather than modules) are considered to form a tree, with <xsl:import> elements acting as the links from a parent to a child in the tree.

The stylesheet tree for the example above is shown in Figure 5-5.

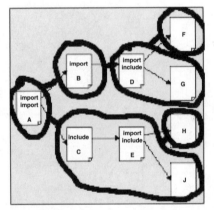

Figure 5-5

The concepts of stylesheet levels, declaration order, and the stylesheet tree have been used to tighten up the specification of how instructions such as <xsl:apply-imports> work. For example, an <xsl:apply-imports> instruction in module J can invoke a template in module H, because H is in a stylesheet layer that is a descendant of the layer that J is in.

Effect of Import Precedence

The import precedence of a declaration affects its standing relative to other declarations of the same type, and may be used to resolve conflicts. The effect is as shown in the table below for each kind of declaration.

Element type	Rules
`<xsl:attribute-set>`	If there are two attribute sets with the same expanded name, they are merged. If there is an attribute that is present in both, then the one from the attribute set with higher import precedence wins. It is a runtime error if there is no clear winner from this process (that is, if there are two or more values for an attribute that have the same precedence, and this is the highest precedence). The XSLT processor has the choice of reporting the error or choosing the one that was specified last (for a more precise definition of what "last" means, see `<xsl:attribute-set>` on page 214)
`<xsl:character-map>`	If there are several `<xsl:character-map>` declarations with the same name, then the one with highest import precedence wins. It is a compile-time error if this leaves no clear winner
`<xsl:decimal-format>`	All the `<xsl:decimal-format>` elements in the stylesheet that share the same name are effectively merged. For each attribute, if the value is explicitly present on more than one `<xsl:decimal-format>` element, then the one with highest import precedence wins. It is an error if there is no clear winner. The XSLT processor has the choice of reporting the error or choosing the one that was specified last
`<xsl:function>`	If there are several `<xsl:function>` declarations with the same name and arity (number of arguments), then the one with highest import precedence wins. It is a compile-time error if this leaves no clear winner
`<xsl:import>` and `<xsl:include>`	No conflicts arise; the import precedence of these elements is immaterial, except in determining the import precedence of the referenced stylesheet module
`<xsl:import-schema>`	If there are several `<xsl:import-schema>` declarations for the same target namespace (or for no target namespace) then the one with highest import precedence wins. If this leaves more than one, then the rules are defined by reference to the XML Schema specifications, which give implementations a great deal of latitude
`<xsl:key>`	All the key definitions are used, regardless of their import precedence. See `<xsl:key>` on page 332 for details
`<xsl:namespace-alias>`	If several aliases for the same stylesheet prefix are defined, the one with the highest import precedence is used. It is a compile-time error if there is no clear winner

Continues

Element type	Rules
`<xsl:output>`	All the `<xsl:output>` elements in the stylesheet that share the same name are effectively merged. In the case of the `cdata-section-elements` and `use-character-maps` attributes, the values from all the `<xsl:output>` elements are merged. For all the other attributes, if the value is explicitly present on more than one `<xsl:output>` element, then the one with highest import precedence wins. It is an error if there is no clear winner. The XSLT processor has the choice of reporting the error or choosing the one that was specified last
`<xsl:strip-space>` and `<xsl:preserve-space>`	If there is more than one `<xsl:strip-space>` or `<xsl:preserve-space>` element that matches a particular element name in the source document, then the one with highest import precedence is used. If this still leaves several that match, each one is assigned a priority, using the same rules as for the **match** pattern in `<xsl:template>`. Specifically, an explicit QName has higher priority than the form «`prefix:*`», which in turn has higher priority than «`*`». The one with highest priority is then used
	It is an error if this leaves more than one match (even if they all give the same answer). The XSLT processor has the choice of reporting this as a runtime error or choosing the one that was specified last
	If there are no matches for an element, whitespace nodes are preserved
`<xsl:template>`	When selecting a template rule for use with `<xsl:apply-templates>`, firstly all the template rules with a matching `mode` are taken. Of these, all those with a `match` pattern that matches the selected node are considered. If this leaves more than one, only those with the highest import precedence are considered. If this still leaves more than one, the one with highest priority is chosen: The rules for deciding the priority are given under `<xsl:template>` on page 450. It is an error if this still doesn't identify a clear winner. The XSLT processor has the choice of reporting the error or choosing the template rule that was specified last. (In practice, several processors output a warning message) In the case of named templates, if there are several `<xsl:template>` declarations with the same `name` attribute, then the one with highest import precedence wins. It is a compile-time error if this leaves no clear winner
`<xsl:variable>` and `<xsl:param>`	If there are several global `<xsl:variable>` or `<xsl:param>` declarations with the same name, then the one with highest import precedence wins. It is a compile-time error if this leaves no clear winner

Usage

The rules for `<xsl:import>` are so pervasive that one would imagine the facility is central to the use of XSLT, rather in the way inheritance is central to writing in Java. In practice, many stylesheets never need to use `<xsl:import>`, but you will almost certainly need it once you start to develop a family of stylesheets to handle a wide range of source document types.

Like inheritance in object-oriented languages, `<xsl:import>` is designed to allow the creation of a library or reusable components, only in this case, the components are modules of stylesheets. And the mechanism works in a very similar way to inheritance. For example, you might have a stylesheet that simply defines your corporate color scheme, as a set of global variables defining color names. Another stylesheet might be defined to produce the basic framesets for your site, referring to these color names to supply the background detail. Now if you want to use this general structure but to vary some detail, for example to modify one of the colors because it clashes with an image you are displaying on a particular page, you can define a stylesheet for this particular page that does nothing apart from redefining that one color. This is illustrated in Figure 5-6.

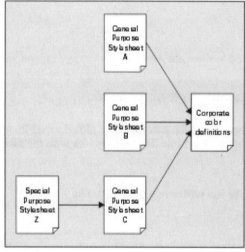

Figure 5-6

Suppose the stylesheet module for corporate color definitions looks like this:

```
<xsl:stylesheet xmlns:xsl="http://www.w3.org/1999/XSL/Transform"
       xmlns:color="http://acme.co.nz/colors"
       version="1.0">
<xsl:variable name="color:blue" select="'#0088ff'"/>
<xsl:variable name="color:pink" select="'#ff0088'"/>
<xsl:variable name="color:lilac" select="'#ff00ff'"/>
</xsl:stylesheet>
```

Now all the general-purpose stylesheets could `<xsl:include>` these definitions (without the need to `<xsl:import>` them unless they are being modified). This makes it easier to maintain the corporate brand image, because things are defined in one place only.

However, there are cases where you would want to depart from the general rule, and you can do so quite easily. If a particular document needs to use stylesheet C, but needs to vary the colors used, you can define stylesheet Z for it, as follows:

```
<xsl:stylesheet xmlns:xsl="http://www.w3.org/1999/XSL/Transform"
        xmlns:color="http://acme.co.nz/colors"
        version="1.0">
<xsl:import href="general-stylesheet-C.xsl"/>
<xsl:variable name="color:lilac" select="'#cc00cc'"/>
</xsl:stylesheet>
```

In fact, this might be the entire stylesheet. In common English, style Z is the same as style C but with a different shade of lilac. Note that all the references to variable «color:lilac» are interpreted as references to the definition in Z, even if the references occur in the same stylesheet module as a different definition of «color:lilac».

As a general principle, to incorporate standard content into a stylesheet without change, use <xsl:include>. If there are definitions you want to override, use <xsl:import>.

Examples

The first example is designed to show the effect of <xsl:import> on variables.

Example 1: Precedence of Variables

This example demonstrates the precedence of global variables when the principal stylesheet module and an imported module declare variables with the same name.

Source

This example can be run with any source XML file.

Stylesheet

The principal stylesheet module is variables.xsl.

```
<?xml version="1.0" encoding="iso-8859-1"?>
<xsl:stylesheet version="1.0"
    xmlns:xsl="http://www.w3.org/1999/XSL/Transform"
    xmlns:acme="http://acme.com/xslt"
    exclude-result-prefixes="acme">

<xsl:import href="boilerplate.xsl"/>
<xsl:output encoding="iso-8859-1" indent="yes"/>

<xsl:variable name="acme:company-name" select="'Acme Widgets Limited'"/>

<xsl:template match="/">
<c><xsl:value-of select="$acme:copyright"/></c>
</xsl:template>

</xsl:stylesheet>
```

The imported stylesheet module is `boilerplate.xsl`.

```xml
<?xml version="1.0" encoding="iso-8859-1"?>
<xsl:stylesheet version="1.0"
                xmlns:xsl="http://www.w3.org/1999/XSL/Transform"
                xmlns:co="http://acme.com/xslt">

<xsl:variable name="co:company-name"
              select="'Acme Widgets Incorporated'"/>

<xsl:variable name="co:copyright"
              select="concat('Copyright © ', $co:company-name)"/>

</xsl:stylesheet>
```

Output

The output of this stylesheet will be:

```xml
<?xml version="1.0" encoding="iso-8859-1" ?>
<c>Copyright © Acme Widgets Limited</c>
```

This is because in the variable declaration of «`$co:copyright`», the reference to variable «`$co:company-name`» matches the declaration of this variable in the principal stylesheet, because this has higher import precedence than the declaration in `boilerplate.xsl`.

The fact that different namespace prefixes are used in the two stylesheets is, of course, irrelevant: The prefix «acme» in the principal stylesheet maps to the same namespace URI as the prefix «co» in `boilerplate.xsl`, so the names are considered equivalent.

This example explicitly specifies `encoding="iso-8859-1"` for both the stylesheet modules and the output. Most of my examples only use ASCII characters, and since the default character encoding UTF-8 is a superset of ASCII, this works fine. This time, though, I've used the copyright symbol «©», which is not an ASCII character, so it's important to specify the character encoding that my text editor uses, which is iso-8859-1 (actually it's the Microsoft variant of it known as Windows ANSI, but this is close enough not to make a difference).

The second example shows the effect of `<xsl:import>` on template rules.

Example 2: Precedence of Template Rules

In this example I shall define a complete stylesheet `standard-style.xsl` to display poems in HTML, and then override one of its rules in an importing stylesheet. The files required are all in the subdirectory `import` in the download file for this chapter.

Source

This example works with the poem that we used in Chapter 1. In the download file it's available as `poem.xml`. It starts like this:

```
<?xml version="1.0"?>
<poem>
<author>Rupert Brooke</author>
<date>1912</date>
<title>Song</title>
<stanza>
<line>And suddenly the wind comes soft,</line>
<line>And Spring is here again;</line>
<line>And the hawthorn quickens with buds of green</line>
<line>And my heart with buds of pain.</line>
</stanza>
etc.
</poem>
```

Stylesheet A

Here is `standard-style.xsl`:

```
<xsl:stylesheet version="1.0"
    xmlns:xsl="http://www.w3.org/1999/XSL/Transform">

<xsl:template match="/">
   <html>
   <head>
   <title><xsl:value-of select="//title"/></title>
   </head>
   <body>

<xsl:apply-templates/>
   </body>
   </html>
</xsl:template>

<xsl:template match="title">
   <h1><xsl:apply-templates/></h1>
</xsl:template>

<xsl:template match="author">
   <div align="right"><i>by </i>
      <xsl:apply-templates/>
   </div>
</xsl:template>

<xsl:template match="stanza">
   <p><xsl:apply-templates/></p>
</xsl:template>

<xsl:template match="line">
   <xsl:apply-templates/><br/>
</xsl:template>

<xsl:template match="date"/>
</xsl:stylesheet>
```

Output A

When you run this stylesheet, the output starts like this (the actual layout may vary, of course, depending on which XSLT processor you use):

```
<html>
    <head>
    <title>Song</title>
    </head>
    <body>
        <div align="right"><i>by </i>Rupert Brooke</div>
        <h1>Song</h1>
        <p>
            And suddenly the wind comes soft,<br>
            And Spring is here again;<br>
            And the hawthorn quickens with buds of green<br>
            And my heart with buds of pain.<br>
        </p>
```

Stylesheet B

Now we want to create a variant of this in which the lines of the poem are numbered. This will act as the principal stylesheet when you want this form of output. Here it is in numbered-style.xsl:

```
<xsl:stylesheet version="1.0"
    xmlns:xsl="http://www.w3.org/1999/XSL/Transform">

<xsl:import href="standard-style.xsl"/>

<xsl:template match="line">
    <xsl:number level="any" format="001"/>  
    <xsl:apply-imports/>
</xsl:template>

</xsl:stylesheet>
```

Note the use of the character reference « » to output a nonbreaking space. In HTML this is normally done by writing « ». You can use this entity reference in the stylesheet if you like (it's simply a symbolic name for the Unicode character #xa0), but only if you declare it as an entity in the DTD. It's usually simpler just to use the numeric character reference.

Output B

This time the output starts like this. Again, the precise format depends on the processor (for example, some processors may output « », or « » instead of « ») but it should look the same when displayed in the browser:

```
<html>
    <head>
    <title>Song</title>
    </head>
```

```
<body>
    <div align="right"><i>by </i>Rupert Brooke</div>
    <h1>Song</h1>
    <p>
        001  
        And suddenly the wind comes soft,<br>
        002  
        And Spring is here again;<br>
        003  
        And the hawthorn quickens with buds of green<br>
        004  
        And my heart with buds of pain.<br>
    </p>
```

All the template rules defined in `standard-style.xsl` are used as normal, except where the current node matches the pattern «`line`». In this situation there are two possible templates that match the node, so the one with higher import precedence is chosen. This is the one in the importing stylesheet module, namely `numbered-style.xsl`. As a result, the lines of the poem are output with a preceding line number, calculated using the `<xsl:number>` instruction, which is described on page 359. The use of `<xsl:apply-imports>` means that once the line number has been output, the line is displayed in the normal way, using the template rule from the `standard-style.xsl` stylesheet.

This use of `<xsl:import>` to customize the presentation produced by a stylesheet is very common. The rules in the importing stylesheet, which vary the standard presentation, are sometimes referred to as a *customization layer*. Sometimes the customization layer corresponds directly to an additional module in the schema or DTD: For example if the schema that you use for press releases is an extended version of the schema used for general company documents, then you will want to write a customization layer over the general-purpose stylesheet to handle the additional features found in press releases.

See Also

`<xsl:include>` on page 328
`<xsl:apply-imports>` on page 184

xsl:import-schema

`<xsl:import-schema>` is a top-level declaration used to identify a schema containing definitions of types that are referred to in the stylesheet. This declaration is available only in a schema-aware processor.

Changes in 2.0

This element is new in XSLT 2.0.

Format

```
<xsl:import-schema
  namespace? = uri-reference
  schema-location? = uri-reference />
```

Position

`<xsl:import-schema>` is a top-level declaration, which means that it must appear as a child of the `<xsl:stylesheet>` element. There are no constraints on its ordering relative to other declarations in the stylesheet.

Attributes

Name	Value	Meaning
namespace optional	URI	The namespace URI of the schema to be imported
schema-location optional	URI	A URI identifying the location of the schema to be imported

Content

None; the element is always empty.

Effect

If the stylesheet contains references to user-defined types, then the schema in which these types are defined must be imported using an `<xsl:import-schema>` declaration. The same applies to user-defined element and attribute declarations.

Importing a schema makes the schema definitions available throughout the stylesheet, not only in the module where they are imported. (This differs from XQuery 1.0, where different modules may import different schemas.)

Importing a schema does not implicitly import other schemas that are referenced from that schema using `<xs:import>`, `<xs:include>`, or `<xs:redefine>`. You should explicitly import every schema document that contains a definition that you want to refer to in the stylesheet.

The XSLT specification defines the way that schema import works in terms of the way that the XML Schema specification defines `<xs:import>`. This leaves a great deal of discretion to the implementation. It is quite likely that an XSLT processor will want to cache schemas somewhere in a compiled form, to avoid analyzing them afresh every time a stylesheet is processed; many systems may also use catalogs or data dictionaries of some kind so that a local copy of a schema can be accessed rather than retrieving it over the internet. The exact way in which the `namespace` and `schema-location` attributes are used is therefore very open-ended. In principle you can specify either or both of these attributes to identify a schema: The `namespace` attribute identifies it according to the `namespace` that the schema is defining (the `targetNamespace` attribute of the `<xs:schema>` element), while the `schema-location` attribute gives a "hint" as to where a copy of the schema might be found.

> *Although the terminology differs, this is not actually any different from the way the* `href` *attribute in* `<xsl:include>` *and* `<xsl:import>` *is handled. Reflecting common practice established with XSLT 1.0, the XSLT specification now recognizes that implementations can provide URI resolvers or catalogs to interpret these URIs, and that it is therefore impossible to be completely prescriptive about their interpretation.*

If the `namespace` attribute is omitted, this acts as a request to import a schema that has no target namespace (that is, a schema for elements that are in no namespace). The `namespace` attribute should not be set to a zero-length string, since this is not a valid namespace URI.

If the `schema-location` attribute is omitted, then it is assumed that the implementation will be able to locate a schema from the knowledge of the target namespace alone.

Any failure that occurs during schema import (for example, failure to locate the requested schema, or an error in the schema itself) is treated as a compile-time error.

If there are multiple `<xsl:import-schema>` declarations for the same target namespace, then the one with highest import precedence is used. Import precedence is explained under `<xsl:import>` on page 314. If this leaves more than one, then the behavior is defined by reference to the XML Schema specification: It's defined to be the same as when a schema document contains more than one `<xs:import>` element for the same namespace. In practice, the schema specification leaves a lot of discretion to implementations on how to handle this. Some implementations may load multiple schema modules and check them for consistency; others (including Saxon) simply take the first one and assume that the others are equivalent.

Consistency rules for schemas extend beyond the question of multiple imports from a single stylesheet. The schema that's imported into the stylesheet must be consistent with the schema used to validate the source document. Since many systems will allow compiled schemas to be cached, probably sharing the cache between many different stylesheets, there is likely to be a more global consistency requirement. In general, it's probably not possible to have two different versions of the same schema (or to put it another way, two different schemas with the same target namespace, or with no target namespace) in use at the same time. The details, however, are left to the implementation.

If a processor that is not schema-aware encounters an `<xsl:import-schema>` declaration, it will report an error. If you want to write stylesheets that work with both schema-aware and non–schema-aware processors, you can achieve this by attaching the attribute «use-when=`"system-property` (`'xsl:schema-aware')='yes')`"» to any element that should be ignored by a non–schema-aware processor (that is, the `<xsl:import-schema>` declaration itself, and any element that uses a «type» or «validation» attribute, or references a schema-defined type).

Usage

It's not necessary to import every schema that has been used to validate an input document. You only need to import the schema if there is code in the stylesheet that actually references the names whose meaning is defined in the schema.

The places where such references may occur are as follows:

❑ In the `type` attribute of `<xsl:element>`, `<xsl:attribute>`, `<xsl:copy>`, `<xsl:copy-of>`, `<xsl:document>`, `<xsl:result-document>`, and the `xsl:type` attribute of literal result elements. This is always a `QName` identifying a top-level type definition, and unless it is one of the built-in types such as `xs:integer`, the schema in which the type is defined must be imported.

❑ In the `as` attribute of `<xsl:variable>`, `<xsl:param>`, `<xsl:with-param>`, `<xsl:function>`, and `<xsl:template>`. The value of this attribute is a description of an XPath type, and is expressed using the `SequenceType` syntax outlined in Chapter 4 (and described more fully in Chapter 9 of *XPath 2.0 Programmer's Reference*). If the `SequenceType` references the name of an atomic type, this will be a `QName` identifying either a built-in type such as `xs:date`, or a top-level simple type definition in a schema. If the latter is the case, the schema must be imported. If the `SequenceType` uses the constructs «`element(N, T)`» or «`attribute(N, T)`» then the rules are slightly more complicated, and are described below.

❑ In an XPath expression anywhere in the stylesheet that uses a `SequenceType`. This construct is used in expressions such as «`$x instance of T`» or «`$x treat as T`». The rules here are the same as for a `SequenceType` appearing in an `as` attribute, as described in the previous item.

❑ In an XPath expression that uses a constructor function for a user-defined atomic type (for example «`mf:part-number('PXW5792')`») or a cast to a user-defined atomic type (for example «`'PXW5792' cast as mf:part-number`»). In both these cases, the type name must be the name of a top-level simple type definition, and the schema containing this type definition must be imported.

❑ If you use the option «`validation="strict"`» or «`validation="lax"`» (or invoke this implicitly using the `default-validation` attribute on the `<xsl:stylesheet>` element), then you may be required to import the schema used to perform this validation, even if there are no explicit references in the stylesheet to the names defined in this schema. The XSLT specification leaves it open to the implementation to use other mechanisms to locate a schema at runtime to perform this validation, but if you import the schema explicitly, then you avoid any dependence on such mechanisms.

When the construct «`schema-element(N)`» or «`schema-attribute(N)`» is used in a `SequenceType`, then N must be the name of a global element or attribute declaration defined in an imported schema. Similarly, when the constructs «`element(N, T)`» or «`attribute(N, T)`» are used, then T must be the name of a simple or complex type defined in an imported schema, unless it is the name of a built-in type. But in these constructs the name N does not need to be present in the schema: this allows reference to local elements and attributes provided they have a global type definition.

For example, if you create an element like this:

```
<temp xsl:type="xs:date">
  <xsl:value-of select="current-date()"/>
</temp>
```

you will later be able to match this using:

```
<xsl:if test="$p instance of element(temp, xs:date)">
```

even though there is no imported schema defining the element name «`temp`».

Examples

This example imports the schema for namespace «http://ns.megacorp.com/hr» from the location «http://schema.megacorp.com/hr/schema.xsd»:

```
<xsl:import-schema
    namespace = "http://ns.megacorp.com/hr"
    schema-location = "http://schema.megacorp.com/hr/schema.xsd"/>
```

The following example imports a no-namespace schema from the file «schema.xsd» in the same directory as the stylesheet:

```
<xsl:import-schema
    schema-location = "schema.xsd"/>
```

The following example imports the schema that defines the structure of XSLT stylesheets. The XSLT processor is expected to know where to find this schema.

```
<xsl:import-schema
    namespace = "http://www.w3.org/1999/XSL/Transform"/>
```

(This import would be useful only in a stylesheet that is designed to process XSLT stylesheets as its input and/or result documents.)

xsl:include

<xsl:include> is a top-level element used to include the contents of one stylesheet module within another. The definitions in the included stylesheet module have the same *import precedence* as those in the including module, so the effect is as if these definitions were textually included at the point in the including module where the <xsl:include> element appears.

Changes in 2.0

There are no changes to the syntax of this instruction in XSLT 2.0. The rules for the href attribute have been reformulated: In effect, the way in which the URI is dereferenced to obtain a stylesheet module is now largely implementation defined. This allows for options such as catalogs or user-specified URI resolvers, as well as implementations that cache or precompile stylesheet modules.

Format

```
<xsl:include
  href = uri-reference~/>
```

Position

<xsl:include> is a top-level declaration, which means that it must appear as a child of the <xsl:stylesheet> element. There are no constraints on its ordering relative to other declarations in the stylesheet.

Attributes

Name	Value	Meaning
href mandatory	URI	The URI of the stylesheet to be included

Like all other XSLT elements, the `<xsl:include>` declaration may also have a «use-when» attribute. This is described in Chapter 3 (see page 122). This can be used in the same way as on `<xsl:import>`: see the example on page 314.

Content

None; the element is always empty.

Effect

The URI contained in the `href` attribute may be an absolute URI or a relative URI. If relative, it is interpreted relative to the base URI of the XML document or external entity containing the `<xsl:include>` element. For example, if a file `main.xsl` contains the element `<xsl:include href="date.xsl"/>` then by default the system will look for `date.xsl` in the same directory as `main.xsl`. You can change this behavior by using the `xml:base` attribute to specify a base URI explicitly, as described in Chapter 2 on page 53.

The URI must identify an XML document that is a valid XSLT stylesheet. The top-level elements of this stylesheet are logically inserted into the including stylesheet module at the point where the `<xsl:include>` element appears. However:

❑ These elements retain their base URI, so anything that involves referencing a relative URI is done relative to the original URI of the included stylesheet. This rule applies, for example, when expanding further `<xsl:include>` and `<xsl:import>` elements, or when using relative URIs as arguments to the `document()` function.

❑ When a namespace prefix is used (typically within a QName, but it also applies to freestanding prefixes such as those in the `xsl:exclude-result-prefixes` attribute of a literal result element), it is interpreted using only the namespace declarations in the original stylesheet module in which the QName occurred. An included stylesheet module does not inherit namespace declarations from the module that includes it. This even applies to QNames constructed at execution time as the result of evaluating an expression, for example an expression used within an attribute value template for the `name` or `namespace` attribute of `<xsl:element>`.

❑ The values of the `version`, `extension-element-prefixes`, `exclude-result-prefixes`, and `xpath-default-namespace` attributes that apply to an element in the included stylesheet module, as well as `xml:lang`, `xml:base`, and `xml:space`, are those that were defined on their own `<xsl:stylesheet>` element, not those on the `<xsl:stylesheet>` element of the including stylesheet module.

The included stylesheet module may use the simplified stylesheet syntax, described in Chapter 3. This allows an entire stylesheet module to be defined as the content of an element such as <HTML>. It is then treated as if it were a module containing a single template, whose match pattern is «/» and whose content is the literal result element.

The included stylesheet module may contain <xsl:include> statements to include further stylesheets, or <xsl:import> statements to import them. A stylesheet must not directly or indirectly include itself.

It is not an error to include the same stylesheet module more than once, either directly or indirectly, but it is not a useful thing to do. It may well cause errors due to the presence of duplicate declarations; in fact, if the stylesheet contains definitions of global variables or named templates, and is included more than once at the same import precedence, such errors are almost inevitable. In some other situations it is implementation-defined whether an XSLT processor will report duplicate declarations as an error, so the behavior may vary from one product to another.

Usage and Examples

<xsl:include> provides a simple textual inclusion facility analogous to the #include directive in C. It provides a way of writing a stylesheet in a modular way so that commonly used definitions can be held in a library and used wherever they are needed.

If you are handling a wide range of different document types, the chances are they will have some elements in common, which are to be processed in the same way regardless of where they occur. For example, these might include standard definitions of toolbars, backgrounds, and navigation buttons to appear on your Web pages, as well as standard styles applied to data elements such as product names, e-mail contact addresses, or dates.

To incorporate such standard content into a stylesheet without change, use <xsl:include>. If there are definitions you want to override, use <xsl:import>.

<xsl:include> is a compile-time facility; it is used to assemble the complete stylesheet before you start executing it. People sometimes ask how to include other stylesheets conditionally at runtime, based on conditions found in the source document. The answer is simple: you can't. It would be like writing a program in Visual Basic that modifies itself as it executes. If you do want different sets of rules to be active at different times, consider using modes, or consider inverting the logic, so that instead of having an all-purpose stylesheet that tries to include different sets of rules on different occasions, you make your principal stylesheet module the one that is most closely tailored to the circumstances, and use <xsl:import> to import the all-purpose rules into it, at a lower import precedence than the specialized rules.

It can make a difference where in your stylesheet the <xsl:include> statement is placed. There are some kinds of objects—notably, template rules—where if there is no other way of deciding which one to use, the XSLT processor has the option of giving priority to the one that occurs last in the stylesheet. This isn't something you can easily take advantage of, because in all these cases the processor also has the option of reporting an error. As a general principle, it's probably best to place <xsl:include> statements near the beginning of the file, because then if there are any accidental overlaps in the definitions, the ones in your principal stylesheet will either override those included from elsewhere, or be reported as errors.

Example: Using `<xsl:include>` with Named Attribute Sets

This example shows the use of `<xsl:include>` to incorporate declarations (in this case of a named attribute set) from one stylesheet module into another.

Source

This example can be used with any source document.

Stylesheet

Consider a principal stylesheet `picture.xsl` that includes a stylesheet `attributes.xsl`, as follows:

```
<xsl:stylesheet version="1.0"
    xmlns:xsl="http://www.w3.org/1999/XSL/Transform">

<xsl:include href="attributes.xsl"/>

<xsl:template match="/">
    <picture xsl:use-attribute-sets="picture-attributes">
       <xsl:attribute name="color">red</xsl:attribute>
    </picture>
</xsl:template>
</xsl:stylesheet>
```

This includes the module `attributes.xsl`:

```
<xsl:stylesheet version="1.0"
    xmlns:xsl="http://www.w3.org/1999/XSL/Transform">

<xsl:attribute-set name="picture-attributes">
    <xsl:attribute name="color">blue</xsl:attribute>
    <xsl:attribute name="transparency">100</xsl:attribute>
</xsl:attribute-set>

</xsl:stylesheet>
```

The named attribute set in the included stylesheet is used exactly as if it were defined in the principal stylesheet, at the point where the `<xsl:include>` statement appears.

Output

The resulting output is:

```
<picture transparency="100" color="red"/>
```

This is because attributes generated using `<xsl:attribute>` override those generated by using a named attribute set; it has nothing to do with the fact that the attribute set came from an included stylesheet.

See Also

`<xsl:import>` on page 312

xsl:key

The `<xsl:key>` element is a top-level declaration used to declare a named key, for use with the `key()` function in expressions and patterns.

Changes in 2.0

The restrictions on using global variables in the `match` and `use` attributes have been eased.

It is now possible to define keys of any data type (for example numbers or dates), and to a specify a collation to be used when deciding whether two string-valued keys match.

The key values for a node can now be evaluated using a sequence constructor contained in the `<xsl:key>` element, as an alternative to using the `use` attribute. This allows the evaluation to invoke templates or other XSLT constructs such as `<xsl:number>`.

Format

```
<xsl:key
   name = qname
   match = pattern
   use? = expression
   collation? = uri>
   <!-- Content: sequence-constructor -->
</xsl:key>
```

Position

`<xsl:key>` is a top-level declaration, which means that it must be a child of the `<xsl:stylesheet>` element. It may appear any number of times in a stylesheet.

Attributes

Name	Value	Meaning
name mandatory	Lexical QName	The name of the key
match mandatory	Pattern	Defines the nodes to which this key is applicable
use optional	Expression	The expression used to determine the value of the key for each of these nodes
collation optional	URI	The name of a collation used to compare string-valued keys

The syntax for a `Pattern` is defined in Chapter 6.

The `use` attribute and the sequence constructor are mutually exclusive: If the `use` attribute is present, the element must be empty, and if it is absent, then there must be a nonempty sequence constructor.

Content

A sequence constructor. This is used as an alternative to the `use` attribute to determine the value of the key.

Effect

The `name` attribute specifies the name of the key. It must be a valid lexical QName; if it contains a namespace prefix, the prefix must identify a namespace declaration that is in scope on the `<xsl:key>` element. The effective name of the key is the expanded name, consisting of the namespace URI and the local part of the name.

The `match` attribute specifies the nodes to which the key applies. The value is a `Pattern`, as described in Chapter 6. If a node doesn't match the pattern, then it will have no values for the named key. If a node does match the pattern, then the node will have zero or more values for the named key, as determined by the `use` attribute.

The simplest case is where the key values are unique. For example, consider the following source document:

```
<vehicles>
<vehicle reg="P427AGH" owner="Joe Karloff"/>
<vehicle reg="T788PHT" owner="Prunella Higgs"/>
<vehicle reg="V932TXQ" owner="William D. Abikombo"/>
</vehicles>
```

In the stylesheet you can define a key for the registration number of these vehicles, as follows:

```
<xsl:key name="vehicle-registration" match="vehicle" use="@reg"/>
```

The `use` attribute specifies an expression used to determine the value or values of the key. This expression doesn't have to select an attribute, like «@reg» in the example above. For example, it could select a child element. If this is a repeating child element, you can create an index entry for each instance. If the `use` attribute isn't supplied, then the sequence constructor is evaluated instead.

The `collation` attribute identifies a collation that will be used when the key value is a string. If no collation is specified, an implementation-defined default collation is used. Collations are discussed under `<xsl:sort>` on page 427. You need to decide whether you want to use a weak collation, in which strings such as «ASCII» and «ascii» are considered equivalent, or a strong collation, in which they are considered to be different. You might also need to consider what language should be used to define the matching rules. One of the options, which might be the best choice when you are comparing strings such as part numbers, is to use the Unicode Codepoint Collation, which considers two strings to be equal only if they use the same Unicode characters, as identified by their codepoint values. You can request this using the collation URI:

```
http://www.w3.org/2003/11/xpath-functions/collation/codepoint
```

The final URI will be determined only when the specification reaches Candidate Recommendation status.

XSLT 2.0 allows the pattern in the `match` attribute, and the expression in the `use` attribute, to reference global variables and to use the `key()` function to access other keys. But the definitions must not be circular: For example, if a key K makes use of the global variable V, then the value of V must not depend in any way on the key K.

The formal rules are as follows. For each node that matches the pattern, the `use` expression or the sequence constructor is evaluated with that node as the context node, and with the context position and context size both set to 1 (one). Then:

❑ The result of evaluating the expression is atomized. Atomization is described in Chapter 2 (page 73); its effect is to extract the typed value of any nodes in the result sequence. Note that the typed value may be a sequence.

❑ Each atomic value in the atomized result contributes one value for the key.

❑ The resulting atomic values can be used to locate the node when supplied in the second argument of the `key()` function. The node is selected by the `key()` function if any of the key values (as established by the procedure just described) is equal to any of the values in the sequence supplied to the `key()` function. The comparison is done using the XPath «eq» operator and is sensitive to the type of the values; if the values are strings, then the selected collation is used.

There is no rule that stops two nodes having the same key value. For example, declaring a key for vehicle registration numbers in the example above does not mean that each registration number must be different. So a node can have more than one key value, and a key value can refer to more than one node.

To describe the rules more formally, each named key can be considered as a set of node-value pairs. A node can be associated with multiple values and a value can be associated with multiple nodes. The value can be of any atomic type. A node-value pair (N, V) is present in this set if node N matches the pattern specified in the `match` attribute, and if the value of the expression in the `use` attribute (or of the sequence constructor), when applied to node N, produces a sequence that after atomization and conversion to the required type contains the value V.

To complicate things a bit further, there can be more than one `<xsl:key>` declaration in the stylesheet with the same name. The set of node-value pairs for the key is then the union of the sets produced by each `<xsl:key>` declaration independently. The import precedence of the key declarations makes no difference. All the `<xsl:key>` declarations with a given name must have the same values for the `collation` attribute, if present.

A key can be used to select nodes in any document, not just the principal source document. This includes a document constructed as a temporary tree. The `key()` function always returns nodes that are in the same document as the context node at the time it is called, or the node supplied in the third argument to the function if present. It is therefore best to think of there being one set of node-value pairs for each named key for each document.

The effect of calling «key(K, V, D)», where K is a key name, V is a string value, and D is a node, is to locate the set of node-value pairs for the key named K in the document containing D, and to return a sequence containing the nodes from each pair where the value is V. If there are several nodes with this value, they are always returned in document order.

If you like to think in SQL terms, imagine a table KEY-VALUES with four columns, KEY-NAME, DOCUMENT, NODE, and VALUE. Then calling «key('K', 'V', 'D')» is equivalent to the SQL statement:

```
SELECT DISTINCT NODE FROM KEY-VALUES WHERE
    KEY-NAME='K' AND
    VALUE='V' AND
    DOCUMENT='D';
```

Usage and Examples

Declaring a key has two effects: It simplifies the code you need to write to find the nodes with given values, and it is likely to make access faster.

The performance effect, of course, depends entirely on the implementation. It would be quite legitimate for an implementation to conduct a full search of the document each time the key() function was called. In practice, however, most implementations are likely to build an index or hash table, so there will be a one-time cost in building the index (for each document), but after this, access to nodes whose key value is known should be very fast.

The <xsl:key> element is usually used to index elements, but in principle it can be used to index any kind of node except namespace nodes.

Keys versus IDs

An alternative to using keys is to use XML-defined IDs. If you have attributes defined in a DTD or schema as being of type ID, you can find an element with a particular ID value using the id() function described in *XPath 2.0 Programmer's Reference*.

Why would you prefer to use keys, rather than relying on ID values? Keys have many advantages:

❑   ID values must be simple attributes of the elements they identify, they cannot be anything more complex.

❑   ID values must be unique.

❑   You cannot have two different sets of ID values in the same document, for example ISBNs and acquisition numbers; if you do, you have to be sure they will not clash with each other.

❑   ID values must take the form of XML names, for example they cannot contain characters such as «/» and «+».

❑   ID values are not recognized in a source document unless it is parsed with a validating XML parser or schema processor that reports attribute types to the XSLT processor. XML parsers are not required to behave in this way, so it is easy to end up with configuration problems that result in IDs not being recognized.

❑   Recognizing ID attributes in temporary trees is particularly troublesome, as it requires the temporary tree to be validated.

Using a Simple Key

The detailed rules for keys seem complicated, but most practical applications of keys are very simple. Consider the following key definition:

```
<xsl:key name="product-code" match="product" use="string(@code)"/>
```

This defines a key whose name is «product-code», and which can be used to find <product> elements given the value of their code attribute. If a product has no code attribute, it won't be possible to find it using this key.

In this example I have deliberately forced the @code attribute to be converted to a string. In the absence of a schema, atomizing the value would normally give a value of type xdt:untypedAtomic. Keys use the rules for the XPath 2.0 eq operator, which treat untyped atomic values as strings. So «key("product-code", "abc")» would perform a string comparison, while «key("product-code", 29)» would be a type error. If the value is a string, then it's known at the time the key is defined that all comparisons will be string comparisons, which gives the system a chance to do the indexing more efficiently.

To find the product with code value «ABC-456», you can write, for example:

```
<xsl:apply-templates select="key('product-code', 'ABC-456')"/>
```

Note that you could just as well choose to index the attribute nodes:

```
<xsl:key name="product-code" match="product/@code" use="."/>
```

To find the relevant product you would then write:

```
<xsl:apply-templates select="key('product-code', 'ABC-456')/.."/>
```

I've used <xsl:apply-templates> here as an example. This will select all the <product> elements in the current document that have code «ABC-456» (I never said it had to be a unique identifier) and apply the matching template to each one in turn, processing them in document order, as usual. I could equally have used any other instruction that uses an XPath expression; for example, I could have assigned the node set to a variable, or used it in an <xsl:value-of> element.

The second argument to the key function is normally a value of the type specified in the as attribute of the <xsl:key> declaration. It won't usually be a literal, as in my example, but is more likely to be a string obtained from somewhere else in the source document, or perhaps supplied as a parameter to the stylesheet. It may well have been passed as one of the parameters in the URL used to select this stylesheet in the first place; for example, a Web page might display a list of available products such as the one in Figure 5-7

Behind each of these buttons shown to the user there might be a URL such as:

```
http://www.cheap-food.com/servlet/product?code=ABC-456
```

You then write a servlet (or an ASP page if you prefer) on your Web server that extracts the query parameter code, and fires off your favorite XSLT processor specifying products.xml as the source

Figure 5-7

document, `show-product.xsl` as the stylesheet, and «ABC-456» as the value to be supplied for the global stylesheet parameter called `prod-code`. Your stylesheet would then look like this:

```
<xsl:param name="prod-code"/>
<xsl:key name="product-code" match="product" use="@code"/>
<xsl:template match="/">
   <html>
   <body>
   <xsl:variable name="product" select="key('product-code', $prod-code)"/>
   <xsl:if test="not($product)">
      <p>There is no product with this code</p>
   </xsl:if>
   <xsl:apply-templates select="$product"/>
   </body>
   </html>
</xsl:template>
```

Multivalued Keys

A key can be multivalued, in that a single node can have several values each of which can be used to find the node independently. For example, a book may have several authors, and each author's name can be used as a key value. This could be defined as follows:

```
<xsl:key name="book-author" match="book" use="author/name"/>
```

The use expression, «author/name», selects more than one node, so the typed value of each of its nodes (that is, the name of each author of the book) is used as one of the values in the set of node-value pairs that makes up the key.

In this particular example, as well as one book having several authors, each author may have written several books, so when you use an XPath expression such as:

```
<xsl:for-each select="key('book-author', 'Agatha Christie')">
```

you will be selecting all the books in which Agatha Christie was one of the authors. What if you want to find all the books in which Alex Homer and David Sussman are joint authors? You can do this using the `intersect` operator provided in XPath 2.0:

```
<xsl:variable name="set1"
    select="key('book-author', 'Alex Homer')"/>
<xsl:variable name="set2"
    select="key('book-author', 'David Sussman')"/>
<xsl:variable name="result"
    select="$set1 intersect $set2"/>
```

You can also supply a sequence of several values as the second argument to the `key()` function. For example, you might write:

```
<xsl:variable name="ac" select="key('book-author', 'Agatha Christie')">
<xsl:for-each select="key('book-author', $ac/author/name)">
```

The result of the `select` expression in the `<xsl:for-each>` instruction is the set of all books in which one of the authors is either Agatha Christie or a co-author of Agatha Christie. This is because `$ac` is the set of all books in which Agatha Christie is an author, so «`$ac/author/name`» is the set of all authors of these books, and using this set of named authors as the value of the key produces the set of books in which *any* of them is an author.

Example: Multivalued Nonunique Keys

This example shows how a node can have several values for one key, and a given key value can identify more than one node. It uses author name as a key to locate <book> elements.

Source

The source file is `booklist.xml`:

```
<booklist>
<book>
    <title>Design Patterns</title>
    <author>Erich Gamma</author>
    <author>Richard Helm</author>
    <author>Ralph Johnson</author>
    <author>John Vlissides</author>
</book>
<book>
    <title>Pattern Hatching</title>
    <author>John Vlissides</author>
</book>
<book>
    <title>Building Applications Frameworks</title>
    <author>Mohamed Fayad</author>
    <author>Douglas C. Schmidt</author>
    <author>Ralph Johnson</author>
</book>
```

```
<book>
    <title>Implementing Applications Frameworks</title>
    <author>Mohamed Fayad</author>
    <author>Douglas C. Schmidt</author>
    <author>Ralph Johnson</author>
</book>
</booklist>
```

Stylesheet

The stylesheet is `author-key.xsl`.

It declares the key and then simply copies the `<book>` elements that match the author name supplied as a parameter. So you can call this stylesheet with a call such as (all on one line):

```
java -jar c:\saxon\saxon7.jar booklist.xml author-key.xsl
                author="Ralph Johnson"
```

Note that parameters containing spaces have to be written in quotes on the command line. The detailed command line syntax for each XSLT processor is different.

```
<xsl:transform
 xmlns:xsl="http://www.w3.org/1999/XSL/Transform"
 version="2.0"
>

<xsl:key name="author-name" match="book" use="author"/>

<xsl:param name="author" required="yes"/>

<xsl:template match="/">
  <xsl:copy-of select="key('author-name', $author)"/>
</xsl:template>

</xsl:transform>
```

Output

With the parameter set to the value «John Vlissides», the output is as follows:

```
<?xml version="1.0" encoding="utf-8" ?>
<book>
    <title>Design Patterns</title>
    <author>Erich Gamma</author>
    <author>Richard Helm</author>
    <author>Ralph Johnson</author>
    <author>John Vlissides</author>
</book>
<book>
    <title>Pattern Hatching</title>
    <author>John Vlissides</author>
</book>
```

Multiple Named Keys

There is nothing to stop you from defining several keys for the same nodes. For example:

```
<xsl:key name="book-isbn" match="book" use="isbn"/>
<xsl:key name="book-author" match="book" use="author/surname"/>
```

This allows you to find a book if either the author or the ISBN is known.

However, it's worth thinking twice before doing this. Assuming the XSLT processor implements the key by building an index or hash table, rather than by searching the whole document each time, you have to weigh the cost of building the index against the cost of finding the information by a search. If your transformation only needs to find a single book using its ISBN number, it might be simpler and faster to write:

```
<xsl:for-each select="//book[isbn='0-13-082676-6']"/>
```

and not use a key at all.

Multiple Definitions for the Same Key

It's also possible to have several <xsl:key> declarations with the same name. For example:

```
<xsl:key name="artist-key" match="book" use="author/name"/>
<xsl:key name="artist-key" match="CD" use="composer"/>
<xsl:key name="artist-key" match="CD" use="performer"/>
```

Now you can use the key() function in an expression such as:

```
<xsl:apply-templates select="key('artist-key', 'Ringo Starr')"/>
```

The set of nodes this returns will be either <book> elements or <CD> elements or a mixture of the two; the only thing you know for certain is that each one will be either a book with Ringo Starr as one of the authors, or a CD with Ringo Starr listed either as the composer or as a performer.

If the use expression were the same in each case, you could simplify this. For example to find books and CDs with a particular publisher, you could write:

```
<xsl:key name="publisher-key" match="book | CD" use="publisher"/>
```

This example uses the union pattern «book | CD», which matches all <book> elements and all <CD> elements. Union patterns are described on page 502 in Chapter 6.

The different definitions do not all need to be in the same stylesheet module; all the key definitions in included and imported stylesheets are merged together regardless of their import precedence.

Using Keys for Grouping

In XSLT 2.0, the new <xsl:for-each-group> instruction (described on page 281) provides facilities for grouping nodes with common values for a grouping key, or for eliminating nodes with duplicate values for a grouping key. In XSLT 1.0, this was a much more difficult problem to solve, and you may well encounter XSLT 1.0 stylesheets that use the workaround for this problem known as Muenchian grouping, named after its inventor, Steve Muench of Oracle.

It shouldn't be necessary to use Muenchian grouping any more in XSLT 2.0. However, since it is widely used and you may have the job of converting stylesheets that use it, or of writing stylesheets that work under both XSLT 2.0 and XSLT 1.0, it's worth understanding how it works.

Say you want to group a list of employees according to their location. Typically, you want two nested loops, in pseudocode:

```
<xsl:for-each (distinct location)>
   <location name="...">
      <xsl:for-each (employee in that location)>
         <employee>
            (details)
         </employee>
      </xsl:for-each>
   </location>
</xsl:for-each>
```

Muenchian grouping uses a key to identify the distinct locations, and then to identify all the employees at a given location. The key is defined like this:

```
<xsl:key name="k" match="employee" use="location"/>
```

To find the distinct locations, scan all the employee elements, and select only those that are the first one in their location. In XSLT 2.0 you would write:

```
<xsl:for-each select="//employee[. is key('k', location)[1]]">
```

The «is» operator wasn't available in XPath 1.0, so this had to be written as:

```
<xsl:for-each select=
   "//employee[generate-id(.) = generate-id(key('k', location)[1])]">
```

The inner loop, which selects all the employees at the same location, is achieved by writing:

```
<xsl:for-each select="key('k', location)">
```

so the final code becomes:

```
<xsl:for-each select=
   "//employee[generate-id(.) = generate-id(key('k', location)[1])]">
   <location name="{location}">
      <xsl:for-each select="key('k', location)">
         <employee>
            <xsl:apply-templates/>
         </employee>
      </xsl:for-each>
   </location>
</xsl:for-each>
```

In XSLT 2.0 this can be rewritten much more readably as:

```
<xsl:for-each=group select="//employee" group-by="location"
   <location name="{current-grouping-key()}">
      <xsl:for-each select="current-group()">
         <employee>
            <xsl:apply-templates/>
         </employee>
      </xsl:for-each>
   </location>
</xsl:for-each>
```

See Also

key() function in Chapter 7, page 572
<xsl:for-each-group> on page 281

xsl:matching-substring

The <xsl:matching-substring> element is used within an <xsl:analyze-string> instruction to indicate the processing that should be applied to substrings of the input string that match the supplied regular expression.

Changes in 2.0

This element is new in XSLT 2.0.

Format

```
<xsl:matching-substring>
   <!-- Content: sequence-constructor -->
</xsl:matching-substring>
```

Position

<xsl:matching-substring> can only appear as a child of an <xsl:analyze-string> element, and it may not appear more than once.

Attributes

None.

Content

A sequence constructor.

Effect

The sequence constructor contained in the `<xsl:matching-substring>` element is evaluated once for each substring of the input string that matches the regular expression. The result of evaluating the sequence constructor is added to the result of the containing `<xsl:analyze-string>` instruction.

Usage and Examples

See `<xsl:analyze-string>` on page 176

See Also

`<xsl:analyze-string>` on page 176
`<xsl:non-matching-substring>` on page 358

xsl:message

The `<xsl:message>` instruction outputs a message, and optionally terminates execution of the stylesheet.

Changes in 2.0

The `terminate` attribute may now be specified as an attribute value template.

The `select` attribute is new in XSLT 2.0.

Format

```
<xsl:message
  select? = expression
  terminate? = { "yes" | "no" }>
  <!-- Content: sequence-constructor -->
</xsl:message>
```

Position

`<xsl:message>` is an instruction. It is always used as part of a sequence constructor.

Attributes

Name	Value	Meaning
select optional	Expression	The expression is evaluated to produce the content of the message
terminate optional	Attribute value template returning «yes» | «no»	The value «yes» indicates that processing is terminated after the message is output. The default is «no»

Content

A sequence constructor. There is no requirement that this should only generate text nodes; it can produce any XML fragment. What happens to any markup, however, is not defined in the standard.

Unlike other elements that allow a `select` attribute and a sequence constructor, in this case they are not mutually exclusive. The results of evaluating the `select` expression and the results of evaluating the sequence constructor are concatenated to form a single sequence.

Effect

The `<xsl:message>` instruction behaves in a similar way to `<xsl:result-document>` described on page 414; it uses the contained sequence constructor (in this case, with the results of evaluating any `select` expression added at the front) to construct a new document node, sends the constructed document to an implementation-defined destination, and returns an empty sequence.

Unlike `<xsl:result-document>`, the `<xsl:message>` element provides no direct control over the destination or format of the result. The intention is that it should be used to produce progress messages, errors and warnings, which are secondary to the purpose of the transformation.

If the `terminate` attribute is omitted, the value «no» is assumed.

The contents of the constructed document (which will often be a simple text node) are output where the user can be expected to see them. The XSLT specification does not actually say where it goes; this is implementation-dependent, and it might be determined by configuration options. The specification suggests an alert box on the screen and a log file as two possible destinations.

If the `terminate` attribute has the value «yes», execution of the stylesheet is abandoned immediately, and any output generated so far is discarded.

Usage

The `<xsl:message>` instruction is generally used to report error conditions detected by the stylesheet logic. An example might be where an element such as `<sales>` is expected to have a numeric value, but is found to have a nonnumeric value:

- ❑ With «`terminate="no"`» (the default), the stylesheet can report the error and continue processing.
- ❑ With «`terminate="yes"`», the stylesheet can report the error and quit.

Before using `<xsl:message>` in a production environment, check what happens to the messages and whether they can be redirected. You need to be particularly clear about whether your messages are intended to be read by the source document author, the stylesheet author, or the end user: This will affect the way in which you write the text of the message.

The output produced by `<xsl:message>` can be unpredictable, because the sequence of execution of a stylesheet is not defined in the standard. For example, some products (including Saxon) defer evaluation of a variable until the variable is first used, which means that the order in which different variables are evaluated is difficult to predict. If evaluation of a variable triggers execution of `<xsl:message>`, the order of the messages may be surprising. Certainly, it can vary from one XSLT processor to another.

A common use of `<xsl:message>` is to generate diagnostic output so you can work out why your stylesheet isn't behaving as expected. This works well with products that have a fairly predictable sequence of execution, but it can be rather bewildering with a processor that does things in a different order from the one you would expect. Placing diagnostics as comments into the result tree (using `<xsl:comment>`) is probably a more flexible solution. Some products, of course, have vendor-defined debugging aids built-in.

> **The Microsoft MSXML parser ignores `<xsl:message terminate="no">` so the message is not reported anywhere. If «`terminate="yes"`» is specified, it generates an error, which can be handled through the script on the HTML page that invoked the transformation.**

Examples

The following example issues a message and quits if the value of the `<sales>` element is non-numeric:

```
<xsl:if test="string(number(sales))='NaN'">
   <xsl:message terminate="yes">
      <xsl:text>Sales value is not numeric</xsl:text>
   </xsl:message>
</xsl:if>
```

Unfortunately there is no mechanism defined in the XSLT standard that allows the location of the error in the source document to be included in the message.

The following example extends this by allowing several such errors to be reported in a single run, terminating the run only after all errors have been reported. It works by assigning a global variable to the set of nodes in error:

```
<xsl:variable name="bad-sales"
              select="//sales[string(number(current()))='NaN']"/>
<xsl:template match="/">
   <xsl:for-each select="$bad-sales">
      <xsl:message>Sales value <xsl:value-of select="."/>
         is not numeric
      </xsl:message>
   </xsl:for-each>
...
   <xsl:if test="$bad-sales">
      <xsl:message terminate="yes">
         <xsl:text>Processing abandoned</xsl:text>
      </xsl:message>
   </xsl:if>
</xsl:template>
```

Localized Messages

XSLT is designed very much with internationalization in mind, and no doubt the requirement to localize message text was discussed by the working group. They clearly decided that no special facilities were needed, and instead included a detailed example in the XSLT 1.0 specification showing how the message text can be localized (output in the user's native language). The example is worth repeating because it shows a general technique.

Messages for a particular language are stored in a file whose name identifies the language, for example German messages might be stored in `messages/de.xml`. The message file might have the structure:

```
<messages>
    <message name="started">Angefangen</message>
    <message name="please-wait"/>Bitte warten!</message>
    <message name="finished"/>Fertig</message>
</messages>
```

A stylesheet that wishes to produce messages in the appropriate local language will need a parameter to identify this language (it might also be obtained via the `system-property()` function described in Chapter 7, on page 581, but not in a portable way). The stylesheet can then get access to the messages file for the appropriate language, and read the messages from there:

```
<xsl:param name="language" select="'en'" as="xs:string"/>
<xsl:template name="output-message">
    <xsl:param name="name"/>
    <xsl:variable name="message-file"
                  select="concat('messages/', $language, '.xml')"/>
    <xsl:variable name="message-text"
                  select="document($message-file)/messages"/>
    <xsl:message>
        <xsl:value-of select="$message-text/message[@name=$name]"/>
    </xsl:message>
</xsl:template>
```

The same technique can, of course, be used for producing localized text to include in the output file from the stylesheet.

See Also

`<xsl:result-document>` on page 414

xsl:namespace

The `<xsl:namespace>` instruction constructs a namespace node that is written to the result sequence. Constructing namespace nodes in this way is not a frequent requirement, but there are situations where it is the only way of getting a required namespace declaration in the output.

Changes in 2.0

This instruction is new in XSLT 2.0.

Format

```
<xsl:namespace
  name = { string }
  select? = expression
<!-- content: sequence-constructor -->
</xsl:namespace>
```

Position

`<xsl:namespace>` is an instruction. It is always used as part of a sequence constructor.

Attributes

Name	Value	Meaning
name mandatory	Attribute value template returning an NCName or a zero-length string	The name of the namespace node (which represents the namespace prefix)
select optional	Expression	Expression to compute the string value of the namespace node (which represents the namespace URI)

Content

If the `select` attribute is present, the element must be empty. Otherwise, it must contain a nonempty sequence constructor.

Effect

The `name` attribute determines the name of the namespace node. This corresponds to the namespace prefix. If the value of the `name` attribute is a zero-length string, the namespace node defines the default namespace. Otherwise, the name must be an NCName (a valid XML name containing no colon). The `name` attribute can be written as an attribute value template, allowing the name to be computed dynamically.

The string value of the namespace node, which represents the namespace URI, is established using either the `select` attribute or the contained sequence constructor. For consistency, this instruction uses the results of evaluating the `select` attribute or sequence constructor in the same way as other instructions such as `<xsl:attribute>` and `<xsl:value-of>`. This means that the result may be a sequence; the sequence is atomized, each item in the atomized sequence is converted to a string, and the resulting strings are concatenated, with an intervening space used as a separator in the case where the `select` attribute is used. Normally, however, the result of the `select` attribute should be a single string.

A zero-length string cannot be used as a namespace URI; so a runtime error occurs if the result of the computation just described is a zero-length string.

Note that a namespace node is not the same thing as a namespace declaration. An element has a namespace node for every namespace that is in scope. A namespace undeclaration, such as «xmlns=""» in XML Namespace 1.0, or «xmlns:z=""», which is allowed by XML Namespaces 1.1, is not represented by a namespace node. Rather, it is represented in the data model by the absence of a namespace node.

Usage and Examples

Although namespace declarations are a special kind of attribute in the surface XML syntax, they are represented quite differently in the XPath data model. This means that you cannot produce namespace declarations in the result document by using <xsl:attribute>, or by any other mechanism that produces attribute nodes.

The namespace declarations produced by the serializer are derived from the namespace nodes that are present in the result tree. However, there isn't a one-to-one mapping between namespace nodes and namespace declarations. An element in the result tree has a namespace node for every namespace prefix that is in scope for this element (even if it's also in scope for the element's parent).

Normally, the namespace nodes needed in a result tree are created automatically.

For namespaces used in the names of elements and attributes, this is guaranteed by the namespace fixup process described under <xsl:element> on page 265. This procedure is invoked whenever an element is created in a result tree, whether by <xsl:element>, a literal result element, or by <xsl:copy> or <xsl:copy-of>. It is the namespace fixup procedure that effectively decides what prefixes to use for these names.

The only difficulties that arise are therefore when you need namespaces to be declared in the result document that are not used in element and attribute names. An example is if you want to output the following:

```
<price xsi:type="xs:decimal">23.50</price>
```

Your document must then contain a namespace declaration that binds the namespace prefix «xs» to the namespace URI «http://www.w3.org/2001/XMLSchema». The serializer will only produce such a declaration if it encounters a namespace node in the result tree that binds this prefix to this URI.

Here is one convenient way to output the above element:

```
<price xsi:type="xs:decimal">
    <xsl:namespace name="xs"
                    select="'http://www.w3.org/2001/XMLSchema'"/>
    <xsl:value-of select="23.50"/>
</price>
```

Note that there is no need to use <xsl:namespace> to produce a namespace declaration that binds the prefix «xsi» to the namespace http://www.w3.org/2001/XMLSchema-instance. Because this namespace is used in an attribute name, the namespace fixup process will ensure that it is declared. In fact, it would be declared in this case even without namespace fixup, because the rules for a literal result element ensure that all namespaces that are in scope for the literal result element in the stylesheet are copied to the result document, and the «xsi» namespace must be in scope here, or the stylesheet fragment would not be valid.

In fact there are four ways that an element in the result tree can acquire namespace nodes:

❑   When an element is copied from a source tree using an `<xsl:copy>` or `<xsl:copy-of>` instruction, its namespace nodes are also copied, unless this is suppressed by writing «copy-namespaces="no"».

❑   When a literal result element is processed, all the namespace nodes that are in scope for this element in the stylesheet are copied to the result tree, unless this is suppressed using the `[xsl:]exclude-result-prefixes` attribute on some containing element. This attribute is described in the entry for `<xsl:stylesheet>` on page 448.

❑   Namespace nodes for namespaces used in element and attribute names are automatically created by the namespace fixup process.

❑   Namespace nodes can be created manually using the `<xsl:namespace>` instruction.

So the `<xsl:namespace>` instruction is needed only if none of the other mechanisms creates the required namespace declaration.

The namespace fixup process does not automatically create namespace nodes in respect of elements or attributes that have QName-valued content, even when there is a schema that describes the content as a QName. The reason for this is to allow namespace fixup and schema validation to operate as separate processes. Suppose that the schema defines the type of attribute `start` as being an `xs:QName`, and that you want to create the attribute «start="my:root"». Schema validation takes the string value of this attribute as input, checks that the namespace prefix «my» is declared, and generates firstly the typed value of this attribute (consisting of the local name «root» and the namespace URI corresponding to prefix «my»), and secondly the type annotation of the attribute as an `xs:QName`. So the namespace node has to be created before schema validation takes place. This means it cannot be done by an automatic namespace fixup process, because at the time namespace fixup takes place, the attribute node has no type annotation, so you don't yet know that it's an `xs:QName`.

If you write a stylesheet that produces an XSLT stylesheet as its output, then it becomes very important to get the right namespace declarations into the output, because XSLT makes heavy use of attributes that contain namespace prefixes: They arise both in attributes such as the `name` attribute of `<xsl:variable>`, `<xsl:template>`, and `<xsl:function>`, and wherever the stylesheet contains XPath expressions. It's worth remarking that there is nothing in the schema for XSLT stylesheets that marks these attributes out as special. Even the `name` attributes that appear to have QName-valued content do not actually have a type of `xs:QName`. This is because although their lexical space is the same as `xs:QName`, the schema processor would expand them incorrectly. XML Schema specifies (in an erratum, actually) that a schema processor, when it comes across an unprefixed `xs:QName` value, will expand it using the default namespace, and this is not the behavior required by XSLT. So these attributes are simply strings, which means it is the application that must choose a namespace prefix, and then create a namespace node to bind this to the correct namespace URI.

The `<xsl:namespace>` instruction adds a namespace node to the result sequence produced by the sequence constructor that it is part of. Normally this result sequence will immediately be used to create the content of an element node. In this case, the attribute and namespace nodes in the sequence need to come before any other nodes. It doesn't matter what order the attributes and namespace nodes are in relative to each other. It is an error if there are two namespace nodes that bind the same namespace prefix to different URIs; this could happen if you create a namespace node manually using `<xsl:namespace>` that clashes with one that is copied automatically from a source document by an `<xsl:copy>` or `<xsl:copy-of>` instruction, or from the stylesheet by a literal result element. This is only really likely to happen in the case of the default namespace. It is permissible to create a default namespace node using `<xsl:namespace>`, but it's probably not a good idea.

Namespace fixup happens after all the namespace nodes from this result sequence have been constructed, and it is constrained to generate prefixes that don't clash with these namespace nodes. If you have created a namespace node for the default namespace (that is, the empty prefix), then the system will have a problem if the element node itself is in the null namespace, because an element in the null namespace has to use the empty prefix, and it will no longer be available. This can cause a runtime failure.

See Also

`<xsl:attribute>` on page 201.
`<xsl:element>` on page 260.

xsl:namespace-alias

The `<xsl:namespace-alias>` element allows a namespace used in the stylesheet to be mapped to a different namespace used in the output. It is most commonly used when writing transformations that produce an XSLT stylesheet as their output.

Changes in 2.0

The rules for generating namespace prefixes have been made stricter.

Format

```
<xsl:namespace-alias
    stylesheet-prefix = prefix | "#default"
    result-prefix = prefix | "#default"/>
```

Position

`<xsl:namespace-alias>` is a top-level declaration, which means it must be a child of the `<xsl:stylesheet>` element. It may be repeated any number of times in a stylesheet.

Attributes

Name	Value	Meaning
stylesheet-prefix mandatory	NCName | «#default»	A namespace prefix used in the stylesheet
result-prefix mandatory	NCName | «#default»	The prefix of the corresponding namespace to be used in the output

Content

None. The `<xsl:namespace-alias>` element is always empty.

Effect

The `<xsl:namespace-alias>` element affects the treatment of namespaces on literal result elements.

Normally, when an element node is output by processing a literal result element, the output element name will have the same local part, the same prefix, and the same namespace URI as those of the literal result element itself. It isn't guaranteed that it should have the same prefix, but it usually will. The same applies to the attributes of the literal result element. The namespace nodes on the literal result element must be copied unchanged to the result tree, using the same prefix and namespace URI. (The XSLT specification states that when processing a literal result element, all the namespaces that are in scope for the element in the stylesheet, with certain defined exceptions, will also be present in the output, even if they aren't used. Redundant namespace nodes can be suppressed by using the `xsl:exclude-result-prefixes` attribute. For more details on this, see the section *Literal Result Elements*, on page 106 in Chapter 3.)

Suppose you want the output document to be an XSLT stylesheet. Then you need to create elements such as `<xsl:template>` that are in the XSLT namespace. However, you can't use `<xsl:template>` as a literal result element, because by definition, if an element uses the XSLT namespace, it is treated as an XSLT element.

The answer is to use a different namespace on the literal result element in the stylesheet, and include an `<xsl:namespace-alias>` declaration to cause this to be mapped to the XSLT namespace when the literal result element is output. So your literal result element might be `<out:template>`, and you could use an `<xsl:namespace-alias>` element to indicate that the stylesheet prefix «out» should be mapped to the result prefix «xsl».

The `<xsl:namespace-alias>` element declares that one namespace URI, the stylesheet URI, should be replaced by a different URI, the result URI, when literal result elements are output. The namespace URIs are not given directly, but are referred to by using prefixes that are bound to these namespace URIs as a result of namespace declarations that are currently in force. Either one of the namespace URIs may be the default namespace URI, which is referred to using the pseudoprefix «#default». It's an error to use this if there is no default namespace defined.

So although the `<xsl:namespace-alias>` element describes the mapping in terms of prefixes, it is not the prefix that is changed, but the URI.

The substitution of one namespace URI for another affects the names of literal result elements themselves, and the names of all attributes of literal result elements. It also affects the URIs of namespace nodes copied into the result tree from a literal result element. It does not affect elements created using `<xsl:element>`, attributes created using `<xsl:attribute>`, or nodes copied using `<xsl:copy>`.

There was often confusion among XSLT 1.0 users about what namespaces they should expect to find declared in the result document, and different processors handled this differently. In XSLT 2.0, the rules have been clarified. Namespaces find their way from the stylesheet into the result document whenever a literal result element is evaluated. XSLT 2.0 states clearly that if the literal result element has a namespace node with the URI associated with the `stylesheet-prefix` of an `<xsl:namespace-alias>`

instruction, it is not copied to the result tree as it normally would be; if it has a namespace node with the URI associated with the `result-prefix` of an `<xsl:namespace-alias>` instruction, then this namespace node is copied, even if the URI is one such as `http://www.w3.org/1999/XSL/Transform` that would normally not be copied. These rules are designed to produce the result that most users would expect: A literal result element `<out:template>` will produce an element in the result tree that will normally be serialized as `<xsl:template>`; the «xsl» namespace will be declared in the result document, and the «out» namespace will not be declared.

If there are several `<xsl:namespace-alias>` elements that specify the same `stylesheet-prefix`, the one with highest import precedence is used; a compile-time error is reported if there is more than one at the highest import precedence.

The aliasing of namespace URIs applies at the point when a literal result element in the stylesheet is evaluated to create an element node in a result sequence. It applies whether or not this element is written to a final result tree. This means that if you examine a temporary tree into which literal result elements have been copied, the corresponding elements and attributes will use the namespace URI associated with the result prefix, not the stylesheet prefix.

Aliasing of namespaces happens before the namespace fixup process described under `<xsl:element>` on page 265.

Usage and Examples

The main justification for this facility is to enable stylesheets to be written that generate stylesheets as output. This is not as improbable a scenario as it sounds; there are many possible reasons for using this technique, including the following:

❑   There are many proprietary template languages currently in use. Translating these templates into XSLT stylesheets creates an attractive migration route, and there is no reason why these translators should not be written in XSLT.

❑   There may be a continuing need for a template language, which is less complex and powerful than XSLT, for use by nonprogrammers. Again, these simple templates can easily be translated into XSLT stylesheets.

❑   There are some parts of an XSLT stylesheet that cannot easily be parameterized. For example, it is not possible to construct an XPath expression programmatically and then execute it (XSLT is not a reflexive language). The requirement to do this arises when visual tools are developed to define queries and reports interactively. One way of implementing such tools is to construct a customized stylesheet from a generic stylesheet, and again this is a transformation that can be assisted by using XSLT.

❑   You might have developed a large number of stylesheets that all have some common characteristic, for example they might all generate HTML that uses the `<CENTER>` tag. As the `<CENTER>` tag is deprecated, you now want to modify these stylesheets to use `<DIV ALIGN="CENTER">`. Why not write an XSLT transformation to convert them?

❑   There are tools that make it possible to generate XSLT stylesheets from a schema (see for example Schematron at `http://www.ascc.net/xml/resource/schematron/schematron.html`). Since both the schema and the stylesheet are XML documents, this is an XML-to-XML transformation, so it should be possible to write it in XSLT.

In fact, having gone through all the trouble of defining XSLT stylesheets as well-formed XML documents, it would be very surprising if it were impossible to manipulate them using XSLT itself.

However, it is possible to create stylesheets as output without recourse to `<xsl:namespace-alias>`: Just avoid using literal result elements, and use instructions such as `<xsl:element name="xsl:template">` instead. I personally find this approach less confusing, although the stylesheet ends up being more verbose.

There may be other situations where `<xsl:namespace-alias>` is useful. The XSLT specification mentions one, the need to avoid using namespace URIs that have recognized security implications in the area of digital signatures. Another might arise if stylesheets and other documents are held in a configuration management system; there might be a need to ensure that namespaces recognized by the configuration management system, for example to describe the authorship and change history of a document, are not used directly in the stylesheet.

It's also possible to define an alias for the `xml` namespace. For example, the following stylesheet (`xml-space.xsl`):

```
<xsl:transform
   xmlns:xsl="http://www.w3.org/1999/XSL/Transform" version="1.0"
   xmlns:axml="alias">

<xsl:namespace-alias stylesheet-prefix="axml" result-prefix="xml"/>

<xsl:template match="/">
   <doc axml:space="preserve">text</doc>
</xsl:template>

</xsl:transform>
```

produces the following output (regardless of the source document):

```
<?xml version="1.0" encoding="UTF-8"?>
<doc xml:space="preserve">text</doc>
```

This is useful because it gets an «`xml:space="preserve"`» attribute into the result document without affecting the way that whitespace is handled in the stylesheet.

A problem that causes a great deal of confusion with `<xsl:namespace-alias>` is the choice of prefixes in the result. Follow through exactly what happens when you write the stylesheet:

```
<xsl:stylesheet version="1.0"
                xmlns:xsl="http://www.w3.org/1999/XSL/Transform"
                xmlns:oxsl="old.uri">

<xsl:namespace-alias stylesheet-prefix="oxsl" result-prefix="xsl"/>

<xsl:template match="/">
   <oxsl:stylesheet/>
</xsl:template>

</xsl:stylesheet>
```

This transformation executes just one instruction: the `<oxsl:stylesheet>` literal result element. This has two namespace nodes, representing the prefix bindings «xmlns:xsl="http://www.w3.org/1999/XSL/Transform"» and «xmlns:oxsl="old.uri"» (we will ignore the namespace node for the «xml» namespace). The first of these is copied to the result tree, because it matches the `result-prefix`, despite the fact that it would normally be an excluded namespace. The second namespace node is not copied, because its namespace URI («old.uri») is the one referred to by the `stylesheet-prefix` attribute. So the namespace node in the result tree will map the prefix «xsl» to the namespace URI «http://www.w3.org/1999/XSL/Transform».

When the time comes to serialize this result tree, namespace nodes are used to generate namespace declarations, and prefixes are allocated to elements based on the prefixes found in namespace nodes for the element. So the output (ignoring the XML declaration) should be this:

```
<xsl:stylesheet xmlns:xsl="http://www.w3.org/1999/XSL/Transform"/>
```

XSLT 2.0 (unlike 1.0) really doesn't give the implementation any latitude to generate anything else in this situation. In 1.0, there was a general rule that the serializer could add any namespace declarations it chose, and by implication that it could give elements and attributes any prefix that it chose. In 2.0, the namespace fixup process is only allowed to add namespaces if they are actually needed to make the tree consistent, and in this case, they aren't.

Example of <xsl:namespace-alias>

The following example generates an XSLT stylesheet consisting of a single global variable declaration, whose name and default value are supplied as parameters. Although this is a trivial stylesheet, it could be useful when incorporated into another more useful stylesheet using `<xsl:include>` or `<xsl:import>`.

This example is available in the code download as `alias.xsl`.

Source

No source document is required. You can run this with Saxon 7.9 or later using the command:

```
java -jar c:\saxon\saxon7.jar -it main alias.xsl
```

The «-it» option on the command line causes the transformation to start at the template named «main».

Stylesheet

```
<xsl:stylesheet version="1.0"
                xmlns:xsl="http://www.w3.org/1999/XSL/Transform"
                xmlns:xslt="output.xsl">

<xsl:param name="variable-name">v</xsl:param>
<xsl:param name="default-value"/>
<xsl:output indent="yes"/>
```

```
<xsl:namespace-alias
            stylesheet-prefix="xslt"
            result-prefix="xsl"/>

<xsl:template match="/" name="main">
   <xslt:stylesheet version="1.0">
   <xslt:variable name="{$variable-name}">
      <xsl:value-of select="$default-value"/>
   </xslt:variable>
   </xslt:stylesheet>
</xsl:template>

</xsl:stylesheet>
```

Output

If you default the values of the parameters «variable-name» and «default-value», the output is as follows.

```
<?xml version="1.0" encoding="utf-8"?>
<xsl:stylesheet xmlns:xsl="http://www.w3.org/1999/XSL/Transform"
                version="1.0">
   <xsl:variable name="v"/>
</xsl:stylesheet>
```

See Also

Literal Result Elements in Chapter 3, on page 106.

xsl:next-match

The `<xsl:next-match>` instruction allows more than one template rule to be applied to the same node in a source document. When `<xsl:apply-templates>` selects a node, it finds the best match template rule to process this node. Within this template rule, you can use the `<xsl:next-match>` instruction to invoke the next-best matching rule, and so on.

Changes in 2.0

This instruction is new in XSLT 2.0.

Format

```
<xsl:next-match>
  ( <xsl:with-param> | <xsl:fallback> ) *
</xsl:next-match>
```

Position

`<xsl:next-match>` is an instruction, and is always used within a sequence constructor.

Attributes

None.

Content

The element may be empty, or it may contain one or more `<xsl:with-param>` and `<xsl:fallback>` elements. An XSLT 2.0 processor will ignore the `<xsl:fallback>` instructions; they are allowed so that fallback behavior can be defined for use when the stylesheet is processed using an XSLT 1.0 processor. For details, see `<xsl:fallback>` on page 271.

Effect

The effect of the `<xsl:next-match>` instruction is very similar to `<xsl:apply-imports>`. The main difference is that with `<xsl:apply-imports>`, the only template rules that can be invoked are those in imported stylesheet modules. By contrast, `<xsl:next-match>` can invoke other template rules of lower priority in the same stylesheet module, and can also invoke template rules that have lower import precedence because they were imported into the parent stylesheet module earlier than the current template rule.

There is a clear analogy here with object-oriented programming. Writing a template rule that overrides another is like writing a method that overrides a method defined on the superclass. `<xsl:next-match>` behaves analogously to the `super()` function in object-oriented programming languages, allowing the new template rule to refine the behavior of the original template rule, rather than replacing it completely.

`<xsl:next-match>`, like `<xsl:apply-imports>`, relies on the concept of a *current template rule*. A template rule becomes the current template rule when it is invoked using `<xsl:apply-templates>`, `<xsl:apply-imports>`, or `<xsl:next-match>`. Using `<xsl:call-template>` does not change the current template rule. However, using `<xsl:for-each>` makes the current template rule null, until such time as the `<xsl:for-each>` terminates, when the previous value is reinstated. The current template rule is also null while global variables and attribute sets are being evaluated.

Within the stylesheet as a whole, there are potentially several template rules that match the context node. The rules for the `<xsl:apply-templates>` instruction define an ordering of these rules: They are considered first in decreasing order of *import precedence*, then within each import precedence in decreasing order of *priority*, and finally within each priority, by the order of the declarations in the stylesheet (it is actually an error to have two rules with the same priority, but the processor is allowed to ignore this error and select whichever comes last in the stylesheet). At the end of the list is the built-in template rule for the particular kind of node. What `<xsl:next-match>` does is choose the template rule that comes next in this pecking order, after the current template rule.

It is possible to specify parameters to be supplied to the called template, using `<xsl:with-param>` elements contained within the `<xsl:next-match>` element. These work in the same way as parameters for `<xsl:call-template>` and `<xsl:apply-templates>`; if the name of the supplied parameter matches the name of an `<xsl:param>` element within the called template, the parameter will take this value, otherwise it will take the default value supplied in the `<xsl:param>` element. It is not an error to supply parameters that don't match any `<xsl:param>` element in the called template rule, they will simply be ignored. However, if the called template specifies a parameter with «`required="yes"`», then a runtime error occurs if no value is supplied for this parameter.

Usage and Examples

The intended usage pattern behind `<xsl:next-match>` is illustrated by the following example.

One template rule might contain a general-purpose rule for formatting headings, as follows:

```
<xsl:template match="heading" priority="1">
    <xsl:number level="multiple" count="div1|div2|div3" format="1.1"/>
    <a name="{generate-id()}">
       <xsl:value-of select="."/>
    </a>
</xsl:template>
```

Another set of template rules contains specific rules for particular levels of heading:

```
<xsl:template match="div1/heading" priority="2">
    <h1><xsl:next-match/></h1>
</xsl:template>

<xsl:template match="div2/heading" priority="2">
    <h2><xsl:next-match/></h2>
</xsl:template>

<xsl:template match="div3/heading" priority="2">
    <h3><xsl:next-match/></h3>
</xsl:template>
```

These template rules each invoke the first rule using `<xsl:next-match>`, which avoids duplicating the common code in the template rule for each level of heading, and makes it easier to define changes later.

In this example I have made the priorities explicit, but in fact the default priorities could have been used. I always prefer to use explicit priorities when several rules match the same nodes, because it makes it clear to someone reading the stylesheet what your intentions were when you wrote it.

On this occasion there are three specialized rules, each invoking one generalized rule. But there are other problems where the structure can be inverted, so that the general rule invokes the special rule. For example, suppose you want to use a special color to render any inline text element that has the attribute «`highlight="yes"`». You might use a set of template rules like this:

```
<xsl:template match="term" priority="1">
    <i><xsl:apply-templates/></i>
</xsl:template>

<xsl:template match="emph" priority="1">
    <b><xsl:apply-templates/></b>
</xsl:template>
```

```
<xsl:template match="formula" priority="1">
   <code><xsl:apply-templates/></code>
</xsl:template>
```

and then process the `highlight` attribute in a higher priority template rule:

```
<xsl:template match="*[@highlight='yes']" priority="2">
   <span class="highlight"><xsl:next-match/></span>
</xsl:template>
```

Unlike `<xsl:apply-imports>`, where invoking multiple template rules is possible only by defining multiple stylesheet modules, `<xsl:next-match>` allows several rules to be defined within a single module, which is often preferable because it makes the logic more clear.

Note that both `<xsl:next-match>` and `<xsl:apply-imports>` impose the constraint that the two (or more) template rules that match a node in the source tree work on the source node completely independently of each other. Neither rule can see or modify the nodes that the other rule has written to the result tree. This also means that (as the examples above show) the second rule can only create nodes that are children or siblings of the nodes created by the first rule; it cannot create parent nodes.

In some situations, therefore, other solutions might work better. In particular, another design pattern is to use a multipass transformation whereby one template rule creates a temporary tree, which it then processes using a second template rule (perhaps in a different mode). The code tends to look like this:

```
<xsl:template match="diagram">
   <xsl:variable name="temp">
     <div>
         <title><xsl:value-of select="caption"/></title>
         <body><xsl:copy-of select="content"/></body>
     </div>
   </xsl:variable>
   <xsl:apply-templates select="$temp/div"/>
</xsl:template>
```

This design pattern does not require use of `<xsl:next-match>` or `<xsl:apply-imports>`.

See Also

`<xsl:apply-imports>` on page 184
`<xsl:fallback>` on page 271
`<xsl:param>` on page 392
`<xsl:with-param>` on page 488

xsl:non-matching-substring

The `<xsl:non-matching-substring>` element is used within an `<xsl:analyze-string>` instruction to indicate the processing that should be applied to substrings of the input string that appear between the substrings that match the supplied regular expression.

Changes in 2.0

This element is new in XSLT 2.0.

Format

```
<xsl:non-matching-substring>
  <!-- Content: sequence-constructor -->
</xsl:non-matching-substring>
```

Position

`<xsl:non-matching-substring>` can only appear as a child of an `<xsl:analyze-string>` element, and it may not appear more than once.

Attributes

None.

Content

A sequence constructor.

Effect

The sequence constructor contained in the `<xsl:non-matching-substring>` element is evaluated once for each nonempty substring of the input string that appears between two substrings that match the regular expression. The result of evaluating the sequence constructor is added to the result of the containing `<xsl:analyze-string>` instruction.

Usage and Examples

See `<xsl:analyze-string>` on page 176.

See Also

`<xsl:analyze-string>` on page 176
`<xsl:matching-substring>` on page 342

xsl:number

The `<xsl:number>` element performs two functions. It can be used to allocate a sequential number to the current node, and it can be used to format a number for output. These functions are often performed together, but they can also be done separately.

Note that the facilities for number formatting in the `<xsl:number>` element are quite separate from those offered by the `format-number()` function and the `<xsl:decimal-format>` element.

Changes in 2.0

The `select` attribute has been added: This allows a node other than the context node to be numbered.

XSLT 2.0 defines error conditions that must be reported when incompatible attributes are used (for example, `level` and `value` cannot appear together). In XSLT 1.0, redundant attributes were silently ignored. XSLT 2.0 also defines the result of the instruction more precisely in corner cases, for example when there is no node that matches the `from` pattern.

New options have been added in XSLT 2.0 for formatting numbers as words (so you can output «Chapter Three») and as ordinal numbers (so you can output «Fit the First» or «3rd Act»).

Format

```
<xsl:number
  value? = expression
  select? = expression
  level? = "single" | "multiple" | "any"
  count? = pattern
  from? = pattern
  format? = { string }
  lang? = { nmtoken }
  letter-value? = { "alphabetic" | "traditional" }
  ordinal? = { string }
  grouping-separator? = { char }
  grouping-size? = { number } />
```

Position

`<xsl:number>` is an instruction. It is always used within a sequence constructor.

Attributes

Name	Value	Meaning
value optional	Expression	A user-supplied number to be formatted (instead of using a node sequence number)
select optional	Expression	Selects the node whose sequence number is to be output (by default, the instruction numbers the context node)
level optional	«single» | «multiple» | «any»	Controls the way in which a sequence number is allocated based on the position of the node in the tree
count optional	Pattern	Determines which nodes are counted to determine a sequence number
from optional	Pattern	Determines a cut-off point, a point in the document from which sequence numbering starts afresh

Name	Value	Meaning
format optional	Attribute value template, returning a format string, as defined below	Determines the output format of the number
lang optional	Attribute value template, returning a language code, as defined in XML for the `xml:lang` attribute	Indicates a language whose conventions for number formatting should be used
letter-value optional	Attribute value template, returning «alphabetic» | «traditional»	Distinguishes between different numbering schemes used with the same language
ordinal optional	Attribute value template, returning a string	If the attribute is present and is not a zero-length string, it indicates that ordinal numbering is required. For English, a suitable value is «yes»; for inflected languages, it indicates the required ending, for example, «-o» or «-a» in Italian
grouping-separator optional	Attribute value template, returning a single character	A character to be used to separate groups of digits (for example, a comma as a thousand separator)
grouping-size optional	Attribute value template, returning a number	The number of digits in each group, indicating where the grouping-separator should be inserted

For the syntax of a pattern, see Chapter 6.

Content

None, the element is always empty.

Effect

The `<xsl:number>` instruction performs four tasks:

1. Determines a sequence number. This is actually a sequence of integers (to allow section numbers such as 1.16.2); since it is not necessarily a number in the XPath sense, the specification refers to it as the *place marker*.

2. Analyzes the format string into a sequence of format tokens.

3. Formats each part of the place marker using the appropriate format token.

4. Writes the resulting string to the current output destination as a text node.

These steps are considered individually in the following sections.

Determining a Sequence Number

If the `value` attribute is specified, the place marker is obtained by evaluating the expression in the `value` attribute and converting it to a sequence of integers. This is done by atomizing the sequence, calling the `number()` function for each value, then calling the `round()` function, and then casting to an integer. (This rather cumbersome procedure is chosen largely for backwards compatibility reasons.)

If backwards compatibility mode is in effect (that is, if the `version` attribute on the `<xsl:stylesheet>` element or on some other enclosing element is «1.0»), then all items in the sequence after the first are discarded. This is to emulate the behavior of XSLT 1.0.

If the `value` attribute is specified, the `level`, `count`, and `from` attributes must not be specified.

It is an error if any value in the sequence can't be converted to an integer, or produces an integer less than 1, because `<xsl:number>` is designed to handle positive integers. The XSLT processor may treat this error as fatal, or it may produce a fallback representation of the number, using the same conversion rules that apply to the `string()` function. The `<xsl:number>` element is designed for handling the natural numbers that arise from counting nodes, so if you want to handle other cases, it's better to use the `format-number()` function described in Chapter 7, on page 558.

If no `value` attribute is specified, `<xsl:number>` determines a place marker based on the position of a node in a source document. When the `select` attribute is present, the node to be numbered is determined by evaluating the expression contained in this attribute; a type error is reported if the result is anything other than a single node. If the `select` attribute is omitted, the instruction operates on the context node. In this case, an error is reported if the context item is not a node. Either way, we will refer to this node as the *start node*.

The rules for determining the place marker (always a sequence of positive integers) depend on the value of the `level`, `count`, and `from` attributes. If any of these attributes is omitted, the default is as follows:

Attribute	Default value
level	«single»
count	A pattern that matches nodes of the same kind as the start node, and with the same name as the start node if it has a name. As always, names with namespace prefixes are matched using the relevant namespace URI rather than the prefix
from	A pattern that matches the root node of the tree containing the selected node (that is, «/»)

If the `level` attribute is «single» or «any» the place marker will normally contain a single integer; if it is «multiple» then it may contain several integers (for example «3.6.1»). It is also possible for the list to be empty.

The place marker is determined as follows:

level	Rules
single	This is designed for numbering peer nodes at the same level in the structure, for example the bullets in a list of bullets
	First establish a target node. If the start node matches the count pattern, the target node is the start node (this is the normal case). Otherwise the target node is the innermost ancestor of the start node that matches the count pattern. If there is no such node, the place marker is an empty sequence
	Now establish a boundary node. If the from pattern is defaulted, this is the root of the tree (this is by far the most common case: The from attribute is rarely used with «level="single"»). Otherwise, the boundary node is the start node if it matches the from pattern, else it is the innermost ancestor of the start node that matches the from pattern
	If the target node is the boundary node, or is a descendant of the boundary node, the place marker is the number of preceding siblings of the target node that match the count pattern, plus one. For example, if the target node has six preceding siblings that match the count pattern then the sequence number is 7
	If no target node is found, or if the target node is not a descendant-or-self of the boundary node, the place marker is an empty sequence
any	This is designed for numbering nodes that can appear at any level of the structure, for example the footnotes or equations in a chapter of a book
	As a special case, if the start node is a document node, the place marker is an empty sequence
	First form the set of countable nodes. This contains all nodes that can be reached from the start node using the ancestor, preceding, or self axes, provided that they match the count pattern
	Now identify the boundary node. This is the last node (in document order) that can be reached from the start node using the ancestor, preceding, or self axes, and that matches the from pattern. If the from pattern was not specified, this will be the document node
	Exclude from the set of countable nodes all those that are before the boundary node in document order
	If there are no countable nodes, the place marker is an empty sequence; otherwise it is a single integer, equal to the number of countable nodes

Continues

level	Rules
multiple	This is designed to produce a composite sequence number that reflects the hierarchic position of a node, for example «2.17.1»
	First form the set of countable nodes. This contains all nodes that can be reached from the start node using the ancestor-or-self axis, and that match the count pattern
	The boundary node is the same as with «level="single"»
	For each countable node (taking them in document order, that is, outermost first) that has the boundary node on its ancestor-or-self axis, count how many preceding siblings it has that also match the count pattern, and add one for the node itself. The resulting sequence of integers makes up the composite place marker. It is possible for this sequence to be empty

These rules appear complex but in practice most common cases are quite straightforward, as the examples given later in this section demonstrate.

Analyzing the Format String

Once the place marker has been determined, the next stage is to format it into a string.

The place marker, as you have seen, is a list of zero or more positive integers.

The formatting is controlled primarily using the format string supplied in the format attribute. If this is omitted, the default value is «1».

The format string consists of a sequence of alternating formatting tokens and punctuation tokens. Any sequence of consecutive alphanumeric characters is taken as a formatting token, any other sequence is taken as a punctuation token. For example, if the format attribute is «1((a))», this is broken up into a formatting token «1», a punctuation token «((», a formatting token «a», and a punctuation token «))». The term *alphanumeric* is based on Unicode character categories, and is defined to include letters and digits from any language.

In the most common case the place marker is a single number. In this situation, the output string consists of the initial punctuation token if there is one, followed by the result of formatting the number using the first formatting token, and then the final punctuation token if there is one. So if the place marker is «42» and the format attribute is «[1]», then the final output is «[42]».

Where the place marker is a list of numbers, the rules are a little more complex but still have intuitive results, for example if the list of numbers is «3, 1, 6» and the format attribute is «1.1(a)» then the final output is «3.1(f)» (because «f» is the sixth letter in the alphabet). The detailed rules are as follows:

❑ The *n*th formatting token is used to format the *n*th number in the list where possible, using the rules in the following section.

❑ If there are more numbers in the list than formatting tokens, then the excess numbers are formatted using the last formatting token. For example, if the list is «3,1,2,5» and the format attribute is «A.1», then the output will be «C.1.2.5».

- ❏ If there are no formatting tokens, then a formatting token of «1» is used.

- ❏ If there are more formatting tokens than numbers in the list, the excess formatting tokens are ignored.

- ❏ Each number is preceded in the output by the punctuation token that precedes the formatting token used to format this number, if there is one. If there is no preceding punctuation token, and the number is not the first in the list, it is preceded by «.».

- ❏ If the formatting string ends with a punctuation token, this is added to the end of the output string.

Note that if the place marker is an empty sequence, the result will consist of the initial and final punctuation tokens. For example if the format string is «[1]», an empty sequence will be formatted as «[]». The most likely reason for an empty sequence is that no nodes matched the count pattern.

Formatting the Numbers

This section describes how a single number is formatted using a single formatting token to construct a string that will form part of the final output string.

The XSLT specification defines this process only partially. There are some definitive rules, some guidance for the implementor, and many other cases that are left unspecified.

The definitive cases are listed in the table below:

Formatting token	Output sequence
1	1, 2, 3, 4, ...
01	01, 02, 03, ..., 10, 11, 12, ...
	More generally, if the format token is «1» preceded by n zeros, the output numbers will be in decimal notation with a minimum of $n + 1$ digits
other Unicode digits	The above two rules also apply to any other Unicode digits equivalent to 0 and 1, for example Thai or Tamil digits. The number is output using the same family of digits as is used in the formatting token
a	a, b, c, d, ..., x, y, z, aa, ab, ac, ...
A	A, B, C, D, ..., X, Y, Z, AA, AB, AC, ...
i	i, ii, iii, iv, ..., x, xi, xii, xiii, xiv, ...
I	I, II, III, IV, ..., X, XI, XII, XIII, XIV, ...
w	one, two, three, ... ten, eleven (in the chosen language)
W	ONE, TWO, THREE (in the chosen language)
Ww	One, Two, Three (in the chosen language)

The specification doesn't define these sequences in detail, for example it doesn't say how you represent numbers above 1,000 in roman numerals (the Romans themselves had various conventions, such as putting horizontal lines above the letters, or boxes around them—effects that would be difficult to achieve in XML output). The specification does say, however, that if the number is too large to be formatted as requested, it should be output as if the formatting token were «1».

The attributes grouping-separator and grouping-size can be used to control the separation of groups of digits. For example, setting «grouping-separator=" "» (a single space) and «grouping-size="2"» would cause the number 12345 to be output as «1 23 45». The groups will always be formed by counting digits from the right-hand side. If either of these attributes is specified, the other should also be specified.

The ordinal attribute allows you to request ordinal numbers rather than cardinal numbers. For example, with a formatting token of «1» and language set (explicitly or by default) to «en» (English), the value «ordinal="yes"» would produce «1st, 2nd, 3rd, 4th». With the formatting token «Ww», it would produce «First, Second, Third, Fourth». For languages other than English, the correct form of an ordinal number often depends on the noun it is qualifying. In the case of languages where this is simply done by changing the ending, the specification says that the value of the ordinal attribute should be the required ending, for example «ordinal="-e"» or «ordinal="-er"» in German. For other languages with more complicated rules, it's left to the implementer to sort out what to do.

For formatting tokens that aren't included in the table above, the XSLT specification is not prescriptive. It indicates that any formatting token may be used to indicate a sequence starting with this token, provided the implementation supports such a sequence; if the implementation does not support such a sequence, it may format the number using the formatting token «1». So, for example, if an implementation supports the numbering sequence «α, β, γ, δ», you can invoke this sequence with a formatting token of «α».

In case the formatting token does not identify a numbering sequence unambiguously, two attributes are provided to give greater control:

❑ The lang attribute is intended to indicate the target language: for example the sequence starting with a Cyrillic capital letter «A» (x0410 in Unicode) might be different for Russian («lang="ru"») and for Bulgarian («lang="bg"»). The language code is intended to take the same form as the xml:lang attribute defined in the XML specification.

The most obvious case where this changes the output is for the formatting tokens such as «w». For example, if «lang="de"», the output for «w» would become «eins, zwei, drei».

❑ The letter-value attribute is intended for languages such as Hebrew that have several possible sequences starting with the same token. The two permitted values are «alphabetic» and «traditional».

The detailed effect of these attributes is left entirely to the implementer, so you can't expect different products necessarily to behave in the same way. There has been a great deal of discussion on Internet mailing lists about the exact details of certain numbering sequences. With those sequences such as Roman numerals and Hebrew numbering that have a long history, practices have certainly varied at different times and places, so there is no single answer.

All the attributes controlling formatting are attribute value templates, so they can be parameterized using expressions enclosed in curly braces. This is mainly useful if you want to select the values from a localization file based on the preferred language of the current user. To achieve this, you can use the same techniques as described for localizing messages: see <xsl:message> on page 343.

Outputting the Number

The final action of `<xsl:number>` is to write the generated string to the current result sequence, as a text node.

> *The reason it is a text node rather than a string is historical: In XSLT 1.0, instructions always produced nodes. Changing it to a string in XSLT 2.0 would under some circumstances have caused it to be separated from adjacent values by a space character, giving a backwards compatibility problem. In practice, text nodes and strings are nearly always interchangeable.*

If you want to do something else with the number (perhaps to write it as an attribute or to copy it to every page heading), you can save it as the value of a variable, as follows:

```
<xsl:variable name="section-number" type="xs:string">
   <xsl:number/>
</xsl:variable>
```

Writing the value to a variable also allows you to perform further manipulation. For example, if you want to use the traditional numbering sequence for footnotes (*, †, ‡, §, ¶) you cannot do this directly in `<xsl:number>` because these characters are punctuation symbols rather than alphanumerics. What you can do, however, is use conventional decimal numbering and then convert, for example:

```
<xsl:template match="footnote">
<xsl:variable name="footnote-number">
   <xsl:number level="any" from="section"/>
</xsl:variable>
<xsl:value-of select="translate($footnote-number, '12345', '*†‡§¶')"/>
</xsl:template>
```

In practice it might be safer to use character references for these special characters to avoid them being mangled by a text editor that doesn't understand Unicode. The `translate()` function replaces characters in its second argument by the corresponding character in the third argument: It is described in Chapter 10 of *XPath 2.0 Programmer's Reference*.

> *I have dodged a tricky question here, which is that if you want footnote numbers to start at 1 on each page, you can't allocate them until you have paginated the document. Some kinds of numbering are really the domain of XSL Formatting rather than XSL Transformations.*

Usage and Examples

Although the rules for `<xsl:number>` are very general and sometimes complex, most common cases are quite straightforward.

The general rules allow for numbering any kind of node, but in practice the `<xsl:number>` instruction is almost invariably used for numbering elements. So in this section, I'll assume that the selected node is an element.

level="single"

This option (the default) is used to number sibling elements.

The simplest way of using `<xsl:number>` is without any attributes:

```
<xsl:number/>
```

If the current element is the eighth `<item>` element owned by its parent element, say, this will write the text value «8» to the current output destination. Technically, the processor is counting all the elements that match the pattern in the `count` attribute, and the default for the `count` attribute in this case is a pattern that matches `<item>` elements.

For this simple kind of numbering, it is often better to use the `position()` function, particularly if there are many nodes to be numbered. This is because with a typical implementation, each node that is numbered using `<xsl:number>` will result in the preceding siblings being counted, which will take an increasingly long time as the number of siblings increases. With the `position()` function, it is much more likely that the system already knows the position and doesn't have to do any special walking around the tree and pattern matching. Of course, this is only possible where «position()» and `<xsl:number/>` produce the same answer, which will happen when the sequence of nodes being processed using `<xsl:apply-templates>` or `<xsl:for-each>` consists of all the sibling elements of a particular element type.

Another option for numbering is to use the `count()` function, for example «count(preceding-sibling::item)+1». This is often simpler if you want to use the number for further processing, rather than formatting it for output.

The `count` attribute of `<xsl:number>` can be used in two ways.

Firstly, it is useful if there are several different kinds of sibling elements that you want to count. For example, you might have an element containing a mixture of `<item>` and `<special-item>` children, as follows:

```
<shopping-list>
    <item>bananas</item>
    <item>apples</item>
    <special-item>flowers for Grandma</special-item>
    <item>grapes</item>
    <special-item>chocolate for Aunt Maud</special-item>
    <item>cherries</item>
</shopping-list>
```

If you want to number these in a single sequence, you can write:

```
<xsl:template match="item | special-item">
    <xsl:number count="item | special-item"/>
    <xsl:text> </xsl:text>
    <xsl:value-of select="."/><br/>
</xsl:template>
```

which, when you process the `<shopping-list>` element, will result in the output:

```
1 bananas<br/>
2 apples<br/>
3 flowers for Grandma<br/>
4 grapes<br/>
5 chocolate for Aunt Maud<br/>
6 cherries<br/>
```

In this case you could also use «count="*"» to achieve this effect. If you omitted the count attribute, the output would be:

```
1 bananas<br/>
2 apples<br/>
1 flowers for Grandma<br/>
3 grapes<br/>
2 chocolate for Aunt Maud<br/>
4 cherries<br/>
```

because each element is numbered taking into account only other elements with the same name.

Another use of the count attribute is to specify that it is not the context node that should be counted, but an ancestor node. For example, in the template rule for a <title> element you can use <xsl:number> to determine the number of the section that the title belongs to, by writing:

```
<xsl:template match="title">
   <xsl:number count="section"/>
. . .
</xsl:template>
```

This usage is less common, and with XSLT 2.0 the select attribute gives more flexibility, because its value is an expression rather than a pattern. The above example can be written as:

```
<xsl:template match="title">
   <xsl:number select="parent::section"/>
. . .
</xsl:template>
```

The select attribute is particularly handy when you want to construct a cross-reference to a node other than the context node. For example, if your document contains anchors with tags such as <bookmark name="biog"/>, and references to these anchors of the form <ref name="biog"/>, then your stylesheet might expand a reference as follows:

```
<xsl:key name="bm" match="bookmark" select="@name"/>

<xsl:template match="ref">
   <xsl:variable name="target" select="key('bm', @name)/ancestor::div"/>
   <xsl:text>(See section </xsl:text>
   <a href="{generate-id($target)}">
      <xsl:number select="$target"/>
   </a>
   <xsl:text>)</xsl:text>
. . .
</xsl:template>
```

The from attribute is rarely needed with «level="single"». In fact, it's difficult to construct an example that isn't completely artificial.

If you want numbering to start at a value other than 1, or perhaps to proceed in increments other than 1, you can capture the result of <xsl:number> in a variable and manipulate it using XPath expressions.

For example, the following template rule numbers the items in a list starting at an offset passed in as a parameter:

```
<xsl:template match="item">
    <xsl:param name="first-number" select="1"/>
    <xsl:variable name="number"><xsl:number/></xsl:variable>
    <xsl:value-of select="$first-number + $number - 1"/>
. . .
</xsl:template>
```

level="any"

This option is useful when numbering objects within a document that have a numbering sequence of their own, independent of their position within the hierarchic structure. Examples are figures and illustrations, tables, equations, footnotes, and actions from a meeting.

The `count` attribute can usually be defaulted. For example, to number quotations within a document, you can write a template rule such as:

```
<xsl:template match="quotation">
  <table><tr>
  <td width="90%" valign="top">
      <i><xsl:value-of select="."/></i></td>
  <td><xsl:number level="any"/></td>
  </tr></table>
</xsl:template>
```

Again, the `count` attribute is useful when several different element types are included in the same numbering sequence, for example there might be a single sequence that includes both diagrams and photographs.

Note that each evaluation of `<xsl:number>` is quite independent of any previous evaluations. The result depends only on the relative position of the selected element in the source document, and not on how many times the `<xsl:number>` element has been evaluated. So there is no guarantee that the numbers in the output document will be consecutive. In fact, if the output order is different from the input order then the numbers definitely won't be consecutive. If you want to number things based on their position in the output document, you can often achieve this by using the `position()` function. If this isn't adequate, the alternative is to perform a second pass, to add the sequence numbers.

You can do this by writing the result of the first pass to a temporary tree. The following example extracts all the `<glossary-item>` elements from a document, sorts them alphabetically, and numbers them in their output sequence. The variable `glossary` is used to hold the temporary tree. To achieve the same effect with an XSLT 1.0 processor, you would need to use the vendor-specific `node-set()` extension function.

Imagine a source document that contains glossary definitions scattered throughout the document, in the form:

```
<glossary-item>
    <term>XML</term>
    <definition>Extensible Markup Language</definition>
</glossary-item>
```

The relevant template looks like this:

```
<xsl:template name="make-glossary">
  <xsl:variable name="glossary">
    <xsl:for-each select="//glossary-item">
    <xsl:sort select="term"/>
      <xsl:copy-of select="."/>
    </xsl:for-each>
  </xsl:variable>
  <table>
    <xsl:for-each select="$glossary/glossary-item">
    <tr>
      <td><xsl:number format="[1]"/></td>
      <td><xsl:value-of select="term"/></td>
      <td><xsl:value-of select="definition"/></td>
    </tr>
    </xsl:for-each>
  </table>
</xsl:template>
```

In this example, however, the numbers could have been generated equally well on the first pass using the `position()` function.

The `from` attribute is useful for indicating where numbering should restart:

```
<xsl:template match="footnote">
  <xsl:number level="any" from="chapter"/>
  <xsl:text> </xsl:text>
  <xsl:value-of select="."/>
</xsl:template>
```

The above code would number footnotes consecutively within a chapter, starting again at 1 for each chapter.

Example: Numbering the Lines of a Poem

The following example numbers the lines of a poem, showing the number to the right of every third line. Assume the input structure contains a `<poem>` element, a `<stanza>` element, and a `<line>` element: The lines are to be numbered within the poem as a whole, not within each stanza.

Source

This stylesheet can be used with the source file `poem.xml` used in Chapter 1.

Stylesheet

This stylesheet is `poem.xsl`. It uses `<xsl:number>` to get the number of every line, but displays it only every third line, using the «mod» operator to get the remainder when the line number is divided by 3.

```
<xsl:stylesheet version="1.0"
    xmlns:xsl="http://www.w3.org/1999/XSL/Transform">
```

```
<xsl:template match="/">
<html><body>
<p><xsl:apply-templates select="/poem/stanza"/></p>
</body></html>
</xsl:template>

<xsl:template match="stanza">
<p><table><xsl:apply-templates/></table></p>
</xsl:template>

<xsl:template match="line">
<tr>
<td width="350"><xsl:value-of select="."/></td>
<td width="50">
   <xsl:variable name="line-nr">
      <xsl:number level="any" from="poem"/>
   </xsl:variable>
   <xsl:if test="$line-nr mod 3 = 0">
      <xsl:value-of select="$line-nr"/>
   </xsl:if>
</td>
</tr>
</xsl:template>
</xsl:stylesheet>
```

Output

See Figure 5-8

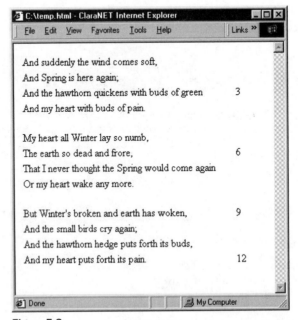

Figure 5-8

level="multiple"

This option is typically used to produce the hierarchic sequence numbers often found in technical or legal documents, for example 1.12.3, or A2(iii).

Note that an alternative way to produce such numbers is to use several calls on <xsl:number> with «level="single"» and different count attributes, for example:

```
<xsl:number count="chapter"/>.<xsl:number count="section"/>
    (<xsl:number count="clause"/>)
```

Another technique, which might be marginally faster, is to evaluate the chapter number once and pass it as a parameter to the template handling the section, and then pass both the chapter number and section number (or their concatenation) as parameters to the template handling each clause.

However, using «level="multiple"» is convenient, and in some cases (particularly with recursive structures, where <section> elements are contained within <section> elements) may be the only way of achieving the required effect.

The count attribute defines which ancestor elements should be included. Usually this is expressed as a union pattern, as in the example below:

```
<xsl:template match="clause">
    <xsl:number
        format="1.1.1. "
        level="multiple"
        count="chapter | section | clause"/>
    <xsl:apply-templates/>
</xsl:template>
```

The effect of the rules is that a composite sequence number will be formed containing one component number for each ancestor (or the element itself) that is a <chapter>, <section>, or <clause>. If the structure is regular, so that chapters, sections, and clauses are neatly nested, each clause will be output preceded by a number such as 1.13.5, where 1 is the chapter number, 13 is the number of the section within the chapter, and 5 is the number of the clause within the section.

If the structure isn't regular, for example if there are sections that don't belong to a chapter, if there are clauses that have sections as siblings at the same level, or if there are sections nested within other sections, then the effects can be surprising, but a careful reading of the rules should explain what's going on.

A problem that sometimes occurs is that the numbering is context-sensitive. For example, within a regular chapter, clauses are numbered 1.2.3, but in an appendix, they are numbered A.2.3. It's possible to achieve this effect by exploiting the fact that the format pattern is an attribute value template; for example, you could write:

```
<xsl:template match="clause">
    <xsl:variable name="format"
            select="if (ancestor::chapter)
                    then '1.1.1. '
                    else 'A.1.1 '"/>
```

```
    <xsl:number
        format="{$format}"
        level="multiple"
        count="appendix | chapter | section | clause"/>
    <xsl:apply-templates/>
</xsl:template>
```

See Also

count() function in XPath 2.0 Programmer's Reference, Chapter 10.
position() function in XPath 2.0 Programmer's Reference, Chapter 10.
format-number() function, in Chapter 7 on page 558
<xsl:decimal-format> on page 251

xsl:otherwise

The <xsl:otherwise> element is used within an <xsl:choose> instruction to indicate the action that should be taken when none of the <xsl:when> conditions is satisfied.

Changes in 2.0

None.

Format

```
<xsl:otherwise>
  <!-- Content: sequence-constructor -->
</xsl:otherwise>
```

Position

<xsl:otherwise> can appear only as a child of an <xsl:choose> element. If it is present at all, it must be the last child of the <xsl:choose> element, and it must not appear more than once.

Attributes

None.

Content

A sequence constructor.

Effect

The sequence constructor of the <xsl:otherwise> element is evaluated if (and only if) none of the <xsl:when> elements in the containing <xsl:choose> element evaluates to true.

Usage and Examples

See <xsl:choose> on page 236.

See Also

<xsl:choose> on page 236
<xsl:when> on page 487

xsl:output

The <xsl:output> element is a top-level declaration used to control the format of the serialized result document. An XSLT stylesheet is processed conceptually in two stages: The first stage is to build a result tree, and the second is to write out the result tree to a serial output file. The <xsl:output> element controls this second stage, which is often referred to as *serialization*.

This second stage of processing, to serialize the tree as an output document, is not a mandatory requirement for an XSLT processor; the standard allows the processor to make the tree available in some other way, for example via the DOM API. A processor that does not write the tree to an output file is allowed to ignore this element. Processors that do provide serialization may also allow the definitions in this element to be overridden by parameters set in the API when the processor is invoked. See Appendix D for details of the JAXP API.

Changes in 2.0

An <xsl:output> declaration may be given a name, allowing a named output format to be defined that can be referenced in an <xsl:result-document> instruction.

An output method has been defined for XHTML.

Several new output options have been added: escape-uri-attributes, include-content-type, normalize-unicode, undeclare-namespaces, and use-character-maps.

Format

```
<xsl:output
  name? = qname
  method? = "xml" | "html" | "xhtml" | "text" | qname-but-not-ncname
  cdata-section-elements? = qnames
  doctype-public? = string
  doctype-system? = string
  encoding? = string
  escape-uri-attributes? = "yes" | "no"
  include-content-type? = "yes" | "no"
  indent? = "yes" | "no"
  media-type? = string
  normalize-unicode? = "yes" | "no"
```

```
omit-xml-declaration? = "yes" | "no"
standalone? = "yes" | "no"
undeclare-namespaces? = "yes" | "no"
use-character-maps? = qnames
version? = nmtoken />
```

Position

`<xsl:output>` is a declaration, which means it must be a child of the `<xsl:stylesheet>` element. It may appear any number of times in a stylesheet.

Attributes

Name	Value	Meaning
name optional	Lexical QName	Defines a name for this output format, so that it can be referenced in an `<xsl:result-document>` instruction
method optional	«xml» | «html» | «xhtml» | «text» | QName	Defines the required output format
cdata-section-elements optional	Whitespace-separated list of lexical QNames	Names those elements whose text content is to be output in the form of CDATA sections
doctype-public optional	string	Indicates the public identifier to be used in the DOCTYPE declaration in the output file
doctype-system optional	string	Indicates the system identifier to be used in the DOCTYPE declaration in the output file
encoding optional	string	Defines the character encoding
escape-uri-attributes optional	«yes» | «no»	Indicates whether URI-valued attributes in HTML and XHTML should be %HH escaped
include-content-type optional	«yes» | «no»	Indicates whether a `<meta>` element should be added to the output to indicate the content type and encoding
indent optional	«yes» | «no»	Indicates whether the output should be indented to indicate its hierarchic structure
media-type optional	string	Indicates the media-type (often called MIME type) to be associated with the output file
normalization-form optional	see below	Indicates whether and how the Unicode characters in the serialized document should be normalized

Name	Value	Meaning
omit-xml-declaration optional	«yes» | «no»	Indicates whether an XML declaration is to be included in the output
standalone optional	«yes» | «no»	Indicates that a `standalone` declaration is to be included in the output, and gives its value
undeclare-namespaces optional	«yes» | «no»	Indicates whether (with XML 1.1 output) namespaces should be undeclared using «`xmlns:p=""`» when they go out of scope
use-character-maps optional	Whitespace-separated list of lexical QNames	A list of the names of `<xsl:character-map>` elements that are to be used for character mapping
version optional	NMtoken	Defines the version of the output format

Content

None, the element is always empty.

Effect

A stylesheet can contain several output format definitions. This is useful if the stylesheet produces multiple result documents, or if it produces different kinds of output on different occasions. One of the output format definitions can be unnamed, and the others are named using a QName in the same way as other stylesheet objects.

An output definition can be split over several `<xsl:output>` elements; all the `<xsl:output>` elements with the same name (specified in the name attribute) constitute one output definition. In this case the attributes defined in these multiple elements are in effect combined into a single conceptual `<xsl:output>` element as follows:

❑ For the `cdata-section-elements` attribute, the lists of QNames supplied on the separate `<xsl:output>` elements are merged—if an element name is present in any of the lists, it will be treated as a CDATA section element.

❑ For the `use-character-maps` attribute, the lists of QNames on the separate `<xsl:output>` elements are concatenated. They are taken in order of the import precedence of the `<xsl:output>` declarations on which they appear, or where two declarations have the same import precedence, in declaration order.

❑ For all other attributes, an `<xsl:output>` element that specifies a value for the attribute takes precedence over one that leaves it defaulted. If several `<xsl:output>` elements specify a value for the attribute, the one with highest import precedence is used. If this leaves more than one value (and even if they are identical), the XSLT processor may either report an error, or use the one that occurs last in the stylesheet.

The concepts of import precedence and declaration order are explained under `<xsl:import>` on page 314.

The `method` attribute controls the format of the output, and this in turn affects the detailed meaning and the default values of the other attributes.

Four output methods are defined in the specification: «xml», «html», «xhtml», and «text». Alternatively, the output method may be given as a QName, which must include a non-null prefix that identifies a namespace that is currently in scope. This option is provided for vendor or user extensions, and the meaning is not defined in the standard. A vendor-defined output method can attach its own interpretations to the meanings of the other attributes on the `<xsl:output>` element, and it can also define additional attributes on the `<xsl:output>` element, provided they are not in the default namespace.

If the `method` attribute is omitted, the output will be in XML format, unless the result tree is recognizably HTML or XHTML. The result tree is recognized as HTML if:

❑ The root node has at least one element child,

❑ The first element child of the root node is named `<html>`, in any combination of upper and lower case, and has a null namespace URI, and

❑ There are no text nodes before the `<html>` element, other than, optionally, a text node containing whitespace only.

The result tree is recognized as XHTML if:

❑ The root node has at least one element child,

❑ The first element child of the root node is named `<html>`, in lower case, and has the namespace URI `http://www.w3.org/1999/xhtml`, and

❑ There are no text nodes before the `<html>` element, other than, optionally, a text node containing whitespace only.

Rules for XML output

When the output method is «xml», the output file will usually be a well-formed XML document, but the actual requirement is that it should be either a well-formed XML external general parsed entity, or a well-formed XML document entity, or both.

An external general parsed entity is something that could be incorporated into an XML document by using an entity reference such as «&doc;». The following example shows a well-formed external general parsed entity that is not a well-formed document:

```
A <b>bold</b> and <emph>emphatic</emph> statement
```

An example of a well-formed document that is not a well-formed external general parsed entity (because it contains a `standalone` attribute) is:

```
<?xml version="1.0" encoding="utf-8" standalone="yes"?>
<p>A <b>bold</b> and <emph>emphatic</emph> statement</p>
```

The rules for document entities and external general parsed entities overlap, as shown in Figure 5-9.

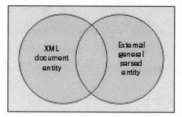

Figure 5-9

Essentially, an XSLT stylesheet can output anything that fits in the darker shaded area, which means anything that is a well-formed XML document entity, a well-formed external general parsed entity, or both.

Well, almost anything:

❏ It must also conform to the XML Namespaces Recommendation.

❏ There is no explicit provision for generating an internal DTD subset, although it can be achieved, with difficulty, by generating text and disabling output escaping, or by using character maps.

❏ Similarly, there is no explicit provision for generating entity references, though this can also be achieved by means of character maps.

In the XML standard, the rules for an external general parsed entity are given as:

```
extParsedEnt ⟹ TextDecl? content
```

while the rule for the document entity is effectively:

```
document ⟹ XMLDecl? Misc* doctypedecl? Misc* element Misc*
```

where `Misc` permits whitespace, comments, and processing instructions.

So the principal differences between the two cases are:

❏ A `TextDecl` (text declaration) is not quite the same thing as an `XMLDecl` (XML declaration), as discussed below.

❏ A document may contain a `doctypedecl` (document type declaration), but an external general parsed entity must not. A document type declaration is the `<!DOCTYPE ... >` header identifying the DTD and possibly including an internal DTD subset.

❏ The body of a document is an `element`, while the body of an external parsed entity is `content`. Here `content` is effectively the contents of an element but without the start and end tags.

The `TextDecl` (text declaration) looks at first sight very much like an XML declaration; for example `<?xml version="1.0" encoding="utf-8"?>` could be used either as an XML declaration or as a text declaration. There are differences, however:

❑ In an XML declaration, the `version` attribute is mandatory, but in a text declaration it is optional.

❑ In an XML declaration, the `encoding` attribute is optional, but in a text declaration it is mandatory.

❑ An XML declaration may include a `standalone` attribute, but a text declaration may not.

The `content` part is a sequence of components including child elements, character data, entity references, CDATA sections, processing instructions, and comments, each of which may appear any number of times and in any order.

So the following are all examples of well-formed external general parsed entities:

```
<quote>Hello!</quote>
<quote>Hello!</quote><quote>Goodbye!</quote>
Hello!
<?xml version="1.0" encoding="utf-8"?>Hello!
```

The following is a well-formed XML document, but it is *not* a well-formed external general parsed entity, both of the `standalone` attribute, and the document type declaration. This is also legitimate output:

```
<?xml version="1.0" encoding="utf-8" standalone="no"?>
<!DOCTYPE quote SYSTEM "hello.dtd">
<quote>Hello!</quote>
```

The following is neither a well-formed XML document nor a well-formed external general parsed entity.

```
<?xml version="1.0" encoding="utf-8" standalone="no"?>
<!DOCTYPE quote SYSTEM "hello.dtd">
<quote>Hello!</quote>
<quote>Goodbye!</quote>
```

It cannot be an XML document because it has more than one top-level element, and it cannot be an external general parsed entity because it has a `<!DOCTYPE>` declaration. A stylesheet attempting to produce this output is in error.

The XSLT specification also places two other constraints on the form of the output, although these are rules for the implementor to follow rather than rules that directly affect the stylesheet author. These rules are:

❑ The output must conform to the rules of the XML Namespaces Recommendation. If the output is XML 1.0, then it must conform to XML Namespaces 1.0, and if it is XML 1.1, then it must conform to XML Namespaces 1.1.

If the output is an XML document, the meaning of this is clear enough, but if it is merely an external entity, some further explanation is needed. The standard provides this by saying that when the entity is pulled into a document by adding an element tag around its content, the resulting document must conform with the XML Namespaces rules.

❑ The output file must faithfully reflect the result tree. This requirement is easy to state informally, but the specification includes a more formal statement of the requirement, which is surprisingly complex.

The rule is expressed by describing what may change when the data model is serialized to XML, and then parsed again to create a new data model. Things that may change include the order of attributes and namespace nodes and the base URI. If the parsing stage does DTD or schema validation, then this may cause new attribute or element values to appear, as specified by the DTD or schema. Perhaps the most significant change is that type annotations on element and attribute nodes will not be preserved. Any type annotations in the data model after such a round trip will be based on revalidation of the textual XML document; the type annotations in the original result tree are lost during serialization.

❑ Serialization never adds attributes such as `xml:base` or `xsi:type`. If you want these present in the output, you must put them in the result tree, just like any other attribute.

Between XSLT 1.0 and XSLT 2.0, there is a change in the way the rules concerning namespace declarations are described. In XSLT 1.0, it was the job of the serializer to generate namespace declarations, not only for namespace nodes explicitly present on the result tree, but also for any namespaces used in the result document, but not represented by namespace nodes. This situation can happen because there is nothing in the rules for `<xsl:element>` and `<xsl:attribute>`, for example, that requires namespace nodes to be created on the tree for the namespace URI used in the names of these nodes. At XSLT 2.0, however, the specification describes a process called namespace fixup, which ensures that an element in a result tree always has a namespace node for every namespace that is used either in the element name or in the name of any of its attributes. This means that it is no longer the responsibility of the serializer to create these namespace declarations. The reason for this change is that with XSLT 2.0, the content of temporary trees (including their namespace nodes) becomes visible to the stylesheet, and the namespace nodes had to be present in the tree to make it usable for further processing. Namespace fixup is described under `<xsl:element>` on page 260.

Although the output is required to be well-formed XML, it is not the job of the serializer to ensure that the XML is valid against either a DTD or a schema. Just because you generate a document type declaration that refers to a specific DTD, or a reference to a schema, don't expect the XSLT processor to check that the output document actually conforms to that DTD. Instead, XSLT 2.0 provides facilities to validate the result tree against a schema before it is serialized, by using the `validation` or `type` attribute on `<xsl:result-document>`.

With the «xml» output method, the other attributes of `<xsl:output>` are interpreted as follows. Attributes that are not applicable to this output method are not included in the table, and they are ignored if you specify them.

Attribute	Interpretation
cdata-section-elements	This is a list of element names, each expressed as a lexical QName, separated by whitespace. Any prefix in a QName is treated as a reference to the corresponding namespace URI in the normal way, using the namespace declarations in effect on the actual `<xsl:output>` element where the `cdata-section-elements` attribute appears; because these are element names, the default namespace is assumed where the name has no prefix

Continues

Attribute	Interpretation
	When a text node is output, if the parent element of the text node is identified by a name in this list, then the text node is output as a CDATA section. For example, the text value «James» is output as «<![CDATA[James]]>», and the text value «AT&T» is output as «<![CDATA[AT&T]]>». Otherwise, this value would probably be output as «AT&T». The XSLT processor is free to choose other equivalent representations if it wishes, for example a character reference, but the standard says that it should not use CDATA unless it is explicitly requested
	The CDATA section may be split into parts if necessary, perhaps because the terminator sequence «]]>» appears in the data, or because there is a character that can only be output using a character reference because it is not supported directly in the chosen encoding
doctype-system	If this attribute is specified, the output file should include a document type declaration (that is, <!DOCTYPE>) after the XML declaration and before the first element start tag. The name of the document type will be the same as the name of the first element. The value of this attribute will be used as the system identifier in the document type declaration
	This attribute should not be used unless the output is a well-formed XML document
doctype-public	This attribute is ignored unless the doctype-system attribute is also specified. It defines the value of the public identifier to go in the document type declaration. If no public identifier is specified, none is included in the document type declaration.
encoding	This specifies the preferred character encoding for the output document. All XSLT processors are required to support the values «UTF-8» and «UTF-16» (which are also the only values that XML parsers are required to support). This encoding name will be used in the encoding attribute of the XML or Text declaration at the start of the output file, and all characters in the file will be encoded using these conventions. The standard encoding names are not case-sensitive
	If the encoding is one that does not allow all XML characters to be represented directly, for example «iso-8859-1», then characters outside this subset will be represented where possible using XML character references (such as «₤»). It is an error if such characters appear in contexts where character references are not recognized (for example within a processing instruction or comment, or in an element or attribute name)
	If the result tree is serialized to a destination that expects a stream of Unicode characters rather than a stream of bytes, then the encoding attribute is ignored. This happens, for example, if you send the output to a Java Writer. It often causes confusion when you use the transformNode() method in Microsoft's MSXML API, which returns the serialized result of the transformation as a string: This is a value of type BSTR, which is encoded in UTF-16 regardless of the encoding you requested in the stylesheet

Attribute	Interpretation
	If you ask for an encoding other than UTF-8 or UTF-16, then the XML rules require that an XML declaration (or text declaration) is written. In this case, requesting «omit-xml-declaration="yes"» has no effect
indent	If this attribute has the value «yes», the idea is that the XML output should be indented to show its hierarchic structure. The XSLT processor is not obliged to respect this request, and if it does so, the precise form of the output is not defined
	There are some constraints on how indentation should be achieved. In effect, it can only be done by adding whitespace-only text nodes to the tree, and these cannot be added adjacent to an existing non–whitespace text node. XSLT 2.0 has introduced a rule that the added text node must be adjacent to an element node, that is, immediately before a start tag or after an end tag (in 1.0, it could be added as a child of an empty element)
	Note that even with these restrictions, adding whitespace nodes to the output may affect the way the recipient interprets it. This is particularly true with mixed content models where an element can have both elements and text nodes as its children
	The processor is not allowed to add whitespace text nodes to the content of an element that has the attribute «xml:space="preserve"»
media-type	This attribute defines the media type of the output file (often referred to as its MIME type). The default value is «text/xml». The specification doesn't say what use is made of this information: It doesn't affect the contents of the output file, but it may affect the way it is named, stored, or transmitted, depending on the environment. For example, the information might find its way into an HTTP protocol header
normalization-form	One of the controversial features of Unicode has always been that it allows the same character to be represented in more than one way. For example, the letter «ç» (lower case «c» with cedilla) can be represented either as a single character (with codepoint x00E7), or as the two codepoints «c» (x0063) and «ِ» (x00B8). This fact causes considerable problems for software that performs comparison, search, and indexing operations on Unicode text. There have been long debates about whether XML should require such characters to be normalized (that is, to require one of these representations and disallow the other). The result of the debate is a compromise: XML 1.1 strongly encourages the use of normalized encodings. It encourages applications to output normalized text, and encourages parsers to provide an option that checks for normalized text, but it does not go so far as to say that non-normalized documents are not well-formed. XSLT 2.0 responds to this by providing an option to serialize the document in Unicode-normalized form. Specify "NFC" for composed normal form, " NFD" for decomposed normal form, any other supported normalization form, or "none" (the default) for no normalization.

Continues

Attribute	Interpretation
	An alternative approach is to make sure that individual text nodes, attribute nodes, and so on are already normalized in the result tree. You can do this by calling the `normalize-unicode()` function, described in *XPath 2.0 Programmer's Reference*, whenever you construct a character string that might not already be normalized
omit-xml-declaration	If this attribute has the value «yes», the XSLT processor should not output an XML declaration (or, by implication, a text declaration; recall that XML declarations are used at the start of the document entity, and text declarations are used at the start of an external general parsed entity)
	If the attribute is omitted, or has the value «no», then a declaration should be output. The declaration should include both the `version` and `encoding` attributes (to ensure that it is valid both as an XML declaration and as a text declaration). It should include a `standalone` attribute only if a `standalone` attribute is specified in the `<xsl:output>` element
	If you select an encoding such as «iso-8859-1», the output may not be intelligible to an XML parser if the XML declaration is omitted. Nevertheless, the specification allows you to omit it, because there are sometimes alternative ways for an XML parser to determine the encoding.
standalone	If this attribute is set to «yes», then the XML declaration will specify «standalone="yes"»
	If this attribute is set to <<no>>, then the XML declaration will specify «standalone="no"»
	If the attribute is omitted, then the XML declaration will not include a `standalone` attribute. This will make it a valid text declaration, enabling its use in an external general parsed entity.
	This attribute should not be used unless the output is a well-formed XML document
undeclare-namespaces	This attribute only comes into effect when you specify «version="1.1"». XML Namespaces 1.1 introduces the ability to "undeclare" a namespace. It's always been possible to undeclare the default namespace, using the syntax «xmlns=" "», but now you can also undeclare a namespace with a specific prefix, using the syntax «xmlns:pfx=" "».
	The result tree created by an XSLT 2.0 processor may have a namespace that is in scope for a particular element, but is not in scope for its children. In fact, this is likely to be a common scenario. The correct way to serialize such a tree is to generate namespace undeclarations on the child elements. However, XSLT 2.0 does not do this by default, because these undeclarations may cause a lot of unwanted clutter in the output document. Instead, you have to request them explicitly by setting this attribute to «yes»

Attribute	Interpretation
use-character-maps	This attribute is used to specify that the serializer should use the named character maps to translate specific characters into the strings given in the character map. For further details, see `<xsl:character-map>` on page 229
version	The version of XML used in the output document. This can be «1.0» or «1.1». The XSLT specification doesn't require either of these versions to be supported: The thinking is that early in the life of XSLT 2.0, many implementations will only support XML 1.0, but in five years time, there may be vendors who would only want to support XML 1.1. As already mentioned, support for a particular version of XML also implies support for the corresponding version of XML Namespaces
	The XPath data model, and therefore the result tree, is not tied to a particular version of XML. It supports the union of what can be represented in XML 1.0 and XML 1.1. This creates the possibility that the result tree uses features that cannot be represented faithfully (or at all) in XML 1.0. If such features are used, the serializer may need to fall back to a 1.0 representation, or if all else fails, report an error

Do remember that the specifications in the `<xsl:output>` element will only be effective if you actually use the XSLT processor to serialize the XML. If you write the output of the transformation to a DOM, and then use a serializer that comes with your DOM implementation (for example by using the `save` method or the `xml` property in the case of the Microsoft DOM implementation), then the `<xsl:output>` specifications will have no effect.

Rules for HTML Output

When the `method` attribute is set to «html», or when it is defaulted and the result tree is recognized as representing HTML, the output will be an HTML file. By default, it will follow the rules of HTML 4.0.

Requesting HTML serialization gives no guarantee that the result will be valid HTML. You can use any elements and attributes you like in the result tree, and the serializer will output them, following the HTML conventions where appropriate, but without enforcing any rules as to which elements can be used where.

HTML is output in the same way as XML, except where specific differences are noted. These differences are:

❑ Certain elements are recognized as empty elements. They are recognized in any combination of upper and lower case. These elements are output with a start tag and no end tag. For HTML 4.0 these elements are:

```
<area>
<base>
<basefont>
<br>
<col>
<frame>
```

```
<hr>
<img>
<input>
<isindex>
<link>
<meta>
<param>
```

❑ The `<script>` and `<style>` elements (again in any combination of upper and lower cases) do not require escaping of special characters. In the text content of these elements, a «<» character will be output as «<», not as «<».

❑ HTML attributes whose value is a URI (for example, the `href` attribute of the `<a>` element, or the `src` attribute of the `<img>` element) are recognized, and special characters within the URI are escaped as defined in the HTML specification. Specifically, non-ASCII characters in the URI should be represented by converting each byte of the UTF-8 representation of the character to «%HH» where HH represents the byte value in hexadecimal. This feature may be suppressed by setting «escape-uri-attributes="no"».

❑ Special characters may be output using entity references such as «é» where these are defined in the relevant version of HTML. This is at the discretion of the XSLT processor; it doesn't have to use these entity names.

❑ Processing instructions are terminated with «>» rather than «?>». Processing instructions are not often used in HTML, but the HTML 4.0 standard recommends that any vendor extensions should be implemented this way, rather than by adding element tags to the language. So it is possible they will be seen more frequently in the future.

❑ Attributes that are conventionally written with a keyword only, and no value, will be recognized and output in this form. Common examples are `<TEXTAREA READONLY>` and `<OPTION SELECTED>`. This is shorthand, permitted in SGML but not in XML, for an attribute that has only one permitted value, which is the same as the attribute name. In XML, these tags must be written as `<TABLE BORDER="BORDER">` and `<OPTION SELECTED="SELECTED">`. The HTML output method will normally use the abbreviated form, as this is the only form that older HTML browsers will recognize.

❑ The special use of the ampersand character in dynamic HTML attributes is recognized. For example, the tag `<TD WIDTH="&{width};">` is correct HTML, though it would not be correct in XML, because of the ampersand character. To produce this output from a literal result element, the tag in the stylesheet would need to be written as `<TD WIDTH="&amp;{{width}};">`: note the double curly braces, to prevent them being interpreted with their special meaning in attribute value templates.

A common source of anxiety with HTML output is the use of ampersands in URLs. For example, suppose you want to generate the output:

```
<a href="http://www.acme.com/search.asp?product=widgets&country=spain>
Spanish Widgets
</a>
```

It's not actually possible to produce this using standard XSLT; the ampersand will always come out as «&». The reason for this is simple: «&», although commonly used and widely accepted, is not actually correct HTML, and according to the standard it must be escaped as «&». All respectable browsers accept the correct escaped form, so the answer is: don't worry about it.

The attributes on the <xsl:output> element are interpreted as follows when HTML output is selected. Attributes not listed are not applicable to HTML, and are ignored.

Attribute	Interpretation
doctype-system	If this attribute is specified, the output file will include a document type declaration immediately before the first element start tag. The name of the document type will be «HTML» or «html». The value of the attribute will be used as the system identifier in the document type declaration
doctype-public	If this attribute is specified, the output file will include a document type declaration immediately before the first element start tag. The name of the document type will be «HTML» or «html». The value of the attribute will be used as the public identifier in the document type declaration
encoding	This specifies the preferred character encoding for the output document
	If the encoding is one that does not allow all XML characters to be represented directly, for example «iso-8859-1», then characters outside this subset will be represented where possible using either entity references or numeric character references. The processor is encouraged not to use such references for characters that are within the encoding, except in special cases such as the nonbreaking space character, which may be output either as itself (it looks just like an ordinary space) or as « », «&#a0;», or « ». It is an error if characters that can't be represented directly appear in contexts where character references are not recognized (for example within a script element, within a comment, or in an element or attribute name).
escape-uri-attributes	This attribute determines whether non-ASCII characters appearing in URI-valued attributes should be escaped using the %HH convention. The default is «yes». Although HTML requires URIs to be escaped in this way, there are several reasons why you might choose to suppress this. Firstly, the URIs might already be in escaped form: You can do the escaping from within the stylesheet, with much greater control, using the escape-uri() function described in *XPath 2.0 Programmer's Reference*. Secondly, browsers do not always handle escaped URIs correctly. This is especially true when the URI is handled on the client side, for example when it invokes JavaScript functions, or when it contains a fragment identifier

Continues

Attribute	Interpretation
include-content-type	If this attribute is set to «yes» (or if it is omitted), the serializer will add a `<meta>` element as a child of the HTML `<head>` element, provided that the result tree contains a `<head>` element. This `<meta>` element contains details of the media type and encoding of the document. You may want to suppress this by specifying the value «no», for example if the stylesheet is copying a document that already includes such an element
indent	If this attribute has the value «yes», the idea is that the HTML output should be indented to show its hierarchic structure. The XSLT processor is not obliged to respect this request, and if it does so, the precise form of the output is not defined
	When producing indented output, the processor has much more freedom to add or remove whitespace than in the XML case, because of the way whitespace is handled in HTML. The processor can add or remove whitespace anywhere it likes so long as it doesn't change the way a browser would display the HTML.
media-type	This attribute defines the media type of the output file (often referred to as its MIME type). The default value is «text/html». The specification doesn't say what use is made of this information; it doesn't affect the contents of the output file, but it may affect the way it is named, stored, or transmitted, depending on the environment. For example, the information might find its way into an HTTP protocol header
normalization-form	This attribute is used in the same way as for the XML output method, described on page 378
use-character-maps	This attribute is used in the same way as for the XML output method, described on page 378
version	The version of HTML used in the output document. It is up to the implementation to decide which versions of HTML should be supported, though all implementations can be expected to support the default version, namely version 4.0

Rules for XHTML Output

An XHTML document is an XML document, so when you specify «method="XHTML"», most of the rules for the XML output method are inherited without change. However, there are special guidelines for serializing XHTML so that it is rendered correctly in browsers that were designed originally to handle HTML; and in addition some of the features of HTML serialization, such as URI escaping and addition of `<meta>` elements, are also applicable to XHTML. So the XHTML output method is essentially a blend of features from the XML and HTML methods.

In fact, the XHTML output method works in the same way as the XML output method (and uses all the `<xsl:output>` attributes that control the XML method) with specific exceptions. These exceptions are:

❑ The way that empty elements are output depends on the way the element is declared in the XHTML DTD. For an element whose content model is empty, such as `<hr>` or `<br>` or `<img>`, the serializer should use an XML empty-element tag, taking care to include a space before the final «/>», so that the tag looks like `<hr />` or `<img src="a.jpeg" />`. For an element that is empty but allowed to have content, such as a `<p>` element, the serializer should use a start tag followed by an end tag, thus: `<p></p>`

❑ The entity reference «'» is not recognized by all browsers, so it should be avoided. It is always possible to use «&#27;» instead.

❑ The serializer needs to take care with whitespace (for example newlines) appearing in attribute values. The specification doesn't say exactly how this should be handled, but it's probably safest, if there is any whitespace other than a single space character, to represent it using numeric character references.

The specification points out that the XHTML DTD requires not only that the `<html>` element is in the namespace «http://www.w3.org/1999/xhtml», but also that this must be the default namespace. This is actually a bit of a fudge. Namespace prefixes are allocated by the namespace fixup process, not by the serializer. If the namespace fixup process has allocated a nondefault prefix to the `<html>` element, there is very little that the serializer can do about it; while the namespace fixup process, of course, isn't supposed to know anything about how the tree will be serialized. In practice, though, this is unlikely to cause problems; XSLT processors don't go out of their way to invent prefixes for namespaces when they don't need to. This is all a messy consequence of the fact that DTDs don't really deal properly with namespaces.

The XHTML output method also inherits two specific features of the HTML output method:

❑ Non-ASCII characters in URI-valued attributes are escaped using the %HH convention, unless you suppress this by specifying «escape-uri-attributes="no"».

❑ A `<meta>` element is added as the child of the `<head>` element, unless you suppress this using «include-content-type="no"».

You can control whether an XML declaration is output using the «omit-xml-declaration» attribute. The XHTML 1.0 specification advises against using an XML declaration, but points out that under the XML rules, it may be omitted only if the encoding is UTF-8 or UTF-16.

Rules for Text Output

When «method="text"», the result tree is output as a plain text file. The values of the text nodes of the tree are copied to the output, and all other nodes are ignored. Within text nodes, all character values are output using the relevant encoding as determined by the `encoding` attribute; there are no special characters such as «&» to be escaped.

The way in which line endings are output (for example LF or CRLF) is not defined; the implementation might choose to use the default line-ending conventions of the platform on which it is running.

The attributes that are relevant to text output are listed below. All other attributes are ignored.

Attribute	Interpretation
encoding	This specifies the preferred character encoding for the output document. The default value is implementation-defined, and may depend on the platform on which it is running If the encoding is one that does not allow all XML characters to be represented directly, for example «iso-8859-1», then any character outside this subset will be reported as an error
media-type	This attribute defines the media type of the output file (often referred to as its MIME type). The default value is «text/plain». The specification doesn't say what use is made of this information: It doesn't affect the contents of the output file, but it may affect the way it is named, stored, or transmitted, depending on the environment. For example, the information might find its way into an HTTP protocol header

Usage

The defaulting mechanisms ensure that it is usually not necessary to include an <xsl:output> element in the stylesheet. By default, the XML output method is used unless the first thing output is an <HTML> element, in which case the HTML output method is assumed.

The <xsl:output> element is concerned with how your result tree is turned into an output file. If the XSLT processor allows you to do something else with the result tree, for example passing it to the application as a DOM Document or as a stream of SAX events, then the <xsl:output> element is irrelevant.

The encoding attribute can be very useful to ensure that the output file can be easily viewed and edited. Unfortunately, though, the set of possible values varies from one XSLT implementation to another, and may also depend on the environment. For example, many XSLT processors are written in Java and use the Java facilities for encoding the output stream, but the set of encodings supported by each Java VM is different. However, support for iso-8859-1 encoding is fairly universal, so if you have trouble viewing the output file because it contains UTF-8 Unicode characters, setting the encoding to iso-8859-1 is often a good remedy.

> If your stylesheet generates accented letters or other special characters, and it looks as if they have come out incorrectly in the output, chances are they are correctly represented in UTF-8, but you are looking at them with a text editor that doesn't understand UTF-8. Either select a different output encoding (such as iso-8859-1), or get a text editor such as jEdit (www.jedit.org) that can work with UTF-8.

The encoding attribute determines how the XSLT processor serializes the output as a stream of bytes, but it says nothing about what happens to the byteslater. If the processor writes to a file, the file will probably be written in the chosen encoding. But if the output is accessed as a character string through an API, or is written to a character field in a database, the encoding of the characters may be changed before you get to see them. A classic example of this effect is the Microsoft `transformNode()` interface (see Appendix C), which returns the result of the transformation as a BSTR string. Because this is a BSTR, it will always be encoded in UTF-16, regardless of the encoding you request. The same thing will happen with the JAXP interface (see Appendix D); if you supply a `StreamResult` based on a `Writer` the encoding then depends on how the particular `Writer` encodes Unicode characters, and the XSLT processor has no control over the matter.

Examples

The following example requests XML output using iso-8859-1 encoding. The output will be indented for readability, and the contents of the `<script>` element, because it is expected to contain many special characters, will be output as a CDATA section. The output file will reference the DTD `booklist.dtd`: Note that it is entirely the user's responsibility to ensure that the output of the stylesheet actually conforms to this DTD, and, indeed, that it is a well-formed XML document.

```
<xsl:output
    method="xml"
    indent="yes"
    encoding="iso-8859-1"
    cdata-section-elements="script"
    doctype-system="booklist.dtd" />
```

The following example might be used if the output of the stylesheet is a comma-separated-values file using US ASCII characters only:

```
<xsl:output
    method="text"
    encoding="us-ascii" />
```

See Also

`<xsl:character-map>` on page 229
`<xsl:result-document>` on page 414

xsl:output-character

The `<xsl:output-character>` element allows a character in the result tree to be mapped to a specific string used to represent this character in the serialized output.

Changes in 2.0

The element is new in XSLT 2.0.

Format

```
<xsl:output-character
    character = char
    string = string />
```

Position

<xsl:output-character> only appears as a child of the <xsl:character-map> element.

Attributes

Name	Value	Meaning
character mandatory	Character	A single XML character; the character that is to be replaced during serialization
string mandatory	String	Any string; the string that is to replace the character during serialization

Content

None. The <xsl:output-character> element is always empty.

Effect

The <xsl:output-character> element defines a mapping for a single character within a character map. The way character maps work is fully described in the entry for the <xsl:character-map> element on page 229.

Note that the character to be replaced, and the string that is to replace it, must consist entirely of valid XML characters, otherwise it would not be possible to represent them in the stylesheet. Also note that any special characters must be escaped using the usual conventions. For example, if you want the ampersand character to be mapped to the string «&ampersand;», write:

```
<xsl:output-character character="&amp;" string="&amp;ampersand;"/>
```

See Also

<xsl:character-map> on page 229

xsl:param

The <xsl:param> element is used either at the top level, to describe a global parameter, or immediately within an <xsl:template> element, to describe a local parameter to a template. It specifies a name for the parameter and a default value, which is used if the caller supplies no value for the parameter.

Changes in 2.0

An `as` attribute has been added to define the required type of the parameter.

A `required` attribute has been added to indicate whether the parameter is mandatory or optional.

A `tunnel` attribute has been added to support the new facility of tunnel parameters.

Format

```
<xsl:param
  name = qname
  select? = expression
  as? = sequence-type
  required? = "yes" | "no"
  tunnel? = "yes" | "no">
  <!-- Content: sequence-constructor -->
</xsl:param>
```

Position

`<xsl:param>` may appear as a top-level declaration (a child of the `<xsl:stylesheet>` element), or as an immediate child element of `<xsl:template>` or `<xsl:function>`. The three kinds of parameters are known as *stylesheet parameters*, *template parameters*, and *function parameters*.

In the case of template parameters and function parameters, `<xsl:param>` elements must come before any other child elements.

Attributes

Name	Value	Meaning
name mandatory	QName	The name of the parameter
select optional	Expression	The default value of the parameter if no explicit value is supplied by the caller
as optional	SequenceType	The required type of the parameter value
required optional	«yes» or «no»	Indicates whether the parameter is optional or mandatory
tunnel optional	«yes» or «no»	Indicates whether the parameter is a tunnel parameter

The SequenceType construct is described in Chapter 4, on page 154, and more fully in Chapter 9 of *XPath 2.0 Programmer's Reference*.

The `required` attribute is available only for stylesheet parameters and template parameters, not for function parameters (function parameters are always mandatory).

The `tunnel` attribute is available only for template parameters.

Content

An optional sequence constructor. If a `select` attribute is present, the element must be empty.

Effect

An `<xsl:param>` element at the top level of the stylesheet declares a global parameter; an `<xsl:param>` element appearing as a child of an `<xsl:template>` element declares a local parameter for that template, and an `<xsl:param>` element appearing as a child of an `<xsl:function>` element declares a local parameter for that function.

The `<xsl:param>` element defines the name of the parameter, and a default value. The default value is used only if no other value is explicitly supplied by the caller. Default values can be supplied for stylesheet parameters and template parameters, but not for function parameters, which must always be supplied in the function call.

An explicit value can be supplied for a template parameter by using the `<xsl:with-param>` element when the template is invoked using `<xsl:apply-templates>`, `<xsl:call-template>`, `<xsl:next-match>`, or `<xsl:apply-imports>`.

For function parameters, values are supplied in the function call. The syntax of function calls is defined in Chapter 5 of *XPath 2.0 Programmer's Reference*. Function calls pass parameters positionally rather than by name; the *n*th argument in the function call is evaluated to provide the value for the *n*th `<xsl:param>` element in the function definition.

The way in which explicit values are supplied for stylesheet parameters is implementation-defined (for example, they may be defined on the command line or through environment variables, or they may be supplied via a vendor-defined API). Information about Microsoft APIs is given in Appendix C, and that about Java APIs in Appendix D.

The Type of the Parameter

The required type of the parameter can be specified using the `as` attribute. For example, «`as="xs:integer"`» indicates that a single integer is expected, «`as="xs:string*"`» indicates that a sequence of strings is expected, and «`as="element()+"`» indicates that the required type is a sequence of one or more element nodes. With a schema-aware processor it is also possible to supply schema-defined types, for example «`as="abc:vehicle-registration"`» indicates that the parameter must be an atomic value conforming to the user-defined simple type `abc:vehicle-registration`, while «`as="schema-element(EVENT)"`» indicates that it must be an element node validated as being either an `EVENT` element or an element in the substitution group of `EVENT`.

If the `as` attribute is omitted, then the supplied value may be of any type.

The value that is actually supplied by the caller must be suitable for the required type. The value is converted if necessary using the standard conversion rules described on page 476, and it is a fatal error if this conversion fails. Because the ability to specify a type on <xsl:param> is new in XSLT 2.0, the conversion is done according to the XPath 2.0 rules—the 1.0 compatibility rules are not used even if the stylesheet version is set to «1.0». In summary, this means that the only conversions allowed are:

❑ Atomization (that is, extraction of the typed values of nodes, when the required type is an atomic value or a sequence of atomic values)

❑ Numeric promotion, for example conversion of xs:integer to xs:double

❑ Casting of xdt:untypedAtomic values (which normally arise as a result of atomizing a node in a document that has not been schema-validated)

If the supplied parameter is the wrong type, then the error may be detected either at compile time or at runtime. With stylesheet parameters the supplied value isn't known until runtime, so this is when the error will occur. The error is more likely to be detected at compile time in the case of calls to named templates or to stylesheet functions.

The as attribute on <xsl:param> also serves a second purpose. Like the as attribute on <xsl:variable>, it is used when the <xsl:param> element has a contained sequence constructor to distinguish whether the default value is the sequence obtained by evaluating the sequence constructor, or the result of building a temporary tree using this sequence to provide the content. For example:

```
<xsl:param name="p">Madrid</xsl:param>
```

declares a parameter whose default value is a temporary tree consisting of a document node, which owns a text node whose string value is «Madrid»; while

```
<xsl:param name="p" as="xs:string">Madrid</xsl:param>
```

declares a parameter whose required type is a single string, and whose default value is the string «Madrid». If you really need to say that the required type is a document node, and to supply a temporary tree as the default value, then you can write it like this:

```
<xsl:param name="p" as="document-node()">
    <xsl:document>Madrid</xsl:document>
</xsl:param>
```

The Default Value of the Parameter

In the case of stylesheet parameters and template parameters, if no value for the parameter is supplied by the caller, a default value is used. The default value of the parameter may be given either by the XPath expression in the select attribute, or by the contents of the contained sequence constructor. If there is a select attribute, the <xsl:param> element should be empty.

The value is calculated in exactly the same way as the value of a variable in <xsl:variable>, and the rules are as given on page 473. Note that the default value need not be a constant; it can be computed in terms of the values of other parameters appearing earlier in the list, and can also depend on information such as the context item and context size.

If there is no select attribute and the sequence constructor is empty, the default value of the parameter is a zero-length string, unless there is an as attribute, in which case the default value is an empty sequence.

If the `required` attribute has the value «yes», then the parameter is mandatory. In this case, it makes no sense to supply a default value, so the `select` attribute must be omitted and the element must be empty. Failing to supply a value for a mandatory parameter is a compile-time error in the case of `<xsl:call-template>`, but a runtime error in all other cases.

The Name of the Parameter

The name of the parameter is defined by the QName given in the `name` attribute. Normally this will be a simple name (such as «num» or «list-of-names»), but it may be a name qualified with a prefix, for example «my:value». If it has a prefix, the prefix must correspond to a namespace that is in scope at that point in the stylesheet. The true name of the parameter, for the purpose of testing whether two names are the same, is determined not by the prefix but by the namespace URI corresponding to the prefix, so two variables «my:value» and «your:value» have the same name if the prefixes «my» and «your» refer to the same namespace URI. If the name has no prefix, it is treated like an attribute name; that is, it has a null namespace URI—it does not use the default namespace URI.

Parameter names are referenced in exactly the same way as variables, by prefixing the name with a dollar sign (for example «$num») and all the rules for uniqueness and scope of names are exactly as if the `<xsl:param>` element was replaced by an `<xsl:variable>` element. The only difference between parameters and variables is the way they acquire an initial value.

Tunnel Parameters

Tunnel parameters are a new facility in XSLT 2.0. They have the property that if a tunnel parameter is passed to a template when it is called, then it is automatically passed on to any further templates called from this template. For example, if template A creates a tunnel parameter and passes it on a call to template B, then when B calls C and C calls D, the tunnel parameter will be passed transparently through all these calls and will be accessible to template D, even if B and C were quite unaware of the parameter.

This feature is very useful when you are customizing a stylesheet. Suppose that D is a template rule that formats equation numbers in roman numerals, and you want to use greek letters instead. You can write a customization layer (an importing stylesheet) that overrides D with a template rule of your own. But suppose you want D sometimes to use greek letters and sometimes roman numerals, how do you pass it this information? Global variables only solve the problem if the choice is constant for all invocations of D during the course of a transformation. Adding parameters to every template en route from your top-level A template to the D template would require overriding lots of template rules in the base stylesheet, which you want to change as little as possible. So the answer is that you write a customized version of the A template that sets a tunnel parameter, and a customized version of D that reads the tunnel parameter, and the intermediate templates B and C don't need to be changed.

The theory behind tunnel parameters is the concept of dynamically scoped variables in functional programming languages such as Lisp.

A tunnel parameter always starts life in an `<xsl:with-param>` element. This may be on any kind of template call that allows parameter passing: specifically, `<xsl:apply-templates>`, `<xsl:call-template>`, `<xsl:apply-imports>`, and `<xsl:next-match>`. For example:

```
<xsl:template match="/">
   <xsl:apply-templates select="body">
      <xsl:with-param name="mq:format-greek" tunnel="yes" select="true()"/>
   </xsl:apply-templates>
```

```
      <xsl:apply-templates select="back">
        <xsl:with-param name="mq:format-greek" tunnel="yes" select="false()"/>
      </xsl:apply-templates>
    </xsl:template>
```

I've put the parameter name in a namespace here, to minimize the risk that it will clash with a parameter added by someone else.

This tunnel parameter will be passed silently up the call stack, through all calls of `<xsl:apply-templates>`, `<xsl:call-template>`, `<xsl:apply-imports>`, and `<xsl:next-match>`, until it reaches a template that is interested in it. This template can declare its interest by including the parameter declaration:

```
<xsl:param name="mq:format-greek" as="xs:boolean" required="yes"
tunnel="yes"/>
```

and can then use the parameter value in the normal way, by referring to it as «$mq:format-greek» within an XPath expression.

Tunnel parameters are not passed through XPath function calls, so if the stylesheet evaluates an XPath expression which in turn calls a stylesheet function, which in turn calls `<xsl:apply-templates>`, then the tunnel parameters will not be accessible in this call. Similarly, they are not available when an attribute set is expanded.

At the point where the parameter enters the tunnel (the `<xsl:with-param>` element) it must have a name that differs from all the other sibling `<xsl:with-param>` elements, whether these are tunnel parameters or not. Similarly, when it emerges from the tunnel (the `<xsl:param>` element) it must have a name that differs from other `<xsl:param>` elements in that template. But where it is being silently passed through intermediate templates, name clashes don't matter: silently passed tunnel parameters are in effect in a different symbol space from explicit parameters.

Tunnel parameters can be of any data type. They can be optional or required parameters, and if optional the receiving template can declare a default value. Reading the tunnel parameter in this way isn't destructive; it will still be passed on to further templates. Specifying a required type or a default value or a required type doesn't change the value that is passed on: For example if the original value is a node, and the receiving template declares it as a string, then the node will be atomized for the purposes of the receiving template, but the value that's passed on will still be a node, unless a new `<xsl:with-param>` element is used to change the value.

Usage

The different kinds of parameters (stylesheet parameters, template parameters, and tunnel parameters) can be used in different ways. These are discussed in the following sections.

Using Stylesheet Parameters

Stylesheet parameters can be used in various ways to control the actions performed by the transformation. For example, they are particularly useful for selecting which part of the source document to process. A common scenario is that the XSLT processor will be running within a Web server. The user request will be accepted by a Java Server Page or by a Java servlet, or indeed by an ASP page, the request parameters will be accepted, and the stylesheet processing will be kicked off using an API defined by each vendor. Generally this API will provide some way of passing the parameters that came from the HTTP request into the stylesheet as the initial values of global `<xsl:param>` elements.

If the API supports it, a global parameter may take a value of any type: not just a string, number, or boolean, but also a node or sequence of nodes. Because the value can contain nodes, this provides another way of supplying secondary source documents for use by the stylesheet, as an alternative to the `document()` function. Many products allow such a parameter to be supplied as a DOM `Document` object.

Where a stylesheet needs to get system-dependent information (for example, the URI of the source document, or the operating system version number) it is often much easier to pass the information as a stylesheet parameter rather than writing extension functions to deliver the information on request.

Wherever you define a global variable, ask yourself whether it would be better to make it a stylesheet parameter instead. The default value of a stylesheet parameter can be used in exactly the same way as a global variable; the only difference is that you have added the ability for the user to change the value from outside.

The new facilities in XSLT 2.0 to declare a stylesheet parameter with «`required="yes"`», and to declare its required type, make stylesheet parameters a lot more robust than they were.

Using Template Parameters

Template parameters are used more often with `<xsl:call-template>` than with `<xsl:apply-templates>`, though they are available to both, and in XSLT 2.0 they can also be used with `<xsl:apply-imports>` and `<xsl:next-match>`. The actual value of the parameter is set by the caller using an `<xsl:with-param>` element. Parameters are often needed by the recursive algorithms used in XSLT to handle lists of items: There are examples of such algorithms under `<xsl:call-template>` on page 220. In XSLT 2.0, however, it is often more convenient to implement such algorithms using `<xsl:function>`.

Declaring the expected type of a parameter, using the `as` attribute, is optional, but I would always recommend it. It provides useful documentation for anyone who has to debug the stylesheet later, as well as trapping errors when the caller provides incorrect parameter values. My experience is that it catches many coding errors that would otherwise have led to incorrect output being generated. In addition, the information is very useful to the XSLT processor itself, as it enables optimized code to be produced. For example, a test such as `<xsl:if test="$p=3">` is very much simpler if it is known in advance that $p will always be an integer, than if the processor has to deal with the possibility of it being a node, a sequence of nodes, a sequence of doubles, or perhaps an `untypedAtomic` value.

Using Tunnel Parameters

Tunnel parameters provide a half-way house between global variables and local template parameters, combining the advantages of both and removing many of the problems of both.

Compared with global variables, their great advantage is that their value can change in the course of the transformation. This doesn't mean that they introduce side effects, because only the caller of a template can set the value, not the callee.

Compared with local parameters, their great advantage is that you don't have to change every template in the stylesheet to pass the values through.

I found a good use case for tunnel parameters in the stylesheet used to generate the XSLT working draft. The XML master version of this document includes entries describing each error condition that can arise. This is used both to generate inline descriptions of the errors in the document body, and to generate a summary of errors in an appendix. Much of the code to handle the two cases is the same, but a few details differ, for example the way that hyperlinks are generated. Traditionally this problem is tackled using modes; however, even with the XSLT 2.0 ability to write a single template rule that works in more than one mode, using modes means that the intermediate template rules need to be aware of the fact that they can be invoked under two different circumstances. They shouldn't need to know this: Only the code that produces different results in the two cases should need to know that there are two possible cases. A tunnel parameter indicating which phase of processing is active solves the problem neatly.

Examples

This section presents two examples showing the use of `<xsl:param>` to define template parameters. The first is a very simple demonstration of how parameters work with `<xsl:call-template>`. The second is a more complicated example, making use of tunnel parameters.

Example: Using <xsl:param> with a Default Value

This example shows a simple named template that defines a parameter and gives it a default value.

Source

This stylesheet works with any XML source file.

Stylesheet

The stylesheet is `call.xsl`.

It contains a named template that outputs the depth of a node (defined as the number of ancestors). The node may be supplied as a parameter; if it is not supplied, the parameter defaults to the current node.

The stylesheet includes a template rule for the document node that invokes this named template, defaulting the parameter, to display the name and depth of every element in the source document.

```
<xsl:transform
  xmlns:xsl="http://www.w3.org/1999/XSL/Transform"
  version="2.0"
>
<xsl:output method="text"/>

<xsl:template match="/">
<xsl:for-each select="//*">
```

```
            <xsl:value-of select="concat(name(), ' -- ')"/>
            <xsl:call-template name="depth"/>;
    </xsl:for-each>
    </xsl:template>

    <xsl:template name="depth">
        <xsl:param name="node" as="node()" select="."/>
        <xsl:value-of select="count($node/ancestor::node())"/>
    </xsl:template>
    </xsl:transform>
```

Output

If the stylesheet is run against the file poem.xml used in Chapter 1, the output is as follows:

```
poem -- 1;
author -- 2;
date -- 2;
title -- 2;
stanza -- 2;
line -- 3;
line -- 3;
line -- 3;
line -- 3;
stanza -- 2;
line -- 3;
line -- 3;
line -- 3;
line -- 3;
stanza -- 2;
line -- 3;
line -- 3;
line -- 3;
line -- 3;
```

Example: Tunnel Parameters

Realistic examples using tunnel parameters tend to involve customization of rather complex stylesheets, such as the DocBook stylesheet suite (http://docbook.sourceforge.net/) produced by Norman Walsh. Unfortunately, explaining such an example would take a full chapter of this book. So we'll make do with a simpler case.

Suppose that you start with the stylesheet play.xsl, which is designed to generate a set of linked HTML files containing the text of one of Shakespeare's plays as marked up by Jon Bosak. I won't present this stylesheet in full, because it's pretty standard, and most of it isn't relevant to the example. The challenge now is to customize this stylesheet so that instead of producing a single rendition of the play, it produces a script for each of the characters appearing in the play, with the lines spoken by the character highlighted. You will do this by producing another stylesheet module, script.xsl, which overrides selected template rules from the original.

Source

This stylesheet can be applied to any of the Shakespeare plays available from `http://metalab.unc.edu/bosak/xml/eg/shaks200.zip`. The examples use `othello.xml`, which is included in the download files for this book.

Output

The existing stylesheet, `play.xsl`, produces a set of HTML files: one file called `play.html`, which acts as a cover sheet and index, and one file for each scene in the play, with names such as `sceneN.html`. You can run it with a command like this:

```
java -jar c:\saxon\saxon7.jar othello.xml play.xsl dir=c:/temp/othello
```

The first page of the output, in the file `play.html`, is shown in Figure 5-10.

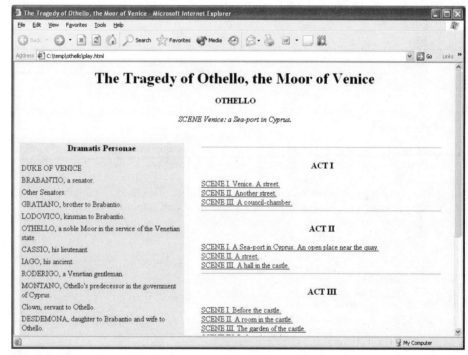

Figure 5-10

In the customized presentation, we want to create an index page that looks like the one shown in Figure 5-11.

This presents an index showing all the speaking parts in the play. Clicking on one of the names brings up a modified version of the front page shown before, in which the titles of the scenes are shown as active links if the character appears in these scenes, or as plain text otherwise. The actual text of the scene should also be modified so that the speaker's lines are highlighted.

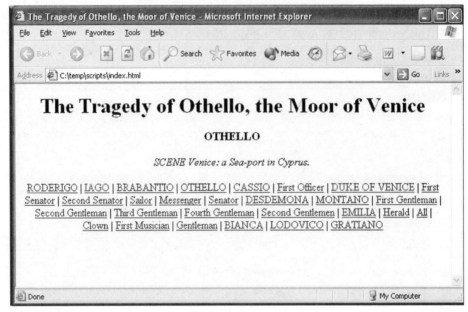

Figure 5-11

Stylesheet

The base stylesheet `play.xsl` is unmodified (it is one that has been included in the Saxon distribution for a while, to illustrate how a stylesheet can create multiple output files).

The customization layer is in the file `scripts.xsl`. This starts by importing `play.xsl`. It then contains a template rule providing the new control logic:

```
<xsl:template match="/">
  <xsl:variable name="play" select="PLAY"/>
  <xsl:result-document href="file:///{$dir}/index.html" format="play">
    <HTML>
    <HEAD><TITLE><xsl:apply-templates select="PLAY/TITLE"/></TITLE>
    </HEAD>
    <BODY BGCOLOR='{$backcolor}'>
        <CENTER>
            <H1><xsl:value-of select="PLAY/TITLE"/></H1>
            <H3><xsl:apply-templates select="PLAY/PLAYSUBT"/></H3>
            <I><xsl:apply-templates select="PLAY/SCNDESCR"/></I>
        <BR/><BR/>
        <P>
          <xsl:for-each select="distinct-values(//SPEAKER)">
            <A HREF="{escape-uri(.,true())}/play.html">
              <xsl:value-of select="."/>
            </A>
            <xsl:if test="position() ne last()"> | </xsl:if>
            <xsl:apply-templates select="$play">
              <xsl:with-param name="speaker" select="." tunnel="yes"/>
```

```
            </xsl:apply-templates>
          </xsl:for-each>
        </P>
        </CENTER>
    </BODY>
    </HTML>
  </xsl:result-document>
</xsl:template>
```

This template creates the index page. It calls the `distinct-values()` function to get a list of speakers appearing in the play, and for each one, it firstly outputs a hyperlink to a `play.html` file in a subdirectory named after the speaker, and then calls `<xsl:apply-templates>` to process the `<PLAY>` element, which is the outermost element in the source file. Crucially, it supplies the name of the speaker as a tunnel parameter to this template.

There are three template rules in the `play.xsl` stylesheet that need to be modified: These are the template for the `<PLAY>` element (because the `play.html` file now has to be placed in a subdirectory), the template for the `<SCENE>` element (which must now generate pages only for those scenes in which the selected speaker appears), and the template for the `<SPEECH>` element (to highlight the lines spoken by the selected speaker). Each of these contains a declaration of the tunnel parameter in an `<xsl:param>` element. Here is the modified template for the `<SCENE>` element:

```
<xsl:template match="SCENE|PROLOGUE|EPILOGUE">
    <xsl:param name="speaker" tunnel="yes" required="yes"/>

    <xsl:variable name="NR">
      <xsl:number count="SCENE|PROLOGUE|EPILOGUE" level="any"/>
    </xsl:variable>
    <xsl:variable name="play" select="ancestor::PLAY/TITLE"/>
    <xsl:variable name="act" select="ancestor::ACT/TITLE"/>
    <xsl:choose>
    <xsl:when test=".//SPEAKER = $speaker">
        <A HREF="scene{$NR}.html">
            <xsl:value-of select="TITLE" />
        </A><BR/>

        <xsl:result-document href=
        "file:///{$dir}/{escape-uri($speaker, true())}/scene{$NR}.html"
          format="scene">
            <HTML>
            <HEAD>
            <TITLE>
              <xsl:value-of select="concat($play, ' ', $act, ': ', TITLE)"/>
            </TITLE>
            </HEAD>
            <BODY BGCOLOR='{$backcolor}'>
            <P>
                <A HREF="play.html"><xsl:value-of select="$play"/>
                </A><BR/>
                <B><xsl:value-of select="$act"/></B><BR/>
            </P>
```

```
                <xsl:apply-templates/>
                </BODY>
                </HTML>
            </xsl:result-document>
        </xsl:when>
        <xsl:otherwise>
            <xsl:value-of select="TITLE"/><BR/>
        </xsl:otherwise>
        </xsl:choose>
    </xsl:template>
```

The modifications here, apart from the addition of the <xsl:param> to declare the tunnel parameter, are the addition of the <xsl:choose> to generate the scene page conditionally, and the choice of file name produced by <xsl:result-document>.

The template rule for the <SPEECH> element becomes:

```
<xsl:template match="SPEECH">
    <xsl:param name="speaker" required="yes" tunnel="yes"/>
    <TABLE><TR>
    <TD WIDTH="160" VALIGN="TOP">
    <xsl:if test="SPEAKER = $speaker">
        <xsl:attribute name="BGCOLOR" select="'cyan'"/>
    </xsl:if>
    <xsl:apply-templates select="SPEAKER"/>
    </TD>
    <TD VALIGN="TOP">
    <xsl:apply-templates select="STAGEDIR|LINE"/>
    </TD>
    </TR></TABLE>
</xsl:template>
```

The changes from the original are addition of the <xsl:param> declaring the tunnel parameter, and the addition of the <xsl:if> instruction that outputs an attribute changing the background color if the selected speaker participates in this <SPEECH> (a <SPEECH> can have more than one <SPEAKER>, the equality test succeeds if any of them match).

The key point about this example is that the original stylesheet has been customized and reused without changing it in any way. Without tunnel parameters, this would have required many more of its template rules to be changed, merely to pass the extra parameter through.

See Also

<xsl:apply-templates> on page 187
<xsl:call-template> on page 220
<xsl:variable> on page 471
<xsl:with-param> on page 488

xsl:perform-sort

The `<xsl:perform-sort>` instruction is used to sort a sequence. If you want to process the items in a sequence in sorted order, you can achieve this by adding `<xsl:sort>` elements to an `<xsl:apply-templates>` or `<xsl:for-each>` instruction. If you just want to sort the sequence, without processing the items individually, this can be done using `<xsl:perform-sort>`.

Changes in 2.0

This instruction is new in XSLT 2.0

Format

```
<xsl:perform-sort
  select? = expression
  <!-- Content: (xsl:sort+, sequence-constructor) -->
</xsl:sequence>
```

Position

`<xsl:perform-sort>` is an instruction, and may be used anywhere within a sequence constructor.

Attributes

Name	Value	Meaning
select optional	Expression	Returns the input sequence to be sorted

Content

The `<xsl:perform-sort>` instruction always contains one or more `<xsl:sort>` elements to specify the sort order.

In addition it may contain a sequence constructor. This is an alternative to the `select` attribute: If the `select` attribute is present, then the `<xsl:perform-sort>` element must contain only `<xsl:sort>` elements. It can also contain `<xsl:fallback>` elements to define what an XSLT 1.0 processor should do when it encounters this instruction in forwards-compatible mode.

Effect

The instruction forms an initial sequence by evaluating the expression in the `select` attribute or the contained sequence constructor, whichever is present. It then sorts this initial sequence to produce a sorted sequence, according to the rules for `<xsl:sort>` which are given on page 423. The result of the `<xsl:perform-sort>` instruction is the sorted sequence.

Usage and Examples

The `<xsl:perform-sort>` instruction is useful when you want to create a sorted sequence in a variable, or as the result of a function. If you want to process items in sorted order you can achieve this using `<xsl:for-each>` or `<xsl:apply-templates>`, but these instructions do not deliver the sorted sequence directly as a value in its own right.

For example, you could define a global variable containing the speakers in a play, sorted alphabetically, by writing:

```
<xsl:variable name="sorted-speakers" as="xs:string*">
  <xsl:perform-sort select="distinct-values(//SPEAKER)">
    <xsl:sort select="."/>
  </xsl:perform-sort>
</xsl:variable>
```

The following function returns the earliest and latest date in a sequence of dates, as a sequence of two dates:

```
<xsl:function name="f:first-and-last">
   <xsl:param name="in" as="xs:date*"/>
   <xsl:variable name="sorted-dates" as="xs:date*">
      <xsl:perform-sort select="$in">
         <xsl:sort select="."/>
      </xsl:perform-sort>
   </xsl:variable>
   <xsl:sequence select="$sorted-dates[1], $sorted-dates[last()]"/>
</xsl:function>
```

See Also

`<xsl:apply-templates>` on page 187
`<xsl:for-each>` on page 276
`<xsl:sort>` on page 423

xsl:preserve-space

The `<xsl:preserve-space>` element, along with `<xsl:strip-space>`, is used to control the way in which whitespace nodes in the source document are handled.

Changes in 2.0

The syntax of a NameTest has been extended to allow the format «*:NCName», which matches all elements with a given local name, in any namespace.

Format

```
<xsl:preserve-space
  elements = tokens />
```

Position

`<xsl:preserve-space>` is a top-level declaration, which means that it must be a child of the `<xsl:stylesheet>` element. There are no constraints on its ordering relative to other declarations.

Attributes

Name	Value	Meaning
elements mandatory	Whitespace-separated list of NameTests	Defines the elements in the source document whose whitespace-only text nodes are to be preserved

The NameTest construct is defined in XPath. NameTests are also used in XSLT patterns, so they are described in Chapter 6 of this book on page 509. A NameTest may be an actual element name, or the symbol «*» meaning all elements, or the construct «prefix:*» meaning all elements in a particular namespace, or the construct «*:local-name» meaning all elements with a given local name, regardless of their namespace.

Content

None, the element is always empty.

Effect

This declaration, together with `<xsl:strip-space>`, defines the way that whitespace-only text nodes in the source document are handled. Unless contradicted by an `<xsl:strip-space>` element, `<xsl:preserve-space>` indicates that whitespace-only text nodes occurring as children of a specified element are to be retained in the source tree.

Preserving whitespace-only text nodes is the default action, so this element only needs to be used where it is necessary to contradict an `<xsl:strip-space>` element. The interaction of the two is explained below.

The concept of whitespace-only text nodes is explained at some length, starting on page 136, in Chapter 3.

This declaration also affects the handling of whitespace-only text nodes in any document loaded using the `document()` function. It does not affect the handling of whitespace-only text nodes in the stylesheet when used in its role as a stylesheet, but it does affect the stylesheet in the same way as any other document if a copy of the stylesheet is loaded using the `document()` function.

The element does not affect whitespace nodes in documents returned as the result of extension functions or passed to the stylesheet as the value of a stylesheet parameter. Also, the element does not affect anything that happens to the source document before the XSLT processor gets to see it, so if you create the source tree using an XML parser that strips whitespace nodes (as Microsoft's MSXML3 does, by default), then specifying `<xsl:preserve-space>` in the stylesheet will not get these nodes back—they are already gone.

A whitespace-only text node is a text node whose text consists *entirely* of a sequence of whitespace characters, these being space, tab, carriage return, and linefeed (`#x20`, `#x9`, `#xD`, and `#xA`). The

`<xsl:preserve-space>` element has no effect on whitespace contained in text nodes that also contain non–whitespace characters; such whitespace is always preserved and is part of the value of the text node.

An XML 1.1 parser will recognize the additional characters «x85» and «x2028» as representing line endings. This means it will convert such characters into «x0A» characters in the data model that XSLT sees. If one of these two characters finds its way into a text node without being converted, which can happen either if they are written as character reference «…» or « » in the source XML or if the tree is built by an XML 1.0 parser, then the XSLT processor will not treat them as whitespace.

Before a node is classified as a whitespace-only text node, the tree is normalized by concatenating all adjacent text nodes. This includes the merging of text that originated in different XML entities.

A whitespace-only text node may either be stripped or preserved. If it is stripped, it is removed from the tree. This means it will never be matched, it will never be copied to the output, and it will never be counted when nodes are numbered. If it is preserved, it is retained on the tree in its original form, subject only to the end-of-line normalization performed by the XML parser.

If a whitespace-only text node has an ancestor with an `xml:space` attribute and the nearest ancestor with such an attribute has the value «`xml:space="preserve"`», then the text node is preserved regardless of the `<xsl:preserve-space>` and `<xsl:strip-space>` elements in the stylesheet.

The `elements` attribute of `<xsl:preserve-space>` must contain a whitespace-separated list of NameTests. The form of a NameTest is defined in the XPath expression language; see Chapter 6, page 509. Each form of NameTest has an associated priority. The different forms of NameTest and their meanings are:

Syntax	Examples	Meaning	Priority
QName	`title` `svg:width`	Matches the full element name, including its namespace URI	0
NCName «`:*`»	`svg:*`	Matches all elements in the namespace whose URI corresponds to the given prefix	−0.25
«`*:`» NCName	`*:address`	Matches all elements with a given local-name, regardless of their namespace	−0.25
«`*`»	`*`	Matches all elements	−0.5

The priority is used when conflicts arise. For example, if the stylesheet specifies:

```
<xsl:strip-space elements="*"/>
<xsl:preserve-space elements="para clause"/>
```

then whitespace-only text nodes appearing within a `<para>` or `<clause>` will be preserved. Even though these elements match both the `<xsl:strip-space>` and the `<xsl:preserve-space>`, the NameTest in the latter has higher priority (0 as compared to −0.5).

An `<xsl:strip-space>` or `<xsl:preserve-space>` element containing several `NameTests` is equivalent to writing a separate `<xsl:strip-space>` or `<xsl:preserve-space>` element for each `NameTest` individually.

A whitespace-only text node is preserved if there is no `<xsl:strip-space>` element in the stylesheet that matches its parent element.

A whitespace-only text node is removed from the tree if there is an `<xsl:strip-space>` element that matches the parent element, and no `<xsl:preserve-space>` element that also matches.

If there is an `<xsl:strip-space>` element that matches the parent element, and also an `<xsl:preserve-space>` element that matches, then the decision depends on the import precedence and priority of the respective rules. Taking into consideration all the `<xsl:strip-space>` and `<xsl:preserve-space>` elements that match the parent element of the whitespace-only text node, the XSLT processor takes the one with highest import precedence (as defined in the rules for `<xsl:import>` on page 312). If there is more than one element with this import precedence, it takes the one with highest priority, as defined in the table above. If there is still more than one, it may either report an error, or choose the one that comes last in declaration order. If the chosen element is `<xsl:preserve-space>`, the whitespace-only text node is preserved on the tree: If it is `<xsl:strip-space>`, it is removed from the tree.

In deciding whether to strip or preserve a whitespace-only text node, only its immediate parent element is considered in the above rules. The rules for its other ancestors make no difference. The element itself, of course, is never removed from the tree: The stripping process will only remove text nodes.

If an individual element has the XML-defined attribute «`xml:space="preserve"`» or «`xml:space="default"`» this overrides anything defined in the stylesheet. These values, unlike `<xsl:preserve-space>` and `<xsl:strip-space>`, do affect descendant elements as well as the element on which the attribute appears. If an `<xsl:strip-space>` doesn't seem to be having any effect, one possible reason is that the element type in question is declared in the DTD to have an `xml:space` attribute with a default value of «`preserve`». There is no way of overriding this in the stylesheet.

Usage

For many categories of source document, especially those used to represent data structures, whitespace-only text nodes are never significant, so it is useful to specify:

```
<xsl:strip-space elements="*"/>
```

which will remove them all from the tree. There are two main advantages in stripping these unwanted nodes:

❑   When `<xsl:apply-templates>` is used with a default `select` attribute, all child nodes will be processed. If whitespace-only text nodes are not stripped, they too will be processed, probably leading to the whitespace being copied to the output destination.

❑   When the `position()` function is used to determine the position of an element relative to its siblings, the whitespace-only text nodes are included in the count. This often leads to the significant nodes being numbered 2, 4, 6, 8, ...

Generally speaking, it is a good idea to strip whitespace-only text nodes belonging to elements that have element content, that is, elements declared in the DTD as containing child elements but no #PCDATA, or declared in a schema to have a complex type with «mixed="no"».

It also usually does no harm to strip whitespace-only text nodes from elements declared as having simple content; that is, elements whose only children are text nodes. In most cases, an element containing whitespace text is equivalent to an empty element, so stylesheet logic can be simplified if elements containing whitespace only are normalized to be empty by removing the text node.

By contrast, stripping whitespace-only text nodes from elements with mixed content, elements declared in the DTD or schema to contain both child elements and #PCDATA, is often a bad idea. For example, consider the element below:

```
<quote>He went to <edu>Balliol College</edu> <city>Oxford</city> to read
<subject>Greats</subject></quote>
```

The space between the <edu> element and the <city> element is a whitespace-only text node, and it should be preserved, because otherwise when the tags are removed by an application that's only interested in the text, the words «College» and «Oxford» will run together.

It's worth noting that many XSLT processors do not physically remove whitespace text nodes from the tree; they only behave as if they did. Whether the nodes are physically removed or whether the processor creates a view of the tree in which these nodes are invisible, whitespace stripping can incur a significant cost. However, if whitespace is stripped while the tree is being built from serial XML input, the performance arguments are reversed: It then becomes cheaper to remove the whitespace nodes than to preserve them. Generally, if whitespace is insignificant then it's best to get rid of it as early as possible.

Examples

To strip whitespace nodes from all elements of the source tree:

```
<xsl:strip-space elements="*"/>
```

To strip whitespace nodes from selected elements:

```
<xsl:strip-space elements="book author title price"/>
```

To strip whitespace nodes from all elements except the <description> element:

```
<xsl:strip-space elements="*"/>
<xsl:preserve-space elements="description"/>
```

To strip whitespace nodes from all elements except those in the namespace with URI http://mednet.org/text:

```
<xsl:strip-space elements="*"/>
<xsl:preserve-space elements="mednet:*"
                    xmlns:mednet="http://mednet.org/text" />
```

See Also

`<xsl:strip-space>` on page 432

xsl:processing-instruction

The `<xsl:processing-instruction>` instruction is used to write a processing instruction node to the result sequence.

Changes in 2.0

A `select` attribute has been added.

Format

```
<xsl:processing-instruction
  name = { NCName }
  select? = expression>
  <!-- Content: sequence-constructor -->
</xsl:processing-instruction>
```

Position

`<xsl:processing-instruction>` is an instruction. It is always used as part of a sequence constructor.

Attributes

Name	Value	Meaning
name mandatory	Attribute value template returning an NCName	The name (target) of the generated processing instruction
select optional	Expression	Used to compute the string value (the data part) of the generated processing instruction

Content

If the `select` attribute is present, the element must be empty. If the `select` attribute is absent, the element may contain a sequence constructor.

Effect

The name of the generated processing instruction (in XML terms, the `PITarget`) is determined by the `name` attribute. This may be expressed as an attribute value template. The name must be valid as a `PITarget` as defined in the XML specification, and XSLT imposes the additional rule that it must be a valid `NCName`, as defined in the XML Namespaces Recommendation. This means it must be an XML

Name that doesn't contain a colon (to make it an NCName) and that isn't the name «xml» in any mixture of upper and lower case (to make it a PITarget).

The specification is quite explicit that <xsl:processing-instruction> cannot be used to generate an XML declaration at the start of the output file. The XML declaration looks like a processing instruction, but technically it isn't one; and the ban on using the name «xml» makes this quite explicit. The XML declaration in the output file is generated automatically by the XSLT processor, and can be controlled to a limited extent using the <xsl:output> element.

The string value of the processing instruction (which corresponds to the data part of a processing instruction in XML terms) is generated using either the select attribute or the contained sequence constructor. If neither is present, the string value of the processing instruction node will be a zero-length string.

The space that separates the PITarget from the data is produced automatically when a processing instruction node is serialized. It is not present in the tree model.

The sequence produced by evaluating the select attribute or the contained sequence constructor is first atomized, and each item in the atomized sequence is then converted to a string. If the select attribute is present, these strings are concatenated with a single space between adjacent strings; if a sequence constructor is used, they are concatenated with no separator. The resulting string forms the string value of the new processing instruction. For more details of this process, including error conditions that can arise, see <xsl:attribute> on page 211, which works in exactly the same way.

The resulting string value must not contain the string «?>», which terminates a processing instruction. Implementations are allowed to trap the «?>» and replace it by «? >» (with an embedded space); unfortunately they are also allowed to report this as an error, so if you want your stylesheet to be portable, you need to make sure this condition can't happen.

The data part of a processing instruction cannot contain character references such as «₤», so it is an error to output any characters that can't be represented directly in the chosen character encoding of the output file. Some processing instructions may accept data that looks like a character reference, but this is an application-level convention, not something defined in the XML standard, so the XSLT processor will never generate such a reference automatically.

Usage

Use this instruction when you want to output a processing instruction.

Processing instructions are not widely used in most XML applications, so you will probably not need to use this instruction very often. They are used even less in HTML, though HTML 4.0 does recommend that any vendor-specific extensions should be implemented this way. In HTML the terminator for a processing instruction is «>» rather than «?>», and this difference is handled automatically during serialization by the HTML output method; see <xsl:output> on page 375.

Note that you cannot generate a processing instruction in the output by writing a processing instruction in the stylesheet. Processing instructions in the stylesheet are ignored completely. You can, however, use <xsl:copy> or <xsl:copy-of> to copy processing instructions from the source tree to the result tree.

Examples

The following example outputs an `<?xml-stylesheet?>` processing instruction at the start of the output file:

```
<xsl:processing-instruction name="xml-stylesheet">
  <xsl:text>href="housestyle.css" type="text/css"</xsl:text>
</xsl:processing-instruction>
```

The generated output is:

```
<?xml-stylesheet href="housestyle.css" type="text/css"?>
```

Writing an XSLT stylesheet that produces an XML document that itself refers to a CSS stylesheet isn't such a crazy thing to do as it might seem. It often makes sense to do the first stage of processing of an XML file on the server, and the second stage on the client (in other words, in the browser). The first stage will extract the data that users want to see—and, most importantly, remove any information they are not allowed to see. The second stage applies the detailed rules for output formatting. The second stage can often be done just as easily with CSS as with XSLT, because anything CSS can't cope with, such as adding or reordering textual content, can be done in the first stage with XSLT.

One point to watch out for in generating an `<?xml-stylesheet?>` processing instruction, and which might well apply to other processing instructions, is the use of pseudoattributes and pseudo character and entity references. The text «`href="housestyle.css"`» in the above example is designed to look like an XML attribute, but it is not actually an XML attribute; it is purely part of the processing instruction data. It is parsed by the application, not by the XML parser. As it is not a true XML attribute, you cannot generate it as an attribute node using the `<xsl:attribute>` instruction; rather, it is generated as text.

The rules for the `<?xml-stylesheet?>` processing instruction are defined in a short W3C Recommendation called *Associating Style Sheets with XML Documents*, available at `http://www.w3.org/TR/xml-stylesheet`. In addition to defining the data part of this processing instruction in the form of pseudoattributes, the rules also allow the use of numeric character references such as «`&#x20A4;`» and predefined entity references such as «`&gt;`» and «`&amp;`». Again, these are not true character references and entity references that the XML parser will recognize, and as a result they will not be generated by the XSLT processor either. If you want to include «`&#x20A4;`» as part of the data of the processing instruction, you can write, for example,

```
<xsl:processing-instruction name="xml-stylesheet">
  <xsl:text>href="housestyle.css" type="text/css" </xsl:text>
  <xsl:text>title="A title containing &amp;#x20A4;" </xsl:text>
</xsl:processing-instruction>
```

Another way of generating this processing instruction, which might be more suitable if the contents are highly variable, is to write a general template that takes the required information as a parameter. This parameter might be supplied in the form of an element:

```
<pi-data name="xml-stylesheet">
  <href>housestyle.css</href>
  <type>text/css</type>
  <title>a title</title>
</pi-data>
```

and the processing instruction might be generated by the template:

```
<xsl:template name="make-pi">
  <xsl:param name="pi-data" required="yes"/>
  <xsl:processing-instruction name="{$pi-data/@name}"
      select="for $att in $pi-data/* return
              concat(name($att), '=&quot;', string($att), '&quot;')"/>
</xsl:template>
```

This does not attempt to deal with the problems that arise if there are special characters in the data that need to be escaped. Note that the space that is needed between pseudoattributes is generated automatically, because each pseudoattribute is produced as one item in the result of the `select` attribute.

xsl:result-document

The `<xsl:result-document>` instruction is used to create a new result tree, and optionally to specify how the result tree should be serialized. The facility allows a transformation to produce multiple result documents, so you can write a stylesheet that splits a large XML file into smaller XML files, or into multiple HTML files, perhaps connected to each other by hyperlinks.

Changes in 2.0

This instruction is new in XSLT 2.0. Many XSLT 1.0 processors provided a similar capability as a proprietary extension, but there are likely to be differences in the detail.

Format

```
<xsl:result-document
  format? = qname
  href? = { uri-reference }
  validation? = "strict" | "lax" | "preserve" | "strip"
  as? = sequence-type>
  <!-- Content: sequence-constructor -->
</xsl:result-document>
```

Position

`<xsl:result-document>` is an instruction, which means it may occur anywhere in a sequence constructor.

Attributes

Name	Value	Meaning
href optional	Attribute value template returning a relative or absolute URI	Defines the location where the output document will be written after serialization
format optional	lexical QName	Defines the required output format

Name	Value	Meaning
validation optional	«strict», «lax», «preserve», or «strip»	Defines the validation to be applied to the result tree
type optional	lexical QName	Defines the schema type against which the document element should be validated

Note: the Working Group has agreed a late addition to this instruction, which allows it to take any of the serialization attributes defined on the `<xsl:output>` element, such as indent and encoding. These attributes can be specified as attribute value templates; they supplement and override those on the output definition named in the format attribute.

Content

The content of the `<xsl:result-document>` element is a sequence constructor.

The `<xsl:result-document>` element may contain an `<xsl:fallback>` element. If it does, the `<xsl:fallback>` element defines the action that an XSLT 1.0 processor will take when it encounters the `<xsl:result-document>` instruction. Note that the fallback processing only applies if the stylesheet is executing in forwards-compatible mode, which will be the case if you set «version="2.0"» on the `<xsl:stylesheet>` element, or «xsl:version="2.0"» on any enclosing literal result element. (XSLT 1.0 processors do not recognize a version attribute on any other element.)

Effect

When the `<xsl:result-document>` instruction is evaluated, a new document node is created, in the same way as for the `<xsl:document>` instruction. The sequence constructor contained in the `<xsl:result-document>` is evaluated to produce a sequence of nodes and items, and this sequence is used to form the content of the document node as described under `<xsl:document>` in the section *The Content of the Document* on page 258. The tree rooted at this document node is referred to as a result tree.

Validation of the result tree also follows the same rules as `<xsl:document>`: See *Validating and Annotating the Document* on page 259. Note that although the validation process (if requested) conceptually creates a result tree in which the elements and attributes are annotated with types, these type annotations will never be seen if the result tree is immediately serialized. But a very useful processing model is to run a series of transformations in a pipeline, where the output of one stylesheet provides the input to the next. The pipeline might also include non-XSLT applications. For example, an XML database product might allow you to run a transformation as part of the process of loading new documents into the database, in which case the result of the transformation might well be captured directly in the database, complete with type information.

The difference between `<xsl:document>` and `<xsl:result-document>` is that `<xsl:document>` adds the new document node to the result sequence, making it available for further processing by the stylesheet, while `<xsl:result-document>` outputs the new document as a final result of the transformation.

What actually happens to the result tree is to some degree system-dependent, and it is likely that vendors will provide a degree of control over this through the processor API.

415

Often, the result tree will be serialized (perhaps as XML or HTML) and written to a file on disk. The format in which it is serialized is then controlled using the `format` attribute, and the location of the file on disk will typically be controlled using the `href` attribute.

If the `format` attribute is present then its value must be a lexical QName, which must match the name of an `<xsl:output>` declaration in the stylesheet. The result tree will then be serialized as specified by that `<xsl:output>` declaration. If there is no `format` attribute then the result tree (assuming it is serialized at all) will be serialized as specified by the unnamed `<xsl:output>` declaration if there is one, or the default serialization rules if not.

The way in which the `href` attribute is used is deliberately left a little vague in the specification, because the details are likely to be implementation-dependent. Its value is a relative or absolute URI. Details of the URI schemes that may be specified are left entirely to the implementation. The specification is also written in such a way that the URI can be interpreted as referring either to the result tree itself, or to its serialized representation. The important thing that the specification says is that it is safe to use relative URIs as links from one output document to another: If you create one result document with «href=`"chap1.html"`» and another with «href=`"chap2.html"`», then the content of the first document can include an element such as `<a href="chap2.html">next chapter</a>` and expect the link to work, whether the result trees are actually serialized or not. The specification achieves this by saying that any relative URI used in the `href` attribute of an `<xsl:result-document>` element is interpreted relative to a *Base Output URI*, which in effect is supplied in the API that invokes the transformation.

> *We are used to thinking of URIs rather like filenames: as addresses of documents found somewhere on the disk. In fact, URIs are intended to be used as unique names for any kind of resource, hence their use for identifying namespaces and collations. Using URIs to identify result trees (which might exist only as a data structure in memory) is no different. Implementations are expected to provide some kind of mechanism in their API to allow the application to process the result tree, given its URI.*

> *One way this might be done is to allow the application, when the transformation is complete, to use a method call such as* `getResultDocument(URI)` *to get a reference to the result tree with a given URI, perhaps returned in the form of a DOM document.*

> *Another possible mechanism would be for the application to supply a resolver or listener object, which is notified whenever a result tree is created.*

The specification of `<xsl:result-document>` is complicated by the fact that it is an instruction that has side effects. The instruction does not return a result (technically, it returns an empty sequence, which means it doesn't affect the result of evaluating the sequence constructor that it is part of). In a pure functional language, side effects are always problematical—though, of course, the only purpose of running any program is to change something in the environment in which it is run. Normally, if a compiler knows that a particular construct will return a particular result, then it can generate code that short cuts the evaluation of this construct. But it would destroy the purpose of `<xsl:result-document>` if it did nothing, just because the compiler already knows what result it will return.

To take an example of how this is a problem in practice, suppose that the stylesheet defined a variable as follows:

```
<xsl:variable name="dummy">
    <xsl:result-document href="hello.xml">
        <hello to="world"/>
    </xsl:result-document>
    <xsl:sequence select="3"/>
</xsl:variable>
```

Now suppose that this variable is never referenced. Is the result document produced, or not? Normally, an XSLT optimizer will avoid evaluating variables that aren't referenced, but this strategy becomes problematic if the evaluation of a variable has a side effect.

The way that the XSLT specification has dealt with this problem is essentially to say that you can only use `<xsl:result-document>` when the sequence constructor you are evaluating is destined to form the content of a result tree. When the stylesheet starts executing, this condition is true for the sequence constructor contained in the first template to be evaluated, and it remains true except when you evaluate `<xsl:variable>` or similar elements such as `<xsl:param>`, `<xsl:with-param>`, and `<xsl:message>`. You also can't use `<xsl:result-document>` while evaluating the result of a stylesheet function defined using `<xsl:function>`, or while computing the content of `<xsl:attribute>`, `<xsl:comment>`, `<xsl:value-of>`, `<xsl:namespace>`, `<xsl:processing-instruction>`, `<xsl:key>`, or `<xsl:sort>`. This restriction is a runtime rule rather than a compile-time rule, for example you can use `<xsl:result-document>` within `<xsl:template>` if the template is called from within `<xsl:element>`, but not if it's called from within `<xsl:variable>`.

XSLT processors are allowed to evaluate instructions in any order. This means that you can't reliably predict the order in which result trees get written. There is a rule preventing a stylesheet from writing two different result trees with the same URI, because if overwriting was allowed, the results would be nondeterministic. There is also a rule saying that it's an error to attempt to write a result tree and then read it back again using the `document()` function: This would be a sneaky way of exploiting side effects and making your stylesheet dependent on the order of execution. In practice, processors may have difficulty detecting this error and you might get away with it.

The fact that order of execution is unpredictable has another consequence: If a transformation doesn't run to completion, because a runtime error occurred (or perhaps because `<xsl:message>` was used with «`terminate="yes"`») then it's unpredictable as to whether a particular result tree was output before the termination. In practice most processors only exploit the freedom to change the order of execution when evaluating variables or functions, so you are unlikely to run into this problem in practice.

Usage

Generating multiple output files is something I have often found useful when doing transformations. A typical scenario is that a weighty publication, such as a dictionary, is managed as a single XML file, which would be far too large to download for a user who only wants to see a few entries. So the first stage in preparing it for human consumption is to split it up into bite-sized chunks, perhaps one document per letter of the alphabet or even one per dictionary headword. You can make these chunks individual HTML pages, but I usually find it's better to do the transformation in two stages: First split the large XML document into several small XML documents, and then convert each of these into HTML independently.

The usual model is to generate one principal output file and a whole family of secondary output files. The principal output file can then serve as an index. Often you'll need to keep links between the files so that you can easily assemble them again (using the `document()` function described on page 532 in Chapter 7), or so that you can generate hyperlinks for the user to follow.

Examples

This feature is often used to break up large documents into manageable chunks. In the section for `<xsl:param>` on page 392 there is an example of a stylesheet that breaks up a Shakespeare play to produce a cover page together with one page per scene. But here we'll illustrate the principle with a much smaller document.

Example: Creating Multiple Output Files

This example takes a poem as input, and outputs each stanza to a separate file. A more realistic example would be to split a book into its chapters, but I wanted to keep the files small.

Source

The source file is `poem.xml`. It starts:

```
<poem>
<author>Rupert Brooke</author>
<date>1912</date>
<title>Song</title>
<stanza>
<line>And suddenly the wind comes soft,</line>
<line>And Spring is here again;</line>
<line>And the hawthorn quickens with buds of green</line>
<line>And my heart with buds of pain.</line>
</stanza>
<stanza>
<line>My heart all Winter lay so numb,</line>
<line>The earth so dead and frore,</line>
...
```

Stylesheet

The stylesheet is `split.xsl`.

We want to start a new output document for each stanza, so we use the `<xsl:result-document>` instruction in the template rule for the `<stanza>` element. Its effect is to switch all output produced by its sequence constructor to a different output file. In fact, it's very similar to the effect of an `<xsl:variable>` element that creates a tree, except that the tree, instead of being a temporary tree, is serialized directly to an output file of its own:

```
<?xml version="1.0"?>
<xsl:stylesheet xmlns:xsl="http://www.w3.org/1999/XSL/Transform"
                version="2.0">

<xsl:template match="poem">
   <poem>
      <xsl:copy-of select="title, author, date"/>
      <xsl:apply-templates select="stanza"/>
   </poem>
</xsl:template>

<xsl:template match="stanza">
   <xsl:variable name="file"
                 select="concat('verse', string(position()), '.xml')"/>
```

```
      <verse number="{position()}" href="{$file}"/>
      <xsl:result-document href="{$file}">
          <xsl:copy-of select="."/>
      </xsl:result-document>
  </xsl:template>
</xsl:stylesheet>
```

To run this example under Saxon, you need to make sure that an output file is supplied for the principal output document. This determines the base output URI, and the other output documents will be written to locations that are relative to this base URI. For example:

```
java c:\saxon\saxon7.jar -o c:\temp\index.xml poem.xml split.xsl
```

This will write the index document to c:\temp\index.xml, and the verses to files such as c:\temp\verse2.xml.

Output

The principal output file contains the skeletal poem below (new lines added for legibility):

```
<?xml version="1.0" encoding="utf-8" ?>
<poem>
<title>Song</title>
<author>Rupert Brooke</author>
<date>1912</date>
<verse number="1" href="verse1.xml"/>
<verse number="2" href="verse2.xml"/>
<verse number="3" href="verse3.xml"/>
</poem>
```

Three further output files verse1.xml, verse2.xml, and verse3.xml are created in the same directory as the principal output file. Here is verse1.xml:

```
<?xml version="1.0" encoding="utf-8" ?>
<stanza>
<line>And suddenly the wind comes soft,</line>
<line>And Spring is here again;</line>
<line>And the hawthorn quickens with buds of green</line>
<line>And my heart with buds of pain.</line>
</stanza>
```

For another version of this example, which uses the element-available() function to test whether the <xsl:result-document> instruction is implemented and takes fallback action if not, see the entry for element-available() on page 542 in Chapter 7.

See Also

<xsl:output> on page 375

xsl:sequence

The `<xsl:sequence>` element is used to deliver an arbitrary sequence, which may contain atomic values, nodes, or a combination of the two. It is the only XSLT instruction (with the exception of `<xsl:perform-sort>`) that can return references to existing nodes, as distinct from newly constructed nodes. Its most common use is to return the result of a stylesheet function.

Despite its name, `<xsl:sequence>` is often used to return a single item.

Changes in 2.0

This instruction is new in XSLT 2.0

Format

```
<xsl:sequence
  select? = expression
  <!-- Content: <xsl:fallback>* -->
</xsl:sequence>
```

Position

`<xsl:sequence>` is an instruction, and may be used anywhere within a sequence constructor. It is often used within `<xsl:function>`, to define the value that the function returns.

Attributes

Name	Value	Meaning
select optional	Expression	Computes the value that the `<xsl:sequence>` instruction will return

Content

The only content permitted is `<xsl:fallback>`. Any contained `<xsl:fallback>` instructions will be ignored by an XSLT 2.0 processor, but can be used to define fallback action for an XSLT 1.0 processor.

Effect

If a `select` attribute is present, then the XPath expression contained in this attribute is evaluated, and the result of the XPath expression is returned as the result of the `<xsl:sequence>` instruction.

If no `select` attribute is present, then the sequence constructor is evaluated, and this provides the result of the `<xsl:sequence>` instruction.

Usage and Examples

This innocent-looking instruction introduced in XSLT 2.0 has far-reaching effects on the capability of the XSLT language, because it means that XSLT instructions and sequence constructors (and hence functions and templates) become capable of returning any value allowed by the XPath data model. Without it, XSLT instructions could only be used to create new nodes in a result tree, but with it, they can also return atomic values and references to existing nodes.

To take an example, suppose you want to set a variable whose value is the numeric value of the `price` attribute of the context node, minus the value of the `discount` attribute if present. In XSLT 1.0 you might have written:

```
<xsl:variable name="discounted-price">
  <xsl:choose>
    <xsl:when test="@discount">
      <xsl:value-of select="@price - @discount"/>
    </xsl:when>
    <xsl:otherwise>
      <xsl:value-of select="@price"/>
    </xsl:otherwise>
  </xsl:choose>
</xsl:variable>
```

This works, but the problem is that the result is not a number, but a temporary tree (in XSLT 1.0 terminology, a result tree fragment) containing a text node that holds a string representation of the number. Not only is this an inefficient way of representing a number, it has also lost the type information, which means that if you use the value in operations that are sensitive to data type, such as comparison or sorting, you might get an unexpected answer.

In XSLT 2.0, using the `<xsl:sequence>` instruction, you can rewrite this as:

```
<xsl:variable name="discounted-price" as="xs:double">
  <xsl:choose>
    <xsl:when test="@discount">
      <xsl:sequence select="@price - @discount"/>
    </xsl:when>
    <xsl:otherwise>
      <xsl:sequence select="@price"/>
    </xsl:otherwise>
  </xsl:choose>
</xsl:variable>
```

Within the `<xsl:when>` and `<xsl:otherwise>` branches, we now use `<xsl:sequence>` rather than `<xsl:value-of>`, to avoid creating a text node that we don't need. Look at the example carefully:

❑ The first `<xsl:sequence>` instruction contains an XPath arithmetic expression. If the source document has a schema, this assumes that the type of `@price` and `@discount` is numeric (typically, `xs:decimal`), and the result of the subtraction will be the same numeric type. If there is no schema, the nodes will be untyped, and the fact that they are used in an arithmetic expression will force the content of the attribute to be converted to an `xs:double`, which means that the result of the subtraction will also be an `xs:double`. The as attribute on the

`<xsl:variable>` element ensures that whatever the numeric type of the result, it will be converted to an `xs:double`.

❑ The second `<xsl:sequence>` instruction simply returns the attribute node `@price` itself. The as attribute on the `<xsl:variable>` element causes the attribute node to be atomized, which extracts its typed value. If there is a schema, the node must be annotated with a numeric type for the conversion to `xs:double` to succeed. If there is no schema, then the string value of the attribute is converted to `xs:double` by casting.

❑ The «`as="xs:double"`» on the `<xsl:variable>` element ensures that a type error will be reported (typically at runtime) if there is no `@price` attribute, or if the content of the `@price` or `@discount` attribute is not numeric. Unlike the `number()` function, casting to `xs:double` gives an error (rather than NaN) if the input is non-numeric.

❑ The first `<xsl:sequence>` instruction could be replaced by `<xsl:copy-of>` without any change in the meaning. When the `select` attribute returns atomic values, `<xsl:sequence>` and `<xsl:copy-of>` have exactly the same effect. If the second `<xsl:sequence>` instruction were replaced by `<xsl:copy-of>`, however, the effect would be subtly different. `<xsl:copy-of>` would create a copy of the attribute node, which is quite unnecessary in this case.

❑ Without the «`as="xs:double"`» on the `<xsl:variable>` element, all our efforts to return a numeric value rather than a temporary tree would be wasted; when `<xsl:variable>` has no `select` or as attribute, it automatically builds a temporary tree whose content is derived from the value returned by its contained sequence constructor.

It would be possible to rewrite this whole construct as:

```
<xsl:variable name="discounted-price" as="xs:double"
    select="if (@discount)
            then @price - @discount
            else @price"/>
```

This illustrates that when you are calculating values, you often have a choice as to whether to do the work at the XPath level or at the XSLT level. My own preference with simple expressions such as this is to use the XPath approach, unless there is a need to use facilities that are only available at the XSLT level, such as the ability to create new nodes, or the more powerful instructions available in XSLT such as `<xsl:number>`, `<xsl:analyze-string>`, or `<xsl:for-each-group>`.

By far the most common use of `<xsl:sequence>` is the evaluation of the result of a stylesheet function, and there are examples of this under `<xsl:function>` on page 300.

The `<xsl:sequence>` instruction also enables template rules to return atomic values, or references to existing nodes. An example of the possibilities this opens up is shown in the section *Simulating Higher Order Functions* on page 198, which shows a generalized function for finding cycles in any XML data source, regardless of how the relationships are represented.

See Also

`<xsl:function>` on page 300.
`<xsl:copy-of>` on page 245.
`<xsl:template>` on page 450.

xsl:sort

The `<xsl:sort>` element is used to define a component of a sort key. It is used within an `<xsl:apply-templates>`, `<xsl:for-each>`, `<xsl:for-each-group>`, or `<xsl:perform-sort>` instruction to define the order in which this instruction processes its data.

Changes in 2.0

The `<xsl:sort>` element may now be used within `<xsl:for-each-group>` and `<xsl:perform-sort>` as well as within `<xsl:apply-templates>` and `<xsl:for-each>`.

The value of the sort key may be calculated using an enclosed sequence constructor, as an alternative to using the `select` attribute.

In XSLT 1.0, `<xsl:sort>` was always used to sort a set of nodes. In 2.0 it is generalized so that it can sort any sequence.

A `collation` attribute has been added to allow the collating sequence for strings to be specified by means of a URI.

Sorting is now sensitive to the data types of the items being sorted. For example, if the sort key values are numeric, they will be compared as numbers rather than as strings.

Format

```
<xsl:sort
  select? = expression
  lang? = { nmtoken }
  order? = { "ascending" | "descending" }
  collation? = { uri }
  case-order? = { "upper-first" | "lower-first" }
  data-type? = { "text" | "number" | qname-but-not-ncname }>
  stable = { "yes" | "no" }
  <!-- Content: sequence-constructor -->
</xsl:sort>
```

Position

`<xsl:sort>` is always a child of `<xsl:apply-templates>`, `<xsl:for-each>`, `<xsl:for-each-group>`, or `<xsl:perform-sort>`. Any number of sort keys may be specified, in major-to-minor order.

When used in `<xsl:for-each>`, `<xsl:for-each-group>`, or `<xsl:perform-sort>`, any `<xsl:sort>` elements must appear before the sequence constructor of the containing element.

When used in `<xsl:apply-templates>`, the `<xsl:sort>` elements can come before or after any `<xsl:with-param>` elements.

Attributes

Name	Value	Meaning
select optional	Expression	Defines the sort key.
order optional	Attribute value template returning «ascending» | «descending»	Defines whether the nodes are processed in ascending or descending order of this key. The default is «ascending»
case-order optional	Attribute value template returning «upper-first» | «lower-first»	Defines whether upper-case letters are to be collated before or after lower-case letters. The default is language-dependent
lang optional	Attribute value template returning a language code	Defines the language whose collating conventions are to be used. The default depends on the processing environment
data-type optional	Attribute value template returning «text» | «number» | QName	Defines whether the values are to be collated alphabetically or numerically, or using a user-defined data type. The default is «text»
collation optional	Attribute value template returning collation URI	The collation URI identifies how strings are to be compared with each other
stable optional	Attribute value template returning «yes» | «no»	This attribute is allowed only on the first `<xsl:sort>` element; if set to «no», it indicates that there is no requirement to retain the original order of items that have equal values for all the sort keys

A number of these attributes can be written as attribute value templates. The context item, context position, and context size for evaluating these attribute value templates are the same as the context for evaluating the `select` attribute of the containing instruction (that is `<xsl:for-each>`, `<xsl:apply-templates>`, `<xsl:for-each-group>`, or `<xsl:perform-sort>`).

Content

The element may contain a sequence constructor. This is used to compute the sort key value, as an alternative to using the `select` attribute. The two are mutually exclusive: If the `select` attribute is present, the element must be empty, and if it is not empty, the `select` attribute must be omitted.

Effect

The list of `<xsl:sort>` elements appearing for example within an `<xsl:apply-templates>` or `<xsl:for-each>` element determines the order in which the selected items are processed. The items are sorted first by the first sort key; any group of items that have duplicate values for the first sort key are then sorted by the second sort key, and so on.

It's useful to start by establishing some clear terminology. There is a tendency to use the phrase *sort key* with several different meanings, often in the same sentence, so to avoid confusion I'll try to stick to the more precise terms that are used in the XSLT specification itself.

❑ A collection of `<xsl:sort>` elements, which together define all the criteria for performing a sort, is called a *sort key specification*.

❑ A single `<xsl:sort>` element within the sort key specification is called a *sort key component*. Often, of course, there will only be one component in a sort key specification.

❑ The result of evaluating a sort key component for one of the items to be sorted is called a *sort key value*.

So if you are sorting by last name and then first name, the sort key specification is "last name, then first name;" the sort key components are "last name" and "first name," and the sort key values are strings such as `"Kay"` and `"Michael"`.

It's also useful to be clear about how we describe the sorting process:

❑ The sequence that provides the input to the sort operation is called the *initial sequence*. In XSLT 1.0 the initial sequence was always a set of nodes in document order, but in 2.0 it can be any sequence of items (nodes or atomic values) in any order.

❑ The sequence that is produced as the output of the sort operation is called (naturally enough) the *sorted sequence*.

The overall rules for the sorting operation are fairly intuitive, but it's worth stating them for completeness:

❑ Given two items A and B in the initial sequence, their relative positions in the sorted sequence are determined by evaluating all their sort key values, one for each component in the sort key specification.

❑ The relative positions of A and B depend on the first pair of sort key values that is different for A and B; the second pair of sort key values needs to be considered only if the first sort key values for the two items are equal, and so on. For example, if you are sorting by last name and then first name, the system will only need to consider the first name for two individuals who have the same last name. I will explain later exactly what it means for one sort key value to be considered equal to another.

❑ Considering only this pair of sort key values, A comes before B in the sorted sequence if A's value for this sort key component is less than B's value, unless «order="descending"» is specified for this sort key component, in which case it comes after B. I will explain later what it means for one sort key value to be "less than" another.

❑ If all the sort key values for A and B are the same, then A and B appear in the sorted sequence in the same relative positions that they had in the initial sequence (the technical term for this is that the sort is *stable*). However, if «stable="no"» is specified on the first `<xsl:sort>` element, this requirement is waived, and the system can return duplicates in any order.

The sort key value for each item in the initial sequence is established by evaluating the expression given in the `select` attribute, or by evaluating the contained sequence constructor. These are mutually exclusive:

If there is a `select` attribute, then the `<xsl:sort>` element must be empty. If neither a `select` attribute nor a sequence constructor is present, the default is equivalent to specifying «`select="."`».

The `select` expression (or sequence constructor) is evaluated for each item, with this item as the context item, its position in the initial sequence as the context position, and with the number of items in the initial sequence as the context size.

This means that if you want to process a sequence in reverse order, you can specify a sort key as:

```
<xsl:sort select="position()" order="descending" />
```

You can also achieve other crafty effects: Try, for example, sorting by «`position() mod 3`». This can be useful if you need to arrange data vertically in a table.

This just leaves the question of how the system decides whether one sort key value is equal to or less than another. The basic rule is that the result is decided using the XPath «`eq`» and «`lt`» operators. These are essentially the same as the «`=`» and «`<`» operators, except that they only compare a single atomic value to another single atomic value, and perform no type conversions other than numeric promotion (which means, for example, that if one operand is an integer and the other is a double, the integer will be converted to a double in order to perform the comparison).

There are several caveats to this general rule:

❑   The «`lt`» operator may raise an error when comparing values of different types (such as a number and a date) or when comparing two values of the same type for which no ordering relation is defined (for example, instances of the type `xs:QName`). If this happens then the XSLT processor has a choice: It can either treat this as a fatal error, or it can continue by assigning an implementation-defined ordering to these items. (This might mean, for example, that if you sort a mixture of strings and numbers, the output will contain all the strings followed by all the numbers, or all the numbers followed by all the strings.)

❑   The `<xsl:sort>` element has an attribute `data-type`. This is only there for backwards compatibility with XSLT 1.0, but you can still use it. If the value of the attribute is «`text`», then the sort key values are converted to strings (using the XPath casting rules) before being compared. If the value is «`number`», then they are cast to the type `xs:double`. The attribute also allows the value to be a prefixed QName, but the meaning of this entirely depends on the implementation. The feature was probably added to XSLT 1.0 to anticipate the use of schema-defined type names such as `xs:date`, and the implementation may allow this usage, but it's not defined in the standard. Instead, if you want to convert the sort key values to a particular type to do the comparison, you can achieve this using a cast or constructor function within the `select` attribute: for example, «`select="xs:date(@date-of-birth)"`».

❑   Another option that has been retained for backwards compatibility with XSLT 1.0 is the ability to supply a sequence of values as the result of the `select` attribute, rather than a single value. XSLT 1.0 allowed the value of the expression to be a node set (a sequence of nodes in document order), and took the string value of the first node in the set as the effective value of the sort key, ignoring any other nodes. This behavior (generalized to any sequence of items) is still available in XSLT 2.0, but only if running in backwards compatibility mode. The `<xsl:sort>` element is in backwards compatibility mode if this element, or an ancestor of this element in the stylesheet module, has a `version` attribute (or `xsl:version` in the case of a literal result element) whose value is «`1.0`». If this is not the case, then supplying a sequence of more than one item as the sort key value will cause an error.

❏ It is possible that evaluating a sort key value will return the empty sequence. XSLT specifies that for sorting purposes, the empty sequence is considered to be equal to itself and less than any other value.

❏ Another possibility is that when evaluating a numeric sort key value, the value will be the special value NaN (not a number). This would happen, for example, if you specify «select="number(@price)"» and the element has no price attribute, or a price attribute whose value is «$10.00» (the «$» sign will cause the conversion to a number to fail). XSLT specifies that for sorting purposes, NaN is considered equal to itself, and less than any other numeric value (but greater than an empty sequence). This is different from the results of using the XPath comparison operators, where «eq» returns false if both operands are NaN.

❏ Last and not least, if the two values are strings, then they are compared using a collation. Collations are a broad subject and so we will devote a separate section to them.

The order attribute specifies whether the order is ascending or descending. Descending order will produce the opposite result of ascending order. This means, for example, that NaN values will appear last rather than first, and also that the effect of the case-order attribute is reversed: If you specify «case-order="upper-first"» with «order="descending"», then *drall* will come before *Drall*.

The final sorted order of the items determines the sequence in which they are processed by the containing <xsl:apply-templates>, <xsl:for-each>, or <xsl:for-each-group> instruction, or the order in which they are returned by the containing <xsl:perform-sort> instruction. While the sorted sequence is being processed, the value of position() will reflect the position of the current item in the sorted sequence.

Collations

When the sort key values to be compared are strings, they are compared using a collation. A collation is essentially a mechanism for deciding whether two strings such as «polish» and «Polish» are considered equal, and if not, which of them should come first.

Choosing the right collation depends on the data that you are sorting, and on the expectations of the users. These expectations vary by country (in Germany, in most modern publications, «ä» is sorted along with «a», but in Sweden, it is sorted after «z») and also vary according to the application. Telephone directories, dictionaries, gazetteers, and back-of-book indexes each have their own rules.

XSLT 2.0 and XPath 2.0 share similar mechanisms for dealing with collations, because they are needed not only in sorting, but also in defining what operators such as «eq» mean, and in functions such as distinct-values(). The assumption behind the design is that many computing environments (for example the Windows operating system, the Java virtual machine, or the Oracle database platform) already include extensive mechanisms for defining and customizing collations, and that XSLT processors will be written to take advantage of these. As a result, sorting order will not be identical between different implementations.

The basic model is that a collation (a set of rules for determining string ordering) is identified by a URI. Like a namespace URI, this is an abstract identifier, not necessarily the location of a document somewhere on the Web. The form of the URI, and its meaning, is entirely up to the implementation. At the time of writing there is talk of IANA (the Internet Assigned Numbers Authority) setting up a register of collation names, but even if this comes to fruition, it will still be up to the implementation to decide whether to support these registered collations or not. Until such time, the best you can do to achieve interoperability is pass the collation URI to the stylesheet as a parameter; the API can then sort out the logic for choosing different collations according to which processor you are using.

The Unicode consortium has published an algorithm for collating strings called the Unicode Collation Algorithm (see `http://www.unicode.org/unicode/reports/tr10/index.html`). Although the XSLT specification refers to this document, it doesn't say that implementations have to support it. In practice, many of the facilities available in platforms such as Windows and Java are closely based on this algorithm. The Unicode Collation Algorithm is not itself a collation, because it can be parameterized. Rather, it is a framework for defining a collation with the particular properties that you are looking for.

You can specify the URI of the collation to be used in the `collation` attribute of the `<xsl:sort>` element. This is an attribute value template, so you can write `<xsl:sort collation= "{$collation-uri}">` to use a collation that has been passed to the stylesheet as a parameter.

There is one collation URI that every implementation is required to support, called the *Unicode codepoint collation* (not to be confused with the Unicode Collation Algorithm mentioned earlier). In the current drafts of the specification this is selected using the URI

    http://www.w3.org/2003/11/xpath-functions/collation/codepoint

but the final URI is likely to change as the specification reaches Recommendation status.

Under the codepoint collation, strings are simply compared using the numeric code values of the characters in the string: If two characters have the same Unicode codepoint they are equal, and if one has a numerically lower Unicode codepoint, then it comes first. This isn't a very sophisticated or user-friendly algorithm, but it has the advantage of being cheap and cheerful. If you are sorting strings that use a limited alphabet, for example part numbers, then it is probably perfectly adequate.

If you specify a collation that the implementation doesn't recognize, then it raises an error. However, the word "recognize" is deliberately vague. An implementation could choose to recognize every possible collation URI that you might throw at it, and never raise this error at all. More probably, an implementation might decide to use parameterized URIs (for example, allowing a component such as «language=fr» to select the target language), and it's then an implementation decision whether to "recognize" a URI that contains invalid or missing parameters.

If you don't specify the collation attribute on `<xsl:sort>`, you can provide a hint as to what kind of collation you want by specifying the `lang` and/or `case-order` attributes. These are retained from XSLT 1.0, which didn't support explicit collation URIs, but they are still available for use in 2.0.

❑   The `lang` attribute specifies the language whose collation rules are to be used (this might be the language of the data, or the language of the target user). Its value is specified in the same way as the standard `xml:lang` attribute defined in the XML specification, for example «lang="en-US"» refers to U.S. English and «lang="fr-CA"» refers to Canadian French.

❑   Knowing the language doesn't help you decide whether upper-case or lower-case letters should come first (every dictionary in the world has its own rules on this), so XSLT makes this a separate attribute, `case-order`. Generally case order will be used only to decide the ordering of two words that compare equal if case is ignored. For example, in German, where an initial upper-case letter can change the meaning of a word, some dictionaries list the adjective *drall* (meaning plump or buxom) before the unrelated noun *Drall* (a swerve, twist, or bias), while others reverse the order. Specifying «case-order="lower-first"» would place *drall* immediately before *Drall*, while «case-order="upper-first"» would have *Drall* immediately followed by *drall*.

Usage

In this section we'll consider two specific aspects of sorting that tend to be troublesome. The first is the choice of a collation, and the second is how to achieve dynamic sorting—that is, sorting on a key chosen by the user at runtime, perhaps by clicking on a column heading.

Using Collations

XSLT is designed to be capable of handling serious professional publishing applications, and clearly this requires some fairly powerful sorting capabilities. In practice, however, the most demanding applications almost invariably have domain-specific collating rules; for instance, the rules for sorting personal names in a telephone directory are unlikely to work well for geographical names in a gazetteer. This is why the working groups decided to make the specification so open-ended in its support for collations.

Collations based on the Unicode collation algorithm generally assign each character in the sort key value a set of weights. The primary weight distinguishes characters that are fundamentally different: «A» is different from «B». The secondary weight distinguishes secondary differences, for example the distinction between «A» and «Ä». The tertiary weight is used to represent the difference between upper and lower case, for example «A» and «a». The way that weights are used varies a little in non-Latin scripts, but the principles are similar.

Rather than looking at each character separately, the Unicode collation algorithm compares two strings as a whole. First it looks to see if there are two characters whose primary weights differ; if so, the first such character determines the ordering. If all the primary weights are the same, it looks at the secondary weights, and it only considers the tertiary weights if all the secondary weights are the same. This means for example that in French, «attache» sorts before «attaché», which in turn sorts before «attachement». The acute accent is taken into account when comparing «attache» with «attaché», because there is no primary difference between the strings, but it is ignored when comparing «attaché» with «attachement», because in this case there is a primary difference.

The `strength` of a collation determines what kind of differences it takes into account. For comparing equality between strings, it is often appropriate to use a collation with weak strength: For example a collation with primary strength will treat «attache» as equal to «attaché». (In French this is not necessarily the right thing to do, as these two words have completely different meanings; but it would be appropriate if there is a high possibility that accents have been omitted from one of the strings.) When sorting, however, it is almost always best to use a collation with high strength, which will take secondary and if necessary tertiary differences into account when there are no primary differences.

Sometimes it is better, rather than defining two separate sort key components, to concatenate the sort key values into a single sort key component. For example, if you define a single sort key component as:

```
<xsl:sort select="concat(last-name, ' ', first-name)"/>
```

this might give better results than

```
<xsl:sort select="last-name"/>
<xsl:sort select="first-name"/>
```

This is because in the second case above, a tertiary difference in the last name is considered more significant than a primary difference in the first name: So «MacMillan Tricia» will sort before

«Macmillan Harold». When the sort key values are concatenated, the difference between «MacMillan» and «Macmillan» is only taken into account when the first names are the same.

Dynamic Sort Keys

The select attribute contains an expression which is evaluated for each node, with the node as the context node, to give the value that determines the node's position in the sequence. There's no direct way of specifying that you want to use different sort keys on different occasions. I've seen people try to write things like:

```
<xsl:param name="sort-key" >
. . .
    <xsl:for-each select="BOOK">
        <xsl:sort select="$sort-key"/>
```

hoping that if $sort-key is set to «TITLE», the elements will be sorted by title, and that if $sort-key is set to «AUTHOR», they will be sorted by author. This doesn't work: The variable $sort-key will have the same value for every <BOOK> element, so the books will always be output in unsorted order. In this case, where the sort key is always a child element of the elements being sorted, you can achieve the required effect by writing:

```
<xsl:sort select="*[local-name()=$sort-key]">
```

Another way of making the sort conditional is to use a conditional expression as the sort key. This is much easier in XSLT 2.0 with the introduction of conditional expressions in XPath:

```
<xsl:sort select="if ($sort-key = 'title') then title
                   else if ($sort-key = 'author') then author
                   else if ($sort-key = 'isbn') then isbn
                   else publisher">
```

If the computation of the sort key is really complicated, you can do it in a sequence constructor rather than in the select attribute. This can even invoke templates or build temporary trees—there are no limits.

There are two other solutions to this problem that are worth mentioning, although both have their disadvantages:

❑　One is to generate or modify the stylesheet before compiling it, so that it includes the actual sort key required. This technique is popular when transformations are executed in the browser, typically under the control of JavaScript code in the HTML page. The stylesheet is then typically loaded from the server and parsed into a DOM document, which can be modified *in situ* before the transformation starts. The disadvantage is that this means recompiling the stylesheet each time it is run: This would probably be an unacceptable overhead if the transformation is running server-side within a Web server.

❑　Another is to use an extension function that permits the evaluation of XPath expressions that have been constructed dynamically, as strings. Such a function, dyn:evaluate(), is defined in the third-party function library at http://www.exslt.org/, and is available in this or a similar form with a number of XSLT processors including Saxon and Xalan.

Examples

I'll start with a couple of simple examples, and then show a full working example that you can download and try yourself.

❑ Example 1: to process all the `<book>` children of the current node, sorting them by the value of the isbn attribute

```
<xsl:apply-templates select="book">
   <xsl:sort select="@isbn"/>
</xsl:apply-templates>
```

❑ Example 2: to output the contents of all the `<city>` elements in the document, in alphabetical order, including each distinct city once only:

```
<ul>
<xsl:for-each select="distinct-values(//city)]">
   <xsl:sort select="."/>
   <li><xsl:value-of select="."/></li>
</xsl:for-each>
</ul>
```

If «select="."» omitted from the `<xsl:sort>` element, the effect would be the same, because this is the default; however, I prefer to include it for clarity.

Example: Sorting on the Result of a Calculation

This example outputs a list of products, sorted by the total sales of each product, in descending order.

Source

This is the file products.xml:

```
<products>
<product name="strawberry jam">
   <region name="south" sales="20.00"/>
   <region name="north" sales="50.00"/>
</product>
<product name="raspberry jam">
   <region name="south" sales="205.16"/>
   <region name="north" sales="10.50"/>
</product>
<product name="plum jam">
   <region name="east" sales="320.20"/>
   <region name="north" sales="39.50"/>
</product>
</products>
```

Stylesheet

`products.xsl` is a complete stylesheet written using the simplified stylesheet syntax, in which the entire stylesheet module is written as a single literal result element. Simplified stylesheets are described in Chapter 3, on page 119.

The `<xsl:sort>` element sorts the selected nodes (all the `<product>` elements) in descending order of the numerical total of the `sales` attribute over all their `<region>` child elements. The total is calculated using the `sum()` function (discussed in *XPath 2.0 Programmer's Reference*, Chapter 10), and displayed using the `format-number()` function (see Chapter 7, page 558).

```
<products xsl:version="2.0"
        xmlns:xsl="http://www.w3.org/1999/XSL/Transform">
<xsl:for-each select="products/product">
    <xsl:sort select="sum(region/@sales)" order="descending"/>
    <product name="{@name}"
            sales="{format-number(sum(region/@sales), '$####0.00')}"/>
</xsl:for-each>
</products>
```

For this to work correctly under XSLT 1.0, you need to add `"data-type="number""` to the `<xsl:sort>` element. This is not needed with XSLT 2.0 because the data type is recognized automatically.

Output

I have added line breaks for readability:

```
<products>
<product name="plum jam" sales="$359.70"/>
<product name="raspberry jam" sales="$215.66"/>
<product name="strawberry jam" sales="$70.00"/>
</products>
```

See Also

`<xsl:apply-templates>` on page 187
`<xsl:for-each>` on page 276
`<xsl:for-each-group>` on page 281
`<xsl:perform-sort>` on page 405

xsl:strip-space

The `<xsl:strip-space>` declaration, along with `<xsl:preserve-space>`, is used to control the way in which whitespace nodes in the source document are handled. The `<xsl:strip-space>` declaration identifies elements in which whitespace-only text nodes are considered insignificant, so they can be removed from the source tree.

Changes in 2.0

The syntax of a NameTest has been extended to allow the format «*:NCName», which matches all elements with a given local name, in any namespace.

Format

```
<xsl:strip-space
    elements = tokens />
```

Position

`<xsl:strip-space>` is a top-level declaration, which means it is always a child of the `<xsl:stylesheet>` element. There are no constraints on where it appears relative to other declarations.

Attributes

Name	Value	Meaning
elements mandatory	Whitespace-separated list of NameTests	Defines elements in the source document whose whitespace-only text nodes are to be removed

The construct NameTest is defined in XPath; because it is used also in XSLT patterns, it is explained in Chapter 6, on page 509.

Content

None, the element is always empty.

Effect, Usage, and Examples

See `<xsl:preserve-space>` on page 406. The two elements `<xsl:strip-space>` and `<xsl:preserve-space>` are closely related, so I have presented the rules and usage guidance in one place.

See Also

`<xsl:preserve-space>` on page 406
`<xsl:text>` on page 459

xsl:stylesheet

The `<xsl:stylesheet>` element is the outermost element of a stylesheet. The synonym `<xsl:transform>` can be used as an alternative.

Changes in 2.0

A new attribute `xpath-default-namespace` has been added, to indicate how unprefixed element names in XPath expressions should be expanded.

A new attribute `default-validation` has been added, to indicate whether and how elements and attributes should be validated if they have no explicit `[xsl:]validation` or `[xsl:]type` attribute.

Format

```
<xsl:stylesheet
  id? = id
  extension-element-prefixes? = tokens
  exclude-result-prefixes? = tokens
  version = number
  xpath-default-namespace? = uri
  default-validation? = "strict" | "lax" | "preserve" | "strip">
  use-when? = expression
  <!-- Content: (xsl:import*, other-declarations) -->
</xsl:stylesheet>
```

Position

`<xsl:stylesheet>` (or its synonym, `<xsl:transform>`) appears as the outermost element of every stylesheet module, except one that uses the *simplified–stylesheet* syntax described on page 119, in Chapter 3. It is used both on a principal stylesheet and on one that is imported or included into another stylesheet.

In addition to being the outermost element of the stylesheet module, the `<xsl:stylesheet>` element is usually the document element of an XML document—but not always; as described in Chapter 3, a stylesheet can also be embedded in another XML document.

Namespace Declarations

There will always be at least one namespace declaration on the `<xsl:stylesheet>` element, typically:

```
xmlns:xsl="http://www.w3.org/1999/XSL/Transform"
```

This is necessary to identify the document as an XSLT stylesheet. The URI part must be written exactly as shown. The prefix «xsl» is conventional, and is used in all XSLT documentation including this book and the standard itself, but you could choose a different prefix if you wanted, for example «XSLT». You would then have to name the element `<XSLT:stylesheet>` instead of `<xsl:stylesheet>`.

You can also make this the default namespace by using the following declaration:

```
xmlns="http://www.w3.org/1999/XSL/Transform"
```

In this case the element name will simply be `<stylesheet>`, and other XSLT elements will similarly be unprefixed, for example `<template>` rather than `<xsl:template>`. Although this works, it is not generally recommended, because the default namespace is then not available for literal result elements. The technique that works best is to reserve the default namespace for literal result elements that you want to go in the default namespace of the output document.

> You may come across a stylesheet that uses the namespace declaration:
> `xmlns:xsl="http://www.w3.org/TR/WD-xsl"`
>
> This is not an XSLT stylesheet at all, but one written in WD-xsl, the working-draft dialect of XSL that Microsoft shipped in 1998 with Internet Explorer 5. This is a very different language, and is not described in this book.

Many stylesheets also need to declare the XML Schema namespace, typically as:

```
xmlns:xs="http://www.w3.org/2001/XMLSchema"
```

This is needed to declare the types of variables or parameters, or use conversions to types such as `xs:integer` and `xs:date`.

Attributes

Name	Value	Meaning
id optional	XML Name	An identifier used to identify the `<xsl:stylesheet>` element when it is embedded in another XML document
version mandatory	Number	Defines the version of XSLT required by this stylesheet. Use «2.0» for a stylesheet that requires XSLT 2.0 features, or «1.0» if you want the stylesheet to be portable between XSLT 1.0 and XSLT 2.0 processors
extension-element-prefixes optional	Whitespace-separated list of NCNames	Defines any namespaces used in this stylesheet to identify extension elements
exclude-result-prefixes optional	Whitespace-separated list of NCNames	Defines any namespaces used in this stylesheet that should not be copied to the output destination, unless they are actually used in the result document
xpath-default-namespace optional	Namespace URI	Defines the namespace URI that is assumed for unprefixed element names and type names occurring in XPath expressions, patterns, and certain other constructs such as the SequenceType in an `as` attribute

Continues

Name	Value	Meaning
default-validation optional	«strict», «lax», «preserve», or «strip»	Defines the validation applied to new element and attribute nodes when the instruction that creates them does not have an [xsl:]validation or [xsl:]type attribute
use-when optional	XPath expression, restricted to use information available at compile time	Defines a condition that must be true if the contents of this stylesheet module are to be included in the stylesheet. It must be possible to evaluate the condition statically, which means it will often consist of a test on the value of the system-property() function

The attributes version, extension-element-prefixes, exclude-result-prefixes, and xpath-default-namespace can be specified on any element in the XSLT namespace. They can also be used on literal result elements, though in this case the attribute must be in the XSLT namespace, to distinguish it from user-defined attributes that are to be copied to the result tree. Collectively these attributes are referred to by names such as [xsl:]version, since they are sometimes namespace-prefixed.

These attributes are described here because they are usually used on the <xsl:stylesheet> element. They are not included in the proforma of other XSLT elements in order to save space.

> The [xsl:]use-when *attribute is more likely to appear on elements in a stylesheet other than the* <xsl:stylesheet> *or* <xsl:transform> *element. This attribute allows you to specify a compile-time conditional expression, and the element on which it appears will be included in the compiled stylesheet only if this condition is true. If the attribute is present on the* <xsl:stylesheet> *or* <xsl:transform> *element and takes the value false, the effect is as if the stylesheet module contained no top-level declarations. This attribute is described in Chapter 3, on page 122.*

In the case of version and xpath-default-namespace, the effective value of the attribute for a particular instruction in the stylesheet is the value on the nearest enclosing element, or the instruction itself, that has a value for this attribute. In the case of extension-element-prefixes and exclude-result-prefixes, the values are cumulative—a namespace is an extension namespace or excluded namespace if it is listed as such on some enclosing instruction.

In practice the most useful place to specify these attributes is often on the <xsl:template> or <xsl:function> declarations, in which case they apply to the body of a template or function.

Content

The <xsl:stylesheet> element may contain XSLT elements referred to as *top-level declarations*. These elements are:

```
<xsl:attribute-set>
<xsl:character-map>
```

```
<xsl:decimal-format>
<xsl:function>
<xsl:import>
<xsl:import-schema>
<xsl:include>
<xsl:key>
<xsl:namespace-alias>
<xsl:output>
<xsl:param>
<xsl:preserve-space>
<xsl:strip-space>
<xsl:template>
<xsl:variable>
```

If there are any `<xsl:import>` elements, they must come before other top-level declarations.

The `<xsl:stylesheet>` element may also contain other elements provided they use a non-null namespace URI that is different from the XSLT namespace URI. If the namespace URI is recognized by the XSLT processor, it may interpret such elements in any way the vendor chooses, provided that the correct functioning of the stylesheet is not affected. If it does not recognize these elements, it should ignore them.

Effect

The rules are described below for each of the attributes.

The id Attribute

This attribute allows an `<xsl:stylesheet>` element to be referenced when it is contained within another XML document.

The precise usage is not defined in the standard, but the expectation is that this id attribute will allow an embedded stylesheet to be referenced in an `<?xml-stylesheet?>` processing instruction. An example is given in Chapter 3 on page 95. The specification points out that for this to work, it may be necessary for the id attribute to be declared in a DTD or schema as having the attribute type ID. However, not all XSLT processors impose this restriction.

The version Attribute

The version attribute defines the version of the XSLT specification that the stylesheet is relying on. At present there are two published versions of the XSLT standard, namely versions 1.0 and 2.0, so this attribute should take one of these two values.

Implementations of XSLT, even if they only implement version 1.0 of the standard, are required to behave in a particular way if the version specified is different from the version that they implement.

❏ If the version attribute is «1.0», an XSLT 1.0 processor must report as errors any elements in the XSLT namespace that it doesn't recognize. For example, if it encounters the element `<xsl:applyTemplate>` it will flag this as an error (because the correct spelling is `<xsl:apply-templates>`). Similarly, an XSLT 2.0 processor must reject unrecognized XSLT elements if the version attribute is set to «1.0» or «2.0».

❏ For an XSLT 1.0 processor, if the version attribute is any other value (including, oddly, a lower value than 1.0), the implementation must assume that the stylesheet is trying to use features defined in some version of XSLT that the software is unaware of. The same rule applies to an XSLT 2.0 processor if the version is greater than 2.0. So if the version attribute is «2.1», and the element <xsl:applyTemplate> appears, the software has to assume that this is a new element defined in version 2.1 of the standard, rather than a misspelling of <xsl:apply-templates>. The XSLT specification calls this *forwards-compatible processing mode*. In this mode, the <xsl:applyTemplate> element will be rejected only if (a) an attempt is made to evaluate it, and (b) it has no <xsl:fallback> child element. If it does have an <xsl:fallback> child element, this will be evaluated in place of the unrecognized parent element. This is described in greater detail under <xsl:fallback> on page 271.

❑ This means that an XSLT 1.0 processor that encounters a stylesheet specifying «version="2.0"», and containing say an <xsl:analyze-string> instruction (which is perfectly legal in XSLT 2.0), will not reject the stylesheet at compile time. Moreover, if the <xsl:analyze-string> instruction has an <xsl:fallback> child element, there will be no runtime error either: The <xsl:fallback> element will be evaluated, and the rest of the <xsl:analyze-string> instruction ignored. This is all a consequence of the way XSLT 1.0 was defined, with forwards compatibility in mind; XSLT 1.0 processors should work this way even if they were written years before the XSLT 2.0 specification was published.

Forwards-compatible mode also affects the handling of other apparent errors. For example if the version attribute is «2.0» (or in the case of an XSLT 1.0 processor, «1.0»), any unrecognized attributes or values of attributes on an XSLT element are reported as errors, but in forwards-compatible mode, such attributes are ignored. Similarly, in forwards-compatible mode a misplaced XSLT element such as <xsl:sort>, if found within a sequence constructor, will not be reported as an error until you try to evaluate it.

The version attribute applies to the entire stylesheet, except any parts contained within an XSLT element that has a version attribute, or a literal result element that has an xsl:version attribute. Its scope is the stylesheet module, not the full stylesheet tree constructed by applying <xsl:include> and <xsl:import> elements.

Note that in XSLT 1.0, the version attribute was allowed only on the <xsl:stylesheet> element, and xsl:version was allowed on literal result elements. In XSLT 2.0 this has been relaxed so version can be specified on any element in the XSLT namespace. If your stylesheet is likely to be executed by an XSLT 1.0 processor, it is best to use it only in the places where it was allowed in XSLT 1.0.

The extension-element-prefixes Attribute

This attribute identifies a set of namespaces used for extension instructions. Extension instructions may be defined by an implementor, a user, or a third party. They can be used anywhere an instruction can be used, that is, within a sequence constructor. If an element is found in a sequence constructor that is not in the XSLT namespace, then it must either be an extension instruction or a literal result element. If its namespace is the same as a namespace identified in the [xsl:]extension-element-prefixes attribute of the containing <xsl:stylesheet> element, of some other containing element, or of the element itself, then it will be treated as an extension instruction, otherwise it will be treated as a literal result element.

The value of the attribute is a whitespace-separated list of prefixes; each of these prefixes must identify a namespace declaration present on the <xsl:stylesheet> element. The default namespace (the namespace declared using the xmlns attribute) may be designated as an extension element namespace by including the pseudoprefix «#default».

The scope of the `extension-element-prefixes` attribute is the stylesheet module, not the full stylesheet tree constructed by applying `<xsl:include>` and `<xsl:import>` elements.

If a namespace is designated as an extension element namespace, then every XSLT processor will recognize that these elements are extension instructions. However, some XSLT processors may be unable to evaluate them. For example, if the namespace `http://www.jclark.com/xt/extensions` is designated as an extension namespace, then both xt and Xalan will recognize that these elements are extensions, but the likelihood is that xt will know how to handle them and Xalan won't. If the processor knows how to evaluate the instruction, it does so; otherwise, it looks to see if the element contains an `<xsl:fallback>` instruction. If it does, the `<xsl:fallback>` instruction is evaluated; otherwise, an error is reported.

It is necessary to designate a namespace as an extension element namespace only to distinguish extension instructions from literal result elements. At the top level of the stylesheet, there is no risk of confusion. Any implementation can define its own top-level elements, using its own namespace, and other implementations will simply ignore these elements, treating them as data. So the `extension-element-prefixes` attribute is not needed to identify top-level elements used as vendor or user extensions. For example, you can use `<msxml:script>` as a top-level declaration, and processors other than Microsoft MSXML3 will probably ignore it (though there is nothing that says they have to).

The exclude-result-prefixes Attribute

This attribute defines a set of namespaces that are *not* to be copied into the result tree.

The XSLT processor is required to produce a correct tree that conforms with the data model (as described on page 48, in Chapter 2) and with the XML Namespaces rules, so you will never find yourself with an output file using namespace prefixes that have not been declared. However, you can easily find yourself with a file containing unnecessary and unwanted namespace declarations, for example, declarations of namespaces that occur on nodes in your source document but are not used in the output document, or namespaces for extension functions that are used only in the stylesheet. These extra namespace declarations usually don't matter, because they don't affect the meaning of the output file, but they can clutter it up. They can also affect validation if you are trying to create a result document that conforms to a particular DTD. So this attribute is provided to help you get rid of them.

More specifically, the XSLT specification requires that when a literal result element in the stylesheet is evaluated, the element is copied into the result tree along with all its namespace nodes, except for the XSLT namespace and any namespace that defines extension instructions. An element has a namespace node for every namespace that is in scope, including namespaces defined on ancestor elements as well as on the element itself, so the namespaces copied over include not only the namespaces defined on the literal result element, and those that are actually used on the literal result element, but even those that are merely *available* for use.

Very often, of course, one literal result element will be a child or descendant of another, and the namespace nodes on the child element will include copies of all the namespace nodes on the parent element. For example, consider the stylesheet below:

```
<xsl:stylesheet version="1.0"
                xmlns:xsl="http://www.w3.org/1999/XSL/Transform"/>

<xsl:template match="/">
```

```
    <acme:document xmlns:acme="http://acme.com/xslt">
      <acme:chapter>
          Once upon a time ...
      </acme:chapter>
    </acme:document>
  </xsl:template>

</xsl:stylesheet>
```

This is represented by the tree shown in Figure 5-12, using the same notation as previously seen in Chapters 2 and 3. Although there are only two namespace declarations, these are propagated to all the descendant elements, so for example the <acme:chapter> element has two namespace nodes even though there are no namespace declarations on the element. (It also has a namespace node for the «xml» namespace, which is not shown in Figure 5-12.)

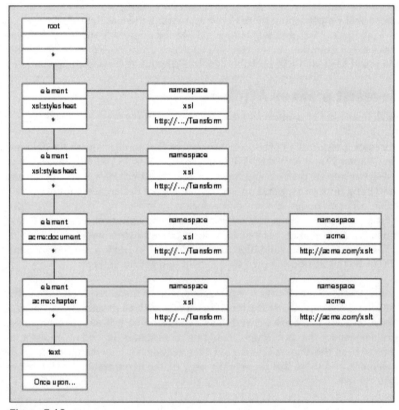

Figure 5-12

The specification says that each literal result element is copied with all its namespace nodes (but excluding the XSLT namespace), so the result tree will resemble Figure 5-13 (again, the «xml» namespace nodes are omitted).

Both elements, <acme:document> and <acme:chapter>, have a namespace node for the «acme» namespace. However, this doesn't mean that the namespace declaration will be repeated unnecessarily in

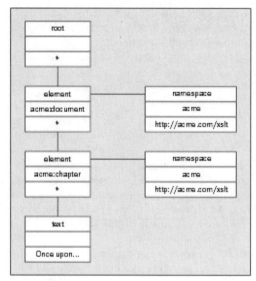

Figure 5-13

the output file: We're talking here about the abstract tree that is created, not the final serialized XML file. Avoiding duplicate namespace declarations is entirely the job of the XSLT serializer, and most serializers will produce the following output, shown indented for clarity:

```
<acme:document xmlns:acme="http://acme.com/xslt">
   <acme:chapter>
      Once upon a time ...
   </acme:chapter>
</acme:document>
```

The `exclude-result-prefixes` attribute isn't present to get rid of duplicate declarations, it's present to get rid of declarations that aren't wanted at all, which is a different matter entirely. For example suppose the stylesheet was like this:

```
<xsl:stylesheet version="1.0"
   xmlns:xsl="http://www.w3.org/1999/XSL/Transform"
   xmlns:var="http://another.org/xslt"
/>


<xsl:variable name="var:x" select="17"/>
<xsl:template match="/">
   <acme:document xmlns:acme="http://acme.com/xslt">
      <acme:chapter>
         Once upon a time ...
      </acme:chapter>
   </acme:document>
</xsl:template>

</xsl:stylesheet>
```

Then although the sequence constructor has not changed, the `<acme:document>` and `<acme:chapter>` elements each now have an extra namespace node, and this will be copied to the output file even though it is unused, resulting in the output:

```
<acme:document xmlns:acme="http://acme.com/xslt"
               xmlns:var="http://another.org/xslt">
   <acme:chapter>
      Once upon a time ...
   </acme:chapter>
</acme:document>
```

Why can't the XSLT processor simply include all the namespaces that are actually used in element and attribute names, and omit the rest? The line of thinking is that many XML applications, like XSLT itself, will use the namespace mechanism to create unique values within their own data. For example, namespace prefixes might be used in attribute values as well as attribute names. The XSLT processor can't distinguish these from ordinary values, so it has to play safe.

So if there are namespaces you don't want in the output tree, you can specify them in the `exclude-result-prefixes` attribute of the `<xsl:stylesheet>` element. The attribute is a list of namespace prefixes, separated by whitespace, and with the option to include the default namespace under the pseudoprefix «#default». If you want more precise control (though it is rarely needed) you can also specify `[xsl:]exclude-result-prefixes` on any element in the stylesheet, remembering that the attribute must be prefixed when it appears on a literal result element, and unprefixed when it appears on an XSLT element. It affects all literal result elements that are textually within its scope.

The prefix, as always, is simply a way of referring to the associated namespace URI: It is the namespace URI that is really being excluded, not the prefix itself. So if the same namespace URI is declared again with a different prefix, it is still an excluded namespace.

The `[xsl:]exclude-result-prefixes` attribute applies only to namespace nodes copied from the stylesheet using literal result elements. It does not affect namespace nodes copied from the source document using `<xsl:copy>` or `<xsl:copy-of>`; these can be suppressed by using the `copy-namespaces` attribute on the instruction itself.

Like the other attributes on the `<xsl:stylesheet>` element, the `exclude-result-prefixes` attribute applies only to elements actually within the stylesheet module, not to those brought in using `<xsl:include>` or `<xsl:import>`.

What happens if you try to exclude a namespace that is actually needed because it is used in the result tree? The XSLT processor is obliged to generate output that conforms to the Namespaces Recommendation, so it will ignore the request to exclude this namespace. Or more accurately, the evaluation of the literal result element will not cause the namespace node to be copied, but the namespace fixup process that comes into play when the element has been constructed will then generate namespace nodes for any namespaces that were missing. Namespace fixup is described under `<xsl:element>` on page 265.

The xpath-default-namespace Attribute

A common source of bewilderment for XSLT 1.0 users is when they see a source document that looks like this:

```
<para>Some text here</para>
```

and they try to match this with a template rule like this

```
<xsl:template match="para">
```

or perhaps to output the value with an expression like this

```
<xsl:value-of select="para"/>
```

and nothing happens. Only with experience do you learn to look near the top of the document for a tell-tale default namespace declaration:

```
<document xmlns="http://www.megacorp.com/ns">
```

Sometimes the default namespace declaration is even more carefully hidden, being placed as a default attribute value in the DTD. The XHTML specification is an example that uses this infuriating technique: hiding in its DTD is the snippet:

```
<!ELEMENT html (head, body)>
<!ATTLIST html
  %i18n;
  id           ID          #IMPLIED
  xmlns        %URI;       #FIXED 'http://www.w3.org/1999/xhtml'
>
```

which has the effect that every element you use in a document that invokes this DTD, an element written as <br/> perhaps, is actually in the namespace «http://www.w3.org/1999/xhtml» although you probably didn't know it.

When you write «match="br"» or «select="br"» in your stylesheet, you are asking for <br> elements in the null namespace, and you will not match <br> elements in any non-null namespace. To match elements in the namespace «http://www.w3.org/1999/xhtml», you first have to declare this namespace in your stylesheet (with a specific prefix):

```
<xsl:stylesheet . . .
    xmlns:xhtml="http://www.w3.org/1999/xhtml">
```

and then use this prefix whenever you refer to elements in this namespace: «match="xhtml:br"» and «select="xhtml:br"».

XSLT 2.0 hasn't found any way of eliminating the frustration of not realizing that the source elements were actually in a namespace, but it has eliminated the tedium of adding all the prefixes to your patterns and XPath expressions once you've realized what the problem is. You can now declare the namespace as being the default namespace for elements in XPath expressions by writing:

```
<xsl:stylesheet . . .
    xpath-default-namespace="http://www.w3.org/1999/xhtml">
```

and the names used in expressions and patterns can then remain unprefixed.

As with other attributes on the <xsl:stylesheet> element, this attribute can also be specified on other elements in the stylesheet, including literal result elements if the attribute is prefixed with the XSLT namespace prefix. This allows you to define a different default XPath namespace in different regions of the stylesheet, which is useful if the stylesheet is processing different source documents. (But it might be simpler in this case to split the stylesheet into different modules.) The attribute affects everything that is textually within its scope, and doesn't extend to included or imported modules.

The value is a namespace URI rather than a prefix, which means that the stylesheet doesn't actually need to declare this namespace. This is convenient because it means the namespace won't be automatically copied into the result document. You can also set it to a zero-length string to restore the default setting, which is that unprefixed names are assumed to refer to elements that are in no namespace.

The XPath default namespace affects unprefixed names appearing in the following contexts:

❑ Element names (but not attribute names) appearing in path expressions: That is, an NCName used as a NameTest in an AxisStep, when the axis is one that selects elements.

❑ Element names used similarly in patterns.

❑ Element names and type names (but not attribute names) used in the SequenceType syntax for defining types, whether the SequenceType syntax is used within an XPath expression, or on its own within an as attribute in the stylesheet

❑ Type names used in an XPath cast expression, for example «cast as part-number ("MF00325Z")».

❑ Type names used in a type attribute in the stylesheet.

❑ Element names used in <xsl:strip-space> and <xsl:preserve-space>.

Note that although the namespace applies to unprefixed names appearing in a cast expression, it does not apply to the names of functions, including constructor functions such as «part-number ("MF00325Z")» where the function name is based on the name of a user-defined type in a schema. With constructor functions the namespace must always be given explicitly; an unprefixed function name can only be used for functions in the core library (that is, standard XSLT and XPath functions).

Another consequence of this rule is that if you import a schema that has no target namespace, you cannot use constructor functions to create instances of the atomic types defined in this schema. Instead, you must use the more long-winded cast syntax. (In fact, this is the main reason that the cast syntax has been retained in the XPath language.)

> *The XPath 2.0 specification refers to a concept called the* default function namespace, *which is the namespace in which unprefixed function names are located. Although XPath allows this to be defined as part of the evaluation context, XSLT does not pass this capability on to the user. When XPath expressions are used in XSLT stylesheets, the default function namespace is always the standard namespace* http://www.w3.org/2003/11/xpath-functions. *This means that calls on standard functions such as* position() *and* last() *never need to be prefixed in XSLT, though you can use a prefix that is bound to the standard namespace if you really want to.*

The default-validation Attribute

Like the other attributes we've been discussing, the default-validation attribute applies to everything that is textually within the stylesheet module. Unlike the other attributes, it can't be overridden with a different declaration on an inner element in the stylesheet. (I don't think there's any good reason for this restriction; it was put there simply to avoid adding unnecessary complexity).

This attribute applies to every instruction in the stylesheet that is allowed to take a `validation` or `type` attribute, but where neither of these attributes is actually present. It also affects literal result elements, which are allowed to take an `xsl:type` or `xsl:validation` attribute, in the same way. The effect is to supply a default value for the `[xsl:]validation` attribute on these instructions or literal result elements.

The possible values of the attribute are «`strict`», «`lax`», «`preserve`», or «`strip`». The meanings of these values are explained under each instruction that takes a `validation` attribute, and vary slightly from one instruction to another, depending on whether it is dealing with single nodes or multiple nodes, elements or attributes.

The use-when Attribute

This attribute is a late addition to the language. The attribute may be specified on any element in the stylesheet (if specified on a literal result element, it is named «`xsl:use-when`») and its value is an XPath expression. Although the full XPath syntax is allowed, the context for evaluation of the expression is severely restricted, which means that the expression cannot refer to anything in the source document or the stylesheet. In practice this means it is restricted to testing the results of functions such as `system-property()`, `function-available()`, and `element-available()`.

The expression is evaluated at compile time, and if its effective boolean value is false, the element on which it appears is effectively excluded from the stylesheet module at compile time. If the attribute is used on the `<xsl:stylesheet>` or `<xsl:transform>` element the effect is slightly different: The element itself is not excluded (because this would make the stylesheet invalid); instead, all the top-level declarations are excluded, so the stylesheet module becomes empty. This is only useful, of course, for an included or imported module.

Usage and Examples

The `<xsl:stylesheet>` element is always the outermost element of the stylesheet (though the stylesheet may be embedded in another document). It will always include:

```
<xsl:stylesheet
        xmlns:xsl="http://www.w3.org/1999/XSL/Transform"
        version="2.0"
>
```

The various possible attributes are considered in the sections that follow.

The id Attribute

If the XSLT processor you are using supports embedding of stylesheets within the source document that they are to transform, then the typical layout will be like this:

```
<?xml version="1.0"?>
<?xml-stylesheet href="#style" type="text/xsl"?>
<!DOCTYPE data [
<!ATTLIST xsl:stylesheet id ID #REQUIRED >
]>
```

```
<data>
...

...
    <xsl:stylesheet id="style" version="2.0"
       xmlns:xsl="http://www.w3.org/1999/XSL/Transform"
    >
    <xsl:include href="module1.xsl"/>
    <xsl:include href="module2.xsl"/>
    <xsl:template match="xsl:*"/>
    </xsl:stylesheet>
</data>
```

Note that when this structure is used, the stylesheet will be presented with the entire source document, including a copy of itself. The stylesheet therefore needs to be written to handle its own elements in an appropriate way, hence the empty template rule that matches all elements in the XSLT namespace.

XSLT 2.0 defines the media type (MIME type) «application/xslt+xml» for XSLT stylesheet modules, but the unofficial usage «text/xsl» is much more widely supported in today's products.

The version Attribute

If your stylesheet only uses features from XSLT 1.0, it is best to specify «version="1.0"» on the <xsl:stylesheet> element. Then it will work with any XSLT processor that conforms to XSLT 1.0 or a later version of the standard.

If the stylesheet uses 2.0 features, you should specify «version="2.0"» on the <xsl:stylesheet> element. An XSLT 2.0 that encounters a stylesheet that specifies «version="1.0"» at the start of the principal stylesheet module is supposed to give you a warning about possible incompatibilities, and then process the stylesheet as if it were a 2.0 stylesheet, but with backwards compatiblity mode switched on. (This doesn't guarantee 100% compatibility, but it's pretty close.)

If your stylesheet says «version="1.0"» this won't stop you using XSLT 2.0 features; an XSLT 2.0 processor isn't expected to look at every construct you use and decide whether it would have been allowed in XSLT 1.0. But for certain specific features, it causes XSLT 2.0 and XPath 2.0 to behave differently. The main examples of this are:

❑   In function calls expecting a string or a number as an argument, a processor running in 1.0 mode will cast the supplied value to a string or number as appropriate. In 2.0 mode, stricter type checking prevails, and you have to do such casts yourself. However, if the argument you supply is a node in a schema-less document (type annotation xs:untyped or xs:untypedAtomic) then a cast will still be performed.

❑   In function calls, if you supply a sequence containing more than one value where a single value is expected, then in 1.0 mode all but the first value will be ignored. In 2.0 mode this is a type error: If you only want to process the first item in the sequence, you must select it explicitly using the predicate «[1]».

❑   Similarly, in certain XSLT contexts, a processor running in 1.0 mode applies the "first item" rule when you supply a sequence of values, but either reports an error, or processes the whole sequence, when in 2.0 mode. The most common example of this is in <xsl:value-of>: If you write <xsl:value-of select="book/author"/> in 1.0 mode then only the first author of the first book will be displayed, while in 2.0 mode this will produce a list of all the authors of all the selected books, space-separated. For more details, see `<xsl:value-of>` on page 465.

XSLT 2.0 allows you to put the `version` attribute on any element in the stylesheet, and at first sight a nice idea would be to flag any template rule that uses XSLT 2.0 features by labeling it with the attribute «version="2.0"». Unfortunately, however, XSLT 1.0 doesn't allow the `version` attribute to appear on the `<xsl:template>` element, so if you want your stylesheet to still work with 1.0, this won't work. A better idea is probably to put all the template rules that depend on XSLT 2.0 in a separate module, and label this module with «version="2.0"» at the `<xsl:stylesheet>` level. Of course, you will still need to provide 1.0 fallback behavior whenever you use a 2.0 construct.

The extension-element-prefixes Attribute

This attribute should be set to a list of all the prefixes you are using for extension instructions in your stylesheet. The most common cases are either to omit it entirely, or to include a single prefix for the namespace used by the vendor of your chosen XSLT processor for their own proprietary extensions. There will always be a namespace declaration for this namespace on the `<xsl:stylesheet>` element as well.

For example, if you are using Saxon:

```
<xsl:stylesheet
          version="2.0"
          xmlns:xsl="http://www.w3.org/1999/XSL/Transform"
          xmlns:saxon="http://saxon.sf.net/"
          extension-element-prefixes="saxon"
          >
```

Don't include the vendor's prefix unless you are actually using their proprietary extensions in the stylesheet. You don't need to include this attribute to use proprietary top-level elements such as `<msxml:script>`, or to use extension functions: You need it only if you want to use vendor-defined instructions within a sequence constructor, where they would otherwise be assumed to be literal result elements.

If your usage of vendor extensions is highly localized within the stylesheet, it is better to identify them using the `xsl:extension-element-prefixes` attribute of the extension element itself, or of a literal result element that surrounds the sequence constructor where the extensions are actually used. This aids portability and makes it easier to see which parts of the stylesheet are standard and which parts use proprietary extensions.

If you want to use extensions supplied by several different vendors, you can list them all in this attribute. An XSLT processor from one vendor won't object to finding another vendor's namespace in the list; it will only object if it is actually asked to evaluate a proprietary instruction that it doesn't understand, and even then if there is an `<xsl:fallback>` child element that defines the fallback behavior it will carry on calmly executing that in place of the unrecognized instruction.

Although extension elements supplied by XSLT product vendors are likely to be the most common case, it's also possible in principle to install third-party extensions or to write your own (however, the APIs for doing so will be different for each vendor). So everything we've said about the vendor's extensions applies equally to your own extensions or those acquired from a third party.

For more information about the extensions provided by various vendors in their products, see the documentation for the relevant product.

An inventive way of using the `extension-element-prefixes` attribute is to flag elements that you want to reserve for debugging or annotation. For example, if you include the following element within a sequence constructor anywhere in the stylesheet, then the normal action will be to output an element to the result tree, showing the current values of the variables $var1 and $var2.

```
<debug:write var1="{$var1}" var2="{$var2}"><xsl:fallback/></debug:write>
```

When you no longer need to use this debugging instruction, you can disable it simply by declaring «debug» as an extension element prefix. This time the `<xsl:fallback/>` action will be taken, because the processor doesn't recognize the extension instruction.

The exclude-result-prefixes Attribute

The simplest way to decide which namespace prefixes to list here is by trial and error. Run the stylesheet, and if the output document contains namespace declarations that clearly serve no useful purpose, add them to the `exclude-result-prefixes` attribute and run the stylesheet again.

The XSLT namespace itself and namespaces used for extension elements will be excluded automatically. However, the stylesheet is also likely to contain references to the schema namespace and perhaps the «xdt» namespaces, which you may not want in your result document. It will also contain any namespace you have used for defining your local stylesheet functions, which you almost certainly don't want in the result document.

A common cause of unwanted namespace declarations finding their way into the result document is where your stylesheet needs to refer to namespaces used in the source document, for example in a template `match` pattern, but where none of these elements is copied into the destination document.

For example:

```
<xsl:stylesheet
        version="2.0"
        xmlns:xsl="http://www.w3.org/1999/XSL/Transform"
        xmlns:po="http://accounting.org/xslt"
        exclude-result-prefixes="po"
>
<xsl:template match="po:purchase-order">
    <order-details>
    ...
    </order-details>
</xsl:template>
</xsl:stylesheet>
```

Here the «po» namespace would be copied into the result document if it weren't for the `exclude-result-prefixes` attribute, because it is in scope when the literal result element `<order-details>` is evaluated.

As with the other `<xsl:stylesheet>` attributes, you don't have to apply the exclusion to the whole stylesheet if you don't want to, you can also apply it to any part of the stylesheet by using the xsl:exclude-result-prefixes attribute on any literal result element. It's probably a good idea in practice to keep the declaration of a namespace and the directive that excludes it from the result document together in one place.

The xpath-default-namespace Attribute

I would recommend always using this attribute if your source documents generally use a default namespace declaration; the value should be the namespace URI of this default namespace declaration. Specifying an xpath-default-namespace will not stop existing code working that uses explicit prefixes to refer to names in this namespace.

One thing to watch out for is that if your stylesheet creates and uses temporary trees, the chances are that these don't use namespaces. Specifying an xpath-default-namespace makes it impossible to refer to names that are in the null namespace, for example elements on such a temporary tree (you can't bind a namespace prefix to the null namespace, unfortunately). In this situation you can override the xpath-default-namespace in the relevant region of your stylesheet by writing «xpath-default-namespace=" "».

If your stylesheet processes multiple source documents of different types, similar considerations apply. In this case it might be clearer to use explicit namespace prefixes for everything.

The default-validation Attribute

This attribute can take the value «strict», «lax», «preserve», or «strip». It affects every literal result element, and every <xsl:element>, <xsl:copy>, <xsl:copy-of> and <xsl:result-document> instruction within the stylesheet module, unless it has its own validation attribute. Unlike the other attributes on <xsl:stylesheet>, this attribute cannot be overridden on an inner element for a region of the stylesheet; it can only be overridden on the actual instruction that uses it.

Specifying «default-validation="strict"» is probably not usually a good idea, because it means that any attempt to create an element or attribute that does not have a global declaration in the schema will cause a failure. All the other three values might be sensible under different circumstances. «lax» means that schema validation will be carried out whenever possible, which is useful if you want to detect the maximum number of errors. «preserve» is useful if source documents carry type annotations and you do not want these to be lost. «strip» is the default value, so specifying it here actually has no effect, but this option is useful if you want the stylesheet to behave as much as possible as a non–schema-aware stylesheet in which source documents are regarded as untyped.

In practice I think that «validation="preserve"» is likely to be the only option that's really useful. Given a schema-aware processor, and a stylesheet whose main job is to copy a selection of the nodes from the source document across to the result document with as few changes as possible, for further transformation by another stylesheet later on in the pipeline, it makes sense to preserve all the existing type annotations. However, check the specification of the individual instructions. <xsl:copy validate="preserve"> probably doesn't do what you imagine. Since <xsl:copy> can completely change the content of an element, the type annotation on the element being copied is no longer reliable, so it isn't retained, even with this option. When a subtree is copied in its entirety, with no changes (typically using <xsl:copy-of>), it makes sense to retain type annotations. As soon as any changes are made, the result can only contain type annotations if you put it through schema validation.

You need to think about whether you actually want the result tree to be validated at all. Validation of the result against a schema can, of course, be very useful, both to detect errors in your stylesheet, and to ensure that the tree is annotated with type information for use by the next process in the pipeline. But there are two reasons you might *not* want this done:

❑   You might actually want to produce a document that's invalid according to the schema. For example, you might have a schema for a university application form that includes required entries for the student's personal details such as name and address. But the purpose of your transformation might be to extract data for statistical purposes in which this personal information is omitted. You can't specify two different schemas for the source document and the result document if they use the same namespace, so you might just have to accept that in this situation, the result document will not validate.

❑   There are probably many transformations where validation of the result adds little value, or where it is simpler to do it as a completely separate process, once the transformation is complete. Just because the facility is available doesn't mean you have to use it.

One thing you might want to try is to have validation switched on while you are doing system testing of your stylesheet, or after you introduce changes, and to have it switched off once everything starts running smoothly. This isn't particularly easy to achieve, but controlling validation from the `<xsl:stylesheet>` level should make it easier than it would be otherwise. But I would be inclined, in this situation, to switch validation on or off at the level of the `<xsl:result-document>` instruction, which is described on page 414.

The use-when Attribute

This attribute is provided to allow you to write stylesheets that are portable across different XSLT processors. For example, you can specify «use-when="system-property('xsl:is-schema-aware')='yes'"» to mark a section of stylesheet code that should be ignored by a processor that is not schema-aware, or you can test the «xsl:vendor» system property to include sections of code that are specific to particular XSLT implementations. You can also use the function-available() function to conditionally include or exclude sections of code based on whether a particular extension function is available in the implementation you are running on.

There are more examples of the use of this attribute in Chapter 3 (see page 122). It can be used on any XSLT element, both declarations (notably `<xsl:include>`, `<xsl:import>`, and `<xsl:import-schema>`), and instructions. Just remember that the expression cannot access the source document, and it cannot access any variables: It is designed only to test properties of the environment in which the stylesheet is compiled.

See Also

`<xsl:transform>` on page 465

xsl:template

The `<xsl:template>` element defines a template for producing output. It may be invoked either by matching nodes against a pattern, or explicitly by name.

Changes in 2.0

It is now possible to define a template rule that matches in multiple modes.

The new `as` attribute allows the type of the result to be defined. Moreover, the new `<xsl:sequence>` instruction means that a template can now return atomic values and references to existing nodes; it is no longer limited to constructing new nodes.

The syntax for patterns has been extended so that a template rule can now match nodes according to their schema-defined type. The match pattern may also now contain references to global variables or parameters.

Nonsensical combinations of attributes are now considered to be errors, for example, specifying `priority` or `mode` when there is no `match` attribute. In XSLT 1.0, such attributes were ignored.

Format

```
<xsl:template
  match? = pattern
  name? = qname
  priority? = number
  mode? = tokens
  as? = sequence-type>
  <!-- Content: (xsl:param*, sequence-constructor) -->
</xsl:template>
```

Position

`<xsl:template>` is a declaration, which means that it always appears as a child of the `<xsl:stylesheet>` element.

Attributes

Name	Value	Meaning
match optional	Pattern	A pattern that determines which nodes are eligible to be processed by this template. If this attribute is absent, there must be a `name` attribute
name optional	lexical QName	The name of the template. If this attribute is absent, there must be a `match` attribute
priority optional	Number	A number (positive or negative, integer or decimal) that denotes the priority of this template, and is used when several templates match the same node
mode optional	list of mode names, or «#all»	The mode or modes to which this template rule applies. When `<xsl:apply-templates>` is used to process a set of nodes, the only templates considered are those with a matching mode
as optional	SequenceType	The type of the sequence produced when this template is evaluated. A type error is reported if the result does not match this type

The construct Pattern is defined in Chapter 6. The construct SequenceType is defined in Chapter 4, and more completely in *XPath 2.0 Programmer's Reference*.

The `mode` and `priority` attributes must not be specified unless the `match` attribute is also specified.

Content

Zero or more `<xsl:param>` elements, followed by a sequence constructor.

Effect

There must be either a `match` attribute, or a `name` attribute, or both.

❑ If there is a `match` attribute, the `<xsl:template>` element defines a template rule that can be invoked using the `<xsl:apply-templates>` instruction.

❑ If there is a `name` attribute, the `<xsl:template>` element defines a named template that can be invoked using the `<xsl:call-template>` instruction.

❑ If both attributes are present, the template can be invoked in either of these ways.

The match Attribute

The match attribute is a `Pattern`, as defined in Chapter 6. The pattern is used to define which nodes this template rule applies to.

When `<xsl:apply-templates>` is used to process a selected set of nodes, each node is processed using the best-fit template rule for this node, as described under `<xsl:apply-templates>` on page 187.

A template is only considered a candidate if the node matches the pattern supplied in the `match` attribute and if the value of the `mode` attribute matches the `mode` attribute of the `<xsl:apply-templates>` instruction (as described below on page 454).

If more than one template rule meets these criteria, they are first considered in order of import precedence (as described under `<xsl:import>` on page 314), and only templates with the highest import precedence are considered further.

If there is still more than one template rule (in other words, if two template rules that both match the node have the same import precedence), they are next considered in order of priority. The priority is either given by the value of the `priority` attribute, described below, or is a default priority that depends on the `match` pattern. The rules for determining the default priority of any pattern are given in Chapter 6, on page 498.

If this leaves one pattern with a numerically higher priority than all the others, this one is chosen. If there are several with the same priority, which is higher than all the others, the XSLT processor has the choice of reporting an error, or choosing from the remaining templates the one that appears last in the stylesheet. Several processors in practice report a warning, which you can ignore if you wish. In my experience, however, this condition often indicates that the stylesheet author has overlooked something.

XSLT 2.0 allows the pattern to contain a reference to a global variable or parameter. This allows a pattern such as «match="part[@number=$param]"», which means that the same pattern will match different nodes on different runs of the stylesheet. But there are rules to prevent circular definitions: Evaluating the variable must not invoke an `<xsl:apply-templates>` instruction, either directly or indirectly.

The name Attribute

The `name` attribute is a lexical QName; that is, a name optionally qualified with a namespace prefix. If there is a prefix, it must correspond to a namespace declaration that is in scope on this element (which means it must be defined either on this element itself, or on the `<xsl:stylesheet>` element). If there is no prefix, the namespace URI is null; the default namespace is not used.

This name is used when the template is invoked using `<xsl:call-template>`. The `name` attribute of the `<xsl:call-template>` element must match the `name` attribute of the `<xsl:template>` element. Two names match if they have the same local part and the same namespace URI, but the prefix can be different.

If there is more than one named template in the stylesheet with the same name, the one with higher import precedence is used; for details, see `<xsl:import>` on page 312. It is an error to have two templates in the stylesheet with the same name and the same import precedence, unless there is another one with the same name and a higher import precedence. This is an error even if the template is never called.

The priority Attribute

The `priority` attribute is a number, for example «17», «0.5», or «-3»: more specifically, an `xs:decimal` as defined in XML Schema, which allows an optional leading minus sign.

The `priority` attribute is used to decide which template to invoke when `<xsl:apply-templates>` is called and there are several possible candidates. For each node selected by the `<xsl:apply-templates>` instruction, a template rule is chosen using the following procedure:

❑   First select all the templates that have a `match` attribute.

❑   From these, select all the templates that match the mode that is used on the call of `<xsl:apply-templates>`. An `<xsl:apply-templates>` instruction uses either a specific mode (identified by a QName), or the default mode (which is unnamed) or it can specify «#current», in which case it uses whatever mode is the current mode at the time. An `<xsl:template>` element can specify a list of modes that it matches (which can include «#default» to indicate that it matches all modes), or it can specify «#all» to indicate that it matches all modes; if it has no `mode` attribute, then it matches only the default mode.

❑   From these, select all those whose pattern matches the selected node.

❑   If there is more than one, select those that have the highest import precedence.

❑   If there is still more than one, select those that have the numerically highest priority.

If there are several matching templates left, and they all have the same import precedence and priority, the XSLT processor can either choose the one that occurs last in declaration order, or report an error. Import precedence and declaration order are described under `<xsl:import>` on page 312.

If there are no templates that match the selected node, the built-in template for the relevant node kind is used. Built-in templates are described under `<xsl:apply-templates>` on page 190.

The rules for determining the default priority for a pattern are given in Chapter 6, on page 498.

Although the default priorities are carefully chosen, they do not guarantee that a highly selective pattern will always have higher priority than a less selective pattern. For example, the patterns «section/para» and «section/para[1]» both have priority +0.5. Similarly, the patterns «attribute(*, xs:integer)» and «attribute(*, xs:decimal)» have the same priority, even though the nodes that match the first pattern are a subset of those that match the second. Choosing your own priorities is therefore a more reliable approach.

The mode Attribute

If the <xsl:template> element has no mode attribute, then it applies only to the default (unnamed) mode, and will be invoked only in response to an <xsl:apply-templates> instruction that uses the default mode. An <xsl:apply-templates> instruction uses the default mode if it has no mode attribute, if its mode attribute has the value «#default», or if its mode attribute has the value «#current» and the current mode is the default mode. The concept of the current mode is explained on page 498.

If the mode attribute is present and has the value «#all», then the template is applicable to all modes.

The mode attribute may also contain a list of modes to which the template is applicable. Each mode is written either as a lexical QName (the actual mode name), or as the token «#default» to indicate that the template is applicable to the default mode.

Mode names are compared using the usual rules for QNames; both names are expanded using the namespace declarations in effect on their respective stylesheet elements (not including any default namespace declaration), and they match if the local name and namespace URI both match.

The mode specified on the <xsl:template> template is *not* automatically propagated to any <xsl:apply-templates> elements within its body. Although it is common practice to process an entire subtree in a single mode, and therefore for a template to continue using the mode it was called in, this is not the default behavior except in the case of built-in templates. However, the current mode can be propagated by explicitly calling <xsl:apply-templates mode="#current"/>.

If you have a mode attribute on a template and there is no <xsl:apply-templates> element with a matching mode anywhere in the stylesheet, this is not an error, though it means the template will never be selected by any <xsl:apply-templates> call. This can be a handy way of commenting out a template rule.

Evaluating a Template

Once an <xsl:template> element is selected for processing, the following occurs:

❑ If called using <xsl:apply-templates>, the context node, context position, and context size are set up as required.

❑ A new stack frame is allocated, to hold a new instance of each local variable defined within the template.

❑ All parameters listed in <xsl:param> elements contained within the <xsl:template> element are evaluated. These <xsl:param> elements must come before any instructions in the content of the template. For each parameter, if a value was supplied by the caller (using an `<xsl:with-param>` element with matching name), this value is assigned to the parameter. If necessary, the supplied values are converted to the required type specified in the as attribute, using the standard conversion rules described on page 476. If the supplied value has the wrong type, an error is reported. If no value was supplied by the caller, then if the `<xsl:param>` element specifies «`required="yes"`» an error is reported; otherwise the default value of the parameter is evaluated. This process is explained in more detail under `<xsl:param>` on page 392.

❑ The sequence constructor is evaluated. This means that the child instructions of the `<xsl:template>` element are evaluated in turn. XSLT instructions and extension elements are processed using their individual rules; literal result elements and text nodes are written to the result sequence.

❑ The result of evaluating the sequence constructor is checked against the type given in the as attribute of the `<xsl:template>` element, if any. If necessary, the value is converted to the required type using the standard conversion rules given on page 476. If the value has the wrong type, a fatal error is reported.

When processing of the sequence constructor is complete, the stack frame containing its local variables is deleted, control returns to the calling template, and the context item, position, and size revert to their previous values. The value produced by evaluating the sequence constructor becomes the return value of the calling `<xsl:apply-templates>`, `<xsl:call-template>`, `<xsl:apply-imports>`, or `<xsl:next-match>` instruction. (If the calling instruction was `<xsl:apply-templates>`, the value is combined with the values delivered by the template rules for other selected nodes.)

The implementation, of course, is free to do things in a different order if it has the same effect. Some products use lazy evaluation, where the parameters are only evaluated when they are first used. Some products also use tail-call optimization, where a recursive template call is deferred until after the stack has been unwound: This reduces the risk of running out of stack space when calls are deeply nested. Such optimizations may show up if you use extension functions that have side effects, or if you use `<xsl:message>` to trace the sequence of execution.

Usage and Examples

We will look first at using template rules, and then I will give some advice on the use of modes. For examples of the use of named templates, see `<xsl:call-template>` on page 220.

Using Template Rules

A *template rule* is an `<xsl:template>` element with a match attribute, which can therefore be invoked using the `<xsl:apply-templates>` instruction.

This rule-based approach to processing is the characteristic way of writing XSLT stylesheets, though it is by no means the only way. Its biggest advantage is that the output for each element type can be defined independently of the context that the element appears in, which makes it very easy to reuse element types in different contexts, or to add new element types to an existing document definition without rewriting the stylesheet templates for all the possible containing elements. A classic example of this approach to processing arises when converting semantic markup in a document to rendition markup, as the following example demonstrates.

Example: Template Rules

This example shows a typical use of template rules to handle narrative text with a free-form structure.

Source

The source file is `soloist.xml`.

In this text featuring the work of a singer, the name of a composer is tagged `<composer>`, the title of a musical work is tagged `<work>`, and the name of a publication is tagged `<publication>`. Sections of text relating to the same performance are marked with a `<performance>` tag. So a fragment of marked up text might read:

```
<cv>
<para>
<performance>
<publication>Early Music Review</publication> said of his debut
    <venue>Wigmore</venue> concert with <group>Ensemble
    Sonnerie</group> in <date>1998</date>: <quote>One of the
finest concerts I have ever heard ... a singer to watch out for</quote>.
</performance>
<performance>
Other highlights include a televised production of
<composer>Bach</composer>'s <work>St. Matthew Passion</work> conducted by
<artist>Jonathan Miller</artist>, in which he played <role>Judas</role>.
</performance>
</para>
</cv>
```

Stylesheet

The stylesheet file is `soloist.xsl`.

In presenting this text to a human reader, the main task is to select typographical conventions to be used for each piece of semantic markup. The designer might choose, for example, to display the titles of works in italics, titles of publications in a sans serif font, and composers' names in the ordinary paragraph font. This could be achieved by the following stylesheet definitions (assuming the output is HTML):

```
<xsl:stylesheet version="1.0"
    xmlns:xsl="http://www.w3.org/1999/XSL/Transform">

<xsl:template match="/">
<html><body>
<xsl:apply-templates/>
</body></html>
</xsl:template>
```

```
<xsl:template match="para">
   <p><xsl:apply-templates/></p>
</xsl:template>

<xsl:template match="publication">
   <font face="arial"><xsl:apply-templates/></font>
</xsl:template>

<xsl:template match="quote">
   <xsl:text/>"<xsl:apply-templates/>"<xsl:text/>
</xsl:template>

<xsl:template match="work">
   <i><xsl:apply-templates/></i>
</xsl:template>

<xsl:template match="role">
   <u><xsl:apply-templates/></u>
</xsl:template>

</xsl:stylesheet>
```

Note that some of the markup is ignored, for example `<artist>`. The default template for elements simply discards the tags and outputs the text, which is exactly what we want here.

Output

If the generated HTML is copied into a word processor, it will look like Figure 5-14.

Early Music Review said of his debut Wigmore concert with Ensemble Sonnerie in 1998: "One of the finest concerts I have ever heard ... a singer to watch out for". Other highlights include a televised production of Bach's *St. Matthew Passion* conducted by Jonathan Miller, in which he played Judas.

Figure 5-14

The great advantage of this approach is that the rules are written making no assumptions about the way the markup tags are nested in the source document. It is very easy to add new rules for new tags, and to reuse rules if an existing tag is used in a new context.

With document structures where the nesting of elements is more rigid, for example in some data interchange files, this very flexible rule-based (or *push*) style of processing may have fewer benefits, and a *pull* programming style using conventional flow-of-control constructs such as `<xsl:for-each>`, `<xsl:if>`, and `<xsl:call-template>` may be preferable. For further discussion of the different design approaches, see Chapter 9.

Using Modes

The classic reason for using modes is to enable the same content to be processed more than once in different ways: For example, the first pass through the document might generate the table of contents, the second pass the actual text, and the third pass an index.

Example: Using modes

The source document is a biography of a singer, in the same format as in the previous example. This time, however, the requirement is to produce at the end of the biography a list of works mentioned in the text.

Source

The source file is `soloist.xml`. See previous example.

Stylesheet

The stylesheet file is `soloist+index.xsl`.

This stylesheet extends the previous one using `<xsl:import>`. After outputting the text as before, it now creates a table listing the singer's performances, completing what information is known about the composer, the work, the date of the performance, and the venue.

The « » characters (better known to HTML authors as a nonbreaking space, « »), are used to ensure that there is something in each table cell: This gives a cleaner appearance in the browser. It would be quite possible to use the entity reference « » in the stylesheet so long as it was properly declared as an XML entity in a `<!DOCTYPE>` declaration at the start of the file.

```
<xsl:stylesheet version="1.0"
    xmlns:xsl="http://www.w3.org/1999/XSL/Transform">

<xsl:import href="soloist.xsl"/>

<xsl:template match="/">
<html><body>
    <xsl:apply-templates/>
    <table bgcolor="#cccccc" border="1" cellpadding="5">
    <tr>
        <td><b>Date</b></td>
        <td><b>Venue</b></td>
        <td><b>Composer</b></td>
        <td><b>Work</b></td>
        <td><b>Role</b></td>
    </tr>
    <xsl:apply-templates mode="index"/>
    </table>
</body></html>
</xsl:template>

<xsl:template match="performance" mode="index">
    <tr>
    <td><xsl:value-of select="date"/> </td>
    <td><xsl:value-of select="venue"/> </td>
    <td><xsl:value-of select="composer"/> </td>
    <td><xsl:value-of select="work"/> </td>
```

```
      <td><xsl:value-of select="role"/> </td>
      </tr>
   </xsl:template>

   </xsl:stylesheet>
```

Output

Using a slightly extended version of the text in the source file, the output is as shown in Figure 5-15:

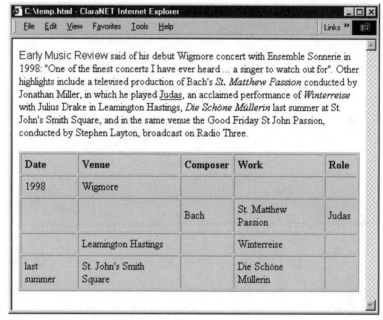

Figure 5-15

See Also

<xsl:apply-templates> on page 187
<xsl:apply-imports> on page 184
<xsl:call-template> on page 220
generate-id() function in Chapter 7, on page 568

xsl:text

The <xsl:text> instruction is used within a sequence constructor to output literal text to the result sequence. The purpose of wrapping an <xsl:text> element around literal text is to ensure that whitespace is preserved.

Changes in 2.0

None.

Format

```
<xsl:text
   disable-output-escaping? = "yes" | "no">
   <!-- Content: character data -->
</xsl:text>
```

Position

<xsl:text> is an instruction. It is always used as part of a sequence constructor.

Attributes

Name	Value	Meaning
disable-output-escaping optional	«yes» | «no»	The value «yes» indicates that special characters in the output (such as «<») should be output as is, rather than using an XML escape form such as «<». The default value is «no»

Content

A text node. The element may also be empty. It must not contain other elements such as <xsl:value-of>.

Effect

Text appearing within a sequence constructor in the stylesheet is copied to the result sequence (in the form of a new text node) whether it is enclosed by <xsl:text> or not. The only direct effect of enclosing text in an <xsl:text> element is that the handling of whitespace is different. A whitespace node appearing in the stylesheet (that is, a text node that consists only of whitespace) is copied to the result tree only if :

❑   it appears within an <xsl:text> element, or

❑   an enclosing element has the attribute «xml:space="preserve"», and this is not overridden by an inner enclosing element specifying «xml:space="default"»

The disable-output-escaping attribute controls whether special characters such as «<» should be escaped (that is, converted to a character reference or entity reference such as «<») if they appear in the text. The default value is «no». The value «yes» may be ignored under some circumstances, for example if the result of the transformation is written to a DOM rather than being serialized as an XML file.

Usage

There are two main reasons for using <xsl:text>, which are to control the output of whitespace, and to disable the escaping of special characters by the serializer. These are discussed in the next two sections.

Whitespace Control

The most obvious case where `<xsl:text>` is useful is to force output of whitespace. An example is given in the XSLT specification. If you write:

```
<xsl:value-of select="first-name"/> <xsl:value-of select="last-name"/>
```

the space between the first name and the last name will be lost, because it is part of a node that contains whitespace only (a single space character). To force a space to appear between the first name and the last name, write:

```
<xsl:value-of select="first-name"/>
<xsl:text> </xsl:text>
<xsl:value-of select="last-name"/>
```

The arrangement on three lines here is purely for readability, but it does not affect the output, because the newline characters are now in whitespace-only nodes that will not be output.

If you find this long-winded, another way of achieving the same effect is to write:

```
<xsl:value-of select="first-name, last-name" separator=" "/>
```

The other aspect of the problem is to prevent the output of unwanted whitespace. Fortunately in HTML output extra whitespace usually doesn't matter, because the browser will ignore it. For XML or text output, however, avoiding unwanted whitespace can be important.

If you are suffering from excess whitespace in your output, the first thing to establish is whether it comes from the source document or from the stylesheet. If the whitespace is adjacent to text copied from the source document, then it probably comes from the source document; but if it is adjacent to text that appears in the stylesheet, then this is the most likely source. Check also that the unwanted whitespace isn't coming from the serializer, by setting `<xsl:output indent="no"/>`.

If the unwanted whitespace comes from the source document, consider using `<xsl:strip-space>` to remove nodes consisting entirely of whitespace, or the `normalize-space()` function to remove leading and trailing spaces around visible text.

The `<xsl:text>` element can be used to suppress unwanted whitespace that originates in the stylesheet. For example, consider the following template:

```
<xsl:template match="stage-direction">
   [ <xsl:value-of select="."/> ]
</xsl:template>
```

The intention here is to output a stage direction enclosed in square brackets. But the text nodes containing the opening and closing square brackets also contain a newline character and several spaces, which will be written to the output destination along with the brackets themselves. To prevent this behavior, the simplest way is to use empty `<xsl:text>` elements before and after, thus:

```
<xsl:template match="stage-direction">
   <xsl:text/>[ <xsl:value-of select="."/> ]<xsl:text/>
</xsl:template>
```

The effect of this is that the extra newlines and spaces now belong to whitespace-only nodes, which are stripped from the stylesheet and ignored.

Note that it is incorrect to use an `<xsl:text>` element around the `<xsl:value-of>` element, as `<xsl:text>` elements must contain text data only. So the following is wrong:

```
<!-- WRONG -->
        <xsl:text>[ <xsl:value-of select="."/> ]</xsl:text>
<!-- WRONG -->
```

Controlling Output Escaping

Normally, when you try to output a special character such as «<» or «&» in a text node, the special character will be escaped in the output file using the normal XML escaping mechanisms. The escaping is done by the serializer: The text node written in the result tree contains a «<» or «&» character, and the serializer translates this into «<» or «&». The serializer is free to represent the special characters any way it wants, for example it can write «<» as «<», «<», or «<![CDATA[<]]>», because these are all equivalent according to the XML standard. The one thing it will not write is «<». So, it doesn't matter how you write the «<» in your input: The serializer sees a «<» and escapes it in the output.

There are several valid reasons why you might not want this behavior. For example:

❑   The output is not XML or HTML at all; it is (say) a data file in comma-separated-values format.

❑   The output is HTML and you want to exploit one of the many HTML quirks where special characters are needed without escaping, for example a «<» sign in a piece of client-side JavaScript on your HTML page.

❑   The output is XML and you want to achieve some special effect that the XSLT processor won't let you do, for example to output an entity reference such as «&current-date;» or a document type declaration containing an entity declaration.

❑   The output is some format that uses angle-bracket syntax but is not pure XML or HTML; for example, ASP pages or Java Server Pages, which both use «<%» and «%>» as delimiters. (If you are generating Java Server Pages, note that these have an alternative syntax that is pure XML; however, this is not widely used.)

If the output is not XML or HTML at all, then rather than using `disable-output-escaping` it is better to set «method="text"» on the `<xsl:output>` element.

The use of `disable-output-escaping` is often discouraged; indeed it is officially deprecated in XSLT 2.0. The underlying reason for this is that it works only if the result tree is being serialized. If the result tree is fed directly into another application, then `disable-output-escaping` has no effect. This happens, for example, in the Netscape browser, where the HTML-structured result tree is used directly by the rendering engine, without first serializing it as text and then re-parsing it. So a stylesheet that depends on `disable-output-escaping` won't always work.

The second reason that the facility is discouraged is that it's often a symptom of careless programming: Its use reveals that the stylesheet author is thinking too much in terms of creating tags in a serialized file, not in terms of creating nodes in a result tree.

Here's an example of a misuse of disabling output escaping that you will often encounter (only in other people's stylesheets, of course). The author wanted to get markup tags into the output document, and they couldn't see how to achieve this with the regular facilities of `<xsl:element>` or literal result elements. For example, the author might have been thinking along these lines:

```
<!-- WRONG -->
<xsl:template match="bullet"/>
    <xsl:if test='not(preceding::*[1][self::bullet])'>
        <ul>
    </xsl:if>
    <li><xsl:value-of select="."/></li>
    <xsl:if test='not(following::*[1][self::bullet])'>
        </ul>
    </xsl:if>
</xsl:template>
<!-- WRONG -->
```

The intended effect here is to output a `<ul>` tag if the preceding element is not a bullet element, and to output a `</ul>` tag when the following element is not a bullet element. Of course it doesn't work, because the `<ul>` and `</ul>` tags are not properly nested: This template will be thrown out by the XML parser before the XSLT processor even gets to look at it.

So their next thought might be to write the tags as text, as follows:

```
<xsl:template match="bullet"/>
    <xsl:if test='not(preceding::*[self::list-item])'>
        <xsl:text disable-output-escaping="yes">&lt;ul&gt;</xsl:text>
    </xsl:if>
    <li><xsl:value-of select="."/></li>
    <xsl:if test='not(following::*[self::list-item])'>
        <xsl:text disable-output-escaping="yes">/&lt;ul&gt;</xsl:text>
    </xsl:if>
</xsl:template>
```

You now have something that is legal XML and indeed legal XSLT, but it's not guaranteed to work under all circumstances. And even if it does work, it's badly written code, because it's cutting against the grain of the language.

With a bit of thought you can usually find a way to achieve the output you want without resorting to such devices.

The first thing is to think in terms of outputting a result tree containing nodes, not a text file containing tags. Don't try to generate the `<ul>` start tag and the `</ul>` end tag as two separate actions; try to generate a `<ul>` element node as a single action, and then generate its children.

In fact, when you see this kind of logic, you can be pretty sure that the problem being tackled is a grouping problem. The solution to a grouping problem always involves two nested loops: In this case an outer loop to generate the `<ul>` element, and an inner loop to generate the `<li>` elements. The solution to this particular grouping problem is shown as the first example of how to use the `group-adjacent` attribute of `<xsl:for-each-group>`, on page 281.

Examples

Here are two simple examples using `<xsl:text>` to control the output of whitespace:

1. Output first-name and last-name, separated by a space:

```
<xsl:value-of select="first-name"/>
<xsl:text> </xsl:text>
<xsl:value-of select-"last-name"/>
```

Another way to achieve the same effect is to use the `concat()` function:

```
<xsl:value-of select="concat(first-name, ' ', last-name)"/>
```

2. Output a comma-separated list of values:

```
<xsl:output method="text"/>
<xsl:template match="book">
    <xsl:value-of select="title"/>,<xsl:text/>
    <xsl:value-of select="author"/>,<xsl:text/>
    <xsl:value-of select="price"/>,<xsl:text/>
    <xsl:value-of select="isbn"/><xsl:text>
</xsl:text>
</xsl:template>
```

The purpose of the empty `<xsl:text/>` elements is to split the comma and the following newline character into separate text nodes; this ensures that the newline character becomes part of a whitespace-only node, and is therefore not copied to the output. The final `<xsl:text>` element ensures that a newline is written at the end of each record.

Another way to achieve this is with the separator attribute of `<xsl:value-of>`:

```
<xsl:value-of select="title, author, price, isbn" separator=","/>
```

The following example is code that you might see used to output an « » entity reference:

```
<xsl:text disable-output-escaping="yes"> </xsl:text>
```

Note that outputting a #xa0 (or #160) character will generally have exactly the same effect, to do this you can simply write:

```
<xsl:text> </xsl:text>
```

Rather than use `disable-output-escaping` in this situation, which will produce an incorrect result if the result tree is not serialized, a better solution is to use character maps. Output the non–breaking-space character as «#xa0;», and then ask for it to be serialized as « » by defining the character map:

```
<xsl:character-map name="nbsp">
    <xsl:output-character character=" " string=" "/>
</xsl:character-map>
```

The character map must then be referenced by specifying:

```
<xsl:output use-character-maps="nbsp"/>
```

See Also

<xsl:character-map> on page 229
<xsl:value-of> on this page 465

xsl:transform

This is a synonym of <xsl:stylesheet>, described on page 433. The two element names may be used interchangeably.

Why is it useful to have two names for the same thing? Probably because it's the easiest way for a standards committee to keep all its members happy. More seriously, the existence of these two names is indicative of the fact that some people see XSLT as being primarily a language for transforming trees, while others see its main role as defining presentation styles. Take your pick.

Format

```
<xsl:transform
  id? = id
  extension-element-prefixes? = tokens
  exclude-result-prefixes? = tokens
  version = number
  xpath-default-namespace? = uri
  default-validation? = "strict" | "lax" | "preserve" | "strip">
  <!-- Content: (xsl:import*, other-declarations) -->
</xsl:transform>
```

See Also

<xsl:stylesheet> on page 433

xsl:value-of

The <xsl:value-of> instruction constructs a text node, and writes it to the result sequence.

Changes in 2.0

In XSLT 2.0 the value to be output can be obtained by evaluating a contained sequence constructor as an alternative to using the select attribute.

A separator attribute has been added, allowing a sequence of values to be output separated by spaces, commas, or any other convenient string.

Format

```
<xsl:value-of
  select? = expression
  separator? = { string }
```

```
            disable-output-escaping? = "yes" | "no">
    <!-- content: sequence-constructor -->
    </xsl:value-of>
```

Position

`<xsl:value-of>` is an instruction. It is always used as part of a sequence constructor.

Attributes

Name	Value	Meaning
select optional	Expression	The value to be output
separator optional	Attribute value template returning a string	A string to be used to separate adjacent items in the output
disable-output-escaping optional	«yes» | «no»	The value «yes» indicates that special characters in the output (such as «<») should be output as is, rather than using an XML escape form such as «<». The default value is «no»

Content

If the `select` attribute is present, the element must be empty. Otherwise, it may contain a sequence constructor.

Effect

The expression is evaluated. In general, this produces a sequence. This sequence is atomized, which causes any nodes in the sequence to be replaced by their typed values.

If the sequence is empty, the result of the `<xsl:value-of>` instruction is a text node containing a zero-length string. Text nodes are allowed to be zero-length so long as they have no parent. But if you try to use a zero-length text node to form the content of an element, the text node disappears in the process.

If the sequence contains a single value, this is converted to a string (by applying the XPath 2.0 casting rules). A new text node is constructed with this string as its value, and the text node is returned as the result of the `<xsl:value-of>` instruction (which usually means it will be written to a result tree). If the sequence (after atomization) contains more than one item, then the effect depends on whether backwards compatibility mode is enabled. This depends on the nearest `version` or `xsl:version` attribute found on a containing element, known as the effective version. If the effective version is less than «2.0», then backwards compatibility mode is in force. However, if there is a `separator` attribute, then the instruction behaves according to the XSLT 2.0 rules regardless of the effective version.

Under the backwards compatibility rules, any item after the first in the sequence is discarded, and the function behaves as if the sequence only contained one item (the rules for this have already been described).

Under the 2.0 rules, each value in the atomized sequence is converted to a string by applying the XPath casting rules, and these strings are concatenated, with the chosen separator inserted between adjacent strings. Unless this concatenated string is zero-length, a new text node is constructed that contains this string as its value, and the text node is returned as the result of the instruction.

The default separator (under the 2.0 rules) is a single space when the `select` attribute is used, or a zero-length string when a sequence constructor is used. This means that

```
<a><xsl:value-of select="1 to 5"/></a>
```

will output

```
<a>1 2 3 4 5</a>
```

but:

```
<a>
  <xsl:value-of>[<xsl:sequence select="1 to 5"/>]</xsl:value-of>
</a>
```

will output:

```
<a>[12345]</a>
```

The `disable-output-escaping` attribute has the same effect as it has with `<xsl:text>`. Special characters such as «<» in the string value of the select expression will be escaped just as if they occurred in literal text, and the `disable-output-escaping` attribute can be used to suppress this in the same way. For details, see `<xsl:text>` on page 459.

Usage

The `<xsl:value-of>` element is the most common way of writing text to a result tree.

The other ways of writing text nodes to the result tree are to include text literally in the stylesheet (perhaps within an `<xsl:text>` instruction) or to use `<xsl:copy>` or `<xsl:copy-of>`. You could generally make do without using `<xsl:value-of>` at all, because `<xsl:value-of select="X" separator="Y"/>` is in most cases equivalent to `<xsl:copy-of select="string-join(X, 'Y')"/>`.
The slight difference between the two is that `<xsl:value-of>` always returns a text node, whereas `<xsl:copy-of>` in this example returns a string; but in most situations, these are interchangeable.

Another alternative is to use `<xsl:apply-templates>` on a text node and rely on the built-in template for text nodes, which is equivalent to `<xsl:value-of select="."/>`.

The `<xsl:value-of>` instruction is often an effective alternative to navigating the source tree recursively using `<xsl:apply-templates>`. For example:

```
<xsl:template match="book">
  <book>
    <publisher><xsl:value-of select="../@name"/></publisher>
    <title><xsl:value-of select="@title"/></title>
    <author><xsl:value-of select="@author"/></author>
    <isbn><xsl:value-of select="@isbn"/></isbn>
```

```
        </book>
    </xsl:template>
```

You will often see `<xsl:value-of>` being used when there is actually no need to create a text node, for example when returning a result from a called template. This is because in XSLT 1.0, there was nothing better available. For example it is common to write a named template that replaces characters in a filename as follows:

```
<xsl:template name="change-filename">
    <xsl:param name="filename"/>
    <xsl:value-of select="translate($filename, '\', '/')"/>
</xsl:template>
```

But in XSLT 2.0 it would be better to return a string rather than a text node:

```
<xsl:template name="change-filename">
    <xsl:param name="filename"/>
    <xsl:sequence select="translate($filename, '\', '/')"/>
</xsl:template>
```

Either way, however, the template can then be called as follows, to get the result into the variable `$new-filename`:

```
<xsl:variable name="$new-filename">
    <xsl:call-template name="change-filename">
        <xsl:with-param name="$old-filename"/>
    </xsl:call-template>
</xsl:variable>
```

The value of variable `$new-filename` is actually a temporary tree, but for all practical purposes it can be treated as a string. In fact, it would be better to declare it as a string:

```
<xsl:variable name="$new-filename" as="xs:string">
    <xsl:call-template name="change-filename">
        <xsl:with-param name="$old-filename"/>
    </xsl:call-template>
</xsl:variable>
```

When the requirement is to return a string, there is no point in creating a text node and then letting the caller extract the string value of the text node. Although it all happens automatically, you are asking the system to do more work than is necessary.

```
The option to use the sequence constructor to obtain the value, rather than
the  select attribute, is provided mainly to make  <xsl:value-of> compatible
with other instructions such as  <xsl:attribute> and  <xsl:comment>. It does
not add any important new capability.
```

Avoiding Surprises

There are two situations in which `<xsl:value-of>` might not give the result you expect.

The first should be less common with XSLT 2.0 than it was with 1.0, but it will still happen in stylesheets that specify «version="1.0"» and thus invoke backwards compatibility mode. This is the fact that only the first item in a sequence is actually output. For example, if the context node is a <book> element and you specify <xsl:value-of select="author"/>, only the first author (in document order) will actually be output. This changes when you specify «version="2.0"»: All the authors are now output, using a single space as the default separator.

Of course, if you have become accustomed to the 1.0 behavior, then the surprise might be the other way around. If your stylesheet specifies <xsl:value-of select="following-sibling::para"/>, then when you change it to say «version="2.0"», the output will contain all the following sibling paragraphs rather than just the first. You can easily correct this by changing it to <xsl:value-of select="following-sibling::para[1]"/>.

The second situation that sometimes causes surprise is typified by the question "Why have all the tags disappeared?" If you use <xsl:value-of> to output an element such as a <para> element that contains complex or mixed content, then it will extract the value of this element as a string. If there are nested elements, for example elements marked up by tags such as <i> or <b>, then these are lost in the course of converting to a string. If you want these tags to appear in the output, then use <xsl:copy-of> to copy the element, not <xsl:value-of>.

This situation may also change in XSLT 2.0 if you use a schema-aware processor. If the select expression selects an element, and the element is described in the schema as having complex element-only content, then atomization will raise a runtime error. For example if the source document contains the element:

```
<book>
    <title>XSLT 2.0 Programmer's Reference</title>
    <author>Michael Kay</author>
    <publisher>Wiley</publisher>
</book>
```

then with a processor that is not schema-aware (or an XSLT 1.0 processor), the instruction <xsl:value-of select="book"/> will produce the output:

```
XSLT 2.0 Programmer's ReferenceMichael KayWiley
```

But with a schema-aware processor, assuming the schema declaration is:

```
<xs:element name="book">
    <xs:complexType>
        <xs:sequence>
            <xs:element name="title" type="xs:string"/>
            <xs:element name="author" type="xs:string"/>
            <xs:element name="publisher" type="xs:string"/>
        </xs:sequence>
    </xs:complexType>
</xs:element>
```

the result will be a runtime error. If you want to concatenate the text nodes within the <book> element then you can still do so, using the string() function, but it's not something that atomization will do automatically for you. This is because, for data-oriented XML, it doesn't usually make sense. With mixed content however (where text and markedup elements can be freely mixed in the content) it does make sense to extract the textual content without the markup, and <xsl:value-of> will do this whether or not there is a schema.

Mixed content is described in the schema using `<xs:complexType mixed="true">`.

Using disable-output-escaping

One technique used quite often is to wrap HTML inside an XML document, for example:

```
<message>
  <header>
    <sent-by>Dept 178</sent-by>
    <recipient>App 263</recipient>
  </header>
  <content type="text/html">
    <![CDATA[
       <html>
          <head><title>An HTML page with unmatched tags</title></head>
          <body>HTML authors are often lazy!<p></body>
       </html>
    ]]>
  </content>
</message>
```

One way you can include the HTML within the XML message is to put it through a program such as Dave Raggett's *html tidy* utility (available from `http://www.w3.org/`), which converts it to well-formed XHTML. But you may not want to risk changing it, so using a CDATA section as shown here is the only alternative. When you do this, however, the «<» and «>» characters are no longer treated as mark up characters, they are now ordinary text. If you try to run an XSLT transformation that outputs the HTML enclosed in this message, these characters will therefore be escaped, typically by writing them as «<» and «>». This isn't what you want; so you can solve the problem by writing:

```
<xsl:template match="content[@type='text/html']">
  <xsl:value-of select="." disable-output-escaping="yes"/>
</xsl:template>
```

But remember that this is likely to work only if the output is serialized by the XSLT processor; it won't work if you write the result to a DOM.

Examples

The table below shows some common ways in which `<xsl:value-of>` is used.

Instruction	Effect
`<xsl:value-of select="."/>`	Output the string value of the current node
`<xsl:value-of select="title"/>`	Output the string value of the first child `<title>` element of the current node
`<xsl:value-of select="sum(@*)"/>`	Output the sum of the values of the attributes of the current node, converted to a string. If there is any non-numeric attribute, the result will be "NaN"
`<xsl:value-of select="$x"/>`	Output the value of variable $x, after converting it to a string

See Also

<xsl:copy-of> on page 245
<xsl:text> on page 459

xsl:variable

The <xsl:variable> element is used to declare a local or global variable in a stylesheet, and to give it a value.

Changes in 2.0

A new attribute, as, has been introduced. This allows the type of the variable to be declared; it also determines whether an <xsl:variable> element containing a sequence constructor will use the value of the sequence to construct a temporary tree, or will simply set the value of the variable to be this sequence.

Format

```
<xsl:variable
  name = qname
  select? = expression
  as? = sequence-type>
  <!-- Content: sequence-constructor -->
</xsl:variable>
```

Position

The <xsl:variable> element may appear either as a top-level declaration (that is, as a child of the <xsl:stylesheet> element), or as an instruction within a sequence constructor.

Attributes

Name	Value	Meaning
name mandatory	lexical QName	The name of the variable
select optional	Expression	An expression that is evaluated to give the value of the variable. If omitted, the value is determined from the contents of the <xsl:variable> element
as optional	SequenceType	Declares the type of the variable. A type error occurs if the value of the expression cannot be converted to this type using the standard type conversions defined below (page 476). In addition, the presence of this attribute on an <xsl:variable> element with nonempty content indicates that the result of evaluating the contained sequence constructor is to be used directly as the value of the variable, rather than being used to construct a temporary tree

The SequenceType construct is outlined in Chapter 4, and described in full detail in Chapter 9 of *XPath 2.0 Programmer's Reference*.

Content

An optional sequence constructor. If a `select` attribute is present, the `<xsl:variable>` element must be empty.

Effect

An `<xsl:variable>` element may appear either at the top level of the stylesheet (in which case it declares a global variable) or as an instruction within a sequence constructor (in which case it declares a local variable).

The Name of the Variable

The name of the variable is defined by a lexical QName. Normally this will be a simple name such as «`city`» or «`total-sales`», but it may be a name qualified with a prefix, for example «`my:value`». If it has a prefix, the prefix must correspond to a namespace that is in scope at that point in the stylesheet. The true name of the variable, for the purpose of testing whether two names are the same, is determined not by the prefix but by the namespace URI corresponding to the prefix: So two variables «`my:value`» and «`your:value`» have the same name if the prefixes «`my`» and «`your`» refer to the same namespace URI. If the name has no prefix, it has a null namespace URI—it does not use the default namespace URI.

The scope of a global variable is the entire stylesheet, including any stylesheets that are included or imported. A global variable may even be referenced before it is declared. The only constraint is that circular definitions are not allowed; if variable x is defined in terms of y, then y may not be defined directly or indirectly in terms of x.

The scope of a local variable is block-structured; it may be referenced in any following sibling element or in a descendant of a following sibling. This is illustrated in Figure 5-16.

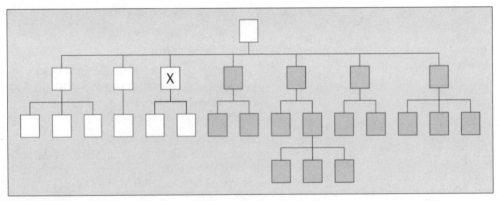

Figure 5-16

The diagram shows, for a variable X, the elements that may contain a reference to X; the shaded elements may refer to X, and the unshaded elements may not. Specifically, a local variable may be referenced in any following sibling element, or in a descendant of a following sibling. It cannot be referenced within its own descendants, and it goes out of scope when the end tag for its parent element is encountered. Unlike global variables, a forwards reference to a local variable is not allowed. If you think of XSLT instructions as being like the statements in a block-structured language such as C, Java, or JavaScript, and the enclosing element as being like a block enclosed in these languages by curly braces, the scope rules will seem very familiar.

Two global variables may have the same name only if they have different *import precedence*; in other words, if one of them was in an imported stylesheet (for further details, see <xsl:import> on page 312). In this case, the definition with higher import precedence wins. Note that the higher precedence definition applies everywhere, even within the imported stylesheet that contains the lower precedence definition. This means it is not a good idea to rely on precedence to resolve accidental name clashes between independently developed modules, it's better to use namespaces.

XSLT 1.0 did not allow a local variable to be defined with the same name as another local variable already in scope. This restriction was there as a way of detecting user errors. The restriction has gone in XSLT 2.0, although there is still a warning in the specification advising that this isn't good practice. In fact, not all XSLT 1.0 processors actually enforced this rule. If a variable reference is used when two or more variables with the matching name are in scope, then the reference is taken to refer to the one whose scope is smallest.

This principle extends to variables declared within an XPath expression. To take an extreme example, it is legal to write:

```
<xsl:variable name="x" select="'A'"/>

<xsl:template match="para">
  <xsl:variable name="x" select="$x, 'B'"/>
  <xsl:variable name="x" select="$x, 'C'"/>
  <xsl:value-of select="for $x in ($x, 'D') return ($x, '+')"/>
</xsl:template>
```

The output of the template will be «A + B + C + D +».

These rules on uniqueness and scope of names apply equally to parameters declared using <xsl:param>; the <xsl:param> instruction is effectively just another way of declaring a variable.

The Value of the Variable

The value of the variable may be given either by the XPath expression in the select attribute, or by the contents of the contained sequence constructor. If there is a select attribute, the <xsl:variable> element should be empty. If there is no select attribute and the sequence constructor is empty, the value of the variable is a zero-length string, unless there is an as attribute, in which case the value is an empty sequence (assuming that the as attribute permits an empty sequence).

The table below summarizes the different ways of specifying the value. The numbers in brackets refer to the numbered paragraphs below the table that explain the option in more detail.

		select present	**select absent**
content present	**as** present	error	Evaluate the content constructor and return its value, checking the type against the as attribute (3)
content present	**as** absent	error	Evaluate the content constructor and use it to build a temporary tree (4)
content absent	**as** present	Evaluate the select expression and return its value, checking the type against the as attribute (1)	Return an empty sequence, provided the as attribute allows an empty sequence (5)
content absent	**as** absent	Evaluate the select expression and return its value (2)	Return a zero-length string (6)

1. If the select attribute is provided, its value must be an XPath expression. This expression is evaluated. The value is checked against the type specified in the as attribute, and if necessary is converted to this type using the standard conversion rules described on page 476. An error occurs if this conversion is not possible. The processor may report this as a compile-time error if it can tell at compile time that the value of the expression will never be convertible to the required type. Otherwise, it will report the error at runtime. For example:

```
<xsl:variable name="pi" select="3.14159" as="xs:double"/>
```

Here the value of the select expression is of type xs:decimal, but the final value of the variable is an xs:double, because the as attribute forces a conversion.

2. If the select attribute is provided without an as attribute, the effect is the same as if «as="item()*"» were specified: No type checking or conversion takes place, and the value may be of any type. For example:

```
<xsl:variable name="pi" select="3.14159e0"/>
```

Here the value of the select attribute is again of type xs:double, but for a different reason: It was written as a double literal, and no conversion has taken place.

3. If a sequence constructor is used with an as attribute, the instructions in the sequence constructor are evaluated. The result sequence is checked against the type specified in the as attribute, and is converted if necessary using the standard conversion rules. Again, an error is reported if the conversion is not possible. For example:

```
<xsl:variable name="n" as="xs:integer">
    <xsl:number/>
</xsl:variable>
```

Here the sequence constructor returns a single text node. The contents of this text node are converted to an integer, which becomes the value of the variable.

4. If a sequence constructor is used with no `as` attribute, a temporary tree is constructed. This is done by creating a new document node, and using the value of the result sequence to form the children of the document node. The detailed rules for constructing the content of the document node are the same as those for the `<xsl:document>` instruction, and are given on page 258. The value of the variable will be the document node at the root of the temporary tree. For example:

```
<xsl:variable name="tree">
   <data>
     <country code="de">Germany</country>
     <country code="fr">France</country>
     <country code="gb">United Kingdom</country>
     <country code="us">United States</country>
   </data>
</xsl:variable>
```

Here the value of the variable is a document node, whose only child is a `<data>` element, which in turn has four `<country>` elements as its children. Temporary trees are described in more detail on page 481.

5. The following example declares a parameter whose default value is an empty sequence:

```
<xsl:param name="codes" as="xs:integer*"/>
```

This option is not very useful for variables, but `<xsl:param>` follows exactly the same rules as `<xsl:variable>`, and it can be useful there.

6. The following example declares a parameter whose default value is a zero-length string:

```
<xsl:param name="input"/>
```

Again, this option is not useful for variables, but `<xsl:param>` follows exactly the same rules as `<xsl:variable>`, and it can be useful there.

Note that if an expression is used to assign a literal string value to a variable, the string literal must be enclosed in quotes, and these quotes are additional to the quotes used around the XML attribute. So to assign the string value «London» to the variable named «city», you can write either of the following:

```
<xsl:variable name="city" select="'London'"/>
<xsl:variable name="city" select='"London"'/>
```

You can also write:

```
<xsl:variable name="city" as="xs:string">London</xsl:variable>
```

A common mistake is to write:

```
<xsl:variable name="city" select="London"/> <!-- WRONG -->
```

This sets the value of «$city» to a sequence containing all the element children of the current node that have element name <London>. This will probably be an empty sequence, so if you use the variable as a string, its value will be a zero-length string. You won't get any error message if you make this mistake, because it's a perfectly valid thing to write, it will just cause your stylesheet to produce the wrong output.

A schema-aware XSLT processor might give you a warning saying that there is no <London> element defined in the schema; but you can't rely on this.

You won't be alone if you make this mistake; there's an example of it in the original XSLT 1.0 specification, which had to be fixed in a subsequent erratum.

You don't need the extra quotes if you want the value to be a number:

```
<xsl:variable name="max-size" select="255"/>
```

Standard Conversion Rules

This section provides the detailed conversion rules used when converting the supplied value of a variable (the result of evaluating its `select` attribute or its sequence constructor) to the type required by the `as` attribute. The same conversion rules are used under a number of other circumstances, such as when values are supplied for stylesheet parameters. They are the same as the *function conversion rules* defined in XPath 2.0, which define what happens when the supplied arguments in a function call differ from the declared types of the parameters, with the exception that the rules described here never use XPath 1.0 backwards compatibility mode. The reason for this is that they are always invoked in contexts where backwards compatibility issues do not arise.

The rules take as input a *supplied value* and a *required type*, and they produce as output a *result value*. The required type has two parts: the *required item type* (for example, integer or element) and the *required cardinality*. The required cardinality may be *exactly-one* (when there is no occurrence indicator in the SequenceType as written) or *zero-or-one*, *zero-or-more*, or *one-or-more*, corresponding to the occurrence indicators «?», «*», and «+».

Instead of returning a result value, the rules may also result in a type error, if the supplied value cannot be converted to the required type.

The rules are as follows:

1. If the supplied value is an instance of the required type, return it as the result value.

2. If the required item type is an atomic type, the supplied value is atomized. Atomization causes each node in the supplied sequence to be replaced by its typed value, while leaving any atomic values in the sequence unchanged. Note that the typed value of a node can itself be a sequence of zero or more atomic values. Elements declared in the schema to have element-only content have no typed value, so this operation can result in an error.

3. Any item in the atomized sequence that is of type `xdt:untypedAtomic` is cast to the required type. Such items are most likely to arise as the result of atomizing a node in a schema-less document. This means, for example, that an attribute such as `@date-of-birth` will be acceptable where the required type is `xs:date`, provided that either (a) the attribute is annotated as an `xs:date` as a result of schema validation, or (b) the attribute is unvalidated and its textual form is acceptable as an `xs:date`.

4. If the required item type is a numeric type (one of `xs:double`, `xs:float`, `xs:decimal`, or `xs:integer`, or a type derived from these by restricting the range of values), then any numeric value in the atomized sequence is promoted to the required numeric type where possible. An integer can be promoted to any other numeric type; a decimal can be promoted to `xs:float` or `xs:double`; and an `xs:float` can be converted to an `xs:double`. However, other conversions

are not possible, for example if the required item type is `xs:integer` but the supplied value is `xs:double`, a type error will be reported.

If, after these conversions, the sequence conforms to the required type, then it is returned as the result value. If not, the system reports a type error. Type errors may be reported at runtime, but if the system can tell in advance that the expression will return a value of the wrong type, then they can also be reported at compile time.

These rules are not as liberal as the rules that were used in XPath 1.0 for type conversions, where, for example, a boolean could be supplied when a string was expected, and it would be treated as the string `"true"` or `"false"`. Because the type system in XSLT 2.0 is so much richer, you have to get used to the idea of thinking about what type of value you are handling, and of doing any necessary conversions yourself, using explicit casts or calls on constructor functions.

Usage

Variables are useful, as in any programming language, to avoid calculating the same result more than once.

Global variables are useful for defining constants, such as a color value, that will be used in many places throughout the stylesheet. They can also be used to extract values from the principal source document.

Unlike variables in many programming languages, *XSLT variables cannot be updated*. Once they are given an initial value, they retain this value until they go out of scope. This feature has a profound effect on the programming style used when a stylesheet needs to do calculations. The subject of *programming without assignment statements* is discussed in detail in Chapter 9.

Examples

Most XSLT variables fall into one of the three categories:

❑ Variables used to avoid repeating a common expression in more than one place. This might be simply to make the code more readable, or to ensure that you only have to make a change in one place if the value changes, or perhaps because it gives a performance benefit.

❑ Variables used to capture context-sensitive information, allowing the variable to be used after the context has changed.

❑ Variables holding a temporary tree (or a result tree fragment as it was known in XSLT 1.0).

In each case the variable might be local or global. I'll show some examples of each kind.

Convenience Variables

Consider this example, which calculates the number of goals scored by, and against, a soccer team.

```
<xsl:variable name="for"
              select="sum($matches/team[.=$this]/@score)"/>
<xsl:variable name="against"
              select="sum($matches[team=$this]/team/@score) - $for"/>
...
<td><xsl:value-of select="$for"/></td>
<td><xsl:value-of select="$against"/></td>
```

This uses two rather complex expressions to construct the variables «for» and «against», which calculate the number of goals scored by, and against, the team identified by the variable «$team».

It would be quite possible in this case to avoid using the variable «against». The expression that calculates its value could equally be written at the point where the variable is used, in the second <xsl:value-of> instruction. The same is true of the «for» variable, though this time the expression would need to be written twice, in both places where the variable is used, and this might give a performance penalty. However, these variables are really being used only for clarity; it would be quite possible to write the stylesheet without them.

This is true because nothing can change between the variables being defined and being used. The source document can't change, and the values of the variables $team and $matches can't change. The context (for example the current position in the source document) can change, but in this example (a) it doesn't, and (b) the expressions don't depend on the context anyway.

I call these *convenience variables* because you could get by without them if you had to (though there might be a performance hit). They can be used either as global variables or as local variables. Creating global convenience variables that refer to sets of nodes in the source document is often a useful programming technique, for example:

```
<xsl:variable name="group-A-matches" select="//match[@group='A']"/>
```

These act rather like views in an SQL database.

Variables to Capture Context-Sensitive Values

These variables are most often useful in conjunction with <xsl:for-each>, which changes the context item. Consider the following example:

Example: Using a Variable for Context-Sensitive Values

This example shows how a variable can be used to hold on to information that depends on the context, for use when the context has changed.

Source

The source file is opera.xml. It contains a list of operas and details of their composers.

```xml
<?xml version="1.0"?>
<programme>
    <opera>
        <title>The Magic Flute</title>
        <composer>Mozart</composer>
        <date>1791</date>
    </opera>
    <opera>
        <title>Don Giovanni</title>
        <composer>Mozart</composer>
        <date>1787</date>
    </opera>
```

```
            <opera>
                <title>Ernani</title>
                <composer>Verdi</composer>
                <date>1843</date>
            </opera>
            <opera>
                <title>Rigoletto</title>
                <composer>Verdi</composer>
                <date>1850</date>
            </opera>
            <opera>
                <title>Tosca</title>
                <composer>Puccini</composer>
                <date>1897</date>
            </opera>
            <composer name="Mozart">
                <fullname>Wolfgang Amadeus Mozart</fullname>
                <born>1756</born>
                <died>1791</died>
            </composer>
            <composer name="Verdi">
                <fullname>Guiseppe Verdi</fullname>
                <born>1813</born>
                <died>1901</died>
            </composer>
            <composer name="Puccini">
                <fullname>Giacomo Puccini</fullname>
                <born>1858</born>
                <died>1924</died>
            </composer>
        </programme>
```

Stylesheet

The stylesheet is the file `opera.xsl`. This is a complete stylesheet: It uses the simplified stylesheet syntax described on page 119, in Chapter 3.

The stylesheet contains two nested `<xsl:for-each>` loops. In the outer loop, it sets a variable «c» to the context node (the current composer). In the expression controlling the inner loop, this variable is used. It would not be correct to use «.» in place of «$c», because the `<composer>` element is no longer the context node. In this example it would be possible to use the `current()` function here (this function is described on page 526, in Chapter 7), but there are other cases where a variable is necessary.

```
<html
    xmlns:xsl="http://www.w3.org/1999/XSL/Transform"
    xsl:version="1.0">

<body><center>
    <h1>Programme</h1>
    <xsl:for-each select="/programme/composer">
        <h2><xsl:value-of
            select="concat(fullname, ' (', born, '-', died, ')')"/></h2>
        <xsl:variable name="c" select="."/>
```

```
        <xsl:for-each select="/programme/opera[composer=$c/@name]">
            <p><xsl:value-of select="title"/></p>
        </xsl:for-each>
    </xsl:for-each>
</center></body>
</html>
```

Output

See Figure 5-17.

Figure 5-17

One case where context variables are very useful is when handling multiple source documents.

In any stylesheet that handles multiple source documents, it is useful to include a global variable that refers to the document node of the principal source document, thus:

```
<xsl:variable name="root" select="/"/>
```

This means it is always possible to refer to the source document by using this variable. Without this, when the context node is in a secondary document, there is no way of accessing data from the principal document. For example, the expression «//item» refers to all <item> elements in the same document as the context node. If you actually want all <item> elements in the principal source document, then (provided you have included the global variable declaration above) you can use the expression «$root//item».

If there is a document referenced from the stylesheet, for example to hold look-up data such as messages or tax rates, it is also useful to define this in a global variable, for example:

```
<xsl:variable name="tax-rates" select="document('tax-rates.xml')"/>
```

Temporary Trees

The value of a variable is a temporary tree (or result tree fragment as it was known in XSLT 1.0) if it is defined using the content of the `<xsl:variable>` element rather than the `select` attribute, and if there is no as attribute.

Temporary trees can be divided into two categories: trivial trees and genuine trees.

A trivial temporary tree will only contain a single text node, in which case it behaves almost exactly like a string variable. Here is an example:

```
<xsl:variable name="width">
   <xsl:choose>
      <xsl:when test="@width">
         <xsl:value-of select="@width"/>
      </xsl:when>
      <xsl:otherwise>0</xsl:otherwise>
   </xsl:choose>
</xsl:variable>
```

Such a variable can often be useful for expanding the default value of an attribute. Subsequently the variable `$width` can be used in calculations in place of the attribute `@width`, without worrying about the case where the attribute was omitted. The fact that the variable is technically a tree rather than a string does not affect the way it can be used.

I prefer in such cases to specify the type of the variable explicitly (which means that the type is no longer a document node):

```
<xsl:variable name="width" as="xs:integer">
   <xsl:choose>
      <xsl:when test="@width">
         <xsl:sequence select="@width"/>
      </xsl:when>
      <xsl:otherwise>0</xsl:otherwise>
   </xsl:choose>
</xsl:variable>
```

Or more concisely:

```
<xsl:variable name="width" as="xs:integer"
   select="if (@width) then @width else 0"/>
```

Or perhaps even:

```
<xsl:variable name="width" as="xs:integer" select="(@width, 0)[1]"/>
```

There are several benefits in declaring the type. Firstly, it's good documentation for anyone reading the stylesheet. Secondly, it causes the system to do some error checking for you: If the width isn't an integer, you'll get an appropriate error message. Finally, it's likely to be more efficient. A temporary tree is a rather heavyweight object compared with an integer.

In the example above I substituted `<xsl:sequence>` for `<xsl:value-of>`. In fact either instruction would work (in both examples). The system would carry out any necessary conversions automatically.

481

But in the second example, using `<xsl:value-of>` would create a text node, only to extract its value and convert this to an integer, which is unnecessarily inefficient.

Beginners often try to write this as:

```
<xsl:choose>
   <xsl:when test="@width">
      <xsl:variable name="width" select="@width"/>
   </xsl:when>
   <xsl:otherwise>
      <xsl:variable name="width" select="0"/>
   </xsl:otherwise>
</xsl:choose>
```

This won't work, because when you get to the end tag of the `<xsl:choose>` element, both variable declarations will have gone out of scope!

Tree-valued variables are useful when you use `<xsl:call-template>` or `<xsl:apply-templates>` to calculate a value that you then want to manipulate further. The next example shows how this works in the case of `<xsl:call-template>`, but the same applies equally to `<xsl:apply-templates>`.

Example: Getting the Result of <xsl:call-template> in a Variable

This example calls a general-purpose template to format a list of items. It captures the result of this template in a variable, and then performs further processing on the result.

Source

The source file is the list of operas and composers used in the previous example, `opera.xml`.

Stylesheet

The stylesheet is the file `composers.xsl`.

This stylesheet uses a general-purpose named template («`make-list`») to output a list of names in the form «`A; B; C; and D`». It passes this template a sequence of nodes containing the names of all the composers in the source document. On return from the «`make-list`» template, it extracts the result of this template into a variable (which will be a temporary tree containing a single text node), and passes this variable into the `translate()` function (described in *XPath 2.0 Programmer's Reference*, Chapter 10) to convert the commas to semicolons. The `translate()` function converts its first argument to a string, which in this case extracts the value of the text node from the tree.

```
<xsl:stylesheet
    xmlns:xsl="http://www.w3.org/1999/XSL/Transform"
    version="1.0">

<xsl:template match="/">
    <xsl:variable name="list">
        <xsl:call-template name="make-list">
            <xsl:with-param name="names"
                           select="/programme/composer/fullname"/>
```

```
            </xsl:call-template>
        </xsl:variable>
        This week's composers are:
        <xsl:value-of select="translate($list, ',', ';')"/>
    </xsl:template>

    <xsl:template name="make-list">
        <xsl:param name="names"/>
        <xsl:for-each select="$names">
            <xsl:value-of select="."/>
            <xsl:if test="position()!=last()">, </xsl:if>
            <xsl:if test="position()=last()-1">and </xsl:if>
        </xsl:for-each>
    </xsl:template>

</xsl:stylesheet>
```

Output

This week's composers are:

```
Wolfgang Amadeus Mozart; Guiseppe Verdi; and Giacomo Puccini
```

Most of the examples so far have used trivial trees, those containing a single text node. These can be manipulated to all intents and purposes as if they were strings, with the additional feature that the string will be converted to whatever type is required when it is used. (Technically, the value of the variable is a document node. The standard type conversions will atomize this document node if necessary, which returns a value of type xdt:untypedAtomic, and in contexts where the standard conversion rules are used, such as function calls and XSLT variable initialization, a value of xdt:untypedAtomic will be automatically cast to the required type.) Although convenient, you should be aware that using a trivial temporary tree rather than an atomic value is likely to incur some system overhead.

Genuine (nontrivial) temporary trees have a rather more important role to play. They are needed whenever you require working data that is too complex to hold in a simple sequence. With XSLT 2.0, it is possible to perform any operation on a temporary tree that you can perform on the principal source document, or on a document loaded using the document() function. This greatly increases their usefulness. There are two main categories:

❑   Intermediate results of a multiphase transformation.

    It's often useful to break up a transformation into a sequence of steps, to simplify the logic. A temporary tree can be used as the output of the first phase and the input to the next.

❑   Working data passed as a parameter through template or function calls.

    For example, if you need to create a data structure such as a list of keyword/value pairs, and pass this as a parameter to a function or template, then the best way to construct this data structure is as a tree.

The next example shows a multiphase transformation.

Example: A MultiPhase Transformation

This example performs a transformation in two phases. The first phase starts with a list containing the results of a series of soccer matches, and computes a league table showing the standing of the various teams. The second phase renders this league table in HTML. These are quite separate operations and it's best to keep them separate. In fact, we'll keep them completely separate by using different stylesheet modules and different modes.

Source

The source document is `soccer.xml`. It contains the results of individual matches. Here are the first few:

```
<results group="A">
<match>
<date>10-Jun-98</date>
<team score="2">Brazil</team>
<team score="1">Scotland</team>
</match>
<match>
<date>10-Jun-98</date>
<team score="2">Morocco</team>
<team score="2">Norway</team>
</match>
<match>
<date>16-Jun-98</date>
<team score="1">Scotland</team>
<team score="1">Norway</team>
</match>
...
</results>
```

Stylesheet

The first phase of the transformation calculates a league table. This is in module `league.xsl`, shown below:

```
<xsl:transform
  xmlns:xsl="http://www.w3.org/1999/XSL/Transform"
  version="2.0"
>

<xsl:variable name="teams" select="distinct-values(//team)"/>
<xsl:variable name="matches" select="//match"/>

<xsl:template match="results">
<league>
  <xsl:for-each select="$teams">
    <xsl:variable name="this" select="."/>
    <xsl:variable name="played" select="count($matches[team=$this])"/>
    <xsl:variable name="won"
         select="count($matches[team[.=$this]/@score gt
                               team[.!=$this]/@score])"/>
```

```
        <xsl:variable name="lost"
             select="count($matches[team[.=$this]/@score lt
                                    team[.!=$this]/@score])"/>
        <xsl:variable name="drawn"
             select="count($matches[team[.=$this]/@score eq
                                    team[.!=$this]/@score])"/>
        <xsl:variable name="for"
             select="sum($matches/team[.=current()]/@score)"/>
        <xsl:variable name="against"
             select="sum($matches[team=current()]/team/@score) - $for"/>

        <team name="{.}" played="{$played}" won="{$won}" drawn="{$drawn}"
             lost="{$lost}" for="{$for}" against="{$against}"/>

    </xsl:for-each>
  </league>
</xsl:template>

</xsl:transform>
```

Since we're talking about usage of `<xsl:variable>` here, it's worth drawing attention to the way this example uses variables. There are a couple of global variables to define the list of teams and the list of matches. Since the stylesheet only contains one template, these variables could equally well have been local, but making them global reflects the fact that they are potentially reusable. Within the template, the variable $this is set to the context item so that it can be used within predicates, where the context item will have changed. Then the computation is done entirely within a sequence of local variable declarations. This is a very characteristic programming style. Finally, the template outputs one `<team>` element for each team, with attributes indicating the number of matches won and lost, the goals scored, and so on.

The second stylesheet renders the league table into HTML. It's quite straightforward:

```
<xsl:transform
 xmlns:xsl="http://www.w3.org/1999/XSL/Transform"
 version="2.0"
>

<xsl:import href="league.xsl"/>

<xsl:variable name="league">
  <xsl:apply-templates select="results"/>
</xsl:variable>
```

Note the variable here to capture the result of the first phase of processing. The value of this variable will be a document node containing the `<league>` element created by the previous stylesheet.

```
<xsl:template match="/">
<html>
  <head><title>League Table</title></head>
  <body>
    <h1>League Table</h1>
    <xsl:copy-of select="$league"/>
    <table border="2" cellpadding="5">
```

```
      <thead>
        <th>Team</th>
        <th>Played</th>
        <th>Won</th>
        <th>Lost</th>
        <th>Drawn</th>
        <th>For</th>
        <th>Against</th>
      </thead>
      <tbody>
      <xsl:for-each select="$league/league/team">
        <tr>
          <td><xsl:value-of select="@name"/></td>
          <td><xsl:value-of select="@played"/></td>
          <td><xsl:value-of select="@won"/></td>
          <td><xsl:value-of select="@lost"/></td>
          <td><xsl:value-of select="@drawn"/></td>
          <td><xsl:value-of select="@for"/></td>
          <td><xsl:value-of select="@against"/></td>
        </tr>
      </xsl:for-each>
      </tbody>
    </table>
  </body>
</html>
</xsl:template>

</xsl:transform>
```

Output

The output of the stylesheet is shown in Figure 5-18.

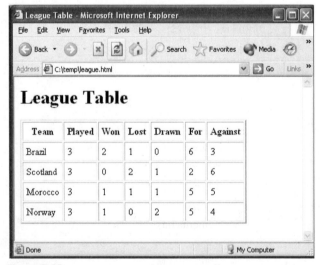

Figure 5-18

See Also

<xsl:param> on page 392

xsl:when

The <xsl:when> element always appears as a child of <xsl:choose>. It defines a condition to be tested and the action to be performed if the condition is true.

Changes in 2.0

None.

Format

```
<xsl:when
  test = expression>
  <!-- Content: sequence-constructor -->
</xsl:when>
```

Position

<xsl:when> is always a child element of <xsl:choose>. There must be at least one <xsl:when> element within an <xsl:choose> element.

Attributes

Name	Value	Meaning
test mandatory	Expression	The boolean condition to be tested

Content

A sequence constructor.

Effect

The <xsl:choose> element is evaluated as follows:

❑ The first <xsl:when> element whose test expression has an effective boolean value of true is selected; subsequent <xsl:when> elements are ignored regardless of the value of their test expression.

❑ If none of the <xsl:when> elements has a test expression that is true, the <xsl:otherwise> element is selected. If there is no <xsl:otherwise> instruction, no element is selected.

❑ The sequence constructor contained in the selected child element (if any) is evaluated in the current context: that is, the effect is as if the relevant sequence constructor appeared in place of the <xsl:choose> instruction.

Any XPath expression may be evaluated to obtain an effective boolean value. In brief, the rules are:

❑ If the value of the expression is an empty sequence, the effective boolean value is false.

❑ If the value of the expression is a single atomic value, the effective boolean value is `false` if the value is a zero-length string, the boolean value `false`, a number (integer, decimal, float, or double) equal to zero, or the special value NaN (not a number). Otherwise the effective boolean value is `true`.

❑ If the value of the expression contains a node, the effective boolean value is `true`.

❑ If the value of the expression is a sequence of two or more items, the effective boolean value is `true`.

The `test` expression in a `<xsl:when>` element after the selected one is not evaluated. This means it is safe to write code such as this:

```
<xsl:choose>
  <xsl:when test="not($x castable as xs:integer)">
    <xsl:sequence select="-1"/>
  </xsl:when>
  <xsl:when test="xs:integer($x) lt 0">
    <xsl:sequence select="-1"/>
  </xsl:when>
  <xsl:otherwise>
    <xsl:sequence select="xs:integer($x)"/>
  </xsl:otherwise>
</xsl:choose>
```

The conversion to an integer will not be attempted, and cannot therefore cause a failure, if the condition in the first `<xsl:when>` is true.

Usage and Examples

See `<xsl:choose>` on page 236

See Also

`<xsl:choose>` on page 236
`<xsl:otherwise>` on page 374
`<xsl:if>` on page 309

xsl:with-param

The `<xsl:with-param>` element is used to set the values of parameters when calling a template, either when using `<xsl:call-template>`, or when using `<xsl:apply-templates>`. It can also be used with `<xsl:apply-imports>` and with `<xsl:next-match>`.

Changes in 2.0

The `<xsl:with-param>` element can now be used as a child of `<xsl:apply-imports>` or `<xsl:next-match>`.

The `as` and `tunnel` attributes have been added.

When used with `<xsl:call-template>`, XSLT 2.0 defines compile-time errors if there is mismatch between the parameters supplied in the call and the parameters declared for the target `<xsl:template>` element.

Format

```
<xsl:with-param
   name = qname
   select? = expression
   as? = sequence-type
   tunnel? = "yes" | "no">
   <!-- Content: sequence-constructor -->
</xsl:with-param>
```

Position

`<xsl:with-param>` is always a child of `<xsl:apply-templates>`, `<xsl:call-template>`, `<xsl:apply-imports>`, or `<xsl:next-match>`.

Attributes

Name	Value	Meaning
name mandatory	QName	The name of the parameter
select optional	Expression	The value of the parameter to be supplied to the called template
as optional	SequenceType	Defines the type of the value
tunnel optional	«yes» or «no»	Indicates whether this is a tunnel parameter

Content

An optional sequence constructor. If a `select` attribute is present, the `<xsl:with-param>` element should be empty.

Effect

The `<xsl:with-param>` element assigns a value to a parameter. The value of the parameter can be used within the called template.

The value of the parameter is established in exactly the same way as for the `<xsl:variable>` element. That is, the value is obtained by evaluating the `select` expression if present, or the contained sequence constructor if not.

If the called template has an `<xsl:param>` element whose name matches that of the `<xsl:with-param>` element, then the value assigned to the `<xsl:with-param>` element is available within the template. If the called template has no such parameter, the value is ignored, except when using `<xsl:call-template>`, when this is an error. In the case of `<xsl:apply-templates>`, the parameter value is available in each of the templates that is called (one per selected node). The parameter is effectively evaluated once only—it will have the same value for each of these templates.

The name of the parameter is defined by a lexical QName. Normally this will be a simple name such as «city» or «total-sales», but it may be a name qualified with a prefix, for example «my:value». If it has a prefix, the prefix must correspond to a namespace that is in scope at that point in the stylesheet. The true name of the parameter, for the purpose of matching it with an `<xsl:param>` element in the called template, is determined not by the prefix but by the namespace URI corresponding to the prefix; so the name «my:value» will match a parameter declared as «your:value» if the prefixes «my» and «your» refer to the same namespace URI. If the name has no prefix, it has a null namespace URI—it does not use the default namespace URI.

It is an error for two sibling `<xsl:with-param>` elements to have the same name, after namespace prefixes are replaced with namespace URIs. In other words, you can't supply two values for the same parameter.

The `<xsl:with-param>` element does not actually declare a variable, so there is no problem if the name is the same as that of a variable that is currently in scope. In fact it is quite normal to pass a parameter in the form:

```
<xsl:with-param name="current-user" select="$current-user"/>
```

This is used to ensure that the variable «$current-user» in the called template has the same value as the variable «$current-user» in the calling template.

If the as attribute is present, then the supplied value of the parameter is converted to the specified type using the same rules as for `<xsl:variable>`. There is no requirement that this type must be identical to the declared type of the corresponding `<xsl:param>`: For example the `<xsl:with-param>` might specify «as="xs:byte"» when the `<xsl:param>` specifies «as="xs:integer"». This means that potentially two conversions may take place, from the type of the supplied value as calculated by the select expression, to the type declared in the as attribute of `<xsl:with-param>`, to the type declared in the as attribute of the corresponding `<xsl:param>`. In each case the standard conversion rules are used, as described in the entry for `<xsl:variable>` on page 476.

The option «tunnel="yes"» allows the parameter to be set up as a tunnel parameter. Tunnel parameters are described in the entry for `<xsl:param>` on page 396, with a worked example on page 400.

Usage and Examples

Parameters to templates take on considerable significance in XSLT because variables cannot be updated. This means that many tasks that in conventional programming languages are done by updating variables in a loop are done instead in XSLT using recursive calls and parameters. The consequences of this are explained in Chapter 9, and there are some detailed examples of the technique in Chapters 11 and 12.

Examples of recursive calls are also included in this chapter under <xsl:call-template> on page **000**.

See Also

<xsl:apply-imports> on page 184
<xsl:apply-templates> on page 187
<xsl:call-template> on page 220
<xsl:param> on page 392

Summary

This was a long chapter, but I hope you agree that every page was worth it! We have examined all of the XSLT elements in detail and have provided working examples to bolster your understanding of how they are used.

The next chapter describes the syntax of patterns, which are used in the match attribute of <xsl:template>, and in various other XSLT elements, to define conditions for matching nodes.

6

Patterns

A pattern defines a condition that a node must satisfy in order to be selected. The most common use of patterns is in the `match` attribute of `<xsl:template>`, where the pattern says which nodes the template rule applies to. For example, `<xsl:template match="abstract">` introduces a template rule that matches every `<abstract>` element. This chapter defines the syntax and meaning of XSLT patterns.

Patterns are used in just six places in an XSLT stylesheet:

❑ In the `match` attribute of `<xsl:template>`, to define the nodes in a source document to which a template applies

❑ In the `match` attribute of `<xsl:key>`, to define the nodes in a source document to which a key definition applies

❑ In the `count` and `from` attributes of `<xsl:number>`, to define which nodes are counted when generating numbers

❑ In the `group-starting-with` and `group-ending-with` attributes of `<xsl:for-each-group>`, to identify a node that acts as the initial or final node in a group of related nodes

Most of the patterns found in stylesheets are simple and intuitive. For example:

Pattern	Meaning
`title`	Matches any `<title>` element
`chapter/title`	Matches any `<title>` element whose parent is a `<chapter>` element
`speech[speaker="Hamlet"]`	Matches any `<speech>` element that has a child `<speaker>` element whose value is «Hamlet»
`section/para[1]`	Matches any `<para>` element that is the first `<para>` child of a `<section>` element

The rules for the more complex patterns, however, are quite technical—so I'm afraid some of the explanations in this chapter are not going to be easy reading.

Patterns are defined in terms of the name, type, and content of a node, and its position relative to other nodes in the tree. To understand how patterns work you therefore need to understand the tree model (described in Chapter 2) and the different kinds of node.

Patterns look very similar to XPath expressions, and it turns out that they are closely related. However, patterns and expressions are not quite the same thing. In terms of its syntax, every pattern is a valid XPath expression, but not every XPath expression is a valid pattern. It wouldn't make any sense to use the expression «2+2» as a pattern, for example—which nodes would it match?

> *The full rules for expressions are given in XPath 2.0 Programmer's Reference. Expressions are defined in the XPath 2.0 Recommendation, which allows them to be used in contexts other than XSLT stylesheets. For example, XPath expressions are used in the XPointer specification to define hyperlinks between documents, and they are used in some Document Object Model (DOM) implementations as a way for applications to navigate around the DOM data structure. Patterns, however, are local to the XSLT Recommendation, and they are found only in stylesheets.*

It would have been quite possible for XSLT to define both the syntax and the meaning of patterns quite independently of the XPath rules for expressions, but this would risk unnecessary inconsistency. What the XSLT language designers chose to do instead was to define the syntax of patterns in such a way that every pattern was sure to be a valid expression, and then to define the formal meaning of the pattern in terms of the meaning of the expression.

Look at the simplest pattern in the earlier examples, «title». If «title» is used as an expression, it's an abbreviation for «./child::title», and it means "select all the <title> children of the context node." How do we get from that to a definition of the pattern «title» as something that matches all <title> elements?

The section *The Formal Definition* gives the formal definition of patterns in terms of expressions. In practice, it's easier to think of most patterns as following their own rules—rather like the intuitive examples listed earlier—and referring to the formal definition only to resolve difficult cases. So I'll follow the formal explanation with an informal definition that's not only more intuitive, but also closer to the way most implementations are likely to work.

When patterns are used in template rules, we need to consider what happens if the same node is matched by more than one pattern. This situation is discussed in the section *Conflict Resolution*.

A new feature of the XPath 2.0 data model is that it is possible to create nodes in a tree whose root node is not a document node. Such trees cause additional complications for the semantics of pattern matching. The section *Matching Parentless Nodes* explains how these nodes are handled.

The bulk of the chapter is then devoted to an explanation of the syntax of patterns, and the usage of each syntactic construct that can appear in a pattern.

Changes in XSLT 2.0

The syntax of patterns is probably the area of the specification that has changed least between XSLT 1.0 and XSLT 2.0. However, because many capabilities of patterns are picked up implicitly by virtue of the way they are defined in terms of expressions, they benefit automatically from many of the new features in XPath 2.0.

The most notable facility this introduces is the ability to match nodes according to their schema-defined type. For example, you can match all date-valued attributes with the pattern «match="attribute(*, xs:date)"», and you can match all elements in the substitution group of the event element with the pattern «match="schema-element(event)"».

There are also some changes in the semantics of patterns, designed to cope with the complications introduced by parentless element and attribute nodes.

In XSLT 1.0 there were three restrictions on the content of a predicate used in a pattern. All three restrictions have been removed in XSLT 2.0.

❑   When a pattern was used in the match attribute of <xsl:template> or <xsl:key>, the predicate was not allowed to contain any references to variables. This was to prevent circular definitions. XSLT 2.0 allows variable references, provided that they do not introduce a circular definition.

❑   For the same reasons, when a pattern was used in the match attribute of <xsl:template> or <xsl:key>, XSLT 1.0 did not allow the predicate to use the key() function. Again, this rule has been replaced with a more permissive rule that says you can use the key() function provided it doesn't introduce a circularity.

❑   In XSLT 1.0, patterns were not allowed to use the current() function (described on page 526 in Chapter 7) within a predicate. XSLT 2.0 allows this, and defines that within a pattern, current() refers to the node that is being tested against the pattern.

The Formal Definition

The XSLT specification defines the way patterns are evaluated in terms of the XPath expression that is equivalent to the pattern. We've already seen that every pattern is a valid XPath expression. In fact, the rules are written so that the only XPath expressions that can be used as patterns are those that return a sequence of nodes. The idea is that you should be able to decide whether a node matches a pattern by seeing whether the node is in the sequence returned by the corresponding expression.

This then raises the question of context. The result of the XPath expression «title» is all the <title> children of the context node. Does that include the particular <title> element we are trying to match, or not? It obviously depends on the context. Since we want the pattern «title» to match every <title> element, we could express the rule by saying that the node we are testing (let's call it N) matches the pattern «title» if we can find a node (A, say) anywhere in the document, which has the property that when we take A as the context node and evaluate the expression «title», the node N will be selected as part of the result. In this example, we don't have to look very far to find node A: in fact, only as far as the parent node of N.

So the reason that a <title> element matches the pattern «title» is that it has a parent node, which when used as the context node for the expression «./child::title», returns a sequence that includes that <title> element. The pattern might be intuitive but, as you can see, the formal explanation is starting to get quite complex.

In an early draft of the XSLT 1.0 specification, the rules allowed almost any path expression to be used as a pattern. For example, you could define a pattern «ancestor::*[3]», which would match any node that was the great grandparent of some other node in the document. It turned out that this level of generality was neither needed nor possible to implement efficiently, and so a further restriction was imposed, that the only axes you could use in a pattern were the child and attribute axes (the various axes are explained in Chapter 7 of *XPath 2.0 Programmer's Reference*). A consequence of this is that the only place where the XSLT processor has to look for node *A* (the one to use as a context node for evaluating the expression) is among the ancestors of the node being matched (*N*), including *N* itself.

This brings us to the formal definition of the meaning of a pattern. For the moment let's ignore the complications caused by parentless nodes; I return to these page 500 later.

> **The node $N matches a pattern PAT if $N is a member of the sequence selected by the expression «root($N)//(PAT)».**

The way this rule is expressed has changed since XSLT 1.0, but the effect is the same. It has become possible to simplify the rule as a result of the generalization of path expressions that has happened in XPath 2.0. In XPath 1.0, XPath expressions such as «//(a|b)» or «//(/a)» were not allowed, so this rule would have made many patterns illegal.

Let's see what this rule means. We start with a node $N that we want to test against the pattern. First we find the root node of the tree containing $N. Then we look for all the descendant-or-self nodes of this root node, which means all the nodes in the tree except for attributes and namespaces. For each one of these nodes, we evaluate the pattern as if it were an XPath expression, using that node as the context node. If the result includes the original node $N, we have a match.

Let's see how this rule works by testing it against some common cases:

❑ If the pattern is «title», then a node matches the pattern if the node is included in the result of the expression «root(.)//(title)», which is the same as «//title». This expression selects all <title> elements in the document, so a node matches the pattern if and only if it is a <title> element.

❑ If the pattern is «chapter|appendix», then a node matches the pattern if it is selected by the expression «root(.)//(chapter|appendix)». This expression is equivalent to «//chapter | //appendix», and matches all <chapter> and <appendix> elements in the document.

❑ If the pattern is «/», then a node matches if it is selected by the expression «root(.)//(/)». This rather strange XPath expression selects the root node of every descendant of the root node, and then eliminates duplicates: so it is actually equivalent to the expression «/», which selects the root node only. (There are complications if the root node is not a document node, for example if it is a parentless element. I will cover these complications later in the chapter.)

❑ If the pattern is «chapter/title» then a node matches if it is selected by the expression «root(.)//(chapter/title)», which selects all <title> elements that are children of <chapter> elements.

❑ If the pattern is «para[1]» then a node matches if it is selected by the expression «root(.)//(para[1])», which selects any <para> element that is the first <para> child of its parent.

❑ If the pattern is «id('S123')» then a node matches if it is selected by the expression «root(.)//(id('S123'))», which is equivalent to the expression «id('S123')», and selects the element with an ID value of «S123».

This means there is a theoretical algorithm for testing whether a given node N matches a pattern P, as follows: for each node, starting from N and working through its ancestors up to the root node, evaluate P as an XPath expression with that node as the context node. If the result is a sequence of nodes containing N, the pattern matches; otherwise keep trying until you get to the root.

XSLT processors don't usually use this algorithm, it's there only as a way of stating the formal rules. The processor will usually be able to find a faster way of doing the test—which is just as well, since pattern matching would otherwise be prohibitively expensive.

Although the formal rules usually give the answer you would expect intuitively, there can be surprises. For example, you might expect the pattern «node()» to match any node; but it doesn't. The equivalent expression, «//(node())» is short for «root(.)/descendant-or-self::node()/child::node()», and the only nodes that this can select are nodes that are children of something. Since document nodes, attribute nodes, and namespace nodes are never children of another node (see the description of the tree model on page 48 in Chapter 2), they will never be matched by the pattern «node()».

Patterns Containing Predicates

The formal equivalence of patterns and expressions becomes critical when considering the meaning of predicates (conditions in square brackets), especially predicates that explicitly or implicitly use the position() and last() functions.

For example, the pattern «para[1]» corresponds to the expression «root(.)//(para [position()= 1])». This expression takes all the <para> children of the context node, and then filters this sequence to remove all but the first (in document order). So the pattern «para[1]» matches any <para> element that is the first <para> child of its parent. Similarly the pattern «*[1][self::para]» matches any element that is the first child of its parent and that is also a <para> element, while «para[last()!=1]» matches any <para> element that is a child of an element with two or more <para> children.

An Informal Definition

The formal rules for a pattern such as «book//para», because they are written in terms of expressions, encourage you to think of the pattern as being evaluated from left to right, which means finding a <book> element and searching for all its <para> descendants to see if one of them is the one you are looking for.

An alternative way of looking at the meaning of this expression, and the way in which most XSLT processors are likely to implement the pattern-matching algorithm, is to start from the right. The actual logic for testing a node against the pattern «book//para» is likely to be along the lines:

❑ Test whether this is a <para> element. If not, then it doesn't match.

- ❑ Test whether there is a `<book>` ancestor. If not, then it doesn't match.

- ❑ Otherwise, it matches.

If there are predicates, these can be tested en route, for example to evaluate the pattern «speech [speaker='Hamlet']», the logic is likely to be the following:

- ❑ Test whether this is a `<speech>` element. If not, then it doesn't match.

- ❑ Test whether this element has a `<speaker>` child whose typed value is «Hamlet». If not, then it doesn't match.

- ❑ Otherwise, it matches.

Most patterns can thus be tested by looking only at the node itself and possibly its ancestors, its attributes, and its children. The patterns that are likely to be the most expensive to test are those that involve looking further afield.

For example, consider the pattern «para[last() - 1]», which matches any `<para>` element that is the last but one `<para>` child of its parent. Most XSLT processors, unless they have an exceptionally good optimizer, are going to test whether a particular `<para>` element matches this pattern by counting how many children the parent element has, counting how many preceding `<para>` siblings the test `<para>` has, and comparing the two numbers. Doing this for every `<para>` element that is processed could get a little expensive, especially if there are hundreds of them with the same parent. With the patterns «para[1]» or «para[last()]» you've a slightly better chance that the processor will figure out a quicker way of doing the test, but it would be unwise to rely on it.

If you write a stylesheet with a lot of template rules, then the time taken to find the particular rule to apply to a given node can make a significant difference. The exact way in which different XSLT processors do the matching may vary, but one thing you can be sure of is that patterns containing complex predicates will add to the cost.

Conflict Resolution

When a pattern is used in the definition of a template rule, it is possible that several patterns may match the same node. There are rules for resolving this conflict, which are described in the section *Choosing a Template Rule* in the entry for `<xsl:apply-templates>` in Chapter 5 page 189. One of the factors these rules take into account is the *default priority* of the pattern, which is determined from the way it is written.

The default priority is decided according to the following rules. A numerically higher value indicates a higher priority. Note that some of the priorities are fractional, and some are negative.

If the pattern is a union of two or more patterns («P1 | P2»), then the processor treats it as if there were two completely separate template rules specified, one for P1 and one for P2, and it calculates the default priority of P1 and P2 independently, using the rules in the table.

If the pattern starts with an axis specifier («child::», «attribute::», or «@») this does not affect the priority.

Pattern Syntax	Default Priority

`document-node(schema-element(`*QName*`))`
`document-node(element(`*QName*`,`*QName*`))`
`schema-element(`*QName*`)`
`element(`*QName*`,`*QName*`)`
`schema-attribute(`*QName*`)`
`attribute(`*QName*`,`*QName*`)`
	+0.25

QName
`document-node(element(`*QName*`))`
`document-node(element(*,`*QName*`))`
`element(`*QName*`)`
`element(*,`*QName*`)`
`attribute(`*QName*`)`
`attribute(*,`*QName*`)`
`processing-instruction(`*Literal*`)`
`processing-instruction(`*NCName*`)`
	0.0

NCName`:*` `*:`*NCName*	- 0.25

`/`
`document-node()`
`document-node(element())`
`document-node(element(*))`
`element()`
`element(*)`
`attribute()`
`attribute(*)`
`text()`
`comment()`
`processing-instruction()`
`node()`
	- 0.5

Otherwise	+0.5

These default priorities are carefully chosen to reflect the selectivity of the pattern:

❑ The patterns «node()» and «text()» and «*» are not very selective at all; they match any node of the right node kind, so they have a low priority of -0.5.

❑ Patterns of the form «abc:*» or «@xyz.*» are more selective; they will match element or attribute nodes belonging to a particular namespace only, so they have a higher priority than the previous category. Patterns such as «*:abc» are also placed in this category, because they are less specific than a pattern that fully specifies the node name, but more specific than one that specifies only the kind of node.

❑ Patterns such as «title» or «@isbn» are the ones most commonly encountered; their default priority of 0.0 reflects the fact that in terms of selectivity, they are typical. Other patterns that specify the kind of node as well as its name fall into the same group. Patterns that specify the schema type of the node without specifying its name, for example «element(*, pers:employee)» are placed at the same level because they might be more or less specific than a pattern specifying the node name.

❑ Patterns that specify both the node name and its schema type, for example «attribute(@code, mf:part-number)» are more specific than those that specify only the name or the type, so they get a priority of +0.25.

❑ Patterns that provide a more specific context, for example «book[@isbn]» or «chapter/ title» or «para[1]» have a higher priority, so they will be chosen in preference to templates whose patterns are respectively «book», «title», or «para». Note however that this category can also include patterns that turn out not to be very selective at all, for example «//node()».

All these values are chosen to leave you free to allocate your own priorities as natural numbers, for example «1», «2», «3:», and such templates will always be chosen ahead of those with a system-allocated default priority.

You may find that stylesheets are easier to understand and less error prone if you avoid relying on default priorities, and use explicit priorities whenever you have more than one template rule that can match the same node.

Although the default priorities are carefully chosen, they do not guarantee that a highly selective pattern will always have higher priority than a less selective pattern. For example, the patterns «section/para» and «section/para[1]» both have priority +0.5. Similarly, the patterns «attribute(*, xs:integer)» and «attribute(*, xs:decimal)» have the same priority, even though the nodes that match the first pattern are a subset of those that match the second. Choosing your own priorities is therefore a more reliable approach.

A complete description of the conflict resolution rules, including the role played by the default priority of the pattern, is described under <xsl:apply-templates> page 189 in Chapter 5.

Matching Parentless Nodes

In XSLT 1.0, every node belonged to a tree with a document node at its root. In fact, since the root was always the same kind of node, this kind of node was known as a root node rather than a document node. This has changed in XSLT 2.0: you can now have elements, or even attributes and text nodes, that have no parent. For example, if you write:

```
<xsl:variable name="seq" as="element()*">
  <e>2</e>
  <f>5</f>
  <g>9</g>
</xsl:variable>
```

then the value of the variable $seq is a sequence of three element nodes. These element nodes have no parent, and they are therefore not siblings of each other. The XPath expression «$seq/e» will not select anything, because none of the three nodes in $seq has a child element whose name is «e». If you want to select the «e» element, you should write «$seq[self::e]».

A tree may thus be rooted at an element node rather than a document node, and this affects the rules for pattern matching. Two consequences of parentless elements complicate the rules.

The first consequence has to do with error handling. In XPath, using an expression such as «/» or «//book» is an error if the context item is in a tree whose root is not a document node. The same applies to the id() and key() functions. This could mean that if you wrote <xsl:apply-templates select="$seq"/>, where $seq is a sequence of parentless elements, then as soon as the system tried to match it against a template rule specifying <xsl:template match="/">, a runtime error would occur. This would happen, of course, only if the processor took the naïve approach of matching every node against every pattern in the stylesheet, and even then only if it took the formal approach of evaluating the equivalent XPath expression. In practice, neither the user nor the implementer would be very happy if this was defined to be an error, so the specification includes a (very ad-hoc) rule saying that the system never attempts to match a parentless node against a pattern starting with «/» or key() or id(), and therefore never hits this error condition.

More generally, runtime errors can also occur when evaluating a predicate in a pattern. For example, matching the pattern «//book[@price div 0 = 0]» could cause a runtime error (division by zero). The spec is open ended about these; it makes it clear that whether or not a particular error is ever reported will depend on the order in which the processor chooses to test the different patterns, and even then, on its evaluation strategy for a particular pattern.

The other problem that occurs with parentless nodes is that using the definition as we have it so far, the pattern «match="e"» means «match="child::e"», and would match an <e> element only if it is a child of something. The Working Group decided that this would be just too confusing, and resolved that the pattern «e» should match every <e> element whether or not it has a parent. Similarly, «chapter/para» should match every <para> whose parent is a <chapter>, whether or not the <chapter> has a parent.

The way that the formal definition of patterns has been bent to meet this requirement is somewhat tortuous. It is done by introducing two new axes, child-or-top and attribute-or-top, and using these axes in the first step of a RelativePathPattern in place of the usual child and attribute axes. The child-or-top axis selects the children of the context node, unless the context node is a parentless element, text node, comment, or processing instruction, in which case it selects the parentless context node itself. Similarly, the attribute-or-top axis selects the context node itself if it is a parentless attribute node. Given these two extra axes, the equivalence between patterns and XPath expressions continues to hold. (These axes, of course, are purely notional. You can't use them explicitly either in an XPath expression or in a pattern.)

Note that this refinement does not apply to patterns starting with «/». The pattern «//book», which in XSLT 1.0 matched exactly the same nodes as the pattern «book», now has a slightly different meaning: it selects only <book> elements that are descendants of a document node. It will not select a parentless <book> element, or a <book> element in a tree whose root is a parentless element. This, incidentally, means that «match="//book"» is quite likely to be less efficient than «match="book"», since the system now has to check what kind of node is at the root of the tree.

The Syntax of Patterns

The rest of this chapter gives the detailed syntax rules for patterns.

The indented hierarchy that follows shows the overall structure of the rules. Constructs marked with the symbol § are defined in *XPath 2.0 Programmer's Reference*.

```
Pattern
    PathPattern
        RelativePathPattern
            PatternStep
                PatternAxis
                NodeTest
                Predicates
                    Expr §
        IdKeyPattern
            Literal §
            VariableReference §
```

The rules are presented in top-down order, starting with the `Pattern` construct itself.

The production rules use the same syntax notation that is used to define the syntax of XPath expressions in *XPath 2.0 Programmer's Reference*. The entry for each construct defines the syntax using a BNF notation, it describes the meaning of the construct in a section headed *Effect*, and then includes sections relating to the *Usage* of the construct, followed by *Examples*. The BNF uses chevrons to enclose literal symbols, but is otherwise conventional: alternatives are indicated using «|», repetition by «*», and optional constructs by «?».

Pattern

This is the top-level construct for the XSLT Pattern syntax. A pattern defines a condition that is either true or false for any given node in a document. The syntax for a `Pattern` is a subset of the syntax for a `UnionExpr` (and therefore for an `Expr`) in the XPath expression syntax.

Syntax

Expression	Syntax
Pattern	*PathPattern* | *Pattern* «|» *PathPattern*

A `Pattern` is either a `PathPattern` or a sequence of `PathPatterns` separated by the union operator «|».

The syntax of a `PathPattern` is given on the next page.

Effect

A node matches a `Pattern` if it matches any of the `PathPatterns` contained in the `Pattern`.

Usage

Although «|» is technically a union operator, it is simpler to read it as «or»; a node matches the pattern "A|B" if it matches either A or B or both.

In patterns, the «|» operator can be used only at the top level. XPath 2.0 allows expressions such as «(chap|appendix)/title», but this is not a valid pattern. The required effect can be achieved by writing «chap/title|appendix/title», or «title[parent::chap|parent:: appendix]».

Examples

`TITLE`	«TITLE» is a `PathPattern`, so it is also a `Pattern`
`preface|chapter|` `appendix`	A node matches this pattern if it is a `<preface>` element, a `<chapter>` element, or an `<appendix>` element
`/|*`	A node matches this pattern if it is either a document node or an element node

PathPattern

A `PathPattern` states conditions that a node must satisfy based on its name, its node kind, its position relative to other nodes, and/or its ID and key values.

This construct is a subset of the `PathExpr` construct in the XPath grammar.

Syntax

Expression	Syntax

`PathPattern`	`RelativePathPattern|`
	`«/» RelativePathPattern?|`
	`«//» RelativePathPattern|`
	`IdKeyPattern`
	`((«/»|«//»)RelativePathPattern)?`

This production rule is the way the syntax is defined in the XSLT specification. However, the following equivalent production rule may be easier to understand, and corresponds with the description in the *Usage* section discussed later.

Expression	Syntax

`PathPattern`	`«/»|`
	`RelativePathPattern|`
	`«/» RelativePathPattern|`
	`«//» RelativePathPattern|`
	`IdKeyPattern|`
	`IdKeyPattern «/» RelativePathPattern|`
	`IdKeyPattern «//» RelativePathPattern`

The syntax of a `RelativePathPattern` (page 505) and that of an `IdKeyPattern` (page 518) are described later.

Effect

The syntax rule reproduced earlier from the XSLT specification can be better understood by listing the seven different kinds of `PathPattern`, as follows:

Construct	Meaning
«/»	Matches a document node.
RelativePathPattern	Matches a node that can appear anywhere in the document. Example: «book/chapter/title» matches any <title> element whose parent is a <chapter> element that is a child of a <book> element.
«/» RelativePathPattern	Matches a node via a defined path from a document node. Example: «/book/title» matches a <title> element that is a child of a <book> element whose parent is a document node.
«//» RelativePathPattern	Matches a node that can appear anywhere in the document. The inclusion of the leading «//» rules out nodes in trees that don't have a document node at their root. It also affects the default priority of a template rule that uses this pattern. The default priority of a pattern comes into play when two template rules match the same node: for details, see the description of <xsl:template> in Chapter 5 page 450. Example: «//title» matches any <title> element within a tree that is rooted at a document node.
IdKeyPattern	Matches a node with a given ID attribute or key value. For example, «id('A001')» matches an element with an ID attribute whose value is «A001».
IdKeyPattern «/» RelativePathPattern	Matches a pattern defined relative to the children of a node with a given ID attribute or key value. For example, «id('A001')/title» matches the <title> child of an element with an ID attribute whose value is «A001».
IdKeyPattern «//» RelativePathPattern	Matches a pattern defined relative to the descendants of a node with a given ID attribute or key value. For example, «id('A001')//title» matches any <title> element that is a descendant of an element with an ID attribute whose value is «A001».

Usage

The pattern «/» matches any document node. This means that if you have several trees (which will be the case in a stylesheet that uses the document() function described on page 532 in Chapter 7, or the doc() function described in *XPath 2.0 Programmer's Reference*), the pattern «/» will match the document nodes of each one. This makes it difficult to write different template rules to match the document nodes of different trees. There are a few ways around this problem:

❑ If your documents are of different types (that is, if they use different schemas, or different top-level elements in the same schema) then you can distinguish them using a pattern such as «document-node(schema-element(invoice))» or «document-node(schema-element(purchase-order))». These constructs are described page 513 later in the chapter.

- ❑ You can use different modes to process each tree (see the description of `<xsl:apply-templates>` page 187 in Chapter 5).

- ❑ You can start the processing of secondary documents at the element node immediately below the root. A pattern such as «/item» will match an item element that is an immediate child of the document node. This kind of pattern is often useful when your stylesheet is dealing with multiple source documents, because it allows you to distinguish them by the name of the document element.

The pattern «/@width» is legal but meaningless; it would match a width attribute of the document node, but as the document node cannot have attributes, there is no such node.

To match every `<para>` element, use the pattern «para» in preference to «//para». The latter will work (except in non-document trees) but its default priority is different, and it may be less efficient. For the other kinds of PathPattern, see RelativePathPattern (on this page) and IdKeyPattern (page 518) discussed later.

Examples

Construct	Meaning
/	Matches a document node.
/*	Matches the outermost element node in a document (the document element). In the case of a tree that is not well formed (see page 50 in Chapter 2), it matches any element whose parent is a document node.
/booklist	Matches any `<booklist>` element whose parent is a document node.
//book	Matches any `<book>` element that has a document node as an ancestor.
book	Matches any `<book>` element.
element(*, mfg:invoice)	Matches any element annotated as conforming to the schema-defined type mfg:invoice.
attribute(*, xs:date)	Matches any attribute annotated as an xs:date, including subtypes of xs:date.
id('figure-1')	Matches an element with an ID attribute having the value 'figure-1'.
id('figure-1')//*	Matches any descendant element of an element with an ID attribute having the value 'figure-1'.
key('empnr', '624381')/@dob	Matches the dob attribute of an element having a value '624381' for the key named empnr.

RelativePathPattern

A RelativePathPattern consists of a PatternStep defining conditions that a node must satisfy, optionally preceded by a RelativePathPattern that a parent or ancestor node must satisfy (the syntax puts it the other way around, but the effect is the same, and it's easier to think of it from right to left). The syntax for a RelativePathPattern is a subset of the syntax for a RelativePathExpr in the XPath Expression language.

Syntax

Expression	Syntax
RelativePathPattern	PatternStep| PatternStep «/» RelativePathPattern| PatternStep «//» RelativePathPattern

A RelativePathPattern is thus a sequence of one or more PatternSteps separated by either of the operators «/» (is-parent-of) or «//» (is-ancestor-of).

The syntax of a PatternStep is described page 567 later in the chapter.

Effect

Because in practice patterns are likely to be evaluated from right to left, it's easier to explain the semantics if we rearrange the syntax, as follows.

Expression	Syntax
RelativePathPattern	PatternStep| RelativePathPattern «/» PatternStep| RelativePathPattern «//» PatternStep

With the first form, PatternStep, a node matches the pattern if it satisfies the conditions (node name, node kind, and predicates) defined in the PatternStep. The simplest and most common form of PatternStep is simply an element name, for example «title».

With the second form, RelativePathPattern «/» PatternStep, a node matches the pattern if it satisfies the conditions (node name, node kind, and predicates) defined in the PatternStep, and if its parent node matches the RelativePathPattern. This RelativePathPattern may in turn include conditions that the parent node's parent or ancestor nodes must satisfy.

With the third form, RelativePathPattern «//» PatternStep, a node matches the pattern if it satisfies the conditions (node name, node kind, and predicates) defined in the PatternStep, and if it has an ancestor that matches the RelativePathPattern. This RelativePathPattern may in turn include conditions that the ancestor node's parent or ancestor nodes must satisfy.

Usage

Notice that although there is an equivalence between RelativePathPattern in the pattern language and RelativePathExpr in the expression language, the meaning of a RelativePathPattern is most easily explained by examining the PatternSteps from right to left, starting at the node being tested and working up through its ancestors, if necessary; this is despite the fact that the meaning of a RelativePathExpr is explained by considering the Steps from left to right, starting at the context node. It's likely that most implementations will adopt a strategy similar to the algorithm as I've explained it here.

Generally speaking, there is no point in making patterns any more selective than is necessary. For example, if a <row> element always appears as a child of <table>, then there is no point in specifying the pattern as «table/row»—you might just as well use the simpler pattern «row».

In theory, everything you can do in a RelativePathPattern could be done in a single PatternStep, since the pattern «A/B» means exactly the same as «B[parent::A]», and the pattern «A//B» means exactly the same as «B[ancestor::A]». However, where several steps are present, the form using «/» and «//» operators is a lot easier to read.

Examples

Construct	Meaning
title	This is a PatternStep, and therefore the simplest form of RelativePathPattern. It selects any <title> element.
section/title	This is a RelativePathPattern consisting of two PatternSteps joined by the «/» (is-parent-of) operator. It matches a <title> element whose parent is a <section> element.
chapter//footnote	This is a RelativePathPattern consisting of two PatternSteps joined by the «//» (is-ancestor-of) operator. It matches a <footnote> element that is a descendant of a <chapter> element.
chapter/section//footnote	A more complex RelativePathPattern that matches any <footnote> element that is a descendant of a <section> element that is a child of a <chapter> element.
chapter[1]//footnote	This pattern matches every <footnote> element in the first chapter (more strictly, in a <chapter> that is the first child <chapter> of its parent).

PatternStep

A PatternStep defines conditions that an individual node must satisfy: typically some combination of the node name, node kind, schema type, and a set of boolean or numeric predicates. The syntax for a PatternStep is a subset of the syntax for an AxisStep in the XPath expression language.

Syntax

Expression	Syntax
PatternStep	PatternAxis? NodeTest-Predicates
PatternAxis	«child» «::»| «attribute» «::»| «@»
NodeTest	NameTest|KindTest
NameTest	QName| «*»| NCName «:*»| «*:» NCName
Predicates	(«[» Expr «]») *

The syntax of *KindTest* is given page 510 later. The constructs *QName*, *NCName*, and *Expr* are all defined in the XPath 2.0 grammar, and are described in *XPath 2.0 Programmer's Reference*.

Effect

To describe the effect of a PatternStep we'll look at each of its components separately: first the PatternAxis, then the two kinds of NodeTest, that is, NameTests and KindTests, and finally the Predicates.

The PatternAxis

The PatternAxis may take the form «attribute::» (abbreviated «@») or «child::» (abbreviated to nothing: «»). In general, if no PatternAxis is specified, the child axis is assumed; the only exception is that when the NodeTest is an AttributeTest (for example, «attribute(*)»), the attribute axis is assumed.

In the formal rules for evaluating a pattern, the steps in a RelativePathPattern are evaluated from left to right, and the choice of axis determines whether this step looks at the children or the attributes of the nodes found in the previous step.

Looking at it informally, it is simplest to think of the axis specifier as simply a way of saying what kind of node is required.

❑ If the child axis is used and the NodeTest is a NameTest (for example, «title», «*», or «svg:*»), then we are looking for an element node.

❑ If the child axis is used and the NodeTest is a KindTest (for example, «comment()» or «text()»), then we are looking for that kind of node. If the NodeTest is «node()», then we are looking for any node on the child axis: specifically, elements, text nodes, comments, or processing instructions. Note that the pattern «node()», which is short for «child::node()» will not match document nodes, attributes, or namespace nodes, because these nodes never appear as the child of another node.

❑ If the attribute axis is used and the NodeTest is a NameTest (for example «@title», «@*», or «@svg:*»), then we are looking for an attribute node.

❑ If the attribute axis is used and the `NodeTest` is a `KindTest` (for example, «@schema-attribute(xml:space)»), then we are looking for nodes on the attribute axis. Of course, the only nodes found on the attribute axis are attribute nodes. The patterns «@comment()» and «@text()» are not illegal, but they are pointless, because the attribute axis cannot contain comments or text nodes. However, the `NodeTest` «@node()» looks for any node on the attribute axis, so it is equivalent to «@*».

If the `PatternStep` is the first `PatternStep` in a top-level `RelativePathPattern`, then it matches parentless nodes as if they had a parent. For example, the `PatternStep` «child::title» or «title» will match a `<title>` element that has no parent node, and the `PatternStep` «schema-attribute(xml:space)» will match an xml:space attribute that has no parent element.

The only two axes that are available directly in a pattern are the child and attribute axes. However, testing for the presence of related nodes on a different axis can be done in the predicate of the `PatternStep`. Any expression can be used in the predicate, and so all axes are available. For example:

```
caption[preceding-sibling::*[1]][self::figure]
```

matches a `<caption>` element whose immediately preceding sibling element is a `<figure>` element.

The NameTest

A `NameTest` such as «*» or «prefix:*» is purely testing the name of the node. This works whether or not there is a schema. There are four forms:

❑ A lexical QName such as «title». or «mfg:invoice» must match both the local name and the namespace URI of the node. If the QName has a prefix, then it is expanded using the namespace declarations on surrounding elements in the stylesheet; if not, the XPath default namespace is used. The XPath default namespace can be set using the [xsl:]xpath-default- namespace attribute, which is described in the entry for `<xsl:stylesheet>` in Chapter 5, page 442.

❑ The `NameTest` «*» matches any node of the principal node kind for the axis.

❑ The `NameTest` «prefix:*» matches any node whose name is in a particular namespace. There must be a declaration for this namespace (of the form «xmlns:prefix="uri"») on some enclosing element in the style-sheet module, and the namespace is the one with the corresponding URI.

❑ The `NameTest` «*:local-name» matches any node with the specified local name, regardless of its namespace. This includes nodes whose name is not in any namespace.

In all these cases, a `NameTest` matches nodes only of the principal node kind for the selected axis. This means that if the `PatternAxis` is «@» or «attribute::», the `NameTest` selects attribute nodes with the given name; otherwise, it matches element nodes only.

Patterns that match nodes by name are extremely common and work well with many kinds of document. If you find yourself writing a pattern with many alternatives, for example

```
match="b | i | u | sub | sup | s"
```

then (if you are using a schema-aware processor) it may be worth asking yourself what these elements have in common. One possibility is that they are all members of the same substitution group defined in the schema: in this case, you may be able to replace the pattern with one such as «match="schema-element(inline)"». Another possibility is that the elements all have the same internal structure. In this case they are likely to conform to the same type definition in the schema, so you can replace the list of elements by a pattern of the form «match="element(*, inline-type)"».

If the list includes most of the members of a substitution group, or most elements conforming to a given type, then you could consider excluding the unwanted ones with a predicate, for example «match="schema-element(inline)[not(self::schema-element(span))]"». Alternatively, if the pattern is being used to define a template rule, simply define another template rule with higher priority to catch the exceptions.

A pattern of the form «prefix:*», which matches all the elements (or attributes) in a particular namespace, is often useful if all that you want to do is exclude such elements from the result tree. An empty template rule takes the form:

```
<xsl:template match="svg:*" xmlns:svg="http://www.w3.org/2000/svg"/>
```

This example causes all subtrees rooted at an element in the namespace http://www.w3.org/2000/svg to be excluded from the result. (This is the namespace for the W3C Scalable Vector Graphics specification: see http://www.w3.org/TR/SVG11/)

«*:local-name» patterns are new in XSLT 2.0. They should be used with care, because in principle the names in one namespace bear no relationship to names in a different namespace: for example, the «xsl:sequence» element in the XSLT namespace is quite unrelated to the «xs:sequence» element in the XML Schema namespace. However, there are cases where you might need to write a stylesheet that handles several namespaces that are variants of each other, in which many of the elements are common to more than one namespace. This construct can be very useful in this situation.

The KindTest

Whereas a NameTest is designed to match nodes primarily by their name, a KindTest matches specific kinds of nodes. In the case of element and attribute nodes, it also allows matching against the type annotation attached to the node as a consequence of schema validation.

The syntax of a KindTest, copied from the XPath specification, is as follows:

Expression	Syntax
KindTest	DocumentTest| ElementTest| AttributeTest| TextTest| PITest| CommentTest| AnyKindTest
DocumentTest	«document-node» «(» ElementTest? «)»
ElementTest	BasicElementTest| SchemaElementTest

Expression	Syntax
BasicElementTest	«element» «(» (ElementNameOrWildCard («,» TypeName «?»?)?)? «)»
SchemaElementTest	«schema-element» «(» QName «)»
AttributeTest	BasicAttributeTest| SchemaAttributeTest
BasicAttributeTest	«attribute» «(» (AttributeNameOrWildcard («,» TypeName)?)? «)»
SchemaAttributeTest	«schema-attribute» «(» QName «)»
TextTest	«text» «(» «)»
PITest	«processing-instruction» «(» (NCName| StringLiteral)? «)»
CommentTest	«comment» «(» «)»
AnyKindTest	«node» «(» «)»
NodeName	QName| «*»
TypeName	QName| «*»

A KindTest is used to define the kind of node that is required and, optionally, information about its schema-defined type.

Let's take the simple cases first:

❑ «text()» matches any text node.

❑ «comment()» matches any comment node.

❑ «node()» matches any node whatsoever (but remember that on its own, it means «child::node()», which searches only for nodes that are children of something).

❑ «processing-instruction()» matches any processing instruction node.

❑ «processing-instruction(NCName)» matches any processing instruction node with the given name (the name of a processing instruction is referred to in the XML Specification as the *PITarget*). For compatibility with XPath 1.0, the NCName may be written in quotes as a StringLiteral.

❑ «document-node()» matches any document node.

❑ «element()» matches any element node. This can also be written as «element(*)».

❑ «attribute()» matches any attribute node. This can also be written as «attribute(*)».

Now things start to get more complicated, because the other kinds of `KindTest` are concerned with testing for specific types of node as defined in a schema. In general, you will use these `KindTests` only to match nodes in documents that have been validated against a schema.

KindTests for Element Nodes

Let's look first at the options for matching element nodes:

❑ «element(QName)» matches any element node whose name is the given QName. As a pattern, this is exactly the same as writing the QName on its own. (The reason for providing this syntax is that a `KindTest` is allowed in contexts other than patterns, for example in the «as» attribute of an <xsl:param> element.)

❑ «schema-element(QName)» is used to test for an element that matches a top-level element declaration in the schema identified by the given QName. It's an error to use this form unless you have imported a schema containing this top-level element declaration. For example, if you write «element(mfg:invoice)», then the schema for the «mfg» namespace must have been imported, and must include a top-level element declaration of the form «xs:element name="invoice"».

The element is considered to match if two conditions are satisfied:

❑ its name is either the same as the QName, or the name of an element defined in the schema to be a member of the substitution group with the named element as its head.

❑ the type of the element node, identified from its type annotation, matches the type defined for this element declaration in the schema. This rule is there because a schema can allow the same name to be used in different contexts with different type definitions.

❑ «element(*, QName)» is used to test for an element whose type annotation indicates that it has been successfully validated against the schema-defined type definition identified by the QName. The QName can identify a built-in type such as «xs:dateTime», or a type (which may be a simple type or a complex type) that is the subject of a named type definition in an imported schema. The test will match any element that has a type annotation that refers to the named type, or a type derived from the named type by restriction or by extension.

❑ If the element includes the attribute «xsi:nil="true"» then it will match this `KindTest` only if the QName is followed by the symbol «?». This extra test is necessary because without it, the system would not be able to make any assumptions about the contents of the element, since xsi:nil essentially allows an element to have no content even when the schema would otherwise require it.

❑ The `KindTest` «element(QName, QName)» is essentially a combination of «element (QName)» and «element(*, QName)». This tests both the name of the node and its type: the name must match the first QName, or the name of one of the elements in its substitution group, and the type annotation must match the second QName (which must be the name of a top-level type definition in an imported schema). Again, if the element includes the attribute «xsi:nil="true"» then it will match this `KindTest` only if the second QName is followed by the symbol «?».

KindTests for Attribute Nodes

`KindTests` for attribute nodes follow the same format as those for element nodes, with minor variations. The same options are available, though in practice they are likely to be used rather differently. For example, global attribute declarations are not used very often in XML Schema, and matching against the names of a top-level simple type definition is probably a more likely scenario.

- ❑ «attribute(QName)» matches any attribute whose name matches the given QName: as a pattern, this means exactly the same as @QName or attribute::QName.

- ❑ «schema-attribute(QName)» is used to test for an attribute that matches a top-level attribute declaration in the schema identified by the given QName. It's an error to use this form unless you have imported a schema containing this top-level attribute declaration. The attribute is considered to match if two conditions are satisfied:

  - ❑ its name is the same as the QName

  - ❑ the type of the attribute node, identified from its type annotation, matches the type defined for this attribute declaration in the schema

- ❑ «attribute(*, QName)» is used to test for an attribute whose type annotation indicates that it has been successfully validated against the schema-defined simple type definition identified by the QName. The QName can identify a built-in type such as «xs:dateTime», or a type (it will always be a simple type) that is the subject of a named type definition in an imported schema. The test will match any attribute that has a type annotation that refers to the named type, or a type derived from the named type by restriction. For example, the KindTest «attribute(*, xs:date)» matches any attribute whose type (as established by schema validation) is xs:date.

- ❑ The KindTest «attribute(QName, QName)» is essentially a combination of «attribute(QName)» and «attribute(*, QName)». This tests both the name of the node and its type: the name must match the first QName, and the type annotation must match the second QName (which must be the name of a top-level simple type definition in an imported schema).

KindTests for Document Nodes

The document-node() KindTest can take an argument that is an element() or schema-element() KindTest: it then matches any document node that has the specified kind of element as its only element child. For this KindTest to work, the document must be a well-formed document in the sense that the document node has exactly one element node as a child, and no text node children, and the element node must have been validated against a schema. Here are two examples.

Construct	Meaning
document-node (schema-element(mfg:invoice))	Matches the document node at the root of a well-formed document whose outermost element has been validated against the top-level element declaration named «invoice» in the schema for the namespace associated with the prefix «mfg», or an element in the substitution group headed by the «invoice» element. This schema must have been imported into the stylesheet.
document-node (element(*, fin:movement))	Matches the document node at the root of a well-formed document whose outermost element has the type annotation «fin:movement», or a type derived from this by restriction or extension. The schema for the namespace associated with the prefix «fin» must have been imported into the stylesheet.

Using KindTests

The simple KindTests comment(), processing-instruction(), and text() are used whenever you want to match one of these kinds of node. These are used comparatively rarely. For example, it's unusual to define a template rule that matches text nodes: usually a stylesheet will either copy text nodes unchanged, or suppress them from the output, and the choice is usually controlled from the template rule for the containing element node.

The default template rule for comment nodes causes them to be discarded; if you want to copy comment nodes to the output, you can achieve this by adding the template rule.

```
<xsl:template match="comment()"><xsl:copy/></xsl:template>
```

However, this will work only if the template rule used to process the containing element issues the instruction <apply-templates/> to process all its children.

The [schema-]element() and [schema-]attribute() KindTests are most useful when you a processing a source document that has been validated against a schema, especially when the schema is fairly complex. It allows you to define a generic rule for a whole class of elements or attributes. There are a number of ways such a class can be identified, and the approach you use will depend on the design of your schema:

❑   Identifying the elements or attributes by type, using the syntax «element(*, QName)» or «attribute(*, QName)» is useful for processing elements and attributes that have simple content. For example, if all elements containing monetary amounts are identified as being of type «money», then you can define a template rule with the pattern «match="element(*, money)"» that contains the formatting logic for values of this type. This will also work if the schema defines subtypes derived by restricting the money type, for example a subtype that restricts the values to be positive sums of money.

❑   Where the schema defines many elements that share the same complex type, the syntax «element(*, QName)» can again be useful to define generic logic that applies to all elements of this type. For example, a schema for retail banking might define a generic type «movement» that represents all movements of money from one account to another. A template rule declared with «match="element(*, QName)"» will match all elements declared with this type, or with a type derived from it.

❑   You need to be aware that in choosing a template rule, the system takes no account of the type hierarchy in the schema. If direct-debit is defined as a subtype of movement, this does not mean that the template rule defined with «match="element(*, direct-debit)"» takes priority over the rule with «match="element(*, movement)"». You need to allocate explicit priorities in the stylesheet to make sure that the right rule is invoked.

❑   If subtypes have been defined by extending the base type, then it can often be useful to invoke processing of the extensions by using the <xsl:next-match> instruction, described in Chapter 5. The template rule for the base type can process all the contents that are common to all instances of the type, while the template rule for an extended type needs to process only those contents that are included in the extension.

❑   Sometimes substitution groups are used to define a collection of similar elements. Whereas types identify elements or attributes with common content, substitution groups identify elements that are interchangeable in terms of where they can appear in a document. The content of different elements in a substitution group might be completely different, in which case it is probably not very useful to define a template rule that processes all the elements in the group. More commonly, however, the elements in a substitution group will have some content in common, for example all elements in the substitution group of <event> might have attributes time and place. In this case a pattern such as «schema-element(event)» can be used to process this common content.

❑ Patterns that match all elements in a substitution group can be especially useful in contexts other than <xsl:template>. For example, suppose a genealogy database allows a <person> element to contain any number of <event> elements among its children, and that elements such as <birth>, <death>, <baptism>, and <burial> are defined as elements within the substitution group for <event>. In this case, if you want to number the events for a particular person you can use <xsl:number count="schema-element(event)"/>.

Predicates

The form of a Predicate is defined in the XPath expression language: it is any expression enclosed in square brackets. For example «[speaker='Hamlet']», or «[@width > 100]», or «[*]», or «[1]». A PatternStep may include any number of predicates. These are additive—a node must satisfy all the predicates if it is to match.

There are two kinds of predicate: those that depend on the node's position relative to its siblings, and those that don't. A positional predicate is one whose value is a number, or one that uses the functions position() or last(); all others are nonpositional. For example, the predicates «[1]», «[position()!=1]», and «[last()-1]» are all positional predicates, whereas «[@name='Tokyo']» and «[*]» are nonpositional.

For a nonpositional predicate, its meaning is that the PatternStep matches a node only if the *effective boolean value* of the predicate is true. The concept of effective boolean value is defined in XPath, and is summarized in the entry for <xsl:if> on page 309 in Chapter 5. For example, the predicate «[@security ='secret']» is true when the node has a security attribute whose value is 'secret', so any PatternStep that uses this predicate will fail if the node has no security attribute or if the security attribute has any value other than 'secret'.

For a positional predicate, the meaning of the predicate can be deduced from the formal rules given at the start of this chapter. However, it is easier to understand their meaning by using informal rules. A numeric predicate such as «[1]» or «[last()-1]» is equivalent to the boolean predicate «[position()=1]» or «[position()=last()-1]». So to evaluate a positional predicate, we need to know what position() and last() are.

The use of positional predicates with the attribute axis doesn't make much sense, because the order of attributes is undefined (though I did see one stylesheet that was using «@*[1]» to match the first attribute, and «@*» to match the others, which is perfectly legitimate so long as you realize that it's unpredictable which of the attributes will be the first). In the following description, I'll assume that you're using the child axis.

If there is only one predicate in the PatternStep, or if this predicate is the first, then:

❑ last() is the number of siblings of the node being tested that satisfy the NodeTest (including the node itself). For example, if we are testing a <para> element against the pattern «para [last()=1]», then last() is the number of <para> elements that are children of the parent of the <para> element being tested. This pattern will match any <para> element that is the only <para> child of its parent.

❑ position() is the position of the node being tested among these siblings, taking them in document order and counting from one. So «para[1]», which means «para[position() =1]», will match any <para> element that is the first <para> child of its parent element, in document order.

Note that it is the position of the node relative to its siblings that counts, not the position in the sequence you are processing the nodes. For example, suppose you want to process all the <glossary-entry> elements in a document, in alphabetical order. You can write:

```
<xsl:apply-templates select="//glossary-entry">
     <xsl:sort/>
<xsl:apply-templates>
```

Then suppose you have the following two template rules.

```
<xsl:template match="glossary-entry[1]">
. . .
</xsl:template>
<xsl:template match="glossary-entry">
. . .
</xsl:template>
```

The first template rule will be used for any <glossary-entry> that is the first <glossary-entry> child of its parent. Not, as you might expect, the first <glossary-entry> in alphabetical order, nor even the first <glossary-entry> element in the document. If you want to apply different processing to the <glossary-entry> that is first in alphabetical order, the way to do it is as follows.

```
<xsl:template match="glossary-entry">
   <xsl:choose>
     <xsl:when test="position()=1">
         . . .
     </xsl:when>
     <xsl:otherwise>
         . . .
     </xsl:otherwise>
   </xsl:choose>
</xsl:template>
```

This is because the context position within the body of the template rule is the position of the node in the list of nodes being processed, whereas the result for deciding whether a node matches a pattern is the same regardless of the processing context.

If there are several predicates in the PatternStep, then position() and last() in predicates after the first apply to the nodes that survived the previous predicates. So «speech[speaker='Hamlet'] [1]» matches a <speech> element that is the first <speech> element among its siblings, counting only those <speech> elements in which one of the <speaker>s is Hamlet.

The `position()` and `last()` functions relate to children of the same parent even when the «//» operator is used. For example, «chapter//footnote[1]» matches any `<footnote>` element that is a descendant of a `<chapter>` element and that is the first `<footnote>` child of its parent. There is no simple way to write a pattern that matches the first `<footnote>` element in a `<chapter>`, because the relevant expression «(chapter//footnote)[1]» is not a valid pattern. (Why not? No good reason, it's just that the spec doesn't allow it.)

If you do need to write a template rule for the first `<footnote>` element in a `<chapter>`, the cleanest solution is probably to write your own function. You can invoke this in a predicate within the pattern, for example «match="footnote[test:position-in-chapter(.)=1]». The definition of the function might look like this.

```
<xsl:function name="test:position-in-chapter" as="xs:integer">
  <xsl:param name="in" as="element()"/>
  <xsl:number level="any" from="chapter"/>
</xsl:function>
```

Positional predicates in patterns need to be used with some attention to performance. Writing a template with the match pattern «para[last()-1]», for example, seems a sensible way to define the processing for the penultimate paragraph of a section. However, a simplistic XSLT processor will expand this predicate to «para[position()=last()-1]», and evaluate it by first determining the position of the current paragraph in its section, then finding the total number of paragraphs in the section, and comparing the two. If the number of paragraphs in a section is large, this could be a very expensive operation. An optimized XSLT processor will find a better strategy, but if performance is critical it would be worth doing some measurements.

Examples

The following table provides some examples of PatternSteps.

Construct	Meaning
`child::title`	Matches elements named `<title>`.
`title`	Short form of «child::title».
`attribute::title`	Matches attributes named `<title>`.
`@title`	Short form of «attribute::title».
`*[@width]`	Matches an element node that has an attribute named `width`.
`text()[starts-with(.,'The')]`	Matches a text node whose text content starts with the characters «The».
`p[@code][position() &lt; 10]`	Matches a `<p>` element that is among the first nine `<p>` elements of its parent that have a `code` attribute.
`p[position() &lt; 10][@code]`	Matches a `<p>` element that is among the first nine `<p>` elements of its parent and that has a `code` attribute.

Continues

Construct	Meaning
`*[not(@code = preceding-sibling::*/@code)]`	Matches an element node provided that it does not have a code attribute with the same value as the code attribute of any preceding sibling element.
`comment()`	Matches any comment node.
`@comment()`	This matches comment nodes that are found on the attribute axis of their parent node. Since the attribute axis contains attribute nodes only, this condition can never be satisfied; nevertheless, it is a legal `PatternStep`.

IdKeyPattern

This construct allows a pattern to be matched only if the node being tested (or one of its ancestors) has a specified ID attribute or key value.

This construct is a subset of the `FunctionCall` construct in an Expression, described in *XPath 2.0 Programmer's Reference*. The only function calls that can be used in a pattern (except within predicates) are the `id()` and `key()` functions, and these can be used only with arguments that are literals or variable references.

The `id()` function is an XPath function and is described in Chapter 10 of *XPath 2.0 Programmer's Reference*. The `key()` function is exclusive to XSLT, and is described on page 572 in Chapter 7.

Syntax

Expression	Syntax
`IdKeyPattern`	«id» «(» Value «)»| «key» «(» StringLiteral «,» Value «)»
`Value`	Literal|VariableReference

For both the `id()` and `key()` functions, the required value of the ID or key can be specified as either a literal or a variable reference (in the form «$» QName). For the `id()` function, the only kind of literal that makes sense is a string literal (for example «"E-102"»). For the key function, numeric literals also make sense if the key values are numeric. It is not possible to supply literals for other data types, for example `xs:date` values.

With the `key()` function, the first argument is the name of the key. This must be specified as a string literal, and it must match the name of a key defined in the stylesheet.

Usage

This facility provides an equivalent to the ability in Cascading Style Sheets (CSS) to define a style for a specific node in the source document. It can be used:

❑ If for a particular source document you want to use a general-purpose stylesheet, but want to override its behavior for certain selected nodes, you can write a stylesheet that imports the general-purpose one, and then write the overriding rules in the form of templates that match specific identified elements in the source document.

❑ Sometimes the source document is generated dynamically from a database. Perhaps there is something in the source document you want to highlight, say the search term that was used to locate this record. You could flag this item while generating the source document by giving it a special ID attribute value known to the stylesheet.

In practice, this construct isn't as useful as it might seem. Even though XSLT 2.0 has made it a lot more flexible by allowing the value to be specified as a variable (which in general is likely to be a stylesheet parameter), this form of pattern still achieves nothing that can't be achieved just as easily with a predicate, and is unlikely to be any more efficient.

For example, if <book> elements are keyed on their ISBN property, which is implemented as a child element, then the following declarations are equivalent:

Using a direct pattern match:

```
<xsl:template match="book[isbn='1-861002-68-8']">
```

Using a key definition:

```
<xsl:key name="isbn-key" match="book" use="isbn"/>
<xsl:template match="key('isbn-key', '1-861002-68-8')>
```

Of course there may be a performance difference between the two, but this depends on how the XSLT processor is implemented. There is certainly no intrinsic reason why the predicate should be less efficient.

Examples

id('figure1')	Matches a node with an ID attribute equal to the string 'figure1'. An attribute is an ID attribute if it is defined in the Document Type Definition (DTD) or schema as having type ID (the name of the attribute is irrelevant).
key('empnr', $pers)	Matches a node having a value of $pers for the key named «empnr», where $pers is typically a stylesheet parameter.

The following example shows how this feature can be used in a stylesheet.

Example: Using the key() Pattern to Format a Specific Node

This example shows how to use the key() pattern to format one selected node differently from the others. The selected node will be specified by a style-sheet parameter.

Source

The source document, itinerary.xml, is a tour itinerary.

```
<itinerary>
<day number="1">Arrive in Cairo</day>
<day number="2">Visit the Pyramids at Gaza</day>
<day number="3">Archaelogical Museum at Cairo</day>
<day number="4">Flight to Luxor; coach to Aswan</day>
<day number="5">Visit Temple at Philae and Aswan High Dam</day>
<day number="6">Cruise to Edfu</day>
<day number="7">Cruise to Luxor; visit Temple at Karnak</day>
<day number="8">Valley of the Kings</day>
<day number="9">Return flight from Luxor</day>
</itinerary>
```

Stylesheet

Let's start with a straightforward stylesheet, itinerary.xsl, to display this itinerary.

```
<?xml version="1.0" encoding="iso-8859-1"?>
<xsl:stylesheet version="1.0"
      xmlns:xsl="http://www.w3.org/1999/XSL/Transform">

<xsl:template match="/">
  <html>
    <head>
      <title>Itinerary</title>
    </head>
    <body><center>
      <xsl:apply-templates select="//day"/>
    </center></body>
  </html>
</xsl:template>

<xsl:template match="day">
  <h3>Day <xsl:value-of select="@number"/></h3>
  <p><xsl:apply-templates/></p>
</xsl:template>
</xsl:stylesheet>
```

Now let's specialize this by importing it into another stylesheet, today.xsl, which displays the activities for a selected day in red.

```
<?xml version="1.0" encoding="iso-8859-1"?>
<xsl:stylesheet
      version="2.0"
```

```
            xmlns:xsl="http://www.w3.org/1999/XSL/Transform"
            xmlns:xs="http://www.w3.org/2001/XMLSchema">

  <xsl:import href="itinerary.xsl"/>

  <xsl:param name="highlight-day" as="xs:integer" required="yes"/>
  <xsl:key name="day-number" match="day" use="xs:integer(@number)"/>

  <xsl:template match="key('day-number', $highlight-day)//text()">
      <font color="red"><xsl:value-of select="."/></font>
  </xsl:template>

  </xsl:stylesheet>
```

To run this stylesheet using Saxon, enter the command line:

```
java net.sf.saxon.Transform -t itinerary.xml today.xsl highlight-day=5
```

Note that this example requires Saxon 7.9 or later (earlier versions do not support numeric keys).

Output

The resulting output is as follows, when the $highlight-day parameter is set to 5.

```
<html>
    <head>
        <META http-equiv="Content-Type" content="text/html;
charset=utf-8">
        <title>Itinerary</title>
    </head>
    <body>
        <center>
            <h3>Day 1</h3>
            <p>Arrive in Cairo</p>
            <h3>Day 2</h3>
            <p>Visit the Pyramids at Gaza</p>
            <h3>Day 3</h3>
            <p>Archaelogical Museum at Cairo</p>
            <h3>Day 4</h3>
            <p>Flight to Luxor; coach to Aswan</p>
            <h3>Day 5</h3>
            <p><font color="red">
               Visit Temple at Philae and Aswan High Dam</font></p>
            <h3>Day 6</h3>
            <p>Cruise to Edfu</p>
            <h3>Day 7</h3>
            <p>Cruise to Luxor; visit Temple at Karnak</p>
            <h3>Day 8</h3>
            <p>Valley of the Kings</p>
            <h3>Day 9</h3>
            <p>Return flight from Luxor</p>
        </center>
    </body>
</html>
```

> While this example shows one way of using this feature, I have to admit that it's not very convincing. You could achieve the same effect by writing the relevant pattern as «day[@number=5]», without the need to introduce a key at all.

Summary

This chapter described the syntax and meanings of patterns, whose main use in an XSLT stylesheet is to define which template rules apply to which nodes in the source document, but which are also used in the <xsl:key>, <xsl:number>, and <xsl:for-each-group> elements.

Patterns, although their syntax is a subset of that for XPath expressions, are evaluated in a different way to expressions, though we saw that the formal rules express the meaning of a pattern in terms of the corresponding expression.

The next chapter describes the library of standard functions that can be used within XPath expressions in a stylesheet

XSLT Functions

This chapter describes all the standard functions included in the XSLT 2.0 specifications for use in XPath expressions. These functions are XSLT-specific additions to the standard XPath 2.0 function library, which is described in *XPath 2.0 Programmer's Reference*. The functions defined in the XPath specification are also summarized in Appendix B.

The description of each function includes its name, a brief description of its purpose, a list of the arguments it expects and the value it returns, the formal rules defining what the function does, and finally usage advice and examples.

> *If you are using XPath in a context other than XSLT, you should be aware that the functions described in this chapter will not be available.*

The syntax and semantics of a function call are described as part of the XPath expression syntax in *XPath 2.0 Programmer's Reference*. A function call can be used anywhere within an expression, so long as it returns the proper type of value expected in the context where it appears. For example, on the right-hand side of the «/» operator, a function call must return a sequence that consists entirely of nodes. Similarly, within a function call, the values supplied as arguments can be any XPath expression, subject only to the rules on data types.

The functions in this chapter are arranged in alphabetical order so you can find them quickly if you know what you're looking for. In case you only know the general area you are interested in, you may find the following quick reference useful .

Function	Purpose	Page
current()	Returns the current item in the stylesheet	526
current-group()	Returns the contents of the current group of items being processed by `<xsl:for-each-group>`	529
current-grouping-key()	Returns the value of the key value shared by all the items in the current group	530

Continues

Function	Purpose	Page
document()	Loads an external document identified by URI	532
element-available()	Tests whether a given XSLT or extension instruction is available for use	542
format-date()	Formats an xs:date value	548
format-dateTime()	Formats an xs:dateTime value	550
format-number()	Formats a number	558
format-time()	Formats an xs:time value	562
function-available()	Tests whether a given function is available for use	564
generate-id()	Generates a unique identifier for a node	568
key()	Locates nodes given the value of a key declared using <xsl:key>	572
regex-group()	Returns a captured subgroup within a string matched using <xsl:analyze-string>	580
system-property()	Returns information about the implementation	581
unparsed-entity-public-id()	Returns the public identifier of an unparsed entity within a source document	584
unparsed-entity-uri()	Returns the system identifier of an unparsed entity within a source document	585
unparsed-text()	Reads the content of an external text file identified by its URI	587

All these functions are technically in the same namespace as the core XPath functions. This namespace is currently defined by the URI http://www.w3.org/2003/11/xpath-functions but this will change in subsequent drafts, until XPath is issued as a Candidate Recommendation. This namespace is conventionally used with the prefix «fn». However, within XSLT stylesheets, this namespace is the default namespace for function calls, so these functions can always be called without specifying a prefix. This distinguishes them clearly from user-defined functions, which always carry a namespace prefix.

When these functions are called, the supplied arguments are converted to the required type in the standard way defined by the XPath 2.0 function calling mechanism. The details of this depend on whether XPath 1.0 backwards compatibility is activated or not, which in turn depends on the value of the [xsl:]version attribute on the innermost containing element that has such an attribute.

❑   If the effective version is «2.0» or greater, then the standard conversion rules listed under <xsl:variable> (page 476) in Chapter 5 are used. These rules permit only the following kinds of conversion:

     ❑   Atomization of nodes to extract their numeric values

- ❑ Promotion of numeric values to a different numeric type, for example xs:integer to xs:double

- ❑ Casting of a value of type xdt:untypedAtomic to the required type. Such values generally arise by extracting the content of a node that has not been schema validated

❑ If the effective version is «1.0», then two additional conversions are allowed:

- ❑ If the required type is xs:string or xs:double (perhaps with an occurrence indicator of «?»), then the first value in the supplied sequence is converted to the required type using the string() or number() function as appropriate, and other values in the sequence are discarded.

- ❑ If the required type is node() or item() (perhaps with an occurrence indicator of «?»), then when the supplied value contains more than one item, all items except the first are ignored.

So, even though the function signature might give the expected type of an argument as xs:string, say, the value you supply can be a node containing a string, or a node whose value is untyped (because it has not been validated using a schema). With 1.0 compatibility mode on, you can also supply values of other types, for example an xs:integer or an xs:anyURI, but when compatibility mode is off, you will need to convert such values to an xs:string yourself, which you can achieve most simply by calling the string() function.

The function descriptions use a common structure wherever possible. This includes the following subsections:

- ❑ The *name* of the function is followed by a very brief statement of the purpose of the function, sometimes with a quick example.

- ❑ The section *Changes in 2.0* summarizes any significant changes in the function since XSLT 1.0.

- ❑ The *Signature* section includes a table listing the names and types of the arguments, with the meaning of each argument. It also defines the type of the result. Note that technically, functions are identified by their name and arity, so the document() function with two arguments is a different function from document() with one argument. However, the core function library has been designed so that different functions with the same name are always closely related, so it is simpler to describe these as two variants of the same function, in which the second argument is optional.

- ❑ The *Effect* section says what the function does, with each possible combination of input arguments.

- ❑ The *Usage* section contains advice on how the function can be used.

- ❑ The *Examples* section contains examples showing the function in use. Where appropriate, the examples are merged with the *Usage* section.

- ❑ The *See Also* section points you to other relevant information in this book or in *XPath 2.0 Programmer's Reference*.

For some functions (notably document()), the description of the function is subdivided into a number of modes of use, each with its own *Effect*, *Usage*, and *Examples* subsections.

current

The `current()` function returns a single item, the item that is the context item at the point in the stylesheet where the XPath expression containing this function call is called.

Changes in 2.0

The function has been generalized so it may return any item (a node or an atomic value), not only a node.

The function may now be used within an XSLT pattern.

Signature

There are no arguments.

	Data type	Meaning
Result	`item()`	*The item that is the context item at the outermost level of the XPath expression containing the function call.*

Effect

At any point in the processing of a stylesheet, there is generally a context item. The XPath expression « . », if it is used as a stand-alone expression within a stylesheet, will always select the context item and will return the same result as the expression `current()`. Within an XPath expression, the context item may change: for example, within a predicate, the context item is the item being tested using the predicate. The result of the `current()` function, however, is the same wherever it is used within an expression. This makes it useful within predicates, as a way of referring to the item that would have been the context item at the outermost level.

This is best explained by example. The following example processes all `<part>` elements that have a `code` attribute whose value is the same as the `code` attribute of the element that is the context item at the point where the instruction is evaluated.

```
<xsl:apply-templates select="//part[@code = current()/@code]"/>
```

Another way of writing this would be:

```
<xsl:apply-templates select="for $c in . return //part[@code = $c/@code]"/>
```

and in fact this substitution is completely general; any complete XPath expression that references the `current()` function could be replaced by one in which a variable is bound to the value of « . » at the outermost level of the expression, and the call on `current()` is replaced by a reference to that variable.

The context item in a stylesheet is established as follows:

- ❑ When evaluating a global variable, the context item is the initial context item, supplied by the calling application (it may be undefined if no initial context item has been supplied). Usually, this will be the document node of the main input document.

- ❑ When `<xsl:apply-templates>` is used to process a selected set of nodes, each selected node in turn becomes the context item. So when a template rule is invoked, the context item is always the node that caused that template rule to be selected. On return from `<xsl:apply-templates>`, the context item reverts to its previous value.

- ❑ When `<xsl:for-each>` is used to process a selected sequence of items, each selected item in turn becomes the context item. When the `<xsl:for-each>` loop completes, the context item reverts to its previous value.

- ❑ When a stylesheet function is called from within an XPath expression, the context item is undefined. This means that any attempt to reference «.» or `current()` will raise an error.

- ❑ The `<xsl:for-each-group>` and `<xsl:analyze-string>` instructions also change the context item: for details, see the description of these instructions in Chapter 5.

- ❑ All other instructions, including `<xsl:call-template>` and `<xsl:apply-imports>`, leave the context item unchanged.

When the `current()` function is used in a pattern, it refers to the node that is being matched against the pattern. For example, the pattern «part[ancestor::*/@code != current()/@code]» matches all part elements that have an ancestor with a code attribute that differs from the code attribute on the element itself.

Usage

The reason the `current()` function is provided is to allow you to determine the XSLT context item when it is different from the XPath context item—specifically, inside a predicate. The XPath context item can always be determined using the path expression «.».

The most common situation where `current()` is useful is when you want to follow a cross-reference from the context node to some other node. For example, the expression «//department[deptNr = current()/@dept]» finds a `<department>` element referenced from the dept attribute of the context item (which might be an `<employee>` element).

Example

The following example shows the use of `current()` in a predicate.

Example: current()

This example lists the books in a catalog; in the description of each book, it also lists other books in the same category.

Source

The source document is `booklist.xml`.

```
<booklist>
<book category="S">
    <title>Number, the Language of Science</title>
    <author>Danzig</author>
</book>
<book category="FC">
    <title>The Young Visiters</title>
    <author>Daisy Ashford</author>
</book>
<book category="FC">
    <title>When We Were Very Young</title>
    <author>A. A. Milne</author>
</book>
<book category="CS">
    <title>Design Patterns</title>
    <author>Erich Gamma</author>
    <author>Richard Helm</author>
    <author>Ralph Johnson</author>
    <author>John Vlissides</author>
</book>
</booklist>
```

Stylesheet

The stylesheet is `list-books.xsl`. It processes all the books in an `<xsl:for-each>` loop, and for each one it displays the title and the first author. Then it looks for other books in the same category. Here it uses the predicate «`[./@category = current()/@category]`», which is true if the `category` attribute of the context element is the same as the `category` attribute of the current element. The context element is the one being tested; the element returned by `current()` is the one whose entry is being displayed. It also tests that these two elements are distinct elements, using the condition «`not(. is current())`». In this case, you could also get away with writing «`.!=current()`», which tests whether the two nodes have a different string value, but it can be a more expensive test, and it doesn't mean quite the same thing.

```
<xsl:transform
 xmlns:xsl="http://www.w3.org/1999/XSL/Transform"
 version="2.0"
>
<xsl:template match="/">
  <html><body>
    <xsl:variable name="all-books" select="//book"/>
    <xsl:for-each select="$all-books">
      <h1><xsl:value-of select="title"/></h1>
      <p><i>by </i><xsl:value-of select="author[1]"/>
        <xsl:if test="count(author)!=1"> and others</xsl:if>
      </p>
      <xsl:variable name="others"
        select="$all-books[./@category=current()/@category and
```

```
                          not(. is current())]"/>
            <xsl:if test="$others">
              <p>Other books in this category:</p><ul>
              <xsl:for-each select="$others">
                  <li><xsl:value-of select="title"/></li>
              </xsl:for-each>
              </ul>
            </xsl:if>
        </xsl:for-each>
    </body></html>
</xsl:template>

</xsl:transform>
```

Output

The output of the transformation is as follows.

```
<html>
    <body>
        <h1>Number, the Language of Science</h1>
        <p><i>by </i>Danzig
        </p>
        <h1>The Young Visiters</h1><p><i>by </i>Daisy Ashford
        </p>
        <p>Other books in this category:</p>
        <ul>
          <li>When We Were Very Young</li>
        </ul>
        <h1>When We Were Very Young</h1>
        <p><i>by </i>A. A. Milne
        </p>
        <p>Other books in this category:</p>
        <ul>
          <li>The Young Visiters</li>
        </ul>
        <h1>Design Patterns</h1>
        <p><i>by </i>Erich Gamma and others
        </p>
    </body>
</html>
```

current-group

The current-group() function returns the set of items making up the group that is currently being processed using the <xsl:for-each-group> instruction.

Changes in 2.0

This function is new in XSLT 2.0.

Signature

There are no arguments.

	Data type	Meaning
Result	`item()*`	*A sequence of items, specifically the sequence that is being processed in the current iteration of an* `<xsl:for-each-group>` *instruction.*

Effect

When the stylesheet starts executing, there is no current group; the `current-group()` function then returns an empty sequence.

The `<xsl:for-each-group>` instruction, described in Chapter 5, page 281, takes as input a sequence of items (called the population) and a grouping expression or pattern. It allocates each item in the population to zero or more groups of items, and then processes each group in turn. While it is processing each group, the `current-group()` function returns the sequence of items that participate in that group.

The `current-group()` function does not need to be called textually within the `<xsl:for-each-group>` instruction. Its scope is dynamic, and the current group remains available in called templates unless another nested `<xsl:for-each-group>` instruction is evaluated. On completion of an `<xsl:for-each-group>` instruction, it reverts to its previous value.

The `current-group()` function can also be called while evaluating the sort key in an `<xsl:sort>` element contained within the `<xsl:for-each-group>` instruction. This affects the order in which groups are processed. In this context, `current-group()` refers to the group whose sort key is being calculated. For example, to sort groups in order of decreasing size, write `<xsl:sort select="count (current-group())" order="descending"/>`.

On entry to a stylesheet function, the current group is an empty sequence.

Usage and Examples

See `<xsl:for-each-group>` on page 281 in Chapter 5.

See Also

`<xsl:for-each-group>` on page 281 in Chapter 5.
`current-grouping-key()`—the next entry in this chapter.

current-grouping-key

The `current-grouping-key()` function returns the value of the grouping key that defines the group currently being processed using the `<xsl:for-each-group>` instruction. The grouping key is the value of the expression in the `group-by` or `group-adjacent` attribute. When grouping is done using patterns, there is no current grouping key.

Changes in 2.0

This function is new in XSLT 2.0.

Signature

There are no arguments.

	Data type	Meaning
Result	`xdt:anyAtomicType?`	*This is the value of the* `group-by` *or* `group-adjacent` *expression that is shared by all the items in the current group. The return type indicates that the grouping key can be of any atomic type, for example* `xs:string`, `xs:decimal`, *or* `xs:date`. *When there is no current group, the function returns an empty sequence.*

Effect

When the stylesheet starts executing, there is no current grouping key; the `current-grouping-key()` function then returns an empty sequence.

The `<xsl:for-each-group>` instruction, described in Chapter 5, page 281, takes as input a sequence of items called the population and a grouping expression or pattern. If the grouping criteria are defined using the `group-by` or `group-adjacent` attributes, then while each group is being processed, the `current-grouping-key()` function returns the grouping key value that characterizes that group.

If the grouping criteria are defined using the `group-starting-with` or `group-ending-with` attributes of `<xsl:for-each-group>`, the current grouping key is an empty sequence.

The `current-grouping-key()` function does not need to be called textually within the `<xsl:for-each-group>` instruction. Its scope is dynamic, and the current grouping key remains available in called templates unless another nested `<xsl:for-each-group>` instruction is evaluated. On completion of an `<xsl:for-each-group>` instruction, it reverts to its previous value.

The `current-grouping-key()` function can also be called while evaluating the sort key in an `<xsl:sort>` element contained within the `<xsl:for-each-group>` instruction. This affects the order in which groups are processed. In this context, `current-grouping-key()` refers to the group whose sort key is being calculated. For example, to sort groups in descending order of their grouping key, write `<xsl:sort select="current-grouping-key()" order="descending"/>`.

On entry to a stylesheet function, the current grouping key is an empty sequence.

Usage and Examples

The following example groups a set of books by the name of the author. For each author, a section heading is displayed giving the name of the author, followed by a list of the books written by this author. The authors are sorted by name. A book that has several authors will be listed more than once.

```
<xsl:for-each-group select="//book" group-by="author">
  <xsl:sort select="current-grouping-key()"/>
  <h2><xsl:value-of select="current-grouping-key()"/></h2>
  <xsl:apply-templates select="current-group()"/>
</xsl:for-each-group>
```

See Also

`<xsl:for-each-group>`, page 281 in Chapter 5.

document

The `document()` function finds an external XML document by resolving a URI reference, parses the XML into a tree structure, and returns its root node. It may also be used to find a set of external documents, and it may be used to find a node other than the root by using a fragment identifier in the URI.

For example, the expression «`document('data.xml')`» looks for the file `data.xml` in the same directory as the stylesheet, parses it, and returns the root node of the resulting tree.

Changes in 2.0

XPath 2.0 defines a simplified version of the `document()` function called `doc()`. The full `document()` function is retained as an XSLT function for backwards compatibility with XSLT 1.0.

The specification of the function has been generalized to allow the first argument to be an arbitrary sequence of URIs, and it has also become less prescriptive, to allow greater freedom to configure the way in which the URI is interpreted and the way in which the retrieved documents are parsed.

Signature

Argument	Data type	Meaning
href	`item()*`	A sequence, which may contain values of type `xs:string` or `xs:anyURI`, or nodes containing such values. These URIs are used to locate the documents to be loaded.
base (optional)	`node()`	If the argument is present, it must be a node. The base URI of this node is used for resolving any relative URIs found in the first argument.
Result	`node()*`	*A sequence of nodes, in document order. In the common case where a single URI is specified, and this URI contains no fragment identifier, the result will normally be a single document node.*

Effect

In brief, the document() function locates an XML document, using a URI. The resulting XML document is parsed and a tree is constructed. On completion, the result of the document() function is the document node of the new document.

If a sequence of URIs is provided, rather than a single URI, then the result is a sequence of document nodes. If a URI contains a fragment identifier, then the result may be an element node rather than a document node. The details are described in the following sections.

I will describe the effect of the function by considering three separate cases, which reflect different ways of determining a base URI to use for resolving relative URIs. However, first a word about URIs and URLs, which are terms I use rather freely throughout this section.

Resolving the URI

The XSLT specification always uses the term URI: Uniform Resource Identifier. The concept of a URI is a generalization of the URLs (Uniform Resource Locators) that are widely used on the Web today and displayed on every cornflakes packet. The URI extends the URL mechanism, which is based on the established Domain Name System (with its hierarchic names such as www.ibm.com and www.cam.ac.uk), to allow other global naming and numbering schemes, including established ones such as ISBN book numbers and international telephone numbers. While URIs are a nice idea, the only ones that really enable you to retrieve resources on the Web are the familiar URLs. This is why the terms URI and URL seem to be used rather interchangeably in this section and indeed throughout the book. If you read carefully, though, you'll see that I've tried to use both terms correctly.

The way URIs are used to locate XML documents, and the way these XML documents are parsed to create a tree representation, is not defined in detail. In fact, the XSLT document() function defines this process in terms of the XPath doc() function, and the XPath doc() function essentially says that it's a piece of magic performed by the context of the XPath expression, not by the XPath processor itself. This reflects the reality that when you are using an application programming interface (API) such as the Java JAXP interface or the System.Xml.Xsl class in Microsoft's .NET, you can supply your own code that maps URIs to document nodes in any way you like. (The relevant class is called URIResolver in JAXP, XmlResolver in .NET.) This might not even involve any parsing of a real XML file; for example, the URIResolver might actually retrieve data from a relational database, and return an XML document that encapsulates the results of the query.

There's an expectation, though, that most XSLT processors—unless running in some kind of secure environment—will allow you to specify a URL (typically one that starts «http:» or «file:») that can be dereferenced in the usual way to locate a source XML document, which is then parsed. The details of how it is parsed, for example whether schema or Document Type Definition (DTD) validation is attempted and whether XInclude processing is performed, are likely to depend on configuration settings (perhaps options on the command line, or properties set via the processor's API). The language specification leaves this open ended.

A URI used as input to the document() function should generally identify an XML document. If the URI is invalid, or if it doesn't identify any resource, or if that resource is not an XML document, the specification leaves it up to the implementation to decide what to do: it can either report the error, or ignore that particular URI. Implementations may go beyond this, for example if the URI identifies an

HTML document they may attempt to convert the HTML to XML—this is all outside the scope of the W3C specifications.

A URI can be relative rather than absolute. A typical example of a relative URI is data.xml. Such a URI is resolved (converted to an absolute, globally unique URI) by interpreting it as relative to some base URI. By default, a relative URI that appears in the text of an XML document is interpreted relative to the URI of the document (or more precisely, the XML entity) that contains it, which in the case of the document() function is usually either the source document or the stylesheet. So if the relative URI data.xml appears in the source document, the system will try to find the file in the same directory as the source document, while if it appears in the stylesheet, the system will look in the directory containing the stylesheet. The base URI of a node in an XML document can be changed using the xml:base attribute, and this will be taken into account. In addition, the document() function provides a second argument so that the base URI can be specified explicitly, if required.

The actual rule is that the href argument may be a sequence of nodes or atomic values. In the case of a node in this sequence, the node may contain a URI (or indeed, a sequence of URIs), and if such a URI is relative then it is expanded against the base URI of the node from which it came. In the case of an atomic value in the sequence, this must be an xs:string or xs:anyURI value, and it is expanded using the base URI of the stylesheet.

The expansion of relative URIs exploits the fact that in the XPath data model, described on page 53 in Chapter 2, every node has a base URI. (Don't confuse this with the namespace URI, which is quite unrelated.) By default, the base URI of a node in the source document or the stylesheet will be the URI of the XML document or entity from which the node was constructed. In some cases, for example when the input comes from a Document Object Model (DOM) document or from a relational database, it may be difficult for the processor to determine the base URI (the concept does not exist in the DOM standard). What happens in this situation is implementer defined. Microsoft, whose MSXML3 processor is built around its DOM implementation, has extended its DOM so it retains knowledge of the URI from which the document was loaded.

With XSLT 2.0, you can override the default rules for establishing the base URI of a node by using the xml:base attribute of an element. This attribute is defined in a W3C Recommendation called *XML Base* (http://www.w3.org/TR/xmlbase/); it is intended to fulfill the same function as the <base> element in HTML. If an element has an xml:base attribute, the value of the attribute must be a URI, and this URI defines the base URI for the element itself and for all descendants of the element node, unless overridden by another xml:base attribute.

The URI specified in xml:base may itself be a relative URI, in which case it is resolved relative to the base URI of the parent of the element containing the xml:base attribute (that is, the URI that would have been the base URI of the element if it hadn't had an xml:base attribute).

With XSLT 2.0, it is also possible that the node used to establish the base URI for the document() function will be a node in a temporary tree created as the value of a variable. Normally, the base URI for such a node will be the base URI of the <xsl:variable> (or <xsl:param>, or <xsl:with-param>) element that defines the temporary tree. But if an element in the stylesheet has an xml:base attribute, that defines the base URI in the same way as for a source document.

If several calls on the document() function use the same URI (after expansion of a relative URI into an absolute URI), then the same document node is returned each time. You can tell that it's the same node because the «is» operator returns true: «document('a.xml') is document('a.xml')» will always be true. If you use a different URI in two calls, then you may or may not get the same document node back: «document('a.xml') is document('A.XML')» might be either true or false.

A fragment identifier identifies a part of a resource: for example, in the URL http://www.wrox.com/booklist#april2004, the fragment identifier is april2004. In principle, a fragment identifier allows the URI to reference a node or set of nodes other than the root node of the target document; for example, the fragment identifier could be an XPointer expression containing a complex expression to select nodes within the target document. In practice though, this is all implementation defined. The interpretation of a fragment identifier depends on the media type (often called MIME type) of the returned document. Implementations are not required to support any particular media types (which means they are not required to support fragment identifiers at all). Many products support a simple fragment identifier consisting of a name that must be the value of an ID attribute in the target document, and support for XPointer fragment identifiers is likely to become increasingly common now that a usable XPointer specification has finally been ratified.

Parsing the Document

Once the URI has been resolved against a base URI, the next steps are to fetch the XML document found at that URI, and then to parse it into a tree representation. The specification says very little about these processes, which allows the implementation considerable freedom to configure what kind of URLs are acceptable, and how the parsing is done. It is not even required that the resource starts life as XML: an implementation could quite legitimately return a document node that represents an HTML document, or the results of a database query. If the URL does refer to an XML file, there are still variations allowed in how it is parsed, for example whether DTD or schema validation takes place, and whether XInclude references are expanded. A vendor might provide additional options such as the ability to strip comments, processing instructions, and unreferenced namespaces. You need to check the documentation for your product to see how such factors can be controlled.

The specification does say that whites-pace-only nodes are stripped following the same rules as for the source document, based on the <xsl:strip-space> and <xsl:preserve-space> declarations in force. This is true even if the document happens to be a stylesheet.

URIs Held in Nodes

For a simple case such as «document(@href)», the result is a single node, namely the root node of the document referenced by the href attribute of the context node.

More generally, the argument may be a sequence of nodes, each of which contains a sequence of URIs. The result is then the sequence obtained by processing each of these in turn. For example, «document(//@href)» returns the sequence of documents located by dereferencing the URIs in all the href attributes in the original context document. The result is returned in document order of the returned nodes (a somewhat academic concept since they will usually be different documents). The result is not necessarily in the order of the href attributes, and duplicates will be eliminated.

If any of the nodes contains a relative URI, it will be resolved relative to the base URI of that node. The base URI of a node is established using the rules given on page 53. In fact, each node in the supplied sequence could potentially have a different base URI.

This all sounds terribly complicated, but all it really means is that if the source document contains the link «data.xml», then the system will look for the file data.xml in the same directory as the source document.

These rules also cover the case where the argument is a reference to a variable containing a temporary tree, for example:

```
<xsl:variable name="index">index.xml</xsl:variable>
<xsl:for-each select="document($index)">
. . .
</xsl:for-each>
```

In this case relative URI «index.xml» is resolved relative to the base URI of the `<xsl:variable>` element in the stylesheet, which is generally the URI of the stylesheet module itself.

Usage

A common use of the `document()` function is to access a document referenced from the source document, typically in an attribute such as `href`. For example, a book catalog might include links to reviews of each book, in a format such as:

```
<book>
    <review date="1999-12-28" publication="New York Times"
                              text="reviews/NYT/19991228/rev3.xml"/>
    <review date="2000-01-06" publication="Washington Post"
                              text="reviews/WPost/20000106/rev12.xml"/>
</book>
```

If you want to incorporate the text of these reviews in your output document, you can achieve this using the `document()` function. For example:

```
<xsl:template match="book">
    <xsl:for-each select="review">
        <h2>Review in <xsl:value-of select="@publication"/></h2>
        <xsl:apply-templates select="document(@text)"/>
    </xsl:for-each>
</xsl:template>
```

As the argument `@text` is a node, the result will be the root node of the document whose URI is the value of the `text` attribute, interpreted relative to the base URI of the `<review>` element, which (unless it comes from an external XML entity or is affected by an `xml:base` attribute on some ancestor node) will be the same as the URI of the source document itself.

Note that in processing the review document, exactly the same template rules are used as we used for the source document itself. There is no concept of particular template rules being tied to particular document types. If the review document uses the same element tags as the book catalog, but with different meanings, this can potentially create problems. There are two possible ways round this:

❏ *Namespaces*: use a different namespace for the book catalog and for the review documents.

❏ *Modes*: use a different mode to process nodes in the review document, so that the `<xsl:apply-templates>` instruction in the example would become:

```
<xsl:apply-templates select="document(@text)" mode="review"/>
```

You might find that even if the element names are distinct, the use of modes is a good discipline for maintaining readability of your stylesheet. For more detail on modes, see `<xsl:apply-templates>` (page 187) and `<xsl:template>` (page 450) in Chapter 5.

Another useful approach, which helps to keep your style.sheet modular, is to include the templates for processing the review document in a separate stylesheet incorporated using `<xsl:include>`.

Example: Using the document() Function to Analyze a Stylesheet

A stylesheet is an XML document, so it can be used as the input to another stylesheet. This makes it very easy to write little tools that manipulate stylesheets. This example shows such a tool, designed to report on the hierarchic structure of the modules that make up a stylesheet.

This example uses the `document()` function to examine a stylesheet and see which stylesheet modules it incorporates using `<xsl:include>` or `<xsl:import>`. The modules referenced by `<xsl:include>` or `<xsl:import>` are fetched and processed recursively.

Source

The source is any stylesheet, preferably one that uses `<xsl:include>` or `<xsl:import>`. A file `dummy.xsl` is provided in the code download for the book for you to use as a sample.

Stylesheet

The stylesheet `list-includes.xsl` uses the `document()` function to access the document referenced in the `href` attribute of `<xsl:include>` or `<xsl:import>`. It then applies the same template rules to this document, recursively. Note that the root template is applied only to the initial source document, to create the HTML skeleton page.

```
<xsl:transform
 xmlns:xsl="http://www.w3.org/1999/XSL/Transform"
 version="1.0"
>

<xsl:template match="/">
  <html><body>
    <h1>Stylesheet Module Structure</h1>
    <ul>
    <xsl:apply-templates select="*/xsl:include |  */xsl:import"/>
    </ul>
  </body></html>
</xsl:template>

<xsl:template match="xsl:include |  xsl:import">
    <li><xsl:value-of select="concat(local-name(),'s ',@href)"/>
    <xsl:variable name="module" select="document(@href)"/>
    <ul>
    <xsl:apply-templates
```

```
               select="$module/*/xsl:include  |   $module/*/xsl:import"/>
        </ul>
        </li>
    </xsl:template>

    </xsl:transform>
```

Output

The output for the dummy.xsl stylesheet is as shown in Figure 7-1.

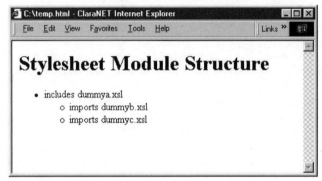

Figure 7-1

URIs as Atomic Values

As an alternative to supplying a URI that is held in the content of a node, the first argument may supply a URI as an atomic string. For convenience, the function accepts both xs:string and xs:anyURI types, as well as untyped atomic values. (Untyped atomic values are unlikely to arise in practice, since they normally arise only from atomizing a node in a schema-less document, and if you supply a node as an argument to the document() function, then the rules that apply are those in the previous section, *URIs Held in Nodes*.)

The first argument may be evaluated to produce a single atomic value containing a URI, or a sequence of them. It is even possible to mix atomic values and nodes in the input sequence; nodes are processed as described in the previous section, and atomic values as described here.

The most common case is a URL hard-coded in the stylesheet, for example «document('tax-rates.xml')».

Another common case is «document('')», which refers to the stylesheet itself. This construct was often used with XSLT 1.0, where it provided a convenient way to maintain lookup tables in the stylesheet itself. It is likely to be less common with XSLT 2.0, since the ability to hold a temporary tree in a global variable is usually much more convenient. The URI may be supplied as an xs:string, an xs:anyURI, or an untyped atomic value, and in each case is converted to a string. (XSLT 1.0 also allowed it to be supplied as a boolean or an integer, which creates a theoretical backwards incompatibility—but since converting a boolean or number is unlikely to yield a useful URL, the point is rather academic.)

The string is treated as a URI reference; that is, a URI optionally followed by a fragment identifier separated from the URI proper by a «#» character. If it is a relative URI, it is treated as being relative to the base URI of the stylesheet element that contains the expression in which the function call was encountered. This will normally be the URI of the principal stylesheet document, but it may be different if `<xsl:include>` or `<xsl:import>` was used, or if pieces of the stylesheet are contained in external XML entities, or if the base URI of any relevant element in the stylesheet has been set explicitly by using the `xml:base` attribute.

Again, all this really means is that relative URLs are handled just like relative URLs in HTML. If you write «`document('tax-rates.xml')`» in a particular stylesheet module, then the system looks for the file `tax-rates.xml` in the same directory as that stylesheet module.

If the string is an empty string, then the document referenced by the base URI is used. The XSLT specification states that «`document('')`» will return the root node of the stylesheet. Strictly speaking, however, this is true only if the base URI of the XSL element containing the call to the `document()` function is the same as the system identifier of the stylesheet module. If the base URI is different, perhaps because the stylesheet has been built up from a number of external entities, or because the `xml:base` attribute has been used, the object loaded by «`document('')`» will not necessarily be the current stylesheet module; in fact, it might not be a well-formed document at all, in which case an error will be reported.

> The specification refers to RFC2396 (`http://www.ietf.org/rfc/rfc2396.txt`) for the definitive interpretation of the use of a zero-length relative URI to refer to the containing document. This is actually a nifty piece of buck-passing, since there has been some debate as to what exactly RFC2396 means in this case. Whereas in all other cases the RFC talks about resolving a relative URI against a base URI, in this case it talks about using the "current document," a concept that some people claim is a different thing. This means there is disagreement as to whether `xml:base` should affect the meaning of this particular relative URI.

If the call is contained in a stylesheet brought in using `<xsl:include>` or `<xsl:import>`, it returns the root node of the included or imported stylesheet, not that of the principal stylesheet document.

Usage

With XSLT 1.0, this form of the `document()` function was very useful for handling data used by the stylesheet for reference information: for example, lookup tables to expand abbreviations, message files in different languages, or the text of the message of the day, to be displayed to users on the login screen. Such data can either be in the stylesheet itself (referenced as «`document('')`»), or be in a separate file held in the same directory as the stylesheet (referenced as «`document('messages.xml')`») or a related directory (for example «`document('../data/messages.xml')`»).

With XSLT 2.0, it is no longer necessary to use a secondary document for these purposes, because the data can be held in a tree-valued variable in the stylesheet and accessed directly. However, it may in some cases be more convenient to maintain the data in a separate file (for example, it makes it easier to generate the data periodically from a database), and in any case you may still want to write stylesheets that work with XSLT 1.0 processors, especially if you want the transformation to happen client-side. So I'll show the XSLT 1.0 technique first, and then show how the same problem can be tackled in XSLT 2.0.

XSLT allows data such as lookup tables to appear within any top-level stylesheet element, provided it belongs to a non-default namespace.

Example: A Lookup Table in the Stylesheet

This example uses data in a lookup table to expand abbreviations of book categories. Two techniques are shown: in the first example the lookup table is held in the stylesheet; in the second example it is held in a separate XML document.

Source

This is the `booklist.xml` file we saw earlier.

```
<booklist>
<book category="S">
     <title>Number, the Language of Science</title>
     <author>Danzig</author>
</book>
<book category="FC">
     <title>The Young Visiters</title>
     <author>Daisy Ashford</author>
</book>
<book category="FC">
     <title>When We Were Very Young</title>
     <author>A. A. Milne</author>
</book>
<book category="CS">
     <title>Design Patterns</title>
     <author>Erich Gamma</author>
     <author>Richard Helm</author>
     <author>Ralph Johnson</author>
     <author>John Vlissides</author>
</book>
</booklist>
```

Stylesheet

The stylesheet is `list-categories.xsl`. It processes each of the <book> elements in the source file and, for each one, finds the <book:category> element in the stylesheet whose code attribute matches the category attribute of the <book>. Note the use of `current()` to refer to the current book; it would be wrong to use «.» here, because «.» refers to the context node, which is the <book:category> element being tested.

```
<xsl:transform
  xmlns:xsl="http://www.w3.org/1999/XSL/Transform"
  version="1.0"
  xmlns:book="books.uri"
  exclude-result-prefixes="book"
>

<xsl:template match="/">
  <html><body>
    <xsl:for-each select="//book">
      <h1><xsl:value-of select="title"/></h1>
```

```
          <p>Category: <xsl:value-of
                       select="document('')/*/book:category
                       [@code=current()/@category]/@desc"/>
          </p>
     </xsl:for-each>
   </body></html>
</xsl:template>
<book:category code="S" desc="Science"/>
<book:category code="CS" desc="Computing"/>
<book:category code="FC" desc="Children's Fiction"/>
</xsl:transform>
```

Output

The output of this stylesheet is as follows.

```
<html>
   <body>
      <h1>Number, the Language of Science</h1>
      <p>Category: Science</p>
      <h1>The Young Visiters</h1>
      <p>Category: Children's Fiction</p>
      <h1>When We Were Very Young</h1>
      <p>Category: Children's Fiction</p>
      <h1>Design Patterns</h1>
      <p>Category: Computing</p>
   </body>
</html>
```

XSLT 2.0 Stylesheet

Now, let's modify this stylesheet to take advantage of XSLT 2.0 facilities. It's renamed list-categories2-0.xsl. It isn't a big change; the lines that are different are shown with a shaded background.

```
<xsl:transform
 xmlns:xsl="http://www.w3.org/1999/XSL/Transform"
 version="2.0"
 xmlns:book="books.uri"
 exclude-result-prefixes="book"
>

<xsl:template match="/">
  <html><body>
    <xsl:for-each select="//book">
       <h1><xsl:value-of select="title"/></h1>

       </p>
    </xsl:for-each>
  </body></html>
</xsl:template>
```

```
            <category code="S" desc="Science"/>
            <category code="CS" desc="Computing"/>
            <category code="FC" desc="Children's Fiction"/>

    </xsl:transform>
```

Supplying an Explicit Base URI

This section discusses what happens when the second argument to the document() function is supplied. In this instance, instead of using the containing node or the stylesheet as the base for resolving a relative URI, the base URI of the node supplied as the second argument is used. In other words, if a node in href contains a relative URL such as «data.xml», the system will look for the file data.xml in the directory containing the XML document from which the node in $base was derived.

The value of the second argument must be a single node. For example, the call «document (@href, /)» will use the root node of the source document as the base URI, even if the element containing the href attribute was found in an external entity with a different URI.

Usage

This option is not one that you will need to use very often, but it is there for completeness. If you want to interpret a URI relative to the stylesheet, you can write, for example:

```
document(@href, document(''))
```

This works because the second argument returns the root node of the stylesheet, which is then used as the base URI for the relative URI contained in the href attribute.

With the extended function library that XPath 2.0 makes available, an alternative is to resolve the relative URI yourself by calling the resolve-uri() function, which is described in *XPath 2.0 Programmer's Reference*. This allows you to resolve a relative URI against any base URI, which does not have to be the base URI of any particular node.

See Also

id() in *XPath 2.0 Programmer's Reference* (*Chapter 10*).
key() page 572.
resolve-uri() in *XPath 2.0 Programmer's Reference* (*Chapter 10*).

element-available

This function is used to test whether a particular XSLT instruction or extension element is available for use.

For example, the expression «element-available('xsl:text')» returns true.

Changes in 2.0

None.

Signature

Argument	Data type	Meaning
name	xs:string	The name of the element being tested. The string must take the form of a QName.
Result	*xs:boolean*	*true if the named element is available for use as an instruction in a template, false otherwise*

Effect

The first argument must take the form of a QName: that is, an XML name with an optional namespace prefix that corresponds to a namespace declaration that is in scope at the point in the stylesheet where the element-available() function is called.

If this namespace declaration identifies the XSLT namespace http://www.w3.org/1999/XSL/ Transform, then the function returns true if the name is the name of an XSLT-defined *instruction*, and false otherwise.

The instructions defined in XSLT 1.0 were as follows.

```
<xsl:apply-imports>
<xsl:apply-templates>
<xsl:attribute>
<xsl:call-template>
<xsl:choose>
<xsl:comment>
<xsl:copy>
<xsl:copy-of>
<xsl:element>
<xsl:fallback>
<xsl:for-each>
<xsl:if>
<xsl:message>
<xsl:number>
<xsl:processing-instruction>
<xsl:text>
<xsl:value-of>
<xsl:variable>
```

In the XSLT 2.0 specification, several new instructions have been added to this list.

```
<xsl:analyze-string>
<xsl:document>
<xsl:for-each-group>
<xsl:next-match>
<xsl:perform-sort>
<xsl:namespace>
<xsl:result-document>
<xsl:sequence>
```

Instructions are XSLT elements that can appear directly within a sequence constructor. Top-level XSLT declarations such as `<xsl:template>` and `<xsl:key>` are not instructions, so in theory they should return `false` (but don't rely on it: at least one popular processor, Microsoft MSXML3, seems to return `true` for all XSLT elements). The same applies to elements such as `<xsl:param>`, `<xsl:with-param>`, `<xsl:sort>`, `<xsl:when>`, and `<xsl:otherwise>`, that can appear only in specific contexts and not anywhere in a sequence constructor.

If the prefix of the QName identifies any namespace other than the XSLT namespace, then the function returns `true` if and only if the XSLT processor has an implementation available for the named instruction: that is, if this element can be used as an instruction in a sequence constructor, rather than being treated simply as a literal result element.

Note that the result of the `element-available()` function does not depend on whether the namespace has been designated as an extension namespace by using the `[xsl:]extension-element-prefixes` attribute. If the XSLT processor has an implementation of the instruction available, the function should return `true` whether or not it is currently in a designated extension namespace.

If the QName has no prefix, the default namespace (declared using «`xmlns="some.uri"`») is used. This is one of the few cases where this happens, and the reason is that the name is always an element name: the default namespace applies only to elements.

However, if the QName expands to a name with a null namespace URI, the result of the function will always be false. This is because both XSLT instructions and extension elements will always have a non-null namespace URI.

In principle, you can construct the value of the argument as a runtime expression, rather than supplying it as a string literal. I can't think of any possible reason why it might be useful to do this, but implementers have to allow for the possibility.

Usage and Examples

There are two ways to use this function: it can be used to test for XSLT elements introduced in a later version of XSLT, and it can be used to test for the presence of vendor or third-party extensions.

Testing for Features Available in Later XSLT Versions

The ability to test whether a particular XSLT instruction is available was introduced in XSLT 1.0, but it becomes useful only now that version 2.0 of the specification is available. It was intended to come into its own when later versions of the specification introduced new instructions. As we've seen, the XSLT 2.0 specification introduces several new instructions. If you want to use an instruction such as `<xsl:next-match>` that became available only in a particular version of XSLT, then you can test to see whether it is available with your chosen XSLT processor before using it. If it is not available, you can either use `<xsl:if>` to avoid executing it, or use the `<xsl:fallback>` mechanism to cope with its absence.

So why was the function specified as part of version 1.0? The answer is obvious when you think about it: you want to write a stylesheet that uses version 2.0 features, so you call `element-available()` in order to fail gracefully if you're running with an XSLT processor that supports version 1.0 features only. However, this will work only if the version 1.0 XSLT processor supports the `element-available()` function, which is why it was specified from the start. This is an unusually thoughtful piece of forward planning: the XSLT designers didn't want to get into the same kind of forwards-compatibility problems that have bedeviled HTML. Of course, it still means that if you want your stylesheet to run with XSLT processors that support different levels of the language, you will have to write and test conditional code in your stylesheet, but at least the capability is there.

In principle, you can test whether a version 1.0 instruction is available on the basis that there may be subset implementations around; unfortunately, this will work only if the subset implementation includes the `element-available()` function, which is not guaranteed; it tends to be one of the things that implementers leave till last.

Note that if you write a stylesheet that uses features in XSLT version 2.0, and if you want to run it with an XSLT 1.0 processor, then you must specify «version="2.0"» on the `<xsl:stylesheet>` element, or «xsl:version="2.0"» on some literal result element, even if you write an `<xsl:if>` test using `element-available()` to avoid executing the relevant code. If you specify «version="1.0"», then any use of new XSLT 2.0 elements is flagged as an error even if the code is never executed.

Here is an example that tests to see whether the new XSLT 2.0 facility to produce multiple output documents is available by testing `element-available('xsl:result-document')`. If it isn't available, you can use an alternative approach: for example, you can use the proprietary syntax for this functionality offered by your chosen XSLT 1.0 processor.

Example: Creating Multiple Output Files

This example takes a poem as input, and outputs each stanza to a separate file. A more realistic example would be to split a book into its chapters, but I wanted to keep the files small. The example is written to work with Saxon version 6.x (which implements XSLT 1.0) and also with any processor that conforms to the XSLT 2.0 specification.

Source

The source file is `poem.xml`. It starts:

```
<poem>
<author>Rupert Brooke</author>
<date>1912</date>
<title>Song</title>
<stanza>
<line>And suddenly the wind comes soft,</line>
<line>And Spring is here again;</line>
<line>And the hawthorn quickens with buds of green</line>
<line>And my heart with buds of pain.</line>
</stanza>
```

```
<stanza>
<line>My heart all Winter lay so numb,</line>
<line>The earth so dead and frore,</line>
. . .
```

Stylesheet

The stylesheet is in file split.xsl. The part to look at is the <xsl:choose> instruction, where each branch calls element-available() to test whether a particular instruction is available, before calling that instruction.

Note that «saxon» is defined as an extension element prefix, so the <saxon:output> element is recognized as an instruction. The <xsl:stylesheet> element specifies «version="2.0"» so that an XSLT 1.0 processor will not reject <xsl:result-document> as an error.

```
<?xml version="1.0"?>
<xsl:stylesheet xmlns:xsl="http://www.w3.org/1999/XSL/Transform"
    version="2.0">

<xsl:template match="poem">
    <poem>
        <xsl:copy-of select="title"/>
        <xsl:copy-of select="author"/>
        <xsl:copy-of select="date"/>
        <xsl:apply-templates select="stanza"/>
    </poem>
</xsl:template>
<xsl:template match="stanza">
    <xsl:variable name="file"
                  select="concat('verse', string(position()), '.xml')"/>
    <verse number="{position()}" href="{$file}"/>
    <xsl:choose>
    <xsl:when test="element-available('xsl:result-document')">
        <xsl:result-document href="{$file}">
            <xsl:copy-of select="."/>
        </xsl:result-document>
    </xsl:when>
    <xsl:when test="element-available('saxon:output')"
            xmlns:saxon="http://icl.com/saxon">
        <saxon:output file="{$file}"
            xsl:extension-element-prefixes="saxon">
            <xsl:copy-of select="."/>
        </saxon:output>
    </xsl:when>
    <xsl:otherwise>
        <xsl:message terminate="yes"
            >Cannot write to multiple output files</xsl:message>
    </xsl:otherwise>
    </xsl:choose>
</xsl:template>

</xsl:stylesheet>
```

Output

Provided the stylesheet is run with one of the processors that support the required capability, the principal output file will contain the following skeletal poem (new lines added for legibility).

```xml
<?xml version="1.0" encoding="utf-8" ?>
<poem>
<title>Song</title>
<author>Rupert Brooke</author>
<date>1912</date>
<verse number="1" href="verse1.xml"/>
<verse number="2" href="verse2.xml"/>
<verse number="3" href="verse3.xml"/>
</poem>
```

Three further output files verse1.xml, verse2.xml, and verse3.xml are created in the same directory as this outline. Here is verse1.xml:

```xml
<?xml version="1.0" encoding="utf-8" ?>
<stanza>
<line>And suddenly the wind comes soft,</line>
<line>And Spring is here again;</line>
<line>And the hawthorn quickens with buds of green</line>
<line>And my heart with buds of pain.</line>
</stanza>
```

To run this using Saxon 7.x (which implements XSLT 2.0), use a command line of the form:

```
java -jar c:\MyJava\saxon7.jar -t -o c:\temp\outline.xml poem.xml
split.xsl
```

With this command line, the output files will all be written to the directory c:\temp. The `<saxon:output>` instruction in Saxon 6.x works slightly differently: it will write the files verseN.xml to the current directory, not necessarily to the directory containing the outline.xml file.

Note that in this stylesheet, all the information needed to evaluate the `<xsl:when>` conditions is available at compile time. A good XSLT processor will generate code only for the path that is actually going to be executed.

You can't use element-available() to test whether the XSLT 2.0 element `<xsl:import-schema>` is available, because this is a declaration rather than an instruction, and a conformant XSLT 2.0 processor should therefore return false (the same result as an XSLT 1.0 processor). If you use this element in an XSLT 1.0 stylesheet, an error will be reported if you specify «version="1.0"» on the `<xsl:stylesheet>` element, but if you specify «version="2.0"» then an XSLT 1.0 processor will ignore the `<xsl:import-schema>` element, under the rules for forwards-compatible processing. Instead you can test whether the XSLT processor you are using is schema aware using the system-property() function (described on page 581 in this chapter) together with the use-when attribute described in the entry for `<xsl:stylesheet>` in Chapter 5.

Testing for Vendor Extensions

The second way of using the function is to test for vendor or third-party extensions. If you know that a particular extension instruction is present in some implementations and not others, you can use the `element-available()` test to see whether it is present, and again use either `<xsl:if>` or `<xsl:fallback>` to handle the situation when it isn't.

For example, the Saxon product provides an extension instruction to output an entity reference. This is available under both Saxon 6.x and Saxon 7.x, which use different namespaces and therefore need to be treated as different processors. If you're not using Saxon, you can achieve the same effect by using `disable-output-escaping`. So to output « » you could write:

```
<xsl:choose xmlns:saxon6="http://icl.com/saxon"
            xmlns:saxon7="http://saxon.sf.net/">
<xsl:when test="element-available('saxon6:entity-ref')">
    <saxon6:entity-ref name="nbsp"
                       xsl:extension-element-prefixes="saxon6"/>
</xsl:when>
<xsl:when test="element-available('saxon7:entity-ref')">
    <saxon7:entity-ref name="nbsp"
                       xsl:extension-element-prefixes="saxon7"/>
</xsl:when>
<xsl:otherwise>
    <xsl:text disable-output-escaping="yes"> </xsl:text>
</xsl:otherwise>
</xsl:choose>
```

An alternative to using the `element-available()` function is to use the `<xsl:fallback>` mechanism described in Chapter, 3 page 136. An `<xsl:fallback>` element allows you to define what processing should occur if its containing instruction isn't available. The two mechanisms are essentially equivalent. A possible limitation of `<xsl:fallback>` is that it can only be used within an element that permits element children: it could not be used, for example, within `<xsl:copy-of>` as currently defined. However, all the new instructions in XSLT 2.0 have been designed so that `<xsl:fallback>` can be used as a child element.

See Also

function-available() page 564.
system-property() page 581.
`<xsl:fallback>` in Chapter 5, page 271.

format-date

The `format-date()` function is used to output a date in human-readable format. It may also be used to obtain information derived from the date, for example the day of the week on which a particular date falls.

Changes in 2.0

This function is new in XSLT 2.0.

Signature

Argument	Data type	Meaning
date	xs:date?	The date to be formatted.
picture	xs:string	A picture string identifying the components to be output and the format in which they are output.
language (optional)	xs:string?	A string following the same rules as the xml:lang attribute in XML, to indicate the language to be used for formatting the date. For example, «en» indicates English, «de» German, and «es» Spanish.
calendar (optional)	xs:string?	A string giving a code for the calendar to be used for formatting the date.
country (optional)	xs:string?	A code identifying the country associated with the date, for example the country in which the dated event took place.
Result	*xs:string?*	*The formatted date.*

The last three arguments are optional, but they must either all be supplied, or all be omitted. That is, the function must be called either with two arguments or with five. Calling it with two arguments is equivalent to supplying an empty sequence « ( ) » for each of the last three arguments; an empty sequence for any of these arguments invokes the default value.

Effect

If the date argument is an empty sequence, then the result is an empty sequence.

The picture string may contain a number of component specifiers, identifying the components to be output. These are described in detail under format-dateTime(), in the following section. If the picture argument includes component specifiers that are not appropriate to a date value (for example, the hours, minutes, and seconds components) then the processor may either report a runtime error, or simply ignore those components.

Apart from this, the effect of the function is the same as that of casting the supplied date value to an xs:dateTime (which gives the xs:dateTime representing 00:00:00 on that date), and calling format-dateTime() with the same value of the $picture argument, and the same value of the $format argument if it is present.

Usage and Examples

The main use of this function is in producing a date formatted for human readers. For example:

```
format-date(xs:date('1999-11-16'), '[D] [MNn] [Y]')
```

typically produces the output:

```
16 November 1999
```

This is assuming that the default calendar is the Gregorian calendar, and that the default language is English.

The function can also be used to reformat dates into non-ISO formats where these are required by the target document design. For example, in the United States it is not uncommon to find XML documents in which dates are encoded as MMDDYY, rather than using the XML Schema (and ISO 8601) format YYYY-MM-DD. This output can be produced using a call such as follows.

```
format-date(xs:date('1999-11-16'), '[M01][D01][Y01]')
```

Full details of the picture string and of the three arguments language, calendar, and country are provided under format-dateTime() in the following section.

See Also

format-dateTime() in the following section.

format-dateTime

The format-dateTime() function returns a formatted representation of a date and time, as a string.

Changes in 2.0

This function is new in XSLT 2.0.

Signature

Argument	Data type	Meaning
dateTime	xs:dateTime?	The date and time to be formatted.
picture	xs:string	A picture string identifying the components to be output and the format in which they are output.
language (optional)	xs:string?	A string following the same rules as the xml:lang attribute in XML, to indicate the language to be used for formatting the date and time. For example, «en» indicates English, «de» German, and «es» Spanish.
calendar (optional)	xs:string?	A string giving a code for the calendar to be used for formatting the date.

Argument	Data type	Meaning
country (optional)	xs:string?	A code identifying the country associated with the date and time, for example the country in which the dated event took place.
Result	xs:string?	*The formatted date and time.*

The last three arguments are optional, but they must either all be supplied, or all be omitted. That is, the function must be called either with two arguments or with five. Calling it with two arguments is equivalent to supplying an empty sequence «()» for each of the last three arguments; an empty sequence for any of these arguments invokes the default value.

Effect

If the dateTime argument is an empty sequence, then the result is an empty sequence.

The Picture Argument

The picture argument consists of a string containing so-called variable markers enclosed in square brackets. Characters outside the square brackets are literal characters to be copied to the result; variable markers within the square brackets indicate components of the date and time to be added to the output string, and the format in which they are to be displayed.

If square brackets are needed as literal characters in the result they should be doubled.

For example, if the picture is given as «[D1]/[M1]/[Y1{4}]» then the date 1 February 2002 will be displayed as «1/2/2002».

Each variable marker consists of a *component specifier* identifying which component of the date or time is to be displayed; an optional *formatting token*; an optional *presentation modifier*; and finally, an optional *width modifier*, preceded by a comma if it is present.

The components of the date and time are identified by the following letters.

Letter	Component	Default Format
Y	Year	Four digits
M	Month of year	Numeric 1–12
D	Day of month	Numeric 1–31
d	Day of year	Numeric 1–366
F	Day of week	Name of day (language dependent)
W	Week of year	Numeric 1–53
w	Week of month	Numeric 1–5

Continues

Letter	Component	Default Format
H	Hour (24 hours)	Numeric 00–23
h	Hour (12 hours)	Numeric 1–12
P	A.M. or P.M.	Alphabetic (language dependent)
m	Minutes in hour	Numeric 00–59
s	Seconds in minute	Numeric 00–59
f	Fractional seconds	Numeric, one decimal place
Z	Timezone	Numeric, for example +08:00
z	Timezone	GMT+n
C	Calendar	Name of calendar, for example «Old Style»
E	Era	Text or abbreviation describing the baseline from which the year is calculated, for example A.D. or the name of a monarch

The formatting token consists of one or more additional letters or digits. The value can be either a formatting token recognized by the `<xsl:number>` instruction (see page 359 in Chapter 5), or one of the values «N», «n», or «Nn» indicating that the component is to be output by name. Ignoring values such as «a» and «A» that are unlikely to be useful, at least in English, this leaves the following as examples of the possibilities.

Character	Resulting Format	Example
1	Decimal numeric format with no leading zeroes: 1, 2, 3, . . .	1, 2, 3
01	Decimal format, two digits: 01, 02, 03, . . .	01, 02, 03
Other Unicode digit	Decimal numeric format, using the set of Unicode digits in which the given digit represents the value one.	١, ٢, ٣, ٤, ٥
i	Roman numerals	i, ii, iii, iv
I	Roman numerals	I, II, III, IV
N	Name of component, in upper case	MONDAY, TUESDAY
n	Name of component, in lower case	monday, tuesday
Nn	Name of component, in title case (for example Monday)	Monday, Tuesday
W	Number expressed in upper case words	ONE, TWO, THREE
w	Number expressed in lower case words	one, two, three
Ww	Number expressed in title case words	One, Two, Three

Two presentation modifiers are recognized:

Character	Resulting Format
t	Indicates so-called traditional numbering. The meaning of this depends on the language; it is intended to produce the same effect as «letter-value="traditional"» in <xsl:number>. The requirement most often cited is for Hebrew numbering.
o	Indicates ordinal numbering. For example, «1o» gives 1st, 2nd, 3rd ..., while «wo» gives first, second, third, and «Wwo» gives First, Second, Third. All these examples are of course language dependent: the language is controlled using the language argument.

Not all combinations of these make sense, but the specification leaves it very open to implementations how to interpret combinations other than the obvious ones. The golden rule for this function is that it is never supposed to raise an error—if it doesn't understand the format that you asked for, it should output the date in some fallback format.

The width modifier, if present, indicates how many digits or letters should be included in the result. It takes the form «,m» or «,m-n», where m is a number giving the minimum width, or «*» to indicate no minimum, and n is the maximum width, or «*» to indicate no maximum. If n is omitted, it is assumed to be equal to m.

Specifying leading zeros in the formatting token is regarded as a shorthand for the width modifier: for example, «01» is a shorthand for «1,2-2». For most numeric fields, the width specified controls whether leading zeroes are output: if the minimum width is 2, then the value 8 will be output as 08. The year field is treated specially: a maximum width of 2 indicates that the century should be omitted. The fractional seconds are also handled differently: the minimum and maximum width indicates the minimum and maximum number of decimal places to be output.

For named fields, such as the name of the month and the day of the week, the width modifier controls the choice of abbreviations. For example, specifying «3-3» requests abbreviations that are exactly three characters long. The specification doesn't say exactly how the abbreviations should be chosen; some systems might use a dictionary of abbreviated forms (for example JLY for July), while others might use simple truncation of the full name. Names should be padded to the minimum length if they are shorter.

The Language Argument

The language argument defines the language to be used for those parts of the output date that are language dependent. The most obvious examples are the names of the days of the week and the months of the year: for example, if the value is «en» then a date might be output as «Sunday 13 December 1987», while with «de» (the code for German) the same date would be «Sonntag 13 Dezember 1987». The choice of language is also likely to affect the way the ordinal numbers are represented («4th» in English, «4.» in German, and «4ème» in French), and the choice of words or abbreviations equivalent to the English «p.m.» and «A.D.».

Since the variety of calendars and numbering schemes that implementations might support is completely open ended, it's quite possible that the language attribute might be used in other ways than these, for example to decide between «IV» and «IIII» as the representation of the number 4 in Roman numerals.

Implementations are not required to support any particular languages, and the set of languages that are supported is likely to depend on the choice of calendar.

The Calendar Argument

The World Wide Web Consortium takes its name very seriously, and bends over backwards to ensure that it caters for every different society on the planet. While most of the western world, and much of the eastern world, now uses the Gregorian calendar first introduced in the sixteenth century, there are many other calendars still in use.

The XSLT specification defines the following codes that you can use to represent different calendars.

Code	Calendar
AD	Anno Domini (Christian Era)
AH	Anno Hegirae (Muhammedan Era)
AME	Mauludi Era (solar years since Mohammed's birth)
AM	Anno Mundi (Jewish Calendar)
AP	Anno Persici
AS	Aji Saka Era (Java)
BE	Buddhist Era
CB	Cooch Behar Era
CE	Common Era
CL	Chinese Lunar Era
CS	Chula Sakarat Era
EE	Ethiopian Era
FE	Fasli Era
ISO	ISO 8601 calendar
JE	Japanese Calendar
KE	Khalsa Era (Sikh calendar)
KY	Kali Yuga
ME	Malabar Era
MS	Monarchic Solar Era
NS	Nepal Samwat Era
OS	Old Style (Julian Calendar)
RS	Rattanakosin (Bangkok) Era
SE	Saka Era

Code	Calendar
SH	Mohammedan Solar Era (Iran)
SS	Saka Samvat
TE	Tripurabda Era
VE	Vikrama Era
VS	Vikrama Samvat Era

This looks like a pretty impressive list, but before you get too excited that your favorite calendar is in the list, you should be aware that there is no requirement for implementations to support all these. And even if a calendar is supported, there are snags that you need to be aware of.

The date-formatting functions assume that the date and/or time will be represented using the data types defined in XML Schema, which are based on the ISO 8601 specification. This doesn't mean that you have to be using a schema to take advantage of them, because you can always construct an instance of one of these data types using a call to a constructor function, for example «xs:date("1999-11-16")». It does mean, however, that you have to ensure that your dates and times are in ISO format before you can use these functions. If your XML documents contain dates in nonstandard formats such as «16 NOV 99» or «11/16/1999», then you are going to have to convert them first to the ISO format. And the same is true if your dates are in a different calendar.

> *A very common use of these functions is simply to output the current date: for example,*
> «format-dateTime(current-dateTime(),...)». *In this case you don't have to worry about whether the supplied date is in the correct ISO format and calendar: it always will be.*

If the calendar argument selects a calendar other than the Gregorian calendar, then the date is translated into that calendar before extracting the relevant component. Not all calendars include concepts directly equivalent to months and weeks (for example, some calendars use lunar months), but most have concepts that are sufficiently similar for this to work. In practice, the handling of non-Gregorian calendars is likely to vary depending on your implementation and is only very loosely described in the XSLT specification.

The numbering of days of the week and weeks of the year may vary from one country or language to another. If you want predictable results, select the «ISO» calendar in the calendar argument. The results will then follow the rules in ISO 8601:

❑ Days of the week are numbered from 1 (Monday) to 7 (Sunday).

❑ Weeks of the year are numbered so that week 1 is the Monday-to-Sunday week that includes the first Thursday of the year. The days before week 1 fall in week 52 or 53 of the previous year.

❑ ISO 8601 does not define a numbering for weeks within a month. You will have to see what your implementation returns.

It's important to understand the distinction in XML Schema between the value space of a data type and the lexical space. The value space for xs:date simply contains one data point for every day in the history of the world, past, present, and future (within limits, but they need not concern us). It's not meaningful to ask whether these data points are represented as integers or strings or to ask what format they are in—or to get to the point, it's not meaningful to ask what calendar they are in. There is a data point representing the day when the Great Fire of London started, and you can represent this data point using any calendar you like. So the value space of dates in XML Schema is calendar neutral.

The same is not true of the lexical space. The lexical representation of dates in XML Schema uses the Gregorian calendar. In fact, it uses the Gregorian calendar even to represent dates that occurred long before the Gregorian calendar was invented: this is referred to as the *proleptic* Gregorian calendar (ISO 8601 calls it "prolaptic," but that appears to be an error). This simply projects the Gregorian calendar backwards in time. This is really no different from our use of "B.C." dates: we are using a representation of dates that is unrelated to the way those same dates were represented in contemporary records.

This means that if you want to use a non-Gregorian calendar, you have to be very careful. For example, if you are storing a historical document that records that the Great Fire of London broke out on September 2, 1666, then if you want to represent this correctly using the xs:date data type you need to know how to convert it into a Gregorian date. In fact, the correct lexical representation of this date is «1666-09-12», as there was then a 10-day difference between the Julian and Gregorian calendars. (Although the Gregorian calendar was introduced in 1585, Britain has always been slow to pick up European ideas, and did not adopt it until 1752.)

If you now want to format this date using the Julian calendar, you can do so by specifying «OS» in the calendar argument. This will produce the correct output («Sunday 2nd Sept 1666») only if you represented the date correctly in the value space. If you were careless, and created the date by writing «xs:date("1666-09-02")», then the formatted output will be «Thursday 23rd Aug 1666».

I suspect what this means in practice is that if you need to use non-Gregorian calendars, the support provided in XSLT 2.0 may not actually be sufficient for your needs; it allows you to convert dates from the Gregorian calendar to a different calendar, but does not provide a conversion in the reverse direction. There are software utilities available to do that, which could be integrated as extension functions, but if you use them then you may well find that they also offer date formatting capability that is better than that offered by your XSLT processor.

If you ask for a date to be formatted using a calendar that hasn't been implemented, the system will output the date using a calendar of its own choosing (you can be fairly certain this will be the Gregorian calendar) but adding to the output a tag indicating that it is a different calendar from the one that was requested.

The inclusion of «ISO» as a calendar name in this list has a special purpose. Sometimes, you want to format the date not in order to present the information to a human reader, but to pass information to other software. The format-date() function, for example, is the only way available in standard XSLT of finding out the day of the week or the week number in the year. If you want to determine whether a given date is a Sunday, then it would be unfortunate if you had to test the result against a language-dependent string. If you choose ISO as the calendar, then you can do this test as:

```
<xsl:variable name="is-Sunday" as="xs:boolean"
        select="format-date(current-date(), 'F1', (), 'ISO', ()) = '7'"/>
```

This is because the ISO 8601 standard specifies numeric representations of the days of the week from Monday (1) to Sunday (7). Similarly, you can get the ISO week number by writing:

```
<xsl:value-of select="format-date(current-date(), 'W', (), 'ISO', ())"/>
```

ISO week numbers (which in some countries are widely used in project planning and similar applications) are chosen so that week 1 is the Monday-to-Sunday week that includes 4th January. Week 1 may thus start before or after 1st January, but always starts on a Monday.

The Country Argument

The country argument allows you to indicate the country associated with the date and time being formatted. For example, if the date and time refer to the death of Erasmus, which took place on July 12, 1536 in Basel, Switzerland, then you can set the country argument to «ch», which is the ISO country code for Switzerland. The system can use this information to assist in converting Gregorian dates to a date in the chosen calendar, since with many non-Gregorian calendars, different variants of the calendar were in use in different places at different times. For example, although in the old Julian calendar the day and the month were synchronized across much of Europe, New Year's day varied in different countries, so the year number might be different from one country to another.

In some cases, such as the Islamic calendar, the start of a day is tied to sunrise or sunset, so accurate conversion of a date into another calendar requires not only knowledge of the time of day, but also knowledge of where the event took place.

More prosaically, the country code might be used to determine the abbreviated names of timezones. Names such as EST and PST are recognized in the US, but not necessarily in other English-speaking countries.

The value of the country argument is expected to be an ISO country code, but the use that the system makes of the information is entirely implementation defined. You can always supply an empty sequence as the value of this argument.

Usage and Examples

Here are some examples showing how the date 2003-11-03 might be formatted using various values of the picture argument, assuming the use of the English language and the Gregorian calendar.

Picture	Output
[D]/[M]/[Y]	3/11/2003
[M]/[D]/[Y]	11/3/2003
[MNn] [Do], [Y] [E]	November 3rd, 2003 A.D.
[Y]-[M,2]-[D,2]	2003-11-03
[MN] [YI]	NOVEMBER MMIII
[Y][[week [W]:[FNn]]]	2003[week 45:Monday]

The following examples show how the time 09:30:02.26-05:00 might be formatted, under the same assumptions. It is possible, of course, to output date and time components at the same time, using a single picture.

Picture	Output
`[H01].[m01]`	09.30
`[h].[m01] [P]`	9.30 A.M.
`[H01]:[m01]:[s01].[f001] [ZN]`	14:30:02.327 EST

See Also

`format-date()` page 548.
`format-time()` page 562.

format-number

The `format-number()` function is used to convert numbers into strings for display to a human user. It is also useful when converting to legacy formats that require a number to occupy a fixed number of character positions. The format of the result is controlled using the `<xsl:decimal-format>` declaration.

For example, the expression «`format-number(12.5, '$#0.00')`» returns the string «`$12.50`».

Changes in 2.0

In XSLT 1.0, the effect of the function was defined by reference to the Java JDK 1.1 specifications. This created problems because the JDK 1.1 description left many details underspecified, and later versions of the JDK not only clarified the specification, but also added new features. It was therefore decided in XSLT 2.0 to provide a freestanding definition of this function. This is largely compatible with the old JDK 1.1 specification, but the rules are now much more precise, and in corner cases they will not necessarily give the same results as implementations based on the JDK, let alone nonJava implementations. For example, the JDK 1.1 specification did not say how rounding was done. The actual JDK 1.1 implementation used the rule of rounding a final 5 to the nearest even number, and this is the rule that XSLT 2.0 has adopted, but XSLT 1.0 processors might well do rounding differently.

Signature

Argument	Data type	Meaning
value	`xs:double?`	The number to be formatted
picture	`xs:string`	A picture string identifying the way in which the number is to be formatted
format (optional)	`xs:string`	A string in the form of a lexical QName, that identifies an `<xsl:decimal-format>` declaration in the stylesheet, giving further information about the required formatting options
Result	`xs:string?`	*The formatted number*

Effect

The function returns a string value; this is the result of formatting the given value using the format picture supplied in picture, while applying the rules defined in the decimal format named in format if present, or using the default decimal format otherwise.

Although the function signature says that value must be an xs:double, the function calling rules ensure that a value of type xs:float, xs:decimal or xs:integer is equally acceptable.

The decimal-format Name

The format argument, if it is present, must take the form of a lexical QName; that is, an XML name optionally prefixed with a namespace prefix that corresponds to a namespace declaration that is in scope at the point in the stylesheet where the format-number() function is called. There must be an <xsl:decimal-format> element in the stylesheet with the same expanded name, using the namespace URIs rather than prefixes in the comparison.

If the format argument is omitted, the default decimal format is used. A default decimal format can be established for a stylesheet by including an <xsl:decimal-format> element with no name. If there is no unnamed <xsl:decimal-format> element in the stylesheet, the system uses a built-in default format, which is the same as specifying an <xsl:decimal-format> with no attributes.

The Picture String

The structure of the picture string is as follows. Here, and in the text that follows, I will use the default characters for each role: for example «;» as the pattern separator, «.» as the decimal point, «0» as the zero digit, «#» as the optional digit placemarker, and so on. Remember, though, that you can change the characters that are used in each of these roles using the <xsl:decimal-format> declaration.

picture	subpicture («;» subpicture)?
subpicture	prefix? integer («.» fraction)? suffix?
prefix	any characters except special characters
suffix	any characters except special characters
integer	«#»* «0»* (but also allowing «,» to appear)
fraction	«0»* «#»* (but also allowing «,» to appear)

The first subpicture is used for formatting positive numbers. The second (optional) subpicture is used for negative numbers. If only one subpicture is specified, then the subpicture used for negative numbers is the same as the positive subpicture, but with a minus sign added before the prefix. The actual character used for the minus sign depends on the <xsl:decimal-format> declaration.

The prefix and suffix are just literal characters that are output at the start and end of the number. The only real reason to use them, other than simple convenience, is when they are different for positive and negative numbers. For example, you can use this mechanism to implement the accounting convention of displaying negative numbers in parentheses.

If the prefix or suffix includes a «%» sign, the percent sign will be displayed in the place where it appears in the prefix or suffix, and the number will be multiplied by 100. Similarly, you can also use a per-mille sign «‰» in which case the number will be multipled by 1,000.

If the number is one of the special values positive or negative infinity or NaN, then it is displayed using the representation defined in the <xsl:decimal-format> declaration, together with the prefix and suffix. The positive subpicture is used for displaying positive zero and positive infinity, while the negative subpicture is used for negative zero and negative infinity.

The special characters used are as follows.

Special Character	Meaning
zero-digit (default «0»)	A digit will always appear at this point in the result string
digit (default «#»)	A digit will appear at this point in the result string unless it is a redundant leading or trailing zero
decimal-point (default «.»)	Separates the integer and the fraction part of the number
grouping-separator (default «,»)	Separates groups of digits
pattern-separator (default «;»)	Separates the positive and negative subpictures
minus-sign (default «-»)	Minus sign
percent-sign (default «%»)	Multiplies the number by 100 and shows it as a percentage
per-mille (default «‰»)	Multiplies by 1,000 and shows it as per-mille

The original JDK 1.1 implementation had the feature (I use the term politely) that if there was an explicit negative subpicture, it served to specify the negative prefix and suffix only; the number of digits, grouping separators, and other characteristics were all taken from the positive subpicture, and any specification to the contrary in the negative subpicture was ignored. This curiosity was not actually documented in the JDK 1.1 specification, though it was retained (and documented) in JDK 1.2. Since XSLT 1.0 referred explicitly to the JDK 1.1 specification (but not to the JDK 1.1 implementation), it's likely that some XSLT 1.0 processors share this behavior and others do not. XSLT 2.0 does away with it: all aspects of formatting for a negative number depend on the negative subpicture alone.

In the fractional part of the number, a «0» means you will get a digit in that position whatever be its value, while a «#» means you will get a digit only if it is non-zero. You will never get more digits displayed than there are «0» and «#» signs. For example, «.00##» displays a minimum of two and a maximum of four digits after the decimal point. If there are more significant digits in the number than you have asked to be displayed, then the number is rounded. It is rounded to the nearest value that can be displayed, and if it is midway between two such values, it is rounded to the one whose last digit is even. For example, with a picture of «0.00», the value 0.125 is shown as «0.12», while 0.875 is shown as «0.88». This is different from the rounding rule that many of us were taught at school, which always rounds 0.5 upwards, but it is preferred by many statisticians and accountants because it means that numbers are equally likely to be rounded up or down, which avoids introducing bias. If you prefer a different rounding rule, you can always round the number yourself before formatting it.

In the integer part of the picture, that is, on the left of the decimal point if there is one, the rules are slightly different. If there is at least one «#» sign in this part, then the number will be displayed with as many digits as necessary to accommodate its value (but with at least as many digits as there are «0» digits in the picture). If there is no «#» sign in the integer part of the picture, then an error occurs if the number is too big to be displayed: for example, displaying the number 218.5 with a picture of «00.0» is an error. The system is allowed to treat this as a fatal error, but it is also allowed to recover, which it can do by simply ignoring the picture and outputting the value using as many digit positions as it needs.

The `format-number()` function doesn't provide any direct way of space-padding the number so that numbers can be vertically aligned in a column. The simplest way to achieve this effect, though it is rather clumsy, is to format the number, use the `string-length()` function to determine the length of the result, and then add the requisite number of spaces to the front.

The grouping separator («,» by default) is commonly used for thousands, but in some countries for ten thousands. You can specify grouping separators either at regular intervals or at irregular intervals, and they can appear in either the integer part or the fractional part of the number. For example, if you write «#,##0.00» then you will get a grouping separator every three digits to the left of the decimal point, while if you specify «#,##,###,###0.00» then you will get separators at the specified positions only. The rule is that if all your explicit grouping separators are regularly spaced, then the system will add implicit grouping separators when it extends the picture on the left, but if the explicit separators are at irregular intervals, then no implicit separators will be added.

If the picture string is invalid, then the implementation is free either to report an error or to display the number in some fallback representation.

Usage

Note that this facility for formatting numbers is completely separate from the facilities available through the `<xsl:number>` element. There is some overlapping functionality, but the syntax of the pictures is quite unrelated. The `format-number()` function formats a single number, which need not be an integer. `<xsl:number>` is primarily designed to format a list of positive integers. For formatting a single positive integer, either facility can be used.

Examples

The following example shows the result of `format-number()` using the default decimal format. Examples with non-default decimal formats are shown under the `<xsl:decimal-format>` element in Chapter 5, page 251.

Number	Picture String	Result
1234.5	#,##0.00	1,234.50
123.456	#,##0.00	123.46

Continues

Number	Picture String	Result
1000000	#,##0.00	1,000,000.00
-59	#,##0.00	-59.00
1 div 0	#,##0.00	Infinity
1234	###0.0###	1234.0
1234.5	###0.0###	1234.5
.00025	###0.0###	0.0004
.00035	###0.0###	0.0004
0.25	#00%	25%
0.736	#00%	74%
1	#00%	100%
-42	#00%	-4200%
-3.12	#.00;(#.00)	(3.12)
-3.12	#.00;#.00CR	3.12CR

See Also

`<xsl:decimal-format>` page 251 in Chapter 5.
`<xsl:number>` page 359 in Chapter 5.

format-time

The `format-time()` function is used to output a time of day in human-readable format.

Changes in 2.0

This function is new in XSLT 2.0.

Signature

Argument	Data Type	Meaning
time	xs:time?	The time to be formatted.
picture	xs:string	A picture string identifying the components to be output and the format in which they are output.

Argument	Data Type	Meaning
language (optional)	xs:string?	A string following the same rules as the xml:lang attribute in XML, to indicate the language to be used for formatting the date. For example, «en» indicates English, «de» German, and «es» Spanish.
calendar (optional)	xs:string?	A string giving a code for the calendar to be used for formatting the time.
country (optional)	xs:string?	A code identifying the country associated with the time, for example the country in which the timed event took place.
Result	*xs:string?*	*The formatted time.*

The last three arguments are optional, but they must either all be supplied, or all be omitted. That is, the function must be called either with two arguments or with five. Calling it with two arguments is equivalent to supplying an empty sequence «()» for each of the last three arguments; an empty sequence for any of these arguments invokes the default value.

Effect

If the $time argument is an empty sequence, then the result is an empty sequence.

The $picture string may contain a number of component specifiers, identifying the components to be output. These are described in detail in the section format-dateTime(), page 550 earlier in the chapter. If the $picture argument includes component specifiers that are not appropriate to a time value (for example, the year, month, and day components) then the processor may either report a runtime error, or simply ignore those component specifiers.

Apart from this, the effect of the function is the same as that of casting the $time value to an xs:dateTime (which gives the xs:dateTime representing that time on the current date) and calling format-dateTime() with the same value of the $picture argument, and the same value of the $format argument if it is present.

Usage and Examples

The main use of this function is in producing a time formatted for human readers. For example:

```
format-time(xs:time('15:30:00'), '[h].[m01] [Pn]')
```

typically produces the output:

```
3.30 p.m.
```

This is assuming that default language is English.

Full details of the picture string and the other arguments are provided under `format-dateTime()` page 550 earlier in the chapter.

See Also

`format-date()` on page 548.
`format-dateTime()` on page 550.

function-available

This function is used to test whether a particular function is available for use. It can be used to test the availability both of standard system functions and of extension functions.

For example, the expression «`function-available('concat')`» returns `true`.

Changes in 2.0

An optional second argument has been added, giving the arity of the required function.

In XSLT 2.0, except when running in forwards-compatibility mode or backwards-compatibility mode, it is a static error if an XPath expression contains a call on a function that is not available. Therefore, the way in which `function-available()` is used needs to change: instead of calling it using a normal runtime conditional instruction (`<xsl:choose>` or `<xsl:if>`), it should be called in a compile-time conditional expression, using the `[xsl:]use-when` attribute.

Signature

Argument	Data Type	Meaning
name	`xs:string`	The name of the function being tested. The string must take the form of a lexical QName.
arity (optional)	`xs:integer`	The arity (number of arguments) of the function being tested.
Result	`xs:boolean`	*true if the named function is available to be called, false otherwise.*

Effect

The first argument must take the form of a lexical QName: that is, an XML name, with an optional namespace prefix that corresponds to a namespace declaration that is in scope at the point in the stylesheet where the `function-available()` function is called.

If there is no prefix, or if the namespace URI is the standard function namespace `http://www.w3.org/2003/11/xpath-functions` (this URI will change when the specification gets to Candidate Recommendation status), the call tests whether there is a system function with the specified name. The system functions are those defined in the XPath and XSLT Recommendations; vendors are not allowed to supply additional functions in this namespace, nor are they allowed to omit any. So an XSLT processor that conforms to XSLT version 2.0 will return `true` if the name is one of the function names in this chapter (for example «current» or «regex-group») or any of the names of the functions described in Chapter 10 of *XPath 2.0 Programmer's Reference*. This means you can test whether a new XSLT 2.0 function is supported in your XSLT processor by writing, for example:

```
use-when="function-available('regex-group')"
```

If the QName includes a non-null namespace (other than the standard function namespace), the XSLT processor returns `true` if there is a stylesheet function or extension function available with the given name. In general, if `function-available()` returns `false` then you are safe in assuming that a call on the function would fail, and if it returns `true`, then there will be some way of calling the function successfully.

If the second argument to the function is supplied, then `function-available()` returns `true` only if there is a function available with the specified name and the specified number of arguments. When the second argument is omitted, the result is true if there is some function with the required name, regardless of the number of arguments.

There is no way of finding out at runtime what the data types of the arguments should be, which means that knowing a function is available is not enough to ensure that any given call on the function will be successful.

The functions that are considered to be available are those in the static context of the XPath expression containing the call on `function-available()`. If `function-available()` is evaluated from the `use-when` attribute, this includes core XPath and XSLT functions, constructor functions for built-in types, and extension functions. If `function-available()` is evaluated during stylesheet execution, it also includes stylesheet functions (defined using `<xsl:function>`) and constructor functions for types imported from a schema.

Usage

There are two ways of using `function-available()`: it can be used to achieve backwards compatibility when using standard functions defined after version 1.0 of the specification, and it can be used to test for the presence of vendor or third-party extensions.

The ability to test for the existence of stylesheet functions is not particularly useful, though it could in principle be used in one stylesheet module to test whether a function defined in another module has been imported, before calling it.

Testing for the Existence of System-Defined Functions

The ability to test whether a particular system-defined function is available was not especially useful with version 1.0 of the specification. It was designed to come into its own when later versions of the specification were published. If you want to use a function that is newly defined in version 2.0, then you can test to see whether it is available with a particular XSLT processor, before using it. If it is not available, you can use `<xsl:if>` to avoid executing it. Provided that you enable *forwards-compatible mode* by setting the `version` attribute on the `<xsl:stylesheet>` element to `"2.0"`, an XSLT 1.0 processor will not object to the presence of an expression in your stylesheet that calls an unknown function, unless the expression is actually executed.

For example, the function `current-date()` becomes available in XPath 2.0. You can test for its existence by writing:

```
<xsl:if test="function-available('current-date')>
```

For a fuller example, see the end of this section.

In theory, you could test whether a function such as `current-date()` is available by calling «system-property('xsl-version')» and testing whether the result is equal to «2.0». But the reality is that there will be processors that have implemented some of the XPath 2.0 functions but not yet all of them. A processor isn't supposed to return «2.0» as the value of «system-property('xsl: version')» unless it is a fully conformant XSLT 2.0 processor; but if it isn't a fully conformant processor, then you can't be sure whether it follows the rules. So it's better to use the finer-grained check offered by `function-available()`.

Testing for Vendor or Third-Party Extensions

The second way of using `function-available()` is to test for vendor or third-party extensions. If you know that a particular extension function is present in some implementations and not others, you can use the `function-available()` test to see whether it is present, and use the new `use-when` attribute to handle the situation when it isn't.

The `use-when` attribute is a late addition to XSLT 2.0. It provides a way of conditionally including or excluding parts of a stylesheet at compile time, based on a compile-time condition. There are more details of this feature on page 122 in Chapter 3. The compile-time condition is an XPath expression, restricted to operate with a very limited context, which means that it can only access information known at compile time. It cannot, for example, access a source document, or refer to variables. But the context does include the set of extension functions that are available. This is illustrated in the example that follows.

Example 1: Testing for xx:node-set() Extensions

The XSLT 2.0 working draft allows you to use a temporary tree (the value constructed when an `<xsl:variable>` element is not empty) in any context where a node can be used. This feature was not available in XSLT 1.0, which handled temporary trees as a distinct data type, known as a result tree fragment. Many vendors filled the gap by allowing a temporary tree to be converted to a node-set using an extension function (for example `xt:node-set()` or `msxml:node-set()`). If you want to write a stylesheet that is as portable as possible, you need to write code that discovers which of these facilities is available.

The following stylesheet (`node-set-available.xsl`) contains a named template that takes a temporary tree as a parameter, and calls `<xsl:apply-templates>` to process its root node in a particular mode. When running with an XSLT 2.0 processor, it does this simply by passing the tree to

`<xsl:apply-templates>` directly; in other cases, it tries to determine whether one of the proprietary `node-set()` extension functions is available, and uses that.

```
<xsl:stylesheet
          xmlns:xsl="http://www.w3.org/1999/XSL/Transform"
          version="2.0">
<xsl:template name="process-tree-fragment"
          xmlns:msxml="urn:schemas-microsoft-com:xslt"
          xmlns:xt="http://www.jclark.com/xt"
          xmlns:saxon6=" http://icl.com/saxon">
  <xsl:param name="fragment"/>
  <xsl:choose>
    <xsl:when test="number(system-property('xsl:version')) &gt; 1.0">
      <xsl:apply-templates mode="process-fragment"
                            select="$fragment"/>
    </xsl:when>
    <xsl:otherwise use-when="system-property('xsl:version') eq '1.0'">
      <xsl:choose>
        <xsl:when test="function-available('msxml:node-set')">
          <xsl:apply-templates mode="process-fragment"
                                select="msxml:node-set($fragment)"/>
        </xsl:when>
        <xsl:when test="function-available('xt:node-set')">
          <xsl:apply-templates mode="process-fragment"
                                select="xt:node-set($fragment)"/>
        </xsl:when>
        <xsl:when test="function-available('saxon6:node-set')">
          <xsl:apply-templates mode="process-fragment"
                                select="saxon6:node-set($fragment)"/>
        </xsl:when>
        <xsl:otherwise>
          <xsl:message terminate="yes">
            Cannot convert result tree fragment to node-set
          </xsl:message>
        </xsl:otherwise>
      </xsl:choose>
    </xsl:otherwise>
  </xsl:choose>
</xsl:template>
</xsl:stylesheet>
```

This named template can be called as follows, to process all the nodes in the result tree fragment.

```
<xsl:call-template name="process-tree-fragment">
   <xsl:with-param name="fragment" select="$supplied-fragment"/>
</xsl:call-template>
```

The logic here is slightly tortuous. You need to look at it in two different ways: as an XSLT 1.0 stylesheet, and as a 2.0 stylesheet.

As a 1.0 stylesheet, the outer `<xsl:choose>` takes the `<xsl:otherwise>` branch, because the processor version is "1.0." The use-when attribute on the `<xsl:otherwise>` element is ignored: the XSLT 1.0 processor will be operating in forwards-compatible mode, because the stylesheet specifies «version="2.0"», and in forwards-compatible mode, unknown attributes on XSLT elements are ignored. The 1.0 processor then takes one of the branches of the inner <xsl:choose>, depending on which of the xx:node-set() extension functions is available.

As an XSLT 2.0 stylesheet, the outer <xsl:choose> takes the <xsl:when> branch. It completely ignores the <xsl:otherwise> branch, by virtue of the use-when condition. The use-when condition is necessary, because an XSLT 2.0 processor would otherwise report a static (compile time) error when it sees an XPath expression that calls an unknown function such as saxon6:node-set(), even though the function is not actually evaluated at runtime.

When this example is run with an XSLT 2.0 processor, it doesn't actually invoke the function-available() function—which arguably makes it a poor choice of example for this section. The next example attempts to remedy this.

Example 2: Testing Availability of a Java Method

In this example, we'll assume that the stylesheet is always going to run under a particular XSLT 2.0 processor, but that it might run under different Java VMs. We'll suppose the existence of an XSLT 2.0 processor that can run under both JDK 1.3 and JDK 1.4, and we'll suppose that we want to use the Java method «Charset.isAvailable()» in the java.nio.charset package, which is new in JDK 1.4. Under JDK 1.3, we'll behave as if the extension function returned false.

We achieve this by writing two versions of a variable declaration. Only one of them is compiled, based on the value of the use-when attribute.

```
<xsl:variable name="charset-ok"
              as="xs:boolean"
              select="Charset:isAvailable('EUC-JP')"
              xmlns:Charset="java:java.nio.charset.Charset"
              use-when="function-available('Charset:isAvailable', 1)"/>

<xsl:variable name="charset-ok"
              as="xs:boolean"
              select="false()"
              xmlns:Charset="java:java.nio.charset.Charset"
              use-when="not(function-available('Charset:isAvailable', 1))"/>
```

See Also

element-available() on page 542.

generate-id

The generate-id() function generates a string, in the form of an XML Name, that uniquely identifies a node. The result is guaranteed to be different for every node that participates in a given transformation.

For example, the expression «generate-id(..)» might return the string «N015732» when using one XSLT processor, and «b23a1c79» when using another.

Changes in 2.0

None.

Signature

Argument	Data Type	Meaning
node (optional)	node()?	The input node. If the argument is omitted, the context node is used. If an empty sequence is supplied, the zero-length string is returned.
Result	xs:string	*A string value that uniquely identifies the node. This will consist only of ASCII alphanumeric characters, and the first character will be alphabetic. This makes the identifier suitable for use in many contexts, for example as an ID value in an XML document or an HTML anchor.*

Effect

If the node argument is omitted, it defaults to « . », the context item. A type error occurs if this is not a node.

If the node argument is an empty sequence, the function returns a zero-length string.

The function returns an arbitrary string. Within a given transformation, the function will always return the same string for the same node, and it will always return different strings for different nodes: in other words, «generate-id($A) = generate-id($B)» is true if and only if «$A is $B» is true, and this includes the case where the nodes are in different documents.

The generated identifiers are unique within a single execution of the stylesheet. If the same stylesheet is used several times, with the same or different source documents, the function may generate the same identifiers in each run but is under no obligation to do so.

Usage and Examples

In XSLT 1.0, the generate-id() function was often used to determine whether two expressions represented the same node, that is, to compare nodes by identity. XPath 2.0 offers the «is» operator for this purpose, so this usage can be expected to dwindle.

The main intended purpose of the generate-id() function is to create links in the output document. For example, it can be used to generate ID and IDREF attributes in an output XML document, or <a name="X"> and <a href="#X"> pairs in an output HTML document.

Example: Using generate-id() to Create Links

This example takes as input a file `resorts.xml` containing details of a collection of holiday resorts, each of which includes a list of hotels.

Source

```
<resorts>
   <resort>
      <name>Amsterdam</name>
      <details>A wordy description of Amsterdam</details>
      <hotel>
         <name>Grand Hotel</name>
         <stars>5</stars>
         <address> . . . </address>
      </hotel>
      <hotel>
         <name>Less Grand Hotel</name>
         <stars>2</stars>
         <address> . . . </address>
      </hotel>
   </resort>
   <resort>
      <name>Bruges</name>
      <details>An eloquent description of Bruges</details>
      <hotel>
         <name>Central Hotel</name>
         <stars>5</stars>
         <address> . . . </address>
      </hotel>
      <hotel>
         <name>Peripheral Hotel</name>
         <stars>2</stars>
         <address> . . . </address>
      </hotel>
   </resort>
</resorts>
```

Stylesheet

The stylesheet `resorts.xsl` constructs an output HTML page in which the hotels are listed first, followed by information about the resorts. Each hotel entry contains a hyperlink to the relevant resort details. The links for the resorts are generated using `generate-id()` applied to the `<resort>` element.

This is a complete stylesheet that uses the *Simplified Stylesheet* syntax introduced on page 119, in Chapter 3.

```
<html
 xmlns:xsl="http://www.w3.org/1999/XSL/Transform"
 xsl:version="1.0"
>
```

```
<body>
  <h1>Hotels</h1>
  <xsl:for-each select="//hotel">
  <xsl:sort select="number(stars)"
                      order="descending" data-type="number"/>
    <h2><xsl:value-of select="name"/></h2>
    <p>Address: <xsl:value-of select="address"/></p>
    <p>Stars: <xsl:value-of select="stars"/></p>
    <p>Resort: <a href="#{generate-id(parent::resort)}">
          <xsl:value-of select="parent::resort/name"/></a></p>
  </xsl:for-each>

  <h1>Resorts</h1>
  <xsl:for-each select="//resort">
    <h2><a name="{generate-id()}">
        <xsl:value-of select="name"/>
    </a></h2>
    <p><xsl:value-of select="details"/></p>
  </xsl:for-each>
</body>
</html>
```

Notice how generate-id() is used twice, once to generate the identifier of the resort, the next time to generate a link from the hotel.

Output

The following output was obtained using Saxon. I have added some extra indentation to show the structure. A different product will generate different identifiers in the `<a>` elements, but the links will work just as well.

```
<html>
  <body>
    <h1>Hotels</h1>
      <h2>Grand Hotel</h2>
        <p>Address:  . . . </p>
        <p>Stars: 5</p>
        <p>Resort: <a href="#d0e3">Amsterdam</a></p>
      <h2>Central Hotel</h2>
        <p>Address:  . . . </p>
        <p>Stars: 5</p>
        <p>Resort: <a href="#d0e36">Bruges</a></p>
      <h2>Less Grand Hotel</h2>

        <p>Address:  . . . </p>
        <p>Stars: 2</p>
        <p>Resort: <a href="#d0e3">Amsterdam</a></p>
      <h2>Peripheral Hotel</h2>
        <p>Address:  . . . </p>
        <p>Stars: 2</p>
        <p>Resort: <a href="#d0e36">Bruges</a></p>
    <h1>Resorts</h1>
```

```
        <h2><a name="d0e3">Amsterdam</a></h2>
          <p>A wordy description of Amsterdam</p>
        <h2><a name="d0e36">Bruges</a></h2>
          <p>An eloquent description of Bruges</p>
    </body>
</html>
```

There is no inverse function to `generate-id()`: specifically, there is no direct way to find a node if its generated id is known, other than the very inefficient:

```
//node()[generate-id()=$X]
```

If you need to do this, however, you can set up a key definition as follows.

```
<xsl:key name="gid-key" match="*" use="generate-id()"/>
```

Then find the element with a given id value using the expression:

```
key('gid-key', $X)
```

It is important to appreciate that the generated identifiers bear no resemblance to any ID attribute values in the source document, so the nodes cannot be found using the `id()` function.

Also, the ID values generated in one run of the processor may be different from those generated in a subsequent run. You need to bear this in mind if you are using the ID values as hyperlinks. If the transformation is likely to be run more than once, then it isn't safe to reference these ID values from another document, or even to save them as a bookmark in a browser.

See Also

`id()` in *XPath 2.0 Programmer's Reference*.
`key()` on page 572.
«`is`» operator in *XPath 2.0 Programmer's Reference*.

key

The `key()` function is used to find the nodes with a given value for a named key. It is used in conjunction with the `<xsl:key>` element described on page 332 in Chapter 5.

For example, if there is a key definition:

```
<xsl:key name="vreg" match="vehicle" use="@reg"/>
```

then the expression «`key('vreg', 'N498PAA')`» might return the single element `<vehicle reg="N498PAA">`.

Changes in 2.0

The key value can now be of any data type, and is compared according to the rules for that data type. The key definitions in `<xsl:key>` can also now specify a collation to be used for comparing strings.

An optional third argument has been added to identify the document to be searched.

Signature

Argument	Data Type	Meaning
name	xs:string	Specifies the name of the key. The value of the string must be a lexical QName that identifies a key declared using an `<xsl:key>` element in the stylesheet.
value	xdt:anyAtomicType*	Specifies the required value of the key, in a way that depends on the data type. See below.
document (optional)	node()	Identifies the document to be searched. If this argument is omitted, the document containing the context node is searched.
Result	node() *	*The nodes with the required key values, returned without duplicates, and in document order.*

Effect

The first argument must take the form of a lexical QName: that is, an XML name optionally prefixed with a namespace prefix that corresponds to a namespace declaration that is in scope at the point in the stylesheet where the key() function is called. If there is no namespace prefix, the relevant namespace URI is null; the default namespace is not used. There must be an `<xsl:key>` element in the stylesheet with the same expanded QName, using the namespace URIs rather than prefixes in the comparison. If there is more than one `<xsl:key>` element with this name, they are all used: a node is considered to match the key if it matches any of the key definitions with this name.

The second argument is a sequence of atomic values (usually a single atomic value, but this is treated as a sequence of length one). If the value actually supplied in the function call includes nodes, the nodes are atomized to create a sequence of atomic values. The result of the key() function contains every node in the same document as the context node that has at least one key value that is equal to one of the values supplied in this sequence.

The key values can be of any data type. The values of the keys as indexed using `<xsl:key>` will be compared with the keys supplied in the key() function, using the rules of the XPath «eq» operator without any special type conversion: this means for example that if the indexed value is the xs:integer value 23, it will not be retrieved by the call «key('k', '23')», because the integer 23 and the string

573

'23' do not compare equal. Untyped atomic values (values extracted from unvalidated nodes) are treated as strings and can only be compared with strings. If a collation is specified in the <xsl:key> declaration, it will be used when comparing strings, otherwise the default collation will be used.

The optional third argument identifies the document to be searched. This can be any node in the relevant document; it does not need to be the document node. The default value is the context node. Note that with multiple source documents, the resulting nodes will all be in this document, which is not necessarily the same document as the nodes from which the key values were obtained.

When the third argument is omitted, it's an error if there is no context item, or if the context item isn't a node. It's also an error to search in a tree that doesn't have a document node as its root.

Usage and Examples

The key() function is provided to make associative access to nodes (finding the nodes given their content) more convenient and more efficient. Efficiency of course depends entirely on the implementation, but it is likely that most implementations will use some kind of index or hash-table data structure to make the key() function faster than the equivalent path expression using predicates to select the required value.

Another use for keys is that they provide an efficient way of grouping related nodes together. This usage is needed far less under XSLT 2.0, because of the introduction of the <xsl:for-each-group> instruction, but it is still worth your while to understand it.

We will examine these two ways of using keys in turn.

Using Keys to Find Nodes by Value

To locate the <book> elements having J. B. Priestley as the content of one of their <author> child elements, you could write:

```
<xsl:for-each select="//book[author='J. B. Priestley']">
```

However, it is probably more efficient, if this is done frequently in the stylesheet, to define the author name as a key.

```
<xsl:key name="book-author" match="book" use="author"/>
. . .
<xsl:for-each select="key('book-author', 'J. B. Priestley')"/>
```

The key() function normally locates elements in the same document as the context node. When you need to locate elements in a different document, you can identify this in the third argument, for example:

```
<xsl:copy-of select="key('book-author', 'J. B. Priestley', document('a.xml'))"/>
```

The key value is usually supplied as a string, or as an expression that returns a string. In XSLT 2.0 it can also be a value of another atomic type: for example, you can use a number or a date as a key. It does not have to be a single value; you can supply a sequence of strings (or numbers or dates, if that is how the key is defined), and the function will return all the nodes that match any one of the values.

Keys are particularly useful for following cross-references. If you supply the key value as a node, or a sequence of nodes, then the values held in those nodes will be used as the key values. The next example explores this in more detail.

Example: Using Keys as Cross-References

This example uses two source files: the principal source document is a file containing a list of books, and the secondary one (accessed using the `document()` function) contains biographies of authors. The author name held in the first file acts as a cross-reference to the author's biography in the second file, rather like a join in SQL.

Source

The principal source document is an abbreviated version of the `booklist.xml` file.

```
<booklist>
<book category="FC">
    <title>The Young Visiters</title>
    <author>Daisy Ashford</author>
</book>
<book category="FC">
    <title>When We Were Very Young</title>
    <author>A. A. Milne</author>
</book>
</booklist>
```

The secondary source document, `authors.xml`, reads like this. I've included only two authors to keep it short, but the `key()` function would really come into its own if there were hundreds of entries.

```
<authors>

<author name="A. A. Milne">
<born>1852</born>
<died>1956</died>
<biog>Alan Alexander Milne, educated at Westminster School and Trinity
College Cambridge, became a prolific author of plays, novels, poetry,
short stories, and essays, all of which have been overshadowed by his
children's books. </biog>
</author>
<author name="Daisy Ashford">
<born>1881</born>
<died>1972</died>
<biog>Daisy Ashford (Mrs George Norman) wrote <i>The Young Visiters</i>,
a small comic masterpiece, while still a young child in Lewes. It was
found in a drawer in 1919 and sent to Chatto and Windus, who published
```

```
it in the same year with an introduction by J. M. Barrie, who had first
insisted on meeting the author\ in order to check that she was genuine.
</biog>
</author>

</authors>
```

Stylesheet

The stylesheet is in the file author-biogs.xsl. It declares a key to match <author>
elements by their name attribute. This is intended for use with the authors.xml file, though
there is nothing in the key definition to say so.

Note the use of a global variable to reference the secondary source file. It would be possible to
use the document() function each time the file is accessed, and any XSLT processor worthy
of the name would actually read and parse the file only once, but using a variable in my view
makes it easier to see what is going on.

The actual call on the key() function is in the path expression «$biogs/key('biog',
$name)». The purpose of the first step, $biogs, is to switch the context node to the
authors.xml document, because the key() function (when used with two arguments)
always looks in the document containing the context node. The expression could equally
have been written «key('biog', $name, $biogs)».

```
<xsl:transform xmlns:xsl="http://www.w3.org/1999/XSL/Transform"
version="2.0"
>
<xsl:key name="biog" match="author" use="@name"/>
<xsl:variable name="biogs" select="document('authors.xml')"/>
<xsl:template match="/">
  <html><body>

  <xsl:variable name="all-books" select="//book"/>
    <xsl:for-each select="$all-books">
                <!-- for each book in the booklist file -->
      <h1><xsl:value-of select="title"/></h1>
      <h2>Author<xsl:if test="count(author)!=1">s</xsl:if></h2>
      <xsl:for-each select="author">
              <!-- for each author of this book -->
        <xsl:variable name="name" select="."/>
        <h3><xsl:value-of select="$name"/></h3>
              <!--locate the biography by key lookup -->
        <xsl:variable name="auth"
                      select="$biogs/key('biog', $name)"/>
        <p><xsl:value-of
            select="concat($auth/born, ' - ', $auth/died)"/>
        </p>
        <p><xsl:value-of select="$auth/biog"/></p>
      </xsl:for-each>
    </xsl:for-each>
  </body></html>
```

```
    </xsl:template>

    </xsl:transform>
```

Output

The output obtained if you run this stylesheet with the subset of the `booklist.xml` file shown earlier is as follows.

```
<html>
    <body>
        <h1>The Young Visiters</h1>
        <h2>Author</h2>
        <h3>Daisy Ashford</h3>
        <p>1881 - 1972</p>
        <p>Daisy Ashford (Mrs George Norman) wrote The Young Visiters, a
small comic masterpiece, while still a young child in Lewes. It was
found in a drawer in 1919 and sent to Chatto and Windus, who published
it in the same year with an introduction by J. M. Barrie, who had first
insisted on meeting the author in order to check that she was genuine.
</p>
        <h1>When We Were Very Young</h1>
        <h2>Author</h2>
        <h3>A. A. Milne</h3>
        <p>1852 - 1956</p>
        <p>Alan Alexander Milne, educated at Westminster School and
Trinity College Cambridge, became a prolific author of plays, novels,
poetry, short stories, and essays, all of which have been overshadowed
by his children's books.</p>
    </body>
</html>
```

Using Keys for Grouping

Because keys provide an efficient way of retrieving all the nodes that share a common value, they are useful when you need to group nodes with common values in the output.

This technique is sometimes called the Muenchian grouping method, after Steve Muench of Oracle who introduced it. In XSLT 1.0, it was the only way of performing grouping efficiently. In XSLT 2.0, the `<xsl:for-each-group>` construct will usually provide a more convenient solution; however, you will still encounter the Muenchian method used in old stylesheets, and there is no reason why you should not continue to use it.

To solve any grouping problem, you need two nested loops. The outer loop selects one node to act as a representative of each group, typically the first node in document order that is a member of the group. The processing associated with this node outputs information about the group as a whole, typically the common value used to group the nodes together, perhaps with counts or subtotals calculated over the members of the group, plus any necessary formatting. The inner loop then processes each member of the group in turn.

With the Muenchian method, a key is defined on the common value that determines group membership. For example, if all the cities in a country comprise one group, then the key definition will be as follows.

```
<xsl:key name="country-group" match="city" use="@country"/>
```

The outer loop selects one city for each country. The way of doing this is to select all the cities, and then filter out those that are not the first in their country. You can tell that a city is the first one for its country, by comparing it with the first node in the sequence returned by the key() function for that country.

```
<xsl:for-each select="//city[. is key('country-group', @country)[1]]">
```

The «is» operator is new in XPath 2.0. In a 1.0 stylesheet, the equivalent expression would apply generate-id() to both operands, and compare the results using the «=» operator.

Within this loop the code can output any heading it needs, such as the name of the country. It can then start an inner loop to process all the cities in this country, which it can find by using the key once again.

```
<xsl:for-each select="key('country-group', @country)">
```

The following shows a complete example of this technique.

Example: Using Keys for Grouping

This example creates a list of cities, grouped by country.

Source

The source cities.xml is a list of cities.

```
<cities>
    <city name="Paris" country="France"/>
    <city name="Roma" country="Italia"/>
    <city name="Nice" country="France"/>
    <city name="Madrid" country="Espana"/>
    <city name="Milano" country="Italia"/>
    <city name="Firenze" country="Italia"/>
    <city name="Napoli" country="Italia"/>
    <city name="Lyon" country="France"/>
    <city name="Barcelona" country="Espana"/>
</cities>
```

Stylesheet

The stylesheet citygroups.xsl is as follows.

```
<xsl:transform
  xmlns:xsl="http://www.w3.org/1999/XSL/Transform"
  version="2.0"
  >
  <xsl:key name="country-group" match="city" use="@country"/>
```

```
<xsl:template match="/">
  <html><body>
   <xsl:for-each
select="//city[. is key('country-group', @country)[1]]">
      <h1><xsl:value-of select="@country"/></h1>
      <xsl:for-each select="key('country-group', @country)">
         <xsl:value-of select="@name"/><br/>
      </xsl:for-each>
   </xsl:for-each>
  </body></html>
</xsl:template>
</xsl:transform>
```

Output

Viewed in a browser, the output is as shown in Figure 7-2.

Figure 7-2

See Also

<xsl:key> on page 332 in Chapter 5.

id() in *XPath 2.0 Programmer's Reference* (*Chapter 10*).

regex-group

The `regex-group()` function returns a captured substring resulting from matching a regular expression using the `<xsl:analyze-string>` instruction.

Changes in 2.0

This function is new in XSLT 2.0.

Signature

Argument	Data Type	Meaning
group	`xs:integer`	Identifies the captured subgroup that is required. The *n*th captured subgroup provides the string that was matched by the part of the regular expression enclosed by the *n*th left parenthesis.
Result	`xs:string`	*The string that was matched by the nth subexpression of the regular expression.*

Effect

When the `<xsl:analyze-string>` instruction is used to match a string against a regular expression (regex), its `<xsl:matching-substring>` child element is invoked once for each substring of the input string that matches the regular expression. The substring that matched the regex can be referred to within this element as «`.`», because it becomes the context item, and for consistency with other regex languages it is also available as the value of «`regex-group(0)`». Sometimes, however, you need to know not only what the substring that matched the regex was, but which parts of that substring matched particular parts of the regex. The group of characters that matches a particular parenthesized subexpression within the regex is referred to as a *captured group*; and the captured group that matches the *n*th parenthesized subexpression is accessible as the value of «`regex-group(n)`».

The substrings matched by `<xsl:analyze-string>` are available during the execution of the sequence constructor within the `<xsl:matching-substring>` element, including any templates called from instructions within this sequence constructor: that is, the scope is dynamic rather than static.

Note that it is only the `<xsl:analyze-string>` instruction that makes captured groups available. They are not made available by the regex functions described in *XPath 2.0 Programmer's Reference*, that is `matches()`, `replace()`, and `tokenize()`.

Usage and Examples

The `regex-group()` function is always used together with the `<xsl:analyze-string>` instruction, described in Chapter 5, page 176.

For example, suppose you are analyzing a comma-separated-values file containing lines like this.

```
423,"Barbara Smith","General Motors",1996-03-12
```

Given this line as the content of variable $in, you might analyze it using the code:

```
<xsl:analyze-string select="$in" regex='("([^"]*?)")|([^,]+?),'>
  <xsl:matching-substring>
    <cell>
      <xsl:value-of select="regex-group(2)"/>
      <xsl:value-of select="regex-group(3)"/>
    </cell>
  </xsl:matching-substring>
</xsl:analyze-string>
```

The regex here has two alternatives. The first alternative, «("([^"]*?)")», matches a string enclosed in quotes. The second alternative, «([^,]+?),», matches a sequence of non-comma characters followed by a comma. If a string within quotes is matched, then the characters between the quotes are matched by the «[^"]*?» part of the regex. This appears after the second «(» in the regex, so the string that it matches is available as «regex-group(2)». If a nonquoted string is matched, it is matched by the «[^,]+?» part, which appears after the third «(» in the regex, and is therefore available as «regex-group(3)». Rather than work out whether group 2 or group 3 was matched, the XSLT code simply outputs both: the one that was not matched will be a zero-length string, so it is simpler to copy it to the output than to write the conditional code to find out whether it was actually matched.

A full stylesheet containing this example is shown under the unparsed-text() function (page 587).

See Also

<xsl:analyze-string> on page 176 in Chapter 5.

system-property

The system-property() function returns information about the processing environment.

For example, with a processor that implements XSLT version 2.0, the expression «system-property('xsl:version')» returns 2.0.

Changes in 2.0

Several new system properties have been defined in XSLT 2.0.

The result of the function is now always a string. In XSLT 1.0 (although the spec was not a hundred percent clear on the point) the «xsl:version» system property was returned as a number.

Signature

Argument	Data Type	Meaning
name	`xs:string`	Specifies the name of the system property required. The value of the string should be in the form of a lexical QName that identifies a system property. If there is no system property with this name, the function returns a zero-length string.
Result	`xs:string`	*The value of the requested system property.*

Effect

The supplied argument is converted into an expanded name using the namespace declarations in scope for the stylesheet element that contains the call on `system-property()`.

There are several system properties that every implementation must support. These are all in the XSLT namespace, and are listed as follows. The first three were available in XSLT 1.0, the others are new in XSLT 2.0.

System Property	Value
`xsl:version`	A number giving the version of XSLT implemented by the processor. For conformant XSLT processors, this will be 1.0 or 2.0. For processors that provide a partial implementation, or an implementation of intermediate working drafts, other versions may be returned. It's a good idea to write your stylesheet on the assumption that new XSLT versions may be introduced in the future.
`xsl:vendor`	A string identifying the vendor of the XSLT processor. In practice it will sometimes also identify the product name, but the actual value is implementation defined. For Microsoft's MSXML3 product, the value is simply «Microsoft».
`xsl:vendor-url`	A string: the URL of the vendor's Web site. For example, MSXML3 returns «http://www.microsoft.com»
`xsl:product`	This property is new in XSLT 2.0. It is intended to identify the product name of the XSLT processor, for example «Xalan» or «Saxon».
`xsl:product-version`	This property is new in XSLT 2.0. It is intended to identify which version of the XSLT processor is being used, for example «7.6.5». If there are several variants of a

System Property	Value
	product (for example Xalan-C and Xalan-J), it is up to the implementer whether the variant is returned as part of the product name or as part of the product version.
`xsl:is-schema-aware`	This property returns the string «yes» or «no», depending on whether the XSLT 2.0 processor is schema aware or not.
`xsl:supports-serialization`	This property returns the string «yes» or «no», depending on whether the XSLT 2.0 processor supports serialization or not.
`xsl:supports-backwards-compatibility`	This property returns the string «yes» or «no», depending on whether the XSLT 2.0 processor supports running in backwards-compatibility mode. A processor that does not support this mode will report an error if «version="1.0"» is specified. In the early life of XSLT 2.0 it is likely that all implementations will support this mode, but the Working Group felt that once XSLT 2.0 has become fully established in the market, vendors should be allowed to make a commercial decision as to whether or not their customers still needed this feature.

Any additional system properties returned by this function are implementer defined. Any implementer-defined properties should be in a namespace specific to the vendor.

Usage

The `system-property()` function can be used to determine details about the processor running the stylesheet, either for display purposes (for example, to produce a comment in the generated output), or to apply conditional logic.

Generally, it is best to avoid using this function to test whether particular features are available, unless there is no other way of doing so. The functions `function-available()` and `element-available()` and the `<xsl:fallback>` instruction often serve this need better, and the forwards-compatibility features described on page 124, in Chapter 3 can be used to ensure that a stylesheet can work with processors that implement an older dialect of XSLT.

However, there are some cases where testing «`system-property('xsl:version')`» is the only practical way of discovering whether a feature is available. For example, the XSLT 2.0 working draft introduces the ability to use a tree-valued variable (or a result tree fragment, as it is known in XSLT 1.0) as a document node, in contexts such as `<xsl:for-each>` and `<xsl:apply-templates>`. Since this feature does not introduce any new functions or XSLT elements, the only practical way to test whether it is available is to check the XSLT version supported.

Examples

The following code outputs a documentary comment into the generated HTML.

```
<HTML>
   <xsl:comment>
     Generated using XSLT stylesheet abc.xsl
     using <xsl:value-of select="system-property('xsl:product')"/>
     version <xsl:value-of select="system-property('xsl:product-version')"/>
   </xsl:comment>
   . . .
```

See Also

element-available() page 542.
function-available() on page 564.
<xsl:fallback> on page 271 in Chapter 5.

unparsed-entity-public-id

The unparsed-entity-public-id() function gives access to the public identifier of unparsed entities declared in the DTD of the source document.

Changes in 2.0

This function is new in XSLT 2.0.

Signature

Argument	Data Type	Meaning
name	xs:string	Specifies the name of the unparsed entity required. The value of the string should be an XML *Name*.
Result	xs:string	*The public identifier of the unparsed entity with the given name, if there is one. Otherwise, a zero-length string.*

Effect

This function operates on the document containing the context node. An error is reported if the context item is undefined, or if it is not a node, or if it is a node in a tree whose root is not a document node.

If the document containing the context node includes an unparsed entity whose name is equal to the supplied string, and if the unparsed entity has a public identifier (signaled by the PUBLIC keyword in XML) then the public identifier is returned. In all other cases, it returns a zero-length string.

Usage

Unparsed entities are one of the more rarely used features of XML; they derive from SGML, and this explains why people who use unparsed entities are also inclined to use public identifiers to refer to them. Public identifiers were designed to tackle the same problem as URNs, namely to provide a way of giving unique names to objects, without becoming locked in to the location where the object can be found. They are often used in conjunction with Oasis catalogs.

Note that it is the public identifier of the unparsed entity that is returned, not the public identifier of the notation named in its NDATA clause. The data model does not provide any information about notations.

Examples

For example, if the DTD contains the declaration:

```
<!ENTITY weather-map SYSTEM "weather.jpeg"
    PUBLIC "-//MEGACORP//WEATHER/" NDATA JPEG>
```

then the expression «unparsed-entity-public-id('weather-map')» returns the public identifier «-//MEGACORP//WEATHER/».

See Also

unparsed-entity-uri() in the following section.

unparsed-entity-uri

The unparsed-entity-uri() function gives access to declarations of unparsed entities in the DTD of the source document.

For example, if the DTD contains the declaration:

```
<!ENTITY weather-map SYSTEM "weather.jpeg" NDATA JPEG>
```

then the expression «unparsed-entity-uri('weather-map')» returns the URI «weather.jpeg», expanded to an absolute URI by applying the base URI for the DTD.

Changes in 2.0

None.

Signature

Argument	Data Type	Meaning
name	`xs:string`	Specifies the name of the unparsed entity required. The value of the string should be an XML *Name*.
Result	`xs:string`	*A string containing the URI (the system identifier) of the unparsed entity with the given name, if there is one. Otherwise, a zero-length string.*

Effect

This function operates on the document containing the context node. An error is reported if the context item is undefined, or if it is not a node, or if it is a node in a tree whose root is not a document node.

If the document containing the context node includes an unparsed entity whose name is equal to the supplied string, then the system identifier for this unparsed entity is returned. In all other cases, it returns a zero-length string.

If the system identifier is given in the source XML as a relative URI, the XSLT processor should expand it into an absolute URI before returning it.

Usage

An unparsed entity is an entity defined in the DTD using a declaration of the form:

```
<!ENTITY weather-map SYSTEM "weather.jpeg" NDATA JPEG>
```

It's the NDATA (meaning "not XML data") that makes it an unparsed entity; and because it is an unparsed entity, it can't be referenced using a normal entity reference of the form «&weather-map;» but must instead be referenced by name in an attribute of type ENTITY or ENTITIES, for example <forecast map="weather-map">.

If you're using a schema-aware XSLT processor, and the document has been validated against a schema that defines the map attribute as being of type xs:ENTITY, then you can process the attribute using a rule such as:

```
<xsl:template match="attribute(*, xs:ENTITY)">
    <img src="{unparsed-entity-uri(.)}"/>
</xsl:template>
```

Without a schema, you are simply expected to know that the map attribute is of type xs:ENTITY, and expected to pick up the attribute value in a call such as «unparsed-entity-uri(@map)». This call returns the absolute URI of the actual resource, that is, something like «file:///c:/documents/forecasts/weather.jpeg».

XSLT provides no way of finding out the notation name («JPEG» in our example) or the URI for the notation, so even if you have a schema that flags the attribute as one that contains an unparsed entity reference, you still have to know what kind of reference you are expecting.

This is not exactly in the spirit of section 4.4.6 of the XML specification, which states: "When the name of an unparsed entity appears as a token in an attribute of declared type ENTITY or ENTITIES, a validating processor must inform the application of the system and public (if any) identifiers for both the entity and its associated notation." However, unparsed entities are hardly XML's most widely used feature, so it is unsurprising that XSLT support for them should be incomplete.

The rules in the XSLT specification don't explicitly state this, but in practice, if you use a nonvalidating XML parser to process the source document, the parser isn't obliged to pass information to the XSLT processor about unparsed entities declared in the external subset of the DTD, and the `unparsed-entity-uri()` function is therefore likely to return a zero-length string. If this happens, try using a validating XML parser—assuming of course that the source document is valid.

Examples

Given the entity definition

```
<!ENTITY weather-map SYSTEM "weather.jpeg" NDATA JPEG>
```

and the entity reference

```
<FORECAST MAP="weather-map"/>
```

the following code will insert an `<IMG>` element into the HTML output.

```
<xsl:template match="FORECAST">
   <IMG HREF="{unparsed-entity-uri(@MAP)}"/>
</xsl:template>
```

See Also

Trees, not Documents, in Chapter 2, page 44.

unparsed-text

The `unparsed-text()` function returns the content of an external file in the form of a string.

Changes in 2.0

This function is new in XSLT 2.0.

Signature

Argument	Data Type	Meaning
href	`xs:string`	The URI of the external text file to be loaded.
encoding (optional)	`xs:string`	The character encoding of the text in the file.
Result	`xs:string`	*The textual content of the file.*

Effect

This function is analogous to the `document()` function described on page 532, except that the file referenced by the URI is treated as text rather than as XML. The file is located and its textual content is returned as the result of the `unparsed-text()` function, in the form of a string.

The value of the `href` argument is a URI. It mustn't contain a fragment identifier (the part marked with a «#» sign). It may be an absolute URI or a relative URI; if it is relative, it is resolved against the base URI of the stylesheet. This is true even if the relative URI is contained in a node in a source document. In this situation it is a good idea to resolve the URI yourself before calling this function. For example, if the URI is in an attribute called `src` then the call might be «`unparsed-text(resolve-uri(@src, base-uri(@src)))`». The `resolve-uri()` function is described in *XPath 2.0 Programmer's Reference*; its first argument is the relative URI, and the second argument is the base URI used to resolve it.

The optional `encoding` argument specifies the character encoding of the file. This can be any character encoding supported by the implementation; the only encodings that an implementation must support are UTF-8 and UTF-16. The system will not necessarily use this encoding: the rules for deciding an encoding are as follows, and are based on the rules given in the XLink recommendation:

❑ First, the processor looks for so-called external encoding information. This typically means information supplied in an HTTP header, but the term is general and could apply to any metadata associated with the file, for example WebDAV properties.

❑ Next, it looks at the media type (MIME type), and if this identifies the file as XML, then it determines the encoding using the same rules as an XML parser (for example, it looks for an XML declaration, and if there is none, it looks for a byte order mark). Why would you use this function, rather than `document()`, to access an XML document? The thinking is that it is quite common for one XML document to act as an envelope for another XML document that is carried transparently in a CDATA section, and if you want to create such a composite document, you will want to read the payload document without parsing it.

❑ Next, it uses the `encoding` argument if this has been supplied.

❑ If there is no `encoding` argument, it tries to use UTF-8 encoding.

Various errors can occur in this process. In most cases there is a defined recovery action, so the processor has an option of treating the error as fatal or struggling on. Some processors will provide configuration options that pass this choice on the user. If the file identified by the URI cannot be found, the fallback action is to return a zero-length string. If the file contains characters that are invalid in XML (this applies to most control characters in the range x00 to x1F under XML 1.0, but only to the null character x00 under XML 1.1) then the invalid characters are substituted by the special Unicode character xFFFD, which is specifically intended for such purposes. If the file is found, but the bytes in the file cannot be decoded into characters using the encoding chosen by following the earlier rules, this is a fatal error.

Usage and Examples

There are a number of ways this function can be used, and I will show three. These are as follows:

❑   Up-conversion: that is, loading text that lacks markup in order to generate the XML markup

❑   XML envelope/payload applications

❑   HTML boilerplate generation

Up-Conversion

Up-conversion is the name often given to the process of analyzing input data for structure that is implicit in the textual content, and producing as output an XML document in which this structure is revealed by explicit markup. I have used this process, for example, to analyze HTML pages containing census data, in order to clean the data to make it suitable for adding to a structured genealogy database. It can also be used to process data that arrives in non-XML formats such as comma-separated values or EDI syntax.

The unparsed-text() function is not the only way of supplying non-XML data as input to a stylesheet; it can also be done simply by passing a string as the value of a stylesheet parameter. But the unparsed-text() function is particularly useful because the data is referenced by URI, and accessed under the control of the stylesheet.

XSLT 2.0 is much more suitable for use in up-conversion applications than XSLT 1.0. The most important tools are the <xsl:analyze-string> instruction, which enables the stylesheet to make use of structure that is implicit in the text, and the <xsl:for-each-group> instruction, which makes it much easier to analyze poorly structured markup. These can often be used in tandem: in the first stage in processing, <xsl:analyze-string> is used to recognize patterns in the text and mark these patterns using elements in a temporary tree, and in the second stage, <xsl:for-each-group> is used to turn flat markup structures into hierarchic structures that reflect the true data model.

Here is an example of a stylesheet that reads a comma-separated-values file and turns it into structured markup.

Example: Processing a Comma-Separated-Values File

This example is a stylesheet that reads a comma-separated-values file, given the URL of the file as a stylesheet parameter. It outputs an XML representation of this file, placing the rows in a <row> element and each value in a <cell> element. It does not attempt to process a header row containing field names, but this would be a simple extension.

Input

This stylesheet does not use any source XML document. Instead, it expects the URI of an ordinary text file to be supplied as a parameter to the stylesheet.

This is what the input file `names.csv` looks like.

```
123,"Mary Jones","IBM","USA",1997-05-14
423,"Barbara Smith","General Motors","USA",1996-03-12
6721,"Martin McDougall","British Airways","UK",2001-01-15
830,"Jonathan Perkins","Springer Verlag","Germany",2000-11-17
```

Stylesheet

This stylesheet `analyze-names.xsl` uses a named template `main` as its entry point: a new feature in XSLT 2.0.

To run this under Saxon, you will need Saxon 7.9 or a later release. The command for running the stylesheet looks like this.

```
java -jar saxon7.jar -it main analyze-names.xsl input-uri=names.csv
```

The `-it` option here indicates that processing should start without an XML source document, at the named template `main`.

The stylesheet first reads the input file using the `unparsed-text()` function, and then uses two levels of processing using `<xsl:analyze-string>` to identify the structure. The first level (using the regex «\n») splits the input into lines. The second level is explained more fully under the description of the `regex-group()` function on page 580: it extracts either the contents of a quoted string, or any value terminated by a comma, and copies this to a `<cell>` element.

```
<?xml version="1.0"?>
<xsl:stylesheet xmlns:xsl="http://www.w3.org/1999/XSL/Transform"
    xmlns:xs="http://www.w3.org/2001/XMLSchema"
    version="2.0">

<xsl:param name="input-uri" as="xs:string"/>
<xsl:output indent="yes"/>

<xsl:template name="main">
  <xsl:variable name="in"
                select="unparsed-text($input-uri, 'iso-8859-1')"/>
  <table>
  <xsl:analyze-string select="$in" regex="\n">
    <xsl:non-matching-substring>
      <row>
      <xsl:analyze-string select="." regex='("([^"]*?)")|([^,]+?),'>
        <xsl:matching-substring>
          <cell>
              <xsl:value-of select="regex-group(2)"/>
              <xsl:value-of select="regex-group(3)"/>
          </cell>
        </xsl:matching-substring>
      </xsl:analyze-string>
```

```
            </row>
          </xsl:non-matching-substring>
        </xsl:analyze-string>
        </table>
    </xsl:template>

    </xsl:stylesheet>
```

Output

The output is as follows.

```
<?xml version="1.0" encoding="UTF-8"?>
<table xmlns:xs="http://www.w3.org/2001/XMLSchema">
    <row>
        <cell>123</cell>
        <cell>Mary Jones</cell>
        <cell>IBM</cell>
        <cell>USA</cell>
    </row>
    <row>
        <cell>423</cell>
        <cell>Barbara Smith</cell>
        <cell>General Motors</cell>
        <cell>USA</cell>
    </row>
    <row>
        <cell>6721</cell>
        <cell>Martin McDougall</cell>
        <cell>British Airways</cell>
        <cell>UK</cell>
    </row>
    <row>
        <cell>830</cell>
        <cell>Jonathan Perkins</cell>
        <cell>Springer Verlag</cell>
        <cell>Germany</cell>
    </row>
</table>
```

XML Envelope/Payload Applications

It is not uncommon to find structures in which one XML document is wrapped in a CDATA section inside another. For example:

```
<envelope>
  <header>... </header>
  <payload>
     <![CDATA[<target-document>...</target-document>]]>
  </payload>
</envelope>
```

I don't normally recommend this as a good way of designing nested structures. In general, it is usually better to nest the structure directly, without using CDATA. That is, to use:

```
<envelope>
  <header>... </header>
  <payload>
      <target-document>...</target-document>
  </payload>
</envelope>
```

But sometimes you don't get to design the documents yourself; and there are some advantages for the CDATA approach, such as the ability for the payload document to include a DOCTYPE declaration.

Handling such structures in XSLT is not easy: the payload document is presented as a single text node, not as a tree of element nodes. However, the unparsed-text() function makes it much easier to output such structures. All you need to do is:

```
<xsl:output cdata-section-elements="payload"/>
<xsl:template match="/">
<envelope>
  <header>... </header>
  <payload>
      <xsl:value-of select="unparsed-text('payload.xml')"/>
  </payload>
</envelope>
```

HTML Boilerplate Generation

Generally, it is best to think of HTML in terms of a tree of element and text nodes, and to manipulate it as such in the stylesheet. Occasionally, you may need to process HTML that is not well formed, and cannot easily be converted into a well-formed structure. For example, you may be dealing with a syndicated news feed that arrives in HTML, whose format is sufficiently unpredictable that you don't want to rely on tools that automatically turn the HTML into structured XHTML. You might want to output the HTML news stories embedded in your own XSLT-generated pages.

An option in such cases is to treat the HTML as unparsed text rather than as a tree of nodes. You can read the HTML news feed using the unparsed-text() function and you can output it to the serialized result, using the disable-output-escaping option, provided your processor supports this.

```
<xsl:value-of select="unparsed-text('news.html')"
             disable-output-escaping="yes"/>
```

Remember when you use disable-output-escaping that not all processors support the feature, and that it works only if the output of the stylesheet is serialized. You can't always tell whether the output is going to be serialized or not: for example, if you run a transformation in Internet Explorer, the output HTML is serialized and then reparsed before being displayed, but if you run the same transformation in the Netscape browser, the result tree is passed directly to the rendering engine, bypassing the serialization stage. This means that disable-output-escaping doesn't work with a client-side transformation in Netscape.

See Also

`<xsl:analyze-string>` on page 176 in Chapter 5.

Summary

This chapter described the functions that are added to the core library by the XSLT specification. Information about the functions provided by XPath 2.0 is available in *XPath 2.0 Programmer's Reference*.

This chapter brings the reference part of this book to a close. You now have what I hope is a definitive reference guide to the XSLT language. The following chapters are designed to help you put the language to work, developing real-world applications. In Chapter 8, we look at the rules for writing XSLT extension functions.

8

Extensibility

The previous three chapters covered all the facilities defined the XSLT language. This chapter discusses what happens when you need to stray beyond the XSLT 2.0 language specification. It's concerned with questions such as:

❑ What extensions are vendors allowed to provide?

❑ How much are implementations allowed to vary from each other?

❑ How can your write your own extensions?

❑ How can you write stylesheets that will run on more than one vendor's XSLT processor?

There is some interesting history here. The draft XSLT 1.1 specification defined a general mechanism for calling extension functions written in any language, and then defined detailed interfaces for Java and JavaScript (or ECMAScript, to give it its vendor-neutral name). This specification was published as a working draft, but was subsequently withdrawn. There were a number of reasons for this, one of which was simply that events were overtaken by the more ambitious XSLT 2.0 initiative. But part of the reason was that the proposals for standardizing extension function interfaces attracted heavy public criticism (see http://xml.coverpages.org/withdraw-xslScript.html). It's difficult in retrospect to summarize the arguments that were waged against the idea, but they probably fell into three categories: some people thought extension functions were a bad idea in principle and should not be encouraged; some people disapproved of singling out two languages (Java and JavaScript) for special treatment; and some people felt that the W3C shouldn't be putting language bindings into the core XSLT specification, the job should be done in separate specifications preferably produced by a different organization.

The result of this minor furor is that there is no defined interface for writing extension functions, either in XSLT 1.0 or in XSLT 2.0. However, conventions have emerged at least for XSLT 1.0 (the draft 1.1 specification was influenced by these conventions, and in turn exerted its own influence on the products, despite being abandoned) and it is worth giving these some space.

What Vendor Extensions Are Allowed?

The XSLT 2.0 language specification makes no distinction between what vendors are allowed to do, and what users and third parties are allowed to do. For example, it says that the set of languages supported by the format-date() function is implementation defined. This can be interpreted in two ways:

❑ Vendors can support as many or as few languages as they think their target market requires.

❑ Vendors are allowed (but not required) to provide localization mechanisms that enable users or third parties to extend the set of supported languages.

Nowhere in the XSLT specification does it say that implementers must provide facilities for users to define their own extensions. Many implementations will choose to do so, but to find out what extensibility is permitted by the language, we need to look at two things: firstly, the set of information that is defined to be part of the context or environment, and secondly, the features of the language whose behavior is implementation defined. There are detailed lists of these features in the W3C specification, but they fall into a few broad categories.

❑ Some features of the language are optional, in the sense that conformant processors are not required to provide them. For example, a processor can choose not to implement schema-aware processing, and it can choose not to implement the disable-output-escaping attribute or the namespace axis in XPath.

❑ Interfaces between the XSLT processor and the outside world are generally implementation defined. This includes the mechanisms for invoking the XSLT processor and delivering its results, the mechanism for reporting errors, and the details of how URIs are interpreted in constructs such as <xsl:include>, <xsl:import>, <xsl:import-schema>, and the document() and doc() functions.

❑ The XSLT vocabulary is extensible in five key areas. In each of these cases, the vendor can extend the vocabulary and, if they wish, they can also enable users or third parties to extend it:

    ❑ *Extension functions*: The set of functions that can be called from XPath expressions, and any mechanisms for adding additional functions, are implementation defined, so long as any functions outside the language-defined core are in a separate namespace.

    ❑ *Extension instructions*: The set of instructions that can appear in a sequence constructor is extensible, so long as the namespace used for any extension instructions is declared in the stylesheet in an «extension-element-prefixes» attribute.

    ❑ *Extension attributes*: Additional attributes can be added to any XSLT element, so long as they are in a separate namespace. There are rules limiting the effect that such attributes may have: essentially, they must not change the result of the transformation except to the extent that the W3C specification leaves the result explicitly implementation defined.

    ❑ *Extension declarations*: Additional top-level declarations can be defined in the stylesheet, provided that the element name is in a separate namespace. These are subject to the same constraints as extension attributes.

    ❑ *Extension types*: Additional types can be made available. This feature is defined primarily so that extension functions can return application-oriented objects (for example, a sql:connect() function might return an object of type sql:databaseConnection), but there are no limits on how the facility might be used.

❑ The set of collations that can be used for sorting and comparing strings is implementation defined.

❑ Many localization attributes, for example those used to control the formatting of dates and numbers, have an implementation-defined range of possible values.

When the specification says that the behavior of a particular feature is *implementation-defined*, this places an onus on the vendor of a conformant product, to describe in the product documentation what choices they have made. There are also some features of the language that are *implementation dependent*: the difference here is that vendors are not expected to document the exact behavior of the product. An example of an implementation-dependent feature is the maximum depth of recursion that is permitted. This will depend on a great many factors outside the software vendor's direct control, so it's not reasonable to expect a definitive statement.

Extension Functions

Extending the library of functions that can be called from XPath expressions has proved to be by far the most important way in which vendors extend the capability of the language, and so we will concentrate most of our attention on this particular extensibility mechanism.

When Are Extension Functions Needed?

There are a number of reasons you might want to call an extension function from your stylesheet:

❑ You might want to get data held externally, perhaps in a database or in an application.

❑ You may need to access system services that are not directly available in XSLT or XPath. For example, you might want to use a random number generator, or append a record to a log file.

❑ You might want to perform a complex calculation that is cumbersome to express in XSLT, or that performs poorly. For example, if you are generating SVG graphics, you might need to use trigonometric functions such as sin() and cos(). This situation arises far less with XSLT 2.0 than it did in 1.0, because the core function library is so much richer, especially in its ability to do string manipulation and date/time arithmetic. But if the function you need is out there in some Java library, it's no crime to call it.

❑ A more questionable use of external functions is to get around the "no side effects" rule in XSLT, for example to update a counter. Avoid this if you can; if you need such facilities, then you haven't yet learned to think about solving problems in the way that is natural for XSLT. More on this in the next chapter.

There are two ways of using extension functions in XSLT. You can write your own extension functions, or you can call extension functions that already exist. These functions might be provided by your XSLT vendor, or they might come from a third-party library such as the EXSLT library found at http://www.exslt.org/ (many EXSLT functions provide capabilities that are no longer needed in 2.0, but some of them, such as the mathematical functions, are still very relevant).

Many vendors designed the interfaces for Java and JavaScript so that the extensive class libraries available in both these languages would be directly accessible to the stylesheet, with no further coding required. This is certainly true for mathematical functions, string manipulation, and date handling. Which language you choose to use to write extension functions is a matter of personal choice, though it will be heavily constrained by the XSLT processor you are using. With a Java-based processor such as

Saxon or Xalan-J, the natural choice is to write extension functions in Java. With Microsoft processors, the natural choice is a .NET language such as C#. If you are using the 4XSLT processor, it is probably because your favorite language is Python. Processors written in C or C++ tend to require a more complex procedure for linking extension functions, if they are supported at all.

When Are Extension Functions not Needed?

There is probably a tendency for newcomers to XSLT to write extension functions simply because they haven't worked out how to code the logic in an XSLT stylesheet function. Slipping back into a programming language you have used for years, rather than battling with an unfamiliar one, is always going to be tempting when you have deadlines to meet. It's understandable, but it's not the right thing to do.

There are other wrong reasons for using extension functions. These include:

❑ Believing that an XSLT implementation of the logic is bound to be slower: Don't believe this until you have proved it by measurement. Dimitre Novatchev has written XSLT functions that do numerical computations in XSLT (calculating square roots, for example) and has found that the performance can be quite acceptable. In some cases, the XSLT logic is intrinsically slower, but this may not matter, because it avoids the overhead of switching languages.

❑ Supplying external data to the stylesheet: The best way to supply information to the stylesheet is in the form of a stylesheet parameter. Another good way is to provide the data in the form of an XML document, in response to a call on the document() function (many processors allow you to write logic that intercepts the URI supplied to the document() function, or you could use a URI that invokes a servlet or a Web service).

❑ Achieving side effects: There are some side effects that are reasonably acceptable, for example writing messages to a log file—these are basically actions that do not affect the subsequent processing of the stylesheet, where the order of events is not critically important. But trying to get round the no-side-effects rule in other ways is nearly always the wrong thing to do, though it can be very tempting. Sooner or later the optimizer will rearrange your code in a way that stops your extension function working.

❑ Using XSLT as a job control language: I have seen stylesheets that consist entirely of calls to external services, effectively using XSLT as a scripting language to invoke a sequence of external tasks. XSLT wasn't designed for this role, and the fact that order of execution in XSLT is undefined makes it a very poor choice of tool for this job. Use a shell script language, or the ant utility.

Calling Extension Functions

Extension functions are always called from within an XPath expression. A typical function call looks like this:

```
my:function($arg1, 23, string(title))
```

The name of an extension function will always contain a namespace prefix and a colon. The prefix («my» in this example) must be declared in a namespace declaration on some containing element in the stylesheet, in the usual way. The function may take any number of arguments (zero or more), and the parentheses are needed even if there are no arguments. The arguments can be any XPath expressions; in our example, the first argument is a variable reference, the second is a number, and the third is a function call. The arguments are passed to the function by value, which means that the function can never modify the values of the arguments (though if you pass nodes, the function may be able to modify the contents of the nodes). The function always returns a result.

We'll have more to say about the data types of the arguments, and the data type of the result, in due course.

What Language Is Best?

Many processors offer only one language for writing extension functions (if indeed they allow extension functions at all) so the choice may already be made for you. Some processors offer a choice, for example Xalan supports both Java and JavaScript, while Microsoft supports any of the usual scripting languages, for example JScript and VBScript.

Generally, I'd suggest using the native language for your chosen processor: for example Java for Oracle, Saxon, and Xalan-J; JScript for MSXML3; Python for 4XSLT. If you want to use your stylesheet with more than one processor, write one version of the extension function for each language.

Client-Side Script

If you are generating HTML pages, your stylesheet can put anything it likes in the HTML page that it is generating. This includes <script> elements containing JavaScript code to be executed when the HTML page is displayed.

Don't get confused between this kind of script, and script that is executed in your stylesheet during the course of the transformation. It's especially easy to get the two confused when the transformation itself is running within the browser. Remember that stylesheet extension functions are always called using function calls in XPath expressions, while you are generating the HTML to be displayed. HTML <script> is always called in response to browser events such as the user clicking on a button.

Binding Extension Functions

When you call «my:function()» from within an XPath expression, the XSLT processor needs to find a suitable function to call. This process is called *binding*. The XSLT specification does not define how the binding is done, but two mechanisms have become popular, which I call explicit binding and implicit binding. Explicit binding uses a top-level declaration in the stylesheet (under a vendor-specific namespace) to define where specific functions or collections of functions are to be found, while implicit binding relies solely on the name of the function, typically using the namespace URI to identify a collection of functions, and the local name to identify the specific function within that collection.

Explicit Binding

Two popular processors that use an explicit binding technique are MSXML and Xalan. It's also available in Saxon, but rarely used.

MSXML uses a special top-level element <msxsl:script> to define extension functions, which may be written in a variety of languages, though JavaScript is the most popular.

Here is an example stylesheet that uses an extension written in VBScript, just to be different. The implementation of the function is written inline within the <msxsl:script> element.

Example: Using VBScript in an MSXML3 Stylesheet

This example shows a stylesheet that converts dimensions in inches to the equivalent in millimeters.

Source

The source file is `inches.xml`. Double-click on it in Windows Explorer to invoke the stylesheet.

```
<?xml version="1.0" encoding="iso-8859-1"?>
<?xml-stylesheet type="text/xsl" href="to-mm.xsl"?>
<dimensions>
The size of the picture is <inches>5</inches> by
<inches>12</inches>.
</dimensions>
```

Stylesheet

The stylesheet is `to-mm.xsl`.

It contains a simple VBScript function within an `<msxsl:script>` element, and invokes this as an extension function from the template rule for the `<inches>` element.

```
<xsl:stylesheet
    xmlns:xsl="http://www.w3.org/1999/XSL/Transform"
    version="1.0"
    xmlns:extra="urn:extra-functions"
>
<msxsl:script xmlns:msxsl="urn:schemas-microsoft-com:xslt"
        language="VBScript"
        implements-prefix="extra"
>

Function ToMillimetres(inches)
   ToMillimetres = inches * 25.4
End Function

</msxsl:script>

<xsl:output method="html"/>

<xsl:template match="/" >
<html><body><p>
   <xsl:apply-templates/>
</p></body></html>
</xsl:template>

<xsl:template match="inches">
   <xsl:text> </xsl:text>
   <xsl:value-of select="format-number(extra:ToMillimetres(number(.)),
                    '0.00')"/>
```

```
    <xsl:text>mm </xsl:text>
</xsl:template>

</xsl:stylesheet>
```

Output

The following text is displayed in the browser:

```
The size of the picture is 127.00mm by 304.80mm.
```

Note that this doesn't work in Netscape, which doesn't recognize the `<msxsl:script>` element.

These scripts can call COM objects named in the system registry in the usual way. However, if the stylesheet is running in the browser, the user's security settings may prevent your script from instantiating a client-side object.

Of course, this example uses an extension function to do something that could be trivially done within an XSLT 2.0 stylesheet function.

JavaScript and VBScript are both dynamically typed languages, which made them a good fit with XSLT 1.0 and XPath 1.0. However, it's easy to get tripped up by the fact that the function calling conventions aren't always what you expect. For example, both in XPath 1.0 and in 2.0, if a function in the core library such as `starts-with()` expects a string, then you can supply an attribute node, and the value of the attribute will be extracted automatically (in XPath 2.0 this process is called *atomization*). JavaScript doesn't declare the types of function parameters, which means that no such conversion is possible: if you supply an attribute node, that's what the JavaScript code will see, and if it was expecting a string, it will probably fail.

The Xalan product also supports JavaScript extension functions using a similar mechanism, but this time the binding element is `<xalan:script>`, where the «xalan» prefix represents the URI `http://xml.apache.org/xslt`. Several `<xalan:script>` elements can be grouped together in a `<xalan:component>` element.

There's nothing to stop you having an `<msxsl:script>` declaration and a `<xalan:script>` declaration in the same stylesheet. An XSLT processor is required to ignore top-level declarations in an unknown namespace, so each processor will ignore the declaration that's intended for the other. This means you can have two implementations of the same extension function in your stylesheet, one for use when you're running MSXML, another for use when running Xalan.

Implicit Binding

Most of the Java XSLT processors (Saxon, Xalan, jd.xslt, Oracle, xt) also support an implicit binding of extension functions to Java methods. This is generally based on the idea that the namespace URI used in the function identifies the Java class, and the local name of the function corresponds to the method name.

For example, the following stylesheet can be used in Saxon to calculate a square root.

Example: An Extension Function to Calculate a Square Root

This example shows a stylesheet that returns the square root of a number in the source document.

Source

The source document is `sqrt.xml`:

```
<number>2.0</number>
```

Stylesheet

The stylesheet is `sqrt.xsl`.

```
<xsl:transform
  xmlns:xsl="http://www.w3.org/1999/XSL/Transform"
  xmlns:xs="http://www.w3.org/2001/XMLSchema"
  exclude-result-prefixes="xs"
  version="2.0">

<xsl:template match="number">
  <result>
    <xsl:value-of select="Math:sqrt(xs:double(.))"
                  xmlns:Math="java:java.lang.Math"/>
  </result>
</xsl:template>

</xsl:transform>
```

Output

```
<?xml version="1.0" encoding="UTF-8"?>
<result>1.4142135623730951</result>
```

This stylesheet calls an external function `Math:sqrt()`, where the namespace prefix «Math» is bound to the namespace URI «java:java.lang.Math». Saxon recognizes namespace URIs beginning with «java:» as special—the part of the URI after the «java:» is interpreted as a Java class name. The processor loads this Java class and looks to see whether it contains a static method called «sqrt» that can take an argument that is a double. It does, so this method is called, and the result is taken as the return value from the function call.

Although each of the Java XSLT processors supports implicit bindings of Java methods to extension functions in much this kind of way, the details vary from one processor to another, and it may be difficult to write code that is completely portable across processors. In particular, processors are likely to vary in how they map between the XPath data types and Java data types. This is especially true if the Java class contains several methods of the same name, but with different argument types (method overloading). To find out the detail of how each processor handles this, you will need to consult the documentation for your specific product.

Most of what I've said so far about extension functions applies equally to XSLT 1.0 and XSLT 2.0. In fact, most of the processors mentioned do not yet have an XSLT 2.0 version. So it remains to be seen how vendors will tackle the challenge of mapping the much richer type system in XSLT 2.0 to Java classes.

Many XSLT 1.0 processors allow a call on a Java method to return a wrapped Java object, which can then be supplied as an argument to another extension function. For example, you might have a function `sql:connect()` that returns an object of type "SQL connection," and another function `sql:query()` that accepts a SQL connection as its first argument. In XSLT 1.0, with its limited type system, this object is generally modeled using a single extra data type "external object." With XSLT 2.0, it is possible to go further than this and implicitly import any number of user-defined types into the stylesheet. Saxon takes this to its logical extreme, and implicitly imports the whole of the Java class hierarchy, mapping class names into the namespace `http://saxon.sf.net/java-type`. The result is that (assuming the prefix «class» is bound to this namespace) you can declare a variable such as:

```
<xsl:variable name="connection" as="class:java.sql.Connection"
              select="sql:connect(...)"/>
```

This means that these external objects can be used with complete type safety, because the Java class hierarchy has been mapped to the XSLT/XPath type hierarchy.

Generally, processors map the common data types into their obvious equivalent in the external programming language. For example, in Java, an `xs:double` maps to a Java `double`; an `xs:string` to a `String`; an `xs:boolean` to a Java `boolean`; and so on. The `xs:integer` type is a little tricky because XML Schema doesn't define its maximum range; Saxon maps it to a Java `long`, but other products may make a different choice, for example «java.math.BigInteger». Bindings for the more common data types are defined in the Java Architecture for XML Binding (JAXB, see `http://java.sun.com/xml/downloads/jaxb.html`) and it's quite likely that these will be adopted by XSLT vendors, though they were not originally defined for that purpose. This doesn't currently cover the less common types like `xs:gYearMonth`, where you can certainly expect variations between products. However, there is an initiative in the Java Community Process to complete the mappings between Java classes and XML Schema data types (watch out for a package called `javax.xml.datatype` in JDK 1.5) and this may lead to further harmonization between XSLT processors.

With XSLT 1.0 (and in the draft XSLT 1.1 specification) most XSLT processors naturally followed the *weak typing* approach of implicitly converting the supplied parameters in the XPath function call to the required type declared in the Java method. Current releases of Saxon still follow this approach. However, it would be more logical to switch to a stricter model aligned with the XPath 2.0 function calling rules, where only very limited conversions between the supplied value and the required type are supported.

When the values passed to an extension function are nodes, rather than atomic values, the data mapping issues become more complicated. The accepted standard for manipulating XML trees in most languages is the DOM, and it's likely that many processors will offer extension functions the ability to manipulate nodes using the DOM interface, even though the DOM does not match the XSLT/XPath data model particularly well. This is discussed in the next section.

Chapter 8

XPath Trees and the DOM

We haven't got space in this book for a detailed description of the DOM interface, but most readers will already have come across it in some form, and it is described in detail in most good books on XML. The DOM provides an object model (and therefore an API) for navigating and manipulating XML data in tree form. Many XSLT processors allow extension functions to access nodes, using the methods defined in the DOM API.

If you want extension functions to access the XSLT source tree, or a secondary input tree that was loaded using the document () function, or even a temporary tree constructed during the course of the XSLT transformation, then you can generally do this by passing a node as one of the function arguments. The extension function can then manipulate this node, and other related nodes such as its children and parent, as objects in a DOM structure. It may also be possible for an extension function to construct a new tree, and return it (typically as a DOM Document object) to the calling XPath expression, where it can be manipulated as a secondary input tree in the same way as the result of the XSLT document () function. Some products may also allow a DOM that's passed to an extension function to be modified in situ—this is definitely a dubious practice, because it creates a dependency on order of execution, but it's not absolutely prohibited.

The only problem with using the DOM in this way is that there are many small but significant differences between the tree model used by XSLT and XPath, and the tree model defined in the DOM specification. For example, the DOM exposes entity references and CDATA sections, the XPath model doesn't.

This is exacerbated by the fact that there are two different implementation approaches adopted by XSLT vendors: both are perfectly valid and both need to be catered for. Some products, such as Microsoft MSXML3, are DOM oriented. This processor uses a DOM as its internal tree model, and provides the XPath model as a virtual data structure (a view or wrapper) on top of this. This means, for example, that CDATA sections will be physically present on the tree, and XPath operations such as following-sibling will dynamically merge the CDATA contents with the surrounding text nodes. When an extension function is called, such a product will present the native underlying DOM to the called function, CDATA nodes and all. Other products (Saxon is an example, as is the XSLT processor in Microsoft .NET) use an internal data structure that is closely aligned to the XPath model described in Chapter 2. This data structure will have discarded any information that is not needed for XPath processing, such as CDATA sections and entity references. When an external function is called, the situation is now reversed; such a product will provide the DOM interface as a wrapper on top of the native XPath model.

It's impossible to hide all the differences between these two approaches. For example, where the XSLT specifications dictate that white-space nodes must be stripped from the tree, a DOM-oriented product will probably not remove these nodes physically from the tree, but will simply hide them from XPath view. A product that uses a native XPath tree is likely to remove the unwanted white-space nodes from the tree while building the tree. This means that with one approach, the stripped white-space nodes will be present in the DOM as seen by extension functions, and with the other, they will be absent.

Another difference is that with a native XPath tree, adjacent text nodes will be merged (or normalized) into a single node, whereas with a native DOM tree, they may be unnormalized. (Actually, MSXML3 doesn't always normalize text nodes correctly even in the XPath tree view.)

What all this means is that if you want your extension functions to be fully portable between different processors, you have to be aware of these possible differences, and work around them. The following table lists the areas of potential differences between the DOM view and the XPath view.

XPath Node	DOM Node	Correspondence
Document	Document	One to one.
Element	Element	One to one.
Attribute	Attr	The XPath tree never represents namespace declarations as attributes named `xmlns` or `xmlns:*`. The DOM might or might not have such `Attr` nodes. If the source document used entity references within the attribute value, these might or might not be preserved in the DOM. The value of the `getSpecified` property in the DOM is unpredictable.
Text	Text	The DOM text nodes might or might not be normalized. If CDATA sections were used in the original document, CDATA nodes might or might not be present in the DOM. If the source document used entity references within the text value, these might or might not be preserved in the DOM. Whitespace nodes that have been stripped as far as XSLT processing is concerned might or might not be present as text nodes in the DOM.
Processing instruction	Processing instruction	One to one.
Comment	Comment	One to one.
Namespace	N/A	There is no direct equivalent in the DOM to XPath's namespace nodes. It is possible in a DOM for elements and attributes to use namespace URIs that are not declared anywhere on the tree.
N/A	CDATA section	CDATA section nodes may be present on the DOM tree if this is the native data structure used by the processor, but they are unlikely to be present if the processor constructs a DOM from the XPath tree.
N/A	Entity reference	Entity reference nodes may be present on the DOM tree if this is the native data structure used by the processor, but they are unlikely to be present if the processor constructs a DOM from the XPath tree.

When you call methods defined in the DOM, the result will follow the DOM rules, not the XPath rules. For example, in XPath the string value of an element node is the concatenation of all the text content within that element; but in the DOM, the apparently similar `nodeValue()` method returns `null`.

It's not a good idea to attempt to update a DOM that is passed to an extension function. Three things might happen, depending on the implementation:

❑ The attempt to update the DOM may cause an exception.

❑ If the DOM was constructed as a copy of the XPath tree, the updates may succeed, but have no effect on the tree as seen subsequently within the stylesheet.

❑ If the DOM and the XPath tree are different views of the same data, then updates may affect the subsequent XSLT processing. This might cause subsequent failures, for example if nodes have been deleted while the XSLT processor holds references to them.

Constructing a new tree, in the form of a DOM, and returning this to the stylesheet as the result of the extension function, is perfectly OK if the implementation allows it.

These rules for the mapping of XPath trees probably seem rather complicated, and there are certainly lots of potential pitfalls. My own advice would be to steer clear of this area if you possibly can. Navigating around the tree is something you can do perfectly well within XSLT and XPath; you don't need to escape into a different language for this. It's simpler, and usually quite adequate, to pass simple strings and numbers to your extension functions.

If you want to write an extension function that constructs and returns a new tree, you might well find that a simpler alternative is to call the `document()` function and implement a URIResolver (or in .NET, an `XmlResolver`) that takes the URI provided in this call, and returns the relevant data source. The JAXP URIResolver interface is described in Appendix D, and an overview of the .NET transformation API is in Appendix C.

Calling External Functions within a Loop

I wanted to show an example that includes a reasonably realistic stylesheet with multiple calls on extension functions. It turns out that all the examples I used for this in XSLT 1.0 are things that can be done quite straightforwardly with standard facilities in XSLT 2.0. However, with this caveat, I've decided to retain this example to show the principles.

This example is specific to the Saxon processor. It can be made to work with any processor that supports Java extension functions, but it will need minor alterations.

Example: Calling External Functions within a Loop

In this example, we will use a Java `BufferedReader` object to read an external file, copying it to the output one line at a time, each line being followed by an empty `<br/>` element. (The alternative way of doing this would be to read the file using the `unparsed-text()` function described in Chapter 7, and then to break it into its lines using `<xsl:analyze-string>`.)

Source

This stylesheet doesn't need a primary source document.

The real input is a serial file, which can be any text file. For example, the following `hiawatha.txt`:

```
Take your bow, O Hiawatha,
Take your arrows, jasper-headed,
Take your war-club, Puggawaugun,
And your mittens, Minjekahwan,
And your birch-canoe for sailing,
And the oil of Mishe-Nama.
```

Stylesheet

The stylesheet can be downloaded as `reader.xsl`.

First we declare the namespaces we will need. It's often easiest to declare these namespaces on the `<xsl:stylesheet>` element itself. I shall stick to the convention of using the same «`java:*`» URI to identify the name of the Java class, and I will also use the abbreviated class name as the namespace prefix. You won't usually want these namespaces appearing in the result document, so you can suppress them using `exclude-result-prefixes`.

```
<xsl:stylesheet
    xmlns:xsl="http://www.w3.org/1999/XSL/Transform"
    version="2.0"
    xmlns:FileReader="java:java.io.FileReader"
    xmlns:BufferedReader="java:java.io.BufferedReader"
    exclude-result-prefixes="FileReader BufferedReader">
```

The name of the file we want to read from will be supplied as a parameter to the stylesheet.

```
<xsl:param name="filename"/>
```

When we are ready to read the file, we create the `BufferedReader` in a variable. Then we call a template to read the file, line by line.

```
<xsl:template name="main">
<out>
    <xsl:variable name="reader"
            select="BufferedReader:new(FileReader:new($filename))"/>
    <xsl:call-template name="read-lines">
        <xsl:with-param name="reader" select="$reader"/>
    </xsl:call-template>
</out>
</xsl:template>
```

The `read-lines` template reads and outputs the first line of the file, and then calls itself recursively to process the remainder. The `readLine()` method of the `BufferedReader` class returns `null` to indicate that the end of file has been reached, and in Saxon, a Java null is translated to a return value of an empty sequence. So we test whether to continue the recursion using the test «`exists($line)`», which returns `false` when the return value was null.

```
<xsl:template name="read-lines">
    <xsl:param name="reader"/>
    <xsl:variable name="line"
                    select="BufferedReader:readLine($reader)"/>
    <xsl:if test="exists($line)">
        <xsl:value-of select="$line"/><br/>
        <xsl:call-template name="read-lines">
            <xsl:with-param name="reader" select="$reader"/>
        </xsl:call-template>
    </xsl:if>
</xsl:template>
</xsl:stylesheet>
```

Note that this template is tail-recursive: it does no further work after calling itself. This means that a processor that provides tail-call optimization should be able to handle arbitrary long input files. A processor without this feature may fail with a stack overflow, perhaps after reading 500 or 1000 lines of text.

Output

When you run this stylesheet, you need to supply a value for the filename parameter. For example:

```
java net.sf.saxon.Transform -it main reader.xsl filename=hiawatha.txt
```

This command line invokes Saxon without a source document, specifying «main» as the name of the first template to be executed, and «hiawatha.txt» as the value of the «filename» parameter.

The output looks like this, adding newlines for clarity.

```
<?xml version="1.0" encoding="UTF-8"?>
<out>
Take your bow, O Hiawatha,<br/>
Take your arrows, jasper-headed,<br/>
Take your war-club, Puggawaugun,<br/>
And your mittens, Minjekahwan,<br/>
And your birch-canoe for sailing,<br/>
And the oil of Mishe-Nama.<br/>
</out>
```

In this example, the function call does have side effects, because the $reader variable is an external Java object that holds information about the current position in the file being read, and advances this position each time a line is read from the file. In general, function calls with side effects are dangerous, because XSLT does not define the order in which statements are executed. But in this case, the logic of the stylesheet is such that an XSLT processor would have to be very devious indeed to execute the statements in any order other than the obvious one. The fact that the recursive call on the read-lines template is within an <xsl:if> instruction that tests the $line variable means that the processor is forced to read a line, test the result, and then, if necessary, make the recursive call to read further lines.

The next example uses side effects in a much less controlled way, and in this case causes results that will vary from one XSLT processor to another.

Functions with Uncontrolled Side Effects

Just to illustrate the dangers of using functions with side effects, we'll include an example where the effects are not predictable.

Example: A Function with Uncontrolled Side Effects

This example shows how a processor can call extension functions in an unpredictable order, causing incorrect results if the functions have side effects. This can apply even when the extension function is apparently read-only.

Source

Like the previous example, this stylesheet doesn't use a source document.

In this example we'll read an input file containing names and addresses, for example `addresses.txt`. We'll assume this file is created by a legacy application and consists of groups of five lines. Each group contains a customer number on the first line, the customer's name on the second, an address on lines three and four, and a telephone number on line five. Because that's the way legacy data files often work, we'll assume that the last line of the file contains the string «****».

```
15668
Mary Cousens
15 Birch Drive
Wigan
01367-844355
17796
John Templeton
17 Spring Gardens
Wolverhampton
01666-932865
19433
Jane Arbuthnot
92 Mountain Avenue
Swansea
01775-952266
****
```

Stylesheet

We might be tempted to write the stylesheet as follows (`addresses.xsl`), modifying the previous example:

```
<xsl:stylesheet
    xmlns:xsl="http://www.w3.org/1999/XSL/Transform" version="2.0"
    xmlns:FileReader="java:java.io.FileReader"
    xmlns:BufferedReader="java:java.io.BufferedReader"
    exclude-result-prefixes="FileReader BufferedReader">

<xsl:output indent="yes"/>
<xsl:param name="filename"/>
```

```
<xsl:template name="main">
  <xsl:variable name="reader"
             select="BufferedReader:new(FileReader:new($filename))"/>
  <xsl:call-template name="read-addresses">
      <xsl:with-param name="reader" select="$reader"/>
  </xsl:call-template>
</xsl:template>

<xsl:template name="read-addresses">
  <xsl:param name="reader"/>
  <xsl:variable name="line1"
              select="BufferedReader:readLine ($reader)"/>
  <xsl:if test="$line1 != '****'">
    <xsl:variable name="line2"
                select="BufferedReader:readLine($reader)"/>
    <xsl:variable name="line3"
                select="BufferedReader:readLine($reader)"/>
    <xsl:variable name="line4"
                select="BufferedReader:readLine($reader)"/>
    <xsl:variable name="line5"
                select="BufferedReader:readLine($reader)"/>
    <label>
      <address>
        <xsl:value-of select="$line3"/><br/>
        <xsl:value-of select="$line4"/><br/>
      </address>
      <recipient>Attn: <xsl:value-of select="$line2"/></recipient>
    </label>
    <xsl:call-template name="read-addresses">
        <xsl:with-param name="reader" select="$reader"/>
    </xsl:call-template>
  </xsl:if>
</xsl:template>
</xsl:stylesheet>
```

What's the difference? This time we are making an assumption that the four variables
$line2, $line3, $line4, and $line5 will be evaluated in the order we've written them.
There is no guarantee of this. The processor is quite at liberty, for example, not to evaluate a
variable until it is used, which means that $line3 will be evaluated *before* $line2, and
worse still, $line5 (because it is never used) may not be evaluated at all, meaning that
instead of reading a group of five lines from the file, the template will only read four lines
each time it is invoked.

Output

The result, in the case of Saxon, is a disaster.

```
<?xml version="1.0" encoding="UTF-8"?>
<label>
   <address>15 Birch Drive<br/>Wigan<br/>
   </address>
   <recipient>Attn: Mary Cousens</recipient>
```

```
    </label>
    <label>
        <address>John Templeton<br/>17 Spring Gardens<br/>
        </address>
        <recipient>Attn: 17796</recipient>
    </label>
    <label>
        <address>19433<br/>Jane Arbuthnot<br/>
        </address>
        <recipient>Attn: 01666-932865</recipient>
    </label>
    <label>
        <address>01775-952266<br/>****<br/>
        </address>
        <recipient>Attn: Swansea</recipient>
    </label>
```

Saxon doesn't evaluate a variable until you refer to it, and it doesn't evaluate the variable at all if you never refer to it. This becomes painfully visible in the output, which reveals that it's simply not safe for an XSLT stylesheet to make assumptions about the order of execution of different instructions.

This stylesheet might work on some XSLT processors, but it certainly won't work on all.

The correct way to tackle this stylesheet in XSLT 2.0 is to read the whole text using the unparsed-text() function; then to split it into lines using either <xsl:analyze-string> or the tokenize() function; and then to use grouping facilities to split it into groups of five lines each. There is no need for extension functions at all.

This example raises the question of whether there is any way you can write a call to an extension function and be sure that the call will actually be executed, given that the function is one that returns no result. It's hard to give a categorical answer to this because there is no limit on the ingenuity of optimizers to avoid doing work that makes no contribution to the result tree. However, with Saxon today a function that returns no result is treated in the same way as one that returns null, which is interpreted in XPath as an empty sequence. So you can call a void method using:

```
<xsl:sequence select="class:voidMethod()"/>
```

and provided the <xsl:sequence> instruction itself is evaluated, the method will always be called.

Keeping Extensions Portable

As soon as your stylesheet uses extension functions, or other permitted extensions such as extension instructions or extension attributes, keeping it portable across different XSLT processors becomes a challenge. Fortunately, the design of the XSLT language anticipated this problem, and offers some help.

There are a number of interrogative functions that you can use to find out about the environment that your stylesheet is running in. The most important are as follows:

❑ The system-property() function, which allows you to determine the XSLT version supported and the name and version of the XSLT processor itself.

❑ The function-available() function, which allows you to determine whether a particular extension function is available. This is particularly useful when you are using a third-party library such as EXSLT, where the same functions may be available under a number of different XSLT processors.

Use these functions to test whether particular vendor extensions are available before calling them. The best way to do this is using the new «use-when» attribute described in Chapter 3, which allows a section of the stylesheet (perhaps a whole template, perhaps a single <xsl:value-of> instruction) to be conditionally included or excluded from the stylesheet at compile time. For example, the following code sets a variable to the result of the random:random-sequence() function (defined in EXSLT) if it is available, or to the fractional seconds value from the current time if not.

```
<xsl:variable name="random-number"
              select="seconds-from-time(current-time()) mod 1.0e0"
              use-when="not(function-available('random:random-sequence', 2))"
              xmlns:random="http://exslt.org/random"/>
<xsl:variable name="random-number"
              select="random:random-sequence(1, ())"
              use-when="function-available('random:random-sequence', 2)"
              xmlns:random="http://exslt.org/random"/>
```

(In fact, the «use-when» attribute on the first <xsl:variable> declaration is not strictly needed, assuming these are local variables. If the «use-when» attribute on the second variable evaluates to true, this variable will shadow the first variable, and it does no harm for both variables to be present.)

Note that the rules for the «use-when» attribute require it to be a condition that can be evaluated at compile time. It's therefore not permitted in this expression to reference the values of variables or stylesheet parameters, or to access the contents of a source document.

You can use similar techniques to make a stylesheet portable between different XSLT versions. In this case there are additional facilities available, notably the [xsl:]version attribute, which can be attached to any element in the stylesheet. Version compatibility is fully discussed in Chapter 3, on page 123.

Summary

Extension functions are useful to extend the capabilities of XSLT stylesheets. They allow stylesheets to access external system services, and to perform calculations that are difficult or inefficient to achieve in "pure" XSLT and XPath.

There are other extensibility mechanisms in XSLT, including extension instructions, extension declarations, and extension attributes, but extension functions are by far the most widely used, so that's what we concentrated on in this chapter.

In the next chapter, we move away from detailed specifications of interfaces, and look at using the facilities of XSLT to create well-designed stylesheets.

9

Stylesheet Design Patterns

This chapter looks at four common design patterns for XSLT stylesheets.

The concept of design patterns was introduced by Erich Gamma, Richard Helm, Ralph Johnson, and John Vlissides in their classic book *Design Patterns: Elements of Reusable Object-Oriented Software* (Addison-Wesley Publishing, 1995). Their idea was that there was a repertoire of techniques that were useful again and again. They presented 23 different design patterns for object-oriented programming, claiming not that this was a complete list, but that the vast majority of programs written by experienced designers fell into one or more of these patterns.

For XSLT stylesheets, the vast majority of stylesheets I have seen fall into one of four design patterns. These are as follows:

- ❑ Fill-in-the-blanks stylesheets
- ❑ Navigational stylesheets
- ❑ Rule-based stylesheets
- ❑ Computational stylesheets

Again, this doesn't mean that these are the only ways you can write stylesheets, nor does it mean that any stylesheet you write must follow one of these four patterns to the exclusion of the other three. It just means that a great many stylesheets actually written by experienced people follow one of these four patterns, and if you become familiar with these patterns, you will have a good repertoire of techniques that you can apply to solving any given problem.

I describe the first three design patterns rather briefly, because they are not really very difficult. The fourth, the computational design pattern, is explored in much greater depth—not because it is encountered more often, but because it requires a different way of thinking about algorithms than you use with conventional procedural programming languages.

Fill-in-the-Blanks Stylesheets

Many proprietary templating languages have been built up around HTML. The template looks largely like a standard HTML file, but with the addition of extra tags used to retrieve variable data and insert it at a particular point in the HTML data page. The designers of XSLT took care to ensure that in spite of the power of XSLT as a full transformation language, it would still be possible to use it in this simple way, bringing it within the reach of nonprogrammers with HTML authoring skills.

Example: A "Fill-in-the-Blanks" Stylesheet

Here's an example of such a stylesheet. It uses the *simplified stylesheet* syntax, so the `<xsl:stylesheet>` element and the `<xsl:template match="/">` element are implicit.

Input

This XML document, `orgchart.xml`, represents an organization chart showing the senior management of a certain company at a particular date. It is organized as a recursive structure that directly reflects the management hierarchy. You may recognize the names, but the roles are entirely fictitious.

```xml
<?xml version="1.0" encoding="iso-8859-1"?>
<orgchart date="2004-03-31">
<person>
<name>Tim Berners-Lee</name>
<title>Chief Executive Officer</title>
<reports>
    <person>
        <name>Sharon Adler</name>
        <title>Technical Director</title>
        <reports>
            <person>
                <name>Tim Bray</name>
                <title>Chief Engineer</title>
            </person>
            <person>
                <name>James Clark</name>
                <title>Director of Research</title>
            </person>
        </reports>
    </person>
    <person>
        <name>Henry Thompson</name>
        <title>Operations and Finance</title>
    </person>
    <person>
        <name>David Megginson</name>
        <title>Human Resources</title>
    </person>
    <person>
        <name>Steve Muench</name>
        <title>Marketing</title>
    </person>
    <person>
        <name>Scott Boag</name>
```

```
        <title>International</title>
     </person>
  </reports>
</person>
```

Stylesheet

There are many creative ways to display this data; for example, you could use SVG graphics, explorer-style trees implemented in client-side JavaScript, or just indented lists. I'm not trying to teach you any clever HTML tricks, so in this stylesheet (orgchart.xsl) I'll show the data instead as a rather boring table, with one row per person, and three columns for the person's name, their title, and the name of their boss.

```
<html xmlns:xsl="http://www.w3.org/1999/XSL/Transform"
   xsl:version="2.0">
<head>
   <title>Management Structure</title>
</head>
<body>
   <h1>Management Structure</h1>
   <p>The following responsibilities were announced on
      <xsl:value-of select="format-date(/orgchart/@date,
                                 '[D1] [MNn] [Y1]')"/>:</p>
   <table border="2" cellpadding="5">
   <tr>
     <th>Name</th><th>Role</th><th>Reporting to</th>
   </tr>
   <xsl:for-each select="//person">
      <tr>
         <td><xsl:value-of select="name"/></td>
         <td><xsl:value-of select="title"/></td>
         <td><xsl:value-of select="ancestor::person[1]/name"/></td>
      </tr>
   </xsl:for-each>
   </table>
   <hr/>
</body>
</html>
```

The key to this design pattern is that the stylesheet has the same structure as the desired output. Fixed content is included directly in the stylesheet as text or as literal result elements, while variable content is included by means of <xsl:value-of> instructions that extract the relevant data from the source document. Repeated sections of output, typically rows in a table or items in a list, can be enclosed by <xsl:for-each>, and conditional sections by <xsl:if> or <xsl:choose>.

Output

The output of this stylesheet is shown in Figure 9-1.

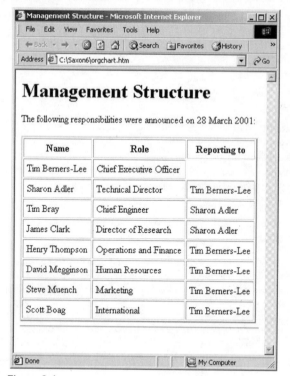

Figure 9-1

This kind of stylesheet makes very limited use of XSLT's power, but it is very similar to a wide variety of proprietary templating languages currently in use. Experience has shown that this kind of stylesheet is easy for experienced HTML authors to write, even if they have no programming training. This is an important consideration, because on many larger Web sites there is a constant need to introduce new page templates at very short notice, and this becomes much easier to achieve if content authors and editors can do the work themselves.

One restriction, of course, is that the input has to come from an XML document. This contrasts with most of the proprietary languages, where the input often comes directly from a relational database. Fortunately all popular relational databases now provide convenient ways to extract data from a database in XML form. Ideally, this doesn't even need to be a serial XML document that has to be re-parsed by the XSLT processor. It will often be possible to transfer the data directly from the database to the XSLT processor in a structured form, for example as a DOM tree in memory or as a SAX event stream. The details of how to do this depend on the database product you are using, and are beyond the scope of this book.

Another approach is to use the document() function (described in Chapter 7, page 532) with a URI that addresses a servlet with parameters to retrieve the required data.

Navigational Stylesheets

Navigational stylesheets are a natural progression from simple fill-in-the-blanks stylesheets.

Like fill-in-the-blanks stylesheets, a navigational stylesheet is still essentially output oriented. However, it is now likely to use named templates or stylesheet functions as subroutines to perform commonly needed tasks; it may use variables to calculate values needed in more than one place, and it may use constructs such as keys, parameters, and sorting.

Whereas a fill-in-the-blanks stylesheet looks like HTML sprinkled with a few extra control statements, a navigational stylesheet (once you look beyond the angle-bracket syntax) has a rather similar structure to a conventional procedural program with variables, conditional statements, for loops, and subroutine calls.

Navigational stylesheets are often used to produce reports on data-oriented XML documents, where the structure of the source document is regular and predictable.

Example: A Navigational Stylesheet

This example shows the use of a navigational stylesheet to produce a very simple sales report.

Input

Suppose the source document, `booklist.xml`, looks like this:

```
<?xml version="1.0" encoding="iso-8859-1"?>
<booklist>
    <book>
        <title>Angela's Ashes</title>
        <author>Frank McCourt</author>
        <publisher>HarperCollins</publisher>
        <isbn>0 00 649840 X</isbn>
        <price>6.99</price>
        <sales>235</sales>
    </book>
    <book>
        <title>Sword of Honour</title>
        <author>Evelyn Waugh</author>
        <publisher>Penguin Books</publisher>
        <isbn>0 14 018967 X</isbn>
        <price>12.99</price>
        <sales>12</sales>
    </book>
</booklist>
```

Stylesheet

The following navigational stylesheet (`booksales.xsl`) produces a report on the total number of sales for each publisher.

```
<xsl:stylesheet
    xmlns:xsl="http://www.w3.org/1999/XSL/Transform"
    xmlns:xs="http://www.w3.org/2001/XMLSchema"
    exclude-result-prefixes="xs"
    version="2.0">

<xsl:key name="pub" match="book" use="publisher"/>
```

We need to declare a variable that refers to the input document, for later use in a named template that has no context node.

```
<xsl:variable name="in" select="/"/>
```

The global variable «$publishers» is a sequence of strings containing one string for each distinct publisher found in the source file. This uses the new distinct-values() function introduced in XPath 2.0.

```
<xsl:variable name="publishers" as="xs:string*"
   select="distinct-values(/booklist/book/publisher)"/>
```

The main template iterates over the distinct publishers using <xsl:for-each>.

```
<xsl:template match="/">
<html>
<head>
   <title>Sales volume by publisher</title>
</head>
<body>
   <h1>Sales volume by publisher</h1>
   <table id="{generate-id(.)}">
      <tr>
         <th>Publisher</th><th>Total Sales Value</th>
      </tr>
      <xsl:for-each select="$publishers">
      <tr>
      <td><xsl:value-of select="."/></td>
      <td><xsl:call-template name="total-sales"/></td>
      </tr>
   </xsl:for-each>
   </table>
</body>
</html>
</xsl:template>
```

Finally, a named template that calculates the total sales for the publisher. The name of the publisher is supplied as an implicit parameter in the context node; however, to make the template more reusable a parameter is declared with this as the default.

```
<xsl:template name="total-sales">
   <xsl:param name="publisher" select="."/>
   <xsl:value-of select="sum($in/key('pub', $publisher)/sales)"/>
</xsl:template>
</xsl:stylesheet>
```

This stylesheet is not very far removed from the fill-in-the-blanks example earlier in the chapter. But because it uses some top-level elements such as <xsl:key> and a named template, it now needs to use the full syntax with an <xsl:stylesheet> element.

Output

```
<html>
   <head>
      <META http-equiv="Content-Type" content="text/html;
```

```
    charset=utf-8">
        <title>Sales volume by publisher</title>
    </head>
    <body>
        <h1>Sales volume by publisher</h1>
        <table>
          <tr>
            <th>Publisher</th>
            <th>Total Sales Value</th>
          </tr>
          <tr>
            <td>HarperCollins</td>
            <td>235</td>
          </tr>
          <tr>
            <td>Penguin Books</td>
            <td>12</td>
          </tr>
        </table>
    </body>
</html>
```

The obvious difference between a fill-in-the-blanks stylesheet and this navigational stylesheet is that the `<xsl:stylesheet>` and `<xsl:template>` elements are now explicit, which makes it possible to introduce other top-level elements, such as `<xsl:key>` and global `<xsl:variable>` elements. More subtly, the range of XSLT features used means that this stylesheet has crossed the boundary from being an HTML document with added control instructions, to being a real program. The boundary, though, is a rather fuzzy one, with no visa required to cross it, so many people who have learned to write simple fill-in-the-blanks stylesheets should be able, as they expand their knowledge, to progress to writing navigational stylesheets of this kind.

Although the use of flow-of-control instructions like `<xsl:if>`, `<xsl:call-template>`, and `<xsl:for-each>` gives such a stylesheet a procedural feel, it does not violate the original concept that XSLT should be a declarative language. This is because the instructions do not have to be executed in the order they are written—variables can't be updated, so the result of one instruction can't affect the next one. For example, it's easy to think of the `<xsl:for-each>` instruction in this example processing the selected nodes in document order and adding them one by one to the result tree; but it would be equally valid for an XSLT processor to process them in reverse order, or in parallel, so long as the nodes are added to the result tree in the right place. That's why I was careful to call this design pattern *navigational* rather than *procedural*. It's navigational in that you say exactly where to find the nodes in the source tree that you want to visit, but it's not procedural, because you don't define the order in which you will visit them.

New features available in XSLT 2.0 and XPath 1.0 greatly increase the scope of what can be achieved with a navigational stylesheet. Many problems that in XSLT 1.0 required complex programming (using the computational design pattern described later in this chapter) can now be tacked within the navigational approach. Examples include grouping problems, and problems that require splitting up of text fields, using delimiters such as commas or newlines, as well as many arithmetic operations such as summing the total value of an invoice. The features that provide this capability include the following:

- ❑ The availability of sequences in the data model, together with the «for» expression in Xpath, to manipulate them.

- ❑ Grouping constructs, including the `<xsl:for-each-group>` instruction in XSLT 2.0 and the `distinct-values()` function in XPath 2.0.

- ❑ Text manipulation facilities, notably the `<xsl:analyze-string>` instruction in XSLT 2.0 and the `replace()` and `tokenize()` functions in XPath 2.0.

- ❑ Aggregation functions such as `avg()`, `min()`, and `max()`.

The ability to write chunks of reusable code in the form of stylesheet functions that can be invoked from XPath expressions, rather than only as templates to be called using XSLT instructions, also helps to make navigational stylesheets much easier to write.

Rule-Based Stylesheets

A rule-based stylesheet consists primarily of rules describing how different features of the source document should be processed, such as "if you find a `<species>` element, display it in italic."

Some would say that this rule-based approach is the essence of the XSLT language, the principal way that it is intended to be used. I would say that it's one way of writing stylesheets, often the best way, but not the only way, and not necessarily the best answer in every situation. It's often strongly recommended in books for beginners, but I think that the main reason for this is that for many beginners the navigational pattern is what comes naturally, because it has a very similar feel to programs written in procedural languages. It's important that every XSLT programmer be comfortable with writing rule-based stylesheets, so it makes sense to teach this approach early on.

Unlike navigational stylesheets, a rule-based stylesheet is not structured according to the desired output layout. In fact, it makes minimal assumptions about the structure of either the source document or the result document. Rather, the structure reads like an inventory of components that might be encountered in the source document, arranged in arbitrary order.

Rule-based stylesheets are therefore most useful when processing source documents whose structure is flexible or unpredictable, or which may change a lot in the future. It is very useful when the same repertoire of elements can appear in many different document structures, so a rule like "display dates in the format *23 March 2004*" can be reused in many different contexts.

Rule-based stylesheets are a natural evolution of CSS and CSS2. In CSS, you can define rules of the form "for this set of elements, use this display rendition." In XSLT, the rules become much more flexible, in two directions: the pattern language for defining which elements you are talking about is much richer; and the actions you can define when the rule is fired are vastly more wide-ranging.

A simple rule-based stylesheet consists of one rule for each element name. The typical rule matches a particular element name, outputs an HTML tag to define the rendition of that element, and calls `<xsl:apply-templates>` to process the child nodes of the element. This causes text nodes within the element to be copied to the output, and nested child elements to be processed each according to its own template rule. In its simplest form, a rule-based stylesheet often contains many rules of the form:

```
<xsl:template match="para">
  <p><xsl:apply-templates/></p>
</xsl:template>
```

This simple rule does a direct replacement of <para> tags by <p> tags. Most real stylesheets do something a bit more elaborate with some of the tags, but they may still contain many rules that are as simple as this one.

XSLT 2.0 introduces the ability to define rules that match elements and attributes by their type, as defined in a schema, rather than simply by their name or context. This makes the technique even more powerful when handling document structures that are highly complex or extensible. For example, you can match all the elements in a particular substitution group with a single template rule, which means that the stylesheet doesn't need to change when new elements are added to the substitution group later. Similarly, you can define a template rule that formats all elements containing part numbers or dates, irrespective of the element or attribute name.

Example: A Rule-Based Stylesheet

Rule-based stylesheets are often used to process narrative documents, where most of the processing consists in replacing XML tags by HTML tags. This example illustrates this by showing how a Shakespeare play can be rendered in HTML.

Input

The input scene2.xml is a scene from a play; Act I, Scene 2 of Shakespeare's *Othello*. It starts like this:

```
<?xml version="1.0" encoding="iso-8859-1" ?>
<SCENE>
    <TITLE>SCENE II. Another street.</TITLE>
    <STAGEDIR>Enter OTHELLO, IAGO, and Attendants with
                torches</STAGEDIR>
    <SPEECH>
        <SPEAKER>IAGO</SPEAKER>
        <LINE>Though in the trade of war I have slain men,</LINE>
        <LINE>Yet do I hold it very stuff o' the conscience</LINE>
        <LINE>To do no contrived murder: I lack iniquity</LINE>
        <LINE>Sometimes to do me service: nine or ten times</LINE>
        <LINE>I had thought to have yerk'd him here under the
                ribs.</LINE>
    </SPEECH>
    <SPEECH>
        <SPEAKER>OTHELLO</SPEAKER>
        <LINE>'Tis better as it is.</LINE>
    </SPEECH>
</SCENE>
```

There are some complications that aren't shown in this sample, but which the stylesheet needs to take account of.

The top-level element is not always a <SCENE>; it might also be a <PROLOGUE> or <EPILOGUE>. The <STAGEDIR> element (representing a stage direction) can appear at any level of nesting: for example, a stage directive can appear between two speeches, between two lines of a speech, or in the middle of a line.

Several people can speak at the same time. In this case a single <SPEECH> element has more than one <SPEAKER>. In general, a <SPEECH> consists of one or more <SPEAKER> elements followed by any number of <LINE> and <STAGEDIR> elements in any order.

Stylesheet

The stylesheet scene.xsl consists of a number of template rules. It starts by declaring a global variable (used simply as a constant) and a rule for the document element.

```
<xsl:stylesheet
    xmlns:xsl="http://www.w3.org/1999/XSL/Transform"
    version="1.0"
>

<xsl:variable name="backcolor" select="'#FFFFCC'" />

<xsl:template match="SCENE|PROLOGUE|EPILOGUE">
   <HTML>
   <HEAD>
      <TITLE><xsl:value-of select="TITLE"/></TITLE>
   </HEAD>
   <BODY BGCOLOR='{$backcolor}'>
      <xsl:apply-templates/>
   </BODY>
   </HTML>
</xsl:template>
```

The appearance of <xsl:value-of> is a rare departure from the purely rule-based pattern, just to prove that none of the patterns has to be used to the exclusion of the others.

The template rule for the <SPEECH> element outputs a table containing one row and two columns: it puts the names of the speakers in the first column, and the lines of the speech, plus any stage directives, in the second, as follows:

```
<xsl:template match="SPEECH">
   <table><tr>
   <td width="160" valign="top">
      <xsl:apply-templates select="SPEAKER"/>
   </td>
   <td valign="top">
      <xsl:apply-templates select="STAGEDIR|LINE"/>
   </td>
   </tr></table>
</xsl:template>
```

The remaining template rules are straightforward. Each of them simply outputs the text of the element, using an appropriate HTML rendition. The only complication, which doesn't actually occur in this particular scene, is that for some elements (<STAGEDIR> and <SUBHEAD>) the HTML rendition is different, depending on the element's context, and so there is more than one rule defined for these elements.

```xml
<xsl:template match="TITLE">
    <h1><center>
    <xsl:apply-templates/>
    </center></h1><hr/>
</xsl:template>
<xsl:template match="SPEAKER">
    <b>
        <xsl:apply-templates/>
        <xsl:if test="not(position()=last())"><br/></xsl:if>
    </b>
</xsl:template>

<xsl:template match="SCENE/STAGEDIR">
    <center><h3>
    <xsl:apply-templates/>
    </h3></center>
</xsl:template>

<xsl:template match="SPEECH/STAGEDIR">
    <p><i>
    <xsl:apply-templates/>
    </i></p>
</xsl:template>

<xsl:template match="LINE/STAGEDIR">
    [ <i>
    <xsl:apply-templates/>
    </i> ]
</xsl:template>

<xsl:template match="SCENE/SUBHEAD">
    <center><h3>
    <xsl:apply-templates/>
    </h3></center>
</xsl:template>

<xsl:template match="SPEECH/SUBHEAD">
    <p><b>
    <xsl:apply-templates/>
    </b></p>
</xsl:template>

<xsl:template match="LINE">
    <xsl:apply-templates/>
    <br/>
</xsl:template>

</xsl:stylesheet>
```

This particular stylesheet doesn't use any XSLT 2.0 features, so I left the version number as «1.0».

Output

The output obtained is shown in Figure 9-2.

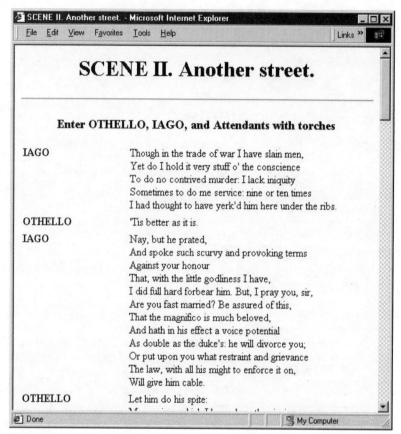

Figure 9-2

Most of the time, a rule-based stylesheet creates a result tree with a structure similar to the source tree—with most of the source text appearing in the same order in the result document, usually with different tags. The closer this describes the transformation you want to do, the closer your stylesheet will be to the example shown above. However, this doesn't mean that the processing has to be purely sequential. You can process chunks of the tree more than once using modes, you can reorder the nodes of the tree, and you can grab data from ancestor nodes, all without deviating from the rule-based design pattern.

The characteristic feature of a rule-based stylesheet is that there is generally one template rule for each class of object found in the source document. I use the term *class* very loosely here: the "classes of object" might correspond to types in a schema, or to element names, or perhaps to element names qualified by their context or content.

Of course it's possible to mix design patterns, particularly if your source document contains a mixture of "data-oriented" and "text-oriented" structures (an example might be a job application form). Then it's quite appropriate to use a navigational pattern for the regular structures and a rule-based pattern for the less regular. For example, I created a Web site that provides information about concert soloists. This contains a mixture of structured data (their name, instrument or voice, photo, and contact details), semistructured data about the performances they have taken part in, and unstructured text. The stylesheet to display the data contains a corresponding mixture of coding styles. The larger and more complex your stylesheet, the more likely it is to contain examples of each of the design patterns.

Computational Stylesheets

Computational stylesheets are the most complex of the four design patterns. They arise when there is a need to generate nodes in the result tree that do not correspond directly to nodes in the source tree. With XSLT 1.0, this happened most commonly when dealing with structure in the source document that is not explicit in its markup. For example:

❑   A text field in the source might consist of a comma-separated list of items that is to be displayed as a bulleted list in the output.

❑   There might be a need to generate `<section>` elements in the output where a section is not explicit in the source, but is defined as comprising an `<h1>` element and all its following sibling elements up to the next `<h1>` element.

With XSLT 2.0, many of these problems can be tackled using new facilities built in to the language: the first of these examples can be handled using `<xsl:analyze-string>`, and the second using `<xsl:for-each-group>`. However, sooner or later you will exhaust the capabilities of these constructs, and need to write a stylesheet in the form of a general-purpose program. Examples of such problems include the following:

❑   Starting a new page (or other unit) when a running total has reached some threshold value

❑   Analyzing graph-structured data, for example to see if it contains any cycles

❑   Creating graphical representations of numeric data using the vector graphics standard SVG as the output format

When you write computational stylesheets you invariably run up against the fact that XSLT does not have an assignment statement, and that it is therefore not possible to write loops in the way you are probably used to in other languages. So you need to understand some of the concepts of *functional programming*, which the following section tries to explain.

Programming without Assignment Statements

Back in 1968, the renowned computer scientist Edsger Dijkstra published a paper under the title *GoTo Statement Considered Harmful*. His thesis, suggesting that programs should be written without goto statements, shattered the world as most programmers saw it. Until then they had been familiar with early dialects of Fortran and Cobol in which the vast majority of decisions in a program were implemented by using a construct that mapped directly to the conditional jump instruction in the hardware: «if *condition* goto *label*». Even the design notation of the day, the ubiquitous flowchart drawn in pencil using a clear plastic template, represented control flow in this way.

Dijkstra argued that structured programs, written using if-then-else and while-do constructs instead of goto statements, were far less likely to contain bugs and were far more readable and therefore maintainable. The ideas were fiercely controversial at the time, especially among practicing programmers, and for years afterwards the opponents of the idea would challenge the structured programming enthusiasts with arguments of the form, "OK, so how do you do *this* without a goto statement?"

Today, however, the battle is won, and the goto statement has been consigned to history. Modern languages like Java don't provide a goto statement, and we no longer miss it.

But for just as long, there has been another group of enthusiasts telling us that assignment statements are considered harmful. Unlike Dijkstra, these evangelists have yet to convince a skeptical world that they are right, though there has always been a significant band of disciples who have seen the benefits of the approach.

This style of coding, without assignment statements, is called *Functional Programming*. The earliest and most famous functional programming language was Lisp (sometimes ridiculed as "Lots of Irritating Superfluous Parentheses"), while more modern examples include ML, Haskell, and Scheme. (See, for example, *Simply Scheme: Introducing Computer Science* by Brian Harvey and Matthew Wright, MIT Press, 1999.)

XSLT is a language without assignment statements, and although its syntax is very different from these languages, its philosophy is based on the concepts of functional programming. It is not a full-fledged functional programming language because you cannot manipulate functions in the same way as data; but in most other respects, it fits into this category of language. If you want to do anything complicated, you must get used to programming without assignment statements. At first, it probably won't be easy: just as early Fortran and Cobol programmers instinctively reached for the goto statement as the solution to every problem, if your background is in languages like C or Visual Basic or even Java you will just as naturally cherish the assignment statement as your favorite all-purpose tool.

So what's wrong with assignment statements, and why aren't they available in XSLT?

The crux of the argument is that it's the assignment statements that impose a particular order of execution on a program. Without assignment statements, we can do things in any order, because the result of one statement can no longer depend on what state the system was left in by the previous statement. Just as the goto statement mirrors the "jump" instruction in the hardware, so the assignment statement mirrors the "store" instruction, and the reason we have assignment statements in our programming languages today is that they were designed to take advantage of sequential von Neumann computers with jump and store instructions. If we want to free ourselves from sequential thinking modeled on sequential hardware architecture, we should find a way of describing what effect we want to achieve, rather than saying what sequence of steps the machine should take in order to achieve it.

The idea of a functional program is to describe the output as a function of the input. XSLT is a transformation language; it is designed to transform an input document into an output document. So, we can regard a stylesheet as a function that defines this transformation: a stylesheet is a function $O=S(I)$ where I is the input document, S is the stylesheet, and O is the output document. Recall the statement made by James Clark at the 1995 Paris workshop, which I quoted in Chapter 1, page 28:

A DSSSL stylesheet very precisely describes a function from SGML to a flow object tree.

This concept clearly remained a key part of the XSLT vision throughout the development of the language. (And, indeed, the flow objects of DSSSL eventually became the Formatting Objects of XSL-FO.)

We're using the word *function* here in something close to its mathematical sense. Languages like Fortran and Visual Basic have borrowed the word to mean a subroutine that returns a result, but the mathematical concept of a function is not that of an algorithm or sequence of steps to be performed, rather it is a statement of a relationship. The square-root function defines a relationship between 3 and 9, namely `3=sqrt(9)`. The essence of a function is that it is a fixed, constant, reliable relationship, and evaluating it doesn't change the world. When you ask me "what's the square root of 9 if you work it out?" I can honestly reply "exactly the same as if I don't." I can say this because square root is a *pure* function, it gives the same answer whoever calls it and however often they call it, and calling it once doesn't change the answer it gives next time; in fact, it doesn't change anything.

The nice property of pure functions is that they can be called any number of times, in any order, and produce the same result every time. If I want to calculate the square root of every integer between zero and a thousand, it doesn't matter whether I start at zero and work up, or start at a thousand and work down, or whether I buy a thousand and one computers and do them all at the same time; I know I will get the same answer. Pure functions have no side effects.

An assignment statement isn't like that. The effect of an assignment statement "if you work it out" is *not* the same as if you don't. When you write «x=x+1;» (a construct, incidentally, which most of us found completely absurd when we were first introduced to programming), the effect depends very much on how often the statement is executed. When you write several assignment statements, for example

```
temp = x;
x = y;
y = temp;
```

then the effect depends on executing them in the right order.

This means, of course, that a pure function can't update external variables. As soon as we allow assignment, we become dependent on doing things in sequence, one step at a time in the right order.

Don't object-oriented languages achieve the same thing, by preventing one object updating data held in another? No, because although they prevent direct writing to private data, they allow the same effect to be achieved by `get()` and `set()` methods. An update to a variable achieved indirectly through a defined interface creates exactly the same dependence on sequence of execution as an update done directly with an assignment statement. A pure function must have no side effects; its only output is the result it returns.

The main reason that functional languages are considered ideal for a stylesheet language (or a tree transformation language, if you prefer) is not so much the ability to do things in parallel or in any order, but rather the ability to do them incrementally. We want to get away from static pages; if you're showing a map of the traffic congestion hotspots in your area, then when the data for a particular road junction changes, you want the map updated in real time, and it should be possible to do this without recalculating and redrawing the whole map. This is only possible if there's a direct relationship—a function—between what's shown at a particular place on the map display and a particular data item in the underlying database. So if we can decompose our top-level stylesheet function, $O=S(I)$, into a set of smaller, independent functions, each relating one piece of the output to one piece of the input, then we have the potential to do this on-the-fly updating.

Another benefit of this incremental approach is that when a large page of XML is downloaded from the network, the browser can start displaying parts of the output as soon as the relevant parts of the input are available. Some XSLT processors already do this: Xalan, for example, runs the transformation in parallel with the XML parsing process. If the stylesheet were a conventional program with side effects, this wouldn't be possible, because the last bit of input to arrive could change everything.

The actual "functions" in XSLT take several forms. The most obvious functions in XSLT 2.0 are the stylesheet functions written using an `<xsl:function>` element. However, templates (both named templates and template rules) also act as functions: the only real difference between an `<xsl:function>` and an `<xsl:template>` is that the former is called from an XPath expression, and the latter from an XSLT instruction.

XSLT template rules and stylesheet functions act as small, independent functions relating one piece of the output to one piece of the input. Functions and template rules in XSLT have no side effects; their output is a pure function of their input. Stylesheet functions follow this model more strictly than templates, because the only input they have is the values of the parameters to the function (plus global variables and the results of functions such as `document()`, which access the context, which cannot vary from one function call to another within a given transformation). Templates are less pure, because they also take the current position in the input document, and other context information, as implicit input parameters. But the principle is the same.

> Technically, functions in XSLT are not completely pure, because they can create nodes with distinct identity. If a function creates and returns a new node `<a/>`, then calling the function twice with the same arguments produces two elements with the same content but with different identity, which means that the expression «f() is f()» will return `false`. Fortunately, it's not too difficult for an optimizer to detect when a function has this characteristic.

It doesn't matter in what order the template rules are executed, so long as we assemble their individual outputs together in the right way to form the result tree. If part of the input changes, then we need to re-evaluate only those template rules that depend on that part of the input, slotting their outputs into the appropriate place in the output tree. In practice, of course, it's not as easy as that, and no one has yet implemented an incremental stylesheet processor that works like this. However, many XSLT processors do take advantage of the freedom to change the order of evaluation, by using a technique known as *lazy evaluation*.

Lazy evaluation means, in general, that expressions are not evaluated until their values are actually needed. This gives two benefits: firstly, it avoids allocating memory to hold the results. (Although modern machines have vast amounts of memory, processing large XSLT documents can be very memory intensive, and the overhead of allocating and de-allocating memory dynamically accounts for a lot of the cost of XSLT processing.) Secondly, lazy evaluation sometimes means that an expression doesn't need to be evaluated at all. To take a simple example, in a function call such as «`string-join($sequence, $separator)`», there is no need to evaluate the second argument unless the first argument is a sequence containing two or more items.

Meanwhile, while the researchers and product developers work out how to optimize XSLT execution using incremental and parallel evaluation, you as a user are left with a different problem: learning how to program without assignment statements. After this rather lengthy digression into computer science theory, in the next section I shall get my feet back on the ground and show you some examples of how to do this.

However, first let's try and separate this from another programming challenge that arose with XSLT 1.0, namely the limited number of data types available. This restriction has been greatly eased in XSLT 2.0, now that arbitrary sequences are available in the data model. In terms of language design principles, the lack of assignment statements and the absence of a rich type system are quite separate matters. With XSLT 1.0, you often hit the two issues together:

❑ The only effect a template could have was via the output it produced (because of the ban on side effects).

❑ And the only output it could produce, if you wanted to process it further, was a character string (because of the limited range of data types available).

However, in XSLT 2.0 it becomes possible for a template to construct an arbitrary sequence or a tree, which can be used as input to further stages of processing. These data structures are about as versatile as you can get, so the second problem is really a thing of the past. With XSLT 1.0, you could often get around the problem by representing complex data in the form of character strings (or by using the `exslt:node-set()` function available in many processors), but the introduction of temporary trees and sequences in XSLT 2.0 greatly reduces the contortions that are necessary to implement complex algorithms in your transformations.

So Why Are They Called Variables?

XSLT, as we have seen, does have variables that can hold values. You can initialize a variable to a value, but what you can't do is change the value of an existing variable once it has been initialized.

People sometimes ask, why call it a variable if you can't vary it? The answer lies in the traditional mathematical use of the word *variable*: a variable is a symbol that can be used to denote different values on different occasions. When I say "area = length × breadth," then *area*, *length*, and *breadth* are names or symbols used to denote values: here, they denote properties of a rectangle. They are variables because these values are different every time I apply the formula, not because a given rectangle is changing size as I watch.

Cheating

Just occasionally, you may feel that programming without assignment statements is too mind-boggling, or too slow. In these cases you may be tempted to cheat.

Most XSLT processors actually allow user-written extension functions to have side effects, and some even describe in their documentation how to exploit this feature to implement a substitute for updateable variables.

The Saxon product goes one step further, and provides an extension element `<saxon:assign>` that allows you to update a variable directly.

Since I've just spent several pages explaining why side-effect-free languages are a "good thing," you might find it surprising that I should put a feature in my own product that destroys the principle at a stroke. I have several excuses:

(a) At the time I did it, XSLT was far less advanced as a functional programming language than it finally became.

(b) I thought that although side-effect-free programming is a good thing in theory, many users wouldn't be ready for it.

(c) I wanted to experiment to see whether the costs (in performance and usability) of the pure functional approach exceeded the benefits, and the best way to do this was to launch a genetically modified variant of the language into the wild and see whether the mutation thrived.

In fact, I hardly ever use `<saxon:assign>`, and the same goes for the vast majority of Saxon users. It has proved a difficult feature to maintain because it prevents certain optimizations, and it probably won't survive in the product much longer. The fact that the feature hasn't been copied in any other XSLT processor (as far as I know) is pretty convincing proof that you can live without it.

These features are a last resort. Most XSLT processors actually do their processing in a predictable way, so you can usually get away with such cheating. If you use a processor that does more optimization, however, then using such extensions might have different side effects from the ones you wanted. You can find yourself, for example, closing a file before you've written to it, because the order of execution of different instructions is not predictable. These facilities are like the PEEK and POKE of early Basic dialects, a messy escape into a lower level of programming, that you should use only if you are desperate. Having said that, there are occasional situations where they can give a dramatic boost to the speed of a stylesheet with performance problems.

Avoiding Assignment Statements

In the following sections I'll look at some of the common situations where assignment statements appear to be needed, and show how to achieve the required effect without them.

Conditional Initialization

This problem has an easy solution, so I shall get it out of the way quickly.

In conventional languages you might want to initialize a variable to zero in some circumstances and to a value of one in others. You might write:

```
int x;
if (zeroBased) {
    x=0;
} else {
    x=1;
}
```

How can you do the equivalent in XSLT without an assignment statement? The answer is simple. Think of the equivalent:

```
int x = (zeroBased ? 0 : 1 );
```

which has its parallel in XSLT 2.0 as:

```
<xsl:variable name="x" select="if ($zeroBased) then 0 else 1">
```

This has become much easier in XSLT 2.0 with the introduction of a conditional expression in XPath. In XSLT 1.0 the nearest equivalent was:

```
<xsl:variable name="x">
    <xsl:choose>
        <xsl:when test="$zeroBased">0</xsl:when>
        <xsl:otherwise>1</xsl:otherwise>
    </xsl:choose>
</xsl:variable>
```

The disadvantage of this, apart from its verbosity, is that when you use the content of `<xsl:variable>` to set its value, rather than the `select` attribute, the value of the variable will always be a tree. This doesn't matter if, as here, you want a string or number, because a tree can easily be converted to a string or number, but it's a problem when what you want is a sequence of nodes from the source document. Using XPath conditional expressions is much more flexible.

Avoid Doing Two Things at Once

Another common requirement for variables arises when you are trying to do two things at once. For example, you are trying to copy text to the output destination, and at the same time to keep a note of how much text you have copied. You might feel that the natural way of doing this is to keep the running total in a variable, and update it as a side effect of the template that does the copying. Similarly, you might want to maintain a counter as you output nodes, so that you can start a new table row after every ten nodes.

Or perhaps you want to scan a set of numbers calculating both the minimum and the maximum value; or while outputting a list of employees, to set a flag for later use if any salary greater than $100,000 was found.

You have to think differently about these problems in XSLT. Think about each part of the output you want to produce separately, and write a function (or template rule) that generates this piece of the output from the input data it needs. Don't think about calculating other things at the same time.

So you need to write one function to produce the output, and another to calculate the total. Write one template to find the minimum, and another to find the maximum.

This might mean writing a little more code, and it might take a little longer because work is being repeated—but it is usually the right approach. The problem of repeated processing can often be solved by using variables for the sequences used as input to both calculations: if you need to use a particular set of nodes as input to more than one process, save that sequence in a variable, which can then be supplied as a parameter to the two separate templates or functions.

An alternative that may occasionally give better performance is to write a template or function that returns a composite result. With XSLT 2.0, it is possible to return a composite result structured either as a sequence or as a tree. The calling code is then able to access the individual items of this sequence, or the individual nodes of the tree, using an XPath expression. For example, the following recursive template, when supplied with a sequence of nodes as a parameter, constructs a tree containing two elements, <min> and <max>, set to the minimum and maximum value of the nodes, respectively. A working stylesheet based on this example can be found in the download file as `minimax.xsl`: it acts as its own source document.

```
<xsl:template name="get-min-and-max">
  <xsl:param name="nodes"/>
  <xsl:param name="best-so-far">
    <min><xsl:value-of select="999999999"/></min>
    <max><xsl:value-of select="-999999999"/></max>
  </xsl:param>
  <xsl:choose>
    <xsl:when test="$nodes">
      <xsl:variable name="new-best-so-far">
      <min>
        <xsl:choose>
          <xsl:when test="$nodes[1] &lt; $best-so-far/min">
            <xsl:value-of select="$nodes[1]"/>
          </xsl:when>
          <xsl:otherwise>
            <xsl:value-of select="$best-so-far/min"/>
          </xsl:otherwise>
        </xsl:choose>
      </min>
      <max>
        <xsl:choose>
          <xsl:when test="$nodes[1] &gt; $best-so-far/max">
            <xsl:value-of select="$nodes[1]"/>
          </xsl:when>
          <xsl:otherwise>
            <xsl:value-of select="$best-so-far/max"/>
          </xsl:otherwise>
        </xsl:choose>
      </max>
      </xsl:variable>
      <xsl:call-template name="get-min-and-max">
        <xsl:with-param name="nodes" select="$nodes[position() &gt; 1]"/>
        <xsl:with-param name="best-so-far" select="$new-best-so-far"/>
      </xsl:call-template>
    </xsl:when>
    <xsl:otherwise>
      <xsl:copy-of select="$best-so-far"/>
    </xsl:otherwise>
  </xsl:choose>
</xsl:template>
```

When you call this template you can let the second parameter, $best-so-far, take its default value:

```
<xsl:variable name="min-and-max">
  <xsl:call-template name="get-min-and-max">
    <xsl:with-param name="nodes" select="//item/price"/>
  </xsl:call-template>
</xsl:variable>
Minimum price is: <xsl:value-of select="$min-and-max/min"/>.
Maximum price is: <xsl:value-of select="$min-and-max/max"/>.
```

One particular situation where it is a good idea to save intermediate results in a variable, and then use them as input to more than one process, is where the intermediate results are sorted. If you've got a large set of nodes to sort, the last thing you want to do is to sort it more than once. The answer to this is to do the transformation in two passes: the first pass creates a sorted sequence, and the second does a transformation on this sorted sequence. If the first pass does nothing other than sorting, then the data passed between the two phases can simply be a sequence of nodes in sorted order. If it does other tasks as well as sorting (perhaps numbering or grouping), then it might be more appropriate for the first phase to construct a temporary tree.

There are actually two ways you can achieve a multistage transformation in XSLT:

❑ Create a temporary tree in which the nodes appear in sorted order. Then use `<xsl:for-each>` or `<xsl:apply-templates>` to process the nodes on this tree in their sorted order. This is similar to the min-and-max example above; it relies on having either XSLT 2.0, or an XSLT 1.0 processor with the `exslt:node-set()` extension function.

❑ Use a sequence of stylesheets (sometimes called a *chain* or *pipeline*): the first stylesheet creates a document in which the nodes are sorted in the right order, and subsequent stylesheets take this document as their input. Such a chain of stylesheets can be conveniently manipulated using the JAXP interface described in Appendix D. The advantage of this approach compared with a single stylesheet is that the individual stylesheets in the chain are easier to split apart and reuse in different combinations for different applications.

Note that neither of these techniques violates the XSLT design principle of "no side effects."

Don't Iterate, Recurse

One of the most common uses of variables in conventional programming is to keep track of where you are in a loop. Whether this is done using an integer counter in a «for» loop, or using an `Iterator` object to process a list, the principle is the same: we have a variable that represents how far we have got and that tells us when we are finished.

In a functional program, you can't do this, because you can't update variables. So instead of writing a loop, you need to write a recursive function.

In a conventional program a common way to process a list of items is as follows.

```
iterator = list.iterator();
while (iterator.hasNext()) {
   item = iterator.next();
   item.doSomething();
}
```

The killer assignment statement is «item = iterator.getNextItem()». This assigns a different value to the item each time, and what's more, it relies on the iterator containing some sort of updateable variable that keeps track of how far it's got.

In a functional program we handle this by recursion rather than iteration. The pseudocode becomes:

```
function process(list) {
    if (!isEmpty(list)) {
        doSomething(getFirst(list));
        process(getRemainder(list));
    }
}
```

This function is called to process a list of objects. It does whatever is necessary with the first object in the list, and then calls itself to handle the rest of the list. (I'm assuming that getFirst() gets the first item in the list and getRemainder() gets a list containing all items except the first). The list gets smaller each time the function is called, and when it finally becomes empty, the function exits, and unwinds through all the recursive calls.

> *It's important to make sure there is a terminating condition such as the list becoming empty. Otherwise, the function will keep calling itself forever—the recursive equivalent of an infinite loop.*

So, the first lesson in programming without variables is to use recursion rather than iteration to process a list. With XSLT, this technique isn't necessary to handle every kind of loop, because XSLT and XPath collectively provide built-in facilities, such as <xsl:apply-templates> and <xsl:for-each> and the «for» expression, that process all the members of a sequence, as well as functions like sum() and count() to do some common operations on sequences; but whenever you need to process a set of things that can't be handled with these constructs, you need to use recursion.

Is recursion expensive? The answer is, not necessarily. Generally, a recursive scan of a sequence using the head/tail method illustrated above has O(n) performance, which means that the time it takes is directly proportional to the size of the list—exactly the same as with a conventional loop. In fact, it's quite possible for a reasonably smart compiler to generate exactly the same code for a recursive procedure as for an iterative one. For example, a common compilation technique with functional programming languages is that of *tail call optimization*, which recognizes that when a function calls itself as the last thing it does (as in the proforma code above) there's no need to allocate a new stack frame or new variables; you can just loop back to the beginning.

Unfortunately, not all XSLT processors implement tail call optimization, which means that a recursive scan of a list can run out of memory, typically after processing 500 or 1,000 items. Among the better-known XSLT 1.0 processors, Saxon and jd.xslt implement tail call optimization, while Xalan and MSXML do not. A programming technique that is often useful in such cases is called *divide-and-conquer* recursion. With head-tail recursion, the function processes one item, and then calls itself to process the rest of the sequence, which means that the maximum depth of recursive calls is equal to the number of items in the sequence. With divide-and-conquer recursion, by contrast, the function calls itself to process the first half of the sequence, and then calls itself again to process the second half. Although the number of function calls is the same, the maximum depth of recursion is now the logarithm of the size of the sequence: for example, to process a sequence of 1,000 items the maximum depth of recursion will be 10. With a little ingenuity, many recursive algorithms that process a sequence of items can be written using this divide-and-conquer approach.

Example: Aggregating a List of Numbers

The following example uses a recursive template to process a whitespace-separated list of numbers.

Input

Suppose, you have a string that holds a white-space-separated list of numbers, for example (12, 34.5, 18.2, 5), and you want to replace this with a cumulative sequence (12, 46.5, 64.7, 69.7) in which each number is the sum of the previous values. An example of an application that might need to do this is a billing application, where the input sequence contains the values of individual transactions, and the output sequence shows a running balance.

This could be done with an XPath expression such as follows:

```
for $i in 1 to count($seq)
    return sum($seq[position() = 1 to $i])
```

However, this involves $n^2/2$ additions, which gets more and more expensive as the size of the sequence increases. It's reasonable to look for a solution that is more scaleable than this.

For the sake of an example, this is the entire content of the document, number-list.xml.

```
<numbers> 12  34. 5  18. 2 5 </numbers>
```

We'll suppose that there is a schema that validates this as a sequence of xs:decimal values, so (unlike XSLT 1.0) we don't need to be concerned with the parsing of the string; we can simply access the typed value of the element as a sequence.

Schema

The schema used to validate this trivial source document is number-list.xsd.

```
<xs:schema xmlns:xs="http://www.w3.org/2001/XMLSchema">

<xs:element name="numbers" type="number-list"/>

<xs:simpleType name="number-list">
  <xs:list itemType="xs:decimal"/>
</xs:simpleType>

</xs:schema>
```

Stylesheet

Here's the recursive stylesheet (in file number-total.xsl):

```
<xsl:stylesheet
    xmlns:xsl="http://www.w3.org/1999/XSL/Transform"
    xmlns:xs="http://www.w3.org/2001/XMLSchema"
    xmlns:f="local-functions.uri"
```

```
        exclude-result-prefixes="xs f"
        version="2.0">

  <xsl:import-schema schema-location="number-list.xsd"/>
  <xsl:function name="f:total-numbers" as="xs:decimal*">
     <xsl:param name="input" as="xs:decimal*"/>
     <xsl:param name="total" as="xs:decimal"/>
     <xsl:if test="exists($input)">
        <xsl:variable name="x" as="xs:decimal"
                       select="$input[1] + $total"/>
        <xsl:sequence select="$x"/>
        <xsl:sequence select="f:total-numbers($input[position()!=1],$x)"/>
     </xsl:if>
  </xsl:function>

  <xsl:template match="/">
     <total values="{f:total-numbers(numbers, 0)}"/>
  </xsl:template>

</xsl:stylesheet>
```

To run this with Saxon, you need the schema-aware version of the product. You can execute the transformation as:

```
java com.saxonica.Transform-val number-list.xml number-total.xsl
```

Notice how closely the function f:total-numbers mirrors the pseudocode structure given earlier.

If the supplied list is empty, the function returns nothing (an empty sequence).

The first time the function is called, it returns the value of the first item in the sequence (obtained by adding the value of this item to the running total, which is initialized to zero). It then calls itself to process the rest of the list, and returns the result of this processing.

Each subsequent time the function is called, it processes the first value in what's left of the input sequence, adds this to the running total that was supplied as a parameter, outputs this value, and then calls itself to process the tail of the sequence.

Eventually, the function will call itself with an empty sequence as the argument, at which point it returns, unwinding the entire stack of function calls.

Output

```
<?xml version="1.0" encoding="UTF-8"?>
<total values="12 46.5 64.7 69.7"/>
```

Here's another example, this time processing a sequence of nodes. XPath provides built-in functions for counting nodes and for totaling their values, but they aren't always flexible enough: sometimes you need to walk round the nodes yourself.

Example: Using Interleaved Structures

XML makes it very easy to represent hierarchic structures, such as the chapters, sections, and paragraphs of a book. But what do you do when there are structures that are nonhierarchic? An example is the text of a play: one way of splitting the text is according to who is speaking, and another way is to follow the meter of the verse. The problem is that lines of verse aren't neatly nested inside speeches, and speeches aren't nested inside lines of verse: the two structures are interleaved. The usual solution to this problem is to use the hierarchic XML tagging to represent one of the structures (say the speeches) and to use empty element tags to mark the boundaries in the other structure.

(Another design approach is referred to as *parallel markup*: the markup for either or both of the structures is held separately from the text itself, using XPointer references to identify the text to which it relates.)

Input

This example (`scene4-3.xml`) is an extract from Shakespeare's *Othello*, Act IV, Scene 3. I have departed from Jon Bosak's markup to show the line endings as they are given in the Arden Shakespeare edition.

```
<?xml version="1.0" encoding="iso-8859-1"?>
<SCENE REF="4.3">
<STAGEDIR>Enter OTHELLO, LODOVICO, DESDEMONA, EMILIA and
attendants</STAGEDIR>

<SPEECH>
<SPEAKER>LODOVICO</SPEAKER>
I do beseech you, sir, trouble yourself no further.<NL/>
</SPEECH>

<SPEECH>
<SPEAKER>OTHELLO</SPEAKER>
O, pardon me: 'twill do me good to walk.<NL/>
</SPEECH>

<SPEECH>
<SPEAKER>LODOVICO</SPEAKER>
Madam, good night; I humbly thank your ladyship.<NL/>
</SPEECH>

<SPEECH>
<SPEAKER>DESDEMONA</SPEAKER>
Your honour is most welcome.
</SPEECH>

<SPEECH>
<SPEAKER>OTHELLO</SPEAKER>
Will you walk, sir?<NL/>
O, Desdemona, --
</SPEECH>
```

```
<SPEECH>
<SPEAKER>DESDEMONA</SPEAKER>
My lord?
</SPEECH>

<SPEECH>
<SPEAKER>OTHELLO</SPEAKER>
Get you to bed<NL/>
on th' instant; I will be returned forthwith<NL/>
dismiss your attendant there: look't be done.<NL/>
</SPEECH>

<SPEECH>
<SPEAKER>DESDEMONA</SPEAKER>
I will, my lord.<NL/>
</SPEECH>
<STAGEDIR>Exeunt Othello, Lodovico, and attendants</STAGEDIR>
</SCENE>
```

Output

Typically, a printed edition of this play is formatted with the kind of layout shown in
Figure 9-3, in which lines that are split across multiple speeches are indented to show their
relationship.

```
DESDEMONA
    Your honour is most welcome.
OTHELLO                              Will you walk, sir?
    O, Desdemona —
DESDEMONA            My Lord?
OTHELLO                        Get you to bed
    On th'instant, I will be returned forthwith
    dismiss your attendant there: look't be done.
```

Figure 9-3

Achieving this format is not easy (especially details such as the omission of a new line if the
indented text fits on the same line as the speaker's name), and it certainly requires a
computational stylesheet to achieve it. Rather than attempt this, I will tackle a simpler
problem, which is to invert the structure so that the primary XML hierarchy shows the lines,
and the start of each speech is tagged by an empty element.

```
<?xml version="1.0" encoding="UTF-8"?>
<scene><title>SCENE III. Another room In the castle.</title>
<stagedir>Enter OTHELLO, LODOVICO, DESDEMONA, EMILIA and
attendants</stagedir>

<speech speaker="LODOVICO"/>
<line>I do beseech you, sir, trouble yourself no further.</line>

<speech speaker="OTHELLO"/>
<line>O, pardon me: 'twill do me good to walk.</line>

<speech speaker="LODOVICO"/>
```

```
<line>Madam, good night; I humbly thank your ladyship.</line>

<speech speaker="DESDEMONA"/>
<line>Your honour is most welcome.

<speech speaker="OTHELLO"/>
Will you walk, sir?</line>
<line>O, Desdemona, --

<speech speaker="DESDEMONA"/>
My lord?

<speech speaker="OTHELLO"/>
Get you to bed</line>
<line>on th' instant; I will be returned forthwith</line>
<line>dismiss your attendant there: look't be done.</line>

<speech speaker="DESDEMONA"/>
<line>I will, my lord.</line>

<stagedir>Exeunt Othello, Lodovico, and attendants</stagedir>
</scene>
```

Stylesheet

I tackle this by processing the text sequentially, using a recursive template. The structure I have followed below is a two-phase approach. The first phase flattens the structure so that both the speech boundaries and the line boundaries are represented by empty elements, appearing as siblings of the text nodes. The result of the first phase is held in the variable $flat. This variable holds a sequence of (parentless) element and text nodes. The second phase then adds the hierarchic structure of <line> elements containing the text and <speech> nodes.

Here is the top-level logic of the stylesheet invert.xsl. Note how the second phase starts by processing only the first node in the sequence $flat.

```
<xsl:stylesheet
    xmlns:xsl="http://www.w3.org/1999/XSL/Transform"
    version="2.0">

<xsl:template match="SPEECH">
    <xsl:variable name="flat" as="node()*">
        <xsl:apply-templates mode="phase1"/>
    </xsl:variable>
    <xsl:apply-templates select="$flat[1]" mode="phase2"/>
</xsl:template>
```

Now the template rules for the first phase, the flattening phase. The important template rule is the first one, which in effect takes the children of the old <SPEECH> element and makes them into following siblings of the new <speech> element.

```
<xsl:template match="SPEECH" mode="phase1">
   <speech speaker="{SPEAKER}"/>
   <xsl:apply-templates/>
</xsl:template>

<xsl:template match="NL" mode="phase1">
   <NL/>
</xsl:template>
<xsl:template match="STAGEDIR" mode="phase1">
   <stagedir>
     <xsl:apply-templates/>
   </stagedir>
</xsl:template>
```

We now have a flat structure containing empty <speech> elements, empty <NL> elements, text nodes, and <stagedir> elements. Phase 2 is structured so a template rule is called once for each node in the sequence $flat. In each case, this template rule calls <xsl:apply-templates> to process the next node in the sequence (and thus, by implication, the rest of the sequence beyond). When an <NL> element is encountered, a new <line> element is written to the result tree, and the following elements generate children of this <line> element. When any other kind of node is encountered, it is simply copied to the result tree at the current level.

```
<xsl:template match="NL" mode="phase2">
   <line>
     <xsl:apply-templates
       select="following-sibling::node()[1][not(self::NL)]"/>
       mode="phase2"/>
   </line>
   <xsl:apply-templates select="following-sibling::node()[1]"/>
</xsl:template>

<xsl:template match="node()" mode="phase2">
   <xsl:copy-of select="."/>
   <xsl:apply-templates
     select="following-sibling::node()[1][not(self::NL)]"/>
</xsl:template>
</xsl:stylesheet>
```

The expression «following-sibling::node()[1][not(self::NL)]» selects the next sibling node, provided it is not an <NL> element; if the next sibling is an <NL> element, it selects an empty sequence.

There is very little that is specific to XSLT 2.0 in this stylesheet, with the exception of the sequence of nodes used as an intermediate variable. The second phase could have been written, without explicit recursion, using <xsl:for-each-group>, but in my view the recursive solution in this case is not really any more difficult.

This stylesheet also demonstrates that recursive processing of a sequence can often be carried out very elegantly, using <xsl:apply-templates>. I find that there is a tendency when writing recursive code to reach straight for <xsl:call-template> (or, in XSLT 2.0, <xsl:function>) when <xsl:apply-templates> can often do the job far better.

Superficially, the logic of this stylesheet doesn't bear much resemblance to the prototypical head/tail recursive structure described earlier. But in fact, this is precisely the underlying structure. There are actually two nested sequences being processed here, each of them using a head/tail recursion. The first sequence is the sequence of lines, where each line is represented in the input by an <NL> element and its following siblings up to the next <NL>. The «match="NL"» template processes the first line of text (which consists of multiple nodes), and then calls itself via <xsl:apply-templates> to process the remaining lines. The second, nested, sequence is the sequence of nodes that follow each <NL> element. In both cases, the test for the terminating condition is implicit, because <xsl:apply-templates> does nothing when the selected node sequence is empty.

Recursion: Summary

By now the principle should be clear. Whenever you need to find something out by processing a sequence of items, write a recursive template that is given the sequence as a parameter. If the sequence isn't empty, deal with the first item, and make a recursive call to deal with the rest of the sequence that follows the first item.

As I mentioned, with XSLT 1.0 there was another problem when doing this, which had nothing to do with the lack of an assignment statement, but was a consequence of the limited range of data types available. The result of a template in XSLT 1.0 was always a temporary tree, and with XSLT 1.0 (without the widely implemented exslt:node-set() extension) there were only two things you could do with the tree: you could copy it to the final result tree, or you could convert it to a string.

With XSLT 2.0, this becomes much easier because a template (or a function) can return an arbitrary sequence, which you can manipulate in any way you like. You can also choose to construct a temporary tree, which can now be manipulated just like an original source document.

For another example that takes advantage of this, see the Knight's Tour in Chapter 12.

Grouping

A common processing task that appears at first sight to need updateable variables is the splitting of data into groups.

Suppose that your source logged cities and their respective countries in the following format:

```
<cities>
   <city name= "CityName" country ="CountryName"/>
... etc ...
</cities>
```

However, you want to list together all cities found in a particular country.

```
<countries>
   <country name="CountryName">
      <city>CityName1</city>
      <city>CityName2</city>
   </country
... etc...
</countries>
```

In other languages, we've probably all written code that achieved similar effects using pseudocode such as this:

```
sortedCities = cities.sortBy("country");
previousCountry = null;
write("<country>")
for each city in sortedCities {
    thisCountry = city.getAttribute("country");
    if (thisCountry != previousCountry) {
        write("</country>\n<country>");
    }
    write("<city>" + city.getAttribute("city") + "</city>");
    previousCountry = thisCountry;
}
write("</country>")
```

In XSLT, of course, this is a nonstarter, for two reasons. Firstly, you need to output a tree, not a text file containing markup tags: this means you can't write the end tag for an element as a separate operation from writing the start tag. Secondly, you can't use assignment statements to spot the change of country as you go through the data.

This kind of problem can nearly always be tackled in XSLT 2.0, using the `<xsl:for-each-group>` construct. In many cases, it can also be handled by writing two nested `<xsl:for-each>` loops (one to execute once per group, the other to execute once per item within each group), using the `distinct-values()` function to select the grouping key values that identify the groups. These problems can therefore be tackled using navigational stylesheets alone.

However, the `<xsl:for-each-group>` construct is a stereotype, a high-level construct designed to tackle a particular class of commonly encountered programming problems. The trouble with stereotype constructs is that there always comes a point where they break down, where the problem falls outside the domain that the stereotype was designed to tackle. The XSL Working Group designed the construct after surveying quite a range of use cases, which means that it's quite hard to come up with examples of things that it won't do, but they are bound to arise.

In addition, even though this book is designed to describe XSLT 2.0, there may well be cases where you want to design a solution that also works under XSLT 1.0. I think it's useful therefore to retain a description of the two principal techniques used for grouping in XSLT 1.0. But I will keep it brief.

All grouping techniques essentially consist of two nested loops, with the structure:

```
<xsl:for-each select=group-representative>
    <group>
        <xsl:for-each member-of-group>
            <item>
                item information
            </item>
        </xsl:for-each>
    </group>
</xsl:for-each>
```

Of course, either of the loops might equally be coded using `<xsl:apply-templates>` or perhaps an XPath «`for`» expression, and sometimes the inner loop will not be a real loop at all, but a call on an aggregation function such as `count()` or `sum()`.

But in all cases, the tricky part in the outer loop, is to select one item that serves to identify the group, and in the inner loop, is to select the remaining items that participate in the same group.

Very often, a call on `distinct-values()` can be used in the outer loop, to select one instance of each distinct value that appears in the input sequence. In XSLT 1.0, there are two ways of achieving the same effect:

❑ The expression «`x[not(@y = preceding-sibling::x/@y)]`» selects all the `<x>` children of the context node whose `@y` attribute is different from that of any preceding `<x>` child.

❑ The expression «`x[. is key('k', @y)[1]]`» selects an `<x>` element if, of all the elements retrieved by the call on «`key('k', @y)`», this is the first one. Unfortunately, the «`is`» operator was not available in XPath 1.0, so instead of writing «`A is B`» to test whether two expressions return the same node, you can write «`generate-id(A) = generate-id(B)`», or «`count(A|B)=1`».

Selecting the remaining elements in the group is generally easier:

❑ In the first case, you can write «`select="../x[@y = current()/@y]"`».

❑ In the second case, you can use the same key again, by writing «`select="key('k', @y)"`».

Of these two techniques, the second is generally more efficient because it takes advantage of the index or hash table built to support the `key()` function. This technique, using keys for grouping, is known as the *Muenchian grouping technique*, after its inventor, Steve Muench of Oracle. A comprehensive guide to Muenchian grouping, including many variants to handle problems such as multilevel grouping, has been produced by Jeni Tennison at `http://www.jenitennison.com/xslt/grouping`.

Another advantage of Muenchian grouping is that it can be used where the grouping expression (the common value that determines whether two nodes belong in the same group) is something other than the string value of a node, as it was in the above example. A typical example is where you want to create alphabetical groups, one for each letter of the alphabet. For example, if you wanted to list the cities alphabetically, with a heading for each initial letter of the alphabet, you could simply use the following key definition.

```
<key name="alpha-group" match="city" use="substring(@name, 1, 1)"/>
```

and apart from this change, the logic of the stylesheet would be much the same.

Summary

This chapter described four design patterns for writing XSLT stylesheets:

❑ Fill-in-the-blanks

❑ Navigational

❑   Rule-based

❑   Computational

The approach to problems in the computational stylesheets may seem unfamiliar, because XSLT is a pure functional programming language, with no assignment statements or other side effects that constrain the order of execution. The result of this is that many of the more complex algorithms need to be written using recursive functions or templates.

10

Case Study: XMLSpec

This is the first of a group of three chapters that aim to show how all the facilities of the XSLT language can work together to solve real XML processing problems of significant complexity. I chose three example applications, with complete stylesheets for handling them. Most of the code is presented in these chapters, but the complete stylesheets, and specimen data files, can be downloaded from the Wrox Web site at http://www.wrox.com/.

As I described in the previous chapter, XSLT has a broad range of applications, and in these three chapters I have tried to cover a representative selection of problems. The three examples I have chosen are as follows:

❑ The first example is a stylesheet for rendering sequential documents: specifically, the stylesheet used for rendering W3C specifications such as the XML and XSLT Recommendations. This is a classic example of the *rule-based* design pattern described on page 620 in Chapter 9.

❑ The second example, in Chapter 11, is concerned with presenting structured data. I chose a complex data structure with many cross-references to illustrate how a navigational stylesheet can find its way around the source tree: the chosen example is a data file containing the family tree of the Kennedys. This example is particularly suitable for demonstrating how stylesheets and schemas can work together.

❑ The final example stylesheet, in Chapter 12, is quite unrealistic, but fun. It shows how XSLT can be used to calculate a knight's tour of the chessboard, in which the knight visits every square without ever landing on the same square twice. This is not the sort of problem XSLT was designed to solve, but by showing that it can be done I hope it will convince you that XSLT has the computational power and flexibility to deal with the many more modest algorithmic challenges that arise in routine day-to-day formatting applications. New features in XSLT 2.0 make this kind of application much easier to write, which means that the stylesheet is almost a total rewrite of the XSLT 1.0 version.

The stylesheet presented in this chapter was written for a practical purpose, not to serve as an example of good programming practice. I wrote in the previous edition of this book that the stylesheet was originally written by Eduardo Gutentag and subsequently modified by James Clark. The stylesheet at that time was around 750 lines long. The current version has grown to over 2,500 lines, and claims as its authors Norman Walsh, Chris Maden, Ben Trafford, Eve Maler, and Henry S.

Thompson. No doubt others have contributed too, and I am grateful to W3C and to these individuals for placing the stylesheet in the public domain. Because the stylesheet has grown so much, and because many of the template rules are quite repetitive, I have omitted much of the detail from this chapter, selecting only those rules where there is something useful to say. But I haven't tried to polish the code for publication—I am presenting the stylesheet as it actually is, warts and all, because this provides many opportunities to discuss the realities of XSLT programming. It gives the opportunity to analyze the code as written and to consider possible ways in which it can be improved. To the individuals whose code I am criticizing, I apologize if this causes them any embarrassment. I do it because I know that all good software engineers value criticism, and these people are all top-class software engineers.

Before embarking on this chapter, I did wonder whether there was any value in presenting in a book about XSLT 2.0 a stylesheet that is written almost entirely using XSLT 1.0. As the chapter progressed, I found that it actually provided a very good opportunity to identify those places where XSLT 2.0 can greatly simplify the code that needs to be written. I hope that it will therefore serve not only as a case study in the use of XSLT 1.0, but also as an introduction to the opportunities offered by the new features in 2.0.

Formatting the XML Specification

In this worked example, we'll study the stylesheet used for formatting the XML specifications themselves. You may have noticed that on the W3C Web site, you can get the specifications for standards such as XML, XSLT, and XPath either in XML format or in HTML. We'll look at a stylesheet for converting the XML Recommendation from its XML form to its HTML form, shown in Figure 10-1.

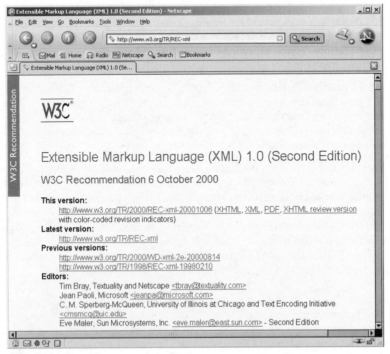

Figure 10-1

The DTDs and stylesheets used for the XSLT, XQuery, and XPath specifications are adapted from the version used for the XML specification, and we'll take a look at the adaptations too.

The download file for this chapter on `http://www.wrox.com/` contains the version of the stylesheet modules that were actually used to publish the last-call working draft of XSLT 2.0 on November 12, 2003. These may differ slightly from the version presented in the text.

This stylesheet is a classic example of the *rule-based* design pattern, which was introduced on page 620 in Chapter 9. It makes minimal assumptions about where all the different elements in the XML source document appear relative to each other, and it allows new rules to be added freely as the document structure evolves.

You'll probably find it helpful while reading this stylesheet to have the XML source document readily accessible. The official version of XML 1.0 Second Edition (the document shown above) is on the Web at `http://www.w3.org/TR/2000/REC-xml-20001006.xml`.

There is also a DTD called `xmlspec.dtd`. You can view the source either in a text editor, or in an XML editor such as XML Spy, or using the default XML viewer in Internet Explorer or Netscape.

Now let's look at the stylesheet, `xmlspec.xsl`.

Preface

Let's start at the beginning:

```
<?xml version="1.0"?>
<xsl:transform xmlns:xsl="http://www.w3.org/1999/XSL/Transform"
               xmlns:saxon="http://icl.com/saxon"
               exclude-result-prefixes="saxon"
               version="1.0">

<!-- ==================================================================== -->
<!-- xmlspec.xsl: An HTML XSL[1] Stylesheet for XML Spec V2.1[2] markup

     Version: $Id: xmlspec.xsl,v 1.42 2003/07/11 17:12:45 NormanWalsh Exp $

     URI:     http://dev.w3.org/cvsweb/spec-prod/html/xmlspec.xsl

     Authors: Norman Walsh (norman.walsh@sun.com)
              Chris Maden (crism@lexica.net)
              Ben Trafford (ben@legendary.org)
              Eve Maler (eve.maler@sun.com)
              Henry S. Thompson (ht@cogsci.ed.ac.uk)

     Date:    Created 07 September 1999
              Last updated $Date: 2003/07/11 17:12:45 $ by $Author:
NormanWalsh$
-->
```

A fairly standard control header. There's a lot of change history as well, which I'll leave out. The stylesheet is an XML document, so it starts with an XML declaration. There's no encoding declaration;

actually, all the characters are ASCII, which means that almost any XML parser should be able to load this document without difficulty.

Note that the <xsl:stylesheet> element specifies «version="1.0"». This doesn't guarantee that the stylesheet makes no use of XSLT 2.0 features, but it's a good clue: it means that when the stylesheet is run on an XSLT 2.0 processor, it will run in backwards-compatibility mode, and when run on an XSLT 1.0 processor, errors will be reported at compile time if any XSLT 2.0 constructs are found. This stylesheet is widely used to produce a whole range of documents, and like most other organizations, W3C wouldn't want its business-critical publishing operation to rely on beta release software. So the main stylesheet does indeed stick to XSLT 1.0. As we'll see later, some of the "overlays" to the stylesheet do take advantage of 2.0.

The reference to the Saxon namespace (in fact the old Saxon 6.5 namespace) in the header turns out to be a red herring. There is no use of this namespace within the body of the document, and the stylesheet has no dependencies on features specific to Saxon or any other XSLT processor. Someone put this in to do some experiments, and forgot to take it out. It does no harm, apart from raising a false alarm about the portability of the stylesheet.

The <xsl:output> element defines the output method as html, and indicates the public identifier of the version of HTML that is being generated, which will be copied into the generated output file. This is good practice. It isn't essential, but of course the W3C wants to produce HTML that conforms to its own recommended practice.

```
<xsl:preserve-space elements="*"/>

<xsl:strip-space elements="
abstract arg attribute authlist author back bibref blist body case col
colgroup component constant constraint constraintnote copyright def
definitions descr div div1 div2 div3 div4 div5 ednote enum enumerator
example exception footnote front gitem glist graphic group header
htable htbody inform-div1 interface issue item itemizedlist langusage
listitem member method module note notice ol olist orderedlist orglist
param parameters prod prodgroup prodrecap proto pubdate pubstmt raises
reference resolution returns revisiondesc scrap sequence slist
sourcedesc spec specref status struct table tbody tfoot thead tr
typedef ul ulist union vc vcnote wfc wfcnote"/>
```

These two elements together indicate that boundary whitespace (whitespace that appears in whitespace-only text nodes) is to be retained for all elements except the long list of elements whose whitespace is to be stripped. The <xsl:preserve-space> element here is actually redundant, since the default is to preserve whitespace anyway. The elements listed for stripping are essentially those that do not allow mixed content in the DTD. It would be nice if there were an easier way of achieving this, but sadly there isn't, not even in XSLT 2.0.

```
<xsl:param name="validity.hacks">1</xsl:param>
<xsl:param name="show.diff.markup">0</xsl:param>
<xsl:param name="additional.css"></xsl:param>
<xsl:param name="additional.title"></xsl:param>
<xsl:param name="called.by.diffspec">0</xsl:param>
<xsl:param name="show.ednotes">1</xsl:param>
<xsl:param name="tabular.examples">0</xsl:param>
<xsl:param name="toc.level" select="5"/>
```

These global parameters allow the behavior of the stylesheet to be customized. Like many publishing organizations, W3C tries hard to maintain a consistent house-style for its publications, and the use of a common DTD and stylesheet goes a long way toward achieving this. However, different publications do have different requirements, so there is a need to manage variety. Sometimes, the authors needed to introduce a new feature in the stylesheet but didn't want to change the way existing documents were rendered, so they put in a parameter to control the new feature. Sometimes, the parameters reflect the needs of different stages in the publication cycle, for example the parameter «show.ednotes» controls whether editorial notes should be shown.

There's no good reason why the last of these parameters uses the `select` syntax while the others all place the value in the content of the `<xsl:param>` element. Generally, I encourage the use of `select` for simple-valued attributes. Placing the value in the content of the element means that the data type is not a simple number or string, but rather a temporary tree, which however much the XSLT processor optimizes it is likely to be a much more heavyweight data structure. The use of «0» and «1» as parameter values, rather than the more obvious `true()` and `false()`, can be justified by the fact that with many XSLT processors, there is no way of supplying boolean parameter values from the command line.

There are two ways these parameters can be set. Either the values can be supplied from the calling application (typically, from the command line), or the parameters can be overridden in an overlay stylesheet. An overlay stylesheet (we'll see examples later) is a stylesheet that imports the main `xmlspec.xsl` stylesheet, and makes modifications or extensions to it. If the parameters were designed to be set in this way only, they could have been defined using `<xsl:variable>` rather than `<xsl:param>`, but using `<xsl:param>` is more versatile because it allows either mechanism to be used.

```
<xsl:key name="ids" match="*[@id]" use="@id"/>
<xsl:key name="specrefs" match="specref" use="@ref"/>
```

The stylesheet uses two key definitions. These are designed to make hyperlinks within the document easier to follow. The first key matches any attribute named «id», on any element, making it easy to find an element with a given «id» attribute. The DTD allows an «id» attribute on any element whatsoever. In fact, it defines the type of the attribute to be «ID», so these elements could also be located using the `id()` function. (Sorry for the overloading of this term!) In fact, the stylesheet avoids the use of the `id()` function altogether, probably because `id()` works correctly only if the document is processed using a validating parser.

The second key definition is a little surprising. A `<specref>` is a cross-reference: it is used wherever the text says something like "See section 8.2." I wouldn't expect to see any code that needs to locate all the cross-references; a more natural usage would be to index the elements that act as the target of a cross-reference. But on examination, it turns out that this key definition is not used. No doubt it is the result of another experiment, and someone forgot to delete it. Again, it does no harm—the chances are that an XSLT processor will completely ignore a key definition if the key is never used.

```
<xsl:output method="html"
    encoding="ISO-8859-1"
    doctype-public="-//W3C//DTD HTML 4.01 Transitional//EN"
    indent="no"/>
```

The `<xsl:output>` declaration indicates how the result tree should be serialized. The stylesheet uses HTML output, using ISO-8859-1 encoding (often called Latin-1). These definitions can again be changed in an overlay stylesheet, or in some cases from the command line (with Saxon, for example, specifying «!indent=yes» on the command line will override the <xsl:output> declaration).

```
<xsl:strip-space elements="author"/>
```

We've already specified <xsl:strip-space> for a long list of elements, including the <author> element, so this declaration has obviously been left in here by mistake. In fact, it's technically an error (and Saxon gives you a warning about it). The XSLT specifications (both 1.0 and 2.0) say that it's an error to have two <xsl:strip-space> or <xsl:preserve-space> declarations for the same element, even if they agree. However, it's one of those errors that the processor is allowed to recover from.

```
<!-- Output a warning for unhandled elements! -->
<xsl:template match="*">
  <xsl:message>
    <xsl:text>No template matches </xsl:text>
    <xsl:value-of select="name(.)"/>
    <xsl:text>.</xsl:text>
  </xsl:message>

  <font color="red">
    <xsl:text>&lt;</xsl:text>
    <xsl:value-of select="name(.)"/>
    <xsl:text>&gt;</xsl:text>
    <xsl:apply-templates/>
    <xsl:text>&lt;/</xsl:text>
    <xsl:value-of select="name(.)"/>
    <xsl:text>&gt;</xsl:text>
  </font>
</xsl:template>
```

This is a useful catchall template rule to make sure that the source document and the stylesheet are consistent with each other. In principle, validating the source document against a DTD should ensure that it contains no surprises. But in practice, DTDs change over time, and there's no way to be sure which version of the DTD was used—indeed, there's no way to be sure that the document was validated at all. So this template rule matches any element for which there is no other more specific template rule in the stylesheet. It produces a message (typically on the console) to indicate that an unexpected element was encountered, and it then copies the offending data to the result document in such a way that the start and end tags will show up visibly in the HTML (in red). This is a good way of helping document authors to correct the error.

```
<!-- Template for the root node. Creation of <html> element could
       go here, but that doesn't feel right. -->
  <xsl:template match="/">
    <xsl:apply-templates/>
  </xsl:template>
```

This template rule is superfluous: it does exactly the same as the built-in template rule for the document node. I don't know why the stylesheet author felt uneasy about including the code to generate the <html> element in this template rule. Perhaps, it was because the template rule for a document node is invoked when processing the root of any document tree, not only the principal source document. If the logic for creating the skeleton of the output HTML goes in the template rule for the outermost element (which in this case is called `<spec>`) then it's less likely to be invoked by accident when temporary trees or secondary input documents are processed.

The remaining rules in the stylesheet are presented in alphabetical order, by element. This is a good way of making sure that any rule can be found quickly. Unfortunately, it also has a drawback, which is that rules that work closely together (for example, the rules for formatting the front matter, or the rules for outputting syntax productions) can be widely separated in the source file. For the purposes of exposition, I've therefore regrouped them according to their logical function. The first group I will consider are the template rules that handle the general outline of the HTML output.

Creating the HTML Outline

The main template rule is evaluated when the `<spec>` element in the source document is encountered. This is always the outermost element of the XML document. It's fairly lengthy, so we'll take it piece by piece.

```
<!-- spec: the specification itself -->
<xsl:template match="spec">
  <html>
    <xsl:if test="header/langusage/language">
      <xsl:attribute name="lang">
        <xsl:value-of select="header/langusage/language/@id"/>
      </xsl:attribute>
    </xsl:if>
```

The code starts by generating the `<html>` element, giving it a «lang» attribute if and only if the source document defines its language in the form `<langusage><language @id="en"/></langusage>`.

```
<head>
  <meta http-equiv="Content-Type" content="text/html; charset=ISO-8859-1"/>
  <title>
    <xsl:apply-templates select="header/title"/>
    <xsl:if test="header/version">
      <xsl:text> </xsl:text>
      <xsl:apply-templates select="header/version"/>
    </xsl:if>
    <xsl:if test="$additional.title != ''">
      <xsl:text> -- </xsl:text>
      <xsl:value-of select="$additional.title"/>
    </xsl:if>
  </title>
  <xsl:call-template name="css"/>
</head>
```

The next stage is to output the `<head>` element. Producing a `<meta>` element giving the media type (or content type) is probably not a very good idea, because the XSLT serializer is required to do this anyway, and this way you will get two such elements, which might not even agree. It's better to leave this to the serializer, which makes sure that the encoding specified in the `<meta>` element is the same as the actual encoding used. With XSLT 2.0, it is possible to suppress the `<meta>` element from the serializer by specifying `<xsl:output include-content-type="no"/>`, but this option is not available in XSLT 1.0.

Most of the above section is concerned with generating the document title (as it appears in the title bar of the browser window). This is a concatenation of the `<title>` and `<version>` elements in the source `<header>` element. Since the HTML title can't contain any markup, I would probably have kept this code simpler, for example the following would work just as well:

```
<title>
  <xsl:value-of select="concat(header/title, ' ', header/version)"/>
</title>
```

which in XSLT 2.0 can be abbreviated further to:

```
<title>
  <xsl:value-of select="header/title, header/version"/>
</title>
```

This simplification ignores the code that allows an additional subtitle to be added after the version number by specifying the stylesheet parameter `$additional.title`.

Note the call on the named template «css», which we'll look at in a moment:

```
        <body>
          <xsl:apply-templates/>
          <xsl:if test="//footnote[not(ancestor::table)]">
            <hr/>
            <div class="endnotes">
              <xsl:text>&#10;</xsl:text>
              <h3>
                <xsl:call-template name="anchor">
                  <xsl:with-param name="conditional" select="0"/>
                  <xsl:with-param name="default.id" select="'endnotes'"/>
                </xsl:call-template>
                <xsl:text>End Notes</xsl:text>
              </h3>
              <dl>
                <xsl:apply-templates select="//footnote[not(ancestor::table)]"
                                 mode="notes"/>
              </dl>
            </div>
          </xsl:if>
        </body>
      </html>
    </xsl:template>
```

The main content of the document is produced by the `<xsl:apply-templates/>` call that immediately follows the `<body>` start tag. This processes the children of the `<spec>` element, using their respective template rules, and generates the output of each of these children independently. There are generally three children: `<header>`, `<body>`, and `<back>`. The header contains front material such as the status section and abstract, the body contains the numbered sections of the document, and the `<back>` element contains the appendices.

I haven't come across a W3C document that uses footnotes or endnotes, which is what the rest of this rule is dealing with. It displays all `<footnote>` elements, other than those found within a `<table>`, as endnotes at the end of the document. A couple of comments on this code:

❑ The XPath expression «//footnote[not(ancestor::table)]» is probably fairly expensive to evaluate, as it involves a scan of the whole document. Since the expression is used twice, it's a natural candidate for a variable.

❑ It's possible that the author imagined that `<xsl:text>&#10;</xsl:text>` would cause the following text to be displayed on a new line. In fact, HTML browsers treat a newline character exactly the same as a space. Alternatively, it's possible that the author simply wanted to create some breaks in the HTML to make it usable in a text editor, without having to switch to `<xsl:output indent="yes"/>`. Either way, it does no harm.

The named template css, which is called from the above template rule, looks like this:

```
    <xsl:template name="css">
      <style type="text/css">
        <xsl:text>
code            { font-family: monospace; }

div.constraint,
div.issue,
div.note,
div.notice      { margin-left: 2em; }

</xsl:text>
        <xsl:if test="$tabular.examples = 0">
          <xsl:text>
div.exampleInner pre { margin-left: 1em;
                       margin-top: 0em; margin-bottom: 0em}
div.exampleOuter {border: 4px double gray;
                  margin: 0em; padding: 0em}
div.exampleInner { background-color: #d5dee3;
                   border-top-width: 4px;
                   border-top-style: double;
                   border-top-color: #d3d3d3;
                   border-bottom-width: 4px;
                   border-bottom-style: double;
                   border-bottom-color: #d3d3d3;
                   padding: 4px; margin: 0em }
div.exampleWrapper   { margin: 4px }
div.exampleHeader { font-weight: bold;
                    margin: 4px}
</xsl:text>
        </xsl:if>
        <xsl:value-of select="$additional.css"/>
      </style>
      <link rel="stylesheet" type="text/css">
        <xsl:attribute name="href">
        <xsl:text>http://www.w3.org/StyleSheets/TR/</xsl:text>

        <xsl:choose>
          <xsl:when test="/spec/@role='editors-copy'">base</xsl:when>
          <xsl:otherwise>
            <xsl:choose>
              <xsl:when test="/spec/@w3c-doctype='wd'">W3C-WD</xsl:when>
```

```
                 <xsl:when test="/spec/@w3c-doctype='rec'">W3C-REC</xsl:when>
                 <xsl:when test="/spec/@w3c-doctype='pr'">W3C-PR</xsl:when>

                 <xsl:when test="/spec/@w3c-doctype='cr'">W3C-CR</xsl:when>
                 <xsl:when test="/spec/@w3c-doctype='note'">W3C-NOTE</xsl:when>
                 <xsl:otherwise>base</xsl:otherwise>
             </xsl:choose>
          </xsl:otherwise>
       </xsl:choose>
       <xsl:text>.css</xsl:text>

     </xsl:attribute>
   </link>
 </xsl:template>
```

This code generates two elements within the HTML <head> element: a <style> element and a <link> element. Together, these define the CSS stylesheet that is used by the browser to render the HTML. This combined use of XSLT and CSS is one that I would very much recommend. It means that the XSLT stylesheet can be concerned with getting the structure of the HTML correct, and can leave the fine detail of fonts and margins to the CSS stylesheet.

Why use both a <link> and a <style>? The <link> contains a reference to a CSS stylesheet stored on the W3C Web server, while the <style> contains local modifications and additions. I suspect that the reason for the split is to do with change control. Changing a CSS stylesheet on the Web server, when there are many documents that refer to it, is a risky thing to do, especially when many of these documents are supposed to be stable specifications. Making minor improvements to the formatting is safer if the modifications affect only new documents, not old. This could be achieved, of course, by introducing a new version of the CSS stylesheet on the server. Perhaps, W3C (like many organizations) has change control processes that made it easier for the XSLT stylesheet authors to introduce the changes locally.

Note how both the <link> and the <style> can be customized. The <link> generates a reference to a CSS stylesheet conditionally, depending on the type of document. The various CSS stylesheets are identical except for the choice of a background image: the stylesheet for Working Drafts, for example, specifies:

```
body {
   background-image: url(http://www.w3.org/StyleSheets/TR/logo-WD);
}
```

while that for Recommendations has:

```
body {
   background-image: url(http://www.w3.org/StyleSheets/TR/logo-REC);
}
```

This image contains the vertical text shown on the top left-hand corner of the displayed page.

The CSS definitions generated within the <style> element include any definitions present in the content of the variable $additional.css. By default, this holds an empty string. However, the variable can be overridden in an overlay stylesheet to define additional CSS display classes, and this is commonly done: for example, the XSLT specification uses extra classes for displaying proforma XSLT element definitions.

Formatting the Document Header

The stylesheet generates the title of the HTML document by accessing the `<title>` element within the `<header>` element of the source XML file. To understand such expressions, you need to take a look at the structure of the `<header>` element in the source document. The actual file contains a lot of material that isn't actually rendered in the HTML: some of this is in the form of XML comments, some in a more structured `<revisiondesc>` element. If you are interested in these things, it contains fascinating snippets such as:

```
<sitem>1997-03-21 : TB : massive changes on plane flight from Chicago to
Vancouver</sitem>
```

(Fascinating for two reasons: first, because I'm sure that Tim Bray would have written that comment differently if he was intending it for a wide audience; second, because it shows that even the authors of the XML specification committed the faux pas of using a private microsyntax within the XML elements, rather than marking up the structure of the entry in the form of three subelements: date, author, and details. This is one of the reasons that regular expression handling in XSLT 2.0 is so valuable. Try sorting these comments first by author, then by date, using XSLT 1.0 alone.)

In abbreviated form, the structure of the XML specification starts like this:

```
<spec w3c-doctype="rec">
    <header>
        <title>Extensible Markup Language (XML) 1.0</title>
        <version>1.0 (Second Edition)</version>
        <w3c-designation>REC-xml-&iso6.doc.date;</w3c-designation>
        <w3c-doctype>W3C Recommendation</w3c-doctype>
        <pubdate>
            <day>&draft.day;</day>
            <month>&draft.month;</month>
            <year>&draft.year;</year>
        </pubdate>

        <publoc>
            <loc href=" url"> url</loc>
            (<loc href="url">XHTML</loc>, <loc href="url">XML</loc>, ...)
        </publoc>
        <latestloc>
            <loc href=" url"> url</loc>
        </latestloc>
        <prevlocs>
            <loc href=" url"> url</loc>
        </prevlocs>

        <authlist>
            <author role="le">
                <name>Tim Bray</name>
                <affiliation>Textuality and Netscape</affiliation>
                <email href="mailto:tbray@textuality.com">
                        tbray@textuality.com</email>
            </author>
```

```
              more authors
        </authlist>
        <abstract>
            <p>The Extensible Markup Language (XML) is a subset of SGML
                          that is completely described in this document...
            </p>
        </abstract>

        <status>
        <p>This document has been reviewed by W3C Members and
                          other interested parties ...</p>

          <p>This document specifies a syntax... It is a product of the W3C
XML Activity, details of which can be found at <loc href=' url'> url</loc>.
<phrase diff="add"><loc role="erratumref" href="http://www.w3.org/XML/xml-
19980210-errata#E100">[E100]</loc> A list of current W3C Recommendations ...
can be found at <loc href=' url'> url</loc>.</p>

          <p>This specification uses the term URI, which is defined by
<bibref ref="Berners-Lee"/>, a work in progress expected to update
<bibref ref="RFC1738"/> and <bibref ref="RFC1808"/>. </p>
        </status>
     </header>
     <body>
        main section of document
     </body>
     <back>
        appendices
     </back>
</spec>
```

Note that some of the tags are structural elements with predictable nesting, while others such as `<loc>` can appear in all sorts of places, including inline within the text.

The next few template rules are all concerned with processing this header:

```
<!-- header: metadata about the spec -->
<!-- pull out information into standard W3C layout -->

<xsl:template match="header">
  <div class="head">
    <xsl:if test="not(/spec/@role='editors-copy')">
      <p>
        <a href="http://www.w3.org/">
          <img src="http://www.w3.org/Icons/w3c_home"
              alt="W3C" height="48" width="72"/>
        </a>
      </p>
    </xsl:if>

    <xsl:text>&#10;</xsl:text>
    <h1>
      <xsl:call-template name="anchor">
```

```
        <xsl:with-param name="node" select="title[1]"/>
        <xsl:with-param name="conditional" select="0"/>
        <xsl:with-param name="default.id" select="'title'"/>
    </xsl:call-template>

    <xsl:apply-templates select="title"/>

    <xsl:if test="version">
    <xsl:text> </xsl:text>
    <xsl:apply-templates select="version"/>
  </xsl:if>
</h1>
<xsl:if test="subtitle">
  <xsl:text>&#10;</xsl:text>
  <h2>
    <xsl:call-template name="anchor">
      <xsl:with-param name="node" select="subtitle[1]"/>
      <xsl:with-param name="conditional" select="0"/>
      <xsl:with-param name="default.id" select="'subtitle'"/>
    </xsl:call-template>
    <xsl:apply-templates select="subtitle"/>
  </h2>
</xsl:if>
<xsl:text>&#10;</xsl:text>

<h2>
  <xsl:call-template name="anchor">
    <xsl:with-param name="node" select="w3c-doctype[1]"/>
    <xsl:with-param name="conditional" select="0"/>
    <xsl:with-param name="default.id" select="'w3c-doctype'"/>
  </xsl:call-template>

  <xsl:apply-templates select="w3c-doctype"/>
  <xsl:text> </xsl:text>

  <xsl:if test="pubdate/day">
    <xsl:apply-templates select="pubdate/day"/>
    <xsl:text> </xsl:text>
  </xsl:if>
  <xsl:apply-templates select="pubdate/month"/>
  <xsl:text> </xsl:text>
  <xsl:apply-templates select="pubdate/year"/>
</h2>

<dl>
  <xsl:apply-templates select="publoc"/>
  <xsl:apply-templates select="latestloc"/>
  <xsl:apply-templates select="prevlocs"/>
  <xsl:apply-templates select="authlist"/>
</dl>

<!-- output the errataloc and altlocs -->
<xsl:apply-templates select="errataloc"/>
```

```
  <xsl:apply-templates select="preverrataloc"/>
  <xsl:apply-templates select="translationloc"/>
  <xsl:apply-templates select="altlocs"/>

<xsl:choose>
  <xsl:when test="copyright">
    <xsl:apply-templates select="copyright"/>
  </xsl:when>
  <xsl:otherwise>

    <p class="copyright">
      <a href="http://www.w3.org/Consortium/Legal/ipr-notice#Copyright">
        <xsl:text>Copyright</xsl:text>
      </a>

        <xsl:text> &#xa9; </xsl:text>
        <xsl:apply-templates select="pubdate/year"/>
        <xsl:text> </xsl:text>
        <a href="http://www.w3.org/">

          <acronym title="World Wide Web Consortium">W3C</acronym>
        </a>
        <sup>&#xae;</sup>
        <xsl:text> (</xsl:text>
        <a href="http://www.lcs.mit.edu/">
          <acronym title="Massachusetts Institute of Technology">
                  MIT</acronym>
        </a>

        <xsl:text>, </xsl:text>
        <a href="http://www.ercim.org/">
          <acronym title="European Research Consortium
                          for Informatics and Mathematics">ERCIM</acronym>
        </a>
        <xsl:text>, </xsl:text>
        <a href="http://www.keio.ac.jp/">Keio</a>
        <xsl:text>), All Rights Reserved. W3C </xsl:text>

        <a
href="http://www.w3.org/Consortium/Legal/ipr-notice#Legal_Disclaimer">
liability</a>
          <xsl:text>, </xsl:text>
          <a
href="http://www.w3.org/Consortium/Legal/ipr-notice#W3C_Trademarks">
trademark</a>
          <xsl:text>, </xsl:text>
          <a
href="http://www.w3.org/Consortium/Legal/copyright-documents">
document use</a>
          <xsl:text> and </xsl:text>

          <a
href="http://www.w3.org/Consortium/Legal/copyright-software">
software licensing</a>
```

```
            <xsl:text> rules apply.</xsl:text>
          </p>
        </xsl:otherwise>
      </xsl:choose>
    </div>
    <hr/>

    <xsl:apply-templates select="notice"/>
    <xsl:apply-templates select="abstract"/>
    <xsl:apply-templates select="status"/>
    <xsl:apply-templates select="revisiondesc"/>
</xsl:template>
```

There's nothing especially complicated here, but the code is worth reading. Note that the template rule controls the ordering of items in the result document (for example, the abstract will always precede the status section, regardless of which comes first in the source XML). However, the formatting of each subsection is delegated to a template rule for that particular element. This is therefore a blend of the *navigational* and *rule-based* design patterns. The generation of HTML anchors is also delegated, this time to a named template with parameters. The template looks like this:

```
<xsl:template name="anchor">
  <xsl:param name="node" select="."/>
  <xsl:param name="conditional" select="1"/>
  <xsl:param name="default.id" select="''"/>
  <xsl:variable name="id">
    <xsl:call-template name="object.id">
      <xsl:with-param name="node" select="$node"/>
      <xsl:with-param name="default.id" select="$default.id"/>
    </xsl:call-template>
  </xsl:variable>
  <xsl:if test="$conditional = 0 or $node/@id">
    <a name="{$id}" id="{$id}"/>
  </xsl:if>
</xsl:template>
```

which in turn calls:

```
<xsl:template name="object.id">
  <xsl:param name="node" select="."/>
  <xsl:param name="default.id" select="''"/>

  <xsl:choose>
    <!-- can't use the default ID if it's used somewhere else in the
document! -->
    <xsl:when test="$default.id != '' and not(key('ids', $default.id))">
      <xsl:value-of select="$default.id"/>
    </xsl:when>

    <xsl:when test="$node/@id">
      <xsl:value-of select="$node/@id"/>
    </xsl:when>
    <xsl:otherwise>
```

```
        <xsl:value-of select="generate-id($node)"/>
      </xsl:otherwise>
    </xsl:choose>
  </xsl:template>
```

The anchor template generates an element of the form `<a name="NNN" id="NNN">`. Generating both attributes helps to ensure maximum portability across different browser versions. If the parameter `$conditional` is set to «1», the template does nothing (actually, it computes an ID value and then ignores it: an example where lazy evaluation will produce performance savings). The actual ID value is taken either from the `@id` attribute of the node passed as a parameter (which defaults to the context node), or from the `$default-id` parameter. Surprisingly, the `$default-id` parameter overrides the `@id` attribute, provided that it is indeed a unique identifier within the source document.

It's instructive to see how much easier this would all be with XSLT 2.0. We could start by rewriting the `object.id` template as a function:

```
<xsl:function name="f:object.id" as="xs:string">
  <xsl:param name="node" as="node()"/>
  <xsl:param name="default.id" as="xs:string"/>
  <xsl:sequence select="
      if ($default.id != '' and not($node/key('ids', $default.id))
         then $default.id
      else if ($node/@id)
         then $node/@id"/>
      else generate-id($node)"/>
</xsl:function>
```

If you prefer, the conditional expression in `<xsl:sequence>` could be written more concisely as:

```
select="($default.id[. != '' and not($node/key('ids',.))],
         $node/@id,
         generate-id($node))[1]"
```

The anchor template can also be turned into a function:

```
<xsl:function name="f:anchor">
  <xsl:param name="node" as="node()"/>
  <xsl:param name="conditional" as="xs:boolean"/>
  <xsl:param name="default.id" as="xs:string"/>

  <xsl:variable name="id" select="f:object.id($node, $default-id)"/>
  <xsl:if test="$conditional = 0 or $node/@id">
    <a name="{$id}" id="{$id}"/>
  </xsl:if>
</xsl:function>
```

and a call on this template, previously written as:

```
<xsl:call-template name="anchor">
    <xsl:with-param name="node" select="w3c-doctype[1]"/>
    <xsl:with-param name="conditional" select="0"/>
    <xsl:with-param name="default.id" select="'w3c-doctype'"/>
</xsl:call-template>
```

can now be rewritten as:

```
<xsl:sequence select="f:anchor(w3c-doctype[1], false(), 'w3c-doctype')"/>
```

Apart from reducing the size of the two templates from 14/15 lines to 10 lines or less, the size of the call is reduced from 5 lines to 1, and since the anchor template is called 18 times in the stylesheet, this reduces the total size of the stylesheet by 82 lines. (I hope your productivity is not measured by the number of lines of XSLT code that you produce.) Some people argue that verbosity is not a problem in itself, but in my view, if you can see the whole of a template or function on the screen at one time, you are likely to understand its logic more quickly and to make fewer mistakes when you modify it.

The only thing you lose by doing this conversion is the ability of the templates to have default parameters. But I'm not entirely sure this is a bad thing: certainly, it's a feature that many languages don't provide.

Creating the Table of Contents

Immediately after the header, the first part of the body of the document is the table of contents. This is generated from within the template rule for the <body> element, and it is controlled by a parameter $toc.level that defines the number of levels in the table of contents: for example, if this is set to «2», then first- and second-level headings will be listed. HTML cannot produce page numbers, so the table of contents instead contains hyperlinks to the headings of the actual sections.

```
<xsl:template match="body">
    <xsl:if test="$toc.level &gt; 0">
      <div class="toc">
        <xsl:text>&#10;</xsl:text>
        <h2>
          <xsl:call-template name="anchor">
            <xsl:with-param name="conditional" select="0"/>
            <xsl:with-param name="default.id" select="'contents'"/>
          </xsl:call-template>
          <xsl:text>Table of Contents</xsl:text>
        </h2>
        <p class="toc">
          <xsl:apply-templates select="div1" mode="toc"/>
        </p>
        <xsl:if test="../back">
          <xsl:text>&#10;</xsl:text>
          <h3>
            <xsl:call-template name="anchor">
              <xsl:with-param name="conditional" select="0"/>
              <xsl:with-param name="default.id" select="'appendices'"/>
            </xsl:call-template>

            <xsl:text>Appendi</xsl:text>
            <xsl:choose>
              <xsl:when test="count(../back/div1 | ../back/inform-div1) > 1">
                <xsl:text>ces</xsl:text>
              </xsl:when>
              <xsl:otherwise>
```

```
            <xsl:text>x</xsl:text>
          </xsl:otherwise>
        </xsl:choose>
      </h3>

      <p class="toc">
        <xsl:apply-templates mode="toc"
                          select="../back/div1 | ../back/inform-div1"/>
        <xsl:call-template name="autogenerated-appendices-toc"/>
      </p>
    </xsl:if>
    <xsl:if test="//footnote[not(ancestor::table)]">
      <p class="toc">
        <a href="#endnotes">
          <xsl:text>End Notes</xsl:text>
        </a>
      </p>
    </xsl:if>
  </div>
  <hr/>
</xsl:if>
<div class="body">
  <xsl:apply-templates/>
</div>
</xsl:template>
```

The <body> template rule generates the table of contents, and then it uses <xsl:apply-templates> to process its own children. The table of contents is produced by applying templates to all the top-level (<div1>) sections and appendices in a special mode «toc», and by generating the headings «Table of Contents», «Appendix» or «Appendices», and «End Notes», as required. There is also provision for referencing appendices that are automatically generated by the stylesheet, for example a glossary or index of error codes.

Let's see how the table of contents is produced. The structure of the <body> element, and also of <back>, consists of a sequence of <div1> elements representing top-level sections, like this.

```
<div1>
    <head>First-level heading</head>
    <p>Some text</p>
    <div2>
        <head>Second-level heading</head>
        <p>Some more text</p>
        <div3>
            <head>Third-level heading</head>
            <p>Lots more text</p>
        </div3>
    </div2>
</div1>
```

Each <div1> element contains a <head> element giving its section title, paragraphs of immediate content, and zero or more <div2> elements containing level-2 subsections. The <div2> elements similarly contain a <head> and zero or more <div3> elements for level-3 subsections, and so on.

In the <back> section, a non-normative appendix is represented by an <inform-div1> element instead of the usual <div1>, but otherwise the structure is the same.

Non-normative *is jargon meaning "for information only, not officially part of the specification."*

The template rule that generates an entry for a top-level section in the table of contents looks like this:

```
<!-- mode: toc -->
<xsl:template mode="toc" match="div1">
  <xsl:apply-templates select="." mode="divnum"/>
  <a>
    <xsl:attribute name="href">
      <xsl:call-template name="href.target">
        <xsl:with-param name="target" select="."/>
      </xsl:call-template>
    </xsl:attribute>
    <xsl:apply-templates select="head" mode="text"/>
  </a>
  <br/>

  <xsl:text>&#10;</xsl:text>
  <xsl:if test="$toc.level &gt; 1">
    <xsl:apply-templates select="div2" mode="toc"/>
  </xsl:if>
</xsl:template>
```

This starts by applying templates to itself with mode divnum: this invokes a template to calculate the section number. We'll take a look at this template rule shortly. The rule then generates an HTML <a> element to produce a hyperlink. The href attribute is generated by calling a named template href.target, with the current node (the <div1> element) as a parameter. The content of the <a> element (the displayed text that the user clicks on) is produced by applying templates to the <head> element, with the special mode text. The stylesheet doesn't actually contain a template rule for this mode; it is used simply to invoke the built-in template rule, which returns the textual content of the <head> element, minus any markup.

The «href.target» template looks like this:

```
<xsl:template name="href.target">
  <xsl:param name="target" select="."/>
  <xsl:text>#</xsl:text>
  <xsl:choose>
    <xsl:when test="$target/@id">
      <xsl:value-of select="$target/@id"/>
    </xsl:when>
    <xsl:otherwise>
      <xsl:value-of select="generate-id($target)"/>
    </xsl:otherwise>
  </xsl:choose>
</xsl:template>
```

To my mind this is crying out to be replaced by an XSLT 2.0 function, something like:

```
<xsl:function name="f:href.target" as="xs:string">
  <xsl:param name="target" as="node()"/>
  <xsl:sequence select="concat('#', ($target/@id, generate-id($target))[1]"/>
</xsl:function>
```

This would allow the code:

```
<a>
  <xsl:attribute name="href">
    <xsl:call-template name="href.target">
      <xsl:with-param name="target" select="."/>
    </xsl:call-template>
  </xsl:attribute>
  <xsl:apply-templates select="head" mode="text"/>
</a>
```

to be rewritten as:

```
<a href="{f:href.target(.)}">
  <xsl:apply-templates select="head" mode="text"/>
</a>
```

If the global parameter $toc.level is greater than one, then the <div2> elements that are children of this <div1> are processed in mode «toc» to generate another level in the table of contents.

The template rule for <div2> elements in mode «toc» and the template rules for further levels such as <div3>, are very similar to the <div1> rule. They differ only in that they apply templates to the next level down (the <div2> template processes the <div3> children, and so on) and in the amount of indentation added before the section number—this is added crudely in the form of four nonbreaking spaces per level, using the instruction:

```
<xsl:text>    </xsl:text>
```

Hexadecimal «a0» (decimal 160) is the Unicode code for the nonbreaking space character, better known to HTML authors as the entity reference « ». This is not available as a built-in entity in XML. It is possible to define it as an entity in the DTD, but the authors of this stylesheet chose to write it explicitly as a numeric character reference.

It wouldn't be difficult to write a parameterized template that handled all the <divN> elements in one rule, but the alternative approach of writing five separate rules is perfectly defensible.

The templates to calculate section numbers have one variant for each level of heading, and also vary depending on whether the section is in the <body> (a main section) or in the <back> matter (an appendix). Here are some of them:

```
<!-- mode: divnum -->
<xsl:template mode="divnum" match="div1">
  <xsl:number format="1 "/>
</xsl:template>

<xsl:template mode="divnum" match="back/div1 | inform-div1">
  <xsl:number count="div1 | inform-div1" format="A "/>
```

```
  </xsl:template>

  <xsl:template mode="divnum" match="div2">
    <xsl:number level="multiple" count="div1 | div2" format="1.1 "/>
  </xsl:template>

  <xsl:template mode="divnum" match="back//div2">
    <xsl:number level="multiple" count="div1 | div2 | inform-div1"
      format="A.1 "/>
  </xsl:template>

  <xsl:template mode="divnum" match="div3">
    <xsl:number level="multiple" count="div1 | div2 | div3"
      format="1.1.1 "/>
  </xsl:template>

  <xsl:template mode="divnum" match="back//div3">
    <xsl:number level="multiple"
      count="div1 | div2 | div3 | inform-div1" format="A.1.1 "/>
  </xsl:template>
```

All these templates work by calling <xsl:number> with appropriate parameters. The default «level="single"» is used for the top-level headings, and «level="multiple"» for all other levels, with a «count» attribute that matches that level and all ancestor levels. The format of the numbering is adjusted for appendices (sections with <back> as an ancestor) to use alphabetic identifiers (A, B, C, ...) for the first component of the number.

Giving a list of alternatives in the count attribute is a common way of doing multilevel numbering. It means, in effect, outputting a sequence number for each ancestor element that is either an <inform-div1>, or a <div1>, or a <div2>, and so on. Like most template rules in a rule-based stylesheet, it doesn't attempt to do any validation: if the input structure is wrong, it will produce some sort of output nevertheless, and it's up to the document author to work out what the problem is. This raises an interesting question that you need to consider when designing your own stylesheets: is it the job of the stylesheet to detect and report on errors in the source document?

The use of <inform-div1> as a separate tag for non-normative appendices was a pretty clumsy design decision, and the stylesheet author has to pay the price here. It would have been much cleaner to give the <div1> element an attribute «normative="no"». Sadly, it is often the case that stylesheet authors have to cope with XML structures that could have been designed better. In XSLT 2.0, if this stylesheet were schema aware, it's likely that <inform-div1> would be in the substitution group of <div1>, and it would then be possible to replace all references to «div1» in these template rules by «schema-element(div1)», which would pick up the <inform-div1> elements automatically.

It would again be possible to make these template rules generic across levels. In fact, the template rule shown above for <div3> elements would produce exactly the right output if it were applied to a <div1> or <div2> element, because of the way that <xsl:number> is defined. The «format» attribute of <xsl:number> can also be parameterized using an attribute value template: in XSLT 2.0 one could write:

```
  <xsl:template mode="divnum" match="div3">
    <xsl:number level="multiple"
```

```
          count="div1 | div2 | div3 | inform-div1"
          format="{if (ancestor::back) then 'A.1.1' else '1.1.1'}"/>
    </xsl:template>
```

However, it does no harm for the stylesheet author to spell things out more explicitly.

The templates for producing section numbers in the table of contents are reused, of course, when producing the section numbers in the body of the document. I'll describe how this is done, in the next section.

Creating Section Headers

We'll now look at the template rules used to format the section headers. These all have the same structure, and they reuse components we have already seen: the named `anchor` template that generates the target of a hyperlink, and the `divnum` mode that produces the section number for any given section. Here are the first two:

```
<xsl:template match="div1/head">
  <h2>
    <xsl:call-template name="anchor">
      <xsl:with-param name="conditional" select="0"/>
      <xsl:with-param name="node" select=".."/>
    </xsl:call-template>
    <xsl:apply-templates select=".." mode="divnum"/>
    <xsl:apply-templates/>
  </h2>
</xsl:template>

<xsl:template match="div2/head">
  <h3>
    <xsl:call-template name="anchor">
      <xsl:with-param name="conditional" select="0"/>
      <xsl:with-param name="node" select=".."/>
    </xsl:call-template>
    <xsl:apply-templates select=".." mode="divnum"/>
    <xsl:apply-templates/>
  </h3>
</xsl:template>
```

It would be entirely possible to use a single generic template by replacing the literal result element <h*N*> with the construct:

```
<xsl:element name="{replace(name(..), 'div', 'h')}">
```

This uses the XPath 2.0 `replace()` function, but the same logic could be written almost as easily by using XPath 1.0 functions such as `concat()` and `substring-after()`. Another way to avoid repetition of code between these templates would be to write separate template rules at the top level, and call a common component to produce the inner content:

```
<xsl:template match="div1/head">
    <h2>
        <xsl:apply-templates select="." mode="head"/>
    </h2>
```

```
    </xsl:template>

    <xsl:template match="div2/head">
        <h3>
            <xsl:apply-templates select="." mode="head"/>
        </h3>
    </xsl:template>

    <xsl:template match="head" mode="head">
        <xsl:call-template name="anchor">
            <xsl:with-param name="conditional" select="0"/>
            <xsl:with-param name="node" select=".."/>
        </xsl:call-template>
        <xsl:apply-templates select=".." mode="divnum"/>
        <xsl:apply-templates/>
    </xsl:template>
```

Yet another approach would be for the common template rule to be invoked using
`<xsl:next-match/>` rather than by using a separate mode.

Formatting the Text

The bulk of the stylesheet is taken up with template rules to process simple textual markup within the
body of the document. Most of these are very straightforward, and to avoid tedious repetition I will show
only a small sample of them.

Probably the most common element is the <p> element, which marks a paragraph, as in HTML:

```
<xsl:template match="p">
  <p>
    <xsl:if test="@id">
      <xsl:attribute name="id">
        <xsl:value-of select="@id"/>
      </xsl:attribute>
    </xsl:if>
    <xsl:if test="@role">
      <xsl:attribute name="class">
        <xsl:value-of select="@role"/>
      </xsl:attribute>
    </xsl:if>
    <xsl:apply-templates/>
  </p>
</xsl:template>
```

You've probably got the message by now that I don't much like unnecessary verbosity. The first thing I
notice about this template rule is that the five lines:

```
<xsl:if test="@id">
   <xsl:attribute name="id">
     <xsl:value-of select="@id"/>
   </xsl:attribute>
</xsl:if>
```

are equivalent to the single line:

```
<xsl:copy-of select="@id">
```

The next is that `<xsl:if>` renames the «`role`» attribute as «`class`», so it's less easy to simplify, though with XSLT 2.0 you can reduce it to:

```
<xsl:if test="@role">
  <xsl:attribute name="class" select="@role"/>
</xsl:if>
```

But the essential structure of this template rule is typical of many others: it translates one element in the source document into one element in the result document, making minor adjustments to the attributes, and then calls `<xsl:apply-templates/>` to process the content of the element. This is the typical style of a rule-based stylesheet. Here are some other simple examples of such rules:

```
<!-- sub: subscript -->
<xsl:template match="sub">
  <sub>
    <xsl:apply-templates/>
  </sub>
</xsl:template>

<!-- term: the actual mention of a term within a termdef -->
<xsl:template match="term">
  <b><xsl:apply-templates/></b>
</xsl:template>

<!-- emph: in-line emphasis -->
<xsl:template match="emph">
  <em><xsl:apply-templates/></em>
</xsl:template>

<!-- rfc2119: identifies RFC 2119 keywords -->
<xsl:template match="rfc2119">
  <strong><xsl:apply-templates/></strong>
</xsl:template>

<!-- item: generic list item -->
<xsl:template match="item">
  <li>
    <xsl:apply-templates/>
  </li>
</xsl:template>

<!-- quote: a quoted string or phrase -->
<!-- it would be nice to use HTML <q> elements, but browser support is
abysmal-->
<xsl:template match="quote">
  <xsl:text>"</xsl:text>
  <xsl:apply-templates/>
  <xsl:text>"</xsl:text>
</xsl:template>
```

```
<!-- affiliation: follows a name in author and member -->
<xsl:template match="affiliation">
  <xsl:text>, </xsl:text>
  <xsl:apply-templates/>
</xsl:template>
```

There are some elements in the XML that are not rendered in the HTML at all, for example:

```
<xsl:template match="revisiondesc">
  <!-- suppressed by default -->
</xsl:template>
```

I generally write empty template rules using the shorter style:

```
<xsl:template match="revisiondesc"/>
```

but one can't criticize this writer for adding a comment to make the intention clear.

The XML specification represents tables in exactly the same way as HTML, except that some additional attributes are permitted. So the template rule's job is essentially to copy the element while adjusting those attributes:

```
<!-- table: the HTML table model adopted wholesale; note however that we -->
<!-- do this such that the XHTML stylesheet will do the right thing. -->
<xsl:template match="caption|col|colgroup|td|tfoot|th|thead|tr|tbody">
  <xsl:element name="{local-name(.)}">
    <xsl:for-each select="@*">
      <!-- Wait: some of these aren't HTML attributes after all... -->

      <xsl:choose>
        <xsl:when test="local-name(.) = 'role'">
          <xsl:attribute name="class">
            <xsl:value-of select="."/>
          </xsl:attribute>
        </xsl:when>
        <xsl:when test="local-name(.) = 'diff'">
          <!-- nop -->
        </xsl:when>

        <xsl:otherwise>
          <xsl:copy>
            <xsl:apply-templates/>
          </xsl:copy>
        </xsl:otherwise>
      </xsl:choose>
    </xsl:for-each>
    <xsl:apply-templates/>
  </xsl:element>

</xsl:template>
```

I think I would have been inclined to handle these attributes using template rules, especially as we've already seen the same code to rename a `role` attribute as a `class` attribute, elsewhere in the stylesheet.

Instead of `<xsl:for-each select="@*">` and the big `<xsl:choose>` instruction, I would write `<xsl:apply-templates select="@*" mode="table-att"/>`, with the three template rules:

```
<xsl:template match="@role" mode="table-att">
   <xsl:attribute name="class" select="."/>
</xsl:template>

<xsl:template match="@diff" mode="table-att"/>

<xsl:template match="@*" mode="table-att">
   <xsl:copy/>
</xsl:template>
```

Producing Lists

The DTD for these documents provides a number of ways of defining lists. For example, an ordered list looks like this:

```
<p>The design goals for XML are:</p>
<olist>
<item><p>XML shall be straightforwardly usable over the
         Internet.</p></item>
<item><p>XML shall support a wide variety of applications.</p></item>
<item><p>XML shall be compatible with SGML.</p></item>
<item><p>It shall be easy to write programs which process XML
         documents.</p></item>
<item><p>The number of optional features in XML is to be kept
           to the absolute minimum, ideally zero.</p></item>
<item><p>XML documents should be human-legible and reasonably
         clear.</p></item>
<item><p>The XML design should be prepared quickly.</p></item>
<item><p>The design of XML shall be formal and concise.</p></item>
<item><p>XML documents shall be easy to create.</p></item>
<item><p>Terseness in XML markup is of minimal importance.</p></item>
</olist>
```

The rule for ordered lists is interesting, because it uses a recursive named template. The aim here is to decide automatically what kind of numbering to apply to nested levels of list: «1, 2, 3» for the outermost level, «a, b, c» for the second level, «i, ii, iii» for the third level, and so on.

```
<!-- olist: an ordered list -->
<xsl:template match="olist">
  <xsl:variable name="numeration">
    <xsl:call-template name="list.numeration"/>
  </xsl:variable>

  <xsl:variable name="type">
    <xsl:choose>
      <xsl:when test="$numeration='arabic'">1</xsl:when>
      <xsl:when test="$numeration='loweralpha'">a</xsl:when>
      <xsl:when test="$numeration='lowerroman'">i</xsl:when>
```

```
          <xsl:when test="$numeration='upperalpha'">A</xsl:when>
          <xsl:when test="$numeration='upperroman'">I</xsl:when>
          <!-- What!? This should never happen -->
          <xsl:otherwise>
            <xsl:message>
              <xsl:text>Unexpected numeration: </xsl:text>
              <xsl:value-of select="$numeration"/>
            </xsl:message>
            <xsl:value-of select="1"/>
          </xsl:otherwise>
        </xsl:choose>
      </xsl:variable>

      <ol class="enum{$type}">
        <xsl:apply-templates/>
      </ol>
</xsl:template>

<xsl:template name="list.numeration">
  <xsl:param name="node" select="."/>
    <xsl:choose>
      <xsl:when test="$node/ancestor::olist">
        <xsl:call-template name="next.numeration">
          <xsl:with-param name="numeration">
            <xsl:call-template name="list.numeration">
              <xsl:with-param name="node" select="$node/ancestor::olist[1]"/>
            </xsl:call-template>
          </xsl:with-param>
        </xsl:call-template>
      </xsl:when>
      <xsl:otherwise>
        <xsl:call-template name="next.numeration"/>
      </xsl:otherwise>
    </xsl:choose>
</xsl:template>

<xsl:template name="next.numeration">
  <xsl:param name="numeration" select="'default'"/>
  <xsl:choose>
    <!-- Change this list if you want to change the order of numerations -->
    <xsl:when test="$numeration = 'arabic'">loweralpha</xsl:when>
    <xsl:when test="$numeration = 'loweralpha'">lowerroman</xsl:when>
    <xsl:when test="$numeration = 'lowerroman'">upperalpha</xsl:when>
    <xsl:when test="$numeration = 'upperalpha'">upperroman</xsl:when>
    <xsl:when test="$numeration = 'upperroman'">arabic</xsl:when>
    <xsl:otherwise>arabic</xsl:otherwise>
  </xsl:choose>
</xsl:template>
```

The recursive call on the «list.numeration» template occurs while calculating a parameter to supply to the «next.numeration» template. The way this works is that if the <olist> element has no <olist> ancestor, it sets the number format to «arabic». If it does have an <olist> ancestor, it calls the «list.numeration» template supplying the first ancestor as a parameter. The «next.numeration» template supplies the next numbering format in the list: if the input is «arabic», the output is «loweralpha», and so on.

I must admit this isn't how I would have written it, though everyone is entitled to their own style. In XSLT 2.0 I would probably define a function:

```
<xsl:function name="f:olist-format" as="xs:string">
    <xsl:param name="node" as="node()"/>
    <xsl:sequence
        select="('1', 'a', 'i', 'A', 'I')[count($node/ancestor::olist)
                                            mod 5 + 1]"/>
</xsl:function>
```

and then write the template rule for <olist> as:

```
<xsl:template match="olist">
    <ol class="enum{$f:olist-format(.)}">
        <xsl:apply-templates/>
    </ol>
</xsl:template>
```

A reduction from 53 lines to 10 can't be all that bad.

Making Cross-References

If you read W3C working drafts and recommendations online, you'll notice that they are very heavily hyperlinked. Terms with special meanings are linked to their definitions; cross-references from one section of the specification to another are represented by hyperlinks; references to other documents are represented first by a link to the bibliography, and then from the bibliography to the external document on the Web if it is available; there are references from a document to previous versions of the document, and so on. In the XML specification, every use of a grammar symbol such as «elementdecl» is linked to the grammar rule where it is defined. Similarly, in the XSLT specification, every use of an XSLT element name such as «xsl:sequence» is linked to its definition. In this section, we will look at the rules that are used to create these links. There are many of these, and I'll pick a selection that illustrates the techniques used.

Let's take the linking of term references to term definitions. Here is an example of a term definition from the XML specification that defines one term and contains two references to terms defined elsewhere in the specification:

```
<p><termdef id="dt-xml-doc" term="XML Document">A data object is an
<term>XML document</term> if it is
<termref def="dt-wellformed">well-formed</termref>, as defined in this
specification. A well-formed XML document may in addition be
<termref def="dt-valid">valid</termref> if it meets certain further
constraints.</termdef></p>
```

(A curious definition, because having said that all XML documents are "well-formed", it seems rather odd to use the phrase *well-formed XML document* in the very next sentence, as if there were any other kind. But we are not here to criticize the prose.)

The `<termdef>` element identifies this as a term definition. The «id» attribute identifies this term definition uniquely within the document. The «term» attribute is the term being defined. This is also tagged using the `<term>` element where it appears in the text. This might appear redundant, but the DTD requires it. There are some cases where the two differ, for example the XML specification states:

```
<p><termdef id="dt-root" term="Root Element">There is exactly one
element, called the <term>root</term>, or document element, no part of
which appears in the <termref def="dt-content">content</termref> of
any other element.</termdef>
```

I'm afraid I've never been sure as to whether the term being defined here is *root* or *root element*.

The `<termref>` element has a «def» attribute that must match the «id» attribute of some `<termdef>`. You find that confusing? Well so do I.

The template rule for the `<termdef>` marks the definition as such, and generates an HTML anchor, like this:

```
<!-- termdef: sentence or phrase defining a term -->
<xsl:template match="termdef">
  <xsl:text>[</xsl:text>
  <a name="{@id}" id="{@id}" title="{@term}">
    <xsl:text>Definition</xsl:text>
  </a>
  <xsl:text>: </xsl:text>
  <xsl:apply-templates/>
  <xsl:text>]</xsl:text>
</xsl:template>
```

The «id» and «name» attributes of the HTML `<a>` element are both used (by various browsers) to identify the element, and the «title» attribute identifies its role: it is not used by a conventional browser, but may be used, for example, by audio browsers.

The corresponding rule for the `<termref>` element generates a link to this anchor:

```
<!-- termref: reference to a defined term -->
<xsl:template match="termref">
  <a title="{key('ids', @def)/@term}">
    <xsl:attribute name="href">
      <xsl:call-template name="href.target">
        <xsl:with-param name="target" select="key('ids', @def)"/>
      </xsl:call-template>
    </xsl:attribute>
    <xsl:apply-templates/>
  </a>
</xsl:template>
```

This calls the named template «href.target» to produce the content of the «href» attribute. We've already seen this named template on page 663. Note the use of the key() function to enable quick access to the target of the link: scanning the whole document, by using an expression such as «//termdef[@id=current()/@def]», would be hopelessly slow.

The other rules that generate internal links are all very similar to this pair.

The links to a section are a little more complex because they require the section number to be computed. In the source XML document, the links look like this:

```
<p>Full definitions of the specific characters in each class
are given in <specref ref="CharClasses"/>.</p>
```

Here, «CharClasses» must match the «id» attribute of an element such as <div1>, <div2>, or <div3>. In fact, quite a range of different elements can act as the target of a <specref>, for example, an <issue> or a <vcnote>. The form of the link depends on the type of target, so the template rule contains a big <xsl:choose> instruction that handles all the possibilities. It reads as follows:

```
<xsl:template match="specref">
<xsl:variable name="target" select="key('ids', @ref)[1]"/>
<xsl:choose>
  <xsl:when test="local-name($target)='issue'">
    <xsl:text>[</xsl:text>
    <a>
      <xsl:attribute name="href">
        <xsl:call-template name="href.target">
          <xsl:with-param name="target" select="key('ids', @ref)"/>
        </xsl:call-template>
      </xsl:attribute>
      <b>
        <xsl:text>Issue </xsl:text>
        <xsl:apply-templates select="key('ids', @ref)" mode="number"/>
        <xsl:text>: </xsl:text>
        <xsl:for-each select="key('ids', @ref)/head">
          <xsl:apply-templates/>
        </xsl:for-each>
      </b>
    </a>
    <xsl:text>]</xsl:text>
  </xsl:when>
```

This code handles the case where the target is an <issue> (used to flag a known problem in a working draft). The «href» attribute is generated using the named template «href.target», as before. The text of the hyperlink contains the issue number and the title (the <head> element) of the issue.

The next section handles <div1>, <div2>, and so on. In this case, the text of the link contains the section number and section heading of the target section. Note the use of <xsl:apply-templates> here, to process an element in a particular mode, to get first the section number and then the section title (from its <head> element):

```
<xsl:when test="starts-with(local-name($target), 'div')">
  <a>
    <xsl:attribute name="href">
      <xsl:call-template name="href.target">
        <xsl:with-param name="target" select="key('ids', @ref)"/>
      </xsl:call-template>
```

```
        </xsl:attribute>
      <b>
        <xsl:apply-templates select="key('ids', @ref)" mode="divnum"/>
        <xsl:apply-templates select="key('ids', @ref)/head" mode="text"/>
      </b>
    </a>
  </xsl:when>
```

Appendices are handled using identical code as normal sections, and the code could have easily been made common by using an «or» in the <xsl:when> condition:

```
<xsl:when test="starts-with(local-name($target), 'inform-div')">
  <a>
    <xsl:attribute name="href">
      <xsl:call-template name="href.target">
        <xsl:with-param name="target" select="key('ids', @ref)"/>
      </xsl:call-template>
    </xsl:attribute>
    <b>
      <xsl:apply-templates select="key('ids', @ref)" mode="divnum"/>
      <xsl:apply-templates select="key('ids', @ref)/head" mode="text"/>
    </b>
  </a>
</xsl:when>
```

Code follows for several more possible target elements, including <vcnote>, <prod>, and <label>, but it's almost identical in each case.

Now, we see something unusual: the template rule does some checking to ensure that the target element is one of the types of element that a <specref> can point to. Generally, this stylesheet does not do much validation of this kind, and it would probably be a good thing if it did more. Many errors in source documents, if they pass the checks performed by the DTD, are detected only because the HTML that's generated turns out to be invalid.

```
<xsl:otherwise>
  <xsl:message>
    <xsl:text>Unsupported specref to </xsl:text>
    <xsl:value-of select="local-name($target)"/>
    <xsl:text> [</xsl:text>
    <xsl:value-of select="@ref"/>
    <xsl:text>] </xsl:text>
    <xsl:text> (Contact stylesheet maintainer).</xsl:text>
  </xsl:message>
  <b>
    <a>
      <xsl:attribute name="href">
        <xsl:call-template name="href.target">
          <xsl:with-param name="target" select="key('ids', @ref)"/>
        </xsl:call-template>
      </xsl:attribute>
      <xsl:text>???</xsl:text>
    </a>
```

```
        </b>
      </xsl:otherwise>
    </xsl:choose>
  </xsl:template>
```

I'm not very fond of tests like «local-name($target)='issue'» or «name($target)= 'issue'». I think it's better to write «test="$target[self::issue]"», because neither of the first two tests properly takes the namespace into account. The fact that both the local-name() and name() tests are incorrect (both allow expanded QNames other than the one that the user was looking for) makes them difficult to optimize. Some systems index elements by name, and it might be impossible to use the index because the condition is capable of matching names in other namespaces.

Setting Out the Production Rules

Now we get to a more interesting area. The XML Recommendation contains syntax production rules, and these are marked up in some detail. A sequence of production rules is contained within a `<scrap>` element, and each rule is a `<prod>` element. Here is an example of a `<scrap>` that contains a single production rule:

```
<scrap lang='ebnf' id='document'>
    <head>Document</head>
    <prod id='NT-document'>
        <lhs>document</lhs>
        <rhs>
            <nt def='NT-prolog'>prolog</nt>
            <nt def='NT-element'>element</nt>
            <nt def='NT-Misc'>Misc</nt>*
        </rhs>
    </prod>
</scrap>
```

This is of course the production rule for an XML document, which appears in the specification as shown in Figure 10-2.

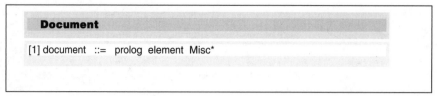

Document

[1] document   ::=   prolog element Misc*

Figure 10-2

In some cases the production rules within a `<scrap>` are grouped into `<prodgroup>` elements, but this grouping is ignored in the output.

Here are the top-level template rules:

```
<!-- scrap: series of formal grammar productions -->
<!-- set up a <table> and handle children -->
<xsl:template match="scrap">
```

```
    <xsl:apply-templates select="head"/>
    <table class="scrap" summary="Scrap">
      <xsl:apply-templates select="bnf | prod | prodgroup"/>
    </table>
</xsl:template>

<!-- create one <tbody> for each group -->
<xsl:template match="prodgroup">
    <tbody>
      <xsl:apply-templates/>
    </tbody>
</xsl:template>

<!-- prod: a formal grammar production -->
<!-- if not in a prodgroup, needs a <tbody> -->
<!-- has a weird content model; makes a table but there are no
     explicit rules; many different things can start a new row -->
<!-- process the first child in each row, and it will process the
     others -->
<xsl:template match="prod">
    <tbody>
      <xsl:apply-templates
        select="lhs |
                rhs[preceding-sibling::*[1][name()!='lhs']] |
                com[preceding-sibling::*[1][name()!='rhs']] |
                constraint[preceding-sibling::*[1][name()!='rhs']] |
                vc[preceding-sibling::*[1][name()!='rhs']] |
                wfc[preceding-sibling::*[1][name()!='rhs']]"/>
    </tbody>
</xsl:template>

<xsl:template match="prodgroup/prod">
    <xsl:apply-templates
      select="lhs |
              rhs[preceding-sibling::*[1][name()!='lhs']] |
              com[preceding-sibling::*[1][name()!='rhs']] |
              constraint[preceding-sibling::*[1][name()!='rhs']] |
              vc[preceding-sibling::*[1][name()!='rhs']] |
              wfc[preceding-sibling::*[1][name()!='rhs']]"/>
</xsl:template>
```

To understand this, let's first ignore the horrendous `select` expression that appears in the last two rules.

❏   The rule for the `<scrap>` element processes the `<head>` element to produce a heading, and then outputs an HTML table, whose contents are generated by processing all the `<prodgroup>` and `<prod>` elements contained in the `<scrap>`.

❏   The rule also allows for a `<scrap>` to contain `<bnf>` elements. However, the document we're working with doesn't contain any, so we can ignore this.

❏   The rules are being rather pedantic by ensuring that the rows of the table are always contained in a `<tbody>` element. In practice, Web browsers don't insist on a `<tbody>` being present, and many HTML authors don't bother writing one, but technically the HTML specification requires it, and the W3C takes great pains to make sure that the documents it publishes are valid HTML. This means that when there is a `<prodgroup>` present, the `<tbody>` is generated at the level of the `<prodgroup>`; when there is a `<prod>` that is not contained in a `<prodgroup>` (that is, it is contained directly in the `<scrap>`), then the `<tbody>` is generated when processing the `<prod>` element; but when a `<prod>` is contained in a `<prodgroup>`, no additional `<tbody>` is produced.

Now let's look at the monster `select` expression. A production rule (`<prod>`) has one left-hand side (`<lhs>`), one or more right-hand sides (`<rhs>`), and one or more annotations (`<vc>`, `<wfc>`, or `<com>`). A `<vc>` element is used to refer to a validation constraint, a `<wfc>` element to refer to a well-formedness constraint, and a `<com>` element to refer to a comment. The XML specification does not use `<constraint>` elements, so we can ignore those.

A rule with one `<lhs>` element, two `<rhs>` elements, and three `<wfc>` annotations would be laid out in an HTML table like this:

[17]	lhs1	::=	rhs1	
			rhs2	wfc1
				wfc2
				wfc3

As the comment says, the `select` expression is processing the children of the `<prod>` element that start a new row: here, lhs1, rhs2, wfc2, and wfc3. More precisely, the selected elements include every `<lhs>` element, any `<rhs>` element that is not immediately preceded by an `<lhs>` element, and any `<vc>`, `<wfc>`, or `<com>` element that is not immediately preceded by an `<rhs>` element. So, this template selects the elements that will start a new row, and calls `<xsl:apply-templates>` to process them.

We'll now look at the template rules that will match these elements. First the `<lhs>`:

```
<!-- lhs: left-hand side of formal productions -->
<xsl:template match="lhs">
  <tr valign="baseline">
    <td>
      <xsl:if test="ancestor-or-self::*/@diff and $show.diff.markup != 0">
        <xsl:attribute name="class">
          <xsl:text>diff-</xsl:text>
          <xsl:value-of select="ancestor-or-self::*/@diff"/>
        </xsl:attribute>
      </xsl:if>
      <xsl:if test="../@id">
        <a name="{../@id}" id="{../@id}"/>
      </xsl:if>
      <xsl:number count="prod" level="any" from="spec" format="[1]"/>
      <xsl:text>   </xsl:text>
    </td>
    <td>
      <xsl:if test="ancestor-or-self::*/@diff and $show.diff.markup != 0">
        <xsl:attribute name="class">
```

```
        <xsl:text>diff-</xsl:text>
        <xsl:value-of select="ancestor-or-self::*/@diff"/>
      </xsl:attribute>
    </xsl:if>
    <code><xsl:apply-templates/></code>
  </td>
  <td>
    <xsl:if test="ancestor-or-self::*/@diff and $show.diff.markup != 0">
      <xsl:attribute name="class">
        <xsl:text>diff-</xsl:text>
        <xsl:value-of select="ancestor-or-self::*/@diff"/>
      </xsl:attribute>
    </xsl:if>
    <xsl:text>   ::=   </xsl:text>
  </td>
  <xsl:apply-templates select="following-sibling::*[1][name()='rhs']"/>
  </tr>
</xsl:template>
```

There's a great deal of clutter in this rule. The code outputs a table row (a `<tr>` element) and the first three cells in that table (`<td>` elements).

For each `<td>` element, there is a six-line `<xsl:if>` instruction that is concerned solely with coloring change-marked sections in the code: changes from one version to the next are marked by the presence of a «diff» attribute on this or some ancestor element, and the coloring happens only if the stylesheet parameter $show.diff.markup is enabled. This clutter could be reduced dramatically by replacing the six lines with a call such as the following, to return the relevant attribute node when required, or an empty sequence otherwise:

```
<xsl:call-template name="handle-diff"/>
```

The first cell contains an optional hyperlink anchor, and a sequence number. The call on `<xsl:number>` using «level="any"» is a good example of how to generate a sequence of numbers that runs through the document. It creates a sequential number for each `<lhs>` element, that is, for each production rule. (Unfortunately, it is actually commented out in the current version of the stylesheet, supposedly because of a bug in one particular XSLT processor, and a less convenient technique is used instead. I decided on this occasion to publish the code as the author would have wanted it to be.)

In the second cell, the template calls `<xsl:apply-templates/>` to process the contents of the `<lhs>` element, which will generally just be the name of the syntactic term being defined. In the third cell it outputs the «::=» that separates the term from its definition. In various places it inserts nonbreaking space characters (« ») to achieve visual separation between the parts of the rule.

After producing these three cells, the template calls:

```
<xsl:apply-templates select="following-sibling::*[1][name()='rhs']"/>
```

This selects the immediately following sibling element, provided it is an `<rhs>` element, and applies the appropriate template rule. Actually, I think the `<lhs>` element is always followed immediately by an `<rhs>` element, so this could have been written rather more straightforwardly as:

```
<xsl:apply-templates select="following-sibling::rhs[1]"/>
```

As I mentioned before, I would normally write the predicate as «[self::rhs]» rather than
«[name()='rhs']» to avoid namespace problems, and more particularly, to allow the optimizer to use
indexes if it can.

As we will see, this <xsl:apply-templates> causes the other two cells to be added to the table row.

So let's look at the template rule for the <rhs> element. There are two cases to consider here: if the <rhs>
immediately follows an <lhs> element, then it will appear in the same table row as the <lhs> element,
but in all other cases, it will appear in a new row of its own, preceded by three empty table cells. I would
probably have chosen to handle these two cases in two separate template rules, distinguishing the first
case using a match pattern such as «match="rhs[preceding-sibling::*[1][self::lhs]]"»,
but the writer of this stylesheet chose to handle both cases in a single rule, like this:

```
<!-- rhs: right-hand side of a formal production -->
<!-- make a table cell; if it's not the first after an LHS, make a
     new row, too -->
<xsl:template match="rhs">
  <xsl:choose>
    <xsl:when test="preceding-sibling::*[1][name()='lhs']">
      <td>
        <xsl:if test="ancestor-or-self::*/@diff and $show.diff.markup != 0">
          <xsl:attribute name="class">
            <xsl:text>diff-</xsl:text>
            <xsl:value-of select="ancestor-or-self::*/@diff"/>
          </xsl:attribute>
        </xsl:if>
        <code><xsl:apply-templates/></code>
      </td>
      <xsl:apply-templates
        select="following-sibling::*[1][name()='com' or
                                        name()='constraint' or
                                        name()='vc' or
                                        name()='wfc']"/>
    </xsl:when>
    <xsl:otherwise>
      <tr valign="baseline">
        <td/><td/><td/>
        <td>
          <xsl:if test="ancestor-or-self::*/@diff and $show.diff.markup != 0">
            <xsl:attribute name="class">
              <xsl:text>diff-</xsl:text>
              <xsl:value-of select="ancestor-or-self::*/@diff"/>
            </xsl:attribute>
          </xsl:if>
          <code><xsl:apply-templates/></code>
        </td>
        <xsl:apply-templates
          select="following-sibling::*[1][name()='com' or
                                          name()='constraint' or
                                          name()='vc' or
                                          name()='wfc']"/>
      </tr>
```

```
        </xsl:otherwise>
      </xsl:choose>
   </xsl:template>
```

Once again, the code is cluttered by the `<xsl:if>` instructions that generate change highlighting when required. It also contains a lot of repetition between the two branches of the `<xsl:choose>`.

What the code does is this:

❑   If the `<rhs>` is to appear on the same row as the `<lhs>`, it outputs a table cell (`<td>` element), colored to reflect any change markings necessary, whose contents are produced by calling `<xsl:apply-templates>` to process the children of the `<rhs>` element. It then calls `<xsl:apply-templates>` to process the following sibling `<vc>`, `<wfc>`, `<constraint>`, or `<com>` element if there is one.

❑   If the `<rhs>` is to appear on a new row, it creates a new table row (`<tr>` element), and within this row it first outputs three blank table cells (`<td>` elements). It then outputs a table cell representing the `<rhs>` element itself, and calls `<xsl:apply-templates>` to process the following sibling element, as in the previous case.

Some people prefer to avoid empty table cells by writing «`<td> </td>`», but that's really necessary only if the table has borders or a background color.

Finally, the last column contains the representation of a `<vc>`, `<wfc>`, `<constraint>`, or `<com>` element if there is one. The rules for these elements are all very similar, and I will show only one of them. The structure is very similar to that for the `<rhs>` element:

```
<!-- vc: validity check reference in a formal production -->
<xsl:template match="vc">
  <xsl:choose>
    <xsl:when test="preceding-sibling::*[1][name()='rhs']">
      <td>
        <xsl:if test="@diff and $show.diff.markup != 0">
          <xsl:attribute name="class">
            <xsl:text>diff-</xsl:text>
            <xsl:value-of select="@diff"/>
          </xsl:attribute>
        </xsl:if>
        <a>
          <xsl:attribute name="href">
            <xsl:call-template name="href.target">
              <xsl:with-param name="target" select="key('ids', @def)"/>
            </xsl:call-template>
          </xsl:attribute>
          <xsl:text>[VC: </xsl:text>
          <xsl:apply-templates select="key('ids', @def)/head" mode="text"/>
          <xsl:text>]</xsl:text>
        </a>
      </td>
```

```
    </xsl:when>
    <xsl:otherwise>
      <tr valign="baseline">
        <td/><td/><td/><td/>
        <td>
          <xsl:if test="@diff and $show.diff.markup != 0">
            <xsl:attribute name="class">
              <xsl:text>diff-</xsl:text>
              <xsl:value-of select="@diff"/>
            </xsl:attribute>
          </xsl:if>
          <a>
            <xsl:attribute name="href">
              <xsl:call-template name="href.target">
                <xsl:with-param name="target" select="key('ids', @def)"/>
              </xsl:call-template>
            </xsl:attribute>
            <xsl:text>[VC: </xsl:text>
            <xsl:apply-templates select="key('ids', @def)/head" mode="text"/>
            <xsl:text>]</xsl:text>
          </a>
        </td>
      </tr>
    </xsl:otherwise>
  </xsl:choose>
</xsl:template>
```

After studying the previous rule, the basic structure should be familiar. But there is some extra code included in this rule, because the <vc> element is represented as a hyperlink to the description of a validity constraint held outside the table itself. The link is represented in the XML by a def attribute, and this is used directly to construct the HTML internal hyperlink. The displayed text of the link is formed by retrieving the element whose ID is equal to this def attribute, and displaying its text.

So much for formatting the production rules! This is by far the most complicated part of this stylesheet; the rest should be plain sailing. But before we move on, we should ask whether all this logic could have been written in a more straightforward way in XSLT 2.0.

I see this problem as an example of a positional grouping problem. Grouping problems are all concerned with turning a one-dimensional sequence of elements into a hierarchy, and the problem of arranging data in a table can often be understood as a grouping problem in which the hierarchic levels are the table, the rows, and the individual cells.

All grouping problems can be solved by answering two questions:

❑ How do you identify an element that can be used to represent the group as a whole (usually the first element of the group)?

❑ How do you then identify the remaining members of the same group?

We already have answers to these questions in the existing stylesheet: the group is a row of the table, and we have an XPath expression that selects elements that will be the first in a new row. The other elements in the row are then the following siblings, up to the next element that's a "new row" element.

So here is my XSLT 2.0 solution to this problem. First, in the two template rules for «match="prod"» and «match="prodgroup/prod"», we'll replace the complicated <xsl:apply-templates> instruction with a simple call on the named template «show.prod», with no parameters. This template looks like this:

```
<xsl:template name="show.prod">
  <xsl:for-each-group select="*" group-starting-with="
               lhs |
               rhs[preceding-sibling::*[1][not(self::lhs)]] |
               com[preceding-sibling::*[1][not(self::rhs)]] |
               constraint[preceding-sibling::*[1][not(self::rhs)]] |
               vc[preceding-sibling::*[1][not(self::rhs)] |
               wfc[preceding-sibling::*[1][not(self::rhs)]]">
    <tr valign="baseline">
       <xsl:apply-templates select="." mode="padding"/>
       <xsl:apply-templates select="current-group()"/>
    </tr>
  </xsl:for-each-group>
</xsl:template>
```

Now, we define a set of simple template rules to produce the empty cells in each row, depending on the type of the first element in the row:

```
<xsl:template match="lhs" mode="padding"/>

<xsl:template match="rhs" mode="padding">
   <td/><td/><td/>
</xsl:template>

<xsl:template match="com|constraint|vc|wfc" mode="padding">
   <td/><td/><td/><td/>
</xsl:template>
```

And finally we provide one template rule for each kind of element, which simply outputs the content of the appropriate cells in the table. There is no longer any need for it to worry about what comes afterwards: that's taken care of by the iteration in the master «show.prod» template.

```
<xsl:template match="lhs">
   <td>
      <xsl:call-template name="show.diff"/>
      <xsl:if test="../@id">
         <a name="{../@id}" id="{../@id}"/>
      </xsl:if>
      <xsl:number count="prod" level="any" from="spec" format="[1]"/>
      <xsl:text>   </xsl:text>
   </td>
   <td>
      <xsl:call-template name="show.diff"/>
      <code><xsl:apply-templates/></code>
   </td>
   <td>
```

```
            <xsl:call-template name="show.diff"/>
            <xsl:text>   ::=   </xsl:text>
        </td>
    </xsl:template>

    <xsl:template match="rhs">
        <td>
            <xsl:call-template name="show.diff"/>
            <code><xsl:apply-templates/></code>
        </td>
    </xsl:template>

    <xsl:template match="vc">
        <td>
            <xsl:call-template name="show.diff"/>
            <a>
                <xsl:attribute name="href">
                    <xsl:call-template name="href.target">
                        <xsl:with-param name="target" select="key('ids', @def)"/>
                    </xsl:call-template>
                </xsl:attribute>
                <xsl:text>[VC: </xsl:text>
                <xsl:apply-templates select="key('ids', @def)/head" mode="text"/>
                <xsl:text>]</xsl:text>
            </a>
        </td>
    </xsl:template>
```

As before, I left out the logic for `<wfc>`, `<com>`, and `<constraint>` elements, to avoid repetition. But I think you'll agree that the `<xsl:for-each-group>` instruction, while still requiring some thought, makes this tricky problem a lot easier to tackle than it was in XSLT 1.0.

For completeness, here is the «show.diff» template:

```
<xsl:template name="show.diff" as="attribute()?">
    <xsl:if test="ancestor-or-self::*/@diff and $show.diff.markup != 0">
        <xsl:attribute name="class"
                       select="concat('diff-', ancestor-or-self::*/@diff)"/>
    </xsl:if>
</xsl:template>
```

Variant Stylesheets

The stylesheet just presented is used for the XML specification. The stylesheets used for the XPath and XSLT specifications are slightly different, because these documents use additional element types beyond those used in the XML specification. In each case, the XML source document has an internal DTD subset that supplements the base DTD with some additional element types. For example, the XPath *Functions and Operators* document uses special tags to mark up function signatures, and the XSLT document has special tags to mark up the proformas used to summarize the syntax of each XSLT element.

In fact, the XSLT 2.0 specification is formatted using a stack of five stylesheet modules, as described in the following sections. The relationship between them is described by the import tree in Figure 10-3.

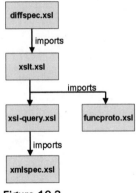

Figure 10-3

diffspec.xsl

This stylesheet module is used to do change marking for the XSLT 2.0 specification. You can see an example of its output at http://www.w3.org/TR/2003/WD-xslt20-20031112/Overview-diff. html.

For historical reasons, change marking is done slightly differently from the way the base XML stylesheet does it: it is derived from the same original code, but has forked. It includes some facilities that aren't in the base specification: for example, the ability to mark each change to say at which internal or external draft each change was introduced, and thus to do change coloring relative to a baseline selected by a stylesheet parameter. For example, a change introduced in draft R might be marked as <phrase diff="add" at="R">new text</phrase>.

The stylesheet module is labeled «version="1.0"» but it actually contains a couple of subtle dependencies on XSLT 2.0, which I will point out as I go along.

The way this stylesheet works is interesting. It contains template rules that override all other rules in the base stylesheet. For example, changes marked as additions («@diff="add"») are handled by this rule:

```
<xsl:template match="*[@diff='chg' and
                        $show.diff.markup='1' and
                        (string(@at) &gt; $baseline or not(@at))]"
              priority="3">
  <xsl:call-template name="diff-markup">
    <xsl:with-param name="diff">chg</xsl:with-param>
  </xsl:call-template>
</xsl:template>
```

This matches every element with the relevant markup, provided that the global parameter $show. diff.markup is enabled.

This is the first place the stylesheet depends on XSLT 2.0. In XSLT 1.0, match patterns in template rules were not allowed to refer to global variables or parameters. This restriction has been lifted in 2.0, and this allows the predicate in the match pattern to refer to two stylesheet parameters, $show.diff.markup and $baseline.

There is also another dependency on XSLT 2.0 in this predicate. Note the condition «string(@at) > $baseline». With XSLT 2.0, if $baseline is "P", then the test «string("R") > "P"» will succeed. With XSLT 1.0, a «>» comparison is always done by converting both operands to numbers. The conversion will produce NaN, and the comparison will be false.

> *To perform the same test in XSLT 1.0, the simplest solution is probably to write* «string-length
> (substring-before($alphabet, @at)) > string-length(substring-
> before($alphabet, $baseline))»*, where* $alphabet *is the string* «ABCDE...XYZ».

Let's look at the named template «diff.markup» to see how this works. The template reads:

```
<xsl:template name="diff-markup">
  <xsl:param name="diff">off</xsl:param>
  <xsl:choose>
    <xsl:when test="ancestor::scrap">
      <!-- forget it, we can't add stuff inside tables -->
      <!-- handled in base stylesheet -->
      <xsl:apply-imports/>
    </xsl:when>
    <xsl:when test="self::gitem or self::bibl">
      <!-- forget it, we can't add stuff inside dls; handled below -->
      <xsl:apply-imports/>
    </xsl:when>
    <xsl:when test="ancestor-or-self::phrase">
      <span class="diff-{$diff}">
        <xsl:apply-imports/>
      </span>
    </xsl:when>
    <xsl:when test="ancestor::p and not(self::p)">
      <span class="diff-{$diff}">
        <xsl:apply-imports/>
      </span>
    </xsl:when>
    <xsl:when test="ancestor-or-self::affiliation">
      <span class="diff-{$diff}">
        <xsl:apply-imports/>
      </span>
    </xsl:when>
    <xsl:when test="ancestor-or-self::name">
      <span class="diff-{$diff}">
        <xsl:apply-imports/>
      </span>
    </xsl:when>
    <xsl:otherwise>
      <div class="diff-{$diff}">
        <xsl:apply-imports/>
      </div>
    </xsl:otherwise>
  </xsl:choose>
</xsl:template>
```

This is pretty pragmatic code, and it almost certainly doesn't handle all possible cases. In effect, it recognizes that the «diff» attribute can occur in three different contexts: contexts where a <span>

element can be added to the HTML, contexts where a `<div>` element can be added to the HTML, and contexts where nothing can be done. In the first two cases, the `<div>` or `<span>` element is added, with a «class» attribute that will invoke a CSS rule to cause the text to be displayed with a background color.

But the magic is in the `<xsl:apply-imports>` instruction, which says that having added a `<div>` or `<span>` element, the stylesheet should go on to process the element exactly as it would have done if the `diffspec.xsl` stylesheet module had not been invoked. The effect of this stylesheet module is thus entirely additive.

The other specifications in the XSLT/XPath/XQuery set use a different technique to produce change markings. For XSLT, the change markup is maintained by hand (and therefore ignores trivial changes considered to be purely editorial). For the other specifications in the family, change markup is generated automatically by a stylesheet that compares two versions of the same document. There is then some manual adjustment of the result to remove obvious flaws, which can easily arise if, for example, two sections are reordered. However, the mechanics of rendering the change markings are essentially the same.

The `diffspec.xsl` stylesheet used for XSLT imports `xslt.xsl`, which handles markup specific to the XSLT specification.

This points up a nice little problem: how would one maintain a `diffspec.xsl` module that could be used as an overlay over a variety of different base stylesheets? To achieve this, the module could not import the underlying module, which means it could not use `<xsl:apply-imports>` to invoke the overridden template rules. In XSLT 2.0, this can be achieved by exploiting `<xsl:next-match>`. Instead of `diffspec.xsl` importing `xslt.xsl`, the `xslt.xsl` module could include `diffspec.xsl` (using `<xsl:include>`), relying on the priority of the rules in `diffspec.xsl` being higher than any rules in `xslt.xsl`. A call on `<xsl:next-match>` in `diffspec.xsl` would then invoke the lower priority rule in `xslt.xsl`.

xslt.xsl

I developed most of this stylesheet module myself in my role as editor of the XSLT 2.0 specification (some parts were inherited from a similar stylesheet produced by James Clark). It refines the features available from the base stylesheet in three main ways:

- ❑ It handles additional markup that is special to the XSLT specification, for example the proformas used for showing the structure of XSLT instructions, and the markup used for describing error conditions.

- ❑ It refines the presentation used for certain constructs, where the default presentation used in the base stylesheet didn't work well for this document. For example, the number of cross-references to other sections of the specification is so great that using a bold font for these became very distracting for the reader, so they were changed to use a normal font. Clearly, such changes need to be made with great discretion, but this is not the right place to discuss typography or editorial policy issues.

- ❑ It automates certain things that were not automated by the base stylesheets. For example, it provides an automatically generated glossary and indexes of error conditions and outstanding issues; it also automates some of the generation of front material and hyperlinks.

In some cases, these changes have had cascading effects. For example, the fact that some sections of the specification are automatically generated means that the stylesheet (in places) operates in two phases. The issues list is generated as a temporary tree using the markup from the `xmlspec` vocabulary, and this is then rendered into HTML by applying the standard template rules. Unfortunately, certain things break when this is done, for example the standard `<specref>` template, shown above on page 674, cannot handle a link from a `<specref>` element in a temporary tree to a target element in the main source document—the use of the `key()` function assumes that both source and target are in the same tree. So, the `xslt.xsl` stylesheet contains a copy of the entire `<specref>` template rule with one line changed.

This is far from ideal, of course. In such cases, it is better to get the base stylesheet changed, but this always takes time and is not possible when timescales are tight. It can then easily happen that differences between versions of the same template gradually accumulate, and it takes constant vigilance to prevent structural decay. This is not really any different, of course, from any other software endeavor.

The `xslt.xsl` stylesheet imports two other stylesheet modules, `funcproto.xsl` and `xsl-query.xsl`

funcproto.xsl

This stylesheet module does a well-defined job: it formats the function signatures used in the XPath *Functions and Operators* specification, and also in the XSLT specification. As with the XML production rules, these function signatures use a highly structured form of markup that is completely independent of the final presentation. For example, here is the function signature for the `format-date()` function:

```
<proto class="xslt" name="format-date" return-type="xs:string"
                                   returnEmptyOk="yes">
  <arg name="value" type="xs:date" emptyOk="yes"/>
  <arg name="picture" type="xs:string"/>
  <arg name="language" type="xs:string" emptyOk="yes"/>
  <arg name="calendar" type="xs:string" emptyOk="yes"/>
  <arg name="country" type="xs:string" emptyOk="yes"/>
</proto>
```

It's worth taking a look at this stylesheet to see how it works (it's available in the downloads for this chapter). There are some interesting features, such as the use of a heuristic calculation that attempts to decide whether to use a single-line format for the function signature, or a multiline format. But I won't include any details here.

xsl-query.xsl

This stylesheet provides a customization of the `xmlspec.xsl` stylesheet that is used by all the specifications in the XSLT/XPath/XQuery family. It provides facilities to support fine-grained cross-references between the different specifications in this family, and to generate appendices such as error listings and glossaries.

Some of these facilities were introduced first in the XSLT specification, and were then adapted for use in other specifications; in some cases, the XSLT specification has changed to use the common capabilities, in other cases it has not. As with any sizable editorial operation, standards and processes are constantly in flux, and at any given point in time, there will be inconsistencies and overlaps. The fact that these exist in this family of stylesheets should actually be taken as positive evidence that the modular structure of the XSLT language can actually support this kind of change, which can never be synchronized totally across the whole organization. Changes are inevitably piloted in one area, then adopted and adapted in another, and at any one time the overall picture may appear slightly chaotic.

Summary

The case study presented in this chapter was of a real family of stylesheets, used for a real application, and not just developed for teaching purposes. It's perhaps slightly atypical in that much of it was written by XML and XSLT experts who developed the languages while they used them. However, it shares with many other projects the fact that the stylesheets were developed over a period of time by different individuals, that they were often working under time pressure, and that they had different coding styles. So, it's probably not that dissimilar from many other stylesheets used in document formatting applications.

The phrase "document formatting" is crucial. The main tasks performed in this stylesheet are applying HTML display styles to different elements, generating hyperlinks, and formatting tables. These are all tasks that lend themselves to using the *rule-based* design pattern.

I think there are three main messages to come out of this study:

❏ Within an application that is doing very simple document formatting ninety percent of the time, it is possible to get benefits by using structured data for small parts of the information that have rich semantics—in this case, examples are the markup used for syntax productions, function prototypes, issue tracking, and error listings. The availability of XSLT really does enable you to use XML to represent the semantics of the data, uninfluenced by the way it is to appear on screen.

❏ Although most of this can be done reasonably easily using XSLT 1.0 facilities, as soon as the data gets complex, XSLT 2.0 features start to make a big impact.

❏ Within any complex publishing operation that's producing a large suite of documents, the key to success is not so much the detail of how individual stylesheets are coded, but rather the overall structure of how many stylesheet modules there are, how they relate to each other, and how change is controlled.

The case study in the next chapter will be a very different kind of application—one that uses a highly structured data, and displays it in a very different form from the way it arrives in the source document.

Case Study: A Family Tree

This chapter presents our second case study. Whereas the XML in the previous example fell firmly into the category of narrative (or document-oriented) XML, this chapter deals largely with data. However, as with many data-oriented XML applications, it is not rigid tabular data, rather it is data with a very flexible structure with many complex linkages and with many fields allowed to repeat an arbitrary number of times; the data can also include structured text (document-oriented XML) in some of its elements.

The chosen application is to display a family tree, and the sample data we will use represents a small selection of information about the family of John F. Kennedy, President of the United States.

Because genealogy is for most people a hobby rather than a business, you may feel this example is a little frivolous. I think it would be a mistake to dismiss it that way, for several reasons:

❑ Genealogy is one of the most popular ways of using the web for millions of people. Catering to the information needs of consumers is a very serious business indeed, and whether consumers are interested in playing games, watching sport, making travel plans, or researching their family trees, the web is in the business of helping them to do so. Genealogy is one of the few areas where web sites have built financial success by asking consumers to pay for content.

❑ Genealogical information presents some complex challenges in terms of managing richly structured data, and these same problems arise in many other disciplines such as geographic information systems, criminal investigation, epidemiology, or molecular biology. Data that fits neatly into rows and columns, to my mind, isn't interesting enough to be worth studying; and what's more, it's likely that the only reason it fits neatly into rows and columns is that a lot of important information has been thrown away in order to achieve that fit. With XML, we can do better.

❑ To write the application shown in this chapter, we have to tackle the problems of converting from non-XML legacy data formats to XML formats, and from one XML data model to another, which are absolutely typical of the data conversion problems encountered in every real-world application.

I could have used an example with invoices and requisitions and purchase orders. I believe that the techniques used in this worked example are equally applicable to many practical commercial problems, but that you will find a little excursion into the world of genealogy a pleasant relief from the day job.

Modeling A Family Tree

Genealogical data is complex for two main reasons:

❑ We want to record all the facts that we know about our ancestors, and many of these facts will not fit into a rigidly predefined schema. For those facts that follow a regular pattern, however, we want to use a structured representation so that we can analyze the data.

❑ The information we have is never complete, and it is never 100% accurate. Genealogy is always work-in-progress, and the information we need to manage includes everything from original source documents and oral evidence to the conjectures of other genealogists (not to mention Aunt Maud) whom we may or may not trust. In this respect it is similar to other investigative applications like crime detection and medical diagnosis.

One caveat before we start. Throughout this book I have been talking about tree models of XML, and I have been using words like parent and child, ancestor and descendant, in the context of these data trees. Don't imagine, though, that we can use this tree structure to represent a family tree directly. In fact, a family tree is not really a tree at all, because most children in real life have two parents, unlike XML elements where one parent is considered sufficient.

The structure of the family tree is quite different from the document tree used to represent it. And in this chapter, words like parent and child have their everyday meaning!

The GEDCOM Data Model

The established standard for representing genealogical data is known as GEDCOM, and data in this format is routinely exchanged between software packages and posted on the Internet. I will show some examples of this format later in the chapter.

In earlier editions of this book I devised my own way of translating this into XML. However, in December 2002 the LDS Church (which maintains the GEDCOM specification) published a beta-release specification of GEDCOM XML, version 6.0. Although this is not yet widely supported by software products, it is this vocabulary that I shall use in this chapter. The specification is available at `http://www.familysearch.org/GEDCOM/GedXML60.pdf`. A great deal of further information about the use of XML in genealogy can be found on the XML Cover Pages at `http://xml.coverpages.org/genealogy.html`.

The GEDCOM XML spec includes a DTD rather than a schema. The DTD has been extracted from the specification and published as a freestanding file at `http://xml.coverpages.org/GEDCOMv60 BetaDTD-Brown.txt`. I have copied this for convenience as file `gedXML.dtd` in the download file for this chapter.

In defining version 6 of GEDCOM, the designers decided to do two things at the same time: to change the syntax of the data representation, so that it used XML instead of GEDCOM's earlier proprietary tagging syntax, and to change the data model, to fix numerous problems that had inhibited accurate data exchange between different software packages for years.

The three main objects in the new model are *individuals*, *events*, and *families*.

It might seem obvious what an individual is, but serious genealogists know that identifying individuals is actually one of the biggest problems: is the Henry Kay who was born in Stannington in 1833 the same individual as the Henry Kay who married Emma Barber in Rotherham in 1855? (If you happen to know, please tell me.)

For this reason, the data is actually centered around the concept of an *Event*. The main events of interest are births, marriages, and deaths, but there are many others: for example, emigration, writing a will, and a mention in a published book can all be treated as events. In earlier times, births and deaths were not systematically recorded, but baptisms and burials were, so these events assume a special importance. Events have a number of attributes:

❑   The date of the event. There are many complexities involved in recording historical dates, due to the use of different calendars, partial legibility, and varying precision.

❑   The place of the event. Again, this is not a simple data element. Places change their names over time, and place names are themselves structured information, with a structure that varies from one country to another. (Some software packages like to pretend that every event happens in a "city", but they are wrong. Even in the limited data used in this chapter, we have two deaths that occurred in the air, over international waters).

❑   The participants in the event. There may be any number of participants, and each has a role. For example, if the event is a marriage, then everyone who is known to have been present at the wedding can be regarded as a participant. Obvious roles include that of the bride, the groom, and the witnesses; but many records also record the names of the father of the bride and the father of the groom, and this information has obvious genealogical significance. Moreover, it's important to record it even if it seems redundant, because it may help to resolve questions that are raised later when conflicting evidence emerges.

❑   Evidence for the event. This includes references to source information recording the event, and may include copies or transcripts of original documents.

Here is an example of an event from the Kennedy data set. I have included some additional information beyond that in the data we are using, to show some of the additional possibilities in the data model.

```
<EventRec Id="F1-6" Type="marriage" VitalType="marriage">
   <Participant>
      <Link Target="IndividualRec" Ref="I1"/>
      <Role>husband</Role>
   </Participant>
   <Participant>
      <Link Target="IndividualRec" Ref="I2"/>
      <Role>wife</Role>
   </Participant>
   <Participant>
      <Link Target="IndividualRec" Ref="I19"/>
      <Role>best man</Role>
   </Participant>
   <Date>12 SEP 1953</Date>
   <Place>
      <PlaceName>
```

```
                <PlacePart Type="country" Level="1">USA</PlacePart>
                <PlacePart Type="state" Level="2">RI</PlacePart>
                <PlacePart Type="city" Level="4">Newport</PlacePart>
            </PlaceName>
        </Place>
    </EventRec>
```

This event is the marriage of John F. Kennedy to Jacqueline Lee Bouvier. Of course, the record only makes sense by following the links to the participating individuals.

The properties of an individual include:

❏   Name (another potentially very complex data element, given the variety of conventions used in different places at different times). This element can be repeated, because a person can have different names at different times.

❏   Gender (male, female, or unknown: the model does not recognize this as an attribute that can change over time)

❏   Personal information: an open-ended set of information items about the person, each tagged with the type of information, optional date and place fields, and the actual information content. Certain types of personal information such as occupation, nationality, religion, and education are specifically recognized in the specification, but the list is completely open-ended.

The third fundamental object in the GEDCOM model is the family. A family is defined as a social group in which one individual takes the role of husband/father, another takes the role of wife/mother, and the others take the role of children. Any of the individuals may be absent or unknown, and the model is flexible as to the exact nature of the relationships: the parents, for example, are not necessarily married, and the children are not necessarily the biological children of the parents. An individual may be a member of several families, either consecutively or concurrently (membership in a family is not governed by dates).

There are actually three ways of representing relationships in the model. One way is through families, as described above. The second is through events: a birth event may record the person being born, the mother, and the father as participants in the event with corresponding roles. For certain key events, there are fixed roles with defined names (*principal*, *mother*, and *father* in this case). The third way is to use the properties of an individual: one can record as a property of an individual, for example, that his godfather was Winston Churchill. These variations are provided to reflect the variety of ways in which genealogical data becomes available. The genealogical research process starts by collecting raw data, which is usually data either about events or about individuals, and gradually builds from this to draw inferences about the identity of individuals and the way in which they relate to each other in families. The model has the crucial property that it allows imprecise information to be captured: for example, you can record that A and B were cousins without knowing precisely how they were related, and you can record that someone was the second of five children without knowing who the other children were. The ability to record this kind of information makes XML ideally suited to genealogical data management.

Apart from individual, event, and family, there are five other top-level object types in the GEDCOM model, but we won't be dealing with them in this chapter:

❏   A *group* is a collection of individuals related in some arbitrary way (for example, the individuals who were staying at a particular address on the night of a census)

❑ A *contact* is typically another genealogist, for example one who collaborates in the research on the individuals in this data set.

❑ A *source* is a document from which information has been obtained, such as a parish register or a will. It might also be a secondary source such as a published obituary.

❑ A *repository* is a place where source documents may be found, for example a library or a web site, or the bottom drawer of your filing cabinet.

❑ An *LDS Ordinance* is an event of specific interest to the Church of Jesus Christ of Latter-day Saints (often called the Mormons), which is the organization that created the GEDCOM standard.

I'm not going to spend time discussing whether this is the perfect way of representing genealogical information. Many people have criticized the data model, either on technical grounds or from the point of view of political correctness. The new model in version 6 corrects many of the faults of the established version, without departing from it as radically as some people would have liked.

I would have liked to see some further changes—for example, some explicit ability to associate personal names with events rather than with individuals (I have an ancestor who is named Ada on her birth certificate, but who was baptized as Edith). But with luck, the amount of change in the GEDCOM model is enough to fix the worst faults, but not so extensive that software products will need wholesale rewriting before they can support it.

Creating a Schema for GEDCOM 6.0

Because genealogical data is a perfect example of semi-structured data (it includes the full spectrum from raw images and sound recordings, through transcribed text, to fully structured and hyperlinked data) it is an ideal candidate for using an XML Schema to drive validation of the data and to produce XSLT stylesheets that are schema-aware. I have therefore produced a schema for a subset of this DTD, which I introduce in the next section.

My first step was to load the DTD into XMLSpy and convert it to a schema. This required a bit ot pre-processing—I found that XMLSpy didn't like the xml:lang attributes defined in the DTD, so I edited them to change the name to xml-lang. The first cut schema produced by XMLSpy is included as rawschema1.xsd. The options I used for the conversion were as shown in Figure 11-1.

However, having chosen these options, I then made many changes to the schema, and in retrospect, I might well have got to the final result just as quickly by choosing a different option. I've included the full schema in the download file gedXML.xsd, but in this chapter I'm only going to show those parts that we are actually using in this application.

The modifications I made to the automatically-generated schema are of two kinds:

❑ Structural changes: for example promoting anonymous types to top-level named types, and using a common type where two elements have the same structure. In particular, I extracted the elements defined as children of the document element <GEDCOM>, for example <IndividualRec> and <EventRec>, and made these into top-level element declarations.

❑ Defining additional constraints that can be expressed in a schema but not in a DTD. I have concentrated my efforts on those elements and attributes that are actually used in this example application.

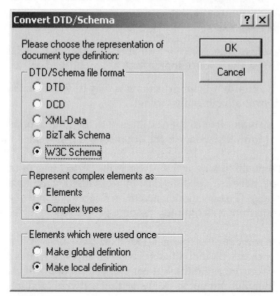

Figure 11-1

An interesting feature of this data is that the schema is very permissive. For example, it specifies a default format for dates in the form «DD MMM YYYY» (such as «18 APR 1924»), which has long been the convention used by genealogists. However, it doesn't insist that the date of an event takes this form. It's quite OK, for example, to replace the last digit of the year by a question mark, perhaps to reflect the fact that the digit is difficult to decipher on an original manuscript. There are certain approved conventions such as preceding the date with «ABT» to indicate that the date is approximate, or «EST» to say that it is estimated, but there are no absolute rules. The golden rule in genealogy is that when you find information in a source document, you should be able to transcribe it as faithfully to the original as you possibly can, and a schema that imposes restrictions on your ability to do this is considered a bad thing. If you find an old church register in which a date of baptism is recorded as *Septuagesima 1582*, then you should be able to enter that in your database. I'll come back to the modeling of dates in the schema on page 700.

In GEDCOM, there is no formal way of linking one file to another. XML, of course, creates wonderful opportunities to define how your family tree links to someone else's. But the linking isn't as easy as it sounds (nothing is, in genealogy) because of the problems of maintaining version integrity between two datasets that are changing independently. So I'll avoid getting into that area, and stick to the model that the whole family tree is in one XML document.

The GEDCOM 6.0 Schema

Let's now take a quick look at some aspects of the XML Schema which I created for GEDCOM 6.0. In principle, because it's converted from the DTD, it covers all aspects of the specification; however in improving the schema to describe the specification more precisely and more usefully, I concentrated on the parts that we are actually using in ths application in this chapter: in particular, the three main object types individual, event, and family, and the three main properties, namely date, place, and personal name.

Individuals

Here is the element declaration for an `<IndividualRec>`:

```xml
<xs:element name="IndividualRec">
  <xs:complexType>
    <xs:sequence>
      <xs:element name="IndivName" type="IndivNameType"
                              minOccurs="0" maxOccurs="unbounded"/>
      <xs:element name="Gender" type="GenderType" minOccurs="0"/>
      <xs:element name="DeathStatus" type="xs:string" minOccurs="0"/>
      <xs:element name="PersInfo" type="PersInfoType"
                              minOccurs="0" maxOccurs="unbounded"/>
      <xs:element name="AssocIndiv" minOccurs="0" maxOccurs="unbounded">
        <xs:complexType>
          <xs:sequence>
            <xs:element name="Link" type="LinkType"/>
            <xs:element name="Association" type="xs:string"/>
            <xs:element name="Note" type="NoteType"
                              minOccurs="0" maxOccurs="unbounded"/>
            <xs:element name="Citation" type="CitationType"
                              minOccurs="0" maxOccurs="unbounded"/>
          </xs:sequence>
        </xs:complexType>
      </xs:element>
      <xs:element name="DupIndiv" minOccurs="0" maxOccurs="unbounded">
        <xs:complexType>
          <xs:sequence>
            <xs:element name="Link" type="LinkType"/>
            <xs:element name="Note" type="NoteType"
                              minOccurs="0" maxOccurs="unbounded"/>
            <xs:element name="Citation" type="CitationType"
                              minOccurs="0" maxOccurs="unbounded"/>
          </xs:sequence>
        </xs:complexType>
      </xs:element>
      <xs:element name="ExternalID" type="ExternalIDType"
                              minOccurs="0" maxOccurs="unbounded"/>
      <xs:element name="Submitter" type="SubmitterType" minOccurs="0"/>
      <xs:element name="Note" type="NoteType"
                              minOccurs="0" maxOccurs="unbounded"/>
      <xs:element name="Evidence" type="EvidenceType"
                              minOccurs="0" maxOccurs="unbounded"/>
      <xs:element name="Enrichment" type="EnrichmentType"
                              minOccurs="0" maxOccurs="unbounded"/>
      <xs:element name="Changed" type="ChangedType"
                              minOccurs="0" maxOccurs="unbounded"/>
    </xs:sequence>
    <xs:attribute name="Id" type="xs:ID" use="required"/></xs:complexType>
</xs:element>
```

IndivName gives the name of the individual. Gender has the obvious meaning; DeathStatus is for
recording information such as "died in infancy" when no specific death event is known. PersInfo allows
recording of arbitrary personal information such as occupation and religion. AssocIndiv is for links to
related individuals where the relationships cannot be expressed directly through Family objects (for

example, links to godparents). DupIndiv is interesting: it allows an assertion that this IndividualRec refers to the same individual as another IndividualRec. This is very useful when combining data sets compiled by different genealogists; merging the two records into one can be very difficult if there are inconsistencies in the data, and it can prove very difficult to unmerge the data later if they are found to be different individuals after all. ExternalID is for reference numbers that identify the individual in external databases; Submitter is the person who created this record; Note is for arbitrary comments; Evidence says where the information came from; Enrichment is for inline documentation such as photographs or transcripts of original documents, and Changed is for a change history of this record.

Most of these fields are optional and repeatable. Something I haven't captured in this schema is that the GEDCOM spec also says the structure is extensible; arbitrary namespaced elements may be inserted at any point in the structure. This is typically used to contain information specific to a particular product vendor, so that GEDCOM can be used to exchange data between users of that product with no loss of information.

I chose to make IndividualRec a top-level element declaration in the schema. This isn't needed for validation, since in a GEDCOM file the IndividualRec will always be a child of the <GEDCOM> element. However, it makes this type available in stylesheets, which is a great convenience: for example, I can write a function whose parameter is declared as <xsl:param name="indi" as="schema-element (IndividualRec)"/>.

Having made IndividualRec a top-level element declaration, there seems to be nothing that would be gained by naming its complex type as a top-level type definition. In general, the only types that are worth naming as top-level types are those that are used in more than one place, or at least look likely to be used in more that one place, and that isn't the case here.

For most of the child elements of IndividualRec, I chose to use a local element declaration referring to a global type. There's nothing absolute about this. In many cases I could equally have used a reference to another global element declaration. Since many elements such as Date and Note appear in more than one place, referring to a global element declaration would make sense, and an accident of the DTD conversion is that this has been done for simple types but not for complex types. When it comes to writing an XSLT stylesheet, it's important that where a data element such as Date appears in several places, it should either use a global element declaration or a global type definition, but one of these is probably sufficient, and either will do.

There are no substitution groups in this model. They aren't needed, because the model has chosen to use generic elements like <PersInfo> rather than specialized types such as <occupation> and <religion>. The need for substitution groups generally arises when there are many elements that are structurally interchangeable.

Events

An event record has this structure:

```
<xs:element name="EventRec">
  <xs:complexType>
    <xs:sequence>
      <xs:element name="Participant" type="ParticipantType"
                                     maxOccurs="unbounded"/>
      <xs:element name="Date" type="DateType" minOccurs="0"/>
```

```
            <xs:element name="Place" type="PlaceType" minOccurs="0"/>
            <xs:element name="Religion" type="xs:string" minOccurs="0"/>
            <xs:element name="ExternalID" type="ExternalIDType"
                                minOccurs="0" maxOccurs="unbounded"/>
            <xs:element name="Submitter" type="SubmitterType" minOccurs="0"/>
            <xs:element name="Note" type="NoteType"
                                minOccurs="0" maxOccurs="unbounded"/>
            <xs:element name="Evidence" type="EvidenceType"
                                minOccurs="0" maxOccurs="unbounded"/>
            <xs:element name="Enrichment" type="EnrichmentType"
                                minOccurs="0" maxOccurs="unbounded"/>
            <xs:element name="Changed" type="ChangedType"
                                minOccurs="0" maxOccurs="unbounded"/>
        </xs:sequence>
        <xs:attribute name="Id" type="xs:ID" use="required"/>
        <xs:attribute name="Type" type="xs:string" use="required"/>
        <xs:attribute name="VitalType" type="VitalTypeType"/>
    </xs:complexType>
</xs:element>
```

Note how many of the fields are the same as those for an IndividualRec. Doing bottom-up data analysis, you would probably come to the conclusion that IndividualRec and EventRec should be defined as extensions of some common abstract type. It wouldn't do any harm to inherit all eight GEDCOM objects from some base type (called GEDCOMObject, say), but I can't say that the stylesheets in this chapter would have benefited from it. Really, an abstract type like this is only useful if there are operations that you want to perform at this level. A practical difficulty is that with XML Schema, types can only be extended by adding fields at the end, whereas here, the shared fields come after the type-specific fields.

Families

The third object type we will look at is the *family*. Here is the definition:

```
<xs:element name="FamilyRec">
  <xs:complexType>
    <xs:sequence>
      <xs:element name="HusbFath" type="ParentType" minOccurs="0"/>
      <xs:element name="WifeMoth" type="ParentType" minOccurs="0"/>
      <xs:element name="Child" type="ChildType"
                            minOccurs="0" maxOccurs="unbounded"/>
      <xs:element name="BasedOn" type="BasedOnType" minOccurs="0"/>
      <xs:element name="ExternalID" type="ExternalIDType"
                            minOccurs="0" maxOccurs="unbounded"/>
      <xs:element name="Submitter" type="SubmitterType" minOccurs="0"/>
      <xs:element name="Note" type="NoteType"
                            minOccurs="0" maxOccurs="unbounded"/>
      <xs:element name="Evidence" type="EvidenceType"
                            minOccurs="0" maxOccurs="unbounded"/>
      <xs:element name="Enrichment" type="EnrichmentType"
                            minOccurs="0" maxOccurs="unbounded"/>
```

```
        <xs:element name="Changed" type="ChangedType"
                            minOccurs="0" maxOccurs="unbounded"/>
      </xs:sequence>
      <xs:attribute name="Id" type="xs:ID" use="required"/>
    </xs:complexType>
  </xs:element>
```

Again, many of the fields are common with the other two object types. The types `ParentType` and `ChildType` play a crucial role in linking the data, so we'd better open them up:

```
<xs:complexType name="ChildType">
  <xs:sequence>
    <xs:element name="Link" type="LinkType"/>
    <xs:element name="ChildNbr" type="xs:positiveInteger" minOccurs="0"/>
    <xs:element name="RelToFath" type="xs:string" minOccurs="0"/>
    <xs:element name="RelToMoth" type="xs:string" minOccurs="0"/>
  </xs:sequence>
</xs:complexType>

<xs:complexType name="ParentType">
  <xs:sequence>
    <xs:element name="Link" type="LinkType"/>
    <xs:element name="FamilyNbr" type="xs:positiveInteger" minOccurs="0"/>
  </xs:sequence>
</xs:complexType>
```

A <ChildType> element represents the participation of an individual in a family in the role of child. The <Link> identifies the individual concerned. The <ChildNbr> represents the position of that child in the family (1 for the eldest child, and so on): this allows for the fact that some of the children may be unknown. <RelToFath> and <RelToMoth> elements allow for detail about the relationship of the child to the father and mother, for example the child may be the natural child of one parent and the adopted child of the other.

The <ParentType> element represents the participation of an individual in a family in the role of parent. The <FamilyNbr> element provides a sequence number, for example it allows you to say that this family is the man's second marriage, which is useful if the dates of the marriages are not known.

Now let's look quickly at the three most common (and difficult) data types used for properties of these objects: dates, places, and personal names.

Dates

As we've seen, GEDCOM allows any character string to be used as a date. However, much of the presentation of data depends on analyzing dates wherever possible. How is this dilemma resolved?

The DateType referenced from the Event record is a complex type, defined like this:

```
<xs:complexType name="DateType">
  <xs:simpleContent>
    <xs:extension base="GeneralDate">
```

```
        <xs:attribute name="Calendar" type="xs:string"/>
      </xs:extension>
    </xs:simpleContent>
  </xs:complexType>
```

That is to say, it is a complex type with simple content: the content is a GeneralDate, and the optional attribute indicates which calendar is used. The GeneralDate can be any character string, but certain formats such as «DD MMM YYYY» are recommended.

As far as validation is concerned, there isn't much point in defining a schema data type for the pattern «DD MMM YYYY». However, it turns out that it can be useful to define this type even if it isn't used for validation. We can define the GEDCOM date format as a union type like this:

```
<xs:simpleType type="GeneralDate">
  <xs:union memberTypes="StandardDate xs:string">
</xs:simpleType>

<xs:simpleType type="StandardDate">
  <xs:restriction base="xs:string">
    <xs:pattern value=
"[0-9]?[0-9]\s(JAN|FEB|MAR|APR|MAY|JUN|JUL|AUG|SEP|OCT|NOV|DEC)\s[0-9]{4}"/>
  </xs:restriction>
</xs:simpleType>
```

This type is meaningless from the point of view of validation—all strings will be considered valid. But the effect is that a date that conforms to the «DD MMM YYYY» pattern will be labeled as a StandardDate, while one that doesn't will be labeled only as an xs:string. This will prove useful when we write our stylesheets, because it becomes very easy to separate standard dates from non-standard dates when we want to perform operations like date formatting and sorting. In fact, I could have usefully split dates into three categories: simple exact dates like «4 MAR 1920»; inexact dates that conform to the GEDCOM syntax, such as «BEF JAN 1866» (meaning some time before January 1866); and arbitrary character strings whose interpretation is left purely to the reader.

Places

Place names have an internal structure, but the structure is highly variable. In many cases components of the place name may be missing, and the part that is missing may be the major part rather than the minor part. For example, you might know that someone was born in Wolverton, England, without knowing which of the three towns of that name it refers to. The GEDCOM schema allows the place name to be entered as unstructured text, but also allows individual components of the name to be marked up using a <PlacePart> element which can carry two attributes: Type, which can take values such as Country, City, or Parish to indicate what kind of place this is, and Level, which is a number that represents the relationship of this part of the place name to the other parts.

Personal Names

As with place names, personal names have a highly variable internal structure. The name can be written simply as a character string (within an <IndivName> element), or the separate parts can be tagged using <NamePart> elements. As with place names, these have a completely open-ended structure. The Type attribute can be used to identify the name part as, for example, a surname or generation suffix, and the Level attribute can be used to indicate its relative importance, for example when used as a key for sorting and indexing.

Creating a Data File

Our next task is to create an XML file containing the Kennedy family tree in the appropriate format. I started by entering the data in a genealogy package, taking the information from public sources such as the web site of the Kennedy museum. The package I use is called *The Master Genealogist*, and like all such software it is capable of outputting the data in GEDCOM 5.5 format. This is a file containing records that look something like this (it's included in the downloads for this chapter as kennedy.ged):

```
0 @I1@ INDI
1 NAME John Fitzgerald/Kennedy/
1 SEX M
1 BIRT
2 DATE 29 MAY 1917
2 PLAC Brookline, MA, USA
1 DEAT
2 DATE 22 NOV 1963
2 PLAC Dallas, TX, USA
2 NOTE Assassinated by Lee Harvey Oswald.
1 NOTE Educated at Harvard University.
2 CONT Elected Congressman in 1945
2 CONT aged 29; served three terms in the House of Representatives.
2 CONT Elected Senator in 1952. Elected President in 1960, the
2 CONT youngest ever President of the United States.
1 FAMS @F1@
1 FAMC @F2@
```

This isn't XML, of course, but it is a hierarchic data file containing tagged data, so it is a good candidate for converting into XML that looks like the document below. This doesn't conform to the GEDCOM 6.0 data model or schema, but it's a useful starting point.

```
<INDI ID="I1">
    <NAME>John Fitzgerald/Kennedy/</NAME>
    <SEX>M</SEX>
    <BIRT>
        <DATE>29 MAY 1917</DATE>
        <PLAC>Brookline, MA, USA</PLAC>
    </BIRT>
    <DEAT>
        <DATE>22 NOV 1963</DATE>
        <PLAC>Dallas, TX, USA</PLAC>
        <NOTE>Assassinated by Lee Harvey Oswald.<BR/></NOTE>
    </DEAT>
    <NOTE>Educated at Harvard University.
Elected Congressman in 1945
aged 29; served three terms in the House of Representatives.
Elected Senator in 1952. Elected President in 1960, the
youngest ever President of the United States.
    </NOTE>
    <FAMS REF="F1"/>
    <FAMC REF="F2"/>
</INDI>
```

Each record in a GEDCOM file has a unique identifier (in this case I1 – that's letter I, digit one), which is used to construct cross-references between records. Most of the information in this record is self-explanatory, except the <FAMS> and <FAMC> fields: <FAMS> is a reference to a <FAM> record representing a family in which this person is a parent, and <FAMC> is a reference to a family in which this person is a child.

The first stage in processing data is to do this conversion into XML, a process which we will examine in the next section.

Converting GEDCOM Files to XML

The obvious way to translate GEDCOM to XML is to write a program that takes a GEDCOM file as input and produces an XML file as output. However, there's a smarter way: why not write a GEDCOM parser which looks just like a SAX-compliant XML parser, so that any program that can handle SAX input can read GEDCOM directly, just by switching parsers? In particular, many XSLT processors can take input from a SAX-compliant parser, so this enables you to feed GEDCOM straight into a stylesheet.

Equally, many XSLT processors can send the result tree to a user-specified ContentHandler in the form of a stream of SAX events, so if we write a SAX2-compatible ContentHandler, our XSLT processor can also output GEDCOM files. This suddenly means we can write stylesheets to transform one GEDCOM file into another, without the hassle of creating an XML file as an intermediate form. An example of such a transformation would be one that removes all the living people from a GEDCOM file.

A SAX2 parser for GEDCOM 5.5 is supplied with the sample files for this chapter on the Wrox web site; it is named GedcomParser. GEDCOM 5.5 uses an archaic character set called ANSEL, so along with GedcomParser is another class, AnselInputStreamReader to translate the ANSEL characters into Unicode.

Similarly, on the output side, there is a SAX2 ContentHandler called GedcomOutputter, which in turn translates Unicode to ANSEL using an AnselOutputStreamWriter. We won't be using this in any of our examples, however. This structure is shown in Figure 11-2.

If you do want to see the XML, you can always feed the GEDCOM into a stylesheet that does an identity transformation, the simplest being identity.xsl:

```
<xsl:transform
    xmlns:xsl="http://www.w3.org/1999/XSL/Transform"
    version="1.0" >

<xsl:template match="/">
    <xsl:copy-of select="."/>
</xsl:template>

</xsl:transform>
```

This is how I created the data file kennedy55.xml which is supplied in the download files.

If you want to convert your own GEDCOM file mytree.ged into XML, you can do it using Saxon by entering the command (all on one line)

```
java net.sf.saxon.Transform -x GedcomParser mytree.ged
identity.xsl >mytree.xml
```

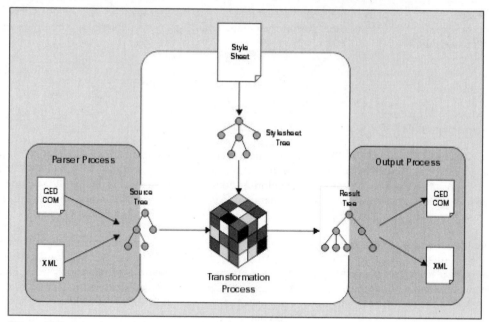

Figure 11-2

The -x option on the command line causes Saxon to use the class GedcomParser as its XML parser. It doesn't matter that this isn't actually parsing XML, it's enough that it implements the SAX2 interface and thus pretends to be an XML parser.

The XML this produces is a direct mechanical translation of the original GEDCOM 5.5 file into XML. It is included in the download files for this chapter as kennedy55.xml. *The next stage in the processing is to convert this so that it conforms to the GEDCOM XML 6.0 schema. This is obviously another job for XSLT. Let's now look at the stylesheet that achieves this conversion, which is in the download as* ged55-to-6 .xsl.

Converting from GEDCOM 5.5 to 6.0

The stylesheet ged55-to-6.xsl doesn't handle the full job of GEDCOM conversion, but it does handle the subset that we're using in this application. It starts like this:

```
<xsl:transform
 xmlns:xsl="http://www.w3.org/1999/XSL/Transform"
 xmlns:xs="http://www.w3.org/2001/XMLSchema"
 version="2.0"
>

<!-- This stylesheet converts from the XML representation GEDCOM 5.5
     to the GEDCOM 6.0 XML beta specification -->
```

```
<xsl:strip-space elements="*"/>
<xsl:output method="xml" indent="yes" encoding="iso-8859-1"/>

<!-- import the schema for the result vocabulary -->

<xsl:import-schema namespace="" schema-location="gedSchema.xsd"/>
```

I'm going to use a schema-aware stylesheet to tackle this conversion. I won't be using a schema for the input vocabulary (because I haven't written one), but I will be using the schema for the result document. I will also be validating the result document against this schema. The main effect of this (for the time being) is that mistakes in the stylesheet that cause incorrect output to be generated are reported immediately, and pinpointed to the line in the stylesheet that caused the error. As I developed this stylesheet, this happened dozens of times before I got it right, and diagnosing the errors proved far easier than using the conventional approach of generating the output, inspecting it for obvious faults, and then running it through a separate validation phase. I'll give some examples of this later on.

This does mean that to run this example yourself, you will need to install a schema-aware processor. At the time of writing, the only schema-aware XSLT 2.0 processor available is the commercial version of Saxon, version 8.0 or later, which you can find at http://www.saxonica.com/. You can easily edit the stylesheet to remove the <xsl:import-schema> declaration and the «validation="strict"» attribute on the <xsl:result-document> instruction, and it will then work with a basic XSLT 2.0 processor. However, later stylesheets in this chapter make rather deeper use of schema-aware transformation.

There is no «namespace» attribute on the <xsl:import-schema> declaration, because the schema has no target namespace.

Top-level processing

We can now get on with the top-level processing logic:

```
<xsl:param name="submitter" select="'Michael Kay'"/>

<xsl:template match="/">
  <xsl:result-document validation="strict">
    <GEDCOM>
      <HeaderRec>
        <FileCreation
          Date="{format-date(current-date(), '[D1] [MN,*-3] [Y0001]')}"/>
        <Submitter>
          <Link Target="ContactRec" Ref="Contact-Submitter"/>
        </Submitter>
      </HeaderRec>
      <xsl:call-template name="families"/>
      <xsl:call-template name="individuals"/>
      <xsl:call-template name="events"/>
      <ContactRec Id="Contact-Submitter">
        <Name><xsl:value-of select="$submitter"/></Name>
      </ContactRec>
    </GEDCOM>
  </xsl:result-document>
</xsl:template>
```

This template rule establishes the outline of the result tree. The containing <GEDCOM> element will contain: a header record, which we generate here and now; then a set of family records, a set of individual records, and a set of events, which must appear in that order; and finally a contact record to indicate the originator of the data set, which must be present because the mandatory <Submitter> element in the header refers to it. The name of the submitter is defined by a stylesheet parameter, so you can set a different value if you use this stylesheet on your own data files. (The reason this field is called «Submitter» is historic: GEDCOM was originally designed so that members of the LDS church could submit details of their ancestors to the church authorities.)

The instruction <xsl:result-document validation="strict"> causes the result tree to be validated. The system will do this by looking in the imported schemas for an element declaration of the outermost element in the result tree (the <GEDCOM> element) and then ensuring that the rest of the result tree conforms to this element declaration. In the case of Saxon, this validation is done on the fly: each element is validated as soon as it is written to the result tree, which means that any validation errors can be reported in relation to the stylesheet instruction that wrote the incorrect data.

In the header I have generated only those fields that are mandatory. These include the file creation date, which must be in the format «DD MMM YYYY». This can easily be generated in XSLT 2.0 using the combination of the current-date() and the format-date() functions. The current-date() function is in XPath, and is described in Chapter 10 of *XPath 2.0 Programmer's Reference*; the format-date() function is in XSLT, and is in Chapter 7 of this book.

Creating family records

The <FamilyRec> elements in the result document correspond one-to-one with the <FAM> elements in the input, except that the event information is not included (it is output separately in <EventRec> elements, later). For example, the input element

```
<FAM ID="F4">
    <HUSB REF="I3"/>
    <WIFE REF="I4"/>
    <CHIL REF="I2"/>
</FAM>
```

is translated to the output element

```
<FamilyRec Id="F4">
    <HusbFath>
        <Link Target="IndividualRec" Ref="I3"/>
    </HusbFath>
    <WifeMoth>
        <Link Target="IndividualRec" Ref="I4"/>
    </WifeMoth>
    <Child>
        <Link Target="IndividualRec" Ref="I2"/>
    </Child>
</FamilyRec>
```

Here is the code to do this:

```
<xsl:template name="families">
  <xsl:apply-templates select="/*/FAM"/>
</xsl:template>
```

```
<xsl:template match="FAM">
  <FamilyRec Id="{@ID}">
    <xsl:apply-templates select="HUSB, WIFE, CHIL"/>
  </FamilyRec>
</xsl:template>

<xsl:template match="FAM/HUSB">
  <HusbFath>
    <Link Target="IndividualRec" Ref="{@REF}"/>
  </HusbFath>
</xsl:template>

<xsl:template match="FAM/WIFE">
  <WifeMoth>
    <Link Target="IndividualRec" Ref="{@REF}"/>
  </WifeMoth>
</xsl:template>

<xsl:template match="FAM/CHIL">
  <Child>
    <Link Target="IndividualRec" Ref="{@REF}"/>
  </Child>
</xsl:template>
```

One point worth noting here is the use of «select="HUSB, WIFE, CHIL"» to ensure that the elements of the family appear in the right order in the output. The GEDCOM 6.0 schema is very strict about the order of elements, whereas GEDCOM 5.5 was more liberal. This expression selects a sequence containing zero-or-one HUSB elements, zero-or-one WIFE elements, and zero-or-more CHIL elements, and processes them in that order.

If the input GEDCOM file is invalid, for example if a FAM contains more than one WIFE element, then the output file will also be invalid, and this will cause a validation error to be reported by the XSLT processor.

Creating individual records

The code for mapping <INDI> records in the source to <IndividualRec> records in the result tree is similar in principle to the code for family records, though a little bit more complicated.

```
<xsl:template name="individuals">
  <xsl:apply-templates select="/*/INDI"/>
</xsl:template>

<xsl:template match="INDI">
  <IndividualRec Id="{@ID}">
    <xsl:apply-templates select="NAME, SEX, REFN, NOTE, CHAN"/>
  </IndividualRec>
</xsl:template>

<xsl:template match="INDI/NAME">
  <IndivName>
    <xsl:analyze-string select="." regex="/(.*?)/">
      <xsl:matching-substring>
```

```
              <xsl:text> </xsl:text>
              <NamePart Type="surname" Level="1">
                <xsl:value-of select="regex-group(1)"/>
              </NamePart>
              <xsl:text> </xsl:text>
          </xsl:matching-substring>
          <xsl:non-matching-substring>
             <xsl:value-of select="."/>
          </xsl:non-matching-substring>
        </xsl:analyze-string>
      </IndivName>
  </xsl:template>
```

Note the code here for extracting the surname from the name using the new `<xsl:analyze-string>` instruction in XSLT 2.0. In GEDCOM 5.5 the surname is tagged by enclosing it between «/» characters; in 6.0, it is enclosed in a nested `<NamePart>` element. The 6.0 specification also allows tagging of other parts of the name, for example as a given name, a title, a generation suffix (such as «Jr») and so on; but as such fields aren't marked up in our source data, we can't generate them.

```
<xsl:template match="INDI/SEX">
  <Gender>
    <xsl:apply-templates/>
  </Gender>
</xsl:template>

<xsl:template match="INDI/REFN">
  <ExternalID Type="REFN" Id="{.}"/>
</xsl:template>

<xsl:template match="INDI/CHAN">
  <Changed Date="{DATE}" Time="00:00"/>
</xsl:template>

<xsl:template match="NOTE">
  <Note>
    <xsl:apply-templates/>
  </Note>
</xsl:template>

<xsl:template match="CONT">
  <xsl:text>&#x0a;</xsl:text>
  <xsl:value-of select="."/>
</xsl:template>
```

The rules for NOTE elements apply to such elements wherever they appear in a GEDCOM file, which is why the patterns specify «match="NOTE"» rather than «match="INDI/NOTE"»; for other elements, the rules may be specific to their use within an `<INDI>` record.

In the original GEDCOM file a NOTE can contain multiple lines, which are arranged like this:

```
1 NOTE Educated at Harvard University. Elected Congressman in 1945
2 CONT aged 29; served three terms in the House of Representatives.
2 CONT Elected Senator in 1952. Elected President in 1960, the
2 CONT youngest ever President of the United States.
```

In the direct conversion to XML, the note appears like this (except that there is no newline before the first
<CONT> start tag):

```
<NOTE>Educated at Harvard University. Elected Congressman in 1945
<CONT>aged 29; served three terms in the House of Representatives.</CONT>
<CONT>Elected Senator in 1952. Elected President in 1960, the</CONT>
<CONT>youngest ever President of the United States.</CONT>
```

The GEDCOM 6.0 specification allows only plain text in a <NOTE> element (it provides other elements for
more complex information, such as a transcript of a will). So the ged55-to-6 conversion stylesheet
preserves the line endings by inserting a newline character wherever a <CONT> element appeared. The
final result is:

```
<Note>Educated at Harvard University. Elected Congressman in 1945
aged 29; served three terms in the House of Representatives.
Elected Senator in 1952. Elected President in 1960, the
youngest ever President of the United States.
</Note>
```

The result isn't always satisfactory, because different genealogy packages that produce GEDCOM 5.5
vary widely in how they handle newlines and whitespace: but it works in this case.

A typical individual record after conversion looks like this:

```
<IndividualRec Id="I2">
   <IndivName>Jaqueline Lee
       <NamePart Type="surname" Level="1">Bouvier</NamePart>
   </IndivName>
   <IndivName>
       <NamePart Type="surname" Level="1">Kennedy</NamePart>
   </IndivName>
   <IndivName>
       <NamePart Type="surname" Level="1">Onassis</NamePart>
   </IndivName>
   <Gender>F</Gender>
   <ExternalID Type="REFN" Id="2"/>
   <Changed Date="13 JAN 2004" Time="00:00"/>
</IndividualRec>
```

GEDCOM 6.0 allows all the parts of an individual's name to be tagged indicating the type of the name,
but it doesn't require it, and in our source data, there isn't enough information to achieve this. The
<ExternalID> allows external reference numbers to be recorded: for example, it might be a stable
reference number used to identify this record in a particular database. As with names, there's no limit on
how many reference numbers can be stored—the idea is that the «Type» attribute distinguishes them.

Creating event records

The event records in the result tree correspond to events associated with individuals and families in the
source data. As we've seen, the 6.0 data model treats events as first-class objects, which are linked to the
individuals who participated in the event.

Our sample data set only includes a few different kinds of event: birth, marriage, divorce, death, and burial, and in the stylesheet we'll confine ourselves to handling these five, plus the other common event of baptism. We also handle the general EVEN tag which is used in GEDCOM 5.5 for miscellaneous events. It should be obvious how the code can be extended to handle other events.

```
<xsl:template name="events">
  <xsl:apply-templates mode="event"
    select="/GED/INDI/(BIRT|BAPM|DEAT|BURI) | /GED/FAM/(MARR|DIV)" />
  <xsl:apply-templates select="/GED/(INDI|FAM)/EVEN"/>
</xsl:template>

<xsl:template match="*" mode="event">
  <xsl:variable name="id">
    <xsl:value-of select="../@ID"/>
    <xsl:text>-</xsl:text>
    <xsl:number count="*"/>
  </xsl:variable>
  <EventRec Id="{$id}">
    <xsl:copy-of select="$event-mapping/*[name()=name(current())]/@*"/>
    <xsl:apply-templates select="." mode="participants"/>
    <xsl:apply-templates select="DATE, PLAC, NOTE"/>
  </EventRec>
</xsl:template>

<xsl:variable name="event-mapping">
  <BIRT Type="birth" VitalType="birth"/>
  <BAPM Type="baptism" VitalType="birth"/>
  <DEAT Type="death" VitalType="death"/>
  <BURI Type="burial" VitalType="death"/>
  <MARR Type="marriage" VitalType="marriage"/>
  <DIV Type="divorce" VitalType="divorce"/>
</xsl:variable>

<xsl:template match="EVEN">
  <xsl:variable name="id">
    <xsl:value-of select="../@ID"/>
    <xsl:text>-</xsl:text>
    <xsl:number count="*"/>
  </xsl:variable>
  <EventRec Id="{$id}" Type="{TYPE}">
    <xsl:apply-templates select="." mode="participants"/>
    <xsl:apply-templates select="DATE, PLAC, NOTE"/>
  </EventRec>
</xsl:template>
```

This code identifies all the subelements of <INDI> and <FAM> that refer to events, and then processes these, creating one <EventRec> in the output for each. The identifier for the event is computed from the identifier of the containing <INDI> or <FAM> element plus a sequence number, and the attributes of the event are obtained from a look-up table based on the original element name. In the 6.0 model, the type of event (for example death or burial) is indicated by the «Type» attribute, whose values are completely open-ended. The optional «VitalType» attribute allows each event to be associated with one of the four key events of birth, death, marriage, and divorce: this means, for example, that the date of publication of an obituary can be used as an approximation for the date of death if no more accurate date is available, and that the announcement of banns can similarly be used to estimate the date of marriage.

The next two templates are used to generate the particpants in an event. The first handles events associated with an individual, the second events associated with a couple (which come from the FAM record):

```
<xsl:template match="INDI/*" mode="participants">
  <Participant>
    <Link Target="IndividualRec" Ref="{../@ID}"/>
    <Role>principal</Role>
  </Participant>
</xsl:template>

<xsl:template match="FAM/*" mode="participants">
  <Participant>
    <Link Target="IndividualRec" Ref="{../HUSB/@REF}"/>
    <Role>husband</Role>
  </Participant>
  <Participant>
    <Link Target="IndividualRec" Ref="{../WIFE/@REF}"/>
    <Role>wife</Role>
  </Participant>
</xsl:template>
```

This leaves the handling of the date and place of the event. Both are potentially very complex information items. Dates, however, have changed little between GEDCOM 5.5 and 6.0, so they can be carried over unchanged.

```
<xsl:template match="DATE">
  <Date><xsl:apply-templates/></Date>
</xsl:template>
```

For the places where events occurred, we can try to be a bit more clever. Many of the events in our data set occurred in the United States, and have a PLAC record of the form «somewhere, XX, USA» where XX is a two-letter code identifying a state. This format is predictable because *The Master Genealogist* captures place names in a structured way and generates this comma-separated format on output. We can recognize places that follow this pattern, and use the regular-expression handling capability of XSLT 2.0 to generate a more structured <Place> attribute. This records the country as USA, and the state as the two-letter code preceding the country name; anything before the state abbreviation is tokenized using commas as the delimiter, and the sequence of tokens is output in reverse order—note the calls on reverse() and tokenize()—using individual <PlacePart> elements in the output.

```
<xsl:template match="PLAC">
  <Place>
    <xsl:choose>
      <xsl:when test="matches(., '^.*,\s*[A-Z]{2},\s*USA\s*$')">
        <xsl:analyze-string select="."
                            regex="^(.*),\s*([A-Z]{{2}}),\s*USA\s*$">
          <xsl:matching-substring>
            <PlaceName>
```

```
                <PlacePart Type="country" Level="1">USA</PlacePart>
                <PlacePart Type="state" Level="2">
                  <xsl:value-of select="regex-group(2)"/>
                </PlacePart>
                <xsl:for-each select="reverse(tokenize(regex-group(1), ','))">
                  <PlacePart Level="{5+position()}">
                    <xsl:value-of select="normalize-space(.)"/>
                  </PlacePart>
                </xsl:for-each>
              </PlaceName>
            </xsl:matching-substring>
            <xsl:non-matching-substring>
              <xsl:message>Error: string "<xsl:value-of select="."/>"
                        does not match regex</xsl:message>
            </xsl:non-matching-substring>
          </xsl:analyze-string>
        </xsl:when>
        <xsl:otherwise>
          <PlaceName><xsl:value-of select="."/></PlaceName>
        </xsl:otherwise>
      </xsl:choose>
    </Place>
  </xsl:template>
```

The effect of these rules is that we end up with event records of the form:

```
<EventRec Id="I2-5" Type="birth" VitalType="birth">
    <Participant>
        <Link Target="IndividualRec" Ref="I2"/>
        <Role>principal</Role>
    </Participant>
    <Date>28 JUL 1929</Date>
    <Place>
        <PlaceName>
            <PlacePart Type="country" Level="1">USA</PlacePart>
            <PlacePart Type="state" Level="2">NY</PlacePart>
            <PlacePart Level="6">Long Island</PlacePart>
            <PlacePart Level="7">Southampton</PlacePart>
        </PlaceName>
    </Place>
</EventRec>
```

The names "Long Island" and "Southampton" are classified as levels 6 and 7 because we don't know enough about them to classify them more accurately: levels up to 5 have reserved meanings, whereas 6 and above are available for arbitrary purposes. The ordering of levels is significant: higher levels are intended to represent a finer granularity of place name, which is why we have reversed the order of the original components of the name.

Debugging the Stylesheet

This completes the presentation of the stylesheet used to convert the data from GEDCOM 5.5 to 6.0 format. I'd like to add some notes, however, from my experience of developing this stylesheet. This was the first time I had developed a real stylesheet using a schema-aware XSLT processor, and it may be worth sharing what I learnt.

Actually, it was the first time anyone had developed a schema-aware stylesheet; the necessary features in Saxon were still hot from the oven while I was writing it.

The vast majority of my errors in coding this stylesheet, unless they were basic XSLT or XPath errors, were detected as a result of the on-the-fly validation of the result document against its schema. These errors included:

- ❑ Leaving out required attributes
- ❑ Misspelling element names (for example, `ExternalId` for `ExternalID`)
- ❑ Generating elements in the wrong order
- ❑ Placing an element at the wrong level of nesting
- ❑ Generating an invalid value for an attribute

With the current version of Saxon, none of these errors are detected at stylesheet compile time, but they are all reported while executing the stylesheet, and in nearly all cases the error message identifies exactly where the stylesheet is wrong. For example, if the code in the initial template is changed to read

```
<Submitter>
    <Link Ref="Contact-Submitter"/>
</Submitter>
```

then the transformation fails with the message:

```
Error at element Link on line 24 of ged55-to-6.xsl:
    Required attribute «Target» is missing
```

This process caught quite a few basic XSLT coding errors. For example, I originally wrote:

```
<xsl:template match="FAM/CHIL">
  <Child>
    <Link Target="IndividualRec" Ref="@REF"/>
  </Child>
</xsl:template>
```

in which the curly braces around «@REF» have been omitted. This resulted in the error message:

```
Error at element Link on line 61 of ged55-to-6.xsl:
    The value '@REF' is not a valid NCName
```

The error message arises because in the absence of curly braces, the system has tried to use «@REF» as the literal value of the «Ref» attribute, and this is not allowed because the attribute is defined in the schema to have type `IDREF`, which is a subtype of `NCName`. An `NCName` cannot contain an «@» character.

Similarly, errors in the picture of the `format-date()` function call were picked up because they resulted in a string that did not match the picture defined in the schema for the `StandardDate` type.

However, schema validation of the result tree will not pick up all errors. I had some trouble, for example, getting the regular expression for matching place names right, but the errors simply resulted in the output file containing an empty `<Place>` element, which is allowed by the schema.

Displaying the Family Tree Data

What we want to do now is to write a stylesheet that displays the data in a GEDCOM file in HTML format. We want the display to look something like the following screenshot (see Figure 11-3).

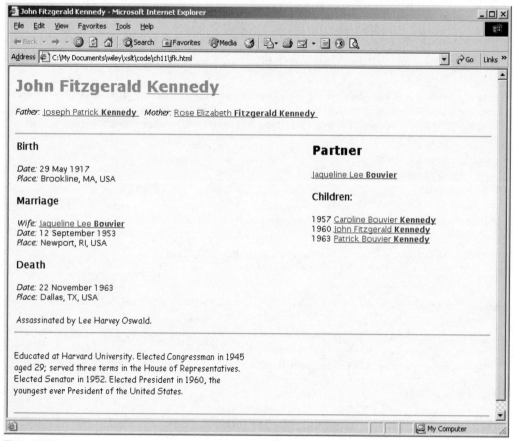

Figure 11-3

This shows all the details of one individual, with links to related individuals so that you can browse around the family tree. Of course one could attempt many more ambitious ways of displaying this data, and I would encourage you to do so: you can start with the small Kennedy data set included in the download for this book, and then continue with any other GEDCOM data set, perhaps one of your own family tree.

Since we will have one HTML page for each individual in the file, we have to think about how to create multiple HTML pages from a single XML input document. There are at least three ways of doing this:

❏ A bulk publishing process, in which you convert the XML input document into a set of HTML pages, and then publish these as static pages on the web server. This has the benefit that you only incur the cost of transformation once. It minimizes your dependence on the facilities available from your Internet Service Provider, and it will work with any browser. However, it can take a lot of space on the server, and can take a long time to upload if you have a slow connection.

❏ Generating HTML pages on demand in the server, using Java servlets or ASP pages. Again this will work with any browser, but this time you need to find an Internet Service Provider who allows you to run servlets or ASP pages.

❏ Downloading the entire XML file to the client, and generating the display there. This has the advantage that the data is only downloaded once, and the user can then browse it at leisure, with no further interaction with the server.

Unfortunately, at the time of writing the two major browsers (Netscape and Internet Explorer) both support XSLT 1.0 transformations, but neither yet supports XSLT 2.0. To get around this problem, I use a fallback stylesheet for this case that uses XSLT 1.0 only.

Another disadvantage is security; you have no way of filtering the data, for example to remove details of living persons, and you have no way to stop your entire XML file being copied by the user (for example, the user can View Source, or can poke around in the browser cache).

The only real difference between the three cases, as far as the stylesheet is concerned, is that the hyperlinks will be generated differently.

We'll handle the differences by writing a generic stylesheet module containing all the common code for the three cases, and then importing this into stylesheets that handle the variations. But we'll start by writing a stylesheet that displays one individual on one HTML page, and then we'll worry about the hyperlinks later.

The Stylesheet

We're ready to write a stylesheet, `person.xsl` that generates an HTML page showing the information relevant to a particular individual. This stylesheet will need to accept the `Id` of the required individual as a stylesheet parameter. If no value is supplied, we'll choose the first `<INDI>` record in the file. Here's how it starts:

```
<xsl:transform
    xmlns:xsl="http://www.w3.org/1999/XSL/Transform"
    xmlns:xs="http://www.w3.org/2001/XMLSchema"
    xmlns:ged="http://www.wrox.com/569090/gedcom"
    xmlns="http://www.w3.org/1999/xhtml"
    exclude-result-prefixes="xs ged"
    version="2.0" >

<!-- import the schema for the GEDCOM 6.0 vocabulary -->

<xsl:import-schema namespace="" schema-location="gedSchema.xsd"/>

<!-- import the schema for the target XHTML vocabulary -->
```

```
<xsl:import-schema namespace="http://www.w3.org/1999/xhtml"
    schema-location="http://www.w3.org/2002/08/xhtml/xhtml1-transitional.xsd"/>

<xsl:output method="xhtml" indent="yes" encoding="iso-8859-1"/>

<!-- parameter to supply the Id of the person to be displayed.
     Default value is the Id of the first person in the data set -->

<xsl:param name="id" select="/*/IndividualRec[1]/@Id" as="xs:string"/>
```

The stylesheet defines four namespaces: the XSLT namespace, the schema namespace, a local namespace which is used only for the functions defined in this stylesheet module, and the XHTML namespace for the result tree. The schema and `ged` namespaces aren't needed in the output file, so the `exclude-result-prefixes` attribute is set to prevent them appearing.

I've chosen to generate the output in XHTML, so I've specified «`method="xhtml"`» in the `<xsl:output>` declaration, and I've imported the XHTML schema. This means that any attempt to generate incorrect XHTML can be reported immediately, as the stylesheet is running, and the offending instruction in the stylesheet can be pinpointed. I decided to use the transitional XHTML schema rather than the strict version of the schema, frankly out of laziness: the strict version is *very* strict indeed, and extra work would be needed on this stylesheet to make its output conform.

There's now a fair bit of preamble before we do any useful work. This is all designed to make the subsequent processing easier and faster. First we define some keys:

```
<!-- keys to allow records to be found by their Id -->

<xsl:key name="indi" match="IndividualRec" use="@Id"/>
<xsl:key name="fam" match="FamilyRec" use="@Id"/>

<!-- a key that locates the family record for a given child -->

<xsl:key name="family-of-child" match="FamilyRec" use="Child/Link/@Ref"/>

<!-- a key that locates the family records for a given parent -->

<xsl:key name="families-of-parent" match="FamilyRec"
use="element(*,ParentType)/Link/@Ref"/>

<!-- a key to allow events to be found for a given individual -->

<xsl:key name="events-for-person" match="EventRec" use="Participant/Link/
@Ref"/>
```

The main purpose of the keys is to make navigation around the structure faster. For a data model like GEDCOM, with many cross-references from one record to another, this can make a big difference. The first two keys allow records to be found given their unique identifiers (they are indexed on their `Id` attributes). The other three keys are there essentially to follow inverse relationships: a family contains links to the children in the family, and the first key enables us quickly to find the family with a link to a given child (in our data there will never be more than one, though GEDCOM allows it: for example a child may be linked both to her birth parents and to her adoptive parents).

Having defined these keys, we now define some functions to make it easier to navigate around the data.

```xsl
<!-- a function to get all the events for a given individual -->

<xsl:function name="ged:events-for-person" as="element(EventRec)*">
  <xsl:param name="person" as="element(IndividualRec)"/>
  <xsl:sequence select="$person/key('events-for-person', $person/@Id)"/>
</xsl:function>

<!-- a function to get the families in which a given individual is a spouse
-->

<xsl:function name="ged:families-of-spouse" as="element(FamilyRec)*">
  <xsl:param name="person" as="element(IndividualRec)"/>
  <xsl:sequence select="$person/key('families-of-parent', $person/@Id)"/>
</xsl:function>

<!-- a function to get all the events for a couple -->

<xsl:function name="ged:events-for-couple" as="element(EventRec)*">
  <xsl:param name="couple" as="element(FamilyRec)"/>
  <xsl:sequence
    select="if ($couple/HusbFath and $couple/WifeMoth)
            then (ged:events-for-person(
                      $couple/key('indi', $couple/HusbFath/Link/@Ref))
                  intersect
                  ged:events-for-person(
                      $couple/key('indi', $couple/WifeMoth/Link/@Ref)))
            else ()"/>

</xsl:function>
```

This checks that the family record does indeed identify a couple (both parents are present), and then finds all the events in which both parties participate—note the use of the `intersect` operator to find the nodes that are present in two given node-sets.

```xsl
<!-- function to get the marriage event for a couple -->

<xsl:function name="ged:marriage-event" as="element(EventRec)?">
  <xsl:param name="couple" as="element(FamilyRec)"/>
  <xsl:variable name="marriage-vitals"
                as="element(EventRec)*"
                select="ged:events-for-couple($couple)[@VitalType='marriage']"
  />
  <xsl:variable name="marriage"
                as="element(EventRec)*"
                select="$marriage-vitals[@Type='marriage']"/>
  <xsl:sequence
    select="if ($marriage)
            then $marriage[1]
            else if ($marriage-vitals)
            then $marriage-vitals[1]
            else ()"/>
</xsl:function>
```

This function is trying to accommodate some of the variety possible in the model. It first finds all the events for the couple (using the previously-defined function) that have the `VitalType` attribute set to «marriage»: this will include events such as engagement or (in older times) the granting of a marriage license. Then it selects the subset of these that are actually «marriage» events. There may still be more than one marriage event for the same couple (these might be different records of the same event, or there may actually have been more than one event, for example a civil marriage and a religious ceremony). So we choose the first marriage event if there is one, or the first event whose `VitalType` is «marriage» if not.

```
<!-- function to get the birth date of an individual -->

<xsl:function name="ged:birth-date" as="element(*,DateType)">
  <xsl:param name="person" as="element(IndividualRec)"/>
  <xsl:variable name="birth-events"
    select="ged:events-for-person($person)[@Type='birth']"/>
  <xsl:sequence
    select="if (exists($birth-events/Date))
            then ($birth-events/Date)[1]
            else (ged:events-for-person($person)[@VitalType='birth']/Date)[1]
"/>
</xsl:function>
```

This function uses similar logic, finding the actual birth event if it exists, or the first event with a `VitalType` of «birth» otherwise.

```
<!-- function to get the estimated marriage date for a couple -->

<xsl:function name="ged:estimated-marriage-date" as="element(*,DateType)">
  <xsl:param name="couple" as="element(FamilyRec)"/>
  <xsl:for-each select="$couple">
    <xsl:variable name="marriage-vitals"
      select="if (HusbFath and WifeMoth)
              then (ged:events-for-person(key('indi', HusbFath/Link/@Ref))
                    intersect
                  ged:events-for-person(key('indi', WifeMoth/Link/@Ref)))
                  [@VitalType='marriage']
              else ()"/>
    <xsl:variable name=      "marriage"
                  as=        "element(EventRec)*"
                  select=    "$marriage-vitals[@Type='marriage']"/>

    <xsl:variable name=      "marriage-date"
                  as=        "element(*, DateType)?"
                  select=    "if ($marriage/Date)
                                then ($marriage/Date)[1]
                              else if ($marriage-vitals/Date)
                                then ($marriage-vitals/Date)[1]
                              else ()"/>

    <xsl:choose>
      <xsl:when test="$marriage-date">
        <xsl:sequence select="$marriage-date"/>
```

```
      </xsl:when>
      <xsl:otherwise>
        <xsl:variable name=    "childbirth-dates"
                      as=      "element(*, DateType)*"
                  select= "Child/Link/@Ref/key('indi',.)/ged:birth-date(.)"/>

        <xsl:for-each select="$childbirth-dates">
          <xsl:sort select="ged:date-sort-key(.)"/>
          <xsl:if test="position() eq 1"><xsl:sequence select="."/></xsl:if>
        </xsl:for-each>
      </xsl:otherwise>
    </xsl:choose>
  </xsl:for-each>
</xsl:function>
```

This function attempts to determine when a couple (identified by a `FamilyRec`) were married. This is done solely so that an individual's partners can be listed in the right order, so the date does not have to be precise. The logic looks complicated, but all it is does is that it finds a dated marriage event if it can, and if it can't, it returns the date of the birth of the oldest child. The call on `ged:date-sort-key()` is a forwards reference to a function that we'll see later.

The body of the function is wrapped in an `<xsl:for-each>` instruction in order to set the context node to the value of the supplied `$couple` argument. It's a matter of personal style, but I find it much more convenient to write path expressions that assume the existence of a context node than to precede every path expression with «`$couple/`».

The next three functions are concerned with date formatting. First a function to convert a date from GEDCOM format into ISO format:

```
<!-- function to convert a standard GEDCOM date (DD MMM YY) to an xs:date -->

<xsl:function name="ged:date-to-ISO" as="xs:date">
  <xsl:param name="date" as="StandardDate"/>
  <xsl:variable name="iso-date">
    <xsl:analyze-string select="$date"
                        regex="\s*([0-9]+)\s+([A-Z]+)\s+([0-9]+)\s*$">
      <xsl:matching-substring>
        <xsl:number value="regex-group(3)" format="0001"/>
        <xsl:text>-</xsl:text>
        <xsl:number value="index-of(('JAN', 'FEB', 'MAR', 'APR', 'MAY', 'JUN',
                                    'JUL', 'AUG', 'SEP', 'OCT', 'NOV', 'DEC'),
                            regex-group(2))" format="01"/>
        <xsl:text>-</xsl:text>
        <xsl:number value="regex-group(1)" format="01"/>
      </xsl:matching-substring>
    </xsl:analyze-string>
  </xsl:variable>
  <xsl:sequence select="xs:date($iso-date)"/>
</xsl:function>
```

This function only works on a date in standard GEDCOM format «DD MMM YYYY». If you pass it a date in an extended form, such as «BEF 1870», the stylesheet will fail with a type error.

I've not attempted here to handle the problems of non-Gregorian calendars (which arise all the time with genealogical data). If the GEDCOM date represents a date in the Julian (or *Old Style*) calendar, then in theory it ought to be shifted by ten or eleven days when converting it to an ISO date, because ISO dates are supposed always to be Gregorian.

```
<!-- function to format a standard GEDCOM date for display -->

<xsl:function name="ged:format-date" as="xs:string">
  <xsl:param name="date" as="StandardDate"/>
  <xsl:sequence select="format-date(ged:date-to-ISO($date), '[D] [MNn] [Y]')"/>
</xsl:function>
```

To format a date into the form «2 January 1931», we first convert the date to standard ISO representation (the xs:date type), and then call XSLT's format-date() function.

```
<!-- function to get a sort key for GEDCOM dates -->

<xsl:function name="ged:date-sort-key" as="xs:string">
  <xsl:param name="date" as="element(*, DateType)"/>
  <xsl:sequence select="
        if (data($date) instance of StandardDate)
          then string(ged:date-to-ISO($date))
          else substring($date, string-length($date)-4)
        "/>
</xsl:function>
```

When we sort on dates, we ideally want to be able to sort standard dates such as «2 JAN 1931» chronologically, but we also want to be able to fit non-standard dates such as «BEF 1870» into the sequence as best we can. To achieve this, I've chosen a sort key that uses the ISO conversion of the date in the case of standard dates (for example, «1931-01-02», and that uses the last four characters otherwise.

Sometimes we just want to display the year:

```
<!-- function to get the year from a GEDCOM date -->

<xsl:function name="ged:get-year" as="xs:string">
  <xsl:param name="date" as="element(*, DateType)"/>
  <xsl:sequence select="substring($date, string-length($date)-4)"/>
</xsl:function>
```

Finally, there's one more function we will be using, which converts a string so that the initial letter is a capital:

```
<!-- a function to capitalize the initial letter of a string -->

<xsl:function name="ged:initial-cap" as="xs:string">
  <xsl:param name="input" as="xs:string"/>
  <xsl:sequence select="concat(upper-case(substring($input, 1, 1)),
                                substring($input, 2))"/>
</xsl:function>
```

And that's the end of the preliminaries. Now we can get on with some actual template rules.

```
<xsl:template match="/">
  <xsl:if test="not(/* instance of schema-element(GEDCOM))">
  <xsl:message terminate="yes">Input document is not a validated GEDCOM 6.0
file</xsl:message>
  </xsl:if>
  <xsl:result-document validation="strict">
    <xsl:variable name="person" select="key('indi', $id)"/>
    <xsl:apply-templates select="$person"/>
  </xsl:result-document>
</xsl:template>
```

The root template rule starts by testing to see if the outermost element of the source document is a GEDCOM element. It doesn't just test the name of the element: the sequence type descriptor «schema-element(GEDCOM)» also checks that the type annotation is appropriate. If the user supplies a source document that hasn't been validated, then this test will fail, even if the document is actually valid; and the stylesheet will proceed no further. If this check weren't present here, some strange and difficult-to-diagnose failures could occur later on, because we are relying on the type annotations being present in the input data.

The entire transformation is then wrapped inside an <xsl:result-document> instruction. This instruction is usually used only when producing multiple result trees, but in this case we're using it for the primary result tree, in order to request validation. It's not actually specifying what the type of the result document must be, only that it must be what it says it is: «validation="strict"» will cause a failure if the outermost element in the result tree isn't defined in some imported schema, or if the result tree isn't valid against that definition. In this case the intent is to check that the result is valid XHTML.

The outline of the HTML page is produced when we process the selected <IndividualRec> element, as one might expect:

```
<xsl:template match="IndividualRec">
  <html>
        <head>
            <xsl:call-template name="css-style"/>
            <xsl:variable name="name">
                <xsl:apply-templates select="IndivName[1]"/>
            </xsl:variable>
            <title><xsl:value-of select="$name"/></title>
        </head>

        <body bgcolor="{if (Gender='M') then 'cyan' else 'pink'}">

            <!-- Show name and parentage -->

            <h1><xsl:apply-templates select="IndivName[1]"/></h1>
            <xsl:if test="IndivName[2]">
              <p>
                <span class="label">Also known as: </span>
                <xsl:for-each select="IndivName[position() ge 2]">
                    <xsl:apply-templates select="."/>
                    <xsl:if test="position() ne last()">, </xsl:if>
                </xsl:for-each>
              </p>
```

```
        </xsl:if>
        <xsl:call-template name="show-parents"/>
        <hr/>

        <table>
        <tr>

            <!-- Show events and attributes -->

            <td width="50%" valign="top">
                <xsl:call-template name="show-events"/>
            </td>
            <td width="20%"/>

            <!-- Show children -->

            <td width="30%" valign="top">
                <xsl:call-template name="show-partners"/>
            </td>
        </tr>
        </table>

        <hr/>

        <!-- Show notes -->

        <xsl:for-each select="Note">
            <p class="text"><xsl:apply-templates mode="note"/></p>
            <xsl:if test="position() eq last()"><hr/></xsl:if>
        </xsl:for-each>

        </body>
    </html>
</xsl:template>
```

This template rule works through the process of generating the output page. Some observations:

❑   The title in the HTML header is generated by first creating a variable, and then copying the value of the variable to the <title> element. This is deliberate, it takes advantage of the standard template rules for generating a personal name, but the <xsl:value-of> instruction then removes the tags such as <b> that appear in the generated name, because these clutter the displayed title in some browsers.

❑   The background color of the page depends on the value of the person's Gender attribute. You might consider this to be an aesthetic abomination, in which case you are welcome to change it, but I left it in because it illustrates another XSLT technique. A more technical criticism is that strict XHTML doesn't allow the <body> element to have a bgcolor attribute: this will be reported as an error if you try to import the strict XHTML schema instead of the transitional one.

❑   The main task of generating the content of the page is split up and delegated to separate named templates, simply for reasons of modularity.

❑   There is no attempt to display all the data that GEDCOM allows to be included in, or referenced from, an <INDI> record, for example citations of sources, multimedia objects such as photographs, etc. If such data is present it will simply be skipped.

I've chosen to use an internal CSS stylesheet to define font sizes and the like, and the task of generating this is delegated to the template named `css-style`. This generates fixed output, as follows:

```xsl
<xsl:template name="css-style">
   <style type="text/css">

   H1 {
       font-family: Verdana, Helvetica, sans-serif;
       font-size: 18pt;
       font-weight: bold;
       color: "#FF0080"
   }

   H2 {
       font-family: Verdana, Helvetica, sans-serif;
       font-size: 14pt;
       font-weight: bold;
       color: black;
   }

   H3 {
       font-family: Lucida Sans, Helvetica, sans-serif;
       font-size: 11pt;
       font-weight: bold;
       color: black;
   }

   SPAN.label {
       font-family: Lucida Sans, Helvetica, sans-serif;
       font-size: 10pt;
       font-weight: normal;
       font-style: italic;
       color: black;
   }

   P,LI,TD {
       font-family: Lucida Sans, Helvetica, sans-serif;
       font-size: 10pt;
       font-weight: normal;
       color: black;
   }

   P.text {
       font-family: Comic Sans MS, Helvetica, sans-serif;
       font-size: 10pt;
       font-weight: normal;
       color: black;
   }

   </style>
</xsl:template>
```

It would have been quite possible, of course, to attach these attributes to the various HTML elements individually, or to incorporate them using XSLT attribute sets, but this way seems cleaner, and shows how

XSLT and CSS can complement each other. In fact, it might have been even better to use an external CSS stylesheet, since a user displaying many of these HTML pages would then get more benefit from caching.

The next template displays the parents of the current individual, as hyperlinks:

```
<xsl:template name="show-parents">
  <xsl:variable name=  "parental-family"
                as=     "element(FamilyRec)?"
                select= "key('family-of-child', @Id)[1]"/>

  <xsl:variable name=  "father"
                as=     "element(IndividualRec)?"
                select= "key('indi', $parental-family/HusbFath/Link/@Ref)"/>

  <xsl:variable name=  "mother"
                as=     "element(IndividualRec)?"
                select= "key('indi', $parental-family/WifeMoth/Link/@Ref)"/>
  <p>
    <xsl:if test="$father">
        <span class="label">Father: </span>
        <xsl:apply-templates select="$father/IndivName" mode="link"/> 
    </xsl:if>
    <xsl:if test="$mother">
        <span class="label">Mother: </span>
        <xsl:apply-templates select="$mother/IndivName" mode="link"/> 
    </xsl:if>
  </p>
</xsl:template>
```

The template starts by locating the `<FamilyRec>` element in which this person appears as a child. It does this using the «family-of-child» key defined earlier. Then it selects the `<IndividualRec>` records for the father and mother, these being the records pointed to by the `<HusbFath>` and `<WifeMoth>` fields of the `<FamilyRec>` record: this time the «indi» key is used.

If the data is not all present, for example if there is no `<FamilyRec>` element, or if the `<FamilyRec>` is missing a `<HusbFath>` and `<WifeMoth>` (no pedigree goes back to infinity), then the «$father» and or «$mother» variables will simply identify an empty sequence. The subsequent `<xsl:if>` instructions ensure that when this happens, the relevant label is omitted from the output.

The actual hyperlinks are generated by using `<xsl:apply-templates>` with «mode="link"»: this gets reused for all the other links on the page, and we'll see later how it works. The « » character reference outputs a non-breaking space. It's actually simpler to do this than to output an ordinary space, which would require an `<xsl:text>` element. If you don't like numeric character references you can define an entity called «nbsp» in the `<!DOCTYPE>` declaration and then use « » in place of « ».

The next named template is used to display the list of events for an individual, such as birth, marriage and death.

```
<!-- Show the events for an individual -->
<xsl:template name="show-events">
```

```
    <xsl:variable name=   "subject"
                  as=     "element(IndividualRec)"
                  select= "."/>

    <xsl:for-each select="ged:events-for-person(.)">
        <xsl:sort select="ged:date-sort-key(Date)"/>
        <h3><xsl:value-of select="ged:initial-cap(@Type)"/></h3>
        <p>
        <xsl:for-each select="Participant[Link/@Ref ne $subject/@Id]">
            <span class="label"><xsl:value-of select="ged:initial-
cap(Role)"/>:
</span>
            <xsl:apply-templates select="Link/@Ref/key('indi',.)/IndivName[1]"
mode="link"/>
            <br/>
        </xsl:for-each>
        <xsl:if test="Date">
            <span class="label">Date: </span><xsl:apply-templates
select="Date"/><br/>
        </xsl:if>
        <xsl:if test="Place">
            <span class="label">Place: </span><xsl:apply-templates
select="Place"/><br/>
        </xsl:if>
        </p>
        <xsl:for-each select="Note">
            <p class="text"><xsl:apply-templates mode="note"/></p>
        </xsl:for-each>

    </xsl:for-each>
</xsl:template>
```

The events are located using the ged:events-for-person() function, and they are presented in an attempt at date order, achieved by calling the ged:date-sort-key() function that we saw earlier.

For each event the template displays the name of the event (in title case, for example «Birth»), the list of participants other than the subject of this page, the date and place of the event, and any notes recorded about the event. In each case this is done by applying the appropriate template rules.

The only part of the HTML display that remains is the right-hand panel, where we show information about a person's partner(s) and children. If multiple partners are recorded for an individual, we use headings such as "Partner 1", "Partner 2"; if there is only one, we omit the number.

The template looks like this:

```
<xsl:template name="show-partners">
  <xsl:variable name=   "subject"
                as=     "element(IndividualRec)"
                select= "."/>

  <xsl:variable name=   "partnerships"
                as=     "element(FamilyRec)*"
```

```
                        select= "ged:families-of-spouse(.)"/>

    <xsl:for-each select="$partnerships">
      <xsl:sort select="ged:date-sort-key(ged:estimated-marriage-date(.))"/>

      <xsl:variable name=    "partner"
                    as=      "element(IndividualRec)?"
                    select=  "key('indi', element(*, ParentType)/Link/@Ref)
except $subject"/>
      <xsl:variable name=    "partner-seq"
                    as=      "xs:integer?"
                    select=  "if (count($partnerships) eq 1)
                              then ()
                              else position()"/>
      <xsl:if test="$partner">
        <h2>Partner <xsl:value-of select="$partner-seq"/></h2>
        <p><xsl:apply-templates select="$partner/IndivName[1]" mode="link"/></p>
      </xsl:if>

      <xsl:if test="Child">
        <h3>Children:</h3>
        <p>
          <xsl:for-each select="Child">
            <xsl:sort select="ChildNbr"/>
            <xsl:sort select="ged:date-sort-key(Link/@Ref/key('indi',.)/ged:
birth-date(.))"/>

            <xsl:variable name=    "child"
                          as=      "element(IndividualRec)"
                          select=  "Link/@Ref/key('indi',.)"/>

            <xsl:value-of select="ged:get-year(ged:birth-date($child))"/>
            <xsl:text> </xsl:text>
            <xsl:apply-templates select="$child/IndivName[1]" mode="link"/><br/>
          </xsl:for-each>
        </p>
      </xsl:if>
    </xsl:for-each>
</xsl:template>
```

As before, we try to list the partners in chronological order, based on the year of marriage. If this isn't known, there's not much we can do about it (I could have tried to use the `<FamilyNbr>` field, but it's not present in the data we are using). For each partnership, we list the partner's name, as a hyperlink, and then the children's names, again as hyperlinks. The children are found from the `<Child>` fields of the `<FamilyRec>` record, and are listed in order of year of birth where this is known.

The next group of template rules is used to create the HTML hyperlinks:

```
<xsl:template match="IndivName" mode="link">
    <a>
      <xsl:attribute name="href">
        <xsl:call-template name="make-href"/>
```

```
        </xsl:attribute>
        <xsl:apply-templates/>
    </a>
</xsl:template>

<xsl:template match="NamePart[@Type='surname']">
    <xsl:text> </xsl:text>
    <span class="surname"><xsl:apply-templates/></span>
    <xsl:text> </xsl:text>
</xsl:template>

<xsl:template name="make-href">
    <xsl:value-of select="concat(../@Id, '.html')"/>
</xsl:template>
```

The «make-href» template is the only place where the form of a link is defined: in this case it consists of a relative URL reference to another HTML file, with a filename based on the individual's Id attribute, for example I27.html. This has been very deliberately isolated into a template all of its own, for reasons that will become clear later.

The stylesheet ends with the template rules for formatting dates, places, and notes:

```
<xsl:template match="PlaceName[PlacePart]">
  <xsl:variable name="sorted-parts" as="element()*">
    <xsl:perform-sort select="PlacePart">
      <xsl:sort select="@Level" order="descending"/>
    </xsl:perform-sort>
  </xsl:variable>
  <xsl:value-of select="$sorted-parts" separator=", "/>
</xsl:template>
```

The above rule sorts the parts of a date by the value of their Level attribute, and then outputs them in a comma-separated list. Note that we no longer need to specify that this is a numeric sort, the system can work this out from the schema.

```
<xsl:template match="Date[data(.) instance of StandardDate]">
  <xsl:value-of select="ged:format-date(data(.))"/>
</xsl:template>

<xsl:template match="Date">
  <xsl:value-of select="."/>
</xsl:template>
```

The above two rules handle standard dates and non-standard dates respectively. We rely on the type annotation to distinguish the two cases. Note the call on «data(.)»: we want to test the type of the simple content of the <Date> element, not the type of the element itself. So we need to call the data() function to get the content.

The final rule, below, is for text nodes within a <Note> element. This uses the <xsl:analyze-string> instruction to replace newline characters by <br/> elements, so that the line endings are preserved in the browser's display.

```
<xsl:template match="text()" mode="note">
  <xsl:analyze-string select="." regex="\n">
    <xsl:matching-substring>
      <br/>
    </xsl:matching-substring>
    <xsl:non-matching-substring>
      <xsl:value-of select="."/>
    </xsl:non-matching-substring>
  </xsl:analyze-string>
</xsl:template>

</xsl:transform>
```

Putting it Together

We've now got a stylesheet that can generate an HTML page for a single chosen individual. We don't yet have a working WEB site!

As I suggested earlier, there are three ways you can work. You can do a batch conversion of the entire data file into a collection of linked static HTML pages held on the web server, you can generate each page on demand from the server, or you can generate pages dynamically at the client. I'll show how to do all three; and in the second case, I'll describe two different implementations of the architecture, one using Java servlets and one using Microsoft ASP pages.

Publishing Static HTML

To generate HTML files for all the individuals in the data file, we need some kind of script that processes each individual in turn and produces a separate output file for each one. Here we can take advantage of the XSLT 2.0 capability to produce multiple output files from one input file. Many XSLT 1.0 products had a similar capability, but unfortunately each product used different syntax.

We'll need a new template for processing the root element, and because this must override the template defined in `person.xsl`, we'll need to use `<xsl:import>` to give the new template higher precedence.

Here is the complete stylesheet, `publish.xsl`, to do the bulk conversion. As well as generating an HTML page for each individual, it also creates an index page listing all the individuals grouped first by surname, then by the rest of the name.

```
<xsl:transform
  xmlns:xsl="http://www.w3.org/1999/XSL/Transform"
  xmlns="http://www.w3.org/1999/xhtml"
  version="2.0"
>
<xsl:import href="person.xsl"/>
<xsl:param name="dir" select="'.'"/>
<xsl:template match="/">
  <xsl:for-each select="*/IndividualRec">
    <xsl:result-document href="{$dir}/{@Id}.html" validation="strict">
      <xsl:apply-templates select="."/>
```

```
      </xsl:result-document>
    </xsl:for-each>
    <xsl:result-document href="{$dir}/index.html" validation="strict">
      <xsl:call-template name="make-index"/>
    </xsl:result-document>
</xsl:template>

<xsl:template name="make-index">
<html>
  <head>
      <title>Index of names</title>
  </head>
  <body>
  <h1>Index of names</h1>
  <xsl:for-each-group select="/*/IndividualRec/IndivName/NamePart[@Level=1]"
                      group-by=".">
    <xsl:sort select="current-grouping-key()"/>
    <h2><xsl:value-of select="current-grouping-key()"/></h2>
    <xsl:for-each select="current-group()">
      <p>
        <xsl:apply-templates select="ancestor::IndividualRec/IndivName[1]"
                             mode="link"/>
      </p>
    </xsl:for-each>
  </xsl:for-each-group>
  </body>
</html>
</xsl:template>
</xsl:transform>
```

You can run this stylesheet using any XSLT 2.0 schema-aware processor. At the time of writing, the only processor that will run this stylesheet as written is the schema-aware version of Saxon, which you can obtain at http://www.saxonica.com/.

You will also need to download the example files from the Wrox web site. Create a new directory, copy the stylesheets and the XML data file into it, make this the current directory, and then run the command:

```
java com.saxonica.Transform -val -t -o index.html kennedy6.xml publish.xsl
```

This assumes that the source files are in the current directory. The -val option is necessary to ensure that the source file is validated against its schema; the -t option is useful because it shows you exactly where the generated output files have been written.

If you want to generate the HTML files in a different directory, you can specify this on the command line, for example:

```
java ... dir=d:\jfk
```

The new directory should fill with HTML files. Double-click on the index.html file, and you should see an index of names. Click on any of the names to see the screen shown on page 714, in glorious color. Then browse the data by following the relationships.

Generating HTML Pages from a Servlet

An alternative to bulk-converting the XML data into static HTML pages is to generate each HTML page on request. This requires execution of a stylesheet on the server, which in principle can be controlled using ASP pages, Java servlets, or even raw CGI programs. However, as many of the available XSLT processors are written in Java, it turns out to be convenient to use servlets.

If you aren't familiar with servlet programming, it's probably best to skip this section, because there isn't space here to start from first principles. There are plenty of good books on the subject.

All the Java XSLT 1.0 processors (there are at least five) implement the JAXP API, which is described in Appendix D. This means you can write a servlet that works with any processor. Although the JAXP API currently only supports XSLT 1.0, there's very little difference at the API level between a 1.0 processor and a 2.0 processor, so you can use this API with minor tweaks to run an XSLT 2.0 processor such as Saxon version 8.

In fact, most of the XSLT processors come with some kind of packaged servlet interface, though it's often best to customize it to suit the particular requirements of the application. As there are a lot of variations depending on the environment you are working in, I won't try to give a complete working solution for this situation, but will just sketch out the design.

A particular feature of this application is that there are lots of requests to get data from the same source document, using the same stylesheet, but with different parameters. So ideally we want to hold both the source document and the stylesheet in memory on the server: we don't want to incur the overhead of parsing and validating the full XML document to display each individual.

We would like to accept incoming requests from the browser in the form:

```
http://www.myserver.com/examples/servlet/GedServlet?tree=kennedy6&id=I1
```

The parameters included in the URL are firstly, the name of the data set to use (we'd like the server to be able to handle several concurrently), and secondly, the identifier of the individual to display.

> When the above URL is included in an XML document, the «&» must be represented as «&». Most HTML browsers will accept either «&» or «&». But strictly, «&» is correct according to the HTML specification, and that is what our stylesheet will actually generate.

So the first thing that we need to do is to generate hyperlinks in this format. We can do this by writing a new stylesheet module that imports person.xsl and overrides the template that generated the hyperlinks. We'll call this ged-servlet.xsl.

The ged-servlet.xsl stylesheet module looks like this. It has an extra parameter, which is the name of the tree we are interested in, because the same servlet ought to be able to handle requests for data from different family trees. And it overrides the «make-href» template with one that generates hyperlinks in the required format:

```
<xsl:transform
    xmlns:xsl="http://www.w3.org/1999/XSL/Transform"
    version="2.0" >

<xsl:import href="person.xsl"/>
<xsl:param name="tree"/>

<xsl:template name="make-href">
    <xsl:value-of select="concat('/examples/servlet/GedServlet?tree=',
                       $tree, '&amp;id=', ../@Id)"/>
</xsl:template>

</xsl:transform>
```

If you configure the servlet in a different location from this, you will need to modify this stylesheet to use a different URL.

The stylesheet and the servlet interface could also be extended to generate an index of names, as in the previous example, but as that's a simple task I'll leave you to work that out for yourself.

More tricky is writing the servlet. The code below uses the JAXP interface with a minor extension to request the XSLT processor to perform validation of source documents.

```
import java.io.*;
import javax.servlet.*;
import javax.servlet.http.*;
import java.util.Hashtable;

import org.w3c.dom.Document;

import javax.xml.parsers.*;
import javax.xml.transform.*;
import javax.xml.transform.stream.*;

import net.sf.saxon.FeatureKeys;

public class GedServlet extends HttpServlet {
```

The init() method of a servlet is called when the servlet is first initialized. In this method we set a couple of system properties. The first property ensures that the XSLT processor we use is the schema-aware version of Saxon. The second property selects Crimson as the XML parser (the tomcat servlet engine comes with its own built-in parser, which causes problems with this example). In a production environment, it would be appropriate to read the values of these system properties from the web.xml configuration file.

```
    public void init(javax.servlet.ServletConfig conf)
    throws javax.servlet.ServletException {
```

```
        super.init (conf);
        System.setProperty("javax.xml.transform.TransformerFactory",
                           "com.saxonica.SchemaAwareTransformerFactory");
        System.setProperty("javax.xml.parsers.SAXParserFactory",
                           "org.apache.crimson.jaxp.SAXParserFactoryImpl");
    }
```

The `service()` method of the servlet responds to an individual request from a user browser. It sets a `StreamSource` to the file identified by the `tree` parameter in the URL. It looks in its local data to see if the compiled stylesheet is already there; if not, it creates it. It then creates a `Transformer`, sets a couple of stylesheet parameters, and calls the JAXP `transform()` method to run the transformation, sending the result to the servlet output destination (which of course causes the result to appear at the browser).

```
/**
 * Respond to an HTTP request
 */

public void service(HttpServletRequest req, HttpServletResponse res)
throws ServletException, IOException
{
    res.setContentType("text/html");

    try {
        String clear = req.getParameter("clear");
        if (clear!=null && clear.equals("yes")) {
            resetData();
        }
        String family = req.getParameter("tree");
        Source source = new StreamSource(
            new File(getServletContext().getRealPath(
                        "/" + family + ".xml")));

        Result result = new StreamResult(res.getOutputStream());

        Templates style = getStyleSheet();
        Transformer transformer = style.newTransformer();
        transformer.setParameter("id", req.getParameter("id"));
        transformer.setParameter("tree", family);
        transformer.transform(source, result);

    } catch (Exception err) {
        PrintStream ps = new PrintStream(res.getOutputStream());
        ps.println("Error applying stylesheet: " + err.getMessage());
    }
}
```

When the stylesheet is first invoked, it is prepared and stored in memory as a `Templates` object. This method causes Saxon to validate the source document by setting the `SCHEMA_VALIDATION` property in the `TransformerFactory`: this attribute is specific to Saxon.

```
/**
 * Get the prepared stylesheet from memory; prepare it if necessary
 */
```

```
    private synchronized Templates getStyleSheet()
    throws TransformerConfigurationException {
        if (stylesheet == null) {
            File sheet = new File(getServletContext().getRealPath(
                                    "/ged-servlet.xsl"));

            TransformerFactory factory = TransformerFactory.newInstance();
            factory.setAttribute(FeatureKeys.SCHEMA_VALIDATION, Boolean.TRUE);
            stylesheet = factory.newTemplates(new StreamSource(sheet));
        }
        return stylesheet;
    }


    /**
     * Reset data held in memory
     */

    private synchronized void resetData() {
        stylesheet = null;
    }

    private Templates stylesheet = null;
}
```

The XML file holding the family tree data must be in a file *tree*.xml where *tree* identifies the specific family tree, in our case kennedy6.xml. This must be in the home directory for the web application containing the servlet, as defined by the configuration parameters for your web server. The two stylesheet modules person.xsl and ged-servlet.xsl , and the schema gedSchema.xsd, must also be in this directory.

The servlet keeps in memory a copy of the compiled stylesheet (the JAXP Templates object): it makes this copy the first time it is needed.

It would also make sense to keep in memory a DOM Document object representing each family tree, but I haven't attempted to do that in this demonstration.

Installing and Configuring the Servlet

To run servlets you need to install a servlet container such as tomcat, available from www.apache.org. For production use, tomcat normally runs as an add-on to the Apache web server, but for testing purposes, it also has an HTTP server of its own built in. There's no space here to go into all the details of installing a servlet container like tomcat, but for quick reference, this section shows where I put the application files to get this example working.

Figure 11-4 shows the directory structure after installing Tomcat 4 (the details, of course, may vary).

Notice the four files in the examples directory: the two XSLT modules, the XML data file, and the XML Schema. Open up the examples directory, and we find the GedServlet.class file, representing the compiled servlet code (see Figure 11-5).

Finally (I won't show you this one), the WEB-INF/lib directory contains the JAR files for the XSLT processor.

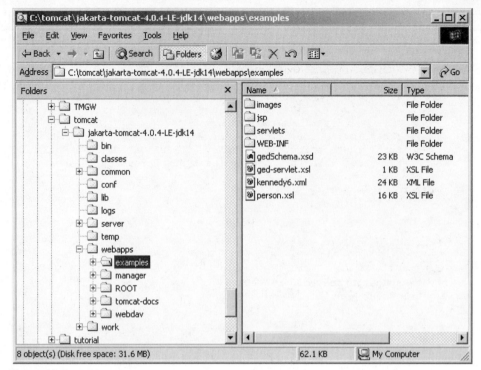

Figure 11-4

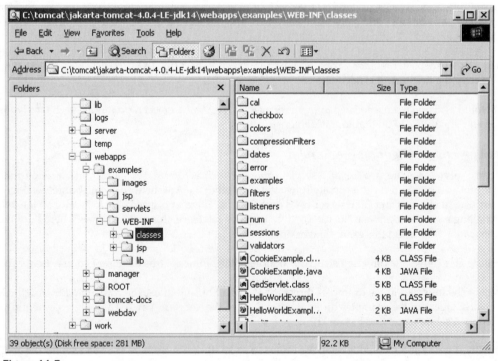

Figure 11-5

To start tomcat up, double-click on the `startup.bat` file in the `bin` directory. This brings up an old-fashioned console that displays progress messages. Then, assuming you have defaulted everything in your configuration, open up your browser and enter the URL:

http://localhost:8080/examples/servlet/GedServlet?tree=kennedy6&id=I1

If things fail (and they probably will—servlets can be delicate animals) then you will probably see a summary message on the browser window, but the detailed diagnostics will be on the Tomcat console, or in its log files. Good luck!

Generating HTML Using ASP Pages

If you work in a Microsoft environment, an alternative to writing Java servlets to perform server-side transformation is to control the process using an ASP page. In this case you have a choice: you can use Microsoft's MSXML3 parser and XSLT processor, or you can use the newer .NET processor. While MSXML3 is best known for its ability to do client-side transformations, it is equally effective as a server-side engine, and many people have reported that its performance is better than the .NET engine. Of course, this may change over time. MSXML3 uses COM interfaces so it can be called from an ASP page in the same way as any other COM object, while the .NET processor (in package `System.Xml.Xsl`) fits more cleanly into the ASP.NET environment. The different APIs to control transformation using the two Microsoft processors are described in Appendix C.

At the time of writing, Microsoft doesn't have an XSLT 2.0 implementation. There have been reports of an XSLT 1.0 processor running on top of their XQuery engine, which could potentially evolve into an XSLT 2.0 processor in the fullness of time. But as this processor doesn't yet exist, I will leave the ASP version of this application as an exercise for the reader.

Generating HTML in the Browser

Finally, let's look at another way to display the family tree: namely, to download the whole XML file to the browser as a single chunk, and then use client-side scripts to invoke stylesheet processing whenever the user clicks on a hyperlink.

The problem with this approach is that at the time of writing, there is no XSLT 2.0 processor available in either Internet Explorer or Netscape: both support XSLT 1.0 client-side transformation, but not yet 2.0. Hopefully this situation will soon change, though there is always a drawback in running client-side applications because not all your users will be using the latest browser versions.

However, this book would not be complete if it didn't show you how to run transformations client-side, and for that purpose I have written an XSLT 1.0 version of the stylesheet.

My first attempt to do this was to produce the 1.0 version of the stylesheet as an overlay on the 2.0 version: that is, I wrote an XSLT 1.0 module in which every top-level declaration in the 2.0 stylesheet that contained constructs that would only run under XSLT 2.0 was replaced by a functionally equivalent 1.0 construct. My thinking was that the forwards compatibility rules in XSLT 1.0 would ensure that no errors were raised because of constructs in the unused part of the stylesheet. Unfortunately, it didn't prove possible to do this. To see why, look at the rule:

```
<xsl:template match="Date[data(.) instance of StandardDate]">
  <xsl:value-of select="ged:format-date(data(.))"/>
</xsl:template>
```

This uses XSLT 2.0 constructs (the `data()` function and the `"instance of"` operator) within the match pattern, and there is no way of overriding this with an XSLT 1.0 template rule in a way that an XSLT 1.0 processor will understand. So one would have to adopt a different strategy: move the shared components to a common module, and import this from modules containing the code that's specific to 1.0 and 2.0 respectively. I didn't want to distort my XSLT 2.0 code to this extent, so I simply copied the common code into the 1.0 module by cut-and-paste to create a freestanding XSLT 1.0 stylesheet, which is named `person10.xsl`. This stylesheet simply leaves out many of the more interesting aspects of the 2.0 version, for example dates are output as they appear in the GEDCOM data, and no attempt is made to sort children or spouses in chronological order.

The next thing we need to do is to adapt the stylesheet to run in the browser. To do this, we need to write an HTML page containing JavaScript to invoke the transformation.

This particular example runs in Internet Explorer 6.

If the XML file is large (family trees produced by serious genealogists often run to several megabytes) then this approach means the user is going to have to wait rather longer to see the first page of data. But the advantage is that once it's downloaded, browsing around the file can be done offline: there is no need to go back to the server to follow each link from one individual to another. This gives the user a lightning-fast response to navigation requests, and reduces the processing load and the number of hits on the server. Another benefit, given that many genealogists only have access to the limited web space provided by a commercial ISP, is that no special code needs to be installed on the server.

This time, the transformation is controlled from JavaScript code on an HTML page `famtree.html`. The page itself reads as follows. The `<script>` elements contain client-side Javascript code.

```
<html>
<head>
   <title>Family Tree</title>
   <style type="text/css">
      ...  as before  ...
   </style>
   <script>
      var source = null;
      var style = null;
      var transformer = null;

      function init() {
         source =
            new ActiveXObject("MSXML2.DOMDocument");
         source.async = false;
         source.load('kennedy.xml');

         style =
            new ActiveXObject("MSXML2.FreeThreadedDOMDocument");
         style.async = false;
         style.load('ms-person.xsl');

         transformer = new ActiveXObject("MSXML2.XSLTemplate");
         transformer.stylesheet = style.documentElement;
         refresh("I1");
      }
```

```
      function refresh(indi) {
          var xslproc = transformer.createProcessor();
          xslproc.input = source;
          xslproc.addParameter("id", indi, "");
          xslproc.transform();
          displayarea.innerHTML = xslproc.output;
      }
    </script>
    <script for="window" event="onload">
        init();
    </script>
  </head>
  <body>
    <div id="displayarea"></div>
  </body>
</html>
```

The CSS style definitions have moved from the XSLT stylesheet to the HTML page, but they are otherwise unchanged.

The init() function on this page is called when the page is loaded. It creates two DOM objects, one for the source XML and one for the stylesheet, and loads these using the relative URLs kennedy.xml and ms-person.xsl. It then compiles the stylesheet into an object which is rather confusingly called an XSLTemplate; this corresponds directly with the TrAX Templates object. Finally it calls the refresh() function to display the individual with identifier I1.

> *I've taken a bit of a short cut here. There's no guarantee that a GEDCOM file will contain an individual with this identifier. A more carefully constructed application would display the first individual in the file, or an index of people.*

The refresh() function creates an executable instance of the stylesheet by calling the createProcessor() method on the XSLTemplate object. It then sets the value of the global id parameter in the stylesheet, and applies the stylesheet to the source document by calling the transform() method. The HTML constructed by processing the stylesheet is then written to the contents of the <div id="displayarea"> element in the body of the HTML page.

We can use the same stylesheet as before, again with modifications to the form of the hyperlinks. This time we want a hyperlink to another individual, I2 say, to take the form:

```
<a href="Javascript:refresh('I2')">Jaqueline Lee Bouvier</a>
```

When the user clicks on this hyperlink, the refresh() function is executed, which causes a new execution of the compiled stylesheet, against the same source document, but with a different value for the id parameter. The effect is that the contents of the page switches to display a different individual.

The ms-person.xsl stylesheet is written by importing the person10.xsl stylesheet presented earlier, and then overriding the aspects we want to change. This time there are two changes: we want to change the form of the hyperlink, and we want to leave out the generation of the CSS style, because the necessary definitions are already present on the HTML page. Here is the stylesheet:

```
<xsl:transform
 xmlns:xsl="http://www.w3.org/1999/XSL/Transform"
 version="1.0"
>

<xsl:import href="person10.xsl"/>

<!-- Change the way hyperlinks are generated -->

<xsl:template name="make-href">
    <xsl:variable name="apos">'</xsl:variable>
    <xsl:value-of
        select="concat('Javascript:refresh(', $apos, ../@Id, $apos, ')')"/>
</xsl:template>

<!-- Suppress the generation of a CSS stylesheet -->

<xsl:template name="css-style"/>

</xsl:transform>
```

One slight infelicity in the resulting stylesheet is that it generates a full HTML page, complete with
<html>, <head>, and <body> elements, and then inserts this as the content of a <div> element within
an existing HTML page. Fortunately Internet Explorer tolerates this abuse of the HTML specification
rather well.

Unfortunately the script shown here works only with Internet Explorer and not with Netscape. If you
want to write the application in a way that is portable between the two browsers, there is a library you
can use to do this: Sarissa, from http://sarissa.sourceforge.net/.

Summary

I hope this little excursion into the strange world of genealogical data models has given you some flavor
of the power of XSLT as a manipulation and reporting tool for complex structured data. We've covered a
lot of ground:

❑   How to navigate your way around complex linked data within an XML document.

❑   Several different ways of generating an interactive view of a large XML data set:

   ❑   Generating lots of static HTML pages in one go at publication time.

   ❑   Generating HTML pages dynamically using either a Java servlet or a Microsoft ASP page.

   ❑   Generating HTML incrementally within the browser.

❑   Using XSLT to transform structured data that wasn't originally in XML format.

The worked example in the next chapter will venture into even stranger territory, using XSLT to solve a
chess problem. While genealogy has demonstrated how XSLT can be used to process complex data, the
chess example will show something of the computational power of the language.

12

Case Study: Knight's Tour

This chapter contains the third (and last) of the XSLT case studies. It shows how XSLT can be used to calculate a knight's tour of the chessboard, in which the knight visits every square without ever landing on the same square twice.

New features in XSLT 2.0 make this kind of application much easier to write, which means that the stylesheet is almost a total rewrite of the XSLT 1.0 version.

Readers of previous editions of this book have reacted differently to this case study. Some have suggested that I should be less frivolous, and stick to examples that involve the processing of invoices and purchase orders, and the formatting of product catalogs. Others have welcomed the example as light relief from the comparatively boring programming tasks they are asked to do in their day job. A third group have told me that this example is absolutely typical of the challenges they face in building real web sites. The web, after all, does not exist only (or even primarily) to oil the wheels of big business. It is also there to provide entertainment.

Whatever your feelings about the choice of problem, I hope that by showing that it can be done I will convince you that XSLT has the computational power and flexibility to tackle any XML formatting and transformation challenge, and that as you study it, you will discover ideas that you can use a wide range of tasks that are more typical of your own programming assignments.

The Problem

The purpose of the stylesheet is to produce a knight's tour of the chessboard, in which each square is visited exactly once, as shown in the illustration overleaf. A knight can move to any square that is at the opposite corner of a 3 × 2 rectangle (Figure 12-1).

The only input to the stylesheet is an indication of the starting square: in modern chess notation, the columns are denoted by the letters a–h starting from the left, and the rows by the numbers 1–8, starting at the bottom. We'll supply the starting square as a parameter to the stylesheet. The stylesheet doesn't need to get anything from the source document. In fact, with XSLT 2.0, there doesn't need to be a source document: the entry point to the stylesheet can be specified as a named template.

We'll build up the stylesheet piece by piece: you can find the complete stylesheet, tour.xsl, on the Wrox web site.

Figure 12-1

The inspiration for this stylesheet came from Oren Ben-Kiki, who published a stylesheet for solving the eight-queens problem. The concept here is very similar, though the details are quite different.

The Algorithm

The strategy for getting the knight round the board is based on the observation that if a square hasn't been visited yet, and if it isn't the knight's final destination, then it had better have at least two unvisited squares that are a knight's move away from it, because there needs to be a way of getting in and another way of getting out. That means that if we can get to a square that's only got one exit left, we'd better go there now or we never will.

This suggests an approach where at each move, we look at all the squares we can jump to next, and choose the one that has fewest possible exits. It turns out that this strategy works, and always gets the knight round the board.

It's possible that this could lead the knight into a blind alley, especially in the case where two of the possible moves look equally good. In this case, the knight might need to retrace its steps and try a different route. In the version of the stylesheet that I published in the previous edition of this book, I included code to do this backtracking, but made the assertion that it was never actually used (though I couldn't prove why). Recently, one of my readers reported that if the knight starts on square f8, it does indeed take a wrong turning at move 58, and needs to retrace its steps. Moreover, this appears to be the only case where this happens.

The place I usually start design is with the data structures. Here the main data structure we need is the board itself. We need to know which squares the knight has visited, and so that we can print out the board at the end, we need to know the sequence in which they were visited. In XSLT 2.0 the obvious choice is to represent the board as a sequence of 64 integers: the value will be zero for a square that has not been visited, or a value in the range 1 to 64 representing the number of the move on which the knight arrived at this square.

In a conventional program this data structure would probably be held in a global variable and updated every time the knight moves. We can't do this in XSLT, because variables can't be updated. Instead, every time a function is called, it passes the current state of the board as a parameter, and when the knight moves, a new copy of the board is created, that differs from the previous one only in the details of one square.

It doesn't really matter which way the squares are numbered, but for the sake of convention we'll number them as shown in Figure 12-2.

0	1	2	3	4	5	6	7
8	9	10	11	12	13	14	15
16	17	18	19	20	21	22	23
24	25	26	27	28	29	30	31
32	33	34	35	36	37	38	39
40	41	42	43	44	45	46	47
48	49	50	51	52	53	54	55
56	57	58	59	60	61	62	63

Figure 12-2

So if we number the rows 0–7, and the columns 0–7, the square number is given as «row * 8 + column + 1», remembering that in XSLT, numbering of the items in a sequence always starts at one.

Having decided on the principal data structure we can decide the broad structure of the program. There are three stages:

1. Prepare the initial data structures (the empty board with a knight placed on it, somewhere)
2. Calculate the tour
3. Display the final state of the board

Calculating the tour involves 63 steps, each one taking the form:

1. Find all the unvisited squares that the knight can move to from the current position
2. For each one of these, count the number of exits (that is, the number of unvisited squares that can be reached from there)
3. Choose the square with the fewest exits, and move the knight there

We're ready to start coding. The tricky bit, as you've probably already guessed, is that all the loops have to be coded using recursion. That takes a bit of getting used to at first, but it quickly becomes a habit.

The Initial Template

Let's start with the framework of top-level elements:

```
<xsl:transform
 xmlns:xsl="http://www.w3.org/1999/XSL/Transform"
 xmlns:xs="http://www.w3.org/2001/XMLSchema"
 xmlns:tour="http://www.wrox.com/5067/tour"
 exclude-result-prefixes="xs tour"
 version="2.0"
>

<xsl:output method="html" indent="yes"/>

<xsl:param name="start" select="'a1'" as="xs:string"/>

<!-- start-column is an integer in the range 0-7 -->

<xsl:variable name="start-column"
   select="number(translate(substring($start, 1, 1),
          'abcdefgh', '01234567'))"/>

<!-- start-row is an integer in the range 0-7, with zero at the top -->

<xsl:variable name="start-row"
   select="8 - number(substring($start, 2, 1))"/>

 . . .

</xsl:transform>
```

All I'm doing here is declaring the global parameter, start, which defines the starting square, and deriving from it two global variables: a row number and column number.

Some observations:

❑ The parameter start has the default value a1. As this is a string-value, it needs to be in quotes; these quotes are additional to the quotes that surround the XML attribute. If I had written «select="a1"», the default value would be the string-value of the <a1> element child of the document root.

❑ The simplest way of converting the alphabetic column identifier (a–h) into a number (0–7) is to use the translate() function, which is described in *XPath 2.0 Programmer's Reference*, in Chapter 10.

❑ The row number is subtracted from 8 so that the lowest-numbered row is at the top, and so that row numbers start from zero. Numbering from zero makes it easier to convert between row and column numbers and a number for each square on the board in the range 0–63.

❑ I haven't yet checked that the supplied start square is valid. I'll do that in the initial template.

Now we can move on to the initial template. In XSLT 2.0 I can define the initial template as a named template, so that it can be invoked directly from the command line, without specifying a source document. However, just in case you're using a processor that doesn't support this capability, it does no harm to define the template with «match="/"» as well.

The root template defines the stages of processing, as follows:

1. Validate the supplied parameter

2. Set up the empty board and place the knight on it at the specified starting square

3. Compute the knight's tour

4. Print out the tour in HTML format

These tasks are all delegated to other templates, so the root template itself is quite simple:

```
<xsl:template name="main" match="/">

    <!-- This template controls the processing.
         It does not access the source document. -->

    <!-- Validate the input parameter -->

    <xsl:if test="not(matches($start, '^[a-h][1-8]$'))">
        <xsl:message terminate="yes"
                     select="Invalid start parameter: try say 'a1' or 'g6'"/>
    </xsl:if>

    <!-- Set up the empty board -->

    <xsl:variable name="empty-board" as="xs:integer*"
        select="for $i in (1 to 64) return 0"/>

    <!-- Place the knight on the board at the chosen starting position -->

    <xsl:variable name="initial-board" as="xs:integer*"
        select="tour:place-knight(1, $empty-board,
                                   $start-row * 8 + $start-column)"/>

    <!-- Evaluate the knight's tour -->

    <xsl:variable name="final-board" as="xs:integer*"
        select="tour:make-moves(2, $initial-board,
                                 $start-row * 8 + $start-column)"/>

    <!-- produce the HTML output -->

    <xsl:call-template name="print-board">
        <xsl:with-param name="board" select="$final-board"/>
    </xsl:call-template>

</xsl:template>
```

Notice the style of coding here, which uses a sequence of variables, each one computed from the value of the previous variable. Each variable is used only once, which means the variables aren't actually necessary: it would be possible to nest all the function calls inside each other, and express the whole calculation using one big XPath expression inside the call to the final print-board template. But in my view, writing the processing logic like this as a sequence of steps makes it much easier to explain what's going on. The «as» clauses, which define the type of each variable, also provide useful documentation. (I also found that while I was writing this code, the type checking provided by the «as» clauses caught many of my errors.)

The code for validating the start parameter uses a simple regular expression. The symbols «^» and «$» match the start and end of the input string, and the body of the regular expression specifies that the string must consist of a single letter in the range [a–h] followed by a single digit in the range [1–8]. If the parameter doesn't match, the stylesheet outputs a message using <xsl:message>, and terminates.

Several of the variables (empty-board, initial-board, and final-board) represent a chessboard containing all or part of a knight's tour. Each of these variables is a sequence of 64 integers in the range 0 to 64. If the square has been visited, it contains a sequence number representing the order of visiting (1 for the start square, 2 for the next square visited, and so on). If the square has not been visited, the value is zero. The type «as="xs:integer*"» is actually much more liberal that this: it doesn't constrain the sequence to be of length 64, and it doesn't constrain the range of values to be 0 to 64. We could define a schema with a user-defined atomic type that allows only integers in the range 0 to 64, but it would seem overkill to import a schema just for this purpose, quite apart from the fact that the stylesheet would then work only with a schema-aware XSLT processor. Even then, restricting the size of the sequence to 64 is not something that the type system can achieve. Although list types can be defined in XML Schema to have a fixed length, this constraint can only be exploited in XSLT when validating an element or attribute node against this list type. Free-standing sequences of atomic values, like the ones being used here, cannot refer to a list type defined in the schema.

In parameters to function calls and in variables, squares on the board will always be represented by an integer in the range 0–63, which is calculated as $row * 8 + $column. When we use the square number to index the sequence that represents the board, we have to remember to add one.

The empty board is first initialized to a sequence of 64 zeroes, and the knight is then placed on its starting square by calling the function place-knight. Let's see how this function works.

Placing the Knight

This is a simple function:

```
<xsl:function name="tour:place-knight" as="xs:integer*">
    <!-- This function places a knight on the board at a given square.
         The returned value is the supplied board, modified to indicate
         that the knight reached a given square at a given move -->
    <xsl:param name="move" as="xs:integer"/>
    <xsl:param name="board" as="xs:integer*"/>
    <xsl:param name="square" as="xs:integer" /><!-- integer in range 0..63 -->
    <xsl:sequence select="
        for $i in 1 to 64 return
            if ($i = $square + 1) then $move else $board[$i]" />
</xsl:function>
```

This function takes three parameters: the number of this move, the current state of the chessboard, and the square on which the knight is to be placed. When it's called from the root template, the move number is always one, and the board is always empty, but I will use the same function again later with different arguments.

What the function does is to copy the whole supplied chessboard before and after the square where the knight is to be placed. This square itself is replaced by the move number. For example, if the tour starts at square a8 (which translates to square zero), then the first call on `place-knight()` will return a sequence containing a one followed by 63 zeroes.

I can't, of course, modify the supplied chessboard in situ. All variables in XSLT are immutable. Instead I create a new board as a modified copy of the original. The result of the function is a sequence representing the new state of the chessboard after placing the knight.

There are various ways the actual calculation of the new board could have been written here. Another possibility would be:

```
<xsl:sequence select="$board[position() = 1 to $square],
                $move,
                $board[position() = $square+2 to 64]"/>
```

and a third option would be:`<xsl:sequence select="insert-before(
                remove($board, $square+1),
                $square+1,
                $move) "/>`

Displaying the Final Board

I'll skip the function that computes the knight's tour for the moment, and describe the relatively easy task of outputting the final result as HTML. Like the rest of the stylesheet, this logic is greatly simplified in XSLT 2.0:

```
<xsl:template name="print-board">

    <!-- Output the board in HTML format -->

    <xsl:param name="board" as="xs:integer*" />

    <html>
    <head>
        <title>Knight's tour</title>
    </head>
    <body>
    <div align="center">
    <h1>Knight's tour starting at <xsl:value-of select="$start"/></h1>
    <table border="1" cellpadding="4" size="{count($board)}">
        <xsl:for-each select="0 to 7">
            <xsl:variable name="row" select="."/>
            <tr>
                <xsl:for-each select="0 to 7">
                    <xsl:variable name="column" select="."/>
                    <xsl:variable name="color"
                        select="if ((($row + $column) mod 2)=1)
                                then 'xffff44' else 'white'"/>
                    <td align="center" bgcolor="{$color}">
                        <xsl:value-of select="$board[$row * 8 + $column + 1]"/>
                    </td>
                </xsl:for-each>
```

```
        </tr>
      </xsl:for-each>
    </table>
  </div>
  </body>
  </html>
</xsl:template>
```

The template contains a little bit of logic to achieve the traditional checkerboard coloring of the squares, using the «mod» operator to test whether the sum of the row number and the column number is a multiple of 2.

The actual content of each square is the move number, extracted from the relevant item in the sequence representing the board.

Finding the Route

So much for the input and output of the stylesheet, now for the substance: the algorithm to calculate the knight's tour.

The basic algorithm we use is that at each move, we consider all the squares we could go to, and choose the one with the fewest exits. For example, if we are on c2 then we could move to a1, e1, a3, e3, b4, or d4, assuming they are all unvisited. Of these, the corner square a1 has only one exit, namely b3, and if we don't visit the corner square now, then we'll never get another chance later. It turns out that this strategy of always visiting the square with least exits nearly always succeeds in generating a complete knight's tour, though in the rare cases where it doesn't, the algorithm is resilient enough to backtrack and try a different route if the first one fails.

The root template makes a call on the function named «make-moves». This function, starting from any given start position, works out all the moves needed to complete the knight's tour. Of course, it does this by recursion: but unlike previous functions which called themselves directly, this one does so indirectly, via another function named «try-possible-moves».

The first thing the «make-moves» template does is to call the template «list-possible- moves» to construct a list of moves that are legal in the current situation. The result of this function, a list of moves, uses a very similar data structure to that of the chessboard itself. The list is represented as a sequence, and each possible move is represented by an integer whose value is the number of the square to which the knight travels. So in Figure 12-3, after move 5 the set of possible moves is the list (3, 19, 28, 30, 23). The list is in no particular order.

Having established the list of possible moves, the function then calls «try-possible-moves» to select one of these moves and execute it.

Here is the function. Its parameters are the number of this move (starting at move 2, because the knight's initial position is numbered 1), the state of the board before this move, and the number of the square on which the knight is currently sitting.

```
<xsl:function name="tour:make-moves" as="xs:integer*">

    <!-- This function takes the board in a given state,
         decides on the next move to make, and then calls itself
```

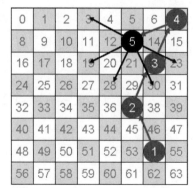

Figure 12-3

```
            recursively to make further moves, until the knight has completed
            his tour of the board. It returns the board in its final state. -->

    <xsl:param name="move" as="xs:integer" />
    <xsl:param name="board" as="xs:integer*" />
    <xsl:param name="square" as="xs:integer" />

    <!-- determine the possible moves that the knight can make -->

    <xsl:variable name="possible-move-list" as="xs:integer*"
        select="tour:list-possible-moves($board, $square)"/>

    <!-- try these moves in turn until one is found that works -->

    <xsl:sequence
        select="tour:try-possible-moves($move,
                                        $board,
                                        $square,
                                        $possible-move-list)"/>

</xsl:function>
```

Finding the Possible Moves

The next function to examine is «list-possible-moves». This takes as input the current state of the board and the position of the knight, and it produces a list of squares that the knight can move to. For a knight in the center of the board there are eight possible squares it can move to (as shown in Figure 12-4): those squares that are either two columns and one row, or two rows and one column, removed from the current row.

However, we have to consider the case where some of these squares are unavailable because they are off the edge of the board, and we also have to eliminate any squares that have already been visited. The logic I have used is simple, if verbose; it simply examines each of the eight candidate squares in turn:

```
<xsl:function name="tour:list-possible-moves" as="xs:integer*">

    <xsl:param name="board" as="xs:integer*" />
```

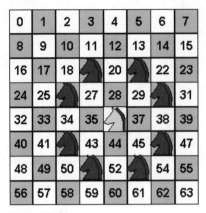

Figure 12-4

```
<xsl:param name="square" as="xs:integer" />

<xsl:variable name="row" as="xs:integer"
    select="$square idiv 8"/>
<xsl:variable name="column" as="xs:integer"
    select="$square mod 8"/>

<xsl:sequence select="
    (if ($row &gt; 1 and $column &gt; 0 and $board[($square - 17) + 1]=0)
        then $square - 17 else (),
    if ($row &gt; 1 and $column &lt; 7 and $board[($square - 15) + 1]=0)
        then $square - 15 else (),
    if ($row &gt; 0 and $column &gt; 1 and $board[($square - 10) + 1]=0)
        then $square - 10 else (),
    if ($row &gt; 0 and $column &lt; 6 and $board[($square - 6) + 1]=0)
        then $square - 6 else (),
    if ($row &lt; 6 and $column &gt; 0 and $board[($square + 15) + 1]=0)
        then $square + 15 else (),
    if ($row &lt; 6 and $column &lt; 7 and $board[($square + 17) + 1]=0)
        then $square + 17 else (),
    if ($row &lt; 7 and $column &gt; 1 and $board[($square + 6) + 1]=0)
        then $square + 6 else (),
    if ($row &lt; 7 and $column &lt; 6 and $board[($square + 10) + 1]=0)
        then $square + 10 else () )"
    />

</xsl:function>
```

An observation: not everyone is happy with the idea of writing a single XPath expression that is 16 lines long in the middle of a stylesheet. Some would prefer to write this code using XSLT instructions, using <xsl:choose>. I'm comfortable with the code as written, but you can express the same logic at the XSLT level if you prefer.

Another approach would be to try and capture all the logic in a single expression, as follows:

```
for $r in (-2, -1, +1, +2),
    $c in (-(3-abs($r)), +(3-abs($r)))
    if ($row+$r = 0 to 7
        and $column+$c = 0 to 7
        and $board[($row+$r)*8 + ($column+$c) + 1] eq 0))
    then ($row+$r)*8 + ($column+$c) + 1
    else ()
```

So having found the possible moves we can make, we need to select one of them and make it. This is the job of the `try-possible-moves` function.

Trying the Possible Moves

At the top level, this function is quite simple. As input it gets the current state of the board, the current position of the knight, the current move, and the list of moves that the knight can make from its current position. If there is at least one move that it can make, then it makes the best move it can find and returns the new state of the board; otherwise, it returns the special value « ( ) » to indicate that it has failed, and that another path needs to be found.

```
<xsl:function name="tour:try-possible-moves" as="xs:integer*" >

    <xsl:param name="move" as="xs:integer" />
    <xsl:param name="board" as="xs:integer*" />
    <xsl:param name="square" as="xs:integer" />
    <xsl:param name="possible-moves" as="xs:integer*" />

    <xsl:sequence
        select="if (count($possible-moves)!=0)
                then tour:make-best-move($move,
                                         $board,
                                         $square,
                                         $possible-moves)
                else ()"/>

        <!-- if there is no possible move, we return the special value ()
             as the final state of the board, to indicate to the caller
             that we got stuck -->
</xsl:function>
```

This depends, of course, on the function `make-best-move()`, which we will look at next. This function is a bit more complex, even though it delegates the task of finding the best move yet again, to another function called `find-best-move()`.

In fact, the first thing that this function does is to call `find-best-move()` to decide which move to make. It then makes a note of all the other possible moves, just in case it needs to backtrack (lazy evaluation comes in handy here: the variable `$other-possible-moves` won't be evaluated unless it's actually needed).

Then the function makes the selected move by placing the knight on the chosen square, using the `place-knight()` function that we saw earlier; and finally it makes a recursive call on `make-moves()`, which we've also seen earlier, to complete the rest of the tour from this new position.

If this final call returns a normal board, then we've finished, and the function exits, unwinding the whole stack down to the initial template, which can now print the final board and quit. However, if the final board is the special value « () », then backtracking is needed. This is done by calling try-possible-moves() with a reduced list of possible moves, that excludes the move that we've found to be a cul-de-sac.

```
<xsl:function name="tour:make-best-move" as="xs:integer*">
    <xsl:param name="move" as="xs:integer" />
    <xsl:param name="board" as="xs:integer*" />
    <xsl:param name="square" as="xs:integer" />
    <xsl:param name="possible-moves" as="xs:integer*" />

    <!-- if at least one move is possible, find the best one -->

    <xsl:variable name="best-move"
        select="tour:find-best-move($board, $possible-moves, 9, 999)"/>

    <!-- find the list of possible moves excluding the best one -->

    <xsl:variable name="other-possible-moves" as="xs:integer*"
        select="$possible-moves[. != $best-move]"/>

    <!-- update the board to make the move chosen as the best one -->

    <xsl:variable name="next-board" as="xs:integer*"
        select="tour:place-knight($move, $board, $best-move)"/>

    <!-- now make further moves using a recursive call,
         until the board is complete -->

    <xsl:variable name="final-board" as="xs:integer*"
        select = "if (count($next-board[.=0])!=0)
                    then tour:make-moves($move+1, $next-board, $best-move)
                    else $next-board"/>

    <!-- if the final board has the special value '()', we got stuck,
         and have to choose the next best of the possible moves.
         This is done by a recursive call. -->

    <xsl:sequence select="
        if (empty($final-board))
        then tour:try-possible-moves($move,
                                     $board,
                                     $square,
                                     $other-possible-moves)
        else $final-board"/>

</xsl:function>
```

Selecting the Best Move

The one thing remaining is to look at the template «find-best-move», which from a set of possible moves chooses the best one, namely the move to the square with fewest exits.

As always, the logic is recursive. We keep track of the best move so far, and the number of exits that the best move so far possesses. If the first move in the list (the *trial move*) is better than the best move so far, it replaces the previous best, and we then call the template to process the other moves in the list. The final output is the best move after examining the whole list.

To find the number of exits for a given move, we create a trial board, and make that move by calling the «place-knight» template described earlier. Using this board, we then call the «list-possible-moves» template, also described earlier, to see what moves would be available after the trial move. We aren't interested in the details of these moves, only in how many there are, which we can find out simply by examining the length of the list.

We can now calculate two variables: the best move so far, and the least number of exits, based on whether the trial move is better than the previous best. If the move is the best one so far, it is output. Finally, the «find-best-move» template calls itself recursively to process the remaining moves in the list. On completion, the value returned by the template is the best move, that is, the square to which the knight should move next.

```
<xsl:function name="tour:find-best-move" as="xs:integer*" >

    <!-- This function finds from among the possible moves,
         the one with fewest exits. It calls itself recursively. -->

    <xsl:param name="board" as="xs:integer*" />
    <xsl:param name="possible-moves" as="xs:integer*" />
    <xsl:param name="fewest-exits" as="xs:integer" />
    <xsl:param name="best-so-far" as="xs:integer" />

    <!-- split the list of possible moves into the first move
         and the rest of the moves -->

    <xsl:variable name="trial-move" as="xs:integer"
        select="$possible-moves[1]"/>
    <xsl:variable name="other-possible-moves" as="xs:integer*"
        select="$possible-moves[position() gt 1]"/>

    <!-- try making the first move -->

    <xsl:variable name="trial-board" as="xs:integer*"
        select="tour:place-knight(99, $board, $trial-move)"/>

    <!-- see how many moves would be possible the next time -->

    <xsl:variable name="trial-move-exit-list" as="xs:integer*"
        select="tour:list-possible-moves($trial-board, $trial-move)"/>

    <xsl:variable name="number-of-exits" as="xs:integer"
        select="count($trial-move-exit-list)"/>

    <!-- determine whether this trial move has fewer exits than
         those considered up till now -->

    <xsl:variable name="minimum-exits" as="xs:integer"
        select="min(($number-of-exits, $fewest-exits))"/>
```

```
    <!-- determine which is the best move (the one with fewest exits)
 so far -->

    <xsl:variable name="new-best-so-far" as="xs:integer"
        select="if ($number-of-exits lt $fewest-exits)
                then $trial-move
                else $best-so-far"/>

    <!-- if there are other possible moves, consider them too,
         using a recursive call. Otherwise return the best move found. -->

    <xsl:sequence
        select="if (count($other-possible-moves)!=0)
                then tour:find-best-move($board, $other-possible-moves,
                                         $minimum-exits, $new-best-so-far)
                else $new-best-so-far"/>

</xsl:function>
```

And that's it.

Running the Stylesheet

To run the stylesheet, download it from the Wrox.com and execute it. No source document is needed. With Saxon, for example, try:

```
java -jar saxon7.jar -it main tour.xsl start=b6 >tour.html
```

This requires Saxon version 7.9 or later. Earlier versions do not allow the «-it» option, which causes execution of the stylesheet to start by calling the named template «main». However, if you want to run the stylesheet with an earlier version of Saxon you can do this simply by supplying a dummy source document, which will not actually be used.

The output of the stylesheet is written to the file tour.html which you can then display in your browser.

The stylesheet requires an XSLT 2.0 processor, so at the time of writing, Saxon is your only choice. If you use a different XSLT 2.0 processor, you will need to consult its documentation to find out how to supply parameters from the command line. If you don't supply a starting square, the tour will start at the a1 square.

Observations

The knight's tour not a typical stylesheet, but it illustrates the computational power of the XSLT language, and in particular the essential part that recursion plays in any stylesheet that needs to do any non-trivial calculation or handle non-trivial data structures. And although you will probably never need to use XSLT to solve chess problems, you may just find yourself doing complex calculations to work out where best to place a set of images on a page, or how many columns to use to display a list of telephone numbers, or which of today's news stories should be featured most prominently given your knowledge of the user's preferences.

So if you're wondering why I selected this example, there are two answers: firstly, I enjoyed writing it, and secondly, I hope it persuaded you that there are no algorithms too complex to be written in XSLT.

The other thing that's worth noting about this stylesheet is how much it benefits from the new features in XSLT 2.0. In the first edition of this book, I published a version of this stylesheet that was written in pure XSLT 1.0: it used formatted character strings to represent all the data structures. In the second edition, I published a revised version that used temporary trees (as promised in the later-abandoned XSLT 1.1 specification) to hold the data structures. The following table shows the size of these three versions (in non-comment lines of code), revealing the extent to which the new language features contribute to making the stylesheet easier to write and easier to read. However it also shows the execution times in milliseconds of each version, using Saxon 7.8, which reveals that my first solution, which used formatted character strings to hold all the data, is actually the fastest:

Version	Data structure	Lines of code	Execution time
1.0	character strings	276	580
1.1	temporary trees	267	1050
2.0	sequences	59	900

The reason that the solution using character strings is the fastest almost certainly reflects the costs associated with memory management. Representing a chessboard as a sequence of 64 integers requires Java to allocate many more objects than when the board is represented as a single string of 192 characters (for each square I used two characters for the knight's position, plus a separator character). A better optimizer might do better, for example by avoiding the cost of copying the whole sequence of 64 integers when placing the knight on a particular square. But this result does suggest that if you want the ultimate in performance and don't mind writing a lot more code, representing a sequence as a structured character string might still be an approach worth considering.

The earlier versions of the stylesheet are included in the download file under the names `tour10.xsl` and `tour11.xsl`. The file `ms-tour11.xsl` is a variant of `tour11.xsl` designed to work with Microsoft's MSXML3 and later processors.

Summary

If you haven't used functional programming languages before, then I hope that this chapter opened your eyes to a different way of programming. It's an extreme example of how XSLT can be used as a completely general-purpose language; but I don't think it's an unrealistic example, because I see an increasing number of cases where XSLT is being used for general-purpose programming tasks. The thing that characterizes XSLT applications is that their inputs and outputs are XML documents, but there should be no limits on the processing that can be carried out to transform the input to the output, and I hope this example convinces you that there are none.

In these last three chapters I've presented three complete stylesheets, or collections of stylesheets, all similar in complexity to many of those you will have to write for real applications. I tried to choose three that were very different in character, reflecting three of the design patterns introduced in Chapter 9, namely:

❑ A rule-based stylesheet for converting a document containing semantic markup into HTML. In this stylesheet, most of the logic was concerned with generating the right HTML display style for each XML element, and with establishing tables of contents, section numbering, and internal hyperlinks, with some interesting logic for laying data out in a table.

❑ A navigational stylesheet for presenting selected information from a hierarchical data structure. This stylesheet was primarily concerned with following links with the XML data structure, and it was able to use the full power of XPath expression to achieve this. This stylesheet also gave us the opportunity to explore some of the systems issues surrounding XSLT; when and where to do the XML-to-HTML conversion, and how to handle data in non-XML legacy formats.

❑ A computational stylesheet for calculating the result of a moderately complex algorithm. This stylesheet demonstrated that even quite complex algorithms are quite possible to code in XSLT once you have mastered recursion. Such algorithms are much easier to implement in XSLT 1.1 than in XSLT 1.0, because of the ability to use temporary trees to hold working data.

XPath 2.0 Syntax Summary

This appendix provides a summary of the XPath 2.0 syntax, for use as a quick reference guide. A full description of each construct is provided in the companion book *XPath 2.0 Programmer's Reference*.

There are four tables:

- ❏ Tokens

    Lists the lexical symbols in the XPath language.

- ❏ Syntax Productions

    Lists the BNF production rules defining the XPath grammar.

- ❏ Operators

    Lists the operators in the XPath language, with their precedence and a quick summary of the effect of each operator.

- ❏ Axes

    Lists the 13 axes used in XPath for navigating a tree.

Appendix B contains a list of all the functions in the core function library.

Tokens

The definition of a *token* that I am using here is a symbol that cannot contain internal separating whitespace.

Symbol	Syntax
IntegerLiteral	Digit+
DecimalLiteral	(«.» Digit+) | (Digit+ «.» Digit*)

Continues

Symbol	Syntax
DoubleLiteral	((«.» Digit+) | (Digit+ («.» Digit*)?)) («e» | «E») («+» | «-»)? Digit+
Digit	[0-9]
StringLiteral	(«"» ([^"])* «"»)+ | («'» ([^'])* «'»)+
Wildcard	«*» | NCName «:*» | «*:» NCName
NCName	*See XML Namespaces Recommendation*
QName	*See XML Namespaces Recommendation*
Char	*See XML Recommendation*

A comment can appear anywhere the separating whitespace can appear. A comment is introduced by «(:» and terminated by a matching «:)». Comments can be nested.

Syntax Productions

These rules mainly use familiar notations: «*» for repetition, parentheses for grouping, «?» to indicate that the preceding construct is optional, and «|» to separate alternatives.

Simple tokens are represented using chevrons, for example «,» in the first rule represents a literal comma.

Sometimes multiple tokens are grouped inside a pair of chevrons, for example «for $» in the third rule. This notation indicates that there are two tokens (whitespace may appear between them) but that the parser needs to recognize both tokens together in order to proceed. The keyword «for» on its own is not enough to recognize a ForExpr, because it might equally well be an element name appearing as a step in a path expression: the parser is therefore looking for the composite symbol consisting of the token «for» followed by the token «$».

Whitespace is always allowed between two tokens, whether these are grouped using chevrons or not. Whitespace is generally required between two tokens in cases where the first character of the second token could otherwise be taken as a continuation of the first token: for example, in the expression «$a - $b» whitespace is required before the «-» (but not after it). There are some exceptions to this rule: for example, whitespace is not required (but is allowed) before the «::» that follows an axis name.

The rules as I have given them here do not correspond exactly with the rules as given in the W3C XPath specification. I have divided some rules and merged others for clarity, to correspond with the way the semantics are presented in *XPath 2.0 Programmer's Reference*. The W3C rules are sometimes distorted by the need to achieve a grammar that is provably nonambiguous, and also by the need to reuse syntactic elements between the XPath and XQuery specifications. I don't have these constraints here, so I can make it more user-friendly.

Symbol	Syntax
Expr	ExprSingle («,» ExprSingle)*
ExprSingle	ForExpr | QuantifiedExpr | IfExpr | OrExpr
ForExpr	«for $» VarName «in» ExprSingle («,» «$» VarName «in» ExprSingle)* «return» ExprSingle
QuantifiedExpr	(«some $» | «every $») VarName «in» ExprSingle («,» «$» VarName «in» ExprSingle)* «satisfies» ExprSingle
IfExpr	«if (» Expr «)» «then» ExprSingle «else» ExprSingle
OrExpr	AndExpr («or» AndExpr)*
AndExpr	ComparisonExpr («and» ComparisonExpr)*
ComparisonExpr	RangeExpr ((ValueComp | GeneralComp | NodeComp) RangeExpr)?
ValueComp	«eq» | «ne» | «lt» | «le» | «gt» | «ge»
GeneralComp	«=» | «!=» | «<» | «<=» | «>» | «>=»
NodeComp	«is» | «<<» | «>>»
RangeExpr	AdditiveExpr («to» AdditiveExpr)?
AdditiveExpr	MultiplicativeExpr ((«+»|«-») MultiplicativeExpr)*
MultiplicativeExpr	UnionExpr ((«*» | «div» | «idiv» | «mod») UnionExpr)*
UnionExpr	IntersectExceptExpr ((«union» | «|») IntersectExceptExpr)*

Continues

Symbol	Syntax
IntersectExceptExpr	InstanceOfExpr ((«intersect» | «except») InstanceOfExpr)*
InstanceofExpr	TreatExpr («instance of» SequenceType)?
TreatExpr	CastableExpr («treat as» SequenceType)?
CastableExpr	CastExpr («castable as» SingleType)?
CastExpr	UnaryExpr («cast as» SingleType)?
UnaryExpr	(«+»|«-»)* PathExpr
PathExpr	(«/» RelativePathExpr?) | («//» RelativePathExpr) | RelativePathExpr
RelativePathExpr	StepExpr ((«/» | «//») StepExpr)*
StepExpr	AxisStep | FilterExpr
AxisStep	(ForwardStep | ReverseStep) PredicateList
FilterExpr	PrimaryExpr PredicateList
PredicateList	Predicate *
Predicate	«[» Expr «]»
PrimaryExpr	Literal | VarRef | ParenthesizedExpr | ContextItemExpr | FunctionCall
Literal	NumericLiteral | StringLiteral
NumericLiteral	IntegerLiteral | DecimalLiteral | DoubleLiteral
VarRef	«$» VarName
Parenthesized Expr	«(» Expr? «)»
ContextItemExpr	«.»

Symbol	Syntax
FunctionCall	FunctionName «(» (ExprSingle («,» ExprSingle)*)? «)»
FunctionName	QName
ForwardStep	(ForwardAxis NodeTest) | AbbrevForwardStep
ReverseStep	(ReverseAxis NodeTest) | AbbrevReverseStep
Abbrev ForwardStep	«@»? NodeTest
Abbrev ReverseStep	«..»
ForwardAxis	«child ::» | «descendant ::» | «attribute ::» | «self ::» | «descendant-or-self ::» | «following-sibling ::» | «following ::» | «namespace ::»
ReverseAxis	«parent ::» | «ancestor ::» | «preceding-sibling ::» | «preceding ::» | «ancestor-or-self ::» |
NodeTest	KindTest | NameTest
NameTest	QName | Wildcard
SingleType	AtomicType «?»?
SequenceType	(ItemType OccurrenceIndicator?) | «empty ( )»
AtomicType	QName
ItemType	AtomicType | KindTest | «item ( )»
Occurrence Indicator	«?» | «*» | «+»
KindTest	DocumentTest | ElementTest | AttributeTest | PITest | CommentTest | TextTest | AnyKindTest
ElementTest	BasicElementTest | SchemaElementTest

Continues

Symbol	Syntax
AttributeTest	BasicAttributeTest | SchemaAttributeTest
Basic ElementTest	«element (» (ElementNameOrWildCard (`«,»` TypeName «?»?) ?) ? «)»
Basic AttributeTest	«attribute (» (AttributeNameOrWildcard (`«,»` TypeName) ?) ? «)»
ElementName OrWildcard	ElementName | «*»
AttributeName OrWildcard	AttributeName | «*»
ElementName	QName
AttributeName	QName
TypeName	QName
Schema ElementTest	«schema-element (» ElementName «)»
Schema AttributeTest	«schema-attribute (» AttributeName «)»
PITest	«processing-instruction (» (NCName | StringLiteral)? «)»
DocumentTest	«document-node (» ElementTest? «)»
CommentTest	«comment ( )»
TextTest	«text ( )»
AnyKindTest	«node ( )»

Operators

The following table lists the XPath operators.

The number on the left indicates the precedence of the operator. A higher number means that the operator binds more tightly. So «A or B and C» means «A or (B and C)».

If two operators have the same precedence, then they are evaluated from left to right. So «A - B + C» means «(A - B) + C».

Precedence	Operator(s)	Meaning
1	«,»	Concatenates two sequences, or forms a sequence from individual items
2	«for»	«for $item in SEQ return f($item)» applies the function f (which might be any expression) to each item in the sequence SEQ, returning the concatenation of the results
2	«some»	«some $item in SEQ satisfies f($item)» returns true if there is at least one item in SEQ for which the function f (which might be any expression) returns true
2	«every»	«every $item in SEQ satisfies f($item)» returns true if there is no item in SEQ for which the function f (which might be any expression) returns false
2	«if»	«if (TEST) then EXPR1 else EXPR2» returns the result of evaluating either expression EXPR1 or expression EXPR2, depending on whether expression TEST is true or false
2	«or»	Boolean disjunction: true if at least one of the operands is true
3	«and»	Boolean conjunction: true if both the operands are true
4	«eq» «ne» «lt» «le» «gt» «ge»	Compares two atomic values. Returns true if the value on the left is equal (or not equal, less than, less than or equal, greater than, or greater than or equal) to the value on the right
4	«=» «!=» «<» «<=» «>» «>=»	Compares two sequences. Returns true if the sequence on the left contains a value that is equal (or not equal, less than, less than or equal, greater than, or greater than or equal) to some value contained in the sequence on the right
4	«is»	Tests whether two expressions return the same node.
4	«<<», «>>»	Tests whether the node returned by the expression on the left precedes or follows the node returned by the expression on the right, in document order
5	«to»	Returns a range of integers, for example «1 to 5»

Continues

Precedence	Operator(s)	Meaning
		returns the sequence «1, 2, 3, 4, 5».
6	«+», «-»	Performs addition or subtraction of two numbers or durations, or adds/subtracts a date/time and a duration, or finds the difference between two dates or times
7	«*», «div»	Multiplies or divides two numbers, or multiplies/divides a duration by a number to give another duration
7	«idiv»	Integer division. Divides two numbers and rounds down to an integer
7	«mod»	Modulus: returns the remainder after dividing the left-hand operand by the right-hand operand and rounding down to an integer
8	«union», «|»	Combines two sequences of nodes to give a new sequence containing any node that is present in either sequence, with duplicates eliminated and sorted into document order
9	«intersect»	Combines two sequences of nodes to give a new sequence containing every node that is present in both the supplied sequences, with duplicates eliminated and sorted into document order
9	«except»	Combines two sequences of nodes to give a new sequence containing every node that is present in the first sequence but not in the second, with duplicates eliminated and sorted into document order
10	«instance of»	Returns true if the value on the left is an instance of the type on the right
11	«treat as»	Asserts that the value on the left is an instance of the type on the right; fails at runtime if it is not
12	«castable as»	Tests whether the value on the left is capable of being converted successfully to the type on the right
13	«cast as»	Converts the value on the left to the type on the right
14	unary «-», unary «+»	Unary minus changes the sign of a number or duration. Unary plus does nothing, provided the value is a number or a duration
15	«/»	«E1/E2» evaluates the expression E2 for every node in the result of evaluating E1, concatenates the results, eliminates duplicates, and sorts the remaining nodes in document order. Applies only to expressions that return nodes

Precedence	Operator(s)	Meaning
15	«//»	Shorthand for «/descendant-or-self::node()/». Loosely, selects the descendants of a node.
16	«[]»	«E1[E2]» selects the items in E1 that satisfy the predicate E2. A numeric predicate «[N]» is shorthand for «[position() = N]»

Axes

Axis	Meaning
self	Selects the context node itself
parent	Selects the parent of the context node
child	Selects the children of the context node
attribute	Selects the attributes of the context node
namespace	Selects the namespaces of the context node
ancestor	Selects the parent, the parent's parent, and so on, recursively
descendant	Selects the children, the children's children, and so on, recursively
ancestor-or-self	Selects the ancestors of the context node together with the context node itself
descendant-or-self	Selects the descendants of the context node together with the context node itself
following-sibling	Selects the children of the context node's parent that follow the context node in document order
preceding-sibling	Selects the children of the context node's parent that precede the context node in document order
following	Selects all nodes that are descendants of a following sibling of an ancestor-or-self of the context node
preceding	Selects all nodes that are descendants of a preceding sibling of an ancestor-or-self of the context node

XPath Function Library

This appendix lists all the standard functions in the core XPath function library.

For each function, I give: its name, a brief description of its purpose, and its signature (that is, a list of the arguments it expects and the value it returns). For expanded descriptions of these functions see Chapter 10 of *XPath 2.0 Programmer's Reference*.

These are not the only functions you can call from an XPath expression:

❑ XSLT 2.0 defines additional functions for use in XPath expressions invoked from XSLT stylesheets. These are listed in Chapter 7 of this book.

❑ So called *constructor functions* are available corresponding to built-in and user-defined atomic types. For example, there is a function called `xs:float()` to create values of type `xs:float`, `xs:date()` to create values of type `xs:date`, and so on. These functions are also available for user-defined atomic types.

❑ User-defined functions may be defined in the stylesheet, using an `<xsl:function>` declaration.

❑ Extension functions written in other languages may be available (see Chapter 8).

❑ Vendor-defined functions may be available. These will be in a namespace controlled by the vendor of the particular product.

abs

The `abs()` function returns the absolute value of a number. For example, «`abs(-3)`» returns 3.

Argument	Data Type	Meaning
input	`Numeric`	The supplied number
Result	`Numeric`	*The absolute value of the supplied number. The result has the same type as the input*

adjust-date/time-to-timezone

This entry describes a collection of three closely related functions: `adjust-date-to-timezone()`, `adjust-dateTime-to-timezone()`, and `adjust-time-to-timezone()`. These functions have the effect of returning an `xs:date`, `xs:time`, or `xs:dateTime`, based on a supplied `xs:date`, `xs:time`, or `xs:dateTime`, modified by adding, removing, or altering the timezone component of the value.

Argument	Data Type	Meaning
input	`xs:date?`, `xs:dateTime?`, or `xs:time?`	The date, time, or dateTime value whose timezone is to be adjusted. The type of this value must correspond to the name of the function invoked, for example in the case of `adjust-time-to-timezone()` it must be an `xs:time` value
timezone (optional)	`xdt:dayTimeDuration`	Specifies the new timezone value. If this argument is omitted, the effect is the same as setting it to the result of the function `implicit-timezone()`
Result	`xs:date?`, `xs:dateTime?`, or `xs:time?`	*The adjusted date, dateTime, or time value.*

avg

The `avg()` function returns the average of a sequence of numbers or durations.

Argument	Data Type	Meaning
sequence	`xdt:anyAtomicType*`	The input sequence. Any untyped atomic values in the input are converted to `xs:double` values. The resulting sequence must consist entirely of numbers, or entirely of durations of the same kind
Result	`xdt:anyAtomicType?`	*The average of the values in the input sequence. This will be a value of the same primitive type as the values in the input sequence. If the input values are `xs:integer` values, the result will be an `xs:decimal`*

base-uri

The `base-uri()` function returns either the base URI from the static context of the XPath expression, or the base URI of a specific node in a document.

Argument	Data Type	Meaning
input-node (optional)	`node()`	The node whose base URI is required

Argument	Data Type	Meaning
Result	`xs:string`	*If the function has no arguments, it returns the base URI from the static context of the XPath expression. If an* `input-node` *is supplied, the function returns the base URI of that node*

boolean

The `boolean()` function calculates the *effective boolean value* of the supplied argument. Every XPath value, of any data type, has an effective boolean value that is either `true` or `false`. The rules for calculating the effective boolean value are given in the entry for `<xsl:if>` in Chapter 5.

Argument	Data Type	Meaning
value	`item()*`	The value whose effective boolean value is required
Result	`xs:boolean`	*The effective boolean value of the argument. This is* `false` *if the supplied value is an empty sequence or if it is a sequence consisting of a single value that is the boolean* `false`, *a number equal to zero, NaN, or a zero-length string; in all other cases, the result is* `true`

ceiling

The `ceiling()` function rounds a supplied number up to the nearest whole number. For example, the expression «`ceiling(33.9)`» returns 34, and «`ceiling(-33.9)`» returns -33.

Argument	Data Type	Meaning
value	`number`	The supplied value
Result	`number`	*The result of rounding* $value *up to the next highest integer. The result has the same primitive data type as the supplied value*

codepoints-to-string

The `codepoints-to-string()` function takes as input a sequence of integers representing the Unicode codepoint values of the characters in a string, and returns the corresponding string. For example, «`codepoints-to-string((65,66,67))`» returns the string `"ABC"`.

Argument	Data Type	Meaning
codepoints	`xs:integer*`	The sequence of codepoints. These must represent

Continues

Argument	Data Type	Meaning
		characters that are valid in XML 1.0 or XML 1.1
Result	`xs:string`	*The string consisting of characters with the given codepoint values*

collection

The `collection()` function returns a sequence of documents, or more generally a sequence of nodes, identified by a URI. The way in which a URI can be used to locate a collection of documents is entirely implementation defined.

Argument	Data Type	Meaning
uri	`xs:string`	A URI that identifies a collection of documents, or nodes within documents
Result	`node()*`	*The sequence of documents, or nodes within documents, identified by the URI*

compare

The `compare()` function is used to compare two strings, and to decide whether they are equal, or if not, which one sorts before the other.

For example, under most collations «`compare("ALPHA", "BETA")`» returns –1.

Argument	Data Type	Meaning
value-1	`xs:string?`	The first string to be compared
value-2	`xs:string?`	The second string to be compared
collation (optional)	`xs:string`	The collation to be used to perform the comparison
Result	`xs:integer?`	*-1 if value-1 is less than value-2 , zero if they are equal, +1 if value-1 is greater than value-2*

concat

The `concat()` function takes two or more arguments. Each of the arguments is converted to a string, and the resulting strings are joined together end-to-end.

For example, the expression «`concat('Jane', ' ', 'Brown')`» returns the string «`Jane Brown`».

This function is unique in that it can take any number of arguments (two or more).

Argument	Data Type	Meaning
value (repeated)	xs:string?	A string to be included in the result
Result	xs:string	*The result of concatenating each of the arguments in turn*

contains

The contains() function tests whether one string contains another as a substring. For example, the expression «contains('Santorini', 'ant')» returns true.

Argument	Data Type	Meaning
value	xs:string?	The containing string
substring	xs:string?	The test string
collation (optional)	xs:string	The collation to be used
Result	xs:boolean	*true if the containing string has a substring that is equal to the test string, false otherwise*

count

The count() function takes a sequence as its argument, and returns the number of items in the sequence. For example, the expression «count((4,5,6))» returns 3.

Argument	Data Type	Meaning
sequence	item()*	The sequence whose items are to be counted
Result	xs:integer	*The number of items in the supplied sequence*

current-date/time

This entry describes a group of three related functions: current-date(), current-dateTime(), and current-time().

These functions take no arguments.

	Data Type	Meaning
Result	xs:date, xs:dateTime, or xs:time	*The date, dateTime, or time at which the transformation is executed. Repeated calls during a single transformation return the same answer each time*

data

The `data()` function returns the atomized value of a sequence. This means that any nodes in the input sequence are replaced by their typed values.

Argument	Data Type	Meaning
sequence	`item()*`	The input sequence
Result	`xdt:anyAtomicType*`	*A sequence based on the input sequence, in which all nodes have been replaced by their typed values*

day-from-date/dateTime

This entry covers two related functions: `day-from-dateTime()` and `day-from-date()`.

These functions extract the day of the month from an `xs:date` or `xs:dateTime` value, as an integer in the range 1 to 31.

Argument	Data Type	Meaning
input	`xs:dateTime?` or `xs:date?`	The value from which the day component is to be extracted. The data type of the supplied argument must correspond to the data type implied by the function name
Result	`xs:integer`	*The day of the month*

days-from-dayTimeDuration

This function extracts the days component of a `dayTimeDuration`, as an integer. For example, if the supplied duration is «PT36H», the result will be 1.

Argument	Data Type	Meaning
input	`xdt:yearMonthDuration`	The value from which the days component is to be extracted
Result	`xs:integer`	*The number of days in the duration, after normalizing it so that 24 hours is represented as one day. The value will be negative if the duration is negative.*

deep-equal

The `deep-equal()` function performs a deep comparison between two sequences:

❑   the items in corresponding positions in each sequence must be deep-equal to each other

❑   if the items are nodes, they are compared by examining their children and attributes recursively

Argument	Data Type	Meaning
sequence-1	`item()*`	The first operand of the comparison
sequence-2	`item()*`	The second operand of the comparison
collation (optional)	`xs:string`	The collation to be used for comparing strings (at any depth)
Result	`xs:boolean`	*true if the sequences are deep-equal, otherwise* `false`

default-collation

The `default-collation()` function returns the URI of the default collation, that is, the collation that is used when no collation is explicitly specified in a function such as `compare()`.

This function takes no arguments.

	Data Type	Meaning
Result	`xs:string`	*The URI of the default collation from the runtime context*

distinct-values

The `distinct-values()` function eliminates duplicate values from a sequence. For example, «`distinct-values((3, 5, 3, 6))`» might return «`(5, 6, 3)`».

Argument	Data Type	Meaning
sequence	`xdt:anyAtomicType*`	The input sequence
collation (optional)	`xs:string`	The collation to be used when comparing values that are strings
Result	`xdt:anyAtomicType*`	*The input sequence, with duplicate values removed. The order of items in the result is undefined*

doc

The `doc()` function retrieves an external XML document by means of a URI, and returns the document node at the root of the tree representation of that XML document. This is a simplified version of the `document()` function available in XSLT.

Argument	Data Type	Meaning
uri	`xs:string?`	The URI of the document to be loaded
Result	`document-node()?`	*The document node of the document identified by this URI*

document-uri

The `document-uri()` function returns a URI associated with a document node.

Argument	Data Type	Meaning
input	`node()`	The document node whose URI is required. If the node is not a document node, the empty sequence is returned
Result	`xs:string?`	*The URI of the document node*

empty

The `empty()` function returns `true` if and only if the argument is an empty sequence. For example, the expression «`empty(//a)`» returns `true` if the context document contains no <a> elements.

Argument	Data Type	Meaning
sequence	`item()*`	The input sequence
Result	`xs:boolean`	*true if the input sequence is empty, otherwise* `false`

ends-with

The `ends-with()` function tests whether one string ends with another string. For example, the expression «`ends-with('17cm', 'cm')`» returns `true`.

Argument	Data Type	Meaning
input	`xs:string?`	The containing string
test	`xs:string?`	The test string
collation (optional)	`xs:string`	A collation URI
Result	`xs:string?`	*true if the input string ends with the test string, otherwise* `false`

error

The error() function can be called when the application detects an error condition; it causes evaluation of the XPath expression as a whole to fail.

Argument	Data Type	Meaning
value (optional)	item()?	The value can be used to identify the error, in an implementation-defined way. If the value is a string, it will probably be used as an error message
Result	*None*	*This function does not return a result; it always raises an error*

escape-uri

The escape-uri() function applies the URI escaping conventions defined in RFC 2396 to an input string. For example, «escape-uri("my document.xml", true())» returns the string «my%20document.xml».

Argument	Data Type	Meaning
value	xs:string	The input string, to which URI escaping is to be applied
escape-reserved	xs:boolean	Set to true if characters with a reserved meaning in URIs (for example «/» and «#») are to be escaped
Result	*xs:string*	*The URI in its escaped form, as a string.*

exactly-one

The exactly-one() function returns its argument unchanged, provided that it is a sequence containing exactly one item. In other cases, it reports an error.

Argument	Data Type	Meaning
value	item()*	The input value. Although the function signature says that any sequence of items is allowed, a runtime error will occur if the number of items is not exactly one
Result	*item()*	*The same as the supplied value, after checking to ensure that it contains a single item*

exists

The exists() function returns true if and only if a supplied sequence contains at least one item.

Argument	Data Type	Meaning
sequence	`item()*`	The input sequence
Result	`xs:boolean`	*true if the input sequence is non-empty, otherwise `false`*

expanded-QName

The `expanded-QName()` function returns a value of type `xs:QName`, given a namespace URI and a local name.

Argument	Data Type	Meaning
namespace	`xs:string`	The namespace URI part of the `xs:QName`, or a zero-length string to construct a QName that is in no namespace
local-name	`xs:string`	The local part of the `xs:QName`. This must conform to the XML rules for an NCName
Result	`xs:QName`	*The newly constructed `xs:QName`*

false

This function returns the boolean value `false`. There are no arguments.

	Data Type	Meaning
Result	`xs:boolean`	*The `xs:boolean` value `false`*

floor

The `floor()` function returns the largest integer value that is less than or equal to the numeric value of the argument. The result has the same data type as the supplied value, for example if the supplied value is an `xs:double` then the result is returned as an `xs:double`.

For example, the expression «`floor(11.3)`» returns the decimal value 11, while «`floor(-11.3)`» returns –12.

Argument	Data Type	Meaning
value	`Numeric`	The supplied number
Result	`Numeric`	*The result of rounding down the supplied number to the integer below. The result has the same primitive data type as the supplied value*

hours-from-dayTimeDuration

This function extracts the hours component of a `dayTimeDuration`, as an integer. For example, if the supplied duration is «PT36H», the result will be 12.

Argument	Data Type	Meaning
input	`xdt:yearMonthDuration`	The value from which the hours component is to be extracted
Result	`xs:integer`	*The number of hours in the duration, after normalizing it so that 60 minutes is represented as one hour and 24 hours is represented as one day. The value will be negative if the duration is negative*

hours-from-time/dateTime

This entry covers two related functions: `hours-from-dateTime()` and `hours-from-time()`.

These functions extract the hour of the day from an `xs:time` or `xs:dateTime` value, as an integer in the range 0 to 23. The value that is returned is in the original (localized) timezone associated with the `time` or `dateTime` value.

Argument	Data Type	Meaning
input	`xs:dateTime?` or `xs:time?`	The value from which the hours component is to be extracted. The data type of the supplied argument must correspond to the data type implied by the function name
Result	`xs:integer`	*The hours component of the time*

id

The `id()` function returns a sequence containing all the elements in the same document as the context node (or as some other specified node), with given ID attribute values.

For example, if the `code` attribute is defined as an ID attribute, then the expression «id('A321-780')» might return the single element `<product code="A321-780">`.

Argument	Data Type	Meaning
values	`xs:string*`	Specifies the required ID values
document (optional)	`node()`	A node identifying the document in which the

Continues

Argument	Data Type	Meaning
		ID values are to be located. If omitted, the document containing the context node is used
Result	`element()*`	*A sequence of nodes, in document order, containing the nodes with the required ID values*

idref

The `idref()` function performs the inverse operation to the `id()` function: it locates all the nodes in a document that contain IDREF or IDREFS values referencing a given ID value.

Argument	Data Type	Meaning
target	`xs:string*`	A sequence of ID values. The function finds all element and attribute nodes of type IDREF or IDREFS that contains a reference to at least one of the ID values in this argument
document (optional)	`node()`	A node identifying the document in which the IDREF(S) values are to be located. If omitted, the document containing the context node is used
Result	`node()*`	*The element and attribute nodes that were found, in document order, without duplicates*

implicit-timezone

The `implicit-timezone()` function returns the value of the implicit timezone from the runtime context. The implicit timezone is used when comparing dates, times, and dateTimes that have no explicit timezone.

This function takes no arguments.

	Data Type	Meaning
Result	`xdt:dayTimeDuration`	*The value of the implicit timezone. For example, «-PT5H» for Eastern Standard Time in the United States*

index-of

The `index-of()` function returns a sequence of integers indicating the positions within a particular sequence where items equal to a specified value occur.

For example, «index-of(("a","b","c"), "b")» returns 2.

Argument	Data Type	Meaning
sequence	xdt:anyAtomicType*	The sequence to be searched
value	xdt:anyAtomicType	The value to be found
collation (optional)	xs:string	The collation to be used when comparing strings
Result	*xs:integer**	*A list containing the positions within the supplied sequence where items that are equal to the specified value have been found*

in-scope-prefixes

The `in-scope-prefixes()` function returns a sequence of strings, representing all the namespace prefixes that are in scope for a given element.

Argument	Data Type	Meaning
element	element()	The element whose in-scope namespaces are to be returned
Result	*xs:string**	*The prefixes of the in-scope namespaces*

insert-before

The `insert-before()` function returns a sequence constructed by inserting an item, or a sequence of items, at a given position within another sequence. For example, «insert-before(("a","b", "c"), 2, "X")» returns «("a", "X", "b", "c")».

Argument	Data Type	Meaning
sequence-1	item()*	The original sequence
position	xs:integer	The position in the original sequence where the new items are to be inserted
sequence-2	item()*	The items that are to be inserted
Result	*item()**	*The constructed sequence*

lang

The `lang()` function tests whether the language of a given node, as defined by the `xml:lang` attribute, corresponds to the language supplied as an argument.

For example, if the node is the element `<para lang="fr-CA">` (indicating Canadian French), then the expression «`lang('fr')`» returns `true`.

Argument	Data Type	Meaning
language	`xs:string`	The language being tested
node (optional)	`node()`	The node whose language is being tested. If the argument is omitted, the function applies to the context node
Result	`xs:boolean`	*true if the language of the context node is the same as, or a sublanguage of, the language being tested*

last

The `last()` function returns the value of the context size. When processing a sequence of items, if the items are numbered from one, `last()` gives the number assigned to the last item in the sequence.

This function takes no arguments.

	Data Type	Meaning
Result	`xs:integer`	*A number, the value of the context size. As the name implies, this is context dependent*

local-name

The `local-name()` function returns the local part of the name of a node, that is, the part of the name after the colon if there is one, or the full name otherwise.

For example, if the context node is an element named `<title>`, the expression «`local-name()`» returns «`title`»; for an element named `<ms:schema>` it returns «`schema`».

Argument	Data Type	Meaning
node (optional)	`node()?`	Identifies the node whose local name is required. If the argument is an empty sequence, the function returns a zero-length string
		If the argument is omitted, the target node is the context node. It is then an error if there is no context item, or if the context item is not a node
Result	`xs:string`	*A string value: the local part of the name of the target node*

local-name-from-QName

The function `local-name-from-QName()` returns the local-name part of an `xs:QName` value. For example if the QName is «`xsl:stylesheet`», it returns the string «`stylesheet`».

Argument	Data Type	Meaning
value	xs:QName?	The xs:QName value whose local-name part is required. If the supplied value is an empty sequence, an empty sequence is returned
Result	*xs:string?*	*The local-name part of the xs:QName*

lower-case

The `lower-case()` function converts upper-case characters in a string to lower-case.

For example, «`lower-case("McAndrew")`» returns `"mcandrew"`.

Argument	Data Type	Meaning
value	xs:string?	The string to be converted
Result	*xs:string?*	*The string with upper-case letters converted to lower-case*

matches

The `matches()` function tests whether a supplied string matches a regular expression. For example, «`matches("PGW867", "[A-Z]{3}[0-9]{3}")`» returns `true`.

Argument	Data Type	Meaning
input	xs:string?	The string to be tested against the regular expression. If an empty sequence is supplied, an empty sequence is returned
regex	xs:string	The regular expression
flags (optional)	xs:string	One or more letters indicating options on how the matching is to be performed. If this argument is omitted, the effect is the same as supplying a zero-length string, which defaults all the option settings. The flags are the same as for the `<xsl:analyze-string>` instruction described on page 176
Result	*xs:boolean?*	*true if the input string matches the regular expression, false if not*

max

The max() function returns the maximum value in a sequence. The input sequence may contain any items that can be compared using the «lt» and «gt» operators. Untyped values are compared as numbers. For example, «max((3,4,5))» returns 5.

Argument	Data Type	Meaning
sequence	xdt:anyAtomicType*	The input sequence
collation (optional)	xs:string	Collation used for comparing strings
Result	xdt:anyAtomicType?	The maximum value found in the input sequence

min

The min() function returns the minimum value in a sequence. The input sequence can contain any items that can be compared using the «lt» and «gt» operators. Untyped values are compared as numbers. For example, «min((3,4,5))» returns 3.

Argument	Data Type	Meaning
sequence	xdt:anyAtomicType*	The input sequence
collation (optional)	xs:string	Collation used for comparing strings
Result	xdt:anyAtomicType?	The minimum value found in the input sequence

minutes-from-dayTimeDuration

This function extracts the minutes component of a dayTimeDuration, as an integer. For example, if the supplied duration is «PT40M30S», the result will be 40.

Argument	Data Type	Meaning
input	xdt: dayTimeDuration	The value from which the minutes component is to be extracted
Result	xs:integer	The number of minutes in the duration, after normalizing it so that 60 seconds is represented as one minute and 60 minutes as one hour. The value will be negative if the duration is negative

minutes-from-time/dateTime

This entry covers two related functions: `minutes-from-dateTime()` and `minutes-from-time()`.

These functions extract the minutes component from an `xs:time` or `xs:dateTime` value, as an integer in the range 0 to 59. The value that is returned is in the original (localized) timezone associated with the time or dateTime value.

Argument	Data Type	Meaning
input	`xs:dateTime?` or `xs:time?`	The value from which the minutes component is to be extracted. The data type of the supplied argument must correspond to the data type implied by the function name
Result	`xs:integer`	*The minutes component of the time*

month-from-date/dateTime

This entry covers two related functions: `month-from-dateTime()` and `month-from-date()`.

These functions extract the month of the year from an `xs:date` or `xs:dateTime` value, as an integer in the range 1 to 12.

Argument	Data Type	Meaning
input	`xs:dateTime?` or `xs:date?`	The value from which the month component is to be extracted. The data type of the supplied argument must correspond to the data type implied by the function name
Result	`xs:integer`	*The month of the year*

months-from-yearMonthDuration

This function extracts the months component of a `yearMonthDuration`, as an integer between −11 and +11. For example, if the supplied argument is «P18M», the result is 6.

Argument	Data Type	Meaning
input	`xdt:yearMonthDuration`	The value from which the months component is to be extracted
Result	`xs:integer`	*The number of months in the duration, after normalizing it so the number of months is less than 12. The value will be negative if the duration is negative*

name

The name() function returns a string in the form of a lexical QName that represents the name of a node. Typically, this will be the name of the node as written in the original XML source document, but the namespace prefix may differ.

For example, if the context node is an element named <ms:schema>, then the expression «name()» will normally return the string «ms:schema».

Argument	Data Type	Meaning
node (optional)	node()?	Identifies the node whose name is required. If the argument is an empty sequence, the function returns a zero-length string
		If the argument is omitted, the target node is the context node. It is then an error if there is no context item, or if the context item is not a node
Result	xs:string	A string value: a QName representing the name of the target node

namespace-uri

The namespace-uri() function returns a string that represents the URI of the namespace in the expanded name of a node. Typically, this will be a URI used in a namespace declaration, that is, the value of an xmlns or xmlns:* attribute in the source XML.

For example, if you apply this function to the outermost element of an XSLT stylesheet by writing the expression «namespace-uri(document(' ')/*)», the result will be the string «http://www.w3.org/1999/XSL/Transform».

Argument	Data Type	Meaning
node (optional)	node()?	Identifies the node whose namespace URI is required. If the argument is an empty sequence, the function returns a zero-length string
		If the argument is omitted, the target node is the context node. It is then an error if there is no context item, or if the context item is not a node
Result	xs:string	The namespace URI of the expanded name of the target node

namespace-uri-for-prefix

The function namespace-uri-for-prefix() returns the namespace URI corresponding to a given namespace prefix, in the in-scope namespaces of a particular element node.

Argument	Data Type	Meaning
prefix	xs:string	The namespace prefix whose corresponding namespace URI is required, or the zero-length string to get the default namespace URI
element	element()	The element node to be examined to find an in-scope namespace declaration for this prefix
Result	*xs:string?*	*The namespace URI corresponding to the given prefix*

namespace-uri-from-QName

The function `namespace-uri-from-QName()` returns the namespace URI part of an `xs:QName` value.

Argument	Data Type	Meaning
value	xs:QName?	The xs:QName value whose namespace URI part is required.
Result	*xs:string?*	*The namespace URI part of the xs:QName. If the supplied value is an empty sequence, an empty sequence is returned. An empty sequence is also returned if the namespace URI part of the value is null, that is, if the QName is in no namespace.*

node-name

The `node-name()` function returns a value of type `xs:QName` containing the expanded name of a node: that is, the namespace URI and local name.

Argument	Data Type	Meaning
input	node()?	The node whose name is required
Result	*xs:QName?*	*The name of the node if it has a name, or an empty sequence if the node has no name*

normalize-space

The `normalize-space()` function removes leading and trailing whitespace from a string, and replaces internal sequences of whitespace with a single space character.

For example, the expression «normalize-space(' x	 y ')» returns the string «x y».

Argument	Data Type	Meaning
value (optional)	xs:string?	The input string. If the argument is omitted, it defaults to the string value of the context item
Result	*xs:string*	*A string obtained by removing leading and trailing whitespace from the input string, and replacing internal sequences of whitespace by a single space character*

normalize-unicode

The `normalize-unicode()` function returns a canonical representation of a string in which different ways of representing the same Unicode character have been reduced to a common representation. This makes it possible to compare two strings accurately.

Argument	Data Type	Meaning
input	xs:string?	The string to be normalized
form (optional)	xs:string	The normalization form to be used
Result	*xs:string?*	*The result of normalizing the string*

not

The `not()` function returns `true` if the effective boolean value of the argument is `false`, and vice versa.

For example, the expression «`not(2+2=4)`» returns `false`.

Argument	Data Type	Meaning
value	item()*	The input value
Result	*xs:boolean*	*`true` if the effective boolean value of the argument is `false`, otherwise `false`*

number

The `number()` function converts its argument to a value of type `xs:double`.

For example, the expression «`number('-17.3')`» returns the `xs:double` value `-1.73e1`.

Argument	Data Type	Meaning
value (optional)	item()?	The value to be converted. If the argument is omitted, the context item is used
Result	xs:double	*A double-precision floating point number: the result of converting the given* value. *If the argument cannot be converted to a number, the function returns NaN (not-a-number)*

one-or-more

The one-or-more() function returns its argument unchanged, provided that it is a sequence containing one or more items. If the input is an empty sequence, it reports an error.

Argument	Data Type	Meaning
value	item()*	The input value. Although the function signature says that any sequence of items is allowed, a runtime error will occur if the number of items is zero
Result	item()	*The same as the supplied value, after checking to ensure that it is not an empty sequence*

position

The position() function returns the value of the context position. When processing a list of items, position() gives the number assigned to the current item in the list, with the first item being numbered as 1. This function takes no arguments.

	Data Type	Meaning
Result	xs:integer	*A number, the value of the context position. As the name implies, this is context dependent*

remove

The remove() function returns a sequence that contains all the items in an input sequence except the one at a specified position.

Argument	Data Type	Meaning
sequence	`item()*`	The input sequence
position	`xs:integer`	The position of the item to be removed
Result	`item()*`	*A sequence containing all the items in the input sequence except the item at the specified position*

replace

The `replace()` function constructs an output string from an input string by replacing all occurrences of substrings that match a supplied regular expression with a given replacement string. The replacement string may include references to captured groups within the input string.

Argument	Data Type	Meaning
input	`xs:string?`	The input string. If an empty sequence is supplied, an empty sequence is returned
regex	`xs:string`	The regular expression. This must not be a regular expression that matches a zero-length string
replacement	`xs:string`	The replacement string
flags (optional)	`xs:string`	One or more letters indicating options on how the matching is to be performed. If this argument is omitted, the effect is the same as supplying a zero-length string, which defaults all the option settings. The flags are the same as for the `<xsl:analyze-string>` instruction described on page 176
Result	`xs:string?`	*The string produced by replacing those substrings of the input string that match the regular expression*

resolve-QName

The `resolve-QName()` function returns a value of type `xs:QName` (that is, an expanded QName consisting of a namespace URI and a local name), taking as input a lexical QName (a string in the form «prefix:local-name» or simply «local-name»), by resolving the prefix used in the lexical QName against the in-scope namespaces of a given element node.

Argument	Data Type	Meaning
lexical-qname	xs:string	The lexical QName whose prefix is to be resolved. It must conform to the syntax of a QName as defined in the XML Namespaces specification (which is the same as the lexical space for an xs:QName defined in XML Schema)
element	element()	An element node whose in-scope namespaces are to be used to resolve the namespace prefix used in the lexical QName
Result	*xs:QName*	*The expanded xs:QName, containing the namespace URI corresponding to the prefix supplied in the lexical QName*

resolve-uri

The `resolve-uri()` function converts a relative URI into an absolute URI by resolving it against a specified base URI.

Argument	Data Type	Meaning
relative-uri	xs:string	The URI to be resolved. If this is an absolute URI, it is returned unchanged; otherwise, it is resolved against the specified base URI
base-uri (optional)	xs:string	The base URI against which the relative URI is to be resolved. If this argument is omitted, the base URI from the static context is used (in XSLT, this is the base URI of the element in the stylesheet). This must be an absolute URI
Result	*xs:string*	*The resulting absolute URI*

reverse

The `reverse()` function returns a sequence in reverse order. For example, «`reverse(1 to 5)`» returns the sequence «`5, 4, 3, 2, 1`».

Argument	Data Type	Meaning
sequence	item()*	The input sequence
Result	*item()**	*A sequence containing the same items as the input sequence, but in reverse order*

root

The root() function returns the root node of the tree containing a specified start node, or the root of the tree containing the context node.

Argument	Data Type	Meaning
start-node (optional)	node()?	A node in the tree whose root is required. If the argument is omitted, it defaults to the context node. It is then an error if the context item is not a node (for example, if it is an atomic value, or if it is undefined)
Result	node()?	*The root of the tree containing the start node*

round

The round() function returns the closest integer to the numeric value of the argument, as an instance of the same primitive data type as the argument. For example, the expression «round(4.6)» returns the xs:decimal value 5.0.

Argument	Data Type	Meaning
value	Numeric	The input value
Result	*Numeric*	*The result of rounding the first argument to the nearest integer, but expressed as a value of the same data type as the input value*

round-half-to-even

The round-half-to-even() function performs rounding to a specified number of decimal places. The rounding algorithm used is to round to the nearest value that has the required precision, choosing an even value if two values are equally close. For example, «round-half-to-even(0.035, 2)» returns 0.04, while «round-half-to-even(4500, -3)» returns 4000.

Argument	Data Type	Meaning
input	Numeric?	The number to be rounded
precision (optional)	xs:integer	If positive, the number of significant digits required after the decimal point. If negative, the number of zeroes required at the end of the integer part of the result
Result	*Numeric?*	*The rounded number. This will have the same data type as the supplied number*

seconds-from-dayTimeDuration

This function extracts the seconds component of a `dayTimeDuration`, as a decimal number (it may include fractional seconds). For example, if the supplied duration is «`-PT73.289S`», the result will be `-13.289`.

Argument	Data Type	Meaning
input	`xdt:` `dayTimeDuration`	The value from which the seconds component is to be extracted
Result	`xs:decimal`	*The number of seconds in the duration, after normalizing it so that 60 seconds is represented as one minute. The value will be negative if the duration is negative*

seconds-from-time/dateTime

This entry covers two related functions: `seconds-from-dateTime()` and `seconds-from-time()`.

These functions extract the seconds component from an `xs:time` or `xs:dateTime` value, as a decimal value usually in the range 0 to 59.999..., unless leap seconds appear.

Argument	Data Type	Meaning
input	`xs:dateTime?` or `xs:time?`	The value from which the seconds component is to be extracted. The data type of the supplied argument must correspond to the data type implied by the function name
Result	`xs:decimal`	*The seconds component of the time, including fractional seconds*

starts-with

The `starts-with()` function tests whether one string starts with another string.

For example, the expression «`starts-with('$17.30', '$')`» returns `true`.

Argument	Data Type	Meaning
input	`xs:string?`	The containing string
test	`xs:string?`	The test string
collation (optional)	`xs:string`	The collation to be used for comparing strings
Result	`xs:string?`	*true if the input string starts with the test string, otherwise false*

string

The string() function converts its argument to a string. When the argument is a node, it extracts the string value of the node; when the argument is an atomic value, it converts the atomic value to a string in a similar way to the xs:string() constructor function.

For example, the expression «string(4.00)» returns the string "4".

Argument	Data Type	Meaning
value (optional)	item()?	The value to be converted. If the argument is omitted, it defaults to the context item
Result	xs:string	*The result of converting the argument to a string*

string-join

The string-join() function returns a string constructed by concatenating all the strings in a supplied sequence, with an optional separator between adjacent strings. For example, «string-join(("a", "b","c"), "|")» returns the string "a|b|c".

Argument	Data Type	Meaning
sequence	xs:string*	The supplied sequence of strings
separator	xs:string	The separator to be used between adjacent strings. If no separator is required, supply a zero-length string for this argument
Result	xs:string	*The result of concatenating the supplied strings and inserting separators*

string-length

The string-length() function returns the number of characters in a string value.

For example, the expression «string-length('Beethoven')» returns 9.

Argument	Data Type	Meaning
value (optional)	xs:string?	The string whose length is required

If the argument is omitted, the string value of the context item is used. If the argument is an empty sequence, the result of the function is 0 (zero) |
| *Result* | xs:string | *A number: the number of characters in the value of the argument* |

string-to-codepoints

The `string-to-codepoints()` function returns a sequence of integers representing the Unicode codepoints of the characters in a string. For example, «`string-to-codepoints("Kay")`» returns the sequence `(75, 97, 121)`.

Argument	Data Type	Meaning
input	xs:string?	The input string
Result	*xs:integer**	*The codepoints of the characters in the input string*

subsequence

The `subsequence()` function returns part of an input sequence, identified by the start position and length of the sub-sequence required.

For example, the expression «`subsequence(("a", "b", "c", "d"), 2, 2)`» returns «`("b", "c")`».

Argument	Data Type	Meaning
sequence	item()*	The input sequence
start	xs:double	The position of the first item to be included in the result
length (optional)	xs:double	The number of items to be included in the result. If this argument is omitted, all items after the start position are included
Result	*xs:string*	*The sequence of items starting at the start position*

substring

The `substring()` function returns part of a string value, determined by character positions within the string. Character positions are counted from one.

For example, the expression «`substring('Goldfarb', 5, 3)`» returns the string «`far`».

Argument	Data Type	Meaning
input	xs:string?	The containing string
start	xs:double	The position in the containing string of the first character to be included in the result string

Continues

Argument	Data Type	Meaning
length (optional)	xs:double	The number of characters to be included in the result string
		If the argument is omitted, characters are taken from the start position up to the end of the containing string.
Result	*xs:string*	*The required substring of the containing string*

substring-after

The substring-after() function returns that part of a string value that occurs after the first occurrence of some specified substring.

For example, the expression «substring-after('print=yes', '=')» returns the string "yes".

Argument	Data Type	Meaning
value	xs:string?	The containing string
substring	xs:string?	The test string
collation (optional)	xs:string	The collation to be used for comparing strings
Result	*xs:string*	*A string containing those characters that follow the first occurrence of the test substring within the containing string*

substring-before

The substring-before() function returns that part of a string value that occurs before the first occurrence of some specified substring.

For example, the value of «substring-before('print=yes', '=')» returns the string "print".

Argument	Data Type	Meaning
value	xs:string?	The containing string
substring	xs:string?	The test string
collation (optional)	xs:string	The collation to be used for comparing strings
Result	*xs:string*	*A string containing those characters that precede the first occurrence of the test substring within the containing string*

subtract-dates/dateTimes...

This entry covers four related functions: `subtract-dates-yielding-yearMonthDuration()`, `subtract-dates-yielding-dayTimeDuration()`, `subtract-dateTimes-yielding-year MonthDuration()`, and `subtract-dateTimes-yielding-dayTimeDuration()`. All three functions return the duration that separates one `date` or `dateTime` from another. If the first argument is chronologically earlier than the second argument, the result is a negative duration. For example, «`subtract-dates-yielding-dayTimeDuration(xs:date('2004-06-01'), xs:date('2004-05-01'))`» returns the duration `P31D`.

Argument	Data Type	Meaning
end-point	`xs:date` or `xs:dateTime`	The end point of an interval
start-point	`xs:date` or `xs:dateTime`	The start point of the interval
Result	*`xdt:dayTimeDuration` or `xdt:yearMonthDuration`*	*The duration between the start point and the end point of the interval*

sum

The `sum()` function calculates the total of a sequence of numeric values or durations.

For example, if the context node is the element `<rect x="20" y="30"/>`, then the expression «`sum(@*)`» returns 50.

Argument	Data Type	Meaning
sequence	`xdt:anyAtomicType*`	The set of items to be totaled
zero-value (optional)	`xdt:anyAtomicType`	The value to be returned when the sequence is empty
Result	*`xdt:anyAtomicType`*	*The total of the values in the sequence*

timezone-from-date/time/dateTime

This entry covers three related functions: `timezone-from-date()`, `timezone-from-dateTime()`, and `timezone-from-time()`.

These functions extract the timezone component from an `xs:date`, `xs:dateTime`, or `xs:time` value, as a value of type `xdt:dayTimeDuration` representing the offset of the timezone from UTC. For example, the timezone «`GMT-5`» is represented as «`-PT5H`».

Argument	Data Type	Meaning
input	`xs:dateTime?` `xs:date?` , or `xs:time?`	The value from which the seconds component is to be extracted. The data type of the supplied argument must correspond to the data type implied by the function name
Result	`xdt:dayTime Duration`	*The timezone component of the* `date`*,* `time`*, or* `dateTime`

tokenize

The `tokenize()` function splits a string into a sequence of substrings, by looking for separators that match a given regular expression. For example, «`tokenize("12, 16, 2", ",\s*")`» returns the sequence «`("12", "16", "2")`».

Argument	Data Type	Meaning
input	`xs:string?`	The input string. If an empty sequence or zero-length string is supplied, the function returns an empty sequence
regex	`xs:string`	The regular expression used to match separators. Note that this must not be a regular expression that matches a zero-length string
flags (optional)	`xs:string`	One or more letters indicating options on how the matching is to be performed. If this argument is omitted, the effect is the same as supplying a zero-length string, which defaults all the option settings. The flags are the same as for the `<xsl:analyze-string>` instruction described on page 176
Result	`xs:string*`	*A sequence whose items are substrings of the input string*

trace

The `trace()` function is used to produce diagnostic output. The format and destination of the output is implementation defined.

Argument	Data Type	Meaning
value	`item()*`	A value that is to be displayed in the diagnostic output
message	`xs:string`	A message that is to be output along with the displayed value
Result	`item()*`	*The value of the first argument, unchanged*

translate

The `translate()` function substitutes characters in a supplied string with nominated replacement characters. It can also be used to remove nominated characters from a string. For example, the result of «`translate('ABC-123', '-', '/')`» is the string «`ABC/123`».

Argument	Data Type	Meaning
value	xs:string?	The supplied string
from	xs:string	The list of characters to be replaced
to	xs:string	The list of replacement characters
Result	*xs:string?*	*A string derived from the supplied string, but with those characters that appear in the second argument replaced by the corresponding characters from the third argument, or removed if there is no corresponding character*

true

This function returns the boolean value `true`. The function takes no arguments.

Data Type	Meaning
Result	*xs:boolean*	*The xs:boolean value true*

unordered

The formal definition of the `unordered()` function is that it returns a sequence that is an arbitrary re-ordering of the sequence provided as its argument. In practice, this is really a pseudo-function: wrapping an expression in a call of `unordered()` tells the XPath processor that you don't care what order the results of that expression are in, which means that the processor might be able to avoid the cost of sorting them into a specific order.

For example, «`unordered(ancestor::*)`» returns the ancestor elements in whatever order the system finds most convenient. (In Saxon, it currently returns them in reverse document order, that is, innermost ancestor first.)

Argument	Data Type	Meaning
sequence	item()*	The supplied sequence
Result	*item()*	*A sequence that contains the same items as the supplied sequence, but in an arbitrary order*

upper-case

The `upper-case()` function converts lower-case characters in a string to upper-case. For example, «`upper-case("Albert Road")`» returns the string `"ALBERT ROAD"`.

Argument	Data Type	Meaning
value	`xs:string?`	The string to be converted
Result	`xs:string?`	*The string with lower-case letters converted to upper-case*

year-from-date/dateTime

This entry covers two related functions: `year-from-dateTime()` and `year-from-date()`.

These functions extract the year from an `xs:date` or `xs:dateTime` value, as an integer. In the case of BC dates, the integer may be negative.

Argument	Data Type	Meaning
input	`xs:dateTime?` or `xs:date?`	The value from which the year component is to be extracted. The data type of the supplied argument must correspond to the data type implied by the function name
Result	`xs:integer`	*The year component of the date*

years-from-yearMonthDuration

This function extracts the years component of a `yearMonthDuration`, as an integer. For example, if the supplied argument is «`-P36M`», the result is `-3`.

Argument	Data Type	Meaning
input	`xdt:yearMonthDuration`	The value from which the years component is to be extracted
Result	`xs:integer`	*The number of years in the duration, after normalizing it so the number of months is less than 12. May be negative*

zero-or-one

The zero-or-one() function returns its argument unchanged, provided that it is a sequence containing no more than one item. In other cases, it reports an error.

Argument	Data Type	Meaning
value	item()*	The input value. Although the function signature says that any sequence of items is allowed, a runtime error will occur if the number of items is more than one
Result	*item()*	*The same as the supplied value, after checking to ensure that it is either an empty sequence or contains a single item*

Microsoft XSLT Processors

This appendix contains summary information about Microsoft's XSLT processors.

At the time of writing, Microsoft does not yet have an XSLT 2.0 processor, so the information in this appendix all relates to its XSLT 1.0 products. In view of this, I am not including a comprehensive specification of Microsoft's APIs, merely an outline of their structure. The reference information can be found in Microsoft's own documentation, or in books that concentrate on XSLT 1.0 processing.

Microsoft offers two families of products, with completely different APIs. The XSLT processor in the MSXML3/4 family comes as standard with Internet Explorer 6, though it is also available as a free-standing component. More recently, the System.Xml classes have become available as part of the .NET framework. This appendix gives a brief outline of both these product families.

The current FAQ page for XSLT on the MSXML4 site gives the following question and answer:

Question: Will MSXML support XSLT 2.0?

Answer: No. MSXML versions 4.0 and later fully implement and support XSL Transformations (XSLT) Version 1.0 (W3C Recommendation November 16, 1999). If your XML application requires a later version of XSLT, Microsoft strongly recommends moving to the newer System.Xml framework classes, because all future XML development efforts will be focused there.

So, you can't say they didn't tell you.

Sadly, there is no corresponding FAQ page that tells you whether and when the System.Xml technology will be enhanced to support XSLT 2.0. However, the unofficial rumors indicate that there are no immediate plans. Microsoft appears to be concentrating its efforts at present on implementing XQuery.

There is general consensus that MSXML3/4 is usually faster than the .NET processor, and that it conforms more closely to the W3C specifications. This situation may change, of course, over time.

MSXML3/4

Microsoft released several versions of the MSXML product. The original beta version 1.0 was quickly superseded by version 2.0, which was supplied with the final release of Internet Explorer 5.

Version 3, MSXML3, was first released in March 2000 and became a production release in October 2000. It is included as a standard part of Internet Explorer 6.

The current version is MSXML4. However, MSXML3 has not been superseded, because it is the last version that retains support for Microsoft's obsolete WD-xsl dialect. WD-xsl was first shipped in 1998 before XSLT 1.0 was finalized, and you still occasionally come across stylesheets written in this variant of the language: You can recognize them because they use the namespace URI `http://www.w3.org/TR/WD-xsl`. (Microsoft still, confusingly, refer to WD-xsl by the name "XSL," which means something quite different in W3C).

You can find download links for both MSXML3 and MSXML4 by going to `http://msdn.microsoft.com/xml`.

MSXML is not just an XSLT processor, it also includes Microsoft's XML parser and DOM implementation. The main difference between MSXML3 and MSXML4 has nothing to do with the XSLT engine; it is concerned with support for XML Schema, which is outside our scope here.

The objects, methods, properties, and events available with the MSXML3 parser are listed in the Help file that comes with the SDK. I have only included here the parts of the interface that are relevant to XSLT and XPath processing.

Objects

The objects of particular interest to XSLT and XPath processing are listed below:

Object	Description
IXMLDOMDocument	The root of an XML document
IXMLDOMNode	Any node in the DOM
IXMLDOMNodeList	A collection of Node objects
IXMLDOMParseError	Details of the last parse error that occurred
IXMLDOMSelection	A selection of nodes
IXSLProcessor	An execution of an XSLT stylesheet
IXSLTemplate	A compiled XSLT stylesheet in memory

These objects are described in the sections that follow.

IXMLDOMDocument and IXMLDOMDocument2

The IXMLDOMDocument class inherits all the properties and methods of IXMLDOMNode.
IXMLDOMDocument2 is a later version of the interface, introducing a few extra properties and methods.
This section lists the additional methods and properties of relevance to XSLT and XPath processing, in
other words, all the methods and properties that are not also present on IXMLDOMNode, which is
described on page 802.

Additional Methods

The methods particularly relevant to XPath and XSLT processing are described in detail below.

The validate() and setProperty() methods actually belong to the IXMLDOMDocument2 interface,
which is an extension to IXMLDOMDocument introduced with the MSXML2 product.

Name	Returns	Description
abort	(Nothing)	When a document is being loaded asynchronously, abort() can be called at any time to abandon the process
load	Boolean	Loads document from the specified XML source. The argument is normally a string containing a URL. Clears out any existing content of the Document object, and replaces it with the result of parsing the XML source. Returns True if successful, False otherwise
loadXML	Boolean	Loads the document from a string containing the text of an XML document. Clears out any existing content of the Document object, and replaces it with the result of parsing the XML string. Returns True if successful, False otherwise
save	(Nothing)	Saves the document to a specified destination. The destination is usually a filename, given as a string. The effect is to serialize the Document in XML format as a file. It is also possible to specify various other objects as a destination, for example, it can be another Document object, in which case the document is duplicated
setProperty	(Nothing)	Sets various system properties. The most important properties are:

Continues

Name	Returns	Description
		SelectionLanguage. This takes the value «XPath» (the MSXML4 default) or «XSLPattern» (the default for MSXML3). This affects the syntax used in the expression passed to the selectNodes() andselectSingleNode() methods. If you want to use XPath 1.0 syntax you must set this property to «XPath». The value «XSLPattern», refers to the old Microsoft-specific WD-xsl dialect
		SelectionNamespaces. The value of this property should be a space-separated list of namespace declarations, for example «xmlns:a='http:// a.com/' xmlns:b='http://b.com/» These define the namespace prefixes that can be used within any expression passed to the selectNodes() and selectSingleNode() methods
validate	(Nothing)	Validates the document, using the current DTD or schema

Additional Properties

Name	Type	Description
async	Boolean	True if the document is to be loaded asynchronously
parseError	IXMLDOMParseError	The last parser error
readyState	Long	Current state of readiness for use. Used when loading asynchronously. The values are Uninitialized (0), Loading (1), Loaded (2), Interactive (3), and Completed (4).
validateOnParse	Boolean	Requests validation of the document against its DTD or schema

IXMLDOMNode

This object represents a node in the document tree. Note that the tree conforms to the DOM model, which is not always the same as the XPath model described in Chapter 2: For example, the way namespaces are modeled is different, and text nodes are not necessarily normalized.

There are subclasses of IXMLDOMNode for all the different kinds of node found in the tree. I have not included descriptions of all these, since they are not directly relevant to XSLT and XPath processing. The only subclass I have included is IXMLDOMDocument, which can be regarded as representing either the whole document or its root node, depending on your point of view.

Methods

The methods available on IXMLDOMNode that are relevant to XSLT and XPath processing are listed below. Most often, these methods will be applied to the root node (the DOM Document object) but they can be applied to any node.

Name	Returns	Description
selectNodes	IXMLDOMNodeList	Executes an XPath expression and returns a list of matching nodes
selectSingleNode	IXMLDOMNode	Executes an XPath expression and returns the first matching node
transformNode	String	Applies a stylesheet to the subtree rooted at this node, returning the result as a string. The argument identifies the XSLT stylesheet. This will usually be a Document, but it may be a Node representing an embedded stylesheet within a Document. The serialized result of the transformation is returned as a string of characters (the <xsl:output> encoding is ignored)
transformNode ToObject	(Nothing)	Applies a stylesheet to the subtree, placing the result into a supplied document or stream. The difference from transformNode() is that the destination of the transformation is supplied as a second argument. This will usually be a Document. It may also be a Stream

Properties

The most useful properties are listed below. Properties whose main purpose is to navigate through the document are not listed here, because navigation can be achieved more easily using XPath expressions.

Name	Type	Description
baseName	String	The local name of the node, excluding any namespace prefix
namespaceURI	String	The namespace URI
nodeName	String	The name of the node, including its namespace prefix if any. Note that unlike the XPath model, unnamed nodes are given conventional names such as "#document", "#text", and "#comment"
nodeTypeStrin	String	Returns the type of node in string form. For example, "element", "attribute", or "comment"
nodeValue	Variant	The value stored in the node. This is not the same as the XPath string-value; for elements, it is always null

Continues

Name	Type	Description
prefix	String	The prefix for the namespace applying to the node
text	String	Text contained by this node (like the XPath string-value)
xml	String	XML representation of the node and its descendants

IXMLDOMNodeList

This object represents a list of nodes. For our present purposes, we are interested in this object because it is the result of the `selectNodes()` method.

An `IXMLDOMNodeList` is returned as a result of the `selectNodes()` method: It contains the list of nodes selected by the supplied XPath expression. You can process all the nodes in the list either by using the `nextNode()` method or by direct indexing using the `item` property.

Methods

Name	Returns	Description
item	IXMLDOMNode	`item(N)` gets the node at position N
nextNode	IXMLDOMNode	Gets the next node
reset	(Nothing)	Resets the current position

Properties

Name	Type	Description
length	Long	Identifies the number of nodes in the collection

IXMLDOMParseError

This object is accessible through the `parseError` property of the `IXMLDOMDocument` interface.

Properties

Name	Type	Description
errorCode	Long	The error code
filepos	Long	The character position of the error within the XML document
line	Long	The line number of the error
linepos	Long	The character position in the line containing the error

Name	Type	Description
reason	String	Explanation of the error
srcText	String	The XML text in error
url	String	The URL of the offending document

IXMLDOMSelection

This object represents a selection of nodes. It is returned as the result of the selectNodes() method when the target document implements the IXMLDOMDocument2 interface.

It's simplest to think of this object as a stored expression that returns a list of nodes on demand. It's rather like a relational view: You don't need to know whether the results are actually stored, or whether they are obtained as required.

This interface extends the IXMLDOMNodeList interface.

Methods

Name	Returns	Description
clone	IXMLDOMSelection	Produces a copy of this IXMLDOMSelection
getProperty	String	Returns the value of a named property such as SelectionLanguage
item	IXMLDOMNode	item(N) gets the node at position N
matches	IXMLDOMNode	Tests whether the given node is a member of the set of nodes (returns null if no match, otherwise the node from which the selection succeeds)
nextNode	IXMLDOMNode	Gets the next node
reset	(Nothing)	Resets the current position

Properties

Name	Type	Description
expr	String	The XPath expression that determines the nodes selected. This can be changed at any time; doing so implicitly resets the current list of nodes, replacing it with a new list
context	IXMLDOMNode	Establishes the context node for evaluating the expression. Changing the context node implicitly resets the current list of nodes, replacing it with a new list
length	Long	Identifies the number of nodes in the collection

IXSLProcessor

An `IXSLProcessor` object represents a single execution of a stylesheet to transform a source document.

The object is normally created by calling the `createProcessor()` method of an `IXSLTemplate` object.

The transformation is achieved by calling the `transform()` method.

Methods

Name	Returns	Description
addParameter	(Nothing)	Sets the value of a stylesheet parameter. The first argument is the local name of the parameter, the second is the parameter value, and the third is the namespace URI (usually ""). The value can be a boolean, a number, or a string, or a `Node` or `NodeList`
reset	(Nothing)	Resets the state of the processor and aborts the current transform
setStartMode	(Nothing)	Sets the initial mode. There are two arguments, representing the local name and the namespace URI parts of the mode name
transform	Boolean	Starts or resumes the XSLT transformation process

transform() ⇒ **Boolean**

This method applies the stylesheet (from which this `XSLProcessor` was derived) to the source document identified in the input property. The result of the transformation is accessible through the `output` property.

If the transformation is completed, the return value is `True`. If the source document is being loaded asynchronously, it is possible for the `transform()` method to return `False`, which means that it needs to wait until more input is available. In this case, it is possible to resume the transformation by calling `transform()` again later. The current state of the transformation can be determined from the `readyState` property.

Properties

Name	Type	Description
input	Variant	XML source document to transform. This is normally supplied as a DOM `Document`, but it may also be a `Node`. The input can also be supplied as an `IStream`
output	Variant	Output of the transformation. If you don't supply an output object, the processor will create a String to hold the output, which you

Name	Type	Description
		can read using this property. If you prefer, you can supply an object such as a DOM `Document`, a DOM `Node`, or an `IStream` to receive the output
ownerTemplate	IXSLTemplate	The `XSLTemplate` object used to create this processor object
readyState	Long	The current state of the transformation. This will be `READYSTATE_COMPLETE` (3) when the transformation is finished
startMode	String	Name of the initial mode. See `setStartMode()` method above
startModeURI	String	Namespace of the initial mode. See `setStartMode()` method above
stylesheet	IXMLDOMNode	The current stylesheet being used

IXSLTemplate

An `IXSLTemplate` object represents a compiled stylesheet in memory. If you want to use the same stylesheet more than once, then creating an `IXSLTemplate` and using it repeatedly is more efficient than using the raw stylesheet repeatedly using `transformNode()`.

Methods

Name	Returns	Description
createProcessor	IXSLProcessor	Creates an `IXSLProcessor` object
		This method should only be called after the stylesheet property has been set to associate the `IXSLTemplate` object with a stylesheet
		It creates an `IXSLProcessor` object, which can then be used to initiate a transformation of a given source document

Properties

Name	Type	Description
stylesheet	IXMLDOMNode	Identifies the stylesheet from which this `IXSLTemplate` is derived

Setting this property causes the specified stylesheet to be compiled; this `IXSLTemplate` object is the reusable representation of the compiled stylesheet.

The DOM `Node` representing the stylesheet will normally be a DOM `Document` object, but it may be an Element representing an embedded stylesheet.

The document identified by the stylesheet property must be a free-threaded document object.

Putting it Together

The example in this section shows one way of controlling a transformation using MSXML from within JavaScript on an HTML page.

Example: Using Client-Side JScript to Transform a Document

This example demonstrates the way that you can load, parse, and transform an XML document using client-side JScript in Internet Explorer 5 or higher. The files are in a folder named `msxml_transform`.

The example shows an HTML page with two buttons on it. The user can click on either of the buttons to select how the data should be displayed. The effect of clicking either button is to apply the corresponding stylesheet to the source XML document.

XML Source

The XML source file for this example is `tables_data.xml`. It defines several tables (real tables, the kind you sit at to have your dinner), each looking like this:

```
<tables>
<table>
    <table-name>Conference</table-name>
    <number-of-legs>4</number-of-legs>
    <table-top-material type="laminate">Ash</table-top-material>
    <table-shape>Oblong</table-shape>
    <retail-price currency="USD">1485</retail-price>
</table>
...
</tables>
```

Stylesheet

There are two stylesheets, `tables_list.xsl` and `tables_catalog.xsl`. Since this example is designed to show the JScript used to control the transformation rather than the XSLT transformation code itself, I won't list them here.

HTML page

The page `default.htm` contains some simple styling information for the HTML page, then the JScript code that loads the XML and XSL documents, checks for errors, and performs the transformation. Notice that the `transformFiles` function takes the name of a stylesheet as a parameter, which allows you to specify the stylesheet you want to use at runtime:

```
<html>
<head>
<style type="text/css">
        body {font-family:Tahoma,Verdana,Arial,sans-serif; font-
size:14px}
        .head {font-family:Tahoma,Verdana,Arial,sans-serif;
                                  font-size:18px; font-weight:bold}
</style>

<script language="JScript">
function transformFiles(strStylesheetName) {

    // get a reference to the results DIV element
    var objResults = document.all['divResults'];

    // create two new document instances
    var objXML = new ActiveXObject('MSXML2.DOMDocument.3.0');
    var objXSL = new ActiveXObject('MSXML2.DOMDocument.3.0');


    // set the parser properties
    objXML.validateOnParse = true;
    objXSL.validateOnParse = true;

    // load the XML document and check for errors
    objXML.load('tables_data.xml');
    if (objXML.parseError.errorCode != 0) {
       // error found so show error message and stop
       objResults.innerHTML = showError(objXML)
       return false;
    }

    // load the XSL stylesheet and check for errors
     objXSL.load(strStylesheetName);
     if (objXSL.parseError.errorCode != 0) {
        // error found so show error message and stop
        objResults.innerHTML = showError(objXSL)
        return false;
    }

    // all must be OK, so perform transformation
    strResult = objXML.transformNode(objXSL);

    // and display the results in the DIV element
    objResults.innerHTML = strResult;
    return true;
 }
```

Provided that there are no errors, the function performs the transformation using the XML file `tables_data.xml` and the stylesheet whose name is specified as the `strStylesheet Name` parameter when the function is called.

The result of the transformation is inserted into the `<div>` element that has the `id` attribute value «divResults». You'll later see where this is defined in the HTML .

If either of the `load` calls fail, perhaps due to a badly formed document, a function named `showError` is called. This function takes a reference to the document where the error was found, and returns a string describing the nature of the error. This error message is then displayed on the page instead of the result of the transformation:

```
function showError(objDocument) {
    // create the error message
    var strError = new String;
    strError = 'Invalid XML file !<BR />'
        + 'File URL: ' + objDocument.parseError.url + '<BR />'
        + 'Line No.: ' + objDocument.parseError.line + '<BR />'
        + 'Character: ' + objDocument.parseError.linepos + '<BR />'
        + 'File Position: ' + objDocument.parseError.filepos + '<BR />'
        + 'Source Text: ' + objDocument.parseError.srcText + '<BR />'
        + 'Error Code: ' + objDocument.parseError.errorCode + '<BR />'
        + 'Description: ' + objDocument.parseError.reason
    return strError;
}


//-->
</script>
```

The remainder of the file is the HTML that creates the visible part of the page. The opening `<body>` element specifies an `onload` attribute that causes the `transformFiles()` function in our script section to run once the page has finished loading:

```
...
</head>
<body onload="transformFiles('tables_list.xsl')">
<p><span class="head">Transforming an XML Document using
      the client-side code</span></p>
...
```

Because it uses the value «tables_list.xsl» for the parameter to the function, this stylesheet is used for the initial display. This shows the data in tabular form.

The next thing in the page is the code that creates the two HTML `<button>` elements, marked `Catalog` and `Simple List`. The `onclick` attributes of each one simply execute the `transformFiles()` function again, each time specifying the appropriate stylesheet name:

```
...
View the tables as a  
<button
onclick="transformFiles('tables_catalog.xsl')">Catalog</button>
  or as a  
<button onclick="transformFiles('tables_list.xsl')">Simple List</button>
<hr />

Finally, at the end of the code, you can see the definition of the
<div> element into which the function inserts the results of the
transformation.
```

```
<!-- to insert the results of parsing the object model -->
<div id="divResults"></div>
</body>

</html>
```

Output

When the page is first displayed, it looks like Figure C-1.

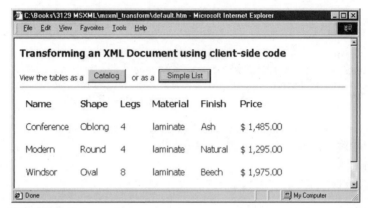

Figure C-1

Click the *Catalog* button, and you will see an alternative graphical presentation of the same data, achieved by applying the other stylesheet.

Restrictions

Microsoft claims full compliance with XSLT 1.0 and XPath 1.0, although there are one or two gray areas where its interpretation of the specification may cause stylesheets to be less than 100% portable. These include:

❑   Handling of whitespace nodes. The normal way of supplying input to Microsoft's XSLT processor is in the form of a DOM, and the default option in MSXML3 for building a DOM is to remove whitespace text nodes as the text is parsed. The result is that `<xsl:preserve-space>` in the stylesheet has no effect, because by the time the XSLT processor gets to see the data, there are no whitespace text nodes left to preserve. If you want conformant behavior in this area, set the `preserveWhitespace` property of the `DOMDocument` object to `True`, before loading the document. The same applies to the stylesheet; if you want to use `<xsl:text>` to control output of whitespace, particularly when generating output in a space-sensitive format such as comma-separated values, then load the stylesheet with `preserveWhitespace` set to `True`.

❑   Normalization of text nodes. XSLT and XPath specify that adjacent text nodes in the tree are always merged into a single node. MSXML3 uses a DOM as its internal data structure, and the DOM does not impose the same rule. Although MSXML3 does a good job at creating a correct XPath view of the underlying DOM tree, this is one area where the mapping is incomplete. The two common cases where adjacent text nodes are not merged are firstly, when one of the text

811

nodes represents the contents of a CDATA section in the source XML, and secondly, when one of them represents the expanded text of an entity reference (other than the built-in entity references such as «<»). This makes it dangerous to use a construct such as <xsl:value-of select="text()"/> because MSXML3 will return only the first of the text nodes, that is, the text up to the start of an entity or CDATA boundary. It's safer to output the value of an element by writing <xsl:value-of select="."/>.

❑ The <xsl:message> instruction has no effect when running a transformation in the browser, unless you specify «terminate="yes"».

System.Xml

System.Xml is the XML infrastructure within Microsoft's .NET framework. It provides support for XML 1.0, XML Namespaces 1.0, XSLT 1.0, XPath 1.0, DOM level 1 and level 2, and XML Schema. Although this package is sometimes referred to as MSXML.NET, Microsoft does not use this terminology. The API is completely different from the older MSXML3/4 products described in the earlier part of this appendix.

Within this framework, the .NET namespace System.Xml.Xsl provides the API for XSLT processing, while System.Xml.Xpath provides the XPath API.

XPathDocument

This class represents a document optimized for XPath and XSLT processing. An instance of this class can be created by directly loading XML from a file:

```
XPathDocument doc = new XPathDocument("source.xml");
```

Other constructors are available, allowing the document to be constructed from a Stream, a TextReader, or an XMLReader. Some of the constructors have a second parameter allowing you to specify whether whitespace text nodes should be stripped or preserved.

An XPathDocument implements the interface IXPathNavigable, described below.

XMLNode

This class represents a node in the .NET implementation of the DOM. Because it supports the DOM data model as well as the XPath data model, it is likely to be less efficient for XPath and XSLT processing than the XPathDocument object.

There are subclasses of XMLNode for the different node kinds, for example XMLElement, XMLAttribute and so on.

This class, like XPathDocument, implements the IXPathNavigable interface. This means that any software written to use the IXPathNavigable interface can use either an XPathDocument or an XMLNode document as the data source.

One of the subclasses of XMLNode is System.Xml.XmlDataDocument, which supports an XML view of data in a relational database. This allows the XSLT processor to run directly against relational data.

IXPathNavigable

This is a very small interface, with a single method, CreateNavigator. This method returns an XPathNavigator object that can be used to process the underlying data, treating it as an implementation of the XPath data model.

For example:

```
XPathDocument doc = new XPathDocument("source.xml");
XPathNavigator nav = doc.CreateNavigator();
```

XPathNavigator

The XPathNavigator object holds a current position within a tree, and provides methods to extract properties of the node at that position, and to move the current position to another related node. If the data source is implemented as an XPathDocument, there is actually no object representing the node itself, which makes the model very efficient because small objects have a high overhead.

Because an XPathNavigator is capable of returning all the information in the XPath data model, it acts as an abstraction of a source document, and any object that implements the XPathNavigator interface can be used as a source document for an XSLT transformation.

XSLTransform

The class System.Xml.Xsl.XslTransform is used to perform an XSLT transformation. The basic sequence of operations is:

❑ Create an XslTransform object.

❑ Use the Load method to load (and compile) the stylesheet.

❑ Use the Transform method to perform the transformation.

There are different variants of the Load method that allow the stylesheet to be loaded by supplying a URL, by nominating an XMLReader to read the stylesheet and perform XML parsing, or by supplying an XPathNavigator or IXPathNavigable that locates the stylesheet within an existing document in memory.

If you want to go through all the stages of loading a stylesheet, you can write:

```
XPathDocument ss = new XPathDocument("stylesheet.xsl");
XPathNavigator nav = doc.createNavigator();
XslTransform trans = new XslTransform();
trans.Load(nav);
```

The options to supply a URL or an XMLReader as input to the Load method can be seen as shortcuts to this process.

The Transform method has a very large number of different overloaded variants. Essentially it takes four arguments: the source document to be transformed, the values supplied for stylesheet parameters, the destination for the result document, and an `XmlResolver` that is used to resolve URI references supplied to the `document()` function. The number of variations of this method is due to the fact that both the source and the destination can be supplied in a number of different ways, and these are supported in all combinations.

❑ The source document can be supplied by giving a URL, or in the form of an `IXPathNavigable` or `XPathNavigator` object.

❑ Stylesheet parameters are supplied in an `XsltArgumentList` object. This allows parameter values to be added using an `AddParam()` method. Parameters of type boolean, number, and string can be supplied using the `Boolean`, `Double`, and `String` classes; a parameter of type node-set can be supplied in the form of an `XPathNavigator`.

❑ The output destination can be given as an `XmlWriter`, a `TextWriter`, or a `Stream`. Alternatively, instead of supplying the output destination as an argument, the `Transform()` method can return an `XMLReader`, which means that the calling application can use the transformation results in the same way as it would use the output of an XML parser.

❑ An `XMLResolver` can be supplied. Like the `URIResolver` in the JAXP interface, this object is used to fetch a document when supplied with a URI. This allows you to implement your own URI schemes or to use your own catalogs to find a local copy of required documents such as stylesheet modules, schemas, or DTDs.

For example:

```
// Load a stylesheet

XslTransform trans = new XslTransform();
trans.Load("stylesheet.xsl");

// Load a source document
XPathDocument source = new XPathDocument("source.xml");

// Set the current date and time as a stylesheet parameter
XsltArgumentList args = new XsltArgumentList();
DateTime now = DateTime.Now;
args.AddParam("date", "", d.ToString());

// Create an XmlTextWriter for the output
XmlTextWriter out = new XmlTextWriter(Console.Out);

// Perform the transformation (no XmlResolver is supplied)
xslt.Transform(source, args, writer, null);
writer.Close();
```

Summary

This appendix summarized the application programming interfaces available for using Microsoft's two XSLT product families: the MSXML3/4 product line, and the `System.Xml` framework classes for .NET. For full information about these APIs, you will need to go to Microsoft's documentation, but the summary given here has hopefully given you a good introduction.

As you've seen, Microsoft doesn't yet offer an XSLT 2.0 processor.

JAXP: The Java API for Transformation

JAXP is a Java API for controlling various aspects of XML processing, including parsing, validation, and XSLT transformation. This appendix concentrates on the transformation API. During its development this was known as TrAX (Transformation API for XML)—you will still see this term used occasionally.

JAXP is well supported by all the Java XML processors. The benefit of JAXP is that it allows you to write Java applications that invoke XSLT transformations without committing your application to a particular XSLT processor. The same program can be used to execute transformations using Saxon, Xalan, Oracle, or jd.xslt. This works so well that I have come across users who were running Saxon when they thought they were using Xalan, or vice versa. It's a good idea to include the following instruction in your initial template so that you avoid this mistake:

```
<xsl:comment>
    Created using <xsl:value-of select="system-property('xsl:vendor')"/>
    on <xsl:value-of select="current-date()"/>
</xsl:comment>
```

The current version is JAXP 1.2, though a version 1.3 is under development for inclusion in JDK 1.5. It doesn't look as if there will be major changes affecting the transformation part of JAXP in the new version, just some tightening up of the specifications in areas that have proved unclear. In particular, the new version does not yet support XSLT 2.0. The most important extensions in JAXP 1.3 are that it supports direct use of XPath, and also schema processing (not just using XML Schema as defined by W3C, but using any schema language, for example Relax NG).

In fact, very few changes to JAXP are needed for XSLT 2.0. When such an upgrade comes, the main extensions are likely to be:

❑   A mechanism for starting the transformation with no source document, and/or by specifying an initial template

❑   The ability to specify an initial mode in which the transformation should start

❏ A definition of how stylesheet parameters of different types should be passed to the `setParameter()` method

❏ Several new constants to define parameters for output serialization

A useful source for information about JAXP is the unofficial JAXP FAQ published by Edwin Goei at `http://xml.apache.org/~edwingo/jaxp-faq.html`.

Notation

To save space, I've used an abbreviated notation in this appendix to indicate the exceptions thrown by each method. A list such as [SAXE, IOE] indicates the exceptions that may be thrown, using the following codes:

Code	Exception class
FCE	`javax.xml.parsers.FactoryConfigurationError`
IAE	`java.lang.IllegalArgumentException`
IOE	`java.io.IOException`
PCE	`javax.xml.parsers.ParserConfigurationException`
SAXE	`org.xml.sax.SAXException`
SAXNRE	`org.xml.sax.SAXNotRecognizedException`
SAXNSE	`org.xml.sax.SAXNotSupportedException`
TCE	`javax.xml.transform.TransformerConfigurationException`
TE	`javax.xml.transform.TransformerException`
TFCE	`javax.xml.transform.TransformerFactoryConfigurationError`

The JAXP Parser API

JAXP 1.2 defines two sets of interfaces: interfaces for XML parsing, in package `javax.xml.parsers`, and interfaces for XML transformation (that is, TrAX) in package `javax.xml.transform` and its subsidiary packages. (JAXP 1.3 adds interfaces for schema validation, for XPath processing, and more.) Although the parser APIs could be regarded as being out of scope for this book, applications will often use both together, so I shall start by quickly reviewing the two parser APIs, covering SAX parsing and DOM parsing.

These interfaces do not supersede the SAX and DOM interfaces, which are described in many XML reference books. Rather, they supplement them with facilities that are lacking in both SAX and DOM, namely the ability to select a SAX or DOM parser to do the processing, and to set options such as specifying whether you want a validating or nonvalidating parser, and whether you want namespace processing to be performed.

I'll look at the two parts of the interface, SAX and DOM, separately.

JAXP Support for SAX

JAXP 1.2 supports SAX2, but remains backwards compatible with earlier versions that supported SAX1. In the interests of brevity, I will leave out the features that are relevant only to SAX1.

javax.xml.parsers.SAXParserFactory

The first thing an application must do is to obtain a SAXParserFactory, which it can do by calling the static method SAXParserFactory.newInstance(). Different vendors of SAX parsers will each implement their own subclass of SAXParserFactory, and this call determines which vendor's parser your application will end up using. If there are several available, the one that is used is based on the following decision process:

1. Use the value of the system property javax.xml.parsers.SAXParserFactory if it is available. You can typically set system properties using the -D option on the Java command line, or by calling System.setProperty() from your application.

2. Look for a properties file $JAVA_HOME/lib/jaxp.properties, and within this file, for the property named javax.xml.parsers.SAXParserFactory.

3. Use the services API, which is part of the JAR specification. This effectively means that the parser that is used will be the first one to be found on your classpath.

It is likely that when you install a particular SAX parser, it will contain a file within its .jar archive that causes that particular parser to be the default, so if you don't do anything to select a specific parser, the one chosen will depend on the order of files and directories on your class path.

The default parser in Sun's JDK 1.4 is the Crimson parser. If you want to use Xerces instead, set the property to the value org.apache.xerces.jaxp.SAXParserFactoryImpl.

Once you have obtained a SAXParserFactory, you can use a number of methods to configure it. Finally, you can call the newSAXParser() method to return a SAXParser. The methods available are as follows. The codes in square brackets indicate the exceptions thrown, according to the table at the start of this appendix.

Method	Description
boolean getFeature(String) [SAXNRE, SAXNSE, PCE]	Determines whether the parser factory is configured to support a particular feature. The names of features correspond to those defined in SAX2 for the XMLReader class
boolean isNamespaceAware()	Determines whether parsers produced using this factory will be namespace aware
boolean isValidating()	Determines whether parsers produced using this factory will perform XML validation
static SAXParserFactory newInstance()[FCE]	Produces a SAXParserFactory for a specific vendor's parser, decided according to the rules given above

Continues

Method	Description
SAXParser newSAXParser() [PCE]	Returns a SAXParser that can be used to perform parsing. This is a wrapper around the SAX2 XMLReader object
void setFeature(String, boolean) [SAXNRE, SAXNSE, PCE]	Sets a particular feature on or off. The names of features correspond to those defined in SAX2 for the XMLReader class
void setNamespaceAware(boolean)	Indicates whether parsers produced using this factory are required to be namespace aware
void setValidating(boolean)	Indicates whether parsers produced using this factory are required to perform XML validation

javax.xml.parsers.SAXParser

A SAXParser is obtained using the newSAXParser() method of a SAXParserFactory. A SAXParser is a wrapper around a SAX2 XMLReader. You can use the getXMLReader() method to get the underlying XMLReader, but in simple cases you won't need to, since you can perform a parse and nominate a handler for all the parsing events using this class alone.

The methods relevant to SAX2 parsers are:

Method	Description
Object getProperty(String) [SAXNRE, SAXNSE]	Gets the named property of the underlying SAX2 XMLReader
XMLReader getXMLReader() [SAXE]	Gets the underlying SAX2 XMLReader
boolean isNamespaceAware()	Determines whether the underlying SAX2 XMLReader is namespace aware
boolean isValidating()	Determines whether the underlying SAX2 XMLReader performs XML validation
void parse(File, DefaultHandler) [IOE, IAE, SAXE]	Parses the contents of the specified file, passing all parsing events to the specified event handler. Normally of course this will not actually be a SAX2 DefaultHandler, but a user-defined subclass of DefaultHandler written to process selected events
void parse(InputSource, DefaultHandler) [IOE, IAE, SAXE]	Parses the contents of the specified SAX InputSource, passing all parsing events to the specified event handler

Method	Description
`void parse(InputStream, DefaultHandler)` `[IOE, IAE, SAXE]`	Parses the contents of the specified `InputStream`, passing all parsing events to the specified event handler. Note that in this case the System ID of the input is unknown, so the parser has no way of resolving relative URIs contained in the XML source
`void parse(InputStream, DefaultHandler, String)` `[IOE, IAE, SAXE]`	Parses the contents of the specified `InputStream`, passing all parsing events to the specified event handler. The third argument contains a System ID that will be used for resolving relative URIs
`void parse(String, DefaultHandler)` `[IOE, IAE, SAXE]`	Parses the XML document identified by the URI in the first argument, passing all parsing events to the specified event handler
`void setProperty(String, Object)` `[SAXNSE, SAXNRE]`	Sets a property of the underlying SAX2 `XMLReader`

JAXP Support for DOM

JAXP 1.2 is aligned with DOM level 2. There are a number of features in DOM level 2 to make navigation easier, but the main advance (and source of complications) is support for XML namespaces.

The DOM interface itself defines methods for constructing a tree programmatically, and methods for navigating around a tree, but it does not define any way of constructing a DOM tree by parsing a source XML document. JAXP is designed to plug this gap.

The architecture of the interface is very similar to the SAX case:

1. First call the static method `DocumentBuilderFactory.newInstance()` to get a `DocumentBuilderFactory` representing one particular vendor's DOM implementation.

2. Then use the `newDocumentBuilder()` method on this `DocumentBuilderFactory` to obtain a `DocumentBuilder`.

3. Finally, call one of the various `parse()` methods on the `DocumentBuilder` to obtain a DOM Document object.

javax.xml.parsers.DocumentBuilderFactory

The first thing an application must do is obtain a `DocumentBuilderFactory`, which it can do by calling the static method `DocumentBuilderFactory.newInstance()`. Different vendors of DOM implementations will each implement their own subclass of `DocumentBuilderFactory`, and this call determines which implementation your application will end up using. If there are several available, the one that is used is based on the following decision process:

1. Use the value of the system property `javax.xml.parsers.DocumentBuilderFactory` if it is available. You can typically set system properties using the −D option on the Java command line, or by calling `System.setProperty()` from your application.

2. Look for a properties file `$JAVA_HOME/lib/jaxp.properties`, and within this file, for the property named

    `javax.xml.parsers. DocumentBuilderFactory`.

3. Use the services API, which is part of the JAR specification. In practice this means that the DOM implementation used will be the first one found on the classpath.

It is likely that when you install a particular DOM implementation, it will contain a file in its `.jar` archive that makes that particular implementation the default, so if you don't do anything to select a specific implementation, the one chosen will depend on the order of files and directories on your class path.

Again, the default parser in Sun's JDK 1.4 is the Crimson parser. If you prefer to use Xerces, set the system property to `org.apache.xerces.jaxp.DocumentBuilderFactoryImpl`.

Once you have got a `DocumentBuilderFactory`, you can use a number of methods to configure it. Finally, you can call the `newDocumentBuilder()` method to return a `DocumentBuilder`. The methods available are:

Method	Description
`Object getAttribute(String)` `[IAE]`	Gets information about the properties of the underlying implementation
`boolean isCoalescing()`	Determines whether the resulting `DocumentBuilder` will merge CDATA nodes into their adjacent text nodes
`boolean isExpandEntityReferences()`	Determines whether the resulting `DocumentBuilder` will expand entity references and merge their content into the adjacent text nodes
`boolean isIgnoringComments()`	Determines whether the resulting `DocumentBuilder` will ignore comments in the source XML
`boolean isIgnoringElement ContentWhitespace()`	Determines whether the resulting `DocumentBuilder` will ignore whitespace in element content
`boolean isNamespaceAware()`	Determines whether the resulting `DocumentBuilder` is namespace aware
`boolean isValidating()`	Determines whether the resulting `DocumentBuilder` will validate the XML source
`DocumentBuilder newDocumentBuilder() [PCE]`	Returns a new `DocumentBuilder` configured as specified by previous calls
`static DocumentBuilderFactory newInstance() [FCE]`	Returns a vendor-specific `DocumentBuilderFactory` selected according to the rules given above
`setAttribute(String, Object)` `[IAE]`	Sets vendor-specific properties on the underlying implementation

Method	Description
void setCoalescing(boolean)	Determines whether the resulting DocumentBuilder will merge CDATA nodes into their adjacent text nodes
void setExpandEntityReferences (boolean)	Determines whether the resulting DocumentBuilder will expand entity references and merge their content into the adjacent text nodes
void setIgnoringComments (boolean)	Determines whether the resulting DocumentBuilder will ignore comments in the source XML
void setIgnoringElementContent Whitespace(boolean)	Determines whether the resulting DocumentBuilder will ignore whitespace in element content
void setNamespaceAware(boolean)	Determines whether the resulting DocumentBuilder is namespace aware
void setValidating(boolean)	Determines whether the resulting DocumentBuilder will validate the XML source

javax.xml.parsers.DocumentBuilder

A DocumentBuilder is always obtained by calling the newDocumentBuilder() method of a DocumentBuilderFactory.

A DocumentBuilder performs the task of parsing a source XML document and returning the resulting instance of org.w3.dom.Document, containing the root of a tree representation of the document in memory.

The source document is specified in similar ways to the input for a SAX parser. This doesn't mean that a DocumentBuilder has to use a SAX parser to do the actual parsing: Some will work this way and others won't. It's defined this way to avoid unnecessary differences between the SAX and DOM approaches.

You might be aware that in the Microsoft DOM implementation, the Document class has a method load() *that parses a source XML file and constructs a Document object. This is a Microsoft extension; there is no corresponding method in the W3C DOM definition. This* DocumentBuilder *class fills the gap.*

The methods available are:

Method	Description
boolean isNamespaceAware()	Indicates whether the parser understands XML namespaces
boolean isValidating()	Indicates whether the parser validates the XML source
Document newDocument()	Returns a new Document object with no content. The returned Document can be populated using DOM methods such as createElement().

Continues

Method	Description
`Document parse(File) [IOE, SAXE, IAE]`	Parses the XML in the supplied file, and returns the resulting `Document` object
`Document parse(InputSource) [IOE, SAXE, IAE]`	Parses the XML in the supplied SAX `InputSource`, and returns the resulting `Document` object
`Document parse(InputStream) [IOE, SAXE, IAE]`	Parses the XML in the supplied `InputStream`, and returns the resulting `Document` object. Note that the System ID of the source document will be unknown, so it will not be possible to resolve any relative URIs contained in the document
`Document parse(InputStream, String) [IOE, SAXE, IAE]`	Parses the XML in the supplied `InputStream`, and returns the resulting `Document` object. The second argument supplies the System ID of the source document, which will be used to resolve any relative URIs contained in the document
`Document parse(String) [IOE, SAXE, IAE]`	Parses the XML in the document identified by the supplied URI, and returns the resulting `Document` object
`void setEntityResolver (EntityResolver)`	Supplies a SAX `EntityResolver` to be used during the parsing
`void setErrorHandler(Error Handler)`	Supplies a SAX `ErrorHandler` to be used during the parsing

The JAXP Transformation API

The previous sections provided a summary of the classes and methods defined in JAXP to control XML parsing. This section covers the classes and methods used to control XSLT transformation.

These classes are designed so they could be used with transformation mechanisms other than XSLT, for example they could in principle be used to invoke XQuery (however, a different API is under development for XQuery, which is likely to have more in common with JDBC). But XSLT is the initial target and is the one we will concentrate on.

There is one other kind of transformation that's worth mentioning, however, and this is an identity transformation in which the result represents a copy of the source. JAXP provides explicit support for identity transformations. These are more useful than they might appear, because JAXP defines three ways of supplying the source document (SAX, DOM, or serial XML) and three ways of capturing the result document (SAX, DOM, or serial XML), so an identity transformation can be used to convert any of these inputs to any of the outputs. For example, it can take SAX input and produce a serial XML file as output, or it can take DOM input and produce a stream of SAX events as output. An implementation of JAXP can also support additional kinds of `Source` and `Result` object if it chooses.

JAXP is also designed to control a composite transformation consisting of a sequence of transformation steps, each defined by an XSLT stylesheet in its own right. To do this, it builds on the SAX2 concept of an

`XMLFilter`, which takes an input document as a stream of SAX events and produces its output as another stream of SAX events. Any number of such filters can be arranged end to end in a pipeline to define a composite transformation.

As with the JAXP `SAXParser` and `DocumentBuilder` interfaces, JAXP allows the specific XSLT implementation to be selected using a `TransformerFactory` object. Typically the XSLT vendors will each provide their own subclass of `TransformerFactory`.

For performance reasons, the API separates the process of compiling a stylesheet from the process of executing it. A stylesheet can be compiled once and executed many times against different source documents, perhaps concurrently in different threads. The compiled stylesheet, following Microsoft's MSXML3 nomenclature, is known as a `Templates` object. To keep simple things simple, however, there are also methods that combine the two processes of compilation and execution into a single call.

The classes defined in the `javax.xml.transform` package fall into several categories:

Category	Class or interface	Description
Principal classes	`TransformerFactory`	Selects and configures a vendor's implementation
	`Templates`	Represents a compiled stylesheet in memory
	`Transformer`	Represents a single execution of a stylesheet to transform a source document into a result
	`SAXTransformerFactory`	Allows a transformation to be packaged as a SAX `XMLFilter`
	`Source`	Represents the input to a transformation
	`Result`	Represents the output of a transformation
Source classes	`SAXSource`	Transformation input in the form of a SAX event stream
	`DOMSource`	Transformation input in the form of a DOM `Document`
	`StreamSource`	Transformation input in the form of a serial XML document
Result classes	`SAXResult`	Transformation output in the form of a SAX event stream
	`DOMResult`	Transformation output in the form of a DOM `Document`

Continues

Category	Class or interface	Description
	StreamResult	Transformation output in the form of a serial XML document (or HTML, or a plain text file)
Helper classes	URIResolver	User-supplied object that takes a URI contained in the stylesheet (for example, in the document() function) and fetches the relevant document as a Source object
	ErrorListener	User-supplied object that is notified of warnings and errors. The ErrorListener notifies these conditions to the user and decides whether to continue processing
	SourceLocator	Used primarily to identify where in the stylesheet an error occurred
	DOMLocator	Subclass of SourceLocator, used when the source was a DOM
	OutputKeys	A collection of constants defining the names of properties for serial output files
Error classes	Transformer ConfigurationException	Generally denotes an error in the stylesheet that is detected at compile time
	TransformerException	A failure occurring in the course of executing a transformation
	TransformerFactory ConfigurationError	A failure to configure the Transformer

In the following sections I will describe each of these classes, in alphabetical order of the class name (ignoring the name of the package).

javax.xml.transform.dom.DOMLocator

A DOMLocator is used to identify the location of an error when the document is supplied in the form of a DOM. This object will normally be created by the processor when an error occurs, and can be accessed using the getLocator() method of the relevant Exception object. It specializes SourceLocator, providing one additional method:

Method	Description
org.w3c.dom.Node getOriginatingNode()	Returns the node at which the error or other event is located

javax.xml.transform.dom.DOMResult

Supplying a DOMResult as the result of a transformation indicates that the output is to be written to a DOM in memory. This object will normally be created by the application, and supplied to the processor as the second argument of the Transformer.transform() method.

The DOMResult identifies a Node (which will generally be a Document or an Element, or possibly a DocumentFragment) to hold the results of the transformation. The children of the root in the result tree will become children of this Node in the DOM. If no Node is supplied by the application, the system will create a Document node, which can be retrieved using getNode().

Many XSLT processors will support DOM output, but it is not mandatory. If the processor does support it, then getFeature(DOMResult.FEATURE) will return true.

If the XSLT stylesheet outputs text using «disable-output-escaping="yes"», then this text will be preceded in the tree by a processing instruction named by the constant Result.PI_DISABLE_OUTPUT_ESCAPING, and followed by another processing instruction named by the constant Result.PI_ENABLE_OUTPUT_ESCAPING.

The DOMResult object holds a reference to the destination Node, and also a String containing a system identifier.

The class has two constructors:

```
DOMResult()
DOMResult(org.w3c.xml.Node)
```

and the following methods:

Method	Description
org.w3c.dom.Node getNode()	Gets the node that will contain the result tree
String getSystemId()	Gets the system identifier (that is, the base URI)
void setNode(org.w3c. dom.Node)	Sets the node that will contain the result tree. It must be a Document, an Element, or a DocumentFragment
void setSystemId(String)	Sets the system identifier (that is, the base URI)

javax.xml.transform.dom.DOMSource

A DOMSource packages a DOM Document as a Source, so it can be supplied as input to a transformation.

The DOMSource object will normally be created by the application, and supplied to the processor as the first argument of the Transformer.transform() method. It can also be used to identify the stylesheet document, in which case it will be supplied as a parameter to TransformerFactory.newTemplates().

It is a good idea to call `setSystemId()` to supply a base URI for the document, so that relative URIs (for example, those used in the `document()` function) can be resolved. The DOM itself does not hold this information, so it must be supplied extraneously.

The `DOMSource` can identify any node in the DOM; it does not have to be the `Document` node. For example, when you use a `DOMSource` to identify a stylesheet, this might be a stylesheet embedded within another document, in which case the `DOMSource` would identify the `<xsl:stylesheet>` element node. When you supply a node other than the `Document` node as input to the `transform()` method, the effect is not specified very clearly, but it is probably intended that it should behave like the `transformNode()` method in MSXML3. This means that the entire document containing the identified node forms the input to the transformation, but the transformation starts by looking for a template rule that matches the specified node, rather than the one that matches the root node.

Note that there are two different ways XSLT processors might handle the supplied document. They might create the XPath tree model as a view or wrapper around the DOM tree, or they might make a copy. The difference between these approaches will become apparent if the stylesheet makes calls to external Java functions that attempt to manipulate the tree as a DOM. It will also, of course, affect performance. Generally, it is best to supply input as a stream or SAX source if you can. Don't construct a DOM specially in order to supply it as input to a transformation, as you might do if you are used to the Microsoft MSXML API. Most implementations will have an internal tree model that is designed to optimize transformation speed, and this will often run several times faster than the same transformation using the DOM.

Not every XSLT processor will support DOM input. If the processor does so, then `getFeature(DOMSource.FEATURE)` will return true.

The class has three constructors:

```
DOMSource()
DOMSource(Node)
DOMSource(Node, String)
```

Its methods are listed below:

Method	Description
`Node getNode()`	Gets the starting node of this `DOMSource`
`String getSystemId()`	Gets the system identifier (that is, base URI) for resolving relative URIs
`void setNode(Node)`	Sets the starting node of this `DOMSource`
`setSystemId(String)`	Gets the system identifier (that is, base URI) for resolving relative URIs

javax.xml.transform.ErrorListener

`ErrorListener` is an interface; if you want to do your own error handling you can write a class that implements this interface and supply it to the `setErrorListener()` methods of the `Transformer`

Factory or Transformer class. The ErrorListener will be notified of both compile-time and runtime errors.

The class is modeled on the SAX ErrorHandler interface, and recognizes three categories of errors: warnings, errors, and fatal errors. After a warning, the transformation can proceed to a successful conclusion; after an error, the processor can continue for the purpose of finding further errors, but in the end it will fail; and after a fatal error, it will stop immediately.

Each method can throw an exception to cause processing to stop immediately, even where the processor is prepared to continue.

Some processors (Xalan in particular) report the output of <xsl:message> to the ErrorListener. If «terminate="no"» is specified, the message is treated as a warning; if «terminate="yes"» is specified, it is treated as a fatal error. JAXP doesn't dictate how <xsl:message> is handled, and other processors do it differently.

If no ErrorListener is supplied, errors will be reported on the standard System.err output stream.

The methods are listed below. The «[TE]» after each method shows that each of them can throw a TransformerException, to terminate processing.

Method	Description
void error(TransformerException) [TE]	Handles an error
void fatalError(TransformerException) [TE]	Handles a fatal error
void warning(TransformerException)[TE]	Handles a warning

javax.xml.transform.OutputKeys

This class defines a set of constant strings used to represent the standard output properties defined in the <xsl:output> element. This list hasn't yet been updated to support the new properties found in XSLT 2.0.

The names of these constants are:

```
CDATA_SECTION_ELEMENTS
DOCTYPE_PUBLIC
DOCTYPE_SYSTEM
ENCODING
INDENT
MEDIA_TYPE
METHOD
OMIT_XML_DECLARATION
STANDALONE
VERSION
```

They correspond in the obvious way to the attributes of the <xsl:output> element.

These constants are useful when you call methods such as getOutputProperty() and setOutputProperty() on the Transformer object.

javax.xml.transform.Result

Result is an interface; it exists as an abstraction of the three classes SAXResult, DOMResult, and StreamResult, which are different ways of representing an XML output destination. This allows any of these different kinds of destination to be supplied as the second argument to the Transformer. transform() method. Implementations can also define other kinds of Result object if they wish.

This class defines the two static constants PI_DISABLE_OUTPUT_ESCAPING and PI_ENABLE_ OUTPUT_ESCAPING which are the names of the processing instructions generated as a result of setting «disable-output-escaping="yes"» on the <xsl:text> or <xsl:value-of> instruction in the stylesheet.

The interface defines two methods, allowing any of the different types of Result to have a system identifier (or base URI):

Method	Description
String getSystemId()	Gets the system identifier
void setSystemId()	Sets the system identifier

javax.xml.transform.sax.SAXResult

Specifying a SAXResult as the output of the transformation causes the result tree produced by the transformation to be fed to a user-supplied SAX2 ContentHandler as a sequence of SAX events, just as if the events came from an XML parser. The SAXResult object holds a reference to this ContentHandler, and also to a String containing a system identifier. (This system identifier might be made available to the ContentHandler code as part of the Locator object, though the specification doesn't make it clear that this is what should happen.)

Many XSLT processors will support SAX output, but it is not mandatory. If the processor does support it, then getFeature(SAXResult.FEATURE) will return true.

There are several potential difficulties with supplying XSLT output to a ContentHandler:

❏ What happens about disable-output-escaping? The JAXP specification solves this by saying that any text output using disable-output-escaping="yes" will be preceded by a processing instruction named by the constant Result.PI_DISABLE_OUTPUT_ESCAPING, and followed by another processing instruction named by the constant Result.PI_ENABLE_ OUTPUT_ESCAPING.

❏ What happens to comments in the result tree? JAXP solves this by allowing the SAXResult to hold a LexicalHandler as well as a ContentHandler. Comments can then be notified to the LexicalHandler.

❏ What happens if the result tree is not a well-formed document? The SAX ContentHandler interface is designed to receive a stream of events representing a well-formed document, and many ContentHandlers will fail (gracefully or otherwise) if they are sent anything else. However, as you saw in Chapter 2, the output of an XSLT transformation needs only to be well-balanced. Unfortunately, the JAXP specification doesn't answer this question. (Saxon allows any sequence of events to be sent to the `ContentHandler`, whether it represents a well-formed sequence or not, unless the additional attribute `saxon:require-well-formed="yes"` is present on the `<xsl:output>` declaration.)

The class has two constructors:

```
SAXResult()
SAXResult(org.xml.sax.ContentHandler)
```

and the following methods:

Method	Description
`org.xml.sax.ContentHandler getHandler()`	Gets the `ContentHandler`
`org.xml.sax.ext.LexicalHandler getLexicalHandler()`	Gets the `LexicalHandler`
`String getSystemId()`	Gets the system identifier (base URI)
`void setHandler (org.xml.sax.ContentHandler)`	Sets the `ContentHandler` that is to receive events representing the result tree
`void setHandler (org.xml.sax.ext.LexicalHandler)`	Sets the `LexicalHandler` that is to receive lexical events (notably, comments) representing the result tree
`void setSystemId()`	Sets the system identifier (base URI)

javax.xml.transform.sax.SAXSource

A `SAXSource` is a `Source`, so it is one of the possible inputs you can supply to the `Transformer.transform()` method (when it represents a source XML document) or to the `TransformerFactory.newTemplates()` method (when it represents a stylesheet).

Essentially, a `SAXSource` is the combination of a SAX parser (`XMLReader`) and a SAX `InputSource`, which can be a URI, a binary input stream, or a character input stream. A `SAXSource` delivers the source document in the form of a stream of SAX events. Usually it will achieve this by parsing XML held in a file or somewhere in memory; but by defining your own implementations of `XMLReader` and/or `InputSource` you can supply the SAX events from anywhere, for example you can generate them as the result of an SQL query or an LDAP directory search.

If no `XMLReader` is supplied, the system will use a default one. It may do this using the rules for the `javax.xml.parsers.SAXParserFactory` class described earlier in this appendix, but this is not guaranteed.

Not every XSLT processor will support SAX input. If the processor does so, then `getFeature (SAXSource.FEATURE)` will return true.

There are three constructors:

```
SAXSource()
SAXSource(InputSource)
SAXSource(XMLReader, InputSource)
```

plus the following methods:

Method	Description
InputSource getInputSource()	Gets the SAX InputSource.
String getSystemId()	Gets the System Identifier used for resolving relative URIs
XMLReader getXMLReader()	Gets the XMLReader (the parser) if one has been set
void setInputSource(org.xml.sax.InputSource)	Sets the SAX InputSource
void setSystemId(String)	Sets a System Identifier that can be used to resolve relative URIs
void setXMLReader(XMLReader)	Sets the XMLReader (the parser) to be used
static org.xml.sax.InputSource sourceToInputSource(Source source)	This static method attempts to construct a SAX InputSource from any kind of Source object. It will return null if this isn't possible

javax.xml.transform.sax.SAXTransformerFactory

This class is a subclass of TransformerFactory that provides three additional facilities:

❑ The ability to construct a SAX ContentHandler (called a TemplatesHandler), which will accept a stream of SAX events representing a stylesheet, and on completion return a Templates object for this stylesheet.

❑ The ability to construct a SAX ContentHandler (called a TransformerHandler) that will accept a stream of SAX events representing a source document, and on completion automatically apply a given stylesheet to that source document.

❑ The ability to construct a SAX XMLFilter based on a particular stylesheet: The XMLFilter performs the same SAX-to-SAX transformation as the equivalent Transformer would perform, but using the interfaces defined for an XMLFilter. This makes it possible to insert this transformation filter into a pipeline of filters.

These are advanced facilities, and they are optional, so not every JAXP processor will support them.

❑ If getFeature(SAXTransformerFactory.FEATURE) returns true, then the implementation's TransformerFactory will be a SAXTransformerFactory.

❑ If getFeature(SAXTransformerFactory.FEATURE_XMLFILTER) returns true, then the two newXMLFilter() methods can be used.

If a `SAXTransformerFactory` is available at all, then it will always be produced as a result of calling `TransformerFactory.newInstance()`.

The class has the following methods, in addition to those of `TransformerFactory`:

Method	Description
`TemplatesHandler newTemplatesHandler()` `[TCE]`	Creates and returns a `TemplatesHandler`. The `TemplatesHandler` can be supplied with a stream of SAX events representing the contents of a stylesheet
`TransformerHandler newTransformerHandler()` `[TCE]`	Creates and returns a `TransformerHandler`. The `TransformerHandler` will perform an identity transformation on the XML source document that is supplied to it in the form of a stream of SAX events
`TransformerHandler newTransformerHandler(Source)` `[TCE]`	Creates and returns a `TransformerHandler`. The `Source` identifies a document containing a stylesheet. The `TransformerHandler` will perform the transformation defined by this stylesheet, on the XML source document that is supplied to it in the form of a stream of SAX events
`TransformerHandler newTransformerHandler(Templates)` `[TCE]`	Creates and returns a `TransformerHandler`. The `Templates` argument identifies a compiled stylesheet. The `TransformerHandler` will perform the transformation defined by this stylesheet, on the XML source document that is supplied to it in the form of a stream of SAX events
`org.sax.xml.XMLFilter newXMLFilter(Source)` `[TCE]`	Creates and returns an `XMLFilter`. The `Source` identifies a document containing a stylesheet. The resulting `XMLFilter` will perform the transformation defined by this stylesheet
`org.sax.xml.XMLFilter newXMLFilter(Templates)` `[TCE]`	Creates and returns an `XMLFilter`. The `Templates` argument identifies a compiled stylesheet. The resulting `XMLFilter` will perform the transformation defined by this stylesheet

javax.xml.transform.Source

`Source` is an interface; it exists as an abstraction of the three classes `SAXSource`, `DOMSource`, and `StreamSource`, which are different ways of representing an XML document. This allows any of these different kinds of object to be supplied as the source document to the `Transformer.transform()` method, or as the stylesheet to the `TransformerFactory.newTemplates()` method.

The interface defines two methods, allowing any of the different types of `Source` to have a system identifier. Specifying a system identifier on a `Source` object is important, because it will be used as the base URI when relative URIs within the `Source` are resolved.

Method	Description
`String getSystemId()`	Gets the system identifier
`void setSystemId()`	Sets the system identifier

javax.xml.transform.SourceLocator

`SourceLocator` is an interface modeled on the SAX `Locator` interface. A `SourceLocator` is used to indicate where in the stylesheet an error occurred. Normally a `SourceLocator` will be produced by the XSLT processor, and the application will access it using the `TransformerException.getLocator()` method.

The methods available are:

Method	Description
`int getColumnNumber()`	Returns the column number of the location if known, or –1 if not
`int getLineNumber()`	Returns the line number of the location if known, or –1 if not
`String getPublicId()`	Returns the public identifier of the document, if available, or `null` if not
`String getSystemId()`	Returns the system identifier of the document, if available, or `null` if not

javax.xml.transform.stream.StreamSource

A `StreamSource` represents XML input in the form of a character or byte stream. It is modeled on the SAX `InputSource` class; the only reason `StreamSource` is necessary is that `InputSource` does not implement the `Source` interface, so it cannot be supplied directly as the input to methods such as `Transformer.transform(Source, Result)`.

Most XSLT processors will support stream input, but it is not mandatory. If the processor does support it, then `getFeature(StreamSource.FEATURE)` will return `true`.

If input is from a byte stream (`InputStream`) or character stream (`Reader`) it is a good idea to call `setSystemId()` to supply a URI for the document, so that relative URIs (for example, those used in the `document()` function) can be resolved. The stream itself does not hold this information, so it must be supplied extraneously.

The constructors are as follows:

```
StreamSource()
StreamSource(java.io.File)
StreamSource(java.io.InputStream)
```

```
StreamSource(java.io.InputStream, String)
StreamSource(java.io.Reader)
StreamSource(java.io.Reader, String)
StreamSource(String)
```

In each case the effect is the same as using the default constructor followed by the relevant setXXX() method. The String argument is always a system identifier for the document.

In my experience the File-to-URI conversion used when you supply a java.io.File object is buggy: It's better to use the File.toURI() method to do the conversion, as this does a better job of handling special characters such as spaces.

The methods are straightforward:

Method	Description
java.io.InputStream getInputStream()	Gets the supplied InputStream
String getPublicId()	Gets the supplied Public Identifier
java.io.Reader getReader()	Gets the supplied Reader
String getSystemId()	Gets the system identifier
void setInputStream(java.io.InputStream)	Supplies an InputStream
void setPublicId(String)	Supplies a Public Identifier
void setReader(java.io.Reader)	Supplies a Reader
void setSystemId(java.io.File)	Supplies a File from which a system identifier can be obtained
void setSystemId(String)	Supplies a system identifier (a URL)

javax.xml.transform.stream.StreamResult

You can supply a StreamResult as the result of a transformation if you want the result tree to be serialized. The format of the resulting file will be XML, HTML, or plain text, depending on the output method defined using <xsl:output> or the Transformer methods setOutputProperty() and setOutputProperties(). With an XSLT 2.0 engine, XHTML output will also be supported.

Note that if you supply a Writer (which represents a stream of characters rather than bytes), then the XSLT processor will ignore the encoding attribute specified on <xsl:output>. The way in which characters are translated to bytes in this situation depends on how the Writer is configured, and not on the XSLT serializer. One consequence of this is that because the Writer knows nothing about XML, it will not be able to replace characters that aren't available in the chosen encoding by XML character references of the form «€».

StreamResult is defined analogously to StreamSource, which in turn is based on the SAX InputSource class. A StreamResult may be a file (represented by a URL or a Java File object), or a character stream (Writer), or a byte stream (OutputStream).

Most XSLT processors will support stream output, but it is not mandatory. If the processor does support it, then getFeature(StreamResult.FEATURE) will return true.

Although the output destination can be expressed as a URI, this must be a writable destination. In practice this usually means it should be a URI that uses the «file:» prefix, but it could potentially be an ftp or WebDAV destination. If you're running the processor in an applet, writing the output to a file is probably not feasible. The specification doesn't say what happens if you supply a relative URI, but since relative URIs are not allowed in a SAX InputSource, on which this class is modeled, it's best to avoid them. Some processors might interpret a relative URI as being relative to the current directory.

The class has constructors for each of the possible output destinations. The constructor for a String expects the string to contain a system identifier (URL).

```
StreamResult()
StreamResult(File)
StreamResult(java.io.OutputStream)
StreamResult(String)
StreamResult(java.io.Writer)
```

The methods are straightforward:

Method	Description
java.io.OutputStream getOutputStream()	Gets the binary output stream
String getSystemId()	Gets the system identifier
java.io.Writer getWriter()	Gets the Writer (character output stream)
void setOutputStream (java.io.OutputStream)	Sets the binary output stream
void setSystemId(java.io.File)	Sets output to go to the specified file, by setting the system identifier to the URL of this file
void setSystemId(String)	Specifies the system identifier of the output, as a URL
void setWriter(java.io.Writer)	Specifies the Writer (character output stream) to receive the output

javax.xml.transform.Templates

A Templates object represents a compiled stylesheet. Compiled stylesheets cannot be saved on a disk, but they are held in memory and can be used as often as required. To use a Templates object to perform a transformation, first create a Transformer by calling its newTransformer() method, then configure the `Transformer` as required (for example, setting its parameters and output properties), and then run the transformation using the `Transformer.transform()` method.

The methods available on the `Templates` object are:

Method	Description
`java.util.Properties` `getOutputProperties()`	Returns a `Properties` object representing the names and values of the output properties defined using `<xsl:output>` elements in the stylesheet. The keys of these properties will be strings defined in the `OutputKeys` class; the values will be the values defined in the stylesheet. Note that output properties that are determined dynamically will not be returned: For example, if the method attribute of `<xsl:output>` is defaulted, the system doesn't know at compile time whether the output will be XML or HTML
`Transformer newTransformer()` `[TCE]`	Creates a `Transformer` object, which can be used to effect the transformation defined in this stylesheet

javax.xml.transform.sax.TemplatesHandler

A `TemplatesHandler` is a SAX `ContentHandler` that treats the stream of SAX events supplied to it as the contents of a stylesheet. When the full document has been supplied, the stylesheet is compiled, and the compiled stylesheet can be retrieved using the `getTemplates()` method.

This provides an alternative to calling `TransformerFactory.newTemplates()` and supplying a `SAXSource` as the source of the stylesheet. The case for using a `TemplatesHandler` arises when the source of the SAX events is something other than a SAX `XMLReader`; for example, when the stylesheet is the output of another transformation, in which case the source of the SAX events is a JAXP `Transformer`. In this situation the `TemplatesHandler` can be wrapped into a `SAXResult` and used as the `Result` of the earlier transformation.

A `TemplatesHandler` is always created using the `newTemplatesHandler()` method of a `SAXTransformerFactory`. It provides the following methods in addition to those defined in the SAX `ContentHandler` interface:

Method	Description
`String getSystemId()`	Gets the system identifier of the stylesheet
`Templates getTemplates()`	Returns the `Templates` object created by compiling the supplied document as a stylesheet

Continues

Method	Description
`void setSystemId()`	Sets the system identifier of the stylesheet. A system identifier is needed if relative URIs (for example in `<xsl:include>` or `<xsl:import>` elements) need to be resolved

javax.xml.transform.TransformerFactoryConfigurationError

A `TransformerFactoryConfigurationError` (the specification writers must be good typists) represents an error in configuring the XSLT processor, as distinct from an error in the stylesheet itself.

Note that this is an `Error` rather than an `Exception`, which means that an application is not expected to take any recovery action.

The only methods available are:

Method	Description
`String getMessage()`	Gets the error message
`Exception getException()`	Gets any nested exception

javax.xml.transform.Transformer

A `Transformer` represents the collection of resources needed to perform a transformation of a `Source` to a `Result`. This includes the compiled stylesheet, the parameter values, and the output properties, as well as details such as an `ErrorListener` and a `URIResolver`.

This interface is analogous to the `IXSLProcessor` class in Microsoft's MSXML3 API.

A `Transformer` is always created by calling the `newTransformer()` method of either the `Templates` object, or the `TransformerFactory` object.

A transformer can be used to perform more than one transformation, but it is not thread-safe: You should not start one transformation until another has finished. If you want to perform several transformations in parallel, obtain several `Transformers` from the same `Templates` object.

The principal method is `transform()`, which takes two arguments, representing the `Source` and the `Result`. There are several different kinds of `Source` defined, and several kinds of `Result`. These are described elsewhere in this appendix.

The full set of methods is as follows. The exception codes `[IAE]` and `[TE]` refer to `IllegalArgumentException` and `TransformerException` respectively.

Method	Description
`void clearParameters()`	Clears all parameter set using `setParameter()`
`ErrorListener getErrorListener()`	Gets the `ErrorListener` for this transformation

Method	Description
`java.util.Properties getOutputProperties() [IAE]`	Gets the output properties defined for this transformation. This will be a combination of those defined in the stylesheet and those defined using `setOutputProperty()` and `setOutput Properties()`
`String getOutputProperty(String) [IAE]`	Gets a specific output property defined for this transformation. The argument should be one of the constants defined in `OutputKeys`, or a vendor-specific property name
`Object getParameter(String)`	Gets the value of a parameter defined for this transformation
`URIResolver getURIResolver()`	Gets the `URIResolver` used for this transformation, or null if none has been supplied
`void setErrorListener(ErrorListener) [IAE]`	Sets the `ErrorListener` to be used to handle errors reported during this transformation
`void setOutputProperties( java.util.Properties) [IAE]`	Sets output properties for the result of this transformation. These properties override any values set using `<xsl:output>` in the stylesheet. The property names will normally be constants defined in `OutputKeys`, or vendor-defined properties, but they can also be user-defined properties provided they are namespace-qualified. Names are namespace-qualified using the «{uri}localname» notation, in the same way as parameters
`void setOutputProperty( String, String) [IAE]`	Sets the value of a specific output property for the result of this transformation
`void setParameter(String, Object)`	Supplies a parameter for the transformation. The first argument corresponds to the parameter name, as defined in a global `<xsl:param>` element in the stylesheet; if this is namespace-qualified, it should be written in the form «{uri}local-name». The second argument is the parameter value. It's not defined in the JAXP 1.2 specification what the mapping from Java objects to XPath data types is: JAXP 1.3 is likely to have more to say on this subject. Using a `String`, a `Double`, a `Boolean`, or a DOM `Node` is likely to work in most processors, but beyond this, it depends on the implementation

Continues

Method	Description
void setURIResolver(URIResolver)	Sets the URIResolver to be used to resolve all URIs encountered during this transformation, especially when evaluating the document() function
void transform(Source, Result) [TE]	Performs the transformation. Source and Result are interfaces, allowing a wide range of different types of Source and Result to be supplied

javax.xml.transform.TransformerConfigurationException

This class defines a compile-time error, generally an error in the stylesheet. It is a subclass of TransformerException and has the same methods as its parent class, TransformerException.

There are several constructors defined, but since this object will usually be created by the XSLT processor itself, I won't list them here.

javax.xml.transform.TransformerException

A TransformerException represents an error that might be detected either at compile-time or at runtime. The exception may contain any or all of the following:

❑ A message explaining the error.

❑ A nested exception, generally containing additional information about this error. (Actually, despite the name getException(), this need not be an Exception object: It can be any Throwable, allowing an Error as well as an Exception.)

❑ A SourceLocator, indicating where in the stylesheet the error occurred.

❑ A cause. This is likely to be the same as the nested exception. Nested exceptions were introduced in JAXP before they became a standard Java feature in JDK 1.4, which is why there are two methods that appear to do the same thing.

There are several constructors defined, but since this object will usually be created by the XSLT processor itself, I won't list them here.

The methods available are:

Method	Description
Throwable getCause()	Gets the cause of the exception, if any
Throwable getException()	Gets the nested exception, if any
String getLocationAsString()	Constructs a String representing the location of the error
SourceLocator getLocator()	Gets the SourceLocator, if any, that identifies where the error occurred

Method	Description
String getMessageAndLocation()	Constructs a String that combines information about the error and information about where it occurred
void initCause(Throwable)	Sets the cause of this exception
void setLocator (SourceLocator)	Sets a SourceLocator identifying where the error occurred

javax.xml.transform.TransformerFactory

Like the SAXParserFactory and DocumentBuilderFactory in the javax.xml.parsers package, described in the first part of this appendix, this factory class enables you to select a specific vendor's XSLT implementation.

The first thing an application must do is obtain a TransformerFactory, which it can do by calling the static method TransformerFactory.newInstance(). Different vendors of XSLT processors will each implement their own subclass of TransformerFactory, and this method call determines which vendor's processor your application will end up using. If there are several available, the one that is used is based on the following decision process:

1. Use the value of the system property javax.xml.transform.TransformerFactory if it is available. You can set system properties using the -D option on the Java command line, or by calling System.setProperty() from your application.

2. Look for a properties file $JAVA_HOME/lib/jaxp.properties, and within this file, for the property named javax.xml.parsers.TransformerFactory.

3. Use the services API, which is part of the JAR specification. This generally means that the first processor found on the classpath will be used.

It is likely that when you install a particular XSLT processor, it will contain a file in its .jar archive that makes that particular processor the default, so if you don't do anything to select a specific processor, the one chosen will depend on the order of files and directories on your class path.

JDK 1.4 includes a copy of Xalan in its core libraries. This doesn't stop you using any of the techniques above to load a different XSLT processor, such as Saxon. What can be slightly tricky, however, is to use a later version of Xalan than the one included with the JDK. The easiest way to achieve this is to copy xalan.jar into a specially recognized directory for endorsed code, such as j2sdk1.4.0/jre/lib/endorsed/xalan.jar.

Once you have got a TransformerFactory, you can use a number of methods to configure it. Finally, you can call the newTemplates() method to compile a stylesheet, or the new Transformer() method to obtain a Transformer directly (if you only want to use the compiled stylesheet once).

The methods available are shown below. As with other methods, the exceptions thrown are indicated by a list of codes, which are explained in the table on page 816 at the start of this appendix.

Method	Description
`Source getAssociatedStyleSheet(Source doc, String media, String title, String charset)` `[TCE]`	Within the XML source document identified by the Source argument, finds the `<?xml-stylesheet ?>` processing instruction corresponding to the `media`, `title`, and `charset` parameters (any of which may be null), and returns a `Source` representing this stylesheet
`Object getAttribute(String)` `[IAE]`	Gets a vendor-specific configuration property
`ErrorListener getErrorListener()`	Gets the default error listener that will be used for transformations. If none has been set, this will be a vendor-supplied `ErrorListener`
`boolean getFeature(String)`	Gets information about the features supported by this implementation. Features are defined by constants within other classes, for example `getFeature(SAXResult.FEATURE)` returns `true` if the processor supports output to a SAX `ContentHandler`
`URIResolver getURIResolver()`	Gets the default `URIResolver` that will be used for transformations
`static TransformerFactory newInstance()` `[TFCE]`	Returns an instance of the vendor-specific `TransformerFactory`, selected according to the rules given above
`Templates newTemplates(Source)` `[TCE]`	Compiles the stylesheet provided in the given `Source`, returning a `Templates` object as a representation of the compiled stylesheet
`Transformer newTransformer()` `[TCE]`	Creates a `Transformer` that will perform an identity transformation
`Transformer newTransformer(Source)` `[TCE]`	A shortcut method equivalent to calling `newTemplates(Source)` `.newTransformer()`
`void setAttribute(String, Object)` `[IAE]`	Sets a vendor-specific configuration property
`void setErrorListener(ErrorListener)` `[IAE]`	Defines the `ErrorListener` to be used for error handling
`void setURIResolver(URIResolver)`	Defines the `URIResolver` to be used for resolving URIs contained in the stylesheet or source document

javax.xml.transform.sax.TransformerHandler

A `TransformerHandler` receives SAX events representing a source document. It performs a transformation on this source document, and writes the results of the transformation to a given `Result` object.

The `TransformerHandler` interface extends three SAX event handling interfaces: the `ContentHandler`, the `LexicalHandler`, and the `DTDHandler` It needs to act as a `LexicalHandler` so that it can handle comments in the source document, and it needs to act as a `DTDHandler` so that it can ignore comments in the DTD and so that it can find out about unparsed entity declarations in the DTD.

Using a `TransformerHandler` is an alternative to creating a `Transformer` and using a `SAXSource` to define the input document. This alternative approach is particularly useful when the source of SAX events is something other than a SAX `XMLReader`. For example, the source of SAX events might be another JAXP transformation, or it might be any other piece of software that allows a `ContentHandler` to be nominated to receive results.

A `TransformerHandler` is always created using the `newTransformerHandler()` method of a `SAXTransformerFactory`.

In addition to the methods defined in the SAX `ContentHandler`, `LexicalHandler`, and `DTDHandler` interfaces, a `TransformerHandler` offers the following methods:

Method	Description
`String getSystemId()`	Gets the system identifier defined for the source document
`Transformer getTransformer()`	Gets the underlying Transformer. This can be used to set parameters and output properties for the transformation
`void setResult(Result)` `[IAE]`	Sets the output destination for the transformation
`void setSystemId(String)`	Sets the system identifier for the source document. This will be used as a base URI to resolve any relative URIs contained in the document

javax.xml.transform.URIResolver

`URIResolver` is an interface; you can write a class that implements this interface and supply it to the `setURIResolver()` method of the `TransformerFactory` or `Transformer` class. When the XSLT processor has to find an XML document using a URI specified in `<xsl:include>`, `<xsl:import>`, or in the `document()` function, it will call any user-supplied `URIResolver` to do the work. The `URIResolver` can treat the URI any way it likes, and it returns the required document as a `Source` object: typically a `SAXSource`, a `DOMSource`, or a `StreamSource`.

For example, if the stylesheet called «`document('db:employee=517541')`», your `URIResolver` could interpret this URI as a database query and return an XML document containing the result as a rowset.

The interface defines only one method:

Method	Description
`Source resolve(String, String)` `[TE]`	The first argument is a relative URI, the second is the base URI against which it is resolved. The method returns a `Source` containing the requested document, or throws a `TransformerException` if it cannot retrieve it. It may also return null, indicating that the default `URIResolver` should be used

Note: There is a practical problem that the JAXP interface does not address, namely the XSLT rule that if you call the `document()` function twice to fetch the same absolute URI, the same document should be returned each time. Since the `URIResolver` accepts the relative URI and base URI as separate arguments, but does not actually return an absolute URI, it's not entirely clear whether it is the responsibility of the processor or the `URIResolver` to enforce this rule, especially when the URI is in a format that the XSLT processor itself does not recognize, as in the example above.

Note also that the arguments are supplied in the opposite order to those of the Java `java.net.URI` class.

Examples

This section provides some simple examples of applications that use the JAXP API in different ways to control a transformation.

Example 1: Transformation Using Files

This example (`FileTransform.java`) performs a single transformation, reading the source document and stylesheet from files, and sending the XML output to another file.

```java
import javax.xml.transform.*;
import javax.xml.transform.stream.*;
import java.io.File;

public class FileTransform {

    public static void main(String[] args) throws Exception {
        String source = new File(args[0]).toURI().toString();
        String style = new File(args[1]).toURI().toString();
        String out = new File(args[2]).toURI().toString();

        TransformerFactory factory = TransformerFactory.newInstance();
        Transformer t = factory.newTransformer(new StreamSource(style));
        t.transform(new StreamSource(source), new StreamResult(out));
    }
}
```

This is a minimal JAXP application.

Note that rather than supply `File` objects to the JAXP `StreamSource` and `StreamResult` constructors, I have converted the files to URIs within the application. Converting file names to URIs is not a straightforward process, and in my experience the `File.toURI()` method is the preferred way of doing it.

The Java examples in this section are provided on the Wrox Web site download for this book in source form only. This is deliberate: You'll learn more if you have to compile them before running them. In particular, you need to have a JAXP-conformant XSLT processor such as Saxon or Xalan properly installed and on your classpath, and if you haven't got this right, you'll get much clearer error messages when you try to compile the code than you get when you try to run it.

Assuming you have installed the Sun Java JDK, you can compile this application by the command:

```
javac FileTransform.java
```

This assumes that the directory containing the Java source file is the current directory. Once you have compiled the code, you can run it from the command line, for example:

```
java FileTransform source.xml style.xsl out.html
```

Of course, this is not a very professionally written application. It will fall over with a stack trace if incorrect arguments are supplied, if either of the input files doesn't exist, or if errors occur during the transformation: But it's a start. My aim in these examples is to show how the main JAXP classes work, not to teach you professional Java programming.

Because some people like to type examples exactly as they are written in the book, the folder containing the Java applications also contains specimen XML and XSL files called `source.xml` and `style.xsl`. So if you make this folder your current directory, you should be able to type the command line above exactly as shown. But, of course, the Java application will handle any source file and any stylesheet.

In my examples, I've supplied relative URIs such as source.xml as arguments. Many of the examples in the JAXP 1.2 specification do the same, and both Saxon and Xalan accept them. But this will probably only work if the SAX parser accepts a relative URI as the system identifier supplied to an InputSource object, despite the fact that the SAX specification states explicitly that it ought to be an absolute URI.

Example 2: Supplying Parameters and Output Properties

This example, `Parameters.java`, enhances the previous example:

❑ It allows a stylesheet parameter to be supplied from the command line.

❑ It modifies the output properties defined in the stylesheet.

❑ It directs the output to `System.out` instead of a file.

The `main()` method of the enhanced application looks like this:

```
public static void main(String[] args) throws Exception {
    String source = new File(args[0]).toURI().toString();
    String style = new File(args[1]).toURI().toString();
    String title = args[2];

    TransformerFactory factory = TransformerFactory.newInstance();
    Transformer t = factory.newTransformer(new StreamSource(style));
    t.setParameter("title", title);
    t.setOutputProperty(OutputKeys.INDENT, "no");
    t.transform(new StreamSource(source), new StreamResult(System.out));
}
```

This version of the program can be run using a command such as the following. The third argument on the command line (written in quotes because it contains spaces) is now a parameter value for the stylesheet, instead of the output file name.

```
java Parameters source.xml style.xsl "New organization structure"
```

Comparing the output with that of the previous example, note that the HTML is no longer indented, and that the contents of the <title> and <h1> elements have changed. And, of course, the output is written to the console this time.

Example 3: Holding Documents in Memory

In this example we will hold both the stylesheet and the source document in memory so they can be used repeatedly. In principle this would allow us to run different source documents past the same stylesheet, or to use different stylesheets to transform the same source document, but in practice, to keep the example simple, we'll use the same source document and stylesheet repeatedly, changing only the parameters to the transformation. We'll do one transformation using each of the parameters supplied on the command line.

To keep the source document in memory, create a DOM. The natural way of doing this would be to use the `DocumentBuilder` class defined in the first section of this appendix; But I'd prefer to stick to using the `javax.xml.transform` interfaces in these examples, so I'll do it in a different way. JAXP makes it very easy to do an identity transform, and to build the DOM, all you need is an identity transform that takes the serial file as input and produces the DOM as output.

You could also keep the stylesheet in memory as a DOM, but this would mean validating and compiling it each time it is used. It's better to keep the compiled stylesheet, that is, the `Templates` object.

The main program of this example (`Repeat.java`) looks like this:

```
public static void main(String[] args) throws Exception {
    String source = new File(args[0]).toURI().toString();
    String style = new File(args[1]).toURI().toString();
```

```
TransformerFactory factory = TransformerFactory.newInstance();

// Build a DOM using an identity transform
Transformer builder = factory.newTransformer();
DOMResult result = new DOMResult();
builder.transform(new StreamSource(source), result);
Document doc = (Document)result.getNode();

// Compile the stylesheet
Templates templates = factory.newTemplates(new StreamSource(style));

// do one transformation for each parameter supplied
for (int i=2; i<args.length; i++) {
    Transformer t = templates.newTransformer();
    System.out.println("======= TITLE = " + args[i] + "=======");
    t.setParameter("title", args[i]);
    t.transform(new StreamSource(source), new StreamResult(System.out));
}
}
```

You can run this application from the command line with a command such as:

```
java Repeat source.xml style.xsl one two three four
```

This will run the transformation four times, producing output HTML with the title set to «one», «two», «three», and «four» in turn.

This application is quite unrealistic, but the same principle of keeping source documents and stylesheets in memory can often be used to achieve significant performance benefits in a servlet environment.

Example 4: Using the <?xml-stylesheet?> Processing Instruction

The previous examples have all specified the source document and the stylesheet separately. However, as you saw in Chapter 3, it is possible for a source XML document to identify its preferred stylesheet using an <?xml-stylesheet?> processing instruction at the start of the source XML. This example shows how to extract the relevant stylesheet using the JAXP API: specifically, the getAssociatedStyle sheet() method provided by the TransformerFactory object.

The main() method of this example (Associated.java) is:

```
public static void main(String[] args) throws Exception {
    String input = new File(args[0]).toURI().toString();
    StreamSource source = new StreamSource(input);

    TransformerFactory factory = TransformerFactory.newInstance();

    // Get the associated stylesheet for the source document
```

```
        Source style = factory.getAssociatedStylesheet(source, null, null, null);

        // Use this to do the transformation

        Transformer t = factory.newTransformer(style);
        t.transform(source, new StreamResult(System.out));
    }
```

Specifying null values for the media, title, and charset arguments of `getAssociatedStylesheet()` selects the default stylesheet for the document. If the document has multiple `<?xml-stylesheet?>` processing instructions it is possible to use these parameters to choose more selectively.

You can run this example with the command:

```
java Associated source.xml
```

Example 5: A SAX Pipeline

It can often be useful to place an XSLT transformation within a SAX pipeline. A pipeline consists of a series of stages, each of which implements the SAX2 interface `XMLFilter`. The filters are connected together so that each filter looks like a SAX2 `ContentHandler` (a receiver of SAX events) to the previous stage in the pipeline, and looks like an `XMLReader` (a supplier of SAX events) to the following stage. Some of these filters might be XSLT filters, others might be written in Java or implemented using other tools.

In our example (`Pipeline.java`) we will use a pipeline that contains a source (the XML parser), three filters, and a sink (a serializer). The first filter will be a Java-written `XMLFilter` whose job is to convert all the element names in the document to upper case, recording the original name in an attribute. The second filter is an XSLT transformation that copies some elements through unchanged and removes others, based on the value of another attribute. The final filter is another Java-written `XMLFilter` that restores the element names to their original form.

I've invented this example for the purpose of illustration, but there is some rationale behind it. In XML, upper case and lower case are distinct, so <b> and <B> are quite distinct element names. But the legacy of HTML means you may sometimes want to do a transformation in which <b> and <B> are handled in the same way. This isn't easy to achieve in XSLT (it's easier in XSLT 2.0, but still clumsy), so do the pre- and postprocessing in Java to get round this.

Start with the two Java-written `XMLFilter` classes. These are written as subclasses of the SAX helper class `XMLFilterImpl`. You only need to implement the `startElement()` and `endElement()` methods; the other methods simply pass the events through unchanged.

The prefilter looks like this. It normalizes the name of the element to lower case, and saves the supplied local name and QName as additional attributes.

```
private class PreFilter extends XMLFilterImpl {

    public void startElement (String uri, String localName,
                              String qName, Attributes atts)
    throws SAXException {
```

```
            String newLocalName = localName.toLowerCase();
            String newQName = qName.toUpperCase();
            AttributesImpl newAtts =
                (atts.getLength()>0 ?
                    new AttributesImpl(atts) :
                    new AttributesImpl());
            newAtts.addAttribute("", "old-local-name",
                        "old-local-name", "CDATA", localName);
            newAtts.addAttribute("", "old-qname",
                        "old-qname", "CDATA", qName);
            super.startElement(uri, newLocalName, newQName, newAtts);
        }

        public void endElement (String uri, String localName,
                                        String qName)
        throws SAXException {
            String newLocalName = localName.toLowerCase();
            String newQName = qName.toUpperCase();
            super.endElement(uri, newLocalName, newQName);
        }
    }
```

The postfilter is very similar; the only difference is that because the original element name is needed by the endElement() code as well as startElement(), the startElement() code (which gets the names from the attribute list) saves them on a stack where endElement can pick them up later.

```
private class PostFilter extends XMLFilterImpl {

    public Stack stack;

    public void startDocument() throws SAXException {
        stack = new Stack();
        super.startDocument();
    }

    public void startElement (String uri, String localName, String qName,
                                    Attributes atts)
    throws SAXException {
        String originalLocalName = localName;
        String originalQName = qName;
        AttributesImpl newAtts = new AttributesImpl();
        for (int i=0; i<atts.getLength(); i++) {
            String name = atts.getQName(i);
            String val = atts.getValue(i);
            if (name.equals("old-local-name")) {
                originalLocalName = val;
            } else if (name.equals("old-qname")) {
                originalQName = val;
            } else {
                newAtts.addAttribute(
                            atts.getURI(i),
                            atts.getLocalName(i),
                            name,
```

```
                              atts.getType(i),
                              val);
            }
        }
        super.startElement(uri, originalLocalName, originalQName, newAtts);
        stack.push(originalLocalName);
        stack.push(originalQName);
    }

    public void endElement (String uri, String localName, String qName)
    throws SAXException {
        String originalQName = (String)stack.pop();
        String originalLocalName = (String)stack.pop();
        super.endElement(uri, originalLocalName, originalQName);
    }
}
```

Now you can build the pipeline, which actually has five components:

1. The XML `parser` itself, which you can get using the `ParserFactory` mechanism described at the start of this appendix.

2. The prefilter.

3. The XSLT transformation, constructed using the stylesheet held in `filter.xsl`.

4. The postfilter.

5. The serializer. The serializer is obtained from the `TransformerFactory` and is actually a `TransformerHandler` that performs an identity transformation with a `StreamResult` as its output.

As with any SAX2 pipeline, the first stage is an `XMLReader`, the last is a `ContentHandler`, and each of the intermediate stages is an `XMLFilter`. Each stage is linked to the previous stage using `setParent()`, except that the `ContentHandler` at the end is linked in by calling `setContentHandler()` on the last `XMLFilter`. Finally, the pipeline is activated by calling the `parse()` method on the last `XMLFilter`, which in our case is the postfilter.

Here is the code that builds the pipeline and runs a supplied source file through it:

```
public void run(String input) throws Exception {
    StreamSource source = new StreamSource(new File(input));
    File style = new File("filter.xsl");

    TransformerFactory factory = TransformerFactory.newInstance();
    if (!factory.getFeature(SAXTransformerFactory.FEATURE_XMLFILTER)) {
        System.err.println("SAX Filters are not supported");
    } else {
        SAXTransformerFactory saxFactory = (SAXTransformerFactory)factory;
        XMLFilter pre = new PreFilter();

        // substitute your chosen SAX2 parser here, or use the
        // SAXParserFactory to get one
        pre.setParent(new com.icl.saxon.aelfred.SAXDriver());
```

```
            XMLFilter filter = saxFactory.newXMLFilter(new StreamSource(style));
            filter.setParent(pre);

            XMLFilter post = new PostFilter();
            post.setParent(filter);

            TransformerHandler serializer = saxFactory.newTransformerHandler();
            serializer.setResult(new StreamResult(System.out));
            Transformer trans = serializer.getTransformer();
            trans.setOutputProperty(OutputKeys.METHOD, "xml");
            trans.setOutputProperty(OutputKeys.INDENT, "yes");
            post.setContentHandler(serializer);
            post.parse(source.getSystemId());
        }
    }
```

For the example I've given the class a trivial main program as follows:

```
    public static void main(String[] args) throws Exception {
        new Pipeline().run(args[0]);
    }
```

And you can execute it as:

```
    java Pipeline mixed-up.xml
```

The results are sent to standard output.

Summary

In this appendix I have given an overview of the JAXP interfaces.

I started, for the sake of completeness, with a quick tour of the JAXP facilities for controlling SAX and DOM parsers, found in package `javax.xml.parsers`.

I then gave detailed descriptions of the classes and methods in the package `javax.xml.transform` and its subsidiary packages.

Finally, I showed some simple examples of JAXP in action, in extremely simple applications.

Saxon

Saxon is an implementation of XSLT 2.0 produced by the author of this book, Michael Kay. Recent releases of Saxon also include an XQuery processor. At the time of writing this appendix, Saxon is the only reasonably complete implementation of XSLT 2.0 available (Oracle and Apache have both made it clear that implementations are underway, but have not yet delivered products).

I will refer to the version of Saxon that implements XSLT 2.0 as Saxon 8.0, though you should check the Web site for details on the latest version as releases are frequent. Saxon 8.0 is available in two variants, corresponding to the two conformance levels defined in the W3C specification. The open-source version is available at http://saxon.sf.net/, and this aims to meet all the requirements for a Basic XSLT Processor—which essentially means an XSLT processor without support for XML Schema. A schema-aware version of the product, which aims to conform to the higher conformance level defined by W3C, is undergoing beta-testing, and will become available as a commercial product from http://www.saxonica.com/.

There is also an older version of Saxon available, version 6.5.3, which implements the XSLT 1.0 specification. The older version is also available at http://saxon.sf.net/. This appendix is concerned only with the XSLT 2.0 processor.

Saxon is written in Java and requires JDK 1.4. It should run successfully on any platform that supports this (or a later) Java release, and there are no other dependencies.

Installing Saxon is simple: Create a suitable directory (say c:\saxon) and unzip the distribution file into this directory. Look for the JAR file containing the saxon classes (for example c:\saxon\saxon8.jar) and add this file to the Java classpath. Remember to add the actual JAR file to the classpath, not the directory that contains the JAR file. (The classpath is an environment variable called CLASSPATH. The way you set this depends on your operating system. Under Windows XP, for example, go to Settings/Control Panel/System/Advanced/Environment Variables. If there is already an environment variable called CLASSPATH, click Edit to change its value, adding the new entries separated by semicolons from the existing entries. Otherwise, click New either under User Variables if you want to change the settings only for the current user, or under System Variables if you want to change settings for all users. Enter CLASSPATH as the name of the variable, and a list of directories and/or .jar files, separated by semicolons, as the value.)

Saxon doesn't include its own XML parser. It will work with any parser that implements SAX2. By default it picks up the Crimson parser, which is a standard component of JDK 1.4.

Invoking the Saxon Processor

Saxon is written in Java, and implements the JAXP API defined in JAXP 1.2, which is described in detail in Appendix D. This allows it to be invoked from a Java application. There is also a command line interface. In addition, Saxon provides a servlet wrapper allowing a stylesheet to be invoked directly from a URL entered at a browser; however, this is more in the nature of a demonstration application than a real part of the product.

There is no graphical user interface; however, Saxon can be used with visual tools such as Stylus Studio (http://www.sonicsoftware.com) or XMLSpy (http://www.xmlspy.com) to provide a friendlier front end.

Using Saxon from the Command Line

If you are using Saxon on a Windows platform (and even more so if you are running on a Mac), then you may not be accustomed to using the command line to run applications. You can do this from the standard MS-DOS console that comes with Windows, but I wouldn't recommend it because it's too difficult to correct your typing mistakes and to stop output scrolling off the screen. It is far better to install a text editor that includes a Windows-friendly command line capability. I use the open-source jEdit editor (from www.jedit.org), mainly because it has good Unicode support. For jEdit you'll need to install the Console plugin, which is an optional component.

You can then run a transformation using Saxon. Assuming all the files are in your current directory, you can use the command

```
java -jar saxon8.jar source.xml style.xsl
```

which will send the output of the transformation to the standard output (that is, to the console window).

This runs the main program contained in the JAR file, which is «net.sf.saxon.Transform» (or «com.saxonica.Transform» for the schema-aware version of the product). You can also invoke this entry point directly, once you have successfully added the JAR file to the classpath, by writing:

```
java net.sf.saxon.Transform source.xml style.xsl
```

You will need to use this form if your stylesheet tries to load extension functions from the classpath.

There are a number of options you can use on the command line. These are written immediately before the name of the source file, for example:

```
java net.sf.saxon.Transform -t -w2 source.xml style.xsl
```

The command line options are as follows:

Option	Description
`-a`	Use the `<?xml-stylesheet?>` processing instruction in the source document to identify the stylesheet to be used. The stylesheet argument should then be omitted
`-c`	Indicates that the stylesheet parameter is not a source XML stylesheet, but a stylesheet that has been previously compiled using the `net.sf.saxon.Compile` command
`-ds` `-dt`	Selects the implementation of the internal tree model. `-dt` selects the "tinytree" model (the default). `-ds` selects the traditional tree model. This is a performance tuning option: The tinytree model is faster to build, and occupies less memory, but is sometimes slower to navigate. The default is `-dt`
`-im mode`	Specifies the initial mode: The transformation will start by looking for a template rule that matches the document node of the source document in the specified mode
`-it template`	Specifies the name of the initial template. The transformation will start by evaluating this named template. In this case, the source filename argument should be omitted (the stylesheet must obtain all the data it needs using the `document()` function, or via stylesheet parameters)
`-l`	Switches line numbering on for the source document. Line numbers are accessible through the extension function `saxon:line-number()`, or from a trace listener. Line numbering will be switched on automatically if the `-T` option is used
`-m classname`	Specifies the full name of a Java class used to process the output of `<xsl:message>` instructions in the stylesheet. Details are available in the Saxon documentation
`-noext`	This option prevents the stylesheet calling extension functions, which is an important security measure if the stylesheet code is untrusted
`-o filename`	Defines a filename to contain the output of the transformation. You must specify this option if the stylesheet creates multiple output files, as the filenames for secondary output files (created using `<xsl:result-document>`) will be interpreted relative to the location of this primary output file
`-r classname`	Specifies the full name of a Java class that implements the JAXP URIResolver interface: This will be used to resolve all URIs used in `<xsl:include>`, `<xsl:import>`, or in the `doc()` and `document()` functions

Continues

Option	Description
-t	This option causes Saxon to display information about the Saxon and Java versions in use, and progress messages indicating which files are being processed and how long the key stages of processing took
-T	Traces execution of the stylesheet. Each instruction is traced as it is executed, identifying the instruction and the current location in the source document by line number. The trace is written to System.err. It is written in the form of an XML document, so if you want to analyze the trace, you can write a stylesheet to do it
-TJ	Traces the loading of Java extension functions. This is a useful debugging aid if you are having problems in this area
-TL classname	Traces execution with a user-defined trace routine. Details are available in the Saxon documentation
-u	Indicates that the names of the source document and stylesheet given on the command line are to be interpreted as URLs rather than file names. (If the names start with «http:» or «file:», this will be assumed automatically)
-v	Requests the XML parser to perform DTD-based validation of all source documents
-val	Performs schema-based validation of all source documents. This option is available only with the schema-aware version of the Saxon product
-wN (where N is 0, 1 or 2)	Indicates how XSLT-defined recoverable errors are to be handled. w0 means recover silently; w1 means output a warning message and continue; and w2 means treat the error as fatal.
-x classname	Defines the XML parser to be used for the source document, and for any additional document loaded using the document() function. The classname must be the name of a parser that implements the SAX2 org.xml.sax.XMLReader interface
-y classname	Defines the XML parser to be used for the stylesheet document, and for any additional stylesheet module loaded using <xsl:include> or <xsl:import>. This parser is also used when parsing a schema. The classname must be the name of a parser that implements the SAX2 org.xml.sax.XMLReader interface

(Why would you want to use different parsers for the source document and the stylesheet? One reason is that the source document might not really be XML; see the GEDCOM example in Chapter 11. Another reason is that you might want to use a validating parser for the source document, but not for the stylesheet.)

You can specify values for global parameters defined in the stylesheet using a `keyword=value` notation; for example:

```
java net.sf.saxon.Transform source.xml style.xsl param1=value1
param2=value2
```

If the parameter names have a non-null namespace, you can use Clark notation for expanded names, for example «`{namespace-uri}local-name`». The parameter values are interpreted as strings. If the string contains a space, you should enclose it in quotes, for example «`param1="John Brown"`».

If you want to pass an XML document as a parameter to the stylesheet, you can do this by prefixing the parameter name with «+» and supplying the name of the XML file as the parameter value. For example:

```
java net.sf.saxon.Transform source.xml style.xsl +lookup=lookup.xml
```

The XML contained in `lookup.xml` will be parsed, and the document node of the resulting tree will be passed to the stylesheet as the value of the stylesheet parameter named «`lookup`».

You can also override `<xsl:output>` attributes using a similar notation, but prefixing the keyword with «!». For example, to get indented output write:

```
java net.sf.saxon.Transform source.xml style.xsl !indent=yes
```

Using Saxon from a Java Application

Saxon can be invoked from a Java application by using the JAXP API, which is described in Appendix D. This allows you to compile a stylesheet into a `Templates` object, which can then be used repeatedly (in series or in multiple threads) to process different source documents through the same stylesheet. This can greatly improve throughput on a Web server. A sample application to achieve this, in the form of a Java servlet, is provided with the product.

Saxon implements the whole of the `javax.xml.transform` package, including the `dom`, `sax`, and `stream` subpackages, both for input and output. It also implements the `SAXTransformerFactory`, which allows you to do the transformation as part of a SAX pipeline.

The `saxon8.jar` package includes a file that has the effect of causing the JAXP `TransformerFactory` to choose Saxon as the default XSLT processor. It can be tricky to ensure that Saxon is loaded, now that JDK 1.4 includes an XSLT implementation (Xalan) as a standard component. The best policy, if you require Saxon because your stylesheet is written in XSLT 2.0, is to select it explicitly. There are several ways this can be achieved:

❑　You can choose Saxon by setting the Java system property named `javax.xml.transform`
`.TransformerFactory` to the value `net.sf.saxon.TransformerFactoryImpl`. Use the

-D option on the Java command when you invoke your application. Note that this goes before the name of the class to be executed:

```
java -Djavax.xml.transform.TransformerFactory=
        net.sf.saxon.TransformerFactoryImpl com.my-com.appl.Program
```

This all goes on one line. In practice of course you won't want to type this more than once, so create a batch file or shell script using your text editor, and invoke this instead.

❏ Create a file called jaxp.properties within the directory $JAVA_HOME/lib (where $JAVA_HOME is the directory containing your Java installation), and include in this file a line of the form key=value, where key is the property key javax.xml.transform .TransformerFactory and value is the Saxon class net.sf.saxon .TransformerFactoryImpl.

❏ Put the call

```
System.setProperty ("javax.xml.transform.TransformerFactory",
                    "net.sf.saxon.TransformerFactoryImpl")
```

in your application, to be executed at runtime. This is the only technique that works if you want to run several different JAXP processors from the same application, perhaps in order to compare their results or to benchmark their performance.

If you want to control the choice of XML parser within your application, or to configure the setting of the XML parser, the best approach is to supply source documents in the form of a SAXSource, which encapsulates the XML parser (an instanceof org.xml.sax.XMLReader) to be used. To do this for documents loaded with the document() function, write your own custom URIResolver.

Saxon Tree Models

Saxon defines an internal interface, the NodeInfo interface, to represent the XPath data model, and it is capable of transforming any data source that supplies an implementation of this interface. There are four implementations of this interface available:

❏ The default is the tinytree, which as the name implies, is optimized for space, but also turns out to be the fastest implementation under many circumstances.

❏ The original model is called the Standard Tree, now something of a misnomer, which is sometimes faster to navigate than the tinytree but takes longer to build and occupies more space.

❏ There is an implementation of NodeInfo that wraps a standard level-2 DOM.

❏ There is another implementation of NodeInfo that wraps a JDOM tree (see www.jdom.org).

If none of these are suitable, you can in principle write your own. For example, you could write an implementation of NodeInfo that fetches the underlying data from a relational database.

Using XPath Expressions in Saxon

It's likely that JDK 1.5 will define a standard interface for executing XPath expressions from Java, but in the absence of a standard, Saxon provides its own API. The relevant classes are in package net.sf .saxon.xpath.

In outline, what you need to do is:

1. Create a JAXP `Source` object, for example:

```
SAXSource source = new SAXSource(new File("source.xml"));
```

2. Create an `XPathEvaluator`:

```
XPathEvaluator xpath = new XPathEvaluator(source);
```

3. If you want to define an expression that contains variables, declare the variables:

```
StandaloneContext sc = StandaloneContext)xpath.getStaticContext();
Variable param = sc.declareVariable("p","");
```

4. Define the XPath expression:

```
XPathExpression search =
                xpath.createExpression("//LINE[contains(., $p)]");
```

5. Set the values of the variables:

```
param.setValue("apple");
```

6. Evaluate the XPath expression:

```
List results = search.evaluate();
```

There are many variations on this theme: For example, you can get the results as an `Iterator` rather than as a `List`, and there is an `evaluateSingle()` method, which is useful when you know the XPath expression will return a single value.

Extensibility

In this section I will describe the facilities Saxon provides for user-written extension functions, and also the way that Saxon handles collations. Following this, I'll look at a few of the extension functions that come ready-supplied with the Saxon product.

For all these extensions, the namespace prefix «saxon» needs to be declared as «xmlns:saxon="http://saxon.sf.net/"».

Writing Extension Functions

Saxon allows you to write extension functions in Java, using mechanisms based on those that were defined in the since-abandoned XSLT 1.1 draft.

An external Java class may be defined using the `<saxon:script>` declaration. So, if you want to use methods in the class `java.util.Date`, you can define:

```
<saxon:script language="java"
               implements-prefix="Date"
               src="java:java.util.Date"/>
```

and then call a method or constructor such as

```
<xsl:variable name="today" select="Date:new()"/>
```

This returns an XPath value that is a wrapper for a Java object of class `java.util.Date`. Saxon maps Java classes into the XPath type hierarchy (as a new kind of atomic value), so you can declare the type of this value as:

```
<xsl:variable name="today" select="Date:new()"
              as="class:java.util.Date"
              xmlns:class="http://saxon.sf.net/java-type"/>
```

There is also a short-cut way of binding Java methods. If the namespace prefix `Date` is bound to a namespace URI such as `java:java.util.Date`, then the `<saxon:script>` element above is implicit. This means that you can make a call such as:

```
<xsl:variable name="today"
              select="Date:new()"
              xmlns:Date="java:java.util.Date"
              as="class:java.util.Date"
              xmlns:class="http://saxon.sf.net/java-type"/>
```

with no further declaration of the external class.

Saxon looks for methods in the specified class that have the right name and the right number of arguments, and if there is more than one, it tries to find the one that is the best fit to the arguments supplied. For convenience, a hyphenated XPath name such as `get-random-number()` is mapped to the camelCased Java name `getRandomNumber()`.

Collations

One of the new features in XSLT 2.0 and XPath 2.0 is that all comparison and sorting of strings can be controlled using collations. This is because the rules for sorting and comparison vary from one language (and one application) to another. Collations are identified using a URI; like namespace URIs, these are not expected to identify real resources on the Web, but simply act as globally unique identifiers.

The specifications say nothing about how collation URIs are established or what they mean, so each product has to devise its own naming scheme. This section explains how it's done in Saxon.

Java offers extensive support for defining collations, so the approach that Saxon adopts is to provide a parameterized URI that identifies an appropriately configured instance of class «java.lang.Collator», which is then used to perform the string comparisons. The collation URI takes the general form:

```
http://saxon.sf.net/collation?keyword=value;keyword=value;...
```

The parameters you are most likely to use are lang, which defines the required language (for example, «lang=sv» selects Swedish), and strength, which defines how sensitive the collation is to minor variations between characters. The four strengths are «primary», «secondary», «tertiary», and «identical». The difference between two different letters, such as «A» and «B», is considered a primary difference; upper case versus lower case is considered a secondary difference; and accents and other diacriticals represent tertiary differences. So a collation with «strength=primary» will ignore both case and accents, while «strength=secondary» will ignore accents but not case. Generally if you are matching words in natural language text, you should use a low-strength collation. But for sorting, a high-strength collation is appropriate: This will ensure that words that differ only in their accents are sorted in the correct way, even though they might compare equal in a search.

For other parameters that you can include in a Saxon collation URI, see the product documentation. If you want the ultimate in control, the collation URI can identify a user-written implementation of the «java.lang.Collator» interface.

Because collation URIs are unlikely to be portable across implementations, it's a good idea to define them as stylesheet parameters. For example, you can define a stylesheet parameter:

```
<xsl:param name="sorting-collation"
  select="'http://saxon.sf.net/collation?lang=de;strength=tertiary'"/>
```

and then use this in a sort, by specifying:

```
<xsl:sort select="value" collation="{$sorting-collation}"/>
```

You could also define the collation using a conditional expression, using the system-property() function to determine which vendor's XSLT processor is currently in use.

The evaluate() Extension

Many of the new facilities included in XSLT 2.0, including multiple output files, grouping facilities, and stylesheet functions, were first pioneered as Saxon extensions. Saxon also copied extensions that were first introduced elsewhere: The ubiquitous node-set() extension function, for example, appeared first in James Clark's xt processor, as did extensions to find the intersection or difference between two node sets. Saxon went further than most XSLT processors in providing a wide range of extensions built in to the product. However, most of these have been superseded by standard features in XSLT 2.0.

The most important extension that remains, which has sadly not made it into XSLT 2.0 even though it has been copied by several other processors, is the ability to evaluate a dynamically constructed XPath expression. This extension has been adopted, in restricted form, as the dyn:evaluate() function within EXSLT (see www.exslt.org). Here I will describe the Saxon implementation of this functionality.

In standard XSLT (even in 2.0), there is no way of constructing an XPath expression at runtime from a string. This makes it difficult to do things that are very familiar to SQL programmers, for example building a query from the values of parameters read from a form, or sorting a table on a column selected by the user. It also makes it impossible to interpret XPath expressions held as part of the text of the source document, perhaps implementing a subset of the XPointer specification for defining links between documents. The Saxon stored expression concept fills this gap: You can use the `saxon:expression()` extension function to create a stored expression from a string, and `saxon:eval()` to evaluate the stored expression; or you can combine these two operations into one using the `saxon:evaluate()` function.

The table below describes these functions in more detail.

Function	Explanation
expression(string)	This function constructs a stored expression from the XPath expression contained in the supplied string. The stored expression can be evaluated later using the `saxon:eval()` function
	If the XPath expression contains namespace prefixes, these are resolved at the time the stored expression is created, not at the time it is subsequently evaluated. (They are always resolved relative to namespaces declared in the stylesheet, which is not ideal when you want to evaluate an XPath expression contained in a source document)
	The expression may contain references to the variables $p1 to $p9. The values of these variables are supplied when the expression is subsequently evaluated
eval(expression, variables...)	This function evaluates a stored expression supplied in the first argument. The stored expression is constructed using the `saxon:expression()` function
	The second and subsequent arguments (which are optional) provide values that will be bound to the variables $p1..$p9 used within the stored expression
	The context node, position, and size for evaluating the expression are those that apply to the stylesheet at the point where `eval()` is called
evaluate(string, variables...)	This function combines the effect of `saxon:expression()` and `saxon:eval()` into a single call: That is, it prepares the expression and immediately evaluates it

Allowing XPath queries to be constructed dynamically gives a number of benefits:

❑ You can construct a query such as «`//book[author="Kay" and publisher="Wrox"]`», from the values of stylesheet parameters supplied at runtime.

❑ You can easily change the sort order used in an `<xsl:sort>` element based on parameters supplied at runtime.

❑ You can allow XPath expressions to be used within the source document, for example to define hyperlinks between documents, and you can write code in your stylesheet to follow these links. (However, there are limitations because of the way the namespace context is established).

❑ You can implement higher order functions in which a function is passed as a parameter to another function.

❑ You can use XPath expressions to define business rules in a separate document.

The following example demonstrates the last of these techniques.

Example: Using saxon:evaluate() to Apply Business Rules

In this example, we imagine a call center that is charging customers for the calls they make. We want to prepare the account for a period, listing all the calls and calculating the total charge.

Source

The list of calls is in the file `calls.xml`, as follows:

```
<calls>
<call date="2001-01-15" time="08.15" duration="17"/>
<call date="2001-01-16" time="10.42" duration="8"/>
<call date="2001-01-18" time="17.42" duration="5"/>
<call date="2001-01-18" time="22.10" duration="06"/>
<call date="2001-01-24" time="12.19" duration="41"/>
<call date="2001-01-25" time="06.40" duration="13"/>
<call date="2001-01-27" time="11.15" duration="26"/>
</calls>
```

We want to put the business rules for calculating the charges in a separate document. Of course, these rules could go in the stylesheet, but this isn't very good practice; mixing business rules and presentation rules in one place doesn't give the right separation of responsibilities. Instead, we'll put the relevant formula in a separate document `tariff.xml`, in the form of an XPath expression. This calculates the total charge, with different rates per minute during the working day and outside office hours:

```
<tariff>
  sum(call[@time &gt;= 08.00 and @time &lt; 18.00]/@duration) * 1.50
+
  sum(call[@time &lt; 08.00 or @time &gt;= 18.00]/@duration) * 2.50
</tariff>
```

Stylesheet

Most of the stylesheet (`account.xsl`) is conventional, and is concerned with displaying the information. When it comes to calculating the total charges, however, the stylesheet reads the XPath expression containing the relevant formula from the `tariff.xml` document, and evaluates it (using `saxon:evaluate()`) in the context of the source document.

```
<?xml version="1.0"?>
<xsl:stylesheet xmlns:xsl="http://www.w3.org/1999/XSL/Transform"
                xmlns:saxon="http://saxon.sf.net/"
                version="1.0">
```

```
<xsl:template match="/">
  <html>
    <head>
      <title>Account for period ending
            <xsl:value-of select="(//@date)[last()]"/></title>
    </head>
    <body>
      <h1>Account for period ending
            <xsl:value-of select="(//@date)[last()]"/></h1>
      <xsl:apply-templates/>
    </body>
  </html>
</xsl:template>

<xsl:template match="calls">
  <table>
    <tr>
      <th width="100">Date</th>
      <th width="100">Time</th>
      <th width="100">Duration</th>
    </tr>
    <xsl:apply-templates/>
  </table>
  <xsl:variable name="total"
              select="saxon:evaluate(document('tariff.xml'))"/>
  <p>Total charges for the period:
      <xsl:value-of select="format-number($total, '$###0.00')"/>
  </p>
</xsl:template>

<xsl:template match="call">
  <tr>
    <td><xsl:value-of select="@date"/></td>
    <td><xsl:value-of select="@time"/></td>
    <td><xsl:value-of select="@duration"/></td>
  </tr>
</xsl:template>

</xsl:stylesheet>
```

(An observation on this stylesheet: This was first written to work with XSLT 1.0. In principle, it could be rewritten to use the facilities for arithmetic on dates, times, and durations provided in XSLT 2.0. However, little would be gained by doing so. Converting the application to use these facilities would require times to be written as «xs:time('08:00: 00')» rather than as «08.00», which would also create a dependency on the declaration of the namespace prefix «xs». Also, multiplying a duration by a number in XPath 2.0 returns a duration, not a cost. Just because the facilities are provided doesn't mean that you have to use them, and in this case, it seems simpler not to.)

To run this stylesheet, make the directory containing the downloaded files for this chapter the current directory, and enter:

```
java -jar c:\saxon\saxon8.jar calls.xml account.xsl >bill.html
```

Output

The output of this stylesheet (bill.html) appears in the browser as shown in Figure E-1.

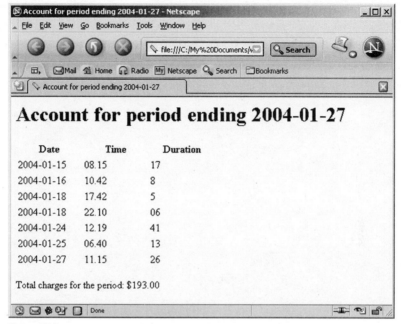

Figure E-1

Summary

This appendix describes how to install and use the Saxon product, and also describes some of the facilities provided by Saxon that go beyond the XSLT 2.0 specification itself.

At the time of writing this appendix, if you want to start taking advantage of XSLT 2.0, Saxon is your only option. I sincerely hope this situation will change in the months after publication.

Backwards Compatibility

This appendix summarizes the areas where XSLT 2.0 is not fully backwards compatible with XSLT 1.0. You can think of the transition from XSLT 1.0 to XSLT 2.0 as happening in three stages, though you may choose to do all three at once:

❏ The first stage takes the stylesheet unchanged, still specifying «version="1.0"», and runs it under an XSLT 2.0 processor instead of an XSLT 1.0 processor.

❏ The next stage is to change the stylesheet to specify «version="2.0"». This has the effect of switching off backwards compatibility mode.

❏ The final stage is to modify the stylesheet to take advantage of new facilities introduced in XSLT 2.0 and XPath 2.0: most notably, the ability to validate the source documents against a schema.

There is potential for transition problems to occur at each of these three stages. The focus in this appendix, however, is on the first two stages, because once you start changing your stylesheet or your application, it's very much under your own control whether existing code keeps working.

In this appendix we'll treat the XSLT changes and the XPath changes together.

Stage 1: Backwards Compatibility Mode

It sounds like a contradiction in terms to say that there are incompatibilities that can occur when you are running in backwards compatibility mode enabled (that is, with a stylesheet that specifies «version="1.0"»), but it is important to remember that even in this mode, you are using the XPath 2.0 data model rather than the XPath 1.0 data model and that this causes some inevitable differences.

We'll first look at the problems that can potentially occur at the XSLT level, and then at the XPath differences.

The First Node Rule

At the XSLT level, most of the incompatibilities relate to the dropping of the rule that you can supply a node set where a single value is expected, and the system will use the first node in the node set.

There are four specific situations where this can arise:

❑ With `<xsl:value-of>`

❑ With attribute value templates

❑ With sort keys

❑ With the `value` attribute of `<xsl:number>`

In all these cases XSLT 1.0 discards any selected node after the first, while XSLT 2.0 normally reports an error. In backwards compatibility mode, however, an XSLT 2.0 processor behaves like an XSLT 1.0 processor.

XPath, in backwards compatibility mode, generally retains the first node rule. This arises for example when calling a function such as `contains()`: If the first argument is a sequence of nodes, this is normally an error, but in backwards compatibility mode, the function is applied to the string value of the first node.

There has been some discussion about whether processors are actually required to report this error. There is a statement in the XPath specification that a processor is never required to do extra work merely in order to look for errors, and it therefore seems acceptable for a processor to display the first node found without taking the trouble to search to see whether there are any more. This question will probably be clarified in the final specifications.

If your stylesheets do fall foul of this change, it's easy to fix. If the current code is, for example, `<xsl:value-of select="//item"/>`, change it to `<xsl:value-of select="(//item)[1]"/>`. Remember to use parentheses where necessary.

Comparing Strings

In XSLT 1.0 testing for equality between two strings performed a strict comparison of the codepoints of the characters in the two strings. There was no flexibility to treat `"XML"` and `"xml"` as being equal. Sorting, however, was left very much up to the implementation: Two different products would likely sort the same set of strings differently. There was no «<» operator to compare strings, and no `min()` or `max()` function.

This changes significantly in XSLT 2.0 and XPath 2.0, though the amount of backwards incompatibility depends to a considerable extent on choices made by the vendor. The «=» operator, when comparing two strings, now uses the default collation. How the default collation is defined is up to the implementer, but it isn't necessarily the Unicode codepoint collation. Nor is it necessarily the same collation as is used by default to support `<xsl:sort>`. One area where products will necessarily be incompatible is that operators such as «<» and «>» in XPath 2.0, when given two strings or two nodes as their arguments, now do a string comparison rather than trying to convert both operands to numbers. This can catch you out with expressions like:

```
<xsl:if test="@price &lt; @margin">
```

Saxon will give you a warning if it encounters such a construct.

Numeric Precision

XPath 2.0 has (in effect) four numeric data types: double, float, decimal, and integer, whereas XPath 1.0 made do with a single type, double. Literals that were interpreted as doubles in XPath 1.0 (such as «3.5» or «17») may be interpreted as decimals or integers in XPath 2.0. This means that arithmetic that was carried out in floating point with XPath 1.0 may be carried out as decimal or integer arithmetic in XPath 2.0. The main thing you are likely to notice as a result is that you no longer get answers like «1.000000000054297», which arose because binary floating point numbers cannot hold all decimal values exactly. It's unlikely that this change will cause any adverse effects. However, if your stylesheets are numerically intensive, then the change in precision of the results could be noticeable.

Very large and very small floating point numbers are now output using scientific notation (or the programmer's variant of scientific notation), for example 1.5E-9. If this output format isn't acceptable, you can use the `format-number()` function to control the format you want.

There are some changes to the specification of `format-number()`. In most cases these are tightening up a specification that was previously rather vague in certain areas, but the result of this is that a conformant XSLT 2.0 may do things differently from the way that your favorite 1.0 processor interpreted the specification. XSLT 1.0 defined this function in terms of the Java JDK 1.1 `DecimalFormat` class, which left many details such as the rounding algorithm unspecified. Later JDK releases tightened this up, but there was no obligation for an XSLT 1.0 processor to implement these clarifications. And in one area the clarification was really formalizing a bug in the implementation: the fact that to a considerable extent, the negative subpicture was ignored when formatting a negative number. XSLT 2.0 has chosen to cut loose from the JDK on this, and now has its own specification for the function, which does not enshrine all the quirks of the Java version.

Other Changes

The previous sections cover the incompatibilities that you are most likely to encounter, but there are one or two other XSLT and XPath changes that are more obscure. There is information on further XPath changes in Appendix C of *XPath 2.0 Programmer's Reference*.

At the XSLT level you may find that the XSLT processor reports as errors some constructs that were previously ignored. For example, it is now an error to have a `mode` or `priority` attribute on an `<xsl:template>` element with no `match` attribute. It is also an error for the stylesheet to contain a call on a named template that doesn't exist (even if the call is never executed), and it's an error for `<xsl:call-template>` to supply a parameter value for a parameter that hasn't been declared on the called template.

You will find a detailed list of further changes in appendixes to the W3C specifications. Most of them are situations where it is extremely unlikely that real stylesheets have been written to depend on the 1.0 behavior, so I won't repeat all these corner cases here.

Stage 2: Setting version="2.0"

The next stage in your transition to XSLT 2.0 is to switch off backwards compatibility mode by setting the `version` attribute in the `<xsl:stylesheet>` element to «2.0». This section looks at what changes you should be prepared for when you do this. I'll assume here that you have fixed any problems that arose during stage 1: for example, that you have added a «[1]» predicate to any node sets used in <xsl:value-of> as suggested above.

At the XSLT level, there should be no further problems, given these assumptions.

In XPath, you will probably find that some expressions that previously worked now fail with type errors. For example, the expression «concat("Chapter", 5)» is no longer allowed, because the arguments to concat() have to be strings. Type errors may also arise because you supply a sequence of items where a singleton is expected. In all such cases, you can get round the problems by doing explicit conversions. For example, you can rewrite the above expression as «concat("Chapter", string(5))».

Stage 3: Adding a Schema

The output that an XSLT 2.0 stylesheet produces for a given source document can change if you validate the source document before transforming it. This section lists some of the changes that might occur:

❑   Processing a source document using a schema will cause attribute nodes with defaulted values to be added to the tree, and will cause element nodes with defaulted values to acquire a value. These extra nodes will be visible to the XSLT stylesheet.

❑   Because data is now typed rather than untyped, errors may be reported. For example if an attribute birthDate is defined in the schema to have type xs:date, then the expression «substring(@birthDate, 1, 4)» will fail with a type error, because the substring() function can be applied only to a string. The remedy is to convert the value to a string explicitly, using the string() function or a cast.

❑   The results of comparisons may change. The most noticeable effect will be with list-valued elements and attributes, where a comparison (using «=» or any of the other general comparison operators) now tests each item in the list of values independently, rather than testing the string value of the containing node as a whole.

❑   The results of sorting may change. For example, if the sort key has type «xs:dayTime Duration», then the values will be compared as durations, not as strings.

Conclusion

XSLT 2.0 is not 100% backwards compatible with version 1.0. Most stylesheets will convert with no changes at all, but a few will need tweaking. Moving a large application from XSLT 1.0 to 2.0 is an exercise that needs to be carefully planned, with detailed regression testing carried out to catch any obscure corner cases that might not show up immediately with the first few test runs.

Glossary

This glossary gathers together some of the more common technical terms used in this book. Most of these terms are defined in the XSLT or XPath specifications, but some of them are borrowed from XML or other standards in the XML family, and one or two have been invented for the purposes of this book. So for each definition, I also tell you where the term comes from.

The definitions in all cases are my own; in some cases the original specifications have a much more formal definition, but in other cases they are surprisingly vague.

Where a definition contains references to other terms defined in the glossary, these terms are written in italic.

ANCESTOR AXIS (*XPATH*)

The ancestor *axis* selects the *parent* of the *context node*, its *parent*, and so on, up to and including the *root node*. This *axis* is a *reverse axis*.

ANCESTOR-OR-SELF AXIS (*XPATH*)

The ancestor-or-self *axis* selects the *context node* followed by all the nodes on the *ancestor axis*. This axis is a *reverse axis*.

ARITY (*XPATH*)

The arity of a *function* is the number of *parameters* defined in the function signature: for example the arity of the function `true()` is zero, while the two versions of the `contains()` function have arity two and three respectively.

ATOMIC VALUE (*XPATH*)

An atomic value is an *item* such as an integer, a *string*, a date, or a *boolean*. Specifically, it is an instance of the class `xdt:anyAtomicType`, which includes all *simple types* (as defined in XML Schema) that are not *list types* or *union types*.

ATOMIZATION (*XPATH*)

Atomization is a process that takes an arbitrary *sequence*, containing a mixture of *nodes* and *atomic values*, and creates a new *sequence* in which each of the nodes is replaced by its *typed value*. Atomic values appearing in the input sequence are retained in the result sequence unchanged.

Glossary

ATTRIBUTE (*XML*)

A name=value pair appearing in an *element*'s start tag, for example «category="grocery"».

ATTRIBUTE AXIS (*XPATH*)

The attribute *axis* selects all the *attributes* of the *context node*. If the *context node* is not an *element*, the *axis* will be empty.

ATTRIBUTE DECLARATION (*SCHEMA*)

An attribute declaration is a *schema component* corresponding to an <xs:attribute> element in a *schema*: it defines constraints on the values of *attributes* having a particular name. It may be a global attribute declaration (if it is defined at the top level of a schema) or a local attribute declaration (if defined within the structure of a *complex type*).

ATTRIBUTE NODE (*XPATH*)

A *node* in a tree that represents an *attribute* in an XML document. There will be an attribute node attached to an *element node* for each *attribute* defined in the start tag of the corresponding *element* in the original XML *document*, other than an attribute acting as a *namespace declaration*. There will also be attribute nodes for attributes given a default value in the *document type definition*. The *string value* of the node is the value of the attribute; its *typed value* is the result of *validating* the string value against the relevant *type definition* in a *schema*.

ATTRIBUTE SET (*XSLT*)

A named collection of <xsl:attribute> *instructions*, which when invoked using the use-attribute-sets attribute of <xsl:element> or <xsl:copy>, or the xsl:use-attribute-sets attribute of a *literal result element*, generates a set of attribute nodes to be added to the result sequence.

ATTRIBUTE VALUE TEMPLATE (*XSLT*)

An attribute value template is an *attribute* in the stylesheet that can contain both fixed and variable parts. The fixed parts are written as ordinary characters, while the variable parts are written between curly braces: for example, «file="{$dir}/{$fname}.html"» would evaluate to «file="out/page.html"» if the variables $dir and $fname have the values «out» and «page» respectively. Attribute value templates can be used for any attribute of a *literal result element*, but on XSLT elements they can be used only for those attributes that explicitly allow them.

AXIS (*XPATH*)

An axis is a direction of travel through the *tree*. Starting from a particular *context node*, an axis defines a list of *nodes* reached from that origin. For example, the *ancestor axis* returns the parent, grandparent, and so on up to the root of the tree, while the *following sibling* axis returns all the nodes that appear after the context node and share the same parent.

Base URI (*XPath*)

Every node has an associated base URI. For an element, this is the absolute URI of the XML external entity containing the element's start and end tags (most often, of course, this will be the document entity). For other node types, it is defined by reference to an associated element node, typically its parent. The base URI of an element can also be set explicitly by using the xml:base attribute. The base URI of a node is used when expanding a relative URI defined in that node, for example a relative URI in an href attribute is considered to be relative to the base URI of the parent element.

Every XPath expression also has a base URI defined as part of its static context. For an XPath expression contained in a stylesheet, this is the base URI of the stylesheet element containing the XPath expression. In non-XSLT contexts, it's up to the host environment to specify a base URI for the expression.

Boolean (*XPath*)

One of the allowed data types for the value of an XPath expression. It takes the value true or false.

Built-In Template Rule (*XSLT*)

A *template rule* that is not explicitly defined in the stylesheet, but that is implicitly available to process a node if there is no explicit template rule that matches it.

Built-In Type (*Schema*)

The XML Schema specification defines a number of built-in *simple types* that are available for use, without any need to declare them in a schema. These include 19 *primitive types* (such as xs:string and xs:date), 20 built-in derived atomic types (including xs:integer and xs:ID), and 3 built-in list types (xs:NMTOKENS, xs:IDREFS, and xs:ENTITIES).

Cast (*XPath*)

An *expression* that converts an *atomic value* of one *type* to an atomic value of a different type.

CDATA Section (*XML*)

A sequence of characters in an XML document enclosed between the delimiters «![CDATA[» and «]]>»; within a CDATA section all characters represent text content rather than markup, except for the sequence «]]>».

Character Reference (*XML*)

A representation of a character using its decimal or hexadecimal Unicode value, for example «
» or «↤». Normally used for characters that are difficult or impossible to enter directly at the keyboard. Character references appear in lexical XML documents, but in the XPath data model they are replaced by the characters that they represent.

CHILD AXIS (*XPATH*)

The child axis selects all the immediate children of the *context node*. These can include elements, text nodes, comments, and processing instructions, but not attributes or namespace nodes. This is a *forwards axis*.

CODEPOINT (*UNICODE*)

A numeric value identifying a Unicode character.

CODEPOINT COLLATION (*XPATH*)

A *collation* that compares and sorts strings strictly according to the numeric values of the *codepoints* making up the characters of the string.

COLLATION (*XPATH*)

A set of rules for comparing strings. A collation can be used to decide whether two strings are equal, to decide how they should be ordered, and to decide whether one string is a substring of another. Different collations are needed to satisfy the needs of different languages or different applications. In XPath and XSLT a collation is identified by a URI. Except for the *codepoint collation*, the URIs used to identify collations are defined by the implementation.

COMMENT (*XML*)

Markup in an XML document that is conventionally used to carry extraneous information that is not part of the document proper. Written between the delimiters «<!--» and «-->».

COMMENT NODE (*XPATH*)

A node in a tree representing an XML *comment*. The *string value* of the node is the text of the comment.

COMPLEX TYPE (*SCHEMA*)

A *schema type* that describes the structure of *elements* that may have *child* elements or *attributes*. If the type permits attributes but not child elements, it is referred to as a complex type with simple content.

CONSTRUCTOR FUNCTION (*XPATH*)

A *function* that constructs an *atomic value* of a particular type. The function has the same name as the target *atomic type*, and always takes a single argument. A constructor function is created automatically for every *atomic type*, including user-defined atomic types. An example of a call on a constructor function is «xs:date("2004-02-29")». The semantics of constructor functions are defined by reference to the rules for *cast* expressions.

Context Item (*XPath*)

The *item* currently being processed; part of the *dynamic context*. Certain XSLT instructions and XPath expressions place a new context item on the stack, and revert to the previous context item when the instruction or expression has been evaluated. The XSLT instructions <xsl:apply-templates> and <xsl:for-each> change the context item, as do the XPath expressions «E1/E2» and «E1[E2]». The context item can be retrieved using the expression «.».

Context Node (*XPath*)

If the *context item* is a *node*, then the context node is the same thing as the context item. If the context item is not a node, then the context node is undefined.

Context Position (*XPath*)

When a *sequence* of *items* is processed in an *expression* of the form «E1/E2» or «E1[E2]», or by an <xsl:for-each> or <xsl:apply-templates> *instruction* in XSLT, each item in the sequence in turn becomes the *context item*, and the context position identifies the position of the context item in the sequence being processed. The context position determines the value of the position() function, and is also used in evaluating a numeric *predicate* such as «[1]».

Context Size (*XPath*)

When a *sequence* of *items* is processed in an *expression* of the form «E1/E2» or «E1[E2]», or by an <xsl:for-each> or <xsl:apply-templates> *instruction* in XSLT, each item in the sequence in turn becomes the *context item*, and the context size identifies the number of items in the sequence being processed. The context size determines the value of the last() function.

Current Mode (*XSLT*)

When a *template rule* is invoked, the *mode* used in the <xsl:apply-templates> *instruction* that invoked it is called the current mode. A further call of <xsl:apply-templates> within this *template rule* can specify «mode="#current"» to continue processing in the current mode.

Current Template Rule (*XSLT*)

When <xsl:apply-templates> selects a *template rule* to process a particular *node*, that template rule becomes the current template rule. It remains the current template rule through calls of <xsl:call-template>, but not through calls of <xsl:for-each>. The current template rule is used only in deciding which template rule to invoke when <xsl:apply-imports> is called.

Data Model (*XPath*)

The data model is a description of the kinds of objects that can be manipulated by XPath *expressions*, and their properties and relationships. Examples of such objects are *sequences*, *items*, *atomic values*, *nodes*, and *trees*. (Sometimes the term *data model* is used loosely to refer to a specific object, such as the tree representation of a particular document).

Declaration (*XSLT*)

A declaration is a top-level *element* in a *stylesheet module* (that is, a *child* element of the `<xsl:stylesheet>` element), other than a user-defined data element, which is ignored by the XSLT processor.

Default Namespace Declaration (*XML*)

This takes the form of an XML *attribute* `xmlns="uri"`. It declares that within its scope, an *element* name with no explicit prefix will be associated with a particular *namespace URI*. The default namespace is used only for element names; other objects with no *prefix* (for example, attributes) have a null namespace URI.

Descendant Axis (*XPath*)

The descendant *axis* selects all the *children* of the *context node*, their children, and so on, in *document order*. This is a *forwards axis*.

Descendant-or-Self Axis (*XPath*)

The descendant-or-self *axis* selects the *context node* followed by all the *nodes* on the *descendant axis*. This is a *forwards axis*.

Document (*XML*)

A parsed entity that conforms to the XML syntax for a `Document` is said to be a *well-formed document*; a document that also obeys the rules in its *document type definition* is said to be *valid*. In XSLT and XPath the term *document* is often used to refer to the *tree* representation of a document: that is, a *document node* together with all the nodes that have this document node as an ancestor.

Document Element (*XML*)

The outermost *element* of a *document*, the one that contains all other elements. The XML standard also refers to this as the root element, but it must not be confused with the *root node* in the XPath tree model: the *root node* is usually the *document node* that is the *parent* of the document element, which represents the document itself.

Document Node (*XPath*)

If the *tree* represents a well-formed XML *document*, the *root node* will be a *document node* with exactly one *element node* as a child, representing the *document element*, and no *text nodes* as children. In other cases it may have zero or more *element node* children, and zero or more *text node* children: I refer to such a document as being *well-balanced*. In both cases the *root node* may also have *comment nodes* and *processing instruction nodes* as children.

DOCUMENT ORDER (*XPATH*)

The *nodes* in a sequence can always be sorted into document order. For elements from the same *document*, document order is the same as the order of the start tags in the original source. In terms of the tree structure, a node is ordered after its preceding siblings, and these are ordered after their parent node. The ordering of attribute and namespace nodes, and of nodes from different source documents, is only partially defined.

DOCUMENT TYPE DEFINITION (DTD) (*XML*)

The definition of the structure of an XML document, or a collection of XML *documents*. May be split into an external subset, held in a separate file, and an internal subset, embedded within the document itself.

DYNAMIC CONTEXT (*XPATH*)

The dynamic context of an XPath *expression* is the total collection of information available to the XPath engine at evaluation time. This includes the *context item*, *context position*, and *context size*, the values of all *variables*, and the contents of all documents that can be accessed by their URI, using functions such as doc() and document().

DYNAMIC ERROR (*XPATH*)

A dynamic error is an error detected during the evaluation phase, as distinct from a *static error*, which is detected at compile time. Technically, *type errors* (which may be detected either at compile time or at runtime) form a separate third category.

Dynamic errors defined in XSLT are classified as being either recoverable or nonrecoverable. In the case of recoverable errors the processor is allowed either to report the error, or to recover in a defined way and continue processing, or both.

EFFECTIVE BOOLEAN VALUE (*XPATH*)

The effective boolean value of an *expression* is used when the expression appears in a context where a choice needs to be made: for example the condition in an XPath conditional *expression* or an XSLT <xsl:if> *instruction*. The effective boolean value of a *sequence* is false if the sequence is empty, or if it contains a singleton *atomic value* that is the *boolean* false, a zero-length string, a number equal to zero, or NaN; in all other cases, the effective boolean value is true.

EFFECTIVE VALUE (*XSLT*)

The effective value of an *attribute* in an XSLT stylesheet is the value after expanding any *attribute value template*: for example given the instruction <xsl:message terminate="{$term}"/>, the effective value of the «terminate» attribute is the value of the $term variable.

Element (*XML*)

A logical unit within an XML document, delimited by start and end tags, for example
`<publisher>Wrox Press</publisher>`; an empty element may also be written in abbreviated form,
for example `<publisher name="Wrox"/>`.

Element Declaration (*Schema*)

An element declaration is a *schema component* that corresponds to an `<xs:element>` *element* in a *schema*:
it defines the structure of *elements* having a particular name. It may be a global element declaration (if it is
defined at the top level of a schema) or a local element declaration (if defined within the structure of a
complex type).

Element Node (*XPath*)

A *node* in a *tree* that represents an *element* in an XML *document*. The *parent* of the element node is either the
containing element or the *document node* of the tree; its *children* are the element nodes, *text nodes*, *comment
nodes*, and *processing instruction nodes* derived from the immediate content of the XML element.

Embedded Stylesheet Module (*XSLT*)

A *stylesheet module* that does not constitute an entire XML *document* in its own right, but is embedded as
an `<xsl:stylesheet>` element within some larger XML (or perhaps non-XML) document.

Empty Sequence (*XPath*)

An empty sequence is a *sequence* containing no *items*.

Entity Reference (*XML*)

A reference to an internal or external *entity*, generally in the form «&name;». Note that numeric references
of the form « » are correctly referred to as *character references* rather than entity references.

Entity (*XML*)

A physical unit of information that may be referenced within an XML *document*. Internal entities are
embedded within the document in its *Document Type Definition*; external entities are generally held as a
separate file. A parsed entity contains text with XML markup; an *unparsed entity* contains binary data. A
general entity contains material for inclusion in the document; a parameter entity contains material for
inclusion in the Document Type Definition.

Expanded QName (*XPath*)

The term QName is sometimes used to mean a QName as written in source XML documents, that is a
construct of the form «prefix:local-name», and it is sometimes used to mean the (namespace-uri,
local-name) pair that this represents. Within the XSLT 2.0 and XPath 2.0 specifications the preferred usage

is *lexical QName* for the first construct, and *expanded QName* for the second. These terms are not consistent across the full range of XML specifications.

There is no standard convention for displaying an expanded QName, though in some interfaces such as JAXP, expanded QNames are written in the form «{namespace-uri}local-name». This is sometimes referred to as Clark notation.

EXPRESSION (*XPATH*)

An XPath construct that can be evaluated to yield a value, which will always be a *sequence* (of *nodes* and/or *atomic values*). In XSLT, expressions are used in many contexts such as the select attribute of <xsl:for-each>, <xsl:value-of>, and <xsl:variable>, and the test attribute of <xsl:if> and <xsl:when>. Expressions are also used between curly braces in *attribute value templates*.

EXTENSION ATTRIBUTE (*XSLT*)

An *attribute* in a vendor- or user-defined *namespace* used on an XSLT *element* in the *stylesheet*. Such attributes may be used to control behavior that would otherwise be implementation defined, or to provide extra control over *serialization*.

EXTENSION INSTRUCTION (*XSLT*)

An *element* within a *sequence constructor* that is defined by a product vendor, a user, or a third party, but otherwise behaves like an XSLT *instruction*. The XSLT specification defines how extension instructions are evaluated but not how they are implemented. In XSLT 1.0, extension instructions were referred to as extension elements.

EXTENSION FUNCTION (*XSLT*)

A *function* defined by a product vendor, a user, or a third party, which can be called from within an XPath *expression*. The XSLT specification defines how extension functions are called but not how they are implemented.

FACET (*SCHEMA*)

A facet is a constraint placed on the values of a *simple type* in the *schema*. For example, the pattern facet (not to be confused with XSLT patterns) constrains the value to match a given regular expression, while the maxInclusive facet defines the largest permitted value.

FINAL RESULT TREE (*XSLT*)

A tree that is constructed by a *stylesheet* and that acts as an output of the transformation (as distinct from a *temporary tree* that can be further processed by the transformation).

FOLLOWING AXIS (*XPATH*)

The following *axis* selects all the *nodes* that follow the *context node* in *document order* with the exception of *attribute* and *namespace* nodes, and the node's own *descendants*. This is a *forwards axis*.

FOLLOWING SIBLING AXIS (*XPATH*)

The following-sibling *axis* selects all the *nodes* that follow the *context node* in *document order* and that share the same *parent* node. This is a *forwards axis*.

FORWARDS AXIS (*XPATH*)

An *axis* containing a sequence of *nodes* that follow the *context node* in *document order*. Within a *predicate* of an axis *step* that uses a forwards axis (for example, «following-sibling::x[3]»), position numbers count the nodes in *document order*.

FUNCTION (*XPATH*)

A procedure that can be called from within an XPath *expression*; it takes arguments and returns a result. Functions cannot be defined using XPath, only invoked from XPath. A function is either a core function defined in the XPath or XSLT recommendations, or a *stylesheet function* defined using an <xsl:function> declaration in XSLT, or an *extension function* provided by the vendor or the user. Functions may also be defined using XQuery. A function has a name (which is a *QName*), a signature defining the types expected for its arguments and the return type, and an implementation.

GLOBAL VARIABLE (*XSLT*)

A *variable* defined in a top-level <xsl:variable> element. Global variables are available anywhere in the *stylesheet* (including in other *stylesheet modules*), unless masked by a *local variable* or *range variable* of the same name, or a global variable of the same name and higher *import precedence*.

ID (*XML*)

An *attribute* of type ID has a value that is unique within the document (that is, different from any other ID attribute). It is an ID by virtue of being declared as such in the *DTD* or *Schema*. It is guaranteed unique only if the document is *valid* (XSLT is not constrained to operate only on valid documents). *Elements* can be accessed using their ID by means of the id() function.

IMPORT PRECEDENCE (*XSLT*)

A *stylesheet module* that is loaded using <xsl:import> has lower import precedence than the *stylesheet module* doing the importing. The import precedence affects all the top-level *declarations* in that stylesheet, and is used when deciding which top-level elements to use. For example, if two *global variables* have the same name, the one with higher import precedence is used.

INITIAL TEMPLATE (*XSLT*)

The first *template* to be evaluated when a *stylesheet* is activated. This may be defined by nominating a *named template* from the invoking API, or it may be selected by applying *template rules* to an initial node supplied in the API (typically, by default, the *document node* of the principal source document).

IN-SCOPE NAMESPACES (*XPATH*)

Any *element node* has a set of *namespace declarations* that are in scope for the element: these are represented by the *namespace nodes* for that element. An XPath *expression* also has a set of in-scope namespaces in its *static context*. For XPath expressions in an XSLT *stylesheet module*, the in-scope namespaces for the expression are the namespaces that are in-scope for the *element* in the *stylesheet* that contains the XPath expression, augmented with the namespace defined in the [xsl:]xpath-default-namespace attribute if present. In non-XSLT contexts, it is up to the host environment to define how the *static context* for an XPath expression is established.

INSTRUCTION (*XSLT*)

One of a number of XSLT *elements* that is permitted to appear directly within a *sequence constructor*, for example <xsl:variable>, <xsl:choose>, and <xsl:message>. Not all XSLT elements are instructions, for example <xsl:param> and <xsl:when> are not: this is because these can appear in a defined context only.

ITEM (*XPATH*)

An item is either an *atomic value* or a *node*.

ITEM TYPE (*THIS BOOK*)

An item type describes the type allowed for *items* within a *sequence*. This is either item(), which allows any item; empty(), which allows nothing; an *atomic type*; or a node type. Node types define the kind of node (for example element, attribute, or comment) plus optionally, constraints on the name of the node and on its *type annotation*, which will always be a *schema type*.

LEXICAL QNAME (*XPATH*)

A *QName* written in its lexical form: either a simple unprefixed name, or a construct of the form «prefix:local-name». See also *expanded QName*.

LIST TYPE (*SCHEMA*)

A *simple type* that allows a space-separated sequence of values to be written. For example, the type xs:NMTOKENS permits the value "red green blue". When an *element* or *attribute* is annotated with a list type, its *typed value* in XPath is a *sequence* containing the individual *items*.

Literal Result Element (*XSLT*)

A literal result element is an element appearing within a *sequence constructor* in a *stylesheet* that is not an XSLT *instruction* or an *extension instruction*. When the sequence constructor is evaluated a new *element node* is added to the result sequence, and its content (which is also a *sequence constructor*) is evaluated to form the content of the newly constructed element.

Local Variable (*XSLT*)

A *variable* defined within a *sequence constructor*. A local variable is accessible only from the following siblings of the `<xsl:variable>` element that defines the variable, and from their descendants. This is analogous to the normal rule in block-structured programming languages.

Mode (*XSLT*)

Modes partition the set of *template rules* in a *stylesheet*, so that the same *nodes* can be processed more than once using different rules each time. The mode named on the call of `<xsl:apply-templates>` must match the mode named on the `<xsl:template>` element that is invoked.

Named Template (*XSLT*)

An `<xsl:template>` element in the *stylesheet* with a name attribute. A named template may be invoked using an `<xsl:call-template>` instruction.

Namespace (*XML Namespaces*)

A named collection of names. The namespace is named using a *URI* (or in the 1.1 specification, an IRI), which is intended to be formed in such a way as to ensure global uniqueness, but which, in practice, may be any string. Within a particular region of a *document*, a namespace is also identified by a shorthand name called a *prefix*; different prefixes can be used to refer to the same namespace in different documents or even within the same document. A name (of an *element* or *attribute* in XML, and of a *variable*, *template*, *function*, *mode*, and so on in XSLT) belongs to a specific namespace, and two names can be considered equivalent only if they belong to the same namespace.

Namespace Axis (*XPath*)

The namespace *axis* selects all the *namespace nodes* belonging to the *context node*. If the context node is not an *element node*, the axis will be empty. For element nodes, there is one *namespace node* for every *namespace* that is in scope for the element, whether it relates to a *namespace declaration* that was defined on this element or on a containing element. This is a *forwards axis*. The namespace axis is retained in XPath 2.0, but is deprecated: applications requiring namespace information should instead use the functions `in-scope-prefixes()` and `namespace-for-prefix()`.

Namespace Declaration (*XML Namespaces*)

A construct in an XML *document* that declares that within a particular region of the document, a given *namespace prefix* will be used to refer to the *namespace* with a particular *URI*. There are two forms of namespace declaration: `xmlns="uri"` to declare the default namespace (the one with a null prefix), and `xmlns:prefix="uri"` to declare a namespace with a non-null prefix. Both are written in the form of XML attributes and apply to the element they are on and all descendant elements, unless overridden.

NAMESPACE FIXUP (*XSLT*)

Namespace fixup is the process of adding *namespace nodes* to a newly constructed *element node* to ensure that all the namespaces actually used by the element are properly declared.

NAMESPACE NODE (*XPATH*)

A *node* in a *tree* that represents the binding of a *namespace prefix* to a *namespace URI*. A namespace node belongs to an element called its *parent*: it applies only to that element and not to any *descendant* elements.

NAMESPACE PREFIX (*XML NAMESPACES*)

A short name used to identify a *namespace* within a particular region of an XML *document*, so called because it is most often used as the prefix of a *lexical QName* (the part before the colon). Different prefixes can be used to identify the same namespace, and in different contexts the same prefix can be used to identify different namespaces.

NAMESPACE URI (*XML NAMESPACES*)

A *URI* used to identify a *namespace*. Namespace URIs are unusual in that there is no actual resource that can be obtained using the URI; the URI is simply a unique identifier. In practice, any string can be used as a namespace URI, though «`http://`» URLs are often used to give some prospect of uniqueness. Technically, the XML Namespaces specification refers to this concept as a *namespace name*, and in version 1.1 the namespace name can be an IRI, which unlike a URI allows non-ASCII characters. However, the term namespace URI is in widespread use despite the fact that practical products allow any string to be used.

NaN (*XPATH*)

Not-a-Number. This is one of the possible values of a *variable* whose data type is float or double. It results from an operation whose result is not numeric, for example «`number('apple')`».

NODE (*XPATH*)

An object forming part of a *tree*. There are seven kinds of node: *attribute nodes, comment nodes, document nodes, element nodes, namespace nodes, processing instruction nodes,* and *text nodes*. Nodes have properties including a name, a *string value*, a *typed value*, and a *base URI*. Every kind of node except a document node may have a *parent* node; document nodes and element nodes may have children; element nodes may have attributes and namespaces.

Node Kind (*XPath*)

Nodes are classified into seven kinds: *attribute nodes, comment nodes, document nodes, element nodes, namespace nodes, processing instruction nodes,* and *text nodes.*

Number (*XPath*)

In XPath 2.0, the term *number* is used as a generic term for the three primitive types decimal, double, and float, and their subtypes (including integer).

Output Method (*XSLT*)

XSLT 2.0 defines four output methods, xml, html, xhtml, and text. The output method controls the way in which the result tree is output (or *serialized*) as a stream of characters or bytes.

Parameter (*XSLT*)

A variable whose value is supplied by the caller. A *stylesheet* parameter is a *global variable* whose value can be set (in a vendor-defined way) when the stylesheet is executed. A *template* parameter is defined within an <xsl:template> element, and its value can be set when the template is invoked using <xsl:apply-templates> or <xsl:call-template>. A *function* parameter is defined within an <xsl:function> element, and is set by evaluating the arguments in an XPath function call.

Parent Axis (*XPath*)

The parent *axis* selects the *node* that is the parent of the *context node*, assuming it has a parent. Since this axis selects at most one node, it doesn't matter whether it is considered as a *forwards axis* or as a *reverse axis*.

Particle (*Schema*)

In the language of XML Schema, a particle is a component part of the definition of the structure of a *complex type*. A particle may be an *element declaration*, or a wildcard that allows elements from defined namespaces, or a sequence or choice compositor with a defined substructure.

Path Expression (*XPath*)

A path expression is an *expression* that selects a *sequence* of *nodes* in a *tree*. It defines a sequence of *steps* that define navigation paths from the *context node* to further nodes. The final result is the sequence of nodes reached by following each of the steps in turn. For example, the path expression «../@code» has two steps: the first step selects the parent of the context node, and the second step selects the «code» attribute of the selected parent. The nodes in the result of a path expression are always returned in *document order*, with duplicates removed.

Pattern (*XSLT*)

A construct that defines a condition that a *node* either satisfies or does not satisfy. The syntax for a pattern is a subset of the syntax for an XPath *expression*. Patterns are used in only four XSLT elements: `<xsl:template>`, `<xsl:key>`, `<xsl:number>`, and `<xsl:for-each-group>`.

Precedence (*XSLT*)

See *Import Precedence*.

Preceding Axis (*XPath*)

The preceding *axis* selects all the *nodes* that precede the *context node* within the same *tree*, with the exception of *attribute* and *namespace* nodes, and the node's own *ancestors*. This is a *reverse axis*.

Preceding Sibling Axis (*XPath*)

The preceding sibling *axis* selects all the *nodes* that precede the *context node* and that share the same parent node. This is a *reverse axis*.

Predicate (*XPath*)

An *expression* used to filter which *nodes* are selected by a particular *step* in a *path expression,* or to select a subset of the *items* in a *sequence*. A boolean expression selects the items for which the predicate is true; a numeric expression selects the item at the position given by the value of the expression, for example «[1]» selects the first item.

Prefix (*XML Namespaces*)

See *Namespace Prefix*.

Primitive Type (*Schema*)

The XML Schema specification defines 19 primitive types. In the XPath model these are defined as subtypes of the abstract type `xdt:anyAtomicType`, which contains all atomic values. The 19 primitive types are `boolean`, `string`, `decimal`, `double`, `float`, QName, anyURI, hexBinary, base64Binary, date, time, dateTime, gYear, gYearMonth, gMonth, gMonthDay, gDay, duration, and NOTATION. XPath in effect adds `untypedAtomic` to this list, representing values that have not been *validated* against any *schema*.

Principal Node Kind (*XPath*)

Every *axis* has a principal *node kind*. For most axes, the principal node kind is *elements*. For the *attribute axis*, the principal node kind is *attribute*, and for the *namespace axis*, it is *namespace*. The principal node kind determines the kind of nodes selected by the node test «*»: for example, «following-siblings::*» selects elements, while «namespace::*» selects *namespace nodes*.

PRIORITY (*XSLT*)

Every *template rule* has a priority. The priority is expressed as a number (which may be a decimal number such as «3.5»). The priority may be specified explicitly, using the `priority` attribute of the `<xsl:template>` element; if it is omitted a default priority is allocated based on the *pattern*. The priority is used to decide which *template rule* to evaluate when several template rules match the same *node*: a rule with numerically higher priority is used in preference to one with lower priority.

PROCESSING INSTRUCTION (*XML*)

An item in an XML *document* that is conventionally used to carry instructions to the software that receives the document and processes it. Written between the delimiters «<?» and «?>». Note that the XML declaration at the start of a document, and the text declaration at the start of an external parsed entity, are not processing instructions even though they use the same delimiters.

PROCESSING INSTRUCTION NODE (*XPATH*)

A *node* in a *tree* representing an XML *processing instruction*.

PROMOTION (*XPATH*)

The type-checking rules for *function* calling in XPath, and also for arithmetic operators and comparison operators, allow numeric values to be used where a different numeric type is expected. The operation of converting the supplied *number* to the required type (for example, integer to double) is known as promotion.

QNAME (*XML NAMESPACES*)

A qualified name. It is either a simple name (an NCName) or a name preceded by a namespace prefix and a colon. See also *lexical QName* and *expanded QName*.

RANGE VARIABLE (*XPATH*)

A *variable* declared in a «for», «some», or «every» expression, which is bound to each *item* in a *sequence* in turn: for example, the variable $i in «for $i in 1 to 5 return $i*$i».

REGULAR EXPRESSION (*XPATH*)

A regular expression is a pattern that *strings* may or may not match. Regular expressions can be used in the three functions matches(), replace(), and tokenize() defined in XPath, and in the `<xsl:analyze-string>` *instruction* in XSLT.

Result Tree (*XSLT*)

The output of a *stylesheet*. A stylesheet defines a transformation from a source tree to a result tree. XSLT 2.0 allows multiple result trees to be created. The final stage of processing is normally to *serialize* the result tree as a stream of characters or bytes: this is controlled by the selected *output method*.

Reverse Axis (*XPath*)

An *axis* containing a *sequence* of *nodes* that precede the *context node* in *document order*. Within a *predicate* of an axis step that uses a reverse axis (for example, «preceding-sibling::x[position() = 1 to 3]»), position numbers count the nodes in reverse *document order*. However, as with any other axis step, the result of the expression is in forwards *document order*. So this *expression* returns the last three «x» nodes before the context node, in document order.

Root Node (*XPath*)

The top-most *node* in a *tree*; any *node* that has no *parent*. In XPath 2.0, any kind of node may be a root node. A root node that represents a complete XML document is now referred to as a *document node*.

Schema (*Schema*)

In this book the term *schema*, unless otherwise specified, always means a schema defined using the W3C XML Schema language. A schema can be regarded as a collection of *element declarations, attribute declarations*, and *type definitions*. A *schema document*, by contrast, is the XML *document* rooted at an <xs:schema> element (which one might regard as containing one module of a schema).

Schema Component (*Schema*)

A generic term for *element declarations, attribute declarations*, and *type definitions*.

Schema Type (*THIS BOOK*)

A type as defined in XML Schema: either a *complex type* or a *simple type*. The type may be named, or it may be anonymous. The term includes both *built-in types* (such as xs:integer) and user-defined types.

Self Axis (*XPath*)

The self *axis* contains a single *node*, the *context node*. It makes no difference whether it is regarded as a *forwards axis* or a *reverse axis*. The *principal node kind* of the self axis is *elements*, which means that when the context node is an *attribute*, an axis *step* of the form «self::*» or «self::xyz» will not select that attribute.

SEQUENCE (*XPATH*)

A sequence in the XPath *data model* is an ordered collection of *items*. The items may be *atomic values* or references to *nodes* in a *tree*. A sequence containing no items is referred to as the *empty sequence*. Sequences have no identity of their own; two sequences containing the same items cannot be distinguished.

SEQUENCE CONSTRUCTOR (*XSLT*)

A sequence of XSLT *instructions, extension instructions, literal result elements,* and *text nodes,* forming the content of an `<xsl:template>` element or of various other elements in the *stylesheet*. When the sequence constructor is evaluated, any *instructions* and *extension instructions* are evaluated according to the rules for each one, while any *literal result elements* and *text nodes* are copied to the result sequence. In most cases the result sequence will be used to form the content of a new node in a result tree, but this depends on the instruction that contains the sequence constructor.

SEQUENCE TYPE (*XPATH*)

A sequence type is a definition that constrains the permitted values of a *sequence*. It has two parts: an *item type,* which constrains the type of the *items* in the sequence, and a cardinality, which constrains the number of items in the sequence. The cardinality may be zero-or-one, exactly-one, zero-or-more, or one-or-more.

SERIALIZATION (*XSLT*)

Serialization is the reverse of parsing: it takes a *document* represented as a *tree* in the XPath *data model,* and converts it into a lexical XML document.

SIMPLE TYPE (*SCHEMA*)

A simple type in XML Schema describes values that can be written as text, with no embedded markup. Simple types divide into *atomic types, list types,* and *union types. Attributes* always have a simple type; the content of an *element* may be either a simple or a *complex type.* XML Schema defines a number of built-in simple types, but further simple types can be defined in a user-written schema.

SIMPLIFIED STYLESHEET MODULE (*XSLT*)

A simplified stylesheet module is a *stylesheet module* consisting solely of a *literal result element* which is evaluated using the root of the source document as the *context node*.

SOURCE DOCUMENT (*XPATH*)

The principal source document is the XML document to which the stylesheet is being applied. Secondary source documents can be loaded using the `document()` function.

Static Context (*XPath*)

The static context of an XPath *expression* is the total collection of information available to the XPath engine at compile time. This includes the *namespace declarations* that are in scope, the names and types of declared *variables*, the *base URI* of the expression, and the *collations* that are available.

Static Error (*XPath*)

A static error is an error detected during the analysis phase, that is, at compile time.

Static Type (*XPath*)

Every *expression* (and subexpression) has a static type. This is a *sequence type*, representing the best possible inference that can be made about the dynamic type of the value that will be returned when the expression is evaluated. For example, the static type of the expression «@*» might be «attribute()*». In an XPath processor that implements strict static typing, a *type error* will be reported if the static type of an expression is not a subtype of the type required by the context in which the expression is used.

Step (*XPath*)

A step is used within a *path expression* to navigate from one *node* to a sequence of related nodes. The most common kind of step is an axis step, which is defined by an *axis*, giving the direction of navigation; a node test, which defines constraints on the type of and names of the target nodes; and zero or more *predicates*, which define arbitrary constraints that the target nodes must satisfy.

String (*XPath*)

One of the allowed data types for the value of an XPath expression. It is a sequence of zero or more Unicode characters (the same character set as is used in XML).

String Value (*XPath*)

Every *node* has a string value. For a *text node* the string value is the textual content; for an *element* it is the concatenation of the string values of its *descendant* text nodes (that is, the textual content of the element after stripping all markup). The string value of a node can be obtained using the `string()` function.

Stylesheet (*XSLT*)

A stylesheet represents the contents of one or more *stylesheet modules*, consisting of a principal stylesheet module and other modules that are reachable from the principal module using `<xsl:include>` and `<xsl:import>` declarations.

Stylesheet Function (*XSLT*)

A *function* defined in a *stylesheet* using an `<xsl:function>` declaration. Like other *functions*, a stylesheet function is called using a function call in an XPath *expression*.

Stylesheet Module (*XSLT*)

A stylesheet module is defined by a single `<xsl:stylesheet>` or `<xsl:transform>` element, usually comprising the whole of an XML document; or it may be a *simplified stylesheet* whose root is a *literal result element* with an `xsl:version` attribute.

Template (*XSLT*)

An `<xsl:template>` element in the *stylesheet*, together with its content. See also *named template*. (XSLT 1.0 had a different definition for this term, but XSLT 2.0 has bowed to popular usage.)

Template Rule (*XSLT*)

An `<xsl:template>` *declaration* in the *stylesheet* with a `match` attribute. A template rule may be invoked using the `<xsl:apply-templates>` *instruction*; for each selected *node*, the appropriate template rule is determined based on a number of criteria including the match *pattern* and the template rule's *import precedence* and *priority*.

Temporary Tree (*XSLT*)

A *tree* constructed in the course of processing a stylesheet, by evaluating a non-empty `<xsl:variable>` element. The value of the *variable* is the *document node* at the root of the temporary tree.

Text Node (*XPath*)

A *node* in a *tree* representing character data (called PCDATA in XML) within an XML *document*. Adjacent text nodes will always be merged into a single node. *Character references* and *entity references* occurring within the original text will have been replaced by their expansions.

Top-level Element (*XSLT*)

An *element* in a *stylesheet* that is an immediate child of the `<xsl:stylesheet>` element.

Tree (*XPath*)

An abstract data structure representing the information content of an XML document. The tree always has a single *root node* (which contrary to the botanical analogy, is always depicted at the top). The structure of nodes in the tree need not follow the rules for a *well-formed* document in XML, for example, there may be several *element nodes* as children of the root. In XPath 2.0 the root of a tree need not be a *document node*. It is possible to have an element node as the root. It is also possible for any other kind of node (for example an attribute node) to be parentless, in which case it acts as the root of a tree in which it is the only node.

TUNNEL PARAMETER (*XSLT*)

A tunnel *parameter* is a parameter to an XSLT *template* that is passed transparently via any called *templates* until eventually the template that actually uses its value receives it.

TYPE (*XPATH*)

In the context of XPath values, the term type means *sequence type*. In the context of nodes validated against a schema, it means *schema type*.

TYPE ANNOTATION (*XPATH*)

Every *element node* and *attribute node* has a type annotation. The type annotation identifies a *schema type*, which may be a *simple type* or a *complex type*. Type annotations are added to nodes as a consequence of *validation* against a *schema*. An element node that has not been validated against any schema is annotated with the special type xdt:untyped, while an attribute node that has not been validated is annotated as xdt:untypedAtomic.

TYPE DEFINITION (*SCHEMA*)

A type definition is a *schema component* that defines a *simple type* or a *complex type*.

TYPED VALUE (*XPATH*)

The typed value of a node is in general a *sequence* of *atomic values*. It represents the result of analyzing the textual content of the *node* against the *schema definition* for that node, during the process of *validation*.

TYPE ERROR (*XPATH*)

A type error occurs when the value used as input to some operation is not of the *type* required by that operation: for example, when a string is used as an argument to an arithmetic operator. Type errors may be detected either at compile time or at runtime. A system that implements strict *static type* checking will report type errors at compile time pessimistically: that is, it will report an error if there is any possibility that the runtime value will have the wrong type.

UNPARSED ENTITY (*XML*)

An unparsed entity is an *entity* declared in the *document type definition* with an associated notation. Such entities are unparsed because they generally contain binary data such as images, rather than XML. Two functions, `unparsed-entity-uri()` and `unparsed-entity-public-id()` are available in XSLT to access the unparsed entities associated with a source document. However, it is not possible to create unparsed entities in a result document.

UNION TYPE (*SCHEMA*)

A union type is a *simple type* that allows a choice of alternatives. For example a union type might allow an attribute to contain either a decimal value, or the string `"N/A"`.

URI (*RFC 2396*)

Uniform Resource Identifier: a generalization of the URLs (Uniform Resource Locators) used to uniquely address resources such as Web pages on the Internet.

VALIDATION (*XSLT*)

Validation in XSLT 2.0 is the process of assessing a *tree* against a *schema*. If the tree is not valid against the schema, the transformation fails; if it is valid, then each *element node* and *attribute node* in the tree acquires a *type annotation* identifying the *schema type* against which it was found to be valid.

VARIABLE (*XPATH*)

A named value. Variables in XPath and XSLT differ from variables in procedural programming language in that there is no assignment statement.

VARIABLE BINDING (*XSLT*)

The declaration of a *variable*, in an `<xsl:variable>` or `<xsl:param>` element, in conjunction with the current value of that variable.

VARIABLE REFERENCE (*XPATH*)

A reference to a *variable* within an *expression*, in the form $name.

WELL-BALANCED (*XML FRAGMENT INTERCHANGE*)

An XML fragment is well-balanced if there is an end tag that matches every start tag. This is a less strict constraint than being *well-formed*: a well-balanced fragment does not have to have a single element that encloses all the others. XSLT and XPath are defined so they will work on any *trees* representing a well-balanced XML fragment. The XML and XSLT standards don't use this terminology; instead they refer to the rules for an *external general parsed entity*.

WELL-FORMED (*XML*)

A *document* is well-formed if it follows the syntax rules in the XML specification. These include the rule that there must be a single outermost *element* that encloses all others. The XML output of an XSLT stylesheet is not required to be well-formed, only to be *well-balanced*.

WHITESPACE (*XML*)

Whitespace is any contiguous sequence of tab, carriage return, newline, and space characters. A whitespace node is a *text node* whose *string value* consists solely of whitespace. (The XML specification spells this as two words, *white space*, but I prefer a single word, because using *white* as a qualifying adjective suggests that white space is to be contrasted with red space and green space, which of course is not the case.)

XPATH 1.0 COMPATIBILITY MODE (*XPATH*)

A mode of executing XPath 2.0 expressions that attempts to provide the maximum possible level of backwards compatibility with XPath 1.0. In XSLT, this mode is selected by specifying «version="1.0"» in the stylesheet.

Index

SYMBOLS

occurrence indicators
*, 156
?, 156
+, 156
operators
«|», 762
«!=», 761
«+», 128, 762
«*», 128, 762
«,», 761
«//», 763
«/», 762
«[]», 763
«<<», 761
«<=», 761
«<», 127, 761
«=», 127, 761
«>=», 761
«-», 762
«>», 761
«>>», 761

A

abort() method (MSXML), 801
abs() function, 765
adjust-dateTime-to-timezone() function, 766
adjust-date-to-timezone() function, 766
adjust-time-to-timezone() function, 766
aggregation functions
avg(), 620, 766
max(), 224, 620, 780
min(), 224, 620, 780
sum(), 634, 793
Ambroziak, Jack, 8
ancestor axis, 77, 763
ancestor-or-self axis, 763
«and», 761
ANSEL character, 703
anyAtomicType, 156
API (Application Programming Interface), 6, 59, 85
Application Programming Interface (API), 6, 59, 85
as attribute, 63, 73, 154, 200
ASP page, 133, 715

ASP.NET, 8, 20
assignment statements, avoiding
avoid doing two things at once, 631
conditional initialization, 630
using recursion, 633
atomization, 73
attribute axis, 77, 763
attribute name at runtime, 213
attribute node for an element, creating, 210
attribute node, 51, 204
attribute normalization (in XML), 137
attribute set for numbering, example of, 218
attribute set names, 217
attribute sets, 214
attribute value templates, 116, 118
attribute whose value is QName, creating, 210
attribute(), 75
attribute-or-top axis, 501
attributes of a node, 53
attributes of literal result element, 110
avg() function, 620, 766

B

backwards compatibility, 123, 126, 865
backwards compatibility mode
comparing strings, 866
first node rule, 865
numeric precision, 867
other changes, 867
strong conversions, 74
base URI for output documents, 59
base URI of a node, 53
base-uri() function, 766
basic processor. See stylesheets and schemas
best move, selecting (Knight's tour example), 750
beyond XSLT 1.0, 31
boolean() function, 310, 767
boundary whitespace, 648
Broadcast Markup Language, 2
BufferedReader object (used in example extension function), 606
built-in atomic types, 157
built-in template rules, 70, 190
<bullet> elements (grouping example), 291

C

calendar argument (of format-date() function), 554
captured groups, 181
Cascading Style Sheets (CSS), 21, 94, 519
«cast as», 762
«castable as», 762
casting, 74
CDATA sections, 57
cdata-section-elements attribute (of <xsl:output>),
    231, 377
ceiling() function, 767
character maps
    choosing characters to map, 233
    limitations of, 235
    used to comment-out elements, example of, 234
    versus disable-output-escaping, 233
child axis, 77, 763
child-or-top axis, 501
children of a node
    choosing, 183
Clark notation (for expanded QNames), 55
Clark, James, 8, 25, 28
client-side script, 599, 808
closure, 7, 44
codepoints-to-string() function, 767
collation attribute, 284, 333
collations, 427, 858
collection() function, 768
COM object, 735
command-line interface, 59
command-line parameters, 85
comma-separated values, 7, 589
comment node, 51
comment(), 75
compare() function, 768
compile time, 122
complex type with complex content, categories of
    element-only content, 149
    empty content, 149
    mixed content, 149
complex type with simple content, 149
computational stylesheets
    assignment statements, 630
    cheating, 629
    grouping, 641
    programming without assignment statements, 625
    variables, 629
concat() function, 117, 768
conditional compilation, 122
conditional expression (XPath 2.0), 35
conflict resolution, 65, 71, 498
constructor functions, 74
contains() function, 769
content of a constructed document, 258
content of a constructed element, 263
ContentHandler interface (SAX2), 46

context
    dynamic context, 78
    static context, 78
context item, 79
context item, changing, 223, 280
context position, 79, 785
context size, 79, 785
controlling sequence of processing, 68
conversion, of types, 73
converting attributes to child elements (example),
    270
copying nodes to and from temporary trees, 247
copy-namespaces attribute, 241, 245, 246
core function library, 130
count() function, 141, 306, 368, 634, 769
country argument (of format-date() function), 557
createProcessor() method (MSXML), 737
creating attributes, different ways of, 208
creating multiple output files, examples of, 418,
    545
cross-references, making, 672
CSS (Cascading Style Sheets), 94, 519
current mode, 190
current template rule, 185
current() function, 526
current-date() function, 85, 769
current-dateTime() function, 769
current-group() function, 283, 286, 529
current-grouping-key() function, 283, 286, 523,
    530
current-time() function, 769
customization layer, 324
cycles in a graph, examples of checking for, 199,
    307

D

data conversion applications, 17
data file, examples of creating
    converting from GEDCOM 5.5 to 6.0, 704
    GEDCOM files to XML, converting, 703
data in tables, arranging, 298
data types
    data types, 74
    expressions, 76
    global, 73
    immutability, 73
    local, 73
    parameters, 74
    temporary trees, 79
data() function, 727, 770
data-oriented XML applications, 691
date, 155
Date:new() (example extension function), 113
Date:toString() (example extension function), 113
day-from-date() function, 770
day-from-dateTime() function, 770

days-from-dayTimeDuration() function, 770
declaration order, 316
declarations
  implementor-defined declarations, 100
  user-defined top-level elements, 101
  XSLT-defined declarations, 99
declarations, XSLT-defined
  <xsl:attribute-set>, 99, 214
  <xsl:character-map>, 99, 229
  <xsl:decimal-format>, 99, 251
  <xsl:function>, 99, 300
  <xsl:import>, 99, 312
  <xsl:import-schema>, 99, 324
  <xsl:include>, 100, 328
  <xsl:key>, 100, 332
  <xsl:namespace-alias>, 100, 116, 350
  <xsl:output>, 100, 375
  <xsl:param>, 100, 392
  <xsl:preserve-space>, 100, 406
  <xsl:strip-space>, 100, 432
  <xsl:template>, 100, 450
  <xsl:variable>, 100, 471
declaring types, 154
deep copy, 249
deep-equal() function, 770
default namespace, 54, 98
default value of stylesheet and template
  parameters, 395
default-collation() function, 771
default priority, 498
default-validation attribute (of xsl:stylesheet), 92,
  168
descendant axis, 763
descendant-or-self axis, 763
design principles (of XSLT language), 29
disable-output-escaping attribute, 233, 460, 466
disable-output-escaping, using, 470
displaying family tree data (Family tree example)
  putting it together, 728
  stylesheet, 715
distinct-values() function, 224, 620, 642, 771
distributed object systems
  COM, 47
  Java, 47
«div», 762
divide-and-conquer recursion, 634
Döbler, Johannes, 8
doc() function, 79, 771
document element, 88
document header, formatting, 655
document node, 49, 51
Document Object Model (DOM), 6, 48, 375, 494
document order, 76, 278
document order. See sorting
Document Style Semantics and Specification
  Language (DSSSL), 27, 627
Document Type Definitions (DTD), 23

document() function to analyze stylesheet,
  example of, 537
document() function, 39, 47, 66, 532
DocumentBuilderFactory.newInstance() method
  (JAXP), 819
document-node() function, 75, 163
document-uri() function, 772
DOM (Document Object Model), 6, 48, 375, 494
DSSSL (Document Style Semantics and
  Specification Language), 27, 627
DTD (Document Type Definitions), 23
DTD information in the tree model, 58
DTD types, 58
duplicate attribute names, 205, 217
duplicate namespace declarations, 114, 350
dyn:evaluate() function (EXSLT), 859
dynamic sort keys, 430

E

EDI messages, 15, 18, 37, 46
effective boolean value, 236, 309, 767
electronic data interchange message, 15, 18, 37,
  46
element node, 51
element nodes within sequence constructor
  extension elements, 103
  literal result elements, 103
  XSLT instructions, 103
element or attribute, 115
element types (in XML Schema), 148
element(), 75
element-available() function, 122, 126, 445, 542
element-only content, 148
  mixed content, 149
  simple content, 148
elements that may appear as children of
  <xsl:stylesheet>
  implementor-defined declarations, 98
  user-defined data elements, 98
  XSLT-defined declarations, 98
embedded stylesheets, 95
empty() function, 772
encoding argument (to unparsed-text() function),
  588
encoding attribute (of xsl:output), 389
ends-with() function, 772
«eq» operator, 284, 761
error handling
  dynamic errors, 71
  static errors, 71
error() function, 773
escape-uri() function, 773
evaluate() extension function (EXSLT), 859
event based interface, 6
event records, creating (Family tree example), 709

«every», 761
exactly-one() function, 773
example of aggregating a list of numbers, 635
example of navigational stylesheet, 617
example of rule-based stylesheet, 621
example of supplying parameters and output
    properties, 843
example of transformation using files, 842
example of using <xsl copy-of> for repeated output
    source, 247
example of using a character-map to comment-out
    elements, 234
example of using an attribute set for numbering,
    218
example of using an extension instruction, 134
example of using client-side JScript to transform a
    document, 808
example of using document() function to analyze
    stylesheet, 537
example of using generate-id() to create links, 570
example of using interleaved structures, 637
example of using keys as cross-references, 575
example of using modes, 194
example of using recursion to process a sequence
    of nodes, 224
example of using recursion to process a sequence
    of strings, 227
examples section. See literal result elements
«except» operator, 209, 762
«except», 762
exclude-result-prefixes attribute, 93, 439
existence of system-defined functions, testing for,
    565
exists() function, 773
expanded content, 231
expanded-QName() function, 774
explicit base URI, supplying, 542
expressions (XPath), 76
extensibility, 128, 595
eXtensible Stylesheet Language (XSL), 21
eXtensible Stylesheet Language Transformations
    (XSLT), 1
extension attributes, 596
extension declarations, 596
extension elements, 118
extension function examples
    calculate a square root, 602
    freeMemory() function, 132
    getRuntime() function, 132
extension functions
    binding, 599
    calling extension functions, 598
    calling external functions within a loop, 606
    calling, 598
    client-side script, 599
    explicit binding, 599
extension instructions, 105, 133, 135

extension types, 596
extension-element-prefixes attribute, 93, 133, 438
extensions, keeping portable
    function-available() function, 612
    system-property() function, 612
external functions within a loop, calling, 606
external general parsed entity, 50

F

false() function, 774
family records, creating, 706
family tree
    case study of, 691–92
    modeling, 692
family tree data, displaying, 714
<FamilyRec> element (Family tree example), 706
features available in later XSLT versions, testing
    for, 544
fill-in-the-blanks stylesheets, 613
final board, displaying (Knight's tour example),
    745
find-best-move() function (Knight's tour example),
    749
finding the route (Knight's tour example), 746
flags (for regular expressions)
    i, 178
    m, 178
    s, 178
    x, 178
floor() function, 774
focus, 78
fold() function (FXSL example), 198
following axis, 763
following-sibling axis, 77, 763
for loop, 223
«for», 761
formal definition of pattern semantics, 495
Format section. See literal result elements
format string (of xsl:number), analyzing, 364
format-date() function
    presentation modifiers, 553
format-dateTime() function, 550
format-number() function, 149, 251, 359, 362,
    558
format-time() function, 562
formatting a list of names, example of, 311
forwards compatibility in XSLT 1.0, 124
forwards-compatibility mode, 105, 123, 566
4xslt, 8
from attribute (of xsl:number), 369
function parameters, 74
function. See programming without assignment
    statements
functional programming, 306, 626
function-available() function, 122, 125, 445, 564

FunctionCall construct (XPath), 518
functions versus named templates, 304
functions with uncontrolled side effects, 609
FXSL library of extension functions, 198

G

«ge», 761
GEDCOM 5.5 to 6.0, converting from, 704
GEDCOM 6.0 schema, 696
GEDCOM data model, 692
GEDCOM files to XML, converting, 703
GEDCOM model, object types of
  contact, 695
  group, 694
  repository, 695
  source, 695
GEDCOM parser, 703
<GEDCOM> element, 706
generate-id() function, 246, 291, 568
generate-id() to create links, example of, 570
generating an attribute conditionally, example of, 211
getXMLReader() method (JAXP), 818
global id parameter, 737
global variables, 73, 99, 622
goto statement, 625
Gregor, 8
group theory, 44
group-adjacent attribute (of xsl:for-each-group)
  using, 290
group-by attribute (of xsl:for-each-group)
  using, 286
group-ending-with attribute (of xsl:for-each-group), 285
grouping consecutive elements by name, example of, 291
grouping, 641
grouping-separator attribute (of xsl:number), 366
grouping-size attribute (of xsl:number), 366
group-starting-with attribute (of xsl:for-each-group), 284
«gt», 761
GUI interface, 59

H

handling flat XHTML documents, example of, 296
handling repeating groups of adjacent elements, example of, 294
head-tail recursion, 224
Hello World example, 10
higher order function, 200
hours-from-dateTime() function, 775
hours-from-dayTimeDuration() function, 775
hours-from-time() function, 775

href attribute
  ?xml:stylesheet?<>, 95
  <xsl:import>, 313
  <xsl:include>, 329
HTML
  boilerplate generation, 592
  files, 2, 728
  in the browser, generating, 735
  internal hyperlink, 682
  outline, creating, 651
  output method, 38, 46, 385
  output page, 132
  pages, 298, 715
  tags, 621
HTML outline, creating, 651
HTML pages from servlet, generating, 730
HTML using ASP pages, generating, 735
<html> element, 46, 61
HTTP
  message, 2
  server, 733
hyperlinks, in HTML output, 47

I

IANA (Internet Assigned Numbers Authority), 427
id attribute, 214, 437
id() function, 58, 335, 775
id/idref constraint, 251
identity constraints (XML Schema)
  <xs:key>, 259
  <xs:keyref>, 259
  <xs:unique>, 259
identity template, 243
«idiv», 762
IdKeyPattern construct, 518
idref attribute, 199
idref() function, 776
if expression (XPath), 35, 227, 236, 310
«if», 761
implementor defined declaration, features of
  binding of extension functions, 100
  collations used for sorting, 100
  details of result-tree serialization, 100
  extension instructions, 100
  localization of messages, 100
implementor defined declarations
  implicit binding, 131, 601
  Java examples, 131
  JavaScript example, 132
  need for, 598
  performance, 83, 129
  purpose of, 129
  side effects, 609
  significance of, 597
  writing, 857

implicit-timezone() function, 776
import precedence
  determining, 314
  effect of, 316
  of template rules, example of, 321
  of variables, example of, 320
import precedence. *See xsl:import*
importing schemas, 168, 325
index-of() function, 776
individual attributes, validating, 167
individual elements, validating, 164
individual records, creating (Family tree example),
  707
informal definition of pattern semantics, 497
InfoSet, 24
init() method (Java servlets), 731, 737
initial mode, 59
initial sequence, 425
initial template, 59, 742
inputs and outputs, multiple, 47
in-scope-prefixes() function, 777
insert-before() function, 777
installing and configuring the servlet, 733
instance methods, 132
«instance of», 159, 762
instructions
  attribute value templates, 116
  extension instructions, 105
  literal result elements, 106
  XSLT instructions, 103
integer, 155
interleaved structures, example of, 637
International Resource Identifier (IRI), 23
Internet Assigned Numbers Authority (IANA), 427
Internet Service Provider, 715
intersect operator, 200, 308, 717
«intersect», 762
introspection, 58
invoking a transformation, 59
IRI (International Resource Identifier), 23
«is», 761
item() function, 525
item(), 75
<item> elements, 214
ItemType construct, 75
IXMLDOMDocument and IXMLDOMDocument2
  (MSXML), 801
IXMLDOMNode (MSXML), methods of
  Document, 803
  selectNodes, 803
  selectSingleNode, 803
  transformNode, 803
  transformNodeToObject, 803
IXMLDOMNode (MSXML), properties of
  baseName, 803
  namespaceURI, 803
  nodeName, 803

nodeTypeString, 803
nodeValue, 803
prefix, 804
text, 804
xml, 804
IXMLDOMNodeList (MSXML), methods of
  item, 804
  nextNode, 804
  reset, 804
IXMLDOMParseError (MSXML), properties of
  errorCode, 804
  filepos, 804
  line, 804
  linepos, 804
  reason, 805
  srcText, 805
  url, 805
IXPathNavigable (.NET), 813
IXSLProcessor object (MSXML), methods of
  addParameter, 806
  reset, 806
IXSLProcessor object (MSXML), properties of
  setStartMode, 806
  transform, 806

J

Java
  APIs, 93
  JAXP interface, 59, 133, 233, 815–850
  Server Pages, 20
  servlets, 20
  XML processors, 815
javax.xml.parsers.DocumentBuilder, 821
javax.xml.parsers.DocumentBuilderFactory
  method, 819
javax.xml.parsers.SAXParser, 818
javax.xml.transform.dom.DOMLocator, 824
javax.xml.transform.dom.DOMResult, 825
javax.xml.transform.dom.DOMSource, 825
javax.xml.transform.ErrorListener, 826
javax.xml.transform.OutputKeys, 827
javax.xml.transform.Result, 828
javax.xml.transform.sax.SAXResult, 828
javax.xml.transform.sax.SAXSource, 829
javax.xml.transform.sax.SAXTransformerFactory,
  830
javax.xml.transform.sax.TemplatesHandler, 835
javax.xml.transform.Source, 831
javax.xml.transform.SourceLocator, 832
javax.xml.transform.stream.StreamResult, 833
javax.xml.transform.stream.StreamSource, 832
javax.xml.transform.Templates, 834
javax.xml.transform.Transformer, 836
javax.xml.transform.TransformerFactory, 839
javax.xml.transform.TransformerFactory
  ConfigurationError, 836

JAXP
  benefits of, 815
  parser API, 816
  support for DOM, 819
  support for SAX, 817
  transform() method, 732, 838
  transformation API, 822
jd.xslt processor, 8, 37, 601
jEdit editor, 852

K

keeping extensions portable, 611
key() function, 280, 332, 495, 572
key() pattern to format specific node, example of,
  520
key/keyref constraint (XML Schema), 251
keys as cross-references, example of, 575
keys for grouping, using, 340, 577, 578
keys to find nodes by value, using, 574
keys versus IDs, 335

L

lang attribute (of xsl:number), 366
lang() function, 777
language argument (of format-date() function),
  553
last() function, 79, 189, 288, 778
lax validation, 162, 207, 250, 259, 268
lazy evaluation, 628
LDAP directory, 44
«le», 761
letter-value attribute (of xsl:number), 366
level attribute (of xsl:number), 727
lexical QName, 174
libxslt, 8
lists, producing, 670
literal result elements
  attributes, 110
  content, 108
  format, 107
  namespaces, 112
  position, 107
load() method (MSXML), 801
loadXML() method (MSXML), 801
local variables, 73
localized messages, 346
local-name() function, 55, 778
local-name-from-QName() function, 779
locating a stylesheet module, 313
looking for cycles among attribute sets, example
  of, 307
lookup table in stylesheet, examples of, 80, 540
lower-case() function, 16, 779
«lt», 761

M

main() method, 844
make-best-move() function (Knight's tour example),
  749
match attribute (of xsl:template), 60, 333, 493
matches() function, 182, 184, 779
matching parentless nodes, 500
max() function, 224, 620, 780
mechanisms to test extension instruction, 135
media attribute, 95
media type (MIME type), 94, 588
MEI (Music Encoding Initiative), 4
method attribute (of xsl:output), 129, 378, 385
methods in Java class library, examples of calling
  Enumeration.hasMoreElements(), 134
  Enumeration.nextElement(), 134
  Properties.getProperty(), 134
  Properties.propertyNames(), 134
  System.getProperties(), 134
Microsoft MSXML parser, 8, 345, 735, 800
Microsoft WD-xsl dialect, 8, 30, 435
Microsoft XSLT processors, 8, 30, 799
MIDI files, 4
MIME type, 94, 588
min() function, 224, 620, 780
minutes-from-dateTime() function, 781
minutes-from-dayTimeDuration() function, 780
minutes-from-time() function, 781
mixed content, 149
«mod», 762
mode attribute (of xsl:apply-templates), 187, 190
modeling family tree example
  GEDCOM 6.0 schema, 696
  GEDCOM data model, 692
  schema for GEDCOM 6.0, creating, 695
modes, 70, 194, 454
modular structure of stylesheet, 84
month-from-date() function, 781
month-from-dateTime() function, 781
months-from-yearMonthDuration() function, 781
Mozilla browser, 8
MSXML, 8, 345, 735, 800
Muenchian grouping, 341, 643
multilevel grouping by value, example of, 288
multiphase transformations, 81
multiple definitions for the same key, 340
multiple named keys, 340
multiple template rules, invoking
  grouping-separator, 361
  grouping-size, 361
  ordinal, 361
multiple-match example (xsl:analyze-string), 183
multivalued keys, 337
multivalued nonunique keys, example of, 338
Music Encoding Initiative (MEI), 4
Music Markup Language, 4

MusicML, 4
MusicXML, 4
MusiXML, 4

N

name of a node, parts of
  local name, 52, 262
  namespace URI, 52, 262
name of a parameter, 396
name() function, 55, 204, 782
named templates and stylesheet functions,
    difference between, 304
names and namespaces, 53
namespace
  aliasing, 115
  attribute, 203, 326
  declaration, 53, 230, 114
  default, 54
  fixup, 204, 264
  literal result element, 112
  node, 51, 55, 113
  nodes, copying, 250
  prefix, declaring, 23, 53
  prefixes, 115
  relative URI, 54
  undeclarations, 23, 114
  URI, 23, 53, 115
  working of, 53
namespace axis, 763
namespaces of a node, 53
namespaces, 22, 53
namespace-uri() function, 782
namespace-uri-for-prefix() function, 782
namespace-uri-from-QName() function, 783
NameTest construct (XPath), 509
navigational design patterns, 619
navigational stylesheets, 616
«ne», 761
.NET
  environment, 8
  framework, 8
Netscape browser, 8
newDocumentBuilder() method (JAXP), 819
newSAXParser() method (JAXP), 818
NewsML format, 2
nillability, 171
node kinds
  attribute, 51, 242
  comment, 51, 243
  document, 51, 242
  element, 51, 242
  namespace, 51, 243
  processing instruction, 51, 243
  text, 51, 242
node(), 75, 525

node, properties of
  attributes, 53
  base URI, 53
  children, 53
  name, 52
  namespaces, 53
  parent, 53
  string value, 52
  type annotation, 52
  typed value, 52
NodeInfo interface (Saxon), 856
node-name() function, 204, 783
node-set() extension function, 81, 370,
    629, 859
nodeValue() method (DOM), 606
non-ASCII characters, 389
non-null namespace URI, 129
normalization
normalize-space() function, 139, 783
normalize-unicode() function, 784
not() function, 784
Novatchev, Dimitre, 198
number format pattern result (xsl:decimal-format),
    256
number() function, 127, 362, 784
numbering the lines of a poem, example of, 371
numbers, formatting, 365
numeric promotion, 73, 395

O

object instances, 131
object-oriented programming language, 184
objects in the new model
  events, 693
  families, 693
  individuals, 693
occurrence indicators, 75, 156
one-or-more() function, 785
<OPTION> element, 211
«or», 761
Oracle processor, 601
ordinal attribute (of xsl:number), 366
output escaping, controlling, 462
output formats, different, 45
outputting the number (xsl:number), 367
override attribute (of xsl:function), 302

P

parallel markup, 637
<param> element, 59
parameterized attribute value, 116
parameters
  function parameters, 74

stylesheet parameters, 74
template parameters, 74
parent axis, 763
parent of a node, 52
parentless nodes, matching, 500
parse() method (JAXP)
parser API, 816
support for DOM, 819
support for SAX, 817
transform() method, 732
transformation API, 822
parsing, 6, 45, 535
path expression, 76
PathPattern, 503
PatternAxis, 508
patterns containing predicates, 497
patterns, meaning of, 493
patterns, overview of, 493
patterns, syntax of
IDKeyPattern, 518
PathPattern, 503
Pattern, 502
PatternStep, 507
RelativePathPattern, 505
PC based Web browser, 2
PDF (Portable Document Format), 2, 46
percent attribute (of xsl:decimal-format), 311
picture argument (of format-date() function), 551
picture string, 253, 559
place of XSLT in the XML family
XSL and CSS, 24
XSLT and XML schemas, 25
XSLT and XML, 22
XSLT and XSL, 21
<Place> attribute (Family tree example), 711
place-knight() function (Knight's tour example), 745
population order, 282
Portable Document Format (PDF), 46
portable stylesheets, writing
conditional compilation, 122
extensibility, 128
version compatibility, 123
position() function, 79, 111, 371, 785
possible moves (Knight's tour example)
finding, 747
trying, 749
Post Schema Validation Infoset (PSVI), 146
precedence. *See* import precedence
preceding axis, 763
preceding-sibling axis, 77, 763
preserve validation, 162, 207, 250, 259, 268
preserveWhitespace property (MSXML), 811
principal stylesheet module, 85
priority (of template rules), 71, 190, 453
priority, default, 498
procedural design patterns, 619

procedural languages
C#, 6
Java, 6
Visual Basic, 6
procedure call, 220
processing instruction node, 51
processing-instruction(), 75
producing lists (XML specification example), 670
programming without assignment statements, 625
progressive rendering, 36
promotion, numeric, 73, 395
pseudo-attributes in <?xml-stylesheet?>
    processing instruction
alternate, 94
charset, 94
href, 94
media, 94
title, 94
type, 94
PSVI (Post Schema Validation Infoset), 146
publishing information to user, process of, 20
publishing static HTML, 728
pull processing, 69
push processing
examples of, 54, 65

Q

QName value space, 210
QName, 130, 203
QName-valued
attribute, creating, 210
content, 349
elements, 210

R

recursion to process a sequence of nodes, 224
recursion to process a sequence of strings, 227
recursion, 223, 306, 633
recursive templates, writing, 224
reflection, 58
refresh() function (Family tree example), 737
regex. *See* <xsl analyze-string> instruction
regex-group() function, 181, 184, 580
regular expression syntax, 179
relational database, 7
RelativePathPattern, 501
RelaxNG, 25
remove() function, 785
replace() function, 182, 184, 620, 786
required attribute (of xsl:param), 301, 393
resolve-QName() function, 786
resolve-uri() function, 787
result document, validating, 160, 259, 415

result tree fragments, 81, 249
result tree
  writing to, 68
reverse() function, 787
Rich Text Format (RTF), 46
root node, 49, 673
root() function, 788
round() function, 362, 788
round-half-to-even() function, 788
round-tripping. See namespace fixup
RTF (Rich Text Format), 46
Rubik's cube, 44
rule based design pattern, 37, 645
rule based stylesheets
  advantages of, 620
  features of, 620
rules for HTML output, 385
rules for text output, 389
running the stylesheet, 11, 752

S

Sablotron, 8
save() method (MSXML), 801
SAX (Simple API for XML), 6
SAX API, 6
SAX filter application, 19
SAX2 API specification, 46
SAX-compliant parser, 703
Saxon
  collations, 858
  command line, 852
  evaluate() extension, 859
  expression() extension, 860
  extension functions, writing, 601, 857
  JAVA API, 855
  installing, 12
  origins, 31
  processor, 8, 851–864
Saxon from a Java application, using, 855
Saxon from the command line, using, 852
Saxon processor, 601
Saxon processor, invoking, 852
Saxon tree models, 856
Saxon
  installing, 12
  origins, 31
Saxon, 8, 12, 31, 851
saxon:expression() extension function, 860
SAXResult class (JAXP), 233
Scalable Vector Graphics (SVG), 244
scene.xsl stylesheet, 622
<SCENE> element, 195
schema for GEDCOM 6.0, creating, 695
schema information in the tree model, 58
schema processor, 140, 161

schema, adding, 868
schema. See also XML Schema
SCHEMA_VALIDATION property (Saxon), 732
schema-aware XSLT processor, 58, 145, 201, 262,
  705, 729
schema-location attribute, 325, 326
schemas, importing, 168, 324, 705, 715
<scrap> element (XML specification example),
  676
seconds-from-dateTime() function, 789
seconds-from-dayTimeDuration() function, 789
seconds-from-time() function, 789
section headers, creating, 666
select
  attribute, 22, 73, 347, 362
  expression, 189
  statement, 236
select attribute, 18, 60
SELECTED attribute, 211
selecting nodes explicitly, example of, 69
selectNodes method (MSXML), 22
self axis, 763
separator attribute, 201, 206
sequence constructor, 60, 64, 106
sequence number, determining, 362
sequence of nodes, 279
sequence type descriptor
  attribute() +, 156
  document-node(), 156
  element(), 156
  node() *, 156
  node(), 156
SequenceType syntax, 74, 301, 327, 444
serialization, 45, 57, 375
service() method (Java servlets), 732
set() method (MSXML), 627
setErrorListener() method (JAXP), 826
setParameter() method (JAXP), 816
setProperty() method, 801
setting out the production rules, 676
SGML (Standard Generalized Markup Language),
  27
SGML-based standard, 27
SGML syntax, 34
showing the ancestors of a node, example of, 279
side effects, 36, 609
Simple API for XML (SAX), 6
simple key, using, 336
simple type definitions, 146
simplified stylesheet. See fill-in-the-blanks
  stylesheets
simplified stylesheets
  advantages of, 119
  examples of, 14, 120
simulating higher order functions, 198
single-level grouping by value, example of, 286
single-match example, 182

SOAP namespaces, 23, 114
«some», 761
sort key
  component, 425
  specification, 425
  value, 425
sorted sequence, 425
sorting on the result of a calculation, example of,
    431
sorting the groups, 285
sorting, 189, 278
source document, 307
source document, validating, 159
<SPEAKER> element, 293
<SPEECH> element, 225
SQL script, 2
SQL Server, 9
sql:connect() function (Saxon), 603
Standard Generalized Markup Language (SGML),
    27
Standard Music Description Language, 4
start node, 362
starts-with() function, 789
static method, 131
strict validation, 161, 207, 250, 259, 268
string value of a node, 52, 138
string() function, 116, 127, 138, 790
string, 155
string-join() function, 790
string-length() function, 790
strings, 116
string-to-codepoints() function, 791
«strip» 162, 207, 250
stripping whitespace nodes, effect of, 141
stylesheet
  debugging, 712
  program, 84
  structure, 83
  tree, 115
stylesheet design patterns
  computational stylesheets, 625
  fill-in-the-blanks stylesheets, 613
  navigational stylesheets, 616
  rule based stylesheets, 620
stylesheet design patterns, 613
stylesheet functions, 129, 224
stylesheet functions, using, 303
stylesheet languages
  Cascading Style Sheets (CSS and CSS2), 24
  XSL (XSLT plus XSL Formatting Objects), 24
stylesheet layer, 316
stylesheet module
  overview of, 119
  principal, 85
stylesheet namespaces
  local, 716
  schema, 716

XHTML, 716
XSLT, 716
stylesheet parameters, 59, 74, 397
stylesheet-prefix attribute, 354
stylesheets and schemas, 145
stylesheets, 85
Stylus Studio, 9
subroutine call, 220
subsequence() function, 791
substitution groups, 150, 151
substring() function, 116, 791
substring-after() function, 792
substring-before() function, 792
subtract-dates-yielding-dayTimeDuration() function,
    793
subtract-dates-yielding-yearMonthDuration()
    function, 793
subtract-dateTimes-yielding-dayTimeDuration()
    function, 793
subtract-dateTimes-yielding-year MonthDuration()
    function, 793
sum() function, 634, 793
super() method (in object-oriented programming),
    184, 356
SVG (Scalable Vector Graphics), 244
SVG namespace, 244
switch statement, 236
syntax of patterns
  syntax, 7, 125
  trees and DOM, 604
  type system, 251
system overview of XSLT, 43
System.Xml (Microsoft .NET), 812
System.Xml.Xsl interface (Microsoft .NET), 133
system-property() function, 122, 124, 125, 346

T

table of contents, example of creating, 661
tables, arranging data in, 298
targetNamespace attribute (XML Schema), 326
template bodies, 84
template parameters, 74, 398
template rules
  built-in, 70
  choosing, 189
temporary tree, 79, 260
temporary tree, validating, 163
Tennison, Jeni, 643
terminate attribute (of xsl:message), 343
test expression, 236, 309
testing availability of a Java method, example of,
    568
testing for node-set() extensions, example of,
    566
Text Encoding Initiative, 4

text node
in a sequence constructor, 64
whitespace-only, 64
text output method, 46, 389
text(), 75
text, formatting, 667
timezone-from-date() function, 793
timezone-from-dateTime() function, 793
timezone-from-time() function, 793
«to», 761
token output sequence, formatting, 365
token symbols (in XPath)
Char, 756
DecimalLiteral, 755
Digit, 756
DoubleLiteral, 756
IntegerLiteral, 755
QName, 756
StringLiteral, 756
Wildcard, 756
tokenize() function, 16, 182, 184, 224, 794
top-level elements, 98
top-level processing, 705
trace() function, 794
Transformation API for XML (TrAX), 815
transformation process
built-in template rules, 70
conflict resolution policy, 71
controlling which nodes to process, 68
modes, 70
push processing, 65
sequence constructors, 61
template rules, 60
transformation, invoking, 59
**transformation process. See system overview of
   XSLT**
transformation processor, 57
transformation sheet. See system overview of XSLT
transformation, invoking, 59
Transformiix, 8
translate() function, 367, 742, 795
TrAX (Transformation API for XML), 815
«treat as», 762
tree construction process, 64
tree model
nodes in tree model, 51
Saxon implementation, 856
XML as tree, 48
true() function, 795
tunnel attribute (of xsl:param), 393
tunnel parameters, 398, 490
type annotation of a node
copying, 250
description, 52
setting and using, 146, 159, 164
type attribute, 160, 161, 201, 207
type conversion, 73, 496

type of the parameter, 394
type system for XSLT
based on XML Schema, 41
typed value of a node, 52

U

unary «+», 762
unary «-», 762
Unicode
characters, 334
codepoint collation, 333
codepoints-to-string() function, 767
collation algorithm, 429
normalization, 232, 383
Private Use Area, 234
string-to-codepoints() function, 791
Uniform Resource Identifier (URI), 22, 533
Uniform Resource Locators (URLs), 533
«union», 762
unordered() function, 795
unparsed-entity-public-id() function, 584
unparsed-entity-uri() function, 585
unparsed-text() function, 587, 611
up-conversion, 589
upper-case() function, 796
URI (Uniform Resource Identifier), 22, 533
URI identifying a namespace, 262
URI, resolving, 533
URIResolver class, 133, 841
URIs as atomic values, 538
URIs held in nodes, 535
URI-valued attributes, 231, 389
URLs (Uniform Resource Locators), 533
Usage section. See literal result elements
use attribute (of xsl:key), 333, 337
use-attribute-sets attribute, 215, 241, 262, 308
use-character-maps attribute, 230
user defined attributes, 124
user defined top-level element
user-defined data elements, 98
XSLT-defined declarations, 98
use-when attribute
using, 85, 89
with named attribute sets, example of, 331

V

validate() method, 802
validating
individual attributes, 167
individual elements, 164
result document, 160
source document, 159
temporary tree, 163

validating and annotating the document, 259

validation attribute, 161, 164, 201

validation attribute, values of
lax, 162
preserve, 162
strict, 161
strip, 162

value attribute, 214, 362

value of a constructed attribute, 206

variables
context, 78
datatypes, 74
expressions, 76
global, 73
immutability, 73
local, 73
parameters, 74
temporary trees, 79

variant stylesheets (XML specification example), 685–688

VBScript in MSXML3 stylesheet, 600

<vc> element (XML specification example), 678

vendor defined attributes, 129

vendor extensions
permissible, 595
testing for, 548, 566

vendor or third-party extensions, testing for, 566

vendor portability, 274

version attribute, 123, 124, 437

version compatibility, 123

VitalType attribute (family tree example), 718

W

WD-xsl, 8, 30, 435

Web browsers
Internet Explorer, 30, 95, 715
Netscape, 95, 715

Web client, 27

Web content, creating
markup, 29
program, 29
script, 29

Web sites, 739

well-balanced fragment, 50

well-formed XML document, 49

while loop, 223

whitespace
control using <xsl:text>, 461
effect of stripping whitespace nodes, 141
in a sequence constructor, 64
in MSXML3, 138
solving whitespace problems, 142

stripping, 432
whitespace nodes in stylesheet, 64, 141

whitespace characters
carriage return, 137
newline, 137
space, 137
tab, 137

whitespace facet in XML Schema
collapse, 138
preserve, 138
replace, 138

whitespace handling, 136

whitespace nodes
in the stylesheet, 64, 141

whitespace problems, solving
too little whitespace, 143
too much whitespace, 142

X

Xalan processor, 8, 601

xdt:anyAtomicType, 62

xdt:dayTimeDuration, 63, 76

xdt:untypedAtomic, 63, 76

xdt:yearMonthDuration, 63, 76

XHTML output method, 46, 388

XML
as a tree, 39, 44, 48
attributes, 44, 55
base attribute, 539
data, 2
documents, 1
element, 24
information set (InfoSet), 24
lang attribute, 695
Namespaces 1.1, 23
namespaces, 22
output method, 46, 378
parser, 6, 137
Query Language, 32
space attribute, 60
specification, formatting, 646
syntax, use of, 34
tags, 621
tree model, 56
vocabulary, 17

XML-based electronic commerce, 2

XML-based model, 19

XML-defined IDs, 335

XML document features, categories of
debatable, 56
definitely insignificant, 56
definitely significant, 56

XML envelope/payload applications, 591

XML parser, 6

XML Query Language, 28

XML Schema, 25, 92, 145, 210
XML Schema, overview of
  elements with attributes and simple content, 148
  elements with element-only content, 150
  elements with mixed content, 149
  processing, 8
  overview of, 145
  rule-based, 37
  types based, 41
  simple type definitions, 146
  substitution groups, 151
XML specification, formatting, 646
XML Spy, 9
XML to HTML, transforming, 1
XML vocabulary, 21, 210
XML, features of
  separating data from presentation, 2
  transmitting data between applications, 2
xml:space attribute, 49
XMLFilter class (JAXP), 823
XMLNode, 812
XMLSpec, case study of, 645–46
XPath
  cast expression, 444
  data model, 147, 163, 204
  doc() function, 533
  engine, 305
  expression language, 7
  expression syntax, 130
  expressions, 76, 101, 125
  function call, 68, 224
  function library, 765
  language, 18
  relationship to XSLT, 21
XPath 2.0 requirements, 33
**xpath-default-namespace attribute, 304,
  442**
XPathDocument (.NET), 812
XPathNavigator object (.NET), 813
XPointer, 21, 860
XQuery, 9, 32, 131, 206
xs:anyURI, 63, 76
xs:boolean, 75
xs:date, 75
xs:dateTime, 75
xs:decimal, 73, 75
xs:double, 73, 75
xs:float() constructor function, 765
xs:float, 73
xs:ID, 73
xs:integer() constructor function, 72
xs:integer, 73, 75
xs:QName, 76, 204
xs:string, 73, 75
xs:time, 75
xs:token, 150
<xsl:apply-imports> instruction, 184

<xsl:apply-templates> instruction
  changes in 2.0, 184
  effect, 185
  format, 184
  usage and examples, 185
xsi:nil attribute, 171
xsi:type attribute, 170
XSL (Extensible Stylesheet Language), 21
XSL and CSS, 24
XSL Formatting Objects (XSL-FO), 21
XSL, capabilities of
  creation of formatting constructs, 29
  definition of reusable formatting macros, 29
  extensible set of formatting objects, 29
  formatting constructs, creating, 25
  formatting of source elements, 29
  source elements, formatting, 24
  writing-direction independent stylesheets,
    29
XSL, history of
  beyond XSLT 1.0, 31
  Microsoft WD-xsl dialect, 8, 30, 435
  prehistory, 26
  Saxon, 31
  XQuery, 32
  XSLT 2.0 and XPath 2.0, 33
<xsl:analyze-string> instruction, 176, 227
<xsl:apply-imports> instruction, 184
<xsl:apply-templates> instruction
  changes in 2.0, 187
  effect, 188
  format, 187
  usage and examples, 193
**<xsl:apply-templates> versus <xsl:for-each>,
  194**
<xsl:attribute> instruction
  changes in 2.0, 201
  effect, 202
  examples, 211
  format, 201
  usage, 208
<xsl:attribute> instruction, attributes of
  name, 202
  select, 202
  separator, 202
  type, 202
  validation, 202
xsl:attribute-set
  changes in 2.0, 214
  effect, 215
  examples, 217
  format, 214
  usage, 217
<xsl:attribute-set> declaration, 214
<xsl:attribute-set> declaration, attributes of
  name, 215
  use-attribute-sets, 215

xsl:call-template
  changes in 2.0, 220
  effect, 221
  format, 220
  usage and examples, 222
<xsl:character-map> declaration
  changes in 2.0, 229
  effect, 230
  format, 229
  usage and examples, 232
xsl:choose
  changes in 2.0, 236
  effect, 236
  examples, 237
  format, 236
  instruction, 213, 227, 236, 237
  usage, 237
xsl:comment
  changes in 2.0, 238
  effect, 239
  examples, 240
  format, 238
  instruction, 238
  usage, 239
xsl:copy
  changes in 2.0, 241
  effect, 242
  examples, 244
  format, 241
  instruction, 205, 216, 240, 350
<xsl:copy>
  attributes of, 241
  changes in 2.0, 245
  copy-namespaces, 241
  effect, 246
  example of, 244
  format, 245
  significance of, 243
  type, 241
  usage and examples, 247
  validation, 241
<xsl:copy-of>
  attributes of
  copy-namespaces, 245
  for repeated output source, example of, 247
  instruction, 245, 350
  select, 245
  type, 245
  validation, 245
xsl:decimal-format
  attributes of
  changes in 2.0, 252
  declaration, 251, 359
  decimal-separator, 252
  digit, 253
  effect, 253
  examples, 255

  format, 252
  grouping-separator, 252
  infinity, 252
  minus-sign, 252
  name, 252
  NaN, 253
  pattern-separator, 253
  percent, 253
  per-mille, 253
  usage, 255
  zero-digit, 253
xsl:document
  changes in 2.0, 257
  effect, 258
  format, 257
  instruction, 257
  usage and examples, 260
xsl:element
  changes in 2.0, 260
  effect, 261
  format, 261
  instruction, 62, 260
  usage and examples, 269
xsl:exclude-result-prefixes attribute, 114
xsl:fallback
  changes in 2.0, 271
  effect, 272
  examples, 274
  format, 271
  instruction, 106, 125, 135, 271
  usage, 273
xsl:for-each
  changes in 2.0, 276
  effect, 277
  format, 277
  instruction, 276
  usage and examples, 279
xsl:for-each-group
  attributes of, 281
  changes in 2.0, 281
  collation, 282
  effect, 282
  format, 281
  group-adjacent, 282
  group-by, 282
  group-ending-with, 282
  group-starting-with, 282
  instruction, 281
  select, 282
  usage and examples, 286
xsl:function
  as, 301
  attributes of
  changes in 2.0, 300
  declaration, 35, 73, 131, 300
  effect, 301
  format, 300

xsl:function (*continued*)
  name, 301
  override, 301
  usage and examples, 303
xsl:if
  changes in 2.0, 309
  effect, 309
  examples, 311
  instruction, 102, 309
  format, 309
  usage, 310
xsl:import
  changes in 2.0, 312
  declaration, 47, 88, 98, 312
  effect, 313
  examples, 320
  format, 312
  usage, 319
xsl:import-schema
  changes in 2.0, 324
  declaration, 163, 168, 324
  effect, 325
  examples, 328
  format, 325
  usage, 326
xsl:include
  changes in 2.0, 328
  declaration, 47, 88, 328
  effect, 329
  format, 328
  usage and examples, 330
**<xsl:include> and <xsl:import>, difference
  between, 88**
xsl:key
  attributes of
  changes in 2.0, 332
  collation, 332
  declaration, 332
  effect, 333
  format, 332
  match, 332
  name, 332
  usage and examples, 335
  use, 332
xsl:matching-substring
  changes in 2.0, 342
  effect, 343
  element, 181, 182, 342
  format, 342
  usage and examples, 343
xsl:message
  changes in 2.0, 343
  effect, 344
  examples, 345
  instruction, 102, 343
  format, 343
  usage, 344

xsl:namespace
  changes in 2.0, 347
  effect, 347
  format, 347
  instruction, 346
  usage and examples, 348
xsl:namespace-alias
  changes in 2.0, 350
  effect, 351
  format, 350
  usage and examples, 352
<xsl:namespace-alias> instruction, 116, 350
xsl:next-match
  changes in 2.0, 355
  effect, 356
  format, 355
  instruction, 355
  usage and examples, 357
xsl:non-matching-substring
  changes in 2.0, 359
  effect, 359
  element, 184, 358
  format, 359
  usage and examples, 359
xsl:number
  attributes of
  changes in 2.0, 360
  count, 360
  effect, 361
  format, 360
  format, 361
  from, 360
  instruction, 359
  lang, 361
  letter-value, 361
  level, 360
  select, 360
  usage and examples, 367
  value, 360
xsl:otherwise
  changes in 2.0, 374
  effect, 374
  element, 237, 374
  format, 374
  usage and examples, 375
xsl:output
  attributes of
  changes in 2.0, 375
  effect, 377
  examples, 391
  format, 375
  usage, 390
<xsl:output> declaration, 46, 375
  cdata-section-elements, 376, 381
  doctype-public, 376, 382
  doctype-system, 376, 382
  encoding, 376, 382

escape-uri-attributes, 376
include-content-type, 376
indent, 376, 383
media-type, 376, 383
method, 376
name, 376
normalization-form, 376, 383
omit-xml-declaration, 377, 384
standalone, 377, 384
undeclare-namespaces, 377, 384
use-character-maps, 377, 385
version, 377, 385
<xsl:output>, attributes of
cdata-section-elements, 376, 381
doctype-public, 376, 382
doctype-system, 376, 382
encoding, 376, 382
escape-uri-attributes, 376
include-content-type, 376
indent, 376, 383
media-type, 376, 383
method, 376
name, 376
normalization-form, 376, 383
omit-xml-declaration, 377, 384
standalone, 377, 384
undeclare-namespaces, 377, 384
use-character-maps, 377, 385
version, 377, 385
xsl:output-character element, 391
changes in 2.0, 391
effect, 392
format, 392
xsl:param
changes in 2.0, 393
effect, 394
element, 99, 356, 392
examples, 399
format, 393
usage, 397
<xsl:param> element, attributes of
as, 393
name, 393
required, 393
select, 393
tunnel, 393
<xsl:param> with a default value, example of, 399
xsl:perform-sort
changes in 2.0, 405
effect, 405
format, 405
instruction, 405
usage and examples, 406
xsl:preserve-space
changes in 2.0, 406
effect, 407

element, 406
examples, 410
format, 406
usage, 409
<xsl:preserve-space> declaration, 406
xsl:processing-instruction, 411
changes in 2.0, 411
effect, 411
examples, 413
format, 411
usage, 412
xsl:result-document
changes in 2.0, 414
effect, 415
examples, 417
format, 414
usage, 417
<xsl:result-document> instruction, 47, 414
xsl:sequence
changes in 2.0, 420
effect, 420
element, 420
format, 420
usage and examples, 421
<xsl:sequence> instruction, 200, 226, 420
xsl:sort
changes in 2.0, 423
effect, 424
examples, 431
element, 423
format, 423
usage, 429
<xsl:sort> attributes of
case-order, 424
collation, 424
data-type, 424
lang, 424
order, 424
select, 424
stable, 424
<xsl:sort> element, 189, 278, 423
xsl:strip-space
changes in 2.0, 433
declaration, 432
effect, usage, and examples, 433
format, 433
<xsl:strip-space> declaration, 432
xsl:stylesheet
changes in 2.0, 434
effect, 437
format, 434
usage and examples, 445
<xsl:stylesheet> element, 91, 433
<xsl:stylesheet> element, attributes of
default-validation, 92, 168
exclude-result-prefixes, 92
extension-element-prefixes, 92

<xsl:stylesheet> element, attributes of (*continued*)
id, 92
<template> declaration, 103
<template> element, 115
<transform>, 98
<value-of> element, 102
<value-of> instruction, 127
<variable> element, 61, 99
<when> element, 236
xpath-default-namespace, 92
xsl:template
changes in 2.0, 451
declaration, 450
effect, 452
format, 451
usage and examples, 455
xsl:text
changes in 2.0, 460
effect, 460
format, 460
instruction, 459
instruction, 114, 459
usage, 460
xsl:transform
element, 91, 465
format, 465
xsl:type
attribute, 166
validation attribute, 166
version attribute, 119
xsl:value-of
changes in 2.0, 465
effect, 466
examples, 470
format, 465
instruction, 465
usage, 467
xsl:variable
changes in 2.0, 471
effect, 472
element, 471
examples, 477
format, 471
usage, 477
xsl:when
changes in 2.0, 487
effect, 487
format, 487
usage and examples, 488
<xsl:when> element, 487
xsl:with-param
changes in 2.0, 489
effect, 489
element, 488
format, 489
usage and examples, 490
[xsl]version attribute, 273

XSL-FO (XSL Formatting Objects), 21
XSLT
engine, 19
forwards compatibility, 274
namespace, 98, 351, 438
overview of, 1
processor, 6, 47, 92, 115, 168
processor, core task of, 43
Recommendation, 46
significance of, 17
stylesheet, 8, 11
template rules, 116
type system, 72
uses of, 4
XSLT (eXtensible Stylesheet Language Transformations), 1
XSLT 1.0 processor, 122
XSLT 1.0 stylesheet, overview of, 9
XSLT 1.0 stylesheets to XSLT 2.0, migration of, 124
XSLT 2.0 and XPath 1.0, features of, 619
XSLT 2.0 as a language
Rule based, 37
types based on XML schema, 41
XML syntax, use of, 34
XSLT 2.0 behavior and XSLT 1.0 behavior, differences between, 126
XSLT 2.0 processor, 122
XSLT 2.0 requirements, 33
XSLT 2.0 stylesheet, 15, 541
XSLT 2.0, changes in, 84, 494
XSLT 2.0, features of, 122
XSLT and SQL
overview of, 7
similarities between, 7
XSLT and XML
relationship between, 18
schemas, 21
XSLT and XML schemas, 25
XSLT and XML, relationship between, 22
XSLT and XPath processing objects (MSXML)
IXMLDOMDocument, 800
IXMLDOMNode, 800
IXMLDOMNodeList, 800
IXMLDOMParseError, 800
IXMLDOMSelection, 800
IXSLProcessor, 800
IXSLTemplate, 800
XSLT and XPath, 21
XSLT and XSL, 21
XSLT defined attributes, 129
XSLT element, 122
XSLT engine, 16
XSLT functions
current() function, 526
current-group() function, 523
current-grouping-key(), 523

document(), 524
element-available(), 524
format-date(), 524
format-number(), 524
format-time(), 524
function-available(), 524
generate-id(), 524
key(), 524
regex-group(), 524
system-property(), 524
unparsed-entity-public-id(), 524
unparsed-text(), 524
XSLT in data conversion, role of, 2
XSLT instructions. See instructions
XSLT processing model, 43
XSLT processor, 5, 39
XSLT processor, core task of, 36
XSLT Recommendation, 38
XSLT stylesheet, 7, 9
XSLT to XML, transformation from, 5
XSLT to XML, transforming
XSLT 1.0 stylesheet, 9
XSLT 2.0 stylesheet, 15
XSLT and SQL, 7
XSLT processors, 8
XSLT transformations, using
data conversion, 17
publishing, 17
XSLT tree model, 6, 48
XSLT version 2.0, features of
extending the scope of applicability, 3

integration across the XML standards family, 3
tactical usability improvements, 3
XSLT, 1
XSLT, overview of
transforming music, 3
version 2.0, 3
XSLT, system overview of
different output formats, 45
multiple inputs and outputs, 47
trees, not documents, 44
XSLT, use of
data conversion applications, 17
publishing, 19
XSLTC, 8
XSLT-defined declarations. See declarations
XSLT-defined elements, 129
XSLT-defined functions, 130
xt processor, 601
xt, 8

Y

year-from-date() function, 796
year-from-dateTime() function, 796
years-from-yearMonthDuration() function, 796

Z

zero-or-one() function, 796